F ∘ I ∘ D ∘ E

XX CONGRESS LONDON

30 October–2 November 2002

President: Lord Slynn of Hadley
Secretary-General: Mads Andenas

Volume 1 National Reports

I. European Union Law and National Constitutions

II. Financial Services in the Era of the Euro and E-Commerce: Does home country control work?

III. Cross Border Mergers in Company Law and Competition Law: Removing the final barriers

BIICL
British Institute of
International and
Comparative Law
www.biicl.org

Published by
The British Institute of International and Comparative Law

British Library Cataloguing in Publication Data
A Catalogue record of this book is available from the British Library

ISBN 0–903067–87–0

Distributed by the British Institute of International and Comparative Law
Charles Clore House, 17 Russell Square, London WC1B 5DR
<http://www.biicl.org>

Typeset by Cambrian Typesetters
Frimley, Surrey
Printed in Great Britain by Biddles Ltd,
Guildford and King's Lynn

F ∘ I ∘ D ∘ E

XX CONGRESS LONDON

30 October – 2 November 2002

Under the gracious patronage of HM the Queen

Welcome by the Rt Hon The Lord Slynn of Hadley, President of FIDE

It is a great pleasure for me to welcome you to the XXth FIDE Congress in London. The FIDE Congress is always a special occasion: it brings together judges, practitioners, and academic lawyers for lively and informed debate on topical issues of European law and for forming new European bonds. The XXth Congress will live up to these expectations as we consider constitutional, financial services, and competition issues in a leading European financial centre. I look forward to reuniting with old friends and making new friends in London in October 2002. The Social Programme will, I am sure, give much enjoyment

The Congress is a bi-annual meeting of the International Federation for European Law (FIDE). It brings together national associations of European law and serves as a forum for the study and development of the European law. This book, and its companion volume to be produced after the Congress, is a most useful record of the preparations and of the proceedings.

GORDON SLYNN

Foreword by the Secretary-General of FIDE

The XX FIDE Congress has three parallel topics:

- European Law and National Constitutions
- Financial Services in the Era of the Euro and E-commerce: Does home control work? and
- Cross Border Mergers in Company Law and Competition Law: Removing the final barriers.

For each topic, national rapporteurs submit reports on the basis of a questionnaire prepared by the General Rapporteur. The Congress constitutes an open forum for lively debate on the issues raised. The debate is directed by the session Chairman and the General Rapporteur, who prepares a general report and conclusions at the end of the Congress. The emphasis is on participation and the sharing of ideas.

In this volume are collected the national reports which reached us in time before we had to go to press. A second volume will include all other reports, and speeches made at the Congress. It will be produced as soon as possible in the new year.

MADS ANDENAS

CONTENTS

VOLUME ONE: REPORTS

I. EUROPEAN UNION LAW AND NATIONAL CONSTITUTIONS

General Rapporteurs
Professor Jaqueline Dutheuil de la Rochere and Professor Dr Ingolf Pernice

II. FINANCIAL SERVICES IN THE ERA OF THE EURO AND E-COMMERCE: DOES HOME COUNTRY CONTROL WORK?

General Rapporteurs
Professor Marc Dassesse and Stuart Isaacs, QC

QUESTIONNAIRE FOR TOPIC I

European Union Law and National Constitutions

General Rapporteurs
Jacquline Dutheil de la Rochère and Ingolf Pernice

One of the subjects discussed at the 17th Congress of FIDE in 1996 was „National constitutional law vis-à-vis European Integration“.[1] What is the point of taking up this theme again, under a slightly different heading? There are at least two answers:

- Important developments have occurred meanwhile. The Treaty of Amsterdam is in force, the Treaty of Nice is due to be ratified, the Charter of Fundamental Rights has solemnly been proclaimed by the Community institutions and the "Declaration on the Future of the Union" adopted in Nice has already opened a broad public discourse on at least four questions which - though the word constitution was not used - address the key issues of what normally would be a constitution: The delimitation of competencies between the European Union and the Member States, the status of the Charter of fundamental rights, the simplification and, therefore, reorganisation, consolidation and unification of the Treaties for the sake of more democracy, and the role of national Parliaments in the "European architecture". Heads of States and other politicians do not hesitate any more to talk about - or even call for - a European constitution, and the European Parliament is one of the most active parts to act in favour of the constitutionalisation of the Treaties to be undertaken until 2004.
- The new constitutional perspective gives the question of the impact of European law on the national constitutions - and vice versa - another dimension. The questionnaire and the discussion of 1996 were mainly concentrated on the conflicts between national constitutional law and European law, and possible solutions thereupon. This time, the focus should be directed more on the constitutional issues of the co-existence, interaction and co-ordinated functioning of the national and European levels of government, to be regarded as one system of governance in the Union. Though new developments in the case law and doctrines on the relation of national and European law shall not be neglected, conceptual

and systemic considerations on the future of the European Union and its constitutional foundations should be given special attention. With a view to the Post-Nice-Process it is important to understand better the present situation of the Union regarding its constitutional foundations and relation to the Member States' constitutions.

The loyalties of the Member States' institutions under Article 10 ECT have been one of the subjects of the XIX F.I.D.E. Congress, Helsinki, in the year 2000. In its conclusions, John Temple Lang points out that "The whole working of the Community system depends on the national authorities fulfilling their role, applying Community law, implementing Community policies, and not adopting national measures, however well-intentioned, which prevent the Community system from working properly".[2] Again, the aim of the present exercise is not to repeat, but to build upon the findings of the earlier Congress. EU-Law and national constitutions seem to be complementary, interlaced and interdependent in substance and institutionally. National authorities have an important function in the EU-system, which is based upon them, and it would be interesting to find out if and how this European function is reflected in the national constitutions and practice.

The following questionnaire aims at bringing together the basic conceptions and the main streams of the national debates on the relation of European and national constitutional law in the perspective of 2004, with a view to merging them into a general European discourse as it seems to be essential for the further development of what may be called the European constitution. It is suggested to divide the reports into three parts, referring to (*a*) an introductory summary of the foundations and conditions of a European constitution under national constitutional law and the ongoing political debate on the preparation of the IGC 2004 (I.), (*b*) an analysis of the present relationship of EU-law and national constitutions including the question of the Member States' constitutional autonomy under the EU-Treaty, the Fundamental rights charter and the European function of national authorities (II.), and (*c*) recommendations in conclusion, from the perspective of the different constitutional conditions in each Member State, for the issues which are on the agenda for the IGC 2004 (III.).

The rapporteurs are, therefore, requested to elaborate answers to the following points and questions, taking the view of their respective country, if possible in the given order and not exceeding thirty pages. This effort should enable the general rapporteurs to produce a comparative analysis which may, together with the national and European reports, provide a useful contribution to the debate opened by the Declarations of Nice and Laeken.

FIDE 2002 QUESTIONNAIRE

I. Introduction: foundations of European constitutionalism
  1. Concept of constitution in the member States
    a. What is a constitution: theoretical concepts and basic notions
    b. The EU/EC architecture and national constitutional traditions
  2. National provisions for the adoption of a "Constitution" of the European Union
    a. Constitutional conditions for and limits to further steps of integration (substance)
    b. Procedural requirements under national constitutional provisions
    c. The role of the citizens: international treaty or European social contract?
  3. The constitution-making process: preparing the IGC 2004 in practice
    a. How is the internal debate on the future of the European Union organised?
    b. What are the key issues and proposals of the leading political groups?

II. Relationship and interaction of EC/EU law and national constitutions today
  1. Member States' constitutional autonomy under European constraints
    a. National identities of the Member States (article 6.3 TEU) as a limit to the extension of the EC/EU competencies (ex. culture, article 151 TEC)
    b. Articles 6.1 and 7 TEU as limits to the constitutional autonomy of the Member States
  2. Common values: the Charter of fundamental rights of the European Union
    a. Does the Charter reflect the basic human rights standards of your constitution and national law?
    b. The Charter as a reference for fundamental rights protection in national courts
    c. The impact of the Charter on the standards referred to in article 6.1 TEU
  3. The question of the supremacy of EC/EU law and its constitutional effects
    a. Supremacy I: community primary law and national constitutional law. Position of national constitutional courts
    b. Supremacy II: community secondary legislation and national constitutional law
    c. Implicit modification of national constitutions by the revision and application of the TEU

4. Institutional interdependence: European functions of national institutions
   a. The national parliaments in the European legislation process: indirect source of legitimacy and responsibilities for implementation
   b. European functions of national administrations: a double mandate for the executive
   c Judicial protection in the European Union through national judges: conflict of loyalties; question of procedural autonomy

III. The role of the regions and local authorities in EU Law
   1. Effects of EU law on the constitutional framework and settlement in relation to regions and local authorities.
   2. Possible consequences for EU law of regionalisation and decentralisation of the kind that goes on in your country.

IV. Conclusions and recommendations for 2004
   1. A new architecture: how should an EU Constitution or EU basic treaty look like?
   2. A Constitution for the European Union: conditions of adoption and amendment; its relations to national constitutions
   3. Merging the constitutional process and enlargement: how to involve the candidates?

REFERENCES

- Jean-Claude PIRIS, L'Union européenne a-t-elle une constitution? Lui en faut-il une? Revue trimestrielle de droit européen 1999 n° 4 p.599
- Robert TOULEMON, Quelle constitution pour l'Europe? Revue du marché commun et de l'Union européenne, n° 448, mai 2001 p. 293
- Ingolf PERNICE, Multilevel constitutionalism and the treaty of Amsterdam: European constitution -making revisited? Common Market Law Review 1999 n° 4 p. 703

NOTES

1 *Viz.* 17th F.I.D.E. Kongress, I - Le droit constitutionnel national et l'intégration européenne. Nationales Verfassungsrecht mit Blick auf die Europäische Integration. National constitutional law vis-à-vis European integration, Berlin 1996, with the questionnaire of *Michel Fromont*.

2 Viz. 18th F.I.D.E. Congress, Helsinke 1-3 June/Juin 2000, The Duties of Co-operation of National Authorities and Courts and the Community Institutions under Article 10 EC, 2000, p. 378.

AUSTRIA

EU Law and National Constitutions—the Austrian Case

Rapporteur
Heribert Franz Koeck[1]

I. INTRODUCTION: FOUNDATIONS OF EUROPEAN CONSTITUTIONALISM

While there exists a common theoretical basis of European constitutionalism, viz. the doctrine of the social contract and the idea of basic human rights and fundamental freedoms, the practical development in the various European countries has considerably differed in time, form, and contents of the respective constitutional instruments. In a very general way, the U.S. constitution of 1787/1789/91, and the constitutional transformations initiated by the French revolution of 1789, may be said to have provided guidance for a similar development all over Europe. Though the process suffered a setback especially between 1815 and 1848, this could not decisively prevent constitutionalism from carrying the day in the second half of the nineteenth century.

Against this background, the foundations of European constitutionalism may be said to derive from the Christian doctrine of the common dignity of man as the image of God and its early application to the relationship between the individual and the State through the doctrine of the common good, from natural law doctrines of different provenience, as, e.g., the naturalistic and the rationalistic approach, and from the contractual theory of the State, having the realisation of the common good more and more regarded as the essential *raison d'être* of the State. The doctrine of the social contract resulted in attempts to bring into written form its basic principles, thus offering a positive legal basis for the organisation of the State, together with the necessary limitations on its powers, including a workable system of checks and balances between its institutions, as well as for the fundamental rights of the individual and the means by which these rights could be secured. In this latter respect, the British tradition, from the Magna Charter to the Bill of Rights, has also exercised some influence.

In contrast to these common foundations of European constitutionalism, there are only very few European countries which may claim to have enjoyed – as has England, or the United Kingdom, respectively – a century-old constitutional continuity; and Britain, too, has experienced stages of revolution, bloody and less so ones, but similar to those in continental Europe, if only about one and a half century earlier.

In the nineteenth and twentieth century, State crises and their political overcoming often resulted in, or went hand in hand with, the enactment of a new constitution whose founding fathers as often as not invoked legal continuity with the previous constitutional regime, and if they did, justification for doing so often remained doubtful. Due to two World Wars in the twentieth century, and the social and political upheavals in their aftermath, a minority only of the Member States of the European Union may claim an unbroken constitutional tradition going back to the nineteenth century, and quite a few constitutions have not yet come to exist for even fifty or so years. If the tradition of European constitutionalism may said to be old enough to deserve reverence, the actual constitutions are often still comparatively young.

1. Concept of constitution in Member States

a. What is a constitution: theoretical concepts and basic notions

(1) In general

The common constitutional tradition in Europe does not rule out the existence of differing constitutional concepts. The smallest denominator is probably a formula that restricts the notion of constitution to those legal rules which provide for a State's basic organisation by setting up the necessary institutions, endowing them with the necessary powers, and regulating the procedures by which they may fulfil their legislative, administrative, and judicial functions. Those who might consider such a constitution to be too formal, will be inclined to add some basic principles describing the State's object and purpose (what is called in Austrian legal terminology *Staatszielbestimmungen*), in order to give to state action some substantive orientation.

As regards everything else, one has to notice a great number of constitutional variations. In some countries, all constitutional norms are, and have to be, embodied in a single document;[2] in others, there exist, besides the Constitution properly so called, a smaller or greater number of additional constitutional laws which give constitutional status to certain particularly important aspects of the country's legal order which nonetheless would not have, of necessity, to form part of the Constitutions. Sometimes, even individual provisions in simple laws may be granted constitutional rank, mainly in order to make more difficult their subsequent revision.

Constitutional laws and constitutional provisions outside the Constitution properly so called make, of course, sense only if constitutional norms enjoy a higher degree of protection against revocation or revision. In fact, this is a fairly common feature, even if the conditions for repealing or revising constitutional rules may vary from country to country, and may not be identical for all norms even within one and the same legal system. Thus, while the adoption (or revocation, as the case may be) of a constitutional rule requires, in general, only a special quorum of parliamentarians present and consenting, in some cases approval by the people in form of a referendum may be necessary. Here, as with regard to the legal system as a whole, recourse to direct democracy may be quite exceptional, rare, or rather usual.

Finally, the effect exercised by constitutional norms on a legal order at large, and, more particularly, on those of its legal rules that do not enjoy constitutional rank, may again differ from country to country. Where parliament is regarded the collective representation of people's sovereignty, and thus sovereign itself, the constitution, and constitutional laws and rules outside of it, will be no more than a programmatic guideline, a recommendation to be considered by, but not binding on, parliamentary power. Where, in contrast, it is not so much the will of the people's representatives in parliament, but the will of the people represented in the constitution that is regarded as truly sovereign, parliament itself will be subject to the principles and rules contained in, and the limits set out by, constitutional law. In the latter case, parliament, if wanting to free itself from the constitutional restraints will have to transform itself from simple to constitutional legislator, provided it is able to rally the necessary majority of its members. Here, again, some constitutions limit, as a matter of principle, the power of parliament to revise it by declaring at least certain constitutional norms to be inalienable.

The question of judicial review, especially that of legislative acts, is a corollary to the relationship between constitutional and other laws. If simple laws have to conform to the constitution, it makes sense that they, or their relevant provisions, may be disregarded and/or declared unconstitutional if incompatible with the former. In some, but not all, continental legal systems, deciding on the unconstitutionality of laws and individual legal rules and declaring those which are at variance with the constitution to be null and void is reserved to special, so-called constitutional, courts, such reservation being considered desirable in order to enhance the principle of legal certainty.

(2) The Austrian position

Austria is a federal State that is composed of nine component states *(Gliedstaaten)*, which are termed *(Bundes-) Länder*. Accordingly, there exists constitutional law on the federal as well as on the state level. Since, however, the internal organisation of a Member State has no direct bearing on its status under EU/EC law, it is here the federal constitution only which is of interest. Thus, the terms "constitution", "constitutional law" etc. as used here refers to the federal constitution.

Austrian constitutional law is widely dispersed. This is caused by the fact that the Austrian Constitution permits the enactment of constitutional law outside the basic instrument, called *Bundes-Verfassungsgesetz* (Federal Constitution) in contrast to the various *Bundesverfassungsgesetze* (federal constitutional laws).[3] The former is distinguished from the latter by the fact that it contains in a systematic manner those provisions which one would normally expect to be contained in a constitution, namely the organisation of the State, with its main organs or institutions, their competences or powers, and the procedures they have to follow when exercising their legislative, administrative, or judicial functions. The *Bundes-Verfassungsgesetz* may therefore be termed the Constitution properly so-called. In contrast, the federal constitutional laws, and the constitutional provisions in laws that are otherwise not of constitutional rank, deal either with an isolated constitutional question or with no constitutional question at all; in the latter case, they are endowed with constitutional rank for the only purpose of making revision or repeal of the particular law or provision more difficult.

All constitutional provisions, whether contained in the Constitution properly so called, or in separate constitutional laws, or in constitutional provisions inserted into "simple" laws, enjoy a higher degree of protection against revision or repeal inasmuch as enacting, revising, or repealing constitutional law require higher quora of presence and consent,[4] and, where a fundamental revision of the Constitution is concerned, approval by referendum. Although the more important constitutional laws and norms are well known,[5] there may exist less important ones that have long been forgotten.[6] For this reason, the consolidation of constitutional law has been regarded desirable for quite some time, but the task is deemed so difficult that this has so far prevented it from being undertaken.

It is still open to discussion whether there exists in Austria, apart from constitutional law in written form, also customary constitutional law. Some authors argue that customary law is no source of Austrian law because the Federal Constitution does not mention practice accompanied by *opinio iuris* as a law-creating procedure. Others would rely on the notion of customary law as a fundamental fact of any legal system,[7] and would claim that – since it could not even be ruled out by constitutional (written) law –

it would not, for its existence, require any positive mentioning therein. Others refer to Kelsen's hypothetical *Grundnorm*[8] (basic norm) that is still used by some as the starting point of constitutional (and over-all legal) theory, which has been formulated in such a way as to consider only an effective system of rules as a legal order. However, the conclusion drawn, namely, that – since a legal system could be considered effective even without containing norms of customary law – there is no need to regard the basic norm as delegating not only written but also non-written law, is not convincing; since even if a legal system could be effective without customary law, there is no reason why it should be regarded less effective with it. Thus, the basic norm, which is anyway no more than a fiction within a particular legal theory, cannot be invoked for the purpose of demonstrating that there may not exist constitutional custom in Austria. Rather, the practice of the main organs within the Austrian constitutional system – the so-called constitutional institutions – is certainly providing guidance for subsequent cases. Since, however, this practice has so far fulfilled the function of interpreting rather than derogating from written constitutional law, the question has never been pressed to its end.[9]

On the other hand, it is a hardly disputed fact that there exists a gap between constitutional law and constitutional reality, and that reality is sometimes even depriving constitutional rules of their original meaning.[10] This has something to do with the strong position held in Austria by the so-called social partners, i.e. the respective organisations of the employers, on the one hand, and of the employees, on the other. The fact that the various segments of the economy are organized in Chambers with compulsory membership[11] has incurred, for Austria, the designation of "Chamber State". Equally, because of the strong position of the political parties, which – through their leaders – control both government and parliament – Austria has become to be called a "Parties' State". Yet, both features, and particularly the latter one, Austria shares with other Member States, and it is fully compatible with a democratic political system.[12]

The Austrian Constitution has originally been conceived as a system of legal rules, and not – as may apply to some other constitutions – as a political declaration. This has not prevented the inclusion, more recently, of new parts that are of a primarily programmatic character the legal effect of which remains doubtful.[13]

While the Austrian Federal Constitution of 1920/29, strongly influenced by the normative system developed by Hans Kelsen in his *Pure Theory of Law*,[14] is formulated, as much as possible, in a politically indifferent manner, it does still contain certain basic principles that characterise Austria as a democratic[15] and liberal,[16] federal[17] and republican[18] State with the rule of law[19] and the respect for human rights and fundamental freedoms.[20] All these principles, which coincide also with the principles of the European Union as proclaimed in article 6 paragraph 1 EU[21], are considered as fundamental to the constitutional system, and any constitutional change that touches them requires approval by referendum. This leads us directly to the next issue.

b. The EU/EC architecture and national constitutional traditions: the Austrian case

The Austrian constitutional system has originally been conceived as a "closed" one. It was self-contained and allowed even international law to be construed as relevant only because, and only inasmuch as, recognised by the Constitution.[22] The basic principles upon which the whole superstructure of Austrian (constitutional and other) law rested, namely democracy, republicanism, federalism, separation of powers, liberalism, and the rule of law (to name the most basic of the basic), were all given a special meaning, which could not be separated from their context within the Austrian Constitution. Thus, from the wording of article 1 B-VG, according to which "Austria is a democratic republic. Her legal order originates in[23] the people",[24] the democratic principle was understood to mean that all legislative acts applicable in Austria would require, as their ultimate basis, the will of the *Austrian* people, and that they would therefore have to be enacted by a legislature elected, not just by a democratically constituted people, but by, and only by, the *Austrian* people.

(1) The Austrian Constitution and accession to the European Union

It was for this very reason that accession to the European Union was considered a fundamental change of the Austrian Constitution and thus required popular approval by referendum.

Since it would have been difficult to subject the Treaty of Accession – an extremely voluminous and complex instrument, including not only the Treaty proper,[25] but also the Act of Accession[26] and the Final Act[27] with numerous Protocols and Declarations[28] – itself to a referendum,[29] the referendum was held[30] about a one-time exception to the rule that fundamental changes in the Constitution require popular approval, and Parliament empowered to approve the Accession Treaty by that procedure which is normally sufficient only in cases where constitutional amendments do not affect the Constitution in a fundamental manner: at least one half of the deputies being present and two-thirds of those present voting in favour. This one-time exception was embodied in a so-called Accession Enabling Act.[31] An additional reason for this somewhat circumstantial procedure was the endeavour to avoid the problem of whether or not a fundamental change of the Constitution might be brought about by an international treaty (and not only by an act or acts of domestic law).[32] Accession was thus (albeit, from a formal point of view, only indirectly) approved by almost two-thirds of the votes cast in the referendum.[33]

Actually, the Austrian internal procedure for approval of accession to the European Union entailed two different fundamental changes to the Constitution. The first one was contained in the Accession Enabling Act and related to the exceptional power of Parliament to bring about the second one, namely the opening (as it has been termed) of the Austrian Constitution for the law of the EU, and of the EC, respectively. This latter, and much more important, because substantive, fundamental change was not brought about by the Accession Enabling Act but only by the subsequent approval given to the Accession Treaty by Parliament.

Only after popular approval having been obtained in the referendum, the Accession Treaty could be formally signed on 24 June 1994, and subjected to the procedure of ratification.[34] Of the two chambers of Parliament, the National Council *(Nationalrat)* gave its consent on 11 November 1994 by 141 votes in favour und 40 against, and the Federal Council on 17 November 1994 by 51 votes in favour and 8 against.[35] The instrument of ratification was deposited with the Italian Government, functioning as depositary, on 24 November 1994. The treaty entered into force on 1 January 1995.[36]

In addition to approving the Accession Treaty, Parliament adopted a so-called Accession Accompanying Act *(Beitritts-Begleitgesetz)*,[37] which brought about additional adaptations of the Constitution that were regarded necessary[38] or desirable.[39]

The fundamental change of the Constitution took effect with the coming into force of the Treaty on Accession. In addition, Austria had to implement numerous directives. They thus took effect upon implementation.[40] In those cases, however, where Austria was in default, the directives, if suited, took direct effect[41] after the time for implementation had expired.

(2) Adaptation of the Austrian Constitution to the requirements of EU membership

Here, mention shall be made only of the most important questions of the relationship between the Austrian legal order and the law of the EU, and of the EC, respectively.[42] It seems useful to deal, on the one hand, with the constitutional basis, and, on the other, with the method, by which EU/EC law is received as part of Austrian law, and, on the other, with the relationship of the former to the latter. In this connection, specific questions of implementation, execution, review, and legal protection have to be tackled.

The Accession Enabling Act had the constitutional effect of, first, unconditionally opening up the Austrian legal order for primary and secondary EU-EC-law. Unconditionally means that there do not exist, at least in principle,[43] any barriers to the reception of EU/EC law into Austrian law. It is for the EU/EC law to determine the ways and means by which it makes use of the opening up of the Austrian legal order.

Second, the Austrian legal order unconditionally recognizes the autonomous operative force of EU/EC law as elaborated in the case law of the ECJ. This is only a consequence of the obligation, connected with accession, of adopting the complete *acquis communautaire*.

Third, EU/EC law exclusively determines the effect taken by EU/EC law within the Austrian domestic legal order. The relevant criteria have to be observed even where EU/EC law leaves the choice of the means of its implementation and execution to Austrian law. Therefore, Austria's institutional, i.e. organisational and procedural, autonomy is a relative one only.

Accession to the European Union was the by far most incisive move in the course of Austria's constitutional development since her revolutionary emergence, after the First World War, as a State separate from the other parts of the former Austro-Hungarian monarchy, her transformation into a republic,[44] and the adoption of the Federal Constitution in 1920.[45] Even if her occupation (or annexation) by Hitler's Germany in 1938 and her resurrection as an independent country in 1945 may be considered politically equally important, there still exists a legal continuity on the basis of the Federal Constitution of 1920, as amended in 1929.

Prior to accession to the EU, Austria's legal order was open for rules of another legal order only in a very restricted manner. Right from the beginning, the Federal Constitution declared customary international law,[46] and international treaties if published in the (Austrian) Official Journal,[47] to be directly applicable in Austria. Since, however, customary international law, as well as treaties not elevated to constitutional rank, are not granted precedence over Austrian law but have to cede even to "simple" laws according to the maxim *lex posterior derogat legi priori* (the Austrian legal norm being always regarded as the later one), the effect of this early opening up of the Austrian legal order remained marginal.[48] In 1981, possibly as a late consequence of the conclusion of two free trade agreements with the EEC and the ECSC in 1972, a new paragraph 2 was inserted into article 9 B-VG, conveying the right of adopting decisions directly legally binding within the Austrian domestic legal order to international institutions.[49] Yet, this transfer of power was meant only for infrequent cases and was not considered a sufficient basis for acceding to the EU, with the profuse legislation emanating, especially, from the EC.[50]

Thus, the EU/EC architecture, which does not know of a separation of power between different organs or institutions, as once depicted by *Montesquieu*, but consists of a number of institutions that perform both legislative and administrative as well as controlling functions, and where the necessary equilibrium between these institutions is maintained through an elaborate system of checks and balances quite different from the traditional separation of power model, has not much in common with the Austrian constitutional structure. This has not, however, been regarded, for Austria's membership in the EU, an obstacle that could not be overcome. The Austrian constitutional order is a strictly positive one and does not know of any principles which could not be abrogated, or at least changed in its scoped, by a decision of the sovereign, i.e. the people, either acting indirectly through its representatives in Parliament, or directly through a referendum. The reinterpretation, by a combination of parliamentary approval and referendum-based enabling act,[51] of the democratic principle, albeit in a manner that did not affect its essence but rather on its Austrian peculiarities,[52] is proof of this.

Thus, from a formal point of view – and the Austrian legal approach is essentially a formal one – there is nothing in the Austrian Constitution that could prevent acceptance of any revision of the EU/EC architecture, as long as it is brought about in the way prescribed by article 48 EU, namely by a treaty among the Member States ratified by all of them after having obtained the necessary approval required under each of the various national constitutional orders.[53] Whether the Austrian Constitution has also a substantive core, and if so, whether it is therefore, to that extent, inalienable and resistant to integration, appears to be an academic question, open to discussion for those who choose to engage in it, but of little, if any, practical importance.[54]

2. *National Provisions for the adoption of a "Constitution" of the European Union*

a. *Constitutional conditions for and limits to further steps of integration (substance)*

The primarily, if not exclusively formal approach taken by the Austrian Constitution, has its direct bearings on the question of possible limits to further steps of integration. From the Austrian point of view, the legal, and, in particular, the constitutional aspect of the matter has to be strictly distinguished from the political, sociological, and any other aspect which forms the subject of the theory of law and state.

Whether, for instance, a "constitution" is more than just the organisational basis of any association of men or States, whether it thus implies so comprehensive a power of that association that its competences for the pursuance of the common good may be said to be, at least in principle, unlimited, and whether possession of such unlimited power is proper only for a State but not for an organisation of States, even a supranational one, is not a legal question. The same holds true for considerations about the relationship between a constitution and the people for the legal order of which it should serve as a basis. Whether a "constitution" is feasible only for a state-like entity because a constitution presupposes a group of human beings who consider themselves as a "people" that gives, as the original constituent power, validity to the entity's constitutional order, or whether all human beings united under a "constitution" are to be considered a "people" regardless of what they feel, think, or desire – whether, in other words, the "people" form the "State" or the "State" (and any similar institution) forms its "people", is a question for scholars of political theory but not for constitutional lawyers. (And even the former may be said to have widely differing opinions in this matter.)

From the Austrian constitutional point of view, any new treaty, whether regrouping or expanding the provisions of those treaties which are presently at the basis of the EU and the EC, respectively, would have to be considered just another revision treaty, and would therefore have to be treated as any other revision treaty in the past.

(1) Precedent Amsterdam Treaty

The revisions brought about by the Treaty of Amsterdam of 1997[55], and those to be effectuated by the Treaty of Nice of 2000/2001[56] after its eventual entering into force, have caused, in the course of the procedure of ratification and for the purpose of the internal approval required, the adoption, by Parliament, of two more Enabling Acts and Accompanying Acts[57].

The National Council adopted the Enabling Act for the ratification of the Amsterdam Treaty as a special federal constitutional law in 1998. Since the Treaty was not considered having the effect of fundamentally changing the Austrian Constitution, there was no need for a referendum.[58] Yet, if the Amsterdam Treaty did not affect the Austrian constitutional order fundamentally, it still did so substantially, namely in the area of security policy. Already on the occasion of accession to the EU, the Austrian Federal Government had declared Austria's permanent neutrality to have been reduced to its hard core: Austria would not enter into any military alliance, would not have foreign troops stationed on Austrian territory, and would not participate in wars between other States.[59] It was generally agreed that the UN was not to be considered a military alliance,[60] measures of collective security not a war,[61] and soldiers under UN mandate[62] not foreign troops.

Yet, Austria's security policy is more closely related to the developments within the framework of the EU; in the course of her accession she had assured her future partner countries that there was nothing in her Constitution that would prevent her from fully participating in the CFSP.[63] Indeed, already then had Austria's obligations to cooperate within the CFSP been at least partly implemented by the Accession Accompanying Act inserting, into the Constitution, a new article 23e, which permits her participation in embargo measures adopted by the EU. If this provision concerned economic sanctions, the taking over, by the EU in the Amsterdam Treaty, of the Petersberg tasks[64] – comprising not only humanitarian and rescue actions but also measures for coping with crises, including military actions for the preservation or restoration of peace[65] – lead to a revision of article 23f of the Austrian Constitution, expressly enabling the country to participate, without restriction, in all measures within the Petersberg tasks. [66]

Against such participation, it would be of no avail to invoke the Constitutional Law on Austria's Permanent Neutrality of 1955[67], because the 1998 revision of article 27f of the Austrian Constitution had insofar a derogatory effect on that Law.[68] Under these circumstances, when the European Council decided, in 1999, to set up a Rapid Reaction Force in order to make the EU capable of quickly coping with crises and taking the necessary measures in fulfilment of the Petersberg tasks, Austria had no constitutional difficulties to declare, at a Capabilities Commitment Conference of Member States held in November 2000 for the purpose of establishing the strength of their respecting contingents, her readiness to place at the disposal of the EU combat troops in a number equal to that of comparable Member States. Austria's participation in operations of the Rapid Reaction Force is fully covered by article 27f B-VG as amended.[69]

(2) Precedent Nice Treaty

Ratification, by Austria, of the Treaty of Nice was brought on its way in 2001, when Parliament gave the necessary approval. To maintain consistency, this was again done in the form of an Enabling Act, which was adopted by the National Council on 17 November 2001.[70]

In contrast to the Accession Treaty of 1994 and the Amsterdam Treaty of 1997, the Nice Treaty does not seem to involve particular material changes of the Austrian Constitution.

(3) Conclusions deriving from the Amsterdam and Nice precedents

For the Austrian Constitution, it would not make any difference whether or not a new treaty embodying a kind of EU/EC "constitution" would be termed "constitution", e.g. the "Constitution of the European Union". Austrian understanding would not restrict application of this term to the constitution of a state, whether unitarian or federal; the basic instrument of the EU/EC may also be termed the Union's/Community's "constitution".

Actually, this Austrian approach does not seem to differ so much from the common understanding of the term "constitution", for past and present doctrine[71] and practice[72] throughout the EU/EC has come to speak of the primary law as of the "constitutional treaties". The meaning of the term "constitution" as it is used in normal language does not seem to transport all those specific connotations, which are attributed to it by this or that school of political theory. Rather, it is open for different application, and its meaning depends primarily on how it is defined. Giving it, first, a restrictive definition, and proving, thereafter, that – because of the definition – it has only a restrictive field of application, is a way of unnecessarily tying oneself. It certainly cannot have a binding effect on others by obliging them to accept the definition and the conclusion deriving from it.

This does not exclude, of course, the possibility that Austrian politicians, and even Austrian constitutional scholars, may, in any future, invoke one or the other principle contained in the Austrian Constitution for the purpose of claiming that a "Constitution" of the EU would be incompatible with this principle. Yet, such a claim would be unfounded for the reasons already propounded, and any such invocation of constitutional principles against the adoption of a constitution for the EU would have to be considered a political manoeuvre using allegedly legal arguments as a welcome pretext for attaining a political goal; because, for the great majority of people, legal arguments are difficult to understand, and even more difficult to refute.

b. Procedural requirements under Austrian constitutional provisions

While the Maastricht Treaty on European Union received its constitutional sanction in Austria under the aggravated conditions of article 50 paragraph 3 B-VG (ie through the Accession Enabling Act approved by referendum and the subsequent approval of the Accession Treaty by the qualified majority of the National Council), it could be argued, with regard to future enlargement and consolidation treaties, that the Accession Enabling Act of 1994 already covers any further steps towards a higher degree of integration, making referenda[73] and perhaps even qualified parliamentary majorities[74] dispensable, and approval under the alleviated conditions of article 50 paragraph 1 B-VG[75] sufficient.[76]

However, the idea of proceeding on this line did not rally much support. For reasons of constitutional systemic uniformity, it was decided to stick to the precedent set on the occasion of accession, and to make use, as a basis for the approval of revision treaties, of the special form of an enabling act, either adopted by Parliament alone or, if a fundamental constitutional change should be involved, by a referendum. This procedure was followed with regard to both the Amsterdam and the Nice Treaty; and any deviation from it in the future is unlikely. This applies also to the approval of an eventual "Constitution of the European Union", which would also have to be regarded, from the point of view of Austria's constitutional law, a kind of revision treaty. Since it would even be possible, by way of referendum, to fully give up Austria's sovereignty and to merge her, with one or more other countries, into a new State, any less incisive restriction of her sovereignty, even by a "Constitution of the European Union", has to be considered constitutionally all the more possible.[77]

While treaties which are concluded by the EU or the EC without participation of the Member States belong to those sources of EU/EC law the provisions of which are received, under certain conditions, in the domestic legal order, so-called mixed treaties, ie those in which not only the EU or the EC but also the Member States take part, require, for conclusion, observance of their constitutional rules. Accordingly, all treaties that affect Austrian constitutional or "simple" law have to be approved by Parliament with the necessary respective majority.

c. *The role of the citizens: international treaty or European social contract?*

This question relates to different aspects of the problem of an eventual "Constitution of the EU". Mention of the role of the citizens refers to the issue of making the EU/EC more comprehensible to the man in the street, which is certainly a political aspect. The alternatives, for a European constitution, of assuming either the character of an international treaty or of a European social contract contain a socio-political as well as a legal aspect; and both should not be mixed up.

(1) The citizens and a Constitution of the European Union

Making the EU/EC more citizen-oriented is certainly a general political desideratum that is shared by Austria. To give the Union, and the Community, respectively, a so-to-say constitutional basis that is more easily comprehensible than the present jumble of "constitutional" treaties with their complex structure, which makes institutional as well as substantive EU/EC law increasingly a kind of secret science accessible only to a restricted number of specialists, is a political goal that is supported by the Austrian government. In this connection, the EU Charter of Fundamental Rights, as approved by the European Council of Nice in December 2000, is regarded a first step, which will display its full importance as soon as it is elevated to the rank of a formal legal instrument from which direct rights and duties derive for the citizens.[78] High expectations are also connected with the eventual drawing up of a catalogue of competences, delimitating, in a clear way, the powers of the EU/EC and those of the Member States.

Austria could also go along with an increase of the legislative power of the EP, even to a point where European legislation would be entrusted to the Council (as a kind of Federal Council or House of States) and to the Parliament (as a House of the Peoples of Europe) on an equal footing. In contrast to the directly elected Parliament, the Council should remain a forum for the governments of the Member States (somewhat similar to the German *Bundesrat*), with weighted voting and the requirement of qualified majority.

Since the members of the Commission are, rightly or not, widely regarded, in the States of their respective nationality, as the countries' personified link to the EU/EC and therefore the rallying point of integration, transforming the Commission into *the* executive organ of the EU/EC and thus to a kind of European government, might also make the Union, and the Community, respectively, more comprehensible, and thus emotionally more acceptable, to the man in the street. Such a European Government, which would – while staying strictly within the framework of primary and secondary law as created, on the one hand, by the Member States, and, on the other, by co-decision of Parliament and Council – act in the sole interest of the EU/EC (an interest that transcends the sum total of the interests of the Member States), might even contribute to the emergence of a European-wide public opinion, which could be the starting point for a development at the end of which there could be something like a European nation, even if this European nation would not be a substitute for, but a special combination of, the nations of the individual Member States.

Proceeding with the elaboration of a legal text or texts that would have to be regarded a European Constitution, or at least part or parts of one, whatever the designation of such an instrument, could initiate a dialectic process by which the constitutional development of the EU/EC and the development of the various nations in Europe into one European nation would be mutually facilitated and enhanced.

(2) Treaty v. social contract

If we understand by the social contract fundamental legal rules adopted by a *pouvoir constituant*, i.e. by an assembly of representatives of the people decided to set up a new commonwealth, whether these fundamental rules are called a constitution, the assembly a convent, and the commonwealth a state or otherwise, the constituent power exercised by the assembly will either be delegated or original. If delegated, it will derive from the former constitution of the same commonwealth, or from the combined constitutional powers of a plurality of commonwealths intending to merge into a single one. If original, it will derive from a revolutionary act by which the people, or its representatives, or those who have the power to effectively claim that they speak for the people, create a new fundamental legal order that has no direct connection with the former one.

Since revolutions are the consequence of serious economic, social, and political crises, it is neither desirable nor likely that a European Constitution, ie a constitution for that part of Europe that is formed by the Member States of the European Union, will emerge from turmoil and revolutionary transformation. Consequently, even if a body the composition of which would permit to speak of a constituent assembly should elaborate the eventual European Constitution, this assembly would have to be empowered by the present holders of supreme power, ie by the Member States, which – while united in a Union – still continue to be essentially sovereign.[79] It is therefore for the Member States to decide, by common consent, about the ways and means of elaborating a Constitution of the European Union. Viewed in this way, it will always be an international treaty that is at the basis of the future constitution.

The question "International treaty or social contract?" comes down to the option, for the Member States, of whether they are going to convoke a constituent assembly with the power of adopting a constitution on its own, or whether such a constitution will be worked out by an intergovernmental conference and laid down in an international treaty. Yet, the question is moot, because the Member States have already made their decision, and have opted for a two-phase procedure – a convent similar to a constituent assembly for the elaboration of a draft constitution but without the power to adopt it, and an intergovernmental conference, which will transform the draft into an international treaty that would have to be adopted by the Member States and ratified according to their respective constitutional requirements.

Option for such a combined procedure, with the accent on the intergovernmental conference, strongly indicates that Member States do not presently intend to transfer the core elements of sovereignty to the EU/EC, and that the process of creation of a European Constitution has the purpose of making more easily understandable the structure and powers of the EU/EC that already exist rather than to substantially transform that structure or essentially enlarge these powers. This coincides with the approach taken by Austria, insofar as the Austrian government believes that, at the time of imminent enlargement, it is more important to secure what has already been reached in the process of European unification and to prevent the EU/EC system from getting diluted. Therefore, attention must be paid to all draft proposals for a European Constitution from the point of view of retaining the *acquis communautaire*, and any attempt to turn back the wheel of the history of integration, on the one hand, as well as to change the present balance between big and small Member States to the detriment of the latter, on the other, has, in the Austrian view, to be strictly opposed.

3. *The constitution-making process: preparing the IGC 2004 in practice*

Austria takes great interest in the process of constitution making and the preparation of the inter-governmental conference envisaged for 2004.[80]

a. How is the internal debate on the future of the European Union organised?

When the European Council of Nice in December 2000 adopted the

"Declaration on the Future of the European Union",[81] Austria started forthwith, on her part, to set in motion an internal debate on the future of the European Union. For this purpose, various initiatives were taken.[82]

On Wednesday 30 May 2001 the first "Round Table on Europe" *("Europarunde")* took place in the "Hofburg" in Vienna. Representatives of all politically relevant institutions, of the states *(Länder),* of the Administrative and the Constitutional Court, of the European Commission, and of the European Parliament, as well as experts in European affairs took part in this discussion. Speakers in the debate were, *inter alia,* Federal Chancellor *Schüssel*, Vice Chancellor *Riess-Passer*, Minister of Foreign Affairs *Ferrero-Waldner*, First President of the Austria National Council *Fischer*, Third President of the National Council *Fasslabend*, Chairmen of parliamentary clubs *Khol* and *Gusenbauer*, President of the Austrian Federal Chamber of Commerce *Leitl,* President of the Constitutional Court *Adamovich*, Advocate-General of the ECJ *Stix-Hackl*, Judge of the European Court of First Instance *Azizi*, Member of the European Parlament *Stenzel*, former Minister for Science *von Einem*, Professors *Schweitzer* and *Hummer*, and Dr. *Gebetsroithner*.

Topics dealt with were the key issues arising for the Union's future development, for example: What do European citizens expect from the Union? How is the division of competence between the Union and the Member States to be organised? And within the Union, how is the division of powers between the institutions to be organised? Should there be a European constitution at all? How should the Charter of Fundamental Rights be related to it? Thus, a broad and intensive discussion process was started by the "*Europarunde*" and, Austria is – as Federal Chancellor *Wolfgang Schüssel* stated in his concluding remarks – the first country in Europe to engage in so extensive a discussion.

On 21 February 2002 the second "Europarunde" took place. The main item under discussion was the European Union Convention,[83] which took up its work on 1 March 2002. Austria also nominated her representatives and deputy representatives for the Convent, viz. *Hannes Farnleitner*, *Caspar Einem*, *Gerhard Tusek*, *Reinhard Bösch*, *Eva Lichtenberger*, *Gerhard Kurzmann*, *Johannes Voggenhuber*, *Reinhard Rack*, and *Maria Berger*, among them two former cabinet ministers and a number of Members of the European Parliament.[84]

b. What are the key issues and proposals of the leading political groups?

In Austria, there exist four political parties that are represented in Parliament and therefore may be considered leading political groups. The government is formed by the Austrian People's Party *(Österreichische Volkspartei)* with Federal Chancellor *Wolfgang Schüssel* and by the Austrian Freedom Party *(Freiheitliche Partei Österreichs)* with Vice-

Chancellor *Elfriede Riess-Passer*. The parties in opposition are the Social-Democratic Party of Austria *(Sozialdemokratische Partei Österreich)* and the Ecological and Alternative Party *(Grüne und Alternative Österreichs,* shortly termed *"Die Grünen")*. Of those, the People's Party and the Social-Democrats support enlargement of the EU as well as its organic development more or less unconditionally, while the Freedom Party inclines to instrumentalising questions and problems of integration for domestic political purposes, and the "Greens" have been converted from fundamental critics to cautious supporters of the EU only since they have found themselves in opposition to the Freedom Party, which they detest for being populist. The position of these four parties may be summarized as follows.[85]

The Austrian People´s Party´s main aim is to achieve a constitution that strictly devides the competences between the European Union and the Member States. Fundamental rights have to play an important role in this Constitution. The establishment of a parallel structure to the European Convention of Human Rights is not seen as a positive element. The Austrian People´s Party does not share the view that national parliaments have not enough weight in the European Union. It is not a duty of the European Union to secure the influence of national parliaments as this lies within the competence of each national constitution, and has been taken care of, in Austria, by article 23 B-VG.[86] There is, of course, a necessity to transform the European Parliament into a Parliament endowed with full competences, as, e.g., in the budgetary field, and with the right of legislative initiative..

The Austrian Freedom Party is in favour of both the Convention and the "Europarunde", both believed to be a good chance for a broad dialogue about the future of the European Union. Strict division of powers between the Member States and the European Union, is considered desirable, as the Freedom Party regards the principle of subsidiarity one of the most important principles of the Union. Stress is laid on the simplification of the constitutional treaties, and the strengthening of the role of national parliaments. Thus, the Freedom Party is not, at least in principle, against an European Constitution, as it hopes that a Constitution would stop the ongoing discussion about the correct division of powers and what it considers the inherent threat of curtailing Member States competences at each Council meeting.

For the Social-Democratic Party of Austria the democratisation of the institutions has to be the first step towards a European Constitution. Citizens must have the opportunity to state their opinion. In addition to that, the Charta of Fundamental Rights has to be part of a European Constitution. Whether this Treaty bears the title "constitution" or not, is not important. The decisive issue, in the view of the Social-Democratic

Party, is the opportunity, for everyone, to pursue his or her rights. In general, the Social-Democratic Party also stresses the importance and the advantages of the European integration process for each individual and for Europe as a whole. The Social-Democratic Party is of the opinion that framing a European constitution would be a means to have democracy take firm roots on the transnational level; thus, the legitimacy of EU policies would be strengthened. In addition, citizens should have the opportunity of political action on the European level. The Social-Democratic Party does not consider necessary a European "state building" process in the traditional sense for the realisation of the project of a European constitution.

The Ecological and Alternative Party is of the opinion that is important to adopt a European Constitution in order to achieve the transition from a nation-based to an Europe-based sense of identity. A European constitution could re-establish the "sovereignty of the people(s)" on the transnational level and should embody their rights of participation and co-determination as well as certain "basic rights".

c. The position of the Austrian government

The position taken by the Austrian government is more or less in line with the views of the People's Party, since a pro-European attitude has been written into the coalition agreement, concluded with the Freedom Party in early 2000. Federal Chancellor *Wolfgang Schüssel* has repeatedly made it quite clear that support for the enlargement of the EU and a positive approach to a sound development of the Union is a *conditio sine qua non* for the continuation of the present coalition.

The position of the Austrian government is reflected in various statements made on a number of occasions. No formal paper has so far been adopted.[87] Yet, the position of the Austrian government may be circumscribed by declaring a Europe that is democratic and citizen-oriented to be a fundamental goal for a European constitution. Austria can be counted among those Member States that favour a Constitution as compared to a mere simplification of the constitutional treaties. The constitution should include the Charta of Fundamental Rights and a catalogue of powers of the EU/EC, and of the Member States, respectively. This attitude is also shown in various initiatives[88] taken by the Austrian government. According to a statement made by Federal Chancellor *Schüssel* in Parliament, the Unions capacity to act speedily, also as regards its CFSP, on the one hand, and the sovereign equality of Member States within the institutional and procedural framework of the EU/EC, appear, apart from securing the fundamental rights of the citizens of the EU, to be the essential issues that have to be dealt with in the course of elaborating a European Constitution.[89]

II. RELATIONSHIP AND INTERACTION OF EU/EC LAW AND NATIONAL CONSTITUTIONS TODAY

Under this heading, a stock taking of the present situation[90] as well as a reflection on what seems to be desirable for the future is imperative. However, as regards the future, it seems preferable to start from the *status quo*, in order to avoid speculations that would have little, if any relationship to European reality.[91]

1. Member States' constitutional autonomy under European constraints

This issue should not be discussed without a prior clarification. Member States' constitutional autonomy is not a value in itself, but has always to be weighed against the advantages deriving from a restriction of that autonomy. The limits placed on external and internal sovereignty correspond to the needs that cause States to conclude international treaties and to set up international or supranational organisations. Limits on sovereignty are the consequence of every international treaty that creates mutual rights and duties for the parties, and is certainly no peculiarity of European integration. There is a great probability that Member States have not, in the past, transferred powers to the EU/EC in an inconsiderate manner and without necessity; this fact once accepted, there is no need to lament the ensuing constraints on their constitutional autonomy. Discussion on Member States' constitutional autonomy and possible European constraints to it have, therefore, to be held in a way that is not right from the beginning overshadowed by prejudices in favour of constitutional autonomy and against constraints on it.

Moreover, any inventory of the present relationship between the EU/EC and the Member States and their constitutions is always *de lege lata.* Nothing can prevent the Member States of revising, in one or the other direction, this relationship; and therefore nothing can be gained, from an analysis of it, for the process *de lege ferenda.*

a. National identities of the Member States as a limit to the extension of the EC/EU competencies

In this context, reference is made to article 6.3 EU, which provides that "[t]he Union shall respect the national identities of its Member States." As concerns culture, the principle is more closely elaborated in article 151 EC, especially paragraphs 1 and 4. The first paragraph calls for respect for the national and regional cultural diversity; and the fourth paragraph goes even further, since the Community undertakes therein not only "to respect" but also "to promote the diversity of its cultures".

If such provisions may be regarded a clear declaration of policy, their legal value must not be overrated. First of all, they must be read in the context of both treaties; this reduces the respect for the national identity of the Member States to an accessory principle, perhaps the most important one, but still only accessory. The European Union was established for the promotion of "peace, security and progress in Europe and in the world",[92] especially for the promotion of "economic and social progress for the[.] peoples [of the Member States]"[93] and for upholding "the principles of liberty, democracy ad respect for human rights and fundamental freedoms and of the rule of law",[94] and, all together, for the creation of "firm bases for the construction of the future Europe",[95] so that the "division of the European continent"[96] may be ended once and for ever. To reach these goals, the preamble of the Treaty on European Union states the desire of the Member States "to deepen the solidarity between their peoples while respecting their history, their culture and their traditions"[97] It appears clearly that respect for the national identity was not the first and foremost end the founding fathers had in view; it is secondary to the other ends listed in the Treaty.

For this reason, the principle of respect for the national identities of the Member States cannot be regarded a limit to the full exercise, by the EU, or the EC, respectively, of the powers conferred on them for the attainment of their object and purpose, including the competencies under article 308 EC. If the latter provision were, as its sometimes is, to be considered as a power for the creation of new powers necessary for achieving the ends for which the Treaties were concluded, it would be correct to say that article 6.3 EU does not even prevent the extension of the EU/EC competencies.[98]

The same is true for the more specific respect for the cultural national and regional diversities. Article 151 itself provides for cooperation of the Member States in the cultural field, either among themselves[99] or with third countries.[100] For the achievement of these (as all other) objectives referred to in article 151 EC, the Council may adopt incentive measures[101] and recommendations.[102] Even if harmonisation of the laws and regulations of the Member States is expressly excluded,[103] they have the obligation of taking into consideration the recommendations issued by the Council; and the latter's incentive measures will also not remain without effect. Moreover, it goes without saying that article 151 EC, the purpose of which is the promotion of the cultural diversity of the Community, cannot be invoked as an absolute barrier against measures taken by the EC for the fulfilment of the great number of other tasks entrusted to it by the Treaty. And here again, it can be shown from its preamble that the respect for cultural diversity belongs, at the best, to the peripheral, not to the central goals of the EC.[104]

If the principle of respect for the national identities of the Member States is no insurmountable obstacle on the level of secondary law, all the more is it no impediment for changes in the area of primary law, and does not prevent any revision of the constitutional treaties that the Member States should see fit. It is a question of political desirability, and not of legal possibility, whether the EU/EC competencies are – notwithstanding the principle of respect for the national identities of the Member States – extended, for instance on the occasion of the adoption of a European Constitution.

The reverse is, of course, also correct. A new Constitution for the Union does not necessarily imply the extension of the powers of the EU, or EC, respectively, unless the term "constitution" is reserved to the fundamental law of an (albeit federal) state that disposes of unlimited powers, at least in principle. But such terminological purity is neither generally accepted in doctrine nor necessary in practice, and is, as was already shown,[105] alien also to everyday legal terminology.

Having said all this, a remark should be made that, even if it seems to be somewhat belated, hits the very core of the question. As it is formulated, the question of Member State identity v. extension of EU/EC competencies already contains, in fact, a *petitio principii,* namely, that national identities of the Member States and the extension of EU/EC competencies are excluding each other. National identities and EU/EC powers are not like communicating containers, where that the rise in the one means a decline in the other. Such an arithmetic approach seems to be somewhat simple-minded; it is not the number of the EU/EC competencies that counts, it is the quality of the construction that is endowed with these powers. Even a highly integrated entity may scrupulously respect, even strengthen, the identities of its component parts; and a far less integrated entity may, if there is no awareness of the need to respect their identities, encroach on them.

The best example is offered by the language question within the EU/EC. For the preservation of the national identities of Member States it is by far more important to recognise the equal status of all languages of all them, present and future, than to retain the requirement of unanimity in the Council in certain fields where certain Member States claim to have a special interest. The prevalence, in the institutions of the EU/EC, of French, right from the beginning, and of French and English, at the present, with little, if any, regard for German, Italian, or Spanish, to name only those other languages which are also spoken by an at least comparable number of citizens of the Union, and the danger of the emergence, or perhaps even ordainment, of a kind of *lingua franca* for the EU/EC, is a much more serious threat to the national identities of Member States than some minor issue of competence. It is to this problem, and, more particularly, to the question of how to secure equal rights to all languages of the Member States, big or small, that the attention of those who rally behind the flag of national identity should be directed.

b. The basic principles of the Union as limits to the constitutional autonomy of the Member States

This issue is but the other side of the coin of whether there may exist, within the constitutional order of the Member States, a so-called integration-resistant core.[106] If this theory speculates about the consequences of the EU/EC violating the very principles on which it is based, articles 6 and 7 EU envisage a Member State that commits a serious and persistent breach of the principles of liberty, democracy, respect for human rights and fundamental freedoms, and the rule of law, which are common to the Member States and the foundation of the Union.[107]

If observance of these principles is part of the *raison d'être* of the Union, and the Community, respectively, it is also the *conditio sine qua non* for admission of a State to the EU/EC, and, if already admitted, for its full participation in their work. Although the procedure, contained in article 7 paragraph 1 EU for the determination of a violation of the just mentioned principles, lacks – in its present version as inserted by the Amsterdam Treaty – the necessary guarantees of the very principle of the rule of law proclaimed in article 6 paragraph 1,[108] and although the amendments provided for in connection with article 7 EU by the Nice Treaty will only partly remedy this situation, the substance of the two articles, taken together, namely, that the said principles may not be violated, by a Member State, with impunity, and that it has therefore to reckon with sanctions, is a matter of course within a political and legal system that wants to be taken seriously.

Basic principles of a community will always have, as a logical consequence, the character of limits on the autonomy of its members. Such limits are no more lamentable than those that are imposed by criminal law upon potential offenders. This is so axiomatic that, in the Austrian view, it has no real bearing on the discussion concerning the issue of a Constitution of the Union, and need not even be brought up in this connection. If these basic principles have a limiting effect on the constitutional autonomy of the Member States, than it is in only a very formal way.

Remains to be pointed out that it is, from a political point of view, detrimental for the development of the EU, with our without a "constitution", if articles 6 and 7, or even the idea behind them, are abused for political reason in order to illegitimately intervene in the internal affairs of a Member State.[109]

2. Common values: the Charter of Fundamental Rights of the European Union

a. Does the Charter reflect the basic human rights standards of the Austrian Constitution and Austria law?

Austria's national catalogue of human rights and fundamental freedoms goes back to 1862, and 1867, respectively. The Law for the Protection of Personal Freedom,[110] the Law for the Protection of the Home,[111] and the Fundamental State Law on the General Rights of the Citizens,[112] have been received by the Federal Constitution of 1920 and are still valid. In addition, the European Convention on Human Rights and Fundamental Freedoms[113] is directly applicable within the Austrian domestic legal system since 1964.[114] Thus, Austrian law has for a long time reflected the highest standards of human rights in Europe.

In addition, Austria is also party to the European Social Charter, which, however, because of the special nature of the rights guaranteed by it, cannot be of the same direct applicability as an instrument embodying the classic civic and political rights.

The Charter of Fundamental Rights of the European Union appears to reflect the basic human rights standards of Austrian constitutional and other law.[115] The fact that it was approved unanimously, and thus also with the consent of Austria, by the European Council in Nice 2000, may, in this regard, serve as *prima facie* evidence. Whether, apart from the question of meeting basic human right standards, the Charter exceeds, or, by the way, lags behind, the exact measure of protection enjoyed by the different kinds of fundamental rights in Austria, it is to early to decide, especially at a time when the legal nature of the Charter within the EU system itself is still open to discussion.

b. The Charter as a reference for fundamental rights protection in national courts

As long as the legal character of the Charter is not clarified, its direct application within Austria's domestic law seems excluded. And even if, perhaps on the occasion of the next revision of the Maastricht Treaty and/or the eventual adoption of a European Constitution, the Charter may be declared to have binding effect, the issue of direct applicability in Austria will depend on whether the Charter is intended to create such an effect and, therefore, to form part of the Union's supranational law, be it within or without the first pillar.[116]

For the time being, the Charter is no more than a compilation of the various categories of fundamental rights in the EU/EC, which the Member States have not yet been ready to elevate to the position of a legally binding instrument, perhaps afraid of opening what some of them may regard as a *Pandora's* box. Since the Charter does not have a legal character, it cannot even be regarded as an authentic basis for the interpretation of Member State law in conformity with EU/EC law.

This is not to say that the Charter is of no relevance at all before Austrian courts (and administrative authorities). At least, it is an interpretation of the European standards concerning human rights and fundamental freedoms, undertaken, in a common effort, by all Member States and therefore having on its side those principles which give authority to it and call for its perusal, as a source of reference, not only by Community institutions but also by the organs of the Member States.

Of course, the timidity of the Member States, which shrank back from granting the Charter a legal character, has made it impossible, for the time being, to regard it a first integral part of a future European Constitution, and does not augur well for a decisive breakthrough in the process of elaborating one.

c. The impact of the Charter on the standards referred to in article 6.1 EU

Had the Charter been adopted as a legally binding instrument and thereby become part of primary EU/EC law, the principles of interpretation would require that both texts – article 6 paragraph 1 EU on the one hand, and the Charter, on the other, – are read in the context of each other. Even if article 6 paragraph 1 EU would have to be regarded a central provision of the Treaty, and the Charter in contrast, an attempt only to elaborate in more detail the (or some of the) conclusions to be drawn from that provision, and if it would therefore always be possible to go back to article 6 paragraph 1 EU itself and to interpret it according to its own merits, it goes without saying that the Charter would exercise, in practice, a considerable influence upon the interpretation of article 6 paragraph 1 EU, because it would provide at least *prima facie* evidence for the understanding the Member States intended those principles to be given.

Being presently no more than a political declaration, the Charter is all the less capable of impairing the principles referred to in article 6 paragraph 1 EU. Yet again, this does not make it devoid of any relevance for construing the principles mentioned there. The general presumption, namely that it is a correct interpretation of the European standards concerning human rights and fundamental freedoms, works also in connection with the EU's basic principles, inasmuch they are elaborated in more detail in the Charter. Therefore, the Charter will also serve as a source of reference for the better understanding of, and substantial consequences deriving from, these principles.

If the case law of the ICJ in connection with the Charter is scarce, not to say practically inexistent, the same is true for the Austrian courts that have not yet come to give an opinion on the relationship between it and the principles mentioned in article 6 paragraph 1 EU.

3. The question of the supremacy of EU/EC law and its constitutional effects

The constitutional effect of the supremacy of EU/EC law is only one aspect of the general question of the EU/EC law's supremacy.

Here, the Austrian position is clear and in conformity with that taken by the ECJ. Accession to the EU by the various consecutive steps dealt with earlier[117] has resulted, *inter alia*, in a reception of EU/EC law into the Austrian domestic legal order. This reception of EU/EC law has also caused a reception of the consequences, for the Austrian legal order, that follow from EU/EC law itself. Among the main consequences – direct applicability, direct effect, and supremacy of EU/EC law where so required –, the principle of supremacy is the most important one. If an Austrian legal norm, whether enacted before or after the coming into being of a norm of EU/EC law that is directly applicable or of direct effect, appears to be incompatible with that norm of EU/EC law, the Austrian courts and administrative authorities must not apply it.

In this connection, reception of EU/EC law has effects on substantive as well as on procedural Austrian law. In the first case, the substantive Austrian norm is substituted by the EU/EC rule relating to the same subject matter. In the second, the procedural requirements of EU/EC law for proceedings before Austrian courts and administrative authorities have to be observed and Austrian procedural rules, if incompatible with these requirements, have to be disregarded.

Reception of the EU/EC law extends not only to its written part but also to the non-written ones. What has been received, is the entire *acquis communautaire*, as it appears from the practice within the EU/EC and particularly from the case law of the ECJ. Reception of the non-written parts of EU/EC law is of special importance in all cases where a limitation of Austria's legal autonomy derives only from principles of the EU/EC law that are but implicitly contained therein and have been formulated only in the course of time. Special mention should be made, in this connection, of the principles of proportionality, of effectiveness, and of equivalence.

Since written EU/EC law is only partly, and in fact only in exceptional cases, published in the Austrian Federal Official Journal *(Bundesge-setzblatt)*, one might speak also of, not reception but adoption of EU/EC law into Austrian domestic law by a command of application resulting from the Accession Treaty approved and published on the bases of the Accession Enabling Act of 1994.[118] Source of reference for EU/EC law is the Official Journal of the European Communities, to be renamed into Official Journal of the European Union after the entering into force of the Nice Treaty. The constitutional treaties, originally not contained in the EC Official Journal, have in the mean time been published therein, as well as in the Austrian Federal Official Journal.

a. *Primary and secondary Community law, the question of primacy, and Austrian constitutional law*

As regards the primacy of Community law, there is no difference, in

Austria, between primary and secondary Community law, on the one hand, and between constitutional and "simple" national law, on the other. Any norm of Community law, whether contained in the constitutional treaties or in the legislative acts of Community institutions, has primacy over any norm of national law, whether contained in the Constitution or in "simple" law. This applies even to the so-called fundamental or basic principles of the Constitution (the so-called *Baugesetze*[119]). Whether there exists an exception to this rule where the so-called integration-resistant core of the Constitution is concerned,[120] is of no practical importance, as long as the EU/EC does not completely degenerate into a system where the Union's own basic principles – democracy, liberty, respect for human rights, and the rule of law – are no longer respected.[121]

b. Implicit modification of national constitutions by the revision and application of the Treaty on European Union

According to the relationship between EU/EC law and domestic law as laid down in the constitutional treaties and established in the case law of the ECJ, a relationship that is governed, first and foremost, by the principles of direct application, or effect, respectively, and of supremacy of EU/EC law where so required by the latter, implicit modification of national constitutions by the revision and application of the Maastricht Treaty are immanent to the system. Whether the same result is reached if the relationship is looked upon from the point of view of domestic, and more specifically, constitutional law of the individual Member State, is a matter to be decided by domestic law. Since, however, the institutional and procedural autonomy of the Member States is limited by the very principle of supremacy of EU/EC law over Member State law, whether constitutional or other, Member States have an obligation to conform, and adapt, their domestic, and therefore also their constitutional law, to the requirements of EU/EC law. In addition, Member States may not invoke, before the ECJ and other EU/EC institutions, their domestic law in order not to comply with the demands of EU/EC law, including the principle of supremacy, and national Courts and administrative authorities, too, would have – even from the point of view of Austrian law – to disregard any norm of national law, constitutional or other, inconsistent with the principles of supremacy and direct application or effect.

Non-compliance with the obligation, existing for a Member State, to bring its domestic law fully in line with the requirements of EU/EC law, would constitute a violation of the constitutional treaties and thus offer a general legal basis for an action pursuant to articles 226 or 227 EC,[122] or, where it is provided for, a special basis for an action pursuant to article 46 EU.[123]

In Austria, revision of the Maastricht Treaty could also bring about a modification of the Constitution by implication, as has in fact been the case with the Amsterdam[124] and the Nice Treaty.[125] Since that opinion among Austrian constitutional scholars, which gives to the constitutional acts performed at the occasion of Austria's accession to the EU the effect of sanctioning all future constitutional modification even without further constitutional measures, has not prevailed, revisions of the Maastricht Treaty call for the observance of the constitutional procedures that are required for changing constitutional law. Therefore, at least qualified approval by Parliament[126] will be necessary; and if the revision of the Maastricht Treaty should be considered as affecting the fundamental principles of the Austrian Constitutions, even a referendum would be required.[127] Yet, since article 48 EU provides for "amendment of the Treaties on which the Unions founded"[128] to be "ratified by all the Member States in accordance with their respective constitutional requirements",[129] no incompatibility between EU/EC law, on the one hand, and Austrian constitutional law, on the other, should arise.

It is probable that approval of future revisions of the Maastricht Treaty, and of an eventual Constitution of the EU, would be done, as in the past,[130] through an Enabling Act.

It is a different question whether, in addition to approving such revision and thereby implicitly modifying the Constitution, the Constitution would also be expressly modifies by amending those of its articles seemingly affected. While this would not, from the point of view of Austrian constitutional law, be absolutely necessary it still might be done for the sake of clarity. The amendments to the Constitution brought about by the Accompanying Acts of 1994[131] and 1999[132] by inserting new articles or changing existing ones, offer a precedent. To expressly modify the relevant articles of the Constitution would also be in accordance with the requirement, existing for the Member States under EU/EC law, to bring in line their national law with EU/EC law as a matter of legal certainty.

4. *Institutional interdependence: European functions of national institutions*

EU/EC law and Member States law influence each other. A distinction can be made between indirect and indirect mutual influence. Indirect influence is exerted, e.g., by national legal traditions in the area of fundamental rights or of the rule of law, traditions which are applied, as principles of law common to the Member States[133] by the ECJ, and thus received into EU/EC law. On the other hand, the European legal standard may also influence the legal standard of the Member States. This can be explained by the fact that the ECJ does not start, when applying fundamental rights or the principle of the rule of law, from the smallest common denominator but rather from the "good European average" or even from a maximum standard, with the consequence of forcing national legal orders that lag behind to follow up when implementing or applying EU/EC law.

a. *The national parliaments in the European legislation process: indirect source of legitimacy and responsibilities for implementation*

(1) In general

European Parliament is sometimes denied the capability to represent the "European people", with the argument that, lacking a collective identity of the citizen of the Union, no such European people would exist. Legitimisation of European legislation would therefore require the inclusion of national parliaments, which represent their respective peoples, into the legislative process on the EU/EC level.

Even if this argument is not considered convincing – a collective consciousness is always more or less a fiction, even in the domestic sphere, a hypothesis that has to be made for the legitimisation of national parliaments, their election and their legislative activities –, a number of Member States, namely Denmark, France, Germany, the United Kingdom, and Austria, have provided for ways and means through which their parliaments may exert some influence on EU/EC legislation. This kind of inclusion of national parliaments into the EU/EC legislative process usually works through a (more or less) binding mandate given by parliament to the Member State's representative in the Council.

Apart from this possible but often not very practicable influence, exerted by national parliaments, on EU/EC decision-making, parliaments may also be included into the process of decision-shaping on EU/EC level. The Commission, when preparing a proposal for a legislative act, works in close contact with experts, both national and transnational, and expert members of national parliaments are certainly not excluded. Moreover, the Commission is bound, by the rules of comitology,[134] to seek advice from the Member States, which gives the latter an opportunity to have their parliaments participate, in one way or the other, in the process of the working out implementing rules for Council regulations.

(2) The Austrian situation

In Austria,[135] participation in "projects within the European Union" is provided for with regard to both federal and state institutions *(Organe des Bundes und der Länder)*. "Projects within the European Union"[136] refers not only to those within the first pillar of the EU, and, in particular, the EC, but also to projects within the CFSP and PJCC.[137]

Participation by the federal government in the legislative process of the EU/EC is not only in conformity with EU/EC law but even required by its system, given the fact that the EU/EC's main legislative organ is the Council, which is composed of government members bound by the decisions of their respective governments. Governmental participation in EU/EC legislation is, thus, not an Austrian particularity, but applies to all Member States. This is not equally true for participation by legislative bodies.

As concerns participation of parliament in the legislative process of the EU/EC, it is primarily the National Council *(Nationalrat)*, representing the people of the Federation as a whole, which is involved. Participation by the Federal Council *(Bundesrat),* representing the people of the individual states *(Länder),* is a rare exception that may be regarded an additional element of federalism supplementing the separately existing possibility of a participation by the states.

In order to give the federal legislative institutions an opportunity to exercise their right of participation, the federal government has an obligation of informing them about all projects within the EU/EC. This duty of information extends not only to projects the subject matter of which comes within the competence of parliament, but is a general obligation that concerns all other projects, too.

Both the National and the Federal Council may give "opinions" (or "comments") addressed to the competent member of the federal government. In all cases where a member of a state government should represent Austria, in the Council, it, too, may be addressee of such an opinion. Opinions may refer to all kinds of "projects within the EU"; as far as they are not binding, they have yet to be taken into consideration.

To have obligatory force, the opinion has to concern "projects" that either would eventually have to be implemented, in Austria, by federal law, or are directed to the adoption, on EU/EC level, of a directly applicable legal act relating to matters otherwise to be regulated by federal law.[138] This comprises not only directives and regulations but also treaties and all other legal acts that could have such an effect. The same applies to decisions taken in the framework of CFSP and PJCC.[139]

The Federal Council may render a binding opinion only if the "project" would have to be implemented by a federal constitutional law limiting the legislative or executive powers of the states *(Länder).*[140] Since these cases are very rare, the provision has not had, so far, any practical effect.

In all cases where the opinion of the National or the Federal Council is binding, this effect extends not only to the Austrian representative in the Council but also to all other instruction-bound Austrian representatives in all other EU/EC bodies. The opinion may only be (fully or partly) disregarded because of compelling reasons of foreign or integration politics.

Whether there exist such reasons, is a matter of discretion to be decided by the Austrian representative in the Council. While he has to inform the National Council of his intention to depart from the course lined out in the opinion,[141] and the National Council may then insist on its opinion, the final decision lies with the Austrian representative in the Council. If he stays within the limits of discretion, he will not incur thereby legal responsibility.[142] This does not exclude, of course, political responsibility; the National Council may adopt a vote of no confidence causing the Minister's resignation.

If the "project" concerns a legal act of the EU/EC that would have the consequence of changing the Austrian constitutional law, the Austrian representative in the Council may depart form the opinion only if the National Council, having been duly informed of the intention to disregard the opinion because of compelling reasons of foreign or integration politics, has not objected within reasonable time. If there should arise a dispute between Government and National Council about the question whether the "project" would cause a change in constitutional law, the Government's view will prevail unless the National Council adopts a vote of no confidence or brings the matter before the Constitutional Court. It would then be for the Court to render the final decision.[143]

In all cases of an opinion adopted by the National Council, whether binding or not, the Austrian representative in the Council has to report to the National Council following adoption of the decision on the EU/EC level. If the representative has departed from the opinion for compelling reasons of foreign or integration politics, the report has to be made "without delay".

Participation by the National Council in "projects within the EU" is exercised through its Main Committee *(Hauptausschuss)*. In 1996, it established a Standing Sub-committee for Matters of European Integration, and delegated to it the necessary powers.[144] A small Working Committee consisting of the Sub-Committee's chairman and one representative from each parliamentary club may, in turn, exercise these powers of the Sub-Committee. If necessary, the Sub-Committee may be convened also at a time when the National Council is not in session.[145] If it thinks fit, the Main Committee may also decide that an EU/EC-related matter be dealt with in the National Council's plenary.

The Federal Council has established a Committee for EU affairs in 1997. This does not bar the Federal Council from adopting an opinion in plenary.

b. European function of national administrations: a double mandate for the executive

According to the principle of institutional autonomy, restricted only by the limitations set by EU/EC law, as, e.g., by the principle of effectiveness, it is up to Austrian law to decide on the institutions that exercise the European function of national administration. When applying EU/EC law, these institutions may also be regarded as exercising a function within the system of EU/EC system, and thus having the character of decentralised EU/EC institutions.[146] This is only the European aspect of a general phenomenon of the relationship between international law and domestic law, termed *dédoublement fonctionnel* by *Georges Scelle*.[147]

If no administrative authority is expressly designated for the application of a rule of EU/EC law, competence is decided by the nearest substantive relationship.

In applying EU/EC law, national administrative authorities have to comply with the EU/EC rules for its application as they appear from the *acquis communautaire*. This means that national administrative authorities have, *ex officio*, to establish the existence of a pertinent rule of EU/EC law, and to apply it even in case that there still exists a national rule to a different effect. Pursuant to the principle of primacy, the national rule, inasmuch as it is incompatible with the rule of EU/EC law, has to be disregarded. Since recourse to the ECJ for a preliminary ruling is not open to administrative authorities, and since EU/EC law requires immediate application, these authorities cannot refer the matter to another (European or national) instance. It is thus for any administrative authority to decide itself on the interpretation of the EU/EC rule and the national rule's compatibility with it.

If the party or parties to the administrative proceedings believe that EU/EC law has not been applied correctly, they may appeal the decision, and will finally end up before the Administrative Court, which the may request a preliminary ruling of the ECJ. If parties do not appeal, an incorrect application of EU/EC law by the administrative authority will stand; the only remedy would then be an action against Austria for violation of the Treaty, to be brought either by another Member State, or by the Commission; for political reasons, however, this is not very likely to happen.

In cases involving EU/EC law, the latter determines the question of who is entitled to appear as a party before the Austrian administrative authority. Generally spoken, the notion of party is wider under EU/EC law than under Austrian law, comprising all physical and juridical persons having a right or interest under EU/EC law.[148]

According to the principle of procedural autonomy, administrative proceedings concerning those rights or interests will follow Austrian rules as long as they are not in conflict with the EU/EC principles of effectiveness or equivalence.

c. *Judicial protection in the European Union through national judges: conflict of loyalties; question of procedural autonomy*

What has been said about the European function of national administrative authorities, applies *mutatis mutandis* also to national courts.[149] It should be noted, in this connection, that the ECJ is also regarded, for the purpose of giving preliminary rulings, as part of the Austrian judicial system. Thus, the Austrian Constitutional Court has held that the right, of the party or parties to proceedings, of accession to a "judge established by law"[150] is violated if the Austrian court of last resort does not make the required request for a preliminary ruling of the ECJ.

"Courts" in the meaning of EU/EC law are all "regular" Austrian courts, and, in addition, special courts and tribunals, as the Constitutional Court, the Administrative Court, the Independent Administrative Senates, the Deciding Senates at the revenue and the customs offices, the Appellate Senates at the central Revenue Authorities in the various states *(Finanzlandesdirektionen)*, the so-called collegial authorities of a judicial character *(Kollegialbehörden mit richterlichem Einschlag)*, the Environment Senate, and the Appellate Senates established pursuant to the Stock Exchange Act.[151]

Inasmuch as EU/EC law does not contain applicable rules of procedure, the principle of procedural autonomy refers to Austrian procedural law. This autonomy is limited only by the principles of effectiveness and equivalence; because of the primacy of EU/EC law, Austrian procedural rules incompatible with these principles must not be applied. Thus, procedural time limits set by Austrian law have to be such as not to make unnecessarily difficult the bringing of claims based on EU/EC law.

Since every market citizen is entitled to be a party to proceedings to the extent necessary for unrestrictedly claiming his or her rights under EU/EC law, and since the notion of "right" is wider in EU/EC law than in Austrian law, there exists a tendency to disregard the difference between the objective aspect of direct applicability and subjective rights, which leads to a qualitative broadening of what has to be regarded a "party".[152] This is demonstrated, in particular, by those cases where EU/EC legal rules, not originally intended for direct application, take direct effect.

According to the principle of effectiveness, Austrian courts and administrative tribunals have to offer a measure of legal protection that is necessary to guarantee the unrestricted application of EU/EC law. Moreover, according to the principle of equivalence, that legal protection must not lag behind the Austrian standard applicable in domestic cases. And according to the principle of primacy of EU/EC law, all Austrian substantive and procedural rules that would be incompatible with these principles would be inapplicable and would have to be disregarded by Austrian courts. This applies even in the cases of restrictions on legal protection that have evidently been intended by the Austrian legislature; these restrictions would have to be disregarded, as, e.g., the Austrian law of non-contractual liability of the State, inasmuch as it does not grant indemnities for wrongful legislative acts. If a legislative act is in violation of EU/EC law, Austria is liable to the market citizens who should be wronged by that act.

Although administrative cases are not, in Austria, referred immediately to courts or tribunals, judicial review of administrative acts is always possible, at least as a last resort.[153]

Courts and administrative authorities have also to grant interim legal protection where required by EU/EC law. This applies in all cases where the right of the market citizen would otherwise be in danger of being frustrated.[154]

Where necessary for the enforcement of EU/EC law, Austria has the obligation to sanction its violation on the part of the market citizens. For this purpose, such violations have to be made statutorily defined offences, either criminal or administrative. The principle of effectiveness requires that procedures be suited to create the necessary effect of deterrence.

Inasmuch as EU/EC law directly applicable or of direct effect is violated by an Austrian organ, inflicting damage to a market citizen, Austria becomes liable.[155] This liability is directly based on EU/EC law, and the claim lies against the Republic of Austria as such, i.e. the Federation. If the violation has been committed, not by a federal but, by a state authority, compensation may have to be made by the state concerned. The principle of effectiveness forbids, however, that such "federalisation" of liability make impossible, unnecessarily difficult, or delayed, the realisation of the claim.

Action for damages has to be brought according to the Public Liability Act *(Amtshaftungsgesetz)*,[156] which is, according to the Constitutional Court,[157] directly applicable also for legislative wrongfulness, while the Supreme Court[158] maintains that it is applicable only by analogy. While the latter position may be considered as disregarding the principle of primacy of EU/EC law, the practical effect of both points of view is the same.

III. THE ROLE OF THE REGIONS AND LOCAL AUTHORITIES IN A EU LAW

Inasmuch as EU/EC law has to be implemented by Austrian legislative acts, the principle of institutional autonomy leaves it to Austria to decide whether implementation is done by constitutional or "simple" law and by federal or state law. The competence for implementation of EU/EC law depends on the distribution of power between the Federation *(Bund)* and the states *(Länder)*.

1. *Effects of EU law on the constitutional framework and settlement in relation to regions and local authorities*

In principle, the EU/EC is does not make special arrangements for federal states. Yet, an amendment to the EC Treaty made by the Maastricht Treaty of 1992 permits Member States to be represented, in the Council, by a member of the government of a component state. In addition, regional entities may, under certain circumstances, bring an action for the review of the legality of acts adopted by EC institutions.

Accession of Austria to the EU has nonetheless resulted in a loss of competences for the component states *(Länder),* without a corresponding right of the latter to participate in EU/EC matters in an adequate manner.[159] The states have received only a limited constitutional compensation through the establishment, by article 23 B-VG, of the so-called procedure for participation of the states.[160] This procedure is also based on an agreement between the Federation and the states pursuant to article 15a B-VG.[161]

According to the just-mentioned agreement between the Federation and the states, the former has the obligation to inform the latter, without delay, of a "project within the EU" that could affect the powers of the states or otherwise be of interested to them.[162]

The participation procedure provides for a right of the states to give an "opinion" (or to make a "comment"), which may either be (so-called) general or (so-called) binding. General comments may be made by each state, within and without the framework of article 23d paragraph 2 B-VG, and have to be taken into due consideration by the Federation.[163]

Binding comments are those that relate to matters coming under the legislative competencies of the states and have been adopted by them "in common". Comments of this kind have to be expressly supported by a majority of the states (ie by at least five of them), with none of the others objecting. In a certain way, this procedure is similar to that used within international organisations for adopting decisions by consensus.[164]

Regular body for the adoption of a common comment is the so-called Integration Conference of the States *(Integrationskonferenz der Bundesländer)*. This conference has been established by agreement among the states and is composed of the state governors, the presidents of the various state legislatures, and the presidency of the Federal Council, the latter without a right to vote. Since, however, the integration conference convenes only rarely, the majority of common comments is made in an informal manner on the level of experts. Yet, the binding character of such informal comments is doubtful. It is thus not the legislatures of the various states that have a say, but only the so-called integration conference of the states in which the state legislatures play only a minor role.

As far as common comments by the states are concerned, they bind all Austrian representatives in EU/EC organs acting under instruction. Departure from such a binding comment is permitted only in cases of compelling reasons of foreign and integration politics. In such a case, the Federation, through the Federal Chancellery, has to inform the states without delay.

Should the Austrian representative in the Council disregard a binding comment made by the states without such compelling reasons, he may be impeached by the combined decision of all nine state parliaments, and tried by the Constitutional Court.

Pursuant to article 23e B-VG, there exists an obligation, for the Federation, to inform the basic units of local government *(Gemeinden)* in all cases that affect their sphere of competences or interests; information has to be made via the Austrian Association of Townships *(Österreichischer Städtebund)* and the Austrian Association of Local Government Units *(Österreichischer Gemeindebund)*. They have a right to make comments; but no binding effect attaches to these comments.[165]

2. *Possible consequences for EU law of regionalisation and decentralisation of the kind existing in Austria*

Although Austria, as one of the Member States of the EU that are organised according to the principle of federalism, welcomes all initiatives by the EU intended to respect the rights and interests of regional and local entities, presently Austria would not seem to advocate an increase of the powers of latter to the detriment of the individual nation States Members of the EU. In particular, the internal constitutional structure of the Member States and the way by which their constitutions provide for participation of regional and local entities in EU affairs is a matter of their institutional autonomy.

The question of regionalism and decentralisation must not be mixed up with that of respect for the rights of ethnic and/or linguistic minorities, which to protect is certainly a matter of common European interest, even if some Member States may not so far have accepted this fact.

IV. CONCLUSIONS AND RECOMMENDATIONS FOR 2004

1. *A new architecture: how should a EU constitution or EU basic treaty look like?*

A European Constitution, whatever its form and designation, should be restricted to those rules that are absolutely necessary for the functioning of the Union. It should therefore only contain provisions establishing the main institutions and defining their powers as well as the procedures by which these competences would have to be exercised. The EU Charter of

Fundamental Rights and provisions on the distribution of powers between the EU/EC and the Member States may come in useful, although the latter may also be deduced from the powers given to the EU/EC institutions, and the former could also exist as a separate instrument if only it were binding on these institutions.

The same applies to the remaining provisions of the constitutional treaties, as they exist today, whether these provisions are of a substantive or of a procedural nature. In any case, it has to be secured that a future European Constitution cannot be construed as curtailing existing powers of the EU/EC; otherwise, it would be a step back rather than forward in European integration. Since it is unlikely that it will possible to formulate a European Constitution is such a way as to exclude any uncertainties about its meaning and thus about the structure and powers of the EU/EC, any such new basic instrument should contain a salvation clause in favour of the present constitutional *acquis communautaire*, in order to avoid unnecessary disputes among Member States as well as between Member States and EU/EC institutions.

Moreover, a European Constitution, if adopted in good faith, should also make the necessary proviso for the ECJ to act as a Constitutional Court of the EU/EC, thereby extending its present powers to all constitutional matters, whether contained in the EU or in the EC Treaty.[166]

2. *A Constitution for the European Union: conditions of adoption and amendment; its relation to national constitutions*

As already discussed *supra*,[167] a future European Constitution will have to be based on a treaty concluded and ratified by the Member States according to present article 48 EU, whether this treaty contains itself the Constitution or empowers a particular body (eg a "convent") to adopt a Constitution with binding effect for all Member States. The procedure for future amendments to such an instrument would also have to be embodied in either the treaty or the constitution based on it.[168]

The relation between a European Constitution and the constitutions of the Member States would have to be the same as that presently existing between the constitutional treaties of the EU/EC and Member State constitutions. Governing principle would have to be the primacy of EU/EC law; and the principles of institutional and procedural autonomy of the Member States would also have to be limited by the EU/EC law's principles of effectiveness and equivalence.

By no means should the adoption of a European Constitution be used to restrict, in any way, the principle of primacy with regard to all other rules of EU/EC law. This could only result in a heavy setback for the cause of integration and might in fact prove disastrous.

3. *Merging the constitutional process and enlargement: how to involve the candidates?*

The question of how to involve the prospective new Member States in the constitutional process should be dealt with in a pragmatic manner. The views of those of them that are likely to accede before the present constitutional process is successfully finished, should be taken into consideration right from the beginning; otherwise, opposition on their part could become a stumble-stone for the adoption of the future European Constitution.

As regards those candidates that will not have become Member States before the conclusion of the constitutional process, they should be heard but not be given a veto in that process, in accordance with the traditional approach taken by the EC, and the EU, respectively, that Non-Members cannot be allowed to participate in the EU/EC's decision making but only in its decision shaping. To deviate from this course could mean to make the constitutional process so complicated as to virtually bring it to naught.

NOTES

[1] Dr. iur. (Vienna), M.C.L. (Ann Arbor), Full Professor of Law, Johannes Kepler University Linz, Institutes of International Law and International Relations, of European Law, and of Environmental Law. Tit. Associate Professor, University of Vienna; Member, Board of Directors, European Studies, Danube University Krems.

The author gratefully acknowledges the support rendered by Dr. Gundula Riepl, Research Assistant, Institute of European Law, Johannes Kepler University Linz, in the preparation and completion of the paper.

[2] Cf, eg, article 79 of the German Constitution *(Bonner Grundgesetz)*.

[3] The formal difference in Austrian legal terminology consists in a hyphen in the term Bundes-Verfassungsgesetz, the Constitution properly so called, while any additional *Bundesverfassungsgesetz* is written without a hyphen. The corresponding abbreviations are B-VG and BVG. Since this way of distinguishing is not available in English terminology, the term Federal Constitution is used here for the *Bundes-Verfassungsgesetz*.

[4] One half of the members of the National Council present and a two-thirds majority of the votes cast, as compared to one third present and absolute majority of votes in the case of "simple" laws.

[5] As constitutional laws outside the constitution proper are numerous it is not possible to classify groups. Very important are those constitutional laws outside the constitution proper which concern human rights, e.g. the *Staatsgrundgesetz vom 21. Dezember 1867 über die allgemeinen Rechte der Staatsbürger*, (Austrian) Federal Official Journal 1867/142, the Convention for the Protection of Human Rights and Fundamental Freedoms 1950, (Austrian) Federal Official Journal Nr 1958/210, changed by 1970/330, 1972/84, 1990/64, 1994/593, 1998/30, or the *Gesetz zum Schutz der persönlichen Freiheit*, (Austrian) Federal Official Journal Nr 1988/684, dating back to 1862. There should also be mentioned those constitutional laws that,

at their time, attempted to cope with particular political problems, both national and international, of a special nature, as, e.g., the *Verbotsgesetz,* (Austrian) Official Journal 1945/13, 1947/25, the *BVG über die Neutralität Österreichs*, (Austrian) Official Journal (Austrian) Official Journal 1955/211, the *BVG über den umfassenden Umweltschutz*, (Austrian) Official Journal 1984/491, or the *BVG für ein atomfreies Österreich*, (Austrian) Official Journal 1999/149. Many laws also contain single paragraphs or sub-paragraphs of constitutional laws only.

[6] For this reason, the present President of the Austrian Constitutional Court, Professor *Ludwig Adamovich*, has stated that nobody can be sure about the full extent of Austrian constitutional law.

[7] Cf Ernst Forsthoff, *Rechtsstaat im Wandel. Verfassungsrechtliche Abhandlungen 1950-1964*, Stuttgart 1964, 23.

[8] Cf Hans Kelsen, *Reine Rechtslehre*, 2nd ed. Vienna 1960, 223 et seqs., 442 et eqs.

[9] It may be for this reason that both the Austrian Administrative Court and the Constitutional Court, together with the Supreme Court forming the *trias* of highest courts in Austria, have rejected customary law as a source of Austrian constitutional law; cf VwSlgNF 6035A, 7873A; VfSlg 8012.

[10] This is accepted even by the Constitutional Court; cf VfSlg 8524.

[11] As, eg, a Labour Chamber, a Chamber of Commerce, a Chamber of Agriculture, but also a Chamber of Attorneys-at-Law, of Medical Doctors, etc. In addition, there exist organisations like the Austrian Labour Union or the Austrian Association of Manufacturers (Industrialists), which have their legal basis in the law on private associations but play nevertheless an important role in political decision shaping.

[12] If, in Austria, the leader of the parliamentary majority is also president of the council of ministers (in Austria constitutional terminology called *Bundeskanzler*), the same holds true for the German Federal Chancellor or for the British Prime Minister, to mention only two other examples. Only a presidential republic like France can experience a situation of a powerful President confronted with a parliament where a different political grouping masters the majority, a situation that will then necessitate a so-called co-habitation.

[13] In this connection, mention may be made of article 9 a of the Federal Constitution containing an avowal of comprehensive national defence including its military aspect, of the federal constitutional law on comprehensive environmental protection, or of the federal constitutional law on a nuclear-free Austria.

[14] 2nd ed. 1960, with several new printings.

[15] Cf article 1 B-VG: „Austria is a *democratic* republic"; cf *Walter/Mayer*, Grundriss des österreichischen Bundesverfassungsrechts, Wien 2000, No 147-152.

[16] Cf *Walter/Mayer*, Grundriss des österreichischen Bundesverfassungsrechts, Wien 2000, No 164.

[17] Cf article 2 B-VG: „Austria is a *federal* state"; cf *Walter/Mayer*, Grundriss des österreichischen Bundesverfassungsrechts, Wien 2000, No 160-161.

[18] Cf article 1 B-VG: „Austria is a democratic *republic*"; cf *Walter/Mayer*, Grundriss des österreichischen Bundesverfassungsrechts, Wien 2000, No 159.

[19] Cf *Walter/Mayer*, Grundriss des österreichischen Bundesverfassungsrechts, Wien 2000, No 165-167.

[20] Cf *Walter/Mayer*, Grundriss des österreichischen Bundesverfassungsrechts, Wien 2000, No 1317.

[21] Cf article 6 paragraph 1 EU: "The Union is founded on the principles of liberty, democracy, respect for human rights and fundamental freedoms, and the rule of law, principles which are common to the Member States."

[22] Cf article 9 paragraph 1, which provides that "[t]he universally recognized rules of international law are considered to be part of federal law." This provision, which had its equivalent in article 4 of the German Constitution of Weimar, recalls William Blackstone's description of the relationship between international law and English law, stating that "international law is part of the law of the land". *Commentaries on the Law of England,* Vol. IV, Oxford 1769, 67.

[23] Or: from.

[24] The verbal translation would be "Her law emanates from the people".

[25] Treaty of the European Union, Official Journal 1992, Nr C 191/1992, 63 consolidated version 1997, Nr C 340/1997, 172.

[26] Act of Accession, Official Journal 1994, Nr C 241/1994, 371.

[27] Final Act, (Austrian) Federal Official Journal Nr 1995/45, 2209.

[28] Cf Official Journal 1995, Nr L 1/1995, 1.

[29] While the text of the Accession Treaty with all its component parts was not officially published before the referendum, copies were available, at all municipal administrations, for those who wanted to make themselves acquainted with its contents.

[30] On 12 June 1994.

[31] Federal Constitutional Law on the Accession of Austria to the European Union) *(Bundesverfassungsgesetz über den Beitritt Österreichs zur Europäischen Union),* (Austrian) Federal Official Journal 1994/744.

[32] Cf Bernd-Christian Funk , *Einführung in das österreichische Verfassungsrecht,* Graz 2000, 129.

[33] Namely by 66,58 per cent of valid votes. The result of the vote was published in: (Austrian) Federal Official Journal 1994/735.

[34] Ratification is a formal act, executed by the head of state, and expressing the final consent of the respective country to being bound by a treaty. Cf. Peter Fischer/Heribert Franz Köck, *Allgemeines Völkerrecht*, 5th ed. Vienna 2000, No 223.

[35] Cf Christoph Thun-Hohenstein/Franz Cede, *Europarecht*, 2nd ed. Vienna 1999, 95.

[36] Together with the Act of Accession, and the Final Act of the Accession Conference. The text of the complete instrument of accession cf in (EC) Official Journnal 1994, Nr C 241/1994, 9 et seqs; (Austrian) Federal Official Journal 1995/45, 2199 at seqs. (Accession Treaty), (EC) Official Journal 1994, Nr C 241/1994, 21 et seqs; (Austrian) Official Journal 1995/45, 2209 et seqs (Act of Accession), and (EC) Official Journal 1994, Nr C 241/1994, 371 et seqs; (Austrian) Federal Official Journal 1995/45, 2545 et seqs (Final Act).

[37] (Austrian) Federal Official Journal 1994/1013. The Constitution proper was amended by inserting, into its First Section, a new Title on "European Union", comprising articles 23a through 23f.

[38] As, eg, article 23a, which deals with the election of the Austrian Members of the European Parliament.

[39] As, eg, article 23d paragraph 2 and article 23e paragraph 2 providing for the possibility, and the extent, of binding the Austrian representative in the Council by decision of the National Council (in rare cases also of the Federal Council) or by concurring opinion of the component states *(Bundesländer)*.

[40] Actually, no State would be able to implement all directives at one and the same time. For this reason, it has to conform its law to the EU/EC legal order well in advance of accession. The fact that Austria had become a member of the European Economic Area as from 1 January 1994, and that she thus had to conform great parts of her law to Community law already then, facilitated this task.

[41] On the question of direct effect of directives under particular circumstances, cf Peter Fischer/Heribert Franz Köck/Margit Hintersteininger, *Europarecht*, 4th ed Vienna 2002, No 1232-1235.

[42] Cf., *inter alia*, Waldemar Hummer (ed.), *Die Europäische Union und Österreich*, Vienna 1994; Gerhart Holzinger, Die Auswirkungen der österreichischen EU-Mitgliedschaft auf das österreichische Verfassungsrecht, 4 *JRP* 1996, 160; Heribert Franz Köck, Die österreichische Bundesverfassung und das Völkerrecht, in: Heribert Franz Köck (Hrsg), *Kritik und Fortschritt im Rechtsstaat – Grundprobleme des österreichischen Bundesverfassungsrechts*, Vienna 1996, 91 et seqs., Waldemar Hummer/Michael Schweitzer (eds.), *Österreich und das Recht der Europäischen Union*, Vienna 1996; Stefan Griller/Heinz-Peter Rill (eds.), *Verfassungsrechtliche Grundfragen der EU-Mitgliedschaft*, Vienna 1997; Josef Aicher/Michael Holoubek/Karl Korinek (eds.), *Gemeinschaftsrecht und Wirtschaftsrecht – Zentrale Probleme des Einwirkens des Gemeinschaftsrechts auf das österreichische Wirtschaftsrecht,* Vienna 2000, 1; Theo Öhlinger/Michael Potacs, *Gemeinschaftsrecht und staatliches Recht,* Vienna 2001.

[43] Some authors contend that there has remained, even after Austria's accession to the EU, what is sometimes called an integration-resistant core (so-called *integrationsfester Kern*) of the Austrian Constitution. Since, however, this core could not comprise more than the very principles avowed by the EU herself in article 6 paragraph 1 EU, the question of an integration-resistant core remains fully hypothetical.

[44] Cf StGBl 1918/5; *Walter/Mayer*, Grundriss des österreichischen Bundesverfassungsrecht, Wien 2000, No 54.

[45] Cf (Austrian) Federal Official Journal 1920, Nr 1/1920.

[46] Cf Article 9 paragraph 1 B-VG, (Austrian) Federal Official Journal Nr 1930/1.

[47] Cf Article 49 B-VG, (Austrian) Federal Official Journal Nr 1930/1.

[48] Of course, if another State would consider itself aggrieved by Austrian law (e.g. if applied to its diplomatic representatives or its nationals sojourning on Austrian territory), it may always have recourse to an international procedure for the purpose of being restored to its rights under international law.

[49] Cf Article 9 paragraph 2 B-VG, (Austrian) Federal Official Journal Nr 1930/1 consolidated by 1981/350.

[50] Fischer/Köck/Hintersteininger, *Europarecht,* 4th ed. Vienna 2002, Section "Österreich und die EU".

[51] Cf *Supra,* I. 1.b. (1).

[52] Cf *supra*, I.1.b. (1).

[53] In fact, it is this constitutional approval, and not the observance of any formal procedure of treaty-making that is decisive, because the Austrian Constitution does not require, for the conclusion of an international treaty, any international formalities not prescribed by international law; and international law is by its very nature not concerned with form but with substance. Thus, the widely held opinion that the Member States of the EU have remained the "lords of the treaties" (*Herren der Verträge)* implies, *inter alia*, that they may revise or terminate them without being bound by the formal requirements provided in this connection by the treaties themselves. Cf *Fischer/Köck/Hintersteininger*, Europarecht, 4th ed Vienna 2002, No 725.

[54] Cf *supra*, fn 40.

[55] Treaty of Amsterdam amending the Treaty on European Union, the Treaties establishing the European Communities and certain related acts, Official Journal 1997 Nr C 340/1997, 1.

[56] Treaty of Nice amending the Treaty on European Union, the Treaties establishing the European Communities and certain related acts, signed at Nice, 26 February 2001, Official Journal 2001 Nr C 80/2001, 1.

[57] Cf (Austrian) Federal Official Journal Nr 1998/76 and Nr 2001/120. Cf. also Theo Öhlinger, Verfassungsrechtliche Aspekte des Vertrags von Amsterdam in Österreich, in: Waldemar Hummer (ed.), *Die Europäische Union nach dem Vertrag von Amsterdam*, Vienna 1998, 297; Christoph Thun-Hohenstein, Der Vertrag von Amsterdam – ausgewählte Rechtsfragen, in: Österreichische Juristenkommission (ed.), *Kritik und Fortschritt im Rechtsstaat. Österreich als Mitglied der Europäischen Union*, Wien 1999, 191; Theo Öhlinger, Die Übernahme des Vertrags von Amsterdam sowie des Rechts der zweiten und dritten Säule in die österreichische Rechtsordnung, in: Waldemar Hummer (ed.), *Rechtsfragen in der Anwendung des Amsterdamer Vertrags*, Wien 2001, 2

[58] The Amsterdam Treaty entered into force on 1 May 1999.

[59] Because of this reduction to a "hard core" some also caustically called the new approach to permanent neutrality "avocado doctrine".

[60] Cf Fischer/Köck, *Das Recht der internationalen Organisationen*, 3rd ed. Vienna 1997, 65.

[61] Cf Fischer/Köck, *Das Recht der internationalen Organisationen*, 3rd ed. Vienna 1997, 198.

[62] Cf Fischer/Köck, *Das Recht der internationalen* Organisationen, 3rd ed. Vienna 1997, 119.

[63] Cf Final Act, (Austrian) Federal Official Journal 1995/45, 2545 et seqs.

[64] Originally, these tasks had been formulated by the WEU in its Petersberg Declaration of 1992; WEU's failure to develop into an effective "sword arm" of the EU caused the latter to take matters in its own hands.

[65] Cf Preben Bonnèn, Die Rolle Österreichs als neutrales und allianzfreies Mitglied der EU in der zukünftigen Entwicklung der GASP bzw. der gemeinsamen Verteidigungspolitik, Vortragsmanuskript, der *Österreichischen Gesellschaft für Landesverteidigung und Sicherheitspolitik* (ed.), Vienna 2000NOTEREF, at 2.

[66] For participation in decisions concerning measures for the preservation of peace, for military actions in cases of crisis, including measures for the restoration

of peace, as well as for the progressive determination of a common defence policy (and eventual closer relations with the WEU, and aspect that, after Nice, seems to have lost its original significance), an understanding has to be reached between the Federal Chancellor and the Minister for Foreign Affairs. Cf Thun-Hohenstein/Cede, *Europarecht,* 260.

[67] (Austrian) Federal Official Journal Nr 1955/211.

[68] Moreover, the reason for which collective action within the UN system had already before been regarded as non incompatible with Austria's permanent neutrality, namely the need for decisive action in the case of crisis, with the purpose of preserving or restoring the peace, is equally applicable to regional collective action, whether carried out under a mandate of the Security Council or without its blessing if blocked by a veto.

[69] Cf *supra*, fn 65.

[70] Bundesverfassungsgesetz über den Abschluss des Vertrages von Nizza, (Austrian) Federal Official Journal Nr 2001/120.

[71] Fischer/Köck/HinterSteininger, *Europarecht*, 4th ed Vienna 2002, No 670–67

[72] Cf only the ECJ's judgment in *Les Verts v Parlament*, Case 294/83, European Court Reports 1986, 1339.

[73] As required, by article 50 paragraph 3, for treaties bringing about a change of the Constitution of a fundamental character.

[74] As required by article 50 paragraph 3, for treaties which bring about constitutional changes.

[75] Article 50 paragraph 1 requires a presence quorum of one third and a consent quorum of "simple", ie absolute, majority.

[76] This would correspond the German constitutional practice based on articles 24 I and 59 II 1 of the Bonner Grundgesetz. See Heribert Franz Köck, *Der Gesamtakt in der deutschen Integrationslehre*, Berlin 1978, 59 f.

[77] This would be a indisputable example for the *argumentum a maiori ad minus*, well known in juridical methodology. – It should be noted that also other treaties having the character of primary EU/EC law, as, e.g., association agreements, if they bring about direct rights and duties not only for the Member States but also for the market citizens, or if they may become of immediate effect, have to obtain parliamentary approval, where necessary also under the aggravated conditions of qualified majority or even a referendum.

[78] Even now, nothing prevents the ECJ from regarding the Charter as evidence of the human rights and fundamental freedoms common to the Member States, as they also appear from their constitutional traditions, the ECHR and the ESCh.

[79] Even though the Member States have transferred, to the EU/EC, certain sovereign powers, and hove not, thus, retained their original sovereignty in its totality, the EU/EC does still not dispose of the essential criterion of a sovereign community, namely the plenitude of power to effectively claim, for itself, all competences necessary to a commonwealth for pursuing the comprehensive common good of its members.

[80] While Austria takes into account the relevant positions of all Member States, public opinion may be said to be influenced, as concerns positions abroad, by German mass media, especially print-media, as, e.g., the *Frankfurter Allgemeine Zeitung*, or *the Süddeutsche Zeitung*, but also by German TV. This is caused by the

common language; for this reason, also some other TV-stations, as the Luxembourg-based RTL, or German Swiss TV, may be rated as sources of information.

[81] Cf. Treaty of Nice amending the Treaty on European Union, the Treaties establishing the European Communities and certa in related acts Declarations Adopted By The Conference. Declaration on the future of the Union, Official Journal Nr C 80/2001, 85.

[82] Since so far a comprehensive, let alone official, summary of the debate, in Austria, on a future European constitution is lacking, resort must be have to semi- or unofficial publications, as the *Parlamentskorrespondenz*, or the Austrian daily newspapers and other periodicals, as, *e.g.*, *Die* Presse, *Der Standard*, the *Salzburger Nachrichten*, the *Oberösterreichische Nachrichten*, or the *Grazer Kleine Zeitung*, which report regurlary and more extensively about related issues.

[83] At its meeting in Laeken in December 2001, the European Council convened a Convention on the future of the European Union. The European Council has appointed Mr Valéry Giscard d'Estaing as Chairman of the Convention and Mr Giuliano Amato and Mr Jean-Luc Dehaene as Vice-Chairmen. In addition to its Chairman and two Vice-Chairmen, the Convention is composed of: 15 representatives of the Heads of State or Government of the Member States (one from each Member State), 13 representatives of the countries that are candidates for accession (one from each candidate country), 30 representatives of the national parliaments of the Member States (two from each Member State), 26 representatives of the national parliaments of the accession candidate countries (two from each candidate country), 16 members of the European Parliament, 2 representatives of the European Commission. The purpose of the Convention is not only to consider key questions about the future development of the European Union but also to identify possible answers. The Convention is devided in three phases. The first phase which should be finished by summer is devoted to a brainstorming about the future of the European Union. After the summer the first drafts on a European Constitution should be finished. The working process on this drafts should be finished in the second half of the year 2003.

[84] Short statements by the Austrian members of the Convent are to be found in the *Salzburger Nachrichten* of 27 February 2002 under the title "Was Österreichs Konvent-Mitarbeiter wollen". More information may be gathered, inter alia, from the Internet, e.g. from http://www.europakonvent.info.

[85] All Austrian Parties represented in Parliament issue regularly information about their stand on European integration in general and the issue of European constitution-making in particular. These informations can be found in the Internet. Cf., e.g., http://www.oevp.at, where an E-Mail Info, No. 68/02, of 28 February 2002 contains Federal Chacellor Schüssel's remarks on a citizen-oriented EU: "Schüssel: Die EU muß sich mit Fragen befassen, die ihre Bürger betreffen!"

[86] Cf. *infra*, II.4.a.

[87] The study for a reform of the constitutional treaties of the EU/EC undertaken, under the auspices of the European University Institute *(Europäisches Hochschulinstitut)* by a Working Group chaired by Claus-Dieter Ehlermann and Yves Mény, with Hervé Bribosia as rapporteur, transmitted to Mr. Romano Prodi, President of the European Commission, on 15 May 2000, the German version of which was done by Christoph U. Schmied and Claus K. Meyer and is entitled "Ein

Basisvertrag für die Europäische Union", may be said to have found some general approval in Austria.

[88] Cf *supra*, I. 3.a.

[89] Cf. *Parlamentskorrespondenz,* 28 February 2002, No. 140.

[90] As regards the Austrian situation, cf., apart from Öhlinger/Potacs, *Gemeinschaftsrecht und österreichisches Recht,* Vienna 2001; also Stefan Griller/Karl Korinek/Michael Potacs (eds.), *Grundfragen und aktuelle Probleme des öffentlichen Rechts* – Essays in honour of Peter Rill, Vienna 1995, 97:

[91] In fact, quite a few, if not the majority of the, authors dealing with the issue of whether, and, if so, what kind of, a European constitution should be worked out, develop ideas that must be regarded aloof from the reality of the EU/EC as an existing and living thing. Yet, any future constitution can only be the organic development of the present state of affairs, because, to remind of the *Schuman's* often quoted remark, Europe cannot be build either in one day or in a single step; and it can certainly not be build on the basis of any abstract design.

[92] Preamble, paragraph 10, EU.

[93] Preamble, paragraph 8, EU.

[94] Preamble, paragraph 3, EU.

[95] Preamble, paragraph 2 second part, EU.

[96] Preamble, paragraph 2 first part, EU.

[97] Preamble, paragraph 5, EU.

[98] Although the correct reading of article 308 EC seems to be that it contains a comprehensive, albeit subsidiary and unspecific, power of the Council to take all measures necessary for attaining object and purpose of the Community in those cases where none of the EC institutions has an express, specific competency, and that therefore article 308 EC does not involve any creation of new powers – cf Fischer/Köck/Hintersteininger, *Europarecht*, 4th ed Vienna 2002, No 891 –, the specific power needed in the particular case has still to be elaborated and circumscribed by the Council; and article 6.3 EU does not prevent it from doing so.

[99] Cf article 151 paragraph 2 EC.

[100] Cf article 151 paragraph 3 EC.

[101] Article 151 paragraph 5 subparagraph 1 EC.

[102] Article 151 paragraph 5 subparagraph 2 EC.

[103] Article 151 paragraph 5 subparagraph 1 EC.

[104] In fact, respect for the cultural diversity of the Member States is not even mentioned in the preamble of the Treaty.

[105] Cf *supra*, I. 1. a. (1).

[106] Cf *supra*, fn 40.

[107] Article 6 paragraph 1 EU.

[108] Cf Heribert Franz Köck/Margit Hintersteininger, Zu den Sanktionen der vierzehn EU-Partnerstaaten gegen Österreich, in: Köck/Hintersteininger (ed), *Europa als Sicherheits- und Wertegemeinschaft*, Vienna 2000, 481.

[109] For this reasons, hope may be expressed that the abortive so-called sanctions against Austria, in connection with the formation of a coalition government with the inclusion of the Freedom Party in early 2000, will remain a one-time sin against the spirit of the European Union.

[110] Bundesverfassungsgesetz vom 29. November 1988 über den Schutze der persönlichen Freiheit, (Austrian) Federal Official Journal Nr 1988/684.
[111] Gesetz zum Schutze des Hausrechtes, (Austrian) Federal Official Journal Nr 1962/88.
[112] Staatsgrundgesetz vom 21. Dezember 1867 über die allgemeinen Rechte der Staatsbürger, (Austrian) Federal Official Journal Nr 1867/142.
[113] Convention for the Protection of Human Rights and Fundamental Freedoms, ETS No 5.
[114] Cf (Austrian) Federal Official Journal Nr 1958/210, changed by 1970/330, 1972/84, 1990/64, 1994/593, 1998/30.
[115] Austria would thus not share the pessimistic views, as, e.g., expressed in Eckhard Pache, Die Europäische Grundrechtecharta – ein Rückschritt für den Grundrechtsschutz in Europa? 36 *EuR* (2001), 475 et seqs.
[116] It goes without saying that appurtenance to the first pillar, and thus reception into EC law, would be a clear indication of the intention to make the Charter directly applicable within Member States. Yet, the Member States are not bound by the present system of the Union, and may very well insert "supranational" and thus directly applicable norms also in any other part of the Treaty. The formal place a rule has been allocated within the framework of the constitutional treaties cannot, therefore, create more than a presumption concerning its direct applicability, and this presumption is refutable.
[117] Cf *supra*, I. 1. b. (1).
[118] Cf *supra*, I. 1. b. (1).
[119] Cf *supra*, I. 1. a. (2).
[120] Cf *supra*, fn 40.
[121] Cf *supra*, II. 1. b.
[122] Cf Fischer/Köck/Hintersteininger, *Europarecht*, 4th ed Vienna 2002, No 1332.
[123] Cf Fischer/Köck/Hintersteininger, *Europarecht*, 4th ed Vienna 2002, No 782.
[124] Cf *supra*, I. 1. 2a. (1).
[125] Cf *supra*, I. 1. 2a. (2).
[126] Cf *supra*, I. 1. 2b.
[127] Cf *supra*, I. 1. 2b.
[128] Article 48 paragraph 1 EU.
[129] Article 48 paragraph 3 EU.
[130] Cf *supra*, I. 2a (1).
[131] Cf *supra*, I. 2.
[132] Cf *supra*, I. 2a. (1).
[133] Sometimes also called European principles of law, being the regional form of the general principles of law as mentioned in article 38 (1) (c) of the ICJ's Statute.
[134] 1999/468/EC: Council Decision of 28 June 1999 laying down the procedures for the exercise of implementing powers conferred on the Commission, Official Journal 1999, Nr L 184/1999, 23.

Declarations on Council Decision 1999/468/EC of 28 June 1999 laying sown the procedures for the exercise of implementing powers conferred on the Commission, Official Journal 1999, Nr C 203/1999, 1.

Agreement between the European Parliament and the Commission on procedures for implementing Council Decision 1999/468/EC of 28 June 1999 laying down the procedures for the exercise of implementing powers conferred on the Commission, Official Journal 2000, Nr L 256/2000 19.

135 For the Austrian situation cf. Margit Körner, Das EU-Begleit-Bundesverfassungsgesetz – Die Mitwirkung der Parlamente von Bund und Ländern bei der Schaffung von neuem EU-Recht, *ÖJBPol* (1994), 513 et seqs.; Theo Öhlinger, Die Mitwirkung des Bundesparlaments sowie der Länder in Österreich an der Entstehung von Europäischem Recht, 11 *ZG* 1996, 57; Heinz Schäffer, Österreichs Beteiligung an der Willensbildung in der Europäischen Union, insbesondere an der europäischen Rechtsetzung, 50 *ZöR* 1996, 3; Theo Öhlinger, Die Mitwirkung des Nationalrates, des Bundesrates und der Länder an der Entstehung von sekundärem Gemeinschaftsrecht, in: Stefan Griller/Heinz-Peter Rill (eds.), *Verfassungsrechtliche Grundfragen der EU-Mitgliedschaft*, Vienna 1997, 1.

136 "Vorhaben im Rahmen der EU"; cf article 23 d B-VG.

137 Cf. also Heinrich Neisser, Die Mitwirkungsbefugnis des Nationalrates im Entscheidungsprozess der Europäischen Union, in: Heinz Schäffer/Walter Berka/Harald Stolzlechner/Josef Werndl (eds.), *Staat – Verfassung – Verwaltung*, Essays in honour of Koja, Vienna 1998, 335; Heinz Peter Rill, Was ist ein "Vorhaben im Rahmen der Europäischen Union"? in: ibid., 391.

138 Cf article 23e paragraph 2 B-VG.

139 This is so because of a reference to article 23e paragraph 2 B-VG contained in article 23f paragraph 2 B-VG – In this connection, doctrine is divided about the question of whether such decisions come under article 23e paragraph 2 or paragraph 3 B-VG, only the latter provision giving an absolute veto to the National Council. Logic demands, however, to assume such an absolute veto only in cases where a matter of Austrian constitutional law is concerned. This is would not be the case, e.g., with regard to all matters where article 27f paragraph 1 B-VG has already derogated from the constitutional aspect of Austria's permanent neutrality by permitting participation in combat operations under EU mandate.

140 Cf article 23e paragraph 6 B-VG in connection with article 44 paragraph 2 B-VG.

141 Cf article 23e paragraph 3 B-VG.

142 In case of doubt, the National Council may institute, against the Minister, procedures pursuant to article 142 paragrah 2 lit c B-VG before the Constitutional Court.

143 Cf. Ignaz Seidl-Hohenveldern, National mandatory orders for voting in the EU/EC council, *Legal Issues of European Integration* (1996), 71

144 Cf. Bernd Wieser, Zur schwierigen Umsetzung der parlamentarischen Beteiligung an der innerstaatlichen Willensbildung in EU-Angelegenheiten; Das Komitee gemäß § 31c Abs 3 GOGNR, 53 *ÖJZ* 1998, 81 et seqs.

145 Cf article 23 paragraph 5 B-VG.

146 Cf., in general, Gerhart Holzinger, Umsetzung und Anwendung des Gemeinschaftsrechts in Österreich, in: Siegfried Magiera/Heinrich Siedentopf (eds.), *Die Zukunft der Europäischen Union*, Berlin 1997, 87; Gregor Obenaus, Gemeinschaftsrechtliche Anforderungen an die österreichische Legistik, 7 *JRP* 1999, 111; Johannes Müller, Allgemeine Umsetzungsprobleme des EU-Rechts auf Landesebene, in: Peter Pernthaler (ed.), Auswirkungen des EU-Rechts auf die Länder, Vienna 1999, 27; Christoph Kleiser, Die Umsetzung von Gemeinschaftsrecht aus legistischer Sicht: Der Umsetzungshinweis, 9 *JRP* 2001,

[147] Cf Fischer/Köck/Hintersteininger, *Europarecht*, 4th ed Vienna 2002, No 840-841.

[148] Cf. in general, Thomas v. Danwitz, Zur Grundlegung einer Theorie der subjektiv-öffentlichen Gemeinschaftsrechte, 49 *DÖV* 1996, 481 et seqs.

[149] Cf. , in general, Thomas Jean Berrang, *Vorbeugender Rechtsschutz im Recht der Europäischen Gemeinschaften*, Baden-Baden 1994; Claus Dieter Classen, *Die Europäisierung der Verwaltungsgerichtsbarkeit*, Tübingen 1996; Günter Hirsch, Kompetenzverteilung zwischen EuGH und nationaler Gerichtsbarkeit, 17 *NVwZ* 1998, 907 et seqs.; especially for the Austrian situation, Christian Kohler, Recht und Rechtsschutz in der Europäischen Union nach dem Beitritt Österreichs, 50 *ÖJZ* 1995, 721 et seqs.; Michael Holoubek, Rechtsschutzpraxis in Vergabesachen, 8 *ecolex* 1997, 200; Michael Potacs, Rechtsschutz beim Vollzug von Gemeinschaftsrecht in Österreich, in: Stefan Griller/Heinz Peter Rill (eds.), *Verfassungsrechtliche Grundfragen der EU-Mitgliedschaft*, Vienna 1997, 127; Meinrad Handstanger, Fragen des Gemeinschaftsrechts in der Judikatur des Verwaltungsgerichtshofes, in: Österreichische Juristenkommission (Hrsg), *Kritik und Fortschritt im Rechtsstaat. Österreich als Mitglied der Europäischen Union*, Geneva-Vienna 1999, 73; Johannes Hengstschläger, Grundrechtsschutz kraft EU-Rechts, 122 *JBl* 2000, 409 et seqs. and 494 et seqs.; Claudio Arturo, Zum Rechtsschutz im Beihilfenrecht, Vienna 2000; Stefan Griller, eds.), *Gemeinschaftsrecht und Wirtschaftsrecht – Zentrale Probleme des Einwirkens des Gemeinschaftsrechts auf das österreichsiche Wirtschaftsrecht*, Vienna 2000, 27; Georg Wilhelm, Rechtsfortbildung im BVergG: Anspruch auf Erfüllungsinteresse, 11 ecolex 2000, 493 et seqs.

[150] As guaranteed by article 83 paragraph 2 B-VG; cf also article 6 paragraph 1 ECHR.

[151] Cf., *inter alia*, Michael Holoubek, Vorlageberechtigung und Vorlageverpflichtung, in: Michael Holoubek/Michael Lang (eds.), Das verwaltungsgerichtliche Verfahren in Steuersachen, Vienna 1999, 45 et seqs.; Meinrad Handstanger, Die Bedeutung des Vorabentscheidungsverfahrens für das verwaltungsgerichtliche Verfahren, in: *ibid.*, 83 et seqs; Gerhart Holzinger, Die Bedeutung des Vorabentscheidungsverfahrens für das verfassungsgerichtliche Verfahren, in: *ibid.*, 65 et seqs.; Gerhart Holzinger, Umsetzung und Anwendung des Gemeinschaftsrechts in Österreich, in: Siegfried Magiera/Heinrich Siedentopf (eds.), *Die Zukunft der Europäischen Union*, Berlin 1997, 87.

[152] Cf *Öhlinger/Potacs*, Gemeinschaftsrecht und staatliches Recht, 2th ed Vienna 2001, 53.

[153] Usually, appeal lies first with a higher administrative instance; but if relief is not granted, a complaint may be made to the Administrative Court, or to the Constitutional Court, respectively, depending on whether violation of a constitutional or only of a "simple" legal norm is claimed. – Cf. also Clemens Jabloner, Anwendungsvorrang des Gemeinschaftsrechts und Verwaltungsgerichtsbarkeit, 50 *ÖJZ* 1995, 921 et seqs.; Peter Vcelouch, Auswirkungen der österreichischen Unionsmitgliedschaft auf den Rechtsschutz vor dem VwGH und dem VfGH, 52 *ÖJZ* 1997, 721 et seqs.; Michael Holoubek, Tatsachen- und Rechtskontrolle, in: Michael Holoubek/Michael Lang (eds.), Das verwaltungsgerichtliche Verfahren in Steuersachen, Vienna 1999, 169 et seqs.

[154] Strangely enough, it is disputed in Austria whether or not interim protection has to be granted also by administrative authorities; but the *ratio* of interim protection, and thus EU/EC law, clearly demands it. Cf. Thomas Keppert, Der Einfluss des Europarechts auf die nationale Gewährung vorläufigen Rechtsschutzes im Bereich des Abgabenrechts, in: Gerald Heidinger/Karl Bruckner (eds.), *Steuern in Österreich – Gestern, heute, morgen*, Hommage of the Fachsenats für Steuerrecht zum 50-Jahr-Jubiläum der Kammer der Wirtschaftstreuhänder, Vienna 1998, 183 et seqs.; Stefan Hoehl, Vorläufiger Rechtsschutz im verwaltungsgerichtlichen Verfahren unter besonderer Berücksichtigung des Europarechts, in: Rudolf Thienel (ed.), Verwaltungsgerichtsbarkeit im Wandel, Vienna 1999, 247 et seqs.; *id.*, *Vorläufiger Rechtsschutz vor dem VwGH unter besonderer Berücksichtigung des Europarechts*, Vienna 1999; Michael Potacs, Vorläufiger Rechtsschutz im verwaltungsgerichtlichen Verfahren – innerstaatliche und gemeinschaftsrechtliche Aspekte, in: Michael Holoubek/Michael Lang (eds.), Das verwaltungsgerichtliche Verfahren in Steuersachen, Vienna 1999, 43 et seqs.; Michael Potacs, Vorläufiger Rechtsschutz, in: *ibid.*, 265 et seqs.

[155] Cf., in general, Robert Rebhahn, Staatshaftung nach dem Recht der Europäischen Gemeinschaft, 118 *JBl* 1996, 749 et seqs.; Bernd-Christian Funk, Staatshaftung auf der Grundlage von Gemeinschaftsrecht, 8 *ecolex* 1997, 553 et seqs.; Waldemar Hummer/Walter Obwexer, Die unmittelbare Wirkung von EG-Richtlinien und die Haftung des Staates für Umsetzungsmängel, in: Stefan Griller/Heinz-Peter Rill (eds.), *Verfassungsrechtliche Grundfragen der EU-Mitgliedschaft*, Vienna 1997, 21 et seqs.; Jens Budischowsky, Schadenersatz wegen Nichtumsetzung von Richtlinien der EG und Amtshaftung, 25 *ÖZW* 1998, 1 et seqs.; *id.*, Staatshaftung und Föderalismus, 9 *ecolex* 1998, 740 et seqs.; Robert Rebhahn, Staatshaftung bei Verletzung von Gemeinschaftsrecht und Umsetzung bin Österreich, in: Österreichische Juristenkommission (Hrsg), *Kritik und Fortschritt im Rechtsstaat. Österreich als Mitglied der Europäischen Union*, Wien 1999, 149 et seqs.; Peter Bußjäger, Zur kompetenzrechtlichen Umsetzung der "Staatshaftung" in Österreich, 11 *ecolex* 2000, 74 et seqs.; Birgit Schoisswohl, Die Grundlagen des Rechtswidrigkeitsurteils in der Staatshaftung wegen Gemeinschafstrechtsverletzung, 11 *ecolex* 2000, 332 et seqs.

[156] Bundesgesetz vom 18. Dezember 1948, womit die Haftung des Bundes, der Länder, der Bezirke, der Gemeinden und der sonstigen Körperschaften und Anstalten des öffentlichen Rechts für den in Vollziehung der Gesetze zugefügten Schaden geregelt wird (Amtshaftungsgesetz), (Austrian) Federal Official Journal Nr 1949/20.

[157] Cf. Öhlinger/Potacs, *Gemeinschaftsrecht und staatliches Recht*, 2th ed Vienna 2001, 176.

[158] Highest of the "regular" courts (i.e. courts of civil or criminal law).

[159] A transfer of powers from the Federation to the states, as originally envisaged for the occasion of accession to the EU, has so far not been carried out.

[160] Cf. Peter Pernthaler, *Das Länderbeteiligungsverfahren an der Europäischen Integration*, Wien 1992; Helmut Schreiner, Die Mitwirkung der Länder im Zuge der EG-Integration, *ÖJBPol* 1992, 183; Heinz Peter Rill, Die Bundesländer und die europäische Integration (EWR und EG), in: Heinz Schäffer/Harald Stolzlechner (eds.), *Reformbestrebungen im österreichischen Bundesstaatssystem*, Vienna 1993;

Heinz Schäffer, Die Länder-Mitwirkung in Angelegenheiten der Europäischen Integration, in: Johannes Hengstschläger/Heribert Franz Köck/Karl Korinek/Klaus Stern/Antonio Truyol y Serra (eds.), *Für Staat und Recht.* Essays in honour of Herbert Schambeck, Berlin 1994, 1002; Peter Pernthaler, Die Auswirkungen einer Mitgliedschaft Österreichs in der Europäischen Union auf die österreichischen Bundesländer, in: Waldemar Hummer (ed.), Die Europäische Union und Österreich, Vienna 1994, 179; Borchmann, Die Mitwirkung der österreichischen Länder in Europaangelegenhgeiten, 5 *EuZW* 1994, 116; Fritz Staudigl/Renate Fischler (eds), *Die Teilnahme der Bundesländer am europäischen Integrationsprozess*, Vienna 1996; Michael Morass, Die Praxis der Bund-Länder-Koordination in der EU-Politik, in: ibid., 85; *Helmut Schreiner*, Das Länderbeteiligungsverfahren in Österreich, 4 *JRP* 1996, 207; Josef Unterlechner, *Die Mitwirkung der Länder am EU-Willensbildungs-Prozess*, Vienna 1997; Johannes Müller, Allgemeine Umsetzungsprobleme des EU-Rechts auf Landesebene, in: Peter Pernthaler (ed.), *Auswirkungen des EU-Rechts auf die Länder*, Vienna 1999, 27; Andreas Rosner, *Koordinationsinstrumente der österreichischen Länder*, Vienna 2000.

161 Vereinbarung zwischen dem Bund und den Ländern über die Mitwirkungsrechte der Länder und Gemeinden in Angelegenheiten der Europäischen Integration, (Austrian) Federal Official Journal 1992/775.

162 Cf article 23d paragraph 1 B-VG.

163 Cf article Art 5 Abs 1 of the agreement between the Federation and the states.

164 Cf Heribert Franz Köck/Peter Fischer, *Das Recht der Internationalen Organisationen,* Vienna 1997, 554 et seq.

165 Cf. Hans Neuhofer, Der Wandel der Gemeindeaufgaben unter Berücksichtigung des EU-Beitritts, in: Herbert Strunz/Christine Fohler-Norek/Karl W. Edtstadler (eds.), *Öffentliche Verwaltung im Wandel*, Vienna 1996, 93.

166 By no means should the idea of a separate European Court of Competences – as proposed by Ulrich Goll and Markus Kenntner, Brauchen wir ein Europäisches Kompetenzgericht. Vorschläge zur Sicherung der mitgliedstaatlichen Zuständigkeit, *EuZW* (2002), 101 et seqs. – be pursued; if the unity of EU/EC law is to be preserved, the ECJ has to remain the one and only "Supreme Court" of the EU/EC. Cf., in this context, Werner Schroeder, Zu eingebildeten und realen Gefahren durch kompetenzüberschreitende Rechtsakte der Europäischen gemeinschaft, 34 *EuR* (1999), 452 et seqs.

167 Cf *supra*, II. 3. b.

168 For related proposals, cf., *inter alia*, the Second report on the reorganisation of the European Union Treaties, submitted to the European Commission on 31 July 2000, elaborated, under the auspices of the European University Institute, by a Working Group chaired by Claus-Dieter Ehlermann and Yves Mény, Hervé Bribosia serving as rapporteur, entitled *Reforming the Treaties' Amendment Procedures.*

SELECTED GENERAL BIBLIOGRAPHY

Hartmut Bauer, Europäisierung des Verfassungsrechts, 122 *JBl* (2000), 750 et seqs.
Bergedorfer Gesprächskreis, *Die Verfassung Europas*, 103. Gesprächskreis 1995

Wolfgang Streitenberger (ed.), *Zum Projekt einer transnationalen europäischen Verfassung*. Die Union 4/98

Tanja A. Börzel and Thomas Risse, *The Post-Nice Agenda of the European Union: What's the Problem, How to Deal With It, and What to Avoid*, European University Institute, 2001

Wolfgang Dix, Charte des droits fondamentaux et Convention. De nouvelles voies pour réformer l'UE?, *Revue du Marché commun et de l'union européenne* (2001), 305 et seqs.

Benita Ferrero-Waldner, *Der weitere Diskussions- und Entscheidungsprozess zur Zukunft der Europäischen Union,* Paper read on the occasion of the Enquête by the Austrian National Council on "Zukunft der Europäischen Union", 20 June 2001

Joschka Fischer, *Vom Staatenverbund zur Föderation – Gedanken über die Finalität der europäischen Integration*, Manuscript of a paper delivered at the Humboldt University Berlin on 12 May 2000

Jochen Abr. Frowein, Die Verfassung der Europäischen Union aus der Sicht der Mitgliedstaaten, 30 EuR (1995), 315 et seqs.

Dieter Grimm, *Braucht Europa eine Verfassung ?* 1995

Jürgen Habermas, *Warum braucht Europa eine Verfassung?* European University Institute, 2001 (Enlarged text of a paper delivered in Hamburg on 26 June 2001, published in DIE ZEIT of 29 June 2001)

Markus Heintzen, Gemeineuropäisches Verfassungsrecht in der Europäischen Union, 32 *EuR* (1997), 1 et seqs.

Frank Hoffmeister, Europäisches Verfassungsrecht nach Amsterdam, in: 34 *EuR* 1999, 280 et seqs.

Peter-Christian Müller-Graff/Eibel Riedel (eds.), *Gemeinsames Verfassungsrecht in der Europäischen Union,* Baden-Baden 1998

Ingolf Pernice, Multilevel Constitutionalism and the Treaty of Amsterdam: European Constitution-Making Revisited?, 36 *CMLR* (1999), 703 et seqs.

Jean-Claude Piris, L'Union européenne a-t-elle une constitution? Lui en faut-il une?, 35 *RTD eur.* (1999), 599 et seqs.; also in German: Hat die Europäische Union eine Verfassung? Braucht sie eine? 35 *EuR* (2000), 311 et seqs.

Johannes Rau, Plädoyer für eine Europäische Verfassung, *Europinformationen,* Address delivered to the European Parlament on 4 April 2001

Gil Carlos Rodrígez Iglesias, Zur "Verfassung" der Europäischen Gemeinschaft, 23 *EuGRZ* (1996), 125 et seqs.

Herbert Schambeck, Über die Idee einer EU-Verfassung, in: Baudenbacher/Mayer/Torggler (eds.), *Ein Leben in Praxis und Wissenschaft.* Essays in honour of Walter Barfuss, Vienna 2002

J.H.H. Weiler, The Reformation of European Constitutionalism, 35 *Journal of Common Market Studies* (1997), 97 et seqs.

Antje Wiener, Constitution-making and Citizenship Practice – Bridging the Democracy Gap in the EU? 35 *Journal of Common Market Studies* (1997), 595 et seqs.

Frank Vibert, *Europe: A Constitution for the Millenium*, Aldershot Hants 1995

Sonja Volkmann-Schluck, *Die Deatte um eine europäische Verfassung*, C.A.P. Working Paper 2001

CYPRUS

L'ordre juridique communautaire et les constitutions nationales

La constitution de Chypre face au débat constitutionnel dans l'Union européenne

Rapporteur
Maître Christos Josephides

I. INTRODUCTION: LES FONDEMENTS DU CONSTITUTIONALISME EUROPEEN

L'inclusion du débat constitutionnel européen dans les travaux du XXème Congrès de la Fédération Internationale pour le Droit Européen-FIDE, qui suit ceux du XVIIème congrès de Berlin en 1996 sur le même thème, témoigne de l'intérêt que portent les Européens sur cette importante question. Car la question est réellement posée : « L'union européenne a-t-elle une Constitution ? Lui en faut une ? » se demande Jean-Claude PIRIS[2]. « De la constitution composée de l'Europe » écrivent Ingolf PERNICE et Frantz C. MAYER[3]. « Quelle Constitution pour quelle Europe ? » s'interroge Robert TOULEMON[4]. Le Parlement Européen revient en permanence à la question dans le cadre de ses travaux depuis le rapport Spinelli de 1984 et le rapport Herman de 1994. Les parlements nationaux s'y intéressent à un très haut degré et développent leur propre problématique. Le rapport du Sénat français présenté par M. le sénateur Hubert HAENEL[5], en juin 2001, et la Décision du Bundesrat[6] prise le 20 décembre 2001, sont deux exemples significatifs de l'intérêt que portent les parlements nationaux à cette question.

Les chefs d'Etat et de Gouvernement des Etats membres de l'Union Européenne (UE) et plus particulièrement ceux des Etats membres les plus grands ont également posé la question, notamment en vue et après le Conseil Européen de Nice en décembre 2000. Le discours de M. Joschka Fischer le 9 mai 2000, celui du Président Chirac devant le Bundestag le 27 juin de la même année, celui du britannique M. Tony Blair à Varsovie le 9 octobre 2000 constituent, s'il en faut, des preuves de l'intérêt porté par les Etats membres sur la problématique constitutionnelle européenne. La conférence donnée le 31 juillet 2002 à Nicosie par l'Italien M. Giuliano Amato[7] en pleine Convention maintient vivant le débat.

La problématique constitutionnelle a naturellement atteint les 13 pays candidats à l'adhésion à l'Union. Le vaste mouvement d'élargissement en perspective, qui portera dès l'année 2004 ou 2005[8] le nombre des Etats membres de 15 à près de 25, apporte au débat constitutionnel des éléments nouveaux qui l'élargissent aux questions de fonctionnement des institutions à 25 d'une part, à un plus grand public venant d'un plus grand nombre d'Etats, d'autre part. L'association des pays candidats à la réflexion sur l'avenir de l'Europe lancée le 28 février 2002 dans le cadre d'une Convention donne une base légitime de leur propre apport. Encore faut-il qu'au moment des conclusions n'apparaissent pas, lors de la Conférence Intergouvernementale de 2004, des phénomènes de différenciation d'idées sur la base du caractère d'Etat membre par opposition à celui de pays candidat. L'Union européenne doit continuer à se développer sur la base de l'idée développée par les pères fondateurs et reprise dans les Traités : une union toujours plus étroite entre les peuples européens.

Chypre, pays candidat avec, en juillet 2002, un très haut degré d'harmonisation de sa législation avec l'acquis communautaire, fera probablement partie des pays candidats dont l'avenir européen en tant qu'Etat membre sera assuré par la décision qui sera prise par le Conseil Européen de Copenhague de décembre 2002. En plus de l'harmonisation de sa législation, l'Etat chypriote a déjà étudié toutes les modifications constitutionnelles qui seront nécessaires pour permettre à ce pays de disposer, au moment de l'adhésion, d'une Constitution conforme au droit communautaire. A ce titre, Chypre participe aux travaux de la Convention sur l'avenir de l'Europe ainsi qu'au débat qui se développe à ce sujet par le monde académique, le monde des affaires, les jeunes etc. L'Association Chypriote pour le Droit Européen[9], en tant que membre associé de la FIDE, propose de partager certaines réflexions produites dans le cadre de la problématique institutionnelle.

1. Le concept de Constitution dans les Etats européens

A l'occasion d'un tel débat, il est important de bien poser le concept de base et son contenu (a), de définir celui ou ceux à qui le concept est destiné (b), de choisir la méthode qui sera suivie (c) et, dans la mesure du possible, oser certaines évaluations sur les évolutions attendues (d). Ce faisant, il faut garder à l'esprit le fait que tous ces éléments sont interdépendants et varient selon les conceptions du droit qui prévalent à telle ou telle période de l'histoire de l'humanité civilisée.

a. Le concept de base et son contenu

La thèse contractualiste attachée à l'idée du contrat social, reprise et développée comme suit par Ingolf PERNICE et Franz MAYER[10] offre une piste intéressante à explorer dans la mesure où elle permet l'analyse selon laquelle les peuples européens peuvent redéfinir leur destin commun:

« La thèse contractualiste explique donc l'Etat comme création, objet de la constitution, mais ne s'y limite pas. La constitution peut être le texte créateur d'autres formes de communauté dans la mesure où elle est l'expression d'un « contrat social » par lequel un groupe de personnes sur un territoire délimité convient de se donner le statut de citoyen d'un nouvel ordre politique, d'en être les citoyens ou « le peuple », pris dans le sens large de participants, membres ou adhérents qui partagent les mêmes valeurs, telles que consacrées dans la constitution. Et c'est ce « peuple » qui, par son pouvoir constituant, se crée des institutions et procédures, droits et obligations propres pour accomplir certaines tâches et fonctions dans l'intérêt de tous. « Pas plus de pouvoir public que la constitution n'en institue » : c'est l'essentiel d'une définition générale et démocratique de la notion de constitution. Elle a l'avantage de ne pas dépendre, essentiellement, de l'existence d'un Etat, elle exclut l'existence d'une autorité publique légitime en dehors d'une constitution, et elle permet de concevoir la constitution comme l'expression d'un accord aussi sur d'autres formes et structures composées et non unitaires d'organisation politique, soit supra ou infra-étatique. La notion de constitution, ainsi définie, légitime et limite les pouvoirs confiés aux institutions de la communauté qu'elle fonde. »

Partant de cette thèse et, sans exclure « l'existence de toute autorité publique en dehors d'une constitution », nous proposons de retenir le concept de base et le contenu d'une constitution pour l'Union européenne comme étant celui d'un contrat social librement établi entre les individus (citoyens) et l'autorité publique organisée pour administrer leurs relations sur la base de règles fondamentales destinées à garantir l'exercice de leurs droits et devoirs respectifs. Il est le lien et constitue le fondement même de la légitimité de l'exercice du pouvoir public et le moyen de contrôle de cet exercice par ceux à qui il se destine. Il peut être renégocié à tout moment pour rendre compte de toute évolution significative des conceptions sociales et juridiques relatives à la vie en société organisée. En ce sens, le concept est vivant et évolutif.

b. Les destinataires de la constitution

Le besoin de constitution apparaît donc le plus souvent lorsqu'il y réunion de deux éléments constitutifs :

- un large groupe d'individus libres, partageant des valeurs communes qui couvrent de larges expressions de la vie en communauté,
- une volonté affirmée du groupe d'établir, de façon démocratique et dans

un esprit d'égalité, des règles de coexistence libre et créative sur un espace déterminé et souverain appartenant au groupe.

Le concept de base ainsi défini détermine logiquement ceux à qui il est destiné qui ne peuvent être autres que les individus, les citoyens qui composent le groupe et qui souhaitent asseoir leurs relations sur une légitimité incontestée.

Dans un système de relations plus large et plus complexe, comme celui de l'Union européenne, les destinataires de la Constitution seront toujours les citoyens. S'agissant d'une Union d'Etats et de peuples, les Etats eux même en tant que partie prenante dotée d'un rôle démocratique actif seront aussi destinataires de la Constitution. Ainsi, l'Etat membre sera à la fin du processus membre fondateur et destinataire de la Constitution européenne, sans pour autant perdre, à son niveau, le caractère d'un ensemble de normes constitutionnelles qui ont, elles aussi, pour destinataire final le citoyen européen, le peuple européen en formation. Le peuple, quant à lui, disposera de deux références constitutionnelles, l'une nationale et l'autre européenne, qui seront complémentaires à l'instar de la citoyenneté européenne (voir article 17 TCE) qui complète la citoyenneté nationale.

c. Le choix de la méthode

La méthode, en partie contestée, qui sera finalement choisie pour l'élaboration d'un texte de caractère constitutionnel ne sera pas étrangère au produit final de la réflexion engagée. La simple révision des traités actuels en vue de les rendre plus clairs et par conséquent plus accessibles à ceux à qui ils sont destinés, emprunte la voie classique de la Conférence Intergouvernementale précédée par les conclusions de la Convention. Le texte ainsi produit sera adopté par un Conseil européen et la procédure nationale dans chaque Etat membre et au niveau de l'Union, une fois terminée de façon positive, accorderont au nouveau traité une légitimité accrue. Une telle révision pourra notamment intégrer dans le texte du traité la Charte des Droits Fondamentaux proclamée à Nice et lui attribuer ainsi expressément un caractère juridique de rang constitutionnel au sens donné par la Cour de Justice qui, dans son arrêt « Les Verts »[11], qualifie le traité de « charte constitutionnelle ».

La méthode qui conduira à l'étude et à l'adoption d'une constitution au sens le plus couramment compris en Europe est toute différente. Une « Constituante » pourra proposer un texte de constitution et ensuite les peuples des Etats membres, soit par voie parlementaire, soit par référendum pourront l'adopter. La même question d'unanimité se posera dans les mêmes conditions que pour l'adoption de toute révision des traités. La Convention lancée à Bruxelles le 28 février 2002 avec des représentants venant des Etats membres, des pays candidats, et des Institutions européennes finira par présenter ses propositions en mars 2003. L'avenir de l'Europe et la procédure à suivre seront ainsi tracés pour permettre à la Conférence Intergouvernementale d'en débattre. Elle pose ainsi un premier jalon sur le long parcours de la « constitutionnalisation » de l'évolution de l'Union Européenne.

d. Les évolutions attendues

L'Europe d'aujourd'hui n'a pas été faite en un jour. Plus de la moitié d'un siècle a été nécessaire pour parvenir à l'équilibre institutionnel existant et à l'équilibre connu du partage des compétences entre Etats membres et les institutions de l'Union. La citoyenneté européenne est déjà une réalité[12] et le système communautaire *sui generis* a établi sa propre spécificité en tant que système fondé sur la prééminence du doit, qui fixe un nouvel ordre juridique distinct des droits nationaux et qui protège les droits de l'homme et des libertés fondamentales. La Charte des droits fondamentaux constitue une référence qui orientera les débats sur l'avenir de l'Europe.

A l'instar du passé, l'avenir de l'Europe se fera pas par pas. Le vaste élargissement prévu pour les années 2004 ou 2005[13], combiné avec une nouvelle forme de traités simplifiés, qualifiés de « traités constitutionnels » ou de « constitution », auront pour effet l'efficacité et la démocratie, deux caractéristiques du mouvement vers l'objectif des pères fondateurs : une union toujours plus étroite entre les peuples.

Le peuple chypriote dans son ensemble aspire à ce rapprochement. L'élargissement de l'Union vers Chypre et vers d'autres pays candidats, et la participation de leurs représentants à la Convention sur l'avenir de l'Union contribuent à la réalisation du projet des pères fondateurs. La Constitution chypriote devra néanmoins s'adapter, comme cela est d'ailleurs prévu par une importante étude du Service Juridique de la République, aux principes démocratiques communautaires qui lui permettront d'être en plein accord avec les principes démocratiques généralement en vigueur dans les ordres constitutionnels des Etats membres, qui deviendront aussi formellement les principes constitutionnels de l'Union Européenne.

e. Le concept de Constitution à Chypre

La constitution chypriote est la loi suprême de la République (article 179). Elle est marquée par la colonisation[14] et elle a la particularité d'être une constitution octroyée au peuple chypriote par d'autres que le peuple lui-même. La constitution chypriote a été préparée à la fin de la période coloniale dans le cadre de l'Accord de Zurich du 11 février 1959 signé entre la Grèce et la Turquie, en l'absence de représentants du peuple chypriote, et de l'Accord de Londres qui a suivi huit jours plus tard et signé le 19 février 1959[15]. La rédaction de la Constitution, dont la structure et les principaux éléments étaient imposés par les Accords de Zurich et de Londres, a été réalisée par une Commission[16] mixte mise en place par l'Accord de Londres et composée de représentants des gouvernements grec et turc et des communautés chypriotes grecque et turque. Un professeur suisse de droit constitutionnel à l'Université de Lausanne y apportait ses services de conseiller juridique.

Le rôle de la Commission constitutionnelle était celui de la préparation du projet de la Constitution de la future République de Chypre. Dans cette tâche, elle devait notamment tenir compte et « observer scrupuleusement » les éléments contenus dans les documents de la Conférence de Zurich et de mener à bien sa tâche « en accord avec les principes » posés par ladite Conférence.

Comme le précise l'ancien *Attorney General* de la République de Chypre C. TORNARITIS « la Constitution est entrée en vigueur le 16 août 1960, lors de la création de la République de Chypre sans avoir été votée soit par le peuple chypriote directement, soit par ses représentants dûment élus pour cet objet constitués en Assemblée »[17].

Ainsi la Constitution chypriote est une constitution octroyée au peuple chypriote sur l'initiative du pouvoir colonial, acte qui rappelle les temps révolus des monarques condescendant de doter leurs sujets de chartes de droits et devoirs. Elle a été créée par des tiers et allouée au peuple chypriote dans son ensemble, sans que le peuple soit appelé à y donner formellement son accord, soit directement par l'expression du suffrage universel, soit indirectement par des représentants élus en Assemblée Constituante[18], ce qui maintient des doutes sérieux quant à son assise démocratique.

Pour D.G. LAVROFF[19] « ... la procédure suivie constitue incontestablement une anomalie au regard du droit international... les accords de Londres sont à notre connaissance, les seuls qui aient élaboré une Constitution applicable à un Etat tiers ». Ceci constitue une première particularité de fond[20].

De même la Constitution, au moment de son entrée en vigueur était accompagnée de deux traités internationaux cités dans la Constitution même (article 181). Ces traités y sont annexés et sont dotés de force constitutionnelle. Il s'agit :

- du Traité de Garantie[21] entre la République de Chypre d'une part, la Grèce, la Turquie et le Royaume Uni, d'autre part.
- du Traité d'Alliance[22] entre la République de Chypre, la Grèce et la Turquie visant à protéger Chypre contre toute attaque ou agression contre l'indépendance ou l'intégrité territoriale et la sécurité de la République.

Par ailleurs, au moment de l'entrée en vigueur de la Constitution, le « Traité d'Etablissement » signé entre le Royaume-Uni, la Grèce, la Turquie et la République de Chypre accordait au Royaume Uni deux bases militaires souveraines et des facilités pour l'usage du territoire de la République par les forces britanniques. Ainsi, à la proclamation de l' « indépendance » de Chypre une Constitution a été octroyée au peuple chypriote dans les conditions ci-dessus, et il a été soustrait à ce peuple une partie de son territoire national pour le maintenir sous l'autorité de l'ancien Etat colonial.

Ce phénomène des trois traités annexés à, ou accompagnant la Constitution, constitue la deuxième particularité de la Constitution. En outre, les trois Traités ci-dessus mentionnés sont en principe toujours en vigueur et deux d'entre eux ont rang constitutionnel (article 181 de la Constitution) et font ainsi partie du corps de la Constitution. L'*Attorney General* Alecos Markides qualifie la Constitution de la République de Chypre de Constitution « rigide, détaillée et complexe »[23]. Dans ces conditions, il est aisé d'imaginer les effets bienfaiteurs de l'intégration Chypre à l'Union européenne notamment en matière constitutionnelle.

2. *Dispositions nationales pour l'adoption d'une « Constitution » pour l'Union européenne : le cas de Chypre, Etat candidat*

La Constitution chypriote, introduite dans les conditions ci-dessus décrites, n'a pas retenu de dispositions nationales relatives à l'adoption d'une « Constitution » de l'Union européenne. La question de légitimité de l'intégration de Chypre à l'Union européenne ayant été posée par la Turquie[24], trois professeurs de droit international, James CRAWFORD[25] de l'Université de Cambridge, Gerhard HAFNER de l'Université de Vienne et Alain PELLET de l'Université de Paris X – Nanterre conclurent en 1997 et en 2001 que la Constitution de Chypre et plus particulièrement l'article 1, paragraphe 2 du Traité de Garantie, l'article 50 de la Constitution de 1960 et/ou l'article 170 de la Constitution n'interdisaient pas à Chypre « de devenir membre de l'Union européenne ».

Le traité d'adhésion de Chypre à l'Union européenne en tant que traité international sera singé après accord donné par le Conseil des Ministres et ratifié par la Chambre des Représentants (article 169.2). A défaut d'amendement de la Constitution, il aura une valeur infra constitutionnelle et supra législative dès son entrée en vigueur (article 169.3). Toute révision des Traités en vue d'adoption d'une « constitution » de l'Union empruntera cette voie constitutionnellement prévue, sans pour autant exclure la possibilité offerte par le référendum qui, bien que n'étant pas prévu par la Constitution, n'en constitue pas moins une voie démocratique permettant au peuple de s'exprimer de façon directe sur d'importantes questions d'ordre national.

La société civile chypriote est très fermement attachée à l'idée et à l'intégration européenne. Au delà des aspects formels de la signature et de la ratification du traité d'adhésion tels qu'ils sont prévus par la Constitution, la société civile conçoit l'idée d'une Constitution de l'Union comme un contrat social établi sur la base de la thèse exposée par Ingolf Pernice et Frantz C. Meyer réaménagée. (voir ci-dessus)

3. Le processus de préparation d'une constitution – la Conférence Intergouvernementale de 2004

Dans la mesure où l'on admet que la Convention sur l'avenir de l'Europe constitue une démarche visant notamment à la production d'une constitution[26] ou à défaut à un « traité constitutionnel » on peut estimer que le produit principal de la Conférence Intergouvernementale sera la proposition d'un texte de Constitution / d'un traité constitutionnel pour l'Union.

a. L'organisation du débat interne à Chypre sur l'avenir de l'Union européenne

Le débat interne de la République de Chypre sur l'avenir de l'Europe a été organisé à divers niveaux par différents instances nationales dans un souci de la plus large implication de la société civile à la réflexion. La Chambre des Représentants (Assemblée Nationale chypriote) a pris l'initiative de l'organisation d'une série de débats sur l'avenir de l'Europe avec la participation de la société civile et a produit une réflexion sur la mise en place d'un mécanisme de diffusion de l'information faisant appel aussi bien à des moyens classiques de diffusion (conférences, support papier, activités diverses) qu'à des moyens d'informatique/télématique dont l'internet.

D'autres institutions, dont l'Université de Chypre (Chaire Jean Monnet) et divers établissements d'enseignement supérieur, l'Institut Européen de Chypre, l'Association Chypriote pour le Droit européen (FIDE), la Chambres de Commerce et d'Industrie et les Syndicats des travailleurs ont organisé des conférences-débats, ont participé à des débats radiophoniques et télévisés, ont produit des articles dans la presse locale et ont généralement contribué et continuent de contribuer à la diffusion de la problématique sur l'avenir de l'Europe.

b. Les questions essentielles et les propositions

Les questions clefs et les propositions résultant du débat chypriote sur l'avenir de l'Europe se développent autour des thèmes suivants : (a) Le rôle des parlements nationaux dans l'Europe de demain, (b) La dimension culturelle de l'Europe à venir, (c) Europe et jeunesse : Questions et

Aspirations, (d) Le fonctionnement des institutions européennes de demain et le partage des compétences et pouvoirs, et (e) Pouvoirs locaux-subsidiarité.

Les propositions soumises dans le cadre du premier thème peuvent se résumer comme suit : Meilleure information des citoyens et développement de leur engagement dans les affaires de l'Union grâce à un plus grand rôle qui devra être attribué aux parlements nationaux et au Parlement Européen dans la nouvelle architecture de l'Union. L'Europe des citoyens et l'intégration européenne ne pourront se faire que si le déficit démocratique diminue, et la légitimité et la transparence sauvegardées. Pour y parvenir, une série de mesures pratiques et concrètes sont proposées. Celles-ci concernent plus particulièrement la création de commissions parlementaires composées à la fois de parlementaires venant des Parlements nationaux et du Parlement européen, la transparence des travaux du Conseil, l'accord du Parlement national sur le choix du Commissaire de l'Etat respectif, une relation plus étroite entre les parlements nationaux et les Organisations Non Gouvernementales, une information plus suivie des Parlements nationaux et de la société civile, la participation élargie des parlements nationaux dans la préparation de la Conférence Intergouvernementale de 2004 et de celles qui en suivront, et autres propositions ayant pour objectif une information plus large des Parlements nationaux et de la société civile rendant leur participation au devenir européen plus attrayante et plus effective.

Dans le cadre de la discussion sur la dimension culturelle de l'Europe de demain le partage de valeurs communes telles que la stabilité politique, la démocratie, la légitimité, l'état de droit, les droits de l'homme, la protection des minorités, la tolérance et l'acceptation mutuelle doivent venir compléter l'Europe du Marché Commun. L'institution et le renforcement de la citoyenneté européenne contribuent à la création auprès des citoyens d'un sentiment d'appartenance à l'édifice européen en construction et à l'identité commune d'Européens, qui n'est pas une simple notion juridique mais correspond à un concept de nature politique et culturelle. La double appartenance culturelle nationale et européenne doit être sauvegardée et encouragée. Afin de permettre la coopération culturelle entre les différents peuples européens, les programmes communautaires d'échanges culturels devront se multiplier, avec l'accent porté aux pays candidats. La protection des minorités et la préservation de l'identité européenne face à la domination américaine devront également faire partie de la réflexion sur l'Europe de demain.

La question des institutions et du partage des pouvoirs doit se régler dans le cadre de la problématique relative à la question « Quelle Europe voulons-nous et dans quel but ? ». Il n'y aura pas d'Europe forte, prête à jouer le rôle qui lui revient dans le monde si l'Europe ne dispose pas les moyens d'une politique de défense et de sécurité propre. Sur le plan interne, le citoyen devra se sentir proche des institutions. Tout nouveau transfert de compétences des Etats vers l'Union doit se faire dans le cadre d'un échange qui doit sauvegarder la légitimité et la transparence et dans le respect du principe de subsidiarité et de proximité.

Les thèmes d'éducation, d'emploi, de participation au devenir européen intéressent les jeunes qui doivent être introduits d'une façon ou d'une autre dans le processus de prise de décision et de son contrôle démocratique. Une Europe forte sur le plan international est nécessaire pour lui permettre d'intervenir efficacement dans la recherche de solutions en Palestine, à Chypre et ailleurs dans le monde.

Les autorités locales, démocratiquement élues sont plus proches des problèmes et des préoccupations quotidiennes des citoyens et l'application pratique du principe de subsidiarité doit en tenir compte pour conduire au transfert de compétences au niveau le plus proche des citoyens. Entre l'Union et les Etats membres le partage des compétences devra être repensé sur la base du principe de subsidiarité et de celui de proximité.

II. DROIT COMMUNAUTAIRE ET DROIT INSTITUTIONNEL NATIONAL

Pour les Etats membres il s'agit de deux ordres constitutionnels complémentaires vivants qui se développent simultanément selon les cas l'un par rapport à l'autre et l'un à côté de l'autre ou parallèlement l'un à l'autre. Il n'en va pas de même pour les pays candidats dont les ordres constitutionnels se sont institués et développés indépendamment de l'évolution constitutionnelle de l'Union.

1. L'autonomie constitutionnelle des Etats membres et les contraintes européennes

S'agissant d'une union à la fois d'Etats et de peuples, vu d'un pays candidat, la disposition de l'article 6.3 TUE n'apparaît pas nécessaire. Elle se dégage d'une manière ou d'une autre de la répartition formelle des compétences et de l'exercice réel des pouvoirs respectifs. De même, l'article 151 TCE est particulièrement précis pour normalement exclure toute introduction intempestive de l'Union dans les affaires, ici les affaires culturelles, des Etats membres. L'Union vient en aide aux Etats membres, avec l'accord unanime des Etats membres.

De même, partant du principe constaté par la CJCE que les Etats membres partagent les mêmes valeurs constitutionnelles dans les matières concernées par l'article 6.1 et qui sont le fondement même d'un Etat démocratique, on peut difficilement considérer une situation dans laquelle la constitution d'un

Etat membre pourrait dévier de ces principes fondamentaux avec ledit Etat continuant à participer au fonctionnement de l'Union. C'est pourquoi l'introduction des dispositions de l'article 6.1 dans le corps du Traité n'a de sens que si les dispositions de l'article 7 sont portées au même rang dans la hiérarchie des normes juridiques de l'Union, ce qui est fait. Les critères de Copenhague relatifs à l'Etat de droit et aux valeurs démocratiques que doivent partager le pays candidats ne sauraient être mis de côté après l'adhésion à l'Union. Les transformations profondes que doivent connaître les constitutions des pays candidats en vue de leur adhésion au système juridique de l'Union déterminent par analogie les limites de l'autonomie des Etats membres dans leurs initiatives constitutionnelles d'ordre national. En effet, le corps des valeurs communes des Etats membres ne saurait devenir déficitaire sans atteindre les fondements et les objectifs de l'Union retenus par les articles 1 et 2 du TUE qui constituent en même temps la raison d'être de l'Union.

2. Valeurs communes : la Charte des droits fondamentaux de l'Union Européenne

La République de Chypre est dotée d'un système juridique fondé sur l'Etat de droit et les principes démocratiques communs dans les Etats membres de l'Union. Chypre, Etat européen[27], partage les valeurs communes des Etats membres et, grâce à la Constitution, aux différents traités et protocoles internationaux relatifs aux droits de la personne humaine, ratifiés par la loi de la République dont la Convention européenne de sauvegarde des droits de l'homme et des libertés fondamentales, qui a une valeur supra législative et infra constitutionnelle, combinés avec un ensemble de lois protecteur des droits de la personne, peut être considérée comme un Etat où la Charte reflète en grande partie des droits fondamentaux déjà protégés.

Il existe néanmoins certains droits prévus dans la Charte, et plus spécialement ceux liés à la citoyenneté de l'Union qui, et pour cause, ne font pas encore partie du système juridique chypriote.

a. La protection des droits de l'homme et des libertés fondamentales

La partie II de la Constitution est exclusivement consacrée aux droits fondamentaux de l'homme et à ses libertés fondamentales.

Le rang constitutionnel de la protection et le système judiciaire dans son ensemble assurent aux citoyens un niveau de protection élevé analogue à celui des systèmes de protection en vigueur dans tout Etat démocratique et en particulier dans le système de l'Union européenne, incluant notamment la Charte des droits fondamentaux.

b. Un rang élevé de protection

La place réservée aux droits fondamentaux et à leur protection par la Constitution d'une part et l'étendue de ces droits d'autre part, démontrent la volonté de leur assurer une efficacité juridique de première importance.

La Partie II de la Constitution comprend 30 articles (articles n° 6 à 35) et a pour titre « Sur les droits fondamentaux et libertés ». Elle est située immédiatement après les « Dispositions générales » qui définissent notamment le caractère de la République de Chypre, le rôle de la Constitution, le drapeau de la République, les langues officielles et autres clauses constitutionnelles de caractère général. Il s'agit par conséquent d'une matière constitutionnelle située en très bonne place pour constituer le cœur et l'une des grandes priorités de la Constitution.

L'étendue des droits fondamentaux et des libertés de rang constitutionnel est plus large dans la Constitution de la République de Chypre que celle retenue dans la Convention européenne de Sauvegarde des Droits de l'Homme et des Libertés Fondamentales et dans d'autres constitutions[28]. Tous les droits garantis par la Convention[29] sont également garantis par la constitution. En plus, il existe des droits qui sont mieux garantis par la Constitution et d'autres qui, sans être sauvegardés par la Convention, sont sauvegardés par la Constitution.

Dans l'exposé des droits fondamentaux et libertés garantis on remarque aisément, moyennant souvent une simple translation numérique, due aux « dispositions générales de la Constitution » (articles 1 à 5) et à l'introduction d'articles supplémentaires dans la Constitution, une similitude et une analogie dans la présentation des droits garantis par la Convention et par la Constitution. Ainsi, par exemple, le droit à la vie protégé par l'article 2 de la Convention et figurant à l'article 2 de la Charte figure à l'article 7 de la Constitution. S'y ajoute le droit à l'intégrité physique de la personne. (Article 3 de la Charte) L'interdiction de la soumission à la torture et à des peines ou traitements inhumains ou dégradants figure respectivement à l'article 3 de la Convention, à l'article 4 de la Charte et à l'article 8 de la Constitution chypriote. L'interdiction de la soumission à l'esclavage et la servitude est retenue à l'article 4 de la Convention et à l'article 10 de la Constitution, légèrement différente dans l'article 5 de la Charte, et ainsi de suite. Il en est de même pour tous les droits et libertés sauvegardées par la Convention. Ils sont également sauvegardés par la Constitution dans des articles analogues moyennant, nous l'avons vu, une simple translation numérique.

En plus des articles de la Constitution qui sont la reproduction au mot par mot des articles de la Convention européenne des droits de l'homme relatifs aux mêmes droits garantis, la Constitution de la République de Chypre contient dans sa partie II nombre de dispositions relatives à la protection d'autres droits qui ne sont pas protégés par la Convention.

Pour énoncer les droits garantis, la partie II de la Constitution comprend 30 articles alors que la Convention européenne en comprend 17 et cette différence s'explique notamment par la présence dans la Constitution d'articles relatifs à des droits qui ne figurent pas dans la Convention. Le nombre d'articles de la Charte (54) s'explique par le fait que certains des droits y contenus sont sauvegardés par la loi nationale, au lieu d'avoir un rang constitutionnel, comme par exemple la protection des données à caractère personnel (article 8 de la Charte), le droit à l'asile (article 18 de la Charte), ou les droits de l'enfant (article 24 de la Charte), ces derniers étant protégés par la loi de ratification de la Convention de New York sur les droits de l'enfant signée le 20 novembre 1989.

Ainsi, et sans ignorer les articles portant le germe d'une discrimination entre citoyens selon leur appartenance à l'une ou l'autre des deux communautés grecque et turque reconnue par la Constitution[30], le rang constitutionnel des droits et libertés fondamentales place la Constitution à un bon niveau de protection de standard européen. En fait, les dispositions de la Constitution de la République de Chypre relatives à la protection des droits fondamentaux sont davantage proches des dispositions constitutionnelles d'autres Etats démocratiques de l'Europe que de celles de la Convention Européenne qui constitue, elle, un standard minimum institué, et en principe respecté, dans tous les Etats membres du Conseil de l'Europe. La Charte des Droits fondamentaux vient réduire cet écart.

Dans la pratique, le système judiciaire assure une protection effective aux droits et libertés juridiquement sauvegardées par la Constitution.

La ratification de la Convention européenne des droits de l'homme par la République de Chypre[31] et l'acceptation de la compétence de la Cour Européenne des Droits de l'Homme pour les requêtes individuelles d'une part, la protection constitutionnelle de la Cour Suprême[32] et l'organisation du système juridictionnel qui en dépend, d'autre part, constituent deux facteurs importants pour la protection effective des droits et libertés fondamentales. L'adhésion de Chypre à l'Union Européenne et l'attribution à la Charte de la valeur de référence juridique, permettront au juge chypriote de considérer celle-ci comme référence supplémentaire pour la protection des droits fondamentaux. Chypre n'est pas Etat membre de l'Union et le juge chypriote n'est pas tenu d'appliquer la Charte qui en tout état de cause, à ce stade, n'a pas valeur juridique, ni pour les Etats membres ni pour les Etats candidats à l'adhésion à l'Union.

La présentation détaillée, article par article, des droits retenus par la Charte, présente un avantage certain et un inconvénient non négligeable par rapport à l'article 6.1 TUE. L'avantage réside dans le fait que les droits et libertés prennent corps grâce à la concrétisation produite par la Charte et le citoyen européen connaît avec précision les droits auxquels il peut faire appel. L'inconvénient réside dans les limites imposées par tout catalogue figé de droits. Une formulation générale, comme celle de l'article 6.1 TEU rend l'évolution plus vivante car elle tient compte du mouvement de la vie. L'existence de la Charte ne nuit pas à l'article 6.1 TEU et l'article 6.1 TEU continuera de permettre à la Charte d'évoluer pour prendre en considération les nouveaux droits que la vie fera naître dans le chef des citoyens l'Union Européenne de demain.

3. *La question de primauté du droit communautaire et ses effets constitutionnels : le cas de Chypre*

Au stade des négociations d'adhésion de la République de Chypre à l'Union Européenne la question de la primauté du droit communautaire dans son ensemble face à la Constitution de l'Etat chypriote n'a pas produit de débat réel et la Cour Suprême de Chypre, qui a également la fonction de Cour constitutionnelle, n'a pas eu à prendre position. Dans l'attente de la signature et de la ratification de l'acte d'adhésion de Chypre à l'Union, l'article 179.1 qui retient que « La Constitution est la loi suprême de la République » garde toute sa vigueur. Notons néanmoins que l'article 179.1 ne figure pas parmi les articles cités dans l'article 182 qui, aux termes de la Constitution, ne peuvent pas être amendés.

La place des traités internationaux dans la hiérarchie des normes juridiques chypriotes est donnée par l'article 169(3) de la Constitution de 1960 qui retient que « les traités conventions et accords... auront force supérieure par rapport à toute loi interne... sous réserve de réciprocité... ». Cette disposition constitutionnelle couvre toute loi antérieure ou postérieure au traité international. Ainsi, en l'absence de toute référence à l'Union européenne, la hiérarchie des normes dans l'ordre juridique chypriote est la suivante : 1. la Constitution, 2. les traités internationaux, et 3. la loi interne ordinaire[33]. En considérant que l'article 179 pourra être amendé pour tenir compte de l'adhésion de Chypre à l'Union, on peut estimer que cette hiérarchie des normes pourra placer la norme européenne en situation de primauté. Le problème demeurera néanmoins face à l'article 61 de la Constitution, qui retient que la Chambre des Représentants exerce le pouvoir législatif « en toutes matières », article qui figure à l'article 182, et ne peut pas par conséquent être amendé.

La Constitution chypriote devra donc être profondément révisée afin d'éviter tout conflit juridique dans l'application du TUE et des TCE. La technique envisagée est, selon le Procureur Général de la République de Chypre, celle de l'article 29(5) de la Constitution de l'Irlande qui permet la coexistence de la Constitution irlandaise avec l'ordre juridique communautaire tout en assurant la primauté de ce dernier. Le Procureur Général se référant à la Constitution irlandaise, retient que :

« The most interesting provision, for our purposes, though is Article 29(5) which provides that: No provision of this Constitution invalidates laws enacted, acts done or measures adopted by the State which are necessitated by the obligations of membership of the European Union or by the Communities or by institutions thereof, or by bodies competent under the Treaties establishing the Communities, from having the force of law in the State".

The adoption of such an amendment would cover the actual accession of the Republic to the Union as well as the transfer of national legislative and treaty-making powers to the EU institutions, thus dealing with the potential problems posed by article 61 of the 1960 Constitution". [34]

Dans cette perspective d'adhésion le recours au referendum, sur la base du principe du peuple souverain peut également être envisagé pour ce qui concerne les articles cités à l'article 182. Il est retenu par l'*Attorney General.* Pour les amendements partiels, relatifs aux articles qui ne figurent pas à la liste de l'article 182, la Chambre des Représentants est admise sous sa forme actuelle par la Cour Constitutionnelle, sur la base du droit de nécessité, de procéder par voie législative aux amendements nécessaires[35]. Les voix des 2/3 des membres actuels de l'Assemblée sont suffisants pour voter ces amendements de la Constitution. Trois amendements constitutionnels ont déjà été votés (articles 111, 63 et 65) sans aucune référence à l'adhésion à l'Union. En juillet 2002 un important quatrième amendement de la Constitution a été voté en vue de l'harmonisation de la Constitution avec l'acquis communautaire en matière d'indépendance de la Banque Centrale[36].

4. *Interdépendance institutionnelle : fonctions européennes des institutions nationales*

Le pouvoir exécutif est attribué, dans l'ordre constitutionnel chypriote, au Président de la République et au Conseil des Ministres. Le Président et le vice-président de la République disposent, en vertu de l'article 50 de la Constitution un droit de veto sur toute décision de politique extérieure. Il est clair que ce droit ne peut être exercé que par le Président ou le Vice-Président en fonction et non par la Communauté qu'il représente. Dans la situation actuelle, le retrait volontaire du Vice-Président constitue un fait qui l'empêche d'assurer ses prérogatives constitutionnelles, rend les dispositions relatives au droit de veto inopérantes et, en vertu de la décision[37] de la Cour de Justice des Communautés Européennes dans l'affaire « ANASTASIOU », les problèmes résultant de la de facto division de l'île sont de la compétence exclusive de la République de Chypre, qui est le seul Etat internationalement reconnu.

En matière de législation, la qualité de Chypre Etat candidat à l'adhésion, étend le rôle du Parlement national à l'adoption de toute la législation existante de l'Union dans un but d'harmonisation à l'acquis communautaire d'une part, et à sa participation aux travaux de la Convention sur l'avenir de l'Europe d'autre part. La question de l'harmonisation comprend notamment les mesures nécessaires à la réalisation des buts et objectifs de la législation. Cette même qualité de la République de Chypre conduit l'exécutif chypriote à la mobilisation de toutes ses forces pour la négociation des conditions d'adhésion et pour la préparation des projets de lois qui sont soumis au Parlement national dans le cadre de l'effort produit pour réussir l'harmonisation dans les délais de 2002.

Dès l'adhésion de Chypre à l'Union Européenne, la République de Chypre transfèrera ses tribunaux nationaux, sous une hiérarchie judiciaire distincte supra-nationale, celle de la Cour de Justice des Communautés Européennes. Les tribunaux nationaux deviendront des tribunaux de l'Union dans le sens où ils seront chargés de la mise en œuvre du droit de l'Union dans la sphère nationale.

III. LE ROLE DES REGIONS ET DES AUTORITES LOCALES DANS L'ORDER JURIDIQUE ET L'UNION EUROPEENNE

Le concept de l'Union Européenne en tant qu'Union d' Etats et de peuples, accorde une importance relativement limitée aux structures intermédiaires composées des régions et des autorités locales, qui assurent le lien entre l'ensemble des individus (les peuples) et les Etats et, par extension, l'Union. Le principe de subsidiarité, plus généralement utilisé dans le cadre de la problématique Union / Etat, devrait pouvoir se généraliser pour s'étendre à toutes les structures démocratiques intermédiaires entre l'individu, et l'Union.

1. *Application à Chypre*

L'Etat chypriote, tant par sa culture administrative centralisatrice que par sa taille, est un Etat peu décentralisé. De sa structure administrative s'absente totalement le niveau région et le pays s'organise autour de l'Etat qui réunit la quasi-totalité des pouvoirs. Le niveau municipal concerne les communes de plus de 5.000 habitants, qui gèrent un nombre limité d'activités et, surtout, dont le budget dépend en très grande partie des dotations budgétaires annuelles ou exceptionnelles venant de l'Etat. Les autres communes, de moins de 5.000 habitants, dépendent totalement de l'Etat et de ses administrateurs départementaux. Le territoire national est divisé en six départements dont l'un se trouve depuis 1974 totalement et deux autres partiellement sous occupation militaire étrangère. Les représentants de l'Etat dans les départements sont nommés par les Services de l'Etat central sans aucune consultation préalable avec les pouvoirs locaux. Leur légitimité est purement administrative.

Sous l'effet de l'harmonisation avec l'acquis communautaire, l'Etat envisage la création du niveau région en divisant la partie de son territoire placée sous son autorité effective en deux régions dotées de conseils d'élus régionaux capables de participer pleinement à la politique régionale de l'Union. Six représentants régionaux participeront au Comité des Régions de l'Union après l'adhésion. De même, les municipalités et les autres collectivités locales bénéficieront d'un mouvement de décentralisation qui les placera à des niveaux de responsabilités et de moyens analogues à ceux des Etats membres de l'Union. Ainsi, l'adhésion sera l'occasion de décentralisation, de modernisation des structures démocratiques chargées de servir les futurs citoyens européens de Chypre.

IV. CONCLUSIONS ET RECOMMENDATIONS POUR 2004

Le phénomène de mondialisation et la dynamique lancée de l'élargissement d'une part, et le besoin pressant des citoyens européens pour plus de clarté, de transparence et de mécanismes d'adaptation permanente à une réalité politique et sociale en transformation perpétuelle, d'autre part, invitent les Européens à une transformation profonde des structures et du fonctionnement de l'Union. Le débat constitutionnel lancé à Nice en décembre 2000 a été organisé par la déclaration de Laeken en décembre 2001 par le lancement des travaux de la Convention sur l'avenir de l'Europe.

L'objectif semble clair : 1. Une nouvelle répartition des tâches entre l'Union européenne et ses Etats membres, en prenant bien en considération les Parlements nationaux, le niveau de la région et celui des autres collectivités territoriales, doit rapprocher les citoyens des institutions chargées de l'écouter et de le servir. Les principes de subsidiarité, de proportionnalité et de proximité des citoyens seront les guides pour plus de démocratie, pour plus d'efficacité, pour une plus grande satisfaction du citoyen européen. Si l'objectif est clair, force est de constater que sa réalisation l'est beaucoup moins.

2. Une légitimité démocratique accrue de l'Union fondée sur la transparence et la simplification des processus décisionnels, des structures et, par extension, la simplification des traités, rendra l'Union plus performante et plus proche des citoyennes et des citoyens.

3. Une intégration réelle, au bon niveau souhaité de la Charte des droits fondamentaux de l'Union européenne dans les traités, apportera une nouvelle dimension à l'avenir de l'Union qui n'est plus une simple union économique et monétaire mais qui devient progressivement une union

d'Etats de peuples fondée sur les valeurs communes de démocratie, d'Etat de droit, de droits de l'homme en Europe et dans le monde.

Le processus est bien lancé. Pour la première fois dans l'histoire de l'Europe le débat sur un profond remaniement des traités se fait en public en toute transparence, avec la participation de la société civile, qui alimente en idées ses représentants chargés de débattre de l'avenir de l'Europe. Les Etats ne sont plus les seuls maîtres à bord et ceci constitue une bonne évolution dans le processus de la transformation. Car le débat et le processus suivi sont aussi importants que le produit qui en est attendu.

En fait, le produit recherché est inhérent au processus suivi pour assurer sa production. En ce sens, la participation des Etats candidats à l'Union fait disparaître tout phénomène ou tout sentiment réel ou fictif d'arrogance d'Etats membres face à de futurs partenaires. L'idéal des pères fondateurs pour une union toujours plus étroite entre les peuples est présent au débat. On est en droit d'espérer que la nouvelle architecture qui en résultera, sera le reflet fidèle de ce processus démocratique lancé pour porter la réflexion sur l'avenir de l'Europe des Européennes et des Européens.

1. *Une nouvelle architecture : A qui doit ressembler une Constitution ou un traité fondamental de l'Union Européen*

La plupart des Etats européens ont leur Constitution. D'autres ont leur loi fondamentale, d'autres n'ont ni constitution, ni loi fondamentale, sans pour autant qu'on puisse affirmer que l'un ou l'autre dispose d'une base juridique plus démocratique en raison de la qualification constitutionnelle ou non de l'ensemble des normes juridiques qui permettent aux citoyens de se sentir libres, protégés et prospères dans leurs Etats respectifs.

Le système juridique valant dans chaque Etat européen est le reflet de la culture, des traditions démocratiques et des influences extérieures intégrées dans le vécu du peuple de chaque Etat. En décidant de penser leur avenir commun, les peuples européens mettent ensemble leurs cultures et traditions juridiques. Ils en feront sortir un système dont l'architecture devra répondre aux objectifs ci-dessus réunis. Ce faisant, ils auront conscience que l'Europe, telle qu'ils la connaissent ne s'est pas faite en un jour. Ils garderont comme objectif la préparation d'une Constitution mais l'architecture qui en ressortira en 2004 ressemblera davantage à un traité constitutionnel beaucoup plus clair que celui que la Cour de Justice qualifie déjà de « Charte Constitutionnelle »[38], qu'une Constitution telle que cette notion est entendue par la plupart des citoyens européens. Ainsi seront posés des jalons supplémentaires dans la direction d'une nouvelle Convention qui sera la Constituante de la Constitution de l'Union.

La Charte des droits fondamentaux figurera en bonne place dans ce traité constitutionnel, car elle sera appelée à guider l'action de l'Union et l'interprétation des autres dispositions du traité dans l'attente d'une Constitution en bonne et due forme pour l'Union.

2. *Une Constitution pour l'Union européenne : conditions d'adoption et amendements ; ses relations avec les constitutions nationales*

Au moment où l'Union européenne sera prête de se doter d'une constitution telle que cette notion est entendue pour la plupart des citoyens et des peuples de l'Union, le moment sera venu de constater que le niveau d'intégration européenne sera tel pour pouvoir l'adopter. Une Constitution ne pourra être que complémentaire aux constitutions des Etats membres, qui prendront bien soin d'éviter tout conflit de droit entre les deux systèmes de règles juridiques de niveau constitutionnel qui seront simultanément en présence dans les Etats de l'Union. L'adoption d'une Constitution et les amendements éventuels feront intervenir dans un premier temps les Etats membres au niveau du Conseil et les peuples de chacun des Etats, soit directement par referendum, soit par l'intermédiaire des parlements nationaux respectifs. Le principe d'une prise de décision fondée sur une très large majorité d'Etats et de peuples pourra être envisagée par l'abandon définitif du principe de prise de décision à l'unanimité. Un très grand pas sera ainsi fait. Quant à la perspective de l'adoption d'une Constitution pour l'Union par le suffrage universel direct de tous les citoyens européens organisé directement par l'Union européenne, il s'agit d'une perspective lointaine qui nécessite l'existence d'un sentiment d'appartenance très fort qui se confirmera à l'avenir ainsi que l'évolution et le perfectionnement d'un système politique européen qui tirera sa légitimité d'un *démos* européen.

3. *L'implication des Etats candidats à l'Union*

Le prochain élargissement de l'Union à d'autres Etats membres n'est plus qu'une question de temps. La décision est prise à Nice et les négociations sont en cours. En cas de ratification du traité de Nice par tous les Etats membres avant la mi-décembre 2002, le Conseil Européen de Copenhague retiendra les Etats avec lesquels un traité d'adhésion à l'Union, sera signé au printemps 2003 à Athènes. Comme tout Etat européen est en principe qualifié pour poser sa candidature pour l'adhésion à l'Union, de même tout Etat candidat devra être engagé à part égale et dans les mêmes conditions que les Etats membres dans le débat sur l'avenir de l'Union. Car, rappelons-le, le processus devant conduire à la réalisation d'une Constitution est aussi important que le produit, la Constitution elle-même. La participation réelle au processus prépare les esprits et contribue à forger le sentiment d'appartenance au peuple européen, sentiment qui est à la base de l'adoption d'une Constitution pour l'Union en perpétuelle intégration.

ELÉMENTS BIOGRAPHIQUES

Christos JOSEPHIDES est avocat au Barreau de Nicosie. Il est titulaire du Diplôme d'Etudes Approfondies (DEA) Droit communautaire (1991) et du DEA Droit International Public et Organisations Internationales (1992), de l'Université de Paris I – Panthéon Sorbonne. Initiateur, membre fondateur et Secrétaire Général de l'Association Chypriote pour le Droit Européen, membre associé de la Fédération Internationale pour le Droit Européen – FIDE. Détaché au Service Juridique de la République de Chypre, il y a initié la création et la mise en place de la Section « Union européenne », et celle de la Commission d'Harmonisation de la Constitution de la République de Chypre avec l'acquis communautaire, dont il a assuré la coordination. Il a participé à l'harmonisation du secteur Justice et Affaires Intérieures, à celle des chapitres Politique Régionale et Fonds Structurels, Politique Extérieure et de Sécurité Commune, Relations Extérieures. En tant qu'initiateur et animateur de la Commission chargée de l'harmonisation de la législation chypriote relative au secteur de l'aviation civile, il a contribué à la rédaction du projet de loi harmonisée avec l'acquis communautaire. Il est l'auteur d'un grand nombre d'articles dans la presse locale et conférencier de droit communautaire dans divers établissements d'enseignement supérieur et de formation professionnelle.

NOTES

1 Voir éléments biographiques à la fin du texte.

2 PIRIS Jean-Claude, "L'Union Européenne a-t-elle une constitution? Lui en faut une ? », Revue Trimestrielle de droit européen, 35(4), oct-dec 1999, p. 599-635.

3 PERNICE Ingolf, MAYER Frantz, "De la constitution composée", Revue trimestrielle de droit européen, 01.10.2000, n°4, p. 623-647

4 TOULEMON Robert, « Quelle Constitution pour quelle Europe », Revue du Marché commun et de l'Union européenne, no 448, mai 2001, p. 293-294.

5 HAENEL Hubert, Rapport d'Information du Sénat sur l'idée d'une "Constitution pour l'Union européenne, séance du 7 janvier 2001, Sénat, session ordinaire de 2000-2001, n° 363.

6 Résolution du Bundesrat sur la délimitation des compétences dans le cadre du débat sur la réforme et l'avenir de l'Union Européenne, prise lors de sa 771ème séance le 2° décembre 2001.

7 Giuliano Amato: Ancien Premier Ministre italien, vice-Président de la Convention pour l'avenir de l'Europe. Conférence organisée par la Chambre de Commerce et d'Industrie de Chypre, à Nicosie le 31 juillet 2002.

8 Sous réserve de ratification du Traité de Nice par tous les Etats membres.

9 Association créée à Chypre en 1994. Organisation non gouvernementale très active sur la diffusion de l'Idée européenne et du droit communautaire à Chypre.

[10] Pernice Ingolf, supra.

[11] Arrêt du 23 avril 1986, aff. 294/83, rec. p. 1365

[12] Article 17 TCE.

[13] En tenant compte des délais habituels de ratification et de la pratique suivie pour l'entrée en vigueur des traités d'adhésion au 1er janvier de l'année qui suit le dernier acte de ratification, nous estimons que la signature des traités d'adhésion au printemps 2003 reportera l'entrée en vigueur des nouvelles adhésions au 1.1.2005 au plus tôt.

[14] Kypros Chrysostomides, l'Etat de Chypre dans le droit international, Sakkoulas, Athènes 1994, p. 2. « Chypre, pays avec une intense orientation européenne, une administration moderne, et des fondements de démocratie politique n'a pas fait exception en ce qui concerne la mentalité et le comportement colonial à son égard ». En fait la Constitution chypriote qui a été le produit de la fin de la période coloniale est donc de création récente. Elle a été élaborée durant la période 1959-60, et elle est entrée en vigueur le 16 août 1960, jour de la création du nouvel Etat, la République de Chypre, nouvel Etat issu de la colonie britannique du même nom.

[15] L'Accord de Londres intégrait l'Accord de Zurich et était signé par les Ministres des Affaires Etrangères de la Grande Bretagne, de la Grèce et de la Turquie, ainsi que par l'Archevêque Makarios au nom de la communauté chypriote-grecque et par le Dr. Kutchuk au nom de la Communauté chypriote-turque. Pour Michalakis PISSAS, avocat, Conseiller et Secrétaire de Makarios lors de la signature de l'Accord de Londres, les 35 personnalités de la société chypriote invitées pour assister à la signature de l'Accord de Londres n'ont pas eu connaissance par avance du texte proposé à la signature. « En présence de tous ceux là a été signé l'accord sur la base duquel nous avons pris l'engagement d'avoir une Constitution octroyée qui n'a pas été choisie ou votée librement par le peuple mais elle nous a été imposée ». (Simerini, journal chypriote, 29.09.1996)

[16] Le Président actuel de la République de Chypre, M. Glafkos Clerides et le Chef actuel de la Communuté chypriote-turque M. Rauf Denktash étaient respectivement le Chef de la délégation chypriote grecque et turque au sein de la commission constitutionnelle mixte.

[17] G. TORNARITIS, The Constitutional problem of Cyprus, LEGAL NEWS, Nicosia, 1964, "Review of Contemporary Law", Brussels, 1964, pp 981-1007.

[18] Ce traitement particulier de Chypre tranche avec la solution retenue en Israël à la fin du Mandat britannique sur la Palestine, qui fut auparavant province turque de 1917 à 1922, et la création de l'Etat hébreu. Ainsi la Déclaration de l'Indépendance, du 14 mai 1948 proclama l'établissement de l'Etat hébreu et appela pour l'élection d'une Assemblée constituante qui serait responsable pour l'adoption d'une Constitution. Voir Claude KLEIN, Public Law in Israel: A General background, European Public Law, vol. 1, June 1995.

[19] D.G. LAVROFF, Le Statut de Chypre, RGDIP 1961, p. 534.

[20] Pour Savvas S. PAPASAVAS, il existe cinq particularités majeures dans la constitution chypriote : Constitution octroyée, rigide, complexe, antidémocratique et imprégnée d'un esprit séparatiste envers les deux Communautés. Voir, Justice constitutionnelle à Chypre, thèse pour le doctorat en droit, Aix en Provence, 20 décembre 1995.

[21] L'objet du Traité de Garantie était *inter allia* de maintenir l'indépendance, l'intégrité territoriale et la sécurité de la République ainsi que le respect de sa Constitution et d'empêcher l'Union de l'île avec tout autre Etat ou la partition de l'île. Les trois Etats garants devaient donc ainsi assurer une telle indépendance, intégrité territoriale et sécurité de la République et l'état de droit créé par les Articles Fondamentaux de la Constitution. Ce traité s'est avéré inopérant au moment de l'invasion de l'île par l'armée turque en 1974 et par la suite, lors de la séparation en deux de l'île et par l'occupation étrangère (turque) de la partie Nord.

[22] Dans le cadre du Traité d'Alliance des contingents militaires grec et turc devaient stationner à Chypre: 950 hommes composent le contingent grec et 650 hommes composent le contingent turc.

[23] Conférence donnée par l'*Attorney General* de la République de Chypre, M. Alecos Markides, au séminaire « The European Union Law, National Constitutions and Human Rights », Nicosie, 21 mai 2002.

[24] Z.M. NECATIGIL, The Cyprus Question and the Turkish position in International Law, Oxford University Press, 2nd ed. 1996.

[25] Cyprus and European Union Membership, Important Legal Documents, Edited by the Attorney General of Cyprus Alecos Markides, Nicosia, Cyprus 2002.

[26] Pour Giuliano Amato (supra) la Constitution de l'Union devra trouver un nouvel équilibre entre "plus d'Europe" en matière notamment de droits de l'homme, politique extérieure et défense commune, environnement, crime organisé d'une part, et davantage d'autonomie des autorités locales, plus proches des citoyens et de leurs préoccupations quotidiennes d'autre part.

[27] Dans son AVIS relatif à la candidature de Chypre aux Communautés Européennes donné par la Commission le 30 juin 1993 et adopté par le Conseil le 17 octobre 1993, la Commission retient que, au delà de tout doute Chypre a une identité et un caractère européens et a vocation d'appartenir à la Communauté: Commission des CE, JOCE Supp 5/93; CE Bulletin: Supplément 4/93.

[28] Pour l'*Attorney General* Criton G. TORNARITIS: "The range of human rights relating to civil and personal relations guaranteed by the Constitution of the Republic of Cyprus is wider than that of other Constitutions and to a certain extent than that of the European Convention of and the International Covenant on Civil and Political Rights", The human rights as recognized and protected by the law of the Republic of Cyprus, the Cyprus Law Tribune, sixth Year, Paris 4-6.

[29] La Convention européenne de Sauvegarde des Droits de l'Homme et des Libertés Fondamentales fait partie du droit interne depuis la publication de la loi de ratification no 39/62 de 1962. Voir en particulier la décision de la Cour Suprême (en composition plénière) en date du 13 mars 1966 dans l'affaire Anthi Demetriadou v. Conseil des Ministres et autres.

[30] L'article 2(7)(a) de la Constitution impose à la femme mariée d'appartenir à la Communauté de son époux alors que l'article 18(1) garantit « la liberté de pensée, de conscience et de religion » et l'article 28(1) garantit l'égalité de « tous » devant la loi. D'autres articles créent d'autres discriminations selon l'appartenance à l'une ou l'autre des deux communautés reconnues par la Constitution.

[31] Loi n° 39/62 de 1962.

[32] Articles 133 à 164 de la Constitution.

[33] Voir décision de la Cour Suprême du 14 décembre 1993, Municipalité de Limassol, appel n° 5793.

[34] Alecos Markides, The Constitutional Impact of Cyprus's EU Accession, rapport à la Venise Commission, 29.8.2000 et Alecos Markides, The European Union Law, National Constitutions and Human Rights », Conférence délivrée le 21 mars 2002 à Nicosie (supra).

[35] Décision dans l'affaire Attorney General of the Republic v. Imbrahim, (1964) CLR 195.

[36] Modification des articles 47(f), 118 et 119 par la loi N104(I)/2002 publiée et entrée en vigueur le 5 juillet 2002.

[37] Arrêt du 5 juillet 1994, The Queen / Ministry of Agriculture, Fisheries and Food, ex parte S.P. Anastasiou (Pissouri) Ltd, (C 432/92, Rec. PI-3087, point 47).

[38] Arrêt “Les Verts” supra.

GERMANY

EU-Recht und nationales Verfassungsrecht

Deutscher Bericht für die XX. FIDE-Tagung 2002

Rapporteur
Professor Dr Martin Nettesheim

I. EUROPÄISCHER KONSTITUTIONALISMUS IN DEUTSCHLAND[1]

Die verfassungstheoretische Diskussion um Stand und Zukunft der europäischen Integration dreht sich gegenwärtig vor allem um zwei Fragen. Zum einen geht es um die Frage, wie sich der Verbund von EU und Mitgliedstaaten verfassungstheoretisch rekonstruieren und begreifen läßt. Ist die EU in ihrer gegenwärtigen Gestalt eine internationale Organisation, ein Staat oder etwas Drittes? Kann ihre Grundordnung als Verfassung bezeichnet werden? Wird diese Ordnung legitimatorisch von den Mitgliedstaaten getragen, oder kann man heute davon ausgehen, dass es (auch) die EU-Bürger sind, auf die die Ausübung europäischer Hoheitsgewalt zurückzuführen ist? In welchem Verhältnis stehen EU-Grundordnung und nationale Verfassungsordnungen, wie wirken sie aufeinander ein? Die Beantwortung dieser Fragen verlangt zunächst dekriptiv-analytische Arbeit. Wer sich dieser Arbeit annimmt, kommt nicht umhin, als Handwerkszeug zunächst die überkommenen Begrifflichkeiten und Kategorien von Staats- und Verfassungsrecht zu verwenden. Dies führt zu der Merkwürdigkeit, dass auf der einen Seite anerkannt wird, dass der Integrationsprozeß in ein Ergebnis münden wird, das nicht dem Modell des klassischen, unabhängigen Nationalstaats entsprechen wird, zugleich aber der Prozeß mit traditionellen Kategorien beschrieben und erfaßt wird.[2] Inzwischen hat die Diskussion allerdings eine Tiefe und Schärfe gewonnen, die es möglich macht, auf einer Metaebene normativ darüber zu streiten, welche der überkommenen Begriffe und Kategorien revisionsbedürftig sind und durch neue, geeignetere Kategorien zur Erfassung der poststaatlichen Konstellation ersetzt werden müssen. Nicht alle Vorschläge erweisen sich als sinnvoll; manche finden keine Beachtung, weil sie begrifflich zu schwach und zu wenig anschaulich sind; wieder andere haben die Chance, in den allgemeinen Sprachgebrauch überzugehen und so zu einer Grundkategorie einer neuen, auch die supranationalen Gegebenheiten in den Blick nehmenden Verfassungswissenschaft zu werden.

Zum anderen beschäftigt sich der europäische Konstitutionalismus mit der normativen Problematik der Fortwicklung des Integrationsverbands. Dabei geht es zunächst um die Aufgabe der Bewertung des Stands der Integration: Wie sind die verfassungstheoretischen Anforderungen zu formulieren, die an die Grundordnung eines überstaatlichen Hoheitsträgers zu stellen sind? Hat die EU eine Grundordnung, die normativ defizitär ist und nicht den Anforderungen entspricht, die aus legitimatorischer Perspektive an die Ausübung europäischer Herrschaftsgewalt zu richten sind – insbesondere im Hinblick auf Demokratie? In welchen Punkten fällt die Grundordnung der EU hinter diesen Anforderungen zurück? Es schließen sich verfassungspolitische Folgefragen über das weitere Vorgehen an: Welche Schritte können unternommen werden, um etwaige Defizite zu beheben? Muß sich die EU vielleicht gar erst noch eine Verfassung zulegen? Wie müßte diese dann aussehen?

Indem sich die europäische Verfassungsrechtswissenschaft diesen Fragekreisen in den letzten Jahren verstärkt angenommen hat, hat sie ihre Perspektive gewechselt. Die Frage nach der Legitimität europäischer Herrschaftsausübung ist erst relativ spät aufgekommen. Bis weit in die neunziger Jahre des 20. Jahrhunderts hinein ging es der europäischen Verfassungsrechtswissenschaft – aus supranationalem Blickwinkel – um die Beschreibung und Erklärung der Europäische Union und ihres Rechts, allenfalls darüber hinaus um Überlegungen zur Sicherung der einheitlichen und gleichen Wirkung ihres Rechts. Weder beschäftigte sie sich mit dem Aspekt der Verflechtung und des Verbundenseins von europäischen und nationalen Grundordnungen, noch ging es ihr um die Bestimmung der gegenseitigen Abhängigkeiten, Wechselwirkungen und Befruchtungen. Die Legitimität der EU ruhte in ihrem Liberalisierungs- und Integrationsauftrag. Solange sie diesen erfolgreich bewältigte (und hieran bestand jedenfalls in den achtziger Jahren kein Zweifel), stieß ihr Wirken nicht auf legitimatorische Zweifel. Man begnügte sich mit der (output-orientierten) Position, dass sich die Ausübung europäischer Herrschaftsgewalt über die Liberalisierungs- und Harmonisierungsleistung ihres Rechts rechtfertige. – Für Beobachter, die die EU aus nationalem Blickwinkel betrachteten, ging es demgegenüber um die Sicherung überkommener Bestände des Nationalstaates: von der Souveränität über die Herrschaft über die Verträge bis hin zur teilweisen Abwehr des Vorranganspruchs des Europarechts. Auch dieser Sichtweise zufolge bestand kein Grund für legitimatorische Zweifel: Solange über europäische Rechtsetzung im Rat einstimmig entschieden werden mußte, behielten die Mitgliedstaaten im übrigen je einzeln die Kontrolle; das Geschehen in Europa ließ sich als Ausdruck herkömmlicher internationaler Zusammenarbeit rekonstruieren und über national-verfassungsstaatliche Mechanismen legitimieren.

Dass die überkommenen Erklärungsmuster ihren Wert verloren haben, liegt an der explosionsartigen Entwicklung des Integrationsverbandes in der zweiten Hälfte der achtziger und der ersten Hälfte der neunziger Jahre. Zu erinnern ist an die dichte Abfolge von Vertragsänderungen, die mit der Einheitlichen Europäischen Akte in den achtziger Jahren begann und über „Maastricht", die Vergemeinschaftung weiterer Rechtsbereiche im Vertrag von Amsterdam[3] sowie die Reformen durch den Vertrag von Nizza[4] eine ungeheuere Dynamik hervorriefen. Die Schnelligkeit (manche würden von Hastigkeit sprechen) der Veränderungen konnten den Anschein erwecken, dass sich die Mitgliedstaaten zu einer einzigen, andauernden und zeitlich offenen Regierungskonferenz zusammengefunden hätten und so in einem Prozeß dauerhafter Verfassungsgebung das Ziel der Integration anzustreben gewillt seien. Zu verzeichnen war in diesem Prozeß nicht nur ein quantitativer Kompetenzgewinn ungeahnten Ausmaßes. Von vielleicht noch größerer Bedeutung war, dass die EU mit dem Maastricht-Vertrag qualitative Kompetenzen gewann, die ihr staatsähnliche Erscheinung verlieh. Zu denken ist in diesem Zusammenhang insbesondere an die Frühformen der Gemeinsamen Außen- und Sicherheitspolitik sowie die Übernahme der Währungshoheit. Auch der Einstieg in den Bereich der inneren und polizeilichen Sicherheit mag – wenngleich es hier zunächst nur um Formen der Zusammenarbeit ging - zu diesem Bild beigetragen haben. Berücksichtigt man in diesem Zusammenhang auch, dass (1) mehr und mehr Entscheidungen im Integrationsverband mehrheitlich ergingen und daher auch einen Staat binden konnten, der der Entscheidung nicht zugestimmt hat, dass (2) das von der EU gesetzte Recht im nationalen Rechtskreis unmittelbare Wirkung beansprucht und Vorrang vor nationalem Recht hat, und dass (3) in mehr und mehr Rechtsbereichen nationale Rechtsanwender (Verwaltungsbehörden, Gerichte) gleichberechtigt und gleichhäufig supranationales und nationales Recht anwendeten, so ist ohne weiteres erklärlich, warum die überkommenen Erklärungs- und Legitimationsmuster der europäischen Integration zerbrechen mußten – namentlich das klassische Legitimationsmuster auswärtiger Zusammenarbeit. In der englischsprachigen Diskussion ist von einer „Transformation" Europas die Rede, in deutscher Sprache läßt sich von einem Gestaltwandel sprechen.

Europäischer Konstitutionalismus im Deutschland der neunziger Jahre war stark von nationalstaatlich-defensiven Stimmen geprägt. Es waren dies Stimmen, die ihrer Betrachtung die Grundprämisse zugrundelegten, dass der Staat in sich ruhen müßte, über die Verhältnisse in ihm unabhängig und eigenständig entscheiden und hierfür die Verantwortung tragen müßte. Diesen Stimmen mußte es vor dem Hintergrund des Gestaltwandels Europas vor allem darum gehen, die Souveränität des Nationalstaats vor den Einwirkungen des Europarechts in Schutz zu nehmen, Einbrüche in staatliche Besitzstände zu verhindern oder doch jedenfalls zu minimieren und die Letztzuständigkeit des Staates für die rechtlichen, wirtschaftlichen und sozialen Gegebenheiten auf seinem Gebiet zu bewahren. Angesichts des Umstandes, dass der Anspruch des Europarechts, unmittelbare Wirkung und Vorrang vor nationalem Recht zu entfalten, grundsätzlich nicht mehr in Frage gestellt werden konnte, mußte sich die Diskussion materiell um die Grenzen des Vorrangs und institutionell um die Befugnisse der nationalen Organe, gegebenenfalls Europarecht unangewendet lassen zu können, drehen. Viele Überlegungen, die in den neunziger Jahren angestellt wurden, hatten denn auch (wenn man die europäische Perspektive einnahm) den Grundsatz der einheitlichen Wirksamkeit des EU-Rechts oder (wenn man die nationale Perspektive einnahm) die Grenzen des Vorrangs des EU-Rechts zum Gegenstand. Auch der XVII. FIDE Kongress 1996 in Berlin beschäftigte sich mit diesem Verhältnis von mitgliedstaatlichen

Verfassungsordnungen und europäischer Integration[5]. Vor dem Hintergrund der gegensätzlichen axiomatischen Grundpositionen von EuGH und nationalem Verfassungsgerichten konnte es nicht gelingen, eine rechtlich zwingende Lösung zu finden. Inzwischen ist die konstitutionelle Debatte aber über diese Grenzfrage des Verhältnisses zweier Rechtsordnungen hinweggegangen. Nicht mehr der Ausnahmefall einer Kollision, sondern das Regelverhältnis der Kooperation und Koordination steht im Mittelpunkt des verfassungstheoretischen Verhältnisses. Inzwischen ist das Wissen um die Vielfalt der Wechselwirkungen und Abhängigkeiten, die sich mit der einfachen Frage danach beschreiben lassen, wer die Letztentscheidungsgewalt hat, zum Gemeingut geworden. Man ist sich des Umstandes bewußt, dass sich die architektonischen Gegebenheiten in der EU nicht hinreichend mit überkommenen Begriffen wie Vorrang, Hierarchie, Weisung etc. erfassen lassen.

Auch die Diskussion um die (demokratische) Legitimität europäischen Herrschens wurde zunächst vor dem Hintergrund des nationalstaatlichen Legitimitätsparadigmas geführt. Es waren zunächst Verfassungswissenschaftler nationalstaatlicher Provenienz, die der EU ein Demokratiedefizit attestierten und Legitimationsmängel anprangerten. In der Tat kommt man schwerlich umhin, den Entscheidungsprozessen der EU Mangelhaftigkeit zu attestieren, wenn man sie an der Ideenwelt nationalstaatlicher Demokratie mißt. Weder steht hinter der EU-Ordnung bislang die legitimatorische Idee der verfassungsgebenden Gewalt des (eines) Volkes, noch wird die Ordnung bislang von zivilgesellschaftlichen Strukturen getragen, wie sie im Hinblick auf Sprache, Kommunikation, Medienwelt etc. in typischen Nationalstaaten bestehen. Tiefgreifende Unterschiede bestehen auch in der institutionellen Ordnung, wo sich vor allem die Rolle des Europäischen Parlaments so stark von der typischen Rolle eines nationalstaatlichen Parlaments unterscheidet, dass manche dem Parlament bis heute diesen Namen verweigern wollen. Kurz: Wer sich in der Ideenwelt der nationalstaatlichen Demokratie bewegte, mußte die EU – in ihrer Gestalt nach „Maastricht" – für einen in seiner Legitimität äußerst prekären Hoheitsträger ansehen. Als Remedur bot sich aus dieser Perspektive vor allem die umfassende Parlamentarisierung der EU an: von der Aufwertung des Europäischen Parlaments im Prozeß der Bestellung gubernativer Organwalter und im Gesetzgebungsprozeß über die Errichtung einer europäischen Parteienwelt bis hin zur Durchsetzung des Gleichheitsprinzips bei Wahlen. Andere konstatierten zwar schwere demokratische Mängel und hielten eine weitere Demokratisierung für (jedenfalls gegenwärtig) ausgeschlossen, nahmen den Zustand allerdings hin. Erst in jüngster Zeit findet die Frage, ob nicht auch die (ja nicht unabänderlichen, sondern ihrerseits entworfenen und funktional gerechtfertigten) Legitimationsmodelle, an denen gerechtfertigte Herrschaft heute gemessen wird, ihrerseits überprüfungs- und anpassungsbedürftig sind. Könnte es nicht sein, dass im supranationalen Kontext andere Legitimationsmuster zur Anwendung kommen als im staatlichen Kontext? Muß sich nicht auch jene Ideenwelt, die sich im achtzehnten Jahrhundert als Maßstab legitimer Herrschaft herausbildete, im 21. Jahrhundert anpassen und auf veränderte funktionale Bedürfnisse eingehen? Ist vielleicht manche Ausprägung der EU-Institutionenordnung zukunftsmächtiger, als es im Lichte der überkommenen Ideen zunächst den Schein hat?

Es ist in gewisser Weise bedauerlich, dass sich die verfassungstheoretische Diskussion der späten neunziger Jahre dieser Fragen nicht intensiv angenommen hat. Statt dessen rückte die eher formale Problematik europäischer Verfassungsgebung in den Mittelpunkt der Aufmerksamkeit. Damit wurde der zweite Schritt vor dem ersten gemacht, wird über Verfassungsbegriff und Verfassungsinhalte diskutiert, ohne dass zuvor über die dabei anzulegenden Maßstäbe gesprochen wurde. Zu den ganz gängigen Erscheinungen gehört es in diesem Zusammenhang, die Erklärungs- und Legitimationsmuster des liberalen Konstitutionalismus unhinterfragt auf die EU zu übertragen (Verfassungsdokument, Parlamentarismus, Grundrechte, kontraktualistische Legitimationstheorien etc.), ohne deren Leistungsfähigkeit in der poststaatlichen Konstellation zu problematisieren. Die in Nizza feierlich verabschiedete Charta der Grundrechte der Europäischen Union[6] nimmt in diesem Prozeß einen herausgehobenen Platz ein. Dass in einer Zeit, in der traditionelle Wertvorstellungen in der Gesellschaft von Mustern des Ökonomismus und Konsumerismus verdrängt werden, Zweifel an der Leistungsfähigkeit dieser Legitimationsmuster aufkommen müssen, wird dabei verdrängt. Zu den Kennzeichnen der Diskussion gehört auch, als Antwort auf ein Problem die Einrichtung eines „Ausschusses", „Gremiums" oder „Gerichts" zu fordern – so beispielsweise im Hinblick auf die Kompetenzabgrenzung und die Durchsetzung des Subsidiaritätsprinzips. Gängig ist auch die Forderung, Institutionen und Verfahren der nationalen Verfassungsstaatlichkeit auf europäische Ebene zu heben. Nicht unproblematisch erweist sich diese Art des Vorgehens vor allem, weil Aussagen darüber, welche funktionale Leistungsfähigkeit derartige Institutionen und Verfahren in dem andersartigen Kontext der EU aufweisen, schwer fallen (und regelmäßig auch nicht empirisch informiert gemacht werden). Es überrascht vor diesem Hintergrund nicht, dass in dieser Diskussion die Begrifflichkeiten, analytischen Befunde und Reformvorschläge stark voneinander abweichen. Es ist zu bedauern, überrascht aber ebenfalls nicht, dass sich die Diskussion durch hohe Technizität und einen erstaunlichen Grad der Beliebigkeit in der Frage auszeichnet, welche Reformvorschläge lanciert werden.

Die Europäische Union treibt den Prozeß nunmehr durch die in den Anhang des Nizzaer Vertrags aufgenommene Erklärung Nr. 23 zur Zukunft der Europäischen Union voran. Die durch diese Erklärung angestossene Diskussion, der sogenannte „Post-Nizza-Prozess", soll sich vor allem der Problematik der vertikalen Kompetenzabgrenzung, des Status der Grundrechtecharta, der Vereinfachung der Verträge und der Rolle der nationalen Parlamente zuwenden[7]. Der Europäische Rat von Laeken hat einen Konvent einberufen, der von Valery Giscard d'Estaing geleitet wird und Antworten auf diese Zukunftsfragen der Europäischen Union finden soll.[8] Begleitet wird dieser Prozeß von einer öffentlichen Diskussion, an der mitgliedstaatliche Politiker, Wissenschaftler, aber auch die Bürger teilnehmen sollen. Auch die FIDE hat sich der Problematik des Zusammenwirkens von EU-Recht und nationalem Verfassungsrecht erneut angenommen. Der vorliegende Landesbericht erörtert das Verhältnis von EU-Recht zu nationalem Recht aus deutscher Sicht. Er geht zunächst auf die Grundlagen europäischer Verfaßtheit ein (II). Sodann werden das Verhältnis des europäischen Rechts zum deutschen Verfassungsrecht (III) und die Rolle der deutschsprachigen Regionen in Europa näher untersucht (IV). Abschließend sollen einige Empfehlungen aus deutscher Sicht für den Prozeß bis zum Jahre 2004 gegeben werden (V).

II. GRUNDLAGEN DES EUROPÄISCHEN KONSTITUTIONALISMUS

1. Verfassungsbegriff in Deutschland und europäischer Konstitutionalismus

a. Verfassung: Grundbegriffe und theoretische Konzepte des Grundgesetzes

Über lange Zeit verstand man in Deutschland unter „Verfassung" die Beschreibung eines Zustandes, etwa des Zustandes eines Landes, eines Gemeinwesens oder überhaupt irgendeines abgrenzbaren Gegenstandes. Erst im 18. Jahrhundert gewann der Verfassungsbegriff seine normative Bedeutung. Die überkommene, auf empirische Gegebenheiten bezogene Bedeutung des Begriffs „Verfassung" wirkt fort; es ist möglich, nach der „Verfassung der Europäischen Union" zu fragen und so ihren Zustand, ihre Befindlichkeit und Lage zu untersuchen.[9] Im rechtlichen Kontext wird diese Begriffsbedeutung allerdings heute von den die Normativität der Verfassung in den Vordergrund stellenden Bedeutungen überlagert. Es ist wohlbekannt, dass dieser Prozeß der Normativierung des Verfassungsbegriffs dem Verfassungsbegriff seine Mehrdeutigkeit nicht genommen hat. Im Sprachgebrauch der Verfassungswissenschaft lassen sich weiterhin verschiedene Bedeutungsgehalte nachweisen. Verfassung kann ein schriftliches Dokument sein, in dem Rechtssätze formuliert werden; Verfassung kann aber auch die Gesamtheit der Normen sein, die in einem

Grunddokument ihren Niederschlag gefunden haben. Man kann den Verfassungsbegriff normativen Grundordnungen vorbehalten, die bestimmten Legitimationsmustern entsprechen – etwa in der Art, dass Verfassung nur die demokratische Grundordnung ist. Ebenso ist es möglich, den Verfassungsbegriff in umfassender Weise auf Normen, Institutionen und die von diesen geordnete Lebenswelt zu beziehen. Die Vieldeutigkeit des Verfassungsbegriffs ermöglicht es, begriffliche und theoretische Überlegungen zu Semantik und Funktion der verschiedenen Begriffsbedeutungen anzustellen und diese am konkreten Anwendungsfall durchzuspielen. Der erste, allerdings schnell erschöpfte Wert derartiger Reflektionen über Begriffsbedeutungen liegt in der Feststellung, dass ein und derselbe Begriff – je nach Begriffsbedeutung – zur Beschreibung eines Lebenssachverhalts verwandt werden kann – oder eben nicht: Je nach Verfassungsbegriff hat die Europäische Union eine Verfassung – oder auch nicht. Der wissenschaftliche Wert begrifflicher Klärungen kann ferner darin liegen aufzuzeigen, dass scheinbare sachliche Meinungsverschiedenheiten ihre Ursache in der Unterschiedlichkeit begrifflicher Setzung haben. Sie können schließlich auch in konventionelle Vorschläge münden, etwa des Inhaltes, dass es sinnvoller ist, die eine Bedeutung der anderen im rechtswissenschaftlichen Sprachgebrauch vorzuziehen. Der Wert derartiger Reflektionen ist allerdings begrenzt. Man erreicht schnell einen Punkt, an der ein sinnvolles Fortkommen bei der Bearbeitung konkreter Fragestellungen nur dann möglich ist, wenn eine bestimmte Begriffsbedeutung als die im konkreten Kontext verwandte Bedeutung gesetzt wird. Es ist wenig zweckmäßig, die Bedeutung eines Begriffs in der Schwebe zu halten und ihn zugleich in einem konkreten Anwendungskontext zu verwenden. Bei dieser Entscheidung spielen Konvention[10], darüber hinaus vor allem aber funktionale Erwägungen eine Rolle.[11]

aa) Verfassung und Staatlichkeit

In der Verfassungsdiskussion der letzten Jahre[12] erfuhr die Frage, inwieweit der Verfassungsbegriff notwendig auf den Staat bezogen sei, besondere Aufmerksamkeit. Kaum einer anderen begrifflichen Frage wurde so viel Aufmerksamkeit geschenkt. Zurückzuführen dürfte dies vor allem auf den Umstand sein, dass es Verfassungsrechtswissenschaftler besonderer Prominenz waren, die die These vertraten, dass eine Verfassung begriffsnotwendig auf den Staat bezogen sei, dass also von Verfassung nur dort gesprochen werden könne, wo es um Zähmung oder Konstituierung *staatlicher* Herrschaft gehe. Der Staat ist danach vorfindlich, d.h. er ist der Verfassung begrifflich vorgelagert: Die grundlegende Behauptung der Anhänger dieses Verständnisses lautet: „Ohne Staat keine Verfassung“[13]. Eine vergleichbare Festlegung treffen jene Verfassungsrechtler, die in der

Verfassung das Grundstatut des *staatlichen* Gemeinwesens reduzieren und damit den Begriff der Verfassung ebenfalls auf den der Staatsverfassung verengen[14]. Verfassung ist danach ihrerseits keine Voraussetzung von Staatlichkeit, sondern nurmehr von Stabilität[15]. Dieses auf die Hegel´sche Staatsphilosophie zurückgehende[16] staatszentrierte Verständnis von Verfassung läßt die Annahme, es existiere bereits eine europäische Verfassung, ebensowenig zu wie die Behauptung, die EU könne sich in näherer Zukunft eine Verfassung zulegen.[17] Europäische Verfassungsgebung liefe dieser Sichtweise zufolge notwendig auf die Schaffung eines europäischen Superstaates hinaus[18]; sie brächte den Verlust souveräner mitgliedstaatlicher Nationalstaatlichkeit[19] mit sich.

Inzwischen hat sich in Deutschland allerdings eine Sichtweise durchgesetzt, derzufolge der Verfassungsbegriff nicht notwendig auf den Staat bezogen ist. Danach waren es historisch-kontingente Gegebenheiten, die dazu geführt haben, dass in den letzten Jahrhunderten von Verfassung vor allem im Zusammenhang mit staatlicher Gewalt gesprochen wurde. Begriffsnotwendig ist diese Engführung des Verfassungsbegriffs danach allerdings nicht. Eine begriffliche *Loslösung* vom Element der Staatlichkeit ist dem Verfassungsbegriff möglich[20]; er entwickelt sich so zum poststaatlichen Begriff, zum „abstrakten Verfassungsbegriff“[21] oder zum „postnationalen Verfassungsbegriff“[22]. Diesem Verständnis zufolge steht der Weg zur Anerkennung europäischen Verfassungsrechts offen. Europäische Verfassungsgebung bedeutet danach nicht Auflösung von Staatlichkeit schlechthin. Sie bedeutet nur, dass an die Seite eines auf Staatlichkeit gerichteten Verfassungsbegriffs auch ein auf supranationale Herrschaftsgewalt bezogener Begriff treten kann. Dass sich diese Sichtweise relativ schnell hat durchsetzen können, dürfte nicht zuletzt daran liegen, dass die Staatslehre in Deutschland darniederliegt[23] und der Ablösung keinen Widerstand entgegensetzen konnte.[24] Von Bedeutung dürfte schließlich auch sein, dass sich aussagekräftige und gehaltvolle Begriffe zur Bezeichnung der Grundordnung der EU bislang nicht entwickelt haben; derartige Begriffe wären aber notwendig, wollte man auf die Verwendung des Verfassungsbegriffs verzichten.

bb) Verfassung als Zähmung oder Einsetzung von Herrschaft

Versucht man, die im gegenwärtigen Sprachgebrauch verwandten Begriffsbedeutungen zu ordnen, so ist zunächst zwischen jenen Bedeutungen zu unterscheiden, denen zufolge Verfassung vorexistente Herrschaft bindet und zähmt, und jenen Bedeutungen, denen zufolge Verfassung Herrschaft konstituiert und inhaltlich anleitet. Beide Bedeutungen sind miteinander inkompatibel. Der zunächst genannten Sichtweise zufolge treten Verfassungen „von außen“ an eine bereits konstituierte Herrschaftsgewalt heran; Verfassungen konstituieren danach nicht, sondern zähmen und binden Herrschaftsgewalt, die ihre Existenz einem außerhalb der Verfassung liegenden Legitimationsgrund verdankt. Seine größte geschichtliche Bedeutung erlangte dieser Verfassungsbegriff vor allem im Deutschland des neunzehnten Jahrhunderts, darüber hinaus aber auch in England. In beiden Fällen mußte es der politischen Theorie darum gehen, die bereits existente Herrschaftsgewalt des Monarchen rechtlich einzubinden. Diesem Verständnis zufolge sind Verfassungen notwendig normativ; sie sind aber nicht notwendig dem demokratischen Prinzip verpflichtet. Eine bedeutende Rolle kommt hier der Idee des Verfassungsvertrages zu, der zwischen dem Träger der Herrschaftsgewalt und jenen gesellschaftlichen Kräften abgeschlossen wird, die auf Begrenzung, Zähmung und Einbindung der Herrschaftsgewalt dringen. Im Extremfall kann Verfassung hier als Akt der Selbstzähmung des Trägers der Herrschaftsgewalt begriffen werden.

Demgegenüber liegt dem zweitgenannten Verfassungsverständnis das Moment der Konstituierung, der Einsetzung von Herrschaftsgewalt zugrunde. Dieser Sichtweise zufolge verdankt in einem verfaßten Gemeinwesen alle Herrschaftsgewalt ihre Existenz und ihr Dasein der Verfassung. Legale Herrschaftsgewalt, die nicht ihre Grundlage in der Verfassung findet, ist danach bereits nicht vorstellbar; jeder Versuch, außerhalb der Verfassung und jenseits verfassungsrechtlicher Kompetenzen Herrschaftsgewalt auszuüben, muß danach als Verfassungsbruch gewertet werden. Verfassungsgebung ist immer Bruch mit der alten Ordnung und Neuanfang; Verfassung und Revolution sind danach untrennbar miteinander verbunden. Das Verständnis von Verfassung als Form der Konstitution von Herrschaft impliziert mindestens dreierlei, nämlich den *normativen*, den *grundlegenden* und den *umfassenden* Charakter von Verfassung. Alle drei Eigenschaften lassen es zu, Verfassung als einen Normenkomplex zu identifizieren, der „die Einrichtung und Ausübung der Staatsgewalt sowie der Beziehungen zwischen Staat und Gesellschaft grundlegend regelt“[25]. Damit ist Verfassung eine *gewollte Gesamtentscheidung*, die dem sozialen Miteinander zugrunde liegt. Dieser Gesichtspunkt der Gesamtentscheidung bildet den wesentlichen Unterschied zu nicht „verfaßten“ rechtlichen Systemen. Während die *institutio* eine „historisch gewachsene, irgendwie, meist vertraglich geformte, an naturrechtlichen Lehren orientierte oder auch nur tatsächlich sich ergebende Machtverteilung unter den real vorhandenen Kräften“[26] ist,[27] kennzeichnet es die *constitutio*, normativ gebundene Grundorientierung über Herrschaftsverhältnisse zu sein. Zu den funktionalen Anforderungen an eine Verfassung gehört insofern nicht nur, dass sie eine Kompetenzordnung etabliert; sie hat auch Institutionen einzurichten und deren Entscheidungsprozeß zu regeln.[28] Zur verfassungsmäßigen negativen Legitimation von Herrschaft (Freiheit *vor* staatlicher Herrschaft) gesellte sich gleichsam die positive Legitimation hinzu (Freiheit *zu* staatlicher Herrschaft)[29]. Die Verfassung muß zudem eine Antwort auf die Legitimationsproblematik geben; eine Verfassung, die sich nicht mit der Frage der Legitimität ihres Geltungsanspruchs befaßt, steht auf tönernen Füßen. Kein *notwendiger* Bestandteil der Verfassung sind dieser Sichtweise zufolge Grundrechte oder Staatszielbestimmungen; die historische Erfahrung belegt allerdings, dass eine Verfassung die Legitimitätserwartungen im westlich-aufgeklärten Gemeinwesen nur dann erfüllen kann, wenn sie Grundrechtsschutz gewährt und materiell-inhaltliche Festlegungen vornimmt. In diesem materiell angereicherten Sinne ist Verfassung die *freiheitlich* politische Grundordnung des Staates, sie ist „der Inbegriff von in der Regel in einer Verfassungsurkunde niedergelegten Rechtssätzen höchsten Ranges, die die Ordnung des Staates hinsichtlich der grundlegenden Organisation, Form und Struktur regeln sowie das grundlegende Verhältnis zu seinen Bürgern und bestimmte aus Gründen erschwerter Abänderbarkeit in diese übernommene Gegenstände festlegen."[30]. Dieser Verfassungsbegriff hat seine Wurzeln in der Theorie Frankreichs und der Vereinigten Staaten, hat aber im Deutschland des zwanzigsten Jahrhunderts an Bedeutung gewonnen und läßt sich wohl heute als vorherrschend bezeichnen.

cc) Verfassung und Legitimität

Die Mehrdeutigkeit des Verfassungsbegriffs ist ferner darauf zurückzuführen, dass sich im Sprachgebrauch von Politik und Wissenschaft Bedeutungsvarianten nachweisen lassen, denen zufolge jede rechtliche Grundordnung im oben beschriebenen Sinne als Verfassung bezeichnet werden kann, darüber hinaus aber auch solche Varianten existieren, die bestimmte materielle Anforderungen an eine Verfassung stellen. Während der erstgenannten Sichtweise zufolge bereits ein bloßes Organisationsstatut „Verfassung" sein kann, verlangen die zuletzt genannten Positionen die Erfüllung bestimmter Legitimationskriterien. Wird etwa der legitimistische Verfassungsbegriff mit tradierten, am „Staatsvolk" und an der Verfassungstheorie des 19. Jahrhunderts orientierten Gehalten angereichert und werden in diesem Zusammenhang hohe Anforderungen an die demokratische Legitimation der einschlägigen Regeln gestellt, so wird die Europäische Union angesichts ihrer dann defizitären Strukturen kaum verfassungsfähig sein[31]. Unter den Anhängern eines legitimistischen Verfassungsbegriffs herrscht allerdings kein Einverständnis darüber, welche Anforderungen zu formulieren sind. Teilweise ist man der Auffassung, dass von Verfassung nur dann gesprochen werden kann, wenn ein bestimmtes Verfahren der Inkraftsetzung oder ein bestimmter Legitimitätsanspruch (regelmäßig: Rückführbarkeit auf den Willen des verfassungsgebenden Volkes) gegeben sind. Als Verfassung ist eine Grundordnung danach nur dann zu bezeichnen, wenn sie ihre Legitimität im demokratischen Prinzip sucht und sich auf das Prinzip der verfassungsgebenden Gewalt des Volkes stützt, um Existenz und Geltungsanspruch zu begründen. Legitimistische Verfassungsbegriffe formulieren ferner Anforderungen, was die inhaltliche Ausrichtung der gezähmten oder eingesetzten Herrschaftsgewalt angeht: Teilweise fordert man, dass von Verfassung nur dort die Rede sein kann, wo Herrschaft demokratisch rückgebunden wird. So identifiziert etwa *Kägi* als Wesensmerkmal und Hauptaufgabe von Verfassung die Bestimmung der Staatsordnung „von unten". Zentrales Merkmal des modernen Konstitutionalismus ist danach das Demokratieprinzip: „Diese Idee der Selbstgesetzgebung ist es, was die Staats*verfassung* von der (autoritär von oben gesetzten) Staats*ordnung* unterscheidet."[32] Anderer Sichtweise zufolge muß eine Grundordnung jedenfalls bestimmte Werte in Rechtsnormen überführen, Grundrechte begründen, Staatsziele festlegen oder bestimmten Organisationsprinzipen genügen, um die begrifflichen Anforderungen an eine Verfassung zu erfüllen. Der vielleicht berühmteste Niederschlag dieses Verständnisses findet sich in der französischen Erklärung der Menschenrechte von 1789: „Toute société dans laquelle la garantie des droits n´est pas assurée, ni la séparation des pouvoirs déterminée, n´a point de constitution." Es liegt auf der Hand, dass der Verfassungsbegriff in dieser inhaltlichen Aufladung zum politischen Kampfbegriff werden konnte. Schwierigkeiten verbinden sich mit diesem Verständnis, weil es keine Einigkeit über die Kriterien gibt, die als *notwendiger* Maßstab und Inhalt einer Verfassung zu formulieren sind.

dd) Verfassung und Gesellschaft

Bedeutungsvarianten des Verfassungsbegriffs lassen sich auch insoweit nachweisen, als es um den Umfang und die Reichweite des Ordnungsanspruchs der errichteten Grundordnung geht. Dem formalen Verständnis zufolge konstituiert oder zähmt die Verfassung Herrschaft, befaßt sich mit der Ordnung der Herrschaftsausübung und leitet diese an. Den Anspruch einer Ordnung der Gesellschaft beansprucht die Verfassung demgegenüber nicht. Die gesellschaftlichen Verhältnisse liegen dieser Sichtweise zufolge vor oder jenseits des Regelungsanspruchs der Verfassung. Sie sind grundsätzlich dem freien Spiel der gesellschaftlichen Kräfte überlassen. Besteht Ordnungsbedarf, so ist dieser von der demokratisch verantwortlichen Hoheitsgewalt im politischen Prozeß zu befriedigen; die gesellschaftliche Ordnung darf nicht bereits substantiell in der Verfassung vorgeprägt sein. Der formale Verfassungsbegriff weist insofern eine große Affinität zur politischen Theorie des Liberalismus auf.

Demgegenüber gehen die Anhänger eines substantiellen Verfassungsbegriffes davon aus, dass sich der Regelungsanspruch der Grundordnung auch auf die Ordnung der Gesellschaft beziehen muß. Verfassung ist danach umfassende Grundordnung des Gemeinwesens, nicht lediglich konstituierendes Statut für den Träger der Hoheitsgewalt. Verfassung ist nicht lediglich „Staatsverfassung“, sondern auch „Gesellschaftsverfassung“[33]; ihr Regelungsanliegen beschränkt sich nicht auf die Steuerung der Hoheitsgewalt, sondern erstreckt sich auch auf die Ordnung der gesellschaftlichen Verhältnisse mit Blick auf eine Idee des Guten oder Richtigen. Mit diesem Verständnis werden Verfassungsfunktionen im Bezugsfeld Bürger - Staat eingefangen, mittelbar darüber hinaus auch im Bezugsfeld Bürger - Gesellschaft. Verfassung konstituiert danach nicht nur staatliche Macht; sie konstituiert auch *Gesellschaft*, wirkt jedenfalls konstituierend in sie hinein[34]. Konrad Hesse etwa hebt hervor, dass Verfassung nicht auf die Ordnung staatlichen Lebens beschränkt sei. Vielmehr sei sie auch in nicht-staatlichen Lebensbereichen konstituierend fühlbar, wie etwa in Ehe und Familie, Eigentum, Bildung, Freiheit von Kunst und Wissenschaft, Wirken sozialer Gruppen usw. [35] Dem folgend sind daher in Abkehr zu dem engen staatszentrierten Verfassungsbegriff in den Begriff der „Verfassung“ auch die gesellschaftsintegrierenden Bestandteile aufzunehmen. Mit Konrad Hesse bedeutet daher Verfassung nicht etwa die „rechtliche Grundordnung *des Staates*“, sondern die „rechtliche Grundordnung *des Gemeinwesens*“.[36] Besonders in der Rechtsprechung des Bundesverfassungsgerichts zur Werteordnung des Grundgesetzes[37] hat dieses weite Verständnis von Verfassung seinen Niederschlag gefunden. Anhänger dieses Verfassungsverständnisses beschreiben als Verfassungsfunktion die Gewährleistung von „Integration“, interpretieren die Verfassung im Lichte republikanisch-politischer Vorstellungen von Bürgeraktivität und politischem Ethos oder verlangen von ihr die Sicherung des gesellschaftlichen Grundkonsenses.

ee) Verfassung und Identität

Bedeutungsvarianten des Verfassungsbegriffs lassen sich schließlich auch insoweit nachweisen, als es um den Stellenwert der Verfassung im Prozeß der Identitätsbildung geht. Es lassen sich in Deutschland Stimmen nachweisen, die den Begriff der Verfassung einer Grundordnung nur dann zuschreiben wollen, wenn sie identitätsformende oder gar identitätskonstituierende Funktion hat, wenn also die Verfassung auch oder vor allem Kristallisationsfaktor der Identität der Mitglieder des Gemeinwesens darstellt. Diese Sichtweise wird in verschiedenen Spielarten vertreten. Teilweise meint man, dass Verfassungsgebung scheitern müsse und eine Verfassung nicht zu ihrem Sinn kommen könne, wenn sie nicht gesellschaftlichen Sinn, historische Erfahrungen und existentielle Momente des Gemeinwesens in sich trage. Von Verfassung könne daher nur dort gesprochen werden, wo hinter der Verfassung die vorfindliche Geschichtlichkeit des Gemeinwesens stünde, wo die Verfassung Gedächtnis des Gemeinwesens sei. Der Versuch, ein Gemeinwesen durch

Verfassungsgebung erst zu konstituieren, sein Zusammenwachsen im Verfassungsleben zu organisieren, soll danach zum Scheitern verurteilt sein. Funktionalistische Verfassungsgebung kann demzufolge lediglich „Scheinlegitimation" vermitteln. Dieser Sichtweise ist insoweit zuzustimmen, als hinter vielen Verfassungen in der Tat existentielle Erfahrungen stehen, die den Akt der Verfassungsgebung zugleich auch zu einem wesentlichen Element der Identitätsbildung machen. Begrifflich oder historisch notwendig ist dies aber nicht. In einer Zeit, in der sich zu identitätskonstituierenden Faktoren vor allem die Kriterien der wirtschaftlichen und sozialen Stellung, der Konsum- und Freizeitgewohnheiten etc. entwickelt haben, mutet es merkwürdig anachronistisch an, dem Verfassungsbegriff einen Gehalt einschreiben zu wollen, mit dem die einzelnen kaum mehr etwas anfangen können. Auf einer anderen Ebene bewegen sich Ansätze, die die Verfassungsqualität einer Grundordnung mit dem identitätsformenden Kriterium des Verfassungspatriotismus in Verbindung bringen.

ff) Schlußfolgerungen

Die vorstehenden Überlegungen bekräftigen zunächst die Ausgangsfeststellung, dass sich die deutsche Verfassungsrechtswissenschaft nicht eines eindeutigen Verfassungsbegriffs bedient. Je nach Erkenntnisinteresse, verfassungstheoretischem Standpunkt und normativem Anliegen bedient man sich des Begriffs in deutlich unterschiedlicher Bedeutung. Insofern kann es nicht verwundern, dass sich die Diskussion um Stand und Entwicklung der europäischen Integration, um Richtung und Finalität des Prozesses auch und zuerst auf begrifflicher Ebene abspielt. Die letzten Jahre haben allerdings im Begrifflichen zu gewissen Ermüdungserscheinungen geführt. Überwiegend hat sich die Auffassung durchgesetzt, dass die Verwendung eines angereicherten, wenngleich nicht legitimistischen Verfassungsbegriffs[38] sinnvoll ist. Es muß sich um einen Verfassungsbegriff handeln, der auf die Problematik zugeschnitten ist, die sich mit der Einbindung und Legitimierung von Herrschaft im 21. Jahrhundert jenseits des Nationalstaates verbinden (konkreter, aber abstrahierender normativer Verfassungsbegriff)[39]. Vor diesem Hintergrund[40] ist man sich inzwischen weitgehend einig, dass das Primärrecht der EU Verfassungsqualität hat, dass aber unter Zugrundelegung eines substantiell angereicherten Verfassungsbegriffs Defizite bestehen. Die Diskussion hat sich inzwischen der Frage danach zugewandt, wo derartige Defizite zu sehen sind und wie sie zu beseitigen sind. Man erkennt die Verfassungswerdung der Verträge an, fordert aber verfassungsrechtliche Erneuerung und Fortschreibung. Dem bestehenden Primärrecht wird die Qualität einer „de-facto"-Verfassung oder einer „Grundordnung"[41] zugeschrieben; sie wird als Verfassung im formellen Sinne bezeichnet. In einem Atemzug werden allerdings dann immer (und jeweils in Abhängigkeit vom verwandten Verfassungsbegriff) jene Mängel hervorgehoben, die dem Primärrecht „in materieller Hinsicht" anhaften und ihm die Qualität als „vollwertige" und angemessene Verfassung [42] nehmen. In diesem Zusammenhang wird vor allem die Frage danach gestellt, ob es nicht Zeit ist, dass sich die EU eine formelle Verfassungsurkunde zulegt.[43]

b. Die EU/EG - Architektur im Spiegel der deutschen Verfassungslehre

aa) Die Konstitutionalisierung der Verträge

Wer in Deutschland heute über die Gestalt Europas spricht, wird zunächst den als „Konstitutionalisierung" bezeichneten Gestaltwandel der Verträge hervorheben.[44] Dieser Wandel ist so häufig beschrieben worden, dass hier einige Stichpunkte genügen. Zu den wesentlichen Elementen der Konstitutionalisierung gehört zunächst und vor allem die Breite, Dichte und Tiefe der Kompetenz- und Zuständigkeitsnormen. Die EU hat sich auf der Grundlage von EGV, EGKSV, EAGV sowie EUV zu einem Verband entwickelt, der sich in staatsgleicher Weise der Angelegenheiten des Gemeinwesens umfassend annimmt. Sie hat ihre ursprünglichen Auftrag der sektoralen Integration der Wirtschaft längst hinter sich gelassen. Heute hat sie den Auftrag, sich beinahe aller Angelegenheiten des europäischen Gemeinwesens ordnend anzunehmen. Das Primärrecht hat sich vor diesem Hintergrund zur Grundordnung einer Herrschaftsgewalt entwickelt, der ein staatsgleicher, quasi-allumfassender Zuständigkeitsbereich unterfällt. Im Lichte der Kompetenzrechtsprechung des EuGH verfügt die EU dabei nicht nur über die Zuständigkeiten, die ihr in den Verträgen explizit überantwortet werden; sie kann auch dort handeln, wo dies zur Verwirklichung der Ziele und zur Erledigung der übertragenen Aufgaben notwendig ist (implied powers).[45] Den Kompetenznormen des Primärrechts hat der EuGH teilweise ausschließliche Qualität zugeschrieben, mit der Folge, dass den Mitgliedstaaten das Handeln in den betroffenen Sachbereichen selbst dann rechtlich versagt ist, wenn die EU ihrerseits noch keine Regelungen erlassen hat. Im übrigen entfaltet das erlassene Sekundärrecht faktisch „Sperrwirkung" und nimmt so den Mitgliedstaaten in weiten Bereichen ihrer Zuständigkeit die Handlungsmöglichkeit. Vor diesem Hintergrund kommt den Verträgen in kompetenzieller Hinsicht konstitutionelle Qualität zu. – Die Breite der Zuständigkeiten würde den Verträgen allein allerdings noch keine konstitutionelle Qualität verleihen, wenn nicht die EU aufgrund dieser Zuständigkeiten befugt wäre, unmittelbar anwendbares Recht zu setzen und so die Verhältnisse in den Mitgliedstaaten zu regeln. Zwar sind nicht alle Bestimmungen des EU-Rechts unmittelbar anwendbar. Indem der EuGH diese Eignung den Grundfreiheiten und anderen wesentlichen Bestimmungen des EGV, den Verordnungen, Entscheidungen sowie (im

Ausnahmefall der fehlerhaften Umsetzung) den Richtlinien zugesprochen hat, hat das EU-Recht doch eine Durchschlagskraft und Wirkmächtigkeit erlangt, die es rechtfertigt, den diese Rechtsetzungsgewalt begründenden Vertragsnormen in der Breite Verfassungsqualität zuzuschreiben. Dabei ist selbstverständlich zu berücksichtigen, dass die Normen des EU-Rechts im Konfliktfall nationalem Recht vorgehen.

Zu einer Konstitutionalisierung der Verträge hat auch beigetragen, dass Entscheidungen der EU heute in vielen Bereichen mit Mehrheit ergehen – mit der Folge, dass den Mitgliedstaaten kein Vetorecht mehr zusteht und sie mit der Pflicht zur Befolgung von Recht konfrontiert werden, dessen Setzung sie nicht zugestimmt haben.

Konstitutionelle Qualität ist den Verträgen schließlich auch deshalb zuzuschreiben, weil sie sich dem Schutz und der Förderung von Freiheit und Interessen der Bürger in einer Weise angenommen hat, wie sie jener im Nationalstaat strukturell entspricht. In diesem Zusammenhang ist nicht nur der Wille der Unionsbürger zu berücksichtigen, eine grundrechtlich geschützte Freiheitssphäre der Bürger zu respektieren. Auch der Umstand, dass den Bürgern durch Unionsrecht Rechte verliehen werden und ihnen die Möglichkeit gegeben wird, diese Rechte auch unmittelbar (Art. 230 EGV) oder mittelbar (Art. 234 EGV) gerichtlich durchzusetzen, spielt dabei eine Rolle.[46] Die bislang allerdings inhaltlich schwache Unionsbürgerschaft verleiht dem heute einen institutionellen Rahmen.

Gewiß ist in diesem Zusammenhang hervorzuheben, dass sich die Dichte der Konstitutionalisierung in den einzelnen Bereichen des Primärrechts noch deutlich unterscheidet; an die Seite von Sphären, in denen Verfassungsqualität klar und greifbar hervortritt, treten insbesondere im Bereich der zweiten und dritten Säule Sphären, in denen die Verdichtung noch gering ist. Auch hier ist aber ein Druck zur Konstitutionalisierung zu beobachten, wie die „Vergemeinschaftung" von Politikbereichen im Vertrag von Amsterdam belegt. Zudem kommt es auf das Gesamtbild und nicht die Einzelsphären an, und dieses Gesamtbild gibt heute der Konstitutionalisierungsthese Rückhalt.

Es liegt auf der Hand, dass die Erscheinung eines konstitutionalisierten überstaatlichen, zugleich aber nichtstaatlichen Hoheitsträgers die Verfassungswissenschaft vor Herausforderungen stellt und mit Fortschreibungsdruck konfrontiert. Im Zuge der Integration hat sich ein Hoheitsträger herausgebildet, der Recht setzt, ohne Staat zu sein. Der überkommene, seit nunmehr dreihundert Jahren gültige und zum Dogma erhobene Konnex von Staat und Recht, von Staatsgewalt und Rechtsetzung wird dadurch durchbrochen. Regierungsgewalt und Rechtsetzung müssen nunmehr als Erscheinungen begriffen werden, die auch jenseits der Staatlichkeit erfolgen. Die damit verbundenen Schwierigkeiten dürfen allerdings - entgegen gelegentlich geäußerter Befürchtungen – nicht überzeichnet werden: Kategorien wie Kompetenz, Zwang, Recht etc. lassen sich ohne Probleme auch außerhalb staatlicher Kontexte denken. Das Völkerrecht bietet hierfür seit Herausbildung des Konzepts der internationalen Organisation in der zweiten Hälfte des neunzehnten Jahrhunderts genügend Beispiele. Insbesondere war der Rechtsbegriff zu keiner Zeit ausschließlich auf den Staat bezogen. Staatliches Recht genoß zwar vor dem Hintergrund der staatlichen Zwangsgewalt eine besonders prägnante Normativität; an seiner Seite stand aber immer auch Recht, hinter dem diese Gewalt nicht stand, das aber gleichwohl in seiner Existenz und Wirksamkeit als Recht nicht in Zweifel gezogen werden konnte.[47] Es sei daran erinnert, dass sich das Völkerrecht seit Jahrhunderten mit der Frage befaßt, warum *Rechts*normen befolgt werden (müssen), hinter der nicht ein mit Zwangsgewalt ausgerüsteter Hoheitsträger steht. Vor diesem Hintergrund muß hier betont werden, dass es der Verfassungswissenschaft nicht um Neufassung oder Revision, sondern um Fortschreibung überkommener Kategorien in neuartigem Zusammenhang gehen muß. Im Prozeß der Integration mag sich zwar die besondere Nähe (nicht: Einheit) von Staat und Recht relativieren; auch ist sofort einzustehen, dass der Staat sein Monopol für die Ordnung des Politischen verliert. Die Herausforderung der europäischen Verfassungsrechtswissenschaft liegt aber nicht im Begrifflichen oder im Kategoriellen, sondern im Legitimatorischen. Hierauf wird zurückzukommen sein.

bb) Die Verbandsqualität des konstituierten Hoheitsträgers

Während man sich im Hinblick auf die Konstitutionalisierungsthese heute weitgehend einig ist, besteht in der Frage, wer Träger der europäischen Hoheitsgewalt ist, Uneinigkeit. Im wesentlichen lassen sich drei Positionen unterscheiden:[48]

Teilweise ist man der Auffassung, dass das Primärrecht einen einzigen Verband konstituiert, der auf der Grundlage der verschiedenen Verträge handelt.[49] Dieser Sichtweise zufolge gingen die Gemeinschaften mit Inkrafttreten des Maastricht-Vertrages in dem neuen Verband *Europäische Union* auf; der Vertrag bewirkte eine Verschmelzung der bis dahin rechtlich selbstständigen drei Europäischen Gemeinschaften. Es ist seither nur noch die europäische Union, die Handlungsträger ist, wenngleich auf der Grundlage von Kompetenznormen, die ihren Ursprung in verschiedenen Verträgen haben. Dieser Sichtweise zufolge ist Rechtsträger und Zurechnungssubjekt allein die Europäische Union, dies gilt selbst dann, wenn sie unter dem Namen Europäische Gemeinschaft handelt. Diese Sichtweise kommt nicht umhin, der Europäischen Union nach innen Rechtssubjektivität zuzuschreiben; sie muß ihr auch Völkerrechtssubjektivität jedenfalls in den Bereichen zuschreiben, in denen die Verträge (namentlich der EGV) dies ausdrücklich oder implizit vorsehen. Insofern empfiehlt es sich, sämtliche Rechtsakte des einen Verbandes als Unionsrecht zu bezeichnen. Für die Mitgliedstaaten bedeutet dies, dass sie nur noch dem einen Verband Europäische Union angehören können; eine parallele Mitgliedschaft in verschiedenen Verbänden, etwa den Europäischen Gemeinschaften, ist ausgeschlossen.

Teilweise lehnt man aber auch die Fusionsthese ab und ist der Auffassung, dass mit dem Inkrafttreten des Vertrages von Maastricht ein gestufter bzw. gegliederter Verband entstanden ist, in dem die Europäische Union als Rechtsträger mehrere Glieder, die europäischen Gemeinschaften, umschließt.[50] Diesem Rechtsverständnis zufolge agieren auf europäischer Ebene gegenwärtig vier Rechtssubjekte, die die jeweils in den Verträgen zugewiesenen Kompetenzen in eigener Verantwortung wahrnehmen. Dem ausdrücklichen Wortlaut der Verträge zufolge ist der Beitritt allein zur Europäischen Union zulässig; dieser Beitritt schließt dann automatisch und ohne weitere rechtliche Schritte die Mitgliedschaft in den Gliedern ein. Dieser Sichtweise zufolge ist zwischen dem vom Verband "Europäische Union" gesetzten Recht („Unionsrecht") und dem von den Europäischen Gemeinschaften erlassenen Recht („Gemeinschaftsrecht") zu unterscheiden. Überwiegend gehen die Vertreter dieser Positionen davon aus, dass der Europäischen Union keine Völkerrechtssubjektivität zukomme; sie kann danach zwar nach innen rechtssetzend tätig werden, nicht aber nach außen rechtliche Bindungen eingehen.

Einer dritten, in Deutschland vereinzelt vertretenen Sichtweise zufolge ist zwischen den fortbestehenden Europäischen Gemeinschaften und dem durch den Maastricht-Vertrag neu errichteten Bereich der Europäischen Union zu unterschieden. Einige Anhänger dieser Position gehen davon aus, dass seither vier oder fünf Organisationen nebeneinander stehen und vom Unionsvertrag „tempelartig" überdacht werden. Die radikaleren Vertreter dieser Sichtweise wollen einen strikten Grenzstrich zwischen dem Bereich der Europäischen Gemeinschaften und der Sphäre der EU ziehen. Dieser Sichtweise zufolge sollen die Europäischen Gemeinschaften und der Bereich der Europäischen Union weitgehend zusammenhanglos nebeneinander stehen.[51] Die Europäische Union ist danach kein Verband mit mitgliedschaftlicher Struktur, sondern lediglich eine Form der mitgliedstaatlichen intergouvernementalen Zusammenarbeit. Rechtsakte, die in diesem Bereich ergehen, sind nicht Rechtsakte eines supranationalen Verbandes, sondern völkerrechtlich vereinbarte Verträge der Mitgliedstaaten.

Misst man die vorgestellten Positionen an den Vertragsbestimmungen, so erweist sich die drittgenannte Sichtweise als kaum haltbar. Sie läßt sich nur unter klarer Überspielung ausdrücklicher vertraglicher Festlegungen vertreten. Demgegenüber verhalten sich die Vertragsbestimmungen gegenüber den beiden erstgenannten Positionen ambivalenter. Welcher der Positionen in einer derartigen Situation der Vorzug zu geben ist, hängt nicht zuletzt vom methodischen Vorverständnis und funktionalen Anliegen ab. Wer es für ein legitimes Anliegen hält, die im Maastricht-Vertrag angelegte Spaltungstendenz und die damit einhergehenden Gefahren für die Einheit des Integrationsverbands abzuwehren, wird sich eher der erstgenannten Sichtweise zuwenden. Ihr wird man auch den Vorzug geben, wenn man pragmatischen Erwägungen (Vermittelbarkeit der rechtlichen Zusammenhänge; praktischer Nutzwert) Raum gibt. Wer sich demgegenüber in den Traditionen dogmatisch-konstruktivistischer Verfassungstheorie bewegt, wird dem Verständnis der EU als gegliedertem Verband den Vorzug geben. In den letzten Jahren läßt sich jedenfalls im allgemeinen europarechtlichen Schrifttum in Deutschland eine deutliche Hinwendung zur erstgenannten These erkennen.

cc) Die verfassungstheoretische Einordnung des Integrationsverbands: Europa als werdender Staat?

Noch immer besteht in Deutschland keine Einigkeit darüber, wie der Integrationsverband (ungeachtet seiner internen Binnenstruktur) verfassungstheoretisch einzuordnen ist. Die Frage ist nicht nur in terminologischer Hinsicht von Bedeutung. Sie entfaltet ihre Bedeutung vor allem, wenn es darum geht, verfassungstheoretische Typenmerkmale im interpretatorischen Umgang mit den Regeln des EU-Rechts zur Anwendung zu bringen: Die Grundordnung einer internationalen Organisation wird nun einmal anders interpretiert als die Grundordnung eines Staates. Relevanz hat die Frage zudem bei der Beurteilung der inneren Finalität des Integrationsprozesses: Je nach dem, wie man den Verband typologisch einordnet, wird ihm eine bestimmte Entwicklungsrichtung eingeschrieben.[52]

(1) Der Integrationsverband als internationale Organisation

Noch immer spielt in Deutschland eine Sichtweise, derzufolge der Integrationsverband als (wenn auch besonders entwickelte) internationale Organisation anzusehen ist, eine besonders prominente Rolle. Dieser Position zufolge haben die Mitgliedstaaten in den Gründungsverträgen auf völkerrechtlichem Wege eine internationale Organisation gegründet; diese Organisation hat sich von ihren Wurzeln nicht gelöst.[53] Die Beziehungen zwischen der Organisation und ihren Mitgliedstaaten werden zwar grundsätzlich vom Europarecht beherrscht; jenseits und hinter diesen Regeln steht aber das Völkerrecht, das insbesondere im Hinblick auf grundlegende konstitutionelle Fragen (etwa die Frage des Austrittsrechts) zur Anwendung kommt. Wird die Konzeption mit normativem Anspruch vertreten,[54] so mündet sie in die Schlußfolgerung, dass der Integrationsverband keinen legitimatorischen Selbststand erlangen kann. Er bleibt in seinem Wirken von der Zustimmung und Rückbindung seitens der Mitgliedstaaten abhängig; er hat die politische Letztverantwortung der Mitgliedstaaten zu respektieren und darf ihre Souveränität nicht antasten. Der Versuch, sich von der mitgliedschaftlichen Basis rechtlich, politisch oder legitimatorisch abzulösen, muß im Nichts enden, weil es der EU als internationaler Organisation schon strukturell nicht möglich ist, politisch-legitimatorische Wurzeln unmittelbar in der Bevölkerung Europas zu schlagen. Damit verbinden sich institutionelle Folgerungen: Eine weitere Parlamentarisierung der EU würde jedenfalls dann, wenn sie mit einem Bedeutungsverlust der Mitgliedstaaten im Rat einherginge, strukturell delegitimierende Effekte mit sich bringen. Der natürliche Modus europäischer Integration ist danach die intergouvernementale Absprache – auch wenn sie im Rahmen europäischer Organe stattfindet. Diese Sichtweise steht nicht nur hinter der von Paul Kirchhof entwickelten Konzeption des „Staatenverbunds“[55], sondern findet auch im Maastricht-Urteil des BVerfG einen (wenn auch in seiner Reichweite unklaren) Niederschlag. Der Kampf des BVerfG um die Sicherung der mitgliedstaatlichen Kompetenz-Kompetenz findet hier seine Erklärung.

Es liegt auf der Hand, dass dem Integrationsverband aus dieser Perspektive nicht mehr als eine funktional definierte, begrenzte Aufgabenstellung zugewiesen werden kann. Der Integrationsverband darf sich nicht der Gesamtverantwortung für die Angelegenheiten des Gemeinwesens annehmen – dies schon deshalb, weil er sonst in ein staatliches Wesen umschlagen könnte. Mehr als sachlich und gegenständlich klar definierte, in ihrer Teleologie inhaltlich festgelegte Zuständigkeiten dürfen ihm nicht überantwortet werden. Diese Position wurde und wird in Deutschland immer wieder und in immer wieder neuen Fassungen und Nuancen formuliert. Die vielleicht bedeutendste Formulierung fand sie im Verständnis des Integrationsverbands als „Zweckverband funktionaler Integration“[56], der sich der Integration bestimmter Sachbereiche anzunehmen habe und hierin seine Erfüllung finde. Während man teilweise das Element des Politischen im Prozeß der Integration hervorhebt, interpretiert man andernorts die Gehalte des EGV als Ausdruck eines ökonomisch beherrschten, auf Marktfreiheit und Effizienz ausgerichteten Deregulierungsprogramms.[57] Das Element der politischen Entscheidung wird hier weit zurückgeschoben; es sind die Gesetze der ökonomischen Rationalität, die eins zu eins in das Primärrecht eingeschrieben worden sind und so in Europa ein Rechts- und Gesellschaftssystem des wirtschaftlichen Liberalismus zu errichten beanspruchen.[58]

Die verfassungstheoretischen Schlußfolgerungen dieser Position liegen auf der Hand und sind wohlbekannt: Die Tätigkeit des Integrationsverbands kann nur dann als legitim erachtet werden, wenn er die Souveränität der Mitgliedstaaten (Letztentscheidungsmacht) nicht antastet. Was die Entscheidungszuständigkeiten angeht, so hängt viel davon ab, welchen Raum man dem Politischen einräumt: Sieht man Integrationsziele und –wege inhaltlich weitgehend festgelegt, so wird man sich Legitimität vor allem dadurch erhoffen, dass unabhängige und funktionaler Gesetzmäßigkeit entsprechende Organe das im Primärrecht angelegte Programm abarbeiten. Gegen eine Stärkung der Kommission wird man aus dieser Perspektive nichts einzuwenden haben; darüber hinaus ist eine weitere Aufgabenverlagerung auf spezialisierte Einrichtungen und Ämter in Betracht zu ziehen. Die Rolle der im Rat vertretenen Vertreter der Mitgliedstaaten darf nicht geringgeschätzt werden. Ihre Funktion liegt aber weniger in der deliberativen Gestaltung und mehr in der retrospektiven Kontrolle der andernorts getroffenen Entscheidungen. Hebt man demgegenüber das Element des Politischen hervor, so ist die Rolle der Mitgliedstaaten stärker in den Vordergrund zu rücken. Ihre Funktion liegt in diesem Fall weniger im Bereich der Kontrolle und mehr im Bereich der politischen Gestaltung. Je nach normativem Verständnis läßt sich so mehr der Charakter eines Zweckverbands oder mehr der Charakter eines Staatenverbunds hervorheben; zwischen den beiden Extrempolen besteht ein gradueller Übergang.

(2) Der Integrationsverbund als (werdender) Staat

Den verfassungstheoretischen Gegenpol zur Konzeption des Integrationsverbands bildet das Verständnis der EU als (werdender) Staat. Die EU ist dieser Sichtweise zufolge dabei, die Qualität eines Verbands anzunehmen, der sich der Angelegenheiten einer europäischen Gemeinschaft in umfassender Weise annimmt. Dieser Verband ist nicht nur sektoral für bestimmte Politikbereiche zuständig, sondern ebenso Hüter des gesellschaftlichen Allgemeinen wie der überkommene Nationalstaat zu seiner Zeit. Er ist auch nicht lediglich Instrument zwischenstaatlicher Kooperation, sondern selbst Träger von Verantwortung für das Gemeinwohl. Er ruht legitimatorisch in sich selbst, stützt sich auf eine europäische Bürgerschaft, die ihre Interessen teils unmittelbar, teils vermittelt über nationalstaatliche Amtswalter äußert. Er erfüllt seine Aufgaben, indem er sich des Individuums in staatsgleicher Weise annimmt, ihm Rechte verleiht und Pflichten auferlegt sowie seine Lebenswelt ordnet. Gewiß, auch in ihrer normativen Version geht die Theorie europäischer Staatswerdung nicht davon aus, dass der Integrationsverband demnächst *Souveränität* gewinnen wird. Staatsqualität ist aber, wie die Bundesstaatslehre zeigt, nicht notwendig von Souveränität abhängig. Staatsqualität setzt auch nicht notwendig allumfassende Kompetenz voraus; Verfassungsstaatlichkeit der Gegenwart zeigt, dass die den Trägern der Hoheitsgewalt zugewiesenen Kompetenzen immer begrenzt sind. Zwar wird im Regelfall die Kompetenz-Kompetenz in den Händen der Organe des Verbandes liegen, um dessen

Kompetenzen es geht. Art. 79 Abs. 3 GG belegt aber, dass eine Verfassung auch hier Grenzen ziehen kann; und ein Blick in die U.S.-amerikanische Verfassung beweist, dass in bündisch verfaßten Gemeinwesen ein Anteil der Kompetenz-Kompetenz bei den Gliedern liegen kann, ohne dass dies die Staatsqualität des Bundes beeinträchtigen würde. Eine der wesentlichen Thesen dieser Theorie ist es, dass die Frage nach der Finalität der Integration mit der Staatswerdung obsolet wird (oder geworden ist); ein Verband, der sich der Rolle des Hüters des Allgemeinen angenommen hat, ist nicht mehr auf dem Weg, sondern hat sein Ziel erreicht.

Zweifellos wird man zu den wichtigsten frühen Anhängern dieser Theorie Walter Hallstein zählen müssen, der in seiner Vision von Europa als Bundesstaat im Werden Richtung und Ziel bereits klar formuliert hat.[59] Er war allerdings nicht allein. Unter den (politischen und wissenschaftlichen) Wegbegleitern der frühen Integration gab es viele, die das Integrationsprojekt im Lichte der Theorie funktionaler Integration interpretierten und ihm normativ das Ziel der Staatswerdung einschrieben - an dieser Stelle sei lediglich Eberhard Grabitz erwähnt.[60] Schwierigkeiten bei der Verwirklichung der Integrationsziele, vor allem aber politische Überlegungen ließen diese Stimmen später verstummen; man war der Auffassung, dass man mit der Rede von europäischer Staatlichkeit dem Fortkommen der Integration eher schaden als nutzen würde. Zudem lassen sich funktionale und vor allem ideelle Einwände dagegen formulieren, dass die europäische Integration in einer Form enden solle, die im neunzehnten Jahrhundert ihre vollendete Form gefunden hat und im zwanzigsten Jahrhundert Grundlage von unvorstellbarem Unrecht werden konnte. Inzwischen aber hat sich das Bild wieder gewandelt. Zwar sind jene, die von der Staatswerdung Europas sprechen, immer noch in der (deutlichen) Minderheit. Die Zahl derer, die die EU als werdenden Staat behandeln und Fragen an sie herantragen, die nur an einen legitimatorisch in sich selbst ruhenden und für das Allgemein zuständigen Verband gerichtet werden können, nimmt aber deutlich zu. Die wohl deutlichste Stimme unter den Anhängern dieser Position in Deutschland[61] gehört gegenwärtig *Ingolf Pernice*, der dem Verband nicht nur Verfassungsfähigkeit attestiert, sondern auch darauf hinarbeitet, die Legitimationsbasis des Verbands von ihren bisherigen (völkerrechtlich-internationalen) Wurzeln zu lösen und in der Idee einer europäischen Gesellschaft neu zu errichten.

(3) Der Integrationsverband als eigenständige Form neben Staat und internationaler Organisation

Es kann nicht überraschen, dass sich an der Seite der beiden beschriebenen Positionen noch eine dritte Sichtweise herausgebildet hat. Wer die EU nicht lediglich als internationale Organisation ansehen will, zugleich aber der These von der Staatswerdung Europas (aus politischen, ideengeschichtlichen oder funktionalen Gründen) mit Skepsis begegnet, wird vorschlagen, die EU als Herrschaftsform „sui generis" anzusehen. Dieser Herrschaftsform läßt sich das Potential einschreiben, jenseits der bekannten und delegitimierten Formen staatlicher und völkerrechtlicher Verbandsformung Grundlage einer neuen, legitimatorisch und moralisch frischen Form der Vergemeinschaftung zu bilden. In dieser Richtung wurden in Deutschland vor allem Anfang der neunziger Jahre mehrfach Vorstöße unternommen. Genannt seien hier vor allem die Beiträge Armin von Bogdandys, der in der EU eine eigenständige und zukunftsmächtige Form zwischen Staat und internationaler Organisation erblickt.[62] In der verfassungstheoretischen Diskussion konnten diese Vorschläge allerdings nie die ihnen gebührende Bedeutung erlangen. Wer darüber nachdenkt, warum sich diese Sichtweise nicht hat durchsetzen können, kommt nicht umhin festzustellen, dass es bislang noch nicht gelungen ist, das Eigene herauszuarbeiten, das der EU als Ausprägung einer eigenständigen Herrschaftsform (nicht: zwischen Staat und Internationaler Organisation, sondern) an der Seite von Staat und internationaler Organisation zukommen soll. Ohne Zweifel läßt sich der Übergang vom Staat zur internationalen Organisation graduell begreifen; ohne Zweifel auch ließ sich die EU Anfang der neunziger Jahre irgendwo im Übergang verorten. Diese Zwischenstellung als Form „sui generis" auszuweisen, stößt allerdings solange auf Bedenken, wie nicht ein Merkmal herausgearbeitet werden kann, das die EU *neben* Staat und internationale Organisation rückt (ein Merkmal also, das das spezifisch Dritte ausmacht). Dies aber ist bislang nicht geglückt. Einer der Gründe hierfür mag sein, dass Staat und internationale Organisation konzeptionell so offen sind, dass sie Platz für ein Tertium nicht lassen.

(4) Schlußfolgerungen

Vor dem Hintergrund des Entwicklungsstandes, den die EU inzwischen erreicht hat, läßt sich der Verband nicht mehr sinnvoll als Ausprägung des Typs Internationale Organisation betrachten. Man kommt nicht umhin, sie jedenfalls als *werdenden Staat* anzusehen. Für den Berichterstatter liegt sogar die Schlußfolgerung nahe, dass die EU inzwischen die Qualität eines staatlichen Verbandes erlangt hat.[63] Sicherlich wird man eingestehen müssen, dass es diesem Verband (noch) an manchen Merkmalen mangelt, die man traditionellerweise dem klassischen, durch das Völkerrecht allein kooperativ eingebundenen Nationalstaat des neunzehnten oder zwanzigsten Jahrhunderts zuschreibt. Hierbei handelt es sich aber, wie ein schneller Blick auf die Vielfalt der Staatsformen (insbesondere in föderalen Systemen) zeigt, um akzidentielle, nicht um notwendige Merkmale. Bestätigung findet die hier vertretene These vor allem, wenn man sich den Verlauf der weiteren Integration ausmalt. Gewiß sind weitere Kompetenzgewinne der EU denkbar; es fällt allerdings schwer, hier irgendeine Grenzlinie zu ziehen, ab der man dann vom Staat Europa ausgeht. Natürlich kann darüber nachgedacht werden, diese Grenze dort zu verorten, wo der EU Fiskalgewalt eingeräumt oder ihr die ersten Polizei- oder Armeeeinheiten zugeordnet werden. Eine derartige Grenzziehung ist aber willkürlich und beliebig; vieles spricht im übrigen für die Erwartung, dass die meisten Beobachter selbst dann, wenn in einer nächsten Vertragsänderungsrunde die Grundlagen für diese Schritte geschaffen würden, diese Schlußfolgerungen dann wieder hinauszögern würden. Wer sich die Wirkmächtigkeit und den Zuständigkeitsumfang der EU vor Augen führt, tut sich schwer damit, den kompetenziell entkräfteten Ländern der Bundesrepublik Deutschland Staatsqualität zuzuschreiben, dies aber der EU vorzuenthalten. Dass die Erlangung von Souveränität nicht notwendiges Merkmal der Staatsqualität ist, bedarf hier keiner Begründung.

dd) Integrationsverband und Mitgliedstaaten: Europa als konsoziative Föderation

Während man sich in Deutschland in der ersten Hälfte der neunziger Jahre vor allem mit der herrschaftstheoretischen Einordnung der EU befaßte, gewann in der zweiten Hälfte der neunziger Jahre die verfassungstheoretische und -rechtliche Beschreibung des Zusammenspiels von Integrationsverband und Mitgliedstaaten an Bedeutung. Im Kreise derjenigen Beobachter, die die Beschreibung der EU als (wenn auch besonderer) internationaler Organisation für überholt erachteten, stellte man sich die Frage, wie das Verhältnis zwischen dem europäischen Herrschaftsträger und seinen Mitgliedstaaten zu konzipieren ist. Dies war folgerichtig: Die überkommenen Begrifflichkeiten und Konzeptionen des Völkerrechts über das Zusammenspiel von Staat und internationaler Organisation konnten das neu entstandene Verhältnis nicht (oder jedenfalls nicht eins zu eins) erfassen. Aufgrund ihrer Kompetenzbreite und ihrer Rechtsetzungsgewalt steht die EU zu den Mitgliedstaaten in einem Verhältnis, das sich elementar von jenem zwischen einer herkömmlichen internationalen Organisation und ihren Mitgliedstaaten unterscheidet. Ihr Wirken, insbesondere ihre Rechtsetzung wirkt breit und tief in die mitgliedstaatlichen Rechtsordnungen hinein. Die EU ist Produkt mitgliedstaatlicher Entscheidung, zugleich aber verändern sich die Mitgliedstaaten im Integrationsprozeß tiefgreifend. Beinahe zeitgleich wurden zwei Konzeptionen dieses Verhältnisses entwickelt, eine eher formalen und konstruktivistischen Inhalts, eine andere eher materiellen Inhalts.

(1) Die Herausbildung eines Verfassungsverbunds

Große Bedeutung hat in der deutschen Diskussion zunächst die Konzeption des Verfassungsverbunds erlangt, die Ingolf Pernice entwickelt hat. Danach stehen Verfassung und Rechtsordnung des Verbands „Europäische Union“ und der mitgliedstaatlichen Verbände in einem so engen Verhältnis der gegenseitigen Verweisung, der gegenseitigen Anhängigkeit und der Verflechtung, dass man die klassisch-völkerrechtliche Sichtweise (unabhängiger Staat und internationaler Zusammenschluß) überwinden müsse. EU und Mitgliedstaaten sind danach rechtsnormativ in einer Weise zusammengewachsen, dass man sie als Bestandteile eines miteinander zusammengewachsenen Verbundes betrachten müsse. Die zwischen der EU und den Mitgliedstaaten bestehende *Trennung* werde durch den Prozeß des konstitutiven Zusammenwachsens aufgehoben.[64] EU-Rechtsordnung und nationale Rechtsordnung würden miteinander verschmolzen. Die Verflechtung hätte einen Grad erreicht, der es konzeptionell nicht mehr sinnvoll erscheinen liesse, zwischen zwei verschiedenen Rechtsordnungen zu unterscheiden.[65] Die in der Vergangenheit immer wieder auftauchenden Konflikte zwischen dem Geltungsanspruch beider Rechtsordnungen wären damit hinfällig. Im Hinblick auf das Zusammenwachsen der Verfassungen müsse auch von einer einheitlichen „Verfassung Europas“ gesprochen werden, in der EU-Verfassungsrecht und nationale Verfassungen aufgegangen seien. Dies mündet in ein Verfassungsverständnis, in dessen Mittelpunkt die europäische Verfassungsgesamtheit steht, in der die mitgliedstaatlichen Verfassungen und die unionale Verfassung als „Teilverfassungen“ aufgehen („Mehrebenen-Verfassungsverbund“[66]). *Ingolf Pernice* hat mit diesen Überlegungen die verfassungstheoretische Diskussion in kaum zu überschätzender Weise vorangebracht und befruchtet. Der unschätzbare Wert dieser Überlegungen liegt (ungeachtet gelegentlicher Überzeichnungen[67]) in dem Umstand, dass die bislang vorherrschende, einen Antagonismus von EU und Mitgliedstaaten unterstellende Sichtweise überwunden werden konnte. Nicht die Frage des Konflikts, nicht die Frage der gegenseitigen Abgrenzung und des Geländegewinns auf Kosten der jeweils anderen Seite steht für diese Position im Vordergrund?, sondern die gemeinsame, nur im gegenseitigen Zusammenspiel zu verwirklichende Zielsetzung der Verwirklichung eines europäischen Gemeinwohls im „europäischen Verfassungsraum“.[68] Nicht die Frage nach der Souveränität, nach dem Ausnahmefall, steht im Zentrum des Denkens von *Pernice*, sondern der Regelfall der Kooperation. Die europäische Verfassungstheorie hat insofern Anschluß an das Verfassungsdenken in bundesstaatlich gestuften Ordnungen gefunden. Es kann insofern als programmatische Formulierung angesehen werden, wenn Pernice seine Verfassungstheorie als „Mehrebenenkonstitutionalismus“ bezeichnet.[69]

(2) Die föderale Qualität des Verbunds

Mit dem Begriff des Mehrebenenverbundes läßt sich das Element der gegenseitigen Verweisung von EU-Verfassung und nationalem Verfassungsrecht gut einfangen. Über die inhaltlichen Qualitäten des entstandenen Verbundes ist damit allerdings noch keine Aussage getroffen. Auch der gelegentlich verwandte Begriff des regulativen „Mehrebenen*systems*" (gerade wegen seines Abstraktionsgrads und seiner begrifflichen Unbelastetheit) hilft nicht unbedingt weiter[70]. Die wohl überwiegende Auffassung in Deutschland geht heute davon aus, dass das Zusammenspiel von EU und Mitgliedstaaten von föderalen Strukturprinzipien beherrscht wird. Deutlich tritt die föderale Natur vor allem in den jeweiligen Gewährleistungsnormen der Art. 6, 7 EUV und Art. 23 GG hervor. Auch die gegenseitigen Loyalitätspflichten sind in dieser Hinsicht von konstitutiver Bedeutung.

In der Theoriegeschichte des Föderalismus ist eine reiche Vielfalt von Varianten entstanden. Vor diesem Hintergrund ist es nur zu verständlich, dass man sich in der Frage, welchen Grad der Föderalisierung der Verbund bereits erreicht hat, nicht einig ist. Während einige Beobachter dem Verbund bereits eine entwickelte Form des Föderalismus attestieren,[71] sehen andere ihn erst auf dem Weg zur Föderation.[72] Die Zurückhaltung, die im Umgang mit dem Föderalismusbegriff zu beobachten ist, mag nicht zuletzt darauf zurückzuführen sein, dass sich im Verlauf des 19. Jahrhunderts eine Verengung auf die Form der Bundesstaatlichkeit vollzogen hat. Wer sich dieser Begriffstradition verpflichtet fühlt, wird sich jedenfalls dann, wenn die damit einhergehenden Folgerungen (insbesondere: Souveränität des Bundes) nicht gezogen werden sollen, im Umgang mit dem Föderalismusbegriff Zurückhaltung auferlegen. Zwingend ist diese Verengung aber nicht; sie ist lediglich eine – wenn auch in den letzten zweihundert Jahren besonders wichtige – Form des Föderalismus. Arbeitet man die ideengeschichtlichen Wurzeln des Föderalismus heraus, so geht es nicht um Souveränität, sondern um Einheitssicherung und Vielfaltgewähr, um das freie und selbstbestimmte Zusammenwirken verschiedener, vertikal gestufter Verbände. Im Lichte eines solchen Föderalismusbegriffs lassen sich gegen die Bezeichnung des Integrationsverbunds als Föderation keine Einwände erheben. Föderalismus ist ein politisches Ordnungsprinzip, das darauf abzielt, die Existenz und Selbstständigkeit einer Mehrheit politischer Einheiten mit der Zusammenfassung dieser Einheiten in ein höheres Ganzes zu verbinden. Föderalistische Ordnungen sind als mehrstufige politische Systeme zu begreifen, in denen an die Seite der politischen Einheit der Glieder die politische Gesamtexistenz tritt. Föderalismus ist damit Bildung eines Ganzen unter gleichzeitiger Bewahrung der Freiheit der engeren territorialen und personellen Gemeinschaften. Er dient der Selbstbehauptung der Eigenart und der Anerkennung des Eigenrechtes dieser Eigenart. Dies kann nur gelingen, wenn man – allen Unterschieden zum Trotze – im Wertverständnis und in der Formulierung der Interessen auf einen Grundkonsens aufbauen kann. „Freiheit ist dort, wo diese Eigenart nicht durch Unitarismus und Zentralismus negiert, sondern durch

Selbstgesetzgebung (Autonomie) und Selbstverwaltung der engeren Gemeinschaften respektiert und beschützt wird. Diese föderalistische Freiheit ist die Grundbedingung für die Einheit eines vielgestaltigen Staatswesens."[73] In der Existenz einer politischen Gesamtexistenz unterscheiden sich föderalistische Ordnungen vom bloßen vertraglichen Zusammenwirken verschiedener Staaten. Im Fortbestand und der Erhaltung der politischen Einheit der Glieder liegt der Unterschied zwischen Föderalismus und bloßer Dezentralisation. Föderalismus dient der Einheitsbildung in Verschiedenheit; er wirkt auf Integration des Unterschiedlichen im Gemeinsamen hin. Der Prozeß der gegenseitigen Verflechtung hat inzwischen einen Grad erreicht, der es rechtfertigt, den Verbund von EU und Mitgliedstaaten als Föderation zu bezeichnen.

(3) Der Verbund als konsoziative Föderation

Mit der Bezeichnung des Integrationsverbunds als Föderation erschließt man sich den ideellen Gehalt und die Geschichte einer politischen Theorie und kann diese für die Interpretation der Vertragsbestimmungen und die Ausgestaltung der Binnenbeziehungen von EU und Mitgliedstaaten fruchtbar machen. Vor dem Hintergrund des Umstandes, dass die politische Theorie eine Vielzahl föderaler Typen mit je unterschiedlicher Prägung kennt, eröffnen sich dabei allerdings erhebliche Spielräume. Es wäre viel gewonnen, wenn es gelänge, den Typ föderalistischer Verbundenheit, der EU und Mitgliedstaaten kennzeichnet, näher zu kennzeichnen. Die in Deutschland deutlich vorherrschende Auffassung ist in diesem Zusammenhang geneigt, den Integrationsverbund weiterhin (empirisch und normativ) als Ausprägung eines bündisch verfaßten Zusammenschlusses anzusehen. Europäischer Föderalismus läßt sich insofern als *konsoziativer Föderalismus* treffend kennzeichnen („Föderation von Staaten").[74] Anders als im *bundesstaatlichen Föderalismus* fließt die verfassungsgebende Gewalt der Glieder in der konsoziativen Föderation nicht aus der Verfassung des übergreifenden Verbands (hier: der EU); anders als im *bundesstaatlichen Föderalismus* haben die Glieder auch ihre Souveränität bewahrt. Weiterhin liegt die Befugnis zur Verfassungsfortschreibung nach Art. 48 EGV weitgehend, allerdings schon nicht mehr ausschließlich in den Händen der Glieder; auch haben die Mitgliedstaaten im Entscheidungsprozeß der überstaatlichen Ebene eine bestimmende Rolle. Man ist sich im übrigen in der verfassungstheoretischen Diskussion einig, dass diesem Prinzip des konsoziativen Föderalismus im Prozeß der Fortentwicklung der EU normative Qualität zukommt: Europa muß seine bündische Struktur bewahren, muß seine Form als „Föderation von Bürgern und Staaten" erhalten. Einen Umschlag in die Form bundesstaatlichen Föderalismus gilt es, so die ganz überwiegende Auffassung, gegenwärtig zu verhindern.[75] Auf absehbare Zeit bleibt die Grundordnung der EU eine „Vertragsverfassung".

(4) Die Integration des Staates

Es liegt auf der Hand, dass sich die verfassungstheoretische Lage der Mitgliedstaaten im Zuge der Entstehung des föderalen Verbunds tiefgreifend gewandelt hat.[76] Ihre Einbindung in diesen Verbund führt zu weitreichenden Veränderungen im Verfassungsgefüge. Wenn sich das Verfassungsrecht dieser Veränderungen lange nicht bewußt geworden ist, so liegt dies nicht zuletzt an dem Umstand, dass sich die Veränderungen unterhalb der Schwelle der formalen Verfassungstextfortschreibung abspielen. Der Wandel vollzieht sich – wenn er nicht vom verfassungsändernden Gesetzgeber aufgenommen und positiviert wird (so in Art. 23 oder Art. 88 GG) – unterhalb des Verfassungswortlautes und höhlt die Verfassungsordnung quasi von innen aus. Diese Strukturveränderungen sind in den letzten Jahren in Deutschland verstärkt zum Gegenstand verfassungstheoretischer und –rechtlicher Betrachtungen gemacht worden. Dabei geht es nicht mehr nur um die alte Frage, welche Anforderungen das Grundgesetz an den Integrationsverband richtet, und ebenso geht es nicht mehr nur um die Frage, wie der Transfer von Hoheitsrechten vorzunehmen ist und welchen Beschränkungen er unterliegt. An die Stelle dieser einseitigen, auf das mitgliedstaatliche „Geben" abstellenden Sichtweise ist ein vertieftes Verständnis für die Wechselwirkungen, für das „Geben und Nehmen" der Mitgliedstaaten getreten. Eine frühe erste Auseinandersetzung mit der Problematik findet sich im Maastricht-Urteil des BVerfG: Das BVerfG postuliert in dieser Entscheidung, dass es gegen das Demokratieprinzip verstoße, wenn sich im Zuge der Vertiefung der Integration ein Zustand einstelle, in dem den gesetzgebenden Organen in Deutschland keine substantiellen Kompetenzen von Gewicht mehr verbleiben.[77] Die Diskussion hat sich inzwischen geöffnet. Man begreift die Einbindung des Verfassungsstaats in den föderalen Verband als strukturelle Gegebenheit, die durch Strukturnormen abzusichern und zu stabilisieren ist.[78] Andere betrachten die Einbindung als Ausdruck eines Verfassungsprinzips und versuchen, dessen Gehalte normativ zu entfalten.[79] Wer die Idee des föderalen Verbunds inhaltlich auffüllen will, wendet sich Einzelfacetten des Zusammenspiels zu. So wird beispielsweise die Kooperationsoffenheit des Verfassungsstaats problematisiert – sei es über die Gewalten hinweg,[80] sei es im Hinblick auf die Kooperation einzelner Gewalten, sei es in einzelnen Sachbereichen.[81] Besondere Aufmerksamkeit hat die gegenseitige Verflechtung im administrativen Bereich inzwischen erfahren. So konnten inzwischen wertvolle Grundlegungen zur Beschreibung der Lage des „integrierten Staats"[82] gemacht werden. Man kommt allerdings nicht umhin zu konstatieren, dass die Aufbauarbeit zur Errichtung eines neuen, die Verbundenheit von Integrationsverband und Mitgliedstaaten in den Vordergrund stellenden Verfassungsverständnisses noch nicht vollendet ist. Die Entwicklung einer europabezogenen „postnationalen Verfassungstheorie“[83] oder einer „Theorie der Verfassung Europas“[84] steht noch am Anfang, die Neukonzeptionalisierung normativer Verfassungselemente auf europäischer und internationaler Ebene (Beisp.: „Mehrebenenkonzept von *Demos*“[85], Entstehungsbedingungen europäischer Identität[86]) zeichnet sich erst in Umrissen ab. Die bisherigen Erkenntnisse mögen ausreichen, einen *strukturellen Erklärungsansatz* für das Bestehen einer europäischen Verfassung zu liefern, die bestehenden verfassungs*technischen* Inhalte des Primärrechts (Vorrang, unmittelbare Wirkung, „implied powers“ etc.) zu verarbeiten und strukturelle Defizite (Mangel an Transparenz und Überkomplexität der Verträge, Offenheit und Unbestimmtheit von Kompetenznormen etc.) zu erkennen. Inzwischen ist der europäische Konstitutionalismus aber an einem Punkt angekommen, an dem dies nicht mehr ausreicht. Für das neue Zeitalter braucht es mehr - es braucht einen öffentlichen Diskurs um Werte, Legitimität und Demokratie in Europa.

2. Nationale Vorschriften über die Schaffung einer „Verfassung“ der Europäischen Union

Der verfassungsändernde Gesetzgeber hat im Jahre 1992 eine Bestimmung in das Grundgesetz eingefügt, die die Beteiligung der Bundesrepublik Deutschland in der Europäischen Union umfassend regelt und damit als Spezialregelung sowohl dem Art. 24 GG als auch dem Art. 59 Abs. 2 S. 1 GG vorgeht[87]. Die Regelung des Art. 23 GG [88] ist die deutsche verfassungsrechtliche Reaktion auf den grundlegenden „Quantensprung“[89], den die Integration mit dem Vertrag von Maastricht gemacht hat. Sie ist die zentrale Vorschrift des Grundgesetzes, wenn es um die Schaffung formellen europagerichteten Verfassungsrechts geht. Sie begründet in ihrem Abs. 1 S. 1 die verfassungsmäßige Pflicht der Bundesrepublik Deutschland, der Europäischen Union anzugehören und an ihrer Entwicklung teilzunehmen (Staatszielbestimmung „Europäisierung“, „Integrationsklausel“)[90]. Für die Teilnahme in der Europäischen Union setzt die Vorschrift der Bundesrepublik Deutschland materielle Bedingungen und Grenzen (a). Sie enthält zudem verfahrensmäßige Beteiligungsvorschriften, mit denen die im Zuge der europäischen Integration erlittenen Zuständigkeitsverluste kompensiert werden - sowohl der Länder gegenüber dem Bund als auch - auf Bundesebene - des Bundestages und des Bundesrates gegenüber der Bundesregierung (b). Art. 23 GG enthält jedoch keine Vorschriften darüber, wie die Rolle des Bürgers im europäischen Verfassungsprozeß aussehen soll. Insoweit ist vor allem die Frage zu klären, ob schon wegen der Idee eines europäischen Sozialkontraktes ein Mehr oder Anderes als die über den Deutschen Bundestag höchst mittelbare Beteiligung des europäischen Bürgers durch Regierungskonferenzen zu fordern ist (c).

a. Materielle verfassungsrechtliche Bedingungen und Grenzen für weitere Integrationsschritte

Art. 23 Abs. 1 S. 1 GG legt die verfassungsrechtlichen Grundsätze fest, denen die Gestalt der *Europäischen Union* zu entsprechen hat, um der Bundesrepublik eine Beteiligung Deutschlands zu erlauben („Struktursicherungsklausel")[91]. Die Bestimmung verlangt nicht, dass sich die EU eine der grundgesetzlichen Ordnung entsprechende Ordnung zulegt (kein Gebot der Strukturgleichheit). Sie wendet auch nicht die Staatsstrukturnormen des Grundgesetzes eins zu eins, d.h. in ihrer im Grundgesetz für die Bundesrepublik Deutschland verwirklichten Form auf die Union an. Wohl aber verlangt sie von den deutschen Verfassungsorganen die unions*spezifische* positive Verwirklichung der genannten Grundsätze[92]. Dies gilt für jeden dieser Grundsätze, auch wenn sich die Formulierung „im wesentlichen vergleichbar" lediglich auf den gewährleisteten Grundrechtsschutz bezieht[93].

Die Struktursicherungsklausel ist vage und offen formuliert. Dies führt zu erheblichen Interpretationsschwierigkeiten. So verbinden sich mit der Forderung, dass die Union „demokratischen Grundsätzen [...] verpflichtet ist", eine Vielzahl von Zweifelsfragen. Es ist zwar immer wieder zu lesen, dass damit im Sinne des Gedankens der Volkssouveränität (Art. 20 Abs. 2 S. 1 GG) verlangt werde, dass die europäische Hoheitsgewalt (ideell) die Bürger Europas zu repräsentieren habe. Auch liest man, dass sich die Staatsgewalt hinreichend effektiv vom Volk herleiten lassen und ihm gegenüber verantwortet werden müsse[94]. Wie effektiv die Herleitung aber sein muß, ergibt sich daraus noch nicht. Ebenso bleibt unklar, ob es die europäische Bürgerschaft oder die jeweils eigenständigen Völker der Mitgliedstaaten sind, die von Art. 23 GG als Legitimationssubjekt benannt werden. Die Idee der „verfassungsgebenden Gewalt des Volkes" nach Art. 20 Abs. 2 S. 1 GG[95] läßt sich aufgrund ihrer Staatsvolkzentriertheit jedenfalls nicht unmittelbar und anpassungslos auf die Europäische Union anwenden. Im Zusammenhang des Art. 23 GG folgen die Schwierigkeiten eines Mindeststandards nicht so sehr aus der Notwendigkeit, „dass die demokratischen Grundlagen der Union schritthaltend [...] ausgebaut werden" [96] müssen, sondern aus den Schwierigkeiten, den richtigen Maßstab hierfür überhaupt erst einmal zu ermitteln. Eine Möglichkeit, „strukturadäquate Legitimation"[97] in der EU zu erreichen, liegt etwa in der Entwicklung neuer funktional-normativer Begrifflichkeiten von „Volk"[98]. Diese werden sich aber notwendig mit dem tradierten Begriff des deutschen Volkes, der seinerseits im Wandel ist, überlagern. Nur in Anerkennung der tatsächlichen Existenz dieses Problemfelds lassen sich die strukturadäquaten Demokratiebedingungen des Grundgesetzes entwickeln[99].

Ähnliches gilt für die weiteren in Art. 23 GG genannten Grundsätze. So fordert Art 23 GG mit seinem Hinweis auf die „föderativen Grundsätze" nicht etwa die Ausformung der Europäischen Union entsprechend dem deutschen Bundesstaatsmodell, sondern allein die Orientierung am föderativen Prinzip als einem allgemeinen Strukturprinzip[100]. Auch hier wird sich der Gehalt nur im Spannungsfeld zwischen Mindeststandard und unionsspezifischer Verwirklichung ermitteln lassen. Die Aufnahme der „föderativen Grundsätze" dient dabei vor allem der Abwehr europäischer Einheitsstaatlichkeit. Ihr darf aber kein rechtlicher Gehalt verliehen werden, der es verhindert, dass der rechtliche und tatsächliche Zusammenhalt der EU beeinträchtigt würde. Die „föderativen Grundsätze" umfassen dementsprechend im einzelnen die in der Union tatsächlich verwirklichten Strukturen (Unionstreue, Aufteilung der Hoheitsgewalt, klare Kollisionsregeln, Verschränkung der Rechtsordnungen, Unionsaufsicht)[101].

Ausgesprochen unbestimmt erscheint Art. 23 Abs. 1 S. 1 GG auch im Hinblick auf den von ihm geforderten „im wesentlichen vergleichbaren Grundrechtsschutz"[102]. Eine Analyse von gerichtlichen Entscheidungen, etwa der Bananenmarktentscheidung des BVerfG, zeigt, dass es praktisch kaum möglich ist, den Grundrechtsschutz verschiedener Grundrechtsordnungen „im wesentlichen" zu vergleichen. Allein kann es um die Frage gehen, wann ein Einschreiten des BVerfG angesichts der Hoheitsausübung in der Union geboten erscheint, letztlich also um die Frage des verfassungsrechtlich verankerten Mindeststandards[103].

Die absoluten Grenzen weiterer Integrationsschritte ergeben sich aus der sogenannten „Bestandssicherungsklausel" des Art. 23 Abs.1 S. 3[104] i.V.m. Art. 79 Abs. 3 GG[105]. Bei diesen Grenzen handelt es sich im Kern um die Verfassungsidentität Deutschlands[106]. Die Vorschriften der Art. 23 Abs. 1 S. 3, 79 Abs. 3 GG können damit inhaltlich in gewisser Weise als deutsches verfassungsrechtliches Pendant zu Art. 6 Abs. 3 EUV verstanden werden (dazu unten II 1 a). Die Kritik an Art. 23 GG geht davon aus, dieser verstoße in einer weiten Lesart selbst gegen Art. 79 Abs. 3 GG und sei daher verfassungskonform eng auszulegen[107] oder hätte sogar zu seiner Wirksamkeit als „Verfassungsneuschaffung" eines zustimmenden Votums „des Volkes als des „Subjekts der Verfassungsgebenden Gewalt" bedurft, um die legitime deutsche Staatlichkeit zu bewahren[108]. Das BVerfG folgte dieser Haltung in seiner Maastrichtentscheidung jedoch nicht. Zwar wies es bei der Auslegung der Vorschriften besonders auf die Funktion der demokratischen Willensbildung des *Staats*volkes hin und begründete damit die dem Art. 79 Abs. 3 GG zugrundeliegende Grenze der hinreichenden Zuständigkeit; eine Garantie der *Eigenstaatlichkeit Deutschlands* findet sich in dem Urteil allerdings nicht[109]. Im Maastricht-Urteil ging das Gericht davon aus, dass die gegenwärtigen Strukturen der EU dem Gebot hinreichender demokratischer Legitimation gerecht würden. Demokratische Legitimation würde nicht nur über das nationale Zustimmungsgesetz, sondern vor allem über die Stellung der Vertreter der Mitgliedstaaten im Rat hinreichend vermittelt.[110] Diese Annahme habe allerdings nur solange Bestand, wie bei der Interpretation des Primärrechts und im täglichen Entscheidungsleben bestimmte Vorgaben beachtet würden. Zugleich erkennt das BVerfG an, dass ein Prozeß mit Art. 23 GG vereinbar wäre, in dem sich die EU unmittelbar legitimatorisch auf die EU-Bürgerschaft stützt und sich so von der mitgliedstaatlichen Basis ablöst. Dem kompetenziellen Ausbau der EU sind damit Grenzen gesetzt, wenn nicht zugleich eine demokratisch-legitimatorisch stärkere Rückbindung damit einhergeht.[111] Angesichts der immer gegenwärtiger werdenden Realität des offenen und integrierten Verfassungsstaates[112] mutiert der Begriff der souveränen Eigenstaatlichkeit und wird seines ursprünglichen Kerns beraubt[113]. Die integrationsfreundliche Auslegung der Maastrichtentscheidung sieht daher unter Hinweis auf die zunehmend lebendiger werdende europäische Öffentlichkeit[114] in dem Vorbehalt deutscher Staatlichkeit lediglich eine föderalistisch geprägte Struktur- statt einer demokratisch fundierten Substanzgarantie[115].

Zusammenfassend läßt sich feststellen, dass Art. 23 Abs. 1 GG je nach Anknüpfung entweder als „Bremserklausel“ oder als „Integrationshebel“ verstanden wird[116]. Die unterschiedlichen Auffassungen knüpfen an eine unterschiedliche Lesart des Art. 23 Abs. 1 GG an, etwa hinsichtlich der Frage, ob sich eine Garantie deutscher Staatlichkeit aus Satz 1, aus Satz 3 oder aus beiden Sätzen gemeinsam ableiten läßt. So wurde etwa vorgeschlagen, dass Satz 3 „als Beginn einer prozesshaften Entwicklung“ und Satz 1 „als das angestrebte, irgendwann zu erreichende Endstadium“ verstanden werden sollte - eine Auslegung, die die Integrationsoffenheit des Grundgesetzes betont[117]. Nach einer anderen Meinung aber sind Satz 1 und Satz 3 des Art. 23 Abs. 1 GG nur zusammen zu lesen. In diesem Verständnis formulieren sie klarere Grenzen nationaler Staatlichkeit und Verfassungsautonomie[118].

b. Verfahrensvoraussetzungen des Grundgesetzes für weitere Integrationsschritte

Art. 23 GG enthält zudem die Vorschriften über das notwendige Verfahren: Gegenstand des Verfahrens ist die „Übertragung von Hoheitsrechten“. Nach der Integrationsklausel des Art. 23 Abs. 1 S. 2 GG ist es Sache des Bundes, diese Rechte „durch Gesetz“ zu übertragen. Insoweit laufen die Vorschriften der Art. 59 Abs. 2 GG und 24 Abs. 1 GG parallel[119]. Dogmatisch kommen in diesem Zusammenhang die zu Art. 24 GG entwickelten Grundsätze zum Tragen. Danach liegt in der „Übertragung von Hoheitsrechten“ ein zweigliedriger Akt:[120] Es geht zum einen um den Akt der *Kompetenzbegründung*, mit dem der überstaatliche Hoheitsträger mit der Befugnis ausgestattet wird, Hoheitsgewalt setzen zu können. Die Rede von einer „Kompetenzübertragung" ist in diesem Zusammenhang mißverständlich; es geht nicht um substanzhafte Weitergabe oder Delegation, sondern um Neugründung. Zum anderen geht es um die gesetzliche Anordnung, die aus überstaatlicher Quelle stammende Hoheitsgewalt als rechtlich verbindlich zu akzeptieren und im deutschen Verfassungsraum zur Anwendung zu bringen (*Anwendungsbefehl*). Dieser Befehl darf nicht mit einem Transformationsakt gleichgesetzt werden. Gelegentlich ist in diesem Zusammenhang die Rede von einer „Öffnung des Souveränitätspanzers." Es ist umstritten, ob dieser Verzicht widerruflich ist, ob also die „Übertragung von Hoheitsrechten" nach Art. 23 GG eine Teilung der Souveränität und Staatsgewalt bedeutet[121], oder ob, wie von manchen angenommen wird[122], dadurch allein eine „vierte Staatsgewalt" entsteht, die jederzeit zurückgenommen werden kann und dadurch gerade die weitere Einheit moderner Staatlichkeit unterstreicht. Nach letzterer Auffassung bleibt die Integration nach deutschem Verfassungsrecht umkehrbar[123].

Art. 23 GG gilt allein für die Übertragung von Hoheitsrechten auf die „Europäische Union". Für das dogmatische Verständnis der Vorschrift hängt daher viel von der rechtlichen Einordnung der Europäischen Union ab. Es ist im Anschluß an die „Einheitsthese", d.h. an jenes Verständnis, das in der Union einen einheitlichen Verband mit eigener (einheitlicher) Rechtsordnung sieht[124], davon auszugehen, dass auch Art. 23 Abs. 1 S. 2 GG auf die gesamte unionale einheitliche Rechtsordnung anwendbar ist[125]. Die Kritiker dieser These, insbesondere diejenigen, die von der vollständigen Trennung des Rechts des Integrationsverbands in einen gemeinschaftsrechtlichen Teil und einen intergouvernementalen Teil ausgehen, müssen demgegenüber diese Zweiteilung in den Art. 23 GG „hineinlesen" und konsequenterweise zu dem Ergebnis kommen, dass Art. 23 Abs. 1 S. 2 GG entgegen seinem Wortlaut auf die intergouvernementalen Bereiche nicht anwendbar sei[126].

Das Verfahren für die Übertragung von Hoheitsrechten fordert nach den Art. 23 Abs. 1 S. 3 und 79 Abs. 2 GG eine Mehrheit von Zweidritteln der Mitglieder des Bundestages und des Bundesrates, wenn durch die Übertragung das „Grundgesetz seinem Inhalte nach geändert oder ergänzt wird". Hierin kommt die besondere Verfassungsqualität der erschwerten Abänderbarkeit zum Ausdruck („Doppelwirkung der Vertragsänderung")[127]. Jedoch ist die Vorschrift insoweit kritisiert worden, dass Änderungen der vertraglichen Grundlagen der Union und vergleichbare[128] Regelungen dem Inhalt nach immer auch eine Grundgesetzänderung bedeuten[129]. Daher ist vorgeschlagen worden, dass Art. 23 Abs. 1 S. 2 und S. 3 GG als Unterfall des Art. 79 Abs. 2 GG immer zusammenzulesen seien[130]. Die unterschiedlichen Auffassungen hierzu wurden auch bei dem Zustimmungsgesetz zum Vertrag von Nizza wieder relevant, als die Bundesregierung zunächst davon ausging, hierfür reiche nach Art. 23 Abs. 1 S. 2 GG die einfache Mehrheit, sich dann aber durch den Widerstand im Deutschen Bundestag davon überzeugen ließ, dass die Zweidrittelmehrheit nach Art. 23 Abs. 1 S. 3, 79 Abs. 2 GG erforderlich sei.

Unabhängig von diesen Fragen der erforderlichen Mehrheiten zeichnet sich der Art. 23 GG vor allem durch die besonderen Kompensationsregeln für den Bundestag und den Bundesrat nach den Absätzen 2 ff aus. Die Bestimmungen der Absätze 2 und 3 fordern eine besonders frühe Beteiligung des Bundestages, um zu vermeiden, dass dieser nach Unterschrift unter den Vertrag de facto nur noch bejahend zustimmen kann. Jedoch werden die Beteiligungsmöglichkeiten überwiegend als uneffektiv eingeschätzt. Nach Abs. 3 hat die Bundesregierung die Stellungnahmen des Bundestages nach dessen frühestmöglicher Unterrichtung (Abs. 2 S. 2) lediglich zu „berücksichtigen"[131].

Darüber hinaus fordert Art. 23 Abs. 1 S. 2 GG für das Zustimmungsgesetz in jedem Fall die Billigung des Bundesrates[132]. Das Verfahren folgt den Regeln des Art. 23 Abs. 4 bis 6 GG[133]. In diesen Bestimmungen drückt sich die Besorgnis der Länder aus, ihre Kompetenzen im Zuge fortschreitender Integration zu verlieren. Der Bundesrat ist daher nicht nur zu beteiligen, soweit er an einer entsprechenden innerstaatlichen Maßnahme mitzuwirken hätte, sondern vor allem auch, wenn die Länder innerstaatlich zuständig wären (Abs. 4)[134]. Absatz 5 gibt je nach Zuständigkeitsverteilung gestufte Beteiligungsformen des Bundesrates vor (Berücksichtigung (Abs. 5 S. 1) und maßgebliche Berücksichtigung (Abs. 5 S. 2 und 3) der Stellungnahme des Bundesrates). Abs. 6 ermöglicht unter bestimmten Voraussetzungen die Wahrnehmung der unionalen Rechte des Bundes durch einen Vertreter der Länder.

Aus Sicht der Länder und überzeugter Bundesratsföderalisten ist die Vorschrift bis heute eine Enttäuschung[135]. Erst kürzlich etwa hat *Josef Isensee* deutlich gemacht, dass Art. 23 GG die im Unionsrecht angelegte Mediatisierung der Länder nicht kompensieren könne[136]. Art. 23 GG bedeute keine Stärkung[137], sondern eine Schwächung der Länder. Nach Art. 23 Abs. 2 GG wirkten die Länder lediglich „*durch den Bundesrat*" mit[138]. Der Bundesrat sei aber ein Bundesorgan. Verschoben würden daher nicht die Gewichte zwischen Bund und Ländern, sondern lediglich jene zwischen den einzelnen Bundesorganen. Die Mediatisierung der Länder werde auch nicht durch Art. 23 Abs. 6 GG durchbrochen, da der jeweilige Ländervertreter nicht als Vertreter seines Landes, ja nicht einmal als der Vertreter der Länder in ihrer Gesamtheit, sondern lediglich des Mitgliedstaates Deutschland, innerstaatlich also als ein Amtswalter des Bundes fungiere und daher auch dessen Interessen wahrnehmen müsse[139]. Dem entspreche Art. 203 EGV, wenn er je einen Vertreter eines

Mitgliedstaats auf Ministerebene vorsehe. Daraus zieht *Isensee* die Konsequenz, die Bundesregierung behalte das „europapolitische Heft in der Hand“ und der Bund fungiere weiter als Sachwalter der Länder[140].

c. Die Rolle des Bürgers: Internationaler Vertrag oder europäischer Sozialkontrakt?

Die deutsche verfassungstheoretische Diskussion über die Rolle der Bürger zerfällt in zwei Teildiskurse. Zum einen geht es um die Frage, wer Legitimationssubjekt der EU-Herrschaftsgewalt ist (aa). Sodann wird die Frage diskutiert, inwieweit man den Geltungsanspruch des Primärrechts mit der Idee eines europäischen Gesellschaftsvertrags abstützen kann (bb). Schliesslich geht es verfassungspositiv um die Frage der Zustimmung zu Vertragsänderung und Verfassungsgebung (cc). Die Diskurse liegen auf unterschiedlichen Ebenen; sie dürfen nicht miteinander vermischt werden.

aa) Ausübung europäischer Herrschaftsgewalt und Legitimationssubjekt

Es steht heute außer Frage, dass in einem nach demokratischen Gesichtspunkten verfaßten Europa der Bürger Ausgangspunkt der Legitimation von Hoheitsgewalt sein muß[141]. Legitimationssubjekt kann im demokratisch verfaßten Gemeinwesen nur der einzelne sein. Ein anderes Subjekt (etwa Gott, die Natur, ein als überindividuell begriffenes Volk) steht nicht mehr zur Verfügung. Ihren demokratietheoretischen Zusammenhang findet diese Feststellung in der europäisch (oder sogar Welt-)orientierten Emanzipierung des Individuums und dem damit verbundenen gedanklichen Übergang zur die staatliche Souveränität überwindenden Souveränität des Einzelnen[142]. Die Frage ist damit nicht, ob sich die europäische Hoheitsgewalt gegenüber einem europäischen Volk oder den nationalen Völkern zu legitimieren hat. Es geht auch nicht um die Frage, ob die Rückbindung primär am Willen der europäischen Bürger, an jenem der nationalen Bürger oder an beidem anzusetzen hat. Es sind die der europäischen Hoheitsgewalt unterworfenen einzelnen, auf deren Akzeptanz und Zustimmung die europäische Hoheitsgewalt angewiesen ist.

Außer Frage steht aber auch, dass der einzelne seine Zustimmung sowohl in der Rolle als nationaler Staatsbürger und Angehöriger des nationalen Gemeinwesens als auch in der Rolle als Europäer und Angehöriger eines (entstehenden) europäischen Gemeinwesens äußern kann. Legitimationsvermittlung kann insofern sowohl unmittelbar als auch vermittelt über nationalstaatliche Kanäle erfolgen. Bis in jüngere Zeit stand der zweitgenannte Kanal ganz im Vordergrund: Es waren die einzelnen jeweils in ihrer nationalen Verbundenheit, die darüber entschieden, inwieweit sie europäische Hoheitsakte zu billigen bereit waren. Wer diese Perspektive anlegt, muß eine (mit-)entscheidende Rolle nationalstaatlicher

Vertreter im Rat für unverzichtbar erachten. Ebenso unverzichtbar sind Vetopositionen, die es den Mitgliedstaaten ermöglichen, Beschlüsse zu verhindern, die für die nationalstaatlich verbundenen Bürger nicht akzeptabel sind.

Inzwischen zeichnet sich allerdings eine Entwicklung ab, an deren Ende die Herausbildung einer genuin europäischen Identität der Bürger stehen wird. Die Europäer werden sich als Mitglieder eines politischen Gemeinwesens begreifen, das gemeinsame Grundwerte hat, von allen getragene Ziele verfolgt und ein einheitliches Gemeinwohl kennt (substanzielle Ebene). In diesem Gemeinwesen werden Interessengegensätze ausgetragen und Wertkonflikte geschlichtet werden müssen; zugleich aber wird Einigkeit darüber bestehen, dass die Grundwerte respektiert (und nicht von der Mehrheit überspielt) werden. Die Mitglieder des Gemeinwesens werden (ungeachtet ihrer Nationalität) einander mit Respekt, Toleranz und Solidarität begegnen. Begleitet werden wird die Herausbildung dieser Identität von der Entstehung zivilgesellschaftlicher Kommunikationsformen (prozedurale Ebene). Im Zuge der Herausbildung dieser europäischen Identität (sie wird die nationale Identität überlagern, aber nicht verdrängen) wird es möglich sein, die Stellung der direkt legitimierten europäischen Organe im EU-Entscheidungsprozeß aufzuwerten und die Rolle der Mitgliedstaaten zurückzuführen. Dabei handelt es sich um einen graduellen Prozeß, nicht um einen qualitativen Sprung. Angesichts des Umstandes, dass sich gemeinsame europäische Identität nur vor dem Hintergrund konkreter politischer Erfahrung herausbilden wird, wäre im übrigen die Erwartung, dass mit institutionellen Veränderungen so lange gewartet werden muß, bis sich irgend ein Grad von Identität eingestellt hat, illusionär. Selbstverständlich sind Überdehnungen zu verhindern: Kompetenzübertragungen, die sich in einem Bereich bewegen, der bislang noch nicht zum Bezugspunkt der gemeinsamen europäischen Identität geworden ist, sind tunlich zu vermeiden, jedenfalls aber durch mitgliedstaatliche Vetorechte abzusichern.

bb) Geltungsanspruch des Primärrechts und Gesellschaftsvertrag

Auf einer anderen Ebene bewegt sich die Frage, wie der Geltungsanspruch des europäischen Verfassungsrechts begründet werden kann. Das traditionelle Verständnis ist bekannt: Die Bestimmungen des europäischen Verfassungsrechts entfalten Wirkung und beanspruchen Verbindlichkeit, weil sie von den Mitgliedstaaten der EU in Form eines völkerrechtlichen Vertrages in Kraft gesetzt wurden. Dieser Sichtweise zufolge sind (und bleiben) die Mitglieder „Herren der Verträge“: Sie haben die EU ins Leben gerufen und können ihr jederzeit wieder das Lebenslicht ausblasen. Zunehmend erachtet man diese Sichtweise allerdings für normativ unbefriedigend. Dabei spielt nicht nur eine Rolle, dass man mit der Behauptung, die Mitgliedstaaten könnten die EU ja wieder auflösen, auf eine Möglichkeit Bezug nimmt, deren Eintritt quasi ausgeschlossen ist. Der vielleicht noch gewichtigere Grund ist, dass sich die EU legitimatorisch von ihrer mitgliedstaatlichen Basis abzulösen beginnt. Einen ersten Schritt unternahm der EuGH bereits früh, als er postulierte, dass die Rechtsordnung der EU autonom sei.[143] Nachdem die EU inzwischen dazu übergegangen ist, ihre legitimatorische Grundlage unmittelbar in einer (identitär verbundenen) europäischen Bevölkerung zu suchen, verliert die Geltungsbegründung über mitgliedstaatliche Zustimmungsakte zunehmend an Stringenz. Zwar gibt es auch Verfassungen, die als völkerrechtlicher oder völkerrechtsähnlicher Verfassungsvertrag zwischen Subjekten des Völkerrechts geschlossen wurden[144]. Die historische Erfahrung belegt aber, dass sich solche Verfassungen vom Willen der sie einsetzenden Subjekte lösen und eine selbsttragende Begründung, eine Idee der *sie eigenständig begründenden* verfassungsgebenden Gewalt entwickeln. Im Zeitalter demokratischer Herrschaft kann diese Idee nur noch die Idee der verfassungsgebenden Gewalt „des Volkes"[145] sein. Insofern kann es nicht verwundern, sondern ist ideengeschichtlich nur folgerichtig, wenn sich inzwischen erste Stimmen bemerkbar machen, die postulieren, dass der Geltungsgrund des europäischen Verfassungsrechts in einem Sozialkontrakt europäischer Bürger liege oder Ausdruck der Entscheidung des sich eine Verfassung gebenden Volkes sei. Beide Ideen lassen sich ohne Probleme an die EU herantragen. Dass dies inzwischen geschieht, belegt vor allem den Grad verfassungstheoretischer Reife, den die EU inzwischen erlangt hat. Nur schwer abschätzen läßt sich, wie groß der legitimatorische Gewinn derartiger Operationen ist. Es gibt gute Gründe, eher skeptisch zu sein. Zum einen fehlt es im Fall der EU an jener begründungstheoretischen Problemlage, die in vielen Fällen nationaler Verfassungsgebung handgreiflich ist: Dass am Zustandekommen der Verfassung weite Kreise der Bevölkerung nicht beteiligt waren. Das Verfahren des Art. 48 EUV stellt sicher, dass jedem mitgliedstaatlichen Bürger ein Mitspracherecht bei Vertragsänderungen gegeben ist. Zum anderen muß in einer Zeit, in der sich europäische Identität noch wenig verfestigt hat, die Rede von einem europäischen verfassungsgebenden Volk oder einer einen Sozialkontrakt schließenden europäischen Bevölkerung merkwürdig anmuten. Entscheidend dürfte aber sein, dass wir in einer Zeit leben, in der Akzeptanz und Zustimmung der Bevölkerung *im* Verfassungsleben als wesentliche Legitimation für den Geltungsanspruch der Verfassung angesehen werden („Verfassungspatriotismus"). Ideen, denen zufolge eine *vor* der Verfassung stehende Gewalt deren Geltungsanspruch trägt, wirken in einer solchen Zeit kraftlos und schwach. Man mag an den Gehalt derartiger Ideen glauben, dem Berichterstatter fällt dies aber schwer.

cc) Vertragsfortschreibung und Plebiszit

Ein dritter Problemkreis dreht sich um Fragen des positiven Rechts. Über die Mitwirkung des Bürgers im Prozeß der Vertragsänderung oder im Verfahren der Schaffung einer formalen europäischen Verfassung schweigt Art. 23 GG. Bei allen Unterschieden, die der Art. 23 GG insoweit zu anderen Vorschriften des Grundgesetzes aufweist - in einem weicht er nicht von ihnen ab: Die Mitwirkung an der Fortentwicklung der EU geschieht „durch Gesetz“ (Abs. 1 S. 2), also durch die Entscheidung repräsentativer Organe. Die Mitwirkung der deutschen Bürger vollzieht sich mittelbar, in einer dem Grundgesetz typischen repräsentativ-demokratischen Weise[146]. Das Handeln durch Gesetz ist trotz der Formulierung des Art. 20 Abs. 2 S. 2 GG[147] in der grundgesetzlichen Ordnung die Regel, unmittelbare Demokratie durch Abstimmungen hingegen die seltene Ausnahme[148]. Indem die Fortschreibung der europäischen Verfassung in die Hände repräsentativ entscheidender Organe gelegt wird, entscheidet sich das Grundgesetz hier für genau jenen Weg, den es auch in anderen Bereichen geht.

Wenn Art. 23 GG anordnet, dass die Fortschreibung der Verträge innerstaatlich durch Gesetz zu erfolgen hat, so behandelt die Bestimmung Fragen der europäischen Verfassungsgebung wie andere wichtige völkerrechtliche Vertragsschlüsse: Die grundgesetzlichen Vorschriften über die Zustimmung zu völkerrechtlichen Verträgen[149] fordern für diese Zustimmung, genauso wie es Art. 23 GG für die Mitwirkung in Angelegenheiten der Europäischen Union tut, die gesetzliche Form. So bestimmt etwa Art. 59 Abs. 2 GG, die allgemeine Ratifizierungsvorschrift des Grundgesetzes für völkerrechtliche Verträge, dass die Zustimmung zu einem völkerrechtlichen Vertrag „der Form eines Bundesgesetzes“ bedarf. Hinsichtlich der Übertragung von Hoheitsrechten auf zwischenstaatliche Einrichtungen gibt es die Spezialvorschrift des Art. 24 I GG, die, wiederum ähnlich dem Art. 23 Abs. 1 S. 2 GG, die Übertragung „durch Gesetz“ vorschreibt und dies in den Spezialvorschriften der folgenden Absätze auch nicht irgendwelchen Sonderregelungen unterwirft. Man kann also sagen, dass sich Art. 23 GG nicht nur inmitten der für das deutsche Staats- und Verfassungsleben typischen repräsentativ-demokratischen Verfahrensstrukturen bewegt, sondern auch, dass er dadurch, dass er auf die grundlegenden Verfahrensvorschriften über die Zustimmung zu völkerrechtlichen Verträgen zurückgreift, die Europäische Union *insoweit* wie eine klassische völkerrechtliche Organisation behandelt[150]. Im Grundsatz erscheint dies auch konsequent: Es gibt an sich keinen zwingenden Grund, die Mitwirkung der Bürger in Angelegenheiten der europäischen Union *insoweit* anders zu gestalten als die Mitwirkung an der staatlichen Willensbildung im innerstaatlichen Bereich[151].

Gleichwohl wird darüber diskutiert, ob nicht formelle europäische

Verfassungsgebung dem Zustimmungsvotum der Bürger unterworfen werden soll. Verfassungsgebung ist etwas paradigmatisch anderes als einfache Gesetzgebung. Sie ist auch etwas paradigmatisch anderes als die Schaffung von Völkerrecht, etwa durch das Inkraftsetzen völkerrechtlicher Verträge über eine internationale Organisation. Es nimmt denn auch nicht Wunder, dass in diesem Zusammenhang eine Änderung des Vertragsänderungsverfahrens nach Art. 48 EUV vorgeschlagen wurde, insbesondere durch die Hinzufügung neuer Stadien der Vertragsänderung: So wird angeregt, es könne sich in einem Vertragsänderungsverfahren etwa nach einer vorgeschalteten interparlamentarischen Phase der Konsultation zwischen dem EP und den nationalen Parlamenten und einer dem jetzigen Verfahren vergleichbaren (jedoch mit substantieller Beteiligung von Kommission und Europäischem Parlament stattfindenden) intergouvernementalen Phase eine dritte Phase anschließen, die zu einer echten Verfassungsgebung führen könnte, etwa in Form eines (*eines*(!), d.h. eines einheitlichen, möglichst europaweiten) Referendums[152]. Damit würde eine zweite Legitimationsschiene eingeführt, die neben die mitgliedstaatlich vermittelte Zustimmung die von der mitgliedstaatlichen Staatlichkeit abstrahierte Zustimmung stellte[153]. Würde das Grundgesetz trotz seiner repräsentativ-demokratischen Strukturen ein derart modifiziertes Vertragsänderungsverfahren erlauben? Unmittelbare Demokratie durch Abstimmungen verwirklicht das Grundgesetz bislang in nur sehr engen Grenzen (dazu oben). Der Versuch, durch Vertragsfortschreibung die verfassungsrechtlichen Grundlagen einer echten, vom Bürger ausgehenden europäischen Verfassungsgebung zu schaffen, ist an Art. 79 Abs. 3, 20 Abs. 1 und 2 GG[154] zu messen. Direkt-demokratische Ansätze für eine europäische Verfassungsgebung werden darin nicht ausgeschlossen. Die in Art. 20 Abs. 1 und 2 GG niedergelegten Grundsätze verlangen lediglich, das demokratische Prinzip dahin zu verwirklichen, dass alle Staatsgewalt (bzw. im europäischen Kontext: alle Hoheitsgewalt) vom Volke ausgeht. Der in Art. 79 Abs. 3 GG in Bezug genommene Art. 20 Abs. 2 S. 2 GG verlangt, dass die Staatsgewalt vom Volke „in Wahlen und Abstimmungen“ ausgeübt wird[155]. Ein etwa europaweites Referendum ist daher nach deutschem Verfassungsrecht de lege ferenda denkbar.

3. Der Prozeß der Verfassungsgebung: Praktische Vorbereitungen für die Regierungskonferenz 2004

Die deutschen Vorbereitungen für die Regierungskonferenz 2004 stehen in einem Spannungsfeld, an dessen einem Pol der Wunsch steht, an den wesentlichen Strukturen des Vertragsänderungsverfahrens nach Art. 48 EUV festzuhalten und insbesondere die mitgliedstaatliche Vetoposition zu bewahren; den entgegengesetzten Pol bildet der Wunsch vieler europäischer

Politiker[156], die Regierungskonferenz 2004 im Rahmen der Zukunftsdiskussion[157] in einen echten Schritt in Richtung europäischer Verfassungsgebung münden zu lassen. Der vom Europäischen Rat von Laeken einberufene Konvent wird teilweise als Verkörperung der verfassungsgebenden Gewalt in Europa angesehen und so ideell enorm aufgewertet.[158] Im folgenden soll auf Aspekte der Vorbereitung der Regierungskonferenz von deutscher Seite eingegangen werden, insbesondere auf die Organisation der Zukunftsdebatte (a) und die Kernthemen und Vorschläge der führenden politischen Gruppen (b).

a. Wie ist die interne Debatte über die Zukunft der Europäischen Union organisiert?

In Deutschland geben die Strukturen des **Gesetzgebungsverfahrens** (Art. 76 ff, 23 GG) einen ersten Diskussionsrahmen vor. Der Vertrag von Nizza (unter Einschluß seines Anhangs mitsamt der Erklärung Nummer 23 zur Zukunft der Europäischen Union) muß durch den deutschen Gesetzgeber gebilligt werden (Art. 48 Abs. 3 EUV, 23 GG, dazu siehe oben II 2). Schon deshalb findet ein wichtiger Teil der inhaltlichen Diskussion über die Zukunft der Europäischen Union in den deutschen Gesetzgebungsorganen, dem Bundestag (Art. 38 ff GG) und dem Bundesrat (Art. 50 ff GG), statt. Die Protokolle der Lesungen im Bundestag (§ 78 ff GOBT)[159] und der Sitzungen im Bundesrat (15 ff GOBR)[160] vermitteln allerdings nur einen ersten Überblick über die Haltungen der Fraktionen (§ 10 ff GOBT) und Landesregierungen (§ 1 GOBR). Wichtiger sind die Protokolle des Bundestagsausschusses für die Angelegenheiten der Europäischen Union (Europaausschuß, Art. 45 GG, §§ 93 f GOBT, s.o.)[161] und die Europakammer des Bundesrates (Art. 52 Abs. 3a GG, §§ 45a GOBR, s.o.). Diesen Gremien wurden vom Plenum jeweils Gesetzgebungsaufgaben übertragen; sie sind schon von daher der Ort detaillierter Diskussionen zu Einzelfragen.

Noch wichtiger für eine so breite Diskussion wie die über die Zukunft der Europäischen Union ist allerdings die vorgelagerte Meinungsbildung in den **Parteien** selbst. Sowohl normativ (Art. 21 GG, §§ 1 ff Parteiengesetz) als auch in der gelebten Verfassungswirklichkeit haben die Parteien in Deutschland eine herausragende Stellung in der politischen Willensbildung des Volkes. Ein besonderer Blick ist daher auf die innerparteilichen Meinungsbildungsprozesse zu richten. Diese finden vor allem in den Organen der Parteien statt: Nach § 8 Parteiengesetz sind dies vor allem die Mitgliederversammlungen als oberste Organe (im Bundesverband: Parteitage, § 9 Parteiengesetz)) und die Vorstände der Parteien (§ 11 Parteiengesetz). Aufschlußreich sind insoweit nicht nur die Parteiprogramme (§ 9 III 1 Parteiengesetz), sondern vor allem die

Diskussionen, die zur Verabschiedung der Parteiprogramme führen, also insbesondere Leitanträge, Präsidiums- und Vorstandsbeschlüsse und Redebeiträge prominenter Mitglieder.

Ihren aktuellen Höhepunkt erreicht die Diskussion in den öffentlichen **Spontanbeiträgen** einzelner Politiker. Diese Einzelbeiträge enthalten wegen der ihnen eigenen Individualität die bislang detailliertesten Vorstellungen zur zukünftigen Gestalt der europäischen Union und wirken schon von daher tief in die innerparteilichen Meinungsbildungsprozesse hinein. Darüber hinaus haben diese Beiträge aber auch eine Wirkung weit über die Parteien hinaus und werden dadurch am ehesten dem von der Kommission geforderten breiten Denkprozeß gerecht. In dieser spontanen Diskussion liegt am ehesten das, was als öffentlicher Prozeß für die Gestaltung Europas gefordert ist, nämlich die Bewußtwerdung Europas und seiner Bürger als *europäische* Bürger.

Neben der Berufspolitik findet sich ein weiterer Schwerpunkt in der **Wissenschaft**. Sie bereitet der öffentlichen Diskussion durch unzählige Studien den Weg und zeichnet den Gang des Machbaren auf. Zu verweisen ist neben den vielen Einzelstudien vor allem auf die vielen Kongresse und Seminare, die in den letzten Jahren immer wieder mit Schwerpunkt zu den Verfassungsfragen in der Europäischen Union abgehalten worden sind[162]. Die öffentliche Zukunftsdebatte scheint insoweit jedenfalls auch im Delta der Wissenschaft geführt zu werden[163].

b. Welches sind die Kernthemen und Vorschläge der führenden politischen Gruppen?

Im Spannungsfeld zwischen einem auch in den Mitgliedstaaten wachsenden Reformdruck und einer europäisch initiierten Zukunftsdiskussion läßt sich zunächst festhalten, dass allgemeine Einigkeit darüber besteht, dass es einer Verfassungsdiskussion bedarf (Verfassungsdiskussionsnotwendigkeit). Über die Einsicht in die Diskussionsnotwendigkeit hinaus ist man in Deutschland überwiegend der Meinung, dass es auch eines Verfassungsvertrages als solchen bedürfe (Verfassungsvertragsnotwendigkeit). Bundeskanzler Schröder hat dies in der Botschafterkonferenz vom 4. September 2000 wie folgt ausdrückt: „Die europäischen Bürger haben im Angesicht des fortschreitenden europäischen Integrationsprozesses einen Anspruch auf eine präzise und für jedermann verständliche Verfassung"[164]. Das Pendant hierzu aus christdemokratischer Sicht ist unter Punkt 6 (Verfassungsvertrag) der "Vorschläge von CDU und CSU für einen Europäischen Verfassungsvertrag" zu lesen. Darin heißt es: "Alle grundsätzlichen Regelungen, insbesondere diejenigen zur Verteilung der Zuständigkeiten zwischen Europäischer Union und Mitgliedstaaten, zur Finanzverfassung, zu den Institutionen der Europäischen Union und ihren Verfahrensweisen, sollen mit der Grundrechtecharta in einem Verfassungsvertrag (Grundvertrag) zusammengefaßt werden."[165].

In den großen Volksparteien scheint es also nicht mehr darum zu gehen, ob ein Verfassungsvertrag überhaupt geschlossen werden soll, sondern nurmehr noch darum, wie, wann und mit welchen Inhalten dies geschehen soll. Dementsprechend besteht über das weitere *Vorgehen* denn auch im wesentlichen Einigkeit: Der auf dem Europäischen Rat von Laeken einberufene **Konvent** zur Zukunft Europas war schon im Vorfeld unter dem Banner von Transparenzprinzip, Effektivität und Partizipation von allen Parteien im Bundestag begrüßt worden[166]. Bundeskanzler Gerhard Schröder hat in seiner Regierungserklärung vom 18. Okt. 2001 vor dem Deutschen Bundestag die deutsche Position zum Konvent wie folgt zusammengefaßt: "Entscheidend ist für mich die parlamentarische Dimension in der jetzt zu führenden Reformdebatte. Daher wird der institutionelle Kern des Prozesses, der jetzt anläuft, ein Konvent sein, der sich aus den Beauftragten der Staats- und Regierungschefs sowie aus Vertretern der nationalen Parlamente, des Europäischen Parlaments und der Europäischen Kommission zusammensetzt. [...] Dieser Konvent soll Reformoptionen erarbeiten. Die endgültige Entscheidung über die konkreten Reformen muß dann - so sieht es das europäische Vertragswerk vor - einer abschließenden Regierungskonferenz überlassen bleiben." [167] Über die Zielsetzungen des Konvents besteht allerdings keine Einigkeit; überwiegend hält man es nicht für sinnvoll, dass der Konvent bereits einen Verfassungsvertrag vorlegt. Gering sind auch die Erwartungen, dass es kurzfristig zum Abschluß eines derartigen Vertrages kommt.[168]

Umstritten ist auch die Entwicklung in längerer Perspektive. Die Kernthemen der Diskussion sind insoweit die **Kompetenzordnung, das institutionelle Gefüge und die Grundrechte** in der Union. Die bestehenden Positionen sollen im folgenden, gegliedert nach Parteizugehörigkeit, kurz vorgestellt werden, zunächst jene der gegenwärtigen Regierungsparteien, sodann jene der gegenwärtigen Oppositionsparteien:

Die Regierungsparteien: Die **SPD** hat auf ihrem Bundesparteitag in Nürnberg vom 19. bis 23. November 2001 den europapolitischen Leitantrag ("Verantwortung für Europa") des SPD-Vorsitzenden und Bundeskanzlers *Schröder* mit großer Mehrheit angenommen[169]. Danach will die SPD in allgemeinen Worten "ein europäisches System der Gewaltenteilung zwischen EP, Rat und Kommission schaffen, welches den Grundsätzen von demokratischer Legitimität, Effizienz und Transparenz entspricht"[170]. Diese Formulierung wurde vom europapolitischen Sprecher der SPD-Fraktion *Gloser* näher spezifiziert: Nach *Gloser* gehe es dabei vorrangig um den "Ausbau der Europäischen Kommission zu einer starken Exekutive", die "Stärkung des Europäischen Parlaments durch die Ausweitung des Mitentscheidungsverfahrens und die Übertragung der vollen Budgethoheit" und den "Ausbau des Rates zu einer europäischen Staatenkammer"[171]. Rat und Europäisches Parlament sollten nach *Gloser* "zu einem Zweikammernsystem umgebaut werden"[172]. Um dem vor allem französischen Vorwurf eines europäischen Föderalismus nach deutschem Vorbild zu begegnen, kommt nach *Gloser* für eine Übergangszeit ein "öffentlich tagender Rat der Europaminister" in Betracht, "dem eine Koordinierungsfunktion zukäme"[173].Bereits 2004 solle der Kommissionspräsident zudem direkt vom EP gewählt werden[174].

Auf im wesentlichen gleicher Linie liegt die Rede von Bundespräsident Johannes *Rau*, die dieser am 4. April 2001 vor dem EP gehalten hat[175]: Er schlägt darin die Schaffung einer europäischen Verfassung vor, die sich in drei Abschnitten gliedert: Die Charta der Grundrechte als ersten Abschnitt, kompetenzabgrenzende Regeln als zweiten Abschnitt und Regeln über das institutionelle Gefüge als dritten Abschnitt. Ohne den deutschen Föderalismus auf europäischer Ebene durchsetzen zu wollen, sieht *Rau* im Föderalismus *das* europäische Ordnungsprinzip und schlägt daher ebenfalls ein Zweikammernparlament vor (Rat als Staatenkammer, EP als Bürgerkammer). Der Kommissionspräsident solle zudem durch das Parlament gewählt werden. Auch *Rau* unterstreicht die Bedeutung einer europäischen Öffentlichkeit und unterstützt zudem die Idee eines Konvents, ohne jedoch die genaue Rolle eines Konvents näher zu spezifizieren. Auch der nordrhein-westfälische Ministerpräsident Wolfgang *Clement* hat sich in einer Rede vor der Humboldt-Universität Berlin am 12. Februar 2001 in dieser Richtung (Zweikammernparlament, Konvent zur Vorbereitung) geäußert[176]. Zur Kompetenzordnung schlug er vor, drei Kategorien einzuführen, nämlich ausschließliche Kompetenzen der EU, Grundsatzkompetenzen der EU und Ergänzungskompetenzen der EU[177].

In der Partei von **Bündnis 90/DIE GRÜNEN** haben bislang vor allem die Äußerungen von Außenminister *Fischer* Beachtung gefunden, die dieser - ausdrücklich als Privatmann – am 12. Mai 2000 vor der Humboldt-Universität Berlin gehalten hat[178]. *Fischers* Rede gilt allgemein als Anstoß der öffentlichen Verfassungsdiskussion[179]. *Fischer* spricht sich in seiner Rede für einen Verfassungsvertrag aus, der zu einer "vollen Parlamentarisierung in einer Europäischen Föderation" führen solle; in diesem Zusammenhang plädiert er für "ein europäisches Parlament und eine ebensolche Regierung, die tatsächlich die gesetzgebende und die exekutive Gewalt innerhalb der Föderation ausüben". Dabei stellt er fest: "Nur wenn die europäische Integration die Nationalstaaten in eine solche Föderation mitnimmt, wenn deren Institutionen nicht entwertet oder gar verschwinden werden, wird ein solches Projekt trotz aller gewaltigen Schwierigkeiten machbar sein." Um dies zu realisieren, schlägt er ein Zweikammernsystem vor, das die Repräsentanz sowohl der europäischen Bürger als auch der europäischen Nationalstaaten erlaubt: Die erste

Kammer des europäischen Parlamentes soll danach aus gewählten Abgeordneten bestehen, die zugleich Mitglieder der nationalen Parlamente seien, die andere Kammer könne dem US- amerikanischen Senatsmodell oder dem deutschen Bundesratsmodell folgen und so auf die eine oder andere Weise als Staatenkammer fungieren. Zudem schlägt *Fischer* eine europäische Gubernative vor, die sich entweder aus dem jetzigen Rat oder aus der heutigen Kommissionsstruktur, jedoch mit Direktwahl des Präsidenten, fortentwickeln könne. Ferner tritt *Fischer* für eine genaue Kompetenzabgrenzung und die Verankerung der europäischen Grund-, Menschen- und Bürgerrechte ein. Kern von *Fischers* Überlegungen ist die Idee eines „Gravitationszentrums", einer Avantgarde, die sich auf einen „neuen europäischen Grundvertrag" als „Nukleus einer Verfassung der Föderation" einigen könnte.

Die Oppositionsparteien CDU und CSU haben eine gemeinsame Arbeitsgruppe "Europäischer Verfassungsvertrag" unter Leitung von *Wolfgang Schäuble* und *Reinhold Bocklet* eingerichtet. Diese hat am 26. November 2001 in Berlin "Vorschläge von CDU und CSU für einen Europäischen Verfassungsvertrag" vorgelegt[180]. Die Arbeitsgruppe beschäftigt sich darin vorwiegend mit Fragen der Kompetenzabgrenzung und hat zusammenfassend dazu unter anderem ausgeführt: "Die Europäische Union muß im wesentlichen Zuständigkeiten haben für die Außen-, Sicherheits- und Verteidigungspolitik, für einen einheitlichen Binnenmarkt mit funktionierendem wirtschaftlichem Wettbewerb, einheitlicher Außenvertretung und gemeinsamer Währung, eine reformierte Agrarpolitik und – soweit grenzüberschreitende Dimensionen gegeben sind – für Rechtspolitik, innere Sicherheit, Verkehr, Infrastruktur, Umwelt- und Gesundheitsschutz. Ferner sollte die Europäische Union eine Zuständigkeit für grenzüberschreitende Regelungen zur Wahrung der Grundfreiheiten der europäischen Verträge haben, ohne dass daraus eine Regelungskompetenz für die gesamten Sachbereiche hergeleitet werden kann. Demgegenüber sollte grundsätzlich alles, was zu den gewachsenen Traditionen in Zivilisation und Kultur und der sogenannten Zivilgesellschaft gehört, der Zuständigkeit der Mitgliedstaaten vorbehalten bleiben, also z.B. der innere Staatsaufbau der Mitgliedstaaten einschließlich der kommunalen Selbstverwaltung, Familienstrukturen und soziale Sicherheit, Arbeitsmarkt, Zuwanderung, ehrenamtliche und gemeinnützige Organisationsformen und Tätigkeitsbereiche, Bildung, Kultur, Sport."[181]

Aber auch in institutioneller Hinsicht haben sich CDU und CSU weitgehend positioniert: Der Fraktionsvorsitzende der CDU/CSU-Bundestagsfraktion *Friedrich Merz* etwa hat im Vorfeld der Bundestagsdebatte zur Ratifizierung des Vertrages von Nizza zusammenfassend folgendes für den Reformprozeß gefordert[182]: Die Gewährleistung der Erweiterungsfähigkeit der EU rechtzeitig vor der nächsten Wahl zum

Europäischen Parlament (Juni 2004), eine Stärkung der Unionsinstitutionen mit einer klaren Gewaltenteilung, die rechtsverbindliche Verankerung der Grundrechtscharta im EU-Vertrag und eine Präzisierung der Kompetenzabgrenzung zwischen der Europäischen Union und ihren Mitgliedstaaten in einem einfacher strukturierten EU-Vertragswerk. Der Auffassung *Merzens* zufolge sind dazu insbesondere erforderlich: eine parlamentarische Verantwortung der Europäischen Kommission gegenüber dem Europäischen Parlament; die gleichberechtigte Mitentscheidung des Europäischen Parlaments bei allen legislativen Vorhaben; die Wahl des Präsidenten der EU-Kommission durch das Europäische Parlament; eine Reform der Ratsarbeit mit dem Ziel einer höheren Transparenz der Ratsverhandlungen und der weiteren Ausweitung des Prinzips der Mehrheitsentscheidung im Ministerrat.

Über diese Positionen hinaus haben sich einzelne CDU-Mitglieder substantiell zur Verfassungsdebatte geäußert: Im Hinblick auf die Organisation und Funktion des Europäischen Parlaments hat etwa *Friedbert Pflüger*, der Vorsitzende des Bundestagsausschusses für die Angelegenheiten der Europäischen Union, in einer Rede vom 24 April 2001 in der Humboldt-Universität Berlin in bewußter Abgrenzung zu *Joschka Fischer* das von diesem vorgeschlagene Doppelmandat (im europäischen und nationalen Parlament) aus Gründen der Arbeitsbelastung und –organisation abgelehnt. Für wichtiger hält *Pflüger* die "substantielle Beteiligung der Parlamente am europäischen Verfassungsprozeß"[183]. Jedoch tritt auch *Pflüger* (im wesentlichen mit der SPD) für eine (zweite) Staatenkammer nach deutschem Vorbild ein [Rz. 92]. Die Exekutivfunktionen von Rat und Kommission müßten "in einer einzigen europäischen Exekutive gebündelt werden" [Rz. 93]. Ferner müsse des EP in allen Bereichen das Mitentscheidungsrecht erhalten [Rz. 88].

Auf völlig anderer Linie liegen die Vorstellungen des ehemaligen sächsischen Ministerpräsidenten *Kurt Biedenkopf*. In seiner Rede vom 4. Dezember 2000 in der Humboldt-Universität hat er das bislang umfassendste Gegenmodell zu den Vorstellungen der Koalitionsfraktionen vorgetragen. Daher sei hier etwas ausführlicher darauf eingegangen: Sein Ausgangspunkt liegt in der völligen Ablehnung einer Föderation von Nationalstaaten. Sie sei schon deshalb nicht in stabiler Form vorstellbar, weil sich das demokratische Prinzip von allgemeinen und gleichen Wahlen ("one man, one vote") nicht mit der Erhaltung so ungleich großer Nationalstaaten wie in Europa vereinbaren ließe[184]. *Biedenkopfs* zentrale These lautet daher, "dass es eine dauerhafte politische Integration Europas nur geben wird, wenn es uns gelingt, mit ihr und durch die Europäische Union zugleich die Herrschaft der Idee des Nationalstaates zu überwinden" (Rz. 44). Als Mittel hierzu schlägt er vor, ein "Europa der Regionen" zur Grundlage europäischer Verfaßtheit zu machen[185]. Eine europäische

Verfassung müsse nach seiner Auffassung "zulassen, dass die Regionen als eigenständige Einheiten zu den Grundlagen der politischen Gestaltung der Europäischen Union gehören, dass sie sich auch als grenzüberschreitende Regionen bilden können und damit die Grenzen der Mitgliedsstaaten, also der Nationalstaaten durch die Bildung von Euroregionen relativieren, und dass ihnen mit der Gewährung von Regionalautonomie das Recht auf Selbstverwaltung zuerkannt wird, sich ihre Zuständigkeiten nach dem Subsidiaritätsprinzip bestimmen und sie in diesem Rahmen eigenständig handeln und verwalten können" (Rz. 26 ff). Ein derart geprägtes Europa entspreche den ökonomischen, kulturellen und gesellschaftlichen Realitäten (Rz. 34) und sei daher "weit besser als Grundlage für eine Demokratisierung der europäischen Institutionen geeignet als die Nationalstaaten" (Rz. 37). Diesen Überlegungen entsprechend zeigt sich auch Biedenkopf der Idee einer zweiten Kammer offen, will diese jedoch auf der Grundlage der Regionen bilden, etwa durch Ausbau und Weiterentwicklung des Ausschusses der Regionen (Rz. 41).

Damit stellt sich *Biedenkopf* in Widerspruch zu praktisch allen anderen Teilnehmern der öffentlichen Diskussion. Insbesondere setzt er sich der Kritik aus, er wolle einen europäischen Superstaat schaffen ("Die Vereinigten Nationen Europas" (Rz. 44)). Eine solche Kritik würde jedoch an *Biedenkopfs* Vorstellungen im wesentlichen vorbeigehen. Ihm geht es gerade nicht um die Schaffung staatlich-interventionistischer Strukturen, sondern um deren Zurückdrängung in der zukünftigen Gestaltung Europas: Legitimation kann eine europäische Verfassung nach *Biedenkopfs* Auffassung nur durch den Ausbau einer zunehmend abstrakten Ordnung gewinnen, die durch weniger Interventionismus[186] und mehr Wettbewerb die Handlungsmöglichkeiten der Bürger stärkt[187]. Die Antworten auf die drängenden Verfassungsfragen seien dann den dadurch entstehenden evolutiven Klärungs- und Suchprozessen zu überantworten (Rz. 89). In diesem Zusammenhang tritt *Biedenkopf* nachdrücklich für mehr Handlungsfreiheit des Einzelnen in Europa[188] ein.

Es sind diese legitimatorischen Gedankenansätze, die *Biedenkopfs* Position gegenüber der "Superstaat"-Kritik in gewisser Weise unempfindlich machen: Er verläßt damit die formale Ebene der Diskussion um einen europäischen Superstaat nach dem Muster "ja oder nein", indem er die *inhaltliche* Gestaltung von Gemeinwesen und hoheitlichem Handeln in den Mittelpunkt seiner Überlegungen stellt. Die Reduktion des Staatsbegriffs in diesem sozusagen Hayek´schen Sinne einer spontanen Ordnung erlaubt es, die Frage, ob die Union ein Staat sein soll oder nicht, als relativ unbedeutend in den Hintergrund treten zu lassen[189]. Unbedeutend in diesem relativen Sinne wird die Frage nach dem Superstaat allerdings nur jenen sein, die ohnehin mit *Biedenkopf* die Verschlankung hoheitlichen Handelns als notwendig erachten. Für alle anderen bleibt die Diskussion weiter offen.

Zusammenfassend rät *Biedenkopf* daher, dem Wettbewerbsprozeß seine Zeit zu geben und den Verfassungsprozeß nicht zu überfordern[190].

III. GEGENWÄRTIGES VERHÄLTNIS UND INTERAKTION ZWISCHEN EU-RECHT UND DEUTSCHEM GRUNDGESETZ

Vor diesem Hintergrund soll nun das Verhältnis des EU-Rechts zum deutschen Verfassungsrecht untersucht werden. In diesem Zusammenhang wird zunächst auf die konstitutionelle Autonomie Deutschlands unter den europäischen Verträgen eingegangen (II.1). Sodann soll es um die gemeinsamen Werte Europas gehen, wie sie in der von dem Europäischen Rat von Nizza feierlich angenommenen Charta der Grundrechte angelegt sind (II.2). Danach wird die konstitutionelle Bedeutung des Vorrangs des EU-Rechts vor deutschem Recht, insbesondere Verfassungsrecht diskutiert (II.3). Schließlich werden die institutionelle Verschränktheit und Interdependenz von europäischem und deutschem Recht, insbesondere die europäischen Funktionen der deutschen Institutionen dargestellt (II.4).

1. *Die konstitutionelle Autonomie Deutschlands unter europäischen Bindungen*

Ein Verlust konstitutioneller Autonomie vollzieht sich nicht immer, jedenfalls nicht ausschließlich, im Sinne der Übertragung von Hoheitsrechten, wie es der Art. 23 Abs. 1 GG nahelegt. Vielmehr kann auch etwas von dem, was man konstitutionelle Autonomie nennt, in den Mitgliedstaaten verloren gehen, ohne dass es notwendigerweise auf europäischer Ebene sichtbar wieder auftaucht (Beisp. kulturelle Autonomie, dazu sogleich). Umgekehrt kann auch auf europäischer Ebene eine Verfestigung von Strukturen hin zu einer europäischen Verfassungsautonomie entstehen, ohne dass dies fühlbar als Verlust nationaler Verfassungsautonomie wahrgenommen werden muß[191]. In diesem Zusammenhang sind die Art. 6 und 7 EUV zu sehen. Im folgenden sollen die beiden Vorschriften des Art. 6 Abs. 1 und 3 EUV in ihrer konstitutionellen Bedeutung für Deutschland zueinander in Beziehung gestellt werden. Dabei soll es zunächst um die nationale Identität Deutschlands als Kompetenzgrenze nach Art. 6 Abs. 3 EUV gehen (II 1 a), sodann um die Grenzen der Art. 6 Abs. 1 und 7 EUV für die konstitutionelle Autonomie Deutschlands (II 1 b).

a. *Die nationale Identität Deutschlands (Art. 6 Abs. 3 EUV) als Grenze bei der Ausweitung von EU/EG-Kompetenzen*

Die Einführung von Art. 6 Abs. 3 EUV wird in Deutschland gemeinhin als

Maßnahme gedeutet, mit der auf den Kompetenzgewinn der EU und das Heranwachsen einer europäischen Identität (etwa Art. 2, 2. Spiegelstr. EUV und Art. 17 ff. EGV) reagiert worden ist. Sie soll nicht nur den Bestand und die Integrität nationaler Identitäten, sondern auch wachsender regionaler Identitäten (etwa Art. 263 ff. EGV) schützen. In diesem Zusammenhang wird die Bestimmung vor allem als Vorschrift kompetenziellen Inhalts ausgelegt[192]. Als Ausfluß des Grundsatzes der Unionstreue ist sie nach allgemeiner Meinung im Gleichlauf mit den Art. 5 und 10 EGV auszulegen, letzterem, soweit er die Rechtspflicht der *EU* zu mitgliedstaatsfreundlichem Verhalten umfasst[193]. In dieser Auslegung schützt Art. 6 Abs. 3 EUV die Kerngehalte des mitgliedstaatlichen Verfassungslebens - oder, wie *Daniel Thürer* es ausdrückt, den „integrationsfesten Kern der staatlichen Verfassung"[194]. In Deutschland sind dies im wesentlichen die in Art. 79 Abs. 3 GG in Bezug genommenen Grundsätze, also jene Grundsätze, die in Art. 1 und 20 GG niedergelegt sind, sowie die Gliederung des Bundes in Länder und die Mitwirkung der Länder bei der Gesetzgebung. Jenseits dieser in Art. 79 Abs. 3 GG garantierten Strukturen werden darüber hinaus gelegentlich auch weitere Ordnungsstrukturen des Verfassungsrechts zum Kern der nationalen Identität gezählt: die Grundelemente einer einem besonderen Programmauftrag verpflichteten öffentlich-rechtlichen Rundfunkordnung, die kommunale Selbstverwaltung (Art. 28 II GG) oder auch die staatskirchenrechtlichen Garantien (Art. 140 GG i.V.m. 136ff. WRV). Diese Regeln sind Teil der nationalen Identität im Sinne des Art. 6 Abs. 3 EUV, weil sie so grundlegend sind, dass sie „uns" und „unser System" von den „anderen" und „deren Systemen" unterscheiden. Rationalisierbar ist dies kaum. Es wird aber in der Regel als evident erlebt.[195]

In diesem Sinne läßt sich Art. 6 Abs. 3 EUV als Vorschrift verstehen, die die Kompetenznorminterpretation anleitet und als Grenzziehung bei der Handhabung und Nutzung bestehender EU-Kompetenzen zu deuten ist. Die nationale Verfassungsidentität anzutasten ist danach nicht mehr nur nach deutschem Verfassungsrecht (Art. 23 GG), sondern wegen des Art. 6 Abs. 3 EUV auch nach Unionsrecht ausgeschlossen. Indes, es erscheint etwas kurz gegriffen, Art. 6 Abs. 3 EUV auf diese Zielrichtung zu reduzieren und allein als kompetenzbegrenzende Vorschrift zum Schutz der nationalen Verfassungsstrukturen anzusehen: Von *Identität* bräuchte keine Rede zu sein, wenn es *allein* um Kompetenzbegrenzung ginge. Nationale Identität umfaßt weit mehr als die erwähnten Kernbestandteile der nationalen Verfassungs*ordnung*. Auch empirische Gegebenheiten können zu den identitätskonstituierenden Faktoren zählen, wie etwa der Bestand und das Gedeihen der deutschen Sprache (mit der Folge eines Gebots der Gleichberechtigung der deutschen Sprache als Unionschafts- oder Amtssprache). Identität setzt an psychologischen Wahrnehmungstatbeständen an und ist daher ein komplexer, nicht lediglich auf Rechtsstrukturen abstellender Begriff. *Ulrich Haltern* zufolge ist sie multireferentiell, vielschichtig und „polyphon“[196]. Identität knüpft an einen *gemeinsamen* „sense of belonging“[197] an. Sie läuft auf eine individuelle Unterscheidung zwischen dem Eigenen und dem Fremden, also auf die Unterscheidung zwischen „Ich“ und „Du“ hinaus. In kollektiven Zusammenhängen bedeutet Identität die Unterscheidbarkeit zwischen dem „Wir“ und dem „Ihr“[198]. *Josef Weiler* hat zu dem in diesem Zusammenhang entstehenden „Festungsgedenken“ folgendes kritisch zu bedenken gegeben: „We have made little progress if the *us* becomes European (instead of German or French or British) and the *them* becomes those outside the Community or those inside who do not enjoy the priviliges of citizenship.“[199] Vor diesem Hintergrund besteht die Gefahr, dass „nationale Identität“, wie sie in Art. 6 Abs. 3 EUV aufgenommen worden ist, tatsächlich eine Wirkrichtung „dem Europäischen entgegen“ annehmen kann.

Vor diesem Hintergrund geht es gegenwärtig *normativ* darum, die Konstruktion von sich überlagernden, aber nicht miteinander in Konfrontation tretenden Identitäten zu entwickeln. Den einzelnen muß das Bewusstsein vermittelt werden, dass sie zugleich Bürger ihres Staates sind und Europäer. Sie müssen die Einsicht dafür entwickeln, dass sie zur gleichen Zeit Mitglieder einer nationalen Gemeinschaft sein können und einer europäischen Gesellschaft angehören. Dies kann nur gelingen, wenn die jeweils identitätskonstituierenden Merkmale von nationaler und europäischer Identität nicht in Antagonismus und abgrenzender Konfrontation entworfen werden; sie müssen jeweils in sich ruhen und offen genug sein, weitere Identitäten zuzulassen.[200] Dieses Zueinander-in-Gleichlauf-Stehen von nationaler und europäischer Identität ist grundlegend für die Auslegung des Art. 6 Abs. 3 EUV. Sie führt zu dem Ergebnis, dass für „die Annahme einer Gegenläufigkeit oder eines Konkurrenzverhältnisses“ kein Platz sein darf; dieser Annahme normativen Raum zu geben, wäre „systemwidrig“. Die „Tonlage des EUV“ ist durch Art. 6 Abs. 3 EUV zwar verändert, es geht aber noch immer um die „Schaffung einer immer engeren Union der Völker“, und damit „keineswegs um Konkurrenz, sondern um Ergänzung“[201].

Für die Interpretation des Art. 6 Abs. 3 EUV sind daraus die folgenden Schlußfolgerungen zu ziehen. Im Grundsatz hat die EU vor dem Hintergrund der Vorschrift zu respektieren, wie sich die konstituierenden Facetten des sozialen Konstrukts „Identität“ in den Mitgliedstaaten zusammensetzen. Art. 6 Abs. 3 EUV schützt damit sowohl Identitäten, die auf dem Element des Subjektiv-Politischen aufbauen, als auch Identitäten mit Schwerpunkt im Element des Objektiv-Kulturellen[202] und Sprachlichen[203]. Bei dem einzelnen Mitglied einer nationalen Gruppe findet die

Wahrnehmung kollektiver Identität oft in einer Mischung aus beiden Elementen, also aus kultureller Eigenheit *und* politischer Organisation statt. Deutlich wird dies in solchen Begriffsverknüpfungen wie etwa der der „politischen Kultur“ - bedeutet sie primär „Politik“, bedeutet sie primär „Kultur“, bedeutet sie von beidem etwas oder vielleicht etwas völlig anderes? Art. 6 Abs. 3 EGV ist insofern nicht als Bestimmung zu interpretieren, die einer Ausprägung nationaler Identität den Vorzug vor anderen gibt (anders teilweise aber die deutsche Literatur: So stellt etwa *Bleckmann* eher das *kulturelle* Element in den Vordergrund[204], *Hilf* hingegen eher das *subjektiv-politische* Element[205]). Auch schützt Art. 6 Abs. 3 EUV nicht nur einen Identitätsbegriff. Gleichwohl ist die Gewährleistung nach Art. 6 Abs. 3 EUV nicht grenzenlos. Schutzwürdig sind nur solche identitätskonstituierenden Gegebenheiten, die dem Ideal einer komplementären Mehrstufigkeit von nationaler und europäischer Identität nicht widersprechen.

Danach steht es den Mitgliedstaaten insbesondere frei, darzulegen, dass bestimmte Erscheinungen kultureller Natur zu den identitätskonstituierenden Merkmalen gehören und deshalb den Schutz der EU verdienen.[206] Die Politik der EU darf nicht dazu führen, dass der Einzelne aus der Verwurzelung in nationaler und lokaler Kultur gerissen wird.[207] Davon geht auch Art. 151 EGV aus, wenn dessen Abs. 1 *sowohl* die Wahrung der nationalen und regionalen Vielfalt *als auch* die Hervorhebung des gemeinsamen kulturellen Erbes als für die Gemeinschaft bedeutsam normiert. Auch diese Vorschrift macht deutlich, dass es um das *Miteinander* der kulturellen Vielfalt in einem gemeinsamen Europa geht[208]. Ein solcher Ansatz wird dem Telos des Art. 6 Abs. 3 EUV als zwar kompetenzbegrenzender, gleichwohl aber nicht dem Festungsdenken verhafteter Vorschrift gerecht. Er entspricht zudem der aktuellen politiktheoretischen Analyse des Zustandes Europas[209]. In seinem Lichte ist Art. 6 Abs. 3 EUV vor allem Ausdruck eines Unbehagens zu lesen, nationale politische wie kulturelle Autonomie zu verlieren, ohne zugleich eine (jedenfalls kompensatorische) europäische Autonomie zu gewinnen. Peter Häberle spricht in diesem Zusammenhang von „europäischem Kulturpatriotismus“[210].

b. Artikel 6 Abs. 1 und 7 EUV als Grenze der konstitutionellen Autonomie Deutschlands

Dieses Ergebnis wird im Lichte des Art. 6 Abs. 1 EUV deutlich bestätigt: Die nationale Identität ist danach nach Art. 6 Abs. 3 EUV nur insoweit schützenswert, als sie auf Merkmalen beruht, die ihrerseits vor den Anforderungen des Art. 6 Abs. 1 EUV Bestand haben. Art. 6 Abs. 1 EUV enthält (ähnlich wie etwa Art. 20 Abs. 1, 23 Abs. 1 S. 1 GG) Rechtsprinzipien, also Sätze, die so offen sind, dass sie im Weg der

Konkretisierung in konkret-anwendungsfähige Regeln überführt werden müssen.[211] Diese Prinzipien bewegen sich im Allgemeinen, im Bereich der Grundlagen sozialer Organisation, die in einem guten Maß abstrakt bleiben müssen. Sieht man von der Konkretisierung der Gehalte des Menschenrechtsschutzes und der Rechtsstaatlichkeit ab, die in der Judikatur des EuGH bereits erfolgt ist, fehlt es an ausgestaltender Judikatur. Dies wird angesichts der Beschränkungen in Art. 48 d) EUV auf absehbare Zeit wohl auch so bleiben[212]. Daraus folgt jedoch noch nicht, dass die Grundsätze des Art. 6 Abs. 1 EUV nicht konkretisierbar wären. Vielmehr können sie, wie andere unionsrechtliche Grundsätze auch, in befruchtender Auseinandersetzung mit den Verfassungstraditionen der Mitgliedstaaten zum Leben erweckt werden. Dies gilt für jeden Einzelnen der Grundsätze [213].

Art. 6 EUV ist eine der Kernbestimmung des Unionsrechts. Art. 6 Abs. 1 EUV enthält ein an die Mitgliedstaaten gerichtetes Gebot, Mindestanforderungen freiheitlich-demokratischer Verfassungsstaatlichkeit zu gewährleisten (Mindestgewährleistungspflicht, Art. 6 Abs. 1 HS 2 EUV). Die Vorschrift enthält gemeinsame Maßstäbe für Demokratie und Grundrechte, die alle öffentlichen Stellen der EU und ihrer Mitgliedstaaten nicht nur normativ binden, sondern über Art. 7 EUV auch faktisch durchgesetzt werden können. Mit einer 4/5 Mehrheit kann danach die Feststellung getroffen werden, dass die eindeutige *Gefahr* einer schwerwiegenden Verletzung der Grundrechte durch einen MS besteht. Zudem können geeignete Empfehlungen an diesen MS ausgesprochen werden. Diese Regeln legen es nahe, dass Art. 6 und 7 EUV nicht mehr nur Vorschriften nationaler und europäischer Verfaßtheit sind, sondern dass es nunmehr auch und vor allem um eine verschärfte Form der *Politikkontrolle* im Sinne eine „Frühwarnsystems“[214] geht. Kern der Vorschrift ist die Möglichkeit, unter dem Gesichtspunkt des *Schutzes* des Kerngehaltes nationaler Verfassungen gegen MS vorzugehen, sofern deren eigene Schutzmechanismen versagen. Die Bestimmungen der Art. 6 Abs. 1, Art. 7 EUV bilden als Teil eines europäischen „Systems wechselseitiger Verfassungsstabilisierung, wie es den Verfassungsverbund [im Sinne einer wechselseitigen Auffang- und Gegenseitigkeitsordnung] kennzeichnet“[215]. Ein solches Verständnis bringt Grenzen in der nationalen Verfassungsautonomie mit sich und setzt diese sogar voraus, indem es zur Folge hat, dass einzelne Mitgliedstaaten nicht mehr ohne weiteres ausbrechen können. Es ist dies der Kerngehalt der Art. 6 Abs. 1 und 7 EUV. In der Einführung des Schutzmechanismusses liegt die Umwandlung der EU zu einer „Organisation kollektiver Ordnung, die den Kerngehalt der mitgliedstaatlichen Verfassungen gewährleistet“[216]. Art. 6 Abs. 1, Art. 7 EGV ist insofern eine Struktursicherungsklausel, wie sie föderalen Verfassungsordnungen geläufig ist. Der besondere Verfassungscharakter der

Art. 6 Abs. 1, Art. 7 EUV wird gerade in dieser strukturbildenden Funktion deutlich: Es handelt sich um Regeln, die in rationaler und vor allem rechtzeitiger Selbstbegrenzung die zukünftige Ausübung politischer Macht beschränken und auf bestimmte Grundsätze festlegen.[217]

Die EU befindet sich gegenwärtig in einer Debatte darüber, welche Sätze vom Grundwertekonsens in Europa umfaßt werden. Ungeachtet aller Kritik an der verfahrenswidrigen Vorgehensweise der vierzehn Mitgliedstaaten hat insbesondere der „Fall Österreich“[218] die Frage nach Grundkonsens, Wertübereinstimmung und pluralistischer Vielfalt provoziert.[219] Die genannten Grundsätze der Freiheit, Demokratie, Achtung der Menschenrechte und Grundfreiheiten sowie der Rechtsstaatlichkeit können vor dem Hintergrund des Art. 6 Abs. 1, Art. 7 EUV als Kerngehalt „gemeineuropäischen Verfassungsrechts“ angesehen werden. Sie fordern nicht Homogenität ein, wohl aber die Einhaltung liberal-demokratischer *Mindeststandards*. Sie spiegeln jene Festlegungen wieder, die Gegenstand eines sich im Kreise der europäischen Bürgerschaft herausbildenden Grundwertekonsenses sind. Art. 6 Abs. 1, Art. 7 EUV spiegeln wieder, wie groß inzwischen die Gemeinsamkeiten in Europa sind, was jedenfalls die politischen Grundwerte angeht. Gewiß, hierbei handelt es sich nur um einen Grundkonsens, der nicht ausschließt, dass man sich in der europäischen Bürgerschaft in vielen Fragen nicht einig ist. Damit aber läßt sich für die europäische Bürgerschaft nur das konstatieren, was auch für die nationale Bürgerschaft gilt. Vor dem Hintergrund pluralistischer Wertevielfalt fällt es denn auch schwer, von Europa als „Wertegemeinschaft“[220] zu sprechen; diese Begrifflichkeit mutet ebenso merkwürdig an, wie sie im nationalen Kontext heute befremdlich wirkt. Gewiß ist auch, dass sich der Grundkonsens auf materielle Normen, darüber hinaus aber auch („Grundsatz der Demokratie“) auf verfahrensrechtliche Festlegungen bezieht. Wie im Nationalstaat stehen Verfahren im täglichen politischen Geschäft im Vordergrund; läuft dieser Prozeß störungsfrei, wird er nicht in jene Grenzbereiche geraten, in denen existentielle materielle Belange beeinträchtigt zu werden drohen und geltend gemacht werden müssen.[221] Rechtsetzungstätigkeit in Europa ist insofern immer (ebenso wie im Nationalstaat) Ausdruck von Wertvorstellung *und* Produkt eines Verfahrens. Es läuft auf Unmögliches hinaus, diese notwendige Gleichzeitigkeit auseinanderdividieren zu wollen und einen Vorrang des einen vor dem anderen zu behaupten.[222] Außer Frage steht auch, dass die in Art. 6 Abs. 1, Art. 7 EUV getroffenen Festlegungen dem Prozeß der Politik nur einen Rahmen setzen und Leitlinien vermitteln. Insofern wäre es im Hinblick auf Art. 6 Abs. 1, Art. 7 EUV falsch, vom Primärrecht als Wertordnung zu sprechen oder anzunehmen, dass das Produkt europäischer Politik eins zu eins Ausdruck einer Wertordnung sei. Auch dies gilt für das Europarecht ebenso wie für das nationale Recht. Und schließlich besteht auch kein Zweifel daran, dass der Grundkonsens in Europa teils vorfindlich ist und den Rechtsetzungsprozeß steuert, zugleich aber auch Produkt des Rechts ist und von diesem geformt wird.

Ausgangspunkt einer näheren Bestimmung der Homogenitätskriterien, die der Art. 6 Abs. 1 EUV an die einzelnen Mitgliedstaaten richtet, müssen die in Art. 6 Abs. 1 Halbsatz 2 EUV normativ aufgegriffenen Grundwertgehalte der nationalen Verfassungen sein. Diese Gehalte entfalten unmittelbar und direkt keine nach außen gerichtete Normativität: weder „nach oben“ gegenüber der EU noch „zur Seite“ gegenüber den anderen Mitgliedstaaten. Keine Verfassung eines europäischen Mitgliedstaates enthält eine Bestimmung, derzufolge die anderen Mitgliedstaaten der Union den in Art. 6 Abs. 1 EUV genannten Grundsätzen entsprechen müssen[223]. Kaum vorstellbar ist es beispielsweise, dass die Verfassung Dänemarks eine Klausel enthielte, die Anforderungen an den demokratischen Zustand in Deutschland oder Frankreich stellen würde[224]. Horizontale Anforderungen zwischen den Mitgliedstaaten existieren insofern nicht. Art. 6 Abs. 1, Art. 7 EGV greifen die Gehalte der Staatsstrukturnormen der mitgliedstaatlichen Ordnungen auf und verfestigen diese normativ-generalisierend. In der normativen Verfestigung werden diese wieder an die Mitgliedstaaten zurückgerichtet; insofern kommt den Bestimmungen eine Umlenkfunktion zu.[225] So verstanden lassen sich die Grenzen der konstitutionellen Autonomie Deutschlands aus der gemeinsamen Verfassungslage der Mitgliedstaaten der Europäischen Union entwickeln.

2. Gemeinsame Werte: Die Grundrechtecharta der Europäischen Union

Die Idee gemeinsamer liberal-demokratischer Mindeststandards ist ein wesentlicher Anknüpfungspunkt der auf dem Europäischen Rat von Nizza feierlich unterzeichneten Charta der Grundrechte der Europäischen Union[226]. Diese stellt in Satz 1 ihrer Präambel klar, dass die immer engere Union der Völker Europas „auf der Grundlage gemeinsamer Werte“ steht[227]. Für diese Feststellung nimmt sie die Entschlußkraft der Völker Europas in Bezug, auf der Grundlage dieser gemeinsamen Werte „eine friedliche Zukunft zu teilen“. In diesem Zusammenhang wirft die Grundrechtecharta unzählige Einzelfragen auf, die sich im soeben behandelten Bezugsfeld zwischen nationaler Identität auf der einen Seite und europäischem Grundwertekonsens auf der anderen bewegen. Um einige dieser Fragen soll es im folgenden gehen, nämlich zunächst um die Frage, inwieweit die Charta der bestehenden Ausgestaltung des Grundrechtsschutzes in Deutschland entspricht (a), inwieweit sie von deutschen Gerichten in Bezug genommen werden kann (b) und schließlich, inwieweit sie die gerade angesprochenen Standards des Art. 6 Abs. 1 EUV zu beeinflussen vermag (c).

a. Entspricht die Charta der Ausgestaltung des Grundrechtsschutzes nach deutschem Recht?

Die deutsche „Verfassungsrechtsgemeinschaft" ist unter dem Grundgesetz zu einer Art „Grundrechte-Gemeinschaft" geworden[228]. Materiell leitend sind dabei vor allem drei Ideen: die der Würde des Menschen (Art. 1 GG)[229], die der Freiheit des Menschen (Art. 2 GG)[230] und die der Gleichheit des Menschen vor allem Gesetz (Art. 3 GG)[231]. Methodisch geht das Grundgesetz den Weg der Enumeration, in dem es in den Art. 1-19 GG, teilweise aber auch darüber, hinaus einen Grundrechtekatalog festschreibt, der zunächst diese allgemeinen Vorschriften und im Anschluß spezielle Freiheitsrechte enthält. Die in diesem Katalog niedergelegten Grundsätze werden vom Grundgesetz sowohl hinsichtlich ihrer Schutzbereichs- als auch hinsichtlich ihrer Schrankensystematik für so wichtig gehalten, dass jedenfalls die Grundsätze des Art. 1 GG und der in Art. 20 GG angelegten Grundrechtsgehalte mit verfassungsmäßigen Mitteln nicht geändert werden können (Art. 79 Abs. 3 GG).

Vor diesem Hintergrund bedarf es keiner weiteren Begründung, dass die Schaffung einer europäischen Charta der Grundrechte, die sich wie die vorliegende Charta an der Würde des Menschen (vgl. Kapitel 1), an seiner Freiheit (Kapitel 2 und 5) und an seiner Gleichheit (Kapitel 3) orientiert und die Rechte des Menschen im Einzelnen katalogartig enumeriert, der deutschen Verfassungstradition sowohl inhaltlich als auch methodisch zunächst entgegenkommt. Sie bewegt sich im wesentlichen in jenen Bereichen, in denen auch die Grundrechte des Grundgesetzes angesiedelt sind. Anders wäre die Entstehung der Charta unter maßgeblich deutscher Beteiligung auch gar nicht erklärbar[232]: So, wie die deutsche Tradition als Teil der gemeinsamen Verfassungstraditionen der Mitgliedstaaten in die Grundrechterechtsprechung des EuGH eingeflossen ist[233], ist sie auch in die Grundrechtecharta miteingeflossen. Entspräche die Charta nicht im wesentlichen dem deutschen Grundrechtsschutz, gäbe sie es nicht[234].

Nun folgt daraus allerdings nicht, dass es keine Unterschiede zwischen der Grundrechtecharta und dem deutschen Grundrechtsschutz gibt. Entsprechend den Vorgaben des Europäischen Rates von Köln[235] sind neben den gemeinsamen Verfassungstraditionen der Mitgliedstaaten und den in der EMRK garantierten Rechten auch die im Gemeinschafts-/Unionsrecht, in der Europäischen Sozialcharta und in der Gemeinschaftscharta der sozialen Grundrechte der Arbeitnehmer enthaltenen Rechte berücksichtigt worden[236]. Damit vereinigt die Charta „die vielfältigen Traditionen in Europa mit den Errungenschaften von mehr als 50 Jahren politischer Integration".[237] Die enthaltenen Rechte und Grundsätze bilden dadurch eine „bunte Mischung"[238] von Rechten. Schon daraus folgt, dass trotz grundsätzlicher Entsprechungen mit dem

Grundrechtsschutz unter dem deutschen Grundgesetz im Einzelnen doch Unterschiede bestehen müssen. Dies gilt vor allem, wenn man nicht lediglich den Text des Grundgesetzes zum Maßstab nimmt, sondern die Gestalt, die das Grundgesetz in nunmehr fünfzigjähriger Verfassungsrechtsprechung gewonnen hat.

Bei der inhaltlichen Bewertung des von der Charta begründeten Schutzes gilt es auf der einen Seite zu berücksichtigen, dass europäische Grundrechtsgebung zwangsläufig in Zwiesprache mit den Traditionsbeständen der verfassungstheoretischen Moderne und den Grundrechtsstandards anderer Grundrechtsordnungen stattfinden muß. Die EU kann sich von diesen Beständen schon deshalb nicht vollständig lösen, weil hierin das Wissen und die Erfahrungen um typische Gefährdungspotentiale öffentlich-rechtlicher Herrschaft quasi gespeichert werden. Auf der anderen Seite reagieren Grundrechtsbestimmungen jeweils auf konkrete Herausforderungen in Raum und Zeit; eine Grundrechtsordnung muß auf die EU quasi zugeschnitten und ihr im Hinblick auf Struktur, Kompetenzumfang und Wirkmächtigkeit sozusagen „auf den Leib geschneidert“ werden.[239] Hier sind (insbesondere vor dem Hintergrund der Grundrechtsordnung des Grundgesetzes) in der Grundrechtecharta vor allem drei Defizite zu erkennen – Defizite, die deutlich machen, dass es sich bei der Charta um ein Kompromißwerk handelt.

Zu bedauern ist erstens, dass einige Schutzgarantien unterentwickelt sind oder überhaupt nicht in der Charta enthalten sind. Eine Reihe von Rechten gewährleistet die Charta nur im Rahmen des Unionsrechts und der einzelstaatlichen Gepflogenheiten. Die Charta gewährleistet damit Grundrechtsschutz nur *im Rahmen* der Gesetze und nicht gegenüber dem EU-Gesetzgeber oder gegenüber dem EU-Recht durchführenden nationalen Gesetzgeber. Die Grundrechtecharta fällt insoweit gegenüber verfassungsrechtlichen Errungenschaften zurück, die für die meisten nationalen Verfassungen heute selbstverständlich sind. Es handelt sich um einen schwerwiegenden Mangel, dass gerade die unternehmerische Freiheit nur im Rahmen des EG-Rechts und der einzelstaatlichen Rechtsvorschriften gewährleistet wird. Auch die Freiheiten des Art. 9, 14 Abs. 3 oder Art. 28 der Charta werden in problematischer Weise nur im Rahmen der Gesetze gewährleistet. Wieder andere Freiheiten hätten vor dem Hintergrund des Zuschnitts der europäischen Herrschaftsgewalt einer ausdrücklichen Regelung bedurft; es muß als Mangel angesehen werden, dass eine Garantie der Außenwirtschaftsfreiheit fehlt und offenbleibt, ob sie als Teilfreiheit des Art. 16 der Charta (unternehmerische Freiheit) angesehen werden kann. In einem Verband, der funktional und legitimatorisch so sehr auf das Gedeihen der Regionen und Staaten angewiesen ist wie die EU, macht sich zudem das Fehlen von Schutzvorschriften zugunsten der Staaten, Regionen und Kommunen schmerzhaft bemerkbar. Gruppen- und Minderheitsrechte werden nicht gewährt, obgleich gerade die dadurch bewirkte Stabilisierung für das Wirken der EU von erheblicher Bedeutung wäre. In Art. 22 wird zwar die Achtung der Vielfalt der Kulturen, Religionen und Sprachen angesprochen; eine Schutzgarantie zugunsten einzelner Kulturen oder Sprachen enthält die Charta aber nicht. Diese Kritikpunkte müssen ungeachtet des Umstandes geäußert werden, dass sich die Charta in anderen Bereichen als zukunftsgerichtet und modern erweist (z.B. Freiheit der Kommunikation (Art. 7); Schutz personenbezogener Daten (Art. 8)). Wie zurückhaltend die Charta im Übrigen bei der Positivierung neuer Gehalte ist, wird etwa darin deutlich, dass strittige Fragen überwiegend offengelassen werden, etwa die Regelung nicht-reproduktiver Formen des Klonens (Art. 3 Abs. 2 Grundrechtecharta), die Anerkennung gleichgeschlechtlicher Ehe und die Institutsgarantie für Ehe und Familie unabhängig des Geschlechts (Art. 9 Grundrechtecharta) oder auch der geschlechtsunabhängige Mutterschutz (Art. 33 Abs. 2 Grundrechtecharta). In diesen Fällen formuliert die Charta zwar ein normatives Leitbild, lässt dem Gesetzgeber aber ausdrücklich offen, die einschlägigen Fragen in die eine oder andere Richtung zu beantworten[240]. Selbst wenn die Charta geltendes Recht würde, wären diese Rechte daher nicht rechtlich bindender Natur im Sinne der typischen Bindungswirkung eines *Grund*rechts, d.h. im Sinne einer gerade *auch den Gesetzgeber* bindenden (Art. 1 Abs. 3 GG), bestimmte Gehalte ausschließenden Wirkung.

Zu bedauern ist zweitens die Unausgewogenheit der Vorschriften über die Begründung von Leistungsansprüchen gegen die öffentliche Gewalt (Kapitel IV). Insgesamt drückt sich – so ist vorab festzuhalten - in den Bestimmungen der Charta erhebliche Zurückhaltung gegenüber einem Grundrechtsverständnis aus, demzufolge sich wohlfahrtsstaatliche Ziele durch Grundrechtspolitik [241] verfolgen lassen. Zu Recht haben die Mitglieder des „Konvents“ darauf verzichtet, einen grundrechtlichen Anspruch auf Bereitstellung eines Arbeitsplatzes oder einer Wohnung, von Urlaub oder einem Transportmittel („Recht auf Auto“) in die Charta aufzunehmen. Auch das in Art. 14 Abs. 1 der Charta ohne Einschränkung und Konturierung gewährte „Recht auf Bildung“ wird letztlich nicht beim Wort genommen werden können. Systematisch deutet die Stellung dieser Bestimmung im Kapitel „Freiheiten“ darauf hin, dass dieses Recht lediglich das Recht umfaßt, sich selbst im Rahmen der bürgerlichen Freiheit zu bilden. Das ebenfalls in Art. 14 Abs. 1 der Charta ausgesprochene Recht auf Zugang zur beruflichen Aus- und Weiterbildung läßt allerdings auch den Schluß zu, dass es der Vorschrift um Leistungs- und Gewährleistungspflichten der öffentlichen Gewalt geht. Den Anspruch der Einzelnen, ihnen Bildung zu verschaffen, wird die EU allerdings kaum einlösen können; dieser Anspruch ist in einer liberalen Gesellschaftsordnung von der öffentlichen Gewalt ebensowenig zu erfüllen wie ein Anspruch auf Bereitstellung von Arbeit. Man wird nicht umhinkommen, den überschießenden Wortlaut auch dieser Vorschrift zurückzuschneiden. Festzustellen ist, dass die Grundrechtecharta bei der Gewährung wirtschaftlicher und sozialer Leistungsrechte jedenfalls hinter die Standards des Grundgesetzes insofern zurückfällt, als sich inzwischen in der Rechtsprechung des BVerfG ein Anspruch auf Sicherung des Existenzminimums herausgebildet hat.[242]

Als bloßes Trostpflaster für die Anhänger sozialer Grundrechte mutet es an, wenn man sich in der Charta wortreich um eher marginale Gewährleistungen sozialer Sicherheit bemüht. So wird das Recht der Unionsbürger auf „Zugang zu einem unentgeltlichen Arbeitsvermittlungsdienst" geschützt. Im Rahmen der Gesetze (und damit nicht gegenüber dem Gesetzgeber) wird auch das Recht auf Unterrichtung und Anhörung der Arbeitnehmer im Unternehmen – nicht aber ein Anspruch auf Mitbestimmung – gewährleistet. Die Tarifautonomie wird ebenso nur im Rahmen der Gesetze gewährleistet wie der Anspruch auf Leistungen der sozialen Sicherheit. Ohne Zweifel handelt es sich hierbei um Regelungen, deren Aufnahme dem Zwang zur Befriedigung politischer Wünsche und der Abrundung geschuldet wurde, ohne dass sich der Regelungsgegenstand wirklich in einer Gefährdungslage befände. Ist das Recht auf kostenlosen Zugang zur Arbeitsvermittlung wirklich so großen Anfechtungen ausgesetzt, dass hier dem politisch-demokratischen Prozeß verfassungsrechtliche Grenzen gesetzt werden müssen?

Die Konzentration auf sozialstaatliche Garantien wirkt zugleich anachronistisch und rückwärtsgewandt, weil die wirklichen Herausforderungen, die sich bei der grundrechtlichen Einbindung der öffentlichen Gewalt heute stellen, teilweise unbeantwortet bleiben: Die blassen und wenig gehaltvollen Vorschriften über den Schutz der Gesundheit und der Umwelt, über den Schutz der Einzelnen als Verbraucher und als Bezieher öffentlicher Dienstleistungen werden schon deshalb, weil sie keine subjektiven Rechte gewährleisten, kaum praktische Bedeutung entfalten. Grundrechte als Verfahrensgarantien fehlen völlig, obgleich doch die legitimierende Wirkung von Verfahrensbeteiligung inzwischen zum Gemeinplatz geworden ist: Das in Art. 41 begründete und wortreich ausgeschmückte „Recht auf eine gute Verwaltung" gewährt dieses Recht nicht.

Ein dritter Kritikpunkt ist grundrechtsdogmatischer Art. Es hat sich eingebürgert, grundrechts-theoretisch zwischen prima-facie-Garantien und definitiven Garantien zu unterscheiden. *Prima facie* wird die Freiheit des Individuums von einer Grundrechtsordnung garantiert, wenn und soweit sie vom Schutzbereich eines Grundrechtes erfaßt wird. Einen *definitiven* Schutz gewährt die Ordnung aber nur dort, wo sie dem Träger der Herrschaftsgewalt die Möglichkeit eines Eingriffs abschneidet. Es gehört zu den vielleicht schwerwiegendsten Mängeln der Grundrechtecharta, dass sie sich bei der Verleihung der prima-facie-Rechte um Detailgenauigkeit und Präzision bemüht, dann aber bei der Festlegung der Schranken wenig mehr als eine vage und unbestimmte Generalklausel enthält, wonach der Wesensgehalt der Rechte und Freiheiten zu wahren und der Verhältnismäßigkeitsgrundsatz [243] zu beachten ist.[244] Alle Grundrechte werden damit über einen Kamm geschert, eine Differenzierung nach Bedeutung und Gehalt, wie sie durch die Aufnahme qualifizierter Grundrechtsschranken erfolgen könnte, erfolgt nicht. Das Verbot des reproduktiven Klonens ist ebenso einschränkbar wie der Anspruch auf bezahlten Mutterschaftsurlaub; die Charta selbst macht zwischen beiden Rechten keinen Unterschied. Dieser Mangel wiegt um so schwerer, weil schon der Europäische Gerichtshof in seiner Grundrechtsrechtsprechung den Unionsbürgern zwar relativ freizügig prima-facie-Rechte gewährte, der europäischen Hoheitsgewalt dann aber weitreichende Eingriffsbefugnisse zubilligte und so den Wert der Grundrechtsgewährleistung schmälerte. In der fehlenden Schrankensystematik liegt der blinde Fleck des Dokuments.[245]

Fragen wirft die Charta insofern auf, als sie einen **„Modernisierungsschub“** mit sich bringt. Sie beansprucht, im Zeichen „der Weiterentwicklung der Gesellschaft, des sozialen Fortschritts und der wissenschaftlichen und technologischen Entwicklungen“ (Präambel S. 4 HS. 1) zu stehen. Beispiele hierfür sind etwa das in Art. 3 II 4. Spiegelstr. der Grundrechtecharta enthaltene Verbot des reproduktiven Klonens. Dieses Verbot entspricht zwar der Gesetzeslage in Deutchland[246]. Neu ist aber, dass ein solches Verbot nun in einer Grundrechtsvorschrift zu finden ist. Heißt dies, dass sich das Verbot zu einem subjektiven Recht des einzelnen vedichtet? Wer ist Träger dieses Rechts und wem gegenüber besteht es? Es ist zwar festzuhalten, dass auch nach deutschem *Verfassungs*recht das reproduktive Klonen schon nach dem Prinzip der Menschenwürde nach Abs. 1 GG verboten ist. Ein subjektives Recht des Einzelnen folgt daraus allerdings noch nicht[247]. Dogmatische Konsequenzen ergeben sich auch im Zusammenhang mit anderen Rechten, etwa im Bereich der grundgesetzlichen Schutzpflichtenlehre[248]: Wie etwa passt der Schutz vor ungerechtfertigter Entlassung (Art. 30 Grundrechtecharta) zur Dogmatik des Grundgesetzes? Handelt es sich hier um eine Schutzpflicht oder wirkt die Vorschrift ungefähr entsprechend der deutschen mittelbaren Drittwirkung?[249]

Zu erwähnen sind schließlich die in der Charta befindlichen doppelten **Günstigkeitsklauseln**. Zum einen wird bestimmt, dass das Unionsrecht einen weiteren Schutz gewähren kann als die aus der EMRK in die Grundrechtecharta übernommenen Rechte (Art. 52 Abs. 3 S. 2 Grundrechtecharta). Andererseits aber bestimmt Art. 53

Grundrechtecharta, dass alle in der Grundrechtecharta verankerten Rechte einen Mindeststandard bilden, der in keinem Falle unterschritten werden darf, der aber der Anwendung weitergehender Rechte nicht entgegensteht. Im Fall des schlichten Abwehrrechts bedeutet dies kein größeres Problem, wirkt dies doch allein im Verhältnis Bürger - Staat beziehungsweise im Verhältnis Bürger - Europäische Union. Im Fall der mehrpoligen Grundrechtsverhältnisse kann es aber zu dogmatisch schwierigen Einzelfragen kommen, reduziert doch etwa die Begründung einer Schutzpflicht den Status negativus eines potenziellen Störers[250].

Zusammenfassend läßt sich sagen, dass der Schutz der Grundrechtecharta dem Grundrechtsschutz unter dem Grundgesetz weitgehend entspricht, dass aber aufgrund des Kompromisscharakters der Charta schmerzliche Schutzlücken entstehen. Sollte der Charta rechtliche Bindungswirkung zugeschrieben werden, wäre die Rechtsprechung des EuGH, die die Grundrechtecharta teilweise kodifiziert hat (Präambel Abs. 5), weiter zu beobachten. Vieles wird vom Grundrechtsverständnis des EuGH abhängen, insbesondere auch von der Frage, inwieweit der EuGH seine Grundrechterechtsprechung im Lichte der *Vertiefung der Integration*[251] vorantreibt. Divergenzen zum BVerfG würden sich vor allem auftun, wenn sich der EuGH nicht bereitfände, Grundrechtsrechtsprechung als Ausdruck eines umfassenden, die Werte und Interessen der Einzelnen mit hinreichendem Gewicht berücksichtigenden Abwägungsprozesses zu betreiben.[252].

b. Die Grundrechtecharta als Referenz für den Grundrechtsschutz durch deutsche Gerichte

Die Charta der Grundrechte ist natürlich auch in Deutschland gegenwärtig kein geltendes Recht. Weder ist sie in die bestehenden Verträge aufgenommen worden, noch besteht eine allgemeine Bindungswirkung außerhalb der Verträge. Schon von daher kann Art. 10 EGV, eine Vorschrift, die auch der nationale Richter zu beachten hat, nicht eingreifen. Auch eine Vorlage nach Art. 234 EGV an den EuGH würde sich außerhalb des Rechtsprechungsauftrags des EuGH nach Art. 220 EGV bewegen[253]. Eine Selbstbindung nationaler Gerichte, die derjenigen der europäischen Organe vergleichbar wäre[254], besteht von Seiten der nationalen Gerichtsbarkeit nicht und kann - schon wegen der rechtsprechenden Funktion der Gerichtsbarkeit - nicht bestehen.

Es stellt sich aber die Frage, ob die Charta im Rahmen ihres Anwendungsbereichs (Art. 51 Grundrechtecharta)[255] gleichwohl als Referenz in Entscheidungen deutscher Gerichte einfließen kann. Immerhin hat Generalanwalt Tizzano von der Grundrechtecharta ausdrücklich als einem **„substantive point of reference“** gesprochen[256]. Derartige

Bezugnahmen sind (im Kontext rechtsvergleichender Argumentation) denkbar, bislang allerdings – soweit ersichtlich – noch nicht erfolgt. Im Übrigen ist anzunehmen, dass der unmittelbare Einfluss der GRC auch in Zukunft eher gering sein wird[257]. Mittelbar-*faktische* Wirkungen der Grundrechtecharta auf die Entscheidungspraxis deutscher Gerichte[258] sind allerdings in zweierlei Hinsicht denkbar: Einmal kann die Grundrechtecharta gegebenenfalls Einfluss auf Entscheidungen des deutschen Gesetzgebers haben und damit mittelbar dann auch Relevanz für die deutschen Gerichte entfalten. Zum anderen aber könnte sich eine mittelbar-faktische Wirkung aus dem Zusammenspiel von EuGH und deutschen Gerichten ergeben. Auch der EuGH kann sich als Rechtsprechungsorgan zwar nicht so wie die anderen Organe der Europäischen Union an die Grundrechtecharta selbst binden. Er könnte aber auf sie Bezug nehmen, zwar nicht im Sinne einer Inspirationsquelle wie der EMRK, wohl aber im Sinne einer „nachgeordneten Orientierungshilfe[259]. In diesem Fall aber könnte die Notwendigkeit einer Auseinandersetzung in deutschen Gerichten mit der Judikatur des EuGH dann auch die Notwendigkeit der Auseinandersetzung mit der Grundrechtecharta mit sich bringen. Dem Berichterstatter ist ein solcher Fall bislang jedoch nicht bekannt[260].

c. Der Einfluss der Charta auf die Gehalte des Art. 6 Abs. 1 EUV

Es bedarf keiner weiteren Erörterung, dass die Charta im Lichte der Grundrechterechtsprechung des EuGH auszulegen sein wird[261]. Außer Frage steht aber auch, dass die Charta Auswirkungen auf die Auslegung der Grundsätze des Art. 6 Abs. 1 EUV haben wird. Im folgenden soll dies zunächst für den Grundsatz der Demokratie und sodann für den nach Art. 6 Abs. 1 und 2 EUV zu gewährleistenden Grundrechtsschutz erläutert werden - jenen beiden Grundsätzen, zu denen die Grundrechtecharta die thematisch engste Verbindung aufweist.

Zunächst zum Grundsatz der europäischen *Demokratie*: Im verfassungstheoretischen Verständnis lassen sich im Hinblick auf das Verhältnis von Demokratie und Grundrechten zwei große Theorielinien beobachten. Große Bedeutung spielt in Deutschland die „Trennungstheorie“: Danach stehen Demokratie und Grundrechte zwar in Wechselwirkungen, bauen aber auf unterschiedlichen Grundprinzipien auf, knüpfen an unterschiedlichen Subjekten an und stehen damit *nebeneinander*. Für die Bundesrepublik hat Josef Isensee dies wie folgt ausgedrückt: „Im grundgesetzlichen Gemeinwesen fließt Legitimation aus zwei Quellen: aus der Freiheit des einzelnen Menschen und aus dem Willen des Volkes. Die Individualfreiheit findet ihre verfassungsrechtliche Form in den liberalen Grundrechten, der Wille des Volkes die seine in der Demokratie.“[262] Demokratie und Grundrechte stehen danach in der Tat in einem engen

Verhältnis zueinander[263], sind aber voneinander zu trennen. Der entgegengesetzen Sichtweise zufolge ruhen Demokratie und Grundrechte auf der gleichen Basis, knüpfen am gleichen Legitimationssubjekt an, bilden damit die beiden Seiten ein und derselben Sache und sind unlösbar miteinander verbunden. Dieser Sichtweise zufolge ist die Ausübungsmöglichkeit bürgerlicher Freiheiten nicht nur faktische, sondern auch rechtliche Konstitutionsvoraussetzung für die Ausbildung demokratischer Staatlichkeit[264]. Dabei geht es nicht nur um faktische Entstehung willensgetragener Entscheidungen, sondern auch um deren legitimationstheoretische Verankerung. Manfred Zuleeg etwa hat im Anschluss an Ingolf Pernice[265] behauptet: „Die [durch die Grundrechtecharta bewirkte] Verstärkung des Grundrechtsschutzes fördert [...] die Demokratie in Europa“[266].

Nicht anderes kann es in der Europäischen Union sein, mit der Maßgabe allerdings, dass die Funktionsbestimmung des „Volkes“ in Europa naturgemäß viel komplizierter ausfällt als in der Bundesrepublik Deutschland[267]. Dementsprechend wird denn auch das Verhältnis von Grundrechten und Demokratie in der Europäischen Union unter dem unionsspezifischen Aspekt diskutiert, ob es europäischen Grundrechtsschutz angesichts des „Funktionsausfalls“ des Europäischen Parlaments in einem demokratisierenden Sinne sinnvoll überhaupt geben kann[268]. Die leitende These ist in diesem Zusammenhang, dass es sinnwidrig sei, parlamentarische Funktionen durch die Tätigkeit eines grundrechtsschützenden Verfassungsgerichtshofs, etwa des EuGH, zu ersetzen[269]. Zu Recht wird in diesem Zusammenhang darauf hinwiesen, dass die Anwendung der Grundrechtecharta einen Zuwachs von Entscheidungsmacht des EuGH bedeuten würde, ohne dass dieser durch eine Funktionsstärkung des Europäischen Parlaments unter dem Gesichtspunkt der Gewaltenteilung ausgeglichen würde. In diesem Lichte betrachtet würde eine Bindungswirkung der Grundrechtecharta die Demokratie in Europa gegebenenfalls nicht nur stärken, sondern in gewisser Weise auch schwächen, selbst dann, wenn, wie in der Grundrechtecharta, ein eigener Abschnitt mit Bürgerrechtsgarantien eingeführt wird[270].

Eindeutiger bestimmen lassen sich die Beziehungen zwischen der Grundrechtecharta und dem in Art. 6 Abs. 1 EUV niedergelegten Grundsatz der *Achtung der Menschenrechte*, konkretisiert durch den vom EuGH bisher gewährten Grundrechtsschutz. Außer Frage steht zunächst, dass die Grundrechtecharta die Eignung besitzt, den EuGH in ein „Dilemma“ zu bringen: Entweder frustriert er die von den Charta-Befürwortern an ihn gerichteten Erwartungen, oder aber er setzt sich dem Vorwurf aus, jenseits des geltenden Rechts Grundrechtsaktivismus zu betreiben[271]. Zukünftige Schritte des EuGH werden in diesem Spannungsfeld stattfinden. Die bisherige Erfahrung lässt vermuten, dass der EuGH behutsam genug, zugleich aber auch hinreichend mutig und willensstark sein wird, hier einen Mittelweg zu gehen. Vieles spricht in diesem Zusammenhang dafür, dass der EuGH nicht jene grundrechtsaktivisitische Rechtsprechtung betreiben wird, die die Rechtsprechung des BVerfG kennzeichnet. Zugleich wird die Grundrechtecharta für die Grundrechterechtsprechung des EuGH nicht bedeutungslos bleiben. Die Vermutung liegt nahe, dass der EuGH in Zukunft in einer Art Wechselwirkung Ansätze aus seiner eigenen Rechtsprechung im Sinne eines Ping-Pong-Spiels deshalb weiterentwickeln wird, weil sie ihrerseits von den Herren der Verträge in eine Grundrechtecharta aufgenommen und dadurch bekräftigt worden sind. Teilweise begründet man dies mit der Annahme, die Grundrechterechtsprechung des EuGH folge, da sie an den gemeinsamen Verfassungstraditionen orientiert sei, einem sogenannten „Mittelmaßprinzip“, während die Grundrechtecharta dem „Vollständigkeitsprinzip“ diene[272]. Von daher müsse die Grundrechtecharta notwendig dynamisierende Wirkung entfalten. Problematisch ist diese These, weil die Charta sich in vielen Bereichen auch lediglich als Kompromißwerk erweist und Lücken aufweist. Insofern dürften die Anstöße auch weniger von konkreten Einzelbestimmungen der Charta und mehr von dem hinter der Charta stehenden Willen der Mitgliedstaaten ausgehen, den EuGH in seiner Rechtsprechung zu bestärken und zu ermuntern.

Im Ausbau der Grundrechterechtsprechung wird der EuGH allerdings immer auch konfligierende Prinzipien im Blick behalten müssen: Sicher ist beispielsweise, dass das Prinzip der einheitlichen und gleichen Wirksamkeit des Europarechts[273] durch Bestimmungen der Grundrechtecharta nicht ausgehebelt werden und der Vorrang des Europarechts daher keinen Schaden erleiden darf.[274] Die Grundrechtecharta selbst enthält den Hinweis, dass die in Anlehnung an die EMRK und ihre Zusatzprotokolle formulierten Rechte, so wie in der EMRK, als Mindeststandard vorgesehen sind (Art. 52 Abs. 3 S. 1 Grundrechtecharta: „... gleiche Bedeutung und Tragweite...“)[275]. Dies könnte zu Friktionen mit dem Vorrangprinzip führen. Manche dieser Rechte behalten zwar ihren Charakter als Mindeststandard, gehen dabei allerdings über den der EMRK hinaus - oder bieten jedenfalls die Möglichkeit hierzu. Es handelt sich insoweit also um einen höheren Standard als in der EMRK (Art 52 Abs. 3 S. 2 Grundrechtecharta: weitergehender Schutz durch das Unionsrecht). Zu diesen Rechten gehören insbesondere die Versammlungs- und Vereinigungsfreiheit[276], das Recht auf Bildung[277], das Recht auf ein unparteiisches Gericht und Prozesskostenhilfe[278] und das Verbot der Doppelbestrafung[279]. Für die meisten dieser Rechte (wie auch für andere Rechte wie etwa das Verbot der Folter[280]) ist fraglich, ob überhaupt irgendeine Tätigkeit der EU oder ihrer Mitgliedstaaten bei der Durchführung des Unionsrechts[281] in absehbarer Zeit zu erwarten ist. Trotzdem könnte sich aber der Gehalt des in Art. 6 Abs. 1 EUV festgeschriebenen Menschenrechtsbestandes im Fall rechtlicher Verbindlichkeit der Charta, sozusagen überschießend, erweitern. Relevanz könnte dies etwa bei Beitrittsverhandlungen haben. Eine andere Entwicklungslinie ist dort denkbar, wo die Grundrechtecharta explizit Fragen offenläßt, etwa im Bereich des nicht-reproduktiven Klonens[282] oder des Rechts, eine Ehe einzugehen und eine Familie zu gründen[283]. In diesen eindeutigen Fällen der Nichtregelung könnte die Grundrechtecharta insofern Einfluss auf die Rechtsprechung des EuGH nehmen, als sie deutlich macht, dass hier vor eindeutigen Stellungnahmen des Gerichts zunächst darauf zu warten ist, ob sich ein europaweiter gesellschaftlicher Konsens durchzusetzen vermag. Insofern könnte es sich hier um ein deutliches Zeichen an die Richter handeln, mit vorschnellen Entscheidungen in die eine oder andere Richtung besser abzuwarten.

Zusammenfassend wird die Grundrechtecharta damit vor allem symbolische und politische, darüber hinaus aber auch erhebliche rechtliche Wirkungen erzeugen. In diesem Sinne etwa haben Siegbert Alber und Ulrich Widmaier formuliert: Die Grundrechtecharta „ist der Beweis, dass die Union nicht nur eine Wirtschaftsgemeinschaft, sondern auch und besonders eine Rechtsgemeinschaft ist. Die Charta zeigt Werte und Rechte auf. So festigt und verdichtet sie die Rechts-*Gemeinschaft*. Auch wenn die Charta gegenüber dem Bisherigen nicht viel an Neuem oder Zusätzlichem bringt, so macht sie doch erstmals deutlich, dass es der Mensch ist, der im Mittelpunkt auch der europäischen Politik steht."[284]

3. Die konstitutionelle Bedeutung des Vorrangs von EU/EG-Recht

Das Unionsrecht gewinnt seine konstitutionelle Bedeutung nicht zuletzt dadurch, dass es Vorrang nicht nur vor nationalem einfachen Recht, sondern vor allem auch vor nationalem Verfassungsrecht beansprucht[285]. Schon immer verfolgt der EuGH seine Vorrangrechtsprechung[286] mit Konsequenz, Härte und Unbeugsamkeit. Demgegenüber hat das BVerfG seine Rechtsprechung zum Vorrang des Unionsrechts, die jahrzehntelang zwischen Integrationsskepsis, Mißtrauen und Europafreundlichkeit hin- und her pendelte[287] nach einigen im Einzelnen nicht ganz eindeutigen Entscheidungen[288] nun in seinem Beschluss vom 7. Juni 2000 zur Bananenmarkt-Ordnung klargestellt: „Ein deckungsgleicher Schutz in den einzelnen Grundrechtsbereichen des Grundgesetzes durch das europäische Unionsrecht und die darauf fußende Rechtsprechung des EuGH ist nicht gefordert." Vielmehr reiche es aus, wenn „die Rechtsprechung des EuGH einen wirksamen Schutz der Grundrechte gegenüber der Hoheitsgewalt der

Union generell gewährleistet, der dem vom Grundgesetz als unabdingbar gebotenen Grundrechtschutz im Wesentlichen gleich zu achten ist, zumal den Wesensgehalt generell verbürgt."[289] Damit nimmt das BVerfG seinen Prüfungsanspruch so weit zurück, dass gegenwärtig eine Überprüfung von Seiten des BVerfG nahezu ausgeschlossen erscheint[290]. Das BVerfG hat den Vorrang des Unionsrechts und die Prüfungskompetenz des EuGH damit jedenfalls im Grundrechtsbereich umfassend anerkannt. Im folgenden soll zunächst auf die allgemeine verfassungsrechtliche Dimension des derart etablierten Vorrangs unionsrechtlicher Normen eingegangen werden (a), sodann auf die spezifischen Fragen der Modifikation des deutschen Verfassungsrechts durch die Vorgaben und Wirkungen vorrangigen europäischen Vertragsrechts (b).

a. Zur Bedeutung des Vorrangs primären und sekundären Unionsrechts vor nationalem Verfassungsrecht

Nach zutreffender Auffassung des EuGH handelt es sich beim Vorrangprinzip um einen in den Rechtsnormen des Unionsrecht angelegten Geltungsanspruch: Das Unionsrecht überläßt es nicht – anders als das klassische Völkerrecht – dem nationalen Recht, seine normhierarchische Einordnung zu bestimmen, sondern trifft die Entscheidung selbst. Die Mitgliedstaaten haben der EU die Kompetenz, die Geltung ihres Rechts zu bestimmen, in den Gründungsverträgen zugewiesen. Insofern ist es fehlerhaft, die Vorrangregel (oder allgemeiner: die Geltung des EU-Rechts) dem nationalen Recht zuzuschlagen und in dem Rechtsanwendungsbefehl des Zustimmungsgesetzes zu verorten: Gewiß, der unionsrechtliche Vorranganspruch liefe leer, wenn er nicht auf Anerkennung und Zustimmung seitens der nationalen Rechtsordnung stieße (noch haben die Mitgliedstaaten ihre Letztverantwortlichkeit für das in ihrem Rechtskreis geltende Recht bewahrt); Vorrangregel und Anerkennung des Vorranganspruchs müssen aber unterschieden werden.

Man geht gemeinhin davon aus, dass sich im Vorrang des Unionsrechts vor dem mitgliedstaatlichen Recht keine Normenhierarchie auspräge, sondern lediglich eine Kollisionsregel, die das Zusammenspiel zweier aus unterschiedlicher Quelle stammender Rechtsordnungen ordne.[291] Das Prinzip des Anwendungsvorrangs impliziert danach kein normenhierarchisches Über-Unterordnungsverhältnis von europäischem und nationalem Recht. Für den europäischen Verfassungsverbund sei es vielmehr gerade charakteristisch, dass er nicht hierarchisch strukturiert sei[292]. Dies gilt auch für jene Beobachter, die den Integrationsverbund mit dem Bild des „Mehrebenensystem" zu erklären versuchen. Franz Mayer meint beispielsweise, das Bild von unterschiedlichen Ebenen im Mehrebenenmodell sei „nicht zwingend" mit der Vorstellung von Über- und Unterordnung verbunden. So seien Mehrebenenmodelle dahingehend vorstellbar, dass die Ebenen, etwa als Plattformen, nebeneinander in gleicher Höhe stehen könnten. Denkbar seien auch Modelle von Zentrum und Peripherie, Pyramidenmodelle, „Marmorkuchenmodelle“ in Abgrenzung zum Schichtenkuchenmodell usw[293]. Wer der Auffassung ist, dass EU-Recht und nationales Recht heute nur noch Teilbestandteile einer gemeinsamen Rechtsordnung sind, wird darüber hinaus postulieren, dass die nationalen Rechtsordnungen und die europäische Rechtsordnung in eine wechselseitige Auffangordnung ohne Hierarchiestufen *eingebettet* seien, aus der heraus sich sowohl ein Recht des EuGH als auch ein solches des BVerfG ergebe, im Fall eines „Notstands“ einzugreifen.[294] Dieses Verständnis entspricht auf den ersten Blick dem „Kooperationsverhältnis“ zwischen BVerfG und EuGH[295].

Auch wenn man in konstruktiver Hinsicht von einer Gleichordnung ausgeht, wird man doch einräumen, dass es „kaum vorstellbar“ und im übrigen „juristisch auch schwer nachzuvollziehen“ ist, dass ein Gericht eines Mitgliedstaates einen echten Konflikt mit dem EuGH „heraufbeschwöre und die dadurch verursachte Rechtsunsicherheit in Kauf“ nimmt, um dadurch auf die Rechtsprechung des EuGH Einfluss zu nehmen[296]. Faktisch drückt sich darin ein ausgeprägtes Merkmal der Unterordnung aus. Vor diesem Hintergrund sieht sich die oben geschilderte These verstärktem Rechtsfertigungsdruck ausgesetzt. *Ingolf Pernice* nennt insoweit als Grund die „übergeordnete Stellung der Mitgliedstaaten als „Gesetzgeber“ der ihnen wieder „hierarchisch übergeordneten“ Normen“[297]. Allerdings sind die Mitgliedstaaten *nicht alleine*, sondern allenfalls gemeinsam europäischer Gesetz- oder Verfassungsgeber[298]. Eine nationale Verfassungsnorm, die mit einer vorrangigen gemeinschaftsrechtlichen Norm kollidiert, ist aber in aller Regel eine Norm, die sich der betreffende Mitgliedstaat *allein* und völlig autonom gegeben hat. Könnte diese Norm die Behauptung des Anwendungsvorrangs der europäischen Norm „neutralisieren“, dann wäre die gemeineuropäische Verfassungsstabilität aufgehoben[299]. Es können daher nur viele, je nach Verfahrenserfordernis gegebenenfalls nur alle Mitgliedstaaten *gemeinsam* und nur unter Einhaltung des jeweils einschlägigen Verfahrens als Gesetzgeber die Vorrangwirkung einer europäischen Norm aufheben. Wenn dem aber so ist, dann erweist sich das Argument, der Anwendungsvorrang der europäischen Normen begründe *kein hierarchisches System* gemeineuropäischen Verfassungsrechts, *weil* die Mitgliedstaaten sozusagen als Herren der Verträge über den Verträgen stünden, als problematisch[300].

Auch der Hinweis auf ein „Notstandsrecht“ und eine „Notkompetenz“ (nicht zuletzt des BVerfG[301]) hilft in diesem Zusammenhang nicht weiter. Die damit angesprochene Kompetenz hat keine Verankerung im Recht des Verfassungsverbands: Der EU-Vorrangsanspruch gilt unbedingt und ausnahmslos. Es mag ja löblich sein, wenn das BVerfG in diesem Zusammenhang von „Kooperationsverhältnis“ spricht - letztlich macht es dabei aber die Rechnung ohne den Wirt, nämlich den EuGH, der den Vorrang europäischer Normen unabhängig davon einfordern wird, ob nationale Verfassungsgerichte und damit einzelne Mitgliedstaaten im Einzelfall kooperieren *wollen* oder nicht[302]. Übte das BVerfG seine Kompetenz zur Prüfung nach nationalem Recht aus und stellte es einen Verstoß durch das Unionsrecht gegen nationales Rechts entgegen dem EuGH fest, würde es dem Anwendungsvorranganspruch des EU-Rechts widersprechen; dieses Vorgehen wäre nicht Bestätigung des Vorranganspruchs, sondern eine Revolte gegen ihn. Der Umstand aber, dass nationale Gerichte versuchen können, in einem Mehrebenensystem zu revoltieren, kann kaum als Grund für den nicht-hierarchischen Aufbau des Rechtssystems angesehen werden. Dies heisst nicht, dass der EuGH sich nicht an der Rechtsprechung des BVerfG orientieren könnte und in diesem Sinne ein Kooperationsverhältnis entstehen könnte[303]; es heisst lediglich, dass das gegenseitige Verhältnis durch das faktische Entstehen hierarchischer Strukturen geprägt ist[304].

Gegen den Versuch einer Hierarchisierung wird auch eingewandt: „Wer dieses System des Ausgleichs und der Zusammenarbeit in eine Hierarchie umdeutet, verschließt den in der europäischen Integration angelegten Weg zu einer Gewaltenbalance innerhalb der Gerichtsbarkeit.“[305]. Hiergegen ist allerdings geltend zu machen, dass sich eine Gewaltenbalance auch im normenhierarchischen System einstellen kann. *Tatsächliche* Gewaltenbalance steht nicht notwendigerweise im Widerspruch zur *normativen* Annahme einer Rechtsnormenhierarchie. Intellektueller Wettbewerb als Such- und Findungsverfahren ist auch zwischen solchen Richtern nicht ausgeschlossen, die in einem institutionell gewachsenen System der Über- und Unterordnung stehen. Wird dies aktuell nicht deutlich, so liegt dies allein darin, dass die Gerichte, insbesondere das BVerfG, sich jedenfalls nach den Entscheidungs*ergebnissen* in diese Hierarchie weitgehend (und mit guten Gründen) eingefunden haben. Gerade dies ist Ausdruck des „Kooperationsverhältnisses“ [306]. Bräche das BVerfG aus, würde sich dies jedoch ändern. Das Verhältnis zwischen den Gerichten verlöre (gegebenenfalls nur vorübergehend) seine hierarchische Struktur, bis sich eine neue de facto-hierarchische Struktur gefunden hätte. Dass der EuGH sich insoweit unterordnete, erscheint in diesem Zusammenhang allerdings weder wahrscheinlich noch wünschenswert.

Insofern gibt es bereits heute gute Gründe für die Annahme, dass sich EU-Recht und nationales Recht in einem hierarchischen Verhältnis befinden: Anwendungsvorrang der Normen (Supremacy) impliziert eine Hierarchie im Normensystem (Hierarchy);[307] aus EU-verfassungsrechtlicher Sicht kann der umfassende Vorranganspruch nur dahingehend rekonstruiert werden, dass er auf ein hierarchisches Verhältnis hinausläuft. Dass die hierarchisch einander zugeordneten Rechtsnormen aus verschiedener Quelle stammen, steht der Anwendung des Hierarchiekonzepts nicht entgegen. Normenhierarchie bedeutet nicht zwingend, dass die eine Norm ihre Geltung der anderen verdankt.[308] Ebensowenig steht der Annahme einer Hierarchie entgegen, dass es aus Sicht der nationalen Verfassungsgerichte weiterhin gute (national-verfassungsrechtliche) Gründe dafür gibt, im Einzelfall dem Anwendungsanspruch einer Norm des EU-Rechts unter Hinweis auf eine (ihrerseits Vorrang beanspruchende) Norm des nationalen Verfassungsrechts zu widersprechen. Dies bezeugt nur, dass sich EuGH und nationale Verfassungsgerichte in einem Grenzbereich in der Einschätzung der Vorrangregeln nicht einig sind und so zu Unterschieden in der Beurteilung des hierarchischen Verhältnisses kommen. Rechtlich nicht zu bewältigender Streit über die Ordnung der Hierarchie schließt es aber nicht aus, das Konzept der Hierarchie zu verwenden und festzuhalten, dass jedenfalls im Hinblick auf die übergroße Mehrzahl der möglichen Konfliktfälle Einigkeit über den (hierarchischen) Vorrang des EU-Rechts besteht. Nach Auffassung des Berichterstatters hat das Recht des Integrationsverbundes den Umschlag in eine Hierarchie inzwischen vollzogen.

b. *Implizite Modifikation des deutschen Grundgesetzes durch die Revision und Anwendung des Vertrages über die Europäische Union (EUV)*

Unter der Anwendung vorrangigen Unionsrechts wandelt sich das deutsche Recht[309]. Dies gilt natürlich auch für das deutsche Grundgesetz. Dabei sind verschiedene Wandlungsebenen zu unterscheiden. Die sichtbarsten Änderungen sind solche, die zu einer Veränderung des Verfassungstextes führen. Derartige Anpassungen können darauf zurückzuführen sein, dass das Primärrecht im Wege der Vertragsänderung fortgeschrieben wird. Fälle solch expliziter Grundgesetzanpassungen im Zuge der Fortentwicklung des Integrationsprozesses sind vor allem die zum Maastrichtvertrag ergangenen Änderungen[310], also vor allem die Regeln des Art. 23 GG (Beteiligung der Bundesrepublik Deutschland in der Europäischen Union)[311], die des Art. 28 Abs. 1 S. 3 GG (Kommunalwahlrecht für EU-Bürger)[312] und des Art. 88 Abs. 2 GG (Währungswesen)[313]. Diese Änderungen wurden in der Literatur zum Teil scharf kritisiert: Dem deutschen verfassungsändernden Gesetzgeber habe das Recht, eine vom Grundgesetz geforderte wirklich freie Entscheidung zu fällen, nicht wirklich offen gestanden; er habe unter erheblichem europäischem Druck nur noch ein „unfreies Ja“ ausrufen können[314]. Andere wenden (zu Unrecht) ein, diese Änderungen seien zum Teil schon deshalb grundgesetzwidrig, weil es der Sache nach

Verfassungsschöpfungen, nicht Verfassungsänderungen gewesen seien, denen das Volk als pouvoir constituant hätte zustimmen müssen[315]. Ungeachtet dieser Kritik bleibt doch aber festzuhalten, dass es immerhin der deutsche verfassungsändernde Gesetzgeber war, der die neuen Regeln ausdrücklich nach den dafür bestimmten Verfahrensvorschriften beschlossen hat.

Es sind aber nicht nur Vertragsänderungen, die sich in Änderungen des deutschen Grundgesetzes niederschlagen. Teilweise hat auch die Rechtsprechung des EuGH den verfassungsändernden Gesetzgeber dazu veranlaßt, das Grundgesetz zu ändern. Rechtlich notwendig wäre dies nicht; der Vorrang des EU-Rechts würde konfligierende Verfassungsbestimmungen überspielen. Nicht zuletzt aus Gründen der „Verfassungsästhetik" empfielt es sich aber, die Bestimmungen des Grundgesetzes im Einklang mit den Vorgaben des EU-Rechts zu halten. In solchen Fällen ist eine nachträgliche Grundgesetzänderung nicht mehr Ausdruck des freien Willens des Verfassungsgebers, sondern nur noch Ausdruck der Akzeptanz der Rechtsprechung des EuGH[316]. Als Beispiel hierfür ist aus jüngerer Zeit vor allem der Streit um den Zugang von Frauen zum Dienst mit der Waffe in der Bundeswehr zu nennen. In der Sache ging es um die Frage, ob Art. 12a Abs. 4 GG („[Frauen] dürfen auf keinen Fall Dienst mit der Waffe leisten.") sowie die entsprechenden Regelungen des § 1 II Soldatengesetz (SG) und des § 3 a Soldatenlaufbahnverordnung (SLV) gegen Art. 2 Abs. 2 RL 76/207/EWG zur Verwirklichung des Grundsatzes der Gleichbehandlung von Männern und Frauen vestoßen. Der EuGH bejahte in seiner Entscheidung[317] diese Frage, nachdem er zuvor darauf hingewiesen hatte, dass es zwar Sache der Mitgliedstaaten sei, die geeigneten Maßnahmen zur Gewährleistung ihrer inneren und äußeren Sicherheit zu ergreifen, dass dies allerdings derartige Maßnahmen nicht vollständig der Anwendung des Unionsrechts entziehe (Rz. 15 ff.). Mit Gesetz vom 19. Dezember 2000, für das gerade eine (!) Lesung erforderlich war, erhielt Art. 12a Abs. 4 S. 2 GG daraufhin folgende Fassung: „[Frauen] dürfen auf keinen Fall zum Dienst mit der Waffe verpflichtet werden"[318]. Nicht immer hat sich der verfassungsändernde Gesetzgeber zu einem derartigen Schritt entschlossen: Die unter dem Einfluß des Art. 39 Abs. 4 EGV[319] erfolgte Öffnung des Beamtentums für EU-Bürger etwa findet bislang im Grundgesetz keinen ausdrücklichen Niederschlag. In der Bewertung der EU-rechtlich erzwungenen Verfassungsänderungen ist man sich uneins: Teilweise spricht man davon, die in dieser Form erfolgende Europäisisierung der deutschen Verfassung bedeute „einen Verlust an substantieller Einheit."[320] Vieles spricht allerdings dafür, in der EU-rechtlich induzierten Anpassung überholter Regelungen an gewandelte gesellschaftliche Selbstverständnisse einen Gewinn an gesellschaftlicher Einheit zu erblicken. Vor dem Hintergrund von Art. 6 Abs. 3 EUV ist ausgeschlossen, dass sich das EU-Recht in einen Bereich begibt, in dem es die Zerstörung substanzieller gesellschaftlicher Einheit bewirken wird.

Das Grundgesetz läßt implizite Änderungen seiner Bestimmungen nicht zu (Art. 79 Abs. 1 GG). Im Zuge der Entstehung des europäischen Verfassungsverbunds hat die vom Grundgesetz errichtete Ordnung allerdings erhebliche Verändungen erfahren. Stille Veränderungen treten nicht nur dadurch ein, dass Kompetenzverlagerungen nach oben stattfinden und so die bestehenden Zuständigkeiten und Verfahren entwertet werden. Wo grundgesetzliche Regeln im Zuge der Integration angesichts der Autorität der Vorrangrechtsprechung des EuGH unanwendbar werden oder mittels gemeinschaftsrechtskonformer Auslegung einen anderen Gehalt annehmen, nimmt die von diesen Regeln errichtete Ordnung eine neue Form an – und zwar ohne explizite Zustimmung des deutschen verfassungsändernden Gesetzgebers. Die durch den Vertrag von Amsterdam eingeführten Regelungen haben in diesem Zusammenhang hohen Wandlungsdruck entfaltet. Man denke nur etwa an die Vergemeinschaftung des Zuwanderungs- und Asylrechts (Art. 61 ff EGV) und deren Einfluss auf Gehalt und Anwendbarkeit des Art. 16a Abs. 1 GG[321]. Nicht ohne Grund wurde schon davon gesprochen, diese Vergemeinschaftung könne zu einer völligen „Umverteilung einer zentralen Rechtsprechungskompetenz vom BVerfG zum EuGH“ führen[322]. Was dies für die Auslegung des Art. 16a GG heißen wird, kann man bislang nur erahnen. Ein weiteres Beispiel ist die neue Antidikriminierungskompetenz im Vertrag von Amsterdam (Art. 13 EGV)[323] und das auf dieser Grundlage erlassene sogenannte „Antidiskriminierungspaket“[324], dessen Vorschriften für die Auslegung und Anwendung des Art. 3 GG unmittelbar relevant werden können. Man denke insoweit nur etwa an den Diskriminierungsbegriff nach Art. 2 der RL 2000/43/EG oder an die positiven Maßnahmen nach Art. 5 dieser Richtlinie[325]. Schon aus Platzgründen ist es nicht möglich, einen auch nur annähernd vollständigen Überblick über die Bereiche zu geben, in denen die grundgesetzliche Ordnung derartigem Wandlungsdruck ausgesetzt ist.

4. Institutionelle Interdependenz: Europäische Funktionen deutscher Institutionen

Institutionell, organisatorisch und zurechnungstechnisch hat der nunmehr fünfzigjährige Integrationsprozeß nichts daran geändert, dass die Träger deutscher Staatsgewalt weiterhin der deutschen Staats- und Rechtsordnung zuzurechnen sind. Insofern sind sie *nicht* zu europäischen Institutionen geworden. Dies ist deutlich herauszuheben, weil die gemeinhin leicht dahingesagte Rede von der Doppelstellung oder vom „Doppelmandat“ der nationalen Stellen die rechtlichen Zusammenhänge zu verunklaren droht. Richtig ist auf der anderen Seite aber auch, dass die nationalen Stellen ihre

Funktionen (in Gesetzgebung, in der vollziehenden Gewalt und in der Justiz[326]) in funktionaler Abhängigkeit von europäischer Hoheitsgewalt wahrnehmen. Die (Teil-)Rechtsordnungen beeinflussen sich wechselseitig so, dass die Ausübung politischer Herrschaft in ihrer Gesamtheit im Zeichen eines Funktionswandels steht, der auch den Kern nationaler Souveränität berührt[327]. Diese funktionale Abhängigkeit ist nicht in allen drei Bereichen gleichermaßen ausgeprägt. Vielmehr wandelt sich die Funktionswahrnehmung der deutschen Institutionen in aufgabenspezifischer Weise. Normatives Leitbild sind dabei die folgenden Prinzipien: das Prinzip der Rechtstreue, das nationale Stellen ebenso wie die EU-Organe dazu verpflichtet, das an sie gerichtete Recht auch zu beachten; das Prinzip der interinstitutionellen Kooperation, also vor allem der Kooperation der nationalen mit den europäischen Institutionen[328]; sowie das Prinzip des Respekts vor verbliebenen Entscheidungsspielräumen, das eng mit dem Subsidiaritätsprinzip verbunden ist. Im folgenden werden Teilaspekte dessen aus den Bereichen aller drei Gewalten herausgegriffen, zunächst für den der Gesetzgebung (a), sodann für den der Exekutive (b) und schließlich den der Judikative (c).

a. Der Bundestag im Prozeß europäischer Hoheitsausübung: Indirekte Legitimationsquelle und Verantwortlichkeit für die Umsetzung europäischen Rechts

Im Prozeß europäischer Hoheitsausübung kommt den nationalen Parlamenten eine wichtige Doppelfunktion zu: Sie nehmen zunächst weiterhin eine zentrale Rolle bei der Vermittlung demokratischer Legitimation ein. Noch immer steht im Prozeß der Vermittlung von Legitimation – vor allem über die Zustimmung zu den Verträgen und personelle Bestimmungsrechte – die Mitsprache und Kontrolle nationaler Parlamente im Vordergrund[329]. Das BVerfG streicht dies im Maastricht-Urteil deutlich hervor und betont, dass das Unionsrecht dem Demokratieprinzip des Grundgesetzes nicht zuletzt deshalb entspreche, weil ihm der deutsche Bundestag zugestimmt hat[330]. Angesichts des Umstandes, dass sich die Identität der europäischen Bürger weiterhin vor allem in nationalen Zusammenhängen definiert (dazu s.o. II 2), müssen repräsentative Organe, die diesem Verständnis eine Stimme verleihen können, weiterhin an entscheidender Stelle im Prozeß europäischer Hoheitsausübung mitwirken. Erst mit der Entstehung einer hinreichend verfestigten europäischen Identität ist ein Bedeutungsverlust der nationalen Organe (und damit der nationalen Parlamente) hinnehmbar. Im deutschen System der repräsentativen Demokratie heisst dies, dass auf die Vermittlung maßgeblicher Legitimation durch die Mitwirkung des Bundestages weiterhin nicht verzichtet werden kann. An allererster Stelle geschieht diese

Legitimationsvermittlung durch die jeweiligen Zustimmungsgesetze, die zur Entstehung und Änderung des unionalen Primärrechts, also als Teil des Vertragsänderungsverfahrens (vgl. Art. 48 Abs. 3 EUV), ergehen.

Legitimatorische Funktionen hat der deutsche Bundestag allerdings nicht nur im Zusammenhang mit der Zustimmung zur Änderung des unionalen Primärrechts. Er wirkt darüber hinaus insofern mit, als er Einfluß darauf nehmen kann, wer die Bundesrepublik im Rat vertritt (Vermittlung personeller Legitimation). Darüber hinaus steht dem Bundestag nach der grundgesetzlichen Ordnung (Art. 23 Abs. 2 S. 1 GG) die Möglichkeit der sachlich-inhaltlichen Mitsprache bei der Festlegung der deutschen Position und damit eine mittelbare sachlich-inhaltliche Beteiligung an der *Rechtsetzung* der Europäischen Union zu (Vermittlung sachlich-inhaltlicher Legitimation). Allerdings hat der Deutsche Bundestag hier nicht, wie in anderen Bereichen formaler Gesetzgebung[331], die Entscheidungsprärogative. Vielmehr werden die aus dem Demokratieprinzip fließenden Grundsätze über Rolle und Rang parlamentarischer Gesetzgebung (unter Einschluß von Vorrang und Vorbehalt des Gesetzes[332]) im Bereich der rechtssetzenden Tätigkeit der Europäischen Union in erheblichem Umfang überspielt[333]. Dem Grundsatz nach wird die deutsche Mitwirkung an europäischer Rechtsetzung als Form der Ausübung auswärtiger Gewalt angesehen, die in der rechtlichen Verantwortung der Bundesregierung liegt, soweit sie nicht, etwa nach Art. 59 Abs. 2 S. 1 und 24 Abs. 1 GG, dem Deutschen Bundestag übertragen ist[334]. Nur die Grundsatzfragen der auswärtigen Politik sind unter einen allgemeinen Parlamentsvorbehalt gestellt. Dazu aber gehört die Sekundärrechtssetzung grundsätzlich nicht[335]. Vor diesem Hintergrund werden die Mitwirkungsrechte, die dem Bundestag nach Art. 23 GG (über die allgemeinen Mitsprache- und Kontrollmöglichkeiten hinaus) gewährt werden, denn auch vorwiegend als Kompensation gedeutet, und zwar nicht nur hinsichtlich der Länderbeteiligung durch den Bundesrat, sondern gerade auch hinsichtlich der Beteiligung des Bundestages (vgl. allgemein dazu oben II 2 b).

Art. 23 Abs. 2 S. 2 GG verpflichtet die Bundesregierung allerdings lediglich dazu, den Bundestag „zum frühestmöglichen Zeitpunkt zu unterrichten“. Nach Art. 23 Abs. 3 GG hat die Bundesregierung dem Bundestag vor der Mitwirkung an Rechtssetzungsakten der Europäischen Union lediglich „Gelegenheit zur Stellungnahme“ zu geben (S. 1) und diese bei den Verhandlungen lediglich zu berücksichtigen (S. 2). *Verfassungsideell und politisch* läßt sich die Bestimmung deutscher Positionen im europäischen Rechtsetzungsprozeß, in Anlehnung an frühere Gedanken Friesenhahns[336], als kooperativer Prozeß verstehen; danach steht das Recht zur Bestimmung dieser Positionen Parlament und Regierung „zur gesamten Hand“ zu betrachten[337]. Dies kommt der Formulierung der Vorschrift des Art. 23 GG nahe. Die daran angelegte Pflicht der Bundesregierung zur „Berücksichtigung" der Stellungnahme des Bundestages läßt es nicht zu, der Stellungnahme *jede* rechtliche Bedeutung abzusprechen. Eine Verantwortung zur gesamten Hand begründet auf der einen Seite echte Kooperationspflichen, auf der anderen Seite läßt sie dem System aber genügend Flexibilität, um zwischen überwiegend technisch-regulierender europäischer Gesetzgebungstätigkeit und bedeutenderen Grundsatzentscheidungen zu unterscheiden. Die Reichweite der Beteiligungsrechte muß insoweit „fallweise" bestimmt werden, nicht im Sinne inhaltlicher Beliebigkeit, sondern vielmehr im Sinne einer zunehmend sich ausgestaltenden Kooperationspraxis am Maßstab vorhergehender Präzedenzfälle[338].

Verfassungsrechtlich sind die Mitwirkungsrechte des Deutschen Bundestages allerdings so schwach ausgestaltet, dass davon auszugehen ist, dass die Entscheidungsverantwortung für die Verhandlungsführung der deutschen Vertreter im Rat bei der Sekundärrechtssetzung allein bei der Bundesregierung, nicht bei dem Bundestag liegt. Die Bundesregierung ist dem Bundestag mit anderen Worten nicht rechtlich, sondern allein politisch verantwortlich[339]. Daran kann naturgemäß auch die Einrichtung des Bundestagsausschusses für die Angelegenheiten der Europäischen Union (Art. 45 GG) nichts ändern, ist dieser doch lediglich zur „Wahrnehmung" und damit in praktisch-politischer Hinsicht auch zur Effektivierung der Rechte des Bundestages gegenüber der Bundesregierung ermächtigt, nicht jedoch zur Ausweitung. Wie bescheiden allerdings die Kompensation zu Gunsten des Bundestages ausgefallen ist, zeigt sich vor allem darin, dass die zu berücksichtigenden „Stellungnahmen" als schlichte Parlamentsbeschlüsse keine Rechtsverbindlichkeit beanspruchen können[340]. Es wird daher auch diskutiert, ob der Bundestag zur Abhilfe seiner Ohnmacht trotz der Regelungen des Art. 23 Abs. 2 und 3 GG in Angelegenheiten von herausgehobener Bedeutung mittels eines förmlichen Mandatsgesetzes die Regelung des deutschen Verhandlungsbeitrags sozusagen an sich ziehen kann[341]. Angesichts der eindeutigen Regelungen des Art. 23 Abs. 2 und 3 GG scheint dies allerdings vom verfassungsändernden Gesetzgeber gerade nicht gewollt gewesen zu sein.

Auch eine bundestagsfreundliche, sich nahe an der Wortlautgrenze des Art. 23 Abs. 2 und 3 GG bewegende Auslegung wird nicht umhinkommen, festzustellen, dass dem europäischen Sekundärrechtssetzungsprozess durch die Beteiligung des Deutschen Bundestages in *sachlich-inhaltlicher Art* nur überaus schwache demokratische Legitimation vermittelt werden kann[342]. In der komplizierten Welt des integrierten Nationalstaates ist kaum davon auszugehen, dass eine Regierung gerade nur *deshalb* das Vertrauen des Bundestages verliert, weil sie einem Akt auf europäischer Ebene zugestimmt hat, der die Zustimmung der Bundestagsmehrheit nicht genießt. Die

Beschränkung des Deutschen Bundestages auf zu berücksichtigende Stellungnahmen ist umso schwerwiegender, weil der zweite maßgebliche Legitimationsstrang europäischer Sekundärrechtssetzung, die Mitentscheidung durch das Europäischen Parlament, zwar mittlerweile sehr viel stärker ausgeprägt ist, in zentralen Fragenbereichen aber immer noch wichtige Wünsche offen lässt[343]. Die Beschränkung muß zudem vor dem Hintergrund der sich immer weiter ausbreitenden Komitologie kritisch befragt werden.[344]

So ist der Bundestag denn auch vorwiegend bei der *Durchführung* des Unionsrechts befähigt, demokratische Legitimation in sachlich-inhaltlicher Sicht zu vermitteln. Dies gilt vor allem dort, wo ihm bei der Durchführung Entscheidungsspielräume zustehen. Dies ist regelmäßig etwa bei der Umsetzung von Richtlinien der Fall (Art. 249 Abs. 3 EGV).[345] Eine legitimationsvermittelnde Rolle spielt der Bundestag auch dort, wo ihm bei der Durchführung von EU-Recht eigene Entscheidungsfreiheit hinsichtlich der Form und des Mittels im Rahmen der Umsetzung nicht verbleibt[346]. Allein der Umstand, dass der Deutsche Bundestag die Entscheidung des europäischen Gesetzgebers anerkennt und durch Erlaß einer deutschen Durchführungsnorm bestätigt, wirkt legitimationsvermittelnd. Insofern wirkt diese Legitimationsvermittlung durchaus *europäisch*[347]. Indem der Deutsche Bundestag europäische Funktionen erfüllt, vermittelt er Legitimation sozusagen in die europäische Gesetzgebung hinein.

Die Feststellungen zur begrenzten Legitimationsvermittlung durch den Deutschen Bundestag sind allerdings im größeren Zusammenhang zu sehen. Das Demokratiedefizit in der Europäischen Union hat nicht nur spezifische , sondern durchaus auch unspezifische Züge, nämlich solche, die sowohl in der EU als auch in ihren Mitgliedstaaten, ja überhaupt im modernen Staat bestehen. Auf die unspezifischen Züge des Demokratiedefizits der EU (etwa Aufgabenkomplexität, gesellschaftliche Differenzierung, Werteverlust, Externalisierungstrend usw.) hat kürzlich *Gertrude Lübbe-Wolff* hingewiesen[348] und dabei deutlich gemacht, welche Schwierigkeiten auch ein nationales Parlament hat, diesem „Legitimationsschwund“ entgegenzuwirken[349]. Insoweit ordnen sich die normativen Beschränkungen des Art. 23 GG in faktische Zusammenhänge größeren Stils ein.[350]

b. Europäische Funktionen deutscher Verwaltungsbehörden: Ein Doppelmandat der Exekutive

Der Funktionswandel der deutschen Institutionen wird auch im Bereich der vollziehenden Gewalt wahrgenommen und gemeinhin unter dem Gesichtspunkt der „Europäisierung des Verwaltungsrechts“ diskutiert. Damit wird ein Prozeß beschrieben, der nicht nur zu einem Funktionswandel der nationalen Verwaltungsbehörden führt, sondern der auch tiefgreifende Wandlungen des jeweils anzuwendenden institutionellen Rechts sowie des Verfahrens- und des materiellen Verwaltungsrechts mit sich bringt.[351] Der Anpassungsdruck ist nicht auf den Bereich des postiven Rechts begrenzt, sondern macht sich auch im Bereich grundlegender Regelungsansätze und Ordnungsstrukturen[352] sowie auf der Ebene dogmatischer Figuren bemerkbar. Dieser Einfluss macht auch vor jenen Bereichen nicht halt, die außerhalb des Anwendungsbereichs des Unionsrechts liegen. Er durchdringt diese jedenfalls mittelbar insoweit, als sich unterschiedliche Regeln für vergleichbare Verwaltungsvorgänge nicht lange durchhalten lassen. *Friedrich Schoch* sprach schon 1995 in diesem Zusammenhang von einem „ungeahnte[n] faktische[n] Harmonisierungspotential" des EuGH[353] und verwies dabei auf die mittlerweile zum Allgemeinplatz gewordenen Problemfelder der Überlagerung des allgemeinen deutschen Verwaltungsrechts durch das Europarecht[354]. Die Probleme der Europäisierung bestehen in der Sache noch heute, jedoch klären und verfestigen sich ihre Konturen[355]. Es treten allerdings auch immer wieder neue Probleme drängend hinzu[356].

Neben diese tiefgreifende Europäisierung der nationalen Rechtsordnung „von oben" rückt die *horizontale Verwaltungskooperation* zwischen den Mitgliedstaaten zunehmend in den Mittelpunkt des Interesses[357]. Zu denken ist etwa im Bereich des Umweltrechts an den Aufbau europaweiter Verbundgebiete nach den FFH-Richtlinien, im Bereich des Infrastrukturrechts an die Planungsanforderungen für die Schaffung transeuropäischer Netze[358] oder im Bereich des Sicherheits- und Ordnungsrechts an den in Amsterdam beschlossenen Aufbau des „Raums der Freiheit, der Sicherheit und des Rechts"[359] und die polizeiliche und justizielle Zusammenarbeit in Strafsachen unter Titel VI des EUV[360]. Dogmatisch schlägt sich die zur Wahrnehmung der neuen Aufgaben erforderliche horizontale Verwaltungskooperation in völlig neuen Kreationen wie etwa dem sog. „transnationalen Verwaltungsakt"[361] nieder. Wegen des überwiegend dezentralen Vollzugs europäischen Rechts kommt der Verwaltungskooperation eine nicht unerhebliche integrationstheoretische Bedeutung zu. Die stetig steigende horizontale Verschränkung der (weiterhin institutionell der nationalen Ordnung zuzurechnenden) Verwaltungsapparate bewirkt neben der bisher überwiegend diskutierten „Öffnung nach oben" eine zunehmende mitgliedstaatliche „Öffnung zur Seite"[362]: Neben die vertikale Integration tritt dadurch, gleichsam als zweites Strukturelement des europäischen Integrationsprozesses, eine immer stärker werdende Horizontalintegration der Mitgliedstaaten. Das entstehende horizontale Integrationsrecht findet sein Spezifikum darin, dass es zwar kein typisches supranationales Unionsrecht bildet, gleichwohl aber dem - wenn auch überwiegend intergouvernementalen – Europarecht verhaftet bleibt und damit dem klassischen Völkerrecht nicht mehr ohne weiteres zuzurechnen ist (vgl. etwa die Vorschriften über die polizeiliche und justizielle Zusammenarbeit in Strafsachen des Titel VI des EUV).

Der Blick auf die Gesamtheit von nationalem und europäischem Verwaltungsrecht macht in diesem Zusammenhang deutlich, dass zur Entwicklung eines kohärenten Systems dogmatische Überlegungen allein nicht mehr ausreichen. Nationales und europäisches Verwaltungsrecht scheinen in dieser Sicht mittlerweile in eine neue „Phase der Strukturbildung" getreten zu sein, die die „Europäisierungsphase" zwar nicht ablöst, wohl aber überlagert und durchdringt[363]. Mittlerweile wird daher verstärkt über eine übergreifende rechtliche Systembildung in diesem Bereich nachgedacht[364].

c. Rechtsschutz in der Europäischen Union durch nationale Gerichte: Loyalitätskonflikte und Fragen der Verfahrensautonomie

Die Fragen der Europäisierung stellen sich nicht nur im Bereich nationalen Verwaltungsrechts, sondern auch (und vor dem Hintergrund von Art. 234 EGV vielleicht sogar mit besonderer Intensität) in dem der Gerichtsbarkeit. Nicht nur haben die deutschen Gerichte deutsches Recht anzuwenden, das in Umsetzung europäischer Vorgaben entstanden ist. Auch haben sie europäisches Recht anzuwenden, soweit dieses unmittelbare Anwendbarkeit beansprucht und somit im Konfliktfall nationalem Recht vorrangig ist (dazu oben III 3). Der nationale Rechtsanwender hat nationales Recht nicht nur verfassungskonform[365], sondern auch unionsrechtskonform auszulegen, wenn ihm die rechtliche Norm einen Auslegungsspielraum beläßt. In der Rechtsprechung des EuGH sind Fälle nachweisbar, in denen das nationale Gericht nicht nur eine Pflicht zur unionsrechtskonformen *Auslegung* nationalen Rechts traf, sondern eine Pflicht zur europarechtsinduzierten *Fortbildung* nationalen Rechts. Die Konsequenzen dieser Rechtsprechung für den Gewaltenteilungsgrundsatz sind an anderer Stelle erörtert worden[366].

Im Prozess der europäischen Rechtsvereinheitlichung stößt der nationale Richter auf eine Fülle von Problemen, die sich spezifisch aus dem Ineinandergreifen der beiden Rechtsordnungen ergeben[367]. So erzeugen die konkurrierenden Rechtsauffassungen von BVerfG und EuGH im Hinblick auf das Vorrangsprinzip für die Organe der Fachgerichtsbarkeit einen Loyalitätskonflikt. Während das BVerfG grundsätzlich nur nach nationalem Recht entscheidet (Art. 93 GG), übt der EuGH seinen Rechtsprechungsauftrag allein auf dem Gebiet des Unionsrechts aus (vgl. Art 46 EUV, 220 EGV, 136 EAG und 31 EGKS). Für den nationalen Richter stellt sich bei divergierender Rechtsprechung von EuGH und BVerfG die Frage, ob er dem EuGH nach Art. 234 EGV oder dem BVerfG nach Art. 100 GG vorzulegen hat. Die Brisanz dieser Frage zeigt sich vor allem in jenen Fällen, in denen erst der EuGH und dann das BVerfG hintereinander in derselben (!) Sache befasst waren, selbst wenn es im Ergebnis nicht zu einem Konflikt gekommen ist[368]. Weitere Konfliktlagen können entstehen, wenn sonstige Obergerichte ihre Rechtsprechung in Widerspruch zum EuGH und damit letztlich unter Verstoß gegen Art. 10 EGV vorantreiben.

Problemfelder und Anpassungsdruck sind natürlich auch bereichsspezifisch nachweisbar. Dies gilt zunächst und vor allem für den Bereich des Verwaltungsprozesses. Neben der Europäisierung des materiellen Verwaltungsrechts (II 4 b) ist für den nationalen Verwaltungsrichter die Europäisierung des Prozessrechts inzwischen deutlich spürbar[369]; dieser Prozeß wird von der deutschen Rechtswissenschaft mit großer Aufmerksamkeit verfolgt. Ähnlich wie im materiellen Verwaltungsverfahrensrecht entstehen Konflikte zwischen europäischem und nationalem Recht hier regelmäßig dadurch, dass der Regelungsanspruch des EU-Rechts in den Bereich der justiziellen Durchsetzung (Stichwort: einheitliche Wirksamkeit des EU-Rechts) hineinreicht, dort aber auf den (auch unionsrechtlich als Ausfluss des Subsidiaritätsprinzips garantierten) Grundsatz der mitgliedstaatlichen Verfahrensautonomie[370] stößt. Bislang setzt das EU-Recht der mitgliedstaatlichen Autonomie vor allem negativ definierte Grenzen der Verfahrensautonomie[371]. Sie liegen bekanntlich im Diskriminierungs[372]- und Vereitelungsverbot[373]. In Deutschland liegen die Problemfelder vor allem im Bereich der Klagebefugnis[374], der gerichtlichen Kontrolldichte[375] und dem einstweiligen Rechtsschutz[376]. Vor dem Hintergrund der expansiven Rechtsprechung des EuGH kann jedenfalls in diesen Bereichen mittlerweile von einer grundlegenden Neuorientierung des deutschen Verwaltungsprozeßrechts gesprochen werden[377].

Die Europäisierung der Gerichtsbarkeit macht sich daneben auch im Bereich des Privatrechts bemerkbar, hat doch besonders die europäische Privatrechtsvereinheitlichung in den letzten Jahren ungeahnte Ausmaße angenommen[378]. Schon lange geht es nicht mehr nur um die Vereinheitlichung regulatorischen Wirtschaftsrechts. Vielmehr dringt die Rechtsvereinheitlichung mittlerweile in den Kernbereich der nationalen Privatrechtsordnungen vor. Zu denken ist in diesem Zusammenhang vor allem an die Fülle von Richtlinien zum Verbraucherschutz[379] oder allgemein zum Schutz von Teilnehmern im Privatrechtsverkehr[380]. Das gesetzte Sekundärrecht hat der nationale Richter nach dem Ablauf der Umsetzungsfristen seinen Entscheidungen in den gerade genannten Konstellationen mittlerweile genauso selbstverständlich zugrundezulegen wie die allgemeinen Regeln des BGB oder des HGB mit ihren jeweiligen Nebengesetzen. Dabei steht der nationale Richter in einem engen Dialog mit dem EuGH[381]. Es kann daher nicht nur gesagt werden, dass der nationale Zivilrichter mittlerweile zu einem guten Teil auch europäischer

Richter ist, sondern auch, dass der EuGH mittlerweile zu einem guten Teil auch europäischer Zivilrichter geworden ist[382].

Neben den genannten Bereichen europäisiert sich in Ansätzen auch das Strafrecht, obgleich in diesem Bereich die Europäisierung bislang (noch) vor allem unter dem Einfluß der Strassburger Rechtsprechungsorgane steht (vgl. etwa Art. 5 und 6 EMRK) [383].

Zusammenfassend läßt sich feststellen, dass die Europäisierung in alle Bereiche der Rechtsprechung tief vorgedrungen ist. Die beschriebenen Phänomene der Europäisierung stehen allerdings erst an ihrem Anfang. Wie weitgehend die Perspektiven sind, wird etwa deutlich in der Forderung nach einem europäischen „Gemeinrecht der Methode“, also nach einer Vereinheitlichung privatrechtlicher Methodik[384]. In diesen Zusammenhang steht etwa auch der Beschluss des Europäischen Rates von Tampere, in dem es unter Punkt 39 heißt: „Im Bereich des materiellen Zivilrechts bedarf es einer allgemeinen Studie über die Frage, ob zur Beseitigung von Hindernissen für das reibungslose Funktionieren von zivilrechtlichen Verfahren die zivilrechtlichen Vorschriften der Mitgliedstaaten angeglichen werden müssen“. Damit ist der Gedanke eines europäischen Privatgesetzbuches[385] in Ansätzen bis in die europäischen Institutionen vorgedrungen[386]. Hier erschließt sich ein Änderungspotenzial großen Ausmaßes für die Tätigkeit deutscher Richter, zumal die Überlegungen langfristig nicht auf das Zivilrecht beschränkt bleiben dürften.

IV. DIE ROLLE DER DEUTSCHEN REGIONEN, LÄNDER UND GEMEINDEN UND DAS RECHT DER EU

Die Union wirft Grundfragen föderaler Staatenverbindungen auf. Die gilt nicht nur im Verhältnis zwischen den Mitgliedstaaten und der Union, sondern vor allem auch innerhalb der Mitgliedstaaten, jedenfalls dann, wenn sie, wie die Bundesrepublik Deutschland, föderal organisiert sind. Die Bundesrepublik Deutschland steht insoweit vor ganz besonderen Herausforderungen: Unter dem Einfluss der europäischen Integration kommt es zu tiefgreifenden Strukturveränderungen und einem weitgehenden Funktionswandel im System des deutschen Föderalismus. Der Integrationsverbund hat sich jedenfalls im Hinblick auf die bundesstaatlich organisierten Mitgliedstaaten zu einer drei- oder gar vierstufigen Föderation entwickelt. Hierin liegt jedoch nicht notwendig eine Aufhebung oder gar Zerstörung des deutschen Föderalismus. Es muß darum gehen, normative Grundprinzipien zu entwickeln, mit denen die gegenseitige Verschränkung, Überlagerung und - möge man es so nennen - „Verformung“ [387] der jeweiligen Ebenen geordnet und in ein angemessenes Verhältnis gebracht werden können.[388] Dies kann nur gelingen, wenn die untergeordneten Ebenen

(Bund, Länder, Gemeinden) die Funktionsnotwendigkeiten der europäischen Integration respektieren. Es setzt aber auch voraus, dass die übergeordnete Ebene (Union) Respekt vor den föderalen Gegebenheiten in den Mitgliedstaaten zeigt. Die EU darf nicht „landesblind" sein![389] Sie muß die wesentlichen Gehalte des mitgliedstaatlichen Föderalismus zur Kenntnis nehmen und im Rahmen des ihr Möglichen schützen.

Dies ist bislang nur unzureichend geschehen. Noch sind es weiterhin nur die Mitgliedstaaten, die Ansprechpartner der EU sind und in den Organen der EU mitwirken. Diese den völkerrechtlichen Strukturen verhaftete Gegebenheit steht in merkwürdigem Gegensatz zu dem Umstand, dass das politische Geschehen im Integrationsverbund als Innenpolitik zu betrachten ist. Viel weniger als auf die nationale Gesetzgebung haben die Länder Einfluss auf das EU-Recht, weder mittelbar über das Grundgesetz (dazu oben II 2 b und IV 1), noch unmittelbar über das EU-Recht. Die Länder wirken im Ausschuss der Regionen (AdR) mit[390], der seinerseits maßgeblich auf Druck der Länder eingeführt worden ist[391]. Dies wird denn auch als großer Erfolg der Länder gesehen[392]. Allerdings hat der Ausschuß der Regionen nur äußerst geringe Befugnisse. Nach Art. 265 Abs. 1 EGV wird er vom Rat oder von der Kommission, soweit dies vorgeschrieben ist[393], „gehört". Er kann gehört werden, wenn es nicht vorgeschrieben ist. Echte Mitbestimmungsbefugnisse hat er nicht. Damit haben die Länder insgesamt einen geringen, wenngleich tendenziell leicht steigenden Einfluss[394]. Als Beispiel für den europapolitischen Erfolg der Länder wird allgemein etwa die Einfügung des Subsidiaritätsprinzips und die Einrichtung eigener Vertretungen in Brüssel genannt[395]. Als Beispiel für die Schwäche der Länder mag etwa die Zurückstellung der Länderbedenken bei der Grundrechtecharta dienen[396]. Interpretativ kann man der gegenwärtigen Schwäche der Länder nur begrenzt abhelfen: Art. 6 Abs. 3 EUV schützt zwar dem Wortlaut nach die *nationale* Identität der *Mitgliedstaaten*; in einem föderal organisierten Mitgliedstaat können hierzu aber auch regionale Vielfalt, regionale Verhaftung und regionale Identität gehören.

Im folgenden soll der wechselseitige Einfluss untersucht werden, zunächst mit Blick auf die unter dem Unionsrecht sich wandelnde verfassungsrechtliche Stellung der Regionen, Länder und Gemeinden (1.), sodann mit Blick auf den Einfluss der deutschen Länder auf das EU-Recht (2.).

1. Auswirkungen des EU-Rechts auf die verfassungsrechtliche Stellung der deutschen Regionen, Länder und Gemeinden

Die deutschen Länder haben unter dem Grundgesetz eine verfassungsrechtlich stark ausgeprägte Rolle. Sie hat ihre tragende Stütze in der Anerkennung der Staatlichkeit und Verfassungshoheit der Länder[397]. Dabei kommt dem Bund die Doppelfunktion als Gesamt- und als Teilstaat zu[398].

Dem Grundsatz nach, d.h. soweit nichts anderes bestimmt ist, ist die Ausübung der staatlichen Befugnisse Sache der Länder (Art. 30 GG), sowohl im Bereich der Gesetzgebung (Art. 70 GG)[399] als auch in den Bereichen der Verwaltung (Art. 83 GG)[400] und der Rechtsprechung (Art. 92 HS. 2 GG)[401]. Diese Strukturmerkmale finden sich auch in der Finanzverfassung (Art. 104 ff GG)[402]. Die föderale Ordnung hat Verfassungsrang (Art. 20 Abs. 1 GG) und ist im Grundsatz mit verfassungsmäßigen Mitteln nicht zu ändern (Art. 79 Abs. 3 GG). Sie wird durch den verfassungsrechtlich garantierten Grundsatz der kommunalen Selbstverwaltung (Art. 28 Abs. 2 GG) ergänzt.[403]

Die so im Grundgesetz angelegte Ordnung befindet sich in einer Krise. Die Entwicklungen, die den grundgesetzlichen Föderalismus in die Krise geführt haben, sind inzwischen vielfach beschrieben worden. Die Architektur des grundgesetzlichen Föderalismussystems ist in den fünfzig Jahren ihres Bestehens drei großen Verschiebungen ausgesetzt worden – jeweils zu Lasten der Eigenständigkeit und Eigenverantwortlichkeit der Länder. Zu beobachten war erstens ein enormer Schub der Kompetenzverlagerung weg von den Ländern und hin zum Bund. Dieser Schub wurde bereits Anfang der sechziger Jahre von *Konrad Hesse* diagnostiziert und mit dem Begriff der „Unitarisierung“ bezeichnet. Wo die Länder ihre Zuständigkeit behalten hatten, unterwarfen sie sich (zweitens) in mannigfacher Weise Kooperations- und Koordinationsmechanismen. In den Blick fallen dabei nicht nur die in Art. 91a abgesicherten Gemeinschaftsaufgaben und die in Art. 104a Abs. 4 GG vorgesehene Mischfinanzierung (vertikale Verflechtung). Auch zwischen den Ländern entstand ein in seiner Tragweite und Ausdehnung nur schwer zu überblickendes Kooperationsgeflecht (horizontale Verflechtung). Eine Entwertung bundesstaatlicher Strukturen erfolgte schließlich (drittens) im Zuge der europäischen Integration: Die Begründung europäischer Zuständigkeiten beschränkte sich nicht auf Bereiche, in denen nach grundgesetzlicher Rechtslage der Bund zuständig war. Der Ausbau der EU seit Anfang der neunziger Jahre brachte auch tiefe und weitgehende Einschnitte in die Kompetenzbasis der Länder mit sich. Die Länder werden sozusagen von der zweiten Ebene aktiver politischer Gestaltung in eine dritte Ebene „herunterverlagert“[404]. Ihre Existenz erodiert. [405]

Es ist ferner vielfach festgestellt worden, dass sich die Länder ihre Einbußen mit verfassungstechnischen Danaergeschenken haben abhandeln lassen: Mitspracherechte, die den Ländern unter Anwendung des Mehrheitsprinzips das Recht zur Mitbestimmung gewähren, können Eigengestaltung nicht ersetzen. Insofern bedeutete es keinen echten Ausgleich, wenn eine dem Bund eingeräumte Gesetzgebungskompetenzen nur mit Zustimmung des Bundesrates ausgeübt werden durfte. Auch die nach Art. 23 Abs. 3-7 GG eingeräumten Mitspracherechte, mit denen sich die Länder Einfluß auf die Position der Bundesrepublik in EU-Organen sicherten, konnten die Verluste nicht wirklich ausgleichen. Während der Bund für seine im Zuge der Integration zunehmend wahrgenommenen Kompetenzverluste durch eine umfassende Beteiligungsmöglichkeit im Rahmen der europäischen Sekundärrechtssetzung entschädigt wird, bleibt den Ländern keine echte Kompensation: Sie müssen sich mit ihrer nur mittelbaren Beteiligung im Ausschuss der Regionen und ihren Beteiligungsmöglichkeiten nach den Vorschriften des Art. 23 Abs. 2 und 4 bis 7 GG begnügen (dazu schon oben II 2 b). Die „überproporzionale[n] Integrationsopfer der Länder" wurden erst jüngst wieder etwa von Isensee mit folgenden Worten festgestellt: „[D]ie Europäisierung des Staates nach außen [führt] zu einer zusätzlichen Zentralisierung im Innern und zu einer weiteren Machtsteigerung des Bundes. Die Kompetenzminderung verläuft also asymmetrisch."[406]

Einen echten Ausgleich konnten diese Mitspracherechte auch deshalb nicht bewirken, weil sie von Seiten der Gubernative wahrgenommen werden. Der Tausch von Sachkompetenz und Mitspracherecht brachte so eine Marginalisierung der Bedeutung der Landesparlamente sowie eine Entparlamentarisierung der politischen Ordnung in den Ländern mit sich: Spielen die Landesparlamente bei eigenverantwortlicher Gestaltung durch Gesetz eine zentrale Rolle, so scheitern sie beim Versuch einer effektiven Kontrolle der (gubernativen) Ausübung von Mitspracherechten an Transparenzdefiziten[407], an klaren Verantwortungszusammenhängen und sowie an der Existenz mannigfachiger „Sachzwänge". Dass derartige Mitspracherechte aufgrund des Koordinationsbedarfs Ineffizienzen mit sich bringen, ist inzwischen auch Gemeingut. Ob in diesen Veränderungen ein Systemwechsel bzw. Typenübergang zu erblicken ist („Vom dualistisch-separativen Föderalismus zum unitarisch-kooperativen Föderalismus"), wird in der Verfassungswissenschaft unterschiedlich beurteilt. Selbst wenn man der Auffassung ist, dass der grundgesetzliche Föderalismus vor dem Hintergrund der verfassungsrechtlichen Absicherung von Kooperation und Mitsprache schon immer tendenziell kooperativ geprägt war, wird man die Bedeutung dieser Veränderungen nicht verkennen und die Frage nach Zweckmäßigkeit und Richtigkeit der Entwicklung formulieren. Über die Reform*bedürftigkeit* der föderalistischen Ordnung besteht kein Streit; parteiübergreifend ist man sich über die Notwendigkeit einer Reform im Grundsatz einig. Der Ruf nach einer „Revitalisierung bundesstaatlicher Ordnung"[408] ist weit verbreitet. Überlegungen zur Wiederbelebung föderalistischer Strukturen werden nicht nur in Kreisen der Politik und regierungsamtlicher Kommissionen angestellt;[409] auch in Kreisen der Wissenschaft hat man sich der Problematik angenommen und vielfältige Lösungsvorschläge unterbreitet. In der Folge des Urteils des BVerfG vom 11. November 1999 zum Länderfinanzausgleich[410] gewann die Forderung, die Neuordnung der Finanzbeziehungen von Bund und Ländern mit einer Gesamtrevision der föderalen Ordnung zu verbinden, an Prominenz.[411] Man ist sich dabei weitgehend einig, dass sich die gegenwärtigen Mißstände, die Verkrustungen und Defizite des grundgesetzlichen Föderalismus nur durch eine Neugewichtung der föderalen Grundprinzipien erreichen läßt: Gefordert sind eine Stärkung der *Eigenverantwortlichkeit* der Länder sowie eine Förderung der *Effizienz*, zurückzudrängen sind überzogene Erwartungen an *Solidarität* und *Gleichheit*. Wie das genau geschehen soll, ist allerdings unklar und Gegenstand einer lebhaften Diskussion.

Es sind aber nicht nur Strukturveränderungen des mitgliedstaatlichen Föderalismus, die im Zuge der Integration zu beobachten sind. Die Mitgliedschaft föderal gegliederter Staaten in der EU wirft teilweise auch spezifische Probleme auf, etwa im Rahmen des Vollzuges von EU-Recht. Hier ist unklar, wie weit die Aufsichtszuständigkeiten des Bundes bei der Durchführung von EU/EG-Recht gehen: Im Fall des mittelbaren Vollzugs, also insbesondere des Vollzugs umgesetzter Richtlinien, bleibt es bei den allgemeinen Regeln der Art. 83 ff. GG. Sie sind anwendbar, da es sich bei umgesetztem Unionsrecht der Sache nach um Bundesrecht handelt. Anders hingegen ist es im Fall des unmittelbaren Vollzugs von Unionsrecht durch die Landesbehörden. In diesem Fall sind nach bestrittener Auffassung die Art. 83 ff. und 37 GG analog anzuwenden, insbesondere auch die aufsichtsrechtlichen Vorschriften nach Art. 84 Abs. 2 bis 5 GG, da hier die Interessenlage dem Vollzug des Bundesrechts entspricht.[412] Probleme treten beispielsweise auch dann in Erscheinung, wenn es um die Verhängung von Zwangsgeldern nach Art. 228 Abs. 2 EGV geht[413]. Der Mitgliedstaat haftet nach dieser Vorschrift der EU, wenn er trotz eines zuvor durch den EuGH festgestellten Verstoßes nicht die erforderlichen Maßnahmen ergriffen hat. Ähnliche Haftungslagen ergeben sich in Fällen unionsrechtlicher Staatshaftung (nur eben gegenüber dem Einzelnen) und in Fällen, in denen Sanktionen aus Gründen mangelnder Haushaltsdisziplin nach Art. 104 Abs. 11 S. 1 Spiegelstrich 4 EGV (Geldbuße) verhängt werden[414]. In diesen Fällen haftet die Bundesrepublik Deutschland selbst dann, wenn ein Land den Verstoß, etwa die Nichtumsetzung einer Richtlinie oder die Schaffung eines Haushaltsdefizits, maßgeblich zu verantworten hat. Dann stellt sich innerstaatlich das Problem des Regresses des Bundes gegen das Land[415]. Angesichts der gegebenenfalls hohen Haftungsbeträge bedarf es einer klaren Regelung[416]. Für die Regresshaftung bei Verstoß gegen Unionsrecht gibt es bislang aber keine Haftungsvorschriften[417].

Die vorstehenden Beispielsfälle erheben keinen Anspruch auf Vollständigkeit. Sie dienen der Illustration der spezifischen Probleme, die sich ergeben, wenn Außenzuständigkeit im Verhältnis zur EU und interne Rechtsetzungs- oder Durchführungsbefugnis auseinanderfallen. Schon aus

Platzgründen ist eine Vertiefung der damit verbundenen Probleme hier nicht möglich.

2. *Konsequenzen gegenwärtiger Regionalisierung und Dezentralisierung in Deutschland für das Recht der EU*

Man ist sich weitgehend einig, dass in der Bundesrepublik Deutschland Tendenzen der Regionalisierung oder der Dezentralisierung nicht zu beobachten sind[418]. Im Gegenteil hat der Bund über die Jahrzehnte immer mehr Kompetenzen an sich gezogen; alle Versuche, diesen Prozeß aufzuhalten oder gar umzukehren, waren bislang erfolglos. Insofern ergeben sich hier keine Probleme.

V. DIE EUROPÄISCHE VERFASSUNG

Im Zuge der Entwicklung der Europäischen Union seit dem „Quantensprung von Maastricht" hat der Integrationsverbund (EU und Mitgliedstaaten) die Qualität einer konsoziativen Föderation gewonnen. Die EU hat in staatsgleicher Weise die Zuständigkeit für das gesellschaftliche Allgemeine übernommen – ohne allerdings Souveränität zu erlangen. Im Verbund haben sich Strukturen herausgebildet, die in ihrer Wirkweise und Art nur mit jenen einer Föderation verglichen werden können. In dem Verbund haben die Mitgliedstaaten allerdings eine so starke Stellung bewahrt, dass von einer konsoziativen Föderation zu sprechen ist; der Umschlag in eine bundesstaatliche Föderation ist kurzfristig nicht zu erwarten und normativ gegenwärtig auch nicht wünschenswert.

Es liegt auf der Hand, dass im Prozess der Entstehung der Föderation die Frage aufgetaucht ist, ob die gegenwärtige Verfasstheit des Verbunds den normativen Anforderungen entspricht. Dabei geht es sowohl um die Frage, ob Struktur und Inhalt des Primärrechts den Erfordernissen unionaler Verfasstheit entsprechen, als auch um die Frage, ob der Verfassungsbedarf des Verbunds (im Hinblick auf das Zusammenwirken von EU und Mitgliedstaaten und das Zusammenspiel von EU-Verfassung und nationalen Verfassungen) hinreichend befriedigt ist. Vor diesem Hintergrund stellt sich zunächst die Frage, ob eine formelle Bürger-Verfassung oder ein formeller Verfassungsvertrag für Europa sinnvoll ist und wie dieser aussehen soll (1.). Sodann ist zu klären, welches die tatsächlichen Bedingungen in Deutschland für einen europäischen Verfassungsgebungs- und -änderungsprozess sind (2.). Schließlich ist zu erörtern, in welcher Weise die Beitrittskandidaten am europäischen Verfassungsprozess sinnvoll zu beteiligen sind (3.).

1. *Eine neue Architektur: Wie sollte eine EU-Verfassung oder ein EU-Vertrag aussehen?*

Man ist sich in Deutschland inzwischen einig, dass die aktuelle Frage nicht mehr lautet: „Braucht Europa eine Verfassung?". Es geht heute vielmehr um die Frage: „Welche Verfassung braucht Europa?"[419] In der Suche nach Antworten diskutiert man zum einen problemorientierte Änderungsvorschläge (a), zum anderen geht es um die Frage, ob das vertragliche Primärrecht in eine formelle Vertragsverfassung oder gar eine Bürgerverfassung überführt werden soll (b).

a. Sachproblembezogene Reformschritte

Die vier konkreten Problembereiche, die der Europäische Rat von Nizza bezeichnet und zum Gegenstand des Arbeitsauftrags des Konvents zur Zukunft der Europäischen Union gemacht hat, stehen auch in der öffentlichen und wissenschaftlichen Diskussion in Deutschland im Zentrum[420].

Die zukünftige ***Rolle der nationalen Parlamente*** läßt sich vor allem unter dem Gesichtspunkt der Stärkung parlamentarischer Kontrolle diskutieren. Die Befürworter einer Verstärkung der Rolle nationaler Parlamente betonen, dass eine Situation wie die in Deutschland, wo dem Parlament nur geringe Mitwirkungsbefugnisse bei der Sekundärrechtssetzung zugewiesen sind (oben III 4 a), dem Anliegen hinreichender parlamentarisch vermittelter Legitimation europäischen Sekundärrechts abträglich ist. Es müsse die Chance ergriffen werden, im Rahmen der europaweiten Zukunftsdiskussion auch eine nationale Debatte über die Stärkung des Deutschen Bundestages in Angelegenheiten der Europäischen Union zu beginnen. Aus dieser Sicht liegt es nahe, die Beteiligungsrechte der nationalen Parlamente im Prozeß der Sekundärrechtssetzung europaweit zu vereinheitlichen. Ferner ist es danach denkbar, die Kooperation zwischen nationalen Parlamenten und Europaparlament, etwa durch gemeinsame Gremien, weiter zu institutionalisieren. In Betracht komme insbesondere eine stärkere Vernetzung der nationalen Parlamente, die über die bisherige Kooperation der Europaausschüsse der nationalen Parlamente (COSAC) hinausgeht. Möglich wäre dies etwa in der Form eines Kongresses[421], eines Senates oder einer zweiten Kammer mit Befugnissen, die eine Konkurenz zum Europäischen Parlament nicht entstehen lassen[422]. Teilweise will man auch die Stärkung der Rechte des Europäischen Parlamentes mit einer Stärkung der Rolle der nationalen Parlamente verbinden.[423] – Diesen Forderungen sind allerdings Einwände von erheblichem Gewicht entgegenzuhalten. Ein Wiederaufgreifen des Doppelmandats von einzelnen Mitgliedern des Bundestages und des Europäischen Parlamentes, wie

Fischer es gefordert hat, ist angesichts der Erfahrungen, die damit schon gemacht wurden (Arbeitsbelastung, Koordination), nicht sinnvoll. Zudem birgt es die Gefahr, die ohnehin schon starke Auffächerung des Europäischen Parlamentes[424] in nationale Abgeordnetengruppen noch weiter zu verstärken. Der Versuch, eine stärkere institutionelle Verzahnung zu erreichen, bringt Verantwortungsunklarheiten mit sich; der Versuch würde den Prozeß der europäischen Rechtsetzung noch komplizierter und mühsamer machen. Manches spricht daher dafür, die Parlamentarisierung des Rechtsetzungsprozesses der EU nicht durch vertikale Verflechtung, sondern durch horizontale Stärkung des Europäischen Parlaments zu suchen.

Eine Mehrheit der Beobachter in Deutschland fordert, der ***Grundrechtecharta*** den Status rechtsverbindlichen Rechts zuzuschreiben. Dem ist ungeachtet des Umstandes zuzustimmen, dass die Charta Schutzlücken enthält und Defizite aufweist (dazu oben III 2). Die Diskussion, ob man eine Grundrechtecharta wirklich braucht,[425] ist insofern überholt; man sollte nicht auf halben Wege stehen bleiben. Die Überführung in Rechtsverbindlichkeit mag zwar zu Abgrenzungsschwierigkeiten in der parallelen Anwendung von Grundrechtecharta und EMRK führen, diese sind jedoch nicht schwerwiegend. Sie führen auch nicht zu einer Senkung des Schutzniveaus. Da die Charta den europäischen Grundrechtsschutz zwar nicht maßgeblich voranbringt, ihm im wesentlichen aber eben auch nicht schadet, erscheint es daher besser, ihr nun, wo sie schon existiert, auch rechtliche Wirkung zu verleihen. Denn nichts wäre schädlicher für den Integrationsprozess als eine Grundrechtecharta, die vom Bürger als Ausdruck politischer Impotenz wahrgenommen würde. Eine nicht bindende Grundrechtecharta ist in ihrer (negativen) Symbolwirkung nicht zu unterschätzen[426]. Denkbar sind verschiedene Lösungen, der Grundrechtecharta rechtliche Wirkung zu verleihen: als selbständiger Primärrechtsquelle, als Bestandteil des EGV oder als Bestandteil des EUV, etwa im Anschluss an die Grundsätze der Art. 1 bis 7 EUV. Letztere Lösung würde den EUV stärker in Richtung auf ein formales Verfassungsdokument rücken[427], wird doch von einem solchen Dokument regelmäßig erwartet, dass es jedenfalls auch über einen Grundrechtskatalog verfügt.

Ein wichtiger Schritt zur Abhilfe wäre eine klarere ***vertikale Kompetenzabgrenzung*** im gegenwärtigen Verfassungsgefüge. Dabei geht es zum einen um die Problematik, ob sich mit einem Kompetenzkatalog ein Gewinn erzielen ließe. Eine Konkretisierung der Kompetenzbestimmung wird in Deutschland vielfach eingefordert[428]. So wurde etwa vorgeschlagen, für die Kompetenzverteilung primäre und partielle Regelungskompetenzen sowohl der Mitgliedstaaten als auch der EU anhand spezifischer Sachbereiche positiv zu bestimmen[429]. Diesem Vorschlag liegt eine bundesstaatsähnliche Auffassung von der Zuordnung von Kompetenzen an EU und Mitgliedstaaten zugrunde; es wären danach nicht mehr die *Mitglied*staaten, die der EU begrenzte Kompetenzen zuweisen, sondern die EU, deren Verfassung den (Mit-)*Glied*staaten eines bündisch geprägten Integrationsverbunds die Wahrnehmungszuständigkeiten vorbehielte. Eine andere mögliche Variante wäre die Trennung von Kompetenzen nach amerikanischem Vorbild, also die Trennung ganzer Sachbereiche ohne (im Querschnitt dazu stehender) Aufgliederung nach staatlichen Funktionen (Gesetzgebung, Vollzug, Rechtsprechung). Allerdings lässt sich auch ein solches System nicht ohne weiteres auf europäische Verhältnisse übertragen[430], hat die Union als gewachsene Entität mittlerweile doch fast wildwüchsig nach und nach unterschiedlichste Kompetenztypen in einem komplizierten und *funktional* geprägten Prozeß gewonnen. Zudem hat in den USA der Supreme Court seine Zuständigkeit zur Überprüfung von Bundeskompetenzen mittlerweile weitgehend abgegeben, so dass Kompetenzstreitigkeiten überwiegend dem politischen Prozess überlassen bleiben[431] - eine Eigenheit des amerikanischen Föderalismus, die der Europäischen Union mit den in ihr angelegten Traditionen sicher nicht angemessen wäre.

Es werden daher Forderungen nach einem den europäischen Traditionen entsprechenden und in diesem Sinne „nachvollziehbaren" Zuständigkeitsprofil laut[432]. Es wäre dies ein Profil, das zugleich die Zurechenbarkeit politischer Verantwortung verbessert, Machtanhäufung und Überforderung der Unionsorgane begrenzt und Entscheidungsmacht grundsätzlich dort ansiedelt, wo sie am effizientesten und mit der demokratisch stärksten Legitimation ausgeübt werden kann. Möglich erscheint dies vielen Beobachtern nur durch Schaffung eines Kompetenzkataloges[433]. Für die Erhaltung der gegenwärtigen konsoziativ-föderalen Struktur kann ein Kompetenzkatalog allerdings nur dann hilfreich sein, wenn er die Komplexität der gegenwärtigen Ordnung in sich aufnimmt. Selbst dann allerdings beseitigt auch ein Kompetenzkatalog weder die Schwierigkeiten der Abgrenzung noch - wie der deutsche Föderalismus zeigt - die Tendenz zur Zentralisierung. Der Versuch, die Kompetenzen in einem Katalog aufzulisten, fällt im Hinblick auf Bestimmtheit und Abgrenzungsschärfe leicht hinter die Kompetenzgebungstechnik zurück, die seit der Verhandlung von Maastricht üblich ist und zu zwar nicht schönen, aber in ihrer Reichweite doch klaren Verfassungsbestimmungen geführt hat (vgl. z.B. Art. 151 EGV). Zudem kann ein „zu strikter" Kompetenzkatalog die Entwicklungspotenziale der EU auf ihrem Weg zu einer „immer engeren Union der Völker Europas" (Art. 1 Abs. 2 EUV) einschränken. Als sinnvoller Ansatz könnte daher ein Kompetenzkatalog mit positiven Kompetenzzuweisungen und negativen Ausschlusstatbeständen sein, wie ihn *Jürgen Schwarze* vorgeschlagen hat[434]. Eine solche Regelungstechnik findet sich bereits in Ansätzen im Unionsrecht (vgl. z.B. Art. 137 Abs. 6 und 149 Abs. 1 EGV). Sie kombiniert ein Mehr an Flexibilität mit einem Mehr an Eindeutigkeit[435]. Der von *Schwarze* in diesem Zusammenhang vorgeschlagene Vermittlungs- oder Schlichtungsausschuss könnte - anders als der EuGH - neben rechtlichen auch sachliche Überlegungen einfließen lassen. Ob sich die Mitgliedstaaten hierauf allerdings einlassen würden, erscheint fraglich, ist es doch gerade die rechtlich strikte Handhabung des Subsidiaritätsprinzips, die ihnen, jedenfalls nach dem Tabakwerbe-Urteil des EuGH[436], die von ihnen gewollten Freiräume am sichersten zu erhalten scheint.

Im Kompetenzbereich geht es aber nicht nur um die Formulierung von Kompetenznormen. Es geht auch um die Frage, ob nicht bestimmte Kompetenzen, z.B. im Agrarbereich, an die Mitgliedstaaten zurückgegeben werden können. Schließlich geht es darum sicherzustellen, dass die bestehenden Kompetenzen nur dort wahrgenommen werden, wo dies auch sachlich angemessen ist. So sicher auch ist, dass sich die demokratische Legitimation EU-rechtlicher Rechtsetzung durch institutionelle Veränderungen erhöhen ließe (wie etwa die Vereinheitlichung des Wahlverfahrens zum Europäischen Parlament oder eine Ausdehnung des Mitentscheidungsverfahrens nach Art. 251 EUV), so wichtig ist es auch, demokratische Legitimität durch *Beachtung des Subsidiaritätsprinzips*[437] zu sichern. Das Subsidiaritätsprinzip ist darauf ausgelegt, sowohl in den Bereichen der Rechtssetzung und Rechtsanwendung als auch in dem der gerichtlichen Kontrolle beachtet zu werden[438]. Das Prinzip hat, wie alle Rechtsprinzipien, keinen „Alles oder Nichts"-Charakter. Es ist flexibel genug, die in Deutschland vorherrschenden Föderalismusvorstellungen[439] aufzugreifen und für die Struktur des Integrationsverbundes fruchtbar zu machen. Seine strikte Anwendung würde ein System „kooperativer Gewaltenteilung"[440] entstehen lassen. Leider wird das Subsidiaritätsprinzip aber von den Mitgliedstaaten weiterhin nicht ernst genommen, wie eine Vielzahl von Rechtsetzungsvorhaben (etwa im Umweltrecht, aber auch im europäischen Privatrecht) belegt.

Nachgedacht werden muß schließlich auch über eine ***institutionelle Fortentwicklung*** der Europäischen Union. Auch hier konkurrieren eine Vielzahl von Vorschlägen. Wichtig sind in diesem Zusammenhang die Vorschläge, die die Kommission in ihrem Weissbuch „Europäisches Regieren" mit dem Ziel einer Neuausrichtung der Institutionen im Lichte sogenannten „guten Regierens" gemacht hat[441]. Die Vorschläge zielen auf eine Stärkung der demokratischen und bürgerorientierten Legitimation europäischen Regierens ab; sie sehen die Lösung in der stärkeren Einbindung der Zivilgesellschaft. Die Kommission ist der Auffassung, dass Rat und Europäisches Parlament die *Gestaltung der „essentiellen*

Elemente" europäischer Politik übernehmen sollten; sie selbst beansprucht, durch Strategien „offener Koordinierung" und unter Berücksichtigung der Unionsmethode die *Durchführung* übernehmen zu können[442]. Das Weissbuch ist auf harsche Kritik gestoßen, die vor allem daran ansetzt, dass es vom Eigeninteresse der Kommission bestimmt sei und eine Antwort auf die wirklich anstehenden Probleme nicht biete[443]. Es fällt in der Tat auf, dass das technokratisch wirkende „governance"-Modell der Kommission eher auf die Entwicklung effizienter Problembewältigungsstrategien als auf die Beseitigung bestehender Legitimationsdefizite zielt[444]. Doch angesichts der Legitimationsschwierigkeiten, die nicht nur die Union, sondern auch ihre Mitgliedstaaten in der Gestaltung aktueller Politik haben[445], und angesichts der Zurückhaltung der Kommission, dem Konvent in Zukunftsfragen zu sehr vorzugreifen[446], erscheinen die Vorschläge der Kommission so schlecht nicht: In einer so großen Union wie der EU kann etwa die Stärkung sogenannter zivilgesellschaftlicher Netzwerkstrukturen, wie sie die Kommission vorschlägt[447], als erster Schritt in der Tat sinnvoll sein, um die EU ihren Bürgern näher zu bringen[448].

Viele der diskutierten Vorschläge weisen einen erheblichen Grad an Beliebigkeit auf. Einige fordern, die Organstruktur der Europäischen Union in ein föderales Zweikammernsystem fortzuentwickeln(vgl. die Vorschläge dazu im einzelnen oben II 3 b). Derartige Vorschläge sind ihrer Struktur nach dem deutschen Föderalismusmodell entlehnt und treffen auf zum Teil völlig andere Vorstellungen aus anderen Mitgliedstaaten. Andere wiederum (etwa Jospin in einer Rede vom 28. Mai 2001) fordern, das bisherige System beizubehalten und eventuell sogar eine Re-Inter-gouvernementalisierung zu fördern[449]. Manche wollen den Präsidenten der Kommission zum Europäischen Regierungschef aufwerten; andere wiederum wollen das Amt eines Europäischen Präsidenten schaffen und diesem das Recht geben, einen Kommissionspräsidenten zu bestimmen. Vorschläge, den Kommissionspräsidenten direkt von der Europäischen Bürgerschaft zu wählen, gibt es ebenso wie Vorschläge, ein parlamentarisches Regierungssystem zu schaffen und den Kommissionspräsidenten vom Parlament abhängig zu machen. Es fällt schwer, den jeweiligen funktionalen Nutzen auch nur annähernd empirisch zu überprüfen. Der Versuch einer wissenschaftlichen Kritik ist damit beinahe ausgeschlossen.

Eine ***Vereinfachung der Verträge*** ist angesichts der Zersplitterung der gegenwärtigen Verfassung in ein Geflecht ungeschriebener und geschriebener Regeln in verschiedenen Verträgen eine kardinale Aufgabe. Kompliziertheit und Intransparenz des europäischen Rechts gehören zu den wesentlichen Gründen fehlender materieller Legitimation.[450] Nur angesichts dieser Kompliziertheit ist überhaupt zu erklären, dass trotz des Bestehens einer europäischen Verfassung ein formaler europäischer Verfassungsvertrag gefordert wird[451]. Welche Schwierigkeiten allein mit einer „bloßen“ Vereinfachung der Verträge verbunden sind, zeigt sich allerdings schon angesichts der bisher unternommenen Versuche. Einige dieser Versuche beinhalten erhebliche, dann auch von den Mitgliedstaaten zu akzeptierende Änderungen; sie brechen mit dem Bewährten und bringen einen qualitativen Sprung (nach vorne?) mit sich. Teilweise laufen die Vorschläge aber auch nur auf redaktionelle Arbeiten hinaus und bringen insofern keinen wesentlichen Fortschritt im Hinblick auf Transparenz und Legitimation mit sich; ihnen fehlt es an der Fähigkeit zur Vereinfachung des Bestehenden[452]. Innerhalb dieses Spektrums sind in Deutschland in den letzten Jahren vielfache Vorschläge gemacht worden. Der Charme, aber auch das Problem dieser Vorschläge ist, dass es beinahe unmöglich ist, den jeweiligen funktionalen Gewinn einigermaßen realistisch abschätzen zu können.

b. Formalisierung der Verfassungswerdung der Verträge?

Der Schritt von einer wesentlichen Vereinfachung der Verträge zur Annahme einer formellen Verfassung ist klein. Mit dem Begriff der formellen Verfassung soll ein Dokument bezeichnet werden, dass diesen Titel trägt; es kann sich dabei sowohl um eine Vertragsverfassung als auch um eine Bürgerverfassung handeln. Für einen formalen europäischen Verfassungsvertrag tritt in Deutschland eine ganze Riege von Verfassungsrechtlern und Verfassungspolitikern ein. In der Sache handelt es sich dabei keinesfalls um eine völlig neue Debatte. Man denke nur etwa an die beiden Verfassungsentwürfe des Europäischen Parlamentes von 1984 und 1994[453] und die ihnen folgenden Diskussionen über das Thema formeller europäischer Verfassungsgebung.[454] Wenn gleichwohl das Thema eines formalen Verfassungsvertrages jetzt mit Macht auf die Tagesordnung gerückt ist, so liegt dies wohl vor allem an den Herausforderungen, denen sich die EU gegenwärtig gegenüber sieht. Die Einführung der gemeinsamen Währung und das Zusammengehen von Erweiterung und Vertiefung scheinen in der allgemeinen Wahrnehmung nach konzeptionellen Neuentwürfen für die Grundlagen der Europäischen Union geradezu zu rufen[455]. Zudem wollen manche gegenwärtig eine historische Chance sehen, die so nur für kurze Zeit gegeben ist, eine Art Fenster, das bald wieder geschlossen sein kann. Wieder andere wollen jedenfalls die Integrationsdynamik nützen, in der sich die EU gegenwärtig (Amsterdam-Nizza-2004) befindet. Zugunsten der Schaffung einer europäischen Verfassung wird immer auch geltend gemacht, dass nur sie die Möglichkeit biete, die Dinge grundlegend neu zu ordnen. Von wieder anderen wird auf den „ideell geprägten, charismatischen Symbolcharakter“[456] des Verfassungsbegriffs verwiesen; man verspricht sich davon eine Vertiefung der Integration und eine Verfestigung der europäischen Identität.

Diesen Argumenten zum Trotze kann keine Rede davon sein, dass man sich in Deutschland in der Forderung nach europäischer Verfassungsgebung einig ist. Gefahren sieht man zum einen in der Möglichkeit, dass bereits geschlossene Kompromisse wieder neu geöffnet würden und dadurch plötzlich Grundfragen wieder offen wären, ohne dass eine befriedigende Lösung in Sicht wäre. Häufig wird auch geltend gemacht, dass der Begriff der Verfassung Begehrlichkeiten und Erwartungen wecke, die gegebenenfalls auf europäischer Ebene gerade nicht befriedigt werden könnten[457]. Man befürchtet, dass Verfassungsgebung notwendig mit Staatswerdung der Europäischen Union einhergehe; dies aber lehnt man ab. Es sei gerade der staatliche Zusammenhang gewesen, in dem der Begriff der Verfassung mit Leben gefüllt wurde. Es bestünde daher die Gefahr, dass die Benutzung des Begriffs „Verfassung" auf europäischer Ebene nationalstaatlich tradierte Gehalte „mitnehme" (dazu schon oben II 2). Denn Wörter - so auch das Wort von der „Verfassung" - seien „Erfahrungsträger", nicht einfach „Hülsen, die wir beliebig füllen oder leeren können"[458]. Würde dies aber versucht, könnten Enttäuschungen eintreten und erhebliche politische Energie ausgelöst werden, die „zum entscheidenden Zeitpunkt die Mobilisierung der europäischen Öffentlichkeit zu blockieren" drohe[459]. Zu den Einwänden gehört auch, dass man die notwendige Kürze und Transparenz gegenwärtig nicht zu schaffen in der Lage sei: Wenn man eine formale europäische Verfassung schaffen wolle, dann müsse sie in ihren Gehalten kurz, einfach und klar sein[460] und in dieser Weise zum Abbau der bestehenden Defizite an Transparenz, Rechtssicherheit und demokratischer Verantwortlichkeit beitragen[461]. Zu einem solchen Schritt seien die Staaten ob der Tiefe und Breite ihrer gegenwärtigen Interessenkonflikte aber noch nicht willens und zum Schutze der weiterhin national geprägten Identitäten auch nicht befugt.

Wer vor diesem Hintergrund den „politischen Neugründungsakt Europas", wie ihn *Fischer* gefordert hat (vgl. oben II 3 b), nicht im Akt formeller Verfassungsgebung sieht, wird immerhin einräumen, dass eine Fortsetzung der Konstitutionalisierung ohne (formale) Konstitution erforderlich ist, d.h. die weitere „Durchdringung der EU-Grundordnung mit Elementen der Verfassungsidee"[462]. Dieser Sichtweise geht es nicht um einen eruptiven, einmaligen Akt, der Inhalt, Struktur und Ziel der EU dauerhaft festlegt, sondern um die Fortführung eines bewährten Prozesses, innerhalb dessen die Struktur der EU entlang der sich stellenden Probleme schrittweise und kontinuierlich angepaßt wird. Der Aspekt der Langfristigkeit wird etwa hervorgehoben, wenn gesagt wird, die Flexibilität des Ordnungsrahmens des Verbunds sei kein Transitorium und müsse daher erhalten bleiben[463]. Es ist in diesem Sinne die Politik der kleinen Schritte, der „Methode Monnet", wie sie so oft genannt wird, die gegenwärtig der sinnvollere Weg zu sein scheint. Dies heisst allerdings nicht, dass es keine

Neuerungen geben sollte. Es heißt lediglich, dass diese sich auf das politisch Machbare beschränken sollten, um sich den, wie Udo Di Fabio es audrückt, gerade erst entdeckten „praktischen und ästhetischen Reiz einer neu ausbalancierten Ordnung“[464] zu erhalten. Es muß das Ziel sein, den bestehenden Ordnungsrahmen zu erhalten und die Möglichkeit einer Vertiefung der Integration offenzuhalten. Der Ordnungsrahmen darf der Union weder ihr Integrationspotenzial noch ihre (ohne dass das Bild vom Radfahrer heute noch zuträfe) Zukunftsmächtigkeit nehmen. Zum Zerfall der Union führt es zwar nicht, wenn sie einmal innehält und sich ihrer Verfassung und ihrer Ziele besinnt; wohl aber wäre es das Ende, wenn ihre verfassungsrechtlichen Grundlagen ihr die Möglichkeit nähmen, auf neue gesellschaftliche Herausforderungen zu reagieren. Eine europäische Verfassung muss der Union sozusagen die Möglichkeit geben, ihren Weg jenseits der internationalen Organisation und vor der Bundestaatlichkeit weiter zu gehen[465]. Die Union kann auf größerer Ebene nicht das wiederholen, was ihr die Nationalstaaten sozusagen vorgemacht haben, sondern wird eine Entität eigener Art bleiben, eine bestimmte Form des Föderalismus - nicht in ständiger Bewegung auf den Bundesstaat klassischer Prägung zu, ohne diesen je wirklich zu erreichen[466], wohl aber auf einem eigenen Weg der Entfaltung des konsoziativen Föderalismus.

2. Eine Verfassung für die Europäische Union: Bedingungen für die Verfassungsgebung und Verfassungsänderung sowie ihr Verhältnis zum deutschen Grundgesetz

Es ist bekannt, dass es möglich und statthaft ist, eine formale europäische Verfassung durch völkerrechtlichen Vertrag zu schaffen. Sie würde – so die Idee - im Moment ihres Inkrafttretens die Natur als völkerrechtlichen Vertrag verlieren und in eine auf autonomer Grundlage beruhende Grundordnung umschlagen. Viele Beobachter meinen allerdings, dass ein derartiges Dokument hinreichende Legitimität nur dann hätte, wenn es von den europäischen Bürgern verabschiedet worden wäre. Es gilt dieser Sichtweise zufolge, die Bürger im Prozess formaler europäischer Verfassungsgebung partizipieren zu lassen. Die Einrichtung eines Verfassungskonventes hindert weitgehende Partizipation nicht. Sie fördert diese trotz immerhin verstärkter Beteiligungsmöglichkeiten der Bürger aber auch nicht in ausreichendem Maße, wenn das Konventsverfahren allein zur Vorbereitung einer Regierungskonferenz mit anschließender Vertragsänderung nach Art. 48 EUV dient. Hinreichende Partizipation wird vielmehr nur dann erreicht werden, wenn das „Konventsverfahren“ als Vorverfahren zu einem umfassenden, die europäische Bürgerschaft einbeziehenden Verfassungsgebungsprozess verstanden wird. Der üblichen Benutzung des Wortes „Konvent“ entspricht es am ehesten, wenn der entstehende Entwurf der europäischen Bürgerschaft in ihrer Gesamtheit vorgelegt wird[467]. Denkbar ist insoweit etwa eine europaweite Abstimmung. Nur ein solches Verfahren gewährleistet eine angemessene Willensbildung und -äußerung der EU-Bürger in ihrer Gesamtheit.

A rt. 23 GG würde nach wohl überwiegender Auffassung europäische Verfassungsgebung tragen. Art. 23 Abs. 1 S. 2 und 3 GG schreibt für die Änderung der vertraglichen Grundlagen der Europäischen Union, und damit auch für die europäische Verfassungsgebung, allerdings ein Handeln durch Gesetz vor (im einzelnen oben III 2 b). Europäische Verfassungsgebung setzt dieser Bestimmung zufolge daher eine Ratifikation voraus; die Volksabstimmung könnte nur zusätzliche Gültigkeits-bestimmung sein.

3. Der Verfassungsprozess und die Erweiterung: Zur Beteiligung der Beitrittskandidaten

Die Verfassungsgebung in der Union ist primär Sache der Union und ihrer Mitgliedstaaten. Sollte sich die Union eine formale Verfassung geben, so wird sie dies daher unabhängig davon tun, ob einzelnen Beitrittsstaaten Art und Inhalt der Verfassungsgebung im einzelnen behagen oder nicht. Allerdings schließt dies im Grundsatz eine gewisse Beteiligung der Beitrittskandidaten auch schon vor deren Beitritt nicht aus. Im Gegenteil, eine Beteiligung ist wünschenswert: Die Akzeptanz der europäischen Verfassungsregeln wird in der Bevölkerung eines neuen Mitgliedstaates höher sein, wenn sich dessen Organe bereits vor dem Beitritt im Hinblick auf die innere Verfasstheit der Europäischen Union Gehör verschaffen konnten. Eine Beteiligung der Beitrittstaaten ist daher nicht nur für den Beitrittstaat, sondern angesichts der großen Zahl der Beitrittskandidaten gerade auch für die Europäische Union selbst wünschenswert. Wenn die „geographische Finalität" der Europäischen Union[468] - wie *Vedder* es nennt - „ausgereizt" ist, dann wird die Europäische Union nach Bevölkerungszahl um immerhin fast die Hälfte, nach Fläche um sogar mehr als die Hälfte größer sein als heute[469].

Es ist daher zu begrüßen, dass schon in der Erklärung Nr. 23 zur Zukunft der Union festgelegt wurde, dass zur Regierungskonferenz 2004 auch die Bewerberstaaten eingeladen werden - diejenigen, die ihre Beitrittsverhandlungen mit der Union abgeschlossen haben werden, als Teilnehmer, diejenigen, die diese Verhandlungen dann noch nicht abgeschlossen haben werden, als Beobachter[470]. Bedeutsam ist zudem, dass die Beitrittskandidaten auch in den offenen Diskussionsprozess über die Zukunft der Europäischen Union einbezogen werden. Waren auf dem Europäischen Rat von Nizza insoweit die Einzelheiten noch offen[471], hat der Europäische Rat von Laeken nun Klarheit geschaffen: Nach der Erklärung von Laeken zur Zukunft der Europäischen Union sollen die Bewerberländer „umfassend an den Beratungen des Konvents [zur Zukunft Europas] beteiligt" werden; insbesondere sollen sie „in gleicher Weise wie die Mitgliedstaaten vertreten sein (ein Vertreter der Regierung und zwei Mitglieder des nationalen Parlaments)[472]. Dies legt es nahe, in diesem offenen Diskussionsprozess die Vertreter aus den Beitrittsstaaten in gleicher Weise wie die Vertreter aus den Mitgliedstaaten zu beteiligen.

Die Völker der Beitrittskandidaten werden im Konvent aber nicht in gleicher Weise wie die Völker der Mitgliedstaaten behandelt: Die Erklärung von Laeken macht erhebliche Unterschiede zwischen den Bevölkerungen der Beitrittsstaaten und jenen der Mitgliedstaaten: Die Vertreter aus den Beitrittsstaaten sollen in der Weise beteiligt werden, dass sie zwar allseits gefundenen Konsens mittragen können, nicht aber einen Konsens, der sich zwischen den Mitgliedern aus den Mitgliedstaaten abzeichnet, verhindern können. Diesem Vorgehen ist zuzustimmen. Es wäre nicht sachgerecht, dass die Konventsmitglieder aus dem Gebiet der Europäischen Union für sich zu einer bestimmten Frage zu einem Konsens kommen, dann aber eine entsprechende Empfehlung[473] nur deshalb nicht abgeben können, weil der gefundene Konsens von einem oder mehren Konventsmitgliedern aus den Beitrittsstaaten nicht mitgetragen werden kann.

Auf Einwände stößt demgegenüber, dass die Mitglieder aus den Beitrittsstaaten aus dem Präsidium des Konvents ausgeschlossen werden, wie es die Erklärung von Laeken vorsieht. Dem Präsidium fällt die Aufgabe zu, erste Anstöße zu geben und eine erste Arbeitsgrundlage für den Konvent zu erstellen. Diese Arbeitsgrundlage wird für die gesamten Verhandlungen und damit auch für das Ergebnis von besonderer Bedeutung sein. Ferner obliegt es dem Präsidium, Experten nach seiner Wahl zu konsultieren und Ad-hoc-Arbeitsgruppen einzusetzen. Auch die Entscheidungen hierüber können von großer Tragweite für das Ergebnis des Konvents sein. Es wäre daher sachgerecht gewesen, wenigstens einen Vertreter aus den Beitrittsstaaten in das Präsidium zu schicken. Dies wäre Ausdruck des Umstandes gewesen, dass es sich immerhin um die zukünftigen Mitgliedstaaten handelt. Von Bedeutung ist in diesem Zusammenhang auch, dass der Konvent ein Forum sein soll: Der Konvent soll ein strukturiertes Netz von Organisationen regelmäßig über die Arbeiten unterrichten. Es wäre dem Präsidium des Konvents daher anzuraten, auch die spezifischen Organisationen aus den Beitrittsstaaten miteinzubeziehen. Nur wenn die sogenannte „Zivilgesellschaft" in den Beitrittsstaaten in ähnlicher Weise einbezogen wird wie in den Mitgliedstaaten, kann der Konvent auf die so dringend erforderliche Akzeptanz seiner Beschlüsse auch aus den Beitrittsstaaten bauen.

NOTES

[1] Der Verfasser ist Inhaber des Lehrstuhls für öffentliches Recht, Europarecht und Völkerrecht an der Universität Tübingen (mail@nettesheim.org). Ich danke Herrn Ass. jur. Johann Ludwig Duvigneau für wertvolle Hilfe bei der Erstellung dieses Berichts.

[2] „Ist es nicht unser altes Problem, dass wir die Gemeinschaftsentwicklung durch die Brille des nationalen Verfassungsrechts betrachten und uns dann wundern, dass wir in Schwierigkeiten geraten?" So Frowein, Jochen Abr., Die rechtliche Bedeutung des Verfassungsprinzips der parlamentarischen Demokratie für den europäischen Integrationsprozess, 18 EuR 1983, S. 301.

[3] Im Einzelnen Karpenstein, Ulrich, Der Vertrag von Amsterdam im Lichte der Maastrichtentscheidung des BVerfG, 113 DVBl. 1998, S. 942 ff.; Streinz, Rudolf, Der Vertrag von Amsterdam, 20 JURA 1998, S. 57 ff.

[4] Vgl. allgemein zum Vertrag von Nizza nur Fischer, Klemens H., Der Vertrag von Nizza, 2001; Pache, Eberhard, Schorkopf, Frank, Der Vertrag von Nizza, 54 NJW 2001, S. 1377; Wiedmann, Thomas, Der Vertrag von Nizza - Genesis einer Reform, 36 EuR 2001, S. 185; Borchmann, Michael, Der Vertrag von Nizza, 12 EuZW 2001, S. 170; Pinder, John, Der Vertrag von Nizza - Wegbereiter eines föderalen oder intergouvernementalen Europa?, 24 integration 2001, S. 77; Pleuger, Gunter, Der Vertrag von Nizza: Gesamtbewertung der Ergebnisse, 24 integration 2001, S. 1; Kyaw, Dietrich von, Weichenstellungen des EU-Gipfels von Nizza, Internationale Politik 2001, S. 5.

[5] Der deutsche Bericht von Dieter H. Scheuing ist unter dem Titel „Deutsches Verfassungsrecht und europäische Integration" in EuR - Beiheft 1 - 1997, S. 7 abgedruckt.

[6] Überblick statt vieler etwa bei Grabenwarter, Christoph, Die Charta der Grundrechte für die Europäische Union, 116 DVBl. 2001, S. 1; Hilf, Meinhard, Die Charta der Grundrechte der Europäischen Union, Beilage zur NJW 2000, S. 5; Nettesheim, Martin, Die Charta der Grundrechte der Europäischen Union, 25 integration 2002, S. 35.

[7] Speziell hierzu nur CMLR, Editorial Comments: Preparing for 2004, The Post-Nice process, 38 CMLRev. 493; Schneider, Heinrich, Der Post-Nizza-Prozess: ein direkter Anlauf zur Konstitutionalisierung der Europäischen Union?, 24 integration 2001, S. 198; Müller-Graff, Peter-Christian, Der Post-Nizza-Prozess: Auf dem Wege zu einer neuen europäischen Verfassung?, 24 integration 2001, S. 208.

[8] Schlussfolgerungen des Vorsitzes des Europäischen Rates von Laeken, Amhang I: Erklärung von Laeken zur Zukunft der Europäischen Union, unter www.eu.2001.be.

[9] Dieser analytischen Aufgabe unterzieht sich der Bericht nicht, sie wird regelmäßig in Lehrbüchern des Europarechts geleistet.

[10] Es ist grundsätzlich nicht sinnvoll, einem Begriff einen Bedeutungsgehalt zuzuschreiben, der so nicht in der Sprachgemeinschaft bekannt ist.

[11] Vgl nur Hesse, Konrad, Grundzüge des Verfassungsrechts der Bunderpublik Deutschland, 19. Aufl.,, 1993, S. 3: Zur Darstellung des Verfassungsrechts kann nur „nach der heutigen, individuell-konkreten Verfassung gefragt werden" . Stern,

Klaus, Das Staatsrecht der Bundesrepublik Deutschland, Bd. I: Grundbegriffe und Grundlagen des Staatsrechts, Strukturprinzipien der Verfassung, 2. Aufl., 1984, S. 70: „Die Staatsrechtswissenschaft muss *den* Verfassungsbegriff in das Zentrum ihrer Betrachtungen stellen, der für die Bewältigung der ihr gestellten Aufgaben wesentlich ist.".

[12] Siehe vor allem: Grimm, Dieter, Braucht Europa eine Verfassung?, 50 JZ 1995, S. 581; Pernice, Ingolf, Multilevel Constitutionalism and the Treaty of Amsterdam: European Constitution-Making Revisited?, 36 CMLRev. 1999, S. 703 ff.; Häberle, Peter, Gemeineuropäisches Verfassungsrecht, in: Ders., Europäische Rechtskultur, 1994, S. 33 ff.; Böckenförde, Ernst-Wolfgang, Welchen Weg geht Europa?, in: Ders., Staat, Nation, Europa. Studien zur Staatslehre, Verfassungstheorie und Rechtsphilosophie, 1999, S. 68 ff.; Bruha, Thomas / Hesse, Joachim Jens / Nowak, Carsten (Hrsg.), Welche Verfassung für Europa? Erstes interdisziplinäres „Schwarzkopf-Kolloquium" zur Verfassungsdebatte in der Europäischen Union, 2001; Habermas, Jürgen, Die postnationale Konstellation und die Zukunft der Demokratie, in: Ders., Die postnationale Konstellation. Politische Essays, 1998, S. 91 ff.; Habermas, Jürgen, Braucht Europa eine Verfassung? Eine Bemerkung zu Dieter Grimm, in: Ders., Die Einbeziehung des Anderen. Studien zur politischen Theorie, 1996, S. 185 ff.; Frankenberg, Günter, The Return of Contract: Problems and Pitfalls of European Constitutionalism, 6 ELJ 2000, S. 257 ff.; Petersmann, Ernst-Ulrich, Proposals for a Constitutional Theory and Constitutional Law of the EU, 32 CMLRev. 1995, S. 1123 ff.

[13] Kirchhof, Paul, Europäische Einigung und der Verfassungsstaat der Bundesrepublik Deutschland, in: Isensee, Josef (Hrsg.), Europa als politische Idee und als rechtliche Form, 1993, S. 63, 82.

[14] Wie es Grimm etwa tut, der zwar von Verfassung als Grundordnung eines Gemeinwesens ausgeht, dieses aber gleichwohl in Bezug auf die Vorfindlichkeit des Staatlichen reduziert, 50 JZ 1995, S. 581, 582.

[15] Kirchhof, Paul, Europäische Einigung und der Verfassungsstaat der Bundesrepublik Deutschland, in: Isensee, Josef (Hrsg.), Europa als politische Idee und als rechtliche Form, 1993, S. 63, 84.

[16] Für Hegel ist der Staat als „die Wirklichkeit der Sittlichen Idee" das „an und für sich Vernüftige", vgl. Hegel. Georg Wilhelm Friedrich, Grundlinien der Philosophie des Rechts, 1821, S. 398 f (§§ 257 ff); Zum modernen sittlichen Staat vgl. Pauly, Walter, Hegel und die Frage nach dem Staat, 39 Der Staat 2000, S. 381, vor allem 392 ff., Böckenförde, Ernst-Wolfgang, Der Staat als sittlicher Staat, Berlin, 1978.

[17] Grimm, Dieter, Braucht Europa eine Verfassung?, 50 JZ 1995, S. 581; Koenig, Christian, Ist die Europäische Union verfassungsfähig?, 51 DÖV1998, S. 268.

[18] Zur Frage der europäischen Staatlichkeit etwa Oeter, Stefan, Vertrag oder Verfassung: Wie offen läßt sich die Souveränitätsfrage halten?, in: Bruha, Thomas u.a. (Hrsg.), Welche Verfassung für Europa?, 2001, S. 243; Landfried, Christine, Auf dem Weg zu einem europäischen Verfassungsstaat?, in: Bruha, Thomas u.a. (Hrsg.), Welche Verfassung für Europa?, 2001, S. 265.

[19] Eine Behauptung, die praktisch einhellig abgelehnt wird, vgl. zum Meinungsstand nur Busse, Christian, Die völkerrechtliche Einordnung der Europäischen Union, 1999, S. 43.

[20] Zur These, die europäische Verfassung schliesse Elemente von staatlicher Verfassung und internationaler Verfassung (UN-Charta) in sich ein und stehe dadurch sozusagen zwischen ihnen, Thürer, Daniel, Föderalistische Strukturen für Europa - eine zweite Chance der Entfaltung, 23 integration 2000, S. 89, 92.

[21] Hertel, Wolfram, Supranationalität als Verfassungsprinzip, 1999, S. 77 ff. und S. 256, Zusammenfassung, Punkt 5.

[22] Pernice, Ingolf, Europäisches und nationales Verfassungsrecht, 60 VVDStRL 2001, S. 148, 155.

[23] Selbst Josef Isensee leugnet diesen Zustand nicht, wenngleich er auch umso stärker und ohne Umschweife die Rückbeziehung des Verfassungsbegriffs auf den Staat fordert, vgl nur „Staat und Verfassung", in Isensee, Kirchof (Hrsg.), HdBStR, Bd. I, § 13, Rdn. 3: „Paradigmenwechsel [der] Ablösung von „Staat" durch „Verfassung" und „Demokratie"" versus „Staat als Natur der Sache"; ähnlich in : „Gemeinwohl und Staatsaufgaben im Verfassungsstaat", in HdBStR Bd. III, § 57, Rdn. 132.

[24] Zsfd. Hofmann, Hasso, Von der Staatssoziologie zu einer Soziologie der Verfassung?, 54 JZ 1999, S. 1065. Eine ganz andere Frage ist, inwieweit Staatlichkeit selbst sich wandelt; hierzu etwa Denninger, Erhard, Vom Ende nationalstaatlicher Souveränität in Europa, 55 JZ 1998, S. 1121.

[25] Grimm, Dieter, Verfassung, in: Ders., Die Zukunft der Verfassung, 1991, S. 11.

[26] Stern, Klaus, Das Staatsrecht der Bundesrepublik Deutschland, Bd. I, 2. Aufl., S. 61.

[27] Sie läßt sich damit mit dem analytischen Verfassungsbegriff gut erfassen.

[28] Vgl. bereits Jellinek, Georg, Allgemeine Staatslehre, 1914, S. 505: „Die Verfassung des Staates umfaßt demnach in der Regel die Rechtssätze, welche die obersten Organe des Staates bezeichnen, die Art ihrer Schöpfung, ihr gegenseitiges Verhältnis und ihren Wirkungskreis festsetzen, ferner die grundsätzliche Stellung des einzelnen zur Staatsgewalt."

[29] Im einzelnen Starck, Christian, Grundrechtliche und demokratische Freiheitsidee, in: Isensee, Josef und Kirchhof, Paul (Hrsg.), HdBStR, Bd. II, 1987, S. 3; Grabitz, Eberhard, Freiheit und Verfassungsrecht, 1976. Legitimation ist in der westlichen Welt eines der wichtigsten, wenn nicht das wichtigste Thema von Verfassung, vgl. nur Alexander, der es gleich zu Beginn seines verfassungsrechtlichen Diskurses aufbringt: Alexander, Larry, Introduction, in: Ders. (Hrsg.), Constitutionalism, Philosophical Foundations, Cambridge: CUP, 1999, S. 1.

[30] Stern, Klaus, Das Staatsrecht der Bundesrepublik Deutschland, Bd. I, 2. Aufl., S. 78; Eingehend: Ders.: Die Verbindung von Verfassungsidee und Grundrechtsidee zur modernen Verfassung, in: Ders.: Der Staat des Grundgesetzes, Ausgewählte Schriften und Vorträge, hrsg. von Helmut Siekmann, 1992, S. 111.

[31] In Deutschland wird die Legitimationsfrage des Unionsrechts überwiegend im Zusammenhang mit der Frage nach der Staatlichkeit diskutiert, weil der Begriff des „Volkes" nach Art. 20 Abs. 2 S. 1 GG im Sinne von „Staatsvolk" verstanden wird; vgl. etwa BVerfGE 89, 155, 186: „Jedes Staatsvolk ist Ausgangspunkt für eine auf es selbst bezogene Staatsgewalt. Die Staaten bedürfen hinreichend bedeutsamer Aufgabenfelder, auf denen sich das jeweilige Staatsvolk in einem von ihme legitimierten und gesteuerten Prozesspolitischer Willensbildung entfalten kann, um so

dem, was es - relativ homogen - geistig, sozial und politisch verbindet, rechtlichen Ausdruck zu geben." Diese Verknüpfung von Staatlichkeit und Legitimation wird auch in der Literatur deutlich. Beispielhaft hierfür etwa die Argumentation, die Union sei nicht verfassungsfähig, weil ihr *mangels legitimierenden Staatsvolkes* die eigene Staatlichkeit fehle: Koenig, Christian, Ist die Europäische Union verfassungfähig? 51 DÖV 1998, S. 268.

[32] Kägi, Werner, Die Verfassung als rechtliche Grundordnung des Staates, 1945 (Neudruck 1971), S. 49.

[33] Brugger, Winfried (Hrsg.), Legitimation des Grundgesetzes aus Sicht von Rechtsphilosophie und Gesellschaftstheorie, 1996, S. 7.

[34] Zur historischen Entwicklung der Verfassungsfunktionen insoweit Böckenförde, Ernst-Wolfgang, Geschichtliche Entwicklung und Bedeutungswandel der Verfassung, in: Ders., Staat, Verfassung, Demokratie, S. 29, 47 ff.

[35] Hesse, Konrad, Grundzüge des Verfassungsrechts der Bundesrepublik Deutschland,19. Aufl. 1993, § 1 III 1: Rz. 17.

[36] Ibid.; vgl auch Verfassung und Verfassungsrecht, in: Benda, Ernst u.a. (Hrsg.): HdBVR, S. 1, 7 Rz. 10.

[37] Werterechtsprechung, vgl. etwa BVerfGE 6, 55 (72); 10, 59 (81) usw.

[38] Zum ganzen Craig, Paul, Constitutions, Constitutionalism and the European Union, 7 ELJ 2001, S. 125.

[39] Zur Begriffsbildung vgl. zsfd. etwa Bieber, Verfassungsfrage und institutionelle Reform, in: Bruha, Thomas u.a. (Hrsg.), Welche Verfassung für Europa?, 2001, S. 111.

[40] Vgl. auch die Einschätzung von Biaggini, Giovanni, Eine Verfassung für Europa?, in NZZ vom 11./12. November 2000, S. 57: „Dem neuen internationalen Verfasssungsbegriff liegt ein in erster Linie deskriptives Verfassungsverständnis zugrunde."

[41] Tsatsos, Dimitris Th., Die europäische Unionsgrundordnung, 22 EuGRZ 1995, S. 287ff.

[42] Hierzu Weiler, Joseph H.H., European Neo-constitutionalism: In Search of Foundations for the European Constitutional Order, 44 Political Studies 1996, S. 517 ff.

[43] Bruha, Thomas / Hesse, Joachim Jens / Nowak, Carsten, Vorwort, in: Dies (Hrsg.), Welche Verfassung für Europa? Erstes interdisziplinäres „Schwarzkopf-Kolloquium" zur Verfassungsdebatte in der Europäischen Union, Baden-Baden: Nomos 2001, S. 5 ff. .

[44] Die Diskussion um das europäische Verfassungsrecht ist in vollem Gange. Auf der Jahrestagung 2000 der Vereinigung der Deutschen Staatsrechtslehrer etwa wurde das Thema „Europäisches und nationales Verfassungsrecht" zum Beratungsgegenstand gemacht; vgl. neben dem Aufsatz von Pernice die Aufsätze von Huber, Peter M., Lübbe-Wolff, Gertrude und Grabenwarter, Christoph, 60 VVDStRL 2001, S. 148, 194, 246, 290; vgl ferner nur etwa folgende Auswahl überwiegend jüngerer deutschsprachiger Literatur: Argirakos, Dimitros, Eine Verfassung für Europa, 2001, Bruha, Thomas u.a. (Hrsg.), Welche Verfassung für Europa, 2001; Dorau, Christoph, Die Verfassungsfrage der Europäischen Union, Möglichkeiten und Grenzen der europäischen Verfassungsentwicklung nach Nizza, 2001, Peters, Anne, Elemente einer Theorie der Verfassung Europas, 2001;

Frowein, Jochen Abr., Die Verfassung der Europäischen Union aus der Sicht der Mitgliedstaaten, 30 EuR 1995, S. 315, Häberle, Peter, Gemeineuropäisches Verfassungsrecht, 18 EuGRZ 1991, S. 261 ff., Häberle, Peter, Europäische Verfassungslehre in Einzelstudien, 1999; Heitzen, Markus, Gemeineuropäisches Verfassungsrecht in der Europäischen Union, 32 EuR 1997, S. 1; Oeter, Stefan, Europäische Integration als Konstitutionalisierungsprozess, 59 ZaöRV 1999, S. 901; Ronge, Frank, In welcher Verfassung ist Europa - welche Verfassung für Europa?, 2001; Schwarze, Jürgen (Hrsg.), Die Entstehung einer europäischen Verfassungsordnung, Das Ineinandergreifen von nationalen und europäischem Verfassungsrecht, 2000; Schwarze, Jürgen, Auf dem Wege zu einer europäischen Verfassung - Wechselwirkungen zwischen europäischem un nationalem Verfassungsrecht, 114 DVBl. 1999, S. 1677; Schwarze, Jürgen,Bieber, Roland (Hrsg.), Eine Verfassung für Europa, 1984; Walter Hallstein Institut für Europäisches Verfassungsrecht (Hrsg.), Grundfragen der europäischen Verfassungsentwicklung, FCE Bd. I, 2000; Weiler, Joseph J. H., The Constitution of Europe, 2000.

[45] EuGH, Rs. 22/70, Kommission/Rat, Slg. 1971, 263.

[46] Hierzu z.B. Slaughter, Anne-Marie / Stone Sweet, Alec / Weiler, Joseph H.H. (Hrsg.), The European Courts and National Courts – Doctrine and Jurisprudence. Legal Change in Its Social Context, 1998, Part II, S. 227 ff.; Stone Sweet, Alec / Brunell, Thomas L., The European Court, National Judges, and Legal Integration: A Researcher's Guide to the Data Set on Preliminary References in EC Law 1958-98, 6 ELJ 2000, S. 117 ff.; Mare, Thomas de la, Article 177 in Social and Political Context, in: Craig, Paul / Búrca, Gráinne de (Hrsg.), The Evolution of EU Law, 1999, S. 215 ff.

[47] Insofern bedarf es eines Hinweises, daß die Durchsetzung des Unionsrechts in den Händen der Mitgliedstaaten liegt, nicht.

[48] Ausführliche Diskussion bei Pechstein, Matthias/Koenig, Christian, Die Europäische Union, 3. Aufl. 2000, S. 5 ff.

[49] So Bogdandy, Armin von/Nettesheim, Martin, Die Verschmelzung der Europäischen Gemeinschaften in der Europäischen Union, 48 NJW 1995, S. 2324 ff.; Dies., Die Europäische Union: Ein einheitlicher Verband mit eigener Rechtsordnung, 31 EuR 1996, S. 3 ff.

[50] So Dörr, Oliver, Zur Rechtsnatur der Europäischen Union, 30 EuR 1995, S. 334.

[51] So Pechstein, Matthias/Koenig, Christian, Die Europäische Union,3. Aufl. 2000, S. 54 ff.

[52] Es werden gegenwärtig unterschiedliche Systematisierungsvorschläge diskutiert: Nach Marcel Kaufmann (Europäische Integration und Demokratieprinzip,1997, S. 224 ff.) ist zwischen Bundesstaatskonzeption, Zweckverbandslehre und Staatenverbundslehre zu unterscheiden. Armin von Bogdandy (Beobachtungen zur Wissenschaft vom Europarecht, 40 Der Staat 2001, S. 24 ff.) geht von den folgenden drei Konzeptionen aus: Konzeption der internationalen Organisation, föderalistische Konzeption, Zweckverbandslehre.

[53] Wer die EU weiterhin als eine internationale Organisationen völkerrechtlichen Typs ansieht (vgl. z.B. Randelzhofer, Albrecht, Zum behaupteten Demokratiedefizit der Europäischen Gemeinschaft, in: Hommelhoff, Peter/Kirchhof, Paul (Hrsg.), Der

Staatenverbund der Europäischen Union, 1994,S. 39, 40; Steinberger, Helmut, Der Verfassungsstaat als Glied einer europäischen Gemeinschaft, 50 VVDStRL 1991, S. 16; Tomuschat, Christian, in: von der Groeben/Thiesing/Ehlermann (Hrsg.), Kommentar zum EWG-Vertrag, 4. Aufl. 1991, Art. 210, Rdnr. 4; Dörr, Oliver, Zur Rechtsnatur der Europäischen Union, 30 EuR 1995, S. 334; Klein, in: Graf Vitzthum, Wolfgang (Hrsg.), Völkerrecht, 1997, S. 309 f.; Kimminich, Otto, Einführung in das Völkerrecht, 6. Aufl. 1997, 162; guter Überblick bei: Pechstein, Matthias/Koenig, Christian, Die Europäische Union, 3. Aufl. 2000), wird immer zugleich einräumen, dass sich der Verband angesichts seiner Kompetenzbreite und –tiefe sowie seiner Befugnis, unmittelbar wirksame Hoheitsgewalt auszuüben, von den herkömmlichen internationalen Organisationen doch erheblich abhebt und als besondere Form des Staatenbundes anzusehen ist. Chr. Tomuschat beispielsweise hält diese Einordnung schon deshalb für zwingend, weil alles andere die EU auf die Ebene eines Staates höbe (Tomuschat, Cristian, Das Endziel der Europäischen Integration, in: Nettesheim, Martin/Schiera Pierangelo (Hrsg.), Der integrierte Staat, 1999, S. 155, 159).

[54] Es ist natürlich möglich, diese Konzeption zur analystischen Beschreibung der Anfangsjahre der Integration zu verwenden, sodann aber einen Übergang zur etatistischen Konzeption zu konstatieren. Dazu z.B. Everling, Ulrich, Vom Zweckverband zur Europäischen Union: Überlegungen zur Struktur der Europäischen Gemeinschaft, FS Ipsen, 1977, S. 595.

[55] Kirchhof, Paul, Der deutsche Staat im Prozeß der europäischen Integration, in: Josef Isensee/Paul Kirchhof (Hrsg.), HdBStR, Bd. VII, 1992, § 183, S. 855 ff., 876 ff., Rdnrn. 43 ff.; Ders., Das Maastricht-Urteil des Bundesverfassungsgerichts, in: Hommelhoff, Peter/Kirchhof, Paul, (Hrsg.), Der Staatenverbund der Europäischen Union, 1994, S. 11 ff.

[56] Ipsen, Hans P., Europäisches Gemeinschaftsrecht, 1972, S. 196, 1055.

[57] Mestmäcker, Ernst J., Der Kampf ums Recht in der offenen Gesellschaft, Rechtstheorie 1989, S. 273 ff.; ähnlich: Majone, Giandomenico, Europe´s „Democratic Deficit“: The Question of Standards, 4 ELJ 1988, S. 5 ff.

[58] Mestmäcker, Ernst J., Die Wiederkehr der bürgerlichen Gesellschaft und ihres Rechts, 10 RJ 1991, S. 177.

[59] Hallstein, Walter, Der unvollendete Bundesstaat, Düsseldorf: Econ, 1969.

[60] Grabitz, Ebergard, Der Verfassungsstaat in der Gemeinschaft, 92 DVBl. 1977, S. 786.

[61] Vgl. etwa Mancini, Giuseppe Federico, Europe: The Case for Statehood, 4 ELJ 1998, S. 29 ff. (deutsch: Europa: Gründe für einen Gesamtstaat, KritV 1998, S. 386 ff.).

[62] Bogdandy, Armin von, Suprantionale Union als neuer Herrschaftstypus: Entstaatlichung und Vergemeinschaftung in staatstheoretischer Perspektive, 16 integration 1993, S. 210.

[63] Wer diese Begrifflichkeit scheut, kann die EU in zweckmäßiger Weise als „supranationale Integrationsgemeinschaft“ bezeichnen (so Nettesheim, Kommentierung des Art. 249 EGV, in: Grabitz, Eberhard/Hilf, Meinhard (Hrsg.), Kommentar zum EU- und EG-Vertrag, 19. Ergänzungslieferung 2002 (im Erscheinen)). Damit kommt nicht nur zum Ausdruck, dass die Unionsgewalt in staatenähnlicher Weise zur Setzung unmittelbar wirksamen Rechts befugt ist und

dabei einen Kompetenzbereich abdeckt, der jenem traditioneller Staatsgewalt inzwischen entspricht. Der Begriff bringt auch zum Ausdruck, dass es sich bei der Union nicht nur um einen Zweckverband zur Erzielung bestimmter wirtschaftlicher Ziele handelt. Inhalte und Finalität des Primärrechts sind Ausdruck und Verkörperung gemeinsamer politischer Grundwerte; die EU wirkt darauf hin, ein europäisches politisches Gemeinwesen zu errichten, in dem die – weiterhin souveränen und selbst-ständigen Mitgliedstaaten eingebunden und integriert werden.

[64] Pernice sieht inzwischen einen Umfang der Verflechtung als gegeben, der es rechtfertigt, davon zu sprechen, dass die Unterscheidung und Unterscheidbarkeit von Europäischer Verfassung und nationalen Verfassungen aufgehoben worden sei.

[65] Pernice, Ingolf, in: Dreier, Horst (Hrsg.), Grundgesetz Kommentar, 1998, Art. 23 Rdnr. 20. M.E. schießt die Feststellung, europäische Rechtsordnung und nationale Rechtsordnungen wüchsen so miteinander zusammen, dass man sie als einheitliche Rechtsordnung ansehen müsse, über das normative Ziel der Verbundsthese hinaus. Ihrem Ursprung nach lassen sich Normen des europäischen Rechts und solche des nationalen Rechts weiterhin unterscheiden – wie auch diese Unterscheidung im Bundesstaat im Hinblick auf Bundes- und Landesrecht möglich ist.

[66] Vgl. nur Pernice, Ingolf, Multilevel Constitutionalism and the Treaty of Amsterdam: European Constitution-making revisited?, 26 CMLRev 1999, S. 703.

[67] Problematisch beispielsweise die Behauptung, „national administrative bodies are in an ´agency-situation´ regarding the transposition and application of community law, in fact they are part of the European executive and exercising European authority"; Pernice, Ingolf, Multilevel Constitutionalism and the Treaty of Amsterdam. European Constitutional-Making Revisited? 36 CMLR 1999, S. 703 (724). Darin läge eine Verwischung der Verantwortlichkeiten, die aus verfassungstheoretischer und demokratischer Sicht bedenklich wäre. Auch im Bundesstaat wandeln sich die Organe der Gliedstaaten nicht zu Organen des Bundes, wenn sie Bundesrecht ausführen.

[68] Vgl. z.B. Bieber, Roland u.a. (Hrsg.), Europäischer Verfassungsraum, 1995.

[69] Pernice, Ingolf, in: WHI für Europäisches Verfassungsrecht (Hrsg.), Grundfragen der europäischen Verfassungsentwicklung, Bd. 1, 2000, 11; ders., 36 CMRL 1996, 703; vgl. auch Bauer, JBl. 2000, S. 749; Bogdandy, Armin von, A bird´s eye view on the science of European Law, 6 ELJ 2000, S. 208; Schuppert, Gunnar F., in: Klingemann, Hans D./Neidhardt, Friedhelm, Zur Zukunft der Demokratie. Herausforderungen im Zeitalter der Globalisierung, 2000, S. 237; Thürer, Daniel, Föderalistische Verfassungsstrukturen – eine zweite Chance der Entfaltung, 23 Integration 2000, S. 89.

[70] Mayer, Franz C., Kompetenzüberschreitung und Letztentscheidung, Das Maastricht-Urteil des Bundesverfassungsgerichts und die Letztentscheidung über Ultra vires-Akte in Mehrebenensystemen, 2000, S. 51 ff.

[71] Cappelletti, Seccombe, Weiler, General Introduction, in: Dies. (Hrsg.), Integration through Law, Vol 1, Book 1 S. 4; Heckel, Katharina, Der Föderalismus als Prinzip überstaatlicher Gemeinschaftbildung, 1998; Hertel, Wolfram, Supranationalität als Verfassungsprinzip, 1999; von Bogdandy, Armin, Supranationaler Föderalismus als Wirklichkeit und Idee einer neuen Herrschaftsform, 1999.

[72] Fischer, Joschka, Vom Staatenverbund zur Föderation – Gedanken über die Finalität der europäischen Integration, 23 integration 2000, S. 149.

[73] Kägi, Werner, in: Die Juristischen Fakultäten der Schweizer Universitäten (Hrsg.), Die Freiheit des Bürgers im schweizerischen Recht. Festgabe zur 100-Jahr-Feier der Bundesverfassung, 1948, S. 53.

[74] Vgl. Schneider, Heinrich, Alternativen der Verfassungsfinalität: Föderation, Konföderation – oder was sonst? 23 integration 2000, S. 171.

[75] Hierzu die Beiträge von: Pernice, Ingolf/Huber, Peter Michael/Lübbe-Wolff, Gertrude/Grabenwarter, Christoph, Europäisches und nationales Verfassungsrecht, 60 VVDStRL 2001, S. 148/194/246/290 mwN.

[76] Weitsichtig: Tomuschat, Christian, Der Verfassungsstaat im Geflecht der internationalen Beziehungen, 36 VVDStRL 1978, S. 7.

[77] BVerfGE 89, 155. Man mag diese Schlußfolgerung dem Subsidiaritätsprinzip entnehmen; auch läßt sich die Idee der Staatlichkeit Deutschlands fruchtbar machen. Die Herleitung aus dem Demokratieprinzip erweist sich allerdings problematisch. Sie hätte zur Folge, dass die Entwertung der Gesetzgebungskompetenzen der Länder im grundgesetzlichen Föderalismus im Hinblick auf Art. 20 Abs. 2 GG zu thematisieren wäre.

[78] Kaufmann, Marcel, Integrierte Staatlichkeit als Staatsstrukturprinzip, 54 JZ 1999, S. 814; Mosler, Hermann, Die Übertragung von Hoheitsgewalt, in: Isensee, Josef/Kirchhof, Paul (Hrsg.), HdBStR, § 175.

[79] Schmitt-Glaeser, Alexander, Grundgesetz und Europarecht als Elemente Eruopäischen Verfassungsrechts, 1996; Hertel, Wolfgang, Supranationalität als Verfassungsprinzip, 1999.

[80] Hobe, Stephan, Der kooperationsoffene Verfassungsstaat, 37 Der Staat 1998, S. 521.

[81] Vgl. z.B. Hahn, Hugo J. (Hrsg.), Das Währungswesen in der europäischen Integration, 1996, Ders., Das Entstehen der Europawährung – Szenarien ihrer Einführung, 57 JZ 1996, S. 321.

[82] So der Titel des von Martin Nettesheim und Pierangelo Schiera herausgegebenen Sammelbandes „Der Integrierte Staat", 1999.

[83] Pernice, Ingolf, Europäisches und nationales Verfassungsrecht, 60 VVDStRL 2001, S. 148, 154 im Anschluss an Habermas, Jürgen, Die postnationale Konstellation, 1998.

[84] Peters, Anne, Elemente einer Theorie der Verfassung Europas, 2001.

[85] In diese Richtung Franck, Thomas M., Clan and Superclan: Loyality, Identity and Community in Law and Practice, 90 AJIL 1996, S. 359.

[86] Weiler, Joseph J. H., „We will do, and hearken..." , in: Ders., The Constitution of Europe, 1999, S. 1; zum ganzen auch Thürer, Daniel, Föderalistische Strukturen für Europa - eine zweite Chance der Entfaltung, 23 integration 2000, S. 89, 94. So aufschlussreich Weilers These ist, dass erst der Aufschrei von Maastricht der konstitutionelle Moment Europas, oder präziser: dessen Beginn war, so zweifelhaft erscheint doch Weilers symbolträchtiger Rekurs auf das biblische zweite Buch Mose, den Exodus, zu sein, geht es jedenfalls in der lutherischen Fassung in dem zitierten Vers doch nicht so sehr um das „*Nachdenken*" über den zuvor geschlossenen Bund, sondern um dessen *Beachtung* als göttlichem Gesetz: „Und er nahm das Buch des Bundes und las es vor den Ohren des Volkes. Und sie sprachen: Alles was der Herr

gesagt hat, wollen wir tun und *auf ihn höhren.*", Die Bibel nach der Übersetzung Martin Luthers, 2. Buch Mose (Exodus), Kap. 24, Vers 7.

[87] Jarrass, Hans D./Pieroth, Bodo, Grundgesetz, Art. 23, Rdn. 2; Geiger, Rudolf, Die Mitwirkung des deutschen Gesetzgebers an der Entwicklung der Europäischen Union, Zur Auslegung des Art. 23 Ab. 1 Satz 2 und 3 GG, JZ 96, S. 1093; Pechstein, Matthias/Koenig, Christian, Die Europäische Union, 3. Aufl. 2000, Rdnr. 148: „Art. 23 GG [erfasst] nunmehr die Übertragung von Hoheitsrechten auf die gesamte Europäische Union, ohne zwischen den einzelnen Unionssäulen zu unterscheiden"; Allerdings wollen Pechstein/Koenig trotzdem nicht alle Bereiche des Unionsrechts anwendbar sein lassen (Rdnr. 147f); dazu unten I 2 b).

[88] Zur Entstehungsgeschichte vertiefend Schmalenbach, Kirsten, Der neue Europaartikel 23 des Grundgesetzes im Lichte der Arbeit der Gemeinsamen Verfassungskommission, Motive einer Verfassungsänderung, 1996.

[89] Scholz, Rupert, Europäische Union und Verfassungsreform, 46 NJW 1993, S. 1690 mit Hinweis auf die Gemeinsame Verfassungskommission von Bundestag und Bundesrat.

[90] „Zur Verwirklichung eines vereinten Europas wirkt die Bundesrepublik Deutschland bei der Entwicklung der Europäischen Union mit [...]".

[91] „ [...], die demokratischen, rechtsstaatlichen, sozialen und föderativen Grundsätzen und dem Grundsatz der Subsidiarität verpflichtet ist und einen diesem Grundgesetz im wesentlichen vergleichbaren Grundrechtsschutz gewährleistet."

[92] Scholz, Rupert, Art. 23, in: Maunz, Theodor/Dürig, Günter, Grundgesetz. Kommentar (Ergänzungslieferung), Rdnr. 55; Scheuing, Dieter H., Deutsches Verfassungsrecht und europäische Integration" in EuR - Beiheft 1 - 1997, S. 7, 21, Rdn 29.

[93] So auch Scheuing, Dieter H., Deutsches Verfassungsrecht und europäische Integration" in EuR - Beiheft 1 - 1997, S. 7, 21, Rdnr. 29; Im einzelnen Scholz, Rupert, Art. 23, in Maunz, Theodor/Dürig, Günter, Grundgesetz. Kommentar (Ergänzungslieferung), Rdn. 54 ff.; Uhrig Stephanie, Die Schranken des Grundgesetzes für die europäische Integration, 2000, S. 106 ff.

[94] Pernice, Ingolf, Deutschland in der Europäischen Union, in Isensee, Josef/Kirchhof, Paul, HdBStR VIII, § 191, Rdnr. 38.

[95] Dazu Böckenförde, Ernst-Wolfgang, Die verfassungsgebende Gewalt des Volkes - Ein Grenzbegriff des Verfassungsrechts, in: Ders., Staat, Verfassung, Demokratie, 2. Aufl. 1992, S. 90.

[96] BVerfGE 89, 155, LS 3b

[97] Schuppert, Gunnar Folke, Überlegungen zur demokratischen Legitimation des europäischen Regierungssystems, in: Ipsen, Jörn/Schmidt-Jorzig, Edzard (Hrsg.), Rechts, Staat, Gemeinwohl, FS Rauschning, 2001, S. 201, 210.

[98] Augustin, Angela, Das Volk der Europäischen Union, Zu Inhalt und Kritik eines normativen Begriffs, 2000

[99] Allgemein dazu schon Zuleeg, Manfred, Demokratie in der Europäischen Gemeinschaft, 48 JZ 1993, S. 1069; ferner Drexl, Josef u.a. (Hrsg.), Europäische Demokratie, 1999 ; eingehend Kaufmann, Marcel, Europäische Integration und Demokratieprinzip, 1997.

[100] Heckel, Katharina, Der Föderalismus als Prinzip überstaatlicher Gemeinschaftbildung, 1998; Zu einer möglichen politisch-inhaltlichen

Konkretisierung des föderalen Prinzips vergl. Ammon, Günther u.a.(Hrsg.), Föderalismus und Zentralismus: Europas Zukunft zwischen dem deutschen und dem französischen Modell, 1996.

101 Im einzelnen Zuleeg, Manfred, Die föderativen Grundsätze der Europäischen Union, 53 NJW 2000, S. 2847.

102 Vgl Kischel, Uwe, Der unabdingbare grundrechtliche Mindeststandard in der Europäischen Union, Zur Auslegung des Art. 23 Abs. 1 S. 1 GG, 39 Der Staat 2000, S. 523.

103 Nettesheim, Martin, Die Bananenmarktentscheidung des BVerfG: Europarecht und nationaler Mindestgrundrechtsstandard, 23 JURA 2001, S. 686, 691; zum Maßstab Nettesheim, Martin, 21 NVwZ (Im Erscheinen).

104 „Für die Begründung der Europäischen Union sowie für Änderungen ihrer vertraglichen Grundlagen und vergleichbare Regelungen, durch diie dieses Grundgesetz seinem Inhalt nach geändert oder ergänzt wird oder solche Änderungen oder Ergänzungen ernöglicht werden, gilt Art. 79 Abs. 2 und 3.“

105 „Eine Änderung dieses Grundgesetzes, durch welche die Gliederung des Bundes in Länder, die grundsätzliche Mitwirkung der Länder bei der Gesetzgebung oder die in den Art. 1 und 20 niedergelegten Grundsätze [Schutz der Menschenwürde, demokratischer und sozialer Bundesstaat, demokratisches Prinzip, Rechtsstaat, Grundrechtsgewähr]berührt werden, ist unzulässig.“

106 Zur Verfassungsidentität Kirchhof, Paul, Die Identität der Verfassung in ihren unabänderlichen Inhalten, in: Isensee, Josef/Kirchhof, Paul, HdBStR I, § 19, S. 775.

107 Fabio, Udo di, Der neue Art. 23 des Grundgesetzes, Positivierung vollzogenen Verfassungswandels oder Verfassungsneuschöpfung?, 32 Der Staat 1993, S. 191.

108 Grundlegend Murswiek, Dietrich, Maastricht und der Pouvoir Constituant, Zur Bedeutung der verfassungsgebenden Gewalt im Prozess der europäischen Integration, 32 Der Staat 1993, S. 161; vgl. auch Rupp, Hans Heinrich, Muß das Volk über den Vertrag von Maastricht entscheiden?, 46 NJW 1993, S. 38.

109 BVerfGE 89, 155, 186: „Die Staaten bedürfen hinreichend bedeutsamer eigener Aufgabenfelder [...]“.

110 BVerfGE 89, 155, LS 4: „Vermitteln - wie gegenwärtig - die Staatsvölker über die nationalen Parlamente demokratische Legitimation [...]“

111 BVerfGE 89, 155, LS 4: „ [...] sind der Ausdehnung der Aufgaben und Befugnisse vom demokratischen Prinzip her Grenzen gesetzt.“

112 Vgl. nur Fabio, Udo di, Das Recht offener Staaten, 1998; Fabio, Udo di, Der Verfassungsstaat in der Weltgesellschaft, Walter Eucken Institut (Hrsg.), Beiträge zur Ordnungstheorie und Ordnungspolitik 166, 2001; Hobe, Stephan, Der offene Verfassungsstaat zwischen Souveränität und Interdependenz, Eine Studie zur Wandlung des Staatsbegriffs der deutschsprachigen Staatslehre im Kontext internationaler institutionalisierter Kooperation, 1998.

113 Dazu etwa Denninger, Erhard, Vom Ende nationalstaatlicher Souveränität in Europa, 55 JZ 1998, S. 1121; Oeter, Stefan, Souveränität und Demokratie in der „Verfassungsentwicklung“ der Europäischen Union, 55 ZaöRV 1995, S. 659ff.

114 Dazu etwa Häberle, Peter, Gibt es eine europäische Öffentlichkeit, in: Ders., Europäische Verfassungslehre in Einzelstudien, 1999, S. 131.

115 Pernice, Ingolf, Deutschland in der Europäischen Union, in Isensee, Josef/Kirchhof, Paul, HdBStR VIII, § 191, Rdnr. 57.

[116] Dazu Oppermann, Thomas, Nationale Verfassungsautonomie und supranationale Bindung innerhalb der Europäischen Union, in: Battis, Ulrich u.a. (Hrsg.), Das GG im Prozess europäischer und globaler Verfassungsentwicklung, FS Grundgesetz, 2000, S. 117, 130; Schwarze, Jürgen: Ist das GG eine Hindernis auf dem Weg nach Europa?, 54 JZ 1999, S. 637ff.

[117] Everling, Ulrich, Überlegungen zur Struktur der Europäischen Union und zum neuen Europa-Artikel des Grundgesetzes, 108 DVBl., 1993, S. 936, bei Fn. 78.

[118] Scholz, Rupert, Art. 23, in Maunz, Theodor/Dürig, Günter, Grundgesetz, Kommentar, Rdnr. 55, 81ff.

[119] Gewichtige Stimmen haben schon früh die Notwendigkeit des Art. 23 GG mit Blick auf die Union als „zwischenstaatliche Einrichtung" i.S. des Art. 24 GG in Zweifel gezogen, vgl. nur Oppermann, Thomas, Classen, Dieter, Die EG vor der Europäischen Union, in 46 NJW 1993, S. 5, 11 (m.w.N.).

[120] Randelzhofer, Albrecht, Art. 24, in Maunz, Theodor/Dürig, Günter, Grundgesetz. Kommentar, Bd. III, Rdnr. 57ff.

[121] So der EuGH in ständiger Rspr. seit Rs 26/62, Van Gend u. Loos, Slg. 1963, S. 1.

[122] Hobe, Stephan, Der kooperationsoffene Verfassungsstaat, 37 Der Staat (1998), S. 521, 545 (fourth branch of gvt-theorie).

[123] Dagegen aber Frowein: Die Einfügung der (oben I 2) erwähnten Mitwirkungs*verpflichtung* sei wahrhaft „revolutionär", weil sie dazu führe, dass (anders als Art. 24 GG) einmal übertragene Hoheitsrechte nicht einseitig zurückgenommen werden könnten, in Frowein, Jochen Abr., Die Europäisierung des Verfassungsrechts, in Badura, Peter und Dreier, Horst (Hrsg,), Festschrift 50 Jahre Bundesverfassungsgericht, S. 209, 211f. In diese Richtung auch Ipsen, der schon früh (allerdings aus dem europäischen Recht) trotz der Geltung des damaligen Art. 24 GG die Unzulässigkeit eines Austritts herleitetete.

[124] Im einzelnen Bogdandy, Armin von/ Nettesheim, Martin, Die Europäische Union: Ein einheitlicher Verband mit eigener Rechtsordnung, 31 EuR 1996, S. 3.

[125] Etwa Pernice, Ingolf, Art. 23, in Dreier, Horst (Hrsg.), Grundgesetz, Kommentar, 1998, Rdn. 98 ff.

[126] Geiger, Rudolf, Die Mitwirkung des deutschen Gesetzgebers an der Entwicklung der Europäischen Union, Zur Auslegung des Art. 23 Ab. 1 Satz 2 und 3 GG, 51 JZ 96, S. 1093, 1095, Pechstein/Koenig, Die Europäische Union, 3. Aufl. 2000, Rdnr. 147, insoweit in innerem Widerspruch zu der These, Art. 23 GG unterscheide nicht zwischen den einzelnen Säulen, Rdnr. 148.

[127] Pernice, Ingolf, Europäisches und nationales Verfassungsrecht, 60 VVDStRL 2001, S. 148, 179.

[128] Vergleichbare Regelungen" sind insbesondere die „vertragsverlängernden", nicht bloss „vertragsausfüllenden" Evolutivklauseln etwa der Art 269 EGV, 17 Abs. 1 UAbs. 2 EUV, 42 Abs. 2, 48, 49 EUV. Diese sind insbesondere durch ihr nicht vohersehbares potentielles „Eigenleben" gekennzeichnet; hierzu Huber, Peter, M., Europäisches und nationales Verfassungsrecht, 60 VVDStRL 2001, S. 221; Uhrig, Stephanie, Die Schranken des Grundgesetzes für die europäische Integration, 2000, S. 101; Scholz, Rupert, Art. 23, in Maunz, Theodor/Dürig, Günter, Grundgesetz, Kommentar, Bd. III, Rdn. 85.

[129] Unter anderem deshalb wurde die Vorschrift des Art. 23 I 3 GG mit viel Skepsis betrachtet; vgl nur etwa Everling, Ulrich, Überlegungen zur Struktur der Europäischen Union und zum neuen Europa-Artikel des Grundgesetzes, 108 DVBl., 1993, S. 936, hinter FN 75: „Betriebsunfall".

[130] Uhrig, Stephanie, Die Schranken des Grundgesetzes für die europäische Integration, 2000, S. 105; demgegenüber differenzierend nach der Vertragsimmanenz einer Änderung (dann einfache Mehrheit nach Satz 2, sonst Zwei-Drittel-Mehrheit nach Satz 3) Scholz, Rupert, Art. 23, in Maunz, Theodor/Dürig, Günter, Grundgesetz, Kommentar, Bd. III, Rdn. 84.

[131] Vgl. insoweit auch die Regelungen des EUZBBG; zur Wahrnehmung der Rechte des Bundestages Art. 45 GG; zsfd. zum ganzen Scholz, Rupert, Art. 23, in Maunz, Theodor/Dürig, Günter, Grundgesetz, Kommentar, Bd. III, Rdn. 112 ff; vertiefend Hansmeyer, Sandra, Die Mitwirkung des Deutschen Bundestages an der europäischen Rechtssetzung, 2001; zu den aktuellen Entwicklungen Sterzing, Christian, Tidow, Stefan, Die Kontrolle der deutschen Europapolitik durch den EU-Ausschuss des Bundestags - Bilanz und Reformpotenziale, 24 integration 2001, S. 274.

[132] Es handelt sich daher immer um ein „Zustimmungsgesetz" nach Art. 77 IIa GG.

[133] Die Einzelheiten sind im EUZBLG und in der Bund-Länder-Vereinbarung (BLV) näher geregelt. Zur internen Europakammer des Bundesrates vgl. Art. 52 III GG; Zsfd. zum ganzen Scholz, Rupert, Art. 23, in Maunz, Theodor/Dürig, Günter, Grundgesetz, Kommentar, Bd. III, Rdn. 120 ff; Pernice, Ingolf, Art. 23, in Dreier, Horst, Grundgesetzkommentar, Bd. II, 1998, Rdn. 104; vertiefend Paul, Michael, Die Mitwirkung der Bundesländer an der Rechtssetzung der Europäischen Gemeinschaften de lege lata und de lege ferenda, 1996; im Lichte der Entstehungsgeschichte Lang, Ruth, Die Mitwirkungsrechte des Bundesrates und des Bundestages in Angelegenheiten der Europäischen Union gemäß Art. 23 Abs. 2 bis 7 GG, 1997.

[134] Zur Kompetenzverteilung im Bereich der Gestzgebung vgl. Art. 30, 70 ff. GG.

[135] Vgl. schon etwa Breuer, Rüdiger, Die Sackgasse des neuen Europaartikels (Art. 23 GG), 13 NVwZ 1994, S. 417.

[136] Hierzu und zum folgenden Isensee, Josef, Der Bundesstaat - Bestand und Entwicklung, in Badura, Peter und Dreier, Horst (Hrsg.), Festsschrift 50 Jahre Bundesverfassungsgreicht, Bd. II, S. 719, 764 ff.

[137] So aber etwa Schwarze, Jürgen, Das Staatsrecht in Europa, 48 JZ 1993, S. 585; Ossenbühl, Fritz, Maastricht un das Grundgesetz - eine verfassungsrechtliche Wende?, 108 DVBl. 1993, S. 629.

[138] A.A. etwa Pernice, Ingolf, Art. 23, in: Dreier, Horst (Hrsg.), Grunsgesetz, Kommentar, 1998, Rz. 99, 107, der den Schwerpunkt des Absatzes II nicht im Sinne eines „die Länder wirken *durch den Bundesrat* mit" setzt, sondern im Sinne eines *„die Länder wirken* durch den Bundesrat *mit*".

[139] Vgl. insoweit auch § 6 EUZBLG.

[140] Isensee, Josef, Ibid, S. 766: „Die Bestimmungen über die Mitwirkungsrechte sind so vage gefaßt, dass sie die Staatspraxis nicht normativ steuern können; vielmehr entscheidet die Staastspraxis über ihre normative Bedeutung".

[141] Zum Begriff der demokratischen Legitimation: Weiler, Joseph J.H., The Transformation of Europe, in: Ders., The Constitution of Europe, 1999, S. 10, 80 m.w.N.

142 Pernice, Ingolf, Europäisches und nationales Verfassungsrecht, 60 VVDStRL 2001, S. 162f: „Selbstbestimmung des Einzelnen als Element der Menschenwürde: Staat kein Naturgebilde sondern „Zweckverband“, ein „Stück Selbstorganisation der Gesellschaft“; ferner Pernice, Ingolf, Vertragsrevision oder europäische Verfassungsgebung?, FAZ vom 7. Juli 1999, Seite 7 Spalte 2: „Das Verfahren des Vertragsschlusses stösst als solches nicht auf Bedenken. Wichtig ist, dass dieser Vertrag auch als Vertrag zwischen den Bürgern der Mitgliedstaaten bewusster wird, zwischen den Bürgern, die hiermit gleichzeitig die Europäische Union *und sich selbst* in ihrer (neuen zusätzlichen) Identität als Unionsbürger konstituieren und entwickeln.“ [Hervorhebung vom Berichterstatter].

143 Dies ist der Kern dessen, was der EuGH meint, wenn er von einer eigenen Rechtsordnung spricht, die sich vom herkömmlichen Völkerrecht abhebt, vgl EuGH Rs 26/62, Van Gend und Loos, Slg. 1963, S. 1/25; Rs 6/64, Costa/ENEL, Slg. 1964, S. 125/126 f.

144 Dazu Böckenförde, Ernst-Wolfgang, Geschichtliche Entwicklung und Bedeutungswandel der Verfassung, in: Ders., Staat, Verfassung, Demokratie, 2. Aufl., 1992, S. 29, 36: „Verfassung als Vertrag“.

145 Böckenförde, Ernst-Wolfgang, Die verfassungsgebende Gewalt des Volkes- Ein Grenzbegriff des Verfassungsrechts, in Ders., Staat, Verfassung, Demokratie, S. 90; Schneider, Hans-Peter, Die verfassungsgebende Gewalt, in: Isensee, Josef/Kirchhof, Paul (Hrsg.), HdBStR, Bd. VII, § 158, S. 3, 13, Rdn 20.

146 Zur Repräsentativdemokratie nur Böckenförde, Ernst-Wolfgang, Demokratische Willensbildung und Repräsentation, in: Isensee, Josef/Kirchhof, Paul (Hrsg.), HdBStR, Bd. II (2.Aufl.), 1998, S. 29 ff.

147 „[...] vom Volke in Wahlen *und Abstimmungen* [.....] ausgeübt [...]“

148 Vgl. die die Neugliederung des Bundesgebiets und einiger Länder betreffenden Vorschriften der Art. 29 und 118 GG; Zusammenfassend Krause, Peter, Verfassungsrechtliche Möglichkeiten unmittelbarer Demokratie, in: Isensee, Josef/Kirchhof, Paul (Hrsg.), HdBStR Bd. II, 2. Aufl. 1998, § 39, S. 313 mwN. A.A. aber etwa Bleckmann, Albert, Die Zulässigkeit des Volksentscheides nach dem Grundgesetz, in JZ 1978, S. 217 ff; Pieroth, Art. 20, in Jarras/Pieroth, GG, 5. Aufl. 200, Rdn 7. In jüngerer Zeit hat die Diskussion durch die Einführung von Vorschriften über direkte demokratische Beteiligung in vielen Landesverfassungen an Dynamik gewonnen (vgl. Hartmann, Bernd J., Volksgesetzgebung in Ländern und Kommunen, 116 DVBl. 2001, S. 776; Huber, Peter M., Die Vorgaben des Grundgesetzes für kommunale Bürgerbegehren und Bürgerentscheide, 126 AöR 2001, S. 165, 183ff, 202). Aber auch auf Bundesebene wird verstärkt über die Einführung von Elementen direkter Demokratie nachgedacht (vgl. etwa Koalitionsvereinbarung vom 20.10.1998, IX.13 (S. 50) (zitiert bei Hartmann)).

149 Also jene Erklärung, die im Völkerrecht „Ratifikation“ genannt wird, vgl. insoweit Art. 14 der Wiener Vertragsrechtskonvention (WVRK) von 1969.

150 Dies entspricht im übrigen dem gegenwärtigen Stand des Unionsrechts. Die Verträge von Maastricht, Amsterdam und Nizza wurden genauso wie die römischen Verträge als völkerrechtliche Verträge abgeschlossen. Art. 48 EUV ist nach seinem Wortlaut eine typisch völkerrechtliche Vertragsänderungsvorschrift: Die

Regierungen einigen sich über bestimmte vertragliche Regeln, die dann von den Mitgliedstaaten, so wie auch sonst im Völkerrecht üblich, nach ihren verfassungsrechtlichen Vorschriften ratifiziert werden.

[151] Selbst die Kritik, die aus dem Gesichtspunkt der verfassungsgebenden Gewalt des Volkes zu Art. 23 GG formuliert worden ist, hat zwar Anstoß daran genommen, dass Art. 23 GG unter (behauptetem) Verstoß gegen Art. 79 Abs. 3 GG ohne Volksbefragung zustandegekommen ist (dazu oben), nicht jedoch daran, dass Art. 23 Abs. 1 S. 1 GG, einmal im Grundgesetz, die Regelung der Angelegenheiten der Europäischen Union so wie andere Angelegenheiten „durch Gesetz" regelt.

[152] Vgl. Pernice, Ingolf, Vertragsrevision oder europäische Verfassungsgebung?, FAZ vom 7. Juli 1999, Seite 7 Spalte 2.

[153] Der Kreis zwischen der Abstraktion von mitgliedstaatlicher Staatlichkeit als Voraussetzung der Anerkennung europäischen Verfassungsrechts) hin zur Abstraktion von mitgliedstaatlicher Staatlichkeit als Voraussetzung für dessen demokratische Legitimation, den ja das BVerfG schon fordert (vgl. oben 1), wäre damit wieder geschlossen.

[154] Aus abstrakt-verfassungstheoretischer Sicht müsste eine europäische Verfassung, verabschiedet etwa durch eine verfassungsgebende Versammlung oder ein europaweites Referendum, gegebenfalls *garnicht* der Dogmatik des Grundgesetzes entsprechen. Denn sich eine Verfassung zu geben heißt eben, eine sich selbst tragende und legitimierende, wirkmächtige rechtliche Grundordnung zu errichten (s.o. 1). Diese ist im Regelfall in ihrer Wirkmächtigkeit dann eben nicht abhängig von gegebenenfalls vorher bestehenden rechtlichen Ordnungen. Eine solche Position würde aber natürlich vollkommen an den gegenwärtigen Realitäten vorbeigehen. Nach dem gegenwärtigen Diskussionsstand soll sich die zu errichtende europäische Ordnung nicht vollständig selbst tragen, sondern eben nur Teilverfassung im System einer europäischen Verfassungsgesamtheit sein (s.o.).Das heißt natürlichauch, dass sie den nationalen Verfassungen, mit denen sie eine Gesamtheit bilden soll, auch gemäß ist.

[155] Vgl. nur Dreier, Horst, Art. 20 (Demokratie), in Ders. (Hrsg.), Grundgesetz, Kommentar, Bd. II 1998, Rdn. 100 m.w.N.

[156] Überblick auch über die europäische Diskussion bei Fritz-Vannahme, Joachim, Nizza ist nur der Anfang – Als nächstes schreibt Europa seine Verfassung, Die ZEIT vom 7. Dez. 2000, Nr. 50, S. 3¸ Guérot, Ulrike, Eine Verfassung für Europa, Internationale Politik 2001, S. 28.

[157] Mit der gemeinsamen Erklärung von Kommission, Parlament, schwedischer und belgischer Präsidentschaft vom 7. März 2001 "zur Eröffnung der Debatte über die künftige Entwicklung der Europäischen Union" wurde die Diskusson formal eröffnet (im Internet zu finden unter http://europa.eu.int/futurum/documents). Die Diskussion in den Mitgliedstaaten hat sodann wesentliche Vorgaben durch die Mitteilung der Kommission über bestimmte Modalitäten der Debatte über die Zukunft der EU vom 25. April 2001 (KOM (2001) 178 endg.) erhalten: Die Kommission schlägt darin einen dreistufigen Diskussionsprozess vor, nämlich einen offenen (1. Stufe), sodann strukturierten (2. Stufe) Denkprozess, "der der Regierungskonferenz (3. Stufe) vorangehen soll". Zugleich fordert die Komission die Mitgliedstaaten darin auf, die Debatten transparent und interaktiv zu organisieren. Zur Gemeinschaftsmethode: Mitteilung der Kommission über die Zukunft

der Europäischen Union - Europäisches Regieren: Erneuerung der Gemeinschaftsmethode, zu finden im Internet etwa unter www.auswaertiges-amt.de (EU-Politik, Aktuelles, Zukunft, Debatte).

[158] Zum Konventsverfahren als Betätigung der verfassungsgebenden Gewalt allgemein Böckenförde, Ernst-Wolfgang, Die Verfassungsgebende Gewalt des Volkes, Ein Grenzbegriff des Verfassungsrechts, in Ders. Staat, Verfassung, Demokratie, S. 90, 102; Zu konkreten Verbesserungsvorschlägen im Vergleich zum Grundrechtekonvent: Dix, Wolfgang, Grundrechtecharta und Konvent - auf neuen Wegen zur Reform der EU?, in 24 integration 2001, S. 34, 40.

[159] Vgl. etwa die zweite und dritte Beratung des von der Bundesregierung eingebrachten Entwurfs eines Gesetzes zum Vertrag von Nizza vom 26. Februar 2001 (BT 14/6146, 14/7172) vom 18. Oktober 2001 Plenarprotokoll 14/195.

[160] Vgl. etwa Bundesrat, Plenarprotokoll, 769. Sitzung vom 9. Nov. 2001, Tagesordnungspunkt 12 (Gesetz zum Vertrag von Nizza vom 26. Februar 2001).

[161] Vgl. etwa BT 14/6643 vom 6. Juli 2001 (AfEU, Bericht): Mitteilung der Kommission über bestimmte Modalitäten der Debatte über die Zukunft der Europäischen Union; BT 14/6644 vom 6.Juli 2001 (AfEU, Beschlussempfehlung und Bericht): Die Weichen für die Erweiterung der Europäischen Union richtig stellen; BT 14/7172 vom 17.Oktober 2001 (AfEU): Entwurf eines Gesetzes zum Vertrag von Nizza vom 26. Februar 2001. Im AfEU wird eng mit den parlamentarischen Gremien der anderen Mitgliedstaaten zusammengearbeitet, vgl. etwa die Konferenz der Europaausschüsse der nationalen Parlamente (COSAC); dazu etwa Lord Tordoff, The Conference of European Affairs Committees: A Collective Voice for National Parliaments in the European Union, 6 JLS 2000, S. 1.

[162] Vgl. aus den letzten Jahren allein die in folgenden Sammelbänden veröffentlichten, meist interdisziplinären Symposien: 23 integration 2000, Heft 2: Forum – Zukunft der Europäischen Union, 24 integration 2001, Heft 2: Die europäische Verfassung; 60 VVDStRL 2001, S. 148 ff: Europäisches und nationales Verfassungsrecht; Bruha, Thomas u.a., Welche Verfassung für Europa?, Schwarzkopf-Kolloquium, 2001; Ronge Frank, In welcher Verfassung ist Europa – Welche Verfassung für Europa?, ZEI-Symposium, 2001; Schwarze, Jürgen (Hrsg.), Die Entstehung einer europäischen Verfassungsordnung. Das Ineinandergreifen von nationalem und europäischem Verfassungsrecht, , 2000; 17. FIDE-Kongress 1996 in Berlin mit deutschem Landesbericht von Scheuing, Dieter, H., Deutsches Verfassungsrecht und europäische Integration, in EuR Beiheft I, 1997, S. 7; vgl. ferner den etwa 350 Artikel umfassenden Verfassungsentwurf von Dimitrios Argirakos und Peter Lüdemann und den Entwurf vom Europäischen Universitätsinstitut; aus früherer Zeit etwa Schwarze, Jürgen, Bieber, Roland, Eine Verfassung für Europa, 1984.

[163] Deutlich wird dies etwa in der mittlerweile großen Zahl von Beiträgen, mit denen sich Wissenschaftler in allgemein zugänglichen Tages- und Wochenzeitungen zu Wort melden, vgl. nur (Auswahl) Biaggini, Giovanni, Eine Verfassung für Europa?, NZZ vom 11./12. November 2000, S. 57; Holzinger, Katharina und Knill, Christoph, Eine Verfassung für die Europäische Föderation, FAZ vom 29. November 2000, S. 11; Weber, Albrecht, Eine einmalige Chance für eine europäische Verfassungsgebung, FAZ vom 26. August 2000; Landfried, Christine, Die Zeit ist reif – Nur ein europäischer Verfassungsstaat kann das Legitimationsdefizit in der

EU beheben, FAZ vom 9. September 1999, S. 10; Pernice, Ingolf, Vertragsrevision oder europäische Verfassungsgebung?, FAZ vom 7. Juli 1999, S. 7; Fabio, Udo di, Was der Staatenverbund leisten kann, FAZ vom 6. April 1999, S. 11; Nass, Klaus Otto, Ein beliebtes Phantom: Das Demokratiedefizit der EU, FAZ vom 29. März 1999, S. 15; Grimm, Dieter, Ohne Volk keine Verfassung – Eine demokratische EU braucht bessere Institutionen, aber kein Grundgesetz, Die ZEIT vom 18. März 1999, S. 4; European Constitutional Group, Für Europa eine Verfassung der Freiheit, FAZ vom 28. August 1993, S. 11.

164 Zu finden im internet unter www.bundesregierung.de/frameset/index.jsp (Bundeskanzler, Reden und Erklärungen).

165 Vorgelegt am 26. November 2001 in Berlin von der CDU-CSU-Arbeitsgruppe "Europäischer Verfassungsvertrag" unter Leitung von Wolfgang Schäuble und Reinhold Bocklet. Ähnlich auch die Arbeitsgruppe der CDU/CSU-Fraktion zu den Angelegenheiten der Europäischen Union unter Vorsitz von Peter Hintze: "Die CDU/CSU-Bundestagsfraktion will, dass die Europäische Union in den nächsten Jahren einen Verfassungsvertrag gestaltet, der eine klarere Kompetenzabgrenzung zwischen EU einerseits und Mitgliedstaaten andererseits, mehr Demokratie, mehr Transparenz sowie eine klarere Gewaltenteilung zwischen den Organen der Europäischen Union vorsieht", im Internet zu finden unter www.cducsu.de/TextVersion/index.jsp: Arbeitgruppe 14 (Angelegenheiten der Europäischen Union).

166 Zsfd. die Äusserungen in BT 14/7172, S. 14; im einzelnen zudem etwa: **SPD**: Leitantrag, S. 16; Gloser, Günter und Roth, Michael, Verfassungsrecht ist Parlamentsrecht: Eine starke europäische Gemeinschaft braucht starke Volksvertretungen, in FAZ vom 27. August 2001, S. 8: die IGC 2004 soll "vorbereitend und begleitend" sein; **CDU**: Arbeitgruppe 14 (Angelegenheiten der Europäischen Union): enge Anlehnung an Grundrechtekonvent, vgl im einzelnen dazu auch den Antrag der CDU-Fraktion "Europa richtig voranbringen" vom 11.12.2001, BT Drucksache 14/7781; **CSU**: Stoiber in seiner Rede "Eckpunkte des europäischen Reformprozesses vor der Humboldt-Universität am 8.11.2001, S. 18: Notwendigkeit der Einbeziehung der Bürger. **Fraktion Bündnis 90/GRÜNE**: Ein Konvent für Europa mit Papier von MdB Christian Sterzing: Demokratisierung des Integrationsprozesses – Der Konvent, Forderungen an den Europäischen Rat in Laeken im Dezember 2001: weites Mandat, grötmögliche Freiheit in der Themenwahl und weitgehende Einbeziehung der Zivilgesellschaft (Katalysatorfunktion).

167 Zu finden im internet unter www.bundesregierung.de/frameset/index.jsp (Bundeskanzler, Reden und Erklärungen).

168 So geht Aussenminister Joschka Fischer von einem "langfristige[n] Zeitraum, weit jenseits der laufenden Regierungskonferenz" aus. Der europapolitische Sprecher der SPD-Bundestagsfraktion, Günter Gloser, hält in der FAZ vom 27.8.2001 eine "umfassende Parlamentarisierung des institutionellen Gefüges der EU im Rahmen der Regierungskonferenz 2004 [für] unwahrscheinlich". Justizministerin Herta Däubler-Gmelin visiert in ihrer Rede vor der Humboldt-Universität vom 19. Okt. 2000 (Rd. 47) eine Regierungkonferenz 2004 oder sogar früher an, ohne aber konkret einen Verfassungsvertrag zu erwarten.

[169] Zu finden unter www.spd.de; dazu Kreile, Michael, Zur nationalen Gebundenheit europapolitischer Visionen: Das Schröder-Papier und die Jospin-Rede, 24 integration 2001, S. 250.

[170] Vgl. den Leitantrag S. 16, ähnlich: Regierungserklärung von Bundeskanzler Schröder im Deutschen Bundestag am 18 Oktober 2001 (14/195).

[171] In: Die europäische Integration voranbringen: Zum europapolitischen Leitantrag der SPD, in: 24 integration, 2001, S. 303-307.

[172] Gloser, Günter und Roth, Michael, Verfassungsrecht ist Parlamentsrecht: Eine starke europäische Gemeinschaft braucht starke Volksvertretungen, in FAZ vom 27. August 2001, S. 8.

[173] *Ibid.*

[174] *Ibid.*

[175] Zu finden im Internet unter www.europarl.eu.int.

[176] Europa gestalten – nicht verwalten, FCE 3/01, Rz. 28 ff, 31 ff.

[177] Kritsch hierzu Bieber, Roland, Abwegige und zielführende Vorschläge: Zur Kompetenzabgrenzung in der Europäischen Union, 24 integration 2001, S. 308.

[178] Vom Staatenverbund zur Föderation – Gedanken über die Finalität der europäischen Integration, 23 integration 2000, S. 149.

[179] Dazu etwa Müller-Graff, Peter-Christian, Europäische Föderation als Revolutionskonzept im europäischen Verfassungsraum?, 23 integration 2000, S. 157; Schneider, Heinrich, Alternativen zur Verfassungsfinalität: Föderation, Konföderation - oder was sonst?, 23 integration 2000, S. 171; Kohler-Koch, Beate, Ziele und Zukunft der Europäischen Union: Eine Frage der Perspektive, 23 integration 2000, S. 185.

[180] Im Internet unter www.cdu.de (Politik A-Z, Europapolitik).

[181] Unter 1 f), S. 3 f.

[182] Im Internet unter www.cducsu.de/TextVersion/index.jsp: Jetzt Europa stärken und demokratischer gestalten, 16. Oktober 2001. Vertiefend vergleiche den Beschluss des Bundesfachausschusses Europapolitik (Vorsitz Elmar Brok, MdEP): Forderungen der CDU an den europäischen Verfassungsprozess bis 2004. In eine ähnliche Richtung geht auch Edmund Stoiber in seiner Rede "Eckpunkte des europäischen Reformprozesses vor der Humboldt-Universität am 8.11.2001; zu den institutionelle Reformen S. 16ff; i.ü.: Bauplan Europa statt Methode Monnet S. 8.

[183] Rede vor der Humboldt-Universität (WHI) vom 24. April 2001, Die Beteiligung der Parlamente in der Europäischen Verfassungsentwicklung, Rz. 74 – 77 (zu finden unter www.whi-berlin.de).

[184] "Wie die gegenwärtigen Versuche zeigen, ist es fast unmöglich, dem enormen Größenunterschied unter den Nationalstaaten innerhalb der Europäischen Union angemessen Rechnung zu tragen, ohne die kleinen Mitgliedsstaaten zu dominieren oder die auf Mitgliedsstaaten aufbauenden Organe der Europäischen Union zur Handlungsunfähigkeit zu verurteilen." (Rz. 37).

[185] "Durch ein Europa, das auf Regionen aufbaut, können wir die Widersprüche zwischen Nationalstaat und seinem Anspruch einerseits und der kulturellen Wirklichkeit andererseits weit besser überwinden als durch eine Föderation der Nationalstaaten. Mit einem Europa der Regionen bieten wir den kulturellen Identitäten Raum, sich zu entfalten und auch grenzüberschreitend unter einem

europäischen Dach und einer europäischen Handlungseinheit zusammenzufinden, unter einem europäischen Gouvernement, gewissermaßen ausgestattet mit den Kernsouveränitäten, deren Europa unstreitig bedarf und selbstverständlich unterstützt durch die Fortdauer der allerdings zunehmend relativierten Nationalstaaten" (Rz. 29).

[186] "Mehr Aktivitäten im Bereich der Regulierung erhöht den Umfang der Interventionen. Damit vermehren sich die Widersprüchlichkeiten innerhalb des europäischen Rechts und des administrativen Handelns. Denn keine Regierung, auch nicht die Kommission, ist in der Lage, die Auswirkungen einer ständig wachsende Zahl von Interventionen so genau abzuschätzen, dass die Gesamtheit der Interventionen in sich widerspruchsfrei bleibt." (Rz. 76).

[187] "Europa wird sich nur dann in einer politischen Union vereinen, wenn es gelingt, die Bürger der Mitgliedsländer für den Bau Europas zu gewinnen, so dass sie diese historisch einmalige Aufgabe zu der ihren machen. Aufgabe der politischen Klasse ist es nicht, die Bürger mitzunehmen. Von ihr wird erwartet, die europäischen Institutionen in einer Weise zu ordnen, die es den Bürgern Europas erlaubt, am Bau Europa aktiv mitzuwirken, ihn zu erleben und zu gestalten. Solange die Debatten über Entwicklung und Reform der europäischen Institutionen und Politiken geprägt sind durch die noch immer vorherrschende Vorstellung vom Nationalstaat klassischer Prägung mit seiner umfassenden, vielfach vormundschaftlich verstandenen Verantwortung für das Wohl der Bürger, wird es ein Europa der Bürger nicht geben." (Rz. 81).

[188] "Das Subsidiaritätsprinzip gilt als genereller Grundsatz auch für das Verhältnis der staatlichen zur nicht staatlichen Ebene. Seine Anwendung auf die Ordnung Europas erschöpft sich nicht, wie Joschka Fischer meint, in der Ordnung des Verhältnisses zwischen Europäischer Union und den Nationalstaaten."

[189] In jenem Sinne, dass die Frage "Superstaat – ja oder nein" keine übergeordnete Rolle mehr spiele, wenn die inhaltliche Gestaltung stimmt.

[190] "Werden Ergebnisse gefunden, die sich bewährt haben und allgemeine Akzeptanz finden, dann können sie durch Normierung verallgemeinert und gegebenenfalls durch die spätere Verfassung dauerhaft konstituiert werden. Bis dahin bestimmt sich die Verfassung der Europäischen Union durch die Verträge. Durch eine entsprechende Differenzierung ihrer Normen und Regelungen können die konstitutionellen Elemente hervorgehoben, als solche erkennbar gemacht und vom übrigen Normenbestand der Verträge getrennt werden. Eine Verständigung auf dieses Verfahren sollte in jedem Falle jedem Versuch vorausgehen, eine europäische Verfassung zu formulieren. Das Ergebnis wird zeigen, dass die Europäische Union auf absehbare Zeit ohne eine endgültige Verfassung auskommen kann" (Rz. 92).

[191] Als Beispiel dieser Wirkrichtung mag der Übergang der europapolitischen Diskussionen vom Typus der (das Links-Rechts-Spektrum völlig ausseracht-lassenden) Diskussion um ein Mehr/Weniger an europäischer Integration zur immer noch in ihren Anfängen steckenden Diskussion um das Wie der Integration dienen: Hier findet europäische Identitätsfindung statt, ohne dass nationale Identitäten sozusagen beeinträchtigt werden. Zum ganzen Weiler, Joseph J. H., The Transormation of Europe, in: Ders., The Constitution of Europe, 1999, S. 10, 88.f.

[192] Stumpf, Cordula, Art. 6 EUV, in: Schwarze (Hrsg.), EU-Kommentar, 2000 Rdnr. 42; Puttler, Adelheit, Art. 6, in: Calliess, Cristian/Ruffert, Matthias (Hrsg.),

Komm. zu EUV u. EGV, 1999, Rdnr. 190; Bleckmann, Albert, Die Wahrung der nationalen Identität im Unionsvertrag, 52 JZ 1997, S. 265; Hilf, Meinhard, Europäische Union und nationale Identität der Mitgliedstaaten, in: Randelzhofer, Albrecht u.a. (Hrsg.), Gedächtnisschrift Eberhard Grabitz, S. 157; Döhring, Karl, Die nationale „Identität" der Mitgliedstaaten der Europäischen Union, in: Due, Ole u.a. (Hrsg.), Festschrift für Everling Bd. 1, 1995, S. 263 ff; Rupp, Hans Heinrich, Bemerkungen zum europarechtlichen Schutz der „nationalen Identität" der EU-Mitgliedstaaten, in: Arndt, Hans-Wolfgang u.a. (Hrsg.), Völkerrecht und nationales Recht, Festschrift für Walter Rudolf, 2001, S. 174.

[193] Zum Verhältnis kürzlich Moersch, Wolfram, Leistungsfähigkeit und Grenzen des Subsidiaritätsprinzips. Eine rechtsdogmatische und rechtspolitische Studie, 2001, S. 350 ff.

[194] Thürer, Daniel, Föderalistische Strukturen für Europa - eine zweite Chance der Entfaltung, 23 integration 2000, S. 89, 99.

[195] Dabei spielt natürlich der Faktor Zeit eine Rolle. Wäre die Frage etwa, ob Frauen in der Bundeswehr Dienst mit der Waffe tun dürfen, vor einigen Jarzehnten wohl noch überwiegend als Frage nationaler Identität begriffen worden, regen sich in der Öffentlichkeit heute nur noch wenige Stimmen, wenn ausgerechnet der EuGH mit wenigen Worten die Frage endgültig entscheidet; vgl. EuGH, Urteil vom 11.1.2000, Rs. C-285/98, EuZW 2000, S. 211 m. Anm. Stein, Torsten, der ausdrücklich auf die geringe öffentliche Diskussion hinweist; vgl aber auch etwa Scholz, Rupert, RIW 2000, 222.

[196] Haltern, Ulrich R., Europäischer Kulturkampf, Zur Wahrung „nationaler Identität" im Unions-Vertrag , 37 Der Staat 1998, S. 590, 608.

[197] Zur rechtswissenschaftlichen Bedeutung dieses „sense of belonging" Böckenförde, Ernst-Wolfgang, Die Nation, Identität in Differenz, in: Ders., Staat - Verfassung - Europa, 1999, S. 34; Ders., Welchen Weggeht Europa, in: Ders., Staat - Verfassung - Europa, 1999, S. 68, 93. Der Begriff des „sense of belonging" ist, anders als Identität, noch kein rechtswissenschaftlicher Begriff. Die Rechtswissenschaft knüpft angesichts solcher Vorschriften wie des Art. 6 Abs. 3 EUV an diesen Begriff aber an. Sie bedarf daher der Vor-rechtswissenschaftlichen Klärung. Zu politikwissenschaftlichen Identitätsdiskussion um den Begriffdes „sense of belonging" vgl etwa nur Laffan, Brigid, The Politics of Identity and Political Order in Europe, 34 Journal of Common Market Studies 1996, S. 1, Aufsätze bei Viehoff, Reinhold, Segers, Rien T., (Hrsg.), Kultur, Identität, Europa, 1999; empirische Untersuchungen in Marcussen, Martin u.a., Constructing Europe? The evolution of French, British and German nation State identities, 6 Journal of European Public Policy 1999, S. 614.

[198] Durch die zunehmende Zuerkennung verschiedener Bürgerschaften, etwa auch die Zuerkennung der Unionsbürgerschaft, wird auch die in diesem Sinne beschriebene kollektive Identität komplizierter; vgl. Haltern, Ulrich, R., Europäischer Kulturkampf, Zur Wahrung „nationaler Identität" im Unions-Vertrag, 37 Der Staat 1998, S. 590, 608.

[199] Weiler, Joseph J. H., The Transformation of Europe, in: Ders., The Constitution of Europe, 1999, S. 10, 95.

[200] In diese Richtung auch Rupp, Hans Heinrich, Bemerkungen zum europarechtlichen Schutz der „nationalen Identität" der EU-Mitgliedstaaten, in: Arndt,

Hans-Wolfgang u.a. (Hrsg.), Völkerrecht und nationales Recht, Festschrift für Walter Rudolf 2001, S. 174.

[201] Haltern, Ulrich R., 37 Der Staat 1998, S. 620, Stützendes Argument: Art 17 Abs. 1 S. 3 EGV (Unionsbürgerschaft ersetzt nicht nationale Staatsbürgerschaft, sondern ergänzt diese). Zur politologischen Einordnung: Eine extensive Auslegung des Art. 6 Abs. 3 EUV reagiere auf die „Erscheinungsformen der Moderne, indem sie der Union eine prämoderne Therapie" verordne (Haltern, S. 622).

[202] Haltern, Ulrich R., Europäischer Kulturkampf, Zur Wahrung „nationaler Identität" im Unions-Vertrag , 37 Der Staat 1998, S. 590, 594; allerdings mit Hinweis auf die gegenwärtig überall zu findende „Über- und Untersozialisation", und zwar sowohl hinsichtlich der Politik als auch hinsichtlich der Kultur, S. 596.

[203] Dazu etwa Oppermann, Thomas, Reform der EU-Sprachenregelung?, 54 NJW 2001, S. 2663, 2664 m.w.N.

[204] Bleckmann, Albert, Die Wahrung der nationalen Identität im Unionsvertrag, 52 JZ 1997, S. 265, 266. Damit steht er in der Nähe von Böckenförde, der (wenn auch nicht im Zusammenhang mit Art. 6 Abs. 3 EUV) die Rolle der Kultur (in kritischer Auseinandersetzung mit ihrem geschichtlichen Zusammenhang) für den Nationenbegriff betont, in: Die Nation, Identität in Differenz, in: Ders., Staat - Verfassung - Europa, 1999, S. 34; zum Ganzen Häberle, Peter, Europa - eine Verfassungsgemeinschaft?, in: Ronge, Frank (Hrsg.), In welcher Verfassung ist Europa - Welche Verfassung für Europa?, 2001, S. 99, 104.

[205] Hilf, Meinhard, Europäische Union und nationale Identität der Mitgliedstaaten, in: Randelzhofer, Albrecht u.a. (Hrsg.), Gedächtnisschrift für Eberhard Grabitz, S. 157, 163.

[206] Dazu Nettesheim, Martin, Das Kulturverfassungsrecht der EU, 57 JZ 2002, S. 246.

[207] Ørstrøm, Møller, Technology and Culture in a European Context, 1991; Smith, A. D., National Identity and the Idea of European Unity, in Gowan, P., Anderson, P. (Hrsg), The Question of Europe, 1997; zitiert aus Haltern, Ulrich R., Europäischer Kulturkampf, Zur Wahrung „nationaler Identität" im Unions-Vertrag , 37 Der Staat 1998, S. 590, 613, Fn 109 (ablehnend). Mag nach manchen Autoren in diesem Licht auch der antike Weltstaat mit der kulturellen Autonomie seiner entlegenen Provinzen, deren nicht weiter ins Gewicht fallenden politischen Beteiligung und der demzufolge ihm eigenen despotischen Machausübung in der Zentrale aufleuchten, vgl. Böckenförde, Ernst-Wolfgang, Die Zukunft politischer Autonomie, in: Staat, Nation, Europa, 1999, S. 103, 126. Häberle hingegen spricht unter Hinweis auf Wallace vom „neuen Mittelalter", in Häberle, Peter, Europa - eine Verfassungsgemeinschaft?, in: Ronge, Frank (Hrsg.), In welcher Verfassung ist Europa - Welche Verfassung für Europa?, 2001, S. 99, 100.

[208] Für ein Europa der (Rechts-)Kultur Häberle, Peter, Europa als werdende Verfassungsgemeinschaft, 115 DVBl. 2000, S. 840.

[209] Stephan, Rüdiger, Über Kultur und Demokratie in Europa, in: Ronge, Frank (Hrsg.), In welcher Verfassung ist Europa - Welche Verfassung für Europa?, 2001, S. 59, 69.

[210] Häberle, Peter, Europa - eine Verfassungsgemeinschaft?, in: Ronge, Frank (Hrsg.), In welcher Verfassung ist Europa - Welche Verfassung für Europa?, 2001, S. 99, 100.

[211] Vgl. zu Rechtsprinzipien Alexy, Robert, Theorie der Grundrechte, 2. Aufl. 1994, S. 71ff.
[212] So wurden im Vertrag von Nizza die Kompetenzen des EuGH zwar durch einen neuen lit. e) erweitert, allerdings nur hinsichtlich der „reinen Verfahrensbestimmungen des Art. 7" EUV, nicht hinsichtlich des Art. 6 Abs. 1 EUV, vgl. Art. 1 Nr. 15 des Vertrages von Nizza.
[213] Allgemein etwa Luchterhandt, Otto, Verfassungshomogenität und Osterweiterung der EU, in: Bruha, Thomas u.a., Welche Verfassung für Europa?, 2001, S. 125. Zur Konkretisierung des in Art. 6 Abs. 1 EUV verkörperten Demokratieprinzip nach dieser Methode etwa Bleckmann, Albert, Das europäische Demokratieprinzip, 56 JZ 2001, S. 53. Für die Union können diese Grundsätze unter Berücksichtigung deren spezifischer Ausgestaltung allerdings ganz andere Gehalte bekommen, vgl hierzu statt vieler nur etwa Schuppert, Gunnar Folke: Überlegungen zur demokratischen Legitimation des europäischen Regierungssystems, in: Ipsen, Jörn und Schmidt- Jortzig, Edzard (Hrsg.), Recht - Staat - Gemeinwohl, Festschrift für Rauschning, 2001, S. 201, 210: „strukturadäquate Legitimation" der EU. Diese auf die EU selbst bezogenen Überlegungen spielen für die Grenzen mitgliedstaatlicher Verfassungsautonomie aber zunächst keine grosse Rolle.
[214] Beutler, Bengt u.a., Die Europäische Union, Rechtsordnung und Politik, 5. Aufl. 2001, S. 113, Rdn. 144.
[215] Pernice, Ingolf, Europäisches und nationales Verfassungsrecht, 60 VVDStRL 2001, S. 184f: „Art. 6.1 EUV als ius cogens".
[216] Bogdandy, Armin von, Grundrechtsgemeinschaft als Integrationsziel?, 56 JZ 2001, S. 157, 162: „qualitativer Sprung".
[217] Problematisch vor diesem Hintergrund: Schorkopf, Frank, Homogenität in der Europäischen Union - Ausgestaltung und Gewährleistung durch Art. 6 Abs. 1 und 7 EUV, 2000, S. 230, Rz. 406: „Die Verfassungsautonomie und damit die Souveränität der Mitgliedstaaten wird durch den materiellen Gehalt der Homogenitätsklausel eingeschränkt. *Die praktische Bedeutung dieser Schlussfolgerung ist gering, weil die Mitgliedstaaten im Hinblick auf die Geltung des Demokratei- und Rechtsstaatsprinzips sowie den Menschenrechtsschutz freiheitlich verfasst und homogen sind.*[Hervorhebung vom Berichterstatter]"
[218] Dazu etwa Pernthaler, Peter, Hilpold, Peter, Sanktionen als Instrument der Politikkontrolle - der Fall Österreich, 23 integration, 2000, S. 105; Hummer, Waldemar, Obwexer, Walter, Die Wahrung der „Verfassungsgrundsätze" der EU, 11 EuZW 2000, S. 485; Adamovich, Ludwig, Juristische Aspekte der „Sanktionen" der EU-14 und des „Weisenberichts", 28 EuGRZ 2001, S. 89.
[219] Vgl. nur Schneider, Heinrich, Die EU als Wertegemeinschaft, 22 integration, 1999, S. 143; Ders., Österreich in Acht und Bann - ein Schritt zur politisch integrierten „Wertegemeinschaft"?, 23 integration, 2000, S. 120.
[220] Dazu Speer, Benedikt, Die Europäische Union als Wertegemeinschaft, 54 DÖV 2001, S. 980.
[221] Problematisch daher von Bogdandy: „Die Union ist eine politische Gemeinschaft, die sich nur wenig auf einen materiellen Grundkonsens verlassen kann. Umso wichtiger sind die Verfahren, in denen eine zuträgliche Lösung der Konflikte erarbeitet werden kann." (Bogdandy, Armin von, Zweierlei Verfassungsrecht, 39 Der Staat 2000, S. 181; ähnlich Zuleeg, Manfred, What Holds

a Nation Together? Cohesion and Democracy in the United States of America and in the European Union, 45 AJCL 1997, S. 505).

222 Pernice, Ingolf, Europäisches und nationales Verfassungsrecht, 60 VVDStRL 2001, S. 162: „Verfassung ist Ausdruck eines *Wertekonsenses als Verfahrensergebnis* und zugleich Verfahren immer neuer Integration, in dem Differenzen sozialer Gruppen und Widersprüche offengelegt, verhandelt und einer Lösung zugeführt werden"; in eine ähnliche Richtung Leisner, Walter, „Werteverlust", „Wertewandel" und Verfassungsrecht, 56 JZ 2001, S. 313, 317f, der hinter jedem Verfahrensergebnis immer auch eine „durchaus materielle Wervorstellung" sieht (S. 318); zum ganzen auch Rödel, in Gebhardt/Schmalz-Bruns (Hrsg.), Demokratie, Verfassung und Nation, 1994, S. 123 ff, 133.

223 Hierzu schon Ipsen, Hans P., Über Verfassungshomogenität in der Europäischen Gemeinschaft, in Maurer, Hartmut (Hrsg.), Das akzeptierte Grundgesetz, Festschrift für Günter Dürig, 1990, S. 159; Grawert, Rolf, Demokratische Regierungssysteme, Qualitätsanforderungen an die Regierungssysteme der Mitgliedstaaten der Europäischen Union, in: Murswiek, Dietrich u.a. (Hrsg.), Staat - Souveränität - Verfassung, Fetschrift Helmut Quaritsch, 2000.

224 An dieser Stelle sind denn auch Schorkopfs Erkenntnisse ziemlich dünn, vgl. S. 43 bis 45.

225 Jedenfalls dann, wenn man nicht akzeptierte, dass die Gesamtheit den Anforderungen doch entsprechen könne, wenn nur andere Mitgliedstaaten den „Homogenitätsmangel" in dem einen Mitgliedstaat durch ein „Mehr" an Homogenität ausgleichen könnten. Solche Überlegungen im Sinne eines möglichen Ausgleichs erscheinen aber schon wegen des begrifflichen Gehalts von Homogenität nicht sinnvoll. Entweder eine Gesamtheit von Staaten ist in ihren verfassungsrechtlichen Ausgestaltungen homogen oder sie ist es eben nicht. Vgl insoweit etwa nur Maunz, nach dem Homogenität von Verfassungen in der Regel eben dann vorliege, „wenn wesentliche Merkmale bei Ihnen *übereinstimmend* festgestellt oder ausgesagt werden können [Hervorhebung vom Berichterstatter]", in Maunz, Theodor, Verfassungshomogenität von Bund und Ländern, in: Isensee, Josef, Kirchhof, Paul (Hrsg), HdBStR IV, § 95, S. 443, 444.

226 Hierzu Hilf, Meinhard, Die Charta der Grundrechte der Europäischen Union, Beilage zur 53 NJW 2000, S. 5; Schmitz, Thomas, Die EU-Grundrechtecharta aus grundrechtsdogmatischer und grundrechtstheoretischer Sicht, in 56 JZ 2001, S. 833; Magiera, Siegfried, Die Grundrechtecharta der Europäischen Union, 53 DÖV 2000, S. 1017; Calliess, Christian, Die Charta der Grundrechte der Europäischen Union, 12 EuZW 2001, S. 261; Fabio, Udo di, Eine europäische Charta, 55 JZ 2000, S. 737; Knöll, Ralf, Die Charta der Grundrechte der Europäischen Union, 20 NVwZ 2001, S. 392; Tettinger, Peter J., Die Charta der Grundrechte der Europäischen Union, 54 NJW 2001, S. 1010; Szczekalla, Peter, Grundrechte für Europa - Die Europäische Union nach Nizza, 116 DVBl. 2001, S. 345; Grabenwarter, Christoph, Die Charta der Grundrechte für die Europäische Union, 116 DVBl. 2001, S. 1; Baer, Susanne, Grundrechtecharta ante portas, 33 ZRP 2000, S. 361; Häffner, Gerald, Strawe, Christoph, Zuegg, Robert, In der Auseinandersetzung um eine Charta der Grundrechte der Europäischen Union, 33 ZRP 2000, S. 365; Ritgen, Klaus, Grundrechtsschutz in der Europäischen Union, 33

ZRP 2000, S. 371; Lenaerts, Koen und de Smijter, Eddy, A „bill of rights“ for the European Union, 38 CMLRev. 2001, S. 273; Liisberg, Jonas Bering, Does the EU Charter of Fundamental Rights threaten the supremacy of Community Law?, 38 CMLRev. 2001, S. 1171; Steiner, Udo, Richterliche Grundrechtsverantwortung in Europa, in Geis, Max-Emanuel, Lorenz, Dieter (Hrsg.), Staat - Kirche - Verwaltung, Festschrift für Hartmut Maurer, 2001, S. 1005; Rengeling, Hans-Werner, Eine Europäische Charta der Grundrechte - Ausarbeitung, Inhalte, Bindung, in: Ipsen, Jörn, Schmidt-Jortzig, Eberhardt (Hrsg.), Recht - Staat - Gemeinwohl, Festschrift für Dietrich Rauschning, 2001, S. 225; Müller-Graff, Peter-Christian, Europäische Verfassung und Grundrechtecharta: Die Europäische Union als transnationales Gemeinwesen, 23 integration, 2000, S. 34; Schmuck, Otto, Die Ausarbeitung der Europäischen Grundrechtecharta als Element der Verfassungsentwicklung, 23 integration, 2000, S. 48; Leinen, Jo, Schönlau, Justus, Die Erarbeitung der EU-Grundrechtecharta im Konvent: nützliche Erfahrungen für die Zukunft Europas, 24 integration, 2001, S. 26; Dix, Wolfgang, Grundrechtecharta und Konvent - auf neuen Wegen zur Reform der EU, 24 integration, 2001, S. 34; Pernice, Ingolf, Europäische Grundrechtecharta und Konventsverfahren: Zehn Thesen zum Prozess der europäischen Verfassung nach Nizza, 24 integration, 2001, S. 194; von Danwitz, Thomas, Zwischen Symbolismus und Realismus, Die Grundrechtecharta der Europäischen Union, Internationale Politik 2001, S. 37; Nettesheim, Martin, Die Grundrechtecharta der Europäischen Union, 25 integration, 2002, S. 35.

[227] Vgl. hierzu schon die Diskussion oben II 1 b.; vgl zudem Leinen, Jo, Schönlau, Justus, Die Erarbeitung der EU-Grundrechtecharta im Konvent: nützliche Erfahrungen für die Zukunft Europas, 24 integration, 2001, S. 26: „Der diskursive Prozess, in dem der Inhalt des europäischen Erbes an Grundrechten aus einer ganzen Fülle von Quellen herausgearbeitet worden ist, hat gezeigt, welche weitreichenden Gemeinsamkeiten bereits in Europa bestehen.“

[228] Dementsprechend schreibt etwa Stern, Klaus, Das Staatsrecht der Bundesrepublik Deutschland, Bd. III/1, 1988, S. VII: „Staatsrechtswissenschaft ist in einem vom Verfassungsgeber kaum erahnten Maße Grundrechtswissenschaft geworden“.

[229] Die Würde des Menschen begründet zwar kein selbständiges „Grundrecht“, sie ist aber Leitbild aller verfassuungsrechtlichen Regelung: Sie ist unantasbar und „sie zu achten und zu schützen ist Verpflichtung aller staatlichen Gewalt“, im einzelnen BVerfGE 50, 166, 175: Verbot, den Menschen zum „bloßen Objekt des Staates zu machen“; im einzelnen etwa Benda, Ernst, Menschenwürde und Persönlichkeitsrecht, in Ders. u.a. (Hrsg.), HdBVerfR, 2. Aufl. 1994, S. 161.

[230] Die allgemeine Handlungsfreiheit des Art. 2 I GG garantiert in ihrer Ausgestaltung durch das BVerfG (BVerfGE 6, 32 (36); 63, 88 (108f); 74, 129 (151)) dort, wo andere Grundrechte nicht greifen, einen größtmöglichen Schutz der Freiheit des Einzelnen vor staatlichen Eingriffen (Auffangtatbestand); im einzelnen Erichsen, Hans-Uwe, Allgemeine Handlungsfreiheit, in: Isensee, Josef/Kirchhof, Paul (Hrsg.), HdBStR Bd. VI, 2. Aufl. 2001, § 151, S. 1185.

[231] Allgemeiner Gleichheitssatz, im einzelnen etwa Kirchhof, Paul, Der allgemeine Gleichheitssatz, in: Isensee, Josef/Kirchhof, Paul (Hrsg.), HdBStR, Bd. V, 2. Aufl. 2000, S. 837ff.

[232] So ging die Initiative für eine Charta auf dem Europäischen Rat von Köln von

deutscher Seite aus; Präsident des Konvents wurde Roman Herzog, ehemals Präsident des BVerfG.

233 Vgl. hierzu grundlegend Pernice, Ingolf, Grundrechtsgehalte im Europäischen Gemeinschaftsrecht, 1979; Ders., Gemeinschaftsverfassung und Grundrechtsschutz - Grundlagen, Bestand und Perspektiven, 43 NJW 1990, 2409; Rengeling, Hans-Werner, Grundrechtsschutz in der Europäischen Gemeinschaft, 1993; Chwolik-Lanfermann, Grundrechtsschutz in der Europäischen Union, 1994; Iliopoulos-Strangas, Julia (Hrsg.), Grundrechtsschutz im Europäischen Raum, 1993; Quasdorf, Peter, Die Dogmatik der Grundrechte der Europäischen Union, 2001.

234 Zur Frage, ob es einen europäischen Menschenrechtsansatz gibt Leben, Charles, Is there a European Approach to Human Rights?, in: Alston, Philip (Hrsg.), The EU and Human Rights, 1999, S. 69.

235 Schlussfolgerungen des Europäischen Rates von Köln, 15.-16. Oktober 1999, Annex IV: „Nach Auffassung des Europäischen Rates soll diese Charta die Freiheits- und Gleichheitsrechte sowie die Verfahrensgrundsätze umfassen, wie sie in der [EMRK] gewährleistet sind und wie sie sich aus den gemeinsamen Verfassungüberlieferungen der [MS] als allgemeine Rechtsgrundsätze des Gemeinschaftsrechts ergeben. Die Charta soll weiterhin die Grundrechte enthalten, die nurden Unionsbürgern zustehen. Bei der Ausarbeitung der Charta sind ferner wirtschaftliche und soziale Rechte zu berücksichtigen, wie sie in der Europäischen Sozialcharta und in der Gemeinschaftscharta der sozialen Grundrechte der Arbeitnehmer enthalten sind [....].

236 Vgl. etwa Art. 22 Grundrechtecharta (u.a. aus dem Unionsrecht: Art. 6 EUV), Art. 23 Grundrechtecharta (teils aus dem primären Gemeinschaftsrecht: Art. 2, 3, 141 EGV), Art. 27, 30, 33 Grundrechtecharta (überwiegend aus dem sekundären Gemeinschaftsrecht), Art. 26 ff Grundrechtecharta (überwiegend aus der Europäischen Sozialcharta und der Gemeinschaftscharta der sozialen Grundrechte der Arbeitnehmer), Art. 24 Grundrechtecharta (Übereinkommen über die Rechte des Kindes) usw.

237 Vgl. Leinen, Jo, Schönlau, Justus, Die Erarbeitung der EU-Grundrechtecharta im Konvent: Nützliche Erfahrungen für die Zukunft Europas, 24 integration, 2001, S. 26, 30.

238 Grabenwarter, Christoph, Die Charta der Grundrechte für die Europäische Union, 116 DVBl. 2001, S. 1, 12. Dies hat zu einer erheblichen Uneinheitlichkeit der Formulierungen beigetragen. Grabenwarter etwa weist auf die Formulierungsunterschiede zwischen Art. 13 S. 1, Art. 2 Abs. 1, Art. 25, Art. 9, Art. 22 und Art. 37 hin (S. 12, Fn. 96).

239 Vor dem Hintergrund dieser Überlegungen muß betont werden, dass der Beitritt der EU zur EMRK keine zur Entwicklung einer Charta gleichwertige Lösung wäre. Die durch den Strassburger Gerichtshof bewirkte *äußere* Kontrolle kann den Prozeß der inneren Verschränkung von politischen und judikativen EU-Organen nicht ersetzen; dies vor allem, wenn man berücksichtigt, dass die EU eine im Vergleich zur EMRK eigenständige Programmatik und ein durch westeuropäische Verfassungstheorie und –praxis geprägtes Schutzniveau aufweist (oder jedenfalls aufweisen sollte).

240 Ein entsprechender Wille des Konvents ergibt sich schon aus den

Erläuterungen: „weder gestattet noch verboten“ (zu Art. 3 Grundrechtecharta), „weder untersagt noch vorgeschrieben“ (Art. 9 Grundrechtecharta).

[241] Bogdandy, Armin von, The European Union as a Human Rights Organization? Human Rights and the Core of the European Union, 37 CMLRev. 2000, S. 1307.

[242] Zu den sozialen Rechten im einzelnen Meyer, Jürgen, Engels, Markus, Aufnahme von sozialen Grundrechten in die Europäische Grundrechtecharta?, 33 ZRP 2000, S. 368; DeSchutter, Olivier, La contribution de la Charte des droits fondamentaux de l´Union Européenne à la garantie des droits sociaux dans l´ordre juridique communautaire, 12 RUDH 2000, S. 33, 46.

[243] Pache, Eckhard, Der Grundsatz der Verhältnismäßigkeit in der Rechtsprechung der Gerichte der Europäischen Gemeinschaften, 18 NVwZ 1999, S. 1033.

[244] So auch Pache, Eckhard, Die Europäische Grundrechtscharta – ein Rückschritt für den Grundrechtsschutz in Europa?, 36 EuR 2001, 475; vgl. auch Kenntner, Markus, Die Schrankenbestimmungen der EU-Grundrechtecharta: Grundrechte ohne Schutzwirkung? 33 ZRP 2000, S. 423.

[245] Nicht zu verkennen ist, dass auch grundrechtsspezifische Schranken allen semantischen Bemühungen zum Trotze Wertungsspielräume enthalten; ebensowenig ist zu übersehen, dass allen Differenzierungsbemühungen zum Trotze zwischen den unterschiedlichen Grundrechtsschranken (einfacher Gesetzesvorbehalt, qualifizierter Gesetzesvorbehalt, vom Wortlaut her einschränkungslos gewährleistete Grundrechte) nur ein quantitativer, nicht aber ein qualitativer Unterschied besteht; und schließlich ist offenkundig dass die Entscheidung über die Reichweite der definitiven Bestandskraft eines Grundrechts letztlich auf eine Angemessenheitsabwägung zwischen dem Freiheits- oder Leistungsinteresse des einzelnen und dem gegensätzlichen staatlichen Interesse hinausläuft. Gleichwohl macht die Praxis der Grundrechtsrechtsprechung des BVerfG nur zu deutlich, dass die vom Verfassungsgeber mit auf den Weg gegebenen Schrankenformulierungen im abwägungspräjudizierenden Prozeß der Gewichtung von Interessen eine wichtige Rolle spielt.

[246] Vgl. § 6 Embryonenschutzgesetz.

[247] Allgemein dazu Benda, Ernst, Menschenwürde und Persönlichkeitsrecht, in: Ders. u.a. (Hrsg.), HdBVerfR, 2. Aufl. 1994, S. 161.

[248] Hierzu etwa Isensee, Josef, Das Grundrecht als Abwehrrecht und staatliche Schutzpflicht, in: Ders./Kirchhof, Paul, HdBStR V, 1992, § 111, S. 143; vertiefend Hermes, Georg, Das Grundrecht auf Schutz von Leben und Gesundheit, 1987; Dietlein, Johannes, Die Lehre von den grundrechtlichen Schutzpflichten, 1992.

[249] Allerdings stellten sich auch diese Fragen schon vor der Aufnahme in die Grundrechtecharta, nur eben, wie gerade angedeutet, jeweils im Zusammenhang der sekundärrechtlichen Vorschriften aus dem Gemeinschaftsrecht; vgl etwa die RL 77/187/EWG über die Wahrung von Ansprüchen der Arbeitnehmer beim Übergang von Unternehmen und RL 80/987/EWG über den Schutz der Arbeitnehmer bei Zahlungsunfähigkeit des Arbeitgebers.

[250] Allerdings wird es in diesem Zusammenhang nicht notwendig zu schwerwiegenden Grundrechtskollisionen gerade im Bereich des Grundgesetzes kommen, handelt es sich bei den ausdrücklichen Schutzpflichten in der Grundrechtecharta doch überwiegend um so grundsätzliche Fälle wie etwa das Verbot des Menschenhandels (Art: 5 III Grundrechtecharta), das Verbot der Kinderarbeit (Art.

32 Abs. 1 S. 1 Grundrechtecharta) aber auch die Rechte des Kindes (Art. 24 Grundrechtecharta). Eher wird es in diesem Zusammenhang Schwierigkeiten etwa bei Beitrittsverhandlungen, also ausserhalb des Geltungsbereichs des Grundgesetzes, geben können.

[251] Bogdanday, Armin, von Grundrechtsgemeinschaft als Integrationsziel? 56 JZ 2001, S. 157, 166: „Stärkung des europäischen Rechts"; schon früh Frowein, Schulhofer und Shapiro, The Protection ofFundamental Rights as a Vehicle of Integration, in: Cappelletti, M., Seccombe, M. und Weiler, J.H.H. (Hrsg.), Integration Through Law, Berlin, 1984, Bd. I, Buch 3, S. 231.

[252] Weiler etwa weist darauf hin, dass Grundrechterechtsprechung nicht notwendig im Bezugsfeld von Mindestandards stattfindet, sondern dass es um die Ausgestaltung der Werteordnung als ganzer geht, in Weiler, Joseph H.H., Fundamental rights and fundamental boundaries: on the conflict of standards and values in the protection of human rights in the Europeanlegal space, in: Ders., The Constitution of Europe, 1999, S. 102.

[253] Vgl. allerdings den Vorlagebeschluss des Landesgerichts Feldkirch (Östereich) vom 22. Juni 2001 in der Rs C-248/01 (Herrmann Pfanner Getränke GmbH/Republik Österreich), der danach fragt ob eine Offenlegungspflichten beim Jahresabschluss von Unternehmen mit dem Datenschutz und „mit den Grundrechten nach der Europäischen Grundrechtecharta vereinbar" seien (dazu auch Alber, Siegbert, Die Selbstbindung der europäischen Organe an die EU-Charta der Grundrechte, 28 EuGRZ 2001, S. 349, 353).

[254] Hierzu Alber, Siegbert, Die Selbstbindung der europäischen Organe an die EU-Charta der Grundrechte,28 EuGRZ 2001, S. 349.

[255] Die Rechtsprechung des EuGH zur Bindung der Mitgliedstaaten an die Unionsgrundrechte ist in Art. 51 Abs. 1 Grundrechtecharta kodifiziert worden, vgl. nur etwa EuGH C-5/88, Slg. 1989, S. 2609 - Wachauf; Rs. C-368/95, Slg. 1997, S. 3689; grundlegend etwa Weiler, Joseph H.H. und Lockhart, Taking Rights Seriously Seriously. The European Court of Justice and its Fundamental Rights Jurisprudence, 32 CMLRev. 1995, S. 518; Ruffert, Matthias, Die Mitgliedstaaten der EG als Verpflichtete der Gemeinschaftsgrundrechte, 22 EuGRZ 1995, S. 518.

[256] Vgl. GA Tizzano, Schlussanträge vom 8.2.2001 zur Rs. C-173/99 - Broadcasting Entertainment, Cinematographic and Theatre Union (BECTU), Rn. 26 ff, 28; auch GA Alber, Schlussanträge vom 1.2.2001, Rs. C-344/99, TNT Traco, Rn. 94; im einzelenen hierzu: Alber, Siegbert, Die Selbstbindung der europäischen Organe an die EU-Charta der Grundrechte, 28 EuGRZ 2001, S. 349, 351 mwN; Calliess, Christian, Die Charta der Grundrechte der Europäischen Union - Fragen der Konzeption, Kompetenz und Verbindlichkeit, 12 EuZW, S. 261, 267; vgl auch Pernice in Europäische Grundrechtecharta und Konventsverfahren. Zehn Thesen zum Prozess der Europäischen Verfassung nach Nizza, 24 integration 2001, S. 194; Pache, Eckhard, Die europäische Grundrechtscharta - ein Rückschritt für den Grundrechtsschutz in Europa? 36 EuR 2001, S. 475, 485.

[257] Es wird allerdings auf einen Beschluss des spanischen Verfassungsgerichts hingewiesen, in dem dieses auf Artikel 8 der Charta verweist, Beschluss STC 292/2000 vom 30. Nov. 2000, Ziff. II 8, zitiert nach Pernice, Ingolf, Europäische

Grundrechte-Charta und Konventsverfahren: Zehn Thesen zum Prozess der Europäischen Verfassung nach Nizza, 24 integration 2001, S. 196.

[258] Zu einer Typologie normativer und faktischer Wirkungen normativer Texte vgl. am Beisp der EMRK Grabenwarter, Christoph, Europäisches und nationales Verfassungsrecht, in 60 VVDStRL 2001, S. 290, 317ff.

[259] Dazu Schmitz, Thomas, Die EU-Grundrechtecharta aus grundrechtsdogmatischer und grundrechtstheoretischer Sicht, 56 JZ 2001, S. 833, 835.

[260] Mit Spannung dürfte insoweit der Fall in der Rs C-248/01 (Herrmann Pfanner Getränke GmbH/Republik Österreich) erwartet werden (Vorlagebeschluss des Landesgerichts Feldkirch (Östereich) vom 22. Juni 2001 dahin, ob Offenlegungspflichten beim Jahresabschluss von Unternehmen mit dem Datenschutz und „mit den Grundrechten nach der Europäischen Grundrechtecharta vereinbar“ seien (dazu auch Alber, Siegbert, Die Selbstbindung der europäischen Organe an die EU-Charta der Grundrechte, 28 EuGRZ 2001, S. 353).

[261] Vgl. nur Beutler, Bengt u.a., Die Europäische Union, Rechtsordnung und Politik, Nomos, 5. Aufl. 2001, S. 353, Rdn. 639.

[262] Isensee, Josef, Grundrechte und Demokratie, Die polare Legitimation im grundgesetzlichen Gemeinwesen, 20 Der Staat 1981, S. 161, 162.

[263] Starck, Christian, Grundrechtliche und demokratische Freiheitsidee, in: Isensee, Josef/Kirchhof, Paul (Hrsg.), HdBStR Bd. II, 2. Aufl., 1998, S. 3.

[264] Schmitt-Glaeser, Walter, Die grundrechtliche Freiheit des Bürgers zur Mitwirkung an der Willensbildung, in: Isensee, Josef/Kirchhof, Paul (Hrsg.), HdBStR Bd. II, 2. Aufl. 1998, S. 49, Rdn 1f.

[265] Pernice, Ingolf, Eine Grundrechte-Charta für die Europäische Union, 115 DVBl. 2000, S. 847.

[266] Zuleeg, Manfred, Zum Verhältnis nationaler und europäischer Grundrechte, Funktionen einer EU-Charta der Grundrechte, 27 EuGRZ 2000, S. 511, 516.

[267] Eingehend Augustin, Angela, Das Volk der Europäischen Union, Zu Inhalt und Kritik eines normativen Begriffs, 2000.

[268] Pauly, Walter, Strukturfragen des unionsrechtlichen Grundrechtsschutzes, 33 EuR 1998, S. 242, 244 ff.

[269] *Ibid.* S. 246.

[270] Abschnitt V.

[271] Dazu Schmitz, Thomas, Die EU-Grundrechtecharta aus grundrechtsdogmatischer und grundrechtstheoretischer Sicht, 56 JZ 2001, S. 833, 835f.

[272] Nickel, Rainer, Zur Zukunft des Bundesverfassungsgerichts im Zeitalter der Europäisierung, 56 JZ 2001, S. 625, 630.

[273] Nettesheim, Martin, Der Grundsatz der einheitlichen Wirksamkeit des Gemeinschaftsrechts, in: Randelzhofer, Albrecht (Hrsg.), Gedächtnisschrift für Eberhard Grabitz, 1995, S. 447.

[274] Dazu etwa Liisberg, Jonas B., Does the EU Charter ofFundamental Rights threaten the supremacy of Community law?, 38 CMLRev. 2001, S. 1171.

[275] Also die Rechte der Art. 2, 4, 5 Abs. 1 und Abs. 2, 6, 7, 9, 10 Abs. 1, 11, 12 Abs. 1, 14 Abs. 1 und Abs. 2, 17, 19 Abs. 1 und Abs. 2, 47 Abs. 2 und Abs. 3, 48, 49 Abs. 1 und 50 Grundrechtecharta.

[276] Vgl. Art. 12 Abs. 1 Grundrechtecharta.

[277] Vgl. Art. 14 Abs. 1 und Abs. 3 Grundrechtecharta.
[278] Vgl. Art. 47 Abs. 2 und Abs. 3 Grundrechtecharta
[279] Vgl.Art. 50 Grundrechtecharta.
[280] Art. 4 Grundrechtecharta.
[281] EuGH, Slg. I-2925 - ERT.
[282] Vgl. Art. 3 Abs. 2 vierter Spiegelstrich Grundrechtecharta (ausdrücklich offen gelassen; Erläuterung: „Die anderen Formen des Klonens werden von der Charta weder gestattet noch verboten.")
[283] Vgl. Art. 9 Grundrechtecharta (ausdrücklich offen gelassen, Erläuterung: „Es wird „weder untersagt, noch vorgeschrieben, Verbindungen von Personen gleichen Geschlechts den Status der Ehe zu verleihen").
[284] Alber, Siegbert, Widmaier, Ulrich, Die EU-Charta der Grundrechte und ihre Auswirkungen auf die Rechtsprechung, 27 EuGRZ 2000, S. 497, 510.
[285] Vgl. aus dem unübersehbaren Schrifttum nur Ipsen, Hans Peter, Die Bundesrepublik Deutschland in der Europäischen Union, in: Isensee, Josef/Kirchhof, Paul (Hrsg.), HdBStR VII 1992, § 181, S. 767, Rz. 57ff.
[286] EuGH, Urteil vom 15.7.1964, Slg. 1964, S. 1251.
[287] Zusammenfassend mit weiteren Hinweisen statt vieler Grabitz, Eberhard, Art. 164, in Grabitz, Eberhard/Hilf, Meinhard (Maastrichter Fassung), Rz. 26ff.
[288] BVerfGE 95, S. 173 (181) - Tabaketikettierung; 2 BvR 1210/98, 53 NJW 2000, S. 2015 - Alcan.
[289] BVerfGE 102, S. 147 - Bananenmarkt.
[290] Nettesheim, Martin, Der Bananenmarktbeschluß des BVerfG, 23 JURA 2001, S. 686; 21 Nettesheim, Martin, NVwZ 2002 (im Erscheinen); Limbach, Jutta, Die Kooperation der Gerichte in der zukünftigen europäischen Grundrechtsarchitektur, 27 EuGRZ 2000, S. 417; Classen, Dieter, Anmerkung zu BVerfG, Beschluss vom 7.6.2000 - 2 BvL 1/97, 55 JZ 2000, S. 1158, Nicolaysen, Gert, Nowak, Carsten, Teilrückzug des BVerfG aus der Kontrolle der Rechtsmäßigkeit gemeinschaftlicher Rechtsakte: Neuere Entwicklungen und Perspektiven, 54 NJW 2001, S. 1233; _arcevic, Edin Der EuGH als gesetzlicher Richter (Art. 101 Abs. 1 GG), 53 DÖV 2000, S. 941; Caspar, Johannes, Nationale Grundrechtsgarantien und sekundäres Gemeinschaftsrecht, 53 DÖV 2000, S. 349; Lecheler, Helmut, Zum Bananenmarkt-Beschluss des BVerfG, JuS 2001, S. 120; Schmid, Christoph, Ein enttäuschender Rückzug, Anmerkungen zum „Bananenbeschluss" des BVerfG, 20 NVwZ 2001, S. 249; Ost, Emanuel, Europarecht vor dem BVerfG, 20 NVwZ 2001, S. 399.
[291] Zsfd. Peters, Anne, Elemente einer Theorie der Verfassung Europas, 2001, S. 308.
[292] Pernice, Ingolf, Europäisches und nationales Verfassungsrecht, 60 VVDStRL 2001, S. 185.
[293] Mayer, Franz, Kompetenzüberschreitung, 2000, S. 37 mwN.
[294] Pernice, Ingolf, Europäisches und nationales Verfassungsrecht, 60 VVDStRL 2001, S. 185.
[295] VerfGE 89, 155 (175) - Maastrichtvertrag; aus der Sicht des EuGH dazu etwa Rodríguez Iglesias, Gil Carlos, Der EuGH und die Gerichte der Mitgliedstaaten - Komponenten der richterlichen Gewalt in der Europäischen Union, 53 NJW 2000, S. 1889.
[296] Nicolaysen, Gert, Der Streit zwischen dem deutschen Bundesverfassungsgericht

und dem Europäischen Gerichtshof, in: Bruha, Th. u.a. (Hrsg.), Welche Verfassung für Europa?, 2001, S. 91, 106; zum Ganzen vgl. nur Hirsch, Günther, Europäischer Gerichtshof und Bundesverfassungsgericht - Kooperation oder Konfrontation?, 49 NJW 1996, S. 2457ff; aus jüngerer Zeit etwa Schwarze, Jürgen, Das „Kooperationsverhältnis des Bundesverfassungsgerichts mit dem Europäischen Gerichtshof, in: Badura, Peter und Dreier, Horst (Hrsg,), Festschrift 50 Jahre Bundesverfassungsgericht, 2001, S. 223; Nickel, Rainer, Zur Zukunft des Bundesverfassungsgerichts im Zeitalter der Europäisierung, 56 JZ 2001, S. 625.

297 Bei Fußnote 194 unter Hinweis auf Bieber/Salomé, 33 CMLR 1996, S. 907, 912.

298 Sie sind *alle gemeinsam* Gesetzgeber bei Regeln, die dem Einstimmigkeitserfordernis zugrundliegen, zu *vielen, aber ggf. nicht allen* gemeinsam bei Gesetzgebung nach dem Mehrheitsprinzip.

299 Dazu etwa Nicolaysen, Gert, Der Streit zwischen dem deutschen Bundesverfassungsgericht und dem europäischen Gerichtshof, in: Bruha, Th. u.a. (Hrsg.), Welche Verfassung für Europa?, 2001, S. 91, 106.

300 Es ist ohnehin erstaunlich, dass Pernice dieses Argument anführt, zweifelt er doch selbst die Phrase der Mitgliedstaaten als „Herren der Verträge“ an, wenn er ausführt, diese leite in die Irre, da die Mitgliedstaaten „weder Herren, noch Herren der Verträge, ja [....] wie noch zu zeigen sein wird, nicht einmal mehr Herren ihrer eigenen Verfassungen“ seien (60 VVDStRL 2001, S. 171f).

301 Pernice, Iingolf, Europäisches und nationales Verfassungsrecht, 60 VVDStRL 2001, S. 185 bei Fn. 192.

302 Eine andere Frage ist, ob verschiedene Gerichte sich idR aneinander orientieren, etwa der EuGH am BVerfG, und dadurch, sozusagen ungeplant, im Sinne spontaner Organisation miteinander kooperieren. Ein Beispiel hierfür mag das jüngste Urteil des EuGH zur Tabakwerberichtlinie sein (EuGH, 27 EuGRZ 2000, S. 436). Darin hat der EuGH festgestellt, Art. 100a I EGV begründe keine allgemeine Kompetenz und die entsprechende Kompetenzüberschreitung sanktioniert. Es liegt nicht ganz fern, diese Entscheidung jedenfalls auch als Antwort auf die Ausführungen des BVerfG zur Kompetenzüberschreitung („ausbrechenden Rechtsakten“) in dessen Maastrichtentscheidung zu sehen (so auch Nickel, Rainer, Die Zukunft des BVerfG im Zeitalter der Europäisierung, 56 JZ 2001, S. 625, 628). Der Grund für derartige Entscheidungen wird jedenfalls auch in dem gegenseitigen Bemühen zu suchen sein, Entscheidungen aufeinander abzustimmen. Daraus allein folgt aber noch kein irgendwie geartetes „Notstandsrecht“ des BVerfG.

303 Vgl in diesem Sinne - um nur zwei Repräsentanten der beiden Gerichte zu nennen - etwa Limbach, Jutta, Das Bundesverfassungsgericht und der Grundrechtsschutz in Europa, 54 NJW 2001, S. 2913, 2916 und Hirsch, Günter, Der EuGH im Spannungsverhältnis zwischen Gemeinschaftsrecht und nationalem Recht, 53 NJW 2000, S. 1817.

304 Anders wären etwa folgende Ausführungrn Froweins nicht zu verstehen, die dieser angesichts der Bananenmarktentscheidung des BVerfG gemacht hat: „Der rechtsstaaliche Aufbau einer nach föderativen Grundsätzen gestalteten Europäischen Union, die freilich kein Bundesstaat sein kann, muß bedeuten, dass die Entscheidung über die Rechtmäßigkeit und Wirksamkeit eines europäischen Rechtssetzungsaktes einem europäischen Verfassungsgericht zu *bindender*

Letztentscheidung übertragen wird. Dies ist mit dem EuGH geschehen. (Das zeigt, dass [mit Art. 23 GG] das deutsche Verfassungsrecht die Grundlage dafür enthält, dass der EuGH mit Wirkung für alle Mitgliedstaaten die Letztentscheidung über die Gültigkeit von Normen oder Entscheidungen der Gerichte zu treffen hat).", in Frowein, Jochen Abr., Die Europäisierung des Verfassungsrechts, in Badura, Peter und Dreier, Horst (Hrsg,), Festschrift 50 Jahre Bundesverfassungsgericht, S. 209, 214; In eine ähnliche Richtung schrieb Weiler schon 1991: „[A]lthough this has never been stated explicitely, the Court [of the European Communities] has the *„Kompetenz-Kompetenz"* in the Community legal order, i.e. it is the body that determines which norms come within the sphere of application of Community law." in: Weiler, Joseph J.H., The Transformation of Europe, in: Ders., The Constitution of Europe, 1999, S. 10, S. 21. Diese Normenanwendungshierarchie entspricht letztlich einer auch nach Weiler aus einer dem Vorrangprinzip entspringenden Normenhierarchie: „The combination of the two doctrines [of direct effect and supremacy] means that Community norms that produce direct effect are not merely the law of the land but the *„higher law" of the land"* [Hervorhebung vom Berichterstatter], in: Ders.: *Ibid.* S. 22.

[305] Kirchhof, Paul, Die Gewaltenbalance zwischen staatlichen und europäischen Organen, 53 JZ 1998, S. 965, 974.

[306] Zu diesem Rückzug widerum Frowein, der meint, die Bananenmarktentscheidung des BVerfG mache „deutlich, dass die im Maastricht-Urteil von vielen gesehene Wiedereröffnung der Gefahr eines Kollisionskurses zwischen dem Europäischen Gerichtshof und dem Bundesverfassungsgericht im Grundrechtsschutz als überwunden angesehen werden kann"; in Frowein, Jochen Abr., Die Europäisierung des Verfassungsrechts, in Badura, Peter und Dreier, Horst (Hrsg,), Festschrift 50 Jahre Bundesverfassungsgericht, 2001, S. 209, 213; vgl zudem statt vieler Nicolaysen, Gert und Nowak, Carsten, Teilrückzug des BVerfG aus der Kontrolle der Rechtsmäßigkeit gemeinschaftlicher Rechtsakte: Neuere Entwicklungen und Perspektiven, 54 NJW 2001, S. 1233. Die integrationsfreundliche Orientierung des BVerfG bestätigt sich in seinem Beschluss vom 9.1.2001, 115 DVBl. 2000, S. 720: Verstoß gegen die Pflicht der Vorlage an den EuGH nach Art. 234 III EGV ist zugleich ein Verstoß gegen den Grundsatz des gesetzlichen Richters nach Art. 101 I 2 GG; dazu Brenner, Michael, Huber, Peter M., Europarecht und Europäisierung in den Jahren 2000/2001, 116 DVBl. 2001, S. 1013, 1020 und Füßer, Klaus, Durchsetzung der Vorlagepflicht zum EuGH gemäß Art. 234 III EGV, 116 DVBl. 2001, S. 1574.

[307] Detailliert hierzu Peters, Anne, Elemente einer Theorie der Verfassung Europas, 2001, S. 308 ff. mit folgender Schlussfolgerung (S. 767): „Langfristig ist es zur Wahrung der Rechtseinheit unabweisbar, dass die nationalen Gerichte die autoritative Letztentscheidungsbefugnis einer gemeinschaftsrechtlichen Instanz anerkennen (prozedurale Vorranglösung)", kombiniert allerdings mit folgender Aussage (S. 768): „Da der externe Vorrang [...] kein konstitutioneller Vorrang ist, hat seine Unvollkommenheit keinen negativen Einfluß auf die Verfassungseignung des Gemeinschaftsrechts".

[308] Trotz der Föderalisierung des Intergrationsverbund haben EU und Mitgliedstaaten weiterhin je autonome Verfassungsgebungs- und Rechtsetzungsgewalt. Die Verfassungstheorie des Bundesstaates zeigt, dass man Rechtsnormen auch dann hierarchisch zuordnen kann, wenn die dahinterstehenden Träger von Hoheitsgewalt ihre Verfassungsgebungs- und Rechtssetzungsbefugnisse aus Ausdruck jeweils originärer Gewalt begreifen.

[309] Die Kraft zum Wandel der deutschen Rechtsordnung haben auch Urteile des EuGH, die auf einen Ausgangsrechtsstreit in anderen Mitgliedstaaten zurückgehen. Vgl. insoweit nur etwa dei Folgen des jüngeren Urteils des EuGH vom 3. Oktober 2000, 12 EuZW 2001, S. 53 - Simap. Eingehend Rixen, Stephan, Europarechtliche Grenzen des deutschen Arbeitszeitrechts, 12 EuZW 2001, S. 421.

[310] Zsfd. Schwarze, Jürgen, Deutscher Landesbericht, in: Ders. (Hrsg.), Die Entsehung einer europäischen Verfassungsordnung, 2000, S. 109, 147; Bogdandy, Armin von, Zweierlei Verfassungsrecht, 39 Der Staat 2000, S. 163, 165.

[311] Dazu oben I 2 a und b.

[312] Das Kommunalausländerwahlrecht (Art. 20Abs. 2, 28 Abs. 1 S. 3 GG) wurde erst im Rahmen einer *Vertragsänderung* (Art. 19 EGV), nicht etwa durch Mehrheitsentscheidung nach Art 249, 308 EGV geregelt. Die RL 94/80/EG ist in diesem Zusammenhang lediglich als Durchführungsvorschrift zu Art. 19 EGV ergangen, vgl. Schrapper, Ludger, Die Richtlinie 94/80 EG zum aktiven und passiven Kommunalwahlrecht für Unionsbürger, 110 DVBl. 1995, S. 1167 f.

[313] Auch Art. 88 GG wurde nicht wegen vorrangigem Sekundärrecht der EG, sondern im Zuge der Maastrichter Vertragsänderungen (Art. 4 Abs. 2, 105 Abs. 1 ff. EGV) geändert; vgl. nur Pernice, Ingolf, Das Ende der Währungspolitischen Souveränität Deutschlands und das Maastrichturteil des BverfG, in: Due, Ole u.a. (Hrsg.), Festschrift für Ulrich Everling, Bd. 2, 1995, S. 1057.

[314] Vgl. etwa Rupp, Hans H., Grundgesetzänderung durch völkerrechtlichen Vertrag - ein vernachlässigtes Problem des Maastrichtvertrages, in: Ipsen, Jörn u.a. (Hrsg.), Festschrift Heymannsverlag, 1995, S. 499.

[315] Im Einzelnen oben I 2.

[316] Anders liegt es im Fall der neu eingefügten Vorschrift über die Auslieferung Deutscher nach Art. 16 II 2 GG, da diese Regelung nicht unter dem Einfluss des Europarechts im engeren Sinne entstanden ist. Im einzelnen Zimmermann, Andreas, Die Auslieferung Deutscher an Staaten der Europäischen Union und internationale Strafgerichtshöfe, Überlegungen zum neuen Art. 16 Abs. 2 S. 2 GG, 56 JZ 2001, S. 233.

[317] EuGH (Urteil vom 11.1.2000) Rs C-285/98, EuZW 2000, S. 211 - Tanja Kreil. Dazu statt vieler Hirsch, Günter, Der EuGH im Spannungsverhältnis zwischen Gemeinschaftsrecht und nationalem Recht, 53 NJW 2000, S. 1817.

[318] Zum Ganzen Scholz, Rupert, RIW 2000, S. 222; Arndt, Claus, Waffeneinsatz von Frauen bei der Bundeswehr, 53 NJW 2000, S. 1461; Köster, Konstantin und Schröder, Jan, Eine beachtenswerte Kompetenzüberschreitung - Frauen an die Waffe, 54 NJW 2001, S. 273, Götz, Volkmar, Anmerkung, 55 JZ 2000, S. 413, Hirsch, Günter, Der EuGH im Spannungsverhältnis zwischen Gemeinschaftsrecht und nationalem Recht, 53 NJW 2000, S. 1817; Kämmerer, Jörn, Axel, Gleichberechtigung am Gewehrt, 35 EuR 2000, S. 102; Koch, Christiane, Anmerkung, 115 DVBl. 2000, S. 476; Stahn, Carsten, Streitkräfte im Wandel - Zu den Auswirkungen der Urteile Sirdar und Kreil auf das deutsche Recht, 27 EuGRZ 2000, S. 121; Streinz, Rudolf, Frauen an die Front, 115 DVBl. 2000, S. 585; Zuck, Rüdiger, Frauen an die Front?, 53 NJW 2000, S. 1701.

[319] Art. 33 IV iVm 116 GG und die einfachen Beamtengesetzen gerieten unter der Rechtsprechung des EuGH in der Rs. 66/85, Slg. 1986, S. 2121 - Lawrie-Blum - derart unter Druck, dass nur die Neufassung von §§ 7 I Nr 1 BBG und 4 I Nr. 1

BRRG der neuen Rechtslage genüge tun konnte; vgl. allerdings immernoch die alte Fassung des Art. 33 II GG.

[320] Bogdandy, Armin von, Zweierlei Verfassungsrecht, 39 Der Staat 2000, S. 183.

[321] Im einzelnen etwa Schmahl, Stefanie, Die Vergemeinschaftung der Asyl- und Flüchtlingspolitik, 21 ZAR 2001, S. 3.

[322] Nickel, Rainer, Die Zukunft des Bundesverfassungsgerichts im Zeitalter der Europäisierung, 56 JZ 2001, S. 625, 628f.

[323] Dazu im einzelnen Jochum, Georg, Der neue Art. 13 EGV oder „political correctness" auf europäisch?, 32 ZRP 1999, S. 279.

[324] RL 2000/43/EG des Rates vom 29. 6. 2000, ABl. L 180, S. 22; RL 2000/78/EG des Rates vom 27.11.2000, ABl. L 303, S. 16.

[325] Im einzelnen Hailbronner, Kay, Die Antidiskriminierungsrichtlinien der EU, 21 ZAR 2001, S. 254.

[326] Kadelbach, Stefan, Allgemeines Verwaltungsrecht unter europäischem Einfluß, 1999, S. 15 ff.

[327] Vgl. nur MacCormick, Neil, Das Maastricht-Urteil: Souveränität heute, 50 JZ 1995, S. 797.

[328] Huber, Peter M., Europäisches und nationales Verfassungsrecht, 60 VVDStRL 2001, S. 228ff; Kirchhof, Paul, Die Gewaltenbalance zwischen staatlichen und europäischen Organen, 48 JZ 1998, S. 965.

[329] Zum Demokratiedefizit vgl. statt vieler den Sammelband von Drexl, Josef u.a. (Hrsg.), Europäische Demokratie, 1999; vertiefend Höreth, Marcus, Die Europäische Union im Legitimationstrilemma.Zur Rechtfertigung des Regierens jenseits der Staatlichkeit, 1999; Kluth, Winfried, Die demokratische Legitimation der Europäischen Union - eine Analyse der These vom Demokratiedefizit der Europäischen Union aus gemeineuropäischer Verfassungsperspektive, 1995; Groeben, Hans von der, Legitimationsprobleme der Europäischen Gemeinschaft, 1987; speziell zur Rechtssetzung Streinz, Rudolf, Die demokratische Legitimation der Rechtssetzung der Europäischen Gemeinschaft, 6 VBlThü. 1997, S. 73.

[330] S.o. I 2. a

[331] Zum Gesetzesbegriff nur Ossenbühl, Fritz, Gesetz und Recht - Die Rechtsquellen im demokratischen Rechtsstaat, in: Isensee, Josef, Kirchhof, Paul (Hrsg.), HdBStR Bd. III, 2. Aufl. 1996, § 61, S. 281, Rdn. 4 ff.

[332] Dazu Ossenbühl, Fritz, Vorrang und Vorbehalt des Gesetzes, in: Isensee, Josef, Kirchhof, Paul (Hrsg.), HdBStR Bd. III, 2. Aufl. 1996, § 62, S. 315.

[333] Zu den Vorschriften im allgemeinen oben I 2 b.

[334] Im einzelnen Grewe, Wilhelm G., Auswärtige Gewalt, in: Isensee, Josef, Kirchhof, Paul (Hrsg.), HdBStR III, 2. Aufl. 1996, § 77, S. 921, Rdn. 41f.

[335] Vgl. Brenner, Michael, Das Gesetz über die Zusammenarbeit von Bundesregierung und Deutschem Bundestag in Angelegenheiten der Europäischen Union, 2 VBlThü. 1993, S. 196, 198.

[336] Friesenhahn, Ernst, Parlament und Regierung im modernen Staat, 16 VVDStRL 1958, S. 9ff, 37f, 70; vgl dazu auch Menzel, Eberhard, Die auswärtige Gewalt in der Deutung des Bundesverfassungsgerichts, 79 AöR 1953/54, S. 326, 348 ff. und Baade, Hans, Das Verhältnis von Parlament und Regierung im Bereich der auswärtigen Gewalt der Bundesrepublik Deutschland, 1962, S. 118.

[337] So Fuchs, Michael, Art. 23 GG in der Bewährung. Anmerkungen aus der

Praxis, 54 DÖV 2001, S. 233; vertiefend Hansmeyer, Sandra, Die Mitwirkung des deutschen Bundestages and der europäischen Rechtssetzung, 2001, S. 136; a.A. Scholz, Rupert, Art. 23, in Maunz, Theodor/Dürig; Günter, Grundgesetz. Kommentar, Bd. III, Rdn. 99.

338 Vgl. im einzelnen aber die Regeln des EUZBBG.

339 Vgl. insoweit nur Scholz, Rupert, Art. 23, in: Maunz, Theodor/Dürig, Günter, Grundgesetz. Kommentar, Rdn. 98 ff, 112 ff.; Pernice, Ingolf, Art. 23, in Dreier, Horst (Hrsg.), Grundgesetz.Kommentar, Rdn. 105.

340 Scholz, Rupert, Art. 23, in: Maunz, Theodor/Dürig, Günter, Grundgesetz. Kommentar, Rdn.117.

341 Rath, Christian, Die „unionswärtige Gewalt" des deutschen Bundestages, in: ZfParl, Sonderheft 1995, Demokratie in Europa: Zur Rolle der Parlamente, S. 114, 138ff; vorsichtig bejahend Scholz, Rupert, Art. 23, in: Maunz, Theodor/Dürig, Günter, Grundgesetz. Kommentar, Rdn. 118.

342 Daran kann auch die Zusammenarbeit in der Konferenz der Europaausschüsse der nationalen Parlamente (COSAC) nichts ändern.

343 So fehlt es noch immer an der für demokratische Legitimation so wichtigen Zählwertgleichheit von Stimmen aus kleinen und großen Mitgliedstaaten mit der Folge einer „Renationalisierung" des Europäischen Parlamentes. Ferner ist die Mitentscheidung noch immer in zentralen Bereichen nicht ausreichend eingeführt; im einzelnen vgl. kürzlich nur Sobotta, Christoph, Transparenz in den Rechtssetzungsverfahren der Europäischen Union, 2001, S. 51 ff.

344 Zur Komitologie unter dem Gesichtspunkt der parlamentarischen Kontrolle vgl. etwa Haibach, Georg, Komitologie nach Amsterdam - Die Übertragung von Rechtssetzungsbefugnissen im Rechtsvergleich, 90 VA 1999, S. 98, 106; für die politiktheoretischen Bezüge vgl. vor allem Toeller, Annette E. und Hofmann, Herwig C.H., Democracy and the Reform of Comitology, in: Andenas, Mads und Türk, Alexander, Delegated Legislation and the Role of Committees in the EC, 2001, S. 25, Joerges, Christian und Falke, Josef (Hrsg.), Das Ausschußwesen der Europäischen Union. Praxis der Risikoregulierung im Binnenmarkt und ihre rechtliche Verfassung, 2000. Lübbe-Wolff, Gertrude, Europäisches und nationales Verfassungsrecht, 60 VVDStRL 2001, S. 267, bei Fn. 55ff; unterscheidet in echte und unechte Komitologie. Echte Komitologie ist danach durch das Halten der Kommission „an der mitgliedstaatlichen Leine" motiviert und Ausdruck des nur begrenzten Willens der europäischen Völker zur politischen Einheit (S. 268). Unechte Komitologie liegt im Fall der technisch-wissenschaftlichen Ausschüsse vor und hat danach ihre Parallele in den Mitgliedstaaten (Teil des sog. unspezifischen Legitimationsdefizits, s. sogleich). Die Unterscheidung ist hier von Interesse, da im Fall der echten Komitologie das Legitimationsdefizit hinsichtlich der Mitwirkung des Deutschen Bundestages nach Art. 23 Abs. 2 und 3 GG durch Rückverlagerung auf die nationalen Exekutiven sozusagen noch verstärkt wird und dadurch hier in doppelter Schärfe auftritt.

345 Im einzelnen Nettesheim, Martin, Die mitgliedstaatliche Durchführung von EG-Richtlinien, 1999, S. 18ff, 31ff; Danwitz, Thomas von, Normkonkretisierende Verwaltungsvorschriften und Gemeinschaftsrecht, 84 VA 1993, D. 73, 79.

[346] Vgl. etwa EuGH Rs. 48/75, Slg. 1976, S. 497 - Royer (ständige Rechtsprechung)

[347] In diese Richtung auch Pernice, Ingolf, The Role of National Parliaments in the European Union, in Walter Hallstein-Institut (Hrsg.), WHI - Papers 5/01, zu finden im Internet unter www.whi-berlin.de/pernice-parliaments.htm.

[348] Lübbe-Wolff, Gertrude, Europäisches und nationales Verfassungsrecht, 60 VVDStRL (2001), S. 246.

[349] *Ibid.* S. 273 ff.

[350] Vgl. auch Weiler, Joseph J.H., The Transformation of Europe, in: Ders., The Constitution of Europe, 1999, S. 10, 80.

[351] Grundlegend Kadelbach, Stefan, Allgemeines Verwaltungsrecht unter europäischem Einfluß, 1999; Danwitz, Thomas von, Verwaltungsrechtliches System und europäische Integration, 1996; Classen, Claus Dieter, Das nationale Verwaltungsverfahren im Kraftfeld des Europäischen Gemeinschaftsrechts, 31 Die Verwaltung 1998, S. 307; Magiera, Siegfried, Sommermann, Karl-Peter (Hrsg.), Verwaltung in der Europäischen Union, 2000; Schwarze, Jürgen, Deutschland, in: Ders. (Hrsg.), Das Verwaltungsrecht unter europäischem Einfluss, 1996, Rengeling, Werner und Zuleeg, Manfred, Deutsches und Europäisches Verwaltungsrecht, 53 VVDStRL 1994; zu Einzelbereichen etwa Kämmerer, Jörn Axel, Europäisierung des öffentlichen Dienstrechts, 36 EuR 2001, S. 27 m.w.N.; Scheuing, Dieter H., Europäisierung des Verwaltungsrechts: Zum mitgliedstaatlichen Verwaltungsvollzug des EG-Rechts am Beispiel der Rückforderung gemeinschaftsrechtswidriger Beihilfen, 34 Die Verwaltung 2001, S. 107-143. Europäisiertes nationales Verwaltungsrecht ist zu unterscheiden vom europäischen Verwaltungsrecht, also jenem Komplex gemeinschaftsrechtlicher Normen, die Organisation und Verfahren der europäischen Verwaltungsbehörden sowie das von Ihnen anzuwendende materielle Recht betreffen; dazu nur Schwarze, Jürgen, Europäisches Verwaltungsrecht, 1988.

[352] Unter europarechtlichem Einfluss entstehen völlig neue Rechtsgebiete, wie etwa das Vergabe- (§§ 97 ff GWB) und Telekommunikationsrecht (TKG) mit der entsprechenden Neuschaffung von Behörden (§§ 66 ff TKG). Diese handelt dann auch nach völlig neuen Maßstäben: Ulrich Battis etwa weist darauf hin, wie fremd dem deutschen Verwaltungsrecht die Versteigerung von Linzenzen anstelle einer hoheitlichen Vergabe nach Kriterien der Zuverlässigkeit und Sachkunde sind, in: Verwaltungsrecht als konkretisiertes Gemeinschaftsrecht, DÖV 2001, S. 988, 989.

[353] Schoch, Friedrich, Die Europäisierung des Allgemeinen Verwaltungsrechts, 50 JZ 1995, S. 109, 117, Ders., Europäisierung der verwaltungsrechtsordnung, 20 VBlBW (1999), S. 241.

[354] Etwa auf die Pflicht nationaler Behörden, gemeinschaftswidriges nationales Recht unangewendet zu lassen („Lockerung der Gesetzesbindung der Verwaltung (Art. 20 III GG)“), auf die Umsetzung von EG-Richtlinien durch Verwaltungsvorschriften („Modifizierung der Rechtsquellen- und Handlungsformenlehre“), auf die Situation bei der Rückforderung gemeinschaftsrechtswidriger Beihilfen („Minimalisierung des Vertrauensschutzes“), auf die Entwicklung des gemeinschaftsrechtlichen Entschädigungsanspruchs („Überforderung unseres Staatshaftungsrechts“) und auf den einstweiligen Rechtsschutz („faktische Ausserkraftsetzung des nationalen Rechts“). Alle Beispiele in Schoch,

Friedrich, *Ibid.*, S. 111f m.w.N. Die Gegenmeinung sieht in der Europäisierung lediglich eine bereichsspezifische Überlagerung, die den Korpus nationalen Rechts im übrigen unangetastet lasse, vgl. etwa hinsichtlich des vorläufigen Rechtsschutzes Schwarze, Jürgen, Europäische Rahmenbedingungen für die Verwaltungsgerichtsbarkeit, NVwZ 2000, 241, 250f: „spezifische Fallgestaltungen".

[355] Vgl. etwa den Beschluss 2 BvR 1210/98 des BVerfG vom 17. 2. 2000, 53 NJW 2000, S. 2015, in dem es die Rechtsprechung des BVerwG zur Rückforderung gemeinschaftsrechtswidriger Subventionen, insbesondere zu § 48 Abs. 4 S. 1 VwVfG, für rechtmäßig erklärte. Die Rechtsprechung des BVerwG hatte sich an der zuvor in derselben Sache ergangenen Entscheidung des EuGH orientiert (EuGH, Slg. 1997, I-1591 - Alcan), eine Entscheidung, die in Deutschland zu einer heftigen Kontroverse über die Autonomie des nationalen Verfahrensrechts und die Befolgungspflicht von Entscheidungen des EuGH geführt hatte, vgl. dazu nur Scholz, Rupert, Zum Verhältnis von europäischem Gemeinschaftsrecht und nationalem Verwaltungsverfahrensrecht - Zur Rechtsprechung des EuGH im Fall „Alcan", 51 DÖV 1998, S. 261 und Frowein, Jochen Abr., Kritische Bemerkungen zur Lage des deutschen Staatsrechts aus rechtsvergleichender Sicht, 51 DÖV 1998, S. 806. Zu den neueren Entwicklungen in diesen Fragen Brenner, Michael, Huber, Peter M., Europarecht und Europäisierung in den Jahren 2000/2001, 116 DVBl. 2001, S. 1013, 1021; Scheuing, Dieter H., Rechtsprechungsanalyse Europäisierung des Verwaltungsrechts, 34 Die Verwaltung 2001, 107.

[356] Vgl. etwa BVerwG, 19 NVwZ 2000, S. 1039: Nicht jede Kollision mit gemeinschaftsrechtlichen Normen ist als Nichtigkeitsgrund i.S. von § 44 Abs. 1 VwVfG zu behandeln; BverwG, 19 NVwZ 2001, S. 319: Auch ohne glichzeitige Vorlage an den EuGH kann im Revisionsverfahren nach § 94 VwGO ausgesetzt werden, wenn dem EuGH dieselbe Rechtsfrage in einem anderen Verfahren bereits vorgelegt worden ist.

[357] Strukturierend insoweit Schmidt-Aßmann, Eberhard, Verwaltungskooperation und Verwaltungskooperationsrecht in der Europäischen Gemeinschaft, 31 EuR 1996, S. 270.

[358] Art. 154 EGV; allgemein zur Europäisierung des Planungsrechts: Jarass, Hans D., Europäisierung des Planungsrechts, 115 DVBl. 2000, S. 945.

[359] Art. 61 ff. EGV.

[360] Art. 29 EUV.

[361] Dazu Becker, Joachim, Der transnationale Verwaltungsakt, Übergreifendes europäisches Rechtsinstitut oder Anstoß zur Entwicklung mitgliedstaatlicher Verwaltungskooperationsgesetze?, 116 DVBl. 2001, S. 855; Ruffert, Matthias, Der transnationale Verwaltungsakt, 34 Die Verwaltung 2001, S. 453 mit Ausführungen zur Wirksamkeit transnationaler Verwaltungsakte in deutschen Recht S. 472; Neßler, Volker, Der transnationale Verwaltungsakt – Zur Dogmatik eines neuen Rechtsinstituts, 14 NVwZ 1995, S. 863.

[362] Überzeugend Hecker, Jan, Europäisches Verwaltungskiooperationsrecht am Beispiel der grenzüberschreitenden polizeilichen Zusammenarbeit, 36 EuR 2001, S. 826, 841 ff.

[363] Hierzu und zum folgenden Schmidt-Aßmann, Eberhard, Strukturen des Europäischen Verwaltungsrechts: Einleitende Problemskizze, in: Ders, Hoffmann-

Riem, Wolfgang (Hrsg.); Strukturen des Europäischen Verwaltungsrechts, 1999, S. 9, 11.

[364] Danwitz, Tomas von, Systemgedanken eines Rechts der Verwaltungskooperation, in Schmidt-Aßmann, Eberhard und Hoffmann-Riem, Wolfgang (Hrsg.), Strukturen des Europäischen Verwaltungsrechts, 1999, S. 171; Hoffmann-Riem, Wolfgang, Strukturen des Europäischen Verwaltungsrechts - Perspektiven der Systembildung, in Schmidt-Aßmann, Eberhard und Hoffmann-Riem, Wolfgang (Hrsg.), Strukturen des Europäischen Verwaltungsrechts, 1999, S. 317.

[365] Dazu Vosskuhle, Andreas, Theorie und Praxis der verfassungskonformen Auslegung von Gesetzen durch Fachgerichte, 125 AöR 2000, S. 177.

[366] Nettesheim, Martin, Auslegung und Fortbildung nationalen Rechts, 119 AöR 1994, S. 261.

[367] Allgemein Dörr, Dieter u.a. (Hrsg.), Europa als Rechtsgemeinschaft, 1997.

[368] Zu verweisen ist etwa nur auf die oben angesprochenen Fall in der Rechtssache Alcan, wengleich diese Rechtssache nicht im Vorlageverfahren nach Art. 100 Abs. 1 GG an das BVerfG gegangen ist, sondern im Wege der Justizverfassungsbeschwerde nach Art. 93 Abs. 1 Nr. 4a GG, §§ 90ff BVerfGG.

[369] Zur Europäisierung der Verwaltungsgerichtsbarkeit im einzelnen etwa Hirsch, Günter, Europarechtliche Perspektiven der Verwaltungsgerichtsbarkeit, 21 VBlBW 2000, S. 71; Schwarze, Jürgen, Europäische Rahmenbedingungen für die Verwaltungsgerichtsbarkeit, 19 NVwZ 2000, S. 241; Kokott, Juliane, Europäisierung des Verwaltungsprozessrechts, 31 Die Verwaltung 1998, S. 335. Zum Thema Europarecht im deutschen Verwaltungprozess vgl. ferner etwa die Tagung des Verwaltungsgerichts Stuttgart, veröffentlicht in den aktuellen Ausgaben 2000 und 2001 der VBlBW.

[370] Vgl etwa EuGH Slg. 1999, I-223, Rdn. 32 - Upjohn; zudem die 43. Erkl. zum Protokoll über die Anwendung der Grundsätze der Subsidiarität und der Verhältnismäßigkeit im Rahmen des Amsterdamer Vertrags. Der Unterschied zum deutschen Justizföderalismus liegt hier vor allem darin, dass die deutschen Landesgerichte überwiegend bundesrechtliches Prozessrecht anwenden, so dass - anders als bei der Anwendung europäischen Rechts durch mitgliedstaatliche Gerichte - insoweit Rechtseinheit gewährleistet ist.

[371] Allgemein Rodríguez Iglesias, Gil Carlos, Zu den Grenzen der verfahrensrechtlichen Autonomie der Mitgliedstaaten bei der Anwendung des Gemeinschaftsrechts, 24 EuGRZ 1997, S. 289.

[372] Das Diskriminierungsverbot verbietet, dass die Verfahren in den Mitgliedstaaten zum Schutz der durch das Gemeinschaftsrecht verliehenen Rechte nicht ungünstiger gestaltet werden dürfen als die nach nationalem Recht vorgesehenen Klagemöglichkeiten (EuGH Slg. 1999, I -223 - Upjohn).

[373] Das Vereitelungsgebot umfasst, dass effektiver Rechtsschutz zu gewähren ist (EuGH Slg. 1986, S. 1651 - Johnston; EuGHSlg. 1987, 4097 - Heylens) und insbesondere die vom Gemeinschaftsrecht vorgeschriebene Rechtsfolge durch die Ausgestaltung des nationalen Rechts nicht unmöglich gemacht oder übermäßig erschwert werden darf (EuGH Slg. 1997, I-1591 - Alcan).

[374] Es steht vor allem noch immer die Vereinbarkeit der deutschen Schutznormtheorie mit der Rechtsschutzrechtsprechung des EuGH in Frage. Dazu

aus jüngerer Zeit etwa Hölscheidt, Sven, Abschied vom subjektiv-öffentlichen Recht? Zu Wandlungen der Verwaltungsgerichtsbarkeit unter dem Einfluss des Gemeinschaftsrechts, 36 EuR 2001, S. 376, 387 m.w.N. und Halfmann, Ralf, Entwicklungen des Verwaltungsrechtsschutzes in Deutschland, Frankreich und Europa, 91 VA 2000, S. 74). Vgl. im übrigen etwa die Einführung der Vorschriften der §§ 97 un 104ff GWB (subjektives Recht für den Bieter auf Einhaltung der Bestimmungen über das Vergabeverfahren und spezielles Rechtsschutzsystem vor den Vergabekammern mit Beschwerdemöglichkeit zum OLG).

[375] In Deutschland sind sowohl die Auslegung unbestimmter Rechtsbegriffe als auch die Ausschöpfung bestehender Ermessens- und Beurteilungsspielräume durch die deutschen Verwaltung als Ausfluss des Art. 19 Abs. 4 GG im Grundsatz voll überprüfbar, während sich der EuGH in der Regel auf eine bloße Rechtskontrolle beschränkt und lediglich danach fragt, ob der Sachverhalt zutreffend festgestellt, das vorgeschriebene Verfahren eingehalten und das Ermessen nicht missbraucht wurde. Der EuGH steht insoweit eher in der Tradition Frankreichs, wo die Überprüfung durch den Richter (unter Hervorhebung der Leistungsfähigkeit der Exekutive) vorwiegend als Problem der Gewaltenteilung wahrgenommen wird. In Deutschland hingegen gilt die Überprüfung durch den Richter (angesichts der Erfahrungen einer zu starken Exekutive) vorwiegend als Ausdruck effektiven Rechtsschutzes. Insoweit liegen hier auch die Unterschiede deutlicher zutage als im Bereich der Klagebefugnis, obgleich auch in diesem Bereich Annäherungen zwischen deutscher/europäischer Rechtsordnung bestehen (Hilf, NVwZ 2000, S. 249 nennt für die deutsche Seite etwa die Reduzierung der gerichtlichen Prüfdichte in BVerwG, NVwZ 1998, S. 961 (Autobahnausbau) und in BVerwG, NVwZ 1998, 628 (atomare Anlage)).

[376] Die bekannten Konstellationen sind die von EuGH Rs. C-213/89, Slg. 1990, S. I-2433 - *Factortame* (Nichtanwendung einer nationalen Vorschrift, wenn nur diese dem Erlass einer einstweiligen Anordnung entgegensteht); EuGH Verb. Rs. C-143/88 und C-92/89, Slg. 1991, S. I-415 - *Zuckerfabrik Süderdithmarschen* (Bedingungen für die Aussetzung des Vollzugs eines auf Gemeinschaftsrecht beruhenden nationalen Verwaltungsakts); EuGH Rs. C- 465/93, Slg. 1995, S. I-3761 - *Atlanta* (Bedingungen zum Erlass einer einstweiligen Anordnung unter Nichtanwendung von Gemeinschaftsrecht bei Zweifeln an dessen Gültigkeit); EuGH Rs. C-68/95, Slg. 1996, S. I-6065 - *T. Port* (Pflicht zur Zurückweisung eines Antrags auf Erlass einer einstweiligen Anordnung, wenn zum Bestehen des behaupteten Rechts noch eine Kommissionsentscheidung ergehen muss (Verweisung auf den europäischen Rechtsschutz)). Diese Entscheidungen dürfen nicht dahin verstanden werden, dass sie das deutsche Verwaltungsprozessrecht grundsätzlich in Frage stellen, sondern lediglich dahin, dass sie bereichspezifisch den Wettbewerb stärken wollen (gleiche Bedingungen unter Konkurenten) und sich zudem nur in einem sehr eingeschränkten Zusammenhang auswirken; vgl hierzu Schwarze, Jürgen, Europäische Rahmenbedingungen für die Verwaltungsgerichtsbarkeit, 19 NVwZ 2000, S. 251.

[377] Danwitz, Thomas von, Die Eigenverantwortung der Mitgliedstaaten für die Durchführung von Gemeinschaftsrecht, DVBl. 1998, S. 421.

[378] Vgl. nur Taupitz, Jochen, Europäische Privatrechtsangleichung heute und morgen, 1993; Müller-Graff, Peter-Christian (Hrsg.), Gemeinsames Privatrecht in der Europäischen Gemeinschaft, 1993; Müller-Graff, Peter-Christian, Europäisches

Gemeinschaftsrecht und Privatrecht, 46 NJW 1993, S. 13 ff; Micklitz, H.W.; Perspektiven eines Europäischen Privatrechts, 6 ZEuP 1998, S. 253ff; Schulze, Reiner (Hrsg.), Auslegung europäischen Privatrechts und angeglichenen Rechts, 1999; Schulte-Nölke, Hans und Schulze, Reiner (Hrsg.), Europäische Rechtsangleichung und nationale Privatrechte, 1999; Franzen, Martin, Privatrechtsangleichung durch die Europäische Gemeinschaft, 1999; Grundmann, Stefan (Hrsg.), Systembildung und Systemlücken in Kerngebieten des Europäischen Privatrechts, 2000.

379 Vgl. etwa RL 93/13/EWG des Rates über missbräuchliche Klauseln in Verbraucherverträgen; RL 85/577/EWG des Rates betreffend den Verbraucherschutz im Falle von ausserhalb von Geschäftsräumen geschlossenen Verträgen; RL 87/102/EWG des Rates zur Angleichung der Rechts-und Verwaltungsvorschriften der Mitgliedstaaten über den Verbraucherkredit; RL 97/7/EG des Europäischen Parlaments und des Rates über den Verbraucherschutz bei Vertragsabschlüssen im Fernabsatz; RL 99/44/EG des Europäischen Parlaments und des Rates zu bestimmten Aspekten des Verbrauchsgüterkaufs und der Garantien für Verbrauchsgüter.

380 RL 77/187/EWG des Rates zur Angleichung der Rechtsvorschriften der Mitgliedstaaten über die Wahrung von Ansprüchen der Arbeitnehmer beim Übergang von Unternehmen, Betrieben und Betriebsteilen; RL 85/374/EWG des Rates zur Angleichung der Rechts- und Verwaltungsvorschriften der Mitgliedstaaten über die Haftung für fehlerhafte Produkte; RL 90/314/EWG des Rates über Pauschalreisen; RL 94/47/EG des Europäischen Parlaments und des Rates zum Schutz der Erwerber im Hinblick auf bestimmte Aspekte von Verträgen über den Erwerb von Teilnutzungsrechten an Immobilien; RL 97/5//EG des Europäischen Parlaments und des Rates über grenzüberschreitende Überweisungen; RL 97/66/EG des Europäischen Parlaments und des Rates über die Verarbeitung personenbezogener Daten und den Schutz der Privatsphäre im Bereich der Telekommunikation.

381 Rechtsprechungsübersicht der letzten Jahre bei Hakenberg, Waltraud, Gemeinschaftsrecht und Privatrecht. Zur Rechtsprechung des EuGH im Jahre 2000, 9 ZEuP 2001, S. 888; Kohler, Christian und Knapp, Andreas, Gemeinschaftsrecht und Privatrecht. Zur Rechtsprechung des EuGH im Jahre 1999, 9 ZEuP 2001, S. 116.

382 Klauer, Irene, Die Europäisierung des Privatrechts. Der EuGH als Zivilrichter, 1998.

383 Beispielhaft etwa Schomburg, Wolfgang, Die Europäisierung des Verbots doppelter Strafverfolgung - Ein Zwischenbericht, 53 NJW 2000, S. 1833.

384 Vgl. etwa Berger, Klaus P., Auf dem Weg zu einem europäischen Gemeinrecht der Methode, 9 ZEuP 2001, S. 4.

385 Dazu etwa Schwintowski, Hans-Peter, Auf dem Weg zu einem Europäischen Zivilgesetzbuch, 57 JZ 2002, S. 205; Basedow, Jürgen, Das BGB im künftigen europäischen Privatrecht: Der hybride Kodex. Systemsuche zwischen nationaler Kodifikation und Rechtsangleichung, 200 AcP 2000, S. 445; Sonnenberger, Hans Jürgen, Der Ruf unserer Zeit nach einer europäischen Ordnung des Zivilrechts, 53 JZ 1998, S. 982; Timme, Michael, Zu Chancen und Grenzen einer Europäischen Ordnung des Zivilrechts, 33 ZRP, S. 301.

[386] Zur Mitteilung der Kommission Von Bar, Christian, Die Mitteilung der Europäischen Kommission zum Europäischen Vertragsrecht, 2 ZEuP 2001, S. 799.
[387] Heckel, Katharina, Der Föderalismus als Prinzip überstaatlicher Gemeinschaftsbildung, 1998, S. 12.
[388] Vgl. hierzu schon Ipsen, Hans Peter, Als Bundesstaat in der Gemeinschaft, in: Caemmerer, Ernst von (Hrsg.), Probleme des europäischen Rechts, Festschrift für Walter Hallstein, 1966, S. 248; Badura, Peter, Die Kunst der föderalen Form, in Ders. und Scholz, Rupert (Hrsg.), Wege und Verfahren des Verfassungslebens, Festschrift für Peter Lerche, 1993; Thürer, Daniel, Föderalistische Verfassungsstrukturen für Europa - eine zweite Chance der Entfaltung, 23 integration, 2000, S. 89; Hrbek, Rudolf, Die deutschen Länder und das Vertragswerk von Nizza, 24 integration, 2001, S. 102; Müller-Terpitz, Ralf, Die Beteiligung des Bundesrates am Willensbildungsprozess der Europäischen Union, 1999.
[389] Leider zu optimistisch: Wuermeling, Rudolf, Das Ende der „Länderblindheit“: Der Ausschuss der Regionen nach dem neuen EG-Vertrag, 28 EuR 1993, S. 196ff.
[390] Dazu etwa Hasselbach, Kai, Der Ausschuß der Regionen in der Europäischen Union, Heymanns, 1996; Johne, Roland, Vertretung der Landtage im Ausschuss der Regionen, 31 ZParl 2001, S. 103.
[391] Dazu Blanke, Hermann-Josef, vor Art. 263-265, in: GrabitzEberhard/Hilf, Meinhard, Das Recht der Europäischen Union, Kommentar, Bd. II (Ergänzungslieferung), Rdn. 8 ff.
[392] Dazu etwa Weber, Albrecht, Die Bedeutung der Regionen für die Verfassungsstrukturen der EU, in: Ipsen, Jörn, Verfassungsrecht im Wandel, Festschrift Heymanns Verlag, 1995, S. 681; Hrbek, Rudolf, Die deutschen Länder und das Vertragswerk von Nizza, 24 integration 2001, S. 102; Roller, Gerhard, Die Mitwirkung der deutschen Länder und der belgischen Regionen an EG-Entscheidungen, 123 AöR 1998, S. 21ff; Schambeck, Horst, Zur Bedeutung der föderalen und regionalen Dimension in der EU, in: Ruch, Alexander u.a., Festschrift für Martin Lendi, 1998, S. 445.
[393] Zu den Fällen im einzelnen Blanke, Hermann-Josef, Art. 265, in Grabitz, Eberhard/Hilf, Meinhard, Das Recht der Europäischen Union, Kommentar, Bd. II (Ergänzungslieferung), Rdn. 2ff.
[394] Vgl. Johne, Roland, Vertretung der Landtage im Ausschuss der Regionen, 31 ZParl 2001, S. 103, 115.
[395] Hrbek, Rudolf, Die deutschen Länder und das Vertragswerk von Nizza, 24 integration 2001, S. 102 hebt hervor, dass die Länder ein steigendes Selbstbewusstsein hätten. Politisch mag dies so sein, rechtlich hingegen findet es sich in den Verträgen nicht wieder.
[396] Dazu Knöll, Ralf, Die Diskussion um die Grundrechtecharta der Europäischen Union aus dem Blickwinkel der deutschen Länder, 53 NJW 2000, S. 1845.
[397] Im einzelnen Maunz, Theodor, Staatlichkeit und Verfassungshoheit der Länder, in: Isensee, Josef'/Kirchhof, Paul (Hrsg.), HdBStR Bd. IV, 2. Aufl., 2001, § 94, S. 427.
[398] Isensee, Josef, Idee und Gestalt des Föderalismus im Grundgesetz, in: Isensee, Josef'/Kirchhof, Paul (Hrsg.), HdBStR IV, 2. Aufl., 2001 , § 98, S. 517, 562 (rdn. 81 ff).

[399] Rengeling, Hans-Werner, Gesetzgebungszuständigkeit, in: Isensee, Josef'/Kirchhof, Paul (Hrsg.), HdBStR IV, 2. Aufl., 2001, § 100, S. 723.
[400] Blümel, Willi, Verwaltungszuständigkeit, in: Isensee, Josef'/Kirchhof, Paul (Hrsg.), HdBStR IV, 2. Aufl., 2001, § 101, S. 857.
[401] Blümel, Willi, Rechtsprechungszuständigkeit, in: Isensee, Josef'/Kirchhof, Paul (Hrsg.), HdBStR IV, 2. Aufl., 2001, § 102, S. 965.
[402] von Arnim, Hans Herbert, Finanzzuständigkeit, in: Isensee, Josef'/Kirchhof, Paul (Hrsg.), HdBStR IV, 2. Aufl., 2001, § 103, S. 987.
[403] Püttner, Günter, Kommunale Selbstverwaltungm, in: Isensee, Josef'/Kirchhof, Paul (Hrsg.), HdBStR IV, 2. Aufl., 2001, § 107, S. 1171.
[404] Vgl. Bullmann, Udo (Hrsg,), Die Politik der dritten Ebene - Regionen im Europa der Union, 1994.
[405] Vgl. Erbguth, Wilfried, Erosion der Ländereigenstaatlichkeit, Art. 30 GG und unitarische Entwicklungen national - wie gemeinschaftsrechtlichen Ursprungs, in: Jörn Ipsen u.a. (Hrsg.), Verfassungsrecht im Wandel, Fetschrift Carl Heymanns Verlag KG, 1995, S. 549.
[406] Isensee, Josef, Der Bundesstaat - Bestand und Entwicklung, in: Badura, Peter und Dreier, Horst (Hrsg.), Festsschrift 50 Jahre Bundesverfassungsgericht, Bd. II, 2001, S. 719, 752; weniger kritisch Müller-Terpitz, Ralf, Die Beteiligung des Bundesrates am Willensbildungsprozess der Europäischen Union, 1999, S. 40.
[407] Regelmäßig erfolgt die Koordination der Mitsprachberechtigten informell und nichtöffentlich; die Entscheidungsverläufe sind diffus und wenig transparent.
[408] Ministerpräsident des Landes Sachsen Biedenkopf, FAZ vom 17.11.1999, S. 6.
[409] Vgl. z.B. Bundesrat, Abschlußbericht der Kommission Verfassungsreform, „Stärkung des Föderalismus in Deutschland und Europa sowie weitere Vorschläge zur Änderung des Grundgesetzes, BR-Dr. 360/92.
[410] BverfG, 53 NJW 2000, S. 1097.
[411] Ministerpräsident des Landes Baden-Württemberg Teufel, FAZ vom 25.11.1999, S. 4 („Wir haben nun die Chance für einen wirklich großen Wurf.“).
[412] Der Grundatz des Vorbehaltes der Verfassung ist hierdurch nicht verletzt, denn die - nunmehr durch Art. 23 GG vermittelte - Integrationsoffenheit des Grundgesetzes veranlasst erst die Notwendigkeit des mittelbaren Vollzugs, so Isensee, Josef, Der Bundesstaat - Bestand und Entwicklung, in Badura, Peter und Dreier, Horst (Hrsg.), Festsschrift 50 Jahre Bundesverfassungsgreicht, Bd. II, 2001, S. 719, 759f; A.A., nach innerstaatlichen Gesetzgebungskompetenzverteilung differenzierend: Hermes; Georg, Art. 83, in Dreier, Horst, GG, Rdn. 5 ff (gute Zusammenfassung der Kompetenzfrage beim Vollzug m.w.N.).
[413] Vgl. EuGH Rs. C- 387/97, 11 EuZW 2000, S. 531 m. Anm. Karpenstein = 53 NJW 2000, S. 3268 L - Kommission/Griechenland. Im einzelnen zum Problem Karpenstein, Peter und Karpenstein Ulrich, Art. 228, in Grabitz, Eberhard/Hilf, Meinhard, Das Recht der Europäischen Union, Bd. II (Ergänzungslieferung), Rdn. 9ff, 18ff.
[414] Bandilla, Art. 104 EGV, in Grabitz, Eberhard/Hilf, Meinhard, Das Recht der Eeuropäischen Union (Amsterdamer Fassung), Rdn. 36 ff.
[415] Im einzelnen Dederer, Hans-Georg, Regress des Bundes gegen ein Land bei Verletzung von EG-Recht, 20 NVwZ 2001, S. 258.

[416] Böhm, Monika, Der Bund-Länder-Regreß nach Verhängung von Zwangsgeldern durch den EuGH, 53 JZ 2000, S. 382, 387; vertiefend Nopper, Frank, Bund-Länder-Haftung beim fehlerhaften Vollzug von Gemeinschaftsrecht durch die deutschen Länder, 1998.
[417] Für eine analoge Anwendung des Art. 104 V GG Isensee, Josef, Der Bundesstaat - Bestand und Entwicklung, in Badura, Peter und Dreier, Horst (Hrsg.), Festsschrift 50 Jahre Bundesverfassungsgericht, Bd. II, 2001, S. 719, 757ff.
[418] So spielen in Überlegungen zu den „Sezessionisten" in Europa deutsche Gruppen in der Regel keine Rolle, vgl. etwa Luyken, Reiner, Schafft zwei, drei, viele Staaten. Schotten, Basken, Okzitanier ... . Europas Sezessionisten arbeiten an der EU der 61. Eine Vision, in DIE ZEIT vom 15. März 2001, S. 12.
[419] Randelzhofer, Albrecht, Schlussworte II: Verfassungsstaatlichkeit im nächsten Jahrhundert - Chancen für Gemeinsamkeit und Notwendigkeit der Vielfalt, in Battis, Ulrich u.a. (Hrsg.), Das Grundgesetz im Prozess europäischer und globaler Verfassungsentwicklung, 2000, S. 281, 286; vgl. dazu auch Alber, Siegbert, Braucht Europa eine Verfassung? in: Ronge, Frank, In welcher Verfassung ist Europa - Welche Verfassung für Europa, 2001, S. 123.
[420] Zsfd. etwa Schwarze, Jürgen, Europäische Verfassungsperspektiven nach Nizza, 55 NJW 2002, S. 993.
[421] In diese Richtung etwa überlegt Lionel Jospin, wenn er in seiner Rede vom 28. Mai 2001 von einer „Permanenten Konferenz der Parlamente" oder einen „Kongress" spricht, in: Discours, Intervention sur „L´avenir de l´Europe élargie", zitiert nach Kreile, Michael, Zur nationalen Gebundenheit europapolitischer Visionen: Das Schröder-Papier und die Jospin-Rede, in: 24 integration 2001, S. 250.
[422] Zu den Vorschlägen im einzelnen mit weiteren Nachweisen Pernice, Ingolf, The Role of National Parliaments in the European Union, in: Walter Hallstein-Institut, WHI - Papers 5/01, zu finden im Internet unter www.whi-berlin.de/pernice-parliaments.htm.
[423] Dazu Dreier, Horst, Art. 20 (Demokratie), in: Ders., Grundgesetz.Kommentar. Bd. II, 1998, S. 45.
[424] Dazu etwa Corbett, Richard, Jacobs, Francis und Shackleton, Michael, The European Parliament, 4. Aufl., 2000, S. 87ff.
[425] Dazu Alston, Philip, Weiler, Joseph H.H., An „Ever Closer Union" in Need of a Human Rights Policy: The European Union and Human Rights, in: Alston, Philip (Hrsg.), The EU and Human Rights, 1999, S. 3.
[426] Dazu Weiler, Joseph H.H., Does the European Union Truly Need a Charter of Rights?, 6 ELJ 2000, S. 95.
[427] Zu den Vor- und Nachteilen dieser wie auch der anderen möglichen Lösungen vgl. Bertelsmann Europa-Kommission (Vorsitz Werner Weidenfeld), Europas Vollendung vorbereiten, Forderungen an die Regierungskonferenz 2000, S. 28 f., zu finden unter www.cap.uni-muenchen.de/download/europakom.pdf.
[428] Die folgende Darstellung orientiert sich in Teilen an Pernice, Ingolf, Kompetenzabgrenzung im Europäischen Verfassungsverbund, JZ 2000, S. 866, 872 ff.
[429] Fischer, Thomas, Schley, Nicole, Europa föderal organisieren, 1999, S. 145 ff.
[430] Zum Vergleich des US-amerikanischen und des europäischen Modells Hertel, Wolfram, Formen des Föderalismus – Die Beispiele der USA, Deutschlands und

Europas, in: Graf Vitzthum, Wolfgang, Europäischer Föderalismus: Supranationaler, subnationaler und multiethischer Föderalismus in Europa, 2000, S. 13 ff.

[431] Dazu etwa Frowein, Jochen Abr., Konkurierende Zuständigkeit und Subsidiarität. Zur Kompetenzverteilung in bündischen Systemen, in Badura, Peter, Scholz, Rupert (Hrsg.), Wege und Verfahren des Verfassungslebens, Festschrift für Peter Lerche, 1993, S. 401, 403 ff; Trute, Hans-H., Zur Entwicklung des Föderalismus in den vereinigten Staaten von Amerika, 49 ZaöRV 1989, S. 191, 246ff.

[432] Vgl. etwa Giering, Claus, Arbeitsteilung in Europa. Modell für ein nachvollziehbares Zuständigkeitsprofil, CAP, München, S. 3 ff, zu finden im Internet unter http://www.cap.uni-muenchen.de/download/2002_arbeitsteilung_giering.pdf, mit dem Fazit einer notwendigen umfassenden Erneuerung der Vertragsstruktur (S. 15).

[433] Für einen Kompetenzkatalog etwa die Bertelsmann Europa-Kommission (Vorsitz Werner Weidenfeld), Europas Vollendung vorbereiten, Forderungen an die Regierungskonferenz 2000, S. 31, zu finden unter www.cap.uni-muenchen.de/download/europakom.pdf); ausführlich Boeck, Ilka, Die Abgrenzung der Rechtssetzungskompetenzen von Gemeinschaft und Mitgliedstaaten in der Europäischen Union. Zur Notwendigkeit und zu den Vorteilen bzw. Nachteilen der Aufstellung eines Kompetenzkataloges in den Gemeinschaftsverträgen, 2000.

[434] Schwarze, Jürgen, Das schwierige Geschäft mit Europa und seinem Recht, 53 JZ 1998, S. 1077, 1086; vertiefend Ders., Kompetenzverteilung in der Europäischen Union und föderales Gleichgewicht, 110 DVBl. 1995, S. 1265, 1268f; in diesem Sinne auch Everling, Ulrich, Kompetenzordnung und Subsidiarität, in: Weidenfeld (Hrsg.), Reform der EU (1995), S. 166, 173; differenzierend Reich, Dietmar O., Zum Einfluss des Europäischen Gemeinschaftsrechts auf die Kompetenzen der deutschen Bundesländer, 28 EuGRZ 2001, S. 1, 16; kritisch mit Hinweis auf den Ausbau einer bipolaren (statt verschränkten) Kompetenzordnung Bogdandy, Armin von, Bast, Jürgen, Die vertikale Kompetenzordnung der Europäischen Union, 28 EuGRZ 2001, S. 441, 446.

[435] Vor allem dann, wenn, wie Pernice es vogeschlagen hat, eine Regelung für Gegenausnahmen etwa entsprechend dem Art. 308 EGV eingefügt wird, vgl. Pernice, Ingolf, Kompetenzabgrenzung im Europäischen Verfassungsverbund, 55 JZ 2000, S. 866, 874. Allerdings wäre in diesem Zusammenhang zunächst zu klären, wie allgemein die Regelung der Gegenausnahmen zu sein hätte, und ob es sinnvoll ist, eine alle negativen Ausschlusstatbestände gleichermaßen umfassende Regelung einzufügen.

[436] EuGH, Rs C-376/98, Urteil vom 5.Oktober 2000, 27 EuGRZ 2000, S. 436 ff - Deutschland/Parlament und Rat. An dem Willen des EuGH zur strikten Überprüfung der Gesetzgebungszuständigkeit wurden allerdings lange Zweifel laut, vgl. etwa Steinberger, Helmut, Der Verfassungsstaat als Glied einer europäischen Gemeinschaft, 50 VVDStRL 1991, S. 38.

[437] Zum engen Zusammenhang zwischen Legitimation und Subsidiarität Ronge, Frank, Legitimität durch Subsidiarität, 1998. Grundlegend zum Subsidiaritätsprinzip neuerdings Moersch, Wolfram, Leistungsfähigkeit und Grenzen des Subsidiaritätsprinzips. Eine rechtsdogmatische und rechtspolitische Studie 2001.

[438] Einzelheiten bei Bogdandy, Armin von, Bast, Jürgen, Die vertikale Kompetenzordnung der Europäischen Union, 28 EuGRZ 2001, S. 441, 452ff.

[439] Vgl. zur Bedeutung des Subsidiaritätsprinzips aus deutscher Sicht etwa von

Borries, Reimer, Das Subsidiaritätsprinzip im Recht der Europäischen Union, Deutscher Landesbericht für den XVI. FIDE-Kongress 1994 in Rom, 29 EuR 1994, S. 263, insbesondere 298 ff.

[440] Dazu Pernice, Ingolf, Kompetenzabgrenzung im Europäischen Verfassungsverbund, 55 JZ 2000, S. 866, 871.

[441] KOM (2001) 428 endgültig vom 25 7. 2001, S. 40ff.

[442] Ebenda.

[443] So schreibt etwa Fritz Scharpf, das Weissbuch reflektiere „a vision that is defined by the institutional self-interest of the Commission and its opposition to Member States and, at the same time, by a remarkable lack of concern about the real challenges confronting the Union and its Member States", in: Scharpf, Fritz W., European Governance: Common Concerns vs. the Challenge of Diversity, Jean Monnet Working Paper 6/01 (Symposium), zu finden im Internet unter www.jeanmonnetprogram.org.

[444] In diesem Sinne etwa Eriksen, Erik Oddvar, Democratic or technocratic governance?, Jean Monnet Working Paper 6/01 (Symposium), zu finden im Internet unter www.jeanmonnetprogram.org.

[445] Dazu Lübbe-Wolff, Gertrude, Europäisches und nationales Verfassungsrecht, 60 VVDStRL 2001, S. 246, 265.

[446] KOM (2001) 428 endgültig vom 25 7. 2001, S. 11.

[447] KOM (2001) 428 endgültig vom 25 7. 2001, S. 21 f.

[448] In diese Richtung etwa auch Wind, Marlene, The Commission White Paper. Bridging the Gap between the Governed and the Governing?, Jean Monnet Working Paper 6/01 (Symposium), zu finden im Internet unter www.jeanmonnetprogram.org.

[449] Allerdings mit einigen Änderungen (u.a. Ernennung des Kommissionspräsidenten durch die stärksten Fraktionen im EP; Recht des Rates, das EP auf Vorschalg der KOM aufzulösen, Ständiger Rat); vgl. in Discours, Intervention sur „L´avenir de l´Europe élargie", zitiert nach Kreile, Michael, Zur nationalen Gebundenheit europapolitischer Visionen: Das Schröder-Papier und die Jospin-Rede, 24 integration 2001, S. 250.

[450] Im Kern ist dies der Grund etwa für den Vorstoß von Philip Alston und Joseph Weiler für eine umfassende Grundrechtspolitik, den sie in der Einführung zu dem von ihnen herausgegebenen Sammelband „The EU and Human Rights", S. 3ff machen. Hintergrund des Vorschlags ist, dass den europäischen Bürgern nicht die Grundrechte fehlen, sondern dass sie sie nicht kennen und gegebenenfalls nicht durchsetzen können; kritisch hierzu Bogdandy, Armin von, Grundrechtsgemeinschaft als Integrationsziel?, 56 JZ 2001, S. 157.

[451] Vgl. dazu Dorau, Christoph, Bedarf und Inhalt einer Verfassung für die Europäische Union, in: Ronge, Frank (Hrsg.), In welcher Verfassung ist Europa - welche Verfassung für Europa?, 2001, S. 155, 161f.

[452] Vgl. dazu die Vorschläge jeweils von Bogdandy, Armin von, Consolidation of the European Treaties, 33 CMLRev. 1996, S. 1107ff. und Bieber, Roland, Die Vereinfachung der Verträge zur Errichtung der Europäischen Union, 111 DVBl. 1996, S. 1339.

[453] Europäisches Parlament vom 14. Februar 1984, in ABl. EG C 77 vom 13.3.1984 und Europäisches Parlament vom 10. Februar 1994, in ABl. EG C 61/155 vom 28.2.1994.

[454] Vgl. nur Schwarze, Jürgen u.a.(Hrsg.), Eine Verfassung für Europa, 1984; Pernice, Iingolf, Verfassungsentwurf für eine Europäische Union, 19 EuR 1984, S. 126 ff.; Hilf, Meinhard, Eine Verfassung für die Europäische Union, 17 integration 1994, S. 68ff.

[455] Vgl. etwa Weidenfeld, W., Janning, J., Europa vor der Vollendung. Der Qualitätssprung der Integration macht strategische Entscheidungen unausweichlich, in: FAZ vom 3. Juli 1998, S. 8.

[456] Dorau, Christoph, Bedarf und Inhalt einer Verfassung für die Europäische Union, in: Ronge, Frank (Hrsg.), In welcher Verfassung ist Europa - welche Verfassung für Europa?, 2001, S. 155, 165.

[457] Am Beispiel der Grundrechtecharta etwa Weiler, Joseph H.H., Does the European Union Truly Need a Charter of Rights?, 6 ELJ 2000, S. 95.

[458] Vgl. Biaggini, Giovanni, Eine Verfassung für Europa?, in NZZ vom 11./12. November 2000, S. 57.

[459] Oeter, Stefan, Vertrag oder Verfassung: Wie offen lässt sich die Souveränitätsfrage halten?, in Bruha, Th. u.a., Welche Verfassung für Europa?, 2001, S. 243, 264.

[460] Insofern hat der vielbachtete Vorschlag von von Weizäcker, Richard, Dehaene, Jean-Luc, Simon, David, Die institutionellen Auswirkungen der Erweiterung, Bericht an die Europäische Kommission, vom 18.10.1999; kritisch allerdings Huber, Peter M., Europäisches und nationales Verfassungsrecht, 60 VVDStRL 2001, S. 234.

[461] Pernice, Ingolf, Europäisches und nationales Verfassungsrecht, 60 VVDStRL 2001, S. 187 f.

[462] Biaggini, Giovanni, Eine Verfassung für Europa?, in NZZ vom 11./12. November 2000, S. 57, in diesem Sinne auch Oeter, Stefan, Europäische Integration als Konstitutionalisierungsprozess, 59 ZaöRV 1999, S. 901, 912; auch von Bogdandy, Armin, Grundrechtsgemeinschaft als Integrationsziel?, 56 JZ 2001, S. 157, 169 mit Hinweis auf die in diesem Sinne vergleichbare Konstitutionalisierung der deutschen Rechtsordnung durch das Grundgesetz. Zu letzterer eingehend Schuppert, Gunnar Folke und Bumke, Christian, Die Konstitutionalisierung der Rechtsordnung, 2000. Der Vergleich ist ein interessanter Gedanke, nur die Wirkrichtung scheint doch sehr unterschiedlich zu sein.

[463] Vgl Huber, Peter M., Europäisches und nationales Verfassungsrecht, 60 VVDStRL 2001, S. 234. Zur Untermauerung insoweit Weiler, Joseph J. H., The Transformation of Europe, in: Ders., The Constitution of Europe, 1999, S. 10: „ It is not an accident that some of the most successful federations which emerged from seperate polities - the United States, Switzerland, Germany - enjoyed a period as a confederation prior to unification. This does not mean confederation is a prerequisite to federation. It simply suggests that in a federation created by integration rather than by devolution, there must be an adjustment period in which the political boundaries of the new polity become socially *accepted as appropriate* for the larger democratic rules by which the minority will accept the new majority" [Hervorhebung vom Berichterstatter].

[464] Fabio, Udo di, Mehrebenendemokratie in Europa. Auf dem Weg in die komplementäre Ordnung, Vortrag an der Humboldt-Universität zu Berlin am 15. November 2001, S. 7 (zu finden im Internet unter www.whi-berlin.de/difabio.htm).

[465] Zu den politiktheoretischen Anforderungen vgl. etwa Voigt, Stefan, What Constitution for Europe? The Constitutional Question from the Point of View of (Positive) Constitutional Economics, in: Bruha, Thomas u.a. (Hrsg.), Welche Verfassung für Europa?, 2001, S. 41.

[466] So etwa Oeter, Stefan, Vertrag oder Verfassung: Wie offen lässt sich die Souveränitätsfrage halten?, in: Bruha, Thomas u.a. (Hrsg.), Welche Verfassung für Europa?, 2001, S. 243, 252; Schneider, Heinrich, Alternativen der Verfassungsfinalität: Föderation, Konföderation - oder was sonst?, 23 integration 2000, S. 171.

[467] Böckenförde, Ernst-Wolfgang, Die verfassungsgebende Gewalt des Volkes - ein Grenzbegriff des Verfassungsrechts, in: Ders., Staat, Verfassung, Demokratie, 2. Aufl., 1992, S. 90, 102: „[Ein Konvent] unterbreitet den Verfassungstext als Vorschlag *an* das Volk, das selbst über Annahme oder Ablehnung entscheidet" [Hervorhebung Böckenförde].

[468] Art. 49 EUV erlaubt prinzipiell jedem *europäischem* Staat den Beitritt.

[469] Zu den Zahlen im einzelnen Vedder, Christoph, Art. 49, in Grabitz, Eberhard/Hilf, Meinhard, Das Recht der Europäischen Union, Bd. I (Ergänzungslieferung), Rdn. 3.

[470] Vgl. Punkt 8 der Erklärung.

[471] Vgl. Punkt 3 der Erklärung, letzter Satz.

[472] Hierzu und zum folgenden Punkt III (Die Einberufung eines Konvents zur Zukunft Europas) der Erklärung von Laeken zur Zukunft der Europäischen Union; zu finden im Internet unter http://europa.eu.int/futurum/documents.

[473] Nach der Erklärung von Laeken setzen Empfehlungen des Konventes im Abschlussdokument Konsens der Konventsmitglieder voraus, Optionen hingegen können auch ohne Konsens abgegeben werden, allerdings nur unter „Angabe, inwieweit diese Optionen im Konvent Unterstützung gefunden haben".

LITERATURVERZEICHNIS

Adamovich, Ludwig, Juristische Aspekte der „Sanktionen" der EU-14 und des „Weisenberichts", 28 EuGRZ 2001, S. 89

Alber, Siegbert, Braucht Europa eine Verfassung? in: Ronge, Frank, In welcher Verfassung ist Europa - Welche Verfassung für Europa, Baden-Baden: Nomos, 2001, S. 123

Alber, Siegbert, Die Selbstbindung der europäischen Organe an die EU-Charta der Grundrechte, 28 EuGRZ 2001, S. 349

Alber, Siegbert, Widmaier, Ulrich, Die EU-Charta der Grundrechte und ihre Auswirkungen auf die Rechtsprechung, 27 EuGRZ 2000, S. 497

Alexander, Larry, Introduction, in: Ders. (Hrsg.), Constitutionalism, Philosophical Foundations, Cambridge: Cambridge UP, 1999, S. 1

Alston, Philip, Weiler, Joseph H.H., An „Ever Closer Union" in Need of a Human Rights Policy: The European Union and Human Rights, i:n Alston, Philip (Hrsg.), The EU and Human Rights, Oxford: Oxford UP, 1999, S. 3

Ammon, Güntheru.a. (Hrsg.), Föderalismus und Zentralismus: Europas Zukunft zwischen dem deutschen und dem französischen Modell, Baden-Baden: Nomos, 1996

Argirakos, Dimitros, Eine Verfassung für Europa, Heidelberg: Müller, 2001

Arndt, Claus, Waffeneinsatz von Frauen bei der Bundeswehr, 53 NJW 2000, S. 1461

Arnim, Hans Herbert von, Finanzzuständigkeit, in: Isensee, Josef, Kirchhof, Paul (Hrsg.), Handbuch des Staatsrechts der Bundesrepublik Deutschland, Bd. IV: Finanzverfassung – Bundesstaatliche Ordnung, Heidelberg: Müller, 2. Aufl., 1999, § 103, S. 987

Augustin, Angela, Das Volk der Europäischen Union, Zu Inhalt und Kritik eines normativen Begriffs, Berlin: Duncker und Humblot, 2000

Baade, Hans, Das Verhältnis von Parlament und Regierung im Bereich der auswärtigen Gewalt der Bundesrepublik Deutschland, 1962

Badura, Peter, Die Kunst der föderalen Form, in: Ders. und Scholz, Rupert (Hrsg.), Wege und Verfahren des Verfassungslebens, Festschrift für Peter Lerche, München: C.H. Beck, 1993

Baer, Susanne, Grundrechtecharta ante portas, 33 ZRP 2000, S. 361

Bandilla, Art. 104 EGV, in Grabitz, Eberhard/Hilf, Meinhard, Das Recht der EU, München: C.H. Beck (Amsterdamer Fassung, 2001)

Bar, Christian von, Die Mitteilung der Europäischen Kommission zum Europäischen Vertragsrecht, 2 ZEuP 2001, S. 799

Basedow, Jürgen, Das BGB im künftigen europäischen Privatrecht: Der hybride Kodex. Systemsuche zwischen nationaler Kodifikation und Rechtsangleichung, 200 AcP 2000, S. 445

Battis, Ulrich, Verwaltungsrecht als konkretisiertes Gemeinschaftsrecht, 54 DÖV 2001, S. 988

Bauer, Hartmut, Europäisierung des Verfassungsrechts, JBl. 2000, S. 749

Becker, Joachim, Der transnationale Verwaltungsakt, Übergreifendes europäisches Rechtsinstitut oder Anstoß zur Entwicklung mitgliedstaatlicher Verwaltungskooperationsgesetze?, 116 DVBl. 2001, S. 855

Benda, Ernst, Menschenwürde und Persönlichkeitsrecht, in: Ders. u.a. (Hrsg.), Handbuch des Verfassungsrechts der Bundesrepublik Deutschland, Berlin: De Gruyter, 2. Aufl. 1994, S. 161

Berger, Klaus P., Auf dem Weg zu einem europäischen Gemeinrecht der Methode, 9 ZEuP 2001, S. 4

Bertelsmann Europa-Kommission (Vorsitz Werner Weidenfeld), Europas Vollendung vorbereiten, Forderungen an die Regierungskonferenz 2000, www.cap.uni-muenchen.de/download/europakom.pdf.

Beutler, Bengt u.a., Die Europäische Union, Rechtsordnung und Politik, Baden-Baden: Nomos, 5. Aufl. 2001

Biaggini, Giovanni, Eine Verfassung für Europa?, NZZ vom 11./12. November 2000, S. 57

Bieber, Roland u.a. (Hrsg.), Europäischer Verfassungsraum, Zürich, Schulthess, Polygraph. Verl., 1995

Bieber, Roland, Abwegige und zielführende Vorschläge: Zur Kompetenzabgrenzung in der Europäischen Union, 24 integration 2001, S. 308

Bieber, Roland, Die Vereinfachung der Verträge zur Errichtung der Europäischen Union, 111 DVBl. 1996, S. 1339

Bieber, Roland, Verfassungsfrage und institutionelle Reform, in: Bruha, Thomas u.a.(Hrsg.), Welche Verfassung für Europa?, Baden-Baden, Nomos 2001, S. 111

Blanke, Hermann-Josef, Art. 265, in Grabitz, Eberhard/Hilf, Meinhard, Das Recht der Europäischen Union, Kommentar, Bd. II, München: C.H. Beck

Blanke, Hermann-Josef, vor Art. 263 -265, in Grabitz, Eberhard/Hilf, Meinhard, Das Recht der Europäischen Union, Kommentar, Bd. II, München: C.H. Beck

Bleckmann, Albert, Das europäische Demokratieprinzip, 56 JZ 2001, S. 53

Bleckmann, Albert, Die Wahrung der nationalen Identität im Unionsvertrag, 52 JZ 1997, S. 265

Bleckmann, Albert, Die Zulässigkeit des Volksentscheides nach dem Grundgesetz, 33 JZ 1978, S. 217

Blümel, Willi, Rechtsprechungszuständigkeit, in: Isensee, Josef, Kirchhof, Paul (Hrsg.), Handbuch des Staatsrechts der Bundesrepublik Deutschland, Bd. IV: Finanzverfassung – Bundesstaatliche Ordnung, Heidelberg: Müller, 2. Aufl., 1999, § 102, S. 965

Blümel, Willi, Verwaltungszuständigkeit, in: Isensee, Josef, Kirchhof, Paul (Hrsg.),, Handbuch des Staatsrechts der Bundesrepublik Deutschland, Bd. IV: Finanzverfassung – Bundesstaatliche Ordnung, Heidelberg: Müller, 2. Aufl., 1999, § 101, S. 857

Böckenförde, Ernst-Wolfgang, Der Staat als sittlicher Staat, Berlin, 1978

Böckenförde, Ernst-Wolfgang, Demokratische Willensbildung und Repräsentation, in: Isensee, Josef, Kirchhof, Paul (Hrsg.), Handbuch des Staatsrechts der Bundesrepublik Deutschland, Bd. II: Demokratische Willensbildung – Die Staatsorgane des Bundes, 2.Aufl., 1998, S. 29

Böckenförde, Ernst-Wolfgang, Die Nation, Identität in Differenz, in: Ders., Staat, Nation, Europa, Frankfurt a.M.: Suhrkamp, 1999, S. 34

Böckenförde, Ernst-Wolfgang, Die verfassungsgebende Gewalt des Volkes - Ein Grenzbegriff des Verfassungsrechts, in: Ders., Staat, Verfassung, Demokratie, Frankfurt a.M.: Suhrkamp, 2. Aufl., 1992, S. 90

Böckenförde, Ernst-Wolfgang, Die Zukunft politischer Autonomie, in: Staat, Nation, Europa, Frankfurt a.M.: Suhrkamp, 1999, S. 103

Böckenförde, Ernst-Wolfgang, Geschichtliche Entwicklung und Bedeutungswandel der Verfassung, in Ders., Staat, Verfassung, Demokratie, Frankfurt a.M.: Suhrkamp, 2. Aufl. 1992, S. 29

Böckenförde, Ernst-Wolfgang, Welchen Weg geht Europa, in: Ders., Staat, Nation, Europa, Frankfurt a.M.: Suhrkamp, 1999, S. 68

Boeck, Ilka, Die Abgrenzung der Rechtssetzungskompetenzen von Gemeinschaft und Mitgliedstaaten in der Europäischen Union. Zur Notwendigkeit und zu den Vorteilen bzw. Nachteilen der Aufstellung eines Kompetenzkataloges in den Gemeinschaftsverträgen, Baden_Baden: Nomos, 2000.

Bogdandy, Armin von, A bird´s eye view on the science of European Law, 6 ELJ 2000, S. 208

Bogdandy, Armin von, Bast, Jürgen, Die vertikale Kompetenzordnung der Europäischen Union, 28 EuGRZ 2001, S. 441

Bogdandy, Armin von, Beobachtungen zur Wissenschaft vom Europarecht, 40 Der Staat 2001, S. 24.

Bogdandy, Armin von, Consolidation of the European Treaties, 33 CMLRev. 1996, S. 1107

Bogdandy, Armin von, Die Europäische Union als supranationale Föderation, 22 integration 1999, S. 95

Bogdandy, Armin von, Suprantionale Union als neuer Herrschaftstypus: Entstaatlichung und Vergemeinschaftung in staatstheoretischer Perspektive, 16 integration 1993, S. 210

Bogdandy, Armin von, Grundrechtsgemeinschaft als Integrationsziel?, 56 JZ 2001, S. 157

Bogdandy, Armin von, Nettesheim, Martin, Die Europäische Union: Ein einheitlicher Verband mit eigener Rechtsordnung, 31 EuR 1996, S. 3

Bogdandy, Armin von, Supranationaler Föderalismus als Wirklichkeit und Idee einer neuen Herrschaftsform, Baden-Baden: Nomos, 1999

Bogdandy, Armin von, Zweierlei Verfassungsrecht, 39 Der Staat, 2000, S. 181

Böhm, Monika, Der Bund-Länder-Regreß nach Verhängung von Zwangsgeldern durch den EuGH, 55 JZ 2000, S. 382

Borchmann, Michael, Der Vertrag von Nizza, 12 EuZW 2001, S. 170

Borries, Reimer von, Das Subsidiaritätsprinzip im Recht der Europäischen Union, Deutscher Landesbericht für den XVI. FIDE-Kongress 1994 in Rom, 29 EuR 1994, S. 263

Brenner, Michael, Das Gesetz über die Zusammenarbeit von Bundesregierung und Deutschem Bundestag in Angelegenheiten der Europäischen Union, 2 VBlThü. 1993, S. 196

Brenner, Michael, Huber, Peter M., Europarecht und Europäisierung in den Jahren 2000/2001, 116 DVBl. 2001, S. 1013

Breuer, Rüdiger, Die Sackgasse des neuen Europaartikels (Art. 23 GG), 13 NVwZ 1994, S. 417

Bruha, Thomas u.a., Welche Verfassung für Europa?, Schwarzkopf-Kolloquium, Baden-Baden: Nomos, 2001

Bullmann, Udo (Hrsg,), Die Politik der dritten Ebene - Regionen im Europa der Union, Baden-Baden: Nomos, 1994

Busse, Christian, Die völkerrechtliche Einordnung der Europäischen Union, Köln: Heymanns, 1999, S. 43

Callies, Christian, Die Charta der Grundrechte der Europäischen Union, 12 EuZW 2001, S. 261

Cappelletti, Seccombe, Weiler, General Introduction, in Dies. (Hrsg.), Integration through Law, Vol 1: A Political, Legal and Economic Overview, Europe and the American Federal Experience, Book 1, Berlin: De Gruyter, 1986, S. 4

Caspar, Johannes, Nationale Grundrechtsgarantien und sekundäres Gemeinschaftsrecht, 53 DÖV 2000, S. 349

CDU-Bundesfachausschusses Europapolitik (Vorsitz Elmar Brok, MdEP), Forderungen der CDU an den europäischen Verfassungsprozess bis 2004

CDU-CSU-Arbeitsgruppe "Europäischer Verfassungsvertrag" unter Leitung von Wolfgang Schäuble und Reinhold Bocklet: „Vorschläge von CDU und CSU für einen Europäischen Verfassungsvertrag"

CDU-Fraktion "Europa richtig voranbringen" vom 11.12.2001, BT Drucksache 14/7781

Chwolik-Lanfermann, Grundrechtsschutz in der Europäischen Union, Frankfurt a.M., Lang, 1994

Classen, Claus Dieter, Das nationale Verwaltungsverfahren im Kraftfeld des Europäischen Gemeinschaftsrechts, 31 Die Verwaltung 1998, S. 307

Classen, Dieter, Anmerkung zu BVerfG, Beschluss vom 7.6.2000 - 2 BvL 1/97, JZ 2000, S. 1158

Clement, Wolfgang, Europa gestalten – nicht verwalten, FCE 3/01 (zu finden unter www.whi-berlin.de)

CMLR, Editorial Comments: Preparing for 2004, The Post-Nice process, 38 CMLRev. 2001, S. 493

Corbett, Richard, Jacobs, Francis und Shackleton, Michael, The European Parliament, London: Harper, 4. Aufl., 2000

Craig, Paul, Constitutions, Constitutionalism and the European Union, 7 ELJ 2001, p. 125

Danwitz, Thomas von Eigenverantwortung der Mitgliedstaaten für die Durchführung von Gemeinschaftsrecht, 113 DVBl. 1998, S. 421

Danwitz, Thomas von, Normkonkretisierende Verwaltungsvorschriften und Gemeinschaftsrecht, 84 VA 1993, S. 73

Danwitz, Thomas von, Verwaltungsrechtliches System und europäische Integration, Tübingen: Mohr, 1996

Danwitz, Thomas von, Zwischen Symbolismus und Realismus, Die Grundrechtecharta der Europäischen Union, Internationale Politik 2001, S. 37

Danwitz, Tomas von, Systemgedanken eines Rechts der Verwaltungskooperation, in Schmidt-Aßmann, Eberhard und Hoffmann-Riem, Wolfgang (Hrsg.), Strukturen des Europäischen Verwaltungsrechts, Baden-Baden: Nomos, 1999, S. 171

Däubler-Gmelin, Herta, Eine Grundrechtecharta für ein Europa der Bürgerinnen und Bürger, Rede vor der Humboldt-Universität vom 19. Okt. 2000 (zu finden unter www.whi-berlin.de)

DeSchutter, Olivier, La contribution de la Charte des droits fondamentaux de l'Union Européenne à la garantie des droits sociaux dans l'ordre juridique communautaire, 12 RUDH 2000, S. 33

Dederer, Hans-Georg, Regress des Bundes gegen ein Land bei Verletzung von EG-Recht, 20 NVwZ 2001, S. 258

Denninger, Erhard, Vom Ende nationalstaatlicher Souveränität in Europa, 55 JZ 1998, S. 1121

Fabio, Udo di, Das Recht offener Staaten, Tübingen: Mohr Siebeck, 1998

Fabio, Udo di, Der neue Art. 23 des Grundgesetzes, Positivierung vollzogenen Verfassungswandels oder Verfassungsneuschöpfung?, 32 Der Staat 1993, S. 191

Fabio, Udo di, Der Verfassungsstaat in der Weltgesellschaft, Walter Eucken Institut, Beiträge zur Ordnungstheorie und Ordnungspolitik 166, Tübingen: Mohr Siebeck, 2001

Fabio, Udo di, Eine europäische Charta, 55 JZ 2000, S. 737

Fabio, Udo di, Mehrebenendemokratie in Europa. Auf dem Weg in die komplementäre Ordnung, Vortrag an der Humboldt-Universität zu Berlin am 15. November 2001 (zu finden im Internet unter www.whi-berlin.de/difabio.htm).

Fabio, Udo di, Was der Staatenverbund leisten kann, FAZ vom 6. April 1999, S. 11

Bibel, nach der Übersetzung Martin Luthers

Dietlein, Johannes, Die Lehre von den grundrechtlichen Schutzpflichten, Berlin: Duncker und Humblot, 1992

Dix, Wolfgang, Grundrechtecharta und Konvent - auf neuen Wegen zur Reform der EU?, 24 integration 2001, S. 34

Döhring, Karl, Die nationale „Identität" der Mitgliedstaaten der Europäischen Union, in: Due, Ole u.a. (Hrsg.), Festschrift für Ulrich Everling, Bd. 1, Baden-Baden: Nomos, 1995, S. 263

Dorau, Christoph, Bedarf und Inhalt einer Verfassung für die Europäische Union, in Ronge, Frank (Hrsg.), In welcher Verfassung ist Europa - welche Verfassung für Europa?, Baden-Baden: Nomos, 2001, S. 155

Dorau, Christoph, Die Verfassungsfrage der Europäischen Union, Möglichkeiten und Grenzen der europäischen Verfassungsentwicklung nach Nizza, Baden-Baden: Nomos, 2001

Dörr, Dieteru.a. (Hrsg.), Europa als Rechtsgemeinschaft, Baden-Baden: Nomos, 1997

Dörr, Oliver, Zur Rechtsnatur der Europäischen Union, 30 EuR 1995, S. 334

Dreier, Horst, Art. 20 (Demokratie), in Ders., Grundgesetz. Kommentar. Bd. II: Art. 20-82; Tübingen: Mohr, 1998

Drexl, Josef u.a. (Hrsg.), Europäische Demokratie, Baden-Baden: Nomos, 1999

Erbguth, Wilfried, Erosion der Ländereigenstaatlichkeit, Art. 30 GG und unitarische Entwicklungen national - wie gemeinschaftsrechtlichen Ursprungs, in Jörn Ipsen u.a.(Hrsg.), Verfassungsrecht im Wandel, Festschrift Carl Heymanns Verlag KG, Köln: Heymanns, 1995, S. 549

Erichsen, Hans-Uwe, Allgemeine Handlungsfreiheit, in: Isensee, Josef, Kirchhof, Paul (Hrsg.), Handbuch des Staatsrechts der Bundesrepublik Deutschland, Bd. IV: Finanzverfassung – Bundesstaatliche Ordnung, Heidelberg: Müller, 2. Aufl., 2001, § 151, S. 1185

Eriksen, Erik Oddvar, Democratic or technocratic governance?, Jean Monnet Working Paper 6/01 (Symposium), www.jeanmonnetprogram.org.

Europäischer Rat von Laeken, Schlussfolgerungen des Vorsitzes, Anhang I: Erklärung von Laeken zur Zukunft der Europäischen Union, unter www.eu.2001.be.

European Constitutional Group, Für Europa eine Verfassung der Freiheit, FAZ vom 28. August 1993, S. 11

Everling, Ulrich, Kompetenzordnung und Subsidiarität, in: Weidenfeld, Werner (Hrsg.), Reform der Europäischen Union: Materialien zur Revision des Maastrichter Vertrages 1996, Gütersloh: Bertelsmann Stiftung, 1994, S. 166

Everling, Ulrich, Überlegungen zur Struktur der Europäischen Union und zum neuen Europa-Artikel des Grundgesetzes, 108 DVBl. 1993, S. 936

Fischer, Joschka, Vom Staatenverbund zur Föderation – Gedanken über die Finalität der europäischen Integration, 23 integration 2000, S. 149

Fischer, Klemens H. (Hrsg.), Der Vertrag von Nizza, Baden-Baden: Nomos, 2001

Fischer, Thomas, Schley, Nicole, Europa föderal organisieren, Bonn: Europa Union Verlag, 1999

Franck, Thomas M., Clan and Superclan: Loyality, Identity and Community in Law and Practice, in 90 AJIL 1996, S. 359

Franzen, Martin, Privatrechtsangleichung durch die Europäische Gemeinschaft, Berlin: De Gruyter, 1999

Friesenhahn, Ernst, Parlament und Regierung im modernen Staat, 16 VVDStRL 1958, S. 9

Fritz-Vannahme, Joachim, Nizza ist nur der Anfang – Als nächstes schreibt Europa seine Verfassung, Die ZEIT vom 7. Dez. 2000, Nr. 50, S. 3

Frowein, Jochen Abr., Die Europäisierung des Verfassungsrechts, in Badura, Peter und Dreier, Horst (Hrsg,), Festschrift 50 Jahre Bundesverfassungsgericht, Bd. 2, Tübingen: Mohr, S. 209

Frowein, Jochen Abr., Die rechtliche Bedeutung desVerfassungsprinzips der parlamentarischen Demokratie für den europäischen Integrationsprozess, 18 EuR 1983, S. 301

Frowein, Jochen Abr., Die Verfassung der Europäischen Union aus der Sicht der Mitgliedstaaten, 30 EuR 1995, S. 315

Frowein, Jochen Abr., Konkurierende Zuständigkeit und Subsidiarität. Zur Kompetenzverteilung in bündischen Systemen, in Badura, Peter, Scholz, Rupert (Hrsg.), Wege und Verfahren des Verfassungslebens, Festschrift für Peter Lerche, München: C.H. Beck, 1993, S. 401

Frowein, Jochen Abr., Kritische Bemerkungen zur Lage des deutschen Staatsrechts aus rechtsvergleichender Sicht, 51 DÖV 1998, S. 806

Frowein, Schulhofer und Shapiro, The Protection of Fundamental Rights as a Vehicle of Integration, in: Cappelletti, M., Seccombe, M. und Weiler, J.H.H. (Hrsg.), Integration Through Law, Berlin, 1984, Bd. I, Buch 3, S. 231

Fuchs, Michael, Art. 23 GG in der Bewährung. Anmerkungen aus der Praxis, 54 DÖV 2001, S. 233

Füßer, Klaus, Durchsetzung der Vorlagepflicht zum EuGH gemäß Art. 234 III EGV, in 116 DVBl. 2001, S. 1574

Geiger, Rudolf, Die Mitwirkung des deutschen Gesetzgebers an der Entwicklung der Europäischen Union, Zur Auslegung des Art. 23 Ab. 1 Satz 2 und 3 GG, 51 JZ 1996, S. 1093

Giering, Claus, Arbeitsteilung in Europa. Modell für ein nachvollziehbares Zuständigkeitsprofil, CAP, München http://www.cap.uni-muenchen.de/download/2002_arbeitsteilung_giering.pdf

Gloser, Günter und Roth, Michael, Verfassungsrecht ist Parlamentsrecht: Eine starke europäische Gemeinschaft braucht starke Volksvertretungen, in FAZ vom 27. August 2001, S. 8

Gloser, Günter, Die europäische Integration voranbringen: Zum europapolitischen Leitantrag der SPD, 24, integration 2001, S. 303

Götz, Volkmar, Anmerkung, 55 JZ 2000, S. 413

Grabenwarter, Christoph, Die Charta der Grundrechte für die Europäische Union, 116 DVBl. 2001, S. 1

Grabenwarter, Christoph, Europäisches und nationales Verfassungsrecht, 60 VVDStRL 2001, S. 290

Grabitz, Eberhard, Art. 164, in: Grabitz, Eberhard, Hilf, Meinhard, Das Recht der Europäischen Union, Kommentar, Bd. II, München: C.H. Beck (Maastrichter Fassung)

Grabitz, Eberhard, Freiheit und Verfassungsrecht: Kritische Untersuchungen zur Dogmatik und Theorie der Freiheitsrechte, Tübingen: Mohr, 1976

Grabitz, Ebergard, Der Verfassungsstaat in der Gemeinschaft, 92 DVBl. 1977, S. 786Grawert, Rolf, Demokratische Regierungssysteme, Qualitätsanforderungen an die Regierungssysteme der Mitgliedstaaten der Europäischen Union, in:

Murswiek, Dietrich u.a. (Hrsg.), Staat - Souveränität - Verfassung, FS Helmut Quaritsch, Berlin: Duncker und Humblot, 2000
Grewe, Wilhelm G., Auswärtige Gewalt, in: Isensee, Josef, Kirchhof, Paul (Hrsg.), Handbuch des Staatsrechts der Bundesrepublik Deutschland, Bd. III: Das Handeln des Staates, Heidelberg: Müller, 2. Aufl. 1996, § 77, S. 921
Grimm, Dieter, Braucht Europa eine Verfassung?, 50 JZ 1995, S. 581
Grimm, Dieter, Ohne Volk keine Verfassung – Eine demokratische EU braucht bessere Institutionen, aber kein Grundgesetz, Die ZEIT vom 18. März 1999, S. 4
Grimm, Dieter, Verfassung, in Ders., Die Zukunft der Verfassung, Frankfurt a.M.: Suhrkamp, 1991, S. 11
Groeben, Hans von der, Legitimationsprobleme der Europäischen Gemeinschaft, Baden-Baden: Nomos, 1987
Grundmann, Stefan (Hrsg.), Systembildung und Systemlücken in Kerngebieten des Europäischen Privatrechts, Tübingen; Mohr Siebeck, 2000
Guérot, Ulrike, Eine Verfassung für Europa, Internationale Politik 2001, S. 28
Häberle, Peter, Europa - eine Verfassungsgemeinschaft?, in Ronge, Frank (Hrsg.), In welcher Verfassung ist Europa - Welche Verfassung für Europa?, Baden-Baden: Nomos, 2001, S. 99
Häberle, Peter, Europäische Verfassungslehre in Einzelstudien, Baden- Baden: Nomos, 1999
Häberle, Peter, Gemeineuropäisches Verfassungsrecht, 18 EuGRZ 1991, S. 261
Häberle, Peter, Gibt es eine europäische Öffentlichkeit, in: Ders., Europäische Verfassungslehre in Einzelstudien, Baden-Baden: Nomos 1999, S. 131
Habermas, Jürgen, Die postnationale Konstellation - Politische Essays, Frankfurt a.M.: Suhrkamp, 1998
Habermas, Jürgen, Wahrheitstheorien, in: Fahrenbach, Helmut, Wirklichkeit und Reflexion, Festschrift für W. Schulz, 1973
Häffner, Gerald, Strawe, Christoph, Zuegg, Robert, In der Auseinandersetzung um eine Charta der Grundrechte der Europäischen Union, 33 ZRP 2000, S. 365
Hahn, Hugo J. (Hrsg.), Das Währungswesen in der europäischen Integration, Baden-Baden: Nomos, 1996
Hahn, Hugo J., Das Entstehen der Europawährung – Szenarien ihrer Einführung, 51 JZ 1996, S. 321
Haibach, Georg, Komitologie nach Amsterdam - Die Übertragung von Rechtssetzungsbefugnissen im Rechtsvergleich, 90 VA 1999, S. 98
Hailbronner, Kay, Die Antidiskriminierungsrichtlinien der EU, 21 ZAR 2001, S. 254
Hakenberg, Waltraud, Gemeinschaftsrecht und Privatrecht. Zur Rechtsprechung des EuGH im Jahre 2000, 9 ZEuP 2001, S. 888
Halfmann, Ralf, Entwicklungen des Verwaltungsrechtsschutzes in Deutschland, Frankreich und Europa, 91 VA 2000, S. 74
Hallstein, Walter, Der unvollendete Bundesstaat, Düsseldorf: Econ, 1969
Haltern, Ulrich R., Europäischer Kulturkampf, Zur Wahrung „nationaler Identität" im Unions-Vertrag , 37 Der Staat 1998, S. 590
Hansmeyer, Sandra, Die Mitwirkung des Deutschen Bundestages an der europäischen Rechtssetzung, Berlin: Duncker und Humblot, 2001
Hartmann, Bernd J., Volksgesetzgebung in Ländern und Kommunen, 116 DVBl. 2001, S. 776

Hasselbach, Kai, Der Ausschuß der Regionen in der Europäischen Union, Köln: Heymanns, 1996

Heckel, Katharina, Der Föderalismus als Prinzip überstaatlicher Gemeinschaftbildung, Berlin: Duncker und Humblot, 1998

Hecker, Jan, Europäisches Verwaltungskooperationsrecht am Beispiel der grenzüberschreitenden polizeilichen Zusammenarbeit, 36 EuR 2001, S. 826

Hegel, Georg Wilehelm Friedrich, Grundlinien der Philosophie des Rechts, 1821

Heitzen, Markus, Gemeineuropäisches Verfassungsrecht in der Europäischen Union, EuR 1997, S. 1

Hermes, Georg, Das Grundrecht auf Schutz von Leben und Gesundheit, Heidelberg: Müller, 1987

Hermes, Georg, Art. 83, in Dreier, Horst (Hrsg), Grundgesetz. Kommentar, Bd. 3: Art. 83 bis 143, Tübingen: Mohr, 1998

Hertel, Wolfram, Formen des Föderalismus – Die Beispiele der USA, Deutschlands und Europas, in: Vitzthum, Wolfgang Graf, Europäischer Föderalismus: Supranationaler, subnationaler und multiethischer Föderalismus in Europa, Berlin: Duncker und Humblot, 2000, S. 13 ff.

Hertel, Wolfram, Supranationalität als Verfassungsprinzip, Berlin: Duncker und Humblot, 1999

Hesse, Konrad, Grundzüge des Verfassungsrechts der Bunderpublik Deutschland, Heidelberg: Müller, 19. Aufl., 1993

Hilf, Meinhard, Die Charta der Grundrechte der Europäischen Union, Beilage zur NJW 2000

Hilf, Meinhard, Eine Verfassung für die Europäische Union, 17 integration 1994, S. 68

Hilf, Meinhard, Europäische Union und nationale Identität der Mitgliedstaaten, in: Randelzhofer, Albrecht u.a. (Hrsg.), Gedächtnisschrift für Eberhard Grabitz, Beck: München, S. 157

Hirsch, Günter, Der EuGH im Spannungsverhältnis zwischen Gemeinschaftsrecht und nationalem Recht, 53 NJW 2000, S. 1817

Hirsch, Günter, Europäischer Gerichtshof und Bundesverfassungsgericht - Kooperation oder Konfrontation?, 49 NJW 1996, S. 2457

Hirsch, Günter, Europarechtliche Perspektiven der Verwaltungsgerichtsbarkeit, 21 VBlBW 2000, S. 71

Hobe, Stephan, Der kooperationsoffene Verfassungsstaat, 37 Der Staat 1998, S. 521

Hobe, Stephan, Der offene Verfassungsstaat zwischen Souveränität und Interdependenz, Eine Studie zur Wandlung des Staatsbegriffs der deutschsprachigen Staatslehre im Kontext internationaler institutionalisierter Kooperation, Berlin: Duncker und Humblot, 1998

Hoffmann-Riem, Wolfgang, Strukturen des Europäischen Verwaltungsrechts - Perspektiven der Systembildung, in: Schmidt-Aßmann, Eberhard und Hoffmann-Riem, Wolfgang (Hrsg.), Strukturen des Europäischen Verwaltungsrechts, Baden-Baden: Nomos, 1999, S. 317

Hofmann, Hasso, Von der Staatssoziologie zu einer Soziologie der Verfassung?, 54 JZ 1999, S. 1065

Hölscheidt, Sven, Abschied vom subjektiv-öffentlichen Recht? Zu Wandlungen der

Verwaltungsgerichtsbarkeit unter dem Einfluss des Gemeinschaftsrechts, 36 EuR 2001, S. 376

Holzinger, Katharina und Knill, Christoph, Eine Verfassung für die Europäische Föderation, FAZ vom 29. November 2000, S. 11

Höreth, Marcus, Die Europäische Union im Legitimationstrilemma. Zur Rechtfertigung des Regierens jenseits der Staatlichkeit, Baden-Baden: Nomos, 1999

Hrbek, Rudolf, Die deutschen Länder und das Vertragswerk von Nizza, 24 integration 2001, S. 102

Huber, Peter M., Die Vorgaben des Grundgesetzes für kommunale Bürgerbegehren und Bürgerentscheide, 126 AöR 2001, S. 165

Huber, Peter M., Europäisches und nationales Verfassungsrecht, 60 VVDStRL 2001, S. 228

Hummer, Waldemar, Obwexer, Walter, Die Wahrung der „Verfassungsgrundsätze" der EU, 11 EuZW 2000, S. 485

Iliopoulos-Strangas, Julia (Hrsg.), Grundrechtsschutz im Europäischen Raum, Baden-Baden: Nomos, 1993

Ipsen, Hans P., Über Verfassungshomogenität in der Europäischen Gemeinschaft, in Maurer, Hartmut u.a. (Hrsg.), Das akzeptierte Grundgesetz, Festschrift für Günter Dürig, München: C. H. Beck, 1990, S. 159

Ipsen, Hans P., Als Bundesstaat in der Gemeinschaft, in: Caemmerer, Ernst von, Probleme des europäischen Rechts, Festschrift für Walter Hallstein, Frankfurt a.M.: Klostermann, 1966, S. 248

Ipsen, Hans P., Die Bundesrepublik Deutschland in der Europäischen Union, in: Isensee, Josef, Kirchhof, Paul (Hrsg.), Handbuch des Staatsrechts der Bundesrepublik Deutschland, Bd. VII: Normativität und Schutz der Verfassung – internationale Beziehungen, 1992, § 181, S. 767

Ipsen, Hans P., Europäisches Gemeinschaftsrecht, Tübingen: Mohr, 1972

Isensee, Josef, Das Grundrecht als Abwehrrecht und staatliche Schutzpflicht, in: Ders., Kirchhof, Paul (Hrsg.), Handbuch des Staatsrechts der Bundesrepublik Deutschland, Bd. V: Allgemeine Grundrechtslehren, 2. Aufl. 2000, § 111, S. 143

Isensee, Josef, Der Bundesstaat - Bestand und Entwicklung, in Badura, Peter und Dreier Horst (Hrsg.), Festsschrift 50 Jahre Bundesverfassungsgericht, Bd. II, Tübingen: Mohr, 2001, S. 719

Isensee, Josef, Grundrechte und Demokratie, Die polare Legitimation im grundgesetzlichen Gemeinwesen, 20 Der Staat 1981, S. 161

Isensee, Josef, Idee und Gestalt des Föderalismus im Grundgesetz, in: Ders., Kirchhof, Paul (Hrsg.), Handbuch des Staatsrechts der Bundesrepublik Deutschland, Bd. IV: Finanzverfassung – Bundesstaatliche Ordnung, Heidelberg: Müller, 2. Aufl., 2001, § 98, S. 517

Isensee, Josef, Staat und Verfassung, in: Ders., Kirchhof, Paul (Hrsg.), Handbuch des Staatsrechts der Bundesrepublik Deutschland, Bd. I: Grundlagen von Staat und Verfassung, Heidelberg: Müller, 2. Aufl., 1995, § 13

Jabloner, Okresek, Theoretische und praktische Anmerkungen zu Phänomenen des „soft law", 34 ÖZöRV 1983, S. 217

Jarass, Hans D., Europäisierung des Planungsrechts, 115 DVBl. 2000, S. 945

Jarass, Hans D./Pieroth, Bodo, Grundgesetzfür die Bundesrepublik Deutschland: Kommentar, München: C.H. Beck, 6. Aufl. 2002

Jochum, Georg, Der neue Art. 13 EGV oder „political correctness“ auf europäisch?, 32 ZRP 1999, S. 279

Joerges, Christian und Falke, Josef (Hrsg.), Das Ausschußwesen der Europäischen Union. Praxis der Risikoregulierung im Binnenmarkt und ihre rechtliche Verfassung, Baden-Baden: Nomos, 2000

Johne, Roland, Vertretung der Landtage im Ausschuss der Regionen, 31 ZParl 2001, S. 103

Jospin, Lionel, Discours, Intervention sur „L´avenir de l´Europe élargie“, zitiert nach Kreile, Michael, Zur nationalen Gebundenheit europapolitischer Visionen: Das Schröder-Papier und die Jospin-Rede, in 24 Integration 2001, S. 250

Kadelbach, Stefan, Allgemeines Verwaltungsrecht unter europäischem Einfluß, Tübingen: Mohr, 1999

Kägi, Werner, Die Verfassung als rechtliche Grundordnung des Staates, Zürich: Polyhraph. Verl., 1945 (Neudruck 1971)

Kägi, Werner, in: Die Juristischen Fakultäten der Schweizer Universitäten (Hrsg.), Die Freiheit des Bürgers im schweizerischen Recht. Festgabe zur 100-Jahr-Feier der Bundesverfassung, 1948

Kämmerer, Jörn A., Europäisierung des öffentlichen Dienstrechts, 36 EuR 2001, S. 27

Kämmerer, Jörn, A., Gleichberechtigung am Gewehr, in EuR 2000, S. 102

Karpenstein, Peter und Karpenstein Ulrich, Art. 228, in Grabitz, Eberhard/Hilf, Meinhard, Das Recht der Europäischen Union, Bd. II, München: C.H. Beck, 2001

Karpenstein, Ulrich, Der Vertrag von Amsterdam im Lichte der Maastrichtentscheidung des BVerfG, 113 DVBl. 1998, S. 942

Kaufmann, Marcel, Europäische Integration und Demokratieprinzip, Baden-Baden: Nomos, 1997

Kaufmann, Marcel, Integrierte Staatlichkeit als Staatsstrukturprinzip, 54 JZ 1999, S. 814

Kenntner, Markus, Die Schrankenbestimmungen der EU-Grundrechtecharta: Grundrechte ohne Schutzwirkung? 33 ZRP 2000, S. 423

Kimminich, Einführung in das Völkerrecht, Tübingen: Francke (UTB), 6. Aufl. 1997

Kirchhof, Paul, Der allgemeine Gleichheitssatz, in: Isensee, Josef und ders. (Hrsg.), Handbuch des Staatsrechts der Bundesrepublik Deutschland, Bd. V: Allgemeine Grundrechtslehren, 2. Aufl., 2000, S. 837

Kirchhof, Paul, Die Gewaltenbalance zwischen staatlichen und europäischen Organen, JZ 1998, S. 965

Kirchhof, Paul, Die Identität der Verfassung in ihren unabänderlichen Inhalten, in: Isensee, Josef und ders. (Hrsg.), Handbuch des Staatsrechts der Bundesrepublik Deutschland, Bd. I: Grundlagen von Staat und Verfassung, Heidelberg: Müller, 2. Aufl., 1995, § 19, S. 775

Kirchhof, Paul, Europäische Einigung und der Verfassungsstaat der Bundesrepublik Deutschland, in Isensee, Josef (Hrsg.), Europa als politische Idee und als rechtliche Form, Berlin: Duncker und Humblot, S. 63

Kirchhof, Paul, Das Maastricht-Urteil des Bundesverfassungsgerichts, in: Hommelhoff, Peter/Kirchhof, Paul, (Hrsg.), Der Staatenverbund der Europäischen Union, Heidelberg: Müller, 1994Kischel, Uwe, Der unabdingbare grundrechtliche Mindeststandard in der Europäischen Union, Zur Auslegung des Art. 23 Abs. 1 S. 1 GG, 39 Der Staat 2000, S. 523

Klauer, Irene, Die Europäisierung des Privatrechts. Der EuGH als Zivilrichter, Baden-Baden: Nomos, 1998.

Klein, in: Graf Vitzthum (Hrsg.), Völkerrecht, 1997, S. 309 f.

Kluth, Winfried, Die demokratische Legitimation der Europäischen Union - eine Analyse der These vom Demokratiedefizit der Europäischen Union aus gemeineuropäischer Verfassungsperspektive, Berlin: Duncker und Humblot, 1995

Knöll, Ralf, Die Charta der Grundrechte der Europäischen Union, 20 NVwZ 2001, S. 392

Knöll, Ralf, Die Diskussion um die Grundrechtecharta der Europäischen Union aus dem Blickwinkel der deutschen Länder, 53 NJW 2000, S. 1845

Koch, Christiane, Anmerkung, 115 DVBl. 2000, S. 476

Stahn, Carsten, Streitkräfte im Wandel - Zu den Auswirkungen der Urteile Sirdar und Kreil auf das deutsche Recht, 27 EuGRZ 2000, S. 121

Koenig, Christian, Ist die Europäische Union verfassungsfähig?, 51 DÖV 1998, S. 268

Kohler, Christian und Knapp, Andreas, Gemeinschaftsrecht und Privatrecht. Zur Rechtsprechung des EuGH im Jahre 1999, 9 ZEuP 2001, S. 116

Kohler-Koch, Beate, Ziele und Zukunft der Europäischen Union: Eine Frage der Perspektive, 23 integration 2000, S. 185

Kokott, Juliane, Europäisierung des Verwaltungsprozessrechts, 31 Die Verwaltung 1998, S. 335

Köster, Konstantin und Schröder, Jan, Eine beachtenswerte Kompetenzüberschreitung - Frauen an die Waffe, 54 NJW 2001, S. 273

Krause, Peter, Verfassungsrechtliche Möglichkeiten unmittelbarer Demokratie, in: Isensee, Josef, Kirchhof, Paul (Hrsg.), Handbuch des Staatsrechts der Bundesrepublik Deutschland, Bd. II: Demokratische Willensbildung – Die Staatsorgane des Bundes, 2. Aufl. 1998, § 39, S. 313

Kreile, Michael, Zur nationalen Gebundenheit europapolitischer Visionen: Das Schröder-Papier und die Jospin-Rede, 24 integration 2001, S. 250

Kyaw, Dietrich von, Weichenstellungen des EU-Gipfels von Nizza, Internationale Politik 2001, S. 5

Laffan, Brigid, The Politics of Identity and Political Order in Europe, 34 Journal of Common Market Studies 1996, S. 1

Landfried, Christine, Auf dem Weg zu einem europäischen Verfassungsstaat?, in Bruha, Thomas u.a., Welche Verfassung für Europa?, Baden-Baden: Nomos, 2001, S. 265

Lanfried, Christine, Die Zeit ist reif – Nur ein europäischer Verfassungsstaat kann das Legitimationsdefizit in der EU beheben, FAZ vom 9. September 1999, S. 10

Lang, Ruth, Die Mitwirkungsrechte des Bundesrates und des Bundestages in Angelegenheiten der Europäischen Union gemäß Art. 23 Abs. 2 bis 7 GG, Berlin: Duncker und Humblot, 1997

Leben, Charles, Is there a European Approach to Human Rights?, in Alston, Philip, The EU and Human Rights, Oxford: OUP, 1999, S. 69

Lecheler, Helmut, Zum Bananenmarkt-Beschluss des BVerfG, JuS 2001, S.120

Leinen, Jo, Schönlau, Justus, Die Erarbeitung der EU-Grundrechtecharta im Konvent: nützliche Erfahrungen für die Zukunft Europas, 24 integration, 2001, S. 26

Leisner, Walter, „Werteverlust", „Wertewandel" und Verfassungsrecht, 56 JZ 2001, S. 313

Lenaerts, Koen und de Smijter, Eddy, A „bill of rights" for the European Union, 38 CMLRev. 2001, S. 273

Liisberg, Jonas B., Does the EU Charter ofFundamental Rights threaten the supremacy ofCommunity law?, 38 CMLRev. 2001, S. 1171

Limbach, Jutta, Das Bundesverfassungsgericht und der Grundrechtsschutz in Europa, 54 NJW 2001, S. 2913

Limbach, Jutta, Die Kooperation der Gerichte in der zukünftigen europäischen Grundrechtsarchitektur, 27 EuGRZ 2000, S. 417

Lord Tordoff, The Conference of European Affairs Committees: A Collective Voice for National Parliaments in the European Union, 6 JLS 2000, S. 1

Lübbe-Wolff, Gertrude, Europäisches und nationales Verfassungsrecht, 60 VVDStRL 2001, S. 246

Luchterhandt, Otto, Verfassungshomogenität und Osterweiterung der EU, in Bruha, Thomas u.a. (Hrsg.), Welche Verfassung für Europa?, Baden-Baden: Nomos, 2001, S. 125

Luyken, Reiner, Schafft zwei, drei, viele Staaten. Schotten, Basken, Okzitanier... Europas Sezessionisten arbeiten an der EU der 61. Eine Vision, in DIE ZEIT vom 15. März 2001, S. 12

MacCormick, Neil, Das Maastricht-Urteil: Souveränität heute, 50 JZ 1995, S. 797

Magiera, Siegfried, Die Grundrechtecharta der Europäischen Union, 53 DÖV 2000, S. 1017

Magiera, Siegfried, Sommermann, Karl-Peter (Hrsg.), Verwaltung in der Europäischen Union, Berlin: Duncker und Humblot, 2000Majone, Giandomenico, Europe´s „Democratic Deficit": The Question of Standards, 4 ELJ 1988, S. 5 ff.

Mancini, Giuseppe Federico, Europe: The Case for Statehood, 4 ELJ 1998, S. 29 ff. (deutsch: Europa: Gründe für einen Gesamtstaat, KritV 1998, S. 386 ff.)

Marcussen, Martin u.a., Constructing Europe? The evolution of French, British and German nation State identities, in 6 Journal of European Public Policy 1999, S. 614

Mare, Thomas de la, Article 177 in Social and Political Context, in: Craig, Paul / Búrca, Gráinne de (Hrsg.), The Evolution of EU Law, Oxford: OUP, 1999, S. 215

Maunz, Theodor, Staatlichkeit und Verfassungshoheit der Länder, in: Isensee, Josef, Kirchhof, Paul (Hrsg.), Handbuch des Staatsrechts der Bundesrepublik Deutschland, Bd. IV: Finanzverfassung – Bundesstaatliche Ordnung, Heidelberg: Müller, 2. Aufl., 2001, § 94, S. 427

Maunz, Theodor, Verfassungshomogenität von Bund und Ländern, in: Isensee, Josef, Kirchhof, Paul (Hrsg.), Handbuch des Staatsrechts der Bundesrepublik Deutschland, Bd. IV: Finanzverfassung – Bundesstaatliche Ordnung, Heidelberg: Müller, 2. Aufl., 2001, § 95, S. 443

Mayer, Franz C., Kompetenzüberschreitung und Letztentscheidung, Das Maastricht-Urteil des Bundesverfassungsgerichts und die Letztentscheidung über Ultra vires-Akte in Mehrebenensystemen, München: C. H. Beck, 2000

Menzel, Eberhard, Die auswärtige Gewalt in der Deutung des Bundesverfassungsgerichts, 79 AöR 1953/54, S. 326

Mestmäcker, Ernst-J..Der Kampf ums Recht in der offenen Gesellschaft, Rechtstheorie 1989, S. 273

Mestmäcker, Ernst-J., Die Wiederkehr der bürgerlichen Gesellschaft und ihres Rechts, 10 RJ 1991, S. 177Meyer, Jürgen, Engels, Markus, Aufnahme von sozialen Grundrechten in die Europäische Grundrechtecharta?, 33 ZRP 2000, S. 368

Micklitz, H.W.; Perspektiven eines Europäischen Privatrechts, 6 ZEuP 1998, S. 253

Moersch, Wolfram, Leistungsfähigkeit und Grenzen des Subsidiaritätsprinzips. Eine rechtsdogmatische und rechtspolitische Studie, Berlin: Duncker und Humblot, 2001, S. 350

Mosler, Hermann, Die Übertragung von Hoheitsgewalt, in: Isensee, Josef/Kirchhof, Paul (Hrsg.), Handbuch des Staatsrechts der Bundesrepublik Deutschland, Heidelberg: Müller, § 175

Müller-Graff, Peter-Christian (Hrsg.), Gemeinsames Privatrecht in der Europäischen Gemeinschaft, Baden-Baden: Nomos, 1993

Müller-Graff, Peter-Christian, Der Post-Nizza-Prozess: Auf dem Wege zu einer neuen europäischen Verfassung?, 24 integration 2001, S. 208

Müller-Graff, Peter-Christian, Europäische Föderation als Revolutionskonzept im europäischen Verfassungsraum?, 23 Integration 2000, S. 157

Müller-Graff, Peter-Christian, Europäische Verfassung und Grundrechtecharta: Die Europäische Union als transnationales Gemeinwesen, 23 integration, 2000, S. 34

Müller-Graff, Peter-Christian, Europäisches Gemeinschaftsrecht und Privatrecht, NJW 1993, S. 13

Müller-Terpitz, Ralf, Die Beteiligung des Bundesrates am Willensbildungsprozess derEuropäischen Union, Stuttgart: Boorberg, 1999

Murswiek, Dietrich, Grundrechte als Teilhaberechte, soziale Grundrechte, in: Isensee, Josef, Kirchhof, Paul (Hrsg.), Handbuch des Staatsrechts der Bundesrepublik Deutschland, Bd. V: Allgemeine Grundrechtslehren, 2.Aufl. 2000, S. 243

Murswiek, Dietrich, Maastricht und der Pouvoir Constituant, Zur Bedeutung der verfassungsgebenden Gewalt im Prozess der europäischen Integration, 32 Der Staat 1993, S. 161

Nass, Klaus Otto, Ein beliebtes Phantom: Das Demokratiedefizit der EU, FAZ vom 29. März 1999, S. 15

Neßler, Volker, Der transnationale Verwaltungsakt – Zur Dogmatik eines neuen Rechtsinstituts, 14 NVwZ 1995, S. 863

Nettesheim, Martin, Auslegung und Fortbildung nationalen Rechts, 119 AöR 1994, S. 261

Nettesheim, Martin, Die Bananenmarktentscheidung des BVerfG: Europarecht und nationaler Mindestgrundrechtsstandard, 23 JURA 2001, S. 686

Nettesheim, Martin, Die mitgliedstaatliche Durchführung von EG-Richtlinien, Berlin: Duncker und Humblot, 1999

Nettesheim, Martin, Die Zulässigkeit von Verfassungsbeschwerden und Richtervorlagen nach Art. 23 GG, 21 NVwZ 2002 (Im Erscheinen).

Nettesheim, Martin, Die Charta der Grundrechte der Europäischen Union, 25 integration 2002, S. 35

Nettesheim, Martin, Das Kulturverfassungsrecht der EU, 57 JZ 2002, S. 157

Nickel, Rainer, Zur Zukunft des Bundesverfassungsgerichts im Zeitalter der Europäisierung, 56 JZ 2001, S. 625

Nicolaysen, Gert, Der Streit zwischen dem deutschen Bundesverfassungsgericht und dem europäischen Gerichtshof, in Bruha, Thomas u.a. (Hrsg.), Welche Verfassung für Europa?, Baden-Baden: Nomos, 2001, S. 91

Nicolaysen, Gert, Nowak, Carsten, Teilrückzug des BVerfG aus der Kontrolle der Rechtsmäßigkeit gemeinschaftlicher Rechtsakte: Neuere Entwicklungen und Perspektiven, 54 NJW 2001, S. 1233

Nopper, Frank, Bund-Länder-Haftung beim fehlerhaften Vollzug von Gemeinschaftsrecht durch die deutschen Länder, Baden-Baden: Nomos, 1998

Oeter, Stefan, Europäische Integration als Konstitutionalisierungsprozess, 59 ZaöRV 1999, S. 901

Oeter, Stefan, Souveränität und Demokratie in der „Verfassungsentwicklung“ der Europäischen Union, 55 ZaöRV 1995, S. 659

Oeter, Stefan, Vertrag oder Verfassung: Wie offen lässt sich die Souveränitätsfrage halten?, in Bruha, Thomas u.a. (Hrsg.), Welche Verfassung für Europa?, Baden-Baden: Nomos 2001, S. 243

Oppermann, Thomas, Classen, Dieter, Die EG vor der Europäischen Union, 46 NJW (1993), S. 5

Oppermann, Thomas, Nationale Verfassungsautonomie und supranationale Bindung innerhalb der Europäischen Union, in Battis, Ulrich u.a. (Hrsg.), Das GG im Prozess europäischer und globaler Verfassungsentwicklung. Internationales Symposium zum 50jährigen Bestehen des Grundgesetzes 1999, Baden-Baden: Nomos 2000, S. 117

Oppermann, Thomas, Reform der EU-Sprachenregelung?, 54 NJW 2001, S. 2663

Ørstrøm, Møller, Technology and Culture in a European Context, 1991

Ossenbühl, Fritz, Gesetz und Recht - Die Rechtsquellen im demokratischen Rechtsstaat, in: Isensee, Josef, Kirchhof, Paul (Hrsg.), Handbuch des Staatsrechts der Bundesrepublik Deutschland, Bd. III: Das Handeln des Staates, Heidelberg: Müller, 2. Aufl. 1996, § 61, S. 281

Ossenbühl, Fritz, Maastricht un das Grundgesetz - eine verfassungsrechtliche Wende?, 108 DVBl. 1993, S. 629

Ossenbühl, Fritz, Vorrang und Vorbehalt des Gesetzes, in: Isensee, Josef, Kirchhof, Paul (Hrsg.), Handbuch des Staatsrechts der Bundesrepublik Deutschland, Bd. III: Das Handeln des Staates, Heidelberg: Müller, 2. Aufl. 1996, § 62, S. 315

Ost, Emanuel, Europarecht vor dem BVerfG, 20 NVwZ 2001, S. 399

Pache, Eckhard, Schorkopf, Frank, Der Vertrag von Nizza, 54 NJW 2001, S. 1377

Pache, Eckhard, Die europäische Grundrechtscharta - ein Rückschritt für den Grundrechtsschutz in Europa? 36 EuR 2001, S. 475

Paul, Michael, Die Mitwirkung der Bundesländer an der Rechtssetzung der Europäischen Gemeinschaften de lege lata und de lege ferenda, Frankfurt a.M.: Lang, 1996

Pauly, Walter, Hegel und die Frage nach dem Staat, 39 Der Staat 2000, S. 381

Pauly, Walter, Strukturfragen des unionsrechtlichen Grundrechtsschutzes, 33 EuR 1998, S. 242

Pechstein, Matthias,Koenig, Christian, Die Europäische Union, Tübingen: Mohr, 3. Aufl. 2000

Pernice, Ingolf, Art. 23, in Dreier, Horst (Hrsg.), Grundgesetz, Kommentar,Bd. II: Art. 20-82; Tübingen: Mohr, 1998

Pernice, Ingolf, Das Ende der Währungspolitischen Souveränität Deutschlands und das Maastrichturteil des BverfG, in: Due, Ole u.a. (Hrsg.), Festschrift für Ulrich Everling, Bd. 2, Baden-Baden: Nomos, 1995, S. 1057

Pernice, Ingolf, Deutschland in der Europäischen Union, in: Isensee, Josef, Kirchhof, Paul (Hrsg.), Handbuch des Staatsrechts der Bundesrepublik Deutschland, Bd. VIII: Die Einheit Deutschlands, Entwicklung und Grundlagen, Heidelberg: Müller, 1995, § 191

Pernice, Ingolf, Eine Grundrechte-Charta für die Europäische Union, 115 DVBl. 2000, S. 847

Pernice, Ingolf, Europäische Grundrechtecharta und Konventsverfahren: Zehn Thesen zum Prozess der europäischen Verfassung nach Nizza, 24 integration, 2001, S. 194

Pernice, Ingolf, Europäisches und nationales Verfassungsrecht, 60 VVDStRL 2001, S. 148

Pernice, Ingolf, Gemeinschaftsverfassung und Grundrechtsschutz - Grundlagen, Bestand und Perspektiven, 43 NJW 1990, S. 2409

Pernice, Ingolf, Grundrechtsgehalte im Europäischen Gemeinschaftsrecht, Baden-Baden: Nomos, 1979

Pernice, Ingolf, Kompetenzabgrenzung im Europäischen Verfassungsverbund, 55 JZ 2000, S. 866

Pernice, Ingolf, Multilevel Constitutionalism and the Treaty of Amsterdam: European Constitution-making revisited?, 26 CMLRev 1999, S. 703

Pernice, Ingolf, The Role of National Parliaments in the European Union, in Walter Hallstein-Institut (Hrsg.), WHI - Papers 5/01, zu finden im Internet unter www.whi-berlin.de/pernice-parliaments.htm.

Pernice, Ingolf, Verfassungsentwurf für eine Europäische Union, 19 EuR 1984, S. 126

Pernice, Ingolf, Vertragsrevision oder europäische Verfassungsgebung?, FAZ vom 7. Juli 1999, S. 7

Pernthaler, Peter, Hilpold, Peter, Sanktionen als Instrument der Politikkontrolle - der Fall Österreich, 23 integration, 2000, S. 105

Peters, Anne, Elemente einer Theorie der Verfassung Europas, Berlin: Duncker und Humblot, 2001

Pflueger, Friedbert, Die Beteiligung der Parlamente in der Europäischen Verfassungsentwicklung, Rede vor der Humboldt-universität Berlin vom 24. April 2001, zu finden im Internet unter www.whi-berlin.de

Pieroth, Bodo, Art. 20, in: Jarass, Hans D./Pieroth, Bodo, Grundgesetzfür die Bundesrepublik Deutschland: Kommentar, München: C.H. Beck, 6. Aufl. 2002

Pinder, John, Der Vertrag von Nizza - Wegbereiter eines föderalen oder intergouvernementalen Europa?, 24 integration 2001, S. 77

Pleuger, Gunter, Der Vertrag von Nizza: Gesamtbewertung der Ergebnisse, 24 integration 2001, S. 1

Puttler, Adelheit, Art. 6, in: Calliess, Christian/Ruffert, Matthias (Hrsg.),

Kommentar des Vertrages über die Europäische Union und des Vertrages zur Gründung der Europäischen Gemeinschaft, Neuwied: Luchterhand, 1999

Püttner, Günter, Kommunale Selbstverwaltung, in: Isensee, Josef, Kirchhof, Paul (Hrsg.), Handbuch des Staatsrechts der Bundesrepublik Deutschland, Bd. IV: Finanzverfassung – Bundesstaatliche Ordnung, Heidelberg: Müller, 2. Aufl., 2001, § 107, S. 1171

Quasdorf, Peter, Die Dogmatik der Grundrechte der Europäischen Union, Frankfurt a.M.: Lang, 2001

Randelzhofer, Albrecht, Art. 24, Maunz, Theodor/Dürig, Günter, Grundgesetz. Kommentar, Bd. III, München: C.H. Beck, 1992 (Ergänzungslieferung)

Randelzhofer, Albrecht, Zum behaupteten Demokratiedefizit der Europäischen Gemeinschaft, in: Hommelhoff, Peter/Kirchhof, Paul (Hrsg.), Der Staatenverbund der Europäischen Union, Heidelberg: Müller, 1994, S. 39

Randelzhofer, Albrecht, Schlussworte II: Verfassungsstaatlichkeit im nächsten Jahrhundert - Chancen für Gemeinsamkeit und Notwendigkeit der Vielfalt, in Battis, U. u.a., Das Grundgesetz im Prozess europäischer und globaler Verfassungsentwicklung, Internationales Symposium zum 50jährigen Bestehen des Grundgesetzes 1999, Baden-Baden: Nomos, 2000, S. 281

Rath, Christian, Die „unionswärtige Gewalt“ des deutschen Bundestages, in ZfParl, Sonderheft 1995, Demokratie in Europa: Zur Rolle der Parlamente, S. 114

Reich, Dietmar O., Zum Einfluss des Europäischen Gemeinschaftsrechts auf die Kompetenzen der deutschen Bundesländer, 28 EuGRZ 2001, S. 1

Rengeling, Hans-W., Eine Europäische Charta der Grundrechte - Ausarbeitung, Inhalte, Bindung, in: Ipsen, Jörn, Schmidt-Jortzig, Eberhardt, Recht - Staat - Gemeinwohl, Festschrift für Dietrich Rauschning, Köln: Heymanns 2001, S. 225

Rengeling, Hans-W., Gesetzgebungszuständigkeit, in: Isensee, Josef, Kirchhof, Paul (Hrsg.), Handbuch des Staatsrechts der Bundesrepublik Deutschland, Bd. IV: Finanzverfassung – Bundesstaatliche Ordnung, Heidelberg: Müller, 2. Aufl., 2001, § 100, S. 723

Rengeling, Hans-W., Grundrechtsschutz in der Europäischen Gemeinschaft, München: C.H. Beck, 1993

Rengeling, Hans-W., Deutsches und Europäisches Verwaltungsrecht, 53 VVDStRL 1994

Ritgen, Klaus, Grundrechtsschutz in der Europäischen Union, 33 ZRP 2000, S. 371

Rixen, Stephan, Europarechtliche Grenzen des deutschen Arbeitszeitrechts, 12 EuZW 2001, S. 421

Rödel, in Gebhardt/Schmalz-Bruns (Hrsg.), Demokratie, Verfassung und Nation, 1994, S. 123

Rodríguez Iglesias, Gil Carlos, Der EuGH und die Gerichte der Mitgliedstaaten - Komponenten der richterlichen Gewalt in der Europäischen Union, 53 NJW 2000, S. 1889

Rodríguez Iglesias, Gil Carlos, Zu den Grenzen der verfahrensrechtlichen Autonomie der Mitgliedstaaten bei der Anwendung des Gemeinschaftsrechts, 24 EuGRZ 1997, S. 289

Roller, Gerhard, Die Mitwirkung der deutschen Länder und der belgischen Regionen an EG-Entscheidungen, 123 AöR 1998, S. 21

Ronge, Frank, In welcher Verfassung ist Europa – Welche Verfassung für Europa?, ZEI-Symposium, Baden-Baden: Nomos 2001

Ronge, Frank, Legitimität durch Subsidiarität, Baden-Baden: Nomos, 1998

Ruffert, Matthias, Der transnationale Verwaltungsakt, 34 Die Verwaltung 2001, S. 453

Ruffert, Matthias, Die Mitgliedstaaten der EG als Verpflichtete der Gemeinschaftsgrundrechte, 22 EuGRZ 1995, S. 518

Rupp, Hans H., Bemerkungen zum europarechtlichen Schutz der „nationalen Identität" der EU-Mitgliedstaaten, in: Arndt, Hans-Wolfgang u.a. (Hrsg.), Völkerrecht und nationales Recht, Festschrift für Walter Rudolf, München: C.H. Beck, 2001, S. 174

Rupp, Hans H., Grundgesetzänderung durch völkerrechtlichen Vertrag - ein vernachlässigtes Problem des Maastrichtvertrages, in: Ipsen, Jörn u.a. (Hrsg.), Verfassungsrecht im Wandel, Festschrift zum 180jährigen Bestehen der Carl Heymanns Verlag KG, Köln: Heymanns,1995, S. 499

Rupp, Hans Heinrich, Muß das Volk über den Vertrag von Maastricht entscheiden?, 46 NJW 1993, S. 38

_arcevic, Edin Der EuGH als gesetzlicher Richter (Art. 101 Abs. 1 GG), 53 DÖV 2000, S. 941

Schambeck, Horst, Zur Bedeutung der föderalen und regionalen Dimension in der EU, in: Ruch, Alexander u.a. (Hrsg.), Das Recht in Raum und Zeit, Festschrift für Martin Lendi, Zürich: Schulthess, 1998, S. 445

Scharpf, Fritz W., European Governance: Common Concerns vs. the Challenge of Diversity, Jean Monnet Working Paper 6/01 (Symposium) www.jeanmonnetprogram.org.

Scheuing, Dieter H. Deutsches Verfassungsrecht und europäische Integration, in EuR - Beiheft 1 - 1997, S. 7

Scheuing, Dieter H., Europäisierung des Verwaltungsrechts : Zum mitgliedstaatlichen Verwaltungsvollzug des EG-Rechts am Beispiel der Rückforderung gemeinschaftsrechtswidriger Beihilfen, 34 Die Verwaltung 2001, S. 107

Scheuing, Dieter H., Rechtsprechungsanalyse Europäisierung des Verwaltungsrechts, in DV 2001, 107

Schmahl, Stefanie, Die Vergemeinschaftung der Asyl- und Flüchtlingspolitik, 21 ZAR 2001, S. 3

Schmalenbach, Kirsten, Der neue Europaartikel 23 des Grundgesetzes im Lichte der Arbeit der Gemeinsamen Verfassungskommission, Motive einer Verfassungsänderung, Berlin: Dunker und Humblot, 1996

Schmid, Christoph, Ein enttäuschender Rückzug, Anmerkungen zum „Bananenbeschluss" des BVerfG, 20 NVwZ 2001, S. 249

Schmidt-Aßmann, Eberhard, Strukturen des Europäischen Verwaltungsrechts: Einleitende Problemskizze, in: Ders, Hoffmann-Riem, Wolfgang (Hrsg.), Strukturen des Europäischen Verwaltungsrechts, Baden-Baden: Nomos 1999, S. 9

Schmidt-Aßmann, Eberhard, Verwaltungskooperation und Verwaltungs-kooperationsrecht in der Europäischen Gemeinschaft, 31 EuR 1996, S. 270

Schmitt-Glaeser, Alexander, Grundgesetz und Europarecht als Elemente Eruopäischen Verfassungsrechts, Berlin: Duncker und Humblot, 1996

Schmitt-Glaeser, Walter, Die grundrechtliche Freiheit des Bürgers zur Mitwirkung an der Willensbildung, in: Isensee, Josef, Kirchhof, Paul (Hrsg.), Handbuch des Staatsrechts der Bundesrepublik Deutschland, Bd. II: Demokratische Willensbildung – Die Staatsorgane des Bundes, 2. Aufl. 1998, S. 49

Schmitz, Thomas, Die EU-Grundrechtecharta aus grundrechtsdogmatischer und grundrechtstheoretischer Sicht, 56 JZ 2001, S. 833

Schmuck, Otto, Die Ausarbeitung der Europäischen Grundrechtecharta als Element der Verfassungsentwicklung, 23 integration, 2000, S. 48

Schneider, Hans-P., Die verfassungsgebende Gewalt, in: Isensee, Josef, Kirchhof, Paul (Hrsg.), Handbuch des Staatsrechts der Bundesrepublik Deutschland, Bd. VII: Normativität und Schutz der Verfassung – internationale Beziehungen, 1992, § 158, S. 3

Schneider, Heinrich, Alternativen der Verfassungsfinalität: Föderation, Konföderation - oder was sonst?, 23 integration 2000, S. 171

Schneider, Heinrich, Der Post-Nizza-Prozess: ein direkter Anlauf zur Konstitutionalisierung der Europäischen Union?, 24 integration 2001, S. 198

Schneider, Heinrich, Österreich in Acht und Bann - ein Schritt zur politisch integrierten „Wertegemeinschaft"?, 23 integration, 2000, S. 120

Schneider, Heinrich: „Die EU als Wertegemeinschaft", 22 integration 99, S. 143

Schoch, Friedrich, Die Europäisierung des Allgemeinen Verwaltungsrechts, 50 JZ 1995, S. 109

Schoch, Friedrich, Europäisierung der Verwaltungsrechtsordnung, 20 VBlBW 1999, S. 241

Scholz, Rupert, Art. 23, in: Maunz, Theodor/Dürig, Günter, Grundgesetz. Kommentar, Bd. III, München: C.H. Beck, 1992 (Ergänzungslieferung)

Scholz, Rupert, Europäische Union und Verfassungsreform, 46 NJW 1993, S. 1690

Scholz, Rupert, Zum Verhältnis von europäischem Gemeinschaftsrecht und nationalem Verwaltungsverfahrensrecht - Zur Rechtsprechung des EuGH im Fall „Alcan", 51 DÖV 1998, S. 261

Schomburg, Wolfgang, Die Europäisierung des Verbots doppelter Strafverfolgung - Ein Zwischenbericht, 53 NJW 2000, S. 1833

Schorkopf, Frank, Homogenität in der Europäischen Union - Ausgestaltung und Gewährleistung durch Art. 6 Abs. 1 und 7 EUV, Berlin: Duncker und Humblot, 2000, S. 102

Schrapper, Ludger, Die Richtlinie 94/80 EG zum aktiven und passiven Kommunalwahlrecht für Unionsbürger, DVBl. 1995, S. 1167

Schulte-Nölke, Hans und Schulze, Reiner (Hrsg.), Europäische Rechtsangleichung und nationale Privatrechte, Baden-Baden: Nomos, 1999

Schulze, Reiner (Hrsg.), Auslegung europäischen Privatrechts und angeglichenen Rechts, Baden-Baden: Nomos, 1999

Schuppert, Gunnar Folke und Bumke, Christian, Die Konstitutionalisierung der Rechtsordnung. Überlegungen zum Verhältnis verfassungsrechtlicher Ausstrahlungswirkung und Eigenständigkeit des „einfachen" Rechts, Baden-Baden: Nomos, 2000

Schuppert, Gunnar F., Anforderungen an eine europäische Verfassung, in:

Klingemann, Hans D./Neidhardt, Friedhelm, Zur Zukunft der Demokratie. Herausforderungen im Zeitalter der Globalisierung, 2000, S. 237

Schuppert, Gunnar Folke, Überlegungen zur demokratischen Legitimation des europäischen Regierungssystems, in: Ipsen, Jörn, Schmidt-Jorzig, Edzard (Hrsg.), Recht, Staat, Gemeinwohl, Festschrift für Dietrich Rauschning, Köln: Heymanns, 2001, S. 201

Schwarze, Jürgen (Hrsg.), Die Entstehung einer europäischen Verfassungsordnung. Das Ineinandergreifen von nationalem und europäischem Verfassungsrecht, Baden-Baden: Nomos, 2000

Schwarze, Jürgen, Auf dem Wege zu einer europäischen Verfassung - Wechselwirkungen zwischen europäischem un nationalem Verfassungsrecht, 114 DVBl. 1999, S. 1677

Schwarze, Jürgen, Bieber, Roland (Hrsg.), Eine Verfassung für Europa, Baden-Baden: Nomos, 1984

Schwarze, Jürgen, Das „Kooperationsverhältnis des Bundesverfassungsgerichts mit dem Europäischen Gerichtshof, in Badura, Peter und Dreier, Horst (Hrsg,), Festschrift 50 Jahre Bundesverfassungsgericht, Bd. 2, Tübingen: Mohr, 2001, S. 223

Schwarze, Jürgen, Das schwierige Geschäft mit Europa und seinem Recht, 53 JZ 1998, S. 1077

Schwarze, Jürgen, Das Staatsrecht in Europa, 48 JZ 1993, S. 585

Schwarze, Jürgen, Deutschland, in: Ders. (Hrsg.), Das Verwaltungsrecht unter europäischem Einfluss, Baden-Baden: Nomos, 1996

Schwarze, Jürgen, Deutschland, in: Ders. (Hrsg.), Die Entstehung einer europäischen Verfassungsordnung, Baden-Baden: Nomos, S. 109

Schwarze, Jürgen, Europäische Rahmenbedingungen für die Verwaltungsgerichtsbarkeit, 19 NVwZ 2000, S. 241

Schwarze, Jürgen, Europäische Verfassungsperspektiven nach Nizza, 55 NJW 2002, S. 993

Schwarze, Jürgen, Europäisches Verwaltungsrecht, Bd. I und II, Baden-Baden: Nomos,1988

Schwarze, Jürgen, Ist das GG ein Hindernis auf dem Weg nach Europa?, 54 JZ 1999, S. 637

Schwintowski, Hans-Peter, Auf dem Weg zu einem Europäischen Zivilgesetzbuch, 57 JZ 2002, S. 205

Slaughter, Anne-Marie / Stone Sweet, Alec / Weiler, Joseph H.H. (Hrsg.), The European Courts and National Courts – Doctrine and Jurisprudence. Legal Change in Its Social Context, Oxford: Hart, 1998

Smith, A. D., National Identity and the Idea of European Unity, in Gowan, Peter u.a. (Hrsg), The Question of Europe, London: Verso, 1997

Sobotta, Christoph, Transparanez in den Rechtssetzungsverfahren der Europäischen Union, Baden-Baden: Nomos, 2001, S. 51

Sonnenberger, Hans J., Der Ruf unserer Zeit nach einer europäischen Ordnung des Zivilrechts, 53 JZ 1998, S. 982

SPD, Leitantrag für den Bundesparteitag 2001 in Nürnberg, Verantwortung für Europa (zu finden unter www.spd.de)

Speer, Benedikt, Die Europäische Union als Wertegemeinschaft, 54 DÖV 2001, S. 980

Starck, Christian, Grundrechtliche und demokratische Freiheitsidee, in: Isensee, Josef, Kirchhof, Paul (Hrsg.), Handbuch des Staatsrechts der Bundesrepublik Deutschland, Bd. II: Demokratische Willensbildung – Die Staatsorgane des Bundes, 2. Aufl. 1998, , S. 3

Steinberger, Helmut, Der Verfassungsstaat als Glied einer europäischen Gemeinschaft, 50 VVDStRL 1991, S. 38

Steiner, Udo, Richterliche Grundrechtsverantwortung in Europa, in Geis, Max-Emanuel, Lorenz, Dieter (Hrsg.), Staat - Kirche - Verwaltung, Festschrift für Hartmut Maurer, München: Beck 2001, S. 1005

Stephan, Rüdiger, Über Kultur und Demokratie in Europa, in Ronge, Frank (Hrsg.), In welcher Verfassung ist Europa - Welche Verfassung für Europa?, Nomos, 2001, S. 59

Stern, Klaus, Das Grundgesetz im europäischen Verfassungsvergleich, Vortrag, gehalten vor der Juristischen Gesellschaft zu Berlin, Bd. 164, Berlin: De Gruyter, 2000

Stern, Klaus, Das Staatsrecht der Bundesrepublik Deutschland, Bd. I: Grundbegriffe und Grundlagen des Staatsrechts, Strukturprinzipien der Verfassung, München: C.H. Beck, 2. Aufl., 1984

Stern, Klaus, Das Staatsrecht der Bundesrepublik Deutschland, Bd. III: Allgemeine Lehren der Grundrechte, 1: Grundlagen und Geschichte, nationaler und internationaler Grundrechtskonstitutionalismus, juristische Bedeutung der Grundrechte, Grundrechtsberechtigte, Grundrechtsverpflichtete, München: C.H. Beck, 1988

Stern, Klaus, Die Verbindung von Verfassungsidee und Grundrechtsidee zur modernen Verfassung, in Ders.: Der Staat des Grundgesetzes, Ausgewählte Schriften und Vorträge, hrsg. von Helmut Siekmann, Köln: Heymanns, 1992, S. 111

Sterzing, Christian, Tidow, Stefan, Die Kontrolle der deutschen Europapolitik durch den EU-Ausschuss des Bundestags - Bilanz und Reformpotenziale, 24 integration 2001, S. 274

Stoiber, Edmund, Eckpunkte des europäischen Reformprozesses vor der Humboldt-Universität am 8.11.2001 (zu finden im Internet unter www.whi-berlin.de

Stone Sweet, Alec / Brunell, Thomas L., The European Court, National Judges, and Legal Integration: A Researcher's Guide to the Data Set on Preliminary References in EC Law 1958-98, 6 ELJ 2000, S. 117

Streinz, Rudolf, Der Vertrag von Amsterdam, JURA 1998, S. 57

Streinz, Rudolf, Die demokratische Legitimation der Rechtssetzung der Europäischen Gemeinschaft, 6 VBlThü. 1997, S. 73

Streinz, Rudolf, Frauen an die Front, 115 DVBl. 2000, S. 585

Stumpf, Cordula, Art. 6 EUV in: Schwarze, Jürgen (Hrsg.), EU-Kommentar,, Baden-Baden: Nomos, 2000

Szczekalla, Peter, Grundrechte für Europa - Die Europäische Union nach Nizza, 116 DVBl. 2001, S. 345

Taupitz, Jochen, Europäische Privatrechtsangleichung heute und morgen, Tübingen: Mohr, 1993

Tettinger, Peter J., Die Charta der Grundrechte der Europäischen Union, 54 NJW 2001, S. 1010

Thürer, Daniel, Föderalistische Verfassungsstrukturen für Europa - eine zweite Chance der Entfaltung, 23 integration, 2000, S. 89

Timme, Michael, Zu Chancen und Grenzen einer Europäischen Ordnung des Zivilrechts, 33 ZRP2000, S. 301

Toeller, Annette E. und Hofmann, Herwig C.H., Democracy and the Reform of Comitology, in: Andenas, Mads und Türk, Alexander, Delegated Legislation and the Role of Committees in the EC, Den Haag: Kluwer, 2001, S. 25

Tomuschat, Christian, Art. 210, in: von der Groeben/Thiesing/Ehlermann (Hrsg.), Kommentar zum EWG-Vertrag, Baden-Baden: Nomos, 4. Aufl., 1991

Tomuschat, Cristian, Das Endziel der Europäischen Integration, in: Nettesheim, Martin/Schiera Pierangelo (Hrsg.), Der integrierte Staat, Berlin: Duncker und Humblot, 1999, S. 155.

Trute, Hans-H., Zur Entwicklung des Föderalismus in den vereinigten Staaten von Amerika, 49 ZaöRV 1989, S. 191

Tsatsos, Dimitris Th., Die europäische Unionsgrundordnung, 22 EuGRZ 1995, S. 287

Uhrig Stephanie, Die Schranken des Grundgesetzes für die europäische Integration, Berlin: Duncker und Humblot 2000, S. 106

Vedder, Christoph, Art. 49, in: Grabitz, Eberhard, Hilf, Meinhard, Das Recht der Europäischen Union, Kommentar, Bd. I, München: C.H. Beck (Ergänzungslieferung 2000)

Viehoff, Reinhold, Segers, Rien T., (Hrsg.), Kultur, Identität, Europa, Frankfurt a.M.; Suhrkamp, 1999

Voigt, Stefan, What Constitution for Europe? The Constitutional Question from the Point of View of (Positive) Constitutional Economics, in: Bruha, Thomas u.a., Welche Verfassung für Europa?, Baden-Baden: Nomos, 2001, S. 41

Vosskuhle, Andreas, Theorie und Praxis der verfassungskonformen Auslegung von Gesetzen durch Fachgerichte, 125 AöR 2000, S. 177

Walter Hallstein Institut für Europäisches Verfassungsrecht (Hrsg.), Grundfragen der europäischen Verfassungsentwicklung, FCE Bd. I, Baden-Baden: Nomos 2000

Weber, Albrecht, Die Bedeutung der Regionen für die Verfassungsstrukturen der EU, in: Ipsen, Jörn u.a. (Hrsg.), Verfassungsrecht im Wandel, Festschrift zum 180jährigen Bestehen der Carl Heymanns Verlag KG, Köln: Heymanns,1995, S. 681

Weber, Albrecht, Eine einmalige Chance für eine europäische Verfassungsgebung, FAZ vom 26. August 2000

Weidenfeld, W., Janning, J., Europa vor der Vollendung. Der Qualitätssprung der Integration macht strategische Entscheidungen unausweichlich, in: FAZ vom 3. Juli 1998, S. 8

Weiler, Joseph J. H., „We will do, and hearken...“ , in: Ders., The Constitution of Europe: “Do the new clothes have an emperor?” and other essays on European integration, Camridge: CUP, 1999, S. 1

Weiler, Joseph J.H., European Democracy and Its Critics: Polity and System, in: Ders., The Constitution of Europe: “Do the new clothes have an emperor?” and other essays on European integration, Camridge: CUP, 1999, S. 264

Weiler, Joseph J.H., The Transformation of Europe, in: Ders., The Constitution of Europe: “Do the new clothes have an emperor?” and other essays on European integration, Camridge: CUP, 1999, S. 10

Weiler, Joseph J.H., The Constitution of Europe: “Do the new clothes have an emperor?” and other essays on European integration, Camridge: CUP, 1999

Weiler, Joseph J.H. und Lockhart, Taking Rights Seriously Seriously. The European Court of Justice and its Fundamental Rights Jurisprudence, 32 CMLRev. 1995, S. 518

Weiler, Joseph. J.H., Fundamental rights and fundamental boundaries: on the conflict of standards and values in the protection of human rights in the Europeanlegal space, in Ders., The Constitution of Europe: "Do the new clothes have an emperor?" and other essays on European integration, Camridge: CUP, 1999, S. 102

Weiler, Joseph J.H., Does the European Union Truly Need a Charter of Rights?, 6 ELJ 2000, S. 95

Weizäcker, Richard von, Dehaene, Jean-Luc, Simon, David, Die institutionellen Auswirkungen der Erweiterung, Bericht an die Europäische Kommission, vom 18.10.1999

Wiedmann, Thomas, Der Vertrag von Nizza - Genesis einer Reform, 36 EuR 2001, S. 185

Wind, Marlene, The Commission White Paper. Bridging the Gap between the Governed and the Governing?, Jean Monnet Working Paper 6/01 (Symposium), www.jeanmonnetprogram.org.

Wuermeling, Das Ende der „Länderblindheit": Der Ausschuss der Regionen nach dem neuen EG-Vertrag, 28 EuR 1993, S. 196

Zimmermann, Andreas, Die Auslieferung Deutscher an Staaten der Europäischen Union und internationale Strafgerichtshöfe, Überlegungen zum neuen Art. 16 Abs. 2 S. 2 GG, 56 JZ 2001, S. 233

Zuck, Rüdiger, Frauen an die Front?, 53 NJW 2000, S. 1701

Zuleeg, Manfred, Demokratie in der Europäischen Gemeinschaft, 48 JZ 1993, S. 1069

Zuleeg, Manfred, Deutsches und Europäisches Verwaltungsrecht, 53 VVDStRL 1994

Zuleeg, Manfred, Die föderativen Grundsätze der Europäischen Union, 53 NJW 2000, S. 2847

Zuleeg, Manfred, What Holds a Nation Together? Cohesion and Democracy in the United States of America and in the European Union, 45 AJCL 1997, S. 505

Zuleeg, Manfred, Zum Verhältnis nationaler und europäischer Grundrechte, Funktionen einer EU-Charta der Grundrechte, 27 EuGRZ 2000, S. 511

ITALY

EU Law and National Constitution

A Pluralist Constitution for a Pluralist Legal Order?

Rapporteur
Enzo Cannizzaro[1]

I. INTRODUCTION: FOUNDATIONS OF EUROPEAN CONSTITUTIONALISM

1. Concept of Constitution in the Member States

a. Constitution and Constitutionalism in the legal tradition of the MS

The term Constitution assumes a variety of meanings in the different contexts in which it may be employed. In a wide sense, it can be employed to indicate the basic rules of functioning and the fundamental values of whatever institutionalised social body. This wide notion of Constitution deepens its roots in the theoretical premise that the State is not the only existing legal order. Rather a plurality of legal orders exist; in all the cases in which legal relations are established within an institutionalised framework, a legal order is thereby established, having its own rules of functioning and its basic principles and values. In this sense, the term Constitution has been largely used in order to indicate the basic law of political organisation, such as the legal order of free cities, that of the roman empire, the legal order of the church, and alike. More recently, is has been employed in the context of international organisations, of NGO, and of groups and associations of individuals. The term has been largely referred to in order to indicate the fundamental norms of the law of nations, and so on.

From a pluralistic theoretical perspective, such as that to which we are now alluding, a Constitution has also the role of unilaterally establishing the relations with the other existing legal orders, with which, inevitably, the social group has relations. The rules describing the relations between legal orders can differ considerably. Although a general study of this topic falls outside the scope of the present paper, it can be argued that these rules determine the degree to which a certain legal system accepts to interact with other legal systems and accepts a certain interference with its basic functions.

But the term Constitution assumes a more precise legal meaning in the context of an ideal movement commonly called, by assonance, constitutionalism. This notion, more complex by far, serves to indicate the evolutionary process that took place within the political organisation of the absolute State, and was triggered by the claim of participation to the conduct of public affairs by even increasing layers of the population.

In this context, the Constitution is not only the document containing the basic rules concerning the functioning of the system; the Constitution has a political, a symbolic and a legal role. Politically it expresses the democratic legitimacy of the power, distributes competences among different organs and levels of government, preserves individual liberties from interference coming from the exercise of power and determines the balance between public interests and individual liberties. The underlying idea of this new concept is that the Constitution is the only source of the political power, and that no power is unrestricted, but must be exercised within the boundaries expressly or implicitly drawn by it. The Constitution thus expresses symbolically the idea that sovereignty belongs to the people, and is exercised in its name and on the basis of its express or implied grant. The consequence of this is the conceptual unity and comprehensiveness of State sovereignty. But this new concept of Constitution has also a legal meaning. Being the supreme law of the State, the Constitution appears also as the source of every other law, represents the legal background against which all other laws can be reviewed and legal conflicts must be adjudged.

The concept of Constitution is hardly a unitary one; rather, many different notions have developed during the centuries, depending on the different legal traditions and on historical contingencies. However, it is not logically impossible to single out a conceptually unitary nucleus. It sprouts out from the consideration that, despite deep differences, State Constitutions generally discharge some common functions.

First, Constitutions generally have a legitimising effect. They allow participation of the people in the decision-making process, allocate powers and distribute them among different organs and levels of government, establish the rules by which all the powers and functions are to be exerted in the name of the people. In short, they assure the unity of the process of government in a legal environment characterised by the separation of the powers.

Second, they have the scope to transform political conflicts, either between organs and level of government, as well as between competing interests and values, into legal conflicts. This is done by allocating powers and competence, and by establishing appropriate conflict-settling criteria. Thus, legal conflicts are univocally settled with binding effect throughout the whole system. In other words, it assures the unity of the perspective from which one can look at legal conflicts.

Third, they contain the basic values and principles, and establish legal processes through which public interests and individual rights are balanced each other. In singling out which interests and values must be considered as fundamental, and in contributing to establish the legal background against which legal acts must be reviewed, the Constitution has a further unifying effect. The existence of shared values and common interests expresses indeed the cultural homogeneity of the social community.

b. The concept of Constitution in a pluralistic legal environment

The considerations contained in the preceding paragraph tend to convey the idea that the very essence of the Constitution relies on the fact that it synthesises in a single legal act the unity of the State as a politically organised entity. This conclusion is not demented by the existence of entities such as federal States, in which powers are not only distributed among organs, but also among different levels of government. The unity of the federal State as a politically organised entity is generally not questioned, as evidenced also by the fact that in respect to foreign affairs federal States act as a single international subject.

Constitutions not only allocate powers and competence, but contain also rules that aim to settle Quite a different question is to see whether this concept is consistent with the tradition and the needs of the process of European integration. In this regard, a fundamental question arises, that points to the core of the notion of Constitution. Could we think of the European Constitution as an instrument expressing a unitary legal perspective in which issues of legitimacy, democracy, participation, are to be dealt with, and in which conflicts of values and competence are to be solved, with binding effects for all the subjects of the European legal order ? Does, in other words, the making of a European Constitution entail the making of a legal order which has close resemblance to that of a State ?

A look back at the constitutional *acquis* of the European Union proves satisfactorily that there is a strong case for giving a negative answer. The process of making a European Constitution is taking place in quite a different historical and theoretical context, which stresses the uniqueness of this phenomenon in the contemporary constitutional history.

First, the EU does not rest solely on the legitimacy expressed by the popular sovereignty. Quite the contrary, the European Union constitutes a complex system, in which sovereignty does not belong only to the citizens, considered as a comprehensive and unitary body. It also belongs to politically organised entities such as the MS, whose existence is presupposed by the founding Treaties as an essential source of democratic legitimacy. If we look retrospectively at the constitutional *acquis* of the EU we can see that the European legal system is not based on the idea of a sole source of legitimacy, provided by the Constitution, but rather on a pluralistic vision thereof.

Second, the political system of the EU is not self-contained, in the sense that it does not provide for a single legal perspective in which conflicts between different organs and levels of government can be solved with binding effect for the whole system. Rather, each system contains its own conflict-settling rules, which only partially coincide. More precisely, each subsystem, the EU and each of its MS, claims the competence to adjudge ultimately legal conflicts involving the most intimate aspects of its social and political organisation.

Thus there is no generally accepted frame of reference for dealing with the relations between EU law and State law. Member States have accepted to give priority to EU law over their domestic law, but only as long as the conflict does not touch upon aspects considered by them as intimately connected to their sovereignty. In other words, conflicts between EC and MS law fall in two classes. There are conflicts of competence, which are normally settled according to the principle of supremacy of EU law, and there are conflicts involving aspects considered by the MS as pertaining to their sovereignty, for which no generally accepted rule has been explicitly set out. The first class is that of the intra-systemic conflicts, which can be settled according to procedures laid down by the founding Treaties. The latter is that of inter-systemic conflicts, which each entity, the EC/EU and, respectivley, each MS, claims the ultimate competence to settle[2]. This system, while possessing some features of both the monistic and the dualistic theories, does not coincide fully with any of them.

Third, each of the subsystems claims the rights to establish its own set of values and principles, and its own system of protection of individual rights. These systems overlap each other to a certain extent. This may be at the origin of the idea, widely spread over legal and political literature, that the existence of a plurality of systems of human rights protection in Europe, at national, supranational and international level, has created a common European space in which shared values and principles apply. Yet the different systems remain legally autonomous, and this is continuously creating clashes and legal difficulties. Thus, the idea of the existence of a unitary human rights standard against which reviewing the rules of each subsystem must be dismissed.

Summing up, there are serious theoretical difficulties in applying the same notion of Constitution, construed upon the legal model of State constitutionalism, to the legal experience of European integration. These theoretical difficulties mirror the practical consideration that in the context of European integration the Constitution can hardly be construed as the only source of legitimacy in the exercise of governmental authority. The establishment of a European entity is by no means meant to bring about the disappearance of the States as sovereign entities, rather to co-ordinate the exercise of competence by a plurality of partially sovereign entities. It follows that a European Constitution can certainly not be conceived as the sole source of sovereignty in the exercise of governmental power across Europe.

In consequence, we can hardly think of the European Constitution as the supreme law, bestowing legitimacy on and having supremacy over all other European and State laws. This legal consideration acquires also a political meaning as it stresses the political difficulties of realising a monistic conception in a fragmented social body. The only partial social, political and cultural homogeneity of the people of Europe constitutes a formidable obstacle towards the recognition of a unique source of legitimacy expressed by the Constitution and of the conceptual unity of the sovereignty that it expresses.

The fact is that the notion of Constitution that we are accustomed to refer to in the internal legal experience is by nature based on the positivistic assumption that State and law coincide, and is build up upon an idea of a legal system as a unitary and comprehensive system of law. In other words, the idea of Constitution seems to be conceptually linked with that of sovereignty. It is therefore not easy to apply that concept to the emerging idea of the coexistence of a plurality of entities deprived of the plenitude of sovereign powers and endowed with partial competence only, that interfere and overlap each other.

The observations laid down previously put us before a formidable conceptual challenge: whether the notion of Constitution, that implies the unity of the legal system that it is called upon to regulate, is still useful in a pluralistic legal system.

There is a strong case for a positive answer. It is certainly true that the making of a European Constitution challenges the theoretical foundation of traditional constitutionalism. We have to consider, however, that the transfer of competence to the EU has brought about an entity exerting governmental authority, in which therefore requirements of democracy, legitimacy and respect for individual rights apply no less than in State entities. To deny this assumption would imply that MS can circumvent these basic requirements simply by transferring powers to a supranational organisation, or that they are prevented from pooling their sovereign powers, two conclusions that are, for different reasons, equally unsatisfying.

If the EU exerts political power, not unlike the MS, it must logically comply with principles of legitimacy, rule of law and democracy, which are imposed in the legal systems of the MS by the very terms of their constitution. If we assume that the EU exercises governmental authority, we are led to conclude that it needs a Constitution.

To think differently would amount to theorise the existence of a political power not bound by constitutional restraints, a conclusion that, albeit in limited fields, is inconsistent with the foundations of constitutionalism that apply to every MS.

We are then approaching the conclusion that the EU does need a Constitution, which must however be based on conceptual foundations other than those that apply to the Constitution of their MS.

To deal with the constitutional features of the legal process of European integration implies therefore a need to adapt the conceptual structures of constitutionalism to the particular legal nature of the EU. What we need then is a new conception of constitutionalism for a new conception of legal order, which assumes the possible coexistence of a plurality of legal perspectives, each claiming autonomy and possessing its own source of legitimacy and its own set of values and principles. In particular, the tradition of the European integration seems not consistent with the idea of a all-embracing self-contained Constitution, monistically conceived as the source of every power and law. It seems to require a pluralistic conception of Constitution, which rejects the idea of a unitary source of State sovereignty and admits the existence of diverse legal perspectives in which the exercise of political power can be framed.

But is this perspective theoretically tenable and politically viable ? Can we renounce to the unitary frame of reference symbolically depicted by the pyramidal system of law, having at its top the *Grundnorm* in which all other powers find their source and their inherent limitations ? Can a plurality of entities disposing of partial competence replace the concept of completeness that is expressed in the existence of a sovereign Constitution ? Can we seriously conceive a Constitution without a State ? A form of legitimacy without a people in the name of which the power is exercised ? An exercise of power outside the conceptual frame of sovereignty ?

To answer these and other fundamental questions of the constitutionalisation process in the European context falls well beyond the scope of the present paper, that must be restricted in the limits of a national report. An endeavour will be made to deal with some of these issues in the more limited perspective of the Italian national legal order. The following pages are dedicated to the fulfilment of this aim.

2. National provisions for the adoption of a Constitution of the European Constitution

a. Substantial requirement

The making of a European Constitution is not easily reconciled with the existence of National Constitutions that claim to be the only source of political power in the legal order established by them. Modern States are premised on the positivistic assumption that their constitution is the founding legal instrument of the State order, and that no law can be validly produced, outside the procedures established thereby.

However, in many Constitutions drafted in the aftermath of the second world war a trend has taken place to include provisions consenting the transfer of sovereign powers to international organisations, in order to overcome national egoism and build up a new international order based on peace and justice.

These provisions have generally a very limited scope: that of consenting to the transfer of limited, albeit important, competence to supranational organisations, without however substantially altering the legal structure of the nation State. Constitutions containing these type of provisions, though recognising the opportunity to open the national legal order, and to consent to the exercise of governmental powers by external authorities, tend to maintain their ultimate control on the exercise of the transferred powers. The transfer of competence to international organisation thus, while substantially altering the positivistic idea of the coincidence between State and law, and the concomitant idea that the law is necessarily a State-made product, leaves formally untouched the supremacy of the Constitution. Rather this tends to reinforce the idea that the effect of EU-made law within the national legal order is ultimately based on the national Constitution itself.

In the Italian Constitution, the transfer of competence to the EC was originally based on Art. 11; this provision consents to the transfer sovereign powers to international organisations inspired by the scope of realising peace and justice among the nations. Though drafted in view of the adhesion of Italy to the United Nations, the provisions has been relied upon as a sufficient legal basis for ratifying the Rome Treaties and all the subsequent amendments and modifications thereof, including the Maastricht Treaty, establishing a European Union. Thus the process of European integration has been accomplished in force of a very generic Constitutional provision that does not even mention expressly the process of integration in the European regional area.

The singularity of this situation has been periodically noted in legal literature, and the sufficiency of the generic provision of Art. 11 to justify legally a massive transfer of sovereign powers such as that implied by European integration has been called to question. In legal literature and in political circles the need has been consequently advocated for an explicit constitutional provision on European integration. Recently, in the context of a more comprehensive constitutional reform, having the scope of bringing about a certain decentralisation in the relations between State and Regions, a new provision has been introduced in Art. 117, that explicitly includes European integration among the objectives of the National Constitution. Art. 117 contains also some basic rules concerning the supremacy of EC law over ordinary Italian legislation (see below).

The problem therefore arises as to whether these provisions constitute a sufficient legal basis for expressing the will of the Italian State to participate in the making of a European Constitution. The answer probably depends on the nature of the new act. These provisions can not grant the effect of incorporating the Italian constitutional order in the frame of a more comprehensive order, having constitutional character. It is even controversial if such an effect can be obtained at all in the frame of the existing Italian constitutional order. On the other hand, Art. 11 and Art. 117 of the Italian Constitution may constitute a sufficient legal basis for the establishment of a constitutional order of a new type, not aimed at embedding the existing National Constitutions into a monistic perspective, but based on the respect for the constitutional autonomy of the member States.

b. Procedural requirement

The consent of the Italian State to a European Constitution should, in this context, be expressed by the Government, acting under the authorisation of the Parliament, expressed by simple majority. The opportunity should however be considered of involving more directly the people in the process of European Constitution-making. At the present stage, this result could be achieved by authorising the adoption of the Treaty incorporating the European Constitution through a procedure of constitutional revision. This somewhat complex procedure envisages a double decision by the Parliament, expressed at a majority of two thirds of the MP, or expressed at the simple majority of the MP and confirmed by a referendum. It may be opportune to stress that this procedure, albeit implying a more direct popular participation in the process of making a European Constitution, can by no means be confused with a process of direct approval of the text of a European Constitution by the people. We are dealing only with a procedure aimed at expressing the will of the Italian State, in which one of the steps consists of a popular referendum.

c. International treaty or European social contract

The considerations contained in the preceding paragraph lead us to conclude that the adhesion to a treaty incorporating the European Constitution must be done, under the existing constitutional order, by the Italian State, conceived as a politically organised entity. A European social contract, to be concluded among European citizens considered by themselves as autonomous political subjects, and not regrouped in social and political communities such as the MS, is inconsistent with the positive grant of the Italian Constitution. In other words, at the present stage, it is indisputable that the adoption of a European Constitution should be made by the Italian State.

In a different perspective, the text incorporating the European Constitution could well envisage that the adoption by the Member States must be preceded by a referendum to be held under national provisions. This additional requirement would make the establishment of a European Constitution conditional upon the approval by the majority of the citizens within each single MS. By considering the segmented will of the citizens of each MS in an aggregate framework, the result would be analogous, albeit not identical, to that which would be obtained by considering the people of Europe as a unitary political subject. The difference relies clearly in the fact that the simple or the qualified majority of citizens in each single MS is a much heavier requirement than the same majority to be obtained within a unitary political body composed by the sum of these citizens. Nonetheless, the approval of a Constitutional text by the majority of the citizens of each MS would express simultaneously the will of the people as a whole, and the will of the single States, and would endow the Constitution with a more strengthened legitimacy than any other procedural requirement.

3. The Constitution-making process: preparing the IGC 2004 in practice

On this point the present rapporteur is unable to give a comprehensive answer. The debate that is taking place in Italy about the adoption of a European Constitution replicates largely themes and proposals debated in other countries of Europe. There is apparently wide consent among the political parties and the Members of the Convention on the adoption of a minimalist approach, consisting in simplifying the decision-making process, merging the three pillars, preserving the competence of the MS from a too invasive activity of the Union, specifying and embodying in the constitutional text the bill of rights of the Union.

However, beyond this common ground, a great confusion reigns both as to the general objectives of the European Constitution-making process, as well as to the technical knots of this process. A plethora of proposals have been put forward, and continue to be uninterruptedly put forward, some of which are, frankly speaking, technically objectionable and politically untenable. Instead of dwelling on proposals that are, for the great deal, loomed to failure, the present rapporteur prefers rather to focus his analysis on other legal aspects of the European Constitution-making process that have been brought to his attention by this questionnaire.

II. RELATIONSHIP AND INTERACTION OF EC/EU LAW AND NATIONAL CONSTITUTIONS TODAY

1. *Member States' constitutional autonomy under European constraints*

a. National identities of the Member States (Art. 6.3 TEU) as a limit to the extension of the EU/EC competence

Art. 6.3 can hardly be intended as a bar for the transfer of new competence to the Union. According to a different interpretation, more consistent with the wording of the provision and with the intention of its drafters, it simply imposes to the EU Institutions the duty to take into account, in enacting legal acts, the normative and cultural differences of the MS.

Whereas its political effect can hardly be overshadowed, its legal effect is thus particularly weak. Considered jointly with norms of the EC treaty, this provision could well serve as a basis for positive actions aimed at tempering the uniforming effect of some EC policies. It is more doubtful to construe the provision as having also the effect of impairing the validity of specific EC acts. It is to be remarked, *inter alia*, that Art. 6, para. 3, is not mentioned by Art. 46 TUE among the provisions to which the competence of the Court of Justice applies.

Much has been said about the more general effect of this provision on the further development of the EU. Art. 6, para. 3, has been undeniably conceived as a mirror of the present situation, in which the EU does not constitute a new national entity, but rather the supranational dimension of a plurality of national entities. In this perspective, it can be viewed also as a limit to the development of a European statehood, absorbing that of the MS.

Art. 6, para. 1, has ostensibly a more accentuated legal meaning in as far as it corresponds to the provisions of some Constitutions of the MS, which require the EU to be based on democratic principles. Correspondingly Art. 6, para. 1, requires the MS to be based on democracy and respect for human rights. In a comprehensive legal background, this set of provisions can be construed as a unitary requirement of democracy in the political system of the European integration.

The incorporation in the EU Treaty of a norm imposing an obligation to the MS to adopt a political system based on democratic principles and respect for fundamental human rights, has been sometimes considered as a curious incoherence in a system that is ostensibly not centred on these principles. This criticism appears to the present author not fully justified. It is perfectly conceivable that a supranational system considers democracy as an essential requirement for its MS, as entities possessing the features of statehood; the same requirement can apply to the EU only in as much as it is consistent with its supranational character. The problem of democracy consists thus not so much in requiring that the same principles apply to both systems, to the supranational as well as to the national ones; the problem of democracy is rather that of singling out which principles, that apply to the legal orders of the MS, are nonetheless of universal character, and must apply also to the supranational level.

Be that as it may, Art. 6, para. 1, can be reasonably construed as curtailing the effect of the principle of *domaine réservé* (domestic jurisdiction) of the MS. It can be argued that the EU Institutions and the MS, acting singly or jointly, possess, under Art. 6, para. 1, a right to interfere with matters of domestic concern of a Member State in order to ascertain compliance therewith. Should they deem that the respect owed to the principles mentioned in this provision falls below a certain standard, mutually agreed upon, they even possess the right to adopt, outside the institutionalised frame set out by Art. 7 TUE, some means of constraints in order to induce the breaching State to revert its course and to assure full respect of these principles[3].

Viewed from a systemic perspective, Art. 6, para. 1, is of paramount importance in the process of emerging of shared principles and values through reciprocal influence by the MS and the EU Institutions. It may be argued that in the European context, democracy is not only a requirement internal to the single constitutional systems. Given the fact that the institutional dimension of the EU is also based on procedures of decision-making that take place within the legal orders of the MS, the conclusion can be drawn that the full realisation of democracy in the EU context requires that democracy is fully realised within each MS legal order.

This conclusion certainly implies a certain loss of autonomy of the MS conceived as a self-standing legal order. However, Art. 6 para. 1 must not be read in isolation. In the light of a joint consideration of the two provisions of Art. 6 paras. 1 and 3, the impression that the TUE aims at imposing a standardised model of democracy in the European area vanishes. What emerges from this provision, read as a whole, is that some basic requirement in terms of democratic legitimacy must be observed. These basic principles constitute a disincentive for a process of political involution undertaken by individual MS. It could be politically dangerous to draw from these provisions more than that, and adopt an interpretation that would permit a too heavy interference in the choice of single MS of their social and political model.

2. *Common values: the Charter of fundamental rights of the EU*

a. Does the Charter reflect the basic human rights standards of the Italian Constitution and national law ?

The reading of the Charter does not allow a satisfactory answer to this question. Only a certain analogy with constitutional provisions of MS and with the ECHR can be observed. At a formal inquiry as to the rights guaranteed by the Charter one is tempted to conclude that the Charter expresses common values of the European area.

This conclusion appears, however, simplistic. The general assumption that the wording of a document is not necessarily telling about its legal content is particularly true for a bill of rights. By nature, the protection of human rights is a product of a balance of values and interests that can hardly be done in abstract; rather it must be contextualised within a given legal order. It is well known that the Court of Justice of the EC, while claiming to apply, within the EC legal order, principles and values extracted from the common constitutional traditions of the MS, has in fact adapted them in order to make them fit the particular needs of the supranational system.

Thus, comparing the Charter of fundamental rights with the catalogue of fundamental rights incorporated in national Constitutions risks being an uneasy and quite useless intellectual operation. The Charter has been drafted keeping an eye on national orders; it is apparent that some individual rights contained therein are meaningful in a national context more than in the context of the EU legal order. Thus, despite the quite elusive norm contained in Art. 51, limiting the field of application of the Charter to the field of application of EU law[4], the impression is hardly unfounded that the Charter represents an attempt to establish a frame of reference for the entire European area. As such, some endeavours can be registered by national judges to apply provisions of the Charter even to situations falling plainly outside the reach of EU law.

Ostensibly, the drawing up of the Charter represents an attempt to codify fundamental principles and values of the European Area, common to a plurality of legal orders. Codifying these principles is however not easy. Whereas a certain uniformity among the national legal orders of the MS and the ECHU can be registered as to the individual rights to be protected, it is much more difficult to identify a uniform balance between individual rights and public interests. Yet, determining a balance between competing rights and interests is a quite complex operation in which the sensitivities of each single legal order are expressed. In comparison with national legal orders and with the ECHR, the Charter may have strengthened the protection for some interests, to the detriment of some others. For example, in drawing the limits for the power to expel aliens, the Charter has significantly omitted any reference to the right of aliens to have their case reviewed before the measure of expulsion is carried out, a right that, under Protocol n. 7 of the European Convention of human rights, can be limited only when the expulsion is necessary in the interest of public order or is grounded on reasons of national security.

Art. 52 contains a general clause aiming at balancing individual rights and public interests. However it does not enumerate the public interests that can legitimately restrict the individual rights. This gap is particularly to be regretted. The wording of the provision gives the impression that the pursuit of a public interest whatever can curtail the enjoyment of individual rights or interfere therewith. This renders problematic the assessment of the standard of protection of the rights guaranteed by the Charter and can suggest that the Charter, while on the one hand solemnly declaring individual rights to be protected by the EU Institutions and by the MS, guarantees, on the other hand, priority to the scopes of integration. A specification as to the interests that can lawfully justify a restriction of fundamental individual rights in the EU legal order could have been particularly useful in order to dissipate this impression.

The consideration contained in the preceding paragraph can shed some light on the possible utilisation of the Charter as a standard of reference for National Courts. This is well possible in fields connected with EU law. In doing so, national Courts must pay due attention to the fact that the Charter should not be invoked in order to lessen the standard of protection deriving from the application of other instruments of protection of human rights, such as, specifically, the European Convention of human rights. This norm, contained in Art. 53 of the Charter, should imply that, in case that the Charter does not reproduce exactly the balance between individual liberties and public interests established in the ECHR, the Courts must apply the standard of protection that grants greater consideration to the former.

However, it may be difficult to indicate the cases in which the level of protection accorded by the Charter is inferior to that accorded by, say, the ECHR. In the specific case of the freedom of thought, conscience and creed, guaranteed without exception by Art. 10, or the freedom of expression, guaranteed equally without exceptions by Art. 11, it can be difficult to say if the general exception clause of Art. 52 has the effect of restricting these rights to a greater extent than that established under, respectively, Articles 9 and 10 ECHR.

b. The Charter as a reference for fundamental human rights protection in national courts

See above, sub heading a)

c. The impact of the Charter on the standards referred to in Art. 6.1

The main effect of the adoption of the Charter is that of endowing the Union with a catalogue of individual rights. Should the Charter have binding effect, this would fill a gap in the protection of human rights, and would meet the conditions set forth by the German and the Italian Constitutional

Courts for not exercising a judicial review on the acts of the EC. However, for the reasons stated above, it remains controversial that the standard established by the Charter bestows on the protection of individual rights in the EU a satisfying degree of legal certainty. If in other words, the aims of the drafters was that of changing the pre-existing situation, in which legal rules concerning fundamental individual rights were judge-made law, this aim is certainly not completely reached. Even if the Charter were conceived as a binding legal instrument, a great discretion would remain nonetheless open to the Court of Justice as to the precise determination of the content of the individual rights to be protected, and to the balance to be established among competing individual and public interests.

3. *The question of supremacy of EC/EU law and its constitutional effect.*

a. *Supremacy I: community primary law and national constitutional law. Position of National Constitutional Courts*

The relations between EC/EU law and Italian Constitution rest on the principles established by the Constitutional Court in *Frontini* (1973)[5]; principles that have stood the test of time and have remained basically unchanged up to now.

In *Frontini* the Court affirmed that the superiority of EC law over Italian law has constitutional underpinnings, as it is based on the provision of Art. 11 of the Italian Constitution, which authorises the transfer of sovereign powers to international organisations with a view to maintaining and securing peace and justice among nations.

This construction has also the effect of delimiting the supremacy granted to EC law: priority is accorded to EC norms only in so far as they do not conflict with fundamental principles of the national Constitution. In *Frontini*, the Constitutional Court went on by affirming that the transfer of powers to the EC can not imply a changing of the structure and the fundamental principles of the national Constitution under which governmental authority is exercised, nor be freed from the constitutional restraints concerning the protection of individual rights.

Apparently, this conclusion could be read as a reserve of judicial review to be exercised by the Italian Constitutional Court on EC acts. However, the Court mitigated by far the legal consequence that could have theoretically been drawn from the premise, by excluding single EC acts from judicial review. Only norms of the founding treaties, considered to be the source of the power to violate the fundamental principles of the Italian legal order, could be subjected to constitutional review. This possibility is thus restricted to the case of grave and persistent violation of the fundamental principles of the national legal order.

This conclusion, technically not immune from objections, has the advantage of taking simultaneously account of two exigencies that are not easily reconciled. It maintains the idea of the supremacy of the National Constitution over EC law, without however limiting too heavily the autonomy the EC legal system. At the cost of some technical shortcomings, this solution requires a certain structural conformity of the supranational legal order to the National Constitution, without however going so far as to permit a constitutional review of the single legal acts of the EU.

A certain evolution of this system has occurred in *Fragd* (1989)[6]. In a case that presents some analogies with the *Solange II* decision of the German Constitution Court, the Italian Constitutional Court upheld the priority of the European Court of Justice in ruling on the conformity of EC law with fundamental individual rights. EC law can thus be subjected to judicial review by the Italian Constitutional Court only in case of grave and persistent breach of fundamental human rights, not duly repaired by the judicial institutions of the Union.

In a different sense, the Constitutional Court upheld in *Granital* (1984)[7] its competence to rule on the constitutionality of Italian ordinary law that could interfere with the fundamental principles of functioning of the EC legal order. This conclusion, contained in a *dictum* of the decision, seems to imply that, should the constitutional reasons that have originally led to the transfer of powers to the EC/EU fail, these powers could be withdrawn. This conclusion emphasises the constitution-based character of the transfer of sovereignty to the EC, and is ideally set against the conception upheld by the Court of Justice in a number of occasions, according to which the transfer of sovereign powers to the EC is to be considered as irrevocable. It is worth noting that this conclusion is paradoxically contained in a decision that is commonly deemed as the one that has acknowledged priority to EC law over Italian ordinary legislation.

b. Supremacy II. Community legislation and national constitutional law

According to the Italian legal system, there is no difference between primary and secondary EC law as to the relations with the Italian Constitution. This question has been implicitly answered above, subheading a)

4. Institutional interdependence: European functions of national institutions

a. The National Parliaments in the European legislation process: indirect source of legitimacy and responsibility for implementation

Much emphasis has been put, in legal literature, on the role of the Italian

Parliaments in the process of EC decision-making. A look at the practice proves however that the involvement of the Italian Parliament in European matters remains scarce and its impact on the decision-making process of the EC negligible.

In the Italian legal system, the Parliament is entitled to be regularly informed of the state of the EC legislative agenda, and can brief the Government with general guidelines to be taken into account by the Government. The Parliament has also the powers to contribute to the will-making process of the Italian Government in regards to single EC acts by enacting recommendations to be taken in account by the government in the process of negotiations, but having no binding force. The internal rules of the two Houses of the Parliament contain provisions to that regard[8].

No special rule concerns the participation of the Parliament to the decision-making process of the EU. That is to be regretted, due to the particularly restricted role of the European Parliament to the policies of the second and, respectively, third pillar.

The practice of the participation of the Italian Parliament to the legislative process of the EU/EC is particularly disappointing. Only in a handful of cases the Parliament has taken a position concerning specific EC acts, and, even in those cases, it appeared to be quite disinterested in the following-up of its opinions. It does not seem exaggerate to say that the contribution by the Italian Parliament to the shaping of the EC/EU politics appears in practice meaningless.

One reason for this is the chronic apathy of the Parliament for activities and events for which it has neither interest nor technical ability. Nonetheless, there are some misconceptions about the participation of the National Parliament that prevent it from playing a more significant role.

The rules briefly mentioned above, do not distinguish among acts to be adopted by the Council of Ministers, without or even against the will of the European Parliaments, and acts to be adopted on the basis of a process including the participation by the European Parliament. In the former case, the participation by National Parliaments has the essential role of providing for a democratic legitimacy that is lacking within the context of the EU/EC. In the latter, National Parliaments do not fulfil a legitimising function, that would duplicate that expressed within the EU/EC system by the European Parliaments, but pursue the scope of contributing to the process of will-making of the MS. Therefore, it is not unreasonable to think that the participation of the National Parliament to the decision-making process of the EC/EU ought to be selective rather than general and focus on certain areas in which the EU/EC Treaties do not envisage a significant role for the European Parliament: the weaker the role of the European Parliament in the decision-making process of the EC/EU, the stronger the influence exerted by National Parliaments in the internal process of will-making should be[9].

This conclusion rests on the consideration that there is a strong case for assuring the democratic legitimacy in areas in which the decision-making process has essentially intergovernmental character. This need vanishes when the democratic participation is granted through the EP. In other words, the EP and the National Parliament have an interchangeable role in assuring the necessary democratic legitimacy to EU/EC acts: the EP should contribute to the adoption of acts of supranational character, while the National Parliament should rather focus on acts having intrinsically an intergovernmental nature.

In the light of this consideration, the rules mentioned above, that allow the Italian Parliament a theoretical participation to the making of every EC/EU acts without however giving it the practical possibility to do so, appear to be a display of shop window syndrome.

b. The role of national administration and judges

In the present author's view, it is advisable to deal jointly with the two issues relating respectively to the role of national administrations, and of the national judges, that present some conceptual analogies and common features.

Interestingly enough, neither the administrative nor the judicial European Institution are endowed with decentralised branches, but avail themselves with the administrative and judicial organs of the MS.

This system has brought about quite satisfactory results. The EC Institutions have established close ties with national administrations and judges, considered as decentralised branch. National administration and judges have been encouraged to refer to Brussels, and respectively, to Luxembourg, for guidance and assistance in matters of European concern.

Problems of co-ordination nonetheless remain, that should be resolved in view of a more institutionalised and efficient relationship between EC and national institutions. A brief reference to some of them seems opportune.

i) The decentralisation in the application of competition law has brought about the competence of national judges and antitrust authorities to issue decisions on matters falling within the field of application of EC antitrust law. This trend could be accentuated with the reform of Regulation 17/62, that could confer to national judges and antitrust authorities the competence to apply directly art. 81, para. 3. However a difference must be made between judicial and administrative decisions: while the decisions by national judges are automatically recognised in the other MS, decisions by national antitrust authorities are not. This could create serious legal difficulties and prevent to a certain extent the process of decentralisation of EC antitrust law. The recognition of decisions of national authorities acting as decentralised branches of the Commission is strongly to be recommended.

ii) The judicial application of EC law by national judges can, under certain circumstances, interfere with the administrative application by the Commission or by national administration. The Commission and the Court of Justice have elaborated some guidelines for National Judges, which are however mainly of an empirical character and do not give a univocal guidance for every case.

iii) National High Courts are generally reluctant to co-operate with EC judicial Institutions. The failure of national judges to comply with the obligation to refer a case to the Court of Justice is not easily remedied under national law. A remedy under the legal order of the EU/EC appears more appropriate. The possibility for individuals lodging an appeal to the Court of Justice could be considered.

III. THE ROLE OF REGIONS AND LOCAL AUTHORITIES IN EU LAW

1. *Effects of EU law on the constitutional framework and settlement in relation to regions and local authorities*

The Constitutional reform adopted in Italy in 2001 has radically changed the role of regions and local authorities. The Italian State, previously a centralised State, is now more similar to a federal State, though this term is not explicitly employed in the Constitution. Correspondingly, regions and other local entities are called upon to assume a new role in domestic institutional dynamics. The situation is more complex by far for what concerns the involvement of these entities in European affairs.

One could expect that regions and other local entities be called to contribute directly to the decision-making process of the EC/EU, and to implement their acts, in matters falling within their competence.

More precisely, it is reasonable to expect the national position in regard to EC legislation projects would be formed through a procedure of assent between the Government and the Regions in fields falling within a concurring competence, and solely by the Regions in fields falling within their exclusive competence.

Around the same rationale the question of the competence of regions to implement EU/EC acts can be hinged. Italian Regions should be empowered to implement directly EC acts. State's organs have, in force of a specific provision of the Constitution, the power of interfering with the normative competence of the Regions only in order to avoid that default by the Regions would call into question the responsibility of the Italian State.

However, the project of law aimed at implementing the constitutional reform tends to adopt a particularly restrictive interpretation of the role of the Regions.

For what concerns the decision-making process, the pre-existing situation has been substantially maintained. While the competence to form the national position is reserved to the State, even in matters falling within the exclusive competence of the Regions, the Regions are entitled to be kept informed on the legislative agenda of the EC/EU, and have the right to submit to the Government observations and comments.

The State has also the power to legislate in matters falling within the competence of the regions in order to implement EC/EU acts. In this context, only a residuary role is recognised to the regions: that of enacting acts of implementation that can repeal those previously enacted by the State.

These solutions do not seem entirely consistent with the new role recognised by the Constitution to the Regions. They are based on the idea that, in its relations with the EU, the State is necessarily a unitary entity. This assumption would then require that the rules that allocate normative powers and competence internally do not apply in the context of the international relations.

This argument is not logically immune from criticism. The unity of the State in its relations with the EU does certainly not require to disregard the constitutional autonomy recognised internally to entities such as the Regions. Various solutions are at hand, that would permit to assure a unitary line of conduct of the Central State and of its sub-units, without however curtailing so drastically the constitutional autonomy of the latter.

2. Possible consequences for EU law of regionalisation and decentralisation of the kind that goes on in Italy

The founding Treaties were silent on the role of regions and local authorities in the process of integration. In the last decade some changes have been brought about, aimed at strengthening the role of these entities and involving them more closely in the process of decision-making and implementation of EC law. From a general policy perspective, the involvement of local entities in the process of the European integration has been conceived also as an answer to the criticism directed against the construction of a centralist super-state in Europe, and in order to favour instances of decentralisation and subsidiarity.

After a decade, one must frankly admit that, despite the efforts, the results are quite disappointing. The role of regions and other local entities in the legal order of the EU/EC is certainly no adequate to the relevance that they have assumed for domestic matters in the legal order of some MS. As above seen, this has a penalising effect also of the influence that these entities are able to exert on matters of European concern within the legal order of the MS.

In a more general perspective, one should recall that the constitutional autonomy of local entities must be now considered as among the fundamental principles concerning the constitutional organisation of some of the MS. This observation can have relevant consequence on the process of a European Constitution-making, as it emphasises the need to consider the federal structure of some MS among the requirements put forward by National Constitutions for the transfer of sovereign powers to the EU, and consequently, to adapt to it the European institutional dynamics. It is not unreasonable to conclude that the reform of the founding Treaties, and the establishment of a constitutional entity embodying the EU, should recognise the regions and other entities enjoying autonomy under National Constitutions among the actors of the institutions dynamics of Union. Beyond the theoretical relevance, such step would have a practical impact as it would allow the regions to contribute, within the fields of their competence, to the decision-making process of the EU and to be directly responsible for lack of compliance. This would imply, in turn, the necessity of rendering the institutional dynamics of the Union more flexible in order to meet the difference in constitutional structure among the various MS.

IV. CONCLUSIONS AND RECOMMENDATIONS FOR 2002

1. *A new architecture: what should an EU Constitution or EU basic treaty look like*

a. *A Constitution for the European Union: conditions of adoption and amendment: its relations to national constitutions.*

The considerations contained in the above standing paragraphs prompt the impression that the task of a European Constitution is basically the establishment of a legal frame in which a plurality of entities endowed with partial sovereign powers may co-exist. Using the terminology that has been employed from the beginning of the present paper, what the European legal order needs is a pluralist Constitution governing a pluralist legal order. To this end, the consideration of the constitutional *acquis* of the legal experience of the EC/EU may significantly contribute.

Much has been said about how this task can be achieved. While the attention of legal and political analysts has been drawn on points of more general interest, it may be opportune, also for the limited scopes of the present paper, to focus on some issues that have remained, in the view of the present writer, mostly in the shadow.

- *Plurality of the sources of legitimacy in the process of European integration*

Consistently with the asymmetric character of the integration, the European Constitution should be premised on the acknowledgement that there is not, in the European political system, a unitary source of democratic legitimacy. Rather a plurality of sources coexist, each bearing its own legitimacy and contributing in a variety of ways, to reinforce the legitimacy of the system as whole.

Thus, while a process of democratisation of the European system appears opportune, with the corollaries of transparency and accountability that are intimately connaturate to the very essence of democracy, this should not necessarily lead to a unique decision-making process. It would be an error, politically and legally, to replicate on the supranational level the models of democracy of the MS, in which a central role is entrusted to the Parliament, expressing symbolically the will of the Nation.

Even less, should this lead to the direct involvement of the National Parliaments in the European decision-making process. National Parliaments express a fragmented democratic legitimacy, that must be properly expressed in the will-making procedures of the single MS, particularly in those areas in which the EU/EC decision-making procedures do not envisage a significant role for the European Parliament. The asymmetric character of the European integration seems to assign to the National Parliaments a role subsidiary to that of the European Parliament, to be carried out within the legal order to which they respectively belong.

- *Plurality of conflict-settling rules in the relations between European law and domestic law of the MS*

This would lead to the possibility of conceiving a system in which legal conflicts do not necessarily have a univocal legal solution. The point is particularly important in the perspective of a pluralist Constitution. While the European Constitution is expected to state in clear terms the supremacy of the European norms over national legislation, it should leave unprejudiced the problem of the relations between European norms and the Constitutions of the MS.

The Constitutions Courts of the MS have stated clearly that they are unwilling to review on the constitutionality of single European acts, but reserved their ultimate power to pass over the legitimacy of norms that have clearly crossed the boundaries established for European law by the National Constitution, either for reasons of competence, or for protecting fundamental national values. This control of last resort assumes thus a political character and does not touch upon the day-to-day relations between national and European norms, regulated by the principle of supremacy of the latter.

- *Plurality of entities possessing international personality and the need for co-ordination*

The problem with bestowing a legal personality on the EU, absorbing that of the EC, has been widely debated in legal literature. Of course, the recognition of a unique personality of the EU entails the problem of including norms in the Constitution dealing with the delicate question of the co-ordination between the exercise of the competence transferred and the pursuit of the aims assigned to the it. How to deal with such a delicate, but as yet, quite neglected problem is a matter for a different study.

In a different sense, it is not contended, in legal literature, that the establishment of a constitutional entity would not deprive the individual MS of their international legal personality. The transfer of sovereign powers to the EU has fragmented the unitary and comprehensive sovereignty of the MS without however creating an other entity disposing of the plenitude of sovereignty. The EU is empowered to act internationally and to exercise international rights and duties connected with the matters over which it has normative competence internally. The MS have been correspondingly deprived of some international rights and duties, but retain their legal personality, and continue to exercise rights and duties in matters that fall internally within their competence. Moreover, some international rights and duties are possessed jointly by the MS and the EU.

Thus the process of European integration confronts us with a new and quite interesting situation that should be fully appreciated within the conceptual categories of international law. Where international law is based on the existence of full sovereign actors, disposing of the plenitude of powers, the process of European integration is leading to the co-existence of a plurality of international actors, each disposing of some competence, but none disposing of full sovereignty. How to deal with this new situation, and how to adapt to it the conceptual structures of international law constitutes a stimulating intellectual challenge for international law scholars[10].

Yet the issue has not only theoretical, but also practical relevance. The exercise of international rights and duties by individual MS and the exercise of international rights and duties possessed by the EU has created, and continues to create, serious international law problems. The necessity of co-ordinating the international activity of a plurality of partial sovereign actors is a matter for the new Constitutional text.

- *The reversible character of the transfer of powers to the Union and the exit from the system.*

The Court of Justice has affirmed more than once the irreversible character of the transfer of powers to the EC. This has apparently been done in order to strengthen the stability of the system and to bestow on it the character of a constitutional system. There is however no reason for maintaining this requisite and exclude that single MS can recess from the system, even if this would be a cause for a great deal of practical uncertainties. The Constitutional Court of some MS, among which the Italian Constitutional Court, have expressed the view that the participation to the European integration is possible only insofar as this process contributes to the realisation of the aims of the National Constitution. Though theoretical, the possibility of a repatriation of the transferred powers is not constitutionally unthinkable. Moreover, it is argued that the exclusion of the possibility of a lawful exit from the system would lead to deepened conflicts and to endanger the relations between States. In an enlarged Europe, the possibility, albeit theoretical, that a State can recess and pursue its own way outside the frame of the integration would strengthen rather than weaken the stability of the system.

b. *Merging the constitutional process and enlargement: how to involve the candidates.*

To this respect, the present author must confess that he is unable to express a personal view. The solution agreed upon in Laeken, according to which the candidates can participate to the process of elaboration of the European Constitution without however having the power to imbalance the process itself, seems politically wise. In a legal perspective, one can only stress the fact that a massive enlargement such as that envisaged at present, will unavoidably constitute a further obstacle towards a political homogeneity and will consequently stress the need for elaborating new forms of political organisations in a legal environment characterise by the plurality of partial sovereign entities.

NOTES

[1*] Professor of international and EU law, University of Macerata (cannizzaro@unimc.it).

[2] I dealt with this question in my essay *Democrazia e sovranità nei rapporti fra Stati membri e Unione europea*, in *Il diritto dell'Unione europea*, 2000, p. 241.

[3] See Cannizzaro, *Integrazione europea e democrazia degli Stati membri,* in *Istituzioni, mercato e democrazia, Liber amicorum Alberto Predieri*, Giappichelli, Torino, 2002, p. 77.

[4] The ambiguous wording of Art. 51 should not be interpreted as excluding the application of the Charter to MS norms issued outside the sphere of application of EU law, in fields to which nonetheless general principles of EU law apply. Rather the

question remains open as to the application of the Charter to EU norms that are made applicable to purely internal situations of a State in force of a rule of application issued autonomously by that State. A positive answer can be given if one assumes that this rule of application refers to those limitations that are incumbent upon the EU norm in force of the general principles of its legal order.

[5] Decision 27 December 1973 n. 183, *Frontini et al. v. Amministrazione delle Finanze*, Riv. dir. int., 1974, p. 130.

[6] Decision 21 April 1989 n. 232, *Fragd v. Amministrazione delle finanze dello Stato*, Riv. dir. int., 1989, p. 103.

[7] Decision 5 June 1984 n, 170, *Granital v. Amministrazione delle finanze dello Stato,* Riv. dir. int., 1984, p. 360.

[8] See Art. 127 of the Internal Rules of the House of Representatives and Art. 144 of the Internal Rules of the Senate.

[9] See more extensively Cannizzaro, *Democrazia e sovranità nei rapporti fra Stati membri e Unione europea, supra,* note 1.

[10] On this topic, see the various contributions collected in the book *The European Union as an Actor in International Relations* (Cannizzaro ed.), KLI, The Hague, 2002.

LUXEMBOURG

Le Droit Europeen et les Constitutions Nationales

Rapporteur
*Georges Wivenes**

Les rapports entre le processus d'intégration européenne et le droit constitutionnel des Etats membres ont fait l'objet de débats récurrents depuis le début de la construction européenne. Il n'est pas inutile de rappeler brièvement les points forts de ce débat en comparant la situation du Luxembourg à celle des autres Etats européens.

La discussion sur les rapports entre l'ordre juridique national et l'ordre juridique communautaire était particulièrement vive au cours de la décennie 1970 et jusque dans les années 1980. Au regard des positions réservées adoptées par les cours constitutionnelles allemande et italienne[1] vis-à-vis du droit communautaire, la doctrine, notamment en Allemagne, avait mis en exergue les problèmes de la protection des droits fondamentaux ainsi que de la légitimité démocratique du processus décisionnel des Communautés et souligné avec force la nécessaire "congruence structurelle" entre l'ordre juridique communautaire et les ordres juridiques nationaux. En France, les juridictions suprêmes de l'ordre judiciaire et administratif[2] et le Conseil constitutionnel[3] étaient appelés à statuer sur la primauté du droit communautaire et les limites des atteintes à la souveraineté nationale. Dans ce contexte, il n'est pas surprenant que les congrès de la FIDE de 1970 (Berlin), 1973 (Luxembourg) et 1975 (Bruxelles) aient porté sur différents aspects des relations entre les ordres juridiques nationaux et l'ordre juridique communautaire[4].

La conclusion du traité sur l'Union européenne a relancé le débat. Avec l'établissement de l'union monétaire, les Etats membres étaient amenés à renoncer à certaines attributions relevant des droits dits régaliens. La consécration de la notion de citoyenneté européenne et l'octroi du droit de vote aux élections municipales aux ressortissants communautaires ayant fait usage de la liberté de circulation touchent aux fondements mêmes de la conception traditionnelle de la citoyenneté nationale. La mise en place d'une coopération en matière de politique étrangère et de sécurité ainsi que dans le secteur des affaires intérieures et de la justice, même si elle devait s'opérer sur une base essentiellement intergouvernementale, constitue également une étape décisive dans l'abandon de compétences relevant du noyau "dur" de la souveraineté des Etats. Dans la plupart des Etats membres, la ratification du traité de Maastricht a exigé des révisions constitutionnelles, souvent après saisine des Cours constitutionnelles respectives[5].

La problématique des rapports entre l'ordre juridique communautaire et les ordres constitutionnels nationaux a trouvé une nouvelle dimension avec la Conférence intergouvernementale de Nice (décembre 2000), les Conseils européens de Göteborg (juin 2001) et de Laeken (décembre 2001). A Nice, la Conférence intergouvernementale a ouvert la voie à l'élargissement de l'Union, avec la réforme du processus décisionnel, et a adopté la Charte des droits fondamentaux. Parallèlement, dans la déclaration n° 23 relative à l'avenir de l'Union annexée au traité, a été lancé un processus de réflexion sur l'architecture future de l'Union dans la perspective d'une nouvelle conférence intergouvernementale en 2004[6] . Cette réflexion a été poursuivie lors du Conseil européen de Göteborg auquel la présidence suédoise a présenté un rapport relatif au débat sur l'avenir de l'Union européenne. Dans la déclaration de Laeken sur l'avenir de l'Union européenne[7] sont abordées les questions centrales déjà évoquées à Nice, à savoir, "une meilleure répartition et définition des compétences dans l'Union"; "la simplification des instruments de l'Union"; "davantage de démocratie, de transparence et d'efficacité dans l'Union européenne". Pour la première fois dans les conclusions d'un sommet, est posée ouvertement la question d'une constitution de l'Union, dans les termes prudents il est vrai d'une "voie vers une constitution pour les citoyens européens". Une convention est instituée pour "examiner les questions essentielles que soulève le développement futur de l'Union"[8].

Dans la perspective luxembourgeoise, on peut relever que les débats juridiques et politiques des années 1970 et 1980 sur la protection des droits fondamentaux, la légitimité démocratique des Communautés et la congruence structurelle n'ont guère retenu l'attention des milieux politiques et juridiques concernés. La primauté du droit communautaire et son effet direct n'étaient jamais sérieusement mis en cause. La question des limites des atteintes à la souveraineté étatique n'a guère été évoquée. Lors de la ratification du traité de Maastricht, les débats se sont focalisés sur le problème ponctuel de l'octroi du droit de vote aux élections communales aux citoyens communautaires[9]. Pour la première fois depuis la conclusion des traités de Rome, la ratification d'un traité modificatif a impliqué une révision constitutionnelle[10]. Ce n'est qu'à la suite des sommets de Nice et de Laeken que la problématique de la future architecture de l'Union européenne est entrée dans le débat public.

Les travaux du congrès de la FIDE de 1996[11] ont porté, pour l'essentiel, sur les conflits possibles entre ordres constitutionnels nationaux et droit communautaire et se sont ainsi inscrits dans la logique des réflexions menées depuis les débuts de l'intégration européenne. Elargissant cette optique, le questionnaire préparé par les organisateurs du congrès de Londres met l'accent sur la coexistence, l'interaction et l'application coordonnée de "deux niveaux de gouvernance" au sein de l'Union, le niveau communautaire et le niveau national, lesquels sont fortement imbriqués et participeraient tous les deux de la notion de constitution. Il est toutefois évident que le problème d'un conflit éventuel continue à se poser, ne serait-ce que dans la mesure où la constitution nationale peut s'opposer à un régime de "constitution composée" dont l'existence est implicitement reconnue dans le questionnaire. Le questionnaire porte sur une série de points qu'il y a lieu d'aborder dans l'ordre retenu par les auteurs. Il va de soi que les éléments de réponse seront fonction des particularités du système juridique national et des positions adoptées par les milieux juridiques et politiques concernés.

I. LES FONDEMENTS D'UN CONSTITUTIONNALISME EUROPÉEN

2. Le concept de constitution en droit luxembourgeois

Se plaçant dans l'optique du cadre juridique organisé et régi par la constitution, le droit luxembourgeois définit la constitution par rapport à l'Etat. Les trois éléments suivants sont pertinents: la constitution établit les bases de l'Etat, d'où sa fonction de loi fondamentale de l'Etat; elle organise l'Etat en déterminant les autorités publiques et leurs pouvoirs, d'où sa fonction de loi organique de l'Etat; enfin, elle détermine le statut du citoyen dans l'Etat et vis-à-vis des autorités publiques, notamment par la consécration des droits de participation aux affaires publiques et des droits fondamentaux. Dans cette logique, la doctrine luxembourgeoise entend par constitution "la loi fondamentale qui contient les bases constitutives de l'Etat, détermine la forme dans laquelle s'exerce l'autorité publique et garantit les libertés et les droits du citoyen"[12]. Le droit constitutionnel regroupe "l'ensemble des règles fondamentales relatives à l'organisation de l'Etat"[13].

Ces définitions traditionnelles, similaires à celles valant dans les autres systèmes nationaux, méritent certaines précisions. On peut, d'abord, s'attacher à l'examen objectif des dispositions constitutionnelles pour dégager des conclusions quant à la définition du concept de constitution. On peut également essayer de circonscrire le concept de constitution par rapport à celui de loi. Enfin, on peut s'interroger sur le rapport de la constitution avec l'existence même de l'Etat en relation avec le droit international.

- Première observation: L'examen des dispositions constitutionnelles confirme la définition de la constitution comme loi organique fondamentale de l'Etat. La constitution luxembourgeoise définit, dans le chapitre Ier , l'Etat, son territoire et l'institution monarchique; le chapitre II porte sur le second élément constitutif de l'Etat, à savoir la population, dont les droits fondamentaux et les libertés publiques sont consacrés; le chapitre III a trait à la puissance publique sous ses trois aspects, pouvoir exécutif[14], législatif et judiciaire. Dans les chapitres IV à VI sont déterminées les prérogatives des organes de l'Etat, Chambre des Députés, Gouvernement, Conseil d'Etat et organes de justice. Dans ces chapitres, une série de principes fondamentaux trouvent leur expression comme la forme monarchique de l'Etat, le principe de la souveraineté nationale, le régime de la démocratie parlementaire, la séparation des pouvoirs, la protection des droits fondamentaux. Les derniers chapitres VII à XI portent sur des points plus techniques, en particulier sur la force publique et les communes en tant que collectivités territoriales. A l'opposé d'une série de constitutions européennes, la constitution luxembourgeoise ne comporte pas de préambule aux termes duquel le peuple, en sa qualité de constituant originaire, se dote d'une loi fondant et organisant l'Etat ni une déclaration, sous forme de préambule, marquant l'attachement du constituant à certaines valeurs fondamentales.
- Deuxième observation: Les textes constitutionnels ne définissent ni la notion de constitution ni celle de loi[15]. Le concept de loi définit par rapport à la constitution par référence à deux critères, le premier d'ordre fondamental, le second de nature formelle.

La constitution est l'assise juridique de la loi, en ce qu'elle fonde son existence, définit ses éléments constitutifs et détermine son champ d'application. La constitution et la loi se situent dans un rapport hiérarchique dont le mécanisme de contrôle de constitutionnalité est l'expression et le garant. Sous un aspect structurel et temporel, la constitution est première par rapport à la loi.

Formellement, la loi se définit par le processus d'adoption fixé dans la constitution, à savoir comme une norme (à portée générale) votée par la Chambre des députés, sur avis du Conseil d'Etat, sanctionnée et promulguée par le Grand-Duc. A relever que les révisions de la constitution revêtent également la forme d'une loi qui se distingue de la loi ordinaire, moins par son contenu que par la procédure particulièrement complexe à laquelle est soumise son adoption et sa révision. La constitution luxembourgeoise appartient, en effet, à la catégorie des constitutions dites rigides. L'article 114 de la constitution exige que la Chambre des Députés adopte une déclaration de révision des dispositions constitutionnelles; cette déclaration entraîne de plein droit la dissolution de la Chambre et l'élection d'une constituante; celle-ci sera compétente pour voter une loi de révision constitutionnelle en respectant des conditions de quorum et de majorité renforcés prévues à l'article 114 de la constitution[16].

- Troisième précision: L'examen des rapports entre les trois pôles que sont l'Etat, la constitution et le droit international met en évidence certaines spécificités de l'ordre juridique luxembourgeois. A l'opposé d'autres Etats européens, le Grand-Duché n'a pas son fondement juridique originaire dans la constitution, mais dans le droit international. Le Luxembourg, en tant qu'Etat indépendant, a été établi dans l'Acte final du Congrès de Vienne du 9 juin 1815. L'indépendance de l'Etat a été confirmée par le traité de Londres du 19 avril 1839 et consacrée par le traité de Londres du 11 mai 1867 qui a imposé un statut de neutralité. Si l'existence de l'Etat remonte à 1815, la première constitution n'a été adoptée qu'en 1841[17]. Son objet est moins de constituer ou de fonder l'Etat, en tant que sujet de droit national et international, que d'organiser un Etat déjà existant. La fonction constituante ou constitutive, reconnue à la constitution dans la plupart des théories constitutionnelles, se vérifie dès lors davantage par rapport à l'ordre juridique luxembourgeois que par rapport à l'Etat en tant que tel.

Historiquement, le droit international, loin d'apparaître comme une source d'atteintes à la souveraineté nationale, a été compris comme une garantie indispensable de l'existence et de la survie de l'Etat. L'importance attachée, dans l'ordre constitutionnel luxembourgeois, au droit international est mise en évidence par les références expresses que les constitutions successives opèrent au droit international. Ainsi, la première constitution libérale du 9 juillet 1848, la constitution dite réactionnaire du 27 novembre 1856 et la deuxième constitution libérale du 17 octobre 1868, toujours en vigueur malgré de nombreuses modifications, se réfèrent, à propos de la dévolution de la couronne, au traité de Vienne de 1815 et au traité de Londres de 1867[18].

2. Dispositions constitutionnelles nationales et droit européen

Les rapports entre l'ordre constitutionnel national et le droit communautaire sont régis par les articles 1er, 37 et 49bis de la constitution.

1) L'article 1er de la constitution qualifie le Grand-Duché d'Etat démocratique, libre, indépendant et indivisible. La question se pose de savoir si le principe de l'indépendance s'oppose à ce que le Grand-Duché soit privé de certains attributs étatiques traditionnels au profit d'une structure européenne de type fédérale dans laquelle il viendrait s'intégrer en tant qu'entité subordonnée. Il faut reconnaître que, à aucun moment, les limites

éventuelles du processus d'intégration européenne n'ont été sérieusement évoquées en relation avec la nécessaire préservation de l'indépendance de l'Etat. Les débats se sont focalisés sur les transferts d'attributions étatiques précises et sur la question de savoir si ces transferts pouvaient être opérés au titre du seul l'article 49bis de la constitution ou exigeaient une révision constitutionnelle.

2) L'article 37 constitue une disposition classique sur le "treaty making power". Le Grand-Duc, lisez le pouvoir exécutif, fait les traités qui doivent toutefois être approuvés par le pouvoir législatif pour avoir effet. Le pouvoir exécutif, organe représentatif de l'Etat au niveau international, est encore compétent pour exécuter les traités. Cette disposition vaut pour tous les instruments juridiques prenant la forme du traité, sans qu'il y ait lieu de distinguer entre le droit international traditionnel et le droit européen.

Pour l'approbation de traités relevant de l'article 49bis de la constitution, c'est-à-dire ceux qui opèrent des transferts de compétences, la Chambre doit respecter les conditions de quorum et de majorité prévues par l'article 114 de la constitution pour la procédure de révision constitutionnelle. Un tel vote ne saurait toutefois être assimilé à une modification implicite de la constitution.

3) La disposition clé quant à la question des transferts d'attributions souveraines aux Communautés européennes ou à l'Union est l'article 49bis de la constitution. Il prévoit que "l'exercice d'attributions réservées par la Constitution aux pouvoirs législatif, exécutif et judiciaire peut être temporairement dévolu par traité à des institutions de droit international".

Cette modification constitutionnelle est intervenue en 1956, au regard de l'expérience du traité CECA , des négociations du traité instituant la Communauté européenne de défense et des négociations en vue de la conclusion des traités de Rome. Elle prenait exemple sur des dispositions constitutionnelles d'autres Etats membres de la CECA, l'article 11 de la constitution italienne, l'article 24 du Grundgesetz allemand, l'article 63 de la constitution néerlandaise[19]. Les débats au Luxembourg étaient influencés par les discussions se déroulant à la même époque en Belgique et qui ont abouti à l'insertion dans la constitution belge d'un nouvel article 25bis[20] ayant une teneur comparable au texte luxembourgeois.

Rappelons que, lors du débat précédant cette révision constitutionnelle, trois points étaient controversés, l'ampleur de la révision constitutionnelle en ce qui concerne les relations entre le droit international et l'ordre juridique national, la place de la nouvelle disposition dans le texte constitutionnel et la formulation à retenir pour le transfert des attributions étatiques[21].

- Le projet gouvernemental envisageait le droit, pour le pouvoir exécutif, de conclure certains traités sans approbation parlementaire, la possibilité d'approuver, sous des conditions de majorité renforcée, des traités contraires à la constitution et de modifier ainsi implicitement la constitution, la consécration de la primauté du droit international, la reconnaissance des compétences des juridictions internationales et le transfert de l'exercice d'attributions étatiques à des institutions de droit international. L'article 49 bis peut être considéré comme une solution minimale inspirée de l'orientation qui a prédominé en Belgique.

- Le gouvernement avait proposé de rattacher la nouvelle disposition aux textes définissant les pouvoirs du Grand-Duc, compétent pour conclure les traités. Arguant du fait que le transfert d'attributions touchait également aux pouvoirs législatif et judiciaire, la Chambre a rejeté cette proposition. La solution retenue en Belgique de rattacher la disposition sur la dévolution d'attributions étatiques aux textes sur la souveraineté nationale a été écartée au motif que la souveraineté ne peut pas être scindée en volet national et international[22]. Finalement, on a inséré les nouvelles dispositions dans un paragraphe particulier intitulé "des pouvoirs internationaux" qui suit les paragraphes traitant du Grand-Duc, de la législation et de la justice.
- En ce qui concerne le libellé de l'article 49bis, on peut relever que les termes utilisés sont assez stricts. L'article 49bis ne vise que la dévolution de l'exercice d'attributions sans toucher à la question du siège de celles-ci. Le texte parle d'attributions des trois pouvoirs dans l'Etat sans envisager les attributions de l'Etat en tant que tel ni des domaines entiers d'attributions[23]. Le Conseil d'Etat, dans son avis sur le projet de loi de révision constitutionnelle, avait souligné que la souveraineté nationale restait indivisible et n'était pas atteinte en tant que telle. Enfin, la dévolution est censée être temporaire et non pas définitive. A relever toutefois que les critères de l'égalité des parties contractantes à un traité et de la réciprocité proposés par le gouvernement[24] n'ont pas été retenus dans le texte adopté par la Chambre des Députés[25].

Cette formulation stricte du texte ne s'est toutefois pas traduite par une application restrictive dans la pratique. L'article 49bis a servi de fondement juridique à l'approbation de tous les traités européens modifiant les traités originaires et élargissant les compétences des Communautés. Les limites de l'article 49bis ont été évoquées, pour la première fois, lors de la ratification du traité de Maastricht. La question s'est posée de savoir si l'octroi du droit de vote aux élections municipales aux résidents ressortissants communautaires était couvert par l'article 49bis ou s'il fallait procéder à une révision préalable des dispositions constitutionnelles réservant le droit de vote actif et passif aux nationaux[26]. Adoptant une position opposée à celle du Conseil d'Etat belge, le Conseil d'Etat luxembourgeois a considéré que les dispositions du traité sur l'Union européenne relatives au droit de vote aux élections municipales pouvaient s'analyser en un transfert de compétences dans le cadre de l'article 49bis[27] et qu'une adaptation de la constitution pouvait valablement suivre l'engagement international[28].

3. La question d'une "européanisation" de la constitution

La ratification du traité sur l'Union européenne a donné lieu, dans les deux principaux Etats voisins du Luxembourg, l'Allemagne et la France, à des révisions constitutionnelles importantes aux termes desquelles la constitution reconnaît la spécificité des rapports entre l'ordre national et l'ordre juridique européen, par rapport aux relations traditionnelles entre le droit national et le droit international[29].

L'ordre constitutionnel luxembourgeois n'a pas connu un tel "saut qualitatif" pour ce qui est de la perception du processus d'intégration européenne. Le maintien de ces conceptions traditionnelles s'explique par le fait que, contrairement aux expériences en France ou en Allemagne, les limites éventuelles de l'application de l'article 49bis n'ont jamais été sérieusement évoquées. L'abandon des droits de souveraineté monétaire, dans le traité de Maastricht, a constitué un "non-problème" dans la mesure où le Grand-Duché n'a jamais disposé d'une souveraineté totale dans ce domaine[30]. Les discussions en ce qui concerne l'octroi du droit de vote communal aux ressortissants communautaires se sont focalisées, ainsi que nous l'avons vu ci-dessus, sur la question procédurale d'une révision constitutionnelle a priori ou a posteriori. Par ailleurs, contrairement à ce qui s'est passé en Allemagne, l'application du droit communautaire et sa primauté sur le droit national n'ont pas été contestées.

Dans la logique de l'article 49bis, les relations entre le Grand-Duché et les Communautés constituent un "cas de figure" des rapports avec l'ordre juridique international. Ce "cas de figure" revêt, certes, une importance particulière, en ce que la genèse de l'article 49bis ne se comprend que sur la toile de fond de l'unification européenne. Il est encore indiscutable que le processus d'intégration européenne constitue le champ d'application privilégié de l'article 49bis. Il n'en reste pas moins que les relations entre l'ordre national et l'ordre communautaire participent de la nature juridique des rapports entre le droit national et international et que les Communautés revêtent la qualité d'institutions du droit international. Trois problèmes particuliers peuvent, à cet égard, être relevés:

- L'article 49bis prévoit un transfert de l'exercice de compétences des organes de l'Etat vers des institutions de droit international. Le système des compétences dites partagées qui passent du niveau national au niveau communautaire au fur et à mesure que la Communauté devient active dans un secteur déterminé cadre mal avec le principe d'un transfert clair et net de compétences déterminées. Il en va de même, a fortiori, pour des attributions de compétences au titre de l'article 308 (ex-article 235) du traité CE.

- L'article 49bis envisage un partage dans l'exercice des compétences entre le niveau national et le niveau supranational avec une distinction corrélative des organes compétents. Or, ainsi qu'il sera précisé par la suite, le mécanisme actuel de gouvernance à plusieurs niveaux investit les organes nationaux de la mission d'exécuter ou d'appliquer les actes adoptés au niveau communautaire.
- Enfin, l'article 49bis met en relation l'Etat, sujet du droit international, doté de la souveraineté que l'ordre juridique international lui reconnaît, et des institutions de droit international créées par les Etats. Les procédures qu'a suivies, jusqu'à présent, l'intégration européenne, à savoir la conclusion de traités, fondateurs d'abord, modificatifs ensuite, répondent à cette conception. La question se pose toutefois de savoir si un changement radical au niveau de l'approche juridique, concrètement le passage d'un ordre juridique basé sur des traités entre Etats, à un système constitutionnel qui serait mis en place par un acte adopté par les peuples européens ou leurs représentants, ne s'écarterait pas de la logique de l'article 49bis.

4. *Les débats autour de la Conférence intergouvernementale de 2004*

Si l'on analyse les moments forts du débat au Luxembourg sur l'avenir de l'Union européenne, on constate l'approche pragmatique et non doctrinaire des acteurs impliqués, qu'il s'agisse de l'opinion publique, de la presse ou du monde politique.

Les citoyens de l'Union résidant sur le territoire luxembourgeois ont été invités, en automne 2001, à répondre à un questionnaire sur l'Europe établi sous la responsabilité du gouvernement et de la Chambre des Députés[31]. Globalement, la perception de la construction européenne est positive, même si les citoyens participant au sondage n'ont pas préconisé un saut qualitatif majeur dans la construction européenne.

Sur le thème des valeurs de l'Europe, les citoyens ont exprimé un net sentiment d'appartenance à leur pays d'origine, qu'il s'agisse du Grand-Duché ou d'un autre Etat membre. Le sentiment de confiance vis-à-vis de l'Europe s'exprime, notamment, en relation avec les facteurs de paix, de stabilité et de prospérité économique[32].

A propos du fonctionnement de l'Union, 6 intervenants sur 10 doutent de la capacité des représentants de leur pays de peser sur les décisions adoptées au niveau européen. Dans les mêmes proportions, les personnes interrogées font davantage confiance aux instances nationales qu'aux institutions communautaires pour représenter leurs intérêts[33] et préconisent une conduite des politiques sociale, fiscale et agricole au niveau national [34].

Les questions les plus pertinentes, au regard du présent rapport, ont porté sur l'avenir de l'Europe. Les réponses soulèvent des problèmes d'interprétation en ce que les intéressés préconisent à la fois un renforcement des moyens d'action de la Commission et, encore davantage, du Parlement européen, tout en souhaitant que le Conseil des ministres reste la principale instance de décision. De façon plus nette est souhaitée une implication plus forte des parlements nationaux dans le processus décisionnel européen. Les concepts de "constitution européenne" et de "fédération européenne" recueillent l'adhésion de la moitié des personnes interrogées sans que ces notions aient toutefois connu une clarification[35].

b) Si la presse luxembourgeoise se fait régulièrement l'écho des discussions sur la construction de l'Europe, des réflexions plus fondamentales sur l'architecture future de l'Union, le constitutionnalisme ou le rôle de l'Etat national dans l'Union de demain sont l'exception. La même remarque vaut pour la doctrine, peu nombreuse il est vrai, dans le domaine des sciences juridiques et politiques.

Les débats portent, outre les problèmes d'actualité, sur les questions plus traditionnelles de la future structure institutionnelle de l'Union, au regard notamment de la représentation du Grand-Duché dans les institutions communautaires, et de la portée des compétences de l'Union, en relation avec le maintien de "niches de souveraineté" au niveau national.

c) La même attitude, à la fois positive et pragmatique, vis-à-vis de la construction européenne est adoptée par les décideurs politiques. Les grandes familles politiques, chrétienne-sociale, socialiste et libérale, partagent, traditionnellement, la même ambition européenne[36].

Une extension des attributions de l'Union dans les domaines de la politique étrangère et de la sécurité, des affaires intérieures et de la justice, voire une communautarisation de ces matières, sont envisagés favorablement. Il en va de même du renforcement des compétences de la Communauté dans l'union économique et monétaire. Pour des raisons économiques évidentes, une harmonisation des législations fiscales ou bancaires est préconisée dans le cadre de l'Organisation de coopération et de développement économiques. D'une façon plus générale, une détermination progressive et graduelle des compétences des Communautés est préférée à une délimitation rigide définitive; dans cette optique, est souhaité le maintien de l'instrument de l'article 308 du traité CE (ex-article 235)[37]. L'importance du principe de subsidiarité est régulièrement rappelé, même si les réflexions sur son application concrète restent assez vagues.

Si les questions institutionnelles sont souvent présentées comme un "faux débat"[38], les discussions autour de la Conférence intergouvernementale de Nice ont toutefois montré que le Luxembourg, comme d'autres petits Etats membres de la Communauté, reste attaché à une représentation satisfaisante au sein des institutions communautaires[39]. Ce souci n'empêche pas les responsables politiques luxembourgeois d'accepter un renforcement des pouvoirs du Parlement européen par le biais, notamment, d'une extension du mécanisme de la co-décision.

Le débat dit constitutionnel peut être résumé comme suit: Dans toutes les prises de position, les responsables politiques luxembourgeois relèvent la double nature de l'Union, union des Etats et union des peuples, de même que le caractère sui generis de la structure européenne. L'idée d'une constitution future de l'Union n'est pas écartée par principe: Si l'on examine les déclarations politiques, on constate que leurs auteurs visent la simplification des textes des traités, plus particulièrement une séparation des dispositions fondamentales par rapport aux dispositions techniques, la question d'une délimitation plus nette des compétences entre l'Union et les Etats, le statut de la Charte des droits fondamentaux ou encore la question institutionnelle du rôle des parlements nationaux. En même temps est préconisé un ancrage plus fort de la construction européenne dans les constitutions nationales. S'il est régulièrement rappelé que l'Union doit rester une union d'Etats, la question du pouvoir constituant, Etats, Etats et / ou peuple(s) européen(s) n'est pas posée, pas davantage que celle de la nature du document juridique à la base de l'Union, traité traditionnel, traité de nature constitutionnelle adopté avec le Parlement européen ou véritable constitution européenne adoptée par les représentants des peuples[40].

II. RELATIONS ET INTERACTIONS ENTRE LE DROIT EUROPÉEN ET LES CONSTITUTIONS NATIONALES

1. *L'autonomie constitutionnelle des Etats membres au regard des contraintes européennes*

Il faut relever, d'emblée, que le sujet, tel qu'il est libellé, met en lumière une certaine conception des relations entre l'ordre juridique communautaire et les ordres constitutionnels nationaux. L'idée d'une simple autonomie constitutionnelle des Etats vis-à-vis d'un système supérieur implique inéluctablement une référence à un régime fédéral dans lequel le texte de base de la structure fédérale, concrètement la constitution de l'Etat fédéral, détermine le domaine des attributions et les pouvoirs d'action des entités fédérées bénéficiant d'une certaine autonomie interne. Or, dans une optique historique, et en conformité avec les traditions constitutionnelles de tous les Etats membres de la Communauté, l'intégration communautaire a suivi un processus différent. Les Etats membres, sujets du droit international, dotés de la plénitude des compétences, ont accepté de limiter, dans des domaines à l'origine précis, leurs attributions au profit de nouveaux sujets de droit international, les Communautés, créés par des traités auxquels sont et restent parties les Etats. Cela vaut, a fortiori, pour les compétences exercées, selon des méthodes largement intergouvernementales, au niveau de l'Union. Cette analyse juridique n'est pas mise en cause par le fait que le volume des compétences transférées a augmenté avec le temps et a vocation à s'accroître. Elle n'est pas davantage affectée par le respect impérieux de la primauté et de l'effet direct qui constituent des principes traditionnels du droit international. Même si l'on entend dépasser l'approche internationale et se placer dans une perspective constitutionnelle, force est de reconnaître que les Etats membres restent, du moins dans le système actuel, les constituants de la future entité européenne. Il est certain qu'un des enjeux de la prochaine conférence intergouvernementale sera de trouver un équilibre entre le niveau de gouvernance communautaire et le niveau national, dans une structure techniquement complexe. Conférer aux Etats un simple statut d'autonomie dans le cadre de la nouvelle Union constitue une option, mais ne s'impose pas nécessairement au regard de l'acquis communautaire. Il s'agira d'un choix éminemment politique et on peut douter que les dispositions actuelles des articles 6 et 7 du traité sur l'Union revêtent, dans ce processus de réflexion, une importance décisive.

a. L'identité nationale des Etats membres comme limite à l'extension de compétences des Communautés ou de l'Union: l'article 6, paragraphe 3 du traité sur l'Union

L'article 6, paragraphe 3, du traité sur l'Union européenne est à comprendre en relation avec l'abandon de compétences étatiques en matière monétaire et la consécration de la citoyenneté de l'Union. Même si la Cour de justice des Communautés européennes (ci-après: la Cour de justice) avait déjà considéré, de longue date, que les sujets de la Communauté ne sont pas seulement les Etats, mais également leurs ressortissants[41], les milieux politiques et l'opinion publique au Luxembourg ont compris que la consécration, dans le traité, d'une citoyenneté de l'Union marquait un pas décisif dans le dépassement définitif d'une vision purement "internationaliste" de la Communauté.

Ainsi qu'il ressort des discussions dans beaucoup d'Etats membres, notamment en Allemagne, la nature et la portée de l'article 6, paragraphe 3, sont sujettes à controverses. S'agit-il d'une déclaration à valeur symbolique ou politique, d'un principe de nature programmatique ou d'une véritable règle de droit? L'Union doit-elle respecter la qualité étatique des Etats membres ou de ce qu'il est convenu d'appeler les Etats-nations, ce qui interdirait la voie vers une structure fédérale au sens traditionnel du terme? Est-ce que l'article 6, paragraphe 3, peut être considéré comme une norme positive de répartition de compétences entre l'Union et ses membres ou, tout au moins, comme un principe qui doit présider à la répartition des compétences? S'agit-il d'un simple corollaire de l'article 10 du traité CE qui se borne à imposer à l'Union un devoir de coopération loyale avec les Etats membres[42]? Est-ce que le respect des identités nationales ne résume pas à un attachement aux particularités culturelles, linguistiques, politiques, sociales ou sociétales des Etats.

Sans vouloir entrer dans ce débat doctrinal, il me paraît difficile de voir dans l'article 6, paragraphe 3, du traité sur l'Union une norme de droit positif à l'aulne de laquelle serait analysée et contrôlée la répartition des compétences, actuelles et a fortiori futures, entre l'Union et ses Etats membres. Certes, l'article 6, paragraphe 3, fait partie d'un traité juridiquement contraignant et on ne saurait lui dénier toute valeur juridique. Il n'empêche que cette disposition pose un principe programmatique ou directeur, mais ne constitue pas une règle de droit positif permettant de contrôler la répartition actuelle des compétences au sein de l'Union ou de déterminer, pour l'avenir, les limites des attributions de l'Union (ou des Communautés).

Dans le cadre des discussions entourant la ratification du traité sur l'Union au Luxembourg, ni l'article 6, paragraphe 3, ni l'article 151 du traité CE sur le respect des cultures dans leur diversité régionale n'ont été perçus comme des sauvegardes contre un empiètement des Communautés sur des domaines de compétence étatique. Une telle fonction de sauvegarde a été, par contre, reconnue au principe de subsidiarité[43].

A relever que l'article 6, paragraphe 3, (à l'époque article F, paragraphe 1) a été invoqué à l'occasion d'un recours en manquement introduit en 1993 contre le Grand-Duché. Au reproche de la Commission d'imposer des conditions de nationalité pour l'accès aux emplois dans certains secteurs de la fonction publique, le gouvernement luxembourgeois avait répondu par la nécessité de sauvegarder l'identité nationale dans une situation démographique spécifique. La Cour de justice a écarté cet argument en relevant que cet objectif ne saurait justifier l'exclusion générale des ressortissants des autres Etats membres, d'autant plus que ces derniers devaient répondre aux critères de qualification y compris d'ordre linguistique[44].

Au-delà de la problématique particulière luxembourgeoise, l'arrêt est important pour circonscrire la portée de l'article 6, paragraphe 3. D'abord, la Cour de justice qualifie la sauvegarde de l'identité nationale comme but légitime respecté par l'ordre juridique communautaire. Elle fait toutefois état de ce but légitime en tant que tel et ne cite l'article F, paragraphe 1, que dans la mesure où il reconnaît ce but. Ensuite, la sauvegarde de l'identité nationale n'est pas examinée au regard de nouvelles compétences que la Communauté revendiquerait, mais en tant que limite à la liberté de circulation des travailleurs inscrite dans les traités depuis 1958. En toute logique, la Cour de justice réduit le moyen de défense du gouvernement luxembourgeois à une condition de connaissances linguistiques qui serait invoquée comme exigence impérative indistinctement applicable pour justifier une entrave à la liberté de circulation. Même si elle invoque l'article F, paragraphe 1, la Cour reprend, en réalité, le raisonnement suivi dans l'arrêt Groener[45], antérieur au traité de Maastricht, mettant ainsi en évidence que cette disposition n'a pas introduit de nouvelles limites aux compétences communautaires.

b. Le respect des droits fondamentaux en tant que limite à l'autonomie constitutionnelle des Etats: les articles 6, paragraphe 1, et 7 du traité sur l'Union

Le paragraphe 1 de l'article 6 énonce, comme le paragraphe 3, un principe à observer dans le fonctionnement de l'Union. L'article 7 étend ce principe à l'action propre des Etats et instaure un système de sanction politique à l'égard des membres de l'Union qui méconnaîtraient les valeurs visées à l'article 6, paragraphe 1.

Au niveau procédural, ce régime de sanction se distingue fondamentalement du recours en manquement traditionnel devant la Cour de justice en ce qu'il relève d'une démarche politique et non pas juridique. A cet égard, il est proche de mécanismes, aussi contraignants, de suspension des droits d'un Etat membre ou d'exclusion dans d'autres organisations internationales[46].

Dans une optique plus fondamentale, il faut reconnaître que l'article 7, malgré le fait qu'il figure dans un traité juridiquement contraignant, remplit une fonction essentiellement symbolique et tout au plus préventive. Dans le domaine d'application du droit communautaire, la Cour de justice assure la protection des droits de l'homme par le biais des principes généraux de droit communautaire en s'inspirant des traditions constitutionnelles communes des Etats membres et de la Convention européenne à laquelle tous les Etats membres sont parties.

L'article 7 ne précise pas si la violation grave et persistante par un Etat membre des principes énoncés à l'article 6, paragraphe 1, doit se situer dans le champ d'application du droit de l'Union ou peut être intervenue dans la sphère des compétences propres de l'Etat. Le mécanisme de sanction ne peut revêtir une portée propre que si l'Etat est concerné dans l'ensemble de sa sphère de compétences. Force est toutefois de reconnaître que, même dans une telle optique, l'instrument de l'article 7 ne va d'ailleurs pas au-delà de mécanismes de sanction prévus dans d'autres textes internationaux.

L'article 7, en combinaison avec l'article 6, paragraphe 1, soumet les Etats à des principes qui les lient déjà en vertu de dispositions nationales ou internationales souvent antérieures aux traités constitutifs des Communautés ou de l'Union. Les limites à l'autonomie constitutionnelle des Etats membres résultent autant de la nécessité de respecter le "noyau dur constitutionnel national" que représentent les droits fondamentaux et les conventions internationales en la matière que de l'article 7 du traité sur l'Union. Dans une approche pragmatique, on peut d'ailleurs se demander si le conflit suggéré dans ce point du questionnaire ne relève pas de l'hypothèse d'école[47].

2. *Les valeurs communes: la Charte des droits fondamentaux*

a. *La Charte en tant que reflet des standards de protection des droits fondamentaux en droit national*

La constitution luxembourgeoise, dans sa teneur actuelle, remonte à 1868. Le texte de 1868 constitue, à son tour, dans une très large mesure, une reprise de la première constitution libérale de 1848, elle-même fortement inspirée de la constitution belge de 1831. Les articles relatifs aux droits fondamentaux sont restés, pour l'essentiel, inchangés depuis le 19e siècle, sous réserve de la consécration, en 1948, de certains droits naturels de la personne humaine ainsi que de droits économiques et sociaux.

Jusqu'à la création récente d'une Cour constitutionnelle en 1997[48], le juge luxembourgeois, judiciaire ou administratif, n'était pas autorisé à écarter l'application d'une loi pour non-conformité avec la constitution, concrètement pour violation de certains droits fondamentaux. Par contre, le même juge était en mesure de sanctionner la non-conformité de la loi nationale avec un traité international, en se fondant sur les principes bien établis de la primauté et de l'effet direct du traité.

Ces deux facteurs expliquent que le juge national a sauvegardé les droits fondamentaux en se référant, pour l'essentiel, à la Convention européenne à laquelle le Luxembourg est partie contractante depuis 1953[49] ou, dans une moindre mesure, au Pacte international sur les droits civils et politiques de 1966. Certains principes fondamentaux de l'ordre juridique communautaire, qu'il s'agisse de la liberté de circulation, de l'interdiction de toute discrimination en raison de la nationalité, de l'égalité de traitement entre hommes et femmes ou encore des droits inhérents à la citoyenneté de l'Union, sont sauvegardés par le juge national au titre du respect du droit communautaire.

Si l'on examine la Charte sur l'arrière-fond de son processus d'adoption et dans une perspective de droit constitutionnel comparé, on peut considérer ce texte comme un standard commun, par ailleurs élevé, des droits fondamentaux dans l'Union européenne. Au niveau de son contenu, la Charte des droits fondamentaux va largement au-delà des droits consacrés dans la constitution nationale. Son importance, dans une optique juridique, doit toutefois s'analyser au regard de son champ d'application et par rapport à d'autres textes de droit supranational auxquels se réfèrent traditionnellement les juges nationaux[50].

Faut-il rappeler que la Charte est dépourvue de valeur juridique. Par ailleurs, l'article 51, paragraphe 1, limite son champ d'application. La Charte s'adresse aux institutions et aux organes de l'Union dans le respect du principe de subsidiarité. Les Etats membres ne sont visés que dans la mesure où ils mettent en œuvre le droit communautaire[51]. A cet égard, on s'est interrogé, à juste titre, sur la portée de certains droits inscrits dans la Charte qui visent des matières pour lesquelles la Communauté ou l'Union n'ont manifestement aucune compétence. Au paragraphe 2 de l'article 51, les auteurs de la Charte ont pris soin de préciser que la Charte ne saurait entraîner une extension des compétences de la Communauté ou de l'Union au détriment des Etats membres. Ces limites du champ d'application de la Charte relativisent son rôle en tant que standard commun de protection des droits de l'homme dans l'Union, notamment par rapport à la Convention européenne qui constitue une référence commune et juridiquement contraignante pour les droits nationaux et pour l'ordre juridique communautaire, fût-ce par le biais des principes généraux du droit communautaire.

b. La Charte en tant que référence pour la protection des droits fondamentaux, par les juges

Faute de valeur juridique contraignante, la Charte ne saurait constituer un texte de référence pour le juge luxembourgeois. Le statut juridique de la Charte est identique à celui de la Déclaration universelle des droits de l'homme des Nations Unies de 1948 qui, à l'opposé du Pacte sur les droits civile et politiques de 1966, n'est pas invoquée par le juge. On peut, bien sûr, spéculer sur la réaction du juge national à une consécration de la Charte par la Cour de justice. Dans la logique de la primauté du droit communautaire et du respect des arrêts de la Cour de justice, le juge national devrait reconnaître à la Charte la valeur qui lui revient devant le juge communautaire. Au regard de la position réservée adoptée, à ce jour, par la Cour de justice, cette question reste toutefois largement théorique[52].

Il va sans dire que les développements qui précèdent s'inscrivent dans une optique "de lege lata". Dans une perspective "de lege ferenda", il est compréhensible que les tenants d'une constitution de l'Union envisagent la transformation de la Charte en texte juridiquement contraignant. Un tel changement de la qualité juridique du texte, outre le fait qu'il ne s'impose pas pour une protection efficace des droits de l'homme, posera toutefois, avec une acuité nouvelle, le problème des limites de son champ d'application et de ses rapports avec la Convention européenne et avec les constitutions nationales.

c. L'impact de la Charte sur l'application de l'article 6, paragraphe 1

Dans une optique formaliste, on ne peut que constater que l'article 6, paragraphe 1, est antérieur à la Charte. Il s'agit d'une disposition d'un traité international, alors que la Charte est dépourvue de toute valeur juridique. La conférence intergouvernementale de Nice a (logiquement) omis d'insérer une référence à la Charte dans le texte de l'article 6. Se pose, à cet égard, également la question de la relation entre la sauvegarde des droits de l'homme et des libertés, au sens du premier et du deuxième paragraphes de l'article 6 et, au-delà, entre la Charte de l'Union et la Convention européenne visée expressément au paragraphe 2 de l'article 6.

Dans une optique fondamentale, il ne devrait pas y avoir de différence entre les droits consacrés à la Charte et ceux visés à l'article 6, paragraphe 1. L'impact, si on peut utiliser ce concept, se limiterait dès lors à préciser les droits de l'article 6 par référence à certaines formulations de la Charte peut-être plus modernes que celles figurant dans les constitutions nationales ou la Convention européenne.

Les interrogations soulevées par la Charte mettent, une nouvelle fois, en évidence les avantages qu'aurait présentés une adhésion de la Communauté à la Convention européenne, à savoir la soumission à un texte juridiquement contraignant, le respect d'une convention à laquelle sont parties tous les Etats membres et à laquelle se réfère historiquement la Cour de justice, texte par ailleurs expressément évoqué dans le traité sur l'Union[53].

3. La question de la primauté du droit communautaire et ses effets constitutionnels

a. La suprématie du droit communautaire primaire et dérivé sur le droit national en particulier le droit constitutionnel54

L'examen de la jurisprudence luxembourgeoise révèle que les juridictions nationales ont adopté, dès le 19ème siècle, une attitude ouverte à l'égard du phénomène international et ont reconnu, très tôt, la prééminence du droit international sur le droit national en se fondant d'ailleurs, au début, sur le principe de droit civil "pacta sunt servanda"[55]. Cette attitude des juridictions luxembourgeoises s'explique par la conviction que les traités internationaux constituaient la garantie du maintien de l'indépendance de l'Etat. Même s'il faut constater, dans la période de l'entre-deux-guerres, certaines hésitations, les juridictions luxembourgeoises sont revenues, à partir de 1950, à une consécration nette de la règle dite de la hiérarchie[56], en décidant qu'en cas de conflit entre les dispositions d'un traité international et celles d'une loi interne postérieure, la loi internationale devait prévaloir sur la loi interne [57].

Ce principe de la primauté a été appliqué sans discussion aux rapports entre le droit communautaire et le droit national et fondé tant sur l'assimilation du droit communautaire au droit international que sur la spécificité du nouvel ordre juridique communautaire. Ainsi, dans la première décision de renvoi à titre préjudiciel, le juge luxembourgeois a fait prévaloir la décision de saisine de la Cour de justice sur le principe dit de la plénitude de juridiction des tribunaux répressifs au motif que "les lois internationales doivent primer la loi nationale"[58]. Le principe de primauté a été régulièrement rappelé dans des décisions de renvoi et dans des décisions rendues en considération des arrêts de la Cour de justice. Ainsi, la Cour de cassation a estimé que l'article 177 du traité CEE (article 234 actuel du traité CE), comportait pour elle l'obligation de surseoir à toute décision au fond, l'obligation de solliciter l'interprétation de la Cour de justice ayant le caractère d'une véritable question préjudicielle qu'elle ne saurait méconnaître sans violer une loi internationale[59]. Le juge luxembourgeois a également consacré ce principe quand il a appliqué le droit communautaire sans recourir à la procédure préjudicielle[60]. Dans certains cas, il a estimé que, au vu de la jurisprudence constante luxembourgeoise, il n'existe aucune raison de saisir la Cour de justice d'une question préjudicielle s'il s'agit uniquement d'assurer la primauté de la règle communautaire sur la règle nationale non conforme[61].

Un conflit entre le droit communautaire, qu'il s'agisse du droit primaire ou même du droit dérivé, et une disposition constitutionnelle nationale devrait également être réglé en application du principe de la primauté du droit communautaire.

La constitution luxembourgeoise ne contient pas de disposition sur la place du traité ou du droit supranational adopté en vertu d'un traité dans l'ordre juridique interne. Dans la logique de la théorie moniste, la suprématie du droit international est fondée sur la nature même du droit international, le traité étant une loi d'une essence supérieure ayant une origine plus haute que la volonté d'un organe interne[62]. Cette prééminence du droit international vaut également vis-à-vis d'une norme constitutionnelle.

La Cour constitutionnelle n'a pas encore été amenée à se prononcer sur cette question. Le problème ne peut d'ailleurs pas se poser pour les dispositions du droit communautaire primaire, étant donné que la loi d'approbation parlementaire d'un traité est expressément exclue du contrôle de constitutionnalité. Un conflit pourrait toutefois naître à propos d'une loi transposant une directive en droit national. La conformité d'une telle loi avec la constitution pourrait se réduire à un conflit entre la directive et la constitution, notamment dans l'hypothèse où la Cour de justice saisie à titre préjudiciel a confirmé la validité de la directive ou consacré une certaine interprétation de ses dispositions.

Si la question de la primauté du droit international sur le droit constitutionnel n'a pas encore été tranchée par la Cour constitutionnelle, le juge judiciaire s'est clairement prononcé en faveur de cette primauté. Dans un récent arrêt, la Cour d'appel de Luxembourg a consacré la primauté de la Convention européenne sur le droit constitutionnel[63]. Cette solution devrait valoir , a fortiori, pour le droit communautaire, adopté par les institutions communautaires dans un domaine où des attributions étatiques ont été transférées en application de l'article 49bis de la constitution.

b. La modification implicite de la constitution par la révision et l'application du traité de l'Union

En l'état actuel des dispositions constitutionnelles pertinentes, l'approbation parlementaire et la ratification d'un traité "constitutionnel" portant révision ou remplaçant les traités actuels ne saurait entraîner une modification ou révision implicite de la constitution luxembourgeoise[64]. La ratification d'un tel traité ne peut dès lors être faite que si les dispositions modificatives entrent dans le cadre de l'article 49 bis actuel ou si la constitution nationale est amendée. C'est dans cette perspective que s'inscrit l'idée d'une disposition constitutionnelle nouvelle qui, allant au-delà de la logique "internationaliste" de l'article 49 bis, consacre expressément le projet d'intégration européenne et l'insertion de l'Etat et des ses organes dans un système de gouvernance à plusieurs niveaux. Une telle disposition devrait également consacrer le principe que la qualité de sujet de droit international de l'Etat ne peut pas être mise en cause et que des limites au processus d'intégration en découlent.

4. *L'interdépendance institutionnelle: les fonctions européennes des institutions nationales*

L'ordre juridique communautaire se caractérise par la dualité de sa structure. A l'unicité et à la centralisation du droit au niveau de sa création correspond une pluralité au niveau de son application et de sa sanction. En effet, les Communautés, en dehors de quelques rares domaines, tel celui de la concurrence, ne disposent pas d'une structure administrative qui permettrait d'entrer directement en contact avec le citoyen. Ce dernier est touché par le droit communautaire par le biais d'actes nationaux d'exécution, même dans les domaines régis par les règlements pourtant directement applicables.

Il est vrai que ce régime dual n'est pas sans rappeler les structures fédérales et constitue un argument clé pour qualifier l'ordre juridique communautaire de système constitutionnel à plusieurs niveaux. Il faut toutefois se rendre compte que ce régime est "consubstantiel" aux Communautés et qu'il existe dès leur origine sans qu'on en ait déduit la nécessité de doter les Communautés d'un fondement juridique de type constitutionnel.

a. Le rôle des Parlements nationaux dans le processus législatif européen: source indirecte de légitimité et responsabilité pour l'exécution du droit communautaire

Dans le processus décisionnel des Communautés, le rôle des parlements nationaux est confiné à celui d'un exécutant d'actes adoptés à un niveau supra-étatique. L'élection directe du Parlement européen et la séparation des fonctions de parlementaire national et de parlementaire européen ont accentué cette perte d'implication des parlements nationaux.

Leur rôle se limite à contrôler l'activité du gouvernement national au sein du Conseil et à intervenir dans la transposition ou l'application du droit communautaire. Le contrôle de l'exécutif s'opère le plus souvent "a posteriori" sans que le parlement national puisse d'ailleurs faire revenir le gouvernement sur des positions adoptées au Conseil. En ce qui concerne l'application du droit communautaire, il convient de distinguer selon le type d'actes en cause. Les règlements, textes directement applicables, ne requièrent une intervention du législateur national que pour les mesures de sanction; encore le parlement national est-il assujetti, à cet égard, à une obligation de résultat consistant à garantir le plein effet du droit communautaire. La situation est certes plus nuancée pour les directives qui doivent être transposées en droit national. Mais, ici encore, il faut apprécier le rôle des parlements nationaux à sa juste mesure. Dans certains systèmes juridiques nationaux, à l'instar de l'ordre juridique luxembourgeois, la transposition des directives ne se fait pas nécessairement par le biais de la loi, mais peut se satisfaire d'actes réglementaires pris par le seul pouvoir exécutif. En outre, l'instrument juridique de la directive tend à se rapprocher, au niveau de son contenu, du règlement, ce qui confère à la loi nationale de transposition une fonction purement formelle[65].

Dans ce contexte, une des revendications majeures des parlements nationaux, y compris de la Chambre des Députés luxembourgeoise, est d'être associés plus intimement aux procédures décisionnelles communautaires[66]. Cette association devrait se traduire, d'un côté, par un pouvoir d'orientation, voire de direction, du parlement sur l'exécutif représentant l'Etat au Conseil, et, d'autre part, par un développement du partenariat entre les parlements nationaux et le Parlement européen[67]. Il faut toutefois être conscient des limites de telles revendications. Au niveau national, une implication plus forte du parlement national se heurte au principe des constitutions nationales selon lequel l'exécutif représente l'Etat dans les relations internationales. Au niveau de l'Union, une participation des parlements nationaux risque d'alourdir et de ralentir le processus décisionnel communautaire et de provoquer des conflits avec le Parlement européen.

b. Les fonctions européennes des administrations nationales

Fonctionnant d'après le système de la gestion administrative décentralisée, les Communautés font appel aux autorités administratives des Etats membres pour l'exécution du droit communautaire et cela quel que soit le type d'acte communautaire en cause, règlement ou directive. Les gouvernements des Etats membres assument, à cet égard, une fonction double difficilement conciliable avec le principe traditionnel de la séparation des fonctions, celle de (co)-législateur au niveau communautaire et celle d'exécutant au niveau national.

Cette structure a toutefois gouverné l'ordre juridique communautaire dès ses origines, sans poser le problème d'un fondement constitutionnel.

c. La protection judiciaire par les juridictions nationales: conflit de loyauté et problème de l'autonomie procédurale

Selon une formule consacrée, le juge national est juge de droit commun de l'application du droit communautaire. Sa fonction juridictionnelle est le corollaire de la fonction exécutive assumée par l'administration nationale. L'uniformité de l'application du droit communautaire est garantie par le mécanisme particulier de coopération entre le juge national et la Cour de justice que constitue le renvoi préjudiciel en interprétation ou en appréciation de validité du droit communautaire.

Les conflits éventuels entre droit communautaire et droit national, y compris constitutionnel, sont réglés, ainsi qu'il a été exposé ci-dessus, par une application des principes de la primauté et de l'effet direct du droit communautaire. Dans la logique du respect de ces principes, le juge luxembourgeois n'a jamais considéré qu'il se trouvait dans un conflit de loyauté. On peut, par ailleurs, formuler des réserves quant à l'utilisation de ce concept pour caractériser la situation du juge: le juge est placé, non pas devant un conflit de loyauté, mais devant un conflit de normes qui doit être tranché en application des principes de la hiérarchie des normes.

Plus délicate est la question de l'autonomie procédurale nationale.[68] La Cour de justice n'a cessé d'affirmer l'obligation, pour le juge national, d'assurer "l'application pleine et complète" du droit communautaire. Dès lors que l'effet direct d'une disposition de droit communautaire ne suffit pas à "assurer au particulier le bénéfice des droits que lui confère le droit communautaire" il appartient au juge national d'assurer l'effet du droit communautaire[69].Cette mission assignée au juge national se traduit par deux obligations précises.

Le juge national doit, d'abord, respecter le principe de l'équivalence, c'est-à-dire veiller à ce que l'exercice des voies de droit nationales, destinées à sauvegarder les droits issus du droit communautaire, ne soit pas plus difficile que l'exercice des recours visant à garantir les droits conférés par l'ordre juridique national.

Le juge national se voit encore imposer l'obligation de garantir l'effectivité du droit communautaire qui peut être mise en cause quand les procédures nationales rendent impossible ou excessivement difficile le respect des droits conférés au particulier par le droit communautaire[70].

Le respect de ce principe d'effectivité place le juge national dans une situation difficile dans la mesure où il devra éventuellement dépasser le cadre de ses pouvoirs juridictionnels tels que définis par le droit national. Différents problèmes particuliers peuvent être relevés, l'absence de procédures permettant l'accès du justiciable au juge, les limites procédurales à l'invocation des moyens tirés de la violation du droit communautaire, l'impossibilité de sauvegarder le droit communautaire en raison des délais de procédure, la difficulté pour le juge d'ordonner des mesures provisoires afin de garantir l'application du droit communautaire etc. Si l'on examine la jurisprudence, on peut constater que la problématique de l'autonomie procédurale nationale, bien réelle en théorie, n'a pas donné lieu, au Luxembourg, à des conflits dans la pratique, le système procédural national ayant permis, à ce jour, la sauvegarde pleine et entière du droit communautaire.

III. LE RÔLE DES RÉGIONS ET DES AUTORITÉS LOCALES

En raison des particularités d'ordre territorial et démographique, le Luxembourg ne connaît pas une structure fédérale ou décentralisée, de sorte que des commentaires sur la problématique soulevée sous ce point sont forcément limités. Deux remarques devraient toutefois être permises.

La seule collectivité territoriale connue de la constitution luxembourgeoise est la commune[71]. La discussion sur le rôle européen des collectivités sub-étatiques s'est focalisée, notamment en Allemagne, sur les Etats fédérés. Par contre, l'importance des villes et des communes dans les sociétés européennes et dans la future structure de l'Union a été largement passée sous silence. Or, dans une optique de subsidiarité, il conviendra de revoir les fonctions de la collectivité territoriale la plus proche du citoyen qu'est la commune, d'autant plus que cette collectivité assure la participation aux affaires publiques de tous les citoyens de l'Union qui y résident[72].

Par ailleurs, le Grand-Duché, Etat membre de l'Union, participe à un nouveau modèle de coopération supra-étatique, mais infra-communautaire, la "grande région" [73]. La coopération entre entités régionales de différents

Etats membres ouvre aux régions de nouvelles perspectives de nature à renforcer le rôle que le traité sur l'Union leur a déjà reconnu avec la création du comité des régions.

IV. CONCLUSIONS

Toute réflexion sur les perspectives d'avenir de l'Union, et plus concrètement sur une éventuelle nouvelle base constitutionnelle, doit partir du constat de l'acquis communautaire, présuppose une clarification au niveau de l'acception des concepts utilisés et requiert une mise au point des problèmes qui se posent.

La Cour de justice a reconnu, depuis longtemps, que les Communautés ont comme sujets non seulement les Etats mais également leurs ressortissants. Le renforcement du rôle législatif du Parlement européen et la consécration du concept de citoyenneté dans le traité de Maastricht a définitivement consacré cette double nature des Communautés ou de l'Union. La Cour a également reconnu aux traités fondateurs des Communautés, conclus par les Etats, une fonction constitutionnelle [74].

Si l'on entend dépasser le qualificatif de "constitutionnel" réservé aux traités instituant les Communautés ou l'Union, il faudra aborder la question de l'acception plurielle ou unique du terme de constitution. Dans une vision de pluralisme constitutionnel, "chacune des structures – infra-étatiques, para-étatiques, supra- étatiques - a sa propre constitution"[75]. La consécration du concept de constitution pour qualifier les textes de base de l'Union se résumerait dès lors à une question de formulation. Dans une optique plus traditionnelle, qui lie la notion de constitution à celle de l'Etat, doter l'Union d'une constitution signifierait qu'on la fait entrer dans le cadre des structures de nature étatique. Un tel choix suscitera inéluctablement le problème du positionnement des Etats membres par rapport à l'Union dans une structure constitutionnelle à deux niveaux. Le débat risquera toutefois de rester largement théorique sur arrière-plan de conceptions politiques, voire philosophiques, divergentes.

Ainsi qu'il apparaît des discussions qui ont d'ores et déjà eu lieu, y compris au niveau national luxembourgeois, derrière la question constitutionnelle se profilent une série de problèmes ponctuels. Il s'agit, pour l'essentiel, de la délimitation des compétences entre l'Union (y compris les Communautés) et les Etats et de la structure institutionnelle. Sans vouloir sous-estimer l'importance de ces problèmes, il faut reconnaître qu'ils ne sont pas nouveaux, mais ont tout au plus connu une nouvelle acuité avec le développement de l'intégration européenne et le projet d'élargissement.

Pour nombre d'ordres constitutionnels nationaux, y compris pour l'ordre constitutionnel luxembourgeois, les dispositions nationales sur l'abandon de compétences étatiques dans le processus d'intégration européenne sont inadaptées ou, en tout cas, dépassées. Une réflexion sur un ancrage plus clair de la construction européenne et de ses implications dans les constitutions nationales s'impose. Les amendements constitutionnels nationaux pourraient utilement être de la même teneur et devraient trouver un "répondant" au niveau des traités ou d'un nouveau traité "constitutionnel". En ce qui concerne la détermination des compétences, la communautarisation des piliers intergouvernementaux s'imposera à moyen terme. Pour le surplus, l'expérience de la construction européenne met en évidence qu'une délimitation rigide des compétences une fois pour toutes, s'avère impossible. Dès lors, l'approche traditionnelle, consistant à aborder, si nécessaire, les problèmes au niveau de la Communauté devrait continuer à prévaloir. Cette ouverture à un élargissement ponctuel des compétences exercées collectivement ne devrait pas empêcher d'affirmer la nécessaire sauvegarde de la qualité étatique des Etats membres et de donner au principe de subsidiarité une application effective.

En ce qui concerne les questions institutionnelles, la Conférence intergouvernementale de Nice a déjà fixé les orientations essentielles en maintenant le Conseil en tant que principal organe législatif, quitte à introduire, dans la perspective de l'élargissement, un mécanisme de double majorité. Le rôle du Parlement européen trouvera sa confirmation avec l'extension du régime de co-décision. Une des questions clés concerne l'association plus étroite des parlements nationaux au processus décisionnel notamment en tant que réponse aux critiques d'un déficit démocratique.

Les discussions autour du statut juridique à la Charte des droits fondamentaux ne répondent pas à un problème réel au niveau de la protection de ces droits, mais s'inscrivent dans une réflexion de philosophie politique.

La forme juridique sous laquelle toutes ces questions seront réglées, traité traditionnel ou traité complété par un acte d'une assemblée parlementaire européenne constituante, sera finalement secondaire. Cette question de la forme serait seulement pertinente si les Etats devaient définitivement abandonner leur pouvoir constituant à un organe représentatif des peuples européens ou si le principe de l'unanimité des Etats devait être abandonné. Pour l'heure, on s'accorde à admettre que le nouveau traité constitutionnel, pour reprendre l'expression consacrée par le président de la Convention, constituera un instrument classique de droit international qui devra être ratifié, dans chaque Etat, d'après les mécanismes constitutionnels en vigueur. Une ouverture du pouvoir constituant, qui associerait le Parlement européen aux Etats fondateurs, ne devrait pas porter à conséquence.

Plus délicate est l'idée de distinguer, dans le traité constitutionnel entre des dispositions fondamentales et des dispositions techniques et de soumettre la révision de ces dernières à des procédures simplifiées abandonnant, en particulier, l'accord unanime des Etats membres.

NOTES

* Premier avocat général à la Cour supérieure de justice de Luxembourg, chargé de cours au Centre universitaire de Luxembourg

[1] Voir les décisions "Solange-I" du Bundesverfassungsgericht du 29 mai 1974 BverfGE, 37,271 et "Solange- II du 22 octobre 1986 BverfGE 73, 339.
Voir les arrêts de la Corte costituzionale du 27 décembre 1973 , RTDE 1974, 148 et du 22 octobre 1975, RTDE 1976, 396.

[2] Arrêt de la Cour de cassation, chambre mixte, du 24 mai 1975, AJDA 1975, 567
Arrêts du Conseil d'Etat du 1er mars 1968, Syndicat national des fabricants de semoule de France, AJDA 1968, 235;
du 24 octobre 1989, Nicolo, Rec. 190 et du 24 septembre 1990, Boisdet, Rec. 250.

[3] Décisions du Conseil constitutionnel du 19 juin 1970 relative aux ressources propres et du 29-30 décembre 1976 relative à l'élection directe des membres du Parlement européen.

[4] Congrès de la FIDE à Berlin 1970, la coopération entre l'ordre juridique communautaire et les ordres juridiques nationaux; Congrès de la FIDE à Luxembourg 1973, jurisprudence sur les problèmes généraux de l'intégration; Congrès de la FIDE à Bruxelles 1975, droits fondamentaux.

[5] Pour la France, décisions du Conseil constitutionnel des 9 avril 1992, JORF 11 avril 1992, p. 5354; 2 septembre 1992, JORF 3 septembre 1992, p. 12095; 23 septembre 1992, JORF 25 septembre 1992, p. 13337.

Loi constitutionnelle du 25 juin 1992 introduisant dans la constitution française le titre XVI "des Communautés européennes et de l'Union européenne"

Pour l'Allemagne, décision du Bundesverfassungsgericht du 18 octobre 1993, BverfGE 89, 155

Gesetz zur Änderung des Grundgesetzes du 21 décembre 1992, reformulant les articles 23 et suivants, BGBl I, p. 2086.

[6] La déclaration n° 23 relative à l'avenir de l'Union européenne , annexée au traité de Nice, prévoit, au point 5, un "processus (qui) devrait porter, entre autres, sur les questions suivantes:

- ... une délimitation plus précise des compétences entre l'Union européenne et les Etats membres, qui soit conforme au principe de subsidiarité;
- le statut de la Charte des droits fondamentaux de l'Union européenne ...
- simplifier les traités afin qu'ils soient plus clairs et mieux compris, sans en changer le sens;:
- le rôle des parlements nationaux dans l'architecture européenne."

[7] Les conclusions adoptées lors des Conseils européens peuvent être consultées, en version intégrale, sur le site Internet de l'Union européenne.

[8] A noter que, dans son discours "Humboldt" de mai 2000, le ministre allemand des Affaires étrangères, J. Fischer avait présenté sa conception d'une constitution européenne. Cette question a également été au centre du discours du Président français J. Chirac devant le Bundestag en juin 2000.

[9] L'existence et l'intensité des débats s'explique par la situation démographique

particulière du Luxembourg qui comporte une proportion importante de résidents étrangers, dont la grande majorité sont des ressortissants communautaires.

[10] Révision constitutionnelle du 23 décembre 1994 modifiant l'article 9 de la Constitution luxembourgeoise (Mém. A – 116, p. 2732). Alors que la disposition ancienne réservait les droits politiques aux nationaux, le texte nouveau prévoit que "la loi peut conférer l'exercice de droits politiques à des non-Luxembourgeois".

[11] Voir le rapport luxembourgeois présenté par L. Frieden, rapports de la FIDE 1996, p. 344 et ss.

[12] P. Majerus, l'Etat luxembourgeois, Luxembourg 1983, p.23.

[13] P. Pescatore, Introduction à la science du droit, Luxembourg 1978, p. 11. De façon significative, l'auteur, spécialiste de droit international, ajoute aux fonctions de la constitution celle de définir les relations entre l'Etat et les autres entités, en particulier celles du droit international.

[14] La Constitution ne parle pas expressis verbis du pouvoir exécutif, mais vise les prérogatives du Grand-Duc, dont le pouvoir exécutif constitue la prérogative essentielle.

[15] P. Pescatore, Essai sur la notion de la loi, Livre jubilaire du Conseil d'Etat, Luxembourg 1957, p. 365 et ss.

[16] Devant les difficultés qu'engendre cette procédure dans l'hypothèse où la ratification d'un traité international requiert une révision constitutionnelle, des propositions de modification de l'article 114 ont été faites. Voir la proposition de révision n° 4154 du 2 avril 1996 qui visait à prévoir, dans un article 114bis nouveau, la possibilité de procéder de suite à la révision de la Constitution dès lors qu'une disposition d'un traité à approuver est contraire à la Constitution. A la suite de l'avis négatif du Conseil d'Etat quant à une dualité des mécanismes de révision, une nouvelle proposition de révision n° 4765 a été déposée le 13 février 2001. Cette proposition prévoit une modification de l'article 114 en ce sens qu'une révision de la Constitution peut intervenir sans dissolution préalable de la Chambre. Les droits du peuple électeur devraient être sauvegardés par la possibilité de recourir, sous certaines conditions, à un référendum sur la proposition de révision de la Constitution.

[17] Constitution dite d'états octroyée le 12 octobre 1841 par le Roi-Grand-Duc Guillaume Ier. Jusqu'à cette époque, le Luxembourg était administré de fait comme province des Pays-Bas, sous le Grondwet de 1815.

[18] Ces réflexions sont tirées du rapport luxembourgeois présenté à la Conférence des Cours à compétence constitutionnelle de septembre 1997, rapport rédigé par G. Reiland et G. Wivenes, Pasicrisie luxembourgeoise (Pas.) T. 30, p. 33 et ss.

[19] Actuel article 92 de la constitution néerlandaise.

[20] Actuel article 34 de la constitution belge.

[21] Compte-rendu des séances de la Chambre des Députés 1953/1954, volume II, p. 798 et ss; 1955/1956, volume II, p. CLXXIV et ss.

[22] Dans la constitution belge, la disposition sur le transfert d'attributions étatiques suit l'article sur la souveraineté de la nation. Il s'agit des articles 33 et 34 du texte constitutionnel actuel.

[23] Voir Marc Thewes, La constitution luxembourgeosie et l'Europe, Annales de droit luxembourgeois, 1992, p. 65.

[24] Voir à cet égard l'article 55 de la Constitution française et les articles 10 et 11 de la constitution italienne.

[25] Ces réflexions sont tirées de la contribution luxembourgeoise à une étude "Europäische Integration und nationales Verfassungsrecht", Nomos, 1995, pp. 303 à 346, par Georges Wivenes

[26] Voir les travaux préparatoires de la loi d'approbation du traité de Maastricht: l'avis du Conseil d'Etat n°3601-1 du 26 mai 1992 et le rapport de la Commission spéciale de la Chambre des Députés n° 3601-2 du 24 juin 1992.

[27] Le Conseil d'Etat luxembourgeois a considéré que les textes pertinents du traité de Maastricht s'analysent "d'une part en un engagement de l'Etat de prendre dans un délai déterminé les dispositions nécessaires pour atteindre le résultat projeté et, d'autre part, en un transfert de compétence au Conseil de la Communauté à l'effet de concrétiser les modalités requises pour réaliser l'objectif recherché, ce transfert devant s'opérer dans le cadre de l'article 49bis de la Constitution".

Le Conseil d'Etat belge avait souligné que si "l'article 25bis (actuellement article 34, disposition équivalant à l'article 49bis luxembourgeois) permet à un traité auquel la Belgique est partie ou à la loi belge d'attribuer des compétences particulières aux autorités communautaires, ... il ne saurait, par contre, justifier l'octroi aux citoyens européens de droits politiques qui leur permettent de concourir à l'organisation de conseils communaux".

[28] Voir Ernest Arendt, Le traité de l'Union européenne et la Constitution du Grand-duché de Luxembourg, Annales de droit luxembourgeois 1992, p. 35. L'auteur, tout en justifiant la démarche du législateur par des considérations pratiques, qualifie la loi d'approbation parlementaire du traité de Maastricht de loi inélégante.

[29] L'article 23 du Grundgesetz, introduit par la loi de révision constitutionnelle du 21 décembre 1992, consacre l'édification d'une Europe unie comme objectif constitutionnel (Verfassungsziel), souligne les principes fédératifs auxquels est attachée l'Union et rappelle la possibilité de transférer des droits de souveraineté, possibilité déjà prévue dans le texte général ancien de l'article 24.

Le titre XV de la constitution française, introduit par la loi de révision constitutionnelle n° 92-554 du 25 juin 1992, consacre, à l'article 88-1, la participation de la République aux Communautés européennes et à l'Union européenne. Il est précisé que les Etats membres ont choisi "d'exercer en commun certaines de leurs compétences". L'article 88-2 autorise le transfert de compétences pour l'établissement de l'union économique et monétaire ainsi que pour la réalisation de la libre circulation des personnes.

[30] En application de la Convention du 21 juillet 1921 établissant une union économique entre le Grand-Duché et la Belgique, de larges domaines de la souveraineté monétaire étaient exercés par la Belgique avec laquelle le Luxembourg se trouvait en union monétaire.

[31] Sur 89.654 questionnaires envoyés, 9037 ont été retournés, soit 4,8%. 66% des questionnaires ont été dépouillés pour l'analyse. Malgré le nombre peu élevé de réponses, qui met en évidence un certain désintérêt de l'opinion publique par rapport à la problématique, les organisateurs ont considéré que l'échantillon était représentatif pour ce genre d'enquête et permettait de tirer des conclusions valables

Le rapport de synthèse du débat sur l'avenir de l'Europe peut être consulté sur le site Internet du Gouvernement luxembourgeois http://gouvernement.lu

[32] Alors que 73% des personnes interrogées se déclarent attachées à leur pays d'origine, 9 % indiquent appartenir d'abord à l'Europe; 12 % optent pour une appartenance "plurielle", Etat, région, Europe. 60% des intéressés déclarent leur adhésion à l'Europe, 25% expriment leur méfiance. 42% des personnes ayant répondu associent l'Europe à la paix et à la prospérité, 27% à la prospérité économique.

[33] A noter que le gouvernement national, avec 40% de vote de confiance, l'emporte largement et que le Parlement national se situe à peu près au même niveau que le Parlement européen (16,05% pour le Parlement national, 17,74% pour le Parlement européen).

[34] De façon surprenante, la Communauté "l'emporte" pour une série de politiques pour lesquelles elle n'a, pour l'heure, que des compétences limitées ou partagées avec les Etats, la justice (50%), la politique étrangère (51%), l'environnement (54%), la défense (56%), la santé publique (57%), la sécurité alimentaire (69%), la recherche (72%), l'énergie (73%).

[35] 57% souhaitent un renforcement des moyens d'action de la Commission et 67% de ceux du Parlement européen; 57% veulent le statu quo pour le Conseil; 80% souhaitent un rôle plus important pour les Parlements nationaux. L'"idée d'une seconde chambre représentative des Etats recueille l'adhésion de 52% des personnes interrogées. 56% sont favorables à une constitution européenne, 49% à une fédération. L'évaluation de ces résultats est très aléatoire, faute de précision des concepts en cause.

[36] Voir: le discours du Premier Ministre Jean-Claude Juncker "Mes convictions pour l'Europe" à la Maison du Grand-Duché de Luxembourg à Bruxelles en date du 15 mai 2001; la contribution de Madame Lydie Polfer, ministre des Affaires étrangères, au débat sur l'avenir de l'Europe; les interventions de M. Jacques Santer, eprésentant du gouvernement à la Convention sur l'avenir de l'Europe, en date des 21 mars, 15 avril, 24 mai et 6 juin 2002.

Tous ces textes sont publiés sur le site Internet du gouvernement luxembourgeois. Voir les interventions de M. Paul Helminger, député libéral, représentant de la Chambre des Députés à la Convention sur l'avenir de l'Europe en date du 22 mars et de M. Ben Fayot, député socialiste, représentant de la Chambre des Députés à ladite Convention en date des 15 et 16 avril 2002.

[37] Voir le discours du Premier Ministre et les interventions de M. Santer, précités.

[38] Selon le Premier Ministre, " que l'Europe ait deux chambres au niveau de l'échelon législatif ou une chambre, que cette deuxième chambre soit composée de ministres nationaux, que nous appelions la Commission dans le futur exécutif renforcé ou gouvernement européen, cela importe finalement très peu. Mettons-nous d'accord sur ce que nous voulons faire et nous trouverons les institutions qui nous permettront de réaliser ce sur quoi nous nous serons mis d'accord."

Selon le Ministre des affaires étrangères, "les questions institutionnelles ont leur importance, certes. Il faut, toutefois, éviter d'en faire un objectif en soi. Les institutions et les instruments sont les outils au service d'une cause."

[39] Dans le débat d'orientation sur l'évolution de l'Union européenne dans le contexte de la Conférence intergouvernementale, les représentants de tous les groupes parlementaires ont souligné l'importance d'une représentation suffisante du Luxembourg dans toutes les institutions des Communautés.

La Chambre a voté, à l'unanimité, une motion dans laquelle elle se prononce

- pour une Commission se composant d'un national de chaque Etat membre,
- pour un régime de pondération des voix au Conseil dans l'approche d'une double majorité garantissant le respect de la double nature de l'Union , union des Etats et union des peuples,
- pour un maintien de la règle de l'unanimité pour les dispositions à caractère constitutionnel ou institutionnel , la sécurité sociale et la fiscalité,
- pour le maintien du régime actuel de composition de la Cour de Justice et de la Cour des Comptes (compte-rendu des débats de la Chambre des Députés, 7e séance du 26 octobre 2000, pp. 239 et ss, notamment p. 284)

[40] Voir les interventions des membres luxembourgeois de la Convention sur l'avenir de l'Europe, citées ci-dessus. Voir le débat sur la politique étrangère de la Chambre des Députés, 43e et 44e séances du 21 mars 2002, compte-rendu des débats de la Chambre des Députés pp. 1601 et ss.

Dans une motion, adoptée à l'unanimité, la Chambre vise la révision des traités, y compris la question d'une constitution européenne, en exigeant une implication de la société civile, du Parlement européen et des parlements nationaux (p. 1645).

Le Premier Ministre, dans son discours précité, voudrait éviter "l'impression qu'il y aurait une Europe avec une constitution propre et des peuples à côté avec des constitutions nationales" et préconise l'intégration de "l'acquis des négociations ... dans les constitutions nationales".

[41] Arrêt de la Cour de justice du 5 février 1963, Van Gend & Loos, 26/62, Rec. p.1. Il est intéressant de relever que la Cour opère cette qualification pour asseoir ou renforcer l'application, en droit communautaire, d'une institution traditionnelle du droit international, à savoir celle de l'effet direct.

[42] A noter que dans l'ordonnance du 13 juillet 1990, Zwartveld, (C-2/88 Imm, Rec. p. I-3365) la Cour de justice avait déjà consacré une lecture bilatérale de l'obligation de loyauté inscrite à l'article 10 du traité CE.

[43] Ce principe a soulevé, au moment où il a été consacré, de nombreux commentaires, tantôt favorables tantôt hostiles. Voir, pour la doctrine luxembourgeoise, G. Wivenes, Le principe de la subsidiarité, rapport luxembourgeois au XVIe Congrès de la FIDE, Rome 1994, volume I, p. 331,;P. Pescatore, Mit der Subsidiarität leben, Festschrift U. Everling, 1996; F. Thoma, Le principe de subsidiarité en droit communautaire, Publications du Centre universitaire de Luxembourg, 1998.

Il est intéressant de relever que, dans son intervention devant la Convention, le représentant du gouvernement luxembourgeois Jacques Santer se réfère, à nouveau, à ce principe.

[44] Arrêt de la Cour de justice du 2 juillet 1996, Commission c. Grand-Duché de Luxembourg, C-473/93, Rec. p. I- 3207.

[45] Arrêt de la Cour de justice du 28 novembre 1989, Groener, C-379/87, Rec. p. I-3967. Dans cet arrêt, la Cour avait reconnu que des exigences linguistiques spécifiques à un Etat, en l'occurrence l'Irlande, pouvaient, sous certaines conditions, être invoquées comme entraves justifiées à la liberté de circulation.

[46] Voir les articles 5 et 6 de la Charte des Nations Unies ou encore l'article 8 du Statut du Conseil de l'Europe; voir le système de sanction des violations des droits de l'homme instauré dans la Convention européenne.

[47] Le "cas autrichien" est plus que significatif à cet égard.

48 Loi de révision constitutionnelle du 12 juillet 1997 introduisant dans la Constitution l'article 95 ter prévoyant une Cour constitutionnelle qui est saisie à titre préjudiciel pour statuer sur la conformité des lois avec la Constitution; Mémorial A n° 45.

Loi du 27 juillet 1997 portant organisation de la Cour constitutionnelle, Mémorial A n° 58.

49 Voir, parmi une doctrine nombreuse, Jean-Claude Wiwinius, L'application de l'article 6, paragraphe 1, de la Convention de sauvegarde des droits de l'homme et des libertés fondamentales par les juridictions luxembourgeoises, Pasicrisie, T 31, p. 209.

50 Il n'y a pas lieu de commenter, dans le cadre de cette contribution, les réactions, fort divergentes il est vrai, d'auteurs, de journalistes ou d'hommes politiques vis-à-vis du contenu de la Charte. Le fait est que les délégués luxembourgeois à la Convention, auteur de la Charte, l'ont acceptée et que ni le gouvernement ni le Parlement n'ont émis des réserves par rapport aux droits reconnus dans ce texte.

51 Le système prévu dans la Charte ne fait que confirmer la jurisprudence traditionnelle de la Cour d'après laquelle les Etats membres sont tenus au respect des droits fondamentaux protégés dans l'ordre juridique communautaire, lorsqu'ils agissent dans le cadre du droit : Voir les arrêts de la Cour de justice du 13 juillet 1989, Wachauf, 5/88, rec. p. 2609; du 18 juin 1991, ERT, C-260/89, Rec. p. I-2925; du 13 avril 2000, Karlsson, C-292/97, Rec. p. I-2737.

52 Il est vrai que les avocats généraux, dans leurs conclusions, se sont référés à la Carte des droits fondamentaux. On peut citer, en particulier, l'avocat général P. Léger qui, dans ses conclusions dans l'affaire C-353/99 P, considère que la "nature des droits énoncés dans la charte .. interdit de la considérer comme une simple énumération sans conséquence de principes purement moraux". La Cour de justice s'est toutefois abstenue de suivre ses avocats généraux.

53 Dans une déclaration faite, le 26 juin 2002 à l'occasion d'une visite au Conseil de l'Europe, le Premier ministre luxembourgeois s'est prononcé pour la solution d'une adhésion de la Communauté à la Convention européenne.

La conférence intergouvernementale de 2004 pourrait d'ailleurs lever les obstacles constitutionnels à une adhésion que la Cour de justice a relevés dans l'avis 2/94 du 28 mars 1996.

54 Les commentaires qui suivent constituent une version adaptée de la contribution de l'auteur du présent rapport au colloque organisé en décembre 2000 par la Cour de cassation française sur le thème l'application des principes généraux du droit communautaire par les juridictions luxembourgeoises, Pasicrisie T. 31, p. 239

55 Arrêt de cassation de la Cour supérieure de justice du 17 juin 1890, Pas. T. 11, p. 620, qui fait expressément référence au principe de l'exécution des conventions.

56 Pierre Pescatore : L'autorité, en droit interne, des traités internationaux, Pas. T 18, p. 97.

57 Arrêt de cassation de la Cour supérieure de justice du 8 juin 1950, Pas. T. 15, p. 41; arrêt du Conseil d'Etat (CE) du 28 juillet 1951, Pas. T. 15, p. 263.

58 Jugement du 29 mai 1963 du Tribunal d'arrondissement de Luxembourg, décision de renvoi dans l'affaire 101/63, Bulletin Cercle F. Laurent, 1963, n° 8, p. 389.

59 Arrêt de cassation de la Cour supérieure de justice du 12 juin 1969, Pas. T 21,

p. 107; arrêt rendu en considération de l'arrêt de la Cour de justice des CE du 5 juillet 1967, De Moor, 2/67, Rec. p. 256; voir également jugement du tribunal d'arrondissement de Luxembourg, jugement de renvoi dans l'aff. 10/71, qui expose que le droit international doit avoir la primauté sur le droit national interne, de sorte qu'en cas de conflit entre les deux droits ou entre deux normes précises de l'un et de l'autre, le droit communautaire est à appliquer par préférence au droit national interne.

[60] Arrêt du Conseil d'Etat du 21 novembre 1984, Pas. T. 25, p. 174.

[61] Arrêt du Conseil d'Etat du 7 décembre 1978, Pas. T 24, p. 186.

[62] Arrêt de la Cour de cassation de la CSJ du 14 juillet 1954, Pagani, Pas. T. 16, p. 150.

[63] Arrêt de la Cour d'appel, n° 396/01V, du 13 novembre 2001, R. c W. non publié.

La Cour d'appel se prononce comme suit: " étant donné que, une fois le traité approuvé et ratifié conformément aux procédures constitutionnelles et aux règles de droit international, l'Etat est engagé sur le plan international et ne peut pas, en application de la Convention de Vienne sur le droit des traités, invoquer les dispositions de son droit interne pour justifier la non-exécution d'un traité, la norme de droit international conventionnel d'effet direct doit prévaloir sur la norme de droit interne, peu importe sa nature législative ou constitutionnelle".

L'arrêt fait actuellement l'objet d'un pourvoi en cassation.

[64] Voir la proposition de révision de l'article 114 de la Constitution, note de bas de page n° 17.

[65] La position réservée manifestée par la Chambre des Députés luxembourgeoise par rapport à la transposition de la directive 98/44/CE du Parlement européen et du Conseil ,du 6 juillet 1998, relative à la protection juridique des inventions biotechnologiques est une illustration récente de cette problématique. Critiquant le fait que la directive permettrait de breveter le vivant humain, la Chambre a déclaré vouloir s'écarter du texte de la directive au niveau de la loi luxembourgeoise de transposition. Quelle que soit la valeur des arguments éthiques invoqués, cette attitude doit s'analyser, juridiquement, en une méconnaissance du droit communautaire. A l'inverse, si le parlement national assumait son obligation juridique de transposer la directive dans toute sa teneur, pourrait-on raisonnablement considérer qu'il confère au texte communautaire une certaine légitimité?

[66] Lors du débat annuel sur la politique étrangère en 2001, la revendication d'une clarification et d'un renforcement du rôle des parlements nationaux dans la structure de l'Union a été clairement rappelée, ceci notamment pour la future conférence intergouvernementale (voir compte-rendu analytique des débats, 43e et 44e séances, mercredi 21 mars, notamment l'intervention du député Paul Helminger, p. 1618, et la motion présentée par le député Ben Fayot, adoptée à l'unanimité par la Chambre, p. 1645).

Voir également la contribution du député Ben Fayot, en date des 15 et 16 avril 2002, à la Convention sur l'avenir de l'Europe. Pour s'assurer que l'Union respecte l'identité nationale des Etats et n'empiète pas sur les compétences essentielles des membres, le représentant de la Chambre des Députés préconise, pour chaque mission nouvelle de l'Union une discussion et décision "soit dans les parlements nationaux, gardiens de la souveraineté nationale, soit dans une convention ad hoc".

[67] Voir, à cet égard, le rôle de la Conférence des commissions des affaires européennes des Parlements nationaux des Etats membres et du Parlement européen (COSAC), qui a été souligné lors du débat d'orientation sur l'évolution de l'Union européenne dans le contexte de la Conférence intergouvernementale, compte-rendu analytique des débats, 7e séance, 26 octobre 2000, notamment l'intervention de la députée Lydie Err, p. 254.

[68] Les commentaires qui suivent constituent une version adaptée de la contribution de l'auteur du présent rapport au colloque organisé en décembre 2000 par la Cour de cassation française sur l'application des principes généraux du droit communautaire par les juridictions luxembourgeoises, Pasicrisie T. 31, p. 239.

[69] Arrêt de la Cour de justice du 5 mars 1996, Brasserie du pêcheur (C-46/93, Rec. p. I-1029),

[70] Arrêt de la Cour de justice du 15 mai 1986, Johnston (222/84, Rec. p. 1651), relatif au contrôle juridictionnel effectif du principe d'égalité de traitement entre hommes et femmes; arrêt de la Cour de justice du 19 juin 1990, Factortame (C-213/89, Rec. p. I-2433), relatif à la compétence des juridictions nationales pour ordonner des mesures provisoires en cas de renvoi préjudiciel; arrêt du 17 novembre 1991, Francovich (C-6/90 et C-9/90, Rec. p. I-5337) et arrêt du 5 mars 1996, Brasserie du pêcheur, précité, relatifs à la responsabilité de l'Etat pour violation du droit communautaire; arrêt du 16 mai 2000, Shirley Preston (C-78/98, Rec. p. I-3201), où la Cour parle expressément des principes d'effectivité et d'équivalence.

[71] Article 107 de la Constitution.

[72] Dans son intervention devant la Convention, le député Paul Helminger, bourgmestre de la ville de Luxembourg, insiste sur le rôle des autorités locales pour répondre aux problèmes de la société européenne.

[73] Initialement limitée à la Sarre, à la Lorraine et au Luxembourg, sous l'appellation Saar-Lor-Lux, cette structure s'est étendue à la Wallonie (et aux Communautés française et germanophone de Belgique) ainsi qu'à la Rhénanie-Palatinat.

[74] Arrêt de la Cour de justice du 5 février 1963, Van Gend & Loos, 26/62, Rec. p. 1. Selon la formule célèbre, " la Communauté (économique) européenne constitue un nouvel ordre juridique de droit international, au profit duquel les Etats membres ont limité, bien que dans des domaines restreints, leurs droits souverains et dont les sujets sont non seulement les Etats membres mais également leurs ressortissants. ...."

Arrêt de la Cour de justice du 23 avril 1986, Les Verts / Parlement, 294/83, Rec. p. 1339. Dans ce arrêt, la Cour dit que "la Communauté .. européenne est une communauté de droit en ce que ni ses Etats membres ni ses institutions n'échappent au contrôle de la conformité de leurs actes à la charte constitutionnelle de base qu'est le traité ...."

[75] Pierre Pescatore: La constitution, son contenu, son utilité, Revue de droit suisse, 1992, p. 41, plus particulièrement p. 43.

THE NETHERLANDS

European Union Law and National Constitutions

Rapporteur
prof.dr. Constantijn A.J.M. Kortmann

I. INTRODUCTION: FOUNDATIONS OF EUROPEAN CONSTITUTIONALISM

1. Concept of constitution in the Netherlands

a. Theoretical concepts and basic notions

The Netherlands possesses a written, rigid Constitution (Grondwet), originally dating from 1814. It has been amended several times. In 1983, a general revision took place, but its main features still date from 1848. The underlying principles are: constitutional monarchy, representative democracy, separation of powers and checks and balances, decentralisation and, finally, the rule of law (rechtsstaat, Etat de Droit, Rechtsstaat). The Constitution is not preceded by "ideological" or "philosophical" principles or declarations, like popular or people's sovereignty,[1] nor does one find any reference to such principles in the text of the Constitution itself. It has a pragmatic character, comparable to the Danish Grundlov, for example.

According to the dominant doctrine, constitutional law of the Netherlands does not only comprise the Constitution in its formal sense. The following are also deemed to be part of constitutional law: the Charter for the Kingdom (a sort of superconstitution governing the federation-like relationship between the European Netherlands, the Dutch Antilles and Aruba), so-called organic regulations, such as the Provinces Act and the Municipalities Act, judge-made law, constitutional conventions, and parts of international and supranational law, especially Community law and the European Convention on Human Rights.[2]

b. The EU/EC architecture and national constitutional traditions

For a long time, the Netherlands constitutional tradition has been one of openness towards international law.[3] Since a revision of the Constitution in

1953, its text explicitly permits transfers of national competences to international organisations. If such a transfer would deviate from the Constitution, it requires no more than an authorisation by Act of Parliament, approved by a two-thirds majority in both Houses of Parliament. Thus, a prior amendment of the Constitution, although possible, is not required. There have been only three such deviations since 1953. Treaties such as the EEC-Treaty and its later amendments have never required the qualified majority of two-thirds of the votes cast.

Concerning the relationship between international law and domestic law, the Netherlands adheres to a monistic system: international law is "automatically" part of the national legal system. Moreover, according to article 94 of the Constitution, directly applicable international law prevails over all domestic law, including the Constitution.

With respect to EC law, it is commonly accepted that it prevails over domestic law. Even without the articles 93 and 94, governing the relationship between international law and national law, EC law would still be national law and prevail over that law. The famous Van Gend and Loos and Costa ENEL rulings of the Court of Justice of the European Communities have been accepted without significant resistance. So, it can be said that the EC/EU architecture did not and does not meet any serious constitutional obstacle.

2. *National conditions for the adoption of a "Constitution" of the European Union*

a. *Constitutional conditions for and limits to further integration (substance)*

The Netherlands Constitution neither mentions nor protects concepts such as national sovereignty, parliamentary sovereignty or, in German terminology, "Staatlichkeit". Therefore, any treaty could limit or even abrogate national competences and structures. However, depending on the content of the relevant treaty dispositions, it could deviate from (articles of) the Constitution, such as those protecting fundamental rights. In these cases the above mentioned authorisation by a two-thirds majority, or a revision of the Constitution, would be required.

According to several opinions of the Council of State (the principal Government advisory body), and in the opinion of the Dutch Government and Parliament, deviation from the Constitution means deviation from specific articles of the written Constitution. So, arguments based on the history, the nature or the character of the Constitution or of the constitutional order to defend the thesis of deviation from the Constitution are constitutionally neither convincing nor decisive.

b. Procedural requirements under national constitutional provisions

Articles 90 ff. of the Dutch Constitution regulate the treaty-making process from a national perspective. Treaty-making power belongs to the Government (i.e. the King and one or more responsible ministers). In principle, treaties must be approved by Parliament. The approval may be tacit or by Act of Parliament. In the latter case the bill is approved or rejected by an ordinary majority of the votes cast. As said before, a two-thirds majority is required in the case of deviation from the Constitution by the treaty. Nevertheless, the question of whether a treaty contains a deviation from the Constitution is decided by an ordinary majority. So, in practice an ordinary majority in Parliament decides whether the Government is entitled to ratify a treaty, notwithstanding its possible deviation from the Constitution.

c. The role of the citizens: international treaty or European social contract?

Here, the author of this report encounters some difficulty in the questionnaire submitted to him. He supposes that "European social contract" has a meaning similar to that of Rousseau's "contrat social", but Dutch constitutional law is not based – either in positive law, or in the doctrine – on the idea of popular sovereignty. Dutch democracy is basically a representative democracy, although an abrogating consultative referendum is possible since 1 January 2002. This could be used for an Act of Parliament which authorises the ratification of a treaty, whether or not concerning the EC or EU. Outside of this possibility for the exercise of direct democracy, the creation of a "European Constitution" would be based on an international treaty.

3. The constitution-making process: preparing the IGC 2004 in practice

a. How is the international debate on the future of the European Union organised?

The Dutch debate on the future of the European Union is to a great extent purely a governmental and parliamentary one. The Treaties of Maastricht and Amsterdam, although negotiated in the Netherlands, have hardly been discussed in Dutch society. The same is true for the Treaty of Nice. The Council of State in its advice on the Treaty of Nice remarks that the public and political debate on Europe is meagre.[4] One may find articles written by lawyers and (other) experts in reviews on European politics and European law, but they rarely result in fundamental discussions about the EC or EU and their future.[5] So we can concentrate on observations on the activities of the Dutch Government and Parliament and describe how they have proceeded during the last two decades.

Except for the conclusion of treaties as such, no constitutional or legal provision prescribes any co-operation between Government and Parliament concerning the preparation of treaties or intergovernmental conferences. All depends on the free will of both.[6]

During the intergovernmental conferences to prepare the Maastricht Treaty, the Government informed Parliament regularly about the difficulties met and the progress made. Several standing committees of the Tweede Kamer (Dutch House of Commons) held discussions with ministers involved in the conferences, but the draft-treaty was not submitted to Parliament. In the end, the Chambers discussed only the Bill authorising the ratification of the Treaty.

During the preparations of the Treaty of Amsterdam, the Government literally buried Parliament in information, consisting of "verkennende"[7] and other governmental notes and papers. Some of these were debated on the floor, others in (standing) committees. Parliament could not and did not complain of a lack of information or debate. Later on, during the review of the Bill authorising the ratification of the Amsterdam Treaty, the Second Chamber asked the Government more than 400 questions, which were answered within a few months. The conclusion may be that the information and debates concerning both Treaties have been ample and intense. The same is globally true for the Treaty of Nice.

In addition to these procedures, the regular parliamentary activities were and are frequently focused on developments[8] within the EC/EU. The annual debate on the budget provides information about future government policy. Annually, within the framework of the budget, the cabinet delivers a document entitled "De staat van de Europese Unie", which "provides a survey of the financial and policy implications of European decision-making, and an overview of future government policy and the financial consequences for the forthcoming years". Recently, the cabinet added a notice on "De toekomst van de Europese Unie",[9] in which it develops several ideas on the future of the EU.

b. Key issues and proposals of the leading political groups

In May 2002, general elections for the Second Chamber will be called. This enables the author to describe the recent standpoints in the respective (draft) electoral programmes of the main political groups in the Netherlands. These groups are the Socialists (Partij van de Arbeid), the Liberal-Conservatives (Volkspartij voor Vrijheid en Democratie), and the Christian-Democrats (Christen-Democratisch Appel).

The "Partij van de Arbeid" emphasises the need for a clearer distribution of competences between the EU and the Member States based on the subsidiarity principle, more democracy within the EU, and more effective decision-making by decreasing unanimity rules. They call for direct election of the President of the Commission and the introduction of a so-called corrective referendum. It should be possible for the European Parliament to dismiss individual members of the Commission, which in its turn should be enabled to dissolve the European Parliament. All this should finally lead to a European Constitution.

The "Volkspartij voor Vrijheid en Democratie" also emphasises the subsidiarity principle, but is opposed to fixing a distribution of competences between the EU and the Member States. However, with the Socialists, they plead for more effective decision-making by qualified majority voting and a stronger role for the European Parliament. There is no mention of a future European Constitution.

The Christian Democrats consider the EU as a federal Union of states based on such values as democracy, solidarity, justice, equality and durability. The EU must strictly observe the subsidiarity principle, and a clear distinction of competences has to be established. The members of the Commission should be individually responsible and the European Parliament should be competent to dismiss any individual member of the Commission. Decision-making should take place by qualified majority voting in a co-decision procedure with the European Parliament. The electoral programme of the Christian Democrats does not mention a future European Constitution.

This overview of the standpoints of the main political parties would not be complete without referring to the opinion of the actual government.[10] Government opts for a "European Constitution for an effective and democratic Union". Its main elements should be: fundamental rights; a clear distribution of powers based on the subsidiarity principle; simplification of the European treaties and splitting them up into a basic constitutional treaty and a "policy treaty"; further integration; strengthening of the Commission and the European Parliament; individual responsibility of the members of the Commission; direct election of the President of the Commission; more decision-making in the Council by a qualified majority; strengthening of the role of national parliaments within the European architecture.

II. RELATIONSHIP AND INTERACTION OF EC/EU LAW AND THE NETHERLANDS CONSTITUTION TODAY

1. Member States' constitutional autonomy under European constraints

a. National identity of the Netherlands (article 6.3 TEU) as a limit to the extension of EC/EU competences

Article 6.3 TEU is formulated as a barrier against the destruction of the national identity of the Member States by the European Union. It is not an obstacle to the Member States' transferring (many of) their competences to the EC/EU. The significance of this barrier, however, is not at all clear. One of the possible interpretations is that the Member States of the EU must remain "states" and that they may not be transformed into component parts of a federation.[11] The opinion of different Dutch governments on the future of the EC/EU seems to attach little value to such an article. Since the beginning of the EC, the majority of the Dutch politicians have always emphasised the final goal of a European Federation. In a "real" federation, the component parts loose their "state-hood", being subject to a federal Constitution. Whatever the meaning of article 6.3 TEU may be, the Luxembourg Court is not competent to condemn the EU institutions because of a breach of article 6.3 TEU. And under Dutch constitutional law, no judge could forbid the political institutions to give up the identity of the Kingdom by means of a treaty.

b. Articles 6.1 and 7 TEU as limits to the constitutional autonomy of the Netherlands

Theoretically article 6.1 TEU could be considered as a limit to the constitutional autonomy of the Netherlands. But in reality it is not. The Dutch Constitution contains several articles that guarantee freedom (i.e. fundamental rights, independent and impartial administration of justice, free and secret elections), democracy (i.e. direct elections for the Lower House), the respect of fundamental rights (i.e. Chapter 1 of the Constitution). Under the national constitutional and legal system it seems very improbable that the Dutch public authorities should seriously and persistently breach one of the principles mentioned in article 6.1 TEU. One should also take into consideration that the Kingdom of the Netherlands ratified the European Convention on Human Rights which, according to the monistic system concerning international treaties, is automatically part of the Dutch legal system.

2. Common values: the Charter of Fundamental Rights of the European Union

a. Does the Charter reflect the basic human rights standards of the Dutch Constitution and international law?

In the Dutch legal system, human rights are guaranteed by different means. Chapter 1 of the Constitution contains a large number of "classical" and social fundamental rights. Moreover, the European Convention on Human Rights, the European Social Charter, the International Convenant on Civil and Political Rights, and the International Convenant on Economic, Social and Cultural Rights have long been part of the Dutch legal system. Therefore, it can be concluded that there is a significant correlation between the Charter of Fundamental Rights of the European Union and the Dutch protection of human rights.

b. The Charter as a reference for fundamental rights protection in Dutch courts

The Charter is not a treaty in the sense of the Dutch Constitution. So, it does not directly create rights for citizens to be upheld by Dutch courts. Articles 93 and 94 of the Dutch Constitution do not apply to the Charter. Nevertheless, Dutch courts sometimes "create" unwritten fundamental principles which may function as a human right. It is not wholly excluded that Dutch courts could make use of the Charter to "create" or "invent" such unwritten fundamental rights.

c. The impact of the Charter on the standards referred to in article 6.1. TEU

It is difficult to predict if the Charter will have any impact on the standards referred to in article 6.1 TEU. In the opinion of this author the Charter could (and will) be used as a help for the interpretation of article 6.1 TEU.[12]

3. The question of the supremacy of EC/EU law and its constitutional effects

a. Supremacy I: Community primary law and Dutch constitutional law. Position of national constitutional courts

The Netherlands does not possess a constitutional court. Article 120 of the Dutch Constitution forbids any judge to test the constitutionality of Acts of Parliament. On the other hand, article 94 of the Constitution orders every judge (and other public authority) not to apply *any* rule of national law if the application would contravene a self-executing or directly applicable provision of an international treaty or of a binding resolution of an international organisation. So, international law prevails in many cases over all national law, including the Constitution. Concerning primary EC law, the Dutch legal system follows the famous Costa ENEL ruling of the Court of Justice of the European Communities. This implies that all primary EC law is superior to national (constitutional) law. This superiority is generally admitted and has to be guaranteed by all Dutch courts, in compliance with the ECJ Simmenthal ruling.

b. Supremacy II: Community secondary legislation and Dutch constitutional law13

According to the Dutch legal system there is no difference between primary and secondary EC law as to its effects on domestic law. So, all Community law is superior to national (constitutional) law.[14]

c. Implicit modification of the Dutch Constitution by the revision and application of the TEU

According to article 93.3 of the Dutch Constitution, any provision of a treaty that deviates from the Constitution, or which leads to conflicts with it, can be approved by the Chambers of Parliament only if at least two-thirds of the votes cast are in favour. So, in theory, all primary and secondary community law which conflicts or could ultimately conflict with the Constitution, could only be binding on the basis of a qualified majority vote of the Dutch Parliament. But the question *if* there is any conflict with the Constitution is decided by an ordinary majority in both Chambers. Neither the EEC Treaty and its later revisions, nor the TEU have been submitted to the aforementioned special procedure. This means that until today EC law and EU law have been considered to be consistent with Dutch constitutional law. However, Dutch constitutional law has surely been modified by community law in an implicit way. The best example of such a modification is the general acceptance of the Costa ENEL ruling of the Luxembourg Court. Its effect goes further than the rule contained in the aforementioned article 94 of the Dutch Constitution, which only gives priority over Dutch law to self-executing or (directly applicable) provisions of international law. According to the Costa ENEL ruling *all* EC law prevails over Dutch law, which is undoubtedly an important extension of the rule laid down in article 94. A second good example of an implicit modification of the Constitution is the introduction of the euro. Article 106 of the Constitution states that the monetary system shall be regulated by Act of Parliament. Since the creation of the European Monetary Union this article has lost much of its meaning. A third example is the position of the Prime Minister. Under Netherlands constitutional law, he is only the "first among equals". In fact, he plays a primary role in EU policy and often dominates the position of the minister for foreign affairs.

4. Institutional interdependence: European functions of Dutch institutions

a. The Dutch Parliament in the European legislative process: indirect source of legitimacy and responsibilities for implementation

The Dutch Parliament is involved – directly or indirectly – in the European legislative process in four ways. First, the Dutch Parliament has to approve treaties by an ordinary or qualified majority vote (article 91 of the Constitution), be it explicitly or tacitly. Second, some draft decisions of the Council of the European Union have to be approved by the Houses of Parliament before the representative of the Kingdom may give his consent to the decision.[15] Third, the Chambers can exercise their normal competences vis-à-vis a Dutch minister acting in the Council, such as asking written and oral questions and using the right of interpellation (their right to demand an explanation). They can only exercise political pressure on the minister. In this way they may try to legitimise the minister's actions in the Council of the European Union. Fourth, the implementation of EC directives must be mentioned. The form of implementation of directives depends partly on constitutional requirements. In several fields of national policy the Constitution attributes competences only to the legislature, i.e. government and parliament in co-operation. In these cases implementation has to take place wholly by Act of Parliament (wet in formele zin). In other fields the Constitution allows the legislator to delegate its rule-making power to the government (the Crown) or a minister. For reasons of speed and flexibility, many Acts of Parliament have delegated powers to the executive to implement EC directives. Depending on the delegating Act, Parliament preserves special control powers, such as the right to ask for a bill replacing the implementation decree of the Crown or a minister. In the other cases parliament preserves its common powers, such as interpellation, questions and ultimately the budget or the application of the confidence rule, which may lead to the dismissal of the minister concerned.

b. European functions of the Dutch administration: a double mandate for the executive

It is obvious that the Dutch government and especially the ministers act as Dutch and as EU officers. In both capacities they are responsible to the House of Parliament. It is clear that their decision-making in the EU weakens the powers of the Dutch Parliament when the unanimity rule does not apply.[16] Nevertheless, as already said, most political groups in Parliament are favourable to an extension of decision-making by a qualified majority in the Council of the European Union.

c. Judicial protection in the European Union through national judges: conflicts of loyalties; questions of procedural autonomy[17]

Dutch judges have to apply the law, be it Dutch law or EC law. Because of the aforementioned Costa ENEL ruling, they (must) apply EC law as national law and even give it priority over Dutch (constitutional) law. In most cases the Dutch judges faithfully apply primary and secondary

Community law, including rulings of the EC Court, such as the famous Francovich case. Moreover, Dutch judges regularly ask the Court of Justice prejudicial questions, but a general complaint is that many judges are insufficiently proficient in EC law. Measures to improve this situation have recently been taken in the form of judge-tailored courses in Community law.

The question of procedural autonomy becomes more and more pressing. Although the Netherlands has had only a few problems in this field, the harmonisation of the different procedural systems of the Member States seems ineluctable. The doctrine in Comet and Rewe appears to be less and less sufficient to guarantee equal protection for the citizens of the European Union.[18] Unfortunately this problem seems to be given no priority at all by most Dutch lawyers and politicians.

III. THE ROLE OF REGIONS AND LOCAL AUTHORITIES IN EU LAW

1. *Effects of EU law on the constitutional framework in relation to regions and local authorities*[19]

The Netherlands is a so-called decentralised unitary state. The Constitution guarantees the existence of provinces and municipalities (territorially decentralised bodies) and permits the creation of other (territorially or functionally) decentralised entities such as the Water Boards, commodity boards and industry boards.[20] Decentralised bodies may be and are charged with the implementation and execution of Community law, although the responsibility for it vis-à-vis the EC stays with the Kingdom itself. This may cause problems where decentralised bodies do not fulfil their obligations. The core of the problem is that the central government is not empowered to give orders to the decentralised bodies, nor to substitute itself for them.[21] This situation stems from the constitutional arrangements according to which there is no general hierarchy between the central government and the decentralised authorities. The only way to solve the problem is to adopt an Act of Parliament which obliges the decentralised bodies to fulfil the requirements of Community law or which centralises the originally decentralised competences.

Special attention should be given to the supremacy of EC law in relation to the obligation of decentralised authorities to implement or execute Community law. Within the Netherlands (national) legal order, decentralised authorities are subject to the Constitution and other "higher" rules like Acts of Parliament. In implementing or executing EC law, however, the decentralised authorities can be compelled to disapply the aforementioned national legal provisions if their application would contravene EC law. It seems a rather theoretical problem, but it arises in practice.[22]

A different question is the representation of decentralised bodies in the EC decision-making process. No Act of Parliament or other statutory instrument guarantees their presence in "Brussels". Nevertheless, the provinces and municipalities take part in the Committee of the Regions. Of the twelve Netherlands members of the Committee, six represent the provincial executives, another six are representatives of the municipal authorities.[23]

2. *Possible consequences for EU law of Dutch-style regionalisation and decentralisation of the kind that goes on in the Netherlands*

Here, the author of this report can be very brief. In the Netherlands there are no plans to fundamentally change the actual form of state. The subdivision of the state in provinces, municipalities and other decentralised bodies will probably survive for many years.

IV. CONCLUSIONS AND RECOMMENDATIONS FOR 2004

1. *A new architecture: What should an EU Constitution or EU basic treaty look like?*[24]

Under the present circumstances it seems rather improbable that the Member States of the EU will decide to establish a real supranational European Constitution. European federalism of the American or German kind meets strong opposition, so it makes little sense to develop such a structure, but a basic European treaty seems feasible. Partly in line with the ideas of the Netherlands government, the author of this report supports the drafting of a basic treaty[25] which, in a systematic manner and following the structure of many recent European constitutions, would contain:

—a clear, though flexible, distribution of powers between the EU and the Member States;
—a basic regulation of the main EU institutions and their respective general competences such as those relating to legislation, execution and administration of justice;
—a clear hierarchy of statutory instruments;[26]
—a bicameral parliament,[27] based on a parliamentary system as is – broadly speaking – present in the Member States;
—fundamental rights.

The tasks or policy of the institutions of the EU should not be covered by the basic treaty, but laid down in one or more substantive treaties.[28]

2. *A Constitution for the European Union: conditions of adoption and amendment; its relationship with the Netherlands Constitution*

As said before, under the present conditions, an EU Constitution is probably a bridge too far. The EU will continue to find its basis in a (basic) treaty. Nevertheless, the conditions of adoption and amendment as laid down in article 48 TEU could be slightly modified. It should not always be necessary that all Member States agree before an amendment of the Treaty enters into force, as article 48 TEU requires. It is imaginable – for example – that the chapter on fundamental rights be amended by a referendum of the citizens of the EU, on a joint proposal of the Council of the European Union and the European Parliament. Such a system would correspond to a certain degree with the actual constitutional provisions of several Member States, where various amendment procedures exist for the national Constitution,
It would not be necessary to alter the relationship of a basic treaty with the Netherlands Constitution. As is the case now, the basic treaty would be superior to the Netherlands Constitution. The author realises, however, that many Member States of the EU disagree on this issue and continue to consider the national Constitution as the basis of all other law in force on the national territory.

3. *Merging the constitutional process and enlargement: how to involve the candidates?*

This last question of the questionnaire is a little obscure for the author of this report. If it means to ask if the (12) candidates for the EU should be formally involved in the ICT of 2004, the (my) answer would be negative. The actual – constitutional – problems of the EU seem to be already sufficiently complicated for the existing institutions of the EU and its Member States. Moreover, the lack of a long (democratic) constitutional tradition on the part of several candidates would probably hamper the progress of constitutional and institutional reforms. On the other hand, it is clear that the existing institutional framework of the EU is insufficiently tailored to a number of 25 or more Member States. The Nice Treaty appears to be insufficient on this point.[29]

Some defects may be mentioned: the composition of the European Commission (too many members), the complicated voting system of the Council of the European Union, the overload of the judicial institutions, the complicated three-pillar-structure.

To avoid further complications concerning the institutions of the EU, it seems wise and practical to involve representatives of the candidate Member States in the discussions on the future of the EU. Therefore, the "Declaration of Laken" of 25 December 2001 rightly states that the candidate Member States will wholly and under the same conditions as the Member States, participate in the discussions of the Convention on the future of the Union, presided over by Valérie Giscard d'Estaing. But they are – also rightly – not entitled to obstruct an apparent consensus between the existing Member States.

NOTES

[1] See C.W. van der Pot, A.M. Donner, L. Prakke et al., *Handboek van het Nederlandse staatsrecht*, Deventer 2001, p. 600.

[2] See C.A.J.M. Kortmann, *Constitutioneel recht*, Deventer 2001, pp. 27 ff.

[3] See Leonard F.M. Besselink, *An Open Constitution and European Integration*, 17 FIDE Congress, Berlin 1996, pp. 361 ff, SEW 1996, pp. 192 ff.

[4] See TK 2000-2001, 27818 (R 1692), A, p. 4.

[5] There are exceptions, such as the Asser Institute Colloquium on European Law. Session XXX – September 2000. See Alfred E. Kellerman, Jaap W. de Zwaan, Jenö Czuczai (eds.), *EU Enlargement. The Constitutional Impact at EU and National Level*, T.M.C. Asser Press, The Hague 2001.

[6] See N.Y. Del Grasso, *Parlement en Europese Integratie*, Nederlands Parlementsrecht, Monografie 10, Deventer 2000.

[7] Literally: exploring, or surveying.

[8] In this field, the "General Commission for European Affairs" of the Second Chamber plays an important role. See Van der Pot/Donner/Prakke, o.c., pp. 613 ff, with further details. It should be noted that Netherlands legislation does not exclude a double mandate for the European Parliament and the Netherlands States General. Nevertheless, the political parties de facto exclude this.

[9] Literally: The future of the European Union, TK 2000-2001, 27407, no. 9.

[10] See "De toekomst van de Europese Unie", TK 2000-2001, 27407, no. 9.

[11] See R. Barents, L.J. Brinkhorst, *Grondlijnen van Europees Recht*, Deventer 1999, pp. 29, 583.

[12] See E.M.H. Hirsch Ballin, *Een wezenlijke maatstaf voor alle actoren in de Gemeenschap*, SEW 2001, pp. 330 ff.

[13] See C.A.J.M. Kortmann, *Secundair gemeenschapsrecht en de nationale constitutie* (Secondary community law and the national constitution), SEW 1999, pp. 82-88.

[14] See C.W. van der Pot, A.M. Donner, L. Prakke et al., *Handboek van het Nederlandse staatsrecht*, Deventer 2001, pp. 600-603.

[15] See for example articles 3 and 4 of the (draft) Act of approval of the Treaty of Nice, TK 2000-2001, 27818 (R 1692), no. 1-2; Van der Pot/Donner/Prakke, o.c., pp. 611, 612.

[16] See Van der Pot/Donner/Prakke, o.c., pp. 6-11.

[17] See Anne-Marie Van den Bossche, *Europees recht in de kering: over winterbedding, potpolder en schorre*, Antwerpen, Kluwer 2001.

[18] See Anne-Marie Van den Bossche, o.c.; Van der Pot/Donner/Prakke, o.c., p. 620.

[19] See B. Hessel, K.J.M. Mortelmans, *Het recht van de Europese Gemeenschappen en de decentrale overheden in Nederland*, Deventer 1997.

[20] See Constantijn A.J.M. Kortmann, Paul P.T. Bovend'Eert, *Dutch Constitutional law*, The Hague-London-Boston 2000, pp. 43-57.

[21] The government is competent to annul every decision of a decentralised institution, but this does not imply the power to take the decision itself. See further J. Gerards, Naleving van het Europese recht door decentrale overheden: naar een herzien stelsel van toezicht, SEW 2000, pp. 208 ff.

[22] See ECJ, Case 103/88, Fratelli v. Comune di Milano [1989] ECR 1839; Koen Lenaerts, Piet van Nuffel, *Constitutional Law of the European Union*, London 1999, p 397.

[23] See Leonard F.M. Besselink, o.c., SEW 1996, p. 199.

[24] See Ars Aequi-special, *De toekomst van de Europese integratie*, May 2001.

[25] See for more details Ars Aequi-special, o.c., p. 310.

[26] See C.A.J.M. Kortmann, *Het normenstelsel in het gemeenschapsrecht*, SEW 1996, pp. 116 ff.; C.A.J.M. Kortmann, Sources and categories of legal acts – Netherlands, in: Gerd Winter (ed.), *Sources and Categories of European Union Law*, Baden-Baden 1996, pp. 127 ff.

[27] The Netherlands government does not support a bicameral system.

[28] See Walter van Gerven, *Het voor en tegen van een Europese grondwet*, in A.K. Koekkoek (red.), *Bijdragen aan een Europese grondwet*, Deventer 2000, pp. 27 ff.

[29] See Ars Aequi-special, o.c., pp. 312 ff.

SPAIN

Droit de LUE et Constitutions Nationales

Rapporteurs
José Martín y Pérez de Nanclares and Antonio López Castillo***

I. INTRODUCTION: CRÉATION DU CONSTITUTIONNALISME EUROPÉEN

1. Le concept de Constitution dans les Etats membres

A la fin de l'année 1978, alors que l'actuelle Constitution espagnole entrait en vigueur, la doctrine et la pratique occidentales avaient déjà assumé depuis bien longtemps quelque chose qui, quelques années plus tard, avec la chute du mur de Berlin et l'écroulement retentissant du rideau de fer et la consécutive disparition de la politique des blocs, s'est étendu à tout un ensemble de pays qui, grâce au cordon ombilical nourricier du Conseil de l'Europe et d'autres organisations et forums de coopération, ont pu (re)naître au constitutionnalisme démocratique; c'est que l'on ne peut assumer qu'un mode d'organisation de la vie sociale, dans lequel "la souveraineté appartient aux générations vives et dans lequel les relations entre les gouvernants et les gouvernés sont donc régies de façon que ces derniers disposent de domaines réels de liberté qui leur permettent de contrôler effectivement les titulaires occasionnels du pouvoir" [1].

I l n'y a pas de doute que les pays qui viennent de consacrer le constitutionnalisme, ancrés dans le tissu institutionnel de l'Europe qu'ils vont contribuer, au cours des prochaines années, à profiler et à développer, pourront avancer rapidement dans la fondation d'une culture politique démocratique qui, comme c'est bien connu, comprend expressis verbis depuis le Traité d'Amsterdam ce que l'on peut caractériser comme une clause d'ordre public constitutionnel de l'Europe politique in fieri.

Comme il n'y a pas de doute non plus que le modèle européen a eu une grande importance dans le processus de transition du système politique espagnol, qui, à la fin du régime politique de Franco, grâce à la Loi sur la réforme politique (la dénommée "huitième loi fondamentale" [2]), a provoqué la disparition définitive de la dénommée "democratie (organique)", un système idéologiquement limité de représentation, par tiers, des institutions (famille, municipalité et syndicat [vertical] unique) reconnues comme domaines exclusifs d'intégration dans un régime politique qui, au-delà de sa progressive formalisation et institutionnalisation par le biais des "lois fondamentales", reposait au fond, sans interruption depuis la Guerre civile, sur la volonté (quand bien même limitée et progressivement formalisée) du "Chef du Gouvernement de l'Etat espagnol", responsable seulement devant Dieu et l'Histoire [3].

Si dans la tradition du constitutionnalisme qui, malgré le destin différent qui a été le sien d'un côté et de l'autre de l'Atlantique, débute à la fin du XVIIIème siècle on peut affirmer qu'"il n'y a pas d'autre Constitution que la Constitution démocratique", sans autres qualificatifs, on comprendra que la dénommée "democratie organique" de l'Espagne préconstitutionnelle, tout comme les "démocraties populaires" de l'Europe de l'est, n'était qu'un "simple despotisme d'apparence constitutionnelle" [4].

a. Qu'est-ce qu'une Constitution?: concepts théorétiques et notions de base

Comme on peut le déduire de ce qui précède, dans la tradition occidentale qui, sans négliger plusieurs antécédents, débute à la fin du XVIIIème siècle et à laquelle l'Europe appartient, la référence à la "Constitution" ou à l'"ordre constitutionnel" a traditionnellement été réservée aux textes qui régissent essentiellement l'organisation des pouvoirs fondamentaux de l'Etat (à la différence des lois fondamentales qui caractérisent l'ancien régime et les régimes autoritaires contemporains) à travers leur division horizontale (avec des différences qui singularisent plusieurs formes de Gouvernement: présidentielle, parlementaire, conventionnelle, etc...) ou, en cas de décentralisation (politique), à travers leur distribution verticale (modèle fédéral, régional...), et qui reconnaissent et garantissent les droits fondamentaux des individus en tant qu'éléments de la communauté politique inorganique qu'il s'agit d'organiser, et non en fonction de leur appartenance à certaines classes ou en fonction de leurs rôles (la liberté et l'égalité apparaissent ainsi, à l'opposé des libertés-privilèges propres à ce que l'on nomme l'"ancien constitutionnalisme" [5], comme deux éléments étroitement unis) [6].

Ce contenu nucléaire, sans préjudice de l'universalité qu'incarnent les valeurs et les principes constitutionnels expressifs d'un principe général de liberté, apparaît diversement formulé, dans l'espace et dans le temps, comme conséquence du particularisme que suppose sa projection (ici et maintenant). En conséquence, toute Constitution (concrète) poursuit l'objectif d'assurer la liberté dans un cadre politique différentié dont la particularité, au-delà des éléments identitaires (langue) et à caractère symbolique (hymnes, drapeaux, etc...), s'étend au catalogue des droits fondamentaux, tout autant en raison de leurs contenus que de leur régime juridique concret (titulaire; intervention du législateur dans leur développement et leur réglementation; instruments de garantie; etc...), tout comme à la propre organisation (division et distribution) des pouvoirs publics, de façon que, tout en déterminant les sujets, l'objet et les procédures d'adoption des décisions, elle articule un système de sources du droit qui correspond logiquement à la forme politique et de gouvernement concrète adoptée.

Cette diversité (historiquement déterminée) des Constitutions et des ordres constitutionnels est visible, au-delà des contenus typiques déjà mentionnés, si l'on examine les instruments qui servent à garantir leur primauté. Si par exception on peut parler d'une suprématie constitutionnelle sans supralégalité formelle (ainsi, dans le droit britannique, il est traditionnel que la modification de certaines lois ne peut être mise en marche sans dissolution préalable du Parlement), la règle générale est que les normes constitutionnelles ne peuvent être contredites que par l'intermédiaire d'une procédure spécifique de modification établie à cet effet, de façon que toute disposition adoptée sans suivre cette procédure et ne pouvant être interprétée conformément à la Constitution est inconstitutionnelle [7].

En résumé, par "constitutionnelles" on entend "les normes qui régissent les positions juridiques fondamentales des citoyens face à l'Etat, afin de garantir la liberté de l'individu dans une communauté politique organisée, ainsi que la distribution du pouvoir entre les principaux organes de celui-ci; normes qui, étant donné leur caractère fondamental et définitoire du système juridique, ont généralement le caractère de normes supérieures, pour ce qui est de leur rang et de leur force d'obliger" [8].

En ce qui concerne l'évolution du processus européen d'intégration des dernières cinquante années, il semble généralement admis que les Traités, entendus dans un sens large qui comprend l'ensemble des principes généraux du droit qui permettent leur interprétation systématique, constituent la "Constitution" de l'ordre juridique communautaire, laquelle, au fur et à mesure qu'elle s'affirme, renforce, dans un processus d'une certaine façon circulaire, son caractère paramétrique, de façon que sa mise en pratique effective sera d'autant moins mise en question que l'assimilation de ses standards (matériels et procéduraux) à ceux qui, dans le cadre de leurs ordres constitutionnels respectifs, sont développés par les organes juridictionnels (et constitutionnels) des Etats membres, sera claire.

En tant que normes sur la production des normes, en tant qu'expression du partage des compétences, etc... les Traités ont été définis par la jurisprudence communautaire comme une "Charte constitutionnelle" et la doctrine n'a pas hésité à mettre entre guillemets le mot "Constitution" pour illustrer la spécificité du système (supranational) [9].

Les doutes résident donc dans le fait de savoir si l'on peut parler simplement de Constitution à propos des Traités, au-delà de la référence au terme entre "guillemets". Pour que cela puisse être possible, les termes Traité et Constitution devraient être identiques. Dans un sens impropre, cela peut être le cas, mais dans un sens propre, c'est-à-dire, comme expression autonome du consensus de base sur lequel repose une communauté différentiée (sans préjudice de l'existence en son sein de minorités [10]), prima facie ce n'est pas le cas. Cependant, sauf si l'on ne conçoit pas son émergence en dehors d'un processus révolutionnaire, c'est-à-dire, dans le contexte historique dans lequel elle apparaît à la fin du XVIIIème siècle, rien de substantiel ne s'oppose au fait qu'un Traité devienne une Constitution. L'expérience historique le montre et c'est parce qu'on a beaucoup progressé au cours du processus d'intégration européenne dans la "constitutionnalisation" des Traités que l'on met maintenant en avant cette éventualité.

A ce propos, le fait que l'on se trouve devant deux concepts présentant une importante différence peut être significatif; tandis que celui de Constitution est un concept matériel, et en même temps formel, celui de Traité, dans sa généralité, comme celui de Loi, auquel il est traditionnellement assimilé, est essentiellement un concept formel [11]. En conséquence, avant de contraster ses éléments et avant d'analyser son fondement, il n'est pas conseillé de nier la présence dans (un texte qui est formellement) un Traité des aspects qui, dans la tradition du constitutionnalisme occidental de référence, définissent une Constitution. Si ce n'était pas le cas, nous ne ferions que nous autoproclamer vainqueurs d'une bataille avant de l'avoir livrée.

b. L'architecture de l'UE/CE et les traditions constitutionnelles nationales

Une fois dépassée la conception étanche et démodée de l'Etat commercial clos, grâce à la progressive intensification durant la deuxième moitié du siècle dernier des flux et des échanges commerciaux, une société transnationale est apparue, dont la vigueur a pousser les Etats —selon l'expression de García-Pelayo— "à rejoindre des organisations régionales interétatiques (pour) atteindre des objectifs qu'ils ne pourraient pas atteindre par eux-mêmes ni par la voie de simples alliances (addition, mais pas intégration —et donc renforcement— de lignes politiques et de ressources)..." [12].

C'est dans l'évolution du processus d'intégration qui, une fois surmontées les méfiances latentes qu'éveillait le compromis de situer sous l'administration des alliés la disponibilité sur les recours appartenant au sol allemand, débute dans l'Europe de l'après-guerre avec le TCECA [13], que cette modulation du pouvoir public dans les Etats contemporains est la plus visible. Dans le processus d'intégration communautaire, il se produit en effet une réaménagement du pouvoir public dans un espace politique et dans un cadre juridique différentié, auxquels participent les Etats et les citoyens [14].

La question —sur laquelle nous reviendrons plus en avant (paragraphe IV.1)— est de savoir quand et pourquoi des textes qui sont formellement des traités internationaux commencent à être considérés comme une espèce de Constitution (incomplète) ou, par l'intermédiaire d'une paraphrase de l'importante clause de droit public, comme une Charte constitutionnelle d'une Communauté de droit, v. gr. d'une Union (supranationale) [15] d'une nature juridique très controversée [16].

A cet effet, il convient de porter son attention sur l'ensemble des éléments sans lesquels cela n'aurait pas de sens d'insister sur la supranationalité, v. gr. spécificité, de l'Union Européenne, par rapport aux (autres) organisations internationales et par rapport aux formes politiques (décentralisées, v. gr. fédérales) nationales [17].

Ainsi, par rapport aux organisations internationales (typiques), l'UE/CE possède, entres autres éléments de différenciation:

— Une plénitude institutionnelle remarquable à laquelle s'ajoute, au-delà de son "quadripartisme" initial, la complexité qui résulte de réformes successives concernant des institutions dont les membres ont une autonomie décisionnelle qui est garantie au niveau statutaire et qui, en marge de dérives intergouvernementales, atteint toute son intensité quand s'ajoute à ce qui précède la progressive constriction du droit de vote découlant du fait que le système du vote à la majorité (simple, dans les questions de procédure, ou) qualifiée se généralise.

Les Traités ne se sont pas limités à la simple articulation d'organes aux compétences exécutives (à la manière qui était traditionnelle dans les commissions de navigation des principales voies fluviales de l'Europe), ou bien d'arbitrage ou juridictionnels (comme ce fut récemment le cas du Tribunal Pénal International). Au contraire, ils ont construit un système institutionnel (spécifique mais quadripartiste) réunissant l'ensemble des fonctions typiquement "législative", exécutive et judiciaire et dans lequel apparaissent des traits et des caractères proches de ceux propres à un système de séparation des pouvoirs, par un volontarisme inversement proportionnel à l'évolution du processus de 'normalisation' institutionnelle qui, depuis la tentative initiale réalisée par le dénommé Traité de fusion (1967), en passant par la progressive insertion de l'Assemblée dans la procédure budgétaire et —tout particulièrement— par l'Acte électoral européen et, à partir de 1979, l'élection directe du PE, aboutit à l'érection de l'Union Européenne et qui, sur un cadre institutionnel et des dispositions générales communes, dans un processus (ouvert) de révisions successives, se projette sur l'ensemble des institutions et sur les Etats membres;

— Une ampleur croissante des pouvoirs assumés d'une manière finaliste, au cours des avancées successives de l'intégration, dans un nombre croissant de matières, qui, comme c'est bien connu, a stimulé une interprétation extensive des titres de compétences communautaires qui, seulement ces derniers temps, à partir de l'avertissement qu'a supposé l'ATCF allemand du 12 octobre 1993, a connu une certaine modulation [18].

Ils ne se sont donc pas limités à établir des obligations de (ne pas) faire des Etats et, allant au-delà, ils ont réalisé une attribution (de plus en plus) ample de pouvoirs en ce qui concerne les matières les plus diverses, articulant ainsi (d'une manière ouverte, étant donné son finalisme) un partage des compétences entre les CC.EE. et les Etats membres qui, dans certains cas, ne serait-ce que par exception, réussit pratiquement à couvrir la totalité d'un domaine matériel ou qui, sans aller jusque là, s'étend d'ordinaire à la réalisation de fonctions (spécialement) normatives; et

— Comme corollaire, une incidence directe du droit (non comme ensemble de normes, mais comme ordre juridique propre) en vertu d'une construction jurisprudentielle —à laquelle n'a pas été étrangère une étroite coopération avec les juridictions nationales par la voie préjudicielle— qui repose sur l'inférence systémique d'une série d'attributs et de caractères (primauté et effet direct, essentiellement) et qui, mises à part quelques resistances épisodiques, a permis leur application (im)médiate et préférentielle dans l'ensemble de l'espace communautaire [19].

En somme, dans le processus d'intégration communautaire, il se produit, au-delà de tout précédent, une accumulation d'éléments typiques de ce que l'on a nommé la supranationalité et qui a permis de soutenir, en présence de dispositions identiques, un sens et une portée différente selon que l'on les interprète dans le cadre des Traités constitutifs des Communautés européennes ou dans le cadre d'un Traité international (en l'occurence, celui créant un espace économique européen) qui n'est pas d'intégration [20].

D'autre part, en opposition avec les formes politiques (décentralisées, v. gr. fédérales) nationales, il faut signaler que l'UE, en tant que structure politiquement dérivée:

— Ne peut rattacher, et encore moins imputer, l'exercice du pouvoir public en son sein au pouvoir constituant d'un peuple (européen) qui (sans préjudice de nuances précises) n'existe (toujours) pas.

Malgré tout, entre l'existence et l'inexistence d'un peuple, il existe une situation dans laquelle se trouve sans doute l'actuelle UE et de laquelle constitue une évidence l'influence que la citoyenneté de l'Union a sur la production de loyautés politiques superposées et complémentaires dans le corpus constitutionnel qu'articulent les systèmes de l'UE et ses Etats membres [21];

— Ne peut imposer d'une manière coercitive, au-delà de leur volonté manifeste de permanence dans l'organisation, la permanence en son sein des Etats membres par une espèce d'exécution fédérale (imprévue).

Malgré tout, cela n'implique pas la reconnaissance d'un caractère unilatéral auquel renoncent par le biais de l'intégration les Etats membres qui, en ce qui concerne leurs obligations communautaires, ne pourraient prétendre a un régime d'exception, en dehors des cas convenus; et

— Malgré sa vaste dimension, elle n'apparaît toujours pas dotée des fins indéterminées ou générales qui définissent traditionnellement la forme politique nationale.

A ce propos, cependant, il faut tenir compte du sophisme qui, dans une certaine mesure, cache une affirmation (plutôt) fondée pour ce qui est de la forme politique nationale centralisée, mais (d'autant plus) discutable quand le modèle national est décentralisé, car, comme c'est bien connu, la complexion finale et la complexion des compétences dans le cadre d'un Etat (politiquement décentralisé, v. gr.) fédéral résultent de la somme d'une division expressive de la reconnaissance de l'existence d'un système complexe.

Il ne s'agit ni d'une organisation internationale, ni d'un Etat. L'UE possède des éléments divers qui font que toute tentative réductionniste dans un sens ou dans l'autre n'est pas envisageable. L'élément personnel éloigne définitivement l'UE de son origine internationale. Mais l'élément étatique la maintient extramuros des formes politiques (fédérales) nationales. On peut dire qu'il s'agit d'une Union supranationale dont les profils doivent faire l'objet d'une réflexion continue, mais sans perdre de vue la double base (personnelle et étatique) de légitimité qui la caractérise.

2. Prévisions nationales en ce qui concerne l'adoption d'une "Constitution" de l'Union Européenne

La Constitution espagnole ne contient aucune référence expresse à l'éventuelle adoption de la "Constitution" de l'Europe. Dans le texte constitutionnel espagnol, on ne trouve en effet aucune référence explicite à l'Europe, ni même à l'Union (et/ou aux Communautés) Européenne(s). La volonté européiste évidente du constituant espagnol a eu un pâle reflet dans la dubitative référence alternative à une "organisation ou institution internationale" complétée, in fine de l'art. 93 CE, par l'imprécise juxtaposition des "organismes internationaux ou supranationaux".

Cette brièveté expressive ne doit cependant pas être interprétée comme ce qu'elle n'est pas; l'apparence vague ou l'imprécision des textes ne cachent pas une volonté ferme d'incorporation au processus d'intégration européenne en marche, que l'Espagne non démocratique suivait de près et avec intérêt; indépendamment des imprécisions qu'il reçoit de ses modèles (art. 49 CL, 25 bis CB, 24.1 LFB, et...), l'art. 93 CE naît bien sûr pour fonder ex Constitutione l'adhésion espagnole aux Communautés Européennes.

Cela explique sans doute l'absence de conditions substantielles et l'établissement d'une procédure simplifiée, aboutissant à une Loi Organique, sans référendum. Le premier aspect (a), l'établissement de précautions et de conditions matérielles, apparaissait étrange dans le contexte d'un pays prêt à se doter d'un système politique démocratique, semblable à celui dont jouissaient les pays participant à l'aventure de l'intégration, considérée à cette époque comme la meilleure garantie se trouvant à sa portée pour consolider la liberté récemment récupérée. Le deuxième aspect (b) n'a presque pas fait l'objet de discussion au moment de la rédaction de la Constitution. La question relative à l'intervention citoyenne dans le processus d'intégration européenne (c), malgré sa perception comme une garantie, dans la mesure où elle apparaît dans le débat constituant, se confond avec l'exigence occasionnelle du réferendum afin de légitimer une décision particulièrement importante qui, pour cette raison, ne devait pas être confiée seulement aux organes représentatifs; l'inexistence pratique de différences d'opinion entre les forces politiques les plus représentatives et le traitement de droit international constitutionnellement réservé à l'intégration européenne, par le biais de l'art. 93 CE, ont contribué à mantenir très bas le profil d'une question qui réclame une réponse.

a. Des conditions constitutionnelles et des limites relatives aux progrès futurs de l´intégration (substance)

Dans son souci d'"européisation", le constituant espagnol a mis au point une disposition, "de nature organique et procédurale (...) assez complexe" [22], l' art. 93 CE, que la doctrine, malgré l'absence de toute référence à de possibles conditions ou limites constitutionnelles s'appliquant à l'intégration, à l'image de ce qui a aussi été le cas dans le processus exégétique de ses équivalents dans d'autres ordres constitutionnels, soumet à des limites (in)certaines qui se confondent essentiellement avec les bases structurelles du système constitutionnel; c'est-à-dire, avec "la substance de la Constitution qu'incarnent les droits fondamentaux, rattachés à la dignité de la personne, en tant que "fondement de l'ordre politique et de la paix sociale" (art. 10.1 CE), et (avec) les principes qui configurent la forme politique qui les protège et qui les favorise" [23].

Au fur et à mesure que la complexion initiale des compétences nationales se resserre et que les institutions communautaires interviennent progressivement "dans des domaines (qui ne sont plus "restreints" mais) de plus en plus étendus" dans le cadre d'un ordre juridique propre, créé à partir des Traités, et dont les traits essentiels "sont en particulier sa primauté par rapport aux droits des Etats membres, ainsi que l'effet direct de toute une série de dispositions applicables à ses nationaux et à eux-mêmes" [24], il apparaît nécessaire de Constitutione ferenda d'avancer dans le débat sur l'établissement des fondements, des conditions ou des limites de l'institutionnalisation politique du processus d'intégration européenne. Il ne s'agit pas par là d'exprimer une configuration de principe mimétique, en ne tenant pas compte de la singularité structurelle de l'UE, mais d'indiquer qu'une intégration ayant une telle dimension (d'un point de vue quantitatif et qualitatif) ne semble acceptable que dans le cadre partagé du respect des principes sur lesquels repose l'exercice de tout pouvoir public dans les différents ordres constitutionnels.

Analyser les principes qui configurent l'ordre constitutionnel espagnol implique que l'on doive faire une référence, d'une part, aux contenus propres du principe de l'Etat démocratique et de droit et du principe de l'Etat régional.

Il n'est pas nécessaire d'entrer dans le détail [25] de la perte de centralité et de la perte de la signification politique et institutionnelle des *Cortes Generales* ou de la modulation du système constitutionnel des sources du droit et de leurs procédures ou paramètres de contrôle, ni de la modification de l'équilibre des compétences qui découle de l'irruption dans le partage territorial interne d'un nouvel espace de compétences qui se superpose à celui établi conformément la dénommée "Constitution territoriale"[26].

Il suffit d'attirer l'attention sur l'acceptation inéluctable de l'altérité respective qui, en ce qui concerne les Etats, dans la perspective communautaire, s'exprime par le biais du principe dénommé d'autonomie institutionnelle (et procédurale) qui, sans préjudice de sa labilité dans la jurisprudence communautaire, se manifeste dans la perspective interne, en particulier, dans la division: intégration ("*interordinamental*") et réforme —et/ou abrogation, modification, etc...— ("*intraordinamental*")[27]. Compte tenu du fait que, dans un tel cadre, on ne peut exiger pleinement une identité et on ne peut admettre un exercice du pouvoir public qui ne tienne pas compte des exigences —peut-on dire— de l'ordre public constitutionnel, la solution (de compromis) ne peut être que celle de l'exigence (mutuelle) d'une congruence structurelle qui, mises à part les singularités de la structure respective et compte tenu des buts respectifs, assure une équivalence (matérielle et structurelle) qui est en même temps la garantie et la condition de la viabilité d'un processus ouvert d'intégration politique, au cours duquel il faut avancer dans la recherche d'une légitimation propre (à partir de la base solide qu'offre la citoyenneté de l'Union) sans préjudice de la présence (déterminante) d'Etats membres dont l'insertion dans la structure commune doit respecter une entité qui, même si elle n'est pas politiquement insurmontable (il suffit de penser à la modulation qui est le résultat du partage des compétences tracé dans les Traités ou de la portée des traits caractéristiques de l'ordre juridique propre qui découlent de la jurisprudence de la CJ, etc...), doit être considérée, tout au moins, garantie d'un point de vue institutionnel [28], de façon que, tant qu'il persiste et qu'il le veut, le peuple espagnol puisse continuer à se projeter de manière autonome ad intra (autonomie constitutionnelle) et ad extra (indépendance).

Le fait de savoir si cela pourrait rester en l'état dans le cadre d'un (futur) Etat (fédéral) européen, dans la mesure où une telle hypothèse est possible, est une question qui n'a toujours pas été réglée dans la doctrine espagnole.

On peut soutenir la même chose en ce qui concerne le système (constitutionnel) de protection des droits fondamentaux car, compte tenu du fait que la soumission simultanée de la part de l'UE à un ensemble de (15) standards constitutionnels est logiquement impossible —a t-on déjà dit à une autre ocasión—, "le système *interordinamental* de l'intégration, qui repose certainement sur une compatibilité de fond, n'est pas en condition d'assurer son application effective, simultanée et égale si la soumission aux ordres constitutionnels n'est pas considérée comme médiate et indirecte, par l'intermédiaire du flux nourricier des principes, mais comme immédiate et directe aux réglementations constitutionnelles respectives" [29].

Si l'on considère l'intégration —comme dans le cas présent— comme une ouverture *interordinamental* non soumises à d'autres conditions que celles expressément accordées ou permises, contrôlable à chaque nouvelle occasion et, en dernier lieu, révocable, mais non disponible ou malléable à volonté, on devrait partir en tout cas, de constitutione ferenda, du constat qu'indépendamment des insuffisances formelles et des désaccords ponctuels[30], l'intégration (partielle) de contenus constitutionnellement garantis par l'intermédiaire du droit communautaire n'est plus si exceptionnelle [31].

b. Conditions de procédure dans les prévisions constitutionnelles nationales

L'art. 93 de la Constitution espagnole (indépendamment de sa localisation systématique concrète, dans le chapitre III (Des traités internationaux) du Titre III (Des *Cortes Generales*) et sans préjudice de sa structure normative insuffisante) est, depuis l'adhésion initiale aux Communautés européennes, le fondement constitutionnel de la participation espagnole à un processus de "création d'une vraie supranationalité" qui —selon l'expression du sénateur Morán— se concrétise dans une vraie "distribution des compétences entre attributions nationales et supranationales"[32]; l'art. 93, bien que de manière indirecte et confuse, donne quelques informations sur la singularité de ce processus [33], étant donné qu'il identifie un certain type de traités (ceux "attribuant à une organisation ou à une institution internationale l'exercice de compétences dérivées de la Constitution") dont l'autorisation est réservée aux *Cortes Generales* (qui sont aussi chargées, conjointement avec le Gouvernement, par le biais de lois organiques, de "la garantie de l'exécution de ces traités et de celle des résolutions émanant des organismes internationaux ou supranationaux qui bénéficient de ce transfert de compétences")[34].

Et par le biais de lois organiques, les *Cortes Generales* ont autorisé les progrès successifs qui ont été faits dans le processus d'intégration européenne, qui, en ce qui concerne le Royaume d'Espagne, débute par son incorporation aux Communautés européennes, à partir de l'entrée en vigueur, le 1er janvier 1986, du Traité d'"adhesión" signé à Madrid le 12 juin 1985 [35].

A différence de la majorité simple requise en principe pour l'autorisation de la célébration (de la plus grande partie) des Traités internationaux (à caractère politique, militaire, qui affectent l'intégrité territoriale ou les droits et les devoirs du Titre I, qui impliquent des obligations financières, qui entraînent la modification ou l'abrogation d'une loi ou exigent l'adoption de mesures législatives pour leur exécution; pour les autres traités, une information immédiate suffit) [36], l'autorisation des "traités d'intégration" se produit par l'intermédiaire d'un type de loi dont la promulgation (modification ou abrogation) nécessite, ex art. 81.2 de la Constitution espagnole, la majorité absolue du Congrès (176 Députés), lors d'un vote final sur l'ensemble du projet.

A propos de ce précepte "de nature organique et procédurale" (qui est ainsi qualifié, dans la lignée de quelques antécédents (ATC 137/1989), depuis l'ATC 28/1991), il faut faire une double référence: la première relative à la (soi-disant) rigidité de cette procédure d'autorisation, la seconde relative à la nature et à la fonction de cette loi organique.

A partir de la prévision, établie réglementairement, selon laquelle les désaccords entre le Congrès et le Sénat en ce qui concerne la concession de l'autorisation parlementaire pour la célébration des traités ou des accords internationaux prévus par l'art. 94.1 de la Constitution espagnole, peuvent être réglés, après une tentative de concertation dans le sein d'une commission mixte (art. 74.2 de la Constitution espagnole), par la majorité absolue du Congrès, la distance entre les procédures d'autorisation prévues par l'art. 93 et celle prévue par l'art. 94.1 a pratiquement disparu, car s'il est vrai que la majorité absolue est requise ex art. 93 depuis le début, dans les cas ordinaires, même si la majorité simple suffit, c'est la majorité absolue qui peut apparaître nécessaire à la fin [37].

La position du Congrès prévalant dans les deux cas, il ne passera pas inaperçu que, bien que ce soit paradoxal, dans le processus d'autorisation des 'traités d'intégration', le Sénat compte moins de possibilités de faire valoir ses critères, étant donné qu'en cas de désaccord, en l'absence de toute concertation, dans un bref délai, l'expression réitérée de la majorité absolue suffit pour que le Congrès des Députés puisse faire valoir sa position [38]. Un tel déséquilibre sera de moins en moins acceptable au fur et à mesure que le Sénat se transforme effectivement dans la Chambre territoriale qu'il n'est (toujours) pas, malgré le contenu de l'art. 69.1 de la Constitution espagnole[39].

Malgré tout, la situation de facto est toute autre et les majorités atteintes dans chaque Chambre, lors des autorisations successives ex art. 93 de la Constitution espagnole, ont dépassé largement non seulement la majorité absolue (en tout cas, du Congrès) expressément prévue, mais aussi les majorités parlementaires exigées par la Constitution (2/3, dans chacune des Chambres) pour mettre en marche, par le biais de la procédure aggravée (art. 168 de la Constitution espagnole), la modification (totale ou assimilée) de la Constitution.

Il apparaît donc de Constitutione ferenda nécessaire de dépasser l'exigence d'une majorité aussi exiguë par la mise en place d'une procédure pouvant (non seulement permettre, mais aussi) garantir le respect du consensus minimum exigible pour continuer d'avancer (ou peut-être de régresser) dans le processus ouvert d'intégration politique [40].

Entre-temps, bien que la prévision d'un référendum complémentaire de la procédure d'autorisation parlementaire finalement prévue par l'art. 93 de la Constitution espagnole ait été expressément écartée lors de la rédaction de la Constitution, un secteur de la doctrine considère la possibilité (exceptionnelle) de convoquer un référendum consultatif, antérieur à l'autorisation parlementaire du Traité, dans l'hypothèse d'une grave césure politique divisant (pratiquement) en deux moitiés la représentation politique existant dans les Chambres. Il n'y a pas de doute que nous nous retrouverions devant une de ces "décisions politiques d'une importance spéciale" auxquelles fait référence l'art. 92 de la Constitution espagnole [41]; pour le reste, il suffit de renvoyer au prochain paragraphe (I.2.c) du questionnaire.

Rien (d'insurmontable) n'oppose à ce qui précède l'évidence d'une autorisation parlementaire accordée "par l'intermédiaire d'une loi organique", car l'opinion doctrinale généralisée (et assumée depuis la première occasion: L.O. 10/1985) est que l'instrument (L.O.) est une chose et l'objectif une autre: l'autorisation parlementaire mentionnée, de façon que s'il s'agit (bien que formellement) d'une loi (organique), en fait nous nous trouvons (matériellement) devant une résolution parlementaire d'autorisation de la signature d'un type concret de Traité international, par rapport à laquelle cette 'loi organique' remplit une fonction (simplement) instrumentale [42].

Malgré tout, l'expression conjonction de cette référence à la loi (organique) et à des "traités attribuant à une organisation ou à une institution internationale l'exercice de compétences dérivées de la Constitution", au-delà de l'indéfinition de son destinataire [43], sème un doute en ce qui concerne la nature d'une "attribution" que la distinction emphatique entre un transfert (imprévu) de compétences et une simple délégation (prévue) de leur exercice [44], ne contribue pas à dissiper.

Tant que l'on ne le dissipe pas définitivement, par l'établissement d'un fondement constitutionnel inéquivoque de l'intégration européenne, le doute découlant du contenu imprécis de l'art. 93 de la Constitution espagnole peut être levé par le biais de son interprétation à la lumière de la réalité qu'il explique (de manière exclusive jusqu'à récemment): le processus d'intégration européenne. A cet effet, on peut insister sur le caractère insatisfaisant d'une caractérisation qui, loin de surmonter la spécificité et l'autonomie de l'ordre juridique communautaire, de la façon qu'elles sont configurées par la jurisprudence, abonde dans le sens de l'idée de la nature unilatérale d'une volonté nationale qui pourrait hypothétiquement se traduire dans la soumission de ce qui est <transféré/délégué> à des directives, à des règles, à des délais et/ou à des conditions, et même dans sa révocation.

Cependant, l'exercice d'un pouvoir public 'intégré' n'est pas (seulement) l'exercice en commun d'un compositum, découlant de l'addition des compétences transférées ou déléguées. La subsistance d'une mosaïque de pouvoirs constituants (persistants) n'empêche pas à la base la conformation d'un pouvoir public (communautaire) propre, différentié [45].

c. Le rôle des citoyens: traité international ou contrat social européen?

Comme c'est bien connu, au-delà de son efficacité en ce qui concerne la conduite et la réglementation de l'engrenage social, la légitimité d'un système réside dans la confiance qu'il fait naître dans l'esprit des citoyens, dont la loyauté permet le fonctionnement régulier des institutions, sans préjudice de la mise à l'écart occasionnelle des intérêts propres, de façon que la discorde ne découle pas de la divergence et que l'on peut continuer d'avancer dans le sentiment d'appartenance à une communauté compréhensive toujours *in fieri*. Exposé à de multiples facteurs, il s'agit d'un processus graduel et de difficile réduction à volonté.

Ainsi donc, compte tenu du fait qu'un titre de légitimité ne change pas de main d'un jour à l'autre, comme l'acte de vente d'une propriété, il semble discutable que cette question puisse être réglée en affirmant que jusqu'à ce jour, ce sont les Etats membres les "maîtres des Traités", mais à partir de demain ce sera le "peuple européen"; au moins, non sans tomber dans l'(excès d') arbitraire car, même si les (dé)loyautés ne sont pas impossibles, l'expérience politique semble indiquer qu'en matière de légitimité une politique des "pas à pas" peut aussi donner des fruits; en d'autres termes, le gradualisme n'est pas (nécessairement) incompatible avec la (cimentation de la) légitimité.

En conséquence, le débat sur la fonction des citoyens (en passe d'émancipation par rapport à leurs Etats) de légitimation de l'articulation (constitutionnelle) du pouvoir public intégré, compte tenu qu'elle est indispensable, doit se situer dans cette perspective réaliste. Le processus en marche n'est pas la moindre des choses. Il s'agit d'une transformation de l'espace politique européen qui, en ce qui concerne la base de légitimation, devrait éviter de brusques avancées, tout autant qu'une arrangeante paralysie; il suffit d'analyser la longue expérience (confédérale) helvétique pour comprendre jusqu'à quel point il est déraisonnable de prétendre dépasser l'état actuel des choses avec hâte, de manière précipitée. Bien sûr, les Etats membres ne peuvent pas briguer aujourd'hui la disposition exclusive sur les Traités d'intégration; l'UE repose déjà sur ses Etats membres, tout autant que sur ses citoyens; se passer à l'heure actuelle de l'appui national c'est mettre l'UE dans de serieuses difficultés pour poursuivre dans son évolution. C'est sur ce point qu'il faut insister, afin de consolider une double base de légitimité qui, sans méconnaître les conditions et les équilibres sous-jacents à l'Union (de plus en plus) complexe et qui, sans être insurmontables, ne semblent pas pouvoir se réduire à un simple "européisme voluntaire", continue d'avancer dans la projection (croissante) du citoyen de l'UE.

Le citoyen, qui l'est de l'UE dans la mesure où il l'est aussi de l'Etat membre respectif, parce qu'il est citoyen, contribue non seulement, avec les autres, au soutien de l'institution publique représentative de l'ensemble des peuples des Etats membres de l'UE, le PE, mais aussi, conformément au droit dérivé, en reconnaissance de la "communauté" émergente à laquelle il appartient —avec les autres nationaux—, à la légitimation des institutions politiques locales de l'Etat membre de sa résidence.

Cette pluralité de projections de légitimation de la part d'une même personne, dans l'Etat membre propre (mais aussi peut-être (en partie) —avec le temps— dans le cadre d'un autre Etat membre dans lequel on réside) et dans le cadre de l'UE, joue en faveur d'une compatibilité des loyautés personnelles par rapport aux systèmes politiques superposés.

Sans préjudice de la relation de proportionnalité que le degré de flexibilité des loyautés politiques concurrentes présente avec celui de forteresse/labilité de la communauté nationale respective, il semble donc nécessaire de fuir de toute vision idéale et —comme le montre l'experience allemande de l'évolution vers une "pleine constitutionnalisation" par le biais de réformes successives de la (supervisée) Loi Fundamentale de Bonn, dans un premier temps, et, plus tard, grâce à leur projection sur l'ensemble de l'Allemagne (ré)unifiée—, en écartant de faciles sous-estimations de ce qui est "provisoire" et/ou "transitoire" qui renferment dans leur indéfinition un potentiel d'adaptation aux circonstances changeantes pouvant faciliter, bien par la voie de l'exégèse bien par l'intermédiaire de réformes, des transitions difficiles dans une prudente équidistance de maximalismes.

En définitive, la "Constitution de l'Europe" doit donc attendre la naissance du peuple européen, comme conséquence d'une solidarité de fait plus étendue, ou même généralisée, et comme résultat d'un processus qu'il serait insensé de trop accélerer. Ceci n'implique pas qu'il ne faille pas avancer fermement dans la tâche indispensable de 'constitutionnaliser' la forme politique spécifique d'une UE qui —selon ce que l'on vient de dire— se trouve bâtie sur une double base de légitimité; et cela ne doit pas nécessairement attendre.

Cela fait déjà longtemps que les Etats ne peuvent disposer des Traités que par une procédure de réforme expressément prévue à cet effet par l'art. 48 TUE. Cependant, l'entrée en vigueur d'une réforme ou d'un élargissement, comme le montre le dernier épisode danois ou le récent épisode irlandais, se trouve toujours entre leurs mains, tout comme l'abandon (accordé) de l'UE, et cela sans autre prise en considération de l'opinion des nationaux (et citoyens de l'UE) que celle prévue dans l'ordre constitutionnel respectif auquel, à cet effet, le TUE lui-même renvoie.

Il faut néanmoins reconnaître, car l'histoire des systèmes politiques le montre, que les Constitutions "peuvent revêtir différentes formes normatives, y compris celle de traité international"[46]. En outre, dans la mesure où le concept de traité est "purement formel", seulement en fonction de la présence en son sein des éléments typiques d'une Constitution on pourra arriver, dans une étape précise du processus, à une conclusion utile en ce qui concerne le maintien d'une organisation supranationale ou, dans un autre cas, l'émergence d'une organisation (fédérale) nationale [47].

Entre-temps, dans le cadre du débat en cours (renvoi au paragraphe IV.1), il faut souligner la signification qu'a sans doute la participation additionnelle des représentants parlementaires nationaux des citoyens de l'UE à la "Convention", en tout cas ouverte à la contribution citoyenne. On ne peut pas sous-estimer la modulation qu'un tel forum (même si son intervention est limitée à la phase initiale d'étude et d'élaboration de recommandations) produit sur une procédure de réforme du TUE qui, de Constitutione ferenda, pourrait connaître quelques modulations additionnelles (ainsi, par exemple, parce que dans le sens de ce qui a déjà été proposé par le PE antérieurement, on contemple la possible entrée en vigueur des réformes à partir d'un certain nombre de ratifications nationales) [48].

3. La préparation de la CIG'2004 dans la pratique

a. L'organisation du débat sur l'avenir de l'Union Européenne

L'Espagne a présenté plusieurs initiatives afin de développer sa participation à ce débat, conformément à la Déclaration conjointe du 7 mars 2001 des premiers ministres de la Suède et de la Belgique (pays qui assumaient la présidence à cette époque), de la Présidente du Parlement Européen et du Président de la Commission, destinée à promouvoir le débat sur l'avenir de la UE dans les Etats membres. Parmi ces initiatives, il convient de souligner l'importance de la création par le Décret Royal du 13 juillet 2001 d'un organe spécifique, dénommé Conseil pour le débat sur l'avenir de l'Union Européenne, destiné à promouvoir la participation citoyenne à ce débat[49]. Le Conseil est formellement rattaché au Secrétariat Général de la Présidence du Gouvernement, mais il est totalement indépendant du Gouvernement dans l'exercice de ses fonctions (art. 1). L'étendue du débat qui lui est propre se concrétise dans les mêmes quatre points que contient la Déclaration 23 du Traité de Nice (art. 2) et ses principales fonctions sont celles de promouvoir et d'organiser des débats, de fonctionner comme un mécanisme facilitant les relations entre les institutions publiques (y compris les Universités et les centres de recherche) et la société afin de définir les tendances de l'opinion pouvant servir de base aux débats, de rédiger des rapports et d'obtenir l'information nécessaire auprès des institutions européennes, des *Cortes Generales* ou des institutions des Communautés Autonomes (art. 4). Il est composé d'un président, nommé par le Président du Gouvernement, et de dix conseillers jouissant d'un grand prestige dans le domaine politique, social et économique (art. 3)[50].

Les travaux réalisés par le Conseil jusqu'à présent peuvent se classer en deux types. D'une part, il existe un débat simplifié à caractère général destiné à la participation de tous les citoyens par le biais de forums sur internet dans lesquels quatre questions fondamentales sont posées: a quoi sert l'UE?, quelles compétences doit assumer l'UE?, comment doivent apparaître les institutions de l'UE? et est-ce que l'UE doit posséder une constitution?[51]. D'autre part, il existe un débat spécialisé destiné à des domaines concrets de la société espagnole (personnalités, académiciens et associations civiques) qui prend la forme d'un questionnaire de 59 questions relatives au processus de construction européenne et dont les réponses sont gérées par le département de droit constitutionnel de l'université d'Oviedo[52].

D'autre part, le début des travaux de la Convention à partir du 28 février 2002 a donné lieu à de nombreuses initiatives publiques et privées destinées à promouvoir la participation des citoyens à ces travaux.

b. Position des principaux partis politiques

Dans leurs discours publics, les partis politiques espagnols parient clairement sur la marche en avant du processus d'intégration européenne[53]. La particularité la plus importante de ce débat est que la isúente politique sur l'avenir de l'UE, au-delà des quatre points de la Déclaration, tourne essentiellement autour de la position que devraient occuper les régions dans l'architecture de l'UE. Les isúentes positions varient, d'une part, entre les partis politiques qui défendent la situation actuelle de prééminence des Etats dans la structure institutionnelle de l'Union et qui considèrent que la participation des régions doit s'articuler à travers les Etats[54] et, d'autre part, ceux qui réclament une position spécifique des régions ayant des compétences législatives propres, comme c'est le cas des Communautés espagnoles, dans le isú institutionnel de l'Union[55]. Entre les deux positions, par exemple, il y a aussi ceux qui défendent l'articulation (interne) d'une participation de ces Communautés Autonomes dans le Conseil, lorsque les questions débattues concernent leurs compétences propres[56].

II. RELATION ET INTERACTION ENTRE LE DROIT COMMUNAUTAIRE/DROIT DE L'UNION EUROPEENNE ET LES CONSTITUTIONS NATIONALES

1. *L'autonomie constitutionnelle des Etats Membres*

a. L'identité nationale (art. 6.3 TUE) comme limite à l'extension des compétences de la CE/UE

L'incorporation dans le TUE du principe du respect de l'identité nationale des Etats membres par l'Union (art. 6.3 TUE) semble au fond refléter une certaine inquiétude de ces Etats membres devant le possible risque de "desétatisation" et de progressive dissolution des Etats membres dans le cadre du processus européen d'intégration[57]. On pourrait même l'interpréter comme une tentative des Etats membres eux-mêmes de souligner (face à l'Union Européenne et aussi, le cas échéant, face aux régions, *länder*, communautés autonomes...) l'importance que continueront à avoir les Etats au sein d'un processus d'intégration dans lequel la doctrine commence à entrevoir certains éléments de nature clairement fédérale[58], tandis que plusieurs Etats présentent des projets de future Union Européenne de type fédéral[59]. Dans ce contexte, les Etats tentent de souligner par le biais de l'article 6.3 le maintien de leur condition de vrais *Herren der Verträge*. Ce précepte sert à souligner que le but ultime du processus n'est pas de faire disparaître les identités nationales des différents Etats européens et de les fondre dans une identité européenne unique et exclusive[60]. Malgré tout, en réalité, ce principe est beaucoup plus ancien que le TUE lui-même, étant donné qu'il est aussi dans une certaine mesure une manifestation du caractère bidirectionnel du principe classique de loyauté communautaure (coopération loyale) de l'article 10 TCE (ancien art. 5 TCEE)[61], lequel imposait déjà aux institutions communautaires, avant l'introduction de l'article 6.3 TUE, le devoir de tenir compte dans leurs actions des *intérêts vitaux* des Etats membres.[62].; entre lesquels il est possible d'inclure l'identité nationale, comme intérêt dernier.

De la même manière que l'article 6.3 TUE pourraient opérer le principe controversé de subsidiarité (art. 5.2 TCE), analysé de façon exhaustive par la doctrine, et, surtout, en matière culturelle, le mandat qui oblige la Communauté à respecter à tout moment dans ses actions "la diversité nationale et régionale" des Etats membres (art. 151.1 TCE), une question à peine traitée par la doctrine[63]. Néanmoins, la référence au respect de la "diversité nationale et régionale" des Etats membres est selon nous plus rhétorique que vraiment juridique, compte tenu du fait que la nature juridique de la compétence attribuée par les Etats à la Communauté Européenne par le biais de l'article 151.1 est simplement *complémentaire*, c'est-à-dire, elle n'est qu'un simple appui ou complément par rapport à la compétence nationale. Cela signifie que la modestie avec laquelle est attribuée la compétence —la culture reste en réalité une compétence de nature étatique— fonctionne comme une limite qui restreint clairement les interventions de la Communauté Européenne en matière culturelle. Il suffit de rappeler que les initiatives doivent se limiter à des actions programmatiques et à des mesures d'encouragement[64]. Sur le plan politique, elle satisfait non seulement le désir des Etats de préserver leur caractère étatique et leur idiosyncrasie propre, mais aussi, tout au moins dans le cas espagnol, une vieille revendication de certaines Communautés Autonomes (en particulier, du Pays Basque) d'introduire aussi dans les traités constitutifs une référence explicite à la "*diversité régionale*". Grâce à elle, ces Communautés Autonomes trouvent dans les Traités une première base juridique qui leur permet de réclamer que le Droit de l'Union Européenne se fasse l'écho de la nécessité que le processus d'intégration européenne respecte leurs particularités culturelles, par l'intermédiaire, par exemple, de mesures de protection de la langue (basque, catalan, galicien...), ainsi que leurs traditions propres.

D'autre part, il semble évident que le contenu et les valeurs qui constituent le concept d'identité nationale sont différents dans chaque Etat membre. Cependant, à notre connaissance, le Tribunal constitutionnel espagnol (contrairement à d'autres Tribunaux constitutionnels, comme l'allemand[65]) n'a pas déterminé le contenu propre du concept d'identité nationale. Malgré tout, selon nous, on peut bien considérer que tout autant le principe de l'Etat de Droit que le principe démocratique, ainsi que la protection des droits fondamentaux et la survivance de l'Espagne comme un Etat souverain et indépendant, sont des éléments minimums et indispensables de l'identité nationale espagnole.

b. Les articles 6.1 y 7 TUE comme limites à l'autonomie constitutionnelle des Etats membres

En Espagne, les articles 6.1 y 7 TUE, introduits par le Traité d'Amsterdam[66], le second ayant été partiellement modifié par le Traité de Nice à la lumière de l'expérience négative du cas autrichien[67], ne constituent pas, selon nous, des limites à l'autonomie constitutionnelle. Les "principes de la liberté, de la démocratie, du respect des droits de l'homme et des libertés fondamentales et de l'Etat de droit" (art. 6.1 TUE) sont des principes clairement assumés par la Constitution espagnole. Tout autant le préambule de la Constitution (proclamation explicite de la justice et de la liberté, de la vie en commun démocratique, de l'Etat de Droit et de l'exercice des droits de l'homme, comme des principes constitutionnels propres) que son texte articulé, en particulier le titre préliminaire (art. 1) et l'important titre I (art. 10 à 55) relatif aux droits et aux devoirs fondamentaux, reprennent pleinement les principes que présente l'article 6.1 TUE comme des principes "communs aux Etats membres".

On peut faire la même réflexion en ce qui concerne le mécanisme de sanction établi par l'article 7 TUE. Une hypothétique *violation grave et persistante* par l'Espagne des principes prévus par le premier alinéa de l'article 6 TUE supposerait par elle-même une violation de la propre Constitution espagnole. On ne peut donc pas parler d'une limite à l'autonomie constitutionnelle de l'Espagne, mais plutôt d'une parfaite syntonie entre les principes de l'article 6.1 TUE et ceux établis par la Constitution espagnole de 1978. Dans ce contexte, ces préceptes (art. 6.1 et 7 TUE) doivent être considérés comme des facteurs du processus de constitutionnalisation que propose l'Union sur la base d'éléments communs que la Constitution espagnole partage pleinement.

2. Valeurs communes: la Charte des droits fondamentaux de l'Union Européenne

Dans le Préambule de la Charte, d'une manière qui rappelle la devise révolutionnaire classique de 1789 (liberté, egalité, fraternité), la Dignité, la liberté, l'égalité et la solidarité s'identifient comme des valeurs indivisibles et universelles de l'Union Européenne en devenir. Si on y regarde avec plus d'attention, plus de deux siècles s'étant écoulés, à travers le prisme des nuances de rigueur qui, au-delà de l'évolution des définitions, se concrétisent dans la mise à jour du troisième de ses éléments, cette triade est toujours en vigueur et, dans la mesure où un quatrième élément s'ajoute aux antérieurs, on cherche par son biais à apporter une réponse au défi (ainsi qu'à d'autres risques déjà connus) que représente le phénomène tout nouveau du clonage par rapport à la conception même de l'être humain.

a. La Charte reflète t-elle le standard de base des droits de l'homme de la Constitution et des droits nationaux?

Il convient de rappeler que le Titre premier de la Constitution espagnole ("Des droits et des devoirs fondamentaux"), après avoir consacré "la dignité de la personne (...comme) fondement de l'ordre politique et de la paix sociale" (art. 10.1), par le biais d'un long cataloque un large eventail de "Droits et libertés" (chapitre II) et identifie ce qu'il nomme des "principes directeurs de la politique sociale et économique" (chapitre III) [68].

Les "droits et libertés" —affirme l'art. 53.1 de la Constitution espagnole— "sont contraignants pour tous les pouvoirs publics" et leur garantie dépend, d'une part, de la sauvegarde d'un (in)certain "contenu essentiel" qui, en tout cas, réserve leur réglementation (ou leur développement) à la loi ordinaire (ou organique), et de leur protection judiciaire effective —laquelle, en ce qui concerne les "droits fondamentaux et les libertés publiques", s'articule autour d'une "procédure se prévalant des principes de priorité et de déroulement sommaire et, le cas échéant, du recours individuel d'*amparo* devant le Tribunal constitutionnel" (art. 53.2 de la Constitution espagnole) [69]—, et, d'autre part, en ce qui concerne aussi les "droits fondamentaux et les libertés publiques", de la garantie additionnelle qui découle de l'existence d'une procédure aggravée pour ce qui est de leur modification (art. 168.1 de la Constitution espagnole) [70].

En revanche, est bien différent le régime des principes reconnus par le chapitre III, lesquels, étant donné que leur est interdit l'accès à la voie spécifique de l'*amparo* constitutionnel —sauf intégration de leurs contenus dans le principe d'égalité—, "ne pourront être allégués que devant la juridiction ordinaire conformément aux dispositions des lois qui les développent", sans préjudice de leur rôle de source d'inspiration de "la législation positive, la pratique judiciaire et l'action des pouvoirs publics" (article 53.3 de la Constitution espagnole).

Conformément à la recommandation adoptée par le Conseil Européen de Cologne, la "Convention" a préparé une Charte de droits s'articulant en sept chapitres, qui "réaffirme... les droits qui résultent notamment des traditions constitutionnelles et des obligations constitutionnelles communes aux Etats membres, du Traité sur l'Union européenne et des traités communautaires, de la Convention européenne de sauvegarde des droits de l'homme et des libertés fondamentales, des Chartes sociales adoptées par la Communauté et par le Conseil de l'Europe, ainsi que de la jurisprudence de la Cour de justice des Communautés européennes et de la Cour européenne des droits de l'homme"[71]. En tant qu'expression synthétique du consensus ordonnateur de l'ensemble des modèles (communautaires, constitutionnels et de droit international) qu'elle réussit à articuler, il existe dans la Charte certains éléments originaux, tout autant dans leur expression textuelle que dans leur propre signification finale [72].

En conséquence, la correspondance entre le catalogue articulé par le biais de la Charte et le contenu du Titre I de la Constitution —ceci n'est pas étonnant dans un contexte aussi pluriel— ne peut être que relative. Cela ne s'explique pas tant par le fait que ses rédacteurs ne se sont pas limités à une simple refonte de l'ensemble des modèles, en introduisant des éléments nouveaux, en ce qui concerne tout autant la structure de la Charte que ses contenus et son régime juridique propre, ni par le fait qu'elle appararaît comme une actualisation de droits et/ou de principes traditionnellement reconnus dans les catalogues de référence, mais par l'impossibilité logique qui découle de l'existence d'une pluralité de (valeurs et de) principes et de règles qui, sauf communion avec certains des standards en présence, n'est reductible en dernier lieu qu'à travers (leur reconnaissance mutuelle et) leur équivalence.

Dans le cadre d'une systématique singulière (structure en chapitres, le septième et dernier concernant des "dispositions générales" sur lesquelles nous reviendrons d'ici peu et les autres ayant pour titres, en ce qui concerne les quatre premiers, les principes de Dignité, Liberté(s), Egalité et Solidarité, et, en ce qui concerne les deux autres, les mots "Citoyenneté" et "Justice") qui n'existait pas initialement, s'articule une "refonte" plutôt originale, dans la mesure où elle prend en considération, en plus de ceux déclarés dans les textes expressément indiqués par le Conseil de l'Europe [73], d'autres contenus additionnels et complémentaires exprimés dans un ensemble pluriel de dispositions et de normes communautaires, de droit international et nationales [74]. La Charte articule donc un catalogue de droits (et/ou de principes) fondamentaux très étendu, en ce qui concerne ses contenus, et actuel. Dans ce sens, en tant que "mise à jour" de valeurs communes, la Charte devient certainement un point de référence incontournable. Cependant, compte tenu de cette importance, il convient de mettre en lumière certaines imprécisions et ambiguïtés.

En ce qui concerne les contenus déclarés, on peut distinguer grosso modo, d'une part, des droits immédiatement applicables et dont le "contenu essentiel" doit être respecté par le législateur (c'est le cas de plusieurs de ceux énoncés dans les trois premiers chapitres: Dignité, Liberté(s) et Egalité) et, dispersés tout au long du catalogue, des droits de configuration légale (liberté d'entreprise (art. 16) ou droit de négociation et d'actions collectives (art. 28), pour ne donner que deux exemples), et, d'autre part, des principes et/ou -selon l'expression de Rubio Llorente- des devoirs corrélatifs d'aucun droit, et même de simples affirmations de principe ou orientations dont la (re)formulation juridique est très difficile, voir impossible [75].

Dans l'ensemble, une telle séparation de contenus n'est pas complètement étrangère à celle existant dans le catalogue prévu par le Titre I de la Constitution. En conséquence, le degré (relatif) d'équivalence des standards de protection dépend, davantage que des (diverses) expressions textuelles, de l'élaboration effective d'une doctrine (dogmatique) communautaire des droits fondamentaux qui, dépassant la tendance casuistique de l'actuel système prétorien de protection, puisse opposer à l'articulation normative discrétionnaire des politiques communautaires certains contenus minimums (essentiels) exprimant les positions juridiques fondamentales des personnes.

Une telle tâche ne peut être réalisée que grâce à un solide progrès dans la distinction que l'on vient de mettre en lumière entre les vrais droits (nécessitant plus ou moins l'intervention normative mais, en tout cas), en tant que tels, limitant le domaine de discrétion propre au législateur, et les principes et/ou les directives qui, compte tenu de leur généralité et indéfinition, ne font qu'ébaucher des critères d'orientation d'une action politique face à laquelle —à l'instar de ce qui se passe en Espagne avec les dénommés principes directeurs de la politique économique et sociale—, en dehors d'hypothèses extrêmes, il serait difficile d'opposer autre chose que le principe d'égalité. On peut affirmer la même chose en ce qui concerne les cas dans lesquels —comme dans les arts. 34 et 35— la détermination du contenu et de la portée du droit déclaré est renvoyée non seulement à la législation mais aussi aux "pratiques nationales" [76].

Mais il existe d'autres ambiguïtés et imprécisions que la Charte aurait eu beaucoup de difficultés à surmonter. C'est le cas des hypothéses dans lesquelles, en tenant compte des changements sociaux en cours, la Charte est le reflet de son temps, mais pas de la manière passive du miroir qui se limite à reproduire ce que l'on met devant lui, mais avec une prétention normative, en assumant ou en repoussant, dans le cadre des "valeurs... universelles" sur lesquelles se fonde l'Union, les potentialités présentes actuellement (ou de manière imminente) dans la société [77].

En ce qui concerne les "dispositions générales", il est à noter que par rapport à d'autres aspects, abstraction faite de la disparité structurelle des contenus déclarés dans les six autres chapitres, la Charte a choisi une clause générique de limitation applicable à l'ensemble —à la manière suisse par exemple— et non pas une spécification des limites tenant compte de la diversité des contenus déclarés, comme c'est le cas, par exemple, tout au long du Titre I de la Constitution.

En effet, l'art. 52.1 établit une clause générale qui repose sur la quadruple exigence de la réserve de loi et du respect du contenu essentiel, du principe de propotionnalité et des objectifs d'intérêt général et/ou du besoin de protection des droits et des libertés d'autrui.

Par ailleurs, la Charte prétend contribuer à la clarification de la portée des droits reconnus, par l'intermédiaire d'un double renvoi, aux conditions et aux limites définies par les Traités communautaires et sur l'Union par rapport aux droits qui trouvent leur fondement dans ceux-ci (art. 52.2), et au sens et à la portée des droits prévus par la Convention européenne de sauvegarde des droits de l'homme et des libertés fondamentales, faute d'un meilleur standard de droit communautaire (art. 52.3).

Si à ce qui précède on ajoute la condition qui découle, en ce qui concerne l'interprétation autonome de la Charte, de l'exclusion implicite, par l'art. 53, de la limitation ou de la violation des standards respectifs de protection en présence (du droit de l'Union, du droit international, v. gr. de la

Convention européenne de sauvegarde des droits de l'homme et des libertés fondamentales, et des Constitutions des Etats membres), on comprendra l'urgence d'une approche sérieuse de la protection des droits fondamentaux dans l'espace communautaire et de l'UE.

Dans le contexte *interordinamental* de l'intégration, la difficulté que présente un tel croisement de règles de renvoi, même si cela peut sembler paradoxal, ne pourra sans doute être éliminée qu'à travers un solide effort de clarification des compétences, qui, grâce à son potentiel générateur de confiance réciproque, pourrait en outre dégager la voie vers la progressive irradiation des standards (équivalents) de l'Union sur l'ensemble des ordres juridiques [78].

b. *La Charte comme point de référence pour la protection des droits fondamentaux par les tribunaux espagnols*

Il est bien connu que, vu que les Institutions de l'Union se sont limitées lors du Conseil européen de Nice a apposer leur simple signature protocolaire, la Charte des Droits de l'UE, même si elle présente une structure normative typique, n'a pas de force juridique contraignante.

Cependant, ceci n'exclut pas l'importante juridique d'une déclaration de droits qui voit s'ajouter à sa dimension symbolique, comme point de référence actualisé du consensus européen sur les droits (et/ou sur les principes) fondamentaux, la plus-value d'offrir, dans l'attente de sa pleine judiciarisation, un texte achevé qui s'exprime dans "la langue des droits"[79].

On peut donc s'attendre à une présence progressive de la Charte dans les ordres juridiques nationaux (y compris indirectement par l'intermédiaire de la Cour européenne des droits de l'homme). On peut même imaginer que l'existence d'un catalogue de droits fondamentaux de l'Union peut apporter aux Tribunaux (suprêmes et/ou constitutionnels) nationaux des éléments de référence additionnels susceptibles de justifier l'autorestriction face aux normes provenant d'un ordre juridique équivalent. Cela a d'ailleurs déjà été le cas.

Le Tribunal constitutionnel a lui-même pris en considération, en effet, entre autres éléments de référence, la Charte des droits fondamentaux de l'UE, en vertu du mandat d'interprétation des droits fondamentaux déclarés au niveau constitutionnel conformément aux normes correspondantes de droit international; et ceci tout autant avant qu'après sa signature solennelle à la fin de l'année 2000 à Nice.

Lors de la première occasion, par le biais de l'ATC 292/2000, rendu dans le cadre de l'examen de la constitutionnalité de la législation interne relative à la protection des données personnelles, on remarque à la vue du contenu de l'art. 8 de la Charte, entre autres références, l'existence d'une coïncidence en ce qui concerne l'établissement d'un régime juridique de la protection des données personnelles [80].

Après sa signature solennelle, la Charte apparaît une nouvelle fois invoquée dans l'ATC 53/2002, relatif au droit d'asile, qui, afin de permettre son exacte compréhension, met en lumière l'importance que, pour cette institution juridique, "présente la progressive disparition des frontières de l'Union Européenne", tout comme sa progressive configuration "comme droit de l'Union Européenne", en soulignant que la relation qui existe entre l'asile et la sécurité n'aurait pas empêcher la Charte —dont il est pris note de la signature solennelle— d'inclure entre les "Libertés" de son chapitre deuxième, "tout autant le droit d'asile (art. 18) que le droit de ne pas être expulsé, extradé ou renvoyé vers un Etat où il existe un risque sérieux que l'intéressé soit soumis à la peine de mort, à la torture ou à d'autres peines ou traitements inhumains ou dégradants (art. 19). De cette manière —tirant alors une conséquence sur le contrôle de la constitutionnalité de la norme nationale mise en examen par rapport à l'art. 13.4 de la Constitution espagnole—, l'intime relation entre l'asile, le contrôle de l'immigration et la sécurité européenne... ne se produit pas au détriment du droit d'asile mais plutôt en partant de son nécessaire respect dans le sein de l'Union"[81].

c. L'influence de la Charte en ce qui concerne le standard compris dans l'art. 6.1 TUE

Il a été signalé que l'effet de déterminer le contenu et la portée des droits énoncés dans la Charte est déterminant, tout comme la législation, la jurisprudence communautaire.

Un effet potentiel de la Charte des Droits fondamentaux de l'UE est en premier lieu de contribuer à un renforcement (ne serait-ce que modeste) de la légitimité du processus décisionnel communautaire dans la mesure où, au-delà de la tendance casuistique traditionnelle, les institutions impliquées jouent un rôle dans le processus d'élaboration des normes, v. gr. processus législatif, la Commission, en présentant ses initiatives et aussi les colégislateurs, le Conseil et le PE.

S auf mise en question de la (double) légitimité sur laquelle repose le processus actuel (co)décisionnel, il ne semble pas qu'il faille rattacher à la prise en considération de la Charte par les institutions de l'Union une perte d'importance du principe démocratique.

La Charte sert sans doute à renforcer le développement de la jurisprudence communautaire relative aux droits fondamentaux et, dans la mesure où l'art. 6.1 TUE lui offre une reconnaissance formelle, elle finira logiquement par avoir une influence sur les standards qui y sont assumés.

La Charte —a t-il été dit—, même si elle n'est pas en vigueur, présente une texture normative qui, en marge de sa structure différente, comme "soft law" [82], peut être une référence indicative, comme l'indiquent depuis longtemps les conclusions de plusieurs Avocats généraux. La vraie valeur paramétrique de contrôle (de la conformité avec le droit primaire du droit dérivé) ne peut découler, comme il est évident, que de la future entrée en vigueur de la Charte.

En attendant, rien n'enpêche le TJ d'utiliser la Charte afin de déterminer les contenus et la portée du substrat des principes et d'avancer dans leur concrétisation, comme c'est le cas depuis l'arrêt Stauder. On peut souligner dans ce sens que la Charte n'élimine pas, ni même limite, l'activisme de la juridiction communautaire qui, en fonction de l'intensité de la coopération (par le biais de la question préjudicielle) des organes juridictionnels nationaux, pourrait même se voir incité; à cet effet, on doit mettre en lumière la nouvelle potentialité des différentes expressions du principe général d'égalité qui, au-delà du chapitre spécifique de la Charte qui lui est réservé, s'applique à une bonne partie du chapitre suivant ainsi qu'à d'autres aspects de cette même Charte. S'offrent donc à la CJ des possibilités additionnelles dans le cadre d'un activisme dont le sort dépend du sérieux de ses analyses et de la densité de ses paramètres.

Par ailleurs, malgré le fait que la (déficiente) argumentation lui servant de fondement est critiquable, l'importance qu'a sans doute présenté dans le débat (constitutionnel) actuel sur la protection des droits fondamentaux dans le cadre de l'UE le Rapport (RCJ) 2/94 ne devrait pas passer inaperçue, car s'il est bien connu que l'articulation d'un catalogue de droits fondamentaux comme celui énoncé dans la Charte peut précéder, grâce à une habilitation explicite ou sans elle, une future adhésion de l'UE/CE à la Convention européenne de sauvegarde des droits de l'homme et des libertés fondamentales, il n'est pas évident que si la réponse de la CJ avait été autre le débat sur les raisons qui soutiennent l'articulation d'un catalogue propre de droits fondamentaux aurait pu avoir lieu avec la promptitude et l'intensité actuelles.

3. La question de la primauté du Droit Communautaire et ses effets constitutionnels[83]

Comme l'affirmait Araceli MANGAS MARTÍN en 1996 dans sa contribution nationale au XVII Congrès de la FIDE, "les rapports entre le droit espagnol et le Droit Communautaire ont été facilités par une tradition légale, jurisprudentielle et doctrinale favorable à la primauté et à l'efficacité des Traités internationaux (et, par analogie, à leur droit dérivé) auxquels l'Espagne prend part. Cette attitude, qui trouve ses racines dans l'Ecole Espagnole du Droit des Gens (*l'Ecole de Salamanque*), révèle d'un point de vue moniste une nécessité de cohérence dans la conduite interne et externe de l'Etat. Les organes de l'Etat, dans leur activité normative, qu'elle soit interne ou externe, produisent le droit (interne et international) et, pour des raisons de cohérence, ils ne doivent pas contribuer à créer des normes incompatibles"[84].

Conformément à ce point de départ, la Constitution espagnole de 1978 —à partir de maintenant, CE— contient deux dispositions qui revêtent une particulière importance dans cette matière. D'une part, de façon générale, l'article 96.1 de la CE prévoit un mécanisme d'incorporation des traités internationaux à l'ordre juridique interne[85]. D'autre part, la Constitution ne contient pas seulement un précepte général relatif à la conclusion des Traités internationaux qui présentent une importance spéciale (art. 94)[86]. De façon particulière, l'article 93 de la CE prévoit un mécanisme *ad hoc* d'autorisation qui s'applique à la conclusion des traités attribuant des compétences à l'Union Européenne, et contient une acceptation explicite des effets que comporte le Droit Communautaire Européen, en particulier l'effet direct et la primauté[87]. L'inclusion de ces deux préceptes (art. 93 et 96) dans la Constitution espagnole garantit, comme nous le verrons plus en avant, la pleine opérativité du principe capital de la primauté du Droit Communautaire Européen proclamé par la jurisprudence de la CJCE depuis la célèbre affaire *Costa*[88].

a. Droit Communautaire originaire et Droit constitutionnel national. Position du Tribunal constitutionnel

Avant d'analyser la position du Tribunal constitutionnel espagnol (TC) concernant les relations entre le Droit Communautaire originaire et le Droit Constitutionnel national, il convient de préciser que la Constitution de 1978 établit dans son article 95.2[89] un mécanisme de contrôle préalable de constitutionnalité des traités internationaux[90]. Selon ce mécanisme, si le Tribunal constitutionnel considère qu'il existe effectivement une contradiction entre un Traité communautaire et la Constitution, il n'existe que deux possibilités. La première possibilité consiste à modifier la Constitution, conformément à la procédure de révision expressément prévue par elle (art. 166 à 169 de la CE), pour l'adapter à l'exigence imposée par le Traité communautaire dont le texte a déjà été définitivement fixé, mais avant qu'ait été donné le consentement. Cette premiére possibilité est celle que contient l'article 95.1 de la CE, lequel stipule que "la conclusion d'un traité international contenant des dispositions contraires à la Constitution devra être *précédée* d'une révision de celle-ci"[91]. La seconde possibilité est de ne pas donner son consentement par rapport à la conclusion du Traité international. Dans le cas d'un Traité communautaire, cela signifie que le Traité communautaire en question (modifiant les traités constitutifs) ne peut pas entrer en vigueur, ni en Espagne ni dans aucun Etat membre, étant donné que, selon l'article 48 TUE, il faut qu'il soit ratifié par *tous* les Etats membres conformément à leurs normes constitutionnelles respectives. Il s'agit en somme d'un intéressant *mécanisme préventif* destiné à éviter les conflits entre les

Traités communautaires et la Constitution espagnole. Dans la pratique, il n'a été utilisé qu'une seule fois.

En effet, il a été utilisé en 1992 lors de la ratification du Traité de Maastricht. Le Gouvernement se demandait alors si le Traité de Maastricht était compatible avec la Constitution. Plus précisément, il se demandait si le droit d'éligibilité qui était reconnu aux citoyens de l'Union Européenne aux élections municipales par l'ancien article 8B.2 TCE (aujourd'hui par l'article 19.2 TCE) était compatible avec l'article 13.2 de la CE. Cette norme constitutionnelle, dans sa rédaction originaire, ne prévoyait que la possibilité de leur reconnaître un droit de suffrage passif: "Seuls les espagnols seront titulaires des droits reconnus à l'article 23 [droit de vote et d'éligibilité], exception faite, en vertu des critères de réciprocité, des dispositions que pourra établir un traité ou une loi concernant le *droit d'éligibilité* aux les élections municipales".

Face à cette situation, dans une Déclaration particulièrement courte pour ce qui est de son analyse mais limpide dans la réponse relative à la question du Gouvernement, le TC a considéré que l'ancien article 8B.2 TCE (l'actuel art. 19 TCE) entrait effectivement en conflit avec l'article 13.2 de la Constitución[92]. Pour ratifier le TUE, il a fallu finalement mettre en marche une procédure de révision constitutionnelle (la première et la seule dont ait fait l'objet la Constitution espagnole de 1978 jusqu'à présent) grâce à laquelle la rédaction de l'article 13.2 a été modifiée, par l'ajout du terme "et passif", de façon à reconnaître aux étrangers le droit de suffrage passif dans les élections locales. C'est ainsi, dans le cas des "étrangers" appartenant à un Etat membre de l'Union Européenne, grâce au TCE, et, dans le cas des étrangers non communautaires, si tel le décide une loi ou un Traité international conclu avec les Etats tiers en question.

Le TC n'a fait donc que constater cette contradiction directe et explicite entre la Constitution et un Traité communautaire, sans pénétrer dans d'autres questions plus générales et non moins problématiques, comme la consolidation des réformes institutionnelles et monétaires (UEM) qu'impliquait le Traité de Maastricht ou, dans un sens plus général, la création de la "citoyenneté de l'Union".

Après l'entrée en vigueur du Traité communautaire, il n'est évidemment plus possible d'activer le mécanisme préventif prévu par l'article 95.2 de la CE déja cité. Dans cette hypothèse, les conflits hypothétiques entre le Traité et la Constitution nationale doivent être analysés à la lumière de l'article 93 de la CE. Ainsi, si les limites s'appliquant à l'attribution par l'article 93 de compétences à l'Union Européenne sont respectées[93], le principe de la primauté du Droit Communautaire, dans ce cas le Droit originaire, déploie pleinement ses effets. La jurisprudence du TC espagnol a néanmoins connu une certaine évolution. Initialement, dans un arrêt de 1991, qui fut fortement critiqué par la doctrine[94], à juste titre d'ailleurs, il a considéré de façon erronée que les normes communautaires avaient un caractère "infraconstitutionnel"[95], ce qui entravait dans une large mesure la défense du principe de la primauté du Droit Communautaire par rapport à la Constitution. Cependant, plus tard, dans un arrêt prononcé en 1993, le Tribunal constitutionnel corrigea sa première vision on mit au point une jurisprudence plus respectueuse du principe de la primauté. Il a ainsi jugé qu'il s'agissait de normes "non constitutionnelles"[96]; ce que la doctrine considère comme des normes "mégaconstitutionnelles" ou "extraconstitutionnelles"[97]. La jurisprudence du TC espagnol est encore pauvre en ce qui concerne son développement théorique. Mais sur le plan pratique, elle a évité des conflits avec le Droit Communautaire Européen et, en fin de compte, même si elle ne l'accepte pas de façon explicite, elle ne l'a jamais mis en doute.

Il n'est donc pas possible, dans le cas espagnol, en principe, qu'une norme de Droit Communautaire originaire entre en conflit avec le Droit constitutionnel national. Rien n'a changé au cours du dernier lustre par rapport à ce qu'affirmait MANGAS MARTÍN en 1996 devant la FIDE sur cette question. "En realité, il ne peut y avoir de conflit entre le droit constitutionnel et les Traités communautaires (...). La Constitution espagnole n'admet pas que l'Etat espagnol donne son consentment à un traité contraire à ses dispositions. Notre système juridique exige que la contradiction soit éliminée: ou nous n'acceptons pas d'être partie à ce traité ou nous procédons à une réforme de la Constitution espagnole"[98].

En conclusion, les Traités communautaires, une fois ratifiés, sont supérieurs à n'importe quelle norme interne, y compris la propre Constitution, comme conséquence des normes générales relatives aux Traités prévues par les articles 95 et 96 de la CE et, en particulier, grâce à la prévision constitutionnelle *ad hoc* prévue par l'article 93 de la CE en ce qui concerne les Traités communautaires.

b. Droit Communautaire dérivé et Droit Constitutionnel national

En permettant que l'exercice de compétences derivées de la Constitution soit attribué à l'Union Européenne, l'article 93 de la CE accepte que les institutions communautaires puissent élaborer un Droit dérivé, conformément aux attributions de compétences comprises dans les Traités constitutifs et dans le respect des procédures législatives expressément prévus par ces derniers. Il reconnaît de la même manière que le paramètre de légalité de ces normes est le Droit communautaire originaire, et non la Constitution nationale, et que, dans les domaines de compétences communautaires, l'unique juge compétent pour examiner la validité d'une norme de Droit Communautaire dérivé est la Cour de Justice de la CE. Le TC espagnol n'est donc pas compétent pour examiner un hypothétique conflit entre el Droit dérivé et la Constitution.

Ni même dans le domaine des droits fondamentaux le TC jouit d'une possibilité de contrôle. Ainsi, dans un arrêt prononcé en 1991, il a affirmé explicitement qu'"il n'est pas possible de former un recours d'*amparo* contre des normes ou contre des actes des institutions de la Communauté"[99]. C'est aussi à la Cour de Justice des Communautés Européennes qu'il appartient de contrôler la validité de la norme de Droit secondaire mise en question. L'Etat impliqué jouit certes d'une position privilégiée pour former, le cas échéant, le recours en annulation correspondant (art. 230 TCE). Une toute autre question (sur laquelle le TC espagnol ne s'est pas prononcé) est celle de la portée devant être attribuée à l'article 6.2 TUE, en ce qui concerne l'obligation des institutions communautaires de respecter les droits fondamentaux tels qu'ils résultent des "traditions constitutionnelles communes aux Etats membres"[100].

En conclusion, "c'est la Constitution espagnole elle-même (art. 93) qui permet au Droit communautaire originaire et dérivé de déployer pleinement ses principes et l'ensemble de ses effets; c'est par la volonté propre de la Constitution que se produit une substitution des dispositions constitutionnelles, légales et réglementaires par les dispositions des Traités et des actes communautaires"[101].

c. *Modification implicite des constitutions nationales dans la révision et l'application du TUE*

En autorisant la conclusion de traités internationaux attribuant à l'Union Européenne l'exercice de compétences dérivées de la Constitution espagnole, l'article 93 de la CE comporte une ouverture constitutionnelle qui suppose une certaine révision implicite de la Constitution, sans qu'intervienne le mécanime de révision formelle prévu par les articles 166 à 169 de la CE. Par le traité de cession de compétences, la Constitution subit une modification, de façon que —on a dit— celui-ci agit indirectement comme un mécanisme spécial de révision prévu par la propre Constitution[102].

Ainsi, les réformes successives des traités constitutifs (AUE, Traité de Maastricht, Traité d'Amsterdam, Traité de Nice) ont entraîné un progressif élargissement du nombre et de l'intensité des compétences matérielles attribuées à la CE/UE par les Etats membres, dans notre cas par l'Espagne. Pour ne citer que le cas le plus marquant, cela suppose, par exemple, une certaine modification implicite du partage des compétences entre l'Etat central et les Communautés Autonomes prévu par le titre VIII (art. 143 à 158) de la Constitution.

Evidemment, sur un plan plus général (et pour donner un exemple de nature institutionnelle), lorsque l'article 97 de la CE affirme que el "Gouvernement dirige la politique intérieure et extérieure", il semble en découler naturellement, par exemple, que la direction de la politique extérieure de nature économique que réalise le Gouvernement espagnol se trouve sérieusement restreinte par les mesures que les institutions communautaires adoptent dans le cadre de l'exercice de leur compétence exclusive en matière de politique commerciale commune (art. 133 TCE). On peut affirmer la même chose en ce qui concerne les conséquences que provoquent dans le Droit constitutionnel national d'autres dispositions communautaires telles que, par exemple, celles qui régissent l'Union Economique et Monétaire et, par là-même, les larges compétences relatives à la politique monétaire (compétence exclusive de l'Etat selon l'article 149.1 CE), ou en ce qui concerne les conséquences que l'existence même de la Cour de Justice provoque sur la juridiction des juges et des tribunaux nationaux.

Ces modifications implicites de la Constitution espagnole (ou d'autres qu'il est possible de signaler) sont pleinement autorisées et couvertes par la prévision *ad hoc* de l'article 93 de la CE. Il s'agit là de la fonction de ce précepte, et c'est précisément pour cette raison que celui-ci exige une majorité renforcée pour l'approbation des mesures d'attribution de compétences (majorité absolue), ainsi que la modalité législative réservée aux questions qui revêtent une importance constitutionnelle spéciale (loi organique)[103]; bien entendu que cette ouverture n'empêche pas d'entreprende des reformes constitutionnelles ou des modifications normatives en attention aussi tant à la l'autonomie de l'ordre constitutionnell qu'aux exigences juscommunautaires de securité juridique. Si ce n'était pas le cas, la disposition générale que prévoit l'article 94.1 de la CE à propos des traités internationaux revêtant une importance spéciale (loi votée à la majorité simple) aurait suffi[104]. Un tout autre problème est que le TC a évité de se prononcer sur les limites de l'article 93 et, en particulier, sur les limites s'appliquant aux réformes implicites pouvant découler de cette disposition, alors même qu'il avait une excellente occasion de le faire dans le cadre de la Déclaration relative au Traité de Maastricht déjà citée.

4. *Interdépendance institutionnelle: fonctions européennes des institutions espagnoles*

En consonance avec le caractère fonctionnel qui est propre au système de compétences articulé entre les Etats membres et les institutions communautaires, l'application du droit communautaire est en principe le résultat de la collaboration entre les institutions communautaires et les organes (exécutif et judiciaire, mais aussi législatif) nationaux, lesquels, ex art. 10 CE, sont obligés de prêter une coopération loyale qui, dans la jurisprudence communautaire, atteint une intensité semblable à celle qui est propre à la clause typique de loyauté fédérale [105].

De la même manière que ni le "dédoublement fonctionnel" des organes et des autorités nationales dans la mise en pratique des obligations de droit international, ni le développement normatif et/ou l'exécution du droit national (fédéral) par les collectivités (infra)étatiques compétentes, impliquent que l'on doive confondre l'affectation des organes respectifs, on ne doit pas non plus douter du fait que la réalisation de leurs fonctions communautaires ne transforme pas les organes nationaux en institutions communautaires, ni change le titre de leurs compétences respectives [106].

Ce que l'on vient de dire ne nous dispense pas de reconnaître l'importante influence qu'a sur l'autonomie constitutionnelle (et même sur sa propre source de légitimation) cette instrumentalisation communautaire de l'exercice du pouvoir public dans les ordres nationaux respectifs.

a. Le parlement espagnol dans le processus législatif européen: source indirecte de légitimité et responsabilité de son exécution

— Responsabilité de son exécution. Selon l'art. 93 in fine de la Constitution espagnole, "il incombe aux *Cortes generales* ou au Gouvernement, selon les cas, de garantir l'exécution de ces traités (par lesquels est attribué à une organisation international l'exercice de compétences dérivées de la Constitution) et des résolutions émanant des organismes internationaux ou supranationaux qui bénéficient de ce transfert de compétences„.

Cette prévision constitutionnalle expresse, conjointement avec la délégation très étendue que contient la (déjà citée) Loi 47/1985 en faveur du Gouvernement, a situé au premier plan le rôle que joue le Parlement dans les affaires communautaires, en tant que garant et comme organe chargé de l'application (im)médiate des obligations de droit communautaire.

— Sans préjudice de reconnaître l'activisme des Gouvernements dans la correcte application lato sensu du droit communautaire et malgré une formalisation de sa dimension traditionnelle, en tant que forum de délibération et de compromis politiques, dans une proportion inversement proportionnelle à son degré de détail, le Parlement espagnol contribue au développement et à l'application normative du droit communautaire, de manière directe ou indirecte, pourvu qu'il existe une influence communautaire sur les matières réservées a la Loi [107].

On considère d'une part que la législation (d'origine communautaire) représente déjà presque un sixième de l'ensemble de la législation ordinaire. D'autre part, une voie semble s'ouvrir, celle de la délégation en faveur des commissions législatives permanentes (art. 75.2 de la Constitution espagnole [108]), qui, dans la mesure où à la réaction politique du Gouvernement provoquée par la perte de centralité qui s'est intensifiée dans le processus d'intégration européenne vient s'ajouter une révision conceptuelle qui, abondant dans le sens de la spécificité du contexte communautaire face au contexte strictement international, dans la lignée de la caractérisation nuancée de l'ATC 165/1994 [109], permet de franchir l'obstacle que représente l'exclusion du traitement en commission, entre autres, des questions internationales (art. 75.3 de la Constitution espagnole), pourrait bien constituer une alternative (partielle) à la pratique courante de la délégation en faveur du Gouvernement pour l'articulation (ou la refonte) de textes normatifs ayant force de loi et que l'on nomme Décrets législatifs (art. 82-85 de la Constitution espagnole) [110].

— En tant que garant de la correcte exécution des obligations de droit communautaire, ex art. 93, in fine, de la Constitution espagnole, le Parlement ne devient, pas plus que le Gouvernement, titulaire d'une compétence d'application qui, selon la matière et la fonction concrète devant être réalisée, appartiendra à qui possède la compétence selon l'ordre établi.

L'institutionnalisation d'une certaine coopération en matière d'application des obligations communautaires conformément au droit communautaire, dans le respect des compétences respectives de l'Etat et des régions, dans le cadre de la Conférence (sectorielle) décrite dans le paragraphe III du questionnaire [111], a adouci la controverse initiale sur l'éventualité de l'intervention substitutive (mais provisoire) de la part des *Cortes Generales* et sur l'hypothétique (car extrême) utilisation du mécanisme de coertion étatique de la part du Gouvernement qui (une fois épuisée la voie du conflit négatif de compétence), avec l'approbation de la majorité absolue des membres du Sénat, pourrait <<prendre les mesures nécessaires pour la contraindre (Communauté autonome (qui) ne remplit pas les obligations que la Constitution ou les autres lois lui imposent ou qui agit de façon à porter gravement atteinte à l'intérêt général de l'Espagne) à respecter ces obligations ou pour protéger l'intérêt général mentionné>> [112].

Source indirecte de légitimité. Dans l'essentiel, les *Cortes Generales*, composée par le Congrès des Députés et par le Sénat, ainsi que les organes parlementaires équivalents des autres Etats membres, offrent une légitimation au système communautaire grâce à leur intervention dans la procédure d'autorisation de la ratification des Traités sur l'intégration, à l'occasion tout autant de l'adhésion propre ou d'un Etat tiers (Droit primaire lato sensu) que de leur réforme (art. 48 TUE), ou même comme conséquence des modifications complémentaires qui, en marge du caractère simplifié de leur adoption communautaire, procèdent expressément à "recommander leur adoption aux Etats membres conformément à leurs normes constitutionnelles respectives"[113].

Si le Traité d'adhésion constitue le fondement immédiat de l'appartenance et de la soumission du Royaume d'Espagne au droit des Communautés Européennes, originaire et dérivé, l'art. 93 de la Constitution espagnole —disait-on dans l'ATC 28/1991— est son fondement juridique indirect[114]; et conformément à ce précepte, les Chambres ont autorisé par l'intermédiaire de Loi(s) Organique(s), d'une part, l'adhésion espagnole initiale, par le biais de la L.O. 10/1985, du 2 août, et la dénommée quatrième ampliation, par l'intermédiaire de la L.O. 20/1994, du 29 décembre, et, d'autre part, les réformes successives des Traités, par le biais des L.O. 4/1986, du 26 novembre (AUE), 10/1992, du 28 décembre (TUE) et 9/1998, du 16 décembre (TrAmsterdam) [115].

Par ailleurs, le Congrès des Députés et, de manière subsidiaire, le Sénat, dans l'exercice de leur fonction de contrôle, plus indirectement que directement, peuvent soutenir les positions que les membres du Gouvernement défendent dans les formations respectives du Conseil-UE et/ou du Conseil Européen. Même s'il est indéniable que l'intensité d'un tel contrôle parlementaire dépend du degré de différenciation du contexte communautaire face au contexte international —traditionnellement revêche au contrôle parlementaire—[116], il ne faut pas sous-estimer une pratique qui, comme dans les cas danois et britannique par exemple, parvient à imposer à son Gouvernement des mandats de négociation ou même à différer l'adoption d'une décision au sein du Conseil jusqu'à la réalisation d'un examen parlementaire préalable de la question[117].

A différence de ce qui se passe dans d'autres droits, rien d'explicite n'est dit dans le texte constitutionnel espagnol à propos d'une question qui, depuis los préliminaires de l'"adhesión" espagnole aux Communautés Européennes, fait l'objet d'une réglementation établie dans une Loi [118], qui institue une commission mixte Congrès-Sénat qui, depuis 1994, se dénomme "Commission mixte pour l'Union Européenne"[119].

On a l'habitude d'affirmer que, depuis la dernière modification législative, l'insertion des *Cortes Generales* dans la dénommée phase ascendante ou décisionnelle a progressé, en vertu du rapide accès de la "Commission mixte" à des propositions normatives de la Commission-UE qui ne sont pas toujours rapidement disponibles en (bon) castellan [120]. Mais il est vrai que la fonctionnalité de la "Commission mixte", qui n'a pas de compétence législative, ni même d'initiative [121], ne va pas au-delà de la contribution à la discussion publique sur les affaires communautaires, grâce à une action de promotion de la célébration de débats lors des sessions plénières des Chambres, desquels peut découler l'adoption de motions et de propositions non législatives; du contraste éventuel de la concordance des décisions communautaires finalement adoptées avec les propositions préalablement examinées en "commission...", il ne découle bien sûr aucune compensation effective de l'évidente perte de pouvoir décisionnel des *Cortes Generales* dans le cadre d'un processus décisionnel qui, au fur et à mesure que l'on avance dans le vote à la majorité qualifiée et au fur et à mesure qu'intervient le PE à côté du Conseil, comme colégislateur, ne dépend plus seulement du (plus ou moins haut degré de) contrôle des représentants des Gouvernements par leurs Parlements respectifs. En outre, dans une étape ultérieure, la dénommée "comitologie", dans son développement, ajoute à la déconnexion déjà citée des Parlements nationaux celle (additionnelle) du PE.

b. *Fonctions européennes des autorités administratives: un double mandat pour les exécutifs*

A ce propos, on doit se souvenir que, comme l'affirme une doctrine constitutionnelle continue, "la cession de l'exercice de compétences en faveur d'organismes supranationaux n'implique pas que les autorités nationales cessent d'être soumises au droit interne quand elles accomplissent des obligations acquises face à de tels organismes, car ils continuent même dans ces cas à être des pouvoirs publics qui sont soumis à la Constitution et au reste de l'ordre juridique espagnol (article 9.1 CE)"[122].

L'exécution simultanée de leur fonction communautaire et strictement étatique ne serait pas viable en dehors du cadre des relations entre les droits, en vertu desquelles s'impose l'application effective d'un ensemble de dispositions qui, en Espagne, comme dans d'autres pays, ont une telle influence sur l'Administration, dans sa perspective organique, et sur le droit administratif, matériel et de procédure, qu'elles modulent sans doute, sans la priver de sens, cette doctrine constitutionnelle emphatique, si l'on tient compte de l'évidence que "le droit de la Communauté européenne est avant tout constitué de règles de droit administratif..." [123] qui, sans préjudice de l'intervention ordinaire des Administrations nationales, se trouvent soumises à la juridiction (et, en conséquence, au paramètre) communautaires [124].

En ce qui concerne le premier aspect, sans préjudice du fait, comme le souligne la Déclaration n° 43 annexe au Traité d'Amsterdam, que "la mise en oeuvre, sur le plan administratif, du droit communautaire incombe par principe aux Etats membres, conformément à leur régime constitutionnel...", il s'agit, d'une part, d'une adaptation inévitable de leurs structures techniques et décisionnelles destinée à articuler une participation plus efficace dans les tâches d'administration et de gestion qui, hormis "les compétences en matière de surveillance, de contrôle et de mise en oeuvre conférées aux institutions communautaires" (Déclaration préc.) [125], appartiennent normalement à l'Administration nationale; et, d'autre part, il s'agit de l'enrichissement de leur propre organisation institutionnelle, par la création de nouveaux organismes et de nouvelles autorités destinées à se charger de la réalisation des nouvelles tâches d'origine communautaire.

A ce propos, on ne soulignera jamais assez l'effet d'harmonisation européenne indirecte que le développement de leur fonctionnalité communautaire produit dans l'organisation institutionnelle d'instruments administratifs de tradition différente; d'une toute autre nature, mais apparaissant aussi comme une conséquence du processus d'intégration, est la ligne de partage établie par les limites (pas toujours nettes) qui jalonnent les différents pouvoirs et, dans les systèmes politiquement décentralisés, les niveaux de Gouvernement. A cet effet, s'est mise en place une certaine spécialisation dans les matières communautaires qui s'étend, même avec une portée différente, à l'ensemble des Administrations (étatique et régionales), tout autant d'un point de vue sectoriel que transversal.

En outre, en consonance avec la configuration de certaines politiques communautaires, plusieurs organismes et autorités qui n'existaient pas ou qui existaient sous un autre aspect ont été créés; il s'agit ainsi tout autant de la création d'un Ministère (en matière d'environnement) ou d'agences administratives autonomes (en matière d'énergie ou de télécommunications) que de la mise à jour du statut juridique d'organismes traditionnels (Banque d'Espagne) [126] qui, grâce à l'institutionnalisation communautaire[127], prennent une nouvelle dimension.

Le développement de (nouvelles) politiques communautaires, tout comme la dérégulation de certains secteurs économiques, a aussi une influence dans le domaine matériel soumis au droit administratif, qui connaît ainsi de nouveaux ordres sectoriels; en particulier, en matière (de télécommunications, d'industrie, et...) environnementale, en fonction de ses différentes politiques (de conservation et de protection de la nature, de traitement des déchets toxiques et dangereux, de protection et d'amélioration de la qualité de l'atmosphère) [128].

La portée de cette influence est mise en évidence quand, dans le cadre d'un conflit positif de compétences relatif à l'étude d'impact de certains projets, publics et privés, sur l'environnement, le TC reconnaît que "prendre en considération la manière avec laquelle un instrument a été créé par la Directive communautaire peut être non seulement utile mais aussi obligatoire pour lui appliquer correctement le schéma interne de partage des compétences, qui plus est quand l'instrument ou les techniques qui font l'objet du conflit n'ont pas d'antécédents dans le droit interne, comme c'est le cas de la procédure d'étude d'impact, qui, en marge de certains antécédents impropres, constitue un instrument nouveau, qui nous est parvenu grâce au droit communautaire"[129].

En ce qui concerne l'influence du droit communautaire sur la procédure administrative, nous pouvons renvoyer le lecteur à ce qui est dit dans le paragraphe suivant, à propos de l'influence qu'a sur le principe d'autonomie (institutionnelle et) de procédure l'enrichissement progressif des pouvoirs de la juridiction administrative nationale.

Sur un autre plan, de nature paracommunautaire, il faut situer la croissante compartimentation des tâches administratives, essentiellement par rapport aux matières qui (feront et qui) font partie du dénommé troisième pilier, c'est-à-dire, par rapport (au Titre IV TCE et) au Titre VI TUE; lors du passage de Maastricht à Amsterdam, on note qu'en l'absence d'une pleine intégration, les Etats peuvent mettre en marche une harmonisation de leurs dispositions qui, selon la séquence, contribue à l'obtention des objectifs communautaires eux-mêmes [130].

c. Protection judiciaire dans l'UE par les juges nationaux: conflit de loyautés; la question de l'autonomie de procédure

Les organes juridictionnels nationaux contribuent au développement d'un ordre juridique, le droit communautaire, dont le respect a provoqué une modulation extraordinaire de leur fonction judiciaire, d'autant plus visible au fur et à mesure que la jurisprudence communautaire a défini son contenu et au fur et à mesure que sont apparues certaines exigences dont la garantie effective intronise le juge national, qui est toujours formellement un organe du pouvoir judiciaire de l'Etat, comme un organe de plus au service de l'ordre juridique communautaire [131].

Le juge national, appelé depuis les premiers prononcés jurisprudentiels à participer à la difficile tâche d'offrir la plus grande efficacité possible aux dispositions de droit communautaire à l'occasion de la réalisation de sa fonction juridictionnelle, en assumant pleinement les critères de référence et de validité propre à l'ordo iuris qui naît de l'intégration, au-delà de la reconnaissance d'obligations pour les Etats, du pouvoir public dans un cadre institutionnel propre et différent de celui des Etats, s'est vu contraint d'utiliser en même temps un double paramètre de référence et de validité, le droit communautaire et le droit national, quand il s'agit —ce qui n'est pas rare—d'appliquer un droit formellement national mais matériellement communautaire.

Compte tenu qu'il ne faut pas confondre deux plans logiquement détachables ou, dans le cadre de systèmes politiques nationaux lato sensu décentralisés, deux plans manifestement différents, on ne peut pas régler cette situation en considérant simplement le juge national, étant donné son rendement fonctionnel au service du droit communautaire, comme un vrai organe communautaire. Même si certains ont suivi un raisonnement qui consiste à relier exclusivement l'organe judiciaire national au paramètre juscommunautaire, au détriment de celui qui est propre à l'ordre constitutionnel, à peine faut-il préciser que ce raisonnement a été écarté par la jurisprudence constitutionnelle et ne compte aucun appui doctrinal[132].

L'hypothèse selon laquelle le droit communautaire comprend le paramètre constitutionnel ayant été exclue par le TC [133] et compte tenu du fait que ce paramètre ne comprend qu'indirectement, en plus des autres modèles qu'utilise la CJ, un paramètre communautaire qui, comme impossibilité logique, ne peut être identique en même temps à tous les paramètres constitutionnels, il n'est pas possible logiquement de surmonter la double exigence de loyauté qui, pour le juge national, découle du fait qu'il applique en même temps le droit national et le droit communautaire. La situation, logiquement insatisfaisante, n'est surmontable qu'à travers une progressive équivalence de principe des standards nationaux et communautaire[134].

La rationalité de l'intégration, en l'absence d'identité, n'est possible que par une équivalence qui, dans le processus de croissante imbrication communautaire, se reflète, entre d'autres éléments, dans un principe général de coopération ou de loyauté communautaire (art. 10 TCE), duquel la jurisprudence de la CJ a tiré un rendement extraordinaire.

L'art. 234 TCE doit être considéré comme une concrétisation singulière de ce principe général. Compte tenu de l'inexistence d'un ordre hierarchisé, dans l'espace juridique de l'intégration communautaire c'est la coopération judiciaire qui incarne dans la question préjudicielle l'instrument (ordinaire [135]) de garantie de l'unité (tendancielle) de la doctrine et, en conséquence, de la (nécessaire) sécurité juridique. Pleinement conscient de cela, la CJ a développé la potentialité de ladite question, de manière progressive, en relativisant dans un premier temps les exigences de procédure et en étendant la base des organes pouvant la poser, en précisant ensuite les critères spécifiques d'interprétation et de validité et en délimitant à ce propos le rôle respectif des organes juridictionnels nationaux et de la CJ, et, finalement, en mettant en marche le processus de normalisation que réclame la maturité du système, après l'intégration systématique de sa rédaction dans les Traités.

Une fois ce point éclairci, il faut affirmer que l'attitude du juge espagnol, quand il rend compatibles les fonctions relatives à son intégration organique (nationale) et son rendement fonctionnel (au service de l'ordre juridique superposé), est conforme aux exigences de droit communautaire. Indépendamment de son ordre concret (civil, pénal, contentieux administratif ou du travail) et en faisant ici abstraction des nuances dont il serait nécessaire de tenir compte dans une étude spécifique relative à un univers aussi ample afin d'expliquer, par exemple, les raisons de l'activisme des Tribunaux Supérieurs de Justice des Communautés Autonomes ou d'analyser l'important apport de certains juges de première instance, la conduite suivie par l'ensemble des organes juridictionnels espagnols (ce qui, dans la perspective communautaire, concerne aussi des organes qui n'appartiennent pas au Pouvoir judiciaire [136]) peut donc être considérée comme "peu belligérante... par rapport à l'ordre communautaire"[137].

Ceci dit, sans préjudice du refus occasionnel (surtout) du Tribunal Suprême, bien de laisser de côté la soumission à l'ordre juridique national et à ses règles de procédure (c'est le cas, par exemple, lorsque la Troisième Salle, du Contentieux Administratif, du Tribunal Suprême refuse d'inappliquer une loi nationale en vertu d'une application stricte du principe traditionnel de soumission du juge à la loi, que l'on considère renforcé par l'attribution exclusive à la juridiction constitutionnelle de la compétence de rejet de la loi [138]), bien de se passer d'un domaine caractéristique de discrétion qui, de la même manière qu'il a conduit occasionnellement au niveau interne l'interprétation judiciaire de la loi, confiant dans la garantie extrême (ou dans son exigence) assurée par le TC, à des résultats difficilement conciliables avec le partage des compétences découlant de l'existence d'une juridiction constitutionnelle spécifique, peut provoquer au moment de jouer son rôle d'organe juridictionnel au service du droit communautaire, compte tenu du degré moindre de discrétion qui est reconnu ex art. 234 TCE aux organes juridictionnels, une perte d'efficacité des normes comme conséquence d'une résistance qui s'explique plus par la défense (organique) d'un domaine de discrétion que l'on ne veut pas perdre que par le choix en faveur de l'un des deux ordres (national et communautaire) en présence; dans la mesure où, malgré sa flexibilisation croissante dans la jurisprudence de la Cour de Justice, l'exigence de poser la question préjudicielle (d'interprétation et de validité) réduit dans une large mesure ce domaine propre de décision, une telle attitude de refus conduit sûrement au non respect du devoir communautaire spécifique de la juridiction (suprême) espagnole [139].

L'autoexclusion qui, contre le critère flexible de la CJ, aboutit au fait que le TC ne se considère pas comme un organe de garantie du droit communautaire (ATC 28/1991) (compte tenu tout autant de sa nature spécifique constitutionnelle, comme instance suprême (seulement) "en matière de garanties constitutionnelles", que de l'absence d'une attribution explicite de la "compétence pour connaître de la conformité du droit interne au droit communautaire"[140]) ne contribue pas à remédier à cette situation insatisfaisante pour le droit communautaire.

Cependant, cette resistance de principe ne constitue pas complètement une pratique jurisprudentielle, dans laquelle on trouve, en plus de prononcés étrangers à la jurisprudence de la CJ [141], des exemples significatifs d'intégration du paramètre constitutionnel conformément aux dispositions communautaires [142].

Ces manifestations de l'intégration du paramètre communautaire, en tant que tel, et non sur la base imprécise du mandat d'interprétation de la conformité des droit fondamentaux constitutionnellement reconnus en fonction des textes internationaux relatifs à cette matière ratifiés par l'Espagne, dans une ligne jurisprudentielle traditionnelle particulièrement manifeste dans l'ATC 64/1991 [143], peuvent contribuer clairement au respect total de la part de la juridiction ordinaire des exigences communautaires d'interprétation (quand ce n'est pas d'inapplication) du droit national conformément au droit communautaire. Le fait que la doctrine Marleasing soit la conséquence directe d'une question préjudicielle posée par un organe juridictionnel espagnol a pu aussi avoir un certaine influence à cet égard[144].

Sur un autre plan, selon une jurisprudence continue [145], il appartient aux organes juridictionnels nationaux, en vertu du principe de coopération de l'art. 10 TCE, d'assurer la pleine efficacité du droit communautaire par une protection judiciaire effective des justiciables, qui, sans préjudice du principe d'autonomie institutionnelle et de procédure, se matérialise en étendant à l'application du droit communautaire les règles propres de la procédure.

La CJ, consciente des disparités en ce qui concerne l'efficacité du droit communautaire qui pourraient découler d'un tel renvoi aux différentes procédures nationales, d'une part, a indiqué rapidement une voie, celle du rapprochement des dispositions légales, réglementaires ou administratives, qui a déjà été utilisée essentiellement à travers des dénommées "Directives-recours" qui, sans préjudice d'autres matières[146], se caractérisent dans le domaine de la protection des consommateurs par la création de voies de recours en matière de publicité trompeuse, en matière de responsabilité du fait des produits défectueux , en matière de credit à la consommation, en matière de voyages, de vacances et de circuits à forfait ou, enfin, en ce qui concerne les clauses abusives dans les contrats conclus avec les consommateurs [147].

D'autre part, elle a procédé à l'encadrement communautaire de modalités et de dispositions ne devant s'appliquer qu'"en l'absence de réglementation communautaire" (principe de subsidiarité) et qui "ne peuvent être moins favorables que celles qui régissent des recours similaires en droit interne" (principe d'équivalence), "ni être adoptées de façon qu'elles rendent pratiquement impossible l'exercice des droits dont la protection s'impose aux organes juridictionnels nationaux" (principe d'effectivité)[148].

On avance ainsi dans la progressive articulation d'un ordre public minimum commun(autaire) de procédure, indispensable pour assurer l'application effective et simultanée du droit communautaire dans un espace, sauf exceptions, n'ayant pas de règles propres de procédure [149].

Dans ce contexte d'influence communautaire sur un principe d'autonomie (institutionnelle et) de procédure dont le respect l'a amené à exclure de manière expresse les voies alternatives à celles prévues dans le droit national, la CJ a initié une dérive, en se basant sur le (principe général du) droit à la protection judiciaire effective[150], qui va de l'interprétation la plus favorable à la recevabilité des recours, au développement d'une importante dimension préventive de la protection judiciaire communautaire qui, en marge des principes et des traditions constitutionnelles en vigueur dans les Etats membres, l'a amené à défendre la faculté judiciaire d'adoption de mesures provisoires et de sursis dans l'application de la norme nationale attaquée tant que la CJ ne se prononce pas (Factortame), ainsi qu'à appliquer le sursis dans l'exécution d'un acte administratif national sur la base d'un règlement communautaire par rapport auquel est posée une question préjudicielle de validité (Zuckerfabrik), hypothèse dans laquelle lui est même reconnue la faculté de mettre en place des mesures provisoires positives (Atlanta)[151], à condition de ne pas méconnaître ou de ne pas violer le système communautaire des recours (T. Port)[152], en passant par l'articulation d'un principe de responsabilité des pouvoirs publics pour violation préjudiciable des droits des particuliers (Francovich et Bonifaci; Brasserie du Pêcheur et Factortame)[153].

La répercussion de ces progrès communautaires réalisés en matière de protection judiciaire provisoire dans le développement des potentialités inhérentes à un droit constitutionnellement reconnu (art. 24 de la Constitution espagnole), au-delà des cas d'application (im)médiate du droit communautaire, dans la mesure où elle a permis un renforcement des standards constitutionnels de protection judiciaire, est considérable [154].

III. LE ROLE DES REGIONS ET DES COLLECTIVITES LOCALES DANS LE DROIT DE L'UNION EUROPEENE

Depuis la Constitución de 1978, l'Espagne est un Etat qui repose sur une structure décentralisée (*Etat des autonomies*) dans lequel les 17 Communautés Autonomes existantes —à partir de maintenant, CCAA— jouissent de compétences législatives propres dans des domaines déterminés dans chaque cas par leur statut d'autonomie. Les CCAA ont donc assumé avec un caractère exclusif —dans certains cas— et de manière partagée avec l'Etat —dans la majorité des hypothèses— un bon nombre de compétences[155].

L'entrée de l'Espagne dans les Communautés Européennes en 1986 a entraîné l'attribution, par le biais de l'article 93 de la CE, non seulement de compétences de l'Etat central (celles prévues par l'article 149 de la CE), mais aussi, évidemment, de compétences des CCAA (celles prévues par l'art. 148 de la CE et par les statuts d'autonomie). Se pose donc ainsi la question de savoir si les CCAA ont, dans le contexte constitutionnel actuel, la possibilité de projeter sur le plan international —en particulier sur celui de l'Union Européenne— la compétence dont elles sont titulaires dans le cadre national interne.

En principe, la Constitution prévoit que l'Etat jouit d'une compétence exclusive en matière de "relations extérieures" (art. 149.1.3 de la CE), alors qu'elle ne contient aucune disposition relative à l'action extérieure des CC.AA. Nénamoins, la majorité des statuts d'autonomie contiennent des clauses de participation interne des CCAA dans les phases ascendante (formation de la volonté) et descendante (exécution des normes déjà adoptées) des processus normatifs internationaux. Face à cette circonstance, il est indispensable de déterminer la portée concrète que el Tribunal constitutionnel a attribuée à la réserve étatique exclusive concernant la matière des "relations internationales" et le domaine dans lequel, le cas échéant, les CCAA peuvent intervenir. Cette jurisprudence a connu deux phases: une première phase très restrictive pour les CCAA et une seconde plus souple.

Dans la première phase, le Tribunal constitutionnel a maintenu une interprétation très large du concept de "relations internationales", comme compétence exclusive, et, par là-même, une limitation extrême —pratiquement une exclusion— de la possibilité d'intervention des CCAA en matière internationale[156], à tel point qu'un simple *Communiqué de collaboration* entre une Communauté Autonome et un Etat tiers violait l'exclusivité de l'Etat en matière internationale[157]. Cette position extrême, mise en place en 1982, était difficilement compatible avec le fonctionnement des Communautés Européennes, auxquelles l'Espagne appartient depuis 1986. Comme l'affirme la doctrine la plus autorisée depuis le moment même de l'adhésion, si cette jurisprudence aussi restrictive pour les CCAA s'était maintenue, l'"attribution de compétences ne se serait pas produite seulement en faveur des Institutions communautaires, comme le permet l'article 93 de la Constitution, mais aussi en faveur de l'Etat, ce que n'admet ni ne désire l'article 93"[158]. C'est ainsi qu'à partir des années quatre-vingt-dix s'est ouverte une deuxième phase dans laquelle le TC a assoupli sa rigidité antérieure, en considérant que la compétence exclusive de l'Etat en matière extérieure ne comprend que le "noyau dur" de ces relations internationales[159]. Ce noyau est en l'ocurrence constitué par la représentation extérieure (art. 56.1 et 63.1 de la CE), la conclusion de traités internationaux —*ius ad tractatum*— (art. 93 et 94), la responsabilité de l'Etat, la détermination de la position espagnole en matière extérieure (art. 97) et les questions relatives à la nationalité, aux étrangers, au régime douanier, à la nationalisation de navires, au contrôle de l'espace aérien et à l'immatriculation d'aéronefs (art. 149.1. 2, 10, 16 et 20).

En dehors de ce noyau dur, les CCAA peuvent réaliser des activités ayant une projection internationale si ces dernières, en plus d'être nécessaires pour l'exercice de leurs compétences, n'impliquent pas l'exercice d'un *ius contrahendi*, ne donnent pas lieu à l'apparition d'obligations immédiates et actuelles face à des pouvoirs publics étrangers, ne touchent pas la politique extérieure de l'Etat et ne mettent pas en jeu la responsabilité de celui-ci face à des Etats étrangers ou à des organisations internationales ou supranationales[160]. Ainsi, par exemple, il est parfaitement possible d'ouvrir des bureaux permanents à l'étranger (ex. à Bruxelles devant l'UE), de conclure des accords de coopération entre régions (ex. accords de coopération transfrontalière), de réaliser des voyages officiels à l'étranger (ex. des Présidents des CC.AA), de coopérer d'une manière décentralisée en matière de développement (il existe même dans certaines CCAA des lois propres de coopération en matière de développement), de faire partie d'associations internationales de régions (comme l'ARE), etc[161].

Le TC obtient ainsi un équilibre entre la considération constitutionnelle des relations externes comme une compétence exclusive de l'Etat et l'attribution de compétences aux CCAA, dont se charge aussi la propre Constitution. Le Tribunal constitutionnel met aussi au point que le cadre européen ne peut pas être considéré comme un domaine de plus des relations internationales. Plus précisément, dans la polémique affaire sur la constitutionnalité de l'ouverture par la Communauté Autonome du Pays Basque d'un bureau permanent à Bruxelles, le TC a affirmé de façon claire que "lorsque l'Espagne agit dans le cadre des Communautés Européennes, elle le fait dans une structure juridique très différente de celle qui est traditionnelle dans les relations internationales". Et ceci se justifie par le fait que "le développement du processus d'intégration a créé un ordre juridique, l'ordre communautaire, qui, pour l'ensemble des Etats membres des Communautés Européennes, *peut être considéré à certains effets comme 'interne'*"[162].

Conformément à cette importante jurisprudence qui n'a connu aucune variation jusqu'à présent, il est nécessaire de mettre en place des mécanismes capables d'articuler de façon satisfaisante la participation des CCAA dans les questions communautaires. Cette participation doit être envisage de deux points de vue différents; dans la perspective interne du processus de formation de la volonté nationale en matière européenne, et dans la perspective externe de la participation directe des CCAA dans les institutions et dans les organes européens. Cette participation doit respecter en tous cas le principe de coopération institutionnelle et de loyauté constitutionnelle.

1. *Perspective interne*

La participation des CCAA à la formation de la volonté nationale (phase ascendante) en matière communautaire s'articule de deux manières: de façon multilatérale ou bilatérale. Le mécanisme institutionnel habituel de coordination entre l'Etat et les CCAA est de nature multilatérale et fonctionne à travers de ce que l'on appelle les *Conférences Sectorielles*, c'est-à-dire, la réunion des *consejeros* des différentes CCAA et du Ministre ou des Ministres du secteur, présidée par l'un de ces derniers[163]. Parmi elles, la denommée Conférence pour les Affaires Relatives aux Communautés Européennes (CARCE)[164] est chargée de trouver, conformément au principe de coopération, "une solution progressive aux questions que pose la participation des Communautés Autonomes dans l'élaboration et l'application du Droit et des politiques communautaires européennes". Elle est composée des *consejeros* responsables des sujets européens dans les différentes CCAA et elle est présidée par le Ministre des Administrations Publiques[165]. Cette Conférence Sectorielle spécifique intervient dans les matières ne pouvant être confiées à aucune des autres Conférences Sectorielles *ad hoc* existant dans les différentes matières.

Dans la pratique, il est vrai que le mécanisme de la CARCE, selon certaines CCAA, ne fonctionne pas de façon adéquate et apparaît clairement insuffisant[166]. En outre, ces derniers temps, quelques tensions politiques importantes entre plusieurs des CCAA qui la composent et l'Etat sont apparues, au sujet de la possible participation directe des CCAA dans le Conseil[167]. On y détecte même des tensions et d'importantes différences de perception entre les CCAA elles-mêmes, fruit de l'évidente *asymétrie* qui existe entre elles[168].

Il existe aussi une coordination bilatérale, de nature exceptionnelle, entre l'Etat et une Communauté Autonome concrète en ce qui concerne les questions "qui intéressent de façon exclusive une Communauté Autonome ou qui présentent pour elle un aspect singulier en fonction de leur spécificité régionale". On retrouve cette spécificité, par exemple, dans certaines questions fiscales intéressant le Pays Basque et la Communauté Autonome de Navarre (concert économique).

2. *Perspective externe*

Mais la question la plus problématique est sans doute celle relative à la participation de représentants des CCAA dans les institutions et dans les organes communautaires. Il s'agit là d'une question ouverte qui fait actuellement l'objet d'un débat intense et polémique, en particulier en ce qui concerne la participation dans le Conseil. Afin d'étudier cette question, nous allons différencier la présence dans la Représentation Permanente, dans le Conseil, dans les groupes de travail de la Comission, dans l'accès à la CJCE et dans le Comité des Régions.

a. Présence dans la REPER

Depuis le moment même de l'entrée de l'Espagne dans la CE, on a constaté la nécessité de mettre en place des mécanismes susceptibles de permettre un certain type de présence des CCAA dans la Représentation Permanente de l'Espagne devant les Communautés Européennes (REPER). Au cours de la même année 1986, un projet d'Accord entre l'Etat et les CCAA créant un Observateur et un Observateur adjoint (inspiré sur le modèle allemand du *Beobachter*) a été élaboré, mais il n'a pas été conclu.

C'est en 1996 que la CARCE est arrivée à un accord[169] qui prit plus tard la forme d'un Décret Royal créant le poste de *Consejero Autonómico* au sein de la REPER[170]. Il s'agit cependant d'une fonction beaucoup plus modeste que celle d'Observateur. Il s'agit d'un représentant de l'Etat (et non pas des CCAA) dont la fonction se limite à se mettre en rapport avec les bureaux des CCAA à Bruxelles et, en particulier, à canaliser vers les CCAA l'information qui voit le jour dans le cadre communautaire. Dans la pratique, cela ne satisfait pas du tout les revendications des CCAA, même s'il faut bien reconnaître qu'il s'agit d'un progrès par rapport à la situation antérieure à 1996.

b. La (non) présence des Communautés Autonomes dans le Conseil

En étroite relation avec cette question on trouve celle la de la présence directe dans le Conseil. Il n'y a jamais eu dans le Droit Communautaire d'inconvénient à ce que les membres du Conseil permettent que d'autres personnes les accompagnent en représentation des régions. L'article 3.2 du Réglement interne du Conseil l'autorise[171]. Depuis le Traité de Maastricht, on reconnaît même explicitement la possibilité d'une présence directe des représentants régionaux dans le Conseil, pourvu qu'ils occupent un "rang ministeriel" et, surtout, qu'ils "soient habilités à engager la responsabilité du Gouvernement de l'Etat membre" (art. 203 TCE). Dans les Etat possédant une structure complexe, savoir s'il convient de faire usage de cette possibilité et, le cas échéant, d'articuler son fonctionnement, est donc une question de droit interne. En Espagne, plusieurs CCAA revendiquent depuis longtemps l'utilisation de cette possibilité. Le Congrès des Députés s'est lui-même prononcé en 1998 en faveur de cette présence et il existait d'ailleurs un compromis verbal de la mettre en place au cours de l'actuelle législature.

Il existe certes des difficultés techniques pour ce qui est de l'articulation de cette participation. Sur un plan technique et juridique, il n'existe cependant pas de difficultés majeures dans le fait d'articuler un système de participation des CCAA dans le Conseil[172]. En fait, conformément à la Constitution espagnole, seule serait nécessaire une loi de délégation qui, selon l'article 150.2 de la CE, viendrait habiliter les représentants des Communautés Autonomes à engager la responsabilité de l'Etat espagnol dans le sens de l'article 203 TCE. Cela mettrait en cause la considération selon laquelle seul le Gouvernement de l'Etat peut engager la responsabilité de l'Espagne dans le cadre international (*ius contrahendi*)[173]. Il est important de bien se rendre compte du fait qu'il ne s'agit pas d'une présence directe d'*une* Communauté Autonome en vue de la défense de *ses* intérêts propres, mais d'une représentation de l'Etat espagnol. La condition concernant le "rang ministériel" du représentant ne pose quant à elle aucune difficulté, étant donné que tout autant les Présidents des CCAA que les conseillers régionaux occupent, conformément au Droit interne, un tel rang.

Une toute autre question est celle relative à la volonté politique de le faire. Nous ne pensons pas qu'elle existe actuellement dans le Gouvernement. Contrairement à ce qu'ont connu l'Allemagne, l'Autriche ou la Belgique, le Gouvernement espagnol a jusqu'à présent refuser d'accepter une telle possibilité. Du reste, actuellement, il existe une rude polémique au sujet de cette question[174], en particulier dans des CCAA comme celle du Pays Basque[175], mais aussi dans d'autres comme la Catalogne et la Galice.

c. Participation des CCAA dans les groupes de travail de la Commission

Les CCAA ne peuvent évidemment réclamer aucun type de participation directe dans la Commission compte tenu du fait, bien connu par tous, que les membres de cette dernière représentent l'intérêt communautaire et non l'intérêt de l'Etat, ni celui des régions (art. 213 TCE). Par contre, la participation dans les groupes de travail est envisagée. Ainsi, depuis 1997, il existe un accord qui permet la participation de représentants régionaux dans 55 groupes de travail sur les 300 existants. En outre, ont actuellement lieu au sein de la CARCE des débats dont l'objet est d'étudier l'augmentation du nombre de groupes dans lesquels pourraient participer les CCAA.

d. Ius standi des CCAA devant la Cour de Justice

La possibilité d'articuler des mécanismes destinés à pallier la défectueuse situation contentieuse des régions dans le système contentieux communautaire a aussi été envisagée. Leur assimilation à des personnes juridiques dans les recours en annulation (art. 230 TCE) et en manquement (art. 232 TCE) gêne sensiblement la justification de l'intérêt direct et individuel exigé, et certaines Communautés Autonomes ont vu comment était rejeté le recours en annulation formé par elles ou par une autre personne juridique[176] alors qu'elles intervenaient comme partie jointe[177]. Il n'est donc pas étonnant que certaines CCAA réclament une modification des Traités constitutifs destinée à reconnaître une capacité pour agir propre aux régions, par rapport aux actes communautaires intéressant les compétences législatives de celles-ci[178].

Sont aussi apparus dans la pratique plusieurs cas de recours en manquement découlant d'un manquement d'une Communauté Autonome[179], ainsi que de nombreuses questions préjudicielles dans lesquelles étaient impliquées des normes adoptées par les CCAA[180]. Il n'existe pas dans ce domaine de difficultés dignes d'être mises en lumière, étant donné qu'il existe un Accord de 1997 qui articule la participation dans les procédures engagées devant la Cour de Justice. Les problèmes n'apparaissent que dans les seuls cas très particuliers dans lesquels il existe un conflit d'intérêts clair entre l'Etat et une Communauté Autonome[181].

e. Participation des CCAA dans le Comité des Régions

En ce qui concerne le Comité des Régions, il est bien connu que, malgré son nom, celui-ci ne représente pas seulement les intérêts des régions mais aussi ceux des collectivités locales. Ainsi, les 21 membres de la délégation espagnole se répartissent de la manière suivante: 4 pour les collectivités locales, élus par la Fédération Espagnole des Communes et des Provinces, et 17 pour les CCAA, chacune d'entre elles ayant un représentant. Face à sa réglementation actuelle, de nombreuses voix —en particulier les CCAA— réclament une réforme du Comité des Régions. On réclame essentiellement un renforcement de ses compétences actuelles, une reconsidération de la cohabitation en son sein entre les collectivités locales et les collectivités régionales et, dans certains cas, la reconnaissance de sa capacité pour agir devant la Cour de Justice pour qu'il puisse défendre ses (rares) prérogatives.

f) Les CCAA et le principe de su subsidiarité

Il convient de noter, pour terminer, que les CCAA réclament dans de nombreux cas une interprétation plus souple du principe de subsidiarité (art. 5 TCE), de façon que, conformément à la Déclaration annexe au Traité d'Amsterdam de l'Autriche, de l'Allemagne et de la Belgique, il "concerne non seulement les Etats membres mais aussi leurs entités dans la mesure où celles-ci disposent d'un pouvoir législatif qui leur est conféré par le Droit constitutionnel national". Il est symptomatique que, malgré les revendications expresses des CCAA, l'Etat espagnol ait refusé de signer cette déclaration quand il eut la possibilité de le faire.

IV. CONCLUSIONS ET RECOMMANDATIONS POUR 2004

1. Una nouvelle architecture: comment devrait-on voir une Constitution ou un Traité de l'UE?

Dans la longue marche vers la création d'un marché unique, le débat sur la "nouvelle architecture" de l'Europe intégrée ne manque pas d'antécédents. Il n'est pas nécessaire de revenir sur la progressive apparition de la "Constitution matérielle" que la jurisprudence communautaire a su articuler à travers une série d'événements très connus, à partir des prononcés génériques du début des années soixante (Van Gend & Loos, Costa/ENEL, San Michele, etc... [182]).

Bien qu'elles se trouvent sur un autre plan, il fautr aussi souligner l'importance des différentes initiatives qu'ont présentées la Commission et le Parlement tout au long des années soixante-dix et quatre-vingts, par rapport à des aspects concrets (éventuelle adhésion à la Convention européenne de sauvegarde des droits de l'homme et des libertés fondamentales) ou dans une perspective plus ample (déclaration des droits fondamentaux; projet de Constitution). Et au moins depuis la moitié des années quatre-vingts, en fonction des débats préalables et des critiques ultérieures à la réforme-gond que constitue sans doute le dénommé Acte unique européen (AUE), le Conseil (sans préjudice de son centralisme décisionnel, conscient de la dérive que comporterait la réaffirmation de la règle de la majorité qualifiée) s'est lui aussi joint à un débat qui, depuis lors, non seulement n'a pas cessé, mais qui a aussi fait l'objet d'une programmation expresse dans une séquence inédite de (in)décision et de débat qui, comme un calendrier électoral, débute en 1986/87 et va durer jusqu'en 2004 (et au-delà?), et qui se déroule à travers une succession de conférences intergouvernementales débouchant sur des réformes à la portée et au contenu différents et qui, avec l'émergence de l'Union Européenne, ont provoqué la disparition définitive de la tiédeur politique d'un processus d'intégration qui, d'un point de vue économique, a pris un élan décisif avec l'achèvement pratique du programme relatif au marché intérieur et avec la mise en marche additionnelle de la dénommée Union Economique et Monétaire (en particulier, avec l'apparition de la monnaie unique, qui ajoute à sa dimension économique une facette politique qui a aussi une valeur symbolique) et qui, par ailleurs, ont réussi à ébaucher un plan (en particulier, la citoyenneté de l'Union qui, au-delà de la propre organisation institutionnelle, a une certaine influence sur le fondement de la légitimation des institutions (locales) des Etats membres) à partir duquel, s'il existe la volonté politique nécessaire, il est possible d'aller de l'avant dans l'articulation d'une Union politique des Etats et des peuples d'Europe.

En effet, à partir de l'entrée en vigueur du Traité de Maastricht du 1er novembre 1993, une fois ratifié le statut danois (après la célébration d'un deuxième référendum) dans les termes qui découlent de l'éclaircissement en vertu de la toute singulière Décision des représentants des Gouvernements réunis dans le sein du Conseil Européen d'Edimbourg des 11 et 12 décembre 1992... [183], le débat sur la forme politique émergente de l'Europe en cours d'intégration a pris un élan considérable en ce qui concerne son objet, ce qui, dans une large mesure, se manifeste surtout dans l'élargissement du cercle des intervenants à un débat qui, au-delà du domaine étroit des eurocrates et des communautaristes, s'ouvre maintenant à l'ensemble des juristes (pas seulement des publicistes; en particulier, des constitutionnalistes), tout en acquérant une présence croissante dans les forums politiques et, par là-même, dans l'opinion publique.

Depuis lors, le débat a été programmé en fonction de dates fixes par l'intermédiaire de la prévision successive de conférences intergouvernementales périodiques célébrées en 1996 et en 2000 et prévues pour 2004. Mais la singularité d'un tel processus (constituant) ne réside pas seulement là; cette singularité est aussi palpable dans la modulation qui, en ce qui concerne la procédure actuelle de modification, découle de la création, par une décision du Conseil Européen de Laeken, d'un forum politique élargi à sa base, dénommé Convention, qui, conformément à l'expérience accumulée grâce à l'essai préalable d'élaboration de la Charte des droits fondamentaux de l'UE, est chargé du débat et de l'élaboration de propositions en vue de la prochaine modification des Traités, sur lesquelles devra se prononcer la conférence intergouvernementale dans l'exercice de sa capacité décisionnelle reconnue.

Même si la Constitution de l'Europe doit attendre la naissance du peuple européen, dans le sens déjà indiqué de la consolidation d'une loyauté politique se superposant aux loyautés (infra)étatiques, il est nécessaire de clarifier le système actuel afin de consolider la structure "constitutionnelle" d'une Union qui repose sur ses Etats (constitutionnels) et sur les citoyens (de ses Etats et qui sont en même temps ceux de l'UE elle-même).

En ce qui concerne le débat (en marche), nous allons faire quelques références synoptiques que nous allons regrouper selon qu'il s'agisse de questions relatives au fond ou à la forme, en ce qui concerne les (quatre) domaines matériels déjà mis en lumière lors du Conseil de Nice (rôle des parlements nationaux, statut de la Charte des Droits fondamentaux, partage des compétences et réformes institutionnelles...).

a. Exigences de fond: droits fondamentaux et séparation des pouvoirs

— *Droits fondamentaux (statut juridique de la Charte).* Il n'échappera à personne que non seulement la Charte des droits fondamentaux de l'UE ne résout pas le débat qui est apparu à propos de la future adhésion de l'UE/CE à la Convention européenne de sauvegarde des droits de l'homme et des libertés fondamentales, mais qu'elle contribue aussi sans doute, dans une certaine mesure, à l'alimenter [184].

La question la plus immédiate est malgré tout la suivante: que faire de la Charte? Maintenir son caractère actuel de déclaration est une option qui a été pratiquement écartée, eu égard à son effet paralysant dans le processus ouvert de discussion. En partant de l'idée de son insertion ou de sa greffe dans les Traités, indépendamment d'autres possibilités imaginables, l'option qui apparaît est donc celle qui consiste dans son insertion immédiate dans le texte articulé ou dans son insertion indirecte par le biais d'une référence expresse dans l'actuel art. 6.2 TUE.

L'option la plus solide en faveur de la "constitutionnalisation" semble être sans doute celle qui consiste dans son insertion immédiate dans le corps du Traité (consititutionnel) sur l'UE. Il est compréhensible que l'on défende cette option s' l'on fait preuve de ce que l'on pourrait appeler un européisme volontariste. Cependant, dans la perspective réaliste qui est celle du présent dossier, il n'est pas si évident qu'une option de cette nature contribue davantage que d'autres à la consolidation de la structure sur laquelle repose (comme condition) l'UE actuelle (en passe de multiplier pratiquement par deux le nombre d'Etats membres).

Dans cette même ligne de réflexion sereine, on a récemment mis en lumière les difficultés qui pourrait découler, en ce qui concerne la préservation de l'équilibre du système (établi) de protection communautaire des droits fondamentaux, d'une telle articulation de la Charte dans le corps des Traités [185].

— *Séparation des pouvoirs: réformes institutionnelles et rôle des parlements nationaux (et régionaux)? et le système de compétences.*

Réformes institutionnelles et processus décisionnel: la question ouverte de la forme de gouvernement de l'UE.

Ce débat concrétise dans une large mesure les visions les plus générales relatives à la fédéralisation ou à la confédéralisation de l'UE. L'accent est donc mis sur la transformation du Conseil en une deuxième Chambre (des exécutifs), selon le modèle allemand, ou, dans une perspective plus étatiste, on insiste sur le renforcement de la présence gouvernementale. Le débat est aussi alimenté depuis l'intérieur, dans la perspective des institutions elles-mêmes, et l'on comprend ainsi, par exemple, qu'il ressort du débat alimenté par la Commission, à propos de la "gouvernance" [186], une proposition de renforcement de cette institution, etc...

Le débat sur la réforme institutionnelle ne doit cependant pas être considéré seulement comme une simple conséquence instrumentale d'un vague débat sur la forme politique (territoriale) de l'UE; il contient au moins deux autres grandes questions, celle relative au (délicat) processus décisionnel et celle de la forme de gouverment de l'UE, qui, comme nous le verrons, ont des implications importantes en ce qui concerne la rationalisation du système normatif.

Il n'est pas nécessaire d'expliquer pour quelles raisons la réforme du processus décisionnel de l'UE (dans la perspective de son élargissement) est un sujet délicat. On le comprend bien à la vue des débats passionnés qui ont lieu ces derniers temps à propos de la composition définitive de la Commission et, surtout, de la (re)pondération des votes dans le Conseil et à propos de la question (décisive) des minorités de blocage dans le cadre d'un processus qui avance vers la généralisation de la majorité qualifiée. Sans préjudice de la modulation du sens politique du Conseil que comporte l'élargissement de la procédure de codécision, c'est dans cette question que réside la clé du fonctionnement normalisé d'une Union élargie.

Il faut pour cela faire très attention au moment de déterminer le poids (relatif) spécifique du quote-part décisionnel des Etats membres; et ceci parce que nous nous trouvons dans un système qui, par définition, repose sur l'ensemble des peuples des Etats membres et qui, sans préjudice de l'élimitation tendancielle des sectionnements au sein du PE, maintient dans le Conseil une base territoriale qui nous empêche de en tenir compte que des majorités. En conséquence, entre la majorité simple qui s'applique occasionnellement (ainsi, par exemple, dans les questions de procédure) et l'unanimité résiduelle qui, même en dehors du contexte communautaire, connaît certaines modulations (avec, par exemple, l'abstention n'empêchant pas la prise de décisions), le système qui s'impose est celui de la majorité qualifiée à partir de laquelle se forme la minorité de blocage. Celle-ci doit être la règle dans le système de l'UE, mais avec des exceptions; et il ne s'agit pas seulement de préserver le véto (lequel connaîtrait par exemple une importante modulation si l'on ne faisait pas dépendre l'entrée en vigueur des réformes de leur ratification dans tous les pays, comme c'est le cas actuellement).

Il s'agirait donc de rechercher les possibilités de procédure susceptibles de réorienter et de freiner, ou même d'empêcher, l'adoption de décisions violant gravement les intérêts généraux, mais très concrets, des Etats membres [187].

En relation directe avec la question antérieure, se trouve celle relative à la forme de gouvernement de l'UE. Les propositions de réforme qui insistent sur la dérive gouvernementaliste de la Commission et sur la consolidation des profils parlementaires de ses relations avec le PE et qui, au-delà de ces aspects, défendent un renforcement du contrôle du Conseil ordinaire (et européen) par le PE, etc... ne devraient pas perdre de vue l'inconvenance (ou même l'impossibilité) radicale de la parlementarisation d'un système de base (essentiellement) territoriale qui repose sur la pratique du consensus (et, par défaut, de la majorité qualifiée). Un système parlementaire de gouvernement basé sur la majorité simple (et/ou, par défaut, sur la majorité qualifiée) présente des difficultés en ce qui concerne l'acceptation de ses décisions dès lors qu'en présence de sectionnements, se forme une minorité permanente (ce qui est le cas, dans un certain sens, du système espagnol).

La question de la forme de Gouvernement de l'Union n'est donc pas de moindre importance. Les insinuations à propos de l'élection directe d'un Président de l'UE, ainsi que les risques de dérive directoriale qui découlent du débat actuel sur les futures présidences de l'UE, à cause de leurs implications, démontrent qu'il est nécessaire d'organiser un grand débat sur le meilleur (le plus adéquat) système de gouvernement pour la future UE.

Rôle des parlements nationaux (et régionaux)? On ne peut pas ignorer qu'avec l'élection directe des représentants des peuples des Etats dans le PE, les Parlements nationaux se sont vu déplacés vers une position désaxée, ce qui contraste avec la position centrale qu'occupent toujours les membres des Gouvernements, lesquels, face à une telle évidence, se sont vus dans l'obligation de reconnaître par l'intermédiaire d'une Déclaration expresse la nécessité de renforcer leur insertion dans le processus décisionnel [188].

Les résultats insatisfaisants auxquels ont aboutis les différents essais de compensation mis en pratique, d'une part, et leur présence ressuscitée dans la "Convention" [189] qui a élaboré la Charte et qui travaille sur les réformes auxquelles il est fait référence, d'autre part, convergent dans la conviction de la nécessité de repenser leur rôle (celui des Parlements étatiques et infraétatiques) dans le processus décisionnel, d'élaboration du droit (fort ou faible[190]) dans le cadre de l'UE.

La question de savoir s'il faut ou non ajouter à cette plus grande insertion dans (le versant interne) du processus décisionnel une présence directe dans l'organisation institutionnelle de l'UE est particulièrement controversée. Les modèles de deuxième Chambre que l'on trouve dans certains Etats membres pourraient orienter le débat. Ainsi, pour ne donner qu'un exemple, on peut imaginer qu'une fraction du PE pourrait exercer certaines fonctions de deuxième Chambre (en particulier, en jouant un rôle important dans la supervision et dans le contrôle de l'application dans le système du principe de subsidiarité, grâce à l'attribution d'un pouvoir (indiret) d'initiative et d'amendement et, peut-être, grâce aussi à la reconnaissance d'une légitimité (indirecte) lui permettant d'inciter le PE à saisir la CJ à propos du respect dudit principe); les options sont nombreuses, mais il ne s'agit pas ici d'en faire la liste.

En outre, il est clair qu'un tel débat provoquerait, directement ou indirectement, une intensification des revendications des Parlements régionaux (étant donné qu'ils forment le Comité des Régions) qui, par émulation, veulent aussi devenir une deuxième (bis) Chambre; et que pourrait-on alors répondre à ceux qui réclament la création d'une espèce de Conseil fédéral à partir des Conseils actuels?

Il faut donc faire très attention en évitant d'improviser dans un système qui se caractérise par l'existence de délicats (dés)équilibres. La politique des petits pas semble être aussi dans ce domaine la meilleure recette.

Système de compétences. En ce qui concerne la nécessité de délimiter plus précisément le partage des compétences entre l'Union européenne et les Etats membres, dans le respect du principe de subsidiarité, de nombreuses propositions sont apparues au cours de ces derniers mois.

En résumé, on a proposé la création d'un catalogue de compétences [191] pouvant contribuer, d'une manière ou d'une autre, à une délimitation plus adéquate et à une nécessaire (re)définition des compétences dans le domaine de l'UE.

En ce qui concerne la redéfinition, on parle surtout (en particulier dans le droit allemand) de la possible "renationalisation" de politiques qui, à leur coût budgétaire élevé ajoutent le fait d'avoir une influence sur les compétences des Länder. Au-delà du "slogan" (derrière lequel se cachent des préoccupations budgétaires et, en dernier lieu, un désaccord en ce qui concerne les apports des Etats membres), il existe des raisons qui, dans le cadre d'un débat serein, devraient permettre de mieux profiler la concurrence en matière de compétences (par exemple, dans le domaine de la politique agricole commune) ou, plus largement, de consolider le contrôle politique de l'application effective du principe de subsidiarité (et de proportionnalité) [192], dont le potentiel de renationalisation, qui reste à découvrir, se consolidera sûrement si l'on continue à avancer dans la mise en commun de nouveaux domaines, par exemple, en matière de sécurité, de défense, etc...

En ce qui concerne la meilleure délimitation (verticale) des compétences, il est clair qu'un catalogue précis et complet de compétences affecterait dans une large mesure l'actuel équilibre instable d'un système en formation. Entre le catalogue définitif et la situation actuelle, il existe une longue liste de possibilités que l'on devrait épuiser avant d'avancer dans la "fédéralisation" du système.

Le système communautaire de compétences [193], dont les principes directeurs ont été mis en place expressément à l'occasion de la rédaction du Traité de Maastricht (art. 5 TCE actuel), s'est établi essentiellement à travers une jurisprudence activiste qui a provoqué en certaines occasions la réaction de certaines juridictions nationales [194], même si elle a été suivie dans une large mesure. La controverse croissante concernant leur passivité dans le contrôle des interprétation extensives des titres comunautaires de compétence, qui n'a été démentie par la CJ que ces dernières années[195], montre la nécessité d'une réforme des Traités en ce qui concerne la trame (complexe) des compétences basée sur un finalisme qui, dans une large mesure, laisse à l'interprète la définition du système. Compte tenu de l'étendue actuelle des compétences, il est indispensable de progresser fermement dans la clarification et dans la délimitation des compétences (sans nécessité d'abandonner définitivement un certain finalisme), à travers bien sûr une meilleure identification des titres de compétences, en simplifiant et en clarifiant leur structure normative logiquement différente des normes de procédure et des normes directives; et, sans préjudice d'autres idées qui ont déjà été avancées par la doctrine [196], à travers une clarification de l'intensité des compétences (exclusivité ou concurrence; partage ou complémentarité; etc...) qui, prima facie, permette de ne pas confier à l'interprète suprême la détermination du régime (une toute autre chose étant la portée concrète) de la compétence.

b. Exigences de forme: simplification des Traités et rationalisation du système de sources

De la même manière que le substantif Constitution doit attendre, en l'absence d'une légitimation propre (suffisante), il est urgent de procéder à une simplification de portée qui, à partir de la complexe trame des Traités, puisse synthétiser les éléments structurels fondamentaux dans de leur contenu constitutionnel [197]; c'est-à-dire, un Traité qui ajoute à la facette formelle qui lui est propre la dimension matérielle qui découle du terme qui le qualifie. L'existence d'un Traité constitutionnel renforcerait une supralegalité qui est déjà présente dans la nette distinction (formelle) entre la modification des Traités et celle du droit dérivé.

En outre, de la clarification de la structure institutionnelle (du processus décisionnel et de la forme de gouvernement) de l'UE peut sans doute découler une rationalisation minimum du système des sources du droit de l'UE. Non seulement à la vue des nouveaux types normatifs qui sont apparus, à cheval entre les dispositions de droit international et le droit communautaire lui-même, en particulier, en matière de coopération judiciaire et policière pénale, mais aussi compte tenu des déficiences et des carences systématiques qui découlent d'une horizontalité des pouvoirs et qui, au fur et à mesure qu'un (co)législateur apparaît et que l'on avance dans la distinction entre les normes de base et celle de développement et entre les fonctions normative et exécutive, sont de plus en plus visibles. La déclaration relative à la hierarchie des "actes normatifs" communautaires elle-même est un bon exemple l'importance de ces déficiences systématiques, qui sont difficilement tolérables dans le cadre de l'UE.

Tout aussi urgente semble être la tâche, qui correspond davantage à la doctrine qu'à un processus de réforme, qui consiste à formuler des propositions en ce qui concerne la modification de la typologie actuelle des actes communautaires [198]; même si cela peut paraître moins important, il est aussi nécessaire d'écarter quelques inerties (internationalistes), par exemple en ce qui concerne l'expression (vrai capharnaüm) des actes atypiques, derrière laquelle se cachent des manifestations de convention politique institutionnelle, en passant par les plus diverses manifestations (déclarations, résolutions, communications...) et expressions typiques de l'autonomie réglementaire des Institutions. Il s'agirait donc de tirer les conséquences de la spécificité de l'ordre juridique communautaire.

2. *Une Constitution pour l'Union européenne: conditions d'adoption et de révision; ses relations avec les Constitutions nationales*

Nous pouvons renvoyer sur ce point à ce qui a déjà été dit à propos du sujet 'Constitution/Traité'. En théorie, n'importe quelle réforme des Traités pourrait être ratifiée par le biais d'une L.O. (art. 93 CE). Cependant:

— A l'occasion d'une césure politique divisant pratiquement en deux moitiés les représentants politiques du peuple espagnol, conformément à l'art. 92 CE, il faudrait convoquer un référendum préalable à la ratification de la réforme en question; autrement, la légitimité d'une telle réforme serait fragilisée et dépendrait de la formation d'une majorité politique alternative... (la simple majorité absolue ne semble pas suffisante dans des hypothèses d'une telle importance)...

— Si compte tenu de l'importance (matérielle ou de procédure) de la réforme, avant de procéder à sa ratification, on utilisait le mécanisme de contrôle préalable de constitutionnalité des traités internationaux de l'art. 95.2 CE (et 78 LOTC) et si, une fois adoptée la Déclaration correspondante, on décidait de son inconstitutionnalité, il faudrait procéder prálablement à la révision de la Constitution en obtenant des Chambres, en fonction de la procédure de réforme, une majorité aggravée des 3/5 (de manière alternative, 2/3 CD + majorité absolue S) ou des 2/3 (avant et après leur dissolution) de leurs membres, suivi d'un référendum (facultatif dans le cas de l'art. 167 CE); hypothèse dans laquelle il serait choquant de recourir ensuite à la simple majorité absolue de la L.O. de l'art. 93 CE pour autoriser la ratification de la réforme.

A la vue de ce que l'on vient de dire, il semble que l'on ne puisse rien objecter ex Constitutione à la ratification à la majorité absolue de l'art. 93 CE de l'hypothétique modification qui ne ferait plus reposer uniquement la procédure de modification des Traités sur la clause de renvoi aux deux ordres constitutionnels, parce que, et dans la mesure où, celle-ci serait complétée par l'exigence additionnelle d'un prononcé des citoyens de l'UE, par l'intermédiaire d'une consultation directe, dans le cadre d'un référendum. Une telle hypothèse n'exigerait pas, même en l'absence d'une clause d'ouverture plus précise, une prévision expresse dans la propre Constitution.

A fortiori, on ne peut rien objecter non plus à la la modulation de la procédure de révision de l'art. 48 TUE que l'on relie à l'élargissement de la base de légitimité découlant de la composition plurielle de la Convention chargée de réaliser les travaux préparatoires et de formuler des recommandations expresses (autorisées mais non obligatoires) en fonction desquelles, le moment venu, la conférence intergouvernementale devra agir.

3. Processus constitutionnel et élargissement: comment impliquer les pays candidats?

Comme c'est bien connu, la Déclaration n° 23 relative à l'avenir de l'Union prévoit expressément la participation des pays candidats à la conférence intergouvernementale de 2004 en qualité d'observateurs. A cet effet, le Conseil Européen de Laeken a déclaré expressément que ceux-ci pourront prendre part aux délibérations de la Convention..., comme les Etats membres eux-mêmes, par l'intermédiaire des représentants de leurs Gouvernements (1) et de leurs Parlements (2)[199].

L'assimilation de cette présence directe dans la Convention des pays candidats à l'intégration à celle des Etats membres eux-mêmes a ses limites car, même s'ils jouissent du droit à intervenir dans les débats et même si rien en lesempêche de contribuer à la recherche de positions de consensus qui, si elles sont finalement adoptées par la Convention, prennent la forme de "Recommandations", ils ne sont pas en mesure de freiner l'adoption d'une proposition concrète ayant déjà fait l'objet d'un consensus entre les Etats membres; en outgre, leurs représentants restent-ils en dehors du Presidium.

Quoi qu'il en soit, dans la mesure où les Conseils Européens successifs vont prendre note des travaux de la Convention, on ne peut douter de l'effet positif qu'a dans les pays candidats l'invitation à évaluer conjointement avec les Etats membres les possibles réformes. L'invitation traditionnellement envoyée aux pays candidats afin de leur permettre d'être présents (dans une certaine mesure) dans les Conseils Européens immédiatement antérieurs à une intégration embryonnaire, au-delà de son utilité effective, a toujours été considéré comme un geste politique significatif en ce qui concerne la legitimation d'une décision cruciale pour l'avenir des Etats adhérents [200].

NOTES

* Professeur (catedrático) de Droit International Public. Titulaire de la Chaire *Jean Monnet*. Université La Rioja.

** Professeur (profesor titular) de Droit Constitutionnel. Université Autónoma de Madrid.

1 F. RUBIO LLORENTE: "La Constitución como fuente del Derecho", in ídem, *La forma del poder*. Ed. CEC, Madrid, 1993 (1999), p. 87; ídem: Notion "Constitución", in *Enciclopedia Jurídica Básica (EJB)*, Ed. Civitas. Madrid, 1994, p. 1526.

2 *Vid*. F. RUBIO LLORENTE: "El proceso constituyente en España", in ídem, *La forma del...* (cit.), pp. 41, 48.

3 *id*., entre autres, L. LÓPEZ GUERRA: "El derecho constitucional español. Origen y características de la Constitución", in ídem e.a., *Derecho Constitucional I*, Ed. Tirant lo Blanch, Valencia, 1994 (2ème éd.), pp. 22-3: "(...) au cours du régime, une série de "Lois Fondamentales" (jusqu'à sept) sont apparues; ces textes établissaient une organisation institutionnelle, exécutive et législative, et, sans limiter le pouvoir du Général Franco, ils rendaient possible le fonctionnement de l'Etat sans intervention immédiate et directe de celui-ci. En tout cas, il s'agissait de normes concernant surtout des aspects d'organisation, qui excluaient tout autant la participation démocratique que la garantie des droits fondamentaux".

4 Sur le sens de cette expression, *vid*. G. JELLINEK: *Teoría general del Estado* (1890), (trad. Fernando de los Ríos). Buenos Aires, 1973, *passim*.

5 *Vid*., par exemple, H. McILWAIN: *Constitucionalismo antiguo y moderno* (1940), trad. J. J. Solozábal Echavarría (1991), Ed. CEC, Madrid.

6 Selon la formulation synthétique de l'art. 16 de la Déclaration française des droits de l'homme et du citoyen (1789): "Toute societé dans laquelle la garantie des droits n´est pas assurée, ni la séparation des pouvoirs determinée, n´a pas de Constitution".

7 Occasionellement, en l'absence de prévision expresse, la déclaration d'inconstitutionnalité a suivi sans solution de continuité l'épuisement de la potentialité de l'interprétation de la conformité constitutionnelle de la loi (dans une perspective historique, *vid*. P. CRUZ VILLALÓN: *La formación del sistema europeo de control de constitucionalidad 1918-1939*, Ed. CEC, Madrid, 1987, *passim*; plus proche dans le temps et en ce qui concerne le droit communautaire, *vid*. P. DYRBERG: "La Constitución danesa y la Unión Europea II (Comentario a la Sentencia del Tribunal

Supremo danés, de 6 de abril de 1998", in *Revista de Derecho Comunitario Europeo* (RDCE), 4 (1998), pp. 573 et s.).

[8] L. LÓPEZ GUERRA: *Introducción al derecho constitucional*, Ed. Tirant lo Blanch. Valencia, 1994, p. 22.

[9] Dans la doctrine espagnole, *vid.*, entre autres, L. Mª DÍEZ-PICAZO GIMÉNEZ: "Reflexiones sobre la idea de Constitución europea", in *RIE* 1993, p. 533 et s.

[10] De manière générale, *vid.* F. RUBIO LLORENTE: "Mayorías y minoría en el poder constituyente", in ídem, *La forma del poder (Estudios sobre la Constitución)*, Ed. CEC. Madrid, 1993 (1ère éd.), pp. et s.

[11] *Vid.*, dans ce même sens, L. Mª DÍEZ-PICAZO GIMÉNEZ: *Tratados y Constitución, in Ídem: Constitucionalismo de la Unión Europea*, Ed. Civitas. Madrid, 2002, pp. 81, 105.

[12] M. GARCÍA-PELAYO ALONSO: *Las transformaciones del Estado contemporáneo* (1977*)*, Alianza Ed., (3ème éd.), Madrid, 1982, p. 155 (même si "(...) compte tenu du fait que certaines décisions et certaines compétences passent à l'organisation régionale et que d'autres doivent s'exercer dans le cadre et dans les conditions établis par cette dernière..." —précise t-on—, l'autodétermination nationale se transforme en simple coparticipation).

[13] Conclus, à la différence des Traités qui sont apparus plus tard, pour une période de temps limitée (50 ans), le TCECA cessera de produire ses effets cette année (2002).

[14] Ce sont en effet les fondements derniers de la construction jurisprudentielle, basée sur une interprétation systématique et finaliste des Traités (constitutifs), de la toute nouvelle doctrine (Van Gend & Loos; Costa; etc...) de la spécificité du droit communautaire, entendu comme un ordre juridique propre, à cheval entre les ordres juridiques nationaux et le droit international (*vid.*, entre autres, A. LÓPEZ CASTILLO: *Constitución e integración*, Ed. CEC. Madrid, 1996, pp. 9, 10 et s.).

[15] *Vid.* l'important apport d'A. von BOGDANDY: *Supranationale Union als neuer Herrschaftstypus: Entstaatlichung und Vergemeinschaftung in staatstheoretischer Perspektive, in Integration* (1993), pp. 210 et s.

[16] Dans la doctrine espagnole (internationaliste), s'est généralisée (avec des nuances) la thèse des trois piliers (*vid.*, à titre d'exemple, la synthèse expositive de P. ANDRÉS SÁENZ DE SANTAMARÍA *e. a., Introducción al Derecho de la Unión Europea*, Ed. Eurolex. Madrid, 1999 (2ème éd.), pp. 61 et s.; A. MANGAS MARTÍN/D. J. LIÑÁN NOGUERAS: *Instituciones y Derecho de la Unión Europea*, Ed. McGraw Hill. Madrid, 1999.

[17] ur ce point, nous suivons de près A. LÓPEZ CASTILLO: "La Constitución y el proceso de integración europea", in C. Closa (éd.), *La europeización del sistema político español*, Ed. Istmo. Madrid (2001), pp. 127 et s.; ídem, "A propósito de la 'Constitución' de Europa", in *Cuadernos de Alzate* 25 (2001), pp. 81, 82 et s.

[18] *Vid.* DCJ 2/94, du 28 mars 1996 (CEDH); ACJ du 5 octobre 2000, aff. C-376/98 (Directive tabac). Sur l'interprétation de la "Constitución des compétences" découlant du TUE, *vid.*, en espagnol, T. STEIN: "La sentencia del Tribunal constitucional alemán sobre el Tratado de Maastricht..." (trad. J. Martín

Pérez de Nanclares), in *RIE* 21 1994, pp. 745 et s.; A. LÓPEZ CASTILLO: "De integración y soberanía. El Tratado sobre la Unión europea ante la Ley Fundamental alemana", in *REDC* 40 (1994), pp. 207 et s.

[19] *Vid.*, de manière générale, F. RUBIO LLORENTE: "El constitucionalismo de los Estados integrados de Europa (estudio preliminar)", in ídem/M. Daranas, *Constituciones de los Estados de la Unión Europea*, Ed. Ariel. Barcelona, 1997; G. C. RODRÍGUEZ IGLESIAS: "Tribunales constitucionales y derecho comunitario", in *Hacia un nuevo orden internacional y europeo (Livre rédigé en l'honneur du professeur M. Díez de Velasco),* Madrid, 1993, pp. 1175 et s.

[20] *Vid.* DCJ 1/91, du 14 décembre (cfr., entre autres, J. A. VALLE GÁLVEZ: "La especificidad del ordenamiento comunitario...", in *RIE* 1993, pp. 155 et s.; J. DUTHEIL DE LA ROCHÉRE: "L´espace économique européen sous le regard des juges de la Cour de Justice des Communautés européennes", in *RMC (UE),* 360 (1992), pp. 603 et s.

[21] On parle à ce propos de "Verfassungsverbund" (I. PERNICE, "Die dritte Gewalt im europäischen Verfassungsverbund", in *EuR* 1/1996, pp. 27 et s.; ídem: "Europäisches und nationales Verfassungsrecht", in *VVDStRL* (2000), 2001, pp. 148 et s.

[22] DTC, du 1er juillet 1992 (TUE), FJ 4.

[23] Cit. d'A. LÓPEZ CASTILLO: "La Constitución y el proceso de integración", in C. Closa (éd.): *La europeización del sistema político español,* Ed. Istmo. Madrid, 2001, pp. 124, 129 et s.

[24] DCJ 1/91, du 14 décembre, paragraphe 21. Sur le sens et la portée de cette importante décision, *vid.*, entre autres, A. LÓPEZ CASTILLO: *Constitución e integración* (1996) préc., pp. 16 et s., avec des références additionnelles.

[25] A. LÓPEZ CASTILLO: *Constitución e integración* (1996), préc., pp. 313 et s.

[26] Sur le sens de ce concept, *vid.* P. CRUZ VILLALÓN: "La constitución territorial del Estado", dans l'ouvrage collectif: *El Estatuto de Andalucía (I): Las competencias*, Ed. Ariel. Barcelona, 1990, pp. 9 et s.

[27] *Vid.* ATC du 1er juillet 1992 (TUE); *vid.*, à ce propos, P. PÉREZ TREMPS: *Constitución española y Comunidad Europea*, Civitas, Madrid, p. 64.

[28] P. PÉREZ TREMPS: *Constitución española y Comunidad Europea* (1994), p. 92, a parlé avec justesse d' "une espèce de garantie institutionnelle de l'Etat luimême".

[29] A. LÓPEZ CASTILLO: *Constitución e integración* (1996), préc., pp. 388 et s.

[30] En ce qui concerne la question controversée des standards de protection, vid. certaines considérations relatives à son traitement dans les dispositions générales de la Charte des droits fondamentaux de l'UE, dans le paragraphe II.2.a).

[31] *Vid.*, en particulier, ATC 130/1995, 120/1998, d'une part (cfr. P. PÉREZ TREMPS: *Derecho constitucional y derecho comunitario* (1999), préc., p. 22), et, d'autre part, ATC 13/1998 (et VV.PP.).

[32] *Vid.* son intervention que l'on peut lire dans "Constitución española: Trabajos parlamentarios", IV, pp. 4598-9; le Sénateur précisait dans ce même sens que "(...) l'adhésion (espagnole aux Communautés européennes) va au-delà de la célébration classique de traités, et va même au -delà du transfert de souveraineté pouvant avoir lieu dans une Union personnelle des Etats, dans laquelle les juridictions restent intactes, intègres, et ne se confondent pa" (*vid.*, in DSCG (S), nº 69, pp. 3148-9).

[33] Ainsi que l'art. 96.2 de la Constitution espagnole, bien qu'implicitement. Selon nous, l'explication la plus sensée du contenu de l'article 96.2 ("Pour dénoncer les Traités ou les accords internationaux, on suivra la même procédure que celle qui est prévue pour leur approbation à l'article 94") réside dans la prise en considération de l'objectif d'intégration de l'art. 93 de la Constitution espagnole (absence d'une clause permettant de dénoncer des Traités conclus —à l'exception du TCECA— pour une durée illimitée).

[34] Art. 81.2 de la Constitution espagnole: "Les lois organiques seront adoptées, modifiées ou abrogées à la majorité absolue des membres du Congrès, par un vote final sur l'ensemble du projet".

[35] *Vid.* L.O. 10/1985, du 2 août (Traité d'adhésion de l'Espagne); L.O. 4/1986, du 26 novembre (AUE); L.O. 10/1992, du 28 décembre (TrMaastricht); L.O. 20/1994, du 29 décembre (Traité Adhésion/AFS); L.O. 9/1998, du 16 décembre (TrAmsterdam).

[36] *Vid.* art. 94.1 et 2 de la Constitution espagnole; art. 154-160 du Réglement du Congrès des Députés (RCD) et art. 144-7 du Réglement du Sénat (RS).

[37] En définitive —a t-on dit—, l'art. 93 de la Constitution espagnole ne contient pas une procédure d'autorisation renforcée par rapport à celle qu'articule l'art. 94.1 de la Constitution espagnole, mais, en réalité, une procédure d'autorisation différente (A. LÓPEZ CASTILLO: *Constitución e integración* (1996), préc., pp. 208 et s., avec des références additionnelles; A. REMIRO BROTONS: "Artículos 93 y 94. Tratados internacionales", in O. Alzaga (dir.), *Comentarios a las Leyes políticas. Constitución española de 1978*, VII, préc., p. 515).

[38] *Vid.* art. 90.2 de la Constitution espagnole (disposition générale: majorité simple, dans le délai de deux mois) et art. 132.1 RCD (disposition spécifique: majorité absolue, en tout cas).

[39] Il ne l'est pas, dans un sens strict, sauf dans la mesure où, selon l'art. 69.5 de la Constitution espagnole, il est composé résiduellement par des représentants régionaux. Dans l'attente de la réforme constitutionnelle qui corrigera définitivement l'institutionnalisation déficiente de l'Etat régional, quelques progrès ont été faits au niveau réglementaire, grâce à la création (en 1994) dans cette Chambre d'une dénommée "commission générale des Communautés Autonomes" (art. 55-56 bis 8).

[40] *Vid.* A. LÓPEZ CASTILLO: "La Constitución y el proceso de integración europea", in C. Closa (éd.), *La europeización del sistema político español* (2001), préc., pp. 124, 143.

[41] Cfr., entre autres, P. PÉREZ TREMPS: *Constitución española y Comunidad europea* (1994), préc., p. 80; A. LÓPEZ CASTILLO: *Constitución e integración* (1996), préc., pp. 211 et s.

[42] Dans la perspective politique, *vid.* la défense du caractère instrumental de la loi organique de la part du parlementaire MORÁN LÓPEZ in BOCG, n° 156-I, A, du 15 juin 1985, p. 10.184. Dans la doctrine, on peut noter l'analyse très solide de G. C. RODRÍGUEZ IGLESIAS: "Problemas jurídicos de la adhesión de España a la Comunidad Europea", in *Cursos de derecho internacional público de Vitoria-Gasteiz (1984)*, UPV, 1985, pp. 193, 208; ídem, "Rechtsprobleme des Beitritts Spaniens zur Europäischen Gemeinschaft", in J. Schwarze (éd.): *Integrationsrecht. Beiträge zu Recht und Politik der EG...* . Hamburg, 1986, II, pp. 9, 13.

[43] Ainsi, en marge des progrès successifs réalisés dans le cadre du processus d'intégration européenne, cette procédure a été recemment utilisée afin d'autoriser la ratification par le Royaume d'Espagne du Statut du Tribunal Pénal International, par la L.O. 6/2000, du 4 octobre (BOE, du 5 octobre). Toute autre est la nature (formelle et matérielle) des lois organiques 15/1994, du 1er juin (BOE, du 2 juin) et 4/1998, du 1er juillet (BOE, du 2 juillet), promulguées afin d'exécuter les Résolutions 827 (1993) et 995 (1994), du Conseil de Sécurité des Nations Unies, sans préjudice du respect de la réserve constitutionnelle de loi (organique).

[44] *Vid.* ATC, du 1er juillet 1992, FJ 4. Et dans la doctrine, M. HERRERO RODRÍGUEZ DE MIÑÓN: "Constitución española y Unión Europea. Comentarios al artículo 93 de la Constitución española", in *RCG* 26 (1992), pp. 7, 10; M. ARAGÓN REYES: "La Constitución española y el Tratado de la Unión Europea: la reforma de la Constitución", in *REDC* 42 (1994), pp. 9, 15.

[45] *Vid.*, dans le détail, A. LÓPEZ CASTILLO: "La caracterización de la naturaleza jurídica de la atribución-cesión de competencias derivadas de la Constitución: unas consideraciones introductorias", in *REP* 90, 1995 (n° monographique: Closa/López Castillo (coord.), *La reforma...*), pp. 173 et s.

[46] *Vid.* L. Mª DÍEZ-PICAZO GIMÉNEZ: "Tratados y Constitución", in *Constitucionalismo de la Unión Europea,* Ed. Civitas, Madrid, 2002, pp. 81, 106.

[47] L. Mª DÍEZ-PICAZO GIMÉNEZ: "Tratados y Constitución", in *op. cit.,* pp. 104 et s., étude dans laquelle l'auteur rappelle de manière très sensée à propos du possible changement de fondement de l'UE, en partant de l'inexistence d'une division claire entre la Constitution et le Traité "en ce qui concerne leur adoption, leur modification ou leur extinction", que "ce qui est vraiment important ce n'est pas tant la dénomination du document; ce sont surtout son mode d'élaboration et d'adoption, les pouvoirs octroyés aux institutions communautaires, la position des Etats membres, etc." (106).

[48] Pour plus de détails, *vid.* A. LÓPEZ CASTILLO: "A propósito de la "Constitución" de Europa", in *Cuadernos de Alzate*, 25 (2001), pp. 81, 90 et s.

[49] Décret Royal 779/2001 du 5 juillet, créant le Conseil pour le débat sur l'avenir de l'Union Européenne, *BOE* n° 167, du 13 juillet 2001, p. 2542.

[50] La présidence échut à Mr. Álvaro Rodríguez Bereijo, professeur de droit, exprésident du Tribunal constitutionnel et ancien membre de la Convention ayant élaboré la Charte des droits fondamentaux de l'UE.

[51] www.futuroeuropa.es.

[52] http://uniovi.es/%7Econstitucional/derecho/PrincipInf.html.

[53] En ce qui concerne les deux partis majoritaires, pour le Parti Populaire (PP), voir par exemple, les réflexions sur l'"Espagne en Europe et dans le monde" formulées dans son dernier programme électoral; http://www.pp.es/popular/pro-ele-pp.pdf., pp.102-108. Sur la position du Parti Socialiste Ouvrier Espagnol (PSOE), voir http://www.psoe.es/NuevasPoliticas- NuevosTiempos/Documentos/ Elecciones 1999/ManifiestoEuropeo-central.htm. ("Nos compromis en Europe").

[54] Voir, par exemple, le rapport présenté lors du dernier Congrès du Parti Populaire en février et intitulé "L'Etat du XXIème siècle-Les nouvelles responsabilités; http://www.pp.es/ponencias/pon_2aprobada.pdf., en particulier le paragraphe 8.

[55] Cette dernière position est défendue essentiellement par les partis nationalistes du Pays Basque —Parti Nationaliste Basque (PNV)— et de Catalogne —Convergencia i Unió (CiU)— qui réclament la formation, sur le plan interne, d'un Etat plurinational et, sur le plan européen, d'une Union qui tienne compte dans son architecture institutionnelle et politique des régions ayant des compétences législatives propres, voir, par exemple, la Déclaration conjointe de Barcelone du 16 juillet 1998 du PNV, de CiU et du Bloc Nacionaliste Galicien (BNG); http://www.mir.es/oris/paz/docs/treg-03.htm.

[56] Il s'agit de la position que défend actuellement le PSOE. Sur cette question, *vid. infra* III.

[57] Voir par exemple, dans ce sens, A. PUTTLER: "Art. 6 TUE", *in* C. CALLIES, C./M. RUFFERT (éd.), *Kommentar zu EU-Vertrag und EG-Vertrag*, Luchterhand, Neuwied, 1999, pp. 49-119, en particulier p. 113.

[58] Voir von BOGDANDY: "The European Union as a Supranational Federation: A Conceptual Attempt in the Light of the Amsterdam Treaty", *The Columbia Journal of European Law* 2000, p. 27; J. MARTÍN Y PÉREZ DE NANCLARES: "The Federal Elements of the European Union", *Zeitschrift für Europarechtliche Studien* 2001, pp. 595-625; M. ZULEEG: "Die föderativen Grundsätze der Europäischen Union", *Neue Juristische Wochenschrift* 2000, pp. 2846-2851.

[59] Se rappeler, par exemple, du polémique discours prononcé par le Ministre allemand des affaires étrangères, J. FISCHER, en mai 2000, à l'Université von Humbolt de Berlin, à propos de la création d'une "Fédération européenne"; *Agence Europe* du 13.5.2000, p. 3, sur les réactions voir RICCARDI *in Agence Europe* des 22 et 23.5.2000, p. 3. L. JOSPIN a par la suite proposé la mise en place d'une "Fédération d'Etats nationaux", tandis que T. BLAIR critique toute approche de l'Europe comme un *Superstate*. Il semble malgré tout que le secteur doctrinal qui recommande plus de pragmatisme dans ce délicat débat constitutionnel n'a pas tout à fait tort; cfr. S. GRILLER: "Mehr Pragmatismus in der Europäischen Verfassungsdebatte, bitte!", *Europäische Zeitschrift für Wirtschafsrecht* 2002, p. 3.

[60] J. LASO PÉREZ: *La cooperación leal en el ordenamiento comunitario*, Colex, Madrid, 2000, en particulier p. 475.

[61] Dans ce sens, par exemple, M. HILF: "Europäische Union und nationale Identität der Mitgliedstaaten", *Gedächtnisschrift für E. Grabitz*, C.H. Beck, Munich, 1995, pp. 157 et s., en particulier p. 167.

[62] *Vid.* J. MARTÍN Y PÉREZ DE NANCLARES: *El sistema de competencias de la Comunidad Europea*, McGraw Hill, Madrid, 1997, p. 60; cfr. *in extenso XIX Congrès FIDE, Les devoirs de coopération des autorités nationales et des tribunaux et les institutions communautaires en vertu de l'article 10 CE*, Helsinki, 2000.

[63] En Espagne, en ce qui concerne la portée de ce précepte, voir F.J. CARRERA HERNÁNDEZ, F.J.: "La acción cultural de la Comunidad Europea", *Comunidad Europea-Aranzadi* 11/1998, pp. 29-36; J. MARTÍN Y PÉREZ DE NANCLARES: "La atribución de competencia en materia cultural.", *Revista de Instituciones Europeas* 1995, pp. 171-189.

[64] J. MARTÍN Y PÉREZ DE NANCLARES: "Otras competencias comunitarias (II): educación, cultura y salud pública", *in* M. LÓPEZ ESCUDERO/J. MARTÍN Y PÉREZ DE NANCLARES (coord.), *Derecho Comunitario Material*, McGraw Hill, Madrid, 2000, pp. 323-338, aux pp. 330-334.

[65] Cfr., par exemple, BVerfGE 89, 155 (189) où il est fait référence à l'étatisme (*Staatlichkeit*) et à l'indépendance (*Unabhängigkeit*).

[66] J. LASO PÉREZ: "El Tratado de Amsterdam y el respeto de la democracia y los derechos humanos", *Boletín Europeo de la Universidad de La Rioja* 1998, n° 2, pp. 31-41.

[67] Voir J. LASO PÉREZ: "La intervención democrática en la Unión Europea después del asunto austríaco y la reforma del Tratado de Niza", *Boletín Europeo de la Universidad de La Rioja* 2001, n° 7/8, supplément, pp. 45-59.

[68] Pour une vision systématique de la jurisprudence relative à cet aspect, *vid.* par exemple, F. RUBIO LLORENTE *e. a., Derechos fundamentales y principios constitucionales (Doctrina jurisprudencial),* Ed. Ariel. Barcelona, 1995 (2ème édition en préparation).

[69] Ce régime de protection judiciaire qui est propre aux droits et aux libertés reconnues par la Section première du Chapitre II (art. 15-29) s'étend ex art. 53.2 de la Constitution espagnole aux droits à l'égalité (art. 14) et à l'objection de conscience relative à l'ancien service militaire (art. 30.2).

[70] En ce qui concerne l'existence éventuelle de limites implicites à la modification (totale) de la Constitution, eu égard au caractère fondamental de certains droits considérés comme inhérents à la dignité humaine, il n'existe pas d'opinion unanime dans la doctrine espagnole (*vid.* par exemple, J. J. SOLOZÁBAL ECHAVARRÍA: "Principialismo..." préc., in *Anuario Jurídico UAM*, 1999, pp. et s.; M. ARAGÓN REYES: *Constitución y democracia*, Ed. Tecnos. Madrid, 1989, pp. et s.).

[71] Extrait de la Charte, cinquième paragraphe.

[72] *Vid.* sur ce point, A. LÓPEZ CASTILLO: "Algunas consideraciones en torno a la Carta de derechos fundamentales de la UE", in *REP* 113 (2001), pp. 43, 44.

[73] L'Annexe IV de la Décision du Conseil de l'Europe des 3/4 juin 1999 faisait référence, en effet, à la Convention européenne de sauvegarde des droits de l'homme et des libertés fondamentales et aux traditions constitutionnelles communes aux Etats membres, ainsi qu'aux droits de citoyenneté de l'Union et, compte tenu qu'il ne s'agit pas de simples objectifs, aux droits économiques et sociaux énoncés par la Charte sociale européenne et par la Charte communautaire des droits sociaux fondamentaux des travailleurs.

[74] *Vid.*, par exemple, A. LÓPEZ CASTILLO: "Algunas consideraciones en torno a la Carta de derechos fundamentales de la UE", in *REP* 113 (2001), *passim*.

[75] Voir une approche similaire dans F. RUBIO LLORENTE: "La Carta europea de los derechos", in *Claves (de razón práctica)* 122 (2002), pp. 4, 9. En outre, *vid.* ídem, "Mostrar los derechos sin destruir la UE", in *REDC* 64 (2002), pp. 9 et s.; A. LÓPEZ CASTILLO: "Algunas consideraciones en torno a la Carta de derechos fundamentales de la UE", in *REP* 113 (2001), *passim*.

[76] F. RUBIO LLORENTE: "La Carta europea de los derechos", in *Claves (de razón práctica)* 122 (2002), p. 9, note à pied de page n° 36, a qualifié cette référence de "déconcertante, et pas seulement à cause du caractère énigmatique du concept de 'pratique'".

[77] Il s'agirait ainsi, en particulier, de l'interdiction du commerce d'organes corporels et du clonage reproductif que contient l'art. 3.2 (dans une ligne de réflexion semblable, *vid.*, par exemple, F. RUBIO LLORENTE, "La Carta europea de los

derechos", in *Claves (de razón práctica)* 122 (2002), p. 9, note à pied de page n° 30: "il ne s'agit pas d'une limite au pouvoir de l'Etat mais à la liberté de la société civile").

[78] *Vid.*, dans le détail, A. LÓPEZ CASTILLO: "Algunas consideraciones en torno a la Carta de derechos fundamentales de la UE", in *REP* 113 (2001), pp. 65 et s.

[79] *Vid.* L. Mª. DÍEZ-PICAZO GIMÉNEZ: "Glosas a la nueva Carta de derechos fundamentales..." préc., in *Tribunales de Justicia* 5 (2001), p. 22 (où la Charte est décrite "comme une machine complètement achevée qui n'attend que sa mise en marche pour déployer toute sa puissance").

[80] "... La même chose se passe au niveau communautaire par rapport à la Directive 95/46, sur la Protection des personnes physiques, au traitement de données personnelles et à la libre circulation de ces données, ainsi qu'à la Charte des Droits fondamentaux de l'Union Européenne de cette année, dont l'art. 8 reconnaît ce droit, précise son contenu et établit la nécessité de la création d'une autorité pour veiller à son respect. Tous ces textes internationaux coïncident dans l'établissement d'un régime juridique de la protection des données personnelles réglementant l'exercice de ce droit fondamental pour ce qui est de l'obtention de ces données, de l'information des intéressés sur leur origine et leur destination, de la faculté de rectification et d'annulation, ainsi que du consentement au respect en ce qui concerne leur usage et leur cession" (ATC (formation plénière) 292/2000, du 30 novembre, FJ 8).

[81] STC (formation plénière) 53/2002, du 27 février, FJ 3.

[82] *Vid.*, par exemple, R. ALONSO GARCÍA: "El "soft law" comunitario", in *RAP* 154 (2001), pp. 63 et s.

[83] Dans l'abondante littérature portant sur cette question, voir A. MANGAS MARTÍN: *Derecho comunitario europeo y Derecho español*, Tecnos, 2ème éd., Madrid, 1987; *id.*: "La Constitución y la ley ante el Derecho comunitario europeo", *in Revista de Instituciones Europeas* 1991, pp. 587 et s.; S. MUÑOZ MACHADO: *El Estado, el Derecho interno y la Comunidad Europea*, Madrid, 1986; G.C. RODRÍGUEZ IGLESIAS: "Tribunales constitucionales y Derecho Comunitario", *in* AAVV, *Hacia un nuevo orden internacional y europeo. Homenaje al Prof. Díez de Velasco*, Tecnos, Madrid, 1993, pp. 1175 et s.

[84] MANGAS MARTÍN, A.: "Le droit constitutionnel espagnol et l'intégration européenne", *in XVIII FIDE Kongress*, Berlín, 1996, vol. I, pp. 206-230, à la p. 206.

[85] "Les Traités internationaux régulièrement conclus, une fois publiés officiellement en Espagne, font partie de l'ordre juridique interne. Leurs dispositions ne peuvent être abrogées, modifiées ou suspendues que dans la forme prévue par les Traités eux-mêmes ou conformément aux normes générales du droit international". Ainsi, "comme n'importe quel autre Traité international, les Traités communautaires s'intègrent au droit interne à partir de leur entrée en vigueur internationale, et en tant que tels ces Traités sont une source directe et sont pleinement efficaces en droit interne, après leur publication au *Boletín Oficial del Estado* espagnol, ils peuvent créer des droits et des obligations dont peuvent se prévaloir directement les particuliers et pouvant être invoqués devant les organes administratifs et judiciaires": A. MANGAS MARTÍN: *loc. cit.* (Le droit constitutionnel..."), p. 206.

[86] "Avant de s'engager par des traités ou par des accords, l'Etat devra être autorisé

préalablement par les *Cortes Generales*, dans les cas suivants: a) traités à caractère politique; b) traités ou accords à caractère militaire; c) traités ou accords qui affectent l'intégrité territoriale de l'Etat ou les droits et les devoirs fondamentaux établis au titre Ier; d) traités ou accords qui impliquent des obligations financières pour les finances publiques; e) traités ou accords qui entraînent la modification ou l'abrogation d'une loi ou exigent l'adoption de mesures législatives pour leur exécution".

[87] "Une loi organique peut autoriser la conclusion de Traités attribuant à une organisation ou à une institution internationale l'exercice de compétences dérivées de la Constitution. Il incombe aux *Cortes Generales* ou au Gouvernment, selon les cas, de garantir l'exécution de ces Traités et des résolutions émanant des organismes internationaux ou supranationaux qui bénéficient de ce transfert de compétences".

[88] Arrêt du 15 juillet 1964, *Costa/ENEL* (6/64, *Rec.*, p. 1141), p. 1125 et p. 1135. Voir par exemple, G.C. RODRÍGUEZ IGLESIAS/J.P. KEPPENNE: "L'incidence du droit communautaire sur le droit national", *in Mélanges en hommage à Michel Waelbroeck*, Bruylant, Bruxelles, 1999, vol. I., pp. 517-551.

[89] "Le Gouvernement ou l'une ou l'autre Chambre peut faire appel au Tribunal constitutionnel pour qu'il déclare s'il y a ou non contradiction". C'est-à-dire, si l'une des deux Chambres des *Cortes Generales* (Congrès ou Sénat) ou le Gouvernement considère qu'il pourrait exister une contradiction entre la Constitution espagnole et le contenu d'un traité dont le texte a déjà été fixé de manière définitive, mais avant qu'ait été donné le consentement, tout autant les Chambres (n'importe laquelle d'entre elles à la majorité simple) que le Gouvernement peuvent faire appel au Tribunal constitutionnel pour qu'il déclare s'il existe ou non contradiction.

[90] *Vid.* article 78.1 de la Loi Organique du Tribunal Constitutionnel (Loi organique 2/1979, du 3 octobre, *BOE* n° 239, du 5 octobre 1979): "Le Gouvernement ou l'une ou l'autre Chambre peut faire appel au Tribunal constitutionnel pour qu'il se prononce sur l'existence ou sur l'inexistence d'une contradiction entre la Constitution et les stipulations d'un traité international dont le texte a déjà été définitivement fixé, mais avant que l'Etat ait donné son consentement".

[91] Italique ajoutée. Dans ce contexte, il faut souligner l'importante du terme "précédée". Cela veut dire qu'une fois donné le consentement et après l'entrée en vigueur du Traité communautaire, il devient impossible de soumettre à un contrôle de constitutionnalité ce Traité international, lequel fait partie de l'ordre juridique interne.

[92] Déclaration du 1er juillet 1992, *BOE* n° 177 du 24.7.1992, pp. 2-7. Sur cette Déclaration, voir en particulier, l'analyse critique réalisée par A. MANGAS MARTÍN: "La Declaración del TC sobre el art. 13.2 de la Constitución (derecho de sufragio pasivo de los extranjeros): una reforma constitucional innecesaria o insuficiente", *Revista Española de Derecho Internacional* 1992, pp. 381-393.

[93] La question des limites relatives à l'article 93 de la CE est loin d'être pacifique dans la doctrine espagnole. La Constitution est dépourvue de toute référence à de telles limites et ne contient aucune "clause d'éternité" à la manière du controversé article 79.3 de la *Grundgesetz* allemande. Il en découle que l'on accepte généralement l'existence de limites à l'attribution par l'article 93 de compétences à l'Union Européenne, mais il n'existe pas d'accord doctrinal pour ce qui est de leur détermination concrète.

[94] Voir A. MANGAS MARTÍN: "La Constitución y la ley ante el Derecho Comunitario europeo (Comentario a la sentencia del Tribunal Constitucional español 28/1991, de 14 de febrero, sobre la Ley Orgánica del Régimen Electoral General y el Acta relativa a las elecciones al Parlamento Europeo)", *Revista de Instituciones Europeas* 1991, pp. 587-623, en particulier pp. 618-623.

[95] Arrêt du TC 28/1991, du 14 février (*Parlement basque vs. Loi Organique du Régime Electoral Général*), *BOE* du 15.3.1991, Fundement Juridique 5.

[96] Arrêt du TC 180/1993, du 31 mai, (*FOGASA*), *BOE* du 31.5.1993, Fondement Juridique 3.

[97] Voir par exemple, A. MANGAS MARTÍN: "Derecho Comunitario y Derecho español", *in* A. MANGAS MARTÍN/D.J. LIÑÁN NOGUERAS, *Instituciones y Derecho de la Unión Europea*, McGraw Hill, 2ème éd., Madrid, 1999, pp. 255-24, dans p. 265.

[98] A. MANGAS MARTÍN: *loc. cit.* (" Le droit constitutionnel espagnol...."), p. 208.

[99] Arrêt du TC 64/1991, du 22 mars (*APESCO*), *BOE* du 24.4.1991, Fondement Juridique 4. Sur cet arrêt, voir en particulier, M.P. ANDRÉS SÁENZ DE SANTA MARÍA: "Comentario de la sentencia del Tribunal Constitucional 64/1991, de 22 de marzo", *Revista Española de Derecho Internacional* 1991, pp. 451 et s.

[100] En supposant que l'actuelle Charte des droits fondamentaux solennellement proclamée à Nice soit revêtue d'un caractère juridiquement obligatoire lors de la CIG'2004, il sera encore plus difficile de déterminer *de lege ferenda* la portée de son article 53. Compte tenu que celui-ci affirme qu'"aucune des dispositions de la présente charte ne doit être interprétée comme limitant ou portant atteiente aux droits de l'homme et aux libertés fondamentales reconnues (...) par les constitutions des Etats membres", un secteur de la doctrine espagnole considère qu'il pourrait exister une certaine relativisation du principe de la primauté; R. ALONSO GARCÍA: "La Carta de los derechos fundamentales de la Unión Europea", *Gaceta Jurídica de la UE y de la competencia* 2000, nº 192, pp. 15-30, dans p. 15; A. LÓPEZ CASTILLO: "Algunas consideraciones sumarias en torno a la Carta de derechos fundamentales de la UE", *Revista de Estudios Políticos* 2001, pp. 43-73, dans p. 68.

Cependant, un autre secteur doctrinal ne croit pas que ce soit le cas; J. MARTÍN Y PÉREZ DE NANCLARES: "La protección de los derechos fundamentales en la UE: cuestiones pendientes tras la Carta de Niza", *Anuario Jurídico de La Rioja* 2000-2001, pp. 387-427, en particulier pp. 412-414; cfr. en dehors de la doctrine espagnole, LIIESBERG, J.B.: "Does the EU-Charter of Fundamental Rights Threaten the Supremacy of Community Law?", *Common Market Law Review* 2001, pp. 1171-1199.

[101] A. MANGAS MARTÍN: *loc. cit.* ("Le droit constituionnel espagnol..."), p. 209.

[102] i. par exemple, A. MANGAS MARTÍN: *Derecho Comunitario europeo y Derecho español*, Tecnos, 2ème éd., Madrid, 1986, pp. 128-129, note 4. Cfr.. DTC 1 juillet 1992; entre autres M. ARAGÓN REYES: "La constitución española y el Tratado de la Unión Europea: la reforma de la Constitución", in *REDC* 42, 1994, pp. 9 et s.

[103] *Voir* l'article 81 de la CE, lequel énumère les matières réservées à la loi organique, c'est-à-dire "le développement des droits fondamentaux et des libertés publiques, celles qui approuvent les statuts d'autonomie et le régime électoral général ainsi que les autres lois prévues dans la Constitution", telles que, par exemple, les lois, prévues par l'article 93, qui permettent la conclusion de traités comportant l'attribution de compétences à l'Union Européenne. On peut aussi citer les lois qui régissent les bases de l'organisation militaire (art. 8.2), l'institution du défenseur du peuple (art. 54), la restriction de certaines garanties en ce qui concerne les groupes terroristes (art. 55.2), l'initiative populaire législative (art. 87.3), les modalités de référendum (art. 92.3), les fonctions des corps de sécurité de l'Etat (art. 104), le Conseil d'Etat (art. 107), la Cour des comptes (art. 136.4), la constitution des Communautés Autonomes (art. 144), le référendum des statuts d'autonomie (art. 150.2), les compétences financières des Communautés Autonomes (art. 157.3) ou la constitution et le fonctionnement du Tribunal constitutionnel (art. 165).

[104] Voir. *supra*.

[105] Voir, entre autres, A. von BOGDANDY, Art. 5 (antérieur) TCE, in E. Grabitz/M. Hilf (eds.), Kommentar zur Europäischen Union. München, 1994.

[106] *Vid*., à propos des arguments du Procureur, ATC 64/1991, FJ 4 a); *vid*., entre autres, ACJ du 9 mars 1978, aff. 106/77, Simmenthal-II, in Recueil. *Vid*., dans le droit allemand, la proposition doctrinale (isolée) de W. BÜNTEN: *Staatsgewalt und Gemeinschaftshoheit bei der innerstaatlichen Durchführung des Rechts der Europäischen Gemeinschaften durch die Mitgliedstaaten*, Ed. Duncker & Humblot. Berlin, 1977.

[107] *Vid*., entre autres, D. ORDÓÑEZ SOLÍS: *La ejecución del derecho comunitario europeo en España*, Ed. Civitas. Madrid, 1994, pp. 232 et s., 293 et s.; M. CIENFUEGOS MATEO: "Las Cortes españolas ante la integración europea", in C. Closa (éd.): *La europeización del sistema político español*, Ed. Istmo. Madrid, 2001, pp. 197, 200 et s.

[108] Cela a été le cas, par exemple, de la Loi 12/1998, du 28 de avril, qui modifie l'ancienne Loi 13/1994 sur l'autonomie de la Banque d'Espagne.

[109] "(...) on peut considérer que lorsque l'Espagne agit dans le cadre des Communautés Européennes, elle agit dans une structure juridique très différente de la structure traditionnelle des relations internationales. Car le développement du processus d'intégration a créé un ordre juridique, le droit communautaire, qui pour l'ensemble des Etats membres des Communautés Européennes peut être considéré à certains effets comme 'interne'" (FJ 4).

[110] Il faut noter la délégation initiale en faveur du Gouvernement réalisée par la Loi 47/1985, du 27 décembre (art. 1, en relation avec l'annexe), afin de transposer 68 directives et 3 décisions communautaires et d'adapter au droit communautaire 36 lois, en l'espace de 6 mois, ce qui s'est concrétisé dans l'adoption de 15 Décrets législatifs (cfr., entre autres, T. R. FERNÁNDEZ RODRÍGUEZ: "La adaptación del ordenamiento jurídico español al ordenamiento comunitario y la ley de delegación 47/1985, de 27 de diciembre", in *Noticias CEE* 27, 1987, pp. 19 et s.).

Sur l'utilisation de cette pratique dans le cadre de certains ordres juridiques régionaux (Communauté Autonome du Pays Basque, Communauté Autonome de la Catalogne), vid. par exemple les références que l'on trouve dans A. LÓPEZ

CASTILLO: "La creación y ejecución del Derecho comunitario en España", in J. Barnés (coord.): *La Comunidad europea, la instancia regional y la organización administrativa de los Estados miembros,* Ed. Civitas. Madrid, 1993, pp. 135 et s.

[111] Pour une vision synthétique de l'influence (jusqu'alors) du dénommé pouvoir d'intégration sur les Communautés Autonomes, *vid.* en plus du renvoi au paragraphe III, A. LÓPEZ CASTILLO: *Constitución e integración* (1996), préc., pp. 273 et s.; dans une perspective politologique, *vid.* entre autres, C. COLINO CÁMARA: "La integración europea y el Estado autonómico: europeización, estrategias y cambio en las relaciones intergubernamentales", in C. Closa (éd.): *La europeización del sistema político español,* pp. 222 et s.

[112] Art. 155.1 de la Constitution espagnole. A cet effet —précise t-on— "le Gouvernement pourra donner des instructions à toutes les autorités des Communautés autonomes" (art. 155.2 de la Constitution espagnole).

Sans aller jusque là, la polémique relative à la ... des tarifs douaniers découlant de la modification juscommunautaire du régime fiscal initialement accordé à la Communauté Autonome des Canaries fut réglée (après de sérieux désaccords entre les Gouvernements central et régional) par la voie de la négociation politique.

[113] C'est le cas, par exemple, des arts. 21, 190.4 ou 269 TCE.

[114] FJ 4. En conséquence, l'articulation des relations entre les ordres juridiques dans l'espace communautaire, comme on peut le déduire de la jurisprudence de la CJ, réside dans le propre système de droit communautaire, davantage que dans l'art. 93 de la Constitution espagnole (et les autres préceptes s'y rattachant).

[115] La dernière réforme des Traités, réalisée par l'intérmédiaire du TrNice, dépend du résultat du deuxième référendum irlandais.

[116] *Vid.*, entre autres, P. PÉREZ TREMPS: *loc. cit.*

[117] En espagnol cfr., entre autres, J. MATÍA PORTILLA: *Parlamentos nacionales y derecho comunitario*, Ed. CEC. Madrid, 1999.

[118] Au caractère exceptionnel d'une institutionnalisation que l'on connaît seulement dans un Etat membre (Eire), on doit ajouter la singularité qui découle de sa réglementation par le biais d'une loi, et non par l'intermédiaire du (toujours inexistant) Réglement des *Cortes Generales* —sans préjudice du fait que, pour tout ce qui n'est pas prévu, il est prévu un renvoi à l'application subsidiaire du Réglement du Congrès des Députés et qu'une décision des Bureaux des Chambres du 21 septembre 1995 contient les aspects relatifs à son organisation, à ses compétences et à la procédure—.

[119] Loi 47/1985, du 27 décembre, relative à la délégation... (art. 5); Loi 18/1988, du 1er juillet, qui modifie la Loi précédente; Loi 8/1994, du 19 mai (BOE, du 20 mai), qui modifie la Loi précédente.

Sur la composition et les fonctions de la "Commission mixte...", *vid.*, entre autres, J. MATÍA PORTILLA: *Parlamentos nacionales y derecho comunitario* (1999), préc., pp. et s.; et, pour une synthèse, M. CIENFUEGOS MATEO: "Las Cortes españolas...", in C. Closa (éd.): *La europeización del sistema político español* (2001), préc., pp. 210 et s.

[120] *Vid.* à ce propos, Proposition non législative (à l'initiative de tous les Groupes parlementaires) priant le Gouvernement d'exiger à la Commission européenne l'envoi immédiat en castellan de toute proposition législative (*BOCG* (V), Série A, n° 18, du 25 février 1994.

[121] *Vid.*, entre autres, M. CIENFUEGOS MATEO: "La Comisión mixta para la Unión Europea: análisis y balance de una década de actividad en el seguimiento de los asuntos comunitarios", in *GJ-CE*, D-27 (1997), pp. 7 et s.
[122] ATC 64/1991, FJ 4 a).
[123] Cit. de J. SCHWARZE: *Droit administratif européen*, Ed. Bruylant. Luxemburgo 1994, I, p. 8. *Vid.*, aussi, J. SCHWARZE (éd.): *Administrative law under European Influence. On the convergence of the administrative laws of the EU Members States*, Ed. Sweet & Maxwell. London, 1996.
[124] Vid, par exemple, ACJ du 22 juin 1989, aff. C-103/88, F. Constanzo, in Recueil 1839 et s.
[125] A propos des relations de notification et de cooperation à l´occasion de l´application administrative, *vid.*, entre autres, A. M. MORENO MOLINA: *La ejecución administrativa del derecho comunitario*, Ed. M. Pons. Madrid, 1998, pp. 71 et s.
[126] *Vid.*, dans le détail, I. MOLINA ÁLVAREZ DE CIENFUEGOS: "La adaptación a la Unión Europea del poder ejecutivo español", in C. Closa (éd.), *La europeización del sistema político español* (2001), préc., pp. 160 et s.; A. LÓPEZ CASTILLO: "La dirección gubernamental de la política comunitaria", in M. Aragón (dir.), *El Gobierno* (en préparation).
[127] *Vid.*, entre autres, A. BETANCOR RODRÍGUEZ: "La posición del banco central europeo en el sistema institucional comunitario: independencia y equilibrio institucional. El federalismo horizontal en el manejo de la moneda", in *Revista de Estudios Políticos* 90 (Closa/López Castillo (éds.), n° monographique: *La reforma...*), 1995, pp. 267 et s.
[128] *Vid.*, en résumé, N. FONT: "La europeización de la política ambiental: desafíos e inercias", in C. Closa (éd.), *La europeización del sistema político español,* Ed. Istmo. Madrid, 2001, pp. 380, 388 et s.
[129] ATC 13/1998, FJ 3, in fine. A propos de l'encadrement de la procédure d'étude d'impact dans le domaine de la gestion de l'environnement, *vid.* Votes particuliers (VV. PP.) relatifs à l'ATC 13/1998 des Magistrats García Manzano (auquel adhèrent les Magistrats González Campos, Cruz Villalón, Viver Pi-Sunyer et Vives Antón) et Jiménez de Parga y Cabrera.
[130] *Vid.*, simplement à titre d'illustration, G. ISAAC: *Manual de Derecho comunitario general (Droit communautaire général),* 5ème éd. (7ème éd.), Ed. Ariel. Barcelona, 2000, pp. 426 et s.
[131] *Vid.* dans ce sens, entre autres, E. GARCÍA DE ENTERRÍA: "Las competencias y el funcionamiento del Tribunal de Justicia de las Comunidades Europeas. Estudio analítico", in Ídem/J. González Campos/S. Muñoz Machado (dirs.): *Tratado de Derecho comunitario*, Ed. Civitas. Madrid, 1986, pp. 656 et s.
[132] *Vid.* ATC 64/1991, FJ 4.
[133] ATC 28/1991, Elections PE; 64/1991, Apesco; DTC, du 1er juillet 1992, TUE.
[134] *Vid.*, entre autres, G. C. RODRÍGUEZ IGLESIAS: "Problemas jurídicos de la adhesión de España a la Comunidad Europea", in *Cursos de Derecho internacional de Vitoria-Gasteiz (1984),* Ed. UPV, 1985, pp. 193 et s.; A. LÓPEZ CASTILLO: *Constitución e integración* (1996), pp. 9 et s., 313 et s. et 435 et s.
[135] D'une autre nature, pas formellement communautaire mais importante pour l'UE, est la dénommée coopération judiciaire horizontale, qui a une signification

progressive et en vertu de laquelle les Etats, quand bien même dans l'exercice de leurs compétences, réalisent un rapprochement de leurs standards qui, dans la mesure où ceux-ci mettent en lumière des espaces d'équivalence, servent les objectifs communautaires propres tout en déblayant le terrain pour de futurs progrès dans l'intégration (dans des domaines qui ont traditionnellement été pris en considération de manière prioritaire par le droit international privé).

[136] A condition qu'ils aient été créés par une Loi, de manière permanente et avec un caractère de 'juridiction' obligatoire, et qu'ils règlent des litiges dans le cadre d'une procédure contradictoire et conformément au droit (jurisprudence constante depuis ACJ du 30 juin 1966, aff. 61/65, Vaassen, Recueil 395).

En ce qui concerne l'Espagne, il s'agit, d'une part, du Tribunal de Défense de la Concurrence (TDC) et, d'autre part, des dénommés Tribunaux économiques administratifs (essentiellement, mais pas uniquement, TEAC). Vid., respectivement, ACJ du 16 juillet 1992, aff. 67/91, AEB, in Recueil I-4785 et s., et du 1er avril 1993, aff. acc. 260 et 261/91, Diversinte e Interlacta, in Recueil I-1885 et s.

[137] *Vid.* P. PÉREZ TREMPS: *Derecho constitucional y derecho comunitario (brouillon)* 1999, p. 11.

[138] *Vid.*, entre autres, ATS du 8 octobre 1992; et du 30 novembre 1990 (Ar. 3442).

[139] Le nombre de questions préjudicielles (4) effectivement posées par le TS espagnol (jusqu'en 2000) ne paraît pas excessif. *Vid.* aff. 17/92, Fedicine (ACJ du 4 mai 1993, Recueil I-2239 et s.); aff. C-153/97, Grajera Rodríguez (ACJ du 17 décembre 1998, Recueil I-8665 et s.); aff. C-390/99, Canal Satélite Digital (ACJ du , Recueil); aff. C-79/00, Telefónica de España (ACJ , Recueil).

[140] ATC 213/1994, FJ 3 ("(l)a Constitution ne l'a pas configuré... comme un Tribunal "supérieur dans tous les ordres", mais uniquement "en matière de garanties constitutionnelles"... Et ni la Constitution ni une loi organique lui ont attribué... la compétence pour connaître de la conformité du droit interne au droit communautaire, ce qui veut dire que cette compétence doit être considérée comme incorporée dans la compétence générique et privative du Pouvoir Judiciaire").

[141] *Vid.*, entre autres, ATC 180/1993; 45/1996 (A.LÓPEZ CASTILLO: "La jurisprudencia iuscomunitaria del Tribunal Consitucional a doce años de la integración española en las Comunidades Europeas", in *REP* 99 (1998), pp. 189, 211 y 205).

[142] A noter l'interprétation du principe constitutionnel de légalité pénale (art. 25.1 de la Constitution espagnole) par le biais de l'intégration d'une norme pénale en blanc contenue dans la Loi sur la répression de la contrebande (L.O. 7/1982, ultérieurement abrogée par la L.O. 12/1995) conformément aux Règlements communautaires relatifs aux espèces animales protégées. Le TC conclut "qu'une norme de Droit communautaire, originaire ou dérivée, compte tenu de sa primauté dans l'ordre interne, est susceptible de définir l'hypothèse de fait d'une norme pénale, même si celle-ci exige que la norme servant à la compléter se situe au niveau légal (... et signale aussi) qu'il n'est pas rare qu'une norme nationale fasse un renvoi à une disposition communautaire, y compris en matière pénale, comme c'est le cas, par exemple, de manière expresse, dans l'art. 2. 1 f) de la nouvelle Loi Organique" (ATC 120/1998, FJ 4 a).

Il est intéressant de noter aussi l'interprétation du droit constitutionnel d'égalité devant la loi (art. 14 de la Constitution espagnole) conformément au Règlement

2211/1978 du Conseil, relatif à l'Accord de coopération entre la Communauté et le Royaume du Maroc (ATC 130/1995, FFJJ 4-5).

[143] FJ 4 a) "dans la mesure où l'on attaque par la voie de l'*amparo* un acte du pouvoir public qui, ayant été pris en exécution du Droit communautaire, peut violer un droit fondamental, la connaissance d'un tel recours revient à cette juridiction constitutionnelle, indépendamment de la question de savoir si cet acte est valable ou non dans le contexte du droit communautaire européen et sans préjudice de sa valeur conformément à l'article 10.2 CE".

[144] Sur l'application par les juridictions espagnoles de la jurisprudence Marleasing, *vid.* J. DÍEZ-HOCHLEITNER RODRÍGUEZ: "Les Directives communautaires: effets, efficacité, justiciabilité (Rapport espagnol)", in *XVIII Congrès FIDE* (1998), I, 185, 201 et s.

[145] ACJ du 16 décembre 1976, aff. 33/76, Rewe, in Recueil 1976, p. 1989; du 7 juillet 1981, aff. Rewe, 158/80, in Recueil 1981, 1805.

[146] Voir Directive 89/665, du Conseil, du 21 décembre 1989, in DOCE L, 395/33, du 30 décembre 1989 (en matière de passation des marchés publics); Directive 92/13, du Conseil, du 25 février 1992, in DOCE L, 76/14, du 23 mars 1992 (en matière de marchés dans les secteurs de l'eau, de l'énergie, des transports et des télécommunications).

[147] *Vid.*, à ce propos, J. DÍEZ-HOCHLEITNER RODRÍGUEZ: "Les Directives communautaires: effets, efficacité, justiciabilité (Rapport espagnol)", préc., pp. 208 et s.

[148] *Vid.*, entre autres, ACJ, du 16 décembre 1976, aff. 33/76, Rewe préc.; des 16 et 27 mars 1980, aff. 61/79, Denkavit, in Recueil 1205 et s.; du 9 de novembre 1983, aff. 199/82, San Giorgio, in Recueil 3595 et s.; du 29 juin 1988, aff. 240/87, Delville, in Recueil 3513 et ss.

[149] *Vid.*, entre autres, G. C. RODRÍGUEZ IGLESIAS: "Zu den Grenzen der verfahrensrechtlichen Autonomie der Mitgliedstaaten bei der Anwendung des Gemeinschaftsrechts", in *EuGRZ* 24 (1997), pp. 289 et s.

[150] *Vid.* ACJ, du 15 mai 1986, aff. 222/84, Johnston, in Recueil 1681 et s.; du 15 octobre 1987, aff. 222/86, Heylens, in Recueil 4097 et s. *Vid.*, entre autres, A. M. MORENO MOLINA: *La ejecución administrativa del derecho comunitario* (1998), préc., pp. 114, 117 et s.

[151] *Vid.*, entre autres, E. GARCÍA DE ENTERRÍA: *La batalla por las medidas cautelares* (2ème éd.), Ed. Civitas. Madrid, 1995; G. C. RODRÍGUEZ IGLESIAS: "La tutela judicial cautelar en el derecho comunitario", in Ídem/D. J. Liñán Nogueras (dirs.), *El derecho comunitario europeo y su aplicación judicial*, Ed. Civitas. Madrid, 1993, p. 633 et s.

[152] A propos de la controverse allemande qui est à l'origine de cet arrêt de la CJ, *vid.*, entre autres, A. LÓPEZ CASTILLO: "Un nuevo paso en la andadura iuscomunitaria del Tribunal constitucional", préc., in *REDC* 61 (2001), pp. 349 et s.

[153] *Vid.*, de manière générale, R. ALONSO GARCÍA: *La responsabilidad de los Estados miembros por infracción del derecho comunitario*, Ed. Civitas. Madrid, 1997.

[154] *Vid.*, entre autres, E. GARCÍA DE ENTERRÍA: *La batalla por las medidas cautelares* (1995) cit.; M. BACIGALUPO SAGESSE: *La nueva tutela cautelar en el contencioso-administrativo*, Ed. M. Pons. Madrid, 1999.

155 L'article 148 de la CE précise que les CCAA peuvent assumer des compétences dans 22 matières, parmi lesquelles nous pouvons citer l'organisation de leurs institutions de gouvernement autonome; l'aménagement du territoire, l'urbanisme et le logement; les travaux publics qui intéressent la Communauté autonome sur son territoire propre; les chemins de fer et les routes; l'agriculture et l'élevage; la gestion en matière de protection de l'environnement; la pêche; le patrimoine monumental; le développement de la culture et de la recherche; la promotion du tourisme et du sport; la santé et l'hygiène; la surveillance et la protection de leurs édifices et de leurs installations, etc.

156 ATC 44/182 du 8 juillet, *BOE* du 4.8.1982, Fondement Juridique 4.

157 ATC 137/89 du 20 juillet, *BOE* nº 190, du 10.8.1989, Fondement Juridique 3. "Toute Convention ou tout Accord conclus par l'une de ces collectivités [les Communautés Autonomes] avec une organisation internationale, un Etat ou une autre collectivité infraétatique étrangère serait entaché d'inconstitutionnalité, et ceci indépendamment de la compétence que possède la collectivité en question dans le secteur matériel d'activité faisant l'objet du pacte".

158 A. MANGAS MARTÍN: "La participación de las Comunidades Autónomas en la integración europea", *in ib.*/D.J. LINÁN NOGUERAS, *op.cit. (Instituciones y Derecho...)*, pp. 275-289, dans p. 276. Comme le précise le TC, si l'Etat invoquait, "par principe, sa compétence exclusive en matière de relations internationales (art. 149.1.3 CE) pour étendre son domaine de compétences à toute activité portant sur le développment, l'exécution ou l'application des Conventions et des Traités internationaux et, en particulier, du Droit dérivé européen". Si c'était le cas, il se produirait "une aspiration du domaine de compétences que la Constitution et les statuts d'autonomie attribuent aux Communautés Autonomes"; ATC 148/98, du 2 juillet, *BOE* nº 181 du 30.7.1998, Fondement Juridique 4.

159 ATC 54/1990, du 28 mars, *BOE* nº 92 du 17.4.1990; ATC 165/194, du 26 mai, *BOE* nº 151 du 25.6.1994.

160 J.M. SOBRINO HEREDIA: *La acción exterior de las Comunidades Autónomas. Especial referencia a Galicia*, Fundación Galicia Europa, 2001, p. 29; dans le même sens, A. MANGAS MARTÍN: *loc. cit.* ("La participación de..."), p. 275.

161 Pour consulter une liste mise à jour des instruments conclus par les CCAA dans le cadre de leur action extérieure, accompagnée de leur texte, voir C. FERNÁNDEZ DE CASADEVANTE ROMANÍ: *La acción exterior de las Comunidades Autónomas-Balance de una práctica consolidada*, Dilex-Universidad Rey Juan Carlos, Madrid, 2001, pp. 215-777.

162 ATC 165/94, du 26 mai, *cit.* Italique ajoutée. Voir *in extenso* C. FERNÁNDEZ DE CASADEVANTE ROMANÍ: "Comentario a la STC de 26 de mayo de 1994 (Oficina vasca en Bruselas)", *Revista Española de Derecho Internacional* 1994, pp. 717 et s.; F.J. CARRERA HERNÁNDEZ: "La oficina vasca en Bruselas", *Comunidad Europea-Aranzadi* 11/1994, pp. 39 et s.; M. PÉREZ GONZÁLEZ: "La 'onda regional' en Bruselas y el ámbito del poder exterior (comentario a la sentencia del TC 165/1994 de 26 de mayo", *Revista de Instituciones Europeas* 1994, pp. 899 et s.

163 Sur le concept et la nature juridique de ces réunions et pour une évaluation du

système, voir J. CORCUERA ATIENZA.: "La participación intergubernamental sectorial en el sistema autonómico español: las conferencias sectoriales", *in* A. PÉREZ CALVO, A. (coord.), *La participación de las CCAA en las decisiones del Estado*, Tecnos, Madrid, 1997, pp. 49-80.

[164] Loi 2/1997, du 13 mars, *BOE* du 15.3.1997; Réglement interne du 5 août 1997; BOE du 8.8.1997. Malgré le fait que son cadre législatif remonte à 1997, elle fonctionne en réalité depuis 1988. En outre, en 1992, elle a été institutionnalisée par un Accord Politique (du 29.10.1992), auquel le Pays Basque ne prit part qu'en 1995, après que sa revendication de relation bilatérale ait été résolue (voir *infra*).

[165] Comme organe d'appui chargé de préparer les travaux de la CARCE, il existe une *Commission des Coordinateurs des Affaires Communautaires Européennes* composée des Directeurs Généraux des CCAA et du Ministère impliqué (art. 1.3 de la Loi 2/1997).

[166] Il suffit de rappeler qu'au cours de l'année 2001, elle ne s'est réunie que trois fois. Et à deux reprises, sans objet très précis: la première pour analyser les conséquences du Conseil Européen de Nice et la deuxième pour recevoir des informations sur le contenu du Conseil Européen de Laeken la veille de sa tenue. Le fait que la Commission des Coordinateurs ne se soit réunie au cours de ces trois dernières années qu'une fois en 1999 et une autre en 2000 est encore plus révélateur.

[167] *Voir infra.*

[168] A l'existence de différents niveaux de compétences entre les CCAA s'ajoutent d'autres éléments différentiels non négligeables. Certaines CCAA possèdent, en plus de l'espagnol, une langue officielle propre (Catalogne, Galice, Pays Basque...), alors que d'autres ne sont pas dans ce cas. Certaines CCAA possèdent une forte tradition historique qui s'accompagne d'éléments culturels et politiques propres, tandis que d'autres ne sont apparues *ex novo* qu'après la Constitution de 1978. Même leur dimension a des conséquences sur leur manière d'exercer leurs compétences propres dans le cadre européen. Les petites CCAA, comme La Rioja (264.178 habitants), ne peuvent avoir les même moyens ni le même intérêt que d'autres CCAA, beaucoup plus puissantes, comme l'Andalousie (7.340.052 habitants), la Catalogne (6.261.999 habitants), Madrid (5.205.408 habitants) ou le Pays Basque (2.098.596 habitants).

[169] Accord du 22 juillet 1996.

[170] Résolution de la CARCE du 5 décembre 1996, *BOE* n° 302 du 16.12.1996.

[171] Voir A. MANGAS MARTÍN: "La participación institucional de Euskadi en la Unión Europea", vol. coll., *Euskadi en la Unión Europea*, Fundación Sabino Arana, Bilbao, 1994, p. 79.

[172] Voir les études comprises dans le vol. coll.: *La participación de las Comunidades Autónomas en los Consejos de Ministros de la Unión Europea*, Instituto Vasco de Administración Pública, Bilbao, 1998.

[173] ATC 137/1989, du 20 juillet, *cit*, Fondements Juridiques 4 et 5.

[174] Souvenons-nous que s'était formé au sein de la CARCE un groupe de travail *ad hoc* composé de quatre CCAA et dont la fonction était de préparer une proposition. Cependant, lors de la réunion plénière de la CARCE, le représentant de l'Etat refusa catégoriquement une telle possibilité, ce qui suscita une très vive réaction de la part de certaines CCAA, fondamentalement le Pays Basque, la Catalogne et la Galice.

[175] L'affaire du dénommé concert économique suscita une très sérieuse crise insti-

tutionnelle entre l'Etat central et la Communauté Autonome basque; voir *El País* du 31 décembre 2001 et du 2 janvier 2002; *El País* du 12 février 2002.

[176] Décision du TPI du 16 juin 1998, *Communauté Autonome de Cantabrique c. Conseil* (T-238/97, *Rec. P. II-2271).*

[177] Il s'agit de l'affaire dans laquelle le Tribunal de Première Instance déclara inadmissible le recours en annulation formé par un groupe d'armateurs contre un réglement (T-194/91).

[178] La Communauté Autonome basque, par exemple, à réclamé une réforme de ce type dans un document qu'elle présenta lors de la Conférence intergouvernementale de 1996; *vid.* J. MARTÍN Y PÉREZ DE NANCLARES: *La posición de las Comunidades Autónomas ante el Tribunal de Justicia de las Comunidades Europeas (propuestas para una reforma)*, Instituto Vasco de Administración Pública, Oñate, 1996.

[179] Arrêt du 19 novembre 1991, *Commission/ Espagne* (Marais de Santoña) (C-335/90, *Rec.*, p.I-5419); arrêt du 14 septembre 1999, *Commission/Espagne* (guides touristiques) (C-375/97, *Rec.*, p.); arrêt du 1er octobre 1998, *Commission/Espagne* (directive de protection des eaux) (C-71/97, *Rec.*, p. I- 5997).

[180] Il suffit de citer comme cas important l'arrêt du 4 octobre 1991, *Aragonesa de Publicidad* (C-176/90, *Rec.*, p. I-4151)

[181] Ce fut par exemple le cas des dénommées "vacances fiscales" du Pays Basque, au sujet duquel le Tribunal supérieur de justice du Pays Basque posa une question préjudicielle (C-400 y 401/97). La question posée à la Cour était celle de la compatibilité avec le Droit Communautaire d'une norme "*foral*" basque qui, conformément aux larges compétences fiscales dont dispose cette Communauté Autonome, octroyait certaines exonérations fiscales aux entreprises s'établissant sur le territoire du Pays Basque. Ce qui était paradoxal c'est que le requérant dans la procédure principale qui demandait au tribunal national la déclaration d'illégalité de la norme basque en question (l'Etat), était chargé de "defendre" devant la Cour de Justice la légalité communautaire de la norme attaquée. Finalement, la question fut retirée par le Tribunal l'ayant posée et la Cour de Justice des Communautés Européennes n'a pu se prononcer. L'Avocat Général Sacchio avait considéré dans ses conclusions que ces "vacances fiscales" étaient contraires au Droit Communautaire, tout autant au droit d'établissement qu'au régime des aides publiques.

[182] *Vid.*, en résumé, A. LÓPEZ CASTILLO: *Constitución e integración* (1996), chap. I; et, dans le détail, Mª. L. FERNÁNDEZ ESTEBAN: "La noción de Constitución europea en la jurisprudencia del Tribunal de Justicia de las Comunidades Europeas", in *REDC* 40 (1994), pp. 241 et s.

[183] Et une fois dissipé le doute allemand sur la constitutionnalité du TUE, certainement sous réserve de l'interprétation par le TC de la conformité avec la Loi Fondamentale de Bonn (LF) de certaines de ses prévisions, dans les termes qui découlent de son polémique Arrêt Maastricht du 12 octobre 1993 (BVerfGE 9x, xxx et s.). En espagnol, cfr., entre autres, les commentaires d'A. LÓPEZ CASTILLO: "De integración y soberanía. El Tratado sobre la Unión", in *REDC* 40 (1994), pp. 207 et s.; T. STEIN: "La sentencia del Tribunal constitucional alemán sobre el Tratado de Maastricht", in *Revista de Instituciones europeas (RIE),* 1994, pp. 745 et s.

[184] A ce propos, cfr., entre autres, S. WINCKLER: *Der Beitritt der Europäischen*

Gemeinschaftten zur Europäischen Menschenrechtskonvention (2000), *passim*; H. Ch. KRÜGER/J. POLAKIEWICZ: "Vorschläge für ein kohärentes System des Menschenrechtsschutzes in Europa", in *EuGRZ* 4-6/2001, pp. 92 et s.

[185] *Vid.* F. RUBIO LLORENTE: Mostrar los derechos sin destruir la Unión", in *REDC* 64 (2002), pp. 13, 44 et s., et 49 et s. "Avec l'incorporation de la Charte aux Traités, on briserait les liens, que l'heureuse formule mise au point par le Tribunal était parvenue à maintenir, entre les Droits fondamentaux garantis par les Etats et ceux que garantit l'Union comme principes généraux de son droit, et l'on détruirait, sans le remplacer par un autre, le délicat équilibre qui existe actuellement entre la juridiction de l'Union et celle des Etats" (52).

[186] *Vid.* le texte du Livre blanc de la Commission sur la "gouvernance" (COM/2001/0428 final).

[187] A l'image du producteur de plus de 90% du charbon dans l'Allemagne de l'après-guerre (la Rhénanie-du-Nord-Westphalie) qui se plaignait au début de l'intégration européenne de son absence dans la prise décisions, qui n'appartenait qu'au Gouvernement fédéral, on comprendra que le producteur d'un pourcentage très significatif (environ 50%) d'un produit (agricole) concret ou de l'exploitation de certaines ressources (de pêche) ne devrait pas se voir imposée dans le cadre de l'UE une politique (non dans la mesure où celle-ci est favorable à la position relative de producteurs moins importants) sans grave dommage pour la légitimité d'un système de négociation (continue) qui repose sur la pratique du consensus.

[188] Cfr. la Déclaration relative aux missions des Parlements nationaux de l'UE (1992).

[189] Pour une étude de la présence des Parlements nationaux dans la Convention, *vid.* en particulier, J. P. JACQUÉ: "La démarche initiée par le Conseil européen de Cologne", in *RUDH* 1-2/2000, pp. 3, 4.

[190] Sur ces concepts, *vid.*, entre autres, R. ALONSO GARCÍA: "El Soft Law comunitario", in *RAP*, 154 (2001), pp. 63 et s.

[191] *Vid*, entre autres, T. FISCHER/N. SCHLEY: *Organizing a Federal Structure for Europe: An EU Catalogue of Competences* (2000).

[192] *Vid.* A. VON BOGDANDY/J. BAST: "El orden vertical de competencias de la Unión Europea", in E. García de Enterría/R. Alonso García (dirs.), *La encrucijada constitucional de la Unión Europea* (sous presse)..

[193] *Vid.*, entre autres, J. MARTÍN PÉREZ DE NANCLARES: *El sistema de competencias de la Comunidad Europea*, Ed. McGraw Hill. Madrid, 1997.

[194] Ainsi, tout particulièrement, du TCF allemand qui, conformément à sa doctrine du "programme d'intégration" (développée dans ses arrêts Eurocontrol I et Kloppenburg), insiste dans le fameux arrêt Maastricht sur l'idée d'une disponibilité de l'intégration allemande et qui, compte tenu de la possible sortie de l'UE (prémisse majeure), se contente d'affirmer la possible inapplication des dispositions communautaires adoptées en dehors dudit "programme d'intégration" ou, dans d'autres termes, "ultra vires" (prémisse mineur). La question de savoir si la récente Décision (TCF) du 7 juin 2000 a modifié cette réserve de juridiction (subsidiaire) sur le droit communautaire reste sans réponse (*vid.* A. LÓPEZ CASTILLO: "Un nuevo paso en la andadura iuscomunitaria del Tribunal constitucional federal de Alemania. El Auto (Sala segunda) de 7 de junio de 2000", in *REDC* 61 (2001), pp. 349 et s.).

[195] Voir, en particulier, ACJ du 5 octobre 2000, aff. C-376/98 (annulation de la

Directiva 98/43, relative à la publicité du tabac). *Vid.*, entre autres, J. Mª de AREILZA CARVAJAL: "Variaciones sobre la limitación de competencias: la anulación de la directiva del tabaco", in *RDCE* 2/2000, pp. 643 et s.

[196] J. DÍEZ-HOCHLEITNER RODRÍGUEZ: "El futuro del sistema competencial comunitario: algunas propuestas de reforma", in E. García de Enterría/R. Alonso García (dirs.), *La encrucijada constitucional de la Unión Europea* (sous presse).

[197] *Vid.* le document "Un traité fondamental pour l'Union européenne. Étude sur le réorganisation des Traités", sur le site <www.iue.it/RSC/Treaties.html>.

[198] *Vid.*, par exemple, J. DÍEZ-HOCHLEITNER RODRÍGUEZ: "La tipología de los actos comunitarios", in M. Oreja (dir.), *El Tratado de Ámsterdam. Análisis y comentarios*, Ed. McGraw Hill. Madrid, 1998, I, pp. 565 et s.

[199] On trouve une liste des membres de la Convention à l'adresse électronique: <http://european-convention.eu.int/Static.asp?lang=FR&Content=Candidats_Gouv(_Parl)>.

[200] Il n'est pas nécessaire de souligner l'importance politique qu'a eu dans l'Espagne de 1985 l'invitation envoyée au Gouvernement pour connaîter directement et évaluer conjointement, à l'occasion de la réunion du Conseil européen, les propositions de réforme qui étaient alors débattues et qui sont apparues plus tard dans l'AUE.

SWEDEN

European Union Law and National Constitutions

Rapporteurs
Justices Göran Schäder and Mats Melin

I. INTRODUCTION: FOUNDATIONS OF EUROPEAN CONSTITUTIONALISM

1. Concept of constitution in Sweden

a. What is a constitution: theoretical concepts and basic notions

It may first of all be pointed out that there is no one single statute entitled the Swedish Constitution. Instead, there are four laws of a superior nature, together forming the Constitution. The fundamental character of those four laws results from the fact that they are named as such in one of the fundamental laws – the Instrument of Government – and from a common procedure for their adoption. The Instrument of Government of 1974 contains provisions normally found in a constitution, such as a bill of rights and the fundamental provisions for the exercise of public power and for the division of power between the Parliament (the Riksdag), the Cabinet, the courts, public authorities and local government. In the introductory chapter of the Instrument of Government "the fundamental laws of the Realm" are identified as being, other than the Instrument of Government itself, the Act of Succession of 1810 – which regulates the order in which the heirs of the Bernadotte dynasty shall inherit the throne of Sweden, the Freedom of the Press Act of 1949 – which regulates the right to free speech in printed matters and the right of public access to official documents and the Freedom of Expression Act of 1991 – which may be said to apply the principles set out in the Freedom of the Press Act to free speech in other media. When, in the following text, the term constitution is used, we will be referring to the Instrument of Government.

The fundamental characteristics of the Swedish form of government are comprehensively stated in the very first article of the Instrument of Government:

"All public power in Sweden emanates from the people.
Swedish democracy is founded on the freedom of opinion and on universal and equal suffrage. It shall be realised through a representative parliamentary polity and through local self-government.
Public power shall be exercised under the laws."

It is thus clear that the Swedish Constitution is founded on the principle of the sovereignty of the people, exercised through the right of the people to elect representatives to a parliament for the nation as a whole as well as to local assemblies, in free elections preceeded by free public debate. The principle of the sovereignty of the people is, however, already in that same first article balanced by the principle of legality in that public power shall be exercised under the laws.

This delicate balance between the sovereignty of parliament, on the one hand, and the rule of law, on the other, has traditionally been struck in favour of the former. The prevailing view was that the Riksdag, in expressing the will of the electorate, should not unnecessarily be restrained by rules of a mainly formal character. Thus, it was not until the adoption of the totally new Instrument of Government in 1974, with successive amendments in 1976 and 1979, that the Constitution came to contain a Bill of Rights. This reluctance to impose formal constitutional constraints on the powers of parliament was coupled with an attitude of cautious restraint taken by Swedish courts when executing concrete norm control.

There has, however, in recent years been a marked shift in the traditional views favouring parliamentary sovereignty and judicial restraint. This tendency may at least partly be attributed to the Swedish membership of the EU and to the incorporation into national law of the European Convention on Human Rights. Swedish courts now may find themselves obliged, not only to interpret national law in conformity with Treaty obligations, but to actually give precedence to Community law over a provision of national law or to resolve a conflict between a norm of human rights given a precise content by the European Court on Human Rights, on the one hand, and en equally precise provision of national law, on the other. It may also be noted that judicial review in recent years to a larger extent has been carried out – at least by the administrative courts – with regard to general principles of law, such as the principle of proportionality.

It may be mentioned that judicial review is the task of the ordinary courts since there is no constitutional court within the Swedish system.

Among other basic principles in the Instrument of Government, it may be noted that there is only one reference to the fact that Sweden is a monarchy. The King, or the Queen, it is stated, is the Head of State. In his capacity as Head of State, the King is a symbol of the Realm, essentially executing representative functions. He does not possess any decision-making power, not even within the sphere of international relations. Nevertheless, Sweden may be said to be a democratic, parliamentary monarchy.

General elections to the Riksdag are held every four years. The election system is strictly proportional in character, ensuring that each vote in principle carries the same weight. On the same occassion, elections are held to assemblies governing the some 280 municipalities and to the 21 regional county councils, the latter primarily being responsible for the administration of the health care system. Sweden may be said to bear the characteristics of a decentralized, but certainly not federal, state. The details of local government are laid down by ordinary law. In one respect, however, the Constitution expressly confers on the municipalities a fundamental decision-making power, namely that to "impose taxes for the fulfilment of their tasks".

Two particularities of the Swedish system should be mentioned. Firstly, that central state administration is carried out by a large number of independent central administrative authorities, each possessing objective competence within a given area but with the whole country as its sphere of activity. The Cabinet office on the other hand is, by international comparison, relatively small in numbers. According to the Constitution, even though the central administrative authorities naturally in general have a subordinate position vis-à-vis the Cabinet, when they exercise public authority against a private subject or a municipality, they are to act independently within the framework laid down in laws and other statutes. No public authority – not even the Riksdag – may give instructions as to how an administrative authority shall decide in an individual case of such a nature. This typically Swedish separation of powers within the national administration has as one of its effects that a Minister, responsible for one of the ministries into which the Cabinet office is divided, does not possess any decision-making power of his own. In principle, when exercising its different functions the Cabinet adopts all decisions *in corpore*.

Secondly, the transparency of Swedish legislative process and national administration, together with an extensive protection of the freedom of the press, are specific constitutional traits and form an important part of Swedish cultural, political and legal heritage. The essential constitutional elements in this respect are, inter alia, the principle of public access to documents kept by the authorities, the protection being afforded to civil servants giving information to the media, the absolute prohibition of censorship and the principle of one individual – in most cases the publisher – being exclusively legally responsible for the content of a printed material.

b. The EU/EC architecture and national constitutional tradition

The fact that, according to the first article of the Constitution, cited above, "all public power emanates from the people" does not – it was stated in the preparatory works on constitutional amendments to make a Swedish accession to the EU possible – hinder the people from instructing its representatives, the Riksdag, to cooperate with other peoples and to let decisions taken within such a cooperation bind the participating states and their peoples. In other words, when the Riksdag decides to transfer decision-making powers to the Communities and the Swedish Cabinet – accountable to the Riksdag – participates in the use of those powers, the execution of public power may still be said to emanate from the Swedish people. On the other hand, it follows from that very same principle that there is a limit to the possible development of the European cooperation. Thus, it would not be in conformity with the initial provision of the Constitution to let the cooperation develop into the creation of a federal state, the powers of which derive their legitimacy from a mandate given by an European people in common elections. It could safely be assumed that such a development would require extensive changes in the constitutions of all the Member States.

In other words, a Constitution for Sweden as a state within a federation must, in many important respects, have a different content than the present Instrument of Government. Following this line of reasoning, no amendment to or change in the Constitution concerning the fundamental characteristics of the Swedish form of government was deemed to be necessary at the time of the accession.

The protection of fundamental rights was, however, found to be a more problematic area. A few provisions in secondary Community law was identified as limiting certain of the fundamental rights enumerated in the Swedish Bill of Rights (Chapter 2 of the Instrument of Government). Consequently, it would not be possible, in the national Constitution, to prohibit the transfer of decision-making competence which could limit those rights. Furthermore, it would not, as a matter of principle, be possible to – in national adjudication – challenge a Community law provision with reference to the national protection of fundamental rights. Therefore, it was found to be of crucial importance that the protection of fundamental rights provided for by Community law would continue to be upheld.

These considerations resulted in an amendment to the provision of the Constitution making a transfer of competence to the Communities possible (Chapter 10, Article 5 of the Instrument of Government). Thus, according to the Constitution, the Riksdag may transfer decision-making rights to the European Communities "as long as" the Communities have a system of protection of fundamental rights and freedoms "corresponding to" that provided for by the Instrument of Government and by the European Convention on Human Rights. It must be assumed, that the Riksdag, at the time of the Swedish accession and later Treaty revisions, has considered Community law to fulfil that requirement.

Another obvious consequence of the membership of the EU is that it has led to a formal weakning of the position of the Riksdag as the central organ of the State. Binding norms, which according to the Constitution should be decided by the Riksdag, may be adopted by the Council, that is to say by the governments of the Member States. It can hardly be denied that with a membership of the union follows a constitutionally important shift in the balance of power between the legislative and the executive branch of government. This fact poses the further problem of accountability. As a general rule, the Cabinet is accountable to the Riksdag even when acting in the Council. The system of qualified majority vote may, however, limit that accountability. The Riksdag can hardly hold the Cabinet responsible for a decision taken in the Council if the Swedish vote was in the minority.

The Swedish tradition of restraint with regard to judicial review by the courts has, as mentioned above, probably been affected by our membership in the union. That tradition is reflected in the Constitution by a provision worded as follows:

> "If a court, or any other public organ, considers that a provision is in conflict with a provision of a fundamental law or with a provision of any other superior statute, or that the procedure prescribed has been set aside in any important respect when the provision was inaugurated, then such a provision may not be applied. However, if the provision has been approved by the Riksdag or by the Cabinet, the provision may be set aside only if the inaccuracy is manifest."

The requirement of manifest inaccuracy, as it traditionally has been understood in Sweden, is not possible to fully apply when a national court is faced with its obligation to give precedence to Community law over a conflicting provision of domestic law.

Finally, it may be mentioned that certain developments within the third pillar (qualified majority vote, competence of the ECJ, consultation of the European parliament) has contributed to a debate concerning whether or not it in the future is sufficient to allow decision-making powers to be trasferred to the Communities only. The Cabinet has recently proposed that the relevant provision of the Instrument of Government be changed to allow such transfer to "cooperation within the European Union".

2. *National provisions for the adoption of a "Constitution" of the European Union*

a. Constitutional conditions for and limits to further steps of integration (substance)

There is, as of today, only one formal provision with regard to conditions for and limits to further steps of integration, namely Chapter 10, Article 5 of the Instrument of Government, mentioned above, according to which decision-making powers may be transfered to the European Communities. As has been mentioned, there is only one condition for such a transfer: the upholding of a sufficient protection of fundamental rights and freedoms in Community law. It is noteworthy that this provision does not contain any limits as to the type or scope of powers that may be transferred.

Nevertheless, it has been assumed, as has also been mentioned earlier, that the Constitution does not allow a transfer of powers to such an extent that its fundamental characteristics of the Swedish form of government no longer would be valid. In the recent proposal for a change concerning the possible adressee of a transfer of powers, it is also suggested that the Article be amended to explicitly state that a transfer of powers may not concern "the foundations" of the Swedish form of government.

b. Procedural requirements under national constitutional provisions

The Riksdag may decide to transfer decision-making powers to the Communities either by one single decision taken with a three fourths majority or, alternatively, in the manner prescribed for a change of or an amendment to the Constitution.

A change of or an amendment to the Constitution is to be decided by two successive decisions of identical wording by the Riksdag, with a general election held between the two decisions. – In addition, a proposal for a change of the Constitution may be put to a referendum if one third of the members of the Riksdag so decides. The referendum should be held simultaneously with the election for the Riksdag. The proposal is rejected if the majority of those taking part in the referendum vote against it (and the number of voters exceeds half the number of those who registered valid votes in the election to the Riksdag). In all other cases the newly elected Riksdag shall take up the proposal for a second and final consideration.

c. The role of the citizens: international treaty or European social contract

It is probably fair to say that in Swedish constitutional debate emphasis has been put on the fact that the cooperation within the Union is based on international treaties, albeit of a special character. Even if those treaties require decision-making powers to be transferred to the institutions of the Union – and thus establish a direct relation between the Community legislator and the individual citizen – they are nevertheless agreements between the Member States, entered into in basically the same manner as other international treaties. The Contracting States are, regardless of the supranational character of the cooperation instituted by the treaties, free to decide, by common accord, to extend, reduce or otherwise modify the treaties.

3. The constitution-making process: preparing the IGC 2004 in practice

a. How the internal debate on the future of the European Union is organized

A special committee has been appointed and entrusted with the mission to initiate and stimulate a broad debate on issues related to the IGC 2004. Its task has been described as threefolded, namely

- to stimulate a broad, public debate on the European Union, in particular with regard to the forthcoming IGC, to contribute to an increased knowledge among the public on relevant questions concerning the development of the Union and to give room for different views to be heard,
- to establish points of contact between the debate in Sweden and in other European countries, and
- to analyse the issues to be decided by the IGC.

The committee has been instructed to discuss such concepts as constitution, federation, subsidiarity, legitimacy, democratic control, accountability and transparency but also whether what is said to be Swedish objectives – such as environment, food safety, consumer protection and the EU budgetary process – may be enhanced within the IGC.

The committe is expected to fulfil its task by, inter alia, organizing seminars and public hearings, initiating scientific reports and developing a special web-site on the Internet with links to corresponding sites in other countries. The committee will also give economic support to organizations and others who wish to engage in the public debate on the IGC issues. It disposes 15 million SEK for this latter purpose.

The committee has only recently started its work, but it seems clear that it intends to primarily focus on concrete political questions as a basis for a further debate on constitutional and institutional issues.

b. Key issues and proposals of the leading political groups

On 18 October 2001, Prime Minister Göran Persson expressed his views on the further development of the EU in a speech given at the Humboldt University in Berlin. It is interesting to note that in the first part of his speech he focused on what he called some challenges facing the EU from the outside – such as terrorism and global warming – and from inside – such as enlargement, the need to develop a common asylum and migration policy and the need to change the CAP within a reallocation of EU resources. He stressed that he believes that it is important "to try to describe what is ahead, before we proceed to a discussion about changes called for in the institutions and working methods of the Union". One should not, Mr Persson said, "start by building institutional castles. That will only widen the gap between policymakers and citizens".

When, in the final part of his speech, Mr Persson commented on the specific issues on the IGC agenda, he said, with regard to the status of the Charter of Fundamental Rights, that "my view is that the wording of the Charter is not sufficiently precise for incorporating it into the Treaty as it stands. An incorporation must not lead to the undermining of the European Convention on Human Rights. That convention already exists, and the Community should accede to it."

Concerning simplification, the Prime Minister feared that this is not an easy task as far as the treaties are concerned since they represent the compromises Member States have been able to agree upon. With regard to the question of a Constitution for the EU, Mr Persson emphasized that it may be argued that the present Treaties indeed may be seen as a constitution. "The important thing is not whether we need a constitution for the European Union, but rather what kind of constitution we want", he continued, and added

> "It would indeed be an advantage if we could concentrate some of the core rules on decision-making, competences and procedures in one document. But an essential question will be the legal status of that document, and what it will take to amend it. I would not be prepared to accept that a transfer of competence from the national to the European level could be made without ratification by national Parliaments. I doubt that many other Member States would either."

On the issue of a catalogue of competences, Mr Persson agreed that a clearer distinction between national and EU competence would be valuable but emphasized that it must not lead to a dismantling of what the EU has achieved over the years, nor should the Union barter away tools that it may need in the future.

Concerning the role of national parliaments, the Prime Minister maintained that their influence on the policies of the EU "is best exercised through close scrutiny of the Governments as members of the Council."

Finally, Mr Persson made some remarks on the role of, respectively, the Council and the Commission. "The Commission has an important role in looking after the interests of the Union as a whole", he said. However, "we agreed about changes in the appointment of the Commission in Nice...I do not see any need for changing it again". The Council, in Mr Perssons view, is the body that can take the broad and overall decisions needed, and be held accountable by the citizens. The European Council and the Council of Ministers will, he said, continue "to play the central role in the governing of Europe". He added, as an "observation in more general terms" that "I do not think that Member States really wish to make a fundamental change in the balance between Member States on the one hand, and the Commission and the European Parliament on the other".

We have dwelled at some length at this speech by Mr Persson, not only because it is a political statement by the Prime Minister in office, but also because the positions taken may be seen as representative not only of the ruling Social Democratic Party but of a relatively large segment of Swedish political debate. This common attitude may be said to be characterized by a relatively weak interest in the constitutional issues as such of the EU. It is rather a pragmatic attitude, interested in the specifics of different policy areas. When forced to take a stand on different issues of a constitutional or institutional nature, the Swedish reflex is to, basically, find that all is well as it is.

At present (March 2002) only the Liberal Party, relatively small in numbers, has presented a coherent view on the IGC in the form of a proposal for a Constitution of the EU. In 27 articles, it deals with, inter alia, basic principles, the objectives of the Union, citizenship, language, what is exclusive competence of the Union and in which field there is a shared competence, transparency, the institutions etc. The proposal is based on a two chamber legislature and a directly elected Commission president.

Two other political parties, of those holding seats in the Riksdag, represent an opposite view in Swedish political debate. The Left Party and the Environmental Party opposes the Swedish membership of the EU and are, consequently, not likely to advocate a more precise position as to how the Union may be reformed.

II. RELATIONSHIP AND INTERACTION OF EC/EU LAW AND NATIONAL CONSTITUTIONS TODAY

1. *Member States´ constitutional autonomy under European constraints*

a. *National identities of the Member States as a limit to the extension of the EC/EU competencies*

In a strictly legal sense, the identity of a Member State consists in its existence as an autonomous entity under public international law. As stated above, it would not be in conformity with the Swedish constitution to let the EC/EU cooperation develop into the creation of a federal state. It would neither be in conformity with the wording of Article 6.3 TEU to let that happen. But since such a development anyhow would necessitate amendments to the TEU, it is not the Treaty-provision but the Member States themselves that would prevent the creation of the United States of Europe.

In a more political sense, the elements forming the identities of the Member States may differ substantively from one Member State to another.

Broadly speaking, the identity of a Member State lies in its political and cultural heritage.

The Swedish position on the limits to the EC/EU competencies could best be described by quoting the preparatory works to the amendment of the Constitution that preceded the Swedish accession. There it was stressed that the Communities could not be given decision-making power to such an extent that the provisions on the basic principles of the constitution ceased to be valid. The position of the Swedish parliament as the principal organ of the state must not be substantially undermined through the transfer of legislative powers. The Standing Committee on the Constitution - whose report formed the basis for the decision of the Swedish Parliament - emphasized that the area that could not be transfered was not restricted to provisions on the basic principles of the constitution but included also other provisions that upholds fundamental principles in our constitutional system. The committee especially stressed the great importance of the free formation of opinion for the Swedish constitutional system. A precondition for the free formation of opinion to play its important role was according to the committee the public access to documents held by the athorities and the freedom to inform the media. Also the prohibition of censorship, the protection afforded to civil servants who give information to the media, the system of the editors exclusive responsability for the content of printed material and other important principles in the Freedom of the Press Act and in the Fundamental Law on the Freedom of Expression where according to the committee of great importance for the free formation of opinion. The provision that would open for transfer of legislative power to the Communities could therefore not be said to open up possibilities to transfer decision-making that would materially alter those principles without simultaneous amendment of the constitution.

The committee assessed that according to the treaties that Sweden would acceed to as a member of the EU, the decision-making power of the Communities in the fields where the fundamental principles of the Swedish constitutional system would be touched upon was very limited. The legislation on the freedom of the press and on the freedom of expression are - just like the rules on openness - national affairs. The treaties does not give the Community organs any competence to harmonize the rules in those fields of legislation. Another matter is, that within the fields where the institutions have competencies, they sometimes can take decisions that affects e.g. questions of secrecy and openness. The rules the Community institutions may decide must not be given such an extent that they disturb the principles upon which the Swedish legislation on freedom of the press, on freedom of expression and on openness and transparency is built. An alteration of this fact would require an amendment of the treaties. If it in the future came into question to transfer such competencies through amendments of the treaties that directly has freedom of the press and freedom of expression in mind, the committee held that that should not be done without simultaneous amendment of the constitution.

In its treaty on accession to the EU Sweden made a unilateral declaration on openness. It said: Sweden welcomes the ongoing development within the Union towards greater openness and transparency. The principle of openness, especially the right of public access to documents kept by the authorities, and the constitutional protection being afforded to civil servants giving information to the media, are and remains fundamental principles that forms a part of Swedens constitutional, political and cultural heritidge.

The Member States at the time responded by noting that Sweden had made a unilateral declaration on openness and transparency and said that they took it for granted that Sweden as a member of the European Union would fully comply with community law in this respect.

This Swedish sensitivity does not only apply to questions on openness. The fact that Sweden at the constitutional level has a very elaborated legislation on the freedom of the press and on the freedom of expression in other media, can make EC initiatives on e.g. the content of advertisments or counteraction against the concentration of ownership of the press very difficult for Sweden to follow.

Sweden is, as earlier stated, a unitary state with a tradition of strong local self government. From a strictly legal point of view, the right of local self determination is a power delegated to the municipalities by the state. In the political debate however, this has not hindered those who feel that the state is unduly restricting the activities of the municipalities to use constitutional arguments and claim that their constitutional right to self determination is being infringed upon. The same would evidently happen if the restrictions came from the EU.

b. Articles 6.1 and 7 TEU as limits to the constitutional autonomy of the Member States

Those articles shall guarantee that Member States upholds the principles of freedom, democracy, respect for human rights and the rule of law. This quite naturally puts limits to the constitutional autonomy of the Member States. That is their purpose.

2. Common values: the Charter of fundamental rights of the European Union

a. Does the Charter reflect the basic human rights standards of your constitution and national law?

All of the rights and freedoms listed in the Charter can not be found in the

Swedish constitution. But when also ordinary law is taken into account, the level of protection is reflected.

However, articles 51 and 52 of the Charter restricts the impact of the Charter in a way that makes it difficult to assess the importance of it.

b. The Charter as a reference for fundamental rights protection in national courts.

The Charter has to our knowledge never been refered to by any Swedish court. References to the Council of Europe Convention on Human Rights and Fundamental Freedoms are however numerous. If the Charter would be made into a legally binding document, there is in our opinion a risk that that the importance of the Convention would be deteriorated. Since the Convention covers both the application of EC/EU law and national law it has a broader field of application and it ought therefore to remain the most important European document on human rights.

c. The impact of the Charter on the standards referred to in article 6.1 TEU

The Charter will, as it is the EU document on the matter, certainly set the standard for the references in article 6.1 TEU.

3. The Question of the supremacy of EC/EU law and its constitutional effects

a. Supremacy I: community primary law and national constitutional law. Position of national constitutional courts.

When acceding to the EU, Sweden was obliged to make its national legal system, including its constitution, conform with community law. Thorough studies where carried out to accomplish that result. The last constitutional amendment was made in 1998, three years after the accession. That concerned the role of the Bank of Sweden and was made in order to make it possible for Sweden to join the EMU. Sweden has however not yet acceeded to the common currency.

As has been explained earlier, Sweden has no constitutional court. All courts are competent to handle cases where constitutional questions have to be answered. To our knowledge there has however never been any case pending before any Swedish court where there has been argued that there should exist a conflict between community primary law and our constitution. There is therefore no case-law on the matter to report.

b. Supremacy II: community secondary legislation and national constitutional law

When the Swedish constitution was amended in order to open up the possibilities to transfer legislative powers to the EC, the Standing Committee on the Constitution addressed the question on what would happen if the EC-institutions would take a decision that was contrary to the Swedish constitution. If the decision was a directive, the committee said, it could not be implemented in Sweden without a prior amendment of the constitution. The directives presupposes national legislation and the Swedish parliament can not legislate in violation of the constitution. From the community law point of view however, there arises an obligation to amend the constitution. The matter would according to the committee be brought to a head if the EC issued a directly applicable regulation that was in conflict with a provision in the Swedish constitution.

If a provision in a regulation or directive stands out as constitutionally unacceptable, the Swedish position should according to the committee not be to talk about a conflict between community law and national law. The question should instead be if the the EC-institution has had the right to take the decision it has taken with effect for Sweden. In other words, does the act fall within the field where legislative powers has been transfered? If the answer is that it falls outside this field, the act is not valid as community law in Sweden.

The crucial question in this way of reasoning is: Who decides if the act falls outside or within the transfer of powers. The ECJ would strongly argue that they alone can decide that. The German Constitutional Court, by whose ruling on the Maastricht Treaty the Swedish parliamentary committee was strongly influenced, would say that they do it for Germany.

The purpose of the Swedish Parliament when approving this reasoning was not only, or even primarily, to give all Swedish courts the right to assess the validity of community law, but to reserve itself the right to make such an assessment when confronted with the question. They have to our knowledge not yet had the opportunity to do so. Neither has any Swedish court been confronted with the problem.

c. Implicit modification of national constitutions by the revision and application of the TUE

The interpretation of the constitution is not independent of changes in the society where it is to be applied. In that sence, the development of the European Union might very well have an influence on the future interpretation of some of the provisions of the Swedish constitution. It is however difficult to say anything concrete about how that could be the case.

4. Institutional interdependence: European functions of national institutions

a. The national parliaments in the European legislation process: indirect source of legitimacy and responsibilities for implementation

The national parliaments have a very important role to play in the European legislation process. You just have to look at the low polling in the elections to the European Parliament and the total lack of debate on European matters in the Swedish campaigns before the elections to reach the conclusion that the European Parliament does not suffice to give the Union democratic legitimacy. It is therefore essential that the national parliaments are involved.

The implementation of directives through national legislation gives community law a legitimacy that it would not have if only regulations where decided. The actual wording of the law has been decided by someone you can hold responsible in the next national election. The essence of democracy is that it is possible to throw the responsible people out. That is not possible on the European level.

For a government negotiating in Brussels it is also wise to involve the national Parliament in the negotiation process and secure acceptance for its negotiation positions with the parliamentarians. It gives you a stronger position at the negotation table and it also makes the national implementation easier if the parliamentarians has had a finger in the pie.

b. European functions of national administrations: a double mandate for the executive

When acting as a competent authority according to community law a national administrative authority could be said to to have a double mandate: one from its own government and one from the EC/EU. In the end it is however not so complicated. It is not the EC/EU that has appointed the authority. That has been done by the national government. And the national government would be free to appoint another authority to the task if it does not approve of the way it performs. That could never be done by the EC/EU institutions.

But when acting as a European authority the national authority has to follow the rules prescribed by the EC/EU. The prohibition referred to in section 1.a to give instructions to a Swedish authority on how it shall decide in an individual case concerning the exercise of public power against an individual or municipality must however apply also to the EC/EU institution in its dealings with the Swedish authority. Or rather the other way around; the Swedish authority is by the Swedish constitution bound to ignore any such instruction.

c. Judicial protection in the European Union through national judges: conflict of loyalties; questions of procedural autonomy

In theory there should be no problem. As a judge you shall have only one loyalty: that to the law. Not to the legislator, whether he is national or European. In practice it is of course not that simple.

The Swedish judiciary has however not yet been confronted with any seriuos problems of this kind. As stated earlier there has been no cases concerning conflicts between national constitutional law and community law. There has been quite a few cases concerning conflicts between ordinary national law and community law. If it has been assessed that there is such a conflict, the cases have regularly been solved in the favour of community law. The Swedish judges have not in principle shown any reluctance to set aside national law in conflict with community law.

The question of procedural autonomy has not been much discussed. What has been seen as a serious problem however, is the length of the procedings at the ECJ when it handles cases on preliminary rulings. The national court that decides to put a question to the ECJ must also convince itself that the adjudication of the case is not so urgent that it can not be delayed for at least two years. This must make any judge think twice before asking for a preliminary ruling.

III. THE ROLE OF THE REGIONS AND LOCAL AUTHORITIES IN EU LAW

As we have explained above (under I), the local administrative authorities, the municipalities, are many and, consequently, given the size of the Kingdom as a whole, fairly small. They possess the right of taxation and they carry out tasks entrusted to them by law and, to a lesser extent, duties which they have taken upon themselves. The municipalities may certainly not be compared to states within a federal structure. The rules which they apply are those given i laws adopted by the Riksdag.

The municipalities are, of course, in many ways affected by EC law, for example with regard to the rules on public procurement. There are also groups of municipalities – regions – developing contacts with neighbouring regions in other Member States to the extent that we may be witnessing the forming of what in fact can be described as transnational regions, for example in the south of Sweden.

However, we fail to see that the to some extent decentralized structure of the Swedish state may be affected by constitutional developments within the union, nor that the existence of municipalities should lead to any consequences of importance for EU law. A catalogue of competences in an EU Constitution would not, for example, affect an internal division of competences since the national legislative power for all practical purposes is exclusively reserved for the national parliament.

IV. CONCLUSIONS AND RECOMMENDATIONS FOR 2004

1. A new architecture: how should an EU Constitution or EU basic treaty look like?

It seems to us that the fundamental treaties should be subject to an operation of "legal clensing". Their present structure, with its mixture of fundamental rules on general principles of law of the union and its instutions together with rules on the politics of the union within a large number of different policy areas, is far from satisfactory from a legal point of view and, it may be added, may even be said to constitute a problem with regard to the principle of democracy.

An EU Constitution containing the basic objectives of the union and the fundamental rules on general principles of law to be respected, on citizenship of the union, identifying the areas of common policy and giving the basic norms governing the institutions of the union and the division of competences between them would undoubtedly make the structure and legislation of the union more clear, understandable and easy to apply for all of its subjects.

Within the foreseeable future it is probably necessary to chose the more limited approach of just "sorting out" the existing rules of a fundamental character from the present treaties and arranging them in a separate document. Even with such a limited approach it would, in our view, be fair to entitle that document the Constitution of the Union.

On one specific point however, such a document would need to be further elaborated than just inserting articles from the existing treaties. The present Article 255 EC is too general to regulate the right of the citizens to access to documents held by the institutions. The right of access to public documents is not absolute and its real content is determined by the application of rules on secrecy. A constitution of the Union should therefore at least enumerate the general grounds on which a document may be kept secret.

2. A Constitution for the European union: conditions of adoption and amendment; its relations to national constitutions

The adoption of a constitution adding new fundamental rules to those existing in the present treaties, for example introducing a formal Bill of Rights, would, in order to possess the legitimacy for the future of such a document, require a broad general debate and a specific form of adoption involving the peoples, if not the people, of the Union.

If, on the other hand, the more limited approach which we have advocated above is chosen, the constitution may – being an ordinary international treaty – be adopted in the same way as are the fundamental treaties at the present. Even this is of course a somewhat dangerous venture in that rules in a treaty once adopted would have to once again be subject to the different national constitutional procedures necessary for the State to be party to an international agreement. It should be pointed out, however, that with the limited approach no new comptences would be transferred from the Member States to the Union. To the extent that national procedures applicable are dependent on whether or not such a transfer is made (which is the case in Sweden), the national procedure of adoption may be simplified.

On this question it may also be said that if the Member States fear that the advantages of an EU Constitution, even with a limited approach, is impossible to explain to their electorate, then that, regrettably as it may be, is a good final argument for refraining from intiating such a reform.

Even if the main goal of the adoption of a constitution for the Union is to make things clearer, it should also serve the pupose of reserving the present complicated and time-consuming amendment procedures for rules of a fundamental character. Consequently, amendments to the constitution should be decided according to present procedures whereas amendments to treaties – or protocols – on the politics to be pursued within the different areas of common action could be decided according to a simplified procedure not necessarily involving national parliaments in their legislative capacity.

As far as the relations of an EU Constitution to national constitutions are concerned, we are of the opinion that *l'aquis communautaire* in this respect with regard to the present treaties, developed by the ECJ and somewhat reluctantly accepted by the Member States and national courts, would still be valid.

3. Merging the constitutional process and enlargement: how to involve the candidates?

The shaping and adoption of a constitution are naturally tasks for those governed by it. Thus, it is a truism that the actual signing of a constitutional treaty only can be done by those states which are members of the Intergovernmental conference of 2004. This being said, the content of an EU Constitution to be is of course of crucial interest and importance to the candidate countries. Most of them will, at the time of an eventual adoption of the constitution, equally be governed by it. Therefore they need to have a voice in the process leading up to the adoption. Since the Member States have chosen to have the IGC 2004 prepared by a convent – which do not have any legislative or decision-making powers of its own – the candidates indeed have such an opprtunity. They may take part in the Convent as observers and express their opinions on an almost equal footing with the representatives of the present Member States.

SWITZERLAND

EU-Recht und Nationale Verfassungen

Länderbericht Schweiz

Rapporteur
Marianne Freiermuth Abt and Robert Mosters[1]

VORSPANN: AKTUELLE BEZIEHUNGEN SCHWEIZ-EU

Nach der Ablehnung des EWR am 6.12.92 durch Volk und Stände konzentrierte sich die Europapolitik der Schweiz auf bilaterale Verhandlungen in einzelnen Sektoren.

1999 wurden sieben bilaterale Verträge abgeschlossen in den Bereichen Personenverkehr, Landverkehr, Luftverkehr, Landwirtschaft, Forschung, technische Handelshemmnisse und öffentliches Beschaffungswesen[2]. Diese

Abkommen treten in Kraft, sobald sie von allen Mitgliedstaaten ratifiziert worden sind. Im Juli 2001 wurde eine neue Runde bilateraler Verhandlungen eröffnet, die weitere Themen behandeln[3]. Im März 2001 wurde die Volksinitiative "Ja zu Europa!", welche unverzügliche Beitrittsverhandlungen forderte, von Volk und Ständen verworfen. Die Europapolitik der Schweiz wird sich kurzfristig auf die Umsetzung der sieben bilateralen Abkommen konzentrieren (sobald sie in Kraft getreten sind). Mittelfristig sollen weitere bilaterale Verhandlungen geführt werden. Langfristig hält der Bundesrat am Ziel des Beitritts fest, aber zuerst sollen Erfahrungen mit den erzielten Abkommen gesammelt, ihre konkreten Auswirkungen beobachtet und die innenpolitische Unterstützung für dieses Ziel gestärkt werden[4].

A. GRUNDLAGEN

I. Zur schweizerischen Verfassungstradition

1. Kurzer Überblick über die Geschichte der Verfassung

Die Ablehnung äusserer Einflüsse ist keineswegs eine schweizerische Tradition: Man muss sich vor Augen halten, dass die erste Helvetische Vefassung von 1798 eine abgeänderte Version der französischen Direktorialverfassung von 1795 war, die zweite Helvetische Verfassung (welche nie in Kraft trat) auf einem Entwurf des Ersten Konsuls von Frankreich beruhte und die Mediationsakte von 1803 durch Napoleon ausgearbeitet wurde[5]. Letztere überdauerte die Herrschaft von Napoleon nicht, statt Frankreich wurden nach 1812 Österreich, Russland und die deutschen Staaten zu einflussreichen Kräften bei der Neuordnung der Schweiz. Die Drohung der gewaltsamen Intervention durch diese Mächte führte schliesslich zur Schaffung eines Bundesvertrages durch die Tagsatzung. Schliesslich löste die Julirevolution in Frankreich 1830 eine weitere Entwicklung aus, welche 1848 in der Errichtung der Bundesurkunde mündete, welche nicht mehr als blosser Vertrag zwischen den Kantonen entstand, sondern als Verfassung. Auf die Androhung von Österreich, Preussen, Frankreich und Russland zu intervenieren, falls der Bundesvertrag anders als mittels einstimmiger Genehmigung geändert werden sollte, reagierte die Tagsatzung mit einer klaren Zurückweisung dieser Regelungsansprüche von aussen: 1815 sei nur das Gebiet der Eidgenossenschaft garantiert worden, nicht der Bundesvertrag, und die schweizerische Neutralität sei nicht an eine bestimmte Form der Bundeseinrichtung gebunden. Es sei somit Sache der Schweiz zu entscheiden, auf welche Art der Vertrag geändert werden könne. Mit der Verfassung von 1848 war der Übergang vom Staatenbund zum Bundesstaat erreicht. Der Begriff der "Nation" wurde jedoch beispielsweise nicht verwendet, weil er für gewisse Kreise einen zu unitaristischen Charakter hatte. Dies erinnert an die Schwierigkeiten, welche in der heutigen EU-Verfassungsdiskussion Begriffe wie "föderalistischer Bundesstaat" oder "federation of nation-states" auslösen und wo dann versucht wird (oder werden sollte), zu "neutraleren" Begriffen zu finden, was für eine konstruktive Diskussion zwischen sehr heterogenen Parteien notwendig sein dürfte (wie bspw. den Vorschlag, zum Begriff der "community" zurückzukehren[6].

Die zweitletzte Totalrevision der BV datiert von 1874. Wesentliches Ziel war damals, den Bund gegenüber den Kantonen zu stärken (Kompetenzerweiterung für den Bund) und den Staat gegenüber der Kirche. Als grundlegende Neuerung wurde das fakultative Referendum für Bundesgesetze und allgemeinverbindliche Bundesbeschlüsse eingeführt. Die repräsentative Demokratie ging damit für den Bund zu Ende[7]. Weitere direktdemokratische Instrumente fanden in späteren Jahren Eingang in die Verfassung: die Volksinitiative 1891, das Referendum bei Staatsverträgen 1921 (ausgebaut 1977). Seit 1966 versuchte man, eine weitere Totalrevision der Bundesverfassung zustande zu bringen, es kam jedoch nur zu unzähligen Partialrevisionen. 1999 war es jedoch soweit: die "neue" Bundesverfassung wurde angenommen. Sie war als "Nachführung" deklariert und darf als "schöpferische Gesamtbereinigung des geltenden Verfassungsrechts"[8] angesehen werden.

2. *Konzepte und Begriffe*

(a) Charakteristika (einleitende Bemerkungen)

Die Schweiz des 19. Jahrhunderts hatte von der Französischen Revolution staatsrechtliche Ideen wie die Garantie der Freiheitsrechte, die Rechtsgleichheit und das Prinzip der Gewaltenteilung übernommen. Prägendes Element der Schweiz ist vor allem die Verwirklichung direktdemokratischer Instrumente wie Initiative und Gesetzesreferendum. Die Wurzeln der direkten Beteiligung der Bevölkerung[9] an politischen Entscheiden liegen in der Begrenztheit der Gemeinwesen der alten Eidgenossenschaft, diese verfügten bereits über Erfahrungen mit Bürgerversammlungen, Landsgemeinden und dem Prinzip der Mehrheitsentscheidung[10]. Auch heute im Kleinstaat Schweiz hat sich die instinktive Abneigung gegen jegliche Abtretung von Kompetenzen an ein übergeordnetes Organ oder eine supranationale Organisation erhalten[11]. Allerdings führt dies nicht zu einer totalen Abgeschlossenheit. Denn trotz der ursprünglichen Zielsetzung des eidgenössischen Bundesstaates, als Schutzbündnis gegen aussen zu wirken (erster Zweck der Verfassung von 1848 war die Behauptung der Unabhängigkeit des Vaterlandes gegen aussen) und der darauf gegründeten Introvertiertheit[12] enthält die schweizerische Bundesverfassung mehrere Bestimmungen, die ihre grundsätzliche Offenheit für das internationale Recht festlegen. Es sind dies die folgenden:

- Präambel: Solidarität und Offenheit gegenüber der Welt
- Art. 2 (Zweckartikel): Einsatz für eine friedliche und gerechte internationale Ordnung
- Art. 5 Abs. 4: Bekenntnis zum Völkerrecht
- Art. 54 Abs. 2 (Teil Staatsaufgaben): Beitrag zur Linderung von Not und Armut in der Welt, zur Achtung der Menschenrechte und zur Förderung der Demokratie, zu einem friedlichen Zusammenleben der Völker

Das Ziel der Unabhängigkeit (Zweckartikel 2 Abs. 1 und 54 Abs. 2 BV) kann nicht als Pflicht ausgelegt werden, jegliche Abhängigkeit von aussen zu vermeiden und eine isolationistische Haltung einzunehmen, einer Einbindung der Schweiz in die internationale Gemeinschaft steht dieses Ziel nicht entgegen (im Gegenteil, s. unter Punkt 2 d)). Es bildet aber insofern eine Schranke der Integration, als die Aufgabe der Staatlichkeit der Schweiz gegen dieses Verfassungsziel verstossen würde[13].

Ein weiteres Zeichen der Offenheit ist der Grundrechtskatalog, welcher durch internationale Abkommen beeinflusst worden ist. Die Sozialziele werden ähnlich dem Uno Pakt I[14] ausgestaltet und das zwingende Völkerrecht bildet eine materielle Schranke der Verfassungsgebung[15]. In der Grundrechtsrechtsprechung des Bundesgerichts lässt sich der Einfluss europäischen Rechts zudem deutlich ablesen[16]. Die Bundesverfassung enthält allerdings keine eigentliche Öffnungs- oder Integrationsklausel, wie sie heute in verschiedenen EU-Mitgliedstaaten in der Verfassung enthalten sind und die verdeutlichen, dass Hoheitsgewalt teilbar ist[17]. In der BV wird das Verhältnis zur EU nicht erwähnt. Die Einfügung eines "Europa-Artikels" wurde aus politischen Gründen nicht propagiert, um nicht die Ablehnung der ganzen Nachführung der BV zu riskieren[18].

Nebst der Funktion, die Macht des Staates zu begrenzen[19], ist es im Bundesstaat insbesondere Aufgabe der Verfassung, die Kompetenzaufteilung zwischen den verschiedenen Organisationsebenen zu regeln, um sie so der Regelungszuständigkeit des Bundes zu entziehen[20].

(b) Begriff der formellen und der materiellen Verfassung

Die Verfassung im *formellen Sinn* umfasst "die Gesamtheit der Rechtssätze, die in der besonderen Form der Verfassungsgebung erlassen worden sind"[21]. In der Schweiz ist das entsprechende Verfahren in Art. 138 ff. BV vorgesehen. Die Änderungen der Verfassung unterliegen dem obligatorischen Referendum und müssen für ihre Annahme in der Volksabstimmung ein sogenanntes doppeltes Mehr erzielen- nämlich erstens das *Volksmehr,* also die Mehrheit der gültigen Stimmen im ganzen Land, und zweitens das *Ständemehr*, also eine Mehrheit von Kantonen, in denen die Stimmenden die Vorlage angenommen haben (Art. 195 BV). Dies ist auch Folge der erhöhten formellen Geltungskraft der Bundesverfassung und charakterisiert sie als relativ starre Verfassung[22]. Zusätzlich gilt die derogatorische Kraft der Bundesverfassung, dh sie hat Vorrang gegenüber anderen Normen des schweizerischen Rechts. Eine Einschränkung dieses Grundsatzes ergibt sich allerdings aus der unvollkommenen Verfassungsgerichtsbarkeit: Gemäss Art. 191 BV müssen Bundesgesetze angewendet werden, auch wenn sie verfassungswidrig sind.

Verfassung im *materiellen Sinn* stellt auf den Inhalt der Rechtssätze ab und bezeichnet die grundlegenden Normen eines demokratischen Rechtsstaats, wie die Gewaltenteilung, die politischen Rechte und Freiheitsrechte der Bürger und sonstige rechtsstaatliche Garantien[23]. Verfassung im formellen und im materiellen Sinn decken sich nicht in jedem Fall, wie man unschwer an der Schweizerischen Bundesverfassung aufzeigen kann. Etliche Detailbestimmungen der BV gehörten nicht auf Verfassungsstufe, befinden sich aber dort, weil eine Volksinitiative auf Gesetzesebene nicht existiert. Zudem trägt auch die extensive demokratische Auseinandersetzung mit neuen Verfassungsnormen zur Detailtreue einiger Bestimmungen bei[24]. Durch die neue Bundesverfassung konnte eine bessere Übereinstimmung der formellen und der materiellen Verfassung erreicht werden, indem man einige Bestimmungen entfernte, welche nicht in die Verfassung gehörten, und andere, die nur auf Gesetzesstufe oder im Richterrecht verankert waren, in die Verfassung aufgenommen hat[25]. Das Problem der nur auf Verfassungsstufe existierenden Volksinitiative wurde nicht gelöst, insofern ist zu erwarten, dass weiterhin "verfassungsunwürdige" Materien in die Verfassung Eingang finden.

(c) Grundzüge der Verfassung

(aa) Aufbau und Grundzüge allgemein

Die neue Bundesverfassung ist systematisch aufgebaut. Sie besteht aus einer Präambel und sechs Titeln: 1. Allgemeine Bestimmungen, 2. Grundrechte, Bürgerrechte und Sozialziele, 3. Bund, Kantone und Gemeinden, 4. Volk und Stände, 5. Bundesbehörden, 6. Revision der Bundesverfassung und Übergangsbestimmungen.

Der Bundesrat zählt in seiner Botschaft vom 20. November 1996 vier Charakteristika des Bundesstaates Schweiz auf, welche als tragende Prinzipien (Strukturprinzipien) der Bundesverfassung gelten: die halbdirekte Demokratie, das Rechtsstaatsprinzip, das Bundesstaatsprinzip (Föderalismus) und das Sozialstaatsprinzip[26]. Als Hauptfunktion des schweizerischen Verfassungsrechts gilt es, die Willensnation[27] Schweiz mit dem Mittel des Föderalismus zusammenzuhalten. Um der Diversität Rechnung zu tragen und trotz den vielfältigen Unterschieden einen Zusammenhalt zu erreichen, war es notwendig, ein sehr komplexes System zu entwickeln, welches geprägt ist durch die Suche nach einem Konsens und eine pragmatischen Haltung[28]. Besonders gut zu erkennen sind diese zwei Charakteristika in der Einrichtung des Vernehmlassungsverfahrens: Gemäss Art. 147 BV werden bei der Vorbereitung wichtiger Erlasse und anderer Vorhaben von grosser Tragweite sowie bei wichtigen völkerrechtlichen Verträgen die Kantone, die politischen Parteien und die interessierten Kreise zur Stellungnahme eingeladen. Schon in der Ausarbeitungsphase wird somit pragmatisch vorgegangen und ein möglichst breiter Konsens gesucht[29].

Spezifisch ausgebaut im Vergleich zu anderen Staaten sind die direktdemokratischen Mitwirkungsrechte und der Föderalismus[30]. Besonderheiten bietet auch das Regierungssystem[31].

bb) Direkte Demokratie

Die hohe Gewichtung der Mitwirkungs- und Entscheidungsrechte des Volkes in der Schweiz können die Europäisierung und Internationalisierung der Rechtsordnung erschweren[32]. Dieser Tatsache steht auf der anderen Seite natürlich die grosse demokratische Legitimation entgegen, welche den akzeptierten Anpassungen und Änderungen dafür zugrunde liegt. Das schweizerische Verständnis der Volkssouveränität beinhaltet nicht nur die Funktion des Volks (und der Stände) als Verfassungsgeber, sondern anerkennt das Volk als "real handelnde Grösse im Prozess der politischen Sachentscheidung"[33]. Die politischen Rechte im Bund sind in Art.136-142 BV geregelt. Vorgesehen ist die Teilnahme an Nationalratswahlen und Abstimmungen des Bundes sowie die Möglichkeit, Volksinitiativen und Referenden in Bundesangelegenheiten zu ergreifen und zu unterzeichnen.

Allerdings nehmen auch die anderen Staatsorgane, insbesondere die Bundesversammlung, wichtige Befugnisse wahr. Auf diese Weise verbinden sich repräsentative und direkte Demokratie in einzigartiger Weise[34].

cc) Rechtsstaatlichkeit

Art. 5 BV enthält die Grundsätze rechtsstaatlichen Handelns. In erster Linie wird das Legalitätsprinzip verankert und in Abs. 4 die Verpflichtung, das Völkerrecht zu beachten. Eine Verfassungsgerichtsbarkeit gibt es zwar nicht in dem Sinne, dass das Bundesgericht Bundesgesetze wegen Verfassungswidrigkeit für nichtig erklären könnte[35], aber Bundesgesetze werden doch auf die Vereinbarkeit mit der EMRK überprüft, dh die Verfassungsgerichtsbarkeit gegenüber Bundesgesetzen ist zumindest im Geltungsbereich der EMRK eingeführt[36]. Ein Beitritt zur EU würde zu einer Stärkung der Justiz und insbesondere der Verfassungsgerichtsbarkeit führen, denn es ist nicht vorstellbar, dass dem EuGH die Kompetenz zur direkten oder indirekten Überprüfung der Vereinbarkeit des schweizerischen Rechts mit dem Gemeinschaftsrecht zugestanden würde, aber der innerstaatlichen Justiz eine solche Kontrolle versagt bliebe[37].

dd) Bundesstaatlichkeit/Föderalismus

1848 fand der Übergang vom Staatenbund zum Bundesstaat statt. Die Kompetenz-Kompetenz für die Änderung der Bundesverfassung liegt bei den Organen des Bundes. Die Kantone haben aber weiterhin ihre Zuständigkeitsbereiche und sind an der Willensbildung im Bund beteiligt[38]. Sie haben die gleiche Stimmkraft auf Bundesebene, ungeachtet ihrer unterschiedlichen Grösse. Föderalismus ist die verfassungsrechtlich garantierte Autonomie und Mitbestimmung der Gliedstaaten[39]. Grundlage des schweizerischen Föderalismus ist die Überzeugung, dass die kulturelle und sprachliche Vielfalt erhalten werden, Minderheiten geschützt und Bürgernähe geschaffen werden müssen. Diversität ist eines der wichtigsten Ziele des schweizerischen Staats, die Vielfalt soll durch eine weitgehende Selbstbestimmung der Glieder gewährleistet sein. Der Leitspruch "Vielfalt in der Einheit" hat somit hohe Geltungskraft, ein Leitspruch, der auch auf EU-Ebene oft angeführt wird. Auch der Minderheitenschutz und das Schaffen von Bürgernähe sind Anliegen, welche in der EU wichtig sind. Das in der EU ebenfalls propagierte Subsidiaritätsprinzip ist Teil des föderalistischen Aufbaus der Schweiz, staatliche Aufgaben sollen auf der jeweils geeignetsten Ebene - Bund, Kantone, Gemeinden - angegangen werden[40]. Der Föderalismus ist nicht - wie oft behauptet - ein Hindernis für eine Integration der Schweiz in die EU, sondern würde es der Schweiz im Vergleich zu anderen Staaten verfassungsrechtlich erleichtern, sich zu integrieren[41].

ee) Sozialstaatlichkeit

Die Sozialstaatlichkeit durchdringt die gesamte Rechtsordnung (Sozialversicherungssystem, sozialverträgliche Ausgestaltung der Wirtschaftsordnung). Die Sozialziele sind im zweiten Titel der BV zusammengefasst. Das Bundesgericht hat ein verfassungsmässiges Recht auf Existenzsicherung anerkannt. In neueren kantonalen Verfassungen sind Sozialziel-Kataloge enthalten. Die Schweiz ist zudem dem UNO-Pakt von 1966 über wirtschaftliche, soziale und kulturelle Rechte beigetreten[42].

ff) Verfassungsrevision

Charakteristisch für die Weiterentwicklung der Verfassung ist, dass es durch die Elemente der direkten Demokratie (obligatorische Verfassungsabstimmung, Verfassungsinitiativen) und die Auseinandersetzungen bezüglich der Kompetenzverteilung zwischen Bund und Kantonen jeweils zu "detaillierten, dichten, angemessenen

Textschritten" kommt[43]. Explizite materielle Schranken der Verfassungsrevision enthält die BV nicht. Allerdings geht zwingendes Völkerrecht der Bundesverfassung vor (Art. 194 Abs. 2 BV) und stellt insofern eine materielle Schranke dar[44]. Ein enges Verständnis der materiellen Schranken der Verfassungsrevision trägt dazu bei, dass Änderungen möglich sind und die Verfassung als "relativ leicht änderbare Verfassung" in der Tradition der Volkssouveränität nach Jean-Jacques Rousseau angesehen werden kann[45].

d) Zielsetzungen

Die Zielsetzungen der Bundesverfassung sind in ihrem Art. 2 aufgezählt.

Art. 2 Zweck

- Die Schweizerische Eidgenossenschaft schützt die Freiheit und die Rechte des Volkes und wahrt die Unabhängigkeit und die Sicherheit des Landes.
- Sie fördert die gemeinsame Wohlfahrt, die nachhaltige Entwicklung, den inneren Zusammenhalt und die kulturelle Vielfalt des Landes.
- Sie sorgt für eine möglichst grosse Chancengleichheit unter den Bürgerinnen und Bürgern.
- Sie setzt sich ein für die dauerhafte Erhaltung der natürlichen Lebensgrundlagen und für eine friedliche und gerechte internationale Ordnung.

Der Zweckartikel verdeutlicht die klassische Viergliedrigkeit des Staatszwecks: Freiheits-, Sicherheits-, Gemeinschafts- und Wohlfahrtszweck, hinzu kommt der für den Bundesstaat charakteristische Zweck der Integration der Gliedstaaten in eine politische Gemeinschaft. Es gibt keine Hierarchie der Staatszwecke, sie haben grundsätzlich alle dasselbe Gewicht[46]. In erster Linie haben sie eine programmatische und historische Funktion.

Für das hier interessierende Thema dürften insbesondere die die Aussenpolitik prägenden Grundsätze wichtig sein (Art. 2 Abs. 1 und 4 BV, konkretisiert in Art. 54 Abs. 2 BV): Unabhängigkeit, internationale "rule of law", internationale Solidarität und Erhaltung der natürlichen Lebensgrundlagen[47].

Das ehemalige Verfassungsziel "Behauptung der Unabhängigkeit des Vaterlandes gegen aussen" hat eine bedeutende Anpassung an die veränderte Wirklichkeit im Sinne der internationalen Verflechtung erfahren. Insofern hat die fortschreitende europäische Integration dieses Staatsziel geprägt. Eine isolationistische Deutung dieses Ziels kann nun auch deshalb nicht mehr stattfinden, weil die anderen Zielsetzungen klar auf eine Offenheit gegenüber der Welt gerichtet sind. Die Änderung dieses Ziels drängte sich auf, da bei den heutigen Bedrohungen die innere und äussere

Sicherheit nur schwer auseinanderzuhalten sind, was angesichts der Ereignisse des 11. September 2001 noch deutlicher geworden ist.

Auf zwischenstaatlicher Ebene soll eine friedliche internationale Ordnung angestrebt und zum friedlichen Zusammenleben der Völker beigetragen werden. Diese Zielsetzung kann über den engeren Sinn von "friedlich" hinaus in dem Sinne ausgelegt werden, dass sich die Schweiz für Kooperation und engere Beziehungen zwischen den Staaten einsetzen soll[48]. Auch soll gemäss Art. 54 Abs. 2 BV zur Förderung der Demokratie und der Achtung der Menschenrechte beigetragen werden und die Schweiz ist insofern verpflichtet, sich in ihrer Aussenpolitik dafür einzusetzen.

Der Grundsatz der Solidarität (Art. 2 Abs. 4 und 54 Abs. 2 BV) umfasst eine gerechte Gestaltung von internationalen Handelsbeziehungen sowie die Pflicht zur Entwicklungshilfe.

Die internationale Verflechtung und gemeinsame Verantwortung für den Frieden und die Sicherheit sind gewachsen. Dieser veränderten Lage soll die neue Zweckbestimmung Rechnung tragen[49].

Besonders hervorzuheben ist die Aufführung der nachhaltigen Entwicklung als Staatsziel. Damit ist ein Leitbild der Umwelt- und Entwicklungspolitik gemeint, das sowohl die natürlichen, als auch die sozialen und ökonomischen Lebensgrundlagen einschliesst[50]. Dieses neue Ziel entspringt der Erkenntnis, dass die staatliche Gemeinschaft in einer zerstörten Umwelt keine dauerhaften Überlebenschancen hat. Der Gedanke der Verantwortung gegenüber künftigen Generationen ist eng mit der Nachhaltigkeit verknüpft. Diese Ergänzung des aussenpolitischen Zielkatalogs legt den Grundstein für eine Verpflichtung der Schweiz, ihre umweltpolitische Verantwortung auch auf internationaler Ebene wahrzunehmen[51].

3. Völker- und Landesrecht in der Schweiz

In der Schweiz gilt das System des gemässigten Monismus[52], auch wenn die Bundesverfassung keinen expliziten Artikel dazu enthält[53]. Das Völkerrecht gilt somit ohne Transformation ins innerstaatliche Recht, Völker- und Landesrecht werden als einheitliche Rechtsordnung angesehen. Die Normen des Völkerrechts haben grundsätzlich direkte Geltung, wie auch die Grundprinzipien *pacta sunt servanda*, Treu und Glauben und das Verbot, sich zur Rechtfertigung einer Nichterfüllung auf innerstaatliches Recht zu berufen. Damit ist noch nichts gesagt über den Fall eines Konflikts zwischen Völkerrecht und Landesrecht, denn Monismus ist nicht gleichzusetzen mit Vorrang des Völkerrechts[54]. Zwingendes Völkerrecht geht der Bundesverfassung vor (Art. 194 Abs. 2 BV). Insofern stellt es eine Schranke der Verfassungsgebung dar[55]. Das übrige Völkerrecht hat zwar keinen Verfassungsrang, aber das Bundesgericht und die sonstigen rechtsanwendenden Behörden sind daran gebunden (Art. 191 BV spricht davon, dass es "massgebend" sei). Einer völkerrechtlichen Verpflichtung kann sich der Bund auch nicht durch den Erlass abweichenden Landesrechts entziehen[56]. Dieser Grundsatz wurde nun auch in Art. 5 Abs. 4 der neuen Bundesverfassung verankert. Folge davon ist die Verpflichtung aller Staatsorgane, wenn immer möglich eine völkerrechtskonforme Auslegung des Landesrechts (inklusive Verfassungsrecht) vorzunehmen[57]. Wenn dies nicht möglich ist, so muss (i.d.R.) das Bundesgericht entscheiden, welche Norm Vorrang hat. In der Bundesverfassung findet man dazu keine ausdrückliche Regelung. Unbestritten ist, dass das Völkerrecht Vorrang hat vor kantonalem Recht und Erlassen, die unterhalb der Stufe von Bundesgesetzen stehen (bspw. Verordnungen des Bundesrates), auch wenn das Landesrecht später erlassen wurde. Vorrang des Völkerrechts gilt auch in Bezug auf ältere Bundesgesetze. Strittig ist insbesondere das Verhältnis von Völkerrecht zu jüngeren Bundesgesetzen, welche dem Völkerrecht widersprechen, wie auch das Verhältnis zu jüngerem Verfassungsrecht[58].

4. Zur Frage der Souveränität

Der Begriff der Souveränität hat in der Diskussion um einen EU-Beitritt grosse Beachtung erfahren. Dabei handelt es sich um einen Begriff, der sich im Wandel befindet, insofern als das traditionelle Konzept der Unteilbarkeit der Souveränität in Frage gestellt ist[59].

Die Souveränität des Bundes wurde in der Verfassung von 1848 nicht erwähnt. Einerseits wollte man, dass die Quelle der Souveränität beim Volk liegt. Auch sollten nicht allein die Kantone souverän sein, da dem Bund gewisse Souveränitätsbefugnisse ausschliesslich zustanden, wie das Recht Krieg zu erklären, Frieden zu schliessen und Bündnisse oder Staatsverträge abzuschliessen. So entstand als Kompromiss Art. 3 BV: "Die Kantone sind souverän, soweit ihre Souveränität nicht durch die Bundesverfassung beschränkt ist, und üben als solche alle Rechte aus, welche nicht der Bundesgewalt übertragen sind." Man ging somit schon da von einer geteilten Souveränität aus[60].

(a) Souveränität des Volkes

Mit dem Prinzip der Volkssouveränität, einer der Ideen der Französischen Revolution, kam die Schweiz erstmals in Kontakt in der Epoche der Helvetik (1798-1803). Verwirklicht wurde diese Idee teilweise in den Kantonsverfassungen der Regeneration (1830-1848). Das obligatorische Verfassungsreferendum und die repräsentative Demokratie in der einfachen Gesetzgebung waren ihre konkreten Ausformungen.

Demokratie und Volkssouveränität stehen in der Schweiz an hoher Stelle. Auf Bundesebene können die Bürger das Wahlrecht in Anspruch nehmen und durch Verfassungsinitiative und -referendum, Gesetzes- und Staatsvertragsreferendum in Sachfragen Entscheidungen treffen. Eine Gesetzesinitiative fehlt.

Ausdruck der Wichtigkeit dieses Prinzips ist Art. 148 BV, der die Bundesversammlung als oberste Gewalt des Bundes bezeichnet. Dies führt sogar dazu, dass das Rechtsstaatsprinzip eine Einschränkung erfährt in der Ausgestaltung des Art. 191 BV, in dem das Bundesgericht und alle Rechtsanwendungsorgane dazu verpflichtet werden, Bundesgesetze (und von der Bundesversammlung genehmigte Staatsverträge) auch bei Verfassungswidrigkeit anzuwenden.

(b) Souveränität der Kantone?

Die Verfassung von 1848 zeichnete sich dadurch aus, dass die Kantone stark an der Willensbildung des Bundes beteiligt wurden. Einerseits zeigte sich dies in der Zusammensetzung des Ständerates, andererseits am Erfordernis des doppelten Mehr (Bürger und Kantone) für jede Partial- oder Totalrevision der Bundesverfassung. Die Kantone behielten in eingeschränktem Mass ihren Charakter als "Staaten", wenn auch der Bund sich mit der Zeit mittels Auslegung mehr Zuständigkeiten einverleibte, als eigentlich ausdrücklich in der Verfassung verankert waren.

Die Kantone werden zwar in Art. 3 BV immer noch als "souverän" bezeichnet (im Sinn eines "Traditionsanschlusses"[61]), jedoch ist ihre Ausübung staatlicher Gewalt durch die Bundesverfassung vorgegeben und insofern eben keine höchste Staatsgewalt. Da die Kantone aber gewisse originäre Zuständigkeiten ausüben, können sie als teilsouverän bezeichnet werden[62].

Die Kantonszuständigkeiten können durch eine Änderung der Bundesverfassung verändert werden, das Recht der Kantone leitet sich aus der Bundesverfassung ab[63]. Daran ändern auch die in Kantonsverfassungen oft zu lesenden Bezeichnungen des Kantons als "souveräner Staat" nichts. Als souveräne Staaten hätten sie völkerrechtlich ein Sezessionsrecht. Ein solches steht ihnen aber nach schweizerischem Recht nicht zu. Die Kantone sind nur in beschränktem Mass Völkerrechtssubjekte, aber die Bundesverfassung verschafft ihnen immerhin einen relativ grossen Spielraum[64]. Grundlegende Bereiche, in denen die Kantone vorwiegend zuständig sind umfassen die Gewährleistung von öffentlicher Sicherheit und Ordnung im Kanton und das Erziehungs- und Gesundheitswesen. Schliesslich gelten die Kantone weiterhin als Bausteine und Träger der Schweizerischen Eidgenossenschaft[65].

(c) Souveränität des Bundes

Der Bund hat die höchste Staatsgewalt inne. Rechtsetzung, Verwaltung und Justiz werden von den Bundesbehörden ausgeübt. Der Bund kann durch Änderung der unableitbaren Bundesverfassung die Kompetenzaufteilung zwischen sich und den Kantonen verändern, dh er verfügt über die Kompetenz-Kompetenz.

Dieses Souveränitätsverständnis hat aber vor dem Hintergrund der sich immer mehr verflechtenden Welt, insbesondere aber durch das Bestreben, sich nicht vollständig auszugrenzen in Europa (Stichwort autonomer Nachvollzug von EU-Recht und Prüfung der EU-Kompatibilität der schweizerischen Gesetzgebungsvorhaben) eine relativierte Bedeutung.

Natürlich würde durch einen Beitritt auch die Kompetenzverteilung in der Schweiz verändert, die Kompetenzen des Parlaments würden vermindert, während die Regierung den Zuständigkeitsverlust auf nationaler Ebene durch grössere Mitentscheidungsrechte im Rat der EU ausgleichen könnte[66].

Aber auch der indirekte Souveränitätsverlust durch die "freiwillige" Anpassung ist wohl faktisch als bedeutend anzusehen, vergleichbar mit der Einbusse an Souveränität durch die Eingliederung in die EU[67]. Dieser Punkt ist allerdings innerhalb der Schweiz streitig, resp. wird nicht so sehr wahrgenommen und somit ist der Souveränitätsverlust durch einen EU-Beitritt auch immer noch ein schlagkräftiges politisches Argument der EU-Gegner.

5. *Das Verfahren des EU-Beitrittes*

Der Bundesrat vertritt gemäss Art. 184 BV die Schweiz nach aussen und besorgt die auswärtigen Angelegenheiten unter Wahrung der Mitwirkungsrechte der Bundesversammlung. Gestützt auf Art. 184 Abs. 2 BV kann der Bundesrat die Aufnahme von Verhandlungen im Hinblick auf den Abschluss eines internationalen Vertrages beschliessen und diesen unterzeichnen. Der Staatsvertrag muss danach durch die Bundesversammlung (Art. 166 Abs. 2 BV), unter gewissen Umständen durch das Volk oder gar von Volk und Ständen (Art. 140 BV) genehmigt werden. Art. 140 Abs. 1 lit.b BV sieht diesbezüglich vor, dass "der Beitritt zu Organisationen für kollektive Sicherheit oder zu supranationalen Gemeinschaften" der Abstimmung des Volkes und der Stände untersteht. Ein Beitritt der Schweiz würde somit durch einen völkerrechtlichen Vertrag erfolgen[68] und dem obligatorischen Referendum unterstehen. Das Gemeinschaftsrecht als Bestandteil einer autonomen Rechtsordnung würde zum schweizerischen Recht in einem ähnlichen Verhältnis stehen wie das Bundesrecht zum kantonalen Recht[69].

Was würde bei einer Änderung der Gemeinschaftsverträge geschehen? Die Genehmigungspflicht gem. Art. 166 Abs. 2 BV gilt in der Regel auch für die Änderung oder Erneuerung von bestehenden Staatsverträgen. Sie besteht aber nicht für alle Staatsverträge: "(Die Bundesversammlung) genehmigt die völkerrechtlichen Verträge; ausgenommen sind die Verträge, für deren Abschluss auf Grund von Gesetz oder völkerrechtlichem Vertrag der Bundesrat zuständig ist." Grundsätzlich werden die Genehmigungskompetenzen bei Vertragsänderungen gleich beurteilt wie beim Abschluss von Staatsverträgen. Dh nur wenn es sich um eine wesentliche Änderung handelt, muss diese dem Parlament unterbreitet werden, andere Vertragsanpassungen und kleine Vertragsänderungen kann der Bundesrat, abgeleitet aus seiner Kompetenz zum Abschluss von Verträgen, genehmigen[70].

Eine EU-Mitgliedschaft würde jedoch eine neue Situation darstellen und insofern müsste bei den notwendigen Verfassungsänderungen auch die Einführung eines innerstaatlichen Verfahrens bei Änderung oder Ergänzungen der Grundverträge der EG anvisiert werden[71]. Gemäss Art. 140 Abs. 1 lit. b BV untersteht nur der Beitritt zu supranationalen Organisationen dem obligatorischen Referendum, nicht aber die Änderungen eines solchen Staatsvertrags, es sei denn, Zielsetzungen, Tätigkeiten oder die Organisationsstruktur würden sich so sehr ändern, dass sie in ihren Wirkungen einem Neubeitritt gleichkämen[72]. Somit wären wohl erhebliche Kompetenzerweiterungen der Union dem obligatorischen Referendum zu unterstellen. Eine genauere Formulierung und Abgrenzung der verschiedenen Kategorien von Änderungen und der jeweiligen Verfahren wäre im Falle eines Beitritts von Vorteil.

6. *Schlussfolgerung*

Zusammenfassend kann festgehalten werden, dass sich das schweizerische System der direkten Demokratie und des Föderalismus für einen Beitritt eignen[73] und dass sich aus Sicht der Verfassung keine unüberwindbaren Hindernisse stellen würden. Die Verfassung kann jederzeit geändert werden (Art. 192 BV).

Ein EU-Beitritt hätte Auswirkungen auf den Föderalismus[74] (Aufgaben- und Kompetenzverteilung sowie Zusammenarbeit zwischen Bund und Kantonen), die direkte Demokratie (Volksrechte), die Finanzordnung (neuer Finanzausgleich: Neuordnung der Finanzströme zwischen Bund und Kantonen), die Wirtschafts- und Währungspolitik, die Ausländer- und Migrationspolitik, die Aussen- und Sicherheitspolitik sowie die Landwirtschaft. Mit der gegenwärtigen Struktur der EU käme es zu einer Verlagerung von Rechtsetzungskompetenzen vom Parlament auf den Bundesrat. Daher müssten der Austausch und die Zusammenarbeit zwischen Parlament und Bundesrat neu geregelt werden[75]. Zur Regelung dieser sich stellenden Fragen bezüglich einer institutionellen Umgestaltung (Schaffung einer Möglichkeit der Einflussnahme der Bundesversammlung auf die Aktivitäten des Bundesrates in der EU) und anderer verfassungsrechtlicher Änderungen (wie Vorrang des Gemeinschaftsrechts,

Beteiligung der Kantone bei der Ausarbeitung von EU-Recht, Grenzen der Übertragung von Hoheitsrechten) würde sich die Ausarbeitung eines "Europa-Artikels" in der Verfassung anbieten[76]. Insgesamt müssten die wesentlichen Merkmale der schweizerischen Bundesverfassung gewährleistet sein[77].

Auch ohne Beitritt zur EU unterliegt die Bundesverfassung dem Einfluss der Gemeinschaftsrechtsordnung. Die durch den Einfluss der Gemeinschaftsrechtsordnung schon eingetretenen Veränderungen sowie potentielle Auswirkungen des Öffnungsprozesses auf die schweizerischen Verfassungsprinzipien sind Gegenstand einer umfassenden Diskussion in der Lehre[78].

B. EG/EU-RECHT UND SCHWEIZERISCHE VVERFASSUNG: VERHÄLTNIS UND WECHSELWIRKUNGEN

I Verfassungsautonomie der Mitgliedstaaten und Anforderungen des Unionsrechts

Gemäss Art. 6 Abs. 3 EUV achtet die Union die nationale Identität der Mitgliedstaaten. Nach geltender Rechtslage ist die Vorschrift jedoch von der Gerichtsbarkeit des Gerichtshofs ausgenommen[79]. Sie steht aber im Zusammenhang mit anderen Vorschriften wie insbesondere dem Gebot der Gemeinschaftstreue (Art. 10 EGV) und dem Subsidiaritätsprinzip (Art. 5 Abs. 2 EGV), die ihrerseits der Gerichtsbarkeit des EuGH unterfallen[80]. Die Vorschrift entspringt der Sorge vor einer möglichen „Entstaatlichung" und schrittweisen Auflösung der Nationalstaaten im Rahmen der Europäischen Union[81]. Dabei sollen nicht nur der Bestand der Staaten, sondern auch bestimmte ihrer häufig historisch begründeten Eigenheiten und Werte geschützt werden. Die Bestimmung des Inhaltes der nationalen Identität und somit der zu schützenden Werte obliegt in erster Linie den Mitgliedstaaten selbst[82]. Zu fragen ist dabei zunächst nach den verfassungsrechtlichen *Schranken der Verfassungsänderung*, welche der Übertragung von Hoheitsrechten durch die Staaten Grenzen setzt. Die Gefährdung der Identität der Schweiz galt lange als Hindernis für einen Beitritt zu den Europäischen Gemeinschaften oder der EU. „Unsere staatspolitischen Einrichtungen und aussenpolitischen Maximen würden durch einen solchen Schritt in einem Mass beeinflusst, das an die traditionelle Identität unseres Landes rühren würde."[83] Zwar kommt der Bundesrat inzwischen zu dem Ergebnis, dass „die EG-Mitgliedschaft mit unserem Willen vereinbar ist, jene Werte zu bewahren, welche die Schweiz ausmachen"[84], wegen des sprachlich-kulturellen Pluralismus der Schweiz wird die nationale Identität jedoch weniger durch gemeinsame Sprache und Kultur sondern vor allem durch die Besonderheiten des politischen Systems vermittelt. Zwar nennt

Art. 6 Abs. 3 EUV ausdrücklich nur die nationale Identität, zu dieser kann jedoch auch die *föderalistische Struktur* eines Staates in ihrer spezifischen Ausprägung gehören[85]. Dies kann sowohl der Schutz der Eigenständigkeit der Untergliederungen des Staates, als auch der Schutz zentralistisch organisierter Staaten gegen eine zu starke europäisch „verordnete" Stärkung der regionalen Identitäten sein. Neben der föderalistischen Struktur kommt im Falle der Schweiz vor allem der Grundsatz der *Neutralität* als spezifisches Element der zu achtenden nationalen Identität in Betracht.

1. *Materielle Schranken der Verfassungsrevision*

Die Bundesverfassung kann, bei Beachtung der in der BV enthaltenen Revisionsvorschriften, jederzeit ganz oder teilweise revidiert werden[86]. Im Wege der Totalrevision, für die ein erschwertes Verfahren vorgesehen ist, können sämtliche Artikel der alten Verfassung durch eine neue Verfassung ersetzt werden (formelle Totalrevision) oder auch bestehende Institutionen und Organe vollständig umgestaltet werden (materielle Totalrevision)[87]. Abgesehen von der Beachtung der zwingenden Bestimmungen des Völkerrechts[88] sieht die Verfassung keine ausdrücklichen inhaltlichen, „materiellen Schranken" der Verfassungsrevision vor[89]. Ob es solche materiellen Schranken gibt, ist strittig[90]. Als solche werden insbesondere verschiedene Konstruktionsprinzipien der Verfassung angesehen, deren Kernbereich geschützt sein soll, z.B. Grundrechte, Demokratie, die bundesstaatliche Ordnung, Rechtsstaatsgedanke und Gewaltenteilung, Mehrsprachigkeit und Sprachenfreiheit, die staatliche Existenz oder ein Mindestmass sozialer Gerechtigkeit. Es ist jedoch festzustellen, dass die Schweizer Praxis „auf eine weitgehende Verneinung materieller Schranken hinausläuft"[91], worin sich auch ein erhebliches Vertrauen in die Funktionsfähigkeit der schweizerischen „Konsensdemokratie" zeigen dürfte. Auch in der Lehre werden materielle Schranken überwiegend ganz oder weitgehend verneint[92]. Dementsprechend könnten auch nur allenfalls die Kerngehalte der genannten Konstruktionsprinzipien eine Schranke für die Übertragung von Hoheitsrechten auf die EU darstellen. Solche Schranken könnten jedoch Gegenstand eines vor einem Beitritt erlassenen Integrationsartikels in der Verfassung sein.

2. *Föderalismus*

Zu den von der EU zu beachtenden Elementen der nationalen Identität gehört auch die *föderalistische Struktur* eines Mitgliedstaates. Diese ist vor allem durch die verfassungsrechtlich garantierte Autonomie[93] („self rule") und Mitbestimmung[94] („shared rule") der Gliedstaaten gekennzeichnet[95]. Eine Gefahr für die föderalistische Struktur liegt darin, dass die EU in immer mehr Bereichen tätig wird, die nach der nationalen Zuständigkeitsverteilung in die Kompetenz der Gliedstaaten fallen, während die unmittelbare Mitwirkung an der Rechtsetzung und Politik auf der Ebene der EU Sache des Bundes ist[96]. Demgegenüber ist Art. 6 Abs. 3 EUV eine Pflicht der EU zur Beachtung der organisatorischen Eigenständigkeit und Autonomie der Mitgliedstaaten zu entnehmen[97]. Dies spricht zum einen dafür, den Vollzug des Gemeinschaftsrechts und den Erlass der dazu erforderlichen Vorschriften weitgehend den Mitgliedstaaten zu überlassen, da dadurch deren organisatorische Eigenständigkeit weitestmöglich gewahrt werden kann. Die zur Sicherstellung der effektiven Umsetzung des Gemeinschaftsrechts erforderlichen Vorgaben müssen dabei die Grundsätze der Subsidiarität und der Verhältnismässigkeit beachten und somit unter möglichster Schonung der mitgliedstaatlichen organisatorischen Autonomie ergehen. Zum anderen ergeben sich Rücksichtnahmepflichten im Bereich der Gesetzgebung und der sonstigen Entscheidungsfindung auf EU-Ebene, um eine möglichst weitgehende Beteiligung der Gliedstaaten zu ermöglichen. Dies bedeutet insbesondere, dass genügend Zeit für die Beratung und Entschliessung über die Vorhaben zur Verfügung stehen muss und die relevanten Texte in allen Amtssprachen der Union zur Verfügung stehen. Denn während die ausreichende Kenntnis der Arbeitssprachen der EU im Falle der Bundesbehörden häufig gewährleistet sein wird, kann auf der Ebene der Gliedstaaten nicht selbstverständlich davon ausgegangen werden. Dies gilt insbesondere, wenn auch nichtstaatliche Stellen und Personen an der Beratung teilnehmen können sollen, wie es entsprechend dem sog. „Vernehmlassungsverfahren“[98] und gemäss der Tradition der Konsensdemokratie in grossem Masse in der Schweiz der Fall ist, wodurch sowohl zusätzlicher Sachverstand einfliessen als auch die politische Akzeptanz einer Massnahme getestet werden kann, was in einem auf Konkordanz und Konsens ausgerichteten politischen System von zentraler Bedeutung ist. Zu den Gesetzgebungsmaterien, die den Kantonen vorbehalten sind, gehören u.a. die Kultur[99] und die Steuer- und Finanzhoheit[100]. Die Förderung der kulturellen Vielfalt ist eines der Hauptziele der Eidgenossenschaft[101], so dass diese Materie möglichst weitgehend den Mitgliedstaaten (und ihren Gliedstaaten) vorbehalten bleiben sollte, was punktuelle Kompetenzen der EG (wie des Bundes auf staatlicher Ebene[102]) nicht ausschliesst.

3. *Neutralität*

Die *Neutralität* der Schweiz ist kein Staatsziel, sondern (nur) ein Mittel, um die verfassungsrechtlich verankerten Zielsetzungen zu verwirklichen[103]. Zugleich dürfte die Neutralität aber Völkergewohnheitsrecht und auch Verfassungsgewohnheitsrecht darstellen[104]. Diese könnte zwar auch wieder aufgegeben werden, aber dabei sind die völkerrechtlichen Voraussetzungen zu beachten. Inhalt der Neutralitätsverpflichtung ist heute nunmehr die Neutralität im Falle bewaffneter Konflikte souveräner Staaten, die nicht im Zusammenhang mit Massnahmen des Sicherheitsrates nach Art. 39 ff. UN-Charta oder mit Notwehr- bzw. Nothilfemassnahmen nach Art. 51 UN-Charta stehen. Dementsprechend hat sich die Schweiz in den letzten Jahren an den meisten der nach Art. 39 ff. UN-Charta beschlossenen Sanktionen beteiligt und wird auch der Beitritt der Schweiz zur EU nicht (mehr) als unvereinbar mit der Neutralität angesehen[105]. Als Völkergewohnheitsrecht müsste sie auch von der EU (bzw. den anderen Mitgliedstaaten), etwa im Rahmen der GASP, beachtet werden, was jedoch z.B. im Falle einer Kollision mit Beschlüssen im Rahmen der GASP auch durch die Möglichkeit eines opting out geschehen könnte.

II. Gemeinsame Werte: Europäische Grundrechtecharta und schweizerische Grundrechte

„Wenn zwei Verfassungen dasselbe sagen, ist es nicht dasselbe." Dieses geflügelte Wort von Rudolf Smend[106] gilt auch und erst recht für die Grundrechte einer Verfassung. Während die neue schweizerische Bundesverfassung insgesamt und speziell auch hinsichtlich der Grundrechte eine „Nachführung" darstellt, so dass der neue Grundrechtskatalog im wesentlichen dem bisherigen Verfassungsrecht entspricht[107], existiert zu der Grundrechtscharta der EU nur teilweise bereits eine Praxis, indem auf die Rechtsprechung zu einzelnen aus der EMRK oder dem Gemeinschaftsrecht übernommen Gewährleistungen Bezug genommen werden kann[108]. Die im Jahre 2000 in Kraft getretene schweizerische Bundesverfassung enthält einen umfassenden und systematisch geordneten Grundrechtsteil, während die Bundesverfassungen von 1848 und 1874 nur punktuell Grundrechtsgarantien vorsahen[109]. In den Grundrechtskatalog wurden die durch die Rechtsprechung entwickelten ungeschriebenen Grundrechte und die wichtigsten in den für die Schweiz verbindlichen internationalen Kodifikationen (insbesondere EMRK und UNO-Pakte I und II) enthaltenen Gewährleistungen eingearbeitet. Dabei fand die Rechtsprechung sowohl des Bundesgerichts, die sich nicht selten von der Grundrechtsauslegung in anderen Staaten inspiriert[110], als auch des Europäischen Gerichtshofs für Menschenrechte Berücksichtigung[111]. Es erstaunt somit nicht, dass der relativ ausführlich geratene Grundrechtskatalog in vielem Ähnlichkeiten mit der EU-Grundrechtecharta aufweist.

1. Grundrechte und Staatszielbestimmungen

Im Kapitel über die *Grundrechte* (Art. 7-36 BV) befinden sich neben Freiheitsrechten und Rechtsgleichheit auch Verfahrensgarantien und soziale

Grundrechte, so dass der Begriff der Grundrechte den Oberbegriff für alle unmittelbar durch die Verfassung gewährleisteten grundlegenden Rechte des Einzelnen im Staat und gegenüber dem Staat bildet. Die einzelnen politischen Rechte stehen zwar ausserhalb des Grundrechtskapitels in einem eigenem Kapitel „*Bürgerrecht und politische Rechte*" (Art. 37-40 BV), doch wird durch die allgemeine Gewährleistung der politischen Rechte im Grundrechtsteil (Art. 34 BV) klargestellt, dass auch ihnen Grundrechtsqualität zukommt[112]. Ein eigenes Kapitel ist den *Sozialzielen* gewidmet (Art. 41 BV), aus denen jedoch keine unmittelbaren Ansprüche auf staatliche Leistungen abgeleitet werden können (Art. 41 Abs. 4 BV). Es handelt sich dabei um Staatszielbestimmungen, die die sozialstaatliche Ausrichtung der Schweiz konkretisieren und die politischen Instanzen (Bund und Kantone) zum Tätigwerden auf sieben grundlegenden Feldern der Sozialpolitik (soziale Sicherheit, Gesundheitspflege, Schutz der Familie, Bereiststellung von Arbeit und Wohnraum, Bildung und Jugendschutz) verpflichten. Eine zusätzliche Relativierung erfährt die Verpflichtung durch ihre Formulierung: „Bund und Kantone setzen sich in Ergänzung (!) zu persönlicher Verantwortung und privater Initiative dafür ein...", aber nur „im Rahmen... ihrer verfügbaren Mittel". Da es sich dabei nicht um verfassungsmässige Rechte handelt, können die Sozialziele auch nicht mit der staatsrechtlichen Beschwerde zum Bundesgericht geltend gemacht werden[113].

2. Freiheitsrechte

Ebenso wie die EU-Charta hebt der Grundrechtsteil der schweizerischen Verfassung mit dem Bekenntnis zur Würde des Menschen an (Art. 7 BV). Auch die übrigen Gewährleistungen in den ersten beiden Kapiteln der Charta entsprechen weitgehend dem schweizerischen Grundrechtsstandard. Allerdings enthält die Bundesverfassung kein ausdrückliches „Recht auf Bildung"[114], und die Anerkennung und der Umfang eines Rechts auf Zugang zu Bildungseinrichtungen ist umstritten[115]. Nach der Rechtsprechung des Bundesgerichts besteht kein – über den Grundschulunterricht[116] hinausgehendes – Recht auf Bildung, lediglich die Grundsätze der Rechtsgleichheit bzw. des Willkürverbotes sind anwendbar[117]. Dagegen wird in der neueren Rechtslehre auch ein Anspruch auf Zugang zu Bildungseinrichtungen wie Hochschulen vertreten, der jedoch aus Gründen des öffentlichen Wohls (z.B. Dämmung der Gesundheitskosten) eingeschränkt werden könne[118]. Die Eigentumsgarantie (Art. 26 BV) umfasst schliesslich einen Anspruch auf volle Entschädigung bei Enteignungen und Eigentumsbeschränkungen, während die Charta in Anlehnung an das 1. Zusatzprotokoll zur EMRK nur eine „angemessene Entschädigung" gewährt[119].

3. Gleichheitsrechte

Im Bereich der *Rechtsgleichheit* ist für die neue Bundesverfassung wie für die EU-Charta eine moderne und fortschrittliche „Anreicherung" des klassischen Gleichheitssatzes zu konstatieren. So verbietet Art. 8 Abs. 2 BV u.a. Diskriminierungen wegen des Alters, der Sprache, der sozialen Stellung, der Lebensform oder wegen einer Behinderung. Nach Art. 8 Abs. 3 BV sorgt das Gesetz für die rechtliche und tatsächliche Gleichstellung von Mann und Frau „in Familie, Ausbildung und Arbeit". Dieses Egalisierungsgebot erlaubt auch Förderungsmassnahmen, die an das Geschlecht anknüpfen, sofern Dritte nicht in unzumutbarer Weise benachteiligt werden[120]. Dabei kann das Egalisierungsgebot zu dem Diskriminierungsverbot in einem Spannungsverhältnis stehen und unter Umständen eine massvolle geschlechtsspezifische Förderung von Frauen durch den Staat trotz der damt verbundenen Ungleichbehandlung der Männer rechtfertigen oder sogar gebieten[121]. Es ist dabei eine Verhältnismässigkeitsprüfung und eine Interessenabwägung im Sinne praktischer Konkordanz zwischen Gleichbehandlungsgebot und Egalisierungsgebot vorzunehmen[122], so dass eine dem Recht der Charta weitgehend entsprechende Regelung besteht[123]. Im Übrigen gibt es ein verfassungsmässiges Recht auf gleichen Lohn für gleiche Arbeit entsprechend Art. 23 Charta und Art. 141 EGV. Auch ein Kinder- und Jugenschutzartikel findet sich in der neuen Verfassung, wonach diese Anspruch auf besonderen Schutz ihrer Unversehrtheit und auf Förderung ihrer Entwicklung haben[124]. Wegen der vagen Formulierung ist jedoch fraglich, inwieweit damit durchsetzbare Ansprüche auf staatliche Leistungen begründet werden[125].

4. Soziale Grundrechte

Die sozialen Grundrechte der Art. 27 bis 38 Charta („*Solidarität*") finden demgegenüber nur teilweise eine Entsprechung in der schweizerischen Verfassung[126]. Insbesondere gewährt die Verfassung fast keine Leistungsrechte[127]. Sie garantiert die individuelle Koalitionsfreiheit der Arbeitnehmerinnen und Arbeitnehmer sowie der Arbeitgeber und die kollektive Koalitionsfreiheit ihrer Organisationen[128]. Streik und auch Aussperrung sind zulässig, wenn sie Arbeitsbeziehungen betreffen und wenn keine Verpflichtungen entgegenstehen, den Arbeitsfrieden zu wahren oder Schlichtungsverhandlungen durchzuführen. Allerdings sollen diese nur als „ultima ratio" eingesetzt werden[129]. Ein Recht auf Hilfe in Notlagen (Art. 12 BV) gewährt Anspruch auf Hilfe und Betreuung, um ein menschenwürdiges Dasein zu ermöglichen[130]. Bei der Auslegung sind der Grundsatz der Menschenwürde (Art. 7 BV) sowie die internationalrechtlichen Gewährleistungen heranzuziehen[131]. Dabei dürfte der Anspruchsumfang nicht über das zur Sicherung der Menschenwürde Erforderliche hinausgehen, so dass Schutzbereich und Kerngehalt hier zusammenfallen[132]. Im Übrigen besteht lediglich ein Anspruch auf unentgeltliche Rechtspflege und unentgeltlichen Rechtsbeistand[133]. Nach Art. 14 der Bundesverfassung ist schliesslich das Recht auf Ehe und Familie gewährleistet. Allerdings fehlt eine verfassungsrechtliche Gewährleistung entsprechend Art. 33 Abs. 2 Charta, wonach ein grundrechtlicher Kündigungsschutz für Schwangere und das Recht auf Mutterschafts- und Elternurlaub besteht. Abgesehen von den bereits erwähnten Sozialzielen des Art. 41 BV, die keine unmittelbaren Ansprüche begründen und auch nicht mit der staatsrechtlichen Beschwerde zum Bundesgericht geltend gemacht werden können[134], finden sich im übrigen keine verfassungsmässigen sozialen Rechte, wie sie in Art. 27 ff. Charta festgeschrieben sind[135]. Allerdings sind einzelne abwehrrechtliche Gewährleistungen von anderen Grundrechten mit umfasst (z.B. sichere Arbeitsbedingungen und Jugendarbeitsschutz gem. Art. 31 und 32 Charta durch das Recht auf körperliche und geistige Unversehrtheit gem. Art. 10 Abs. 2 BV), und die Staatszielbestimmungen des Gesundheits-, Umwelt- und Verbraucherschutzes sind ausserhalb des Grundrechtskapitels geregelt[136].

Die als „Recht auf eine gute Verwaltung“ in Art. 41 Charta normierten Grundsätze rechtsstaatlichen Handelns sind auch Bestandteil des schweizerischen Rechts, jedoch ist neben den allgemeinen Verfahrensgarantien[137] lediglich ein Anspruch darauf, von den staatlichen Organen ohne Willkür und nach Treu und Glauben behandelt zu werden, als Grundrecht ausgestaltet[138]. Dagegen finden sich die weiteren Grundsätze programmartig in den allgemeinen Bestimmungen und sind nicht als subjektive Rechte formuliert. Terminologisch erscheint bemerkenswert, dass der Begriff von Treu und Glauben, auf den Art. 8 Abs. 2 Charta Bezug nimmt, auch von der neuen Bundesverfassung verwendet und dort allgemein auf rechtsstaatliches Handeln angewendet wird (Art. 5 Abs. 3 und Art. 9 BV).

5. *Grundrechtsschranken*

Die Verfassung enthält ausserdem eine Normierung der Grundrechtsschranken in Art. 36 BV, wonach Einschränkungen von Grundrechten einer gesetzlichen Grundlage bedürfen, einem öffentlichen Interesse oder dem Schutz der Grundrechte Dritter dienen und verhältnismässig sein müssen sowie nicht den Kerngehalt antasten dürfen. Zwar ist diese Regelung auf die Freiheitsrechte zugeschnitten und passt nicht unbedingt auf andere Grundrechte und erst recht nicht auf die Gesetzgebungsaufträge[139], aber sie gibt doch Hinweise für die Reichweite und Einschränkbarkeit der Grundrechte und normiert ein Prüfungsprogramm. Die Formulierung ähnelt der in Anlehnung an die

Rechtsprechung des EuGH[140] getroffenen Regelung in Art. 52 Abs. 1 Charta, wobei letztere in redaktioneller Hinsicht insofern weniger eindeutig erscheint, als nicht deutlich wird, ob die Verhältnismässigkeit im Rahmen der übrigen Einschränkungsvoraussetzungen oder getrennt von diesen als allgemeines Prinzip zu prüfen ist[141]. Es ist jedoch darauf hinzuweisen, dass die Rechtsprechung des EuGH, auf die hier Bezug genommen wird, die Frage des Eingriffs in den Schutzbereich und die Schrankenprüfung tendenziell weniger ausführlich begründet und auch die Grundrechtsschranken wohl eher grosszügiger auslegt als das Bundesgericht[142].

6. *Zusammenfassung des Vergleichs*

Zusammenfassend lässt sich somit festhalten, dass zwischen den Gewährleistungen der Grundrechtscharta und der schweizerischen Bundesverfassung weitgehende Übereinstimmung besteht. Dies gilt insbesondere für die mehrheitlich abwehrrechtlich geprägten Freiheitsrechte und die justiziellen Rechte, aber auch für den um moderne Anreicherungen ergänzten Gleichheitssatz. Dagegen ist der grösste Teil der im Kapitel „Solidarität" geregelten Arbeitnehmerrechte in der Schweiz nicht verfassungsrechtlich verankert und zeigt sich in der Bundesverfassung wie auch in der Praxis des Bundesgerichts eine deutliche Zurückhaltung gegenüber der Zuerkennung sozialer Grundrechte als subjektiver Rechte. Verstärkt wird diese Zurückhaltung durch die Betonung der Verantwortung des Einzelnen an verschiedenen Stellen der Verfassung[143] sowie dadurch, dass Staatszielbestimmungen und Programmsätze ausserhalb des Grundrechtskapitels in der Verfassung angesiedelt sind. Dabei handelt es sich jedoch teilweise zunächst nur um redaktionelle Unterschiede, abzuwarten bleibt insbesondere, inwieweit der Europäische Gerichtshof bei der Anwendung der Charta subjektive soziale Rechte aus den Gewährleistungen ableiten und seine Rechtsprechung zu den Schranken weiterentwickeln wird.

7. *Auswirkungen der Charta in der Schweiz*

Bisher wurde die Charta vom schweizerischen Bundesgericht noch nicht zitiert. Angesichts der traditionell starken Rezeption ausländischer und internationaler Rechtsprechung auf dem Gebiet der Grundrechte durch das schweizerische Bundesgericht[144] ist jedoch anzunehmen, dass die Charta eine wichtige Inspirationsquelle für den Grundrechtsschutz durch die schweizerischen Gerichte bilden wird, zumal da die Charta auf Grund ihrer Entstehungsgeschichte weitgehend den Stand des Grundrechtsschutzes als Teil des „gemeineuropäischen Verfassungsrechts" widerspiegeln dürfte, welches nicht zuletzt über die Europäische Menschenrechtskonvention schon bisher einen bedeutenden Einfluss auf die Anerkennung und Auslegung grundrechtlicher Gewährleistungen in der Schweiz hatte. Auch die Vorschriften und die Auslegung im Gemeinschaftsrecht haben schon heute vielfach Vorbildfunktion auch für die Weiterentwicklung des Grundrechtsschutzes in der Schweiz[145]. Die Charta dürfte des weiteren zu einer weiteren Annäherung und „Europäisierung" der nationalen Rechtsordnungen und der Auslegungspraxis im Bereiche der Grundrechte führen. Dadurch wird sie zu einer Zunahme der den Mitgliedstaaten, aber auch Drittstaaten wie der Schweiz, gemeinsamen Grundsätze beitragen und die in Art. 6 I EUV genannten Standards massgeblich mitbestimmen.

III. Der Vorrang des EU-/EG-Rechts und seine verfassungsrechtlichen Auswirkungen

1. Anerkennung des Vorrangs

Wie bereits dargelegt[146], ist der Vorrang der völkerrechtlichen Verträge vor den Bundesgesetzen sowie dem gesamten kantonalen Recht durch die Rechtsprechung anerkannt, wobei das Bundesgericht es jedoch auch schon abgelehnt hat, ein im Wissen um seine Unvereinbarkeit mit einem völkerrechtlichen Abkommen erlassenes Bundesgesetz für ungültig zu erklären[147]. Da die Begründung dieser Ausnahme vor allem auf die mangelnde Kompetenz des Bundesgerichts zur Kontrolle der Rechtmässigkeit von Bundesgesetzen beruht, dürfte das Ergebnis im Falle einer Kollision mit EG-Recht anders ausfallen, wenn den Gerichten die Befugnis zur Prüfung der Vereinbarkeit mit Gemeinschaftsrecht ausdrücklich in der Verfassung zugestanden wird. Für die Offenheit der Schweiz gegenüber supranationalen Rechtsordnungen spricht nicht zuletzt auch die Durchführung der Europäischen Menschenrechtskonvention, an deren Massstab auch eine konkrete Normenkontrolle der Bundesgesetze durchgeführt wird[148], und die Akzeptanz der Rechtsprechung des Europäischen Gerichtshofs für Menschenrechte[149] sowie die monistische Tradition[150]. Der Vorrang des Gemeinschaftsrechts dürfte bei einer entsprechenden Verankerung in der Verfassung auch für die Kollision mit dem Verfassungsrecht anerkannt werden. Dies dürfte gleichermassen für die Kontrolle der Auslegung des Primärrechts wie für die Gültigkeit und Auslegung sekundärrechtlicher Bestimmungen gelten. Es lässt sich jedoch nicht ausschliessen, dass das Bundesgericht sich eine subsidiäre Kontrolle[151], insbesondere zur Wahrung der Grundrechte, vorbehalten würde[152]. Ergänzend ist darauf hinzuweisen, dass die neuere Rechtsprechung des Bundesgerichts zu einer völkerrechtsfreundlicheren Auffassung zu tendieren scheint, indem Staatsverträge mit menschenrechtlichem Gehalt einen stärkeren Vorrang gegenüber Bundesgesetzen besitzen, als es dem allgemeinen Verhältnis von völkerrechtlichen Verträgen zum nationalen Recht in der Schweiz entspricht[153].

2. *Auswirkungen des Vorrangs auf die direkte Demokratie*

Besondere Auswirkungen hätte der Vorrang des Gemeinschaftsrechts in der Schweiz auf das Institut der direkten Demokratie. Die Auswirkungen eines Beitritts der Schweiz zur Europäischen Union auf die direkte Demokratie sind seit den Verhandlungen zum EWR-Vertrag und dem vom Bundesrat eingereichten Gesuch um die Eröffnung von Beitrittsverhandlungen[154] Gegenstand einer umfangreichen Diskussion[155]. In der Schweiz entscheiden die Stimmbürger auf Bundes- wie auf Kantonsebene durch Referendum und Initiative in grossem Masse direkt über einzelne Sachfragen. Sie können etwa auf Bundesebene selbst einen Vorschlag für eine Verfassungsänderung einbringen (Verfassungsinitiative) oder von den zuständigen Organen beschlossenen Gesetzgebungsakten zustimmen oder diese ablehnen (Verfassungs-, Gesetzes- und Staatsvertragsreferendum). Dabei ist das Referendum entweder obligatorisch (Verfasssungsänderungen; Beitritt zu supranationalen Organisationen oder solchen kollektiver Sicherheit) oder fakultativ (Gesetze, referendumspflichtige Bundesbeschlüsse, gewisse Staatsverträge)[156]. Wegen des Vorrangs des Gemeinschaftsrechts, der für alle staatlichen Organe und natürlich auch für Volk und Stände gilt, wird der Entscheidungsspielraum des nationalen Gesetzgebers eingeschränkt, indem er einerseits kein Recht setzen darf, das mit dem Gemeinschaftsrecht unvereinbar wäre, und andererseits zur Gesetzgebung verpflichtet ist, um die Vorgaben des Gemeinschaftsrechts (insbesondere Richtlinien) in nationales Recht umzusetzen. Die damit für alle Mitgliedstaaten gleichermassen[157] einhergehenden Kompetenzverluste würden in der Schweiz zu einer Einschränkung des Anwendungsbereichs der direkten Demokratie führen. Einerseits würde die Entscheidung über den Erlass von Sekundärrecht und den Abschluss völkerrechtlicher Verträge der EG keinem Referendum unterliegen[158], andererseits müsste sichergestellt werden, dass Initiativen und Referenden nicht zu gemeinschaftsrechtswidrigen Ergebnissen führen. Dazu könnte der Erlass von Umsetzungsvorschriften, bei denen die gemeinschaftsrechtlichen Vorgaben keinen Entscheidungsspielraum lassen, dem Referendum entzogen und eine Prüfung der EG-Rechtskonformität von Initiativen vorgesehen werden[159]. Untersuchungen haben jedoch gezeigt, dass nur ein relativ kleiner Teil der Abstimmungen der letzten Jahre zu Konflikten mit dem Gemeinschaftsrecht geführt hätte[160], so dass das Instrument der direkten Demokratie als solches im Falle eines Beitritts nicht in Frage gestellt wäre[161]. So kommt nun auch der Bundesrat zu dem Ergebnis, dass in den Volksrechten kein unüberwindbares Hindernis für den Beitritt zur EU zu sehen sei[162]. Letztlich aber ist zu beachten, dass Souveränitätsverluste auch ohne Beitritt zur Europäischen Union als Folge der zunehmenden internationalen Interdependenz und der „Globalisierung" zu verzeichnen sind[163]. Insbesondere gegenüber dem Recht der EU ist ein nicht unerheblicher tatsächlicher Souveränitätsverlust durch einen faktischen Anpassungsdruck zu konstatieren, denn „die Vermeidung unnötiger Unterschiede zum europäischen Recht gehört heute zur Standardaufgabe der Gesetzgebung" [164], so dass grosse Teile des Gemeinschaftsrechts im Wege des sogenannten autonomen Nachvollzugs[165] übernommen werden und ausserdem jedes neue Gesetz auf seine Europakompatibilität hin geprüft wird.

IV. Institutionelle Interdependenz: Europäische Funktionen staatlicher Institutionen

Eine Mitgliedschaft der Schweiz in der EU hätte eine Gewichtsverlagerung von der Legislative (Parlament und Volk) zur Exekutive (Bundesrat) zur Folge, da die Staaten bei der Entscheidungsfindung auf EG-Ebene vor allem durch die Regierungen im Rat vertreten werden[166]. Daher sollte nach Möglichkeiten gesucht werden, wie die Einflussnahme des Parlaments auf das Handeln der Regierung im Rahmen der Europäischen Union verstärkt werden kann, um eine möglichst grosse demokratische Legitimation zu gewährleisten und den Verlust der Einwirkungsmöglichkeiten der Stimmbürger und den Machtzuwachs der Exekutive auszugleichen. Dazu böten sich verschiedene Massnahmen an: Bildung je einer Europakommission in den beiden Parlamentskammern, Informations- und Berichtspflichten des Bundesrates gegenüber dem Parlament und den Europakommissionen, Erweiterung des Rechts zur Stellungnahme, Bindung bzw. Berücksichtigungspflicht des Bundesrates an Entscheidungen des Parlaments und ggf. der Europakommissionen[167]. Die verfassungsrechtliche Verankerung geschähe wohl am sinnvollsten in einem Europa- oder Integrationsartikel, wie dies auch in einigen EG-Staaten der Fall ist[168].

Die Beteiligung eines Mitgliedstaates an den Tätigkeiten der Europäischen Union stellt ausserdem gewisse Anforderungen an die *Staatsleitung*, auf die das derzeitige Regierungssystem der Schweiz noch nicht in jeder Hinsicht optimal eingestellt ist[169]. Da der aus sieben Personen bestehende Bundesrat, der als Kollegialorgan die Regierung des Bundes bildet, für eine angemessene Vertretung der Schweiz im Rat der EU zu klein sein dürfte, ist zunächst an eine personelle Erweiterung des Bundesrates oder an eine Ergänzung durch eine zweite Ebene (Delegierte Minister mit politischer Mitverantwortung) zu denken[170]. In die gleiche Richtung gehen jedoch auch Reformüberlegungen, die seit Bestehen des Bundesstaates und verstärkt seit Beginn der 90er Jahre immer wieder und unabhängig von der Frage eines Beitritts zur EU angestellt wurden[171]. Darin wird auch vorgeschlagen, die Kompetenzen des Bundespräsidenten zu erweitern und die Amtszeit von einem auf zwei Jahre zu verlängern[172]. Dies dürfte nicht zuletzt auch für die Mitwirkung im Europäischen Rat von erheblicher Bedeutung sein. Andererseits zeigt auch das Beispiel anderer Mitgliedstaaten, dass ganz verschiedene Regierungssysteme mit der Mitgliedschaft in der Union vereinbar sind.

Die EG ist ein System dezentraler Rechtsanwendung und gewährt den Mitgliedstaaten daher Verfahrensautonomie, die jedoch in mehrfacher Hinsicht durch gemeinschaftsrechtliche Vorgaben Einschränkungen erfährt[173]. Das schweizerische *Rechtsschutzsystem* entspricht bereits weitgehend diesen Vorgaben[174]. Durch die am 12. März 2001 von Volk und Ständen angenommenen Verfassungsänderungen (Justizreform) wird ausserdem eine grundrechtliche Rechtsweggarantie in der Verfassung verankert und die Transparenz des Prozessrechts durch eine Vereinfachung des Rechtsmittelsystems (Einführung einer Einheitsbeschwerde zum Bundesgericht) erhöht.[175] Im Bereich des *Rechtsschutzes* wäre insbesondere noch die umfassende Überprüfung des nationalen Rechts am Massstab des Gemeinschaftsrechts sicherzustellen, insbesondere durch die Möglichkeit, in jedem Verfahren vor dem Bundesgericht eine Verletzung des Gemeinschaftsrechts geltend zu machen [176]. Ein Beitritt zur EU dürfte wohl zu einer Stärkung der Verfassungsgerichtsbarkeit führen, denn es ist kaum vorstellbar, dass die nationalen Gerichte zwar befugt sind, die Bundesgesetze am Massstab des Gemeinschaftsrechts, nicht aber der Verfassung zu prüfen[177]. Dabei wird im Schrifttum auch unabhängig von der integrationspolitischen Perspektive eine allgemeine Stärkung der Verfassungsgerichtsbarkeit auf Bundesebene gefordert[178].

C ROLLE DER KANTONE/BETEILIGUNG DER KANTONE AN DER EUROPAPOLITIK

I. Kurzer Überblick der Zuständigkeiten in der schweizerischen Aussenpolitik

In Bezug auf die schweizerische Aussenpolitik kann grundsätzlich folgendes Bild der Zuständigkeiten skizziert werden:

- Der Bundesrat vertritt die Schweiz nach aussen, er kümmert sich um die Aussenpolitik unter Wahrung der Mitwirkungsrechte der Bundesversammlung.
- Das Parlament nimmt an der Ausgestaltung der Aussenpolitik teil und beaufsichtigt die Beziehungen zum Ausland. Die völkerrechtlichen Verträge müssen für ihre Gültigkeit vom Parlament genehmigt werden (ausser denen, für die der Bundesrat zuständig ist).

- Die Kantone können in ihren Zuständigkeitsbereichen eigene Verträge mit dem Ausland schliessen. Vor Abschluss müssen sie darüber den Bund informieren. Sie nehmen an der Vorbereitung der aussenpolitischen Entscheide des Bundes teil, welche ihre Zuständigkeiten oder wesentlichen Interessen betreffen.
- Das Volk stimmt über den Beitritt zu Organisationen für kollektive Sicherheit oder zu supranationalen Gemeinschaften ab (obligatorisches Referendum; benötigt wird ein Volks- und ein Ständemehr). Es kann mittels eines fakultativen Referendums eine Abstimmung verlangen über unbefristete oder unkündbare internationale Verträge, über den Beitritt zu internationalen Organisationen oder über Abkommen, die eine multilaterale Rechtsvereinheitlichung vorsehen. Das Volk kann auch über eine Initiative eigene aussenpolitische Vorschläge einbringen.

Im Folgenden soll die Rolle der Kantone in vertikaler Hinsicht (gegenüber dem Bund und den Bürgern) und in horizontaler Hinsicht (gegenüber den anderen Kantonen) aufgezeigt, mögliche Veränderungen durch einen EU-Beitritt skizziert sowie "unverzichtbare" Charakteristiken dargestellt werden, welche allenfalls auch für eine zukünftige Ausgestaltung der EU Inspirationsquelle sein könnten[179].

II. Rolle der Kantone

1. Rolle der Kantone im Bund

Ein wichtiger Grundsatz ist die Gleichheit der Kantone, was bedeutet, dass alle Kantone die gleichen Kompetenzen, Rechte und Pflichten untereinander, aber auch im Verhältnis zum Bund haben[180]. Ganz generell wirken die Kantone bei der Gesetzgebung und bei der Umsetzung des Bundesrechts mit.

Die Kantone sind "souverän" gemäss Art. 3 BV, womit v.a. die Eigenständigkeit der Kantone gemeint ist[181]. Die Kantone sind als souveräne Einheiten anzusehen, welche einen Teil ihrer Kompetenzen an den Bund übertragen haben. Es stimmt zwar, dass der Bund die Militärhoheit, Teile des Verkehrswesens, die Regelungskompetenz im Zivilrecht, die wichtigen Aufgaben im Wirtschaftsrecht, in der sozialen Sicherheit und bei der Ordnung der Umweltpolitik sukzessive übernommen hat. Trotzdem ist nicht nur die Aufgabe des Vollzugs des Bundesrechts in der Hand der Kantone verblieben (Art. 46 BV), sondern sie haben eine "beachtliche Fülle von öffentlichen Aufgaben"[182]. Die Kompetenzverteilung beruht auf der grundlegenden Regel, dass der Bund nur zuständig ist in dem Mass, in welchem die Bundesverfassung ihm eine bestimmte Zuständigkeit zuweist. Wenn man Föderalismus als partnerschaftliche Erscheinung auffasst, so kann es nicht genügen, einige verschwindende kantonale Kompetenzen aufrechtzuerhalten, es ist unumgänglich, dass die Kantone an der Art und Weise der Ausübung der Kompetenzen des Bundes beteiligt sind[183]. Der neue Art. 45 BV verschafft den Kantonen ein verstärktes Mitwirkungsrecht. Gemäss Art. 51 BV haben die Kantone eine Verfassungsautonomie. Im Rahmen des Bundesrechts können die Kantone ihre Organisation, die Ziele und Aufgaben der Staatstätigkeit selbst bestimmen. In Art. 47 BV steht neu: "Der Bund wahrt die Eigenständigkeit der Kantone." Diese Eigenständigkeit beruht auf ihrer Autonomie in Organisation, Verfahren und öffentlichen Dienstrecht, sowie ihrer Steuer- und Finanzhoheit[184]. Allerdings durchdringt das Bundesrecht fast alle kantonalen Zuständigkeitsbereiche und ist so mit dem kantonalen Recht verflochten[185]. Auch haben sich im Bundesrecht Verfassungsprinzipien entwickelt, welche die kantonalen Rechtsordnungen prägen und beeinflussen. Immerhin findet die Beeinflussung nicht nur in diese eine Richtung statt, verschiedene Grundrechtsbestimmungen der neuen Bundesverfassung wurden umgekehrt von den Entwicklungen in neueren Kantonsverfassungen inspiriert[186]. Zur Wahrung der Einheit und des Vorranges des Bundesrechts existieren Aufsichts- und Rechtsschutzverfahren Der Vorrang des Bundesrechts führt grundsätzlich zur Nichtigkeit des bundesrechtswidrigen kantonalen Rechts, nicht nur zur Nichtanwendbarkeit, wie dies im Rahmen der EU gegenüber gemeinschaftsrechtswidrigem nationalem Recht der Fall ist[187].

Die Kantone haben gemäss Art. 56 Abs. 1 BV das Recht, in ihren Zuständigkeitsbereichen mit dem Ausland Verträge zu schliessen, wobei diese dem Recht und den Interessen des Bundes und anderer Kantone nicht zuwiderlaufen dürfen. Den Kantonen obliegt die Verpflichtung, den Bund vor Abschluss der Verträge zu informieren. Die Aussenpolitik liegt in der Schweiz in der Kompetenz des Bundes (Art. 54 Abs. 1 BV).

Die Kantone haben aber verschiedene Möglichkeiten, um an der Aussenpolitik des Bundes mitzuwirken, u.a.[188]:

- Staatsvertragsreferendum: Die Möglichkeit, sich mittels eines Referendums an der Entscheidung über einen Staatsvertrag zu beteiligen, ist gering. Sie besteht nur bei einem Beitritt zu Organisationen für kollektive Sicherheit oder zu einer supranationalen Organisation (Art. 140 Abs. 1 BV).
- Vernehmlassungsverfahren: Die Kantone werden bei wichtigen völkerrechtlichen Verträgen zu einer Stellungnahme eingeladen (Art. 147 BV).

Da sich völkerrechtliche Verträge und Verpflichtungen in vermehrtem Mass auch direkt auf kantonale Zuständigkeitsbereiche auswirken, entstand ein gesteigertes Bedürfnis der Kantone, an der Ausgestaltung der jeweiligen

Vereinbarungen vermehrt mitzuwirken. Art. 55 der neuen Bundesverfassung trägt diesem Anliegen Rechnung: die Kantone sollen an der Vorbereitung aussenpolitischer Entscheide, welche ihre Zuständigkeitsbereiche oder wesentliche Interessen betreffen, mitwirken. Sie müssen rechtzeitig und umfassend informiert werden. Diese Grundsätze werden im Bundesgesetz über die Mitwirkung der Kantone an der Aussenpolitik des Bundes, welches am 1. Juli 2000 in Kraft trat, konkretisiert (SR 138.1). Die grundsätzliche aussenpolitische Zuständigkeit des Bundes wird nicht tangiert und die Handlungsfähigkeit in der Aussenpolitik bleibt ausdrücklich vorbehalten. Zweck der Mitwirkung ist einerseits die Berücksichtigung der Kantone und die Wahrung ihrer Zuständigkeiten, andererseits die innenpolitische Abstützung der Aussenpolitik des Bundes. Folgende Formen der Mitwirkung der Kantone sind vorgesehen[189]:

- *Information*: Es besteht eine gegenseitige Informationspflicht von Bund und Kantonen. Der Bund informiert die Kantone rechtzeitig und umfassend über aussenpolitische Vorhaben, die ihre Zuständigkeit oder wesentlichen Interessen berühren (Art. 3 Mitwirkungsgesetz). Dies wird von Seiten des Bundes durch das halbjährliche Vorlegen einer Liste an die Kantone erfüllt[190]. Diese können zusätzliche Auskünfte über sie interessierende Bereiche anfordern. Der Föderalistische Dialog, in dessen Rahmen sich Mitglieder des Bundesrates mit Kantonsvertretern treffen, spielt ebenfalls eine wichtige Rolle des Informationsaustausches.
- *Konsultation* (Art. 4 Mitwirkungsgesetz): Soweit die Kantone dies verlangen, soll der Bund sie bei der Vorbereitung aussenpolitischer Entscheide anhören. Er kann sie auch von sich aus anhören. Bevor der Bund Verhandlungen aufnimmt, hört er die Kantone in der Regel an. Diese Anhörung ergänzt das Vernehmlassungsverfahren zu völkerrechtlichen Verträgen. Die Stellungnahmen der Kantone werden nach dem jeweiligen Grad der Betroffenheit gewichtet; sofern der Bund von den Stellungnahmen abweicht, teilt er den Kantonen die massgeblichen Gründe mit.
- *Mitwirkung bei Verhandlungen* (Art. 5 Mitwirkungsgesetz): Der Bund zieht für die Vorbereitung von Verhandlungsmandaten und in der Regel auch für die Verhandlungen, welche die Zuständigkeiten der Kantone betreffen Kantonsvertreter bei. In andern Fällen kann der Bund sie von sich aus beiziehen. Diese gängige Vorgehensweise hat sich im Bereich der sektoriellen Verhandlungen mit der EU bewährt.

Längerfristig müssten im Falle eines Beitritts institutionalisierte Mitwirkungsverfahren für die Integrations- und Europapolitik eingerichtet werden (ähnlich wie in Deutschland und Österreich)[191]. Besondere

Beachtung müsste dabei der Faktor Zeit erhalten: Die Kantone müssen in Absprache mit dem Bund ein effizientes Aktions- und Reaktionskonzept entwickeln, da der Erlass von Verordnungen und Richtlinien rascher erfolgt als der Abschluss von völkerrechtlichen Verträgen. Aus diesem Grund wäre es wichtig, eine kollektive Mitwirkung der Kantone durch *ein* Organ zu planen, sei es durch den Ständerat (in der aktuellen Form oder umgestaltet) oder durch die Konferenz der Kantone[192]. Die Aufgabenverteilung zwischen Bund und Kantonen und die bundesstaatliche Finanzordnung müssten ebenfalls neu geordnet werden[193].

2. *Rolle in Bezug auf andere Kantone und Regionen (Koordination und Kooperation)*

(a) Zusammenarbeit zwischen Kantonen

Die Kantone sind auf interkantonale Zusammenarbeit angewiesen, um ihre Rolle innerhalb der Schweiz und in Bezug auf die internationale Integration der Schweiz zu erhalten und zu stärken[194].

Nebst den Fachdirektoren-Konferenzen, deren Ziel die Zusammenarbeit und Koordination in einem bestimmten Fachbereich zwischen Kantonen und zwischen Kantonen und dem Bund darstellt, gibt es auch regionale Regierungskonferenzen. Zudem haben die Kantone nach dem EWR-Nein vom 6.12.92 die Konferenz der Kantonsregierungen (KdK) gegründet, um aussen- und integrationspolitische Fragen unter den Kantonen besser zu koordinieren und auf die Aussenpolitik des Bundes abstimmen zu können. Der Konferenz der Kantonsregierungen kommt somit auch in Bezug auf die Europapolitik der Kantone eine besondere Bedeutung zu. In diesem Bereich ist eine gemeinsame Haltung der Kantone wichtig, da die internationale Integration tendenziell die Zuständigkeitsbereiche der Kantone verkleinert. Insofern besteht ein Widerspruch zwischen kantonaler Autonomie und internationaler Integration[195]. Durch interkantonale Zusammenarbeit kann der Machtverlust der Kantone in Grenzen gehalten werden, auch weil damit eine Möglichkeit besteht, die Aussenpolitik des Bundes effizient mitzugestalten.

(b) Kantone und europäischer Regionalismus

Die Kantone beteiligen sich schon seit längerem an der Entwicklung der grenzüberschreitenden EuroRegionen. 15 Kantone sind in 6 EuroRegionen integriert[196]. Diese Kooperationsform dient als Dreh- und Servicestelle für die Lösung grenzüberschreitender Probleme (wie Umweltfragen, Infrastrukturentwicklung, Tourismus). Des Weiteren sind 22 Kantone[197] Mitglieder in der 1985 gegründeten Versammlung der Regionen Europas (VRE). Diese hat ihren Einfluss insbesondere genutzt, um den Ausschuss der Regionen zu etablieren, welcher den Regionen (der Mitgliedstaaten) eine gewisse Mitsprachemöglichkeit in den sie betreffenden EU-

Angelegenheiten verschafft hat. Die VRE setzt sich insbesondere auch für die Entwicklung der interregionalen Zusammenarbeit auf dem gesamten europäischen Kontinent ein[198]. Eine weitere Initiative zur verstärkten grenzüberschreitenden Zusammenarbeit mit den Staaten und Regionen der EU besteht mit dem Programm Interreg III (2000-2006). Der Bundesrat hat per 1.3.2000 das Inkrafttreten des Bundesgesetzes über die Förderung der schweizerischen Beteiligung an der Gemeinschaftsinitiative[199] beschlossen. Das Inkrafttreten erfolgte parallel zum Start der EU-eigenen Initiative, welche neue Möglichkeiten der transnationalen und interregionalen Zusammenarbeit vorsieht.

Der europäische Regionalismus ist einer der Impulse für die Idee der Grossregionen[200] in der Schweiz. Es muss aber nicht zu einem Verschwinden der Kantone kommen, der Regionalismus kann sich auch in verstärkter Kooperation zwischen den Kantonen auswirken[201]. So werden bspw. überkantonale Projekte und deren Finanzierung gemeinsam ausgearbeitet und getragen. Die Koordination und Kooperation zwischen Kantonen, aber auch zwischen Regionen werden sich im Fall eines Beitritts zur EU noch intensivieren. Sogar neue Formen der Zusammenarbeit werden nötig. Als Beispiel dafür sei die Umsetzung der Wasserrahmenrichtlinie[202] genannt, die eine Zusammenarbeit in den jeweiligen Flussgebietseinheiten voraussetzt. Diese Gebiete sind nicht mittels bestimmter Kantons- oder Landesgrenzen, sondern nach Einzugsgebieten definiert[203]. Gemäss der Richtlinie sind innerhalb von Einzugsgebieten in denen der Wassergebrauch grenzüberschreitende Auswirkungen haben kann, alle Massnahmenprogramme für die gesamte Flussgebietseinheit zu koordinieren. Bei Einzugsgebieten, welche auch Grenzen zu Nichtmitgliedstaaten überschreiten, sollen die Mitgliedstaaten (gemäss Art. 3 (5) RL) für eine Koordinierung mit diesen sorgen. So muss also Deutschland bspw. eine Koordinierung mit der Schweiz anstreben in der Flussgebietseinheit "Rhein".

3. *Verhältnis zu den Bürgern*

Das direkteste Verhältnis zum Bürger findet sich auf der dritten Stufe des schweizerischen Föderalismus: der Gemeinden. Diese verfügen über die Gemeindeautonomie, sie legen die Höhe ihrer Steuern und deren Verwendung selbst fest. Die Bürger können an der Gemeindeversammlung Anträge stellen, über Sachgeschäfte abstimmen, Behördenmitglieder wählen, etc. Kleinere Gemeinden suchen die regionale Zusammenarbeit mit anderen Gemeinden für grössere Aufgaben. Entsprechend dem Subsidiaritätsprinzip übernimmt der Kanton diejenigen Aufgaben, welche nicht von den Gemeinden übernommen werden können, so bspw. die Mittelschule und die Universitäten.

Bei einem EU-Beitritt wären vorwiegend Bundeskompetenzen (wie Wirtschafts-, Umwelt- oder Verkehrspolitik) von einer Verlagerung auf die Gemeinschaftsebene betroffen. Die Kantonskompetenzen würden jedoch partiell eingeschränkt, bspw. auf der Ebene der Erziehung und Kultur, des Gesundheitswesens, der Raumplanung, der Berufsdiplome, der Steuern und des Hochschulzugangs[204]. Aufgrund der sektoriellen Abkommen mit der EU von 1999 ergeben sich für die Kantone schon jetzt grosse Änderungen. Das Abkommen über die Personenfreizügigkeit führt zur Anwendung eines grossen Teils der entsprechenden EG-Normen und einem weitgehenden Diskriminierungsverbot[205]. Mit einem Beitritt und der Übernahme des gesamten "acquis communautaire" werden für die Schweiz neue Aufgaben entstehen. Einerseits erhalten die Kantone so neue Wirkungsfelder, andererseits wird für sie durch die Umsetzungs- und Vollzugsaufgaben ein Mehraufwand entstehen.

Als konkretes Beispiel für die Auswirkungen eines EU-Beitritts auf die Kompetenzen der Kantone und ihr Verhältnis zu den Bürgern sei hier die Bildungspolitik angeführt:

Das Schul- und Bildungswesen liegt primär in der Zuständigkeit der Kantone (Art. 62 i.V. m. Art. 19 BV). Die Kantone müssen einen allgemeinen, unentgeltlichen und konfessionell neutralen öffentlichen Grundschulunterricht anbieten. Hinzu kommt die kantonale Mitwirkung auf der Mittelstufe, sowie für die kantonalen Universitäten, kantonalen und interkantonalen Fachhochschulen, die universitäre Forschungsförderung und die Erwachsenenbildung (s. Art. 63, 64, 66, 67 BV). Die kantonale Zuständigkeit liegt hier vorwiegend in den unterschiedlichen Sprach- und Kulturräumen begründet, wobei bundesrechtliche Anforderungen eine gewisse Einheit der Qualität und Anerkennung herstellen[206]. Unter die kantonale Schulhoheit fällt auch die Organisation der Universitäten und die Festlegung der Studiengebühren. Gemäss der Interkantonalen Universitätsvereinbarung bezahlen die Kantone einen bestimmten Betrag pro Studierenden an den jeweiligen Unversitätskanton. Ausländische Studierende mussten z.T. bis das doppelte der Gebühren entrichten (aktuell noch im Tessin) und zahlen in Fribourg, Neuchâtel, Zürich und Sankt Gallen eine höhere Gebühr[207]. Diese Praxis wäre nicht mit Gemeinschaftsrecht vereinbar, da Art. 12 EGV Diskriminierungen aufgrund der Staatsangehörigkeit klar verbietet. Im Fall eines Beitritts sind die Kantone verpflichtet, die bildungspolitischen Massnahmen der Gemeinschaft umzusetzen. Dies stellt offenbar schon für aktuelle Mitgliedstaaten teilweise ein Problem dar[208]. In diesem Bereich würde je nach Bildungsprogramm eine unterschiedlich grosse Veränderung kantonaler Zuständigkeiten bewirkt und allenfalls auch eine Begründung von Koordinationsaufgaben auf Bundesebene[209].

Im Bereich der Anerkennung von Diplomen oder

Ausbildungsabschlüssen werden sich schon durch die bilateralen Verträge zwischen der Schweiz und der EG Änderungen in den Zuständigkeiten (resp. Beschränkungen der Regelungskompetenzen) der Kantone im Bereich der Berufszulassung ergeben, da zur Gewährleistung des freien Personenverkehrs eine umfassende gegenseitige Anerkennung von Diplomen vorgesehen ist[210].

Bei einem Beitritt würden sich gewisse Änderung der Kompetenzen der Kantone nicht vermeiden lassen. Die Kantone hätten jedoch weiterhin die Möglichkeit die Europapolitik in Zusammenarbeit mit dem Bund zu gestalten und ihre Zuständigkeiten und Mitwirkungsrechte wahrzunehmen. Die Beeinträchtigung der Kompetenzen wäre wohl je nach Rechtsgebiet unterschiedlich gross. Eine Veränderung der Kantonsstruktur der Schweiz würde sich nicht primär wegen eines EU-Beitritts aufdrängen, sondern allenfalls im Rahmen von Überlegungen, welche auch ohne weitere Integration hätten angestellt werden müssen.

4. *Einfluss des schweizerischen Föderalismus auf die EU-Rechtsordnung?*

Der schweizerische Föderalismus zeichnet sich insbesondere dadurch aus, dass er nicht nur eine Kompetenzaufteilung im Sinne des Subsidiaritätsprinzips verfolgt, welches auf Effizienz ausgerichtet ist, sondern die möglichst weitgehende Selbstbestimmung der Gliedstaaten anstrebt, die als Garantie für die Förderung der Vielfalt dient. Damit soll insbesondere eine grösse Beteiligung der Bürger und Bürgerinnen sichergestellt werden und insofern beinhaltet dieser Ansatz eine starke identitätsbildende Kraft[211]. Dieser Ansatz könnte dazu dienen, ein "Europa der Bürger" zu erreichen[212], in dem ein europäisches Volk entsteht, im Bewusstsein, dass es sich dabei um eine durch verschiedene Völker und Kulturen zusammengesetzte Identität handelt. Die Legitimität der EU würde einerseits dadurch und andererseits durch die Flexibilität des Vollzugs in den einzelnen Staaten oder Gliedstaaten erhöht[213]. Zur Stärkung der demokratischen Legitimation wird es somit notwendig sein, die Rechtsetzungsverfahren auf Gemeinschaftsebene so auszugestalten, dass Gliedstaaten verstärkt beteiligt werden können. Auch was die direktdemokratischen Instrumente und die direkte Beteiligung der Bürger und Bürgerinnen angeht, könnte die EU vom Erfahrungsschatz der Schweiz profitieren[214].

ZUSAMMENFASSUNG

1. Obwohl die Schweiz nicht Mitglied der EU ist, lassen sich doch vielfältige *Einflüsse des EU-Rechts* auf das nationale Verfassungsrecht

feststellen. Ein Beitritt zur EU würde eine Reihe weiterer Änderungen der schweizerischen Verfassung erforderlich machen, die jedoch zu einem grossen Teil schon aus anderen Gründen Gegenstand von Reformprojekten sind (z.B. Justiz- und Staatsleitungsreform). Dies ist nicht zuletzt auf die veränderten Anforderungen politischer Organisation angesichts zunehmender internationaler Interdependenz und Kooperation sowie auf den „autonomen Nachvollzug" und die staatsvertragliche Übernahme (insb. durch die sektoriellen Abkommen von 1999) von EG-Recht in der Schweiz zurückzuführen. Daneben besteht traditionell ein grosses Interesse an den Lösungen insbesondere in den Nachbarstaaten, welche auch in grossem Umfange rezipiert werden. Insofern steht die neue schweizerische Bundesverfassung im Kontext des gemeineuropäischen Verfassungsrechts[215] und einer „Europäisierung des Verfassungsrechts"[216].

2. Einige *Besonderheiten der Verfassungsordnung* der Schweiz lassen sich insbesondere auf die historische Entwicklung und die besondere sprachliche und kulturelle Situation zurückführen. So dient der ausgeprägte Föderalismus dazu, die Einheit der so komplexen, heterogenen, multiethnischen und multireligiösen Nation durch Autonomie und Mitwirkungsrechte der Kantone zu gewährleisten. Da nicht wie bei anderen Staaten auf die sprachliche und kulturelle Einheit des Landes zurückgegriffen werden kann, haben die politischen Institutionen und insbesondere die direkte Demokratie, daneben aber auch der Föderalismus und die Neutralität, eine besondere Bedeutung für die nationale Identität in der Willensnation Schweiz.
3. Die im Jahre 2000 in Kraft getretene neue Bundesverfassung erlaubt den Beitritt zu supranationalen Organisationen und betont an verschiedenen Stellen die Offenheit für internationales Recht und zwischenstaatliche Kooperation. Einem *Beitritt zur EU* stünden auch nicht die Grundsätze des Föderalismus, der direkten Demokratie oder der Neutralität entgegen. Die nur „nachgeführte" Verfassung enthält jedoch keinen Integrations- oder Europaartikel, ein solcher wäre aber wohl erforderlich im Falle eines Beitritts.
4. *Materielle Schranken der Verfassungsänderung* wurden in der Schweiz, abgesehen von der Beachtung der zwingenden Bestimmungen des Völkerrechts (Art. 139 Abs. 3, 193 Abs. 4 und 194 Abs. 2 BV), bisher gar nicht oder nur sehr zurückhaltend anerkannt. Da dies jedoch auch als Ausdruck des Vertrauens in die gewachsenen politischen Strukturen zu sehen ist, ist es denkbar, dass im Falle eines Beitritts zur EU solche Schranken der Übertragbarkeit von Hoheitsrechten in einem Integrations- oder Europaartikel in die Verfassung aufgenommen würden. Diese dürften jedoch im Wesentlichen nicht über die (Kerngehalte der) in Art. 6 Abs. 1 EUV genannten Verfassungsprinzipien hinausgehen.

5. Der Schutz der nationalen Identität der Mitgliedstaaten gem. Art. 6 Abs. 3 EUV müsste im Falle der Schweiz insbesondere zu einer Berücksichtigung des *Föderalismus* führen. Dabei bestehen einerseits Anforderungen an die Ausgestaltung der Rechtsetzungsverfahren, welche eine effektive Mitwirkung der Kantone ermöglichen müssten (Zeitrahmen; Sprache der vorbereitenden Dokumente etc.), andererseits müssten den Gliedstaaten substanzielle Kompetenzen verbleiben, wobei in der Schweiz der Kulturhoheit (vor allem wegen des Staatsziels der Förderung der kulturellen und sprachlichen Vielfalt) und der Finanz- und Steuerhoheit sowie der Verfahrensautonomie der Kantone im Bereich des Vollzuges besondere Bedeutung zukommt.
6. Der Grundsatz der *Neutralität* ist heute völker- und verfassungsrechtliches Gewohnheitsrecht. Inhalt der Neutralitätsverpflichtung ist jedoch nurmehr die Neutralität im Falle bewaffneter Konflikte souveräner Staaten, die nicht im Zusammenhang mit Massnahmen des Sicherheitsrates nach Art. 39 ff. UN-Charta oder mit Notwehr- bzw. Nothilfemassnahmen nach Art. 51 UN-Charta stehen. Als Völkergewohnheitsrecht müsste sie auch von der EU (bzw. den anderen Mitgliedstaaten), etwa im Rahmen der GASP, beachtet werden, wo es jedoch kaum zu Kollisionen kommen dürfte und diese auch durch die Möglichkeit eines opting out gelöst werden könnten.
7. Im Bereich der *Grundrechte* besteht zwischen den Gewährleistungen der Grundrechtscharta und der schweizerischen Bundesverfassung weitgehende Übereinstimmung. Dies gilt insbesondere für die mehrheitlich abwehrrechtlich geprägten Freiheitsrechte und die justiziellen Rechte, aber auch für den um moderne Anreicherungen ergänzten Gleichheitssatz. Dagegen sind die im Kapitel „Solidarität“ geregelten Arbeitnehmerrechte in der Schweiz grossteils nicht verfassungsrechtlich verankert und zeigt sich in der Bundesverfassung wie auch in der Praxis des Bundesgerichts eine deutliche Zurückhaltung gegenüber der Zuerkennung sozialer Grundrechte als subjektiver Rechte. Verstärkt wird diese Zurückhaltung durch die Betonung der Verantwortung des Einzelnen an verschiedenen Stellen der Verfassung sowie dadurch, dass Staatszielbestimmungen und Programmsätze ausserhalb des Grundrechtskapitels in der Verfassung angesiedelt sind. Dabei handelt es sich jedoch teilweise zunächst nur um redaktionelle Unterschiede, abzuwarten bleibt insbesondere, inwieweit der Europäische Gerichtshof bei der Anwendung der Charta subjektive soziale Rechte aus den Gewährleistungen ableiten und seine Rechtsprechung zu den Schranken weiterentwickeln wird.
8. Der *Vorrang des Gemeinschaftsrechts* gilt bisher noch nicht für die

Schweiz. Es ist jedoch zu erwarten, dass im Falle eines Beitritts zur EU die Anerkennung des Vorrangs durch die Rechtsprechung ohne Schwierigkeiten erfolgen würde. Dafür spricht nicht zuletzt die völkerrechtsfreundliche Verfassung und ihre Auslegung durch das Bundesgericht sowie die Erfahrungen mit der Europäischen Menschenrechtskommission. Es ist jedoch nicht unwahrscheinlich, dass sich das Bundesgericht eine subsidiäre Prüfungsbefugnis, insbesondere zum Schutze der Grundrechte, z.B. an Hand eines Europa- oder Integrationsartikels vorbehalten würde, etwa in Anlehnung an die Rechtsprechung des deutschen Bundesverfassungsgerichts. Wegen des Vorrangs des Gemeinschaftsrechts wäre das Referendum gegen nationale Rechtsakte, die nur gemeinschaftsrechtliche Verpflichtungen umsetzen, zu beschränken. Davon wäre nach bisherigen Studien jedoch nur ein zahlenmässig geringer Teil der Abstimmungen erfasst, so dass die Institution der direkten Demokratie als solche nicht in Frage gestellt wäre.

9. Ein Beitritt der Schweiz zur EU hätte im Bereich der *Institutionen* eine Verlagerung von Befugnissen insbesondere im Bereich der Rechtsetzung von den Kantonen auf den Bund und vom Parlament zur Exekutive zur Folge, da die Staaten im Hauptrechtsetzungsorgan Rat durch Vertreter der Regierung, d.h. des Bundesrates vertreten werden. Um diesen Aufgaben nachkommen zu können, würde sich eine Vergrösserung des bisher siebenköpfigen Bundesrates, der als Kollegialorgan entscheidet, ebenso anbieten wie evtl. eine Stärkung des Bundespräsidenten und die Verlängerung seiner Amtsdauer (z.B. zwei Jahre statt bisher einem Jahr). Zum Ausgleich der Machtverlagerung auf den Bundesrat und der Verringerung des Anwendungsbereichs des Referendums, das gegen EG-Rechtsakte nicht mehr ergriffen werden könnte, wären die Mitwirkungsmöglichkeiten des Parlamentes und der Kantone an der Europapolitik des Bundes zu stärken.

10. Im Bereich des *Rechtsschutzes* wäre insbesondere die umfassende Überprüfung des nationalen Rechts am Massstab des Gemeinschaftsrechts sicherzustellen. Dies dürfte letztlich auch zu einer weiteren Stärkung der Verfassungsgerichtsbarkeit, insbesondere auch durch Prüfung der Verfassungsmässigkeit von Bundesgesetzen, beitragen.

11. Die *Beteiligung der Kantone an der Aussenpolitik* des Bundes dient einerseits der Berücksichtigung der Kantone und der Wahrung ihrer Zuständigkeiten, andererseits der innenpolitischen Abstützung der Aussenpolitik des Bundes. Sie wurde in den letzten Jahren deutlich gestärkt und umfasst eine gegenseitige Informationspflicht von Bund und Kantonen, Konultationen und die Mitwirkung bei Verhandlungen. Die schweizerischen Kantone beteiligen sich an grenzüberschreitenden

regionalen Kooperationen, die auch Materien umfassen, die innergemeinschaftlich in die Zuständigkeit der EG fallen (z.B. Wasserrahmenrichtlinie).

NOTES

[1] Universität Freiburg (CH)

[2] Sektorielle Abkommen zwischen der Schweiz und der Europäischen Gemeinschaft vom 21. Juni 1999, BBl 1999 6489-7110. Im Internet unter : http://www.europa.admin.ch/ba/off/abkommen/d/index.htm. Vgl. hierzu die Botschaft des Bundesrates zur Genehmigung der sektoriellen Abkommen zwischen der Schweiz und der EG vom 23. Juni 1999, BBl 1999 6128 sowie Daniel Thürer/Rolf H. Weber/Roger Zäch (Hrsg.), Bilaterale Verträge Schweiz - EG. Ein Handbuch, Zürich 2002.

[3] Dienstleistungen, Ruhegehälter, verarbeitete Landwirtschaftsprodukte, Umwelt, Statistik, Medien, Berufsbildung, Jugend, Betrugsbekämpfung, Zinsbesteuerung, verbesserte Zusammenarbeit bei der inneren Sicherheit (Polizei, Justiz, Asyl und Migration).

[4] http://www.europa.admin.ch/europapol/expl/pol/d/index.htm (Europapolitik der Schweiz)

[5] S. dazu und zum Folgenden Ursula Abderhalden, Die Elemente des schweizerischen Föderalismusverständnisses, in: Peter Hänni (Hrsg.), Schweizerischer Föderalismus und europäische Integration, Zürich 2000, S. 5 (11-13).

[6] So Piet Dankert, ehemaliger Präsident des Europäischen Parlaments, am "Colloquium on European Integration: History and Perspectives" in Lausanne, 8. Nov. 2001.

[7] BBl 1997 I 14.

[8] S. Alfred Kölz, Geschichtliche Grundlagen, in: Thürer/Aubert/Müller (Hrsg.), Verfassungsrecht der Schweiz/Droit constitutionnel suisse, Zürich 2001, S. 124.

[9] Wobei diese Bevölkerung immer in bestimmten Kreisen bestanden hat: Vor 1798 gab es keine im heutigen Sinn demokratischen Orte, die Geschicke wurden durch Patrizier, Zünfte oder Landsgemeinden bestimmt. Im 17. und 18. Jahrhundert kam es zu einer Aristokratisierung und ein grosser Teil der Bevölkerung wurde von der politischen Willensbildung ausgeschlossen. Allerdings war auch bis tief ins 20. Jahrhundert ein sehr grosser Teil der Bevölkerung von der direkten Mitwirkung auf politischer Ebene ausgeschlossen: Das Frauenstimmrecht wurde erst 1971 auf Bundesebene eingeführt!

[10] S. Alfred Kölz, Geschichtliche Grundlagen, in: Thürer/Aubert/Müller (Hrsg.), Verfassungsrecht der Schweiz/Droit constitutionnel suisse, Zürich 2001, S. 111 ff. m.w.H. zur Verfassungsgeschichte der Schweiz.

[11] Dietrich Schindler, EU-Mitgliedschaft und direkte Demokratie - Das Ausmass der Einbusse an direkter Demokratie, CH-Euro-Bulletin, September-Oktober 1995 oder unter www.europa.admin.ch/eu/info_mat/dossiers/d/democratie.htm

Zur geschichtlichen Entstehung des schweizerischen Föderalismus s. Ursula Abderhalden, Die Elemente des schweizerischen Föderalismusverständnisses, in:

Peter Hänni (Hrsg.), Schweizerischer Föderalismus und europäische Integration, Zürich 2000, S. 5 ff.

[12] Welche sich heute noch teilweise in den Streitigkeiten um das Verhältnis Völkerrecht und Landesrecht manifestiert, s. dazu Alberto Achermann, Der Vorrang des Völkerrechts im schweizerischen Recht, in: Cottier/Achermann/ Wüger/Zellweger (Hrsg.), Der Staatsvertrag im schweizerischen Verfassungsrecht, Bern 2000, S. 33 ff. m.w.N.

[13] Astrid Epiney, Beziehungen zum Ausland, in: Thürer/Aubert/Müller (Hrsg.), Verfassungsrecht der Schweiz/Droit constitutionnel suisse, Zürich 2001, S. 871 (875). Die Autorin führt an, dem Ziel der Unabhängigkeit könne allenfalls auch entnommen werden, dass die Schweiz "im Falle einer Teilnahme an internationalen oder supranationalen Integrationsbestrebungen ein irgendwie geartetes Mitbestimmungsrecht" innehaben müsste, da eine reine "Unterwerfung" nicht verfassungsmässig wäre. Gerade dieser Gedanke könnte zumindest auf der politischen Ebene interessant sein, wenn es darum geht, Überlegungen zum autonomen Nachvollzug anzustellen.

[14] Internationaler Pakt vom 16. Dezember 1966 über wirtschaftliche, soziale und kulturelle Rechte (SR 0.103.1).

[15] Ulrich Häfelin/Walter Haller, Schweizerisches Bundesstaatsrecht, Supplément zur 4. Aufl., Zürich 2000, Rn. 154 a ff., S. 7.

[16] S. dazu Walter Kälin, Integration by Constitutional Review: The Case of the Swiss Federal Tribunal, in: Bieber/Wiedmer (Hrsg.), L'espace constitutionnel européen/Der europäische Verfassungsraum, Zürich 1995, S. 209-223 (218 f.).

[17] Zu den Anforderungen und Grenzen einer solchen Übertragung s. Roland Bieber, Der Verfassungsstaat im Gefüge europäischer und insbesondere supranationaler Ordnungsstrukturen, in: Thürer/Aubert/Müller (Hrsg.), Verfassungsrecht der Schweiz/Droit constitutionnel suisse, Zürich 2001, S. 97 (103 f.).

[18] Für einen solchen Europa-Artikel in der Verfassung (mit konkret formuliertem Vorschlag) Karine Siegwart, Die Kantone und die Europapolitik des Bundes, Diss. Freiburg i.Ue. 1997, S. 228 ff. (236 u. 249).

[19] Jean-François Aubert, Notion et fonctions de la Constitution, in: Thürer/Aubert/Müller (Hrsg.), Verfassungsrecht der Schweiz/Droit constitutionnel suisse, Zürich 2001, S. 3 (14).

[20] Jean-François Aubert, Notion et fonctions de la Constitution, in: Thürer/Aubert/Müller (Hrsg.), Verfassungsrecht der Schweiz/Droit constitutionnel suisse, Zürich 2001, S. 3 (7).

[21] Ulrich Häfelin/Walter Haller, Bundesstaatsrecht, 5. Aufl., 2001, Rn. 15, S. 6.

[22] Ulrich Häfelin/Walter Haller, Schweizerisches Bundesstaatsrecht, 5. Aufl., Zürich 2001, Rn. 31, S. 11.

[23] Ulrich Häfelin/Walter Haller, Schweizerisches Bundesstaatsrecht, 5. Aufl., Zürich 2001, Rn. 17, S. 7.

[24] Ulrich Häfelin/Walter Haller, Schweizerisches Bundesstaatsrecht, 4. Aufl., Zürich 1998, Rn. 21, S. 9.

[25] Ulrich Häfelin/Walter Haller, Schweizerisches Bundesstaatsrecht, 5. Aufl., Zürich 2001, Rn. 23, S. 9.

[26] BBl. 1997 I 15, 16.

[27] S. dazu Hanna Muralt Müller, Willensnation und politische Nation - ein

Zukunftsmodell (Unfähigkeit zur Systemreform?), SZPW/RSSP 1999 (5), Nr. 2, S. 115; Jürg Martin Gabriel, Willensnation als Selbstblockade (Unfähigkeit zur Systemreform?), SZPW/RSSP 1999 (5), Nr. 2, S. 144.

[28] Augustin Macheret, Buts et spécifités du droit constitutionnel suisse, in: Thürer/Aubert/Müller (Hrsg.), Verfassungsrecht der Schweiz/Droit constitutionnel suisse, Zürich 2001, S. 138.

[29] Die Verordnung über das Vernehmlassungsverfahren vom 17.6.1991 (SR 172.062) regelt im Einzelnen, in welchen Fällen eine Vernehmlassung durchgeführt werden soll.

[30] S. die Aufzählung von Besonderheiten des schweizerischen Föderalismus bei Augustin Macheret, in: Thürer/Aubert/Müller (Hrsg.), Verfassungsrecht der Schweiz/Droit constitutionnel suissc, Zürich 2001, S. 139.

[31] Die Regierung besteht aus einem Kollektivorgan, dh sieben Bundesräten, welche gemäss der "Zauberformel" Vertreter der vier stärksten Parteien sind. Allerdings sind die Bundesräte von ihren Parteien praktisch unabhängig und vertreten innerhalb der Kollegialbehörde nie bloss ihre parteipolitischen Interessen. Die Regierungsmacht ist also aufgeteilt auf diese sieben Personen.

[32] So Roger Mallepell, Der Einfluss des Gemeinschaftsrechts auf die schweizerische Gesetzgebung 1993-1995, Swiss Papers on European Integration, Heft 21, Bern 1999, S. 47 f.

[33] BBl 1991 I 15.

[34] BBl 1991 I 15.

[35] Die nicht ausgebaute Verfassungsgerichtsbarkeit wird zunehmend als Mangel angesehen, s. Stephan Breitenmoser, Rechtsstaatlichkeit in der Schweiz, in: Rechtsstaatlichkeit in Europa, Heidelberg 1996.

[36] Alberto Achermann, Der Vorrang des Völkerrechts im schweizerischen Recht, Der Vorrang des Völkerrechts im schweizerischen Recht, in: Cottier/Achermann/Wüger/Zellweger (Hrsg.), Der Staatsvertrag im schweizerischen Verfassungsrecht, Bern 2000, S. 63.

[37] Daniel Thürer, Schweizer Verfassungsordnung vor der Herausforderung durch die europäische Integration: Perspektiven, Prinzipien und heisse Eisen, in: Perspektive Schweiz, Zürich 1998, S. 184.

[38] S. dazu unter III. Beteiligung der Kantone an der Europapolitik.

[39] S. Lidija Basta/Thomas Fleiner, Federalism, Federal State and Decentralisation, in: Federalism and Multiethnic State, The Case of Switzerland, PIFF 16, Freiburg i.Ue. 1996, S. 1 ff.

[40] BBl 1997 I 16.

[41] Dies insbesondere, weil schon eine Tradition der geteilten Souveränität besteht. Vertiefend dazu Thomas Fleiner/Nicole Töpperwien, Chancen und Probleme für den schweizerischen Föderalismus nach einem Beitritt zur Europäischen Union, in: Cottier/Kop_e, Der Beitritt der Schweiz zur Europäischen Union, Zürich 1998, S. 323 ff.

[42] Internationaler Pakt vom 16. Dezember 1966 über wirtschaftliche, soziale und kulturelle Rechte (SR 0.103.1).

[43] Rainer Schweizer, Auswirkungen auf das schweizerische Verfassungsrecht, in: Cottier/Kop_e, Der Beitritt der Schweiz zur Europäischen Union, Zürich 1998, S. 515 (528).

[44] 1996 hat die Bundesversammlung die Asylinitiative "Für eine vernünftige Asylpolitik" (BBl 1992 V 864) wegen Unvereinbarkeit mit zwingendem Völkerrecht für ungültig erklärt, da sie gegen das non-refoulement-Gebot (welches nun in Art. 25 Abs. 3 BV verankert ist) verstiess (BBl 1994 III 1496-1500).

[45] BBl 1997 I 17.

[46] BBl 1997 I 126.

[47] Astrid Epiney, Beziehungen zum Ausland, in: Thürer/Aubert/Müller (Hrsg.), Verfassungsrecht der Schweiz/Droit constitutionnel suisse, Zürich 2001, S. 871 (873).

[48] Astrid Epiney, Beziehungen zum Ausland, in: Thürer/Aubert/Müller (Hrsg.), Verfassungsrecht der Schweiz/Droit constitutionnel suisse, Zürich 2001, S. 871 (876).

[49] Astrid Epiney, Beziehungen zum Ausland, in: Thürer/Aubert/Müller (Hrsg.), Verfassungsrecht der Schweiz/Droit constitutionnel suisse, Zürich 2001, S. 871 (877).

[50] Ulrich Häfelin/Walter Haller, Schweizerisches Bundesstaatsrecht, 5. Aufl., Zürich 2001, Rn. 190, S. 56.

[51] Astrid Epiney, Beziehungen zum Ausland, in: Thürer/Aubert/Müller (Hrsg.), Verfassungsrecht der Schweiz/Droit constitutionnel suisse, Zürich 2001, 2001, S. 871 (877).

[52] Vgl. zum Folgenden Jörg Paul Müller/Luzius Wildhaber, Praxis des Völkerrechts, 3. Aufl., Bern 2001, S. 161 ff. und Alberto Achermann, Der Vorrang des Völkerrechts im schweizerischen Recht, in: Cottier/Achermann/Wüger/Zellweger (Hrsg.), Der Staatsvertrag im schweizerischen Verfassungsrecht, Bern 2000, S. 37 ff.

[53] Art. 5 Abs. 4 BV sagt lediglich, dass Bund und Kantone das Völkerrecht "beachten".

[54] S. zu dieser Diskussion Alberto Achermann, Der Vorrang des Völkerrechts im schweizerischen Recht, in: Cottier/Achermann/Wüger/Zellweger (Hrsg.), Der Staatsvertrag im schweizerischen Verfassungsrecht, Bern 2000, S. 39 f.

[55] Die BV spricht sich nicht aus zu allfälligen weiteren materiellen Schranken der Verfassungsrevision.

[56] BGE 122 II 234 E. 4e, S. 239.

[57] Pierre Tschannen, Verfassungsauslegung, in: Thürer/Aubert/Müller (Hrsg.), Verfassungsrecht der Schweiz/Droit constitutionnel suisse, Zürich 2001, S. 149 (158/159). Zum Verhältnis Verfassungsrecht und Völkerrecht s. Daniel Thürer, Verfassungsrecht und Völkerrecht, in: Thürer/Aubert/Müller (Hrsg.), Verfassungsrecht der Schweiz/Droit constitutionnel suisse, Zürich 2001, S. 179 ff. (sowie nachfolgend unter II).

[58] Immerhin scheint das Bundesgericht in seiner jüngeren Rechtsprechung den Grundsatz des Vorranges des Völkerrechts uneingeschränkt gelten zu lassen, s.. BGE 125 II 417, BGE 122 III 209, BGE 122 II 485 Vgl. zu dieser Streitfrage nachfolgend unter II. Wohl eine Mehrheit der Autoren ist der Ansicht, der Grundsatz des Vorrangs des Völkerrechts liege der BV ungeschrieben zugrunde, so z.B. Giovanni Biaggini, Die Öffnung des Verfassungsstaates, in: FS Hangartner, St. Gallen 1998, S. 957 (964) oder implizit im Sinne einer verfassungsrechtlichen Regel, so Astrid

Epiney, Das Primat des Völkerrechts als Bestandteil des Rechtsstaatsprinzips, Ein Diskussionsbeitrag zur Stellung des Völkerrechts im Verhältnis zum innerstaatlichen Recht, ZBl 95 (1994), S.537 (560 f.).

[59] Vgl. m.w.N. Astrid Epiney/Karine Siegwart/Michael Cottier/Nora Refaeil, Schweizerische Demokratie und Europäische Union, 1998, S. 126. Zur Problematik des Souveränitätsbegriffs Karine Siegwart, Die Kantone und die Europapolitik des Bundes, Diss. Freiburg i.Ue. 1997, S. 21 ff.

[60] Ursula Abderhalden, Die Elemente des schweizerischen Föderalismusverständnisses, in: Peter Hänni (Hrsg.), Schweizerischer Föderalismus und europäische Integration, Zürich 2000, S. 5 (29).

[61] BBl 1997 I 130.

[62] Zur geteilten Souveränität im Bundesstaat Karine Siegwart, Die Kantone und die Europapolitik des Bundes, Diss. Freiburg i.Ue. 1997, S. 25 ff. Zur geteilten Souveränität zwischen den Mitgliedstaaten und der Gemeinschaft Jochen Abr. Frowein, Die Verfassung der Europäischen Union aus der Sicht der Mitgliedstaaten, EuR 1995, S. 315-333 (318).

[63] Ulrich Häfelin/Walter Haller, Schweizerisches Bundesstaatsrecht, 5. Aufl., Zürich 2001, Rn. 933, S. 266.

[64] Ulrich Häfelin/Walter Haller, Schweizerisches Bundesstaatsrecht, 5. Aufl., Zürich 1998, Rn. 944, S. 270.

[65] BBl 1997 I 206. Die Kantone sind somit als mehr als nur unter Bundesaufsicht stehende Vollzugsorgane anzusehen.

[66] Roland Bieber, Der Verfassungsstaat im Gefüge europäischer und insbesondere supranationaler Ordnungsstrukturen, in: Thürer/Aubert/Müller (Hrsg.), Verfassungsrecht der Schweiz/Droit constitutionnel suisse, Zürich 2001, S. 97 (105).

[67] Ebenso Hansjörg Seiler, EG, EWR und schweizerisches Staatsrecht, 1990, S. 92.

[68] Gemäss dem in Art. 49 EUV vorgesehenen Verfahren.

[69] Ulrich Häfelin/Walter Haller, Schweizerisches Bundesstaatsrecht, 5. Aufl., Zürich 2001, Rn. 8, S. 4.

[70] Valentin Zellweger, Die demokratische Legitimation, in: Cottier/Achermann/Wüger/Zellweger (Hrsg.), Der Staatsvertrag im schweizerischen Verfassungsrecht, Bern 2000, S. 371 f.

[71] S. Dietrich Schindler, Verfassungsrecht, in: Schindler/Hertig/Kellenberger/Thürer/Zäch (Hrsg.), Die Europaverträglichkeit des schweizerischen Rechts, Zürich 1990, S. 28 ff.

[72] Dietrich Schindler, Verfassungsrecht, in: Schindler/Hertig/Kellenberger/Thürer/Zäch (Hrsg.), Die Europaverträglichkeit des schweizerischen Rechts, Zürich 1990, S. 26.

[73] "Die halbdirekte, föderalistische Demokratie ist "eurokompatibel" so wie sie ist." Wolf Linder, Erfordert die Mitgliedschaft in der Europäischen Union eine Anpassung des schweizerischen Regierungssystems?, in: Cottier/Kop_e, Der Beitritt der Schweiz zur Europäischen Union, Zürich 1998, S. 427 (445).

[74] Zu den Grundelementen des typisch schweizerischen Föderalismus s. BBl 1997 I 129.

[75] Vertiefend dazu Astrid Epiney/Karine Siegwart/Michael Cottier/Nora Refaeil, Schweizerische Demokratie und Europäische Union, Bern 1998, S. 206 ff.

[76] Vgl. Astrid Epiney/Karine Siegwart/Michael Cottier/Nora Refaeil,

Schweizerische Demokratie und Europäische Union, Bern 1998, S. 338. Kritisch zu dieser "schmerzhaften Lücke" Peter Häberle, Die "total" revidierte Bundesverfassung der Schweiz von 1999/2000, in: Festschrift Hartmut Maurer, Beck 2001, S. 935 (945/946).

[77] Als konkretes Beispiel: Art. 39 BV regelt die demokratische Ordnung von Bund und Kantonen. Der Bund regelt das Stimm- und Wahlrecht und andere politische Rechte des Bundes (s. Art. 142, 149, 150 BV), die Kantone das Stimm- und Wahlrecht und andere politische Rechte in Kantonen und Gemeinden (51 BV). Dieser geteilten Zuständigkeit im Bereich der demokratischen Mitwirkungsrechte müsste auch im Rahmen eines EU-Beitrittes Rechnung getragen werden, wenn die Voraussetzungen für die Wahl des Europäischen Parlaments (insb. die Wahlkreise, s. Art. 189, 190 und 19 Abs. 2 EGV) oder die lokalen Wahlrechte der EU-Bürger (Art. 19 Abs. 1 EGV) festzulegen sind. S. Rainer J. Schweizer, Die revidierte Bundesstaatsverfassung, AJP 6/99, S. 666 (669).

[78] Z.B. Hansjörg Seiler, EG, EWR und schweizerisches Staatsrecht, Bern 1990; Schindler/Hertig/Kellenberger/Thürer/Zäch (Hrsg.), Die Europaverträglichkeit des schweizerischen Rechts, Zürich 1990; Der Einfluss des europäischen Rechts auf die Schweiz, Festschrift für Roger Zäch, Zürich 1999; Peter Hänni (Hrsg.), Schweizerischer Föderalismus und europäische Integration, Zürich 2000; Konferenz der Kantonsregierungen (Hrsg.), Die Kantone vor der Herausforderung eines EU-Beitritts, Zürich 2001; Thomas Cottier/Alwin Kop_e (Hrsg.), Der Beitritt der Schweiz zur Europäischen Union - Brennpunkte und Auswirkungen, Zürich 1998; Epiney/Siegwart/Cottier/Refaeil, Schweizerische Demokratie und Europäische Union, Bern 1998; Veröffentlichungen des Schweizerischen Instituts für Rechtsvergleichung, Band 38: Staatsrechtliche Auswirkungen einer Mitgliedschaft in der Europäischen Union, Zürich 1999.

[79] Art. 46 EUV. Eine Änderung ist auch durch den Vertrag von Nizza nicht vorgesehen.

[80] Vgl. hierzu auch Meinhard Hilf, Europäische Union und nationale Identität der Mitgliedstaaten, in: Randelzhofer u.a. (Hrsg.), GS Grabitz, München 1995, S. 157 (162 f., 169); Bengt Beutler, in: GTE, Art. F EUV, Rn. 21.

[81] Adelheid Puttler, in: Christian Calliess/Matthias Ruffert (Hrsg.), Kommentar zu EU-Vertrag und EG-Vertrag, Neuwied 1999, Art. 6 EUV Rn. 190; Meinhard Hilf, Europäische Union und nationale Identität der Mitgliedstaaten, in: Randelzhofer u.a. (Hrsg.), GS Grabitz, München 1995, S. 157 (161).

[82] Meinhard Hilf, in: Eberhard Grabitz/Meinhard Hilf (Hrsg.), EU, Art. F EUV, Rn. 8.

[83] Bericht des Bundesrates vom 24 August 1988 über die Stellung der Schweiz im europäischen Integrationsprozess, BBl 1988 III 249, 373, Separatdruck S. 125.

[84] Bericht des Bundesrates vom 18. Mai 1992 über einen Beitritt der Schweiz zur Europäischen Gemeinschaft, BBl. 1992 IV, 1 (23); vgl. auch Integrationsbericht 1999 des Bundesrates vom 3. Februar 1999, BBl 1999, 3935 ff., Separatdruck, S. 319 ff.

[85] Adelheid Puttler, in: Christian Calliess/Matthias Ruffert (Hrsg.), Kommentar zu EU-Vertrag und EG-Vertrag, Neuwied 1999, Art. 6 EUV Rn. 194.

[86] Art. 192 Abs. 1 BV.

[87] Grundlegend Jean François Aubert, Traité de Droit constitutionnel suisse,

Neuchâtel 1967, Rn. 352 ff.; siehe auch Ulrich Häfelin/Walter Haller, Schweizerisches Bundesstaatsrecht, 5. Aufl., Zürich 2001, Rn. 1763 ff. m.w.N.

[88] Art. 139 Abs. 3, 193 Abs. 4 und 194 Abs. 2 BV. Dabei handelt es sich um einen autonomen Begriff des schweizerischen Rechts, der im Einzelfall über die von der Völkergemeinschaft unzweifelhaft als ius cogens i.S.v. Art. 53 S. 2 und 64 der Wiener Vertragsrechtskonvention hinausgehen kann. Vgl. hierzu Bundesversammlung, BBl 1996 I 1355 (Non-Refoulement-Gebot) sowie Giovanni Biaggini, Das Verhältnis der Schweiz zur internationalen Gemeinschaft, AJP1999, S. 728 ff.

[89] Im Gegensatz etwa zur „Ewigkeitsgarantie" gem. Art. 79 Abs. 3 des deutschen Grundgesetzes.

[90] Vgl. hierzu und zum Folgenden Luzius Wildhaber , in: Jean François Aubert u.a. (Hrsg.), Kommentar zur Bundesverfassung, Art. 118, Rn. 23 ff. (m.w.N.).

[91] Luzius Wildhaber , in: Jean François Aubert u.a. (Hrsg.), Kommentar zur Bundesverfassung, Art. 118, Rn. 122.

[92] Gegen solche Schranken z.B. Jean François Aubert, Traité de Droit constitutionnel suisse, Neuchâtel 1967, Rn. 324 ff.; François Bellanger, in: Thürer/Aubert/Müller (Hrsg.), Verfassungsrecht der Schweiz/Droit constitutionnel suisse, Zürich 2001, § 79, Rn. 14 f.; Auer/Malinverni/Hottelier, Droit constitutionnel suisse, vol. I, Bern 2000, Rn. 1370; zurückhaltend auch Luzius Wildhaber, in: Jean François Aubert u.a. (Hrsg.), Kommentar zur Bundesverfassung, Art. 118, Rn. 119 ff.; Pierre Tschannen, Eidgenössisches Organisationsrecht, Bern 1997, S. 242.

[93] Art. 47 BV: „Der Bund wahrt die Eigenständigkeit der Kantone." Vgl. auch Art. 51 bis 53 BV.

[94] Zur Mitwirkung der Kantone an der Willensbildung des Bundes vgl. Art. 42 ff. BV.

[95] Lidija Basta/Thomas Fleiner, Federalism, Federal State and Decentralisation, in: Federalism and Multiethnic State, The Case of Switzerland, PIFF 16, Freiburg i.Ue. 1996, S. 1 ff.

[96] Daran ändert auch die Entsendung von Länderministern in den Rat, welche nach Art. 203 Abs. 1 EGV zulässig ist, nichts, da diese eben nicht die Gliedstaaten, sondern den gesamten jeweiligen Mitgliedstaat vertreten.

[97] Astrid Epiney, Gemeinschaftsrecht und Föderalismus, EuR 1994, S. 301 (316).

[98] Konsultationsverfahren als Teil des Gesetzgebungsverfahrens, das staatliche Stellen (Kantone, Behörden etc.) und Private (Verbände etc.) einbezieht und mit dem Vernehmlassungsbericht abschliesst. Vgl. hierzu Art. 147 BV und Verordnung über das Vernehmlassungsverfahren vom 17. Juni 1991, SR 172.062. Siehe ausserdem Luzius Mader, in: Thürer/Aubert/Müller (Hrsg.), Verfassungsrecht der Schweiz/Droit constitutionnel suisse, Zürich 2001, S. 1065 f.

[99] Nach Art. 69 BV sind die Kantone für den Bereich der Kultur zuständig.

[100] Gemäss Art. 129 Abs. 2 Satz 2 BV kann der Bund zwar das Steuersystem und das Verfahren harmonisieren, nicht aber die Steuertarife und die Steuersätze.

[101] Art. 2 Abs. 2 BV.

[102] Gemäss Art. 69 Abs. 2 BV bestehen punktuelle Kompetenzen des Bundes im Bereich der Kultur (Unterstützung „von kulturellen Bestrebungen von gesamtschweizerischem Interesse" sowie die Förderung von „Kunst und Musik, insbesondere im Bereich der Ausbildung"), dabei wird er jedoch ausdrücklich zur

„Rücksicht auf die kulturelle und die sprachliche Vielfalt des Landes" verpflichtet.

[103] Bundesrat, Bericht über die Aussenpolitik der Schweiz in den 90er Jahren mit Anhang: Bericht zur Neutralität, BBl 1994 I 153, 210 ff. Vgl. hierzu und zum Folgenden Astrid Epiney, in: Thürer/Aubert/Müller (Hrsg.), Verfassungsrecht der Schweiz/Droit constitutionnel suisse, Zürich 2001, S. 877 f.; Laurent Goetschel, Die Zukunft der Neutralität im Rahmen der GASP: Widerspruch, Gleichgültigkeit oder Ergänzung?, in: Cottier/Kop_e, Der Beitritt der Schweiz zur Europäischen Union, Zürich 1998, S. 637 ff., jeweils m.w.N.

[104] Vgl. hierzu Walter Kälin, Verfassungsgrundsätze der schweizerischen Aussenpolitik, ZSR 1986 II, S. 249 (330 ff.).

[105] Bundesrat, Bericht über die Aussenpolitik der Schweiz in den 90er Jahren mit Anhang: Bericht zur Neutralität, BBl 1994 I 153, 210 ff.; Astrid Epiney, in: Thürer/Aubert/Müller (Hrsg.), Verfassungsrecht der Schweiz/Droit constitutionnel suisse, Zürich 2001, S. 878; Laurent Goetschel, Die Zukunft der Neutralität im Rahmen der GASP: Widerspruch, Gleichgültigkeit oder Ergänzung?, in: Cottier/Kop_e, Der Beitritt der Schweiz zur Europäischen Union, Zürich 1998, S. 637 (643 f.).

[106] Zitiert nach Peter Häberle, Die Verfassung „im Kontext", in: Thürer/Aubert/Müller (Hrsg.), Verfassungsrecht der Schweiz/Droit constitutionnel suisse, Zürich 2001, S. 17.

[107] Ulrich Häfelin/Walter Haller, Schweizerisches Bundesstaatsrecht, 5. Aufl., Zürich 2001, Rn. 221.

[108] Vgl. hierzu die Nachweise in den Erläuterungen des Präsidiums, abgedruckt in EuGRZ 2000, S. 559 ff.

[109] Vgl. die Übersicht bei Auer/Malinverni/Hottelier, Droit constitutionnel suisse, vol. II, Bern 2000, N 70-76.

[110] S. dazu Daniel Thürer, Verfassungsrecht und Völkerrecht, in: Thürer/Aubert/Müller (Hrsg.), Verfassungsrecht der Schweiz/Droit constitutionnel suisse, Zürich 2001, S. 179 (192 f.); Walter Kälin, Integration by Constitutional Review: The Case of the Swiss Federal Tribunal, in: Bieber/Wiedmer (Hrsg.), L'espace constitutionnel européen/Der europäische Verfassungsraum, Zürich 1995, S. 209-223 (218 f.).

[111] Ulrich Häfelin/Walter Haller, Schweizerisches Bundesstaatsrecht, 5. Aufl., Zürich 2001, Rn. 225.

[112] Ulrich Häfelin/Walter Haller, Schweizerisches Bundesstaatsrecht, 5. Aufl., Zürich 2001, Rn. 223.

[113] Art. 84 ff. des Bundesgesetzes über die Organisation der Bundesrechtspflege (OG). Vgl. dazu nur Ulrich Häfelin/Walter Haller, Schweizerisches Bundesstaatsrecht, 5. Aufl., Zürich 2001, Rn. 1929 ff. m.w.N.

[114] Vgl. Art. 14 Charta. Kritisch zur Anerkennung eines Rechts auf Bildung auf europäischer Ebene z.B. Ingolf Pernice, DVBl 2000, S. 847 (853), Albrecht Weber, NJW 2000, S. 537 (541).

[115] Jörg Paul Müller, Grundrechte in der Schweiz, 3. Aufl. Bern 1999, S. 651 f.

[116] Nach Art. 19 BV besteht ein Anspruch auf ausreichenden und unentgeltlichen Grundschulunterricht.

[117] BGE 120 I 22 E2 S. 24 f. (Anouk Hasler).

[118] Jörg Paul Müller, Grundrechte in der Schweiz, 3. Aufl. Bern 1999, S. 651 f. (m.w.N.).

[119] Art. 17 Abs. 2 S. 2 Charta.

[120] Ulrich Häfelin/Walter Haller, Schweizerisches Bundesstaatsrecht, 5. Aufl., Zürich 2001, Rn. 774 f. Die gleiche Möglichkeit besteht auch für Massnahmen zur Förderung von Behinderten, vgl. Art. 8 Abs. 4 BV.

[121] Ulrich Häfelin/Walter Haller, Schweizerisches Bundesstaatsrecht, 5. Aufl., Zürich 2001, Rn. 788-792.

[122] S. hierzu Georg Müller, in: Jean François Aubert u.a. (Hrsg.), Kommentar zur Bundesverfassung, Art. 4, Rn. 137c; Beatrice Weber-Dürler, Aktuelle Aspekte der Gleichberechtigung von Mann und Frau, ZBJV 128 (1992), S. 357 (368 ff.); dies., in: Thürer/Aubert/Müller (Hrsg.), Verfassungsrecht der Schweiz/Droit constitutionnel suisse, Zürich 2001, S. 672 f. (m.w.N.).

[123] Vgl. Art. 23 Abs. 2 Charta.

[124] Art. 11 BV. Vgl. hierzu Art. 24 und 32 Charta.

[125] So auch Ulrich Häfelin/Walter Haller, Schweizerisches Bundesstaatsrecht, 5. Aufl., Zürich 2001, Rn. 910.

[126] Zu den sozialen Grundrechten in der Schweiz siehe Pascal Mahon, Droits sociaux et réforme de la Constitution, in: Piermarco Zen-Ruffinen/Andreas Auer (Hrsg.), Etudes en l'honneur de Jean-François Aubert, Basel 1996, S. 385 ff.; Margrith Bigler-Eggenberger, Nachgeführte Bundesverfassung: Sozialziele oder Sozialrechte?, in: FS Hangartner, St. Gallen 1998, S. 497 ff.

[127] Allerdings bestehen auch im Falle der Grundrechtscharta noch Unklarheiten vor allem bei den sozialen Rechten bezüglich ihres sachlichen Gehalts und der Abgrenzung von blossen Zielen der Union. Vgl. z.B. Jürgen Schwarze, Der Grundrechtsschutz für Unternehmen in der Europäischen Grundrechtscharta, EuZW 2001, S. 517 (521 f.).

[128] Art. 28 BV. Auch hier standen internationalrechtliche Gewährleistungen Pate, namentlich Art. 11 EMRK, Art. 22 UNO-Pakt II und Art. 8 UNO-Pakt I. Zur Koalitionsfreiheit vgl. z.B. Jörg Paul Müller, Grundrechte in der Schweiz, 3. Aufl. Bern 1999, S. 349 ff. und Ulrich Häfelin/Walter Haller, Schweizerisches Bundesstaatsrecht, 5. Aufl., Zürich 2001, Rn. 566 ff.

[129] Vgl. Art. 28 Abs. 2 BV.

[130] Vgl. Art. 34 Abs. 3 Charta.

[131] Insbesondere Art. 11 UNO-Pakt I. Vgl. hierzu Jörg Paul Müller, Grundrechte in der Schweiz, 3. Aufl. Bern 1999, S. 173 ff.

[132] Jörg Paul Müller, Grundrechte in der Schweiz, 3. Aufl. Bern 1999, S. 178.

[133] Art. 29 Abs. 3 BV.

[134] Vgl. oben.

[135] Die Schweiz hat auch die Europäische Sozialcharta vom 18.10.1961, der eine Reihe der Bestimmungen der Charta nachgebildet sind (vgl. die Erläuterungen des Präsidiums, abgedruckt in EuGRZ 2000, S. 559 ff.) , zwar am 6. Mai 1976 unterzeichnet, aber nicht ratifiziert.

[136] So findet sich z.B. der Grundsatz der Nachhaltigkeit ausser in der Präambel noch in Art. 2, 54, 73 BV, das Ziel des Umweltschutzes in Art. 2 Abs. 4, 74 BV, des Verbraucherschutzes in Art. 97 BV und des Gesundheitsschutzes in Art. 118 BV.

[137] Art. 29 BV. Dieser gewährt Anspruch auf rechtliches Gehör, auf gleiche und gerechte Behandlung sowie auf Beurteilung innert angemessener Frist und gilt für Gerichte Verwaltungsbehörden gleichermassen.

[138] Art. 9 BV.

[139] Ebenso René Rhinow, Die Bundesverfassung 2000, Basel 2000, S. 101.

[140] Vgl. die Erläuterungen des Präsidiums, abgedruckt in EuGRZ 2000, S. 559 (569) m.w.N.

[141] Deutlicher insoweit EuGH Rs. C-292/97, Rn. 45, auf den sich die Erläuterungen des Präsidiums zu Art. 52 Charta berufen, abgedruckt in EuGRZ 2000, S. 559 (569).

[142] Kritisch zur Rechtsprechung des EuGH insoweit Martin Nettesheim, Grundrechtliche Prüfdichte durch den EuGH, EuZW 1995, S. 106 (107); Peter M. Huber, Das Kooperationsverhältnis zwischen BverfG und EuGH in Grundrechtsfragen, EuZW 1997, 517 (521); vgl. auch Pernice, Eine Grundrechte-Charta für die Europäische Union, DVBl 2000, S. 847 (850); Eckhart Pache, Die Europäische Grundrechtscharta, EuR 2001, S. 475 (487 ff.); Armin von Bogdandy, Grundrechtsgemeinschaft als Integrationsziel? Grundrechte und das Wesen der Europäischen Union, in: JZ 2001, S. 157-171; zugleich veröffentlicht als Heft Nr. 115 vom Zentrum für Europäisches Wirtschaftsrecht, Rheinische Friedrichs-Wilhelms-Universität Bonn, S. 1 (26 ff.). Ausführlich hierzu jetzt Michael Vögler, Defizite beim Schutz der Berufsfreiheit durch BVerfG und EuGH, Baden-Baden 2001.

[143] Art. 6 BV: „Jede Person nimmt Verantwortung für sich selber wahr und trägt nach ihren Kräften zur Bewältigung der Aufgaben in Staat und Gesellschaft bei.“. Vgl. auch Art. 12 BV: „Wer in Not gerät und nicht in der Lage ist, für sich selbst zu sorgen...“ sowie Art. 41 Abs. 1 BV: „...in Ergänzung zu persönlicher Verantwortung und privater Initiative...“.

[144] Vgl. nur Daniel Thürer, Verfassungsrecht und Völkerrecht, in: Thürer/Aubert/Müller (Hrsg.), Verfassungsrecht der Schweiz/Droit constitutionnel suisse, Zürich 2001, S. 179 (192 f.); Walter Kälin, Integration by Constitutional Review: The Case of the Swiss Federal Tribunal, in: Bieber/Wiedmer (Hrsg.), L'espace constitutionnel européen/Der europäische Verfassungsraum, Zürich 1995, S. 209-223 (218 f.)..

[145] Vgl. dazu oben die Ausführungen zur Gleichheit von Mann und Frau.

[146] Siehe oben A.I.3.

[147] BGE 99 Ib 39 vom 2. März 1973, S. 44, E. 3 (Schubert); deutsche Übersetzung in Praxis 62, 1973, Nr. 106, S. 392. Vgl. hierzu aus der umfangreichen Literatur nur Alberto Achermann, Der Vorrang des Völkerrechts im schweizerischen Recht, in: Cottier/Achermann/Wüger/Zellweger (Hrsg.), Der Staatsvertrag im schweizerischen Verfassungsrecht, Bern 2000, S. 33 (44 ff.); Daniel Thürer, Verfassungsrecht und Völkerrecht, in: Thürer/Aubert/Müller (Hrsg.), Verfassungsrecht der Schweiz/Droit constitutionnel suisse, Zürich 2001, S. 179 (188 ff.); Nicolas Michel, L'imprégnation du droit étatique par l'ordre juridique international, in: Thürer/Aubert/Müller (Hrsg.), Verfassungsrecht der Schweiz/Droit constitutionnel suisse, Zürich 2001, S. 63 (68 ff.), jeweils m.w.N.

[148] Vgl. hierzu nur Mark E. Villiger, EMRK und UNO-Menschenrechtspakte, in:

Thürer/Aubert/Müller (Hrsg.), Verfassungsrecht der Schweiz/Droit constitutionnel suisse, Zürich 2001, S. 647 ff. m.w.N.

[149] So auch Yvo Hangartner, Schweizerische Nation und europäische Integration, in: Max-Emanuel Geis; Dieter Lorenz (Hrsg.), Staat – Kirche – Verwaltung, Festschrift für Hartmut Maurer, München 2001, S. 949 (955).

[150] Heinrich Koller, Globalisierung und Internationalisierung des Wirtschaftsrechts, in: Schweizerischer Juristenverein, Referate und Mitteilungen, 2000, S. 313 (356).

[151] Etwa entsprechend der Rechtsprechung des deutschen Bundesverfassungsgerichts, vgl. die Urteile BVerfGE 73, 339 ff. (Solange II), 89, 155 ff. (Maastricht) und EuZW 2000, S. 702 ff. (Bananenmarktordnung).

[152] So jedenfalls die Botschaft des Bundesrates zum EWR vom 18. Mai 1992, BBl. 1992 IV, 1 (92). Für eine Ermächtigung des Bundesgerichts, „den Vollzug des EG-Rechts aufzuhalten, sofern der Grundrechtsschutz innerhalb der EG absinken oder im Einzelfall den Kerngehalt von Grundrechten der Bundesverfassung verletzen würde“: Jörg Paul Müller, Grundrechts- und Demokratiedefizite als Legitimationsprobleme der EG – Überlegungen zu einem Beitritt der Schweiz, ZSR 1991, S. 103 (115). Ebenso Thomas Cottier, Recht und Macht im Europäischen Wirtschaftsraum, AJP 1992, S. 1206 (1210), Fn. 50: schliesst „einen punktuellen Vorrang nationaler Grundrechte vor EWR-Recht nicht aus“; Maya Hertig, L'influence de l'adhésion à l'Union européenne sur la protection des droits fondamentaux en Suisse, in: Cottier/Kop_e, Der Beitritt der Schweiz zur Europäischen Union, Zürich 1998, S. 349 (375). A.A. offenbar Jean François Egli, Le Tribunal fédéral face à l'Espace économique européen, in: Olivier Jacot-Guillarmod (Hrsg.), Accord EEE, Commentaires et réflexions, 1992, S. 617 (619). Siehe ausserdem Rainer J. Schweizer, Auswirkungen einer Mitgliedschaft in der Europäischen Union auf das schweizerische Verfassungsrecht, in: Cottier/Kop_e, Der Beitritt der Schweiz zur Europäischen Union, Zürich 1998, S. 515 (542).

[153] BGE 125 II 417 E4c S. 425 (PKK). Vgl. dazu Jörg Paul Müller, Verfassung und Gesetz, recht 2000, S. 123 ff.

[154] Vgl. BBl 1992 III 1185. Mit der Ablehnung des EWR-Beitritts war das Gesuch gegenstandslos geworden und wurde nicht weiter verfolgt.

[155] Vgl. z.B. Jean François Aubert, L'EEE et la démocratie suisse, in: Olivier Jacot-Guillarmod (Hrsg.), Accord EEE, Commentaires et réflexions, 1992, S. 792 ff.; Astrid Epiney/Karine Siegwart (Hrsg.), Direkte Demokratie und Europäische Union, Fribourg 1997; Astrid Epiney/Karine Siegwart/Michael Cottier/Nora Rafaeil, Schweizerische Demokratie und Europäische Union, Fribourg 1998; Pascal Mahon/Christoph Müller, Adhésion de la Suisse à l'Union européenne et démocratie directe, in: Cottier/Kop_e, Der Beitritt der Schweiz zur Europäischen Union, Zürich 1998, S. 449 ff.; Andreas Kellerhals/Andreas Auer/Bertil Cottier/Nicole Mathé/Frank Emmert, Staatsrechtliche Auswirkungen einer Mitgliedschaft in der Europäischen Union, Zürich 1999; Christoph Müller, Direkte Demokratie: Ein Hindernis für einen EU-Beitritt der Schweiz?, in: Martin Bertschi u.a. (Hrsg.), Demokratie und Freiheit, Stuttgart u.a. 1999, S. 229 ff., jeweils m.w.N.

[156] Vgl. z.B. die Übersicht bei Wolf Linder, Schweizerische Demokratie, Bern u.a. 1999, S. 242 ff.

[157] Jean François Aubert, L'EEE et la démocratie suisse, in: Olivier Jacot-

Guillarmod (Hrsg.), Accord EEE, Commentaires et réflexions, 1992, S. 792 (806); Astrid Epiney/Karine Siegwart , Direkte Demokratie und Europäische Union, Fribourg 1997, S. 120; Astrid Epiney, EG, EWR und die Auswirkungen auf die schweizerische Verfassungsgerichtsbarkeit und die direkte Demokratie, SJZ 1992, 261 (271 f.).

[158] Integrationsbericht 1999 des Bundesrates vom 3. Februar 1999, Sonderdruck EDMZ, S. 333.

[159] Astrid Epiney/Karine Siegwart/Michael Cottier/Nora Rafaeil, Schweizerische Demokratie und Europäische Union, Fribourg 1998, S. 332 f.; Heinrich Koller, Globalisierung und Internationalisierung des Wirtschaftsrechts, in: Schweizerischer Juristenverein, Referate und Mitteilungen, 2000, S. 313 (357)

[160] Das Ausmass dieser Einschränkungen wurde in verschiedenen Studien quantitativ und qualitativ untersucht. Vgl. z.B. Integrationsbericht 1999 des Bundesrates vom 3. Februar 1999, Sonderdruck EDMZ, S. 333 ff.; Andreas Kellerhals/Andreas Auer/Bertil Cottier/Nicole Mathé/Frank Emmert, Staatsrechtliche Auswirkungen einer Mitgliedschaft in der Europäischen Union, Zürich 1999; Zusammenfassend Christoph Müller, Direkte Demokratie: Ein Hindernis für einen EU-Beitritt der Schweiz?, in: Martin Bertschi u.a. (Hrsg.), Demokratie und Freiheit, Stuttgart u.a. 1999, S. 229 (242 ff.).

[161] Astrid Epiney/Karine Siegwart/Michael Cottier/Nora Rafaeil, Schweizerische Demokratie und Europäische Union, Fribourg 1998, S. 340 f.; Wolf Linder, Erfordert die Mitgliedschaft in der Europäischen Union eine Anpassun des schweizerischen Regierungssystems?, in: Cottier/Kop_e, Der Beitritt der Schweiz zur Europäischen Union, Zürich 1998, S. 427 (445); Christoph Müller, Direkte Demokratie: Ein Hindernis für einen EU-Beitritt der Schweiz?, in: Martin Bertschi u.a. (Hrsg.), Demokratie und Freiheit, Stuttgart u.a. 1999, S. 229 (245 ff.).

[162] Integrationsbericht 1999 des Bundesrates vom 3. Februar 1999, BBl 1999 3935 (4271) = Sonderdruck EDMZ, S. 332.

[163] Vgl. nur Wolf Linder, Erfordert die Mitgliedschaft in der Europäischen Union eine Anpassun des schweizerischen Regierungssystems?, in: Cottier/Kop_e, Der Beitritt der Schweiz zur Europäischen Union, Zürich 1998, S. 427 (434 ff.).

[164] Heinrich Koller, Der schweizerische Gesetzgeber vor der internationalen Herausforderung: Erfahrungen mit „EUROLEX“ – „SWISSLEX“ – „GATTLEX“, ZBl 1994, S. 241 (252).

[165] Vgl. hierzu nur Wolfgang Wiegand/Marcel Brühlhart, Die Auslegung von autonom nachvollzogenem Recht der Europäischen Gemeinschaft, Swiss papers on European Integration, Bd 23, Bern 1999; Roger Mallepell, Der Einfluss des Gemeinschaftsrechts auf die schweizerische Gesetzgebung 1993-1995, Swiss Papers on European Integration, Bd. 21, Bern 1999; Wolfgang Wiegand, Zur Anwendung von autonom nachvollzogenem EU-Privatrecht, in: Forstmoser/von der Crone/Weber/Zobl (Hrsg.), Festschrift zum 60. Geburtstag von Roger Zäch, Zürich 1999, S. 171 ff.; Bruno Spinner/Daniel Maritz, EG-Kompatibilität des schweizerischen Wirtschaftsrechts: Vom autonomen zum systematischen Nachvollzug, in: Forstmoser/von der Crone/Weber/Zobl (Hrsg.), Festschrift zum 60. Geburtstag von Roger Zäch, Zürich 1999, S. 127 ff.; Bettina Kahil-Wolff/Lars-Gerrit Lüßmann, Die Angleichung des Schweizer Rechts an europäisches Gemeinschaftsrecht am Beispiel des Betriebsübergangs, ZIAS 2000, S. 381 ff.

[166] Vgl. hierzu und zum Folgenden Bernhard Ehrenzeller, Auswirkungen eines EU-Beitritts aud die Bundesversammlung und ihr Verhältnis zum Bundesrat, in: Cottier/Kop_e, Der Beitritt der Schweiz zur Europäischen Union, Zürich 1998, S. 293 ff.; Astrid Epiney/Karine Siegwart/Michael Cottier/Nora Rafaeil, Schweizerische Demokratie und Europäische Union, Fribourg 1998, S. 338 ff., jeweils m.w.N.

[167] So auch Astrid Epiney/Karine Siegwart/Michael Cottier/Nora Rafaeil, Schweizerische Demokratie und Europäische Union, Fribourg 1998, S. 338 ff.; Daniel Thürer, Die schweizerische Bundesversammlung und die Europäische Gemeinschaft – Zu den Chancen einer verstärkten parlamentarischen Legitimierung des europäischen Gemeinschaftsrechts im nationalen Rahmen, in: Parlamentsdienste (Hrsg.), Das Parlament – „Oberste Gewalt des Bundes?“, Festschrift der Bundesversammlung zur 700-Jahr-Feier der Eidgenossenschaft, Bern/Stuttgart 1991, 454 ff.; Bernhard Ehrenzeller, Auswirkungen eines EU-Beitritts auf die Bundesversammlung und ihr Verhältnis zum Bundesrat, in: Cottier/Kop_e, Der Beitritt der Schweiz zur Europäischen Union, Zürich 1998, S. 293 (312 ff.).

[168] Vgl. z.B. Art. 23 des deutschen Grundgesetzes. Siehe hierzu z.B. Ingolf Pernice, Art. 23, in: Horst Dreier (Hrsg.), Grundgesetz-Kommentar, Bd. II, Tübingen 1998.

[169] Vgl. hierzu sowie den Zwischenbericht der von Kurt Eichenberger geleiteten Arbeitsgruppe Führungsstrukturen des Bundes (AGFB) vom 23. November 1991: Notwendigkeiten und Kriterien einer Regierungsreform, Modelle des Regierungssystems, BBl 1992 II 1018 (1042 ff.).

[170] Rainer J. Schweizer, Auswirkungen einer Mitgliedschaft in der Europäischen Union auf das schweizerische Verfassungsrecht, in: Cottier/Kop_e, Der Beitritt der Schweiz zur Europäischen Union, Zürich 1998, S.515 (536).

[171] Für eine Reform im Sinne der zweiten Variante die Botschaft zur Staatsleitungsreform vom 19. Dezember 2001. Vgl. hierzu Raoul Blindenbacher/Peter Hablützel/Bruno Letsch (Hrsg.), Vom Service Public zum Service au Public, Zürich 2000; Martin Kayser/Dagmar Richter, Die neue schweizerische Bundesverfassung, ZaöRV 1999, S. 985 (995 f.); Heinrich Koller, Regierung und Verwaltung, in: Thürer/Aubert/Müller (Hrsg.), Verfassungsrecht der Schweiz/Droit constitutionnel suisse, Zürich 2001, S. 1131 (1149ff.) (m.w.N.).

[172] Martin Kayser/Dagmar Richter, Die neue schweizerische Bundesverfassung, ZaöRV 1999, S. 985 (996).

[173] Vgl. nur Gil Carlos Rodriguez Iglesias, Zu den Grenzen der verfahrensrechtlichen Autonomie der Mitgliedstaaten bei der Anwendung des Gemeinschaftsrechts, EuGRZ 1997, S. 289 ff. Ausführlich Stefan Kadelbach, Allgemeines Verwaltungsrecht unter europäischem Einfluss, Tübingen 1999, S. 110 ff.

[174] Botschaft des Bundesrates zum EWR vom 18. Mai 1992, BBl. 1992 IV, 1 (433 ff.); Botschaft II über die Anpassung des Bundesrechts an das EWR-Recht vom 15. Juni 1992, BBl. 1992 V, 520 (725 ff.).

[175] Ausserdem werden u.a. eine Gesetzgebungskompetenz des Bundes für das Zivil- und das Strafprozessrecht geschaffen und ein Bundesstraf- und ein Bundesverwaltungsgericht errichtet. Vgl. zur Justizreform allgemein Botschaft des Bundesrates über eine neue Bundesverfassung vom 14. Januar 1997, BBl. 1997 I, 1

(487 ff.); Martin Kayser/Dagmar Richter, Die neue schweizerische Bundesverfassung, ZaöRV 1999, S. 985 (992 ff.). Zur Umsetzung auf Gesetzesebene siehe die Botschaft des Bundesrates zur Totalrevision der Bundesrechtspflege vom 28. Februar 2001, BBl. 2001 I, 4207 ff.

[176] Jacot-Guillarmod, Conséquences d'une adhésion à l'Union européenne sur l'organisation judiciaire et le droit procédural suisse, in: Cottier/Kop_e, Der Beitritt der Schweiz zur Europäischen Union, Zürich 1998, S.383 (399 f.).

[177] Daniel Thürer, Schweizer Verfassungsordnung vor der Herausforderung durch die europäische Integration: Perspektiven, Prinzipien und heisse Eisen, in: Perspektive Schweiz, Zürich 1998, S. 184; Andreas Auer, Rückwirkungen der europäischen Integration auf die schweizerische Verfassungsgerichtsbarkeit, SZIER 1991, S. 203 (214 ff.).

[178] Für den Ausbau der Verfassungsgerichtsbarkeit auf Bundesebene z.B. Walter Kälin/Andreas Rieder, Verfassungsgerichtsbarkeit und Demokratie, NZZ vom 22.9.1998, S. 28.

[179] Zur Idee der Modellhaftigkeit der Schweiz s. Georg Kreis, Nach der schweizerischen jetzt die europäische Integration: Zur Idee der schweizerischen Modellhaftigkeit, in: Thürer/Aubert/Müller (Hrsg.), Verfassungsrecht der Schweiz/Droit constitutionnel suisse, Zürich 2001, S. 189 ff.; die Schweiz als Grundlage für ein Modell der zukünftigen Europäischen Union sieht David McKay, Designing Europe.Comparative Lessons from the Federal Experiences, Oxford 2001.

[180] Ulrich Häfelin/Walter Haller, Schweizerisches Bundesstaatsrecht, 5. Aufl., Zürich 2001, Rn. 963, S. 274.

[181] Tobias Jaag, Die Rechtsstellung der Kantone in der Bundesverfassung, in: Thürer/Aubert/Müller (Hrsg.), Verfassungsrecht der Schweiz/Droit constitutionnel suisse, Zürich 2001, S. 473 (477).

[182] Rainer J. Schweizer, Homogenität und Vielfalt im schweizerischen Staatsrecht, in: Thürer/Aubert/Müller (Hrsg.), Verfassungsrecht der Schweiz/Droit constitutionnel suisse, Zürich 2001, S. 161 (162).

[183] Blaise Knapp, La répartition des compétences et la coopération de la Confédération et des cantons, in: Thürer/Aubert/Müller (Hrsg.), Verfassungsrecht der Schweiz/Droit constitutionnel suisse, Zürich 2001, S. 457 (468).

[184] S. mit weiteren Hinweisen zur Reformdiskussion des schweizerischen Föderalismus Rainer J. Schweizer, Homogenität und Vielfalt im schweizerischen Staatsrecht, in: Thürer/Aubert/Müller (Hrsg.), Verfassungsrecht der Schweiz/Droit constitutionnel suisse, Zürich 2001, S. 161 (162/163).

[185] Rainer J. Schweizer, Homogenität und Vielfalt im schweizerischen Staatsrecht, in: Thürer/Aubert/Müller (Hrsg.), Verfassungsrecht der Schweiz/Droit constitutionnel suisse, Zürich 2001, S. 161 (164).

[186] S. dazu Kurt Nuspliger, Wechselwirkungen zwischen neueren Kantonsverfassungen und der Bundesverfassung, in: Die neue Bundesverfassung, Bern 2000, S. 63 (87 ff. m.w.H).

[187] Bundesrecht und kantonales Recht haben schliesslich eine gemeinsame Grundlage in der Bundesverfassung. S. Rainer J. Schweizer, Homogenität und Vielfalt im schweizerischen Staatsrecht, in: Thürer/Aubert/Müller (Hrsg.), Verfassungsrecht der Schweiz/Droit constitutionnel suisse, Zürich 2001, S. 161 (168).

[188] Zur Beteiligung der Kantone an der Aussenpolitik des Bundes siehe auch Dieter

Freiburghaus, Die Schweiz – Der Föderalismus nach der neuen Bundesverfassung und die Mitwirkung der Kantone an der Aussenpolitik, in: Europäisches Zentrum für Föderalismus-Forschung Tübingen, Jahrbuch des Föderalismus 2001, S. 296 (300 ff.).

[189] S. SR 138.1 und www.eda.admin.ch zur Mitwirkung der Kantone an der Aussenpolitik des Bundes.

[190] Die Liste enthält ein Inventar der wichtigsten Auslandaktivitäten der Departemente, s. Botschaft vom 15.12.1997 zum Bundesgesetz über die Mitwirkung der Kantone an der Aussenpolitik des Bundes, BBl 1998 I 1168.

[191] Für Deutschland s. Art. 23 GG.

[192] Ausführlich zur Mitwirkung der Kantone an der Europapolitik im Fall eines Beitritts: Jean-François Aubert, Mitwirkung der Kantone an der europäischen Politik im Falle eines Beitritts der Schweizerischen Eidgenossenschaft zur Europäischen Union, in: Konferenz der Kantonsregierungen (Hrsg.), Die Kantone vor der Herausforderung eines EU-Beitritts, Zürich 2001, S. 159 ff.

[193] Rainer J. Schweizer, Homogenität und Vielfalt im schweizerischen Staatsrecht, in: Thürer/Aubert/Müller (Hrsg.), Verfassungsrecht der Schweiz/Droit constitutionnel suisse, Zürich 2001, S. 161 (175) unter Hinweis auf Konferenz der Kantonsregierungen, Auswirkungen eines EU-Beitritts auf die Kantone, Zürich 2001 (insb. Beiträge von C. Jeanrenaud und R. J. Schweizer).

[194] S. vertiefend Ursula Abderhalden, Möglichkeiten und Grenzen der interkantonalen Zusammenarbeit, Diss. Freiburg i.Ue. 1999.

[195] Ursula Abderhalden, Möglichkeiten und Grenzen der interkantonalen Zusammenarbeit, Diss. Freiburg i.Ue. 1999, S. 131.

[196] Als Beispiel sei das Engagement der Kantone Basel, Baselland und Aargau in der Regio Basiliensis genannt, die als Schweizer Partnerin für die Oberrhein-Kooperation wirkt. Ihr Zweck ist es, von schweizerischer Seite Impulse für die Entwicklung des oberrheinischen Raumes zu einer zusammengehörigen europäischen Grenzregion zu geben und bei deren Realisierung mitzuwirken. (S. unter www.regbas.ch)

[197] Aargau, Basel-Landschaft, Basel-Stadt, Bern, Fribourg, Genève, Graubünden, Jura, Luzern, Neuchâtel, Nidwalden, Obwalden, Schwyz, Solothurn, St. Gallen, Thurgau, Ticino, Uri, Valais, Vaud, Zürich, Zug.

[198] S. www.are-regions-europe.org/

[199] Bundesgesetz vom 8. Oktober 1999 über die Förderung der schweizerischen Beteiligung an der Gemeinschaftsinitiative für grenzüberschreitende, transnationale und interregionale Zusammenarbeit (INTERREG III) in den Jahren 2000-2006 (SR 616.9).

[200] S. vertiefend die Beiträge in: Gregory Neugebauer (Hrsg.), Föderalismus in Bewegung - wohin steuert Helvetia?, Zürich 2000.

[201] Gregory Neugebauer, Vom "Schichttorten-Föderalismus" zum "Marmorkuchen-Föderalismus"?, in: Gregory Neugebauer (Hrsg.), Föderalismus in Bewegung - wohin steuert Helvetia?, 2000, S. 10.

[202] Richtlinie 2000/60/EG zur Schaffung eines Ordnungsrahmens für Massnahmen der Gemeinschaft im Bereich der Wasserpolitik (ABl L 327/1 vom 22.12.2000).

[203] So werden in Deutschland für die zukünftige Bewirtschaftung der Gewässer nach der neuen EG-Wasserrahmenrichtlinie die Strom- und Küstengebiete folgenden

Flussgebietseinheiten zugeordnet: Donau, Maas, Rhein, Ems, Weser, Elbe, Oder, Eider, Schlei/ Trave und Warnow/ Peene.

[204] S. zu weiteren Bereichen Rainer J. Schweizer/Stefan Kohler, Auswirkungen eines EU-Beitritts auf die Aufgaben der Kantone, in: Konferenz der Kantonsregierungen (Hrsg.), Die Kantone vor der Herausforderung eines EU-Beitritts, Zürich 2001, S. 9 (25).

[205] S. Botschaft vom 23. Juni 1999, Ziff. 27 (BBl 1999 V 6309 ff.) und das Bundesgesetz vom 8.10.1999 zum Abkommen über die Freizügigkeit (BBl 1999 VIII 8643 ff.). Zu ersten Analysen betr. die bilateralen Abkommen s. Daniel Felder/Christine Kaddous (Hrsg.), Accords bilatéraux Suisse-UE (Commentaires)/Bilaterale Abkommen Schweiz-EU (Erste Analysen), Basel/Bruxelles 2001.

[206] Rainer J. Schweizer, Homogenität und Vielfalt im schweizerischen Staatsrecht, in: Thürer/Aubert/Müller (Hrsg.), Verfassungsrecht der Schweiz/Droit constitutionnel suisse, Zürich 2001, S. 161 (166).

[207] Vgl. die Tabelle für 2000/2001 unter www.crus.ch (Rektorenkonferenz der Schweizer Universitäten).

[208] S. zu den Schwierigkeiten der deutschen Bundesländer mit diesem Eingriff in die nationale Kompetenzordnung: Rainer J. Schweizer/Stefan Kohler, Auswirkungen eines EU-Beitritts auf die Aufgaben der Kantone, in: Konferenz der Kantonsregierungen (Hrsg.), Die Kantone vor der Herausforderung eines EU-Beitritts, Zürich 2001, S. 9 (31).

[209] Rainer J. Schweizer/Stefan Kohler, Auswirkungen eines EU-Beitritts auf die Aufgaben der Kantone, in: Konferenz der Kantonsregierungen (Hrsg.), Die Kantone vor der Herausforderung eines EU-Beitritts, Zürich 2001, S. 9 (34).

[210] Der Umfang dieser Kompetenzbeschränkung würde durch einen Beitritt nicht umfassender, da die Auswirkungen des Freizügigkeitsabkommens schon denen eines Beitritts entsprechen, was die Einschränkung kantonaler Eigenheiten in Bezug auf berufliche Qualifikationserfordernisse betrifft, so Rainer J. Schweizer/Stefan Kohler, Auswirkungen eines EU-Beitritts auf die Aufgaben der Kantone, in: Konferenz der Kantonsregierungen (Hrsg.), Die Kantone vor der Herausforderung eines EU-Beitritts, Zürich 2001, S. 9 (32). Die Autoren erläutern auch die potentiellen Veränderungen in weiteren Bereichen wie Kultur, polizeiliche Zusammenarbeit, Steuerrecht, Raumplanung, Gesundheitswesen und Sozialpolitik.

[211] Thomas Fleiner/Nicole Töpperwien, Chancen und Probleme für den schweizerischen Föderalismus nach einem Beitritt zur Europäischen Union, in: Thomas Cottier/Alwin Kop_e (Hrsg.), Der Beitritt der Schweiz zur Europäischen Union - Brennpunkte und Auswirkungen, Zürich 1998, S. 323 (325).

[212] S. Daniel Thürer, "Europa der Bürger" und Europa der Krämer", Wenig attraktive Phase des Integrationsprozesses, Neue Zürcher Zeitung Nr. 228 vom 11.12.1997, S. 15 (zit. nach Fleiner/Töpperwien, in: Thomas Cottier/Alwin Kop_e (Hrsg.), Der Beitritt der Schweiz zur Europäischen Union - Brennpunkte und Auswirkungen, Zürich 1998, S. 323 (330).

[213] S. zu möglichen Impulsen des schweizerischen Föderalismus für die EU Thomas Fleiner/Nicole Töpperwien, Chancen und Probleme für den schweizerischen Föderalismus nach einem Beitritt zur Europäischen Union, in: Thomas

Cottier/Alwin Kop_e (Hrsg.), Der Beitritt der Schweiz zur Europäischen Union - Brennpunkte und Auswirkungen, Zürich 1998, S. 323 (340 ff.).

[214] So Heidi Hautala und Bruno Kaufmann, Kleine Meisterstücke für das grosse Europa, Öffentlichkeitsprinzip und Volksrechte?, Neue Zürcher Zeitung, Nr. 281 vom 3.12.2001, S. 7.

[215] Siehe hierzu auch Peter Häberle, Die „total" revidierte Bundesverfassung der Schweiz von 1999/2000, in: Max-Emanuel Geis; Dieter Lorenz (Hrsg.), Staat – Kirche – Verwaltung, Festschrift für Hartmut Maurer, München 2001, S. 935 ff.

[216] So ist es sogar nach Yvo Hangartner, Schweizerische Nation und europäische Integration, in: Max-Emanuel Geis; Dieter Lorenz (Hrsg.), Staat – Kirche – Verwaltung, Festschrift für Hartmut Maurer, München 2001, S. 949 (959) „nicht übertrieben, von einem allmählichen De facto-Beitritt der Schweiz durch schrittweise Annäherung an die Union zu sprechen".

QUESTIONNAIRE FOR TOPIC II

Financial Services in the Era of the Euro and E-Commerce:

Does home country control work?

General Rapporteurs
Professor Marc Dassesse
Stuart Isaacs, QC

INTRODUCTION

The great achievement of the Second Banking Directive[1] was formally to remove most of the regulatory obstacles to the effective exercise of the freedom of establishment and the freedom to provide services in the banking sector on a cross-border basis not already removed by the First Banking Directive 1973[2]. It contains the three related pillars on which the EU's legislation not only in the banking sector but in the financial services field as a whole has been built: mutual recognition of authorisations to carry on business granted by Member States to the institutions concerned; minimum harmonisation of the conditions governing the pursuit of the business of banking and the other businesses concerned; and the principle of "home country control". One of the priorities of the Stockholm European Council in March 2001was home country control for all wholesale markets. The essence of the home country control principle is that an institution remains subject to the exclusive control of the supervisory authorities of its home country, wherever in the Community it operates and whether through branches or by the provision of cross-border services. With the introduction of the Euro and the growth of E-commerce, you are invited to reply to the questions below, in the light of the practice and experience of home country control in your country.

AUTHORISATION

1. What procedures exist for the competent authorities in your country to engage in the "prior consultation" envisaged by Article 7 of the Second Banking Directive on the authorisation of a credit institution which is

(1) a subsidiary of a credit institution authorised in another Member State; (2) a subsidiary of the parent undertaking of a credit institution authorised in another Member State; or (3) controlled by the same persons as control a credit institution authorised in another Member State? Are those procedures formal or informal in nature?

2. Have any and, if so, what problems been experienced with the prior consultation process?
3. Are you aware of any cases where the competent authorities have refused authorisation, in particular in accordance with Article 5? If so, in what circumstances has authorisation been refused?
4. Once authorised by its home country, a credit institution may, in accordance with Article 18, carry on any of the activities listed in the Annex either by the establishment of a branch or by way of the provision of services in any other Member State. In this regard:
   (a) By what legislative or other means have the provisions of Article 18 been given effect in your country?
   (b) How effectively has the home country control principle applied?
   (c) Have there been cases in your country where a credit institution is able to provide (on the strength of its home country authorisation) particular services listed in the Annex which credit institutions subject to supervision by your competent authorities are not authorised to provide? If so, what are those services and has this given rise to any problems in practice?
5. In relation to activities *not* listed in the Annex, with what provisions of your national laws or regulations must a credit institution authorised by another Member State comply?
6. Are there cases where such national laws or regulations may not in fact be compatible with the general provisions of Community law? If so, what are they?

THE GENERAL GOOD

7. Under Article 21, host Member States retain certain powers over credit institutions authorised in another Member State. In this regard:
   (a What are the legal rules adopted in your country in the interest of the general good (see Article 21(5))?
   (b) Have the competent authorities exercised their powers under Article 21(5) and, if so, in what circumstances?
   (c) What are the appeal procedures that exist (see Article 21(6))?
   (d) Have there been cases where a credit institution invoked its right of appeal and, if so, how has the court approached the appeal?

THE ESTABLISHMENT OF BRANCHES

8. What, if any, difficulties been experienced with regard to the establishment of branches by a credit institution, where your country is (a) the home Member State and (b) the host Member State of the institution concerned (see Articles 19 and 21)?

THE PROVISION OF CROSS-BORDER SERVICES

9. What, if any, difficulties been experienced with regard to the provision of cross-border services by a credit institution, where your country is (a) the home Member State and (b) the host Member State of the institution concerned (see Articles 20 and 21)?

THE COMPETENT AUTHORITIES

10. What are the national authorities empowered in your country to supervise credit institutions and which are, therefore, the "competent authorities" for the purposes of the Second Banking Directive?
11. Does the national central bank in your country have an involvement in prudential supervision and, if so, what is its role?
12. What is the view in your country about the need for an integrated supervisory authority for the financial services sector as a whole rather than separate authorities for different parts of it, and why?
13. What is the view in your country about the need for the European Central Bank to play a role in prudential supervision, and why?
14. To what extent, if at all, have those views been influenced by the introduction of the Euro and the growth of E-commerce, and why?
15. What relationship do the competent authorities in your country have with the European Central Bank?
16. How, if at all, has human rights legislation affected the competent authorities in your country?
17. Has the introduction of the Euro highlighted any inadequacies in your country in the supervision of credit institutions and the need for further harmonisation at the EU level?

NOTES

[1] Directive 89/646 *OJ* L 386/1 of 15 December 1989.
[2] Directive 73/183 *OJ* L 194/1 of 16 July 1973.

AUSTRIA

Financial Services in the Era of the Euro and E-Commerce:

Does home country control work?

Rapporteur
*Sektionschef Mag. Alfred Lejsek**

A short remarks in the beginning: The answers to the following questionnaire reflect the supervisory practices of banking supervision by the Austrian Ministry of Finance (MoF), which has been the competent authority until end of March 2002. On 1 April 2002 the reorganisation of financial market supervision entered into force, establishing a single regulator provided with the competence of banking, insurance, securities, stock exchange and pension fund supervision. However, we estimate that there will no changes in supervisory practices, therefore the questionnaire points out the actual treatment of the so-called European passport:

AUTHORISATION

1. What procedures exist for the competent authorities in your country to engage in the "prior consultation" envisaged by Article 7 of the Second Banking Directive on the authorisation of a credit institution which is
   (1) a subsidiary of a credit institution authorised in another Member State;
   (2) a subsidiary of the parent undertaking of a credit institution authorised in another member State; or
   (3) controlled by the same persons as control a credit institution authorised in another Member State? Are those procedures formal or informal in nature?

* Austrian Ministry of Finance

As a general remark, Article 7 of the Second Banking Directive dealing with the authorisation of a credit institution, has been fully implemented by Article 4 par. 5 of the Austrian Banking Act, that states:

"Prior to the granting of a license to a credit institution, the Federal Minister of Finance shall inform the competent authorities of another Member State of the application, if

- *the application pursuant to par. 3 has been filed by a subsidiary of a credit institution within the meaning of the first indent of Art. 1 of Directive 77/780/EEC authorised in another Member State or by an investment firm authorised in another Member State;*
- *the application pursuant of par. 3 has been filed by a subsidiary which is itself a subsidiary of a credit institution within the meaning of the first indent of Art 1 of Directive 77/780/EEC authorised in another Member State or of an investment firm authorised in another Member State;*
- *the credit institution is controlled by the same natural and legal persons as control a credit institution within the meaning of the first indent of Art 1 of Directive 77/780/EEC authorised in another Member State or an investment firm authorised in another Member State."*

According to the Austrian Constitution, all administrative bodies have to meet the principle of legality, therefore the MoF is obliged to keep above-mentioned provisions as a binding regulation.

2. Have any and, if so, what problems been experienced with the prior consultation process?

Concerning the prior consultation process no problems are known.

3. Are you aware of any cases where the competent authorities have refused authorisation, in particular in accordance with Article 5? If so, in what circumstances has authorisation been refused?

We (Ministry of Finance) are not aware of any cases where the competent authority has refused authorisation.

4. Once authorised by its home country, a credit institution may, in accordance with Article 18, carry on any of the activities listed in the Annex either by the establishment of a branch or by way of the provision of services in any other Member State. In this regard:

a) By what legislative or other means have the provisions of Article 18 been given effect in your country?

Art. 18 of 2BCD is implemented by Art. 9 –17 of the Austrian Banking Act.

b) How effectively has the home country control principle applied?

The principle of home country control is applied by the so-called "notification process" between the competent authorities (home and host) and - in addition - by a letter to the credit institution stating that – apart from home country regime – some further legal requirements (general good, "Allgemeininteresse") are applicable. The regulations applicable to foreign EC-branches are enumerated in the Austrian Banking Act, fully comparable with the EC general good rules and cannot be extended by supervisors´ discretion.

c) Have there been cases in your country where a credit institution is able to provide (on the strength of its home country authorisation) particular services listed in the Annex which credit institutions subject to supervision by your competent authorities are not authorised to provide? If so, what are those services and has this given rise to any problems in practice?

No.

5. In relation to activities not listed in the Annex, with what provisions of your national laws or regulations must a credit institution authorised by another Member State comply?

A license has to be granted by the MoF (FMA) in order to conduct activities not listed in the Annex of 2BCD but qualified as banking activities in the meaning of Art. 1 par. 1 of the Austrian Banking Act

6. Are there cases where such national laws or regulations may not in fact be compatible with the general provisions of Community law? If so, what are they?

We don't know of any such cases.

THE GENERAL GOOD

7. Under Article 21, host Member States retain certain powers over credit institutions authorised in another Member State. In this regard:

a) What are the legal rules adopted in your country in the interest of the general good (see Art. 21 par. 5) *credit institutions that conduct activities in Austria through a branch office have to comply with*

Art. 25: liquidity

Art. 31 through 36: consumer protection

Art. 37: valuation of payment transactions

Art. 38: banking secrecy

Art 39 to 4: Duty of diligence and anti –money Laundering provisions

Art. 44 par. 3 through 6: checked accounting statements, transmitted to the MoF,

Art. 60 through 63: provisions for the appointment of (external) bank auditors

Art. 65 par. 3a: liability of above mentioned external bank auditors

Art. 66 through 68: provisions for specific secured saving deposits

Art. 74: monthly and quarterly reports to the Austrian central bank

Art. 75: reports to the Central Credit Register, run by the Austrian central bank

Art. 93 par. 8: possibility of "topping up" within the Austrian deposit guarantee scheme

Art. 94: protection of designation and trade marks

Art. 95 par. 3 and 4: prohibition of employee savings banks

Art. 10 through 18 Securities Supervision Act: investors protection rules acc. to the EU - Investment Services Directive.

credit institutions that exercise the freedom to provide services by conducting activities in Austria have to comply with

Art. 31 through 36: provisions for consumer protection

Art. 37: valuation of payment transactions

Art. 38: banking secrecy

Art 39 to 4: Duty of diligence and anti –money laundering provisions

Art. 66 through 68: provisions for specific secured saving deposits

Art. 75: reports to the Central Credit Register, run by the Austrian central bank

Art. 93 par. 8: possibility of "topping up" within the Austrian deposit guarantee scheme

Art. 94: protection of designation and trade marks

Art. 95 par. 3 and 4: prohibition of employee savings banks

Art. 10 through 18 Securities Supervision Act: investors protection rules acc. to the EU - Investment Services Directive.

The above mentioned Articles may contribute as a legal basis (legal framework) for branch offices and for credit institutions that provide services under the freedom of services in the interest of general good rules.

b) Have the competent authorities exercised their powers under Article 21 par. 5 and, if so, in what circumstances?

No.

c) Have there been cases where a credit institution invoked its right of appeal and, if so, how has the court approached the appeal ?

To the best of our knowledge, no such cases are known.

THE ESTABLISHMENT OF BRANCHES

8. What, if any, difficulties been experienced with regard to the establishment of branches by a credit institution, where your country is (a) the home Member State and (b) the host Member State of the institution concerned (see Articles 19 and 21)?

With regard to the establishment of branches by a credit institution, no difficulties have been experienced.

THE PROVISION OF CROSS BORDER SERVICES

9. What, if any, difficulties been experienced with regard to the provision of cross-border services by a credit institution, where your country is (a) the home Member State and (b) the host Member State of the institution concerned (see Articles 20 and 21)?

With regard to the provision of cross-border services by a credit institution, no difficulties have been experienced. However, there is sometimes uncertainty, whether some kind of advertising or providing services via internet is covered by the freedom to provide services.

THE COMPETENT AUTHORITIES

10. What are the national authorities empowered in your country to supervise credit institutions and which are, therefor, the "competent authorities" for the purposes of the Second Banking Directive?

With regard to the implementation of "competent authorities", the Austrian Banking Act states that "competent authorities shall mean those authorities in the Member States which pursuant to legal or administrative regulations are competent for the supervision of credit institutions or investment firms".

By 1 April 2002 the Financial Market Authority (Finanzmarktaufsichtsbehörde "FMA") is the competent authority and therefore empowered to supervise credit institutions. The FMA is supported by the Oesterreichische Nationalbank (OeNB), the central bank of Austria (i.e. in the field of statistics and on-site inspections of credit and market risks as well as checking banks´ internal models covering market risks, see question 11).

11. Does the national central bank in your country have an involvement in prudential supervision and, if so, what is its role?

Yes; there is an intensive co-operation between MoF, FMA and OeNB in prudential supervision laid down by law:

- *On-site inspections concerning market and credit risks of banks have to be done obligatory by OeNB,*
- *OeNB has to be consulted when FMA issues a formal regulation,*
- *OeNB offers expertise in the field of statistical analysis,*
- *OeNB must be consulted whenever a bank license shall be granted,*
- *the preparation of Memoranda of Understanding laying down the principles of co-operation between supervisory bodies within and outside European Union are jointly prepared by FMA, MoF and OeNB, and*
- *OeNB is the competent authority concerning the supervision of payment systems.*

12. What is the view in your country about the need for an integrated supervisory authority for the financial services sector as a whole rather than separate authorities for different parts of it, and why?

By *1 April 2002 an integrated supervisory authority for banking, insurance, securities, stock exchange and pension fund supervision has been established. Austria follows the trend recognised in the financial markets to establish financial conglomerates and to create financial products in all sectors of the industry, bearing elements of banking and insurance business.*

13. What is the view in your country about the need for the European Central Bank to play a role in prudential supervision, and why?

The role of the ECB in prudential supervision in Europe is discussed in many international fora. We (the MoF) are of the opinion, that the ESCB can play a dominant role in providing statistics and market analysis, , but also in developing instruments of crises management. Nevertheless micro-prudential supervision should be organised at national level, since it will be most effective if it remains as close as possible to the supervised entities: the national regulators have sufficient experience of the regional markets as well as of the supervised entities and - in a very practical sense - they can get in contact with persons and institutions more easily, having the power and instruments for winding up a bank (supported by supervisory measures). Of course much effort has to be done to strengthen co-operation between supervisors, not only within the European Union, but also between supervisors from those third countries where European banks play a dominant role (e.g. in the Central and Eastern European countries).

14. To what extent, if at all, have those views been influenced by the introduction of the Euro and the growth of E-commerce, and why?

The introduction of the Euro accelerated the trend to integrated cross-border financial markets dissolving the frontiers between the bank and insurance industry too. The next step is the creation of a fully integrated financial market as laid down in the Commission´s Financial Services Action Plan, aiming to eliminate the remaining obstacles which are cost intensive for providers of financial services and consumers as well and which hinder effective supervision on a cross-border basis. The growth of e-commerce is part of the framework that is needed for a more developed internal market on the one hand.On the other hand e-commerce will have a major impact on the structure of the domestic market, especially on the channels for offering banking services. We expect that banks will reduce their (domestic) branch network parallel to the growth of products distributed via internet banking.

15. What relationship do the competent authorities in your country have with the European Central Bank?

As financial market supervision is organized within an independent body (FMA) and not integrated in the central bank there is no direct representation of the competent authority in the ECB Council. Nevertheless direct relationship exists in that sense that the FMA (until 1st April 2002 MoF) joins (together with OeNB) meetings of the ECB's Banking Supervision Committee (BSC) and its working groups . Documents prepared by the BSC relevant for banking supervision and generally, policy guidelines issued by ECB, e.g. concerning crisis management, are an integrated part of the Austrian supervisory policy. Furthermore there exists a kind of indirect rela-

tionship due to the close co-operation between the FMA and the OeNB being part of the ESCB. Last but not least draft Austrian legislation which might effect monetary policy in the Euro-Area is communicated to the ECB (acc. to the provisions of the EC-Treaty).

16. How, if at all, has human rights legislation affected the competent authorities in your country?

The European Convention of Human Rights is integral part of the Austrian Constitution to which the relevant legislation for the supervisory process in Austria must comply with.

17. Has the introduction of the Euro highlighted any inadequacies in your country in the supervision of credit institutions and the need for further harmonisation at the EU level?

No.

BELGIUM

Financial Services in the Era of the Euro and E-Commerce:

Does home country control work?

Rapporteur
*Jean-Marc Gollier**

INTRODUCTION

In Belgium, the supervision of the activity of credit institutions is entrusted to the Banking and Finance Commission (hereinafter the "BFC"). The BFC is an autonomous public institution[1] with its own legal personality.

The BFC was created in 1935 in accordance with Royal Decree 185 of 9 July 1935 on the supervision of banks and the rules governing the issue of securities. Title I of the Royal Decree – which remained into force until the Law of 22 March 1993 – sets out the regulatory system governing banks. Title II of the Royal Decree governs the supervision of information in case of offer to the public or listing of securities in Belgium. This title is still applicable.

Between 1935 and 1990, the main tasks of the BFC were (i) to control, on a prudential basis, the activity of credit institutions (banks and, since 1975, also savings banks) in Belgium, and (ii) to control the information published by issuers in public offers of securities and listings on the stock exchange. Since 1957, it also supervises investment funds; since 1967, it is also responsible for supervising the information (both occasional and periodic) published by listed holding companies, as well as the information on their accounts (both solo and consolidated). Since 1989, with the implementation of a comprehensive set of rules on takeover bids and changes in the control of public companies, the BFC supervises compliance with this regulation. Since 1990, it also carries out prudential supervision of the activity of providers of investment services (brokers, investment advisers,

* Avocat honorare, Université Libre de Bruxelles, Chargé de mission auprès de la Commission bancaire et financière.

portfolio managers, introducing brokers) and, since 1995, of the proper organization of stock exchanges.

The Law of 22 March 1993 on the legal status and supervision of credit institutions implemented into Belgian law the rules of the Second Banking Directive.

It is worth mentioning that the Law of 6 April1995 on secondary markets, on the legal status and supervision of investment firms, on intermediaries and investment advisers implemented into Belgian law the ISD.

The Belgian Parliament has recently voted a Law which will deeply reform the Belgian framework for the institutional supervision of financial activities[2]. The primary goals of this reform are (i) to concentrate within the hands of the BFC the tasks pertaining to the supervision of financial markets and financial activities[3], (ii) to bring closer together the BFC and the Belgian insurance supervisor, as many savings products are offered in the form of insurance products and the major Belgian financial conglomerates develop concurrent banking and insurance businesses, (iii) to organize closer collaboration between these two institutions and the central bank and favour synergies between these three institutions.

In recent years, the banking sector has experienced an important wave of concentration. The most original factor is that the concentration has been characterized, in the most important cases, by the creation of alliances between Belgian banking groups and neighbouring banking groups. This is the case in the creation of the Belgian-Dutch "bancassurance" Fortis group and the creation of the Franco-Belgian Dexia group. The creation of these groups, under a consortium or conglomerate structure, has driven the BFC to closely collaborate with its neighbouring supervisors (France, the Netherlands and Luxembourg) and with the insurance supervisors.

The following table (source: Belgian Bankers' Association [ABB]) offers a quick view of the evolution of the Belgian banking sector[4]:

	Banks governed by Belgian law			**Banks governed by foreign law**			
End of period	Belgian majority interest	Foreign majority interest	Total	UE	Other countries	Total	Total
12.1985	100	36	136	14	14	28	164
12.1990	85	37	122	20	15	35	157
12.1995	66	38	104	24	16	40	144
12.1999	47	28	75	30	14	44	119
12.2000	44	28	72	34	13	47	119

In the following pages, we will answer the questionnaire. The answers focus on the practice of the BFC, mainly based on the texts of its annual reports[5]. The questions relating to the relationships between the BFC and the national central bank and their respective roles in monitoring the financial system are currently particular importance in Belgium.

AUTHORISATION

1. Question: *What procedures exist for the competent authorities in your country to engage in the "prior consultation" envisaged by Article 7 of the Second Banking Directive on the authorisation of a credit institution which is (1) a subsidiary of a credit institution authorised in another Member State; (2) a subsidiary of the parent undertaking of a credit institution authorised in another Member State; or (3) controlled by the same persons as control a credit institution authorised in another Member State? Are those procedures formal or informal in nature?*

Answer: The main objectives of Article 7 is to allow the come control authorities (i) to supervise the shareholding of a credit institution which is part of a group including a credit institution located in another Member State and (ii) to prevent any attempt to elude supervision in the home country of that credit institution[6].

Article 101 of the law of 22 March 1993 on the legal status and supervision of credit institutions provides that "*Without prejudice to Articles 97 to 99 [on professional secrecy], the Banking and Finance Commission will co-operate with the supervisory authorities of credit institutions and their financial institution subsidiaries, which are governed by the laws of foreign States, in the supervision of their activities in Belgium, in accordance with the provisions of this Law, as well as in the supervision of the activities of institutions governed by Belgian law in those States.*

Without prejudice to Belgium's obligations resulting from European Community law, the Banking and Finance Commission may, on a reciprocal basis, agree with the supervisory authorities of those States upon the procedures for the co-operation, and upon the rules with regard to the obligations and prohibitions applicable to the business of credit institutions, with regard to the object of and the procedures for the supervision of the credit institutions referred to in paragraph 1, through on-the-spot inspections or otherwise, and with regard to the procedures for the exchange of information laid down in Articles 97 to 99.

Paragraph 2 shall [also] apply to co-operation with the Belgian authorities, organizations and persons referred to in Article 99, §§ 1 and 2".

It is on the basis of this general provision that the BFC has developed consultation processes with EC and non-EC prudential supervisors[7].

The extension of the activities of EC credit institutions in Belgium through the creation of new subsidiaries has been limited. In the vast majority of the cases, such an extension has occurred through the acquisition of control of an existing credit institution in Belgium or through alliances with Belgian credit institutions.

As a matter of practice, Article 7 of the Second Banking Directive has only exceptionally been applied for the *authorization* of a (new) credit institution which is a subsidiary of an EC credit institution, but consultations have been organized in case of change of control of Belgian credit institutions taken over by credit institutions located in other EC Member States.

MOUs have been entered into with Luxembourg, France and the Netherlands to organize consultation and exchange of information between competent authorities, mainly for the purpose of supervision of transnational financial conglomerates the central direction of which is shared amongst managers representing Belgian and respectively French or Dutch interests[8].

The content of these MOUs is harmonized, even though the form of each MOU may differ.

These MOUs organize *inter alia* the supervision of subsidiaries of EU credit institutions. The principle is that each supervisor remains responsible for the socalled "firstline" prudential supervision of each credit institution on an individual basis, and that the fome country control authority of the parent company is responsible for the prudential supervision on a consolidated basis.

A special MOU has been entered into between the BFC, the French *Commission bancaire* and the Luxembourg CSSF for the supervision of the Dexia group, whose holding company is located in Belgium. A Dexia credit institution is located in each country. The Belgian and the French subsidiaries originally focused on retail banking and the provision of banking services to municipalities and local authorities. The MOU provides that the BFC carries out consolidated prudential supervision of the Dexia group and relies on the individual prudential supervision carried out in France and in Luxembourg, respectively[9]. The MOU organizes permanent exchange of information between authorities, as well as half-yearly consultation meetings.

For the prudential supervision of the Fortis group, the MOU specifies that due to consortium structure of the group and the combination of banking, financial and insurance businesses, a complementary prudential supervision of the group taken as a conglomerate has to be organized. The insurance supervisors have also signed an MOU.

The conglomerate supervision is shared by the competent authorities. The coordination of this complementary supervision is ensured by the competent authority responsible for individual supervision of the largest business unit of the group in terms of solvency requirements. For the time being, it is the BFC which is in charge of these tasks[10].

2. **Question:** *Have any and, if so, what problems been experienced with the prior consultation process?*

Answer: No particular problem has been experienced with the prior consultation process.

3. **Question:** *Are you aware of any cases where the competent authorities have refused authorisation, in particular in accordance with Article 5? If so, in what circumstances has authorisation been refused?*

Answer: Article 5 of the Second Banking Directive has been implemented in Article 17 of the Law of 22 March 1993[11], which provides that "*The Banking and Finance Commission will not grant authorization before it has been informed of the identities of the natural or legal persons which own direct or indirect holdings, regardless of whether they confer voting rights, of at least 5% in the credit institution's capital, and of the amounts of capital or voting rights held by these persons. (...)*

The Banking and Finance Commission will refuse authorization if, taking into account the need to ensure the sound and prudent management of a credit institution, it is not satisfied as to the suitability of the natural or legal persons referred to in paragraph 1."

The BFC has, since the entry into force of the Second Banking Directive, refused the authorization only on one occasion[12].

The case related to the creation of a credit institution in Belgium. The promoter and would-be shareholder was a non-EU credit institution which was part of a group which, in addition to a banking activity, also carried out an industrial activity. The own funds of the groups were considered as weak and the solvency ratio of the foreign credit institution (even though complying with its local regulation), was well below the minimum 8% requirement. Moreover, the structure of the group was very complex and many subsidiaries had no audited accounts.

The BFC considers that the financial strength of the shareholders of a credit institution is a decisive element in the assessment of the suitability of these shareholders. Moreover, the structure of the group must not impede supervision of the credit institution.

Considering that the applicants did not meet the suitability test, the BFC refused to authorize the creation of the new credit institution in Belgium.

4. **Question:** *Once authorised by its home country, a credit institution may, in accordance with Article 18, carry on any of the activities listed in the Annex either by the establishment of a branch or by way of the provision of services in any other Member State. In this regard:*

(a) By what legislative or other means have the provisions of Article 18 been given effect in your country?

(b) How effectively has the home country control principle applied?

(c) Have there been cases in your country where a credit institution is able to provide (on the strength of its home country authorisation) particular services listed in the Annex which credit institutions subject to supervision by your competent authorities are not authorised to provide? If so, what are those services and has this given rise to any problems in practice?

Answers:

a) The provisions of the Second Banking Directive relating to the establishment of a branch and to the provision of services have been implemented by Title III of the Law of March 22, 1993[13].

b) The home country control principle is effectively applied in Belgium. As a matter of practice, some EU credit institutions have expressed concern about the administrative burden of reporting for branches located in Belgium[14].

c) We are not aware of cases in Belgium of a credit institution able to provide particular services that Belgian credit institutions are not authorized to provide[15].

5. Question: *In relation to activities not listed in the Annex, with what provisions of your national laws or regulations must a credit institution authorised by another Member State comply?*

Answer: This question has never had to be posed as a matter of prudential supervision. Generally, the intended activities will fit as activities listed in the Annex to the Directive.

6. Question: *Are there cases where such national laws or regulations may not in fact be compatible with the general provisions of Community law? If so, what are they?*

Answer: No.

THE GENERAL GOOD

7. Question: *Under Article 21, host Member States retain certain powers over credit institutions authorised in another Member State. In this regard:*

(a) What are the legal rules adopted in your country in the interest of the general good (see Article 21(5))?

(b) Have the competent authorities exercised their powers under Article 21(5) and, if so, in what circumstances?
(c) What are the appeal procedures that exist (see Article 21(6))?
(d) Have there been cases where a credit institution invoked its right of appeal and, if so, how has the court approached the appeal?

Answer:
(a) The BFC has published a list of rules that it considers have been adopted in the interest of the general good. This list is available on the web site of the Commission (www.cbf.be > documents).

In addition to the prudential rules which remain applicable in Belgian to branches of EU credit institutions, the list contains many provisions of Belgian law applicable to financial transactions which are criminally sanctioned (e.g. prohibition of peddling of securities and of door-to-door sales of securities; regulation on public offers of securities; administrative regulation of leasing activities; consumer credit; money laundering; value dates for wire transfers; information on debt interests in current accounts; market abuse regulation) and the regulation on commercial practices and on information to the consumer.

The list is specifically described as being nonexhaustive.

A specific provision of the Law of 22 March 1993 provides that the BFC may intervene in the conduct of business of a credit institution if it finds that such credit institution has put in place "particular mechanisms" the purpose or effect of which is to facilitate fiscal fraud by third parties[16]. This is not a provision of fiscal law but it is a prudential provision inasmuch as the participation to fiscal fraud may at the least create a reputation risk for the credit institution.

This provision is applicable to branches of EU credit institutions. The BFC considers that the prohibition of the organization of "particular mechanisms" is also applicable to EU credit institutions providing financial services in Belgium without having an establishment in Belgium[17, 18].

(b) The BFC has not taken initiatives to find violations of rules adopted in the interest of the general good.

(c) A decision taken by the BFC to prevent violation of provisions pertaining to the general good (e.g. a decision prohibiting a credit institution from initiating further transactions within Belgium in the contested field) may be appealed against before the Ministry of Finance[19]. An appeal against the decision of the Minister of Finance would be submitted to the State Council, which is the ordinary administrative jurisdiction.

(d) No.

THE ESTABLISHMENT OF BRANCHES

8. Question: *What, if any, difficulties been experienced with regard to the establishment of branches by a credit institution, where your country is (a) the home Member State and (b) the host Member State of the institution concerned (see Articles 19 and 21)?*

Answer: As regards branches of EU credit institutions established in Belgium, the BFC has sometimes experienced difficulties to receive adequate reporting documents. The solution to this problem is generally discussed together with the home country control authority.

THE PROVISION OF CROSS-BORDER SERVICES

9. Question: *What, if any, difficulties been experienced with regard to the provision of cross-border services by a credit institution, where your country is (a) the home Member State and (b) the host Member State of the institution concerned (see Articles 20 and 21)?*

Answer: The BFC has not experienced problems in this field.

THE COMPETENT AUTHORITIES

10. Question: *What are the national authorities empowered in your country to supervise credit institutions and which are, therefore, the "competent authorities" for the purposes of the Second Banking Directive?*

Answer: The Banking and Finance Commission is empowered to supervise credit institutions for the purposes of the Second Banking Directive.

11. Question: *Does the national central bank in your country have an involvement in prudential supervision and, if so, what is its role?*

Answer: The National Bank is the lender in last resort in the banking system. It has intervened in cases of bankruptcy of Belgian credit institutions.

The National Bank participates in the definition and implementation of the monetary policy (through the "Eurogroup").

It is a crucial entity in the process of clearing and netting of payments amongst credit institutions.

The new Law on the supervision of the financial sector and financial services[20] has confirmed that the Belgian National Bank is competent for the oversight of the clearing and settlement systems. This is justified by the fact that this oversight is considered as closely linked to the promotion of the smooth operation of payment systems, which is a basic task of the "Eurosystem".

The prudential supervision of clearing and settlement systems remains the task of the BFC[21].

In a nutshell, the National Bank may be seen as being in charge of "macro-prudential" considerations, i.e. stability of the financial system, while the BFC is entrusted with "micro-prudential" supervision aimed at ensuring the financial stability of individual credit institutions. The latter supervision encompasses, for the supervision of financial conglomerates, aspects relating to systemic risks which are close to "macro-prudential" concerns[22]. Consequently, there are inevitably complementarities and some overlapping between the two institutions.

12. Question: *What is the view in your country about the need for an integrated supervisory authority for the financial services sector as a whole rather than separate authorities for different parts of it, and why?*

Answer: The ambit of the new Law on the supervision of the financial sector and financial services[23] is precisely to create closer cooperation between the three actors of the financial stability, namely the National Bank, the insurance supervisor and the BFC.

The Law does not merge these public institutions, but creates institutional links between them. The King also has the power to decide a merger between the BFC and the insurance supervisor.

As a matter of fact, the creation of "bancassurance" conglomerates has made of this change a necessity.

Moreover, according to the Governor of the National Bank, the transfer of responsibility for the monetary policy to the Governing Council and to the Executive Board of the ECB "has reduced the pertinence of the argument according to which the commingling of the monetary and prudential functions could create conflicts of interests"[24].

13. Question: *What is the view in your country about the need for the European Central Bank to play a role in prudential supervision, and why?*

Answer: No official position has been expressed in this respect in Belgium.

14. Question: *To what extent, if at all, have those views been influenced* *by the introduction of the Euro and the growth of E-commerce, and why?*

[Not applicable].

15. Question: *What relationship do the competent authorities in your country have with the European Central Bank?*

Answer: The BFC participates *inter alia* in the Banking Supervision Committee of the European Central Bank and in the Banking Advisory Committee[25]. The collaboration between the BFC, the ECB and the other central banks is organized in an MOU which aims *inter alia* to achieve greater convergence in the field of supervision of the financial system[26].

16. Question: *How, if at all, has human rights legislation affected the competent authorities in your country?*

Answer: Human rights legislation has significantly affected the manner in which matters which may have criminal or even individual economic implications are investigated and decided upon.

If information gathered during an administrative control, and voluntarily handed over to the BFC, provides evidence of a criminal fact, the BFC must not use such information for the purpose of disciplinary or judicial prosecution against the person who has handed over the information (principle of nonself-incrimination). If an administrative sanction has to be taken by the BFC against a credit institution, the principles of Article 6 of the ECHR often have to be complied with.

The problems encountered in this field are common to all administrative authorities. The French market authority has recently faced significant judicial challenging in this respect.

The European Commission has encountered similar problems in the field of supervision of compliance with competition rules.

These problems should to a large extend be solved by the new Law on the supervision of the financial sector and financial services[27].

17. Question: *Has the introduction of the Euro highlighted any inadequacies in your country in the supervision of credit institutions and the need for further harmonisation at the EU level?*

Answer: No.

NOTES

[1] Also qualified as an "autorité administrative indépendante", in accordance with the

terminology of French administrative doctrine (J. Le Brun, "Les autorités administratives indépendantes : le cas de la Commission bancaire et financière belge, *in* Revue internationale de droit économique, 1997, 183-193; on this concept, see e.g. M. Gentot, Les autorités administratives indépendantes, Montchrestien, 1996; M.-J. Guédon, Les autorités administratives indépendantes, LGDJ, 1991; See also my contribution *in* Les autorités de contrôle des marchés financiers, des assurances et de la concurrence : bilan et perspectives, Bruylant, 2002).

[2] Loi du 2 août 2002 relative à la surveillance du secteur financier et aux services financiers, "Moniteur belge"/"Belgisch Staatsblad" (Belgian Official Gazette) of 4 September 2002. The law as passed by Parliament, but in draft form, is available on the web site of the House of Representatives: http://www.lachambre.be/cgi-bin/docs.bat?l=f&dir=1842 > Doc. 1842/6.

[3] The Law of 1995 had entrusted certain tasks to the market authorities (corporate bodies created within the commercial entities managing the stock exchanges) in the field of supervision of occasional information from listed companies, insider dealing and compliance with codes of conduct. The prudential supervision of financial intermediaries remained in the hands of the BFC.

[4] For other statistics and comments on the Belgian banking sector, see the site of the Belgian Bankers' Association (http://www.abb-bvb.be/gen/en/secteur.html) and the section of the annual report of the BFC relating to the evolution of the sector.

[5] The annual reports of the BFC, in French or in Dutch, are since 1994 available in pdf format on the BFC web site www.cbf.be (references made to these reports in this document relate to the French versions). Most of the circulars are also available on the web site. An unofficial English translation of the Laws of 22 March 1993 and 6 April 1995 are also available on the site.

[6] P. Clarotti, « La coopération administrative entre organes de contrôle bancaire dans la CE », Revue (belge) de la banque, 1993, p. 588, also describing the German-French MOU; see also J.W. Van der Vossen, Division of supervisory responsibilities, cooperation and professional secrecy, *in* Banking and EC Financial Law Commentary, Amsterdam Financial Series, Kluwer, 1992, p. 56.

[7] The exchange of information is organized – as a departure from the principle of secrecy which governs the activity of the BFC - by Article 99 of the Law of 22 March 1993, which provides that "*the Banking and Finance Commission may disclose confidential information on credit institutions to: (...)*

6° public authorities of EC Member States in charge of the supervision of foreign investment firms, insurance undertakings, undertakings for collective investment, companies involved in their activities, or other foreign financial institutions, or in charge of the supervision of the foreign financial markets;(...)

The Banking and Finance Commission may disclose the information set out in paragraph 1 only if the recipient uses it exclusively for the purposes referred to in paragraph 1 or in Article 96, 1°, and as far as the foreign recipients referred to in paragraph 1 are subject to conditions of professional secrecy equivalent to those [applicable to the BFC].(...)

§ 2. (...) the Banking and Finance Commission may also disclose to central banks and other organizations with similar duties, in their capacity as monetary authorities, and to other public authorities in charge of supervision of payment systems, such information as they may need for the exercise of their functions, provided that the information received by virtue of § 2 is subject to the same conditions of professional secrecy as those [applicable to the BFC], and provided that they only disclose the information to other central banks or other organizations with a similar aim, in their capacity as monetary authorities, or to other public authorities in charge of supervision of payment systems, within the same limits and under the same conditions laid down by § 2, or for the same purposes as those referred to in Article 96, 1°.

§ 5. (...) the Banking and Finance Commission may disclose confidential information on credit institutions, to those authorities or organizations referred to in § 1, (...) 6° (...), that are governed by the law of a nonMember State and with which the Banking and Finance Commission has concluded co-operation agreements that provide for exchange of information, inasmuch as the authorities or organizations to which the information is disclosed, are subject to guarantees of professional secrecy, which are at least equivalent to those [applicable to the BFC]".

[8] On the principles of these MOUs: BFC Annual Reports 1991-1992, p. 44-45; 1992-1993, p. 60-62; 1999-2000, p. 147-148; on the tentative alliance between Générale de Banque and ABN-AMRO: BFC Annual Reports 1987-1988, p. 33-34; 1989-1990, p. 52-53; on the supervision of the Fortis group: 1993-1994, p. 44-45; 1995-1996, p. 55-57; on the supervision of the Dexia group: 1996-1997, p. 52-54; 1999-2000, p. 43; 2000-2001, p. 45.

[9] BFC Annual Reports 1999-2000, p. 149 (see also p. 43), and 2000-2001, p. 45.

[10] For more details, see the BFC Annual Report 1995-1996, p. 55-57, and 2000-2001, p. 131-132.

[11] See also Article 24 of the Law for the changes affecting capital structure.

[12] BFC Annual Report 1993-1994, p. 32-33.

[13] See also the BFC's circular B93/1 of 18 February 1993, available in French and in Dutch on the BFC web site.

[14] See also Luxembourg's report. For the justification of the reporting requirements, see circular B93/1.

[15] Up to the implementation of the ISD in Belgium through the Law of 6 April 1995, Belgian banks were not allowed to carry out stock exchange orders. This was reserved for brokers. Since 1988-1989, banks have had the possibility to intervene on the stock exchanges through specialized subsidiaries qualifying as brokers.

[16] Article 57, § 3, of the Law of 22 March 1993.

[17] BFC Annual Reports 1996-1997, p. 23-24; 1997-1998, p. 26-32, in particular p. 28; circular D1 97/9 of 18 December 1997.

[18] For the answer to the question of when a financial service is provided in Belgium, see M. Dassesse, The regulatory implications of the location of financial services under EU law, BJIBFL, 2001, p. 473-478.

[19] Article 57, § 2, of the Law.

[20] See above, footnote 2.

[21] Articles 22 and 23 of the new Law, in particular Article 23, § 4. See also the BFC Annual Report 2000-2001, p. 137 on the MOU entered into by the ECB, national central banks and prudential supervisors on the cooperation in the field of payment systems.

[22] See in that respect the speech to Parliament by the Governor of the National Bank of Belgium on the occasion of the discussion of said law: National Bank of Belgium, http://www.nbb.be/sg/En/homee2.htm > Governor's speeches > 18/06/2002: Bill concerning the supervision of the financial sector and financial services.

[23] See above, footnote 2.

[24] Speech mentioned above, footnote 21, p. 4.

[25] On the role of this committee, see e.g. M. van den Bergh, P. Pearson and R. Smits, Institutional arrangements, *in* Banking and EC Financial Law Commentary, Amsterdam Financial Series, Kluwer, 2001.

[26] See e.g. the BFC Annual Report 2000-2001, p. 112-114. See also, on the "Brouwer Report" on financial stability, the BFC Annual Report 1999-2000, p. 135.

[27] See above, footnote 2. Two laws have in fact been voted separately, for Constitutional purposes. The second one (http://www.lachambre.be/cgi-bin/docs.bat?l=f&dir=1843 > Doc. 1843/4) specifically relates to the organization of recourses against decisions of the BFC and of the Insurance Supervisor (***Loi du 2 août 2002 complétant, en ce qui concerne les voies de recours contre les décisions prises par le ministre, par la CBF, par l'OCA et par les entreprises de marché et en ce qui concerne l'intervention de la CBF et de l'OCA devant les juridictions répressives, la loi du 2 août 2002 relative à la surveillance du secteur financier et aux services financiers et modifiant diverses autres dispositions légales***).

DENMARK

Financial Services in the Era of the Euro and E-Commerce:

Does home country control work?

Rapporteur
*Jesper Lau Hansen**

AUTHORISATION

1. What procedures exist for the competent authorities in your country to engage in the "prior consultation" envisaged by Article 7 of the Second Banking Directive on the authorisation of a credit institution which is (1) a subsidiary of a credit institution authorised in another Member State; (2) a subsidiary of the parent undertaking of a credit institution authorised in another Member State; or (3) controlled by the same persons as control a credit institution authorised in another Member State? Are those procedures formal or informal in nature?

In the office procedure for authorization of a credit institution that is owned or controlled as mentioned above, it is stated, that the officer in charge of processing the application should be aware of the consultation procedure. The officer in charge will normally write the relevant home state authorities asking for comments.

2. Have any and, if so, what problems been experienced with the prior consultation process?

None.

3. Are you aware of any cases where the competent authorities have refused authorisation, in particular in accordance with Article 5? If so, in what circumstances has authorisation been refused?

No.

* Associate Professor in Financial Market Law, University of Copenhagen.

4. Once authorised by its home country, a credit institution may, in accordance with Article 18, carry on any of the activities listed in the Annex either by the establishment of a branch or by way of the provision of services in any other Member State. In this regard:

(a) By what legislative or other means have the provisions of Article 18 been given effect in your country?

Article 18 has been given effect in Danish law by section 6a of the Commercial Banks and Savings Banks, etc. Consolidated Act No. 787 of 4 September 2001 (hereinafter the Banking Act).

(b) How effectively has the home country control principle applied?

Very effectively, as a foreign credit institution may carry on in Denmark with all of the activities mentioned in the annex to the Banking Act that it is authorized to carry on in its home country either by the establishment of a branch, cf. section 6a(1), or by way of the provision of services, cf. section 6a(5), and the said annex is identical with the list of activities annexed to the Second Banking Directive. In Denmark, 19 credit institutions from other member states have established a branch and 192 credit institutions are providing services in 2002. In 1993, only 7 credit institutions had established a branch and 30 were providing services. The Danish Financial Supervisory Authority (in Danish: Finanstilsynet, hereinafter: The Danish FSA) has in three cases refused to let credit institutions establish branches in other Member States. In these cases the credit institutions lacked the necessary experience and organizational skills needed.

c) Have there been cases in your country where a credit institution is able to provide (on the strength of its home country authorisation) particular services listed in the Annex which credit institutions subject to supervision by your competent authorities are not authorised to provide? If so, what are those services and has this given rise to any problems in practice?

No, because a Danish credit institution is allowed to provide all services listed in the annex.

5. In relation to activities not listed in the Annex, with what provisions of your national laws or regulations must a credit institution authorised by another Member State comply?

The activities of a Danish credit institution is limited to certain activities, cf. section 1(3) of the Banking Act, these activities being the performance of functions relating to transactions of money, credit instruments and securities and services associated herewith, cf. section 1(4) of the Banking Act. The credit institution may perform other non-core credit credit-institution activities, however, the Danish Financial Supervisory Authority may decide that such activities should be performed through a subsidiary, cf. section 1a(2) of the Banking Act. Beside the Banking Act, other Danish acts provide for a mutual recognition of foreign financial institutions, notably, the Investment Companies Consolidated Act No. 704 of 17 July 2000 that covers investment business, such as the provision of services in connection with securities transactions on a professional basis; and the Mortgage Credit Consolidated Act No. 768 of 28 August 2001 that covers activities as mortgage credit business, that is, the granting of loans against a registered mortgage on real property on the basis of the issue of mortgage-credit bonds. To the extent that a credit institution of another Member State is authorised to perform activities that fall outside the annexed list to the Second Banking Directive and are not covered by these other acts, the credit institution wanting to perform these activities in Denmark would have to rely on the general principles of community law derived from the freedom of establishment and the freedom to provide services.

6. Are there cases where such national laws or regulations may not in fact be compatible with the general provisions of Community law? If so, what are they?

No.

THE GENERAL GOOD

7. Under Article 21, host Member States retain certain powers over credit institutions authorised in another Member State. In this regard:

(a) What are the legal rules adopted in your country in the interest of the general good (see Article 21(5))?

No specific rules have been adopted, however, the Danish regime on restricting speculation by directors and chief officers of financial institutions serves the same objective. The regime is mandated by Statutory Order No. 1002 of 7 December 2001.

(b) Have the competent authorities exercised their powers under Article 21(5) and, if so, in what circumstances?

The Danish FSA has the legal basis to ban a credit institution from carrying on any activities in Denmark if the credit institution has severely or repeatedly violated any relevant Danish laws. It should off course be done in accordance with the procedures described in the directive. The Danish FSA has never actually done this. With the coming amendment to section 3 of the Financial Business Act No. 501 of 7 June 2001 concerning best practice for credit institutions, such rules will be applicable to credit institutions established in other Member States when providing cross boarder services in Denmark.

(c) What are the appeal procedures that exist (see Article 21(6))?

Decisions made by the Danish FSA according to the Banking Act and the other acts on financial business can be appealed to the Danish Commerce and Companies Appeals Board. Appeal is voluntary, as the complaint may be brought directly before the Danish courts. A decision by the Danish Commerce and Companies Appeals Board may be brought before the Danish courts.

(d) Have there been cases where a credit institution invoked its right of appeal and, if so, how has the court approached the appeal?

No.

THE ESTABLISHMENT OF BRANCHES

8. What, if any, difficulties been experienced with regard to the establishment of branches by a credit institution, where your country is (a) the home Member State and (b) the host Member State of the institution concerned (see Articles 19 and 21)?

Re (a):

Some Danish credit institutions have experienced problems when establishing branches in Germany due to the German investor guarantee. Legally the Danish branch can choose to subscribe to the Danish investor guarantee, but in a competitive market, the Danish branches are forced to choose the German investor guarantee to maintain their competitiveness as the German investor guarantee has a more complete coverage than the Danish counterpart. One competent authority in another Member state has also caused some minor problems. They do not keep sufficient records of notifications, causing them to ask for renotification once every or every other year. This puts an unnecessary burden on the credit institutions and competent authorities involved.

Re (b):

None.

THE PROVISION OF CROSS-BORDER SERVICES

9. What, if any, difficulties been experienced with regard to the provision of cross-border services by a credit institution, where your country is (a) the home Member State and (b) the host Member State of the institution concerned (see Articles 20 and 21)?

No, there have only been minor practical inconveniences, such as lacking precision in the description of the activities that the foreign credit institution is authorised to perform by its home Member State.

THE COMPETENT AUTHORITIES

10. What are the national authorities empowered in your country to supervise credit institutions and which are, therefore, the "competent authorities" for the purposes of the Second Banking Directive?

The competent authority for the purpose of the Second Banking Directive is the Danish FSA, which is the single financial supervisory authority covering all financial businesses. Decisions on supervisory matters of general public importance and supervisory matters which entail significant consequences to financial undertakings and financial holding companies can be referred by the Danish FSA to the Financial Business Council, which is an independent public body established according to the Financial Business Act No. 501 of 7 June 2001.

11. Does the national central bank in your country have an involvement in prudential supervision and, if so, what is its role?

No, the Danish National Bank is not directly involved in prudential supervision, however the Danish National Bank appoints one member to the Danish Financial Business Council, see question 10 *supra*.

12. What is the view in your country about the need for an integrated supervisory authority for the financial services sector as a whole rather than separate authorities for different parts of it, and why?

Denmark was one of the first countries to introduce a single financial supervisory authority for the financial services sector, which is believed to offer a more integrated and efficient supervision at a lower cost.

13. What is the view in your country about the need for the European Central Bank to play a role in prudential supervision, and why?

There is no general consensus, however, the need to secure practical cooperation among national supervisory authorities seems to be reasonably fulfilled by the existing procedures, see question 15 *infra*.

14. To what extent, if at all, have those views been influenced by the introduction of the Euro and the growth of E-commerce, and why?

The introduction of the Euro and the growth of E-commerce has had effects on the cross-border activity on the financial market as well and has thus increased the perceived need to secure practical cooperation among national supervisory authorities.

15. What relationship do the competent authorities in your country have with the European Central Bank?

Denmark has not adopted the Euro. The Danish FSA and the Danish National Bank are members of the Banking Supervision Committee, and a number of its subcommittees. The BSC helps the ECB implement eurorelated decisions as well as provides an important informal forum for discussing the financial sector. The subcommittees deal with a number of issues, *inter alia* financial stability and macro-prudential analysis.

16. How, if at all, has human rights legislation affected the competent authorities in your country?

The European Convention on Human Rights and Fundamental Freedoms has been implemented into Danish law. According to the case law of the European Court on Human Rights, article 6(2) on the presumption of innocence is considered to ban self-incrimination. Thus, in cases where the Danish FSA has reason to believe that rules have been violated and criminal sanctions may be applicable, the Danish FSA is probably restricted in its gathering of information. However, information gathered by the Danish FSA in the normal course of its supervisory activities has been admitted by the courts in criminal proceedings. Further, consumer protection legislation is getting increasing attention in Danish law and, consequently, the Danish FSA has to a certain extent reevaluated its traditional focus, and is increasingly emphasizing consumer protection.

17. Has the introduction of the Euro highlighted any inadequacies in your country in the supervision of credit institutions and the need for further harmonisation at the EU level?

No, as Denmark has not adopted the Euro.

FINLAND

Financial Services in the Era of the Euro and E-Commerce

Rapporteurs
*Markku Lounatvvori and Pirjo Kyyrönen**

AUTHORISATION

1. Question: *What procedures exist for the competent authorities in your country to engage in the "prior consultation" envisaged by Article 7 of the Second Banking Directive (Directive 2000/12/EY Article 12) on the authorisation of a credit institution which is*
(1) a subsidiary of a credit institution authorised in another Member State;
(2) a subsidiary of the parent undertaking of a credit institution authorised in another Member State: or
(3) controlled by the same persons as control a credit institution authorised in another Member State? Are those procedures formal or informal in nature?

Answer: In accordance with section 10 of the Credit Institutions Act, when the organisation applying for the authorisation is a subsidiary of a credit institution authorised in another State belonging to the European Economic Area or a subsidiary of a parent company of such credit institution, an opinion of the supervisory authority of that State shall be requested on the application. The same procedure shall apply if the same natural or legal persons that exercise control over such credit institution exercise control in the organisation applying for the authorisation.

* Financial Supervision Authority. In his capacity as president of the Finnish European Law Association, Mr Matti Kauppi, attorney-at-law, has asked the Financial Supervision Authority (FSA) to complete the questionnaire entitled *Financial Services in the Era of the Euro and E-Commerce*. Please find enclosed the FSA's answers to your questions. For further information on the FSA and its activities, please visit the FSA's website at http://www.rahoitustarkastus.fi.

The FSA has also concluded bilateral Memoranda of Understanding (MoU) with several other EU member states. According to these MoUs, an authorisation as referred to in Article 7 of the Second Banking Directive (Article 12 of the Directive 2000/12/EC) can only be granted subject to prior consultation as set out in the Directive. The consultation takes place in writing.

2. Question: *Have any and, if so, what problems been experienced with the prior consultation process?*

Answer: There have not been any problems.

3. Question: *Are you aware of any cases where the competent authorities have refused authorisation, in particular in accordance with Article 5 (Directive 2000/12/EY Article 7)? If so, under what circumstances has authorisation been refused?*

Answer: There are no such cases.

4. Question: *Once authorised by its home country, a credit institution may, in accordance with Article 18, carry on any of the activities listed in the Annex either by the establishment of a branch or by way of the provision of services in any other Member State. In this regard:*

(a) By what legislative or other means have the provisions of Article 18 been given effect in your country?

Answer: Provisions to this effect have been enacted by the Act on Foreign Credit and Financial Institutions in Finland. Section 3 of the Act provides that a credit institution authorised in a member state of the European Economic Area may set up a branch office in Finland or provide such services in Finland as referred to in section 20 of the Credit Institutions Act and covered by its authorisation. Section 20, paragraph 1, of the Credit Institutions Act, which contains the relevant provisions to this effect, has the following wording:

A credit institution may only carry on operations referred to in this section, or ancillary operations.
The operations of a credit institution shall comprise:
1) acceptance of repayable deposits from the public;
2) other funding;
3) lending and financing as well as other funding;
4) financial leasing;
5) payment transactions;

6) collection of payments;
7) foreign-exchange operations;
8) trustee services;
9) securities trading and other securities business;
10) guarantee services;
11) credit reference services;
12) brokerage operations relating to holdings in a housing company and residential real estate in connection with home-saving; as well as
13) other business comparable to that as referred to in subparagraphs 1 to 12, inclusively.

(b) **Question:** *How effectively has the home country control principle been applied?*

Answer:
The home country control has been applied well.

(c) **Question:** *Have there been cases in your country where a credit institution is able to provide (on the strength of its home country authorisation) particular services listed in the Annex which credit institutions subject to supervision by your competent authorities are not authorised to provide? If so, what are those services and has this given rise to any problems in practice?*

Answer: There have been no such cases. In principle, such cases should not even occur in practice, given the practically identical provisions of the Annex of the applicable Directive and section 20 of the Credit Institutions Act, defining the scope of business that credit institutions may engage in.

5. **Question:** *In relation to activities not listed in the Annex, with what provisions of your national laws or regulations must a credit institution authorised by another Member State comply?*

Answer: Credit institutions may only engage in activities listed in the Annex; also cf. the answer under 4 c, above.

6. **Question:** *Are there cases where such national laws or regulations may not in fact be compatible with the general provisions of Community law? If so, what are they?*

Answer:
There have not been any such cases.

THE GENERAL GOOD

7. ***Question:*** *Under Article 21 (article 22, Directive 2000/12/EY), host Member States retain certain powers over credit institutions authorised in another Member State. In this regard:*
(a) *What are the legal rules adopted in your country in the interest of the general good (see Article 21 (5), Article 22(5); Directive 2000/12/EY)?*

Answer: Below are listed certain legal provisions to be followed in the interest of the general good. These provisions must be observed by all the credit institutions providing services in Finland. The list is not exhaustive.

Credit Institutions Act (1607/93)

Chapter 10 of the Credit Institutions Act includes provisions on customer protection. Section 82 of the Act includes provisions on the marketing of credit institution services. According to these provisions, a credit institution must not give false or misleading information in their marketing materials, nor otherwise resort to procedures that are unfair from the point of view of the customer or contrary to good practice. Any marketing materials, which omit information necessary for the customer to make a fair evaluation of the financial implications of the product, are a1so considered misleading, in all cases.

When a foreign credit institution starts to accept deposits from Finnish customers, it is obliged by law to inform its Finnish customers of the deposit guarantee scheme applied in its home country. The marketing materials must a1so clearly indicate that the Finnish lega1 provisions governing deposit guarantee schemes do not apply to deposits made by Finnish customers in foreign credit institutions.

Under section 83, paragraph 1, of the Credit Institutions Act a credit institution shall not apply a contractual term which does not fall within the scope of the activities of a credit institution or which shall be deemed unreasonable to the customer with regard to its content or the positions or circumstances of the parties. A contractual term shall a1ways be deemed unreasonable if the granting of a loan, the va1idity of an agreement or other contractual terms are dependent on the acquisition or use of goods falling outside the scope of activities of the credit institution to an extent that is inappropriate from the point of view of the customer on the whole or if the right of the customer to enter into contractual relations with another supplier is restricted. Under section 83, paragraph 2, of the Credit Institutions Act, the credit institution shall submit to the *FSA* the terms of standard contracts applied in its operations. For the purpose of monitoring the terms and conditions applied in the financial markets, the

FSA would also appreciate being notified of corresponding terms and conditions applied by branches of foreign credit institutions operating in Finland.

Securities Markets Act (495/1989)

Chapter 4 of the Securities Markets Act governing operations in the securities markets lays down the responsibilities of securities intermediaries, which according to the Act also include foreign credit institutions. Under the provisions of chapter 4, credit institutions are, inter alia, required to draw up written agreements on the provision of investment services, to exercise due diligence in the execution of their customers' orders, to provide such information on the investment services and the securities to which they relate as may have a material impact on the customers' decisions. Investment firms must avoid conflicts of interest and, in the event of such conflicts, treat their customers according to the premises of proper practice. Further, in securities trading and in the provision of investment services, procedures that are contrary to proper practice may not be employed. Chapter 2 of the Securities Markets Act includes a general prohibition against false or misleading marketing of securities, together with provisions on rectification or supplementation of false or misleading information.

(b) **Question:** *Have the competent authorities exercised their powers under Article 21 (5) (Article 22(5); Directive 2000/12/EY) and, if so, in what circumstances?*

Answer: No.

(c) **Question:** *What are the appeal procedures that exist (see Article 21 (6), Article 22 (6); Directive 2000/12/EY))?*

Answer: As mentioned under 7 a) above, chapter 10 of the Credit Institutions Act includes provisions on customer protection. This chapter also includes provisions on imposition of a ban on business activities and referral of such cases to the Market Court. The applicable sections 86 and 87 of the Credit Institutions Act are cited below:

Section 86:
Where necessary from the point of view of customer protection, the Financial Supervision Authority may issue an injunction against a credit institution forbidding it to continue a marketing operation or the use of contract terms violating this section or provisions or orders issued thereunder or to repeat the same or similar marketing operation or use of contract terms.

The Financial Supervision Authority may also order that the injunction as referred to in paragraph 1 shall be interlocutory, in which case the injunction shall remain in force until the matter has been finally resolved.

The Financial Supervision Authority may impose a conditional fine to reinforce the injunction issued. The conditional fine shall be ordered payable by the Market Court.

No appeal shall be allowed against a decision of the Financial Supervision Authority as referred to in paragraphs 1 and 2.

Section 87:
A credit institution may refer a decision of the Financial Supervision Authority as referred to in section 86, paragraph 1 to the Market Court within 30 days from being notified of the decision of the Financial Supervision Authority. Otherwise the decision shall be final.

It should be mentioned that unless otherwise provided in the law (cf. the provisions in chapter 10 on customer protection), a decision taken by the FSA may be appealed to the Supreme Administrative Court. Provisions to this effect are included in section 24, paragraph 1, of the Act on the Financial Supervision Authority cited below:

Section 24
Appeal
A decision made by the Financial Supervision Authority may be appealed to the Supreme Administrative Court in the manner provided for the appellation of decisions of the Council of State or a ministry.

(d) **Question:** *Have there been cases where a credit institution invoked its right of appeal and, if so, how has the court approached the appeal?*

Answer: There have not been any cases.

THE ESTABLISHMENT OF BRANCHES

8. **Question:** *What, if any, difficulties been experienced with regard to the establishment of branches by a credit institution where your country is (a) the home Member State and (b) the host Member State of the institution concerned (see Articles 19 and 21, Articles 20 and 22; Directive 2000/12/EY)?*

Answer: a + b) There haven't been any difficulties.

THE PROVISION OF CROSS-BORDER SERVICES

9. **Question:** *What, if any, difficulties been experienced with regard to the provision of cross-border services by a credit institution, where your country is (a) the home Member State and (b) the host Member State of the institution concerned (see Articles 20 and 21, Articles 21 and 22; Directive 2000/12/EY)?*

Answer: a + b) There haven't been any difficulties.

THE COMPETENT AUTHORITIES

10. **Question:** *What are the national authorities empowered in your country to supervise credit institutions and which are, therefore, the "competent authorities" for the purposes of the Second Banking Directive?*

Answer: Financial markets and financial market participants, including credit institutions, are supervised by the FSA, which is the competent authority for the purposes of the Second Banking Directive.

11. **Question:** *Does the national central bank in your country have an involvement in prudential supervision and if so, what is its role?*

Answer: The Bank of Finland is not involved in prudential supervision. The Bank, nevertheless plays a key role in the oversight of the financial system and in maintaining the reliability and stability of the payment and settlement system.

Under the Treaty establishing the European Community, the Bank of Finland is a full member of the European System of Central Banks (ESCB), which is charged with certain tasks in connection with the financial markets. One of the ESCB's essential tasks is to promote the smooth operation of payment systems. The ECB can provide facilities and issue regulations to ensure efficient and sound clearing and payment systems within the Community and with other countries.

The payment-systems oversight by the national central banks, including the Bank of Finland, and the ECB are based on the ESCB's work in promoting the smooth operation of payment systems. Oversight generally refers specifically to the central bank's task of monitoring payment and settlement systems as a whole from the viewpoint of financial stability and prevention of systemic risks. In addition to overseeing national payment systems, the

ECB and NCBs oversee euro-area-wide payment systems handling large-value private payments for individuals.

Under the Treaty, the ESCB has other tasks besides the basic ones. One of the most important of these is to contribute to the smooth conduct of policies pursued by the competent authorities relating to the prudential supervision of credit institutions and the stability of the financial system. This task is supervisory and relates to the whole ESCB, ie not just the ECB but also the NCBs.

The BoF's status, tasks and powers are prescribed in the Act on the Bank of Finland. As mentioned above, the BoF functions as a part of the ESCB in accord with the Treaty establishing the European Community and the Statute of the European System of Central Banks and of the European Central Bank. In performing the tasks of the ESCB, the BoF acts in accordance with the guidelines and instructions of the ECB.

The BoF's primary tasks under the Act on the Bank of Finland are

- contribute to the execution of monetary policy as defined by the Governing Council of the ECB
- contribute to maintenance of the currency supply and issuance of banknotes
- contribute to holding and management of foreign exchange reserves
- provide for the compilation and publication of statistics as necessary for carrying out its tasks
- participate in maintaining the reliability and efficiency of the payment system and overall financial system and participate in their development.

In order to carry out its tasks, the BoF is empowered to

- grant and obtain credit
- accept and make deposits
- engage in trade in securities, precious metals and foreign exchange
- handle payment transactions and clearing of payments
- engage in other activities in the securities, money and foreign exchange markets
- issue rules and instructions concerning the handling of notes and coins to banks and other monetary institutions and to other similar entities.

The following applies to the division of responsibilities and cooperation between the FSA and the Bank of Finland in the field of financial market supervision.

The FSA operates in connection with the Bank of Finland. It is administratively a part of the central bank but is independent in terms of decision-making. In practical terms, this means that FSA employees are BoF employees, and that FSA personnel and payment services are purchased from the BoF, as are translation and certain training services and internal auditing. In respect of information handling, broad decisions on technical matters and decisions on development of basic services for Bank employees are made by the Bank's Information Technology Department, pursuant to Bank strategy.

The basis for supervisory cooperation between FSA and BoF is oversight. Structural and operational changes occur continually in the international money and capital markets, and the consequences for financial stability are monitored and evaluated jointly by the BoF and FSA. The close relationship between oversight and prudential supervision of institutions generates synergies to the advantage of both bodies.

Primary responsibility for oversight of payment systems rests with the BoF. However, the FSA's prudential supervision also promotes the stability of these systems. This is the case because FSA supervision focuses on the reliability of system participants.

The FSA and BoF have been cooperating in the practical supervision of payment and settlement systems for about five years. Formal cooperation commenced two years when a joint supervisory body was set up. The scope of the cooperation covers, inter alia, cooperative efforts in inspections. A concrete example is an FSA study (incl. a Bank participant) on banks' settlement risks in respect of foreign currency trading as at end-2000. This cooperative project also entailed exchange of information pertinent for the broad oversight function, cooperative analysis of risks associated with payment and settlement systems, as well as cooperative efforts in training.

The banking sector forecast is produced two times a year in a joint effort of the FSA and the Bank's Financial Markets Department. The forecast is linked to the macroeconomic forecast produced by the Bank's Economics Department.

Currently, a member of the Bank's board is serving as chairman of the Board of the FSA.

12. Question: *What is the view in your country about the need for an integrated supervisory authority for the financial services sector as a whole rather than separate authorities for different parts of it, and why?*

Answer: In Finland, the FSA is responsible for the supervision of financial markets, including securities markets, whereas the Insurance Supervision Authority (ISA) is responsible for the supervision of insurance companies and the insurance business. The FSA and the ISA have concluded a Memorandum of Understanding on the principles of supervision, and the composition of their boards is virtually identical. However, the organisation of the supervision of financial markets and the insurance business is debated from time to time, the main issue being whether the sectoral supervision by the FSA and the ISA should be replaced by one integrated supervision authority. The outcome of the most recent debate was a decision by the Finnish Government in February 2002 to continue having two separate authorities.

13. Question: *What is the view in your country about the need for the European Central Bank to play a role in prudential supervision, and why?*

Answer: The FSA finds the current arrangement with Bank of Finland representation on the FSA's board to be highly effective.

14. Question: *To what extent, if at all, have those views been influenced by the introduction of the Euro and the growth of E-commerce, and why?*

Answer: Not at all.

15. Question: *What relationship do the competent authorities in your country have with the European Central Bank?*

Answer: Please cf. the answer 11, above. Furthermore, a representative of the FSA attends the meetings of the Banking Supervisory Committee, and the FSA is represented on ECB expert committees.

16. Question: *How, if at all, has human rights legislation affected the competent authorities in your country?*

Answer: Chapter 2 of the Constitution of Finland contains provisions on basic rights and liberties.

Authorities must take account of and observe these basic rights and liberties in their actions.

The section headings of chapter 2 of the Constitution are:
Chapter 2 - Basic rights and liberties
Section 6 - Equality
Section 7 - The right to life, personal liberty and integrity
Section 8 - The principle of legality in criminal
Section 9 - Freedom of movement
Section 10 - The right to privacy
Section 11 - Freedom of religion and conscience
Section 12 - Freedom of expression and right of access to information
Section 13 - Freedom of assembly and freedom of association

Section 14 - Electoral and participatory rights
Section 15 - Protection of property
Section 16 - Educational rights
Section 17 - Right to one's language and culture
Section 18 - The right to work and the freedom to engage in commercial activity
Section 19 - The right to social security
Section 20 - Responsibility for the environment
Section 21 - Protection under the law
Section 22 - Protection of basic rights and liberties
Section 23 - Basic rights and liberties in situations of emergency

For the English wording of the Constitution of Finland, please visit the website of the Ministry of Justice at http://www.om.fi/constitution.

17. **Question:** *Has the introduction of the Euro highlighted any inadequacies in your country in the supervision of credit institutions and the need for further harmonisation at the EU-level?*

Answer: No.

If you want more information, do not hesitate to contact chief legal councel Mr. Markku Lounatvuori by e-mail; markku.lounatvuori@bof.fi or markku.lounatvuori@rahoitustarkastus.fi.

FRANCE

Financial Services in the Era of the Euro and E-Commerce:

Does home country control work?

Rapporteurs
Madame Catherine Kessedjian and Madame Claire Meunier***
Co-auteur
*Monsieur Frédéric Ecolivet***

INTRODUCTION

En France, l'ensemble des dispositions relatives au secteur bancaire et financiers a été codifié par l'Ordonnance n° 2000-1223 du 14 décembre 2000 et est depuis le 1er janvier 2001 contenu dans le Code monétaire et financier. Cette codification était rendue nécessaire par l'adaptation de la législation française aux directives communautaires, notamment par l'adoption de la loi n° 84-46 du 24 janvier 1984, relative aux établissements de crédit, et par la loi n° 96-597 du 2 juillet 1996 de modernisation des activités financières. Ce Code comporte sept livres dans sa partie législative. La codification de la partie réglementaire n'est pas encore intervenue.

Le livre I de la partie législative regroupe les dispositions qui fondent et organisent l'usage de la monnaie et des moyens de paiement. Le premier article de ce livre est consacré à l'Euro, aux termes duquel «*La monnaie de la France est l'euro. Un euro est divisé cent centimes*». La Banque de France y fait également l'objet d'un titre particulier.

Le livre II est consacré au régime juridique des différentes catégories d'instruments financiers et des produits d'épargne générale liés à un régime fiscal spécifique.

Le livre III définit et organise les services financiers, à savoir les opéra-

* Professeur à l'Université de Paris II
** Avocat, Secrétaire Général d l'AJE
*** Avocat, Cabinet ELJ

tions de banque, les services d'investissement et leurs services connexes, les systèmes de règlement et de livraison d'instruments financiers, le démarchage et le colportage.

Le livre IV organise le fonctionnement des marchés financiers.

Le livre V fixe les règles générales applicables aux établissements de crédit et aux entreprises d'investissement, notamment les conditions d'accès à la profession et les dispositions comptables et prudentielles.

Le livre VI est consacré aux institutions en matière bancaire et financière. Il définit les missions notamment de régulation et de contrôle des autorités bancaires et financières.

Enfin, le livre VII reprend l'ensemble des dispositions des six précédents livres et les adapte à la situation spécifique des territoires d'Outre Mer et collectivités de la zone euro, qui n'appartiennent pas au territoire communautaire.

QUESTIONS 1, 2 ET 3

1. Aux termes de l'article L. 511-22 du Code Monétaire et Financier, l'installation en France d'une succursale par un établissement de crédit originaire d'un autre Etat membre de l'Union Européenne est subordonnée à la réception préalable, par le Comité des établissements de crédit et des entreprises d'investissement (CECEI), des informations relatives à son activité émanant de l'autorité compétente du pays d'origine.

Ainsi l'établissement de crédit doit adresser, avant d'implanter une succursale en France, une déclaration à l'autorité compétente du pays d'origine, indiquant l'Etat membre sur le territoire duquel il envisage d'établir une succursale, les types d'opérations envisagées, la structure de l'organisation de la succursale, l'adresse dans l'Etat d'accueil et le nom des dirigeants responsables de la succursale.

L'absence de communication par l'autorité du pays d'origine au CECEI des informations prévues vaut refus du projet de création d'une succursale. Toutefois, ce refus ne doit pas être discrétionnaire et doit s'appuyer sur des motifs d'ordre prudentiel.

Dès qu'il a reçu toutes les informations, le CECEI délivre un accusé de réception à l'autorité compétente et en avise l'établissement concerné. Celui-ci pourra commencer son activité au plus tard dans un délai de deux mois à compter de la réception de la notification.

Dès réception des informations, le CECEI communique à l'établissement de crédit les dispositions d'intérêt général que la succursale doit respecter dans l'exercice d'activités bancaires en France. Ces dispositions sont énumérées à l'article 5 du Règlement n° 92-13 du 23 décembre 1992, adopté par le Comité de la Réglementation Bancaire et Financière (CRBF).

Dans le cas où l'établissement de crédit étranger entend également exercer en France des services d'investissement, le CECEI transmet au Conseil des Marchés Financiers (CMF) et, le cas échéant, à la Commission des Opérations de Bourse (COB), copie de la notification reçue.

Le CMF, ou la COB, informe l'établissement des règles de bonne conduite et des dispositions d'intérêt général qu'il est tenu de respecter pour garantir la protection des investisseurs et la régularité des opérations.

Si les succursales des établissements originaires d'autres Etats membres sont soumises aux contrôles de l'autorité compétente du pays d'origine, la Commission Bancaire demeure compétente pour surveiller sa situation de liquidité et, plus généralement, le respect des dispositions d'intérêt général.

Les établissements financiers contrôlés à 90% au moins par un établissement de crédit ayant son siège dans un autre Etat membre peuvent dans les mêmes conditions, implanter des succursales en France.

La procédure de consultation préalable est définie par des conventions bilatérales existant depuis 1992 entre les autorités compétentes nationales. Il convient de préciser que le secrétariat du CECEI veille au respect des recommandations du Comité de Bâle, notamment celles qui ont été publiées à la suite de l'affaire de la BCCI.

2. A notre connaissance, aucun problème n'a été rencontré dans la procédure de consultation préalable. Les éventuelles difficultés qui auraient pu survenir n'ont fait l'objet d'aucune publicité. Le CECEI a toutefois regretté, dans un rapport adopté le 20 novembre 1998, l'absence de publicité des règles d'intérêt général dans certains Etats membres qui pénalise les prestataires de service et leurs cocontractants. A cet égard, le CECEI diffuse sur son site les références des textes comportant les règles devant être respectées par les succursales en France.

3. A notre connaissance, aucun refus d'agrément n'a été opposé par l'autorité compétente. Toutefois, l'absence de publicité entourant les décisions du CECEI ne permet pas d'affirmer qu'aucune difficulté n'a été rencontrée. Aucune décision juridictionnelle n'est toutefois signalée dans la presse juridique.

QUESTIONS 4, 5 ET 6

4. Les succursales d'établissements communautaires agréés ont la faculté d'effectuer en France l'ensemble des opérations que ces établissements sont en droit d'effectuer en vertu de leur agrément dans leur Etat d'origine (article L. 511-22 du Code monétaire et financier). Dès lors qu'il en a reçu l'autorisation dans son Etat d'origine, il peut exercer en France n'importe

laquelle des activités dont la liste est annexée à la directive (article L.511-23 du Code monétaire et financier). Toutefois, il ne peut pas exercer sur le territoire français une activité qui ne figurent pas sur la liste, sauf à recevoir un accord explicite des autorités françaises. Le CECEI estime que *«compte tenu du large spectre que recouvre la liste européenne, il est peu probable qu'une telle éventualité se produise»*.

Il a été jugé en matière bancaire qu'en l'absence de la notification prévue à l'article L. 511-22 (c'est-à-dire la notification des informations adéquates par l'autorité compétente de l'Etat d'origine), le défaut de notification n'entraîne pas la nullité du contrat de prêt consenti par une banque étrangère à un emprunteur français (Cour d'Appel de Paris, 17 juin 1999).

En revanche, mais en matière financière et dans le cadre de la libre prestation, la Cour de Cassation a estimé, dans un arrêt de sa chambre criminelle du 11 mai 2000 , que l'activité de démarchage en vue du recueil de fonds et de leur placement sur les marchés nord-américains, activité de réception et de transmission d'ordres pour le compte de tiers, était une activité exclue par l'article 26 de la Loi du 2 juillet 1996 de celles pouvant être fournies par un établissement d'investissement agréé dans un autre Etat membre. En conséquence, l'entreprise de droit allemand et ayant son siège social en Allemagne ne pouvait proposer de tels services en France sans encourir des sanctions pénales.

5. Toutefois, pour pouvoir exercer en France des activités non expressément inscrites dans la liste annexée à la Directive, l'établissement de crédit établi dans un Etat de l'EEE doit en demander préalablement l'autorisation au CECEI. A notre connaissance cette situation ne s'est pas présentée ou n'a pas fait l'objet de publication.

6. Le CECEI estime que la réglementation française, en ce qu'elle a transposé quasiment mot à mot les dispositions des directives européennes est insusceptible de critique sur ce point.

Il convient de souligner à cet égard la grande ouverture du marché français aux établissements de crédit de l'Espace Economique Européen. En effet, selon la liste publiée par le CECEI, on comptait au 31 décembre 2001, 55 succursales d'établissements de crédit de l'EEE exerçant en libre établissement. Ce chiffre est stable depuis 1997. On comptait également 315 établissements de crédit de l'EEE exerçant leur activité en libre prestation de service. CE chiffre est à rapprocher de celui pour l'année 1997 où l'on ne comptait que 167 établissements de crédit. La croissance du nombre des établissements de crédit exerçant en libre prestation démontre le bon fonctionnement de la règle du contrôle par l'Etat d'origine.

QUESTION 7

Si les succursales des établissements de crédit communautaires sont soumises à la surveillance des autorités de leur pays d'origine, elles n'en doivent pas moins respecter les règles de l'Etat d'accueil en matière de liquidité et de politique monétaire, ainsi que les règles d'intérêt général.

En application de l'article L. 511-24 du Code monétaire et financier, les succursales des établissements communautaires ne sont pas soumises «-*aux règlements du Comité de la réglementation bancaire et financière (CRBF), sauf pour les dispositions qui n'ont pas fait l'objet de coordination entre les Etats membres, lorsqu'elles présentent un caractère d'intérêt général ou lorsqu'elles sont relatives à la politique monétaire ou à la liquidité des établissements*». Le CRBF détermine les dispositions de ses règlements qui demeurent applicables aux succursales d'établissements communautaires.

L'article 5 du règlement n° 92-13 du 23 décembre 1992 a défini les règles d'intérêt général que les établissements de crédits originaires d'autres états membres doivent, conformément à la deuxième directive des coordination bancaire, respecter lorsqu'ils effectuent des opérations de banque en France. Ces dispositions d'intérêt général comprennent:

—les normes relatives à l'organisation des services communs (1);
—les règles concernant les conditions d'ouverture des guichets (2);
—les normes concernant la protection de la clientèle, à l'exception des dispositions concernant la garantie des dépôts, qui doit être assurée par un système du pays d'origine (3).

Les règles de bonne conduite et les autres dispositions d'intérêt général que les établissements de crédit originaires d'autres Etats membres doivent respecter lorsqu'ils proposent en France des services d'investissement sont définies par le Conseil des marchés financiers (CMF) et par la Commission des opérations de bourse (COB).

1°) L'organisation des services communs

La loi française reconnaît l'exercice de services communs à la profession bancaire, dont la création résulte soit d'une loi spéciale soit d'un règlement adopté par le Comité de la Réglementation Bancaire et Financière (CRBF). L'exercice de ces services communs à la profession bancaire est une particularité française.

Ces services communs ont pour objet de contribuer au bon fonctionnement du système bancaire. Ils sont actuellement au nombre de 6 et sont gérés par la Banque de France.

1.1. Le fichier central des risques a pour objet de recenser l'ensemble des concours accordés par des établissements de crédit à des personnes morales ou physiques, au titre de leurs activités professionnelles, et de fournir ainsi à tous les établissements une information à jour sur l'endettement total par catégorie de crédits contractés en France de leurs clients actuels ou potentiels. Ce fichier est alimenté par les déclarations mensuelles des établissements de crédit. Il est utilisé par les établissements de crédit en vue d'orienter leur décision de prêt. Il sert également aux autorités monétaires qui disposent d'informations régulières sur la distribution du crédit.

1.2. Le fichier bancaire des entreprises comporte des informations sur plus de 2 millions d'entreprises et plus d'un million de dirigeants. Il permet à la Banque de France d'apprécier la situation financière du secteur productif. Il est également utilisé par la profession bancaire comme source d'informations sur la situation d'un grand nombre d'entreprises ainsi qu'à des fins prudentielles, pour le classement des émetteurs éligibles au titre de la surveillance des risques de marché.

1.3. Le fichier des incidents de paiement sur effets est géré par la Banque de France en application du règlement n°86-08 du 27 février 1986. Ce fichier comporte les incidents de paiement constatés sur des ordres de paiements autres que des chèques, c'est-à-dire sur les lettres de change, les billets à ordre, les effets acceptés ou les obligations cautionnées, dès lors qu'ils concernent des titulaires de comptes exerçant une activité professionnelle non salariée et qu'ils portent sur un montant au moins égal à 1.500 Euros ou à 3.000 Euros selon la nature des instruments. Il est ouvert à tout établissement de crédit qui peut obtenir le relevé des incidents de paiement déclarés au nom d'un même titulaire de comptes.

1.4. Le fichier central des chèques impayés vise, en application de la loi du 30 décembre 1991 et du décret du 22 mai 1992 relatif à la sécurité des chèques et des cartes de paiement, à la prévention de l'émission de chèques sans provisions. Les établissements de crédit sont tenus de communiquer à la Banque de France les incidents de paiement de chèques qui assure la diffusion de ces informations aux établissements de crédits et aux autres institutions tirées de chèques ainsi qu'aux autorités judiciaires. Il recense également par accord avec la profession les décisions de retrait de cartes bancaires justifiées par un usage abusif, et prises par les établissements adhérant au groupement des cartes bancaires CB.

1.5. Le fichier national des chèques irréguliers est géré également par la Banque de France qui recense les déclarations de perte ou de vol de chèques, les coordonnées bancaires de comptes clôturés et celles des comptes d'interdits bancaires ou judiciaires. Ce fichier est alimenté à la fois par les établissements teneurs de comptes et par les services de police et de gendarmerie. Il permet à tout bénéficiaire de chèques de vérifier la régularité de cet instrument de paiement.

1.6. Le fichier national des incidents de remboursement des crédits aux particuliers a été institué par la loi du 31 décembre 1989 dite loi «-SCRIVENER» relative à la prévention et au règlement des difficultés liées au surendettement des particuliers. Ce fichier offre aux établissements de crédit des éléments d'appréciation sur les difficultés rencontrées par les emprunteurs.

2°) Les règles concernant les conditions d'ouverture des guichets

Depuis 1991, tous les établissements sont libres de créer, transformer, transférer, céder ou fermer des guichets permanents ou périodiques. Ils restent toutefois soumis à une obligation de **déclaration à la Banque de France** qui tient un répertoire des guichets permanents. Ce répertoire recense notamment les codes d'identification utilisés par tous les établissements pour la gestion des domiciliations des opérations.

3°) Les règles concernant les opérations traitées avec la clientèle

Les succursales d'établissements de crédit communautaires sont soumises à l'ensemble des règles de protection de la clientèle qui n'ont pas fait l'objet d'une harmonisation communautaire. S'il est difficile de les présenter de manière exhaustive dans le cadre de ce rapport, il est possible d'indiquer quelques unes de ces règles.

3.1. De manière générale les règles sur les opérations effectuées par les établissements de crédit:
Les établissements de crédits sont tenus de porter à la connaissance de leur clientèle et du public les conditions générales de banque qu'ils pratiquent pour les opérations qu'ils effectuent.
Les établissements de crédit doivent respecter des obligations découlant du secret professionnel dont la violation est sanctionnée par les dispositions du Code Pénal.

3.2. Sur les obligations de régler par voie scripturale:
La loi française impose aux particuliers des obligations de règlement par voie scripturale, ainsi le paiement de tous bien ou service d'un montant supérieur à 22.900 Euros doit être effectué par voie de chèque barré ou

par carte de paiement ou de crédit. De même, tout commerçant immatriculé dans le Registre du Commerce et des Sociétés est tenu de se faire ouvrir un compte dans un établissement de crédit. Enfin, les industriels, les commerçants, artisans, agriculteurs ou membres de professions libérales adhérant à des centres de gestion agréés sont soumis à l'obligation d'accepter les règlements par chèque et faire libeller ces chèques à leur ordre et de ne pas les endosser. L'établissement de crédit tiré est tenu de payer tout chèque d'un montant égal ou inférieur à 15 Euros. Ces obligations diverses contraignent les banques à traiter un nombre important de chèques d'un montant faible, sans que le paiement de ce service rendu aux clients soit autorisé. En effet, la loi française prévoit également que les formules de chèques sont mises gratuitement à la disposition du client.

3.3. Le droit au compte:
De même, la loi française a prévu un droit de toute personne à un compte. La Banque de France désigne l'établissement qui devra ouvrir un compte à «*toute personne qui s'est vue refuser l'ouverture d'un compte de dépôt par plusieurs établissements de crédits et qui, de ce fait, ne dispose d'aucun compte*». L'établissement de crédit désigné peut cependant limiter les services liés à l'ouverture de ce compte aux seules opérations de caisse.

3.4. Les opérations sur comptes:
L'établissement de crédit doit déclarer aux services fiscaux l'ouverture et la clôture des comptes de toute nature.
Les conditions de fonctionnement des comptes, la rémunération des dépôts et des placements effectués en France auprès des établissements de crédits, ainsi que les modalités de calcul des taux de placement et la garantie des dépôts sont organisés par des dispositions particulières.
Chaque type de placement assorti d'un régime fiscal spécial (Plan et Compte d'Epargne Logement, Codevi, Livret d'épargne populaire) fait l'objet d'une réglementation particulière.
La rémunération des dépôts en Euro de résidents à vue ou à moins d'un mois de terme est interdite.

3.5. En matière de crédit:
La rémunération servie en France par les établissements de crédits sur les placements offerts au public peut être exprimée par le taux de rendement actuariel annuel. Toute publicité faite en France pour un tel placement doit mentionner ce taux, calculé avant tout prélèvement fiscal.
Si les établissements de crédits ont toute liberté pour déterminer les conditions des concours qu'ils accordent à leurs clients, les concours

assortis d'une aide publique demeurent régis par des dispositions spéciales concernant notamment les conditions de leur attribution, leur taux, leur mode de remboursement et de garanties. De plus, le calcul du Taux Effectif Global (TEG) doit être mentionné par le contrat de prêt. Il est déterminé en tenant compte non seulement des intérêts mais aussi des frais, commissions et rémunération.

En outre, est considéré comme usuraire, donc interdit, tout prêt dont le taux effectif global excède, au moment où il est consentit de plus du tiers, le taux effectif moyen pratiqué au cours du trimestre précédent par les établissements de crédit pour des opérations de même nature comportant des risques analogues, tel que constaté par la Banque de France.

Les établissements de crédit doivent également respecter les règles de bonne conduite de la profession.

La Commission bancaire (CB) est chargée de contrôler le respect par les succursales communautaires des dispositions législatives et réglementaires qui leurs sont applicables. La procédure de sanction a été définie par le décret n° 93-381 du 15 mars 1993. S'il revient aux autorités du pays d'origine de sanctionner les manquements constatés, la CB conserve toutefois la possibilité de prendre des mesures conservatoires en cas d'urgence.

QUESTIONS 8 ET 9

A notre connaissance, il n'y a pas eu de difficultés concernant l'établissement de succursales d'origine française, ni de difficultés rencontrées par un établissement de crédit établi en France exerçant en libre prestation de service.

Toutefois, il est possible que nous ne disposions pas des informations suffisantes pour répondre à une telle question. Il convient de souligner que, si les décisions du CECEI peuvent faire l'objet d'un recours juridictionnel, elles ne sont, en revanche, soumises à aucune obligation de publicité. Il est donc possible que des difficultés soient survenues sans qu'elles puissent être connues du public, dès lors que les décisions, notamment celle de refuser de notifier les informations requises aux autorités compétentes de l'Etat membre d'accueil, n'ont pas fait l'objet d'un recours juridictionnel.

QUESTION 10

Les autorités de surveillance bancaire et financière ont été mises en place par la loi n°84-46 du 24 janvier 1984 relative à l'activité et aux contrôle des établissements de crédit, qui régit la profession bancaire, désormais codifiée.

La compétence de ces autorités a été étendue par la loi n°96-597 du 2 juillet 1996 de modernisation des activités financières, également codifiée, à la tutelle et à la surveillance des activités financières, exercées par les établissements de crédits et par les entreprises d'investissement.

Les autorités de surveillance bancaires et financières sont les suivantes:
Le Ministre chargé de l'économie et des finances,
Le Gouverneur de la Banque de France,
Le Comité de la Réglementation Bancaire et Financière (CRBF),
Le Comité des Etablissements de Crédits et des Entreprises d'Investissement (CECEI),
La Commission Bancaire (CB).

Il convient de noter également deux institutions de régulation propres aux marchés financiers:

La Commission des opérations de bourse (COB)
Le Conseil des marchés financiers (CMF).

Une remarque peut déjà être faite sur la multiplication des organes intervenant en matière bancaire et financière.

1°) En matière bancaire:

Le **Ministre chargé de l'économie et des finances** désigne les membres du CRBF du CECEI et de la CB. Il préside le CRBF et homologue les règlements. Il est représenté au CECEI et à la CB.

Le **Gouverneur de la Banque de France** est membre du CRBF, il préside le CECEI et la CB.

Le **Comité de la réglementation Bancaire et financière** (CRBF) établit, sous réserve des compétences du Comité de la réglementation comptable, la réglementation concernant l'activité des établissements de crédits et fixe, sous réserve des compétences de la Commission des Opérations de Bourse et du Conseil des marchés financiers, et après avis de ces derniers, les règles applicables aux prestataires des services d'investissements.

Le **Comité des Etablissements de Crédit et des Entreprises d'Investissement** (CECEI), délivre les agréments et les autorisations en liaison, le cas échéant, avec le Conseil des Marchés Financiers et la Commission des opérations de bourse et il organise l'accueil des établissements communautaires en France en liaison avec, le cas échéant, avec le Conseil des Marchés Financiers.

La **Commission Bancaire** contrôle le respect par les établissements de crédits les dispositions législatives et réglementaires qui leur sont applicables et sanctionne les manquements constatés. Elle examine les conditions de l'exploitation des établissements de crédit et veille à la qualité de leur situation financière. Elle veille au respecte des règles de bonne conduite de la profession. Elle veille enfin au respect par les prestataires de services d'investissements des règlements du CRBF les concernant.

2°) En matière financière:

La **Commission des opérations de bourse** (COB) est une autorité administrative indépendante chargée de veiller à la protection de l'épargne investie dans les instruments financiers et tous les autres placements donnant lieu à appel public à l'épargne, à l'information des investisseurs et au bon fonctionnement des marchés d'instruments financiers.

Les établissements de crédits ou entreprises d'investissements sont soumis à la COB dans la mesure où un nombre important d'entre eux font publiquement appel à l'épargne, ils interviennent sur les marchés pour le compte de leurs clients ou pour leurs propres comptes, ils exercent des fonctions de Gérants, de dépositaires ou de Distributeurs de parts d'OPCVM.

Enfin, la COB est chargée de réglementer et de surveiller l'exercice des activités financières notamment en matière de gestion pour compte de tiers.

Il appartient à la COB d'approuver les programmes d'activité des établissements de crédits et des entreprises d'investissements qui entendent proposer des services de gestion de portefeuilles pour compte de tiers.

La COB est également associée aux travaux du CRBF et du CECEI notamment lorsque le CRBF doit examiner des prescriptions d'ordre général touchant à l'activité des prestataires de services d'investissement et lorsque au cours des séances du CECEI sont examinées des demandes d'agrément ou d'autorisation présentées par des établissements de crédits ou des entreprises d'investissements qui entendent proposer des services de gestion de portefeuille pour compte de tiers et qui ont soumis à son approbation leur programme d'activité dans ce domaine.

Le **Conseil des Marchés financiers** (CMF) a été créé par la loi de modernisation des activités financières du 2 juillet 1996. Il a pour mission de réglementer et de surveiller non seulement les marchés financiers mais également l'ensemble des activités financières, à l'exception de la gestion pour compte de tiers qui relève de la compétence de la COB. A ce titre, il définit les principes généraux d'organisation et de fonctionnement des marchés financiers. Il est consulté par le CECEI dans la procédure d'agrément des établissements de crédit ou entreprise d'investissement. Il dispose d'un pouvoir de sanction. Ses décisions sont susceptibles de recours devant le Conseil d'Etat français.

QUESTION 11

La Banque de France n'est pas, elle même, directement chargée de réglementer, d'agréer, ou de surveiller les professions bancaires et financières. En revanche, elle est associée à l'exercice de ces responsabilités.

Le Gouverneur de la Banque de France est un des membres du Comité de la Réglementation Bancaire et Financière qui définit les règles de fonctionnement des établissements de crédit et des entreprises d'investissement.

Le Gouverneur de la Banque de France préside également le Comité des établissements de crédits et des entreprises d'investissement chargée de délivrer les agréments et les autorisations individuelles à tous les établissements de crédits.

Le Gouverneur de la Banque de France préside également la Commission Bancaire, instance chargée de surveiller la situation financière des établissements de crédits et des entreprises d'investissement et de sanctionner les éventuelles infractions à la réglementation bancaire et financière. Les moyens nécessaires au fonctionnement de la Commission Bancaire, notamment à l'exercice des contrôles sont apportés par la Banque de France.

La loi confie en outre au Gouverneur de la Banque de France les responsabilités particulières en matière de maintien de la stabilité du système bancaire. Lorsque la situation d'un établissement de crédit le justifie, il peut en effet «*inviter les actionnaires ou les sociétaires de cet établissement à fournir à celui-ci le soutien qui lui est nécessaire*».

Il peut également «*organiser le concours de l'ensemble des établissements de crédits en vue de prendre les mesures nécessaires à la protection des intérêts des opposants et des tiers, au bon fonctionnement du système bancaire ainsi que la préservation du renom de la place*».

Le Gouverneur de la Banque de France est enfin vice président de droit du Conseil national du crédit et du titre. Et il est également représenté à la Commission des opérations de bourses et au Conseil des marchés financiers sans y avoir droit de vote. La Banque de France donne son avis sur les règlements adoptés par ces autorités avant qu'ils soient homologués par le Ministre.

QUESTION 12

A la différence de la Grande Bretagne, les compétences réglementaires en matière bancaire et financière sont éclatées entre diverses institutions. Ces dernières se partagent également des compétences en matière de surveillance et de sanction des opérateurs.

A titre d'exemple, la COB et le CMF se partagent le pouvoir de tutelle en matière d'offre publique, ce qui ne va pas sans poser des difficultés qu'il est demandé au juge de trancher en définissant le champ de compétence de chacune de ces autorités (cf. Arrêt de la Cour d'Appel de Paris du 23 octobre 2001, M. Chasques et M. Morhange c/ SA Liberty Surf Group et S.p.a. Tiscali, P.A. du 5 février 2002, p. 20).

Compte tenu des dualités de prérogatives de la COB et du CMF, détaillées ci-dessus en réponse à la question 10, il a été décidé au début de l'année 2001 de fusionner ces deux organismes, ainsi que le conseil de discipline de la gestion financière, au sein d'une seule autorité administrative indépendante, dénommée autorité des marchés financiers (AMF).

Le Conseil des Ministres du 8 février 2001 a été saisi en ce sens d'un avant-projet de loi réformant les autorités financières dont l'objectif est de réorganiser, non seulement les autorités des marchés financiers, mais également les autorités de régulation des entreprises d'assurance, des établissements de crédit et des entreprises d'investissement.

Le projet de loi définit l'AMF comme une autorité administrative indépendante, dépourvue de la personnalité morale, mais détenant le pouvoir d'ester en justice.

Elle sera composée d'un collège plénier et de deux commissions spécialisées. Le collège plénier sera composé de 15 membres, majoritairement des représentants des grands corps d'Etat (Conseil d'Etat, Cour de Cassation, Cour des Comptes...), mais également de personnalités du monde professionnel (intermédiaires de marchés, sociétés côtées, sociétés de gestion,...).

Un Commissaire du Gouvernement sera nommé, dont la fonction principale sera de veiller à la conformité des décisions de l'AMF aux textes réglementaires et législatifs.

Par ailleurs, le projet de loi instaure deux commissions spécialisées- : la commission des offres publiques et la commission des sanctions.

La commission des offres publiques aura pour fonction de fixer les règles en matière d'offres publiques. Elle sera composée pour partie de membres du collège plénier, et de représentants du monde professionnel.

La commission des sanctions sera quant à elle constituée exclusivement des membres du collège plénier de l'AMF.

L'AMF sera dotée des prérogatives de la COB et du CMF.

Elle interviendra dans trois domaines: l'organisation et le fonctionnement des marchés, les offres publiques et les règles professionnelles qui s'imposent aux acteurs des marchés.

L'AMF aura la possibilité d'adopter des règlements homologués par le Ministre de l'économie. Elle pourra également prendre des décisions générales et individuelles à l'effet de faire respecter sa réglementation.

L'AMF aura des pouvoirs de contrôle et de sanction. Elle disposera d'un pouvoir d'injonction et pourra saisir les tribunaux en la forme des référés.

En revanche, il reviendra à la seule commission des sanctions de prononcer les sanctions à l'encontre des auteurs d'actes contraires à la réglementation de l'AMF ou contraires aux obligations professionnelles.

Une parfaite distinction est ainsi établie entre l'autorité qui sera chargée de poursuivre le manquement à la réglementation des marchés financiers (l'AMF) et celle qui sera chargée de réprimer (la commission des sanctions).

Ainsi, le Président de l'AMF (qui ne pourra pas siéger à la Commission des sanctions) désignera-t-il un Rapporteur au sein du collège plénier afin d'instruire le dossier. Mais, ce Rapporteur ne pourra pas siéger à la commission des sanctions, conformément à la jurisprudence de la Cour de cassation.

Le vote de ce projet de loi devrait intervenir lors de la prochaine session parlementaire, d'ici la fin de l'année 2002.

QUESTION 13

Les gouvernements français successifs n'ont pas manifesté le souhait de développer le rôle de la Banque centrale européenne en matière de contrôle prudentiel. Il ne semble pas que l'actuel gouvernement issu des élections de juin 2002 déroge sur ce point.

QUESTION 14

En France, la croissance du commerce électronique s'est accompagnée du souci d'assurer la protection de l'investisseur et de l'épargnant.

En l'absence de dispositions législatives, nationales ou communautaires, les autorités de marché ont tenté de préciser les règles relatives à la prestation de services financiers sur Internet. Le CMF a ainsi publié en septembre 1999 une décision générale n° 99-07, relative aux «*Intermédiaires offrant un service de réception-transmission ou d'exécutions d'ordres via Internet*».

Dans le cadre de ses pouvoirs réglementaires, la COB a diffusé une Recommandation n° 99-02 relative à «*la promotion ou à la vente de produits de placement collectif ou de services de gestion sous mandat via Internet*».

Pour le CECEI, l'offre de produits financiers sur Internet relève de la libre prestation de service et non du libre établissement.

Les problèmes identifiés sont relatifs à l'offre de produits financiers sur Internet, à la nature de l'information dispensée auprès du public, et à la souscription des placements ou la signature des mandats de gestion.

1°) Les problèmes relatifs à l'offre:

Du fait du caractère transnational d'Internet, deux problèmes sont susceptibles de se poser: des résidents étrangers peuvent avoir accès aux sites proposant des produits financiers réservés aux résidents français (il faut envisager l'hypothèse d'un site, offshore ou non, référençant des produits financiers non agréés sur le territoire français). En outre, la promotion d'instruments financiers par le biais d'Internet est susceptible d'être qualifiée d'appel public à l'épargne.

1.1. L'offre de produits Français à des non résidents: la nécessaire conformité de l'offre avec les réglementations locales:
Le caractère transnational d'Internet aboutit à toucher un public non visé a priori par la promotion financière organisée sur le site, avec le risque, parfois, d'être en défaut avec les réglementations nationales.
La difficulté est donc de déterminer si les informations diffusées sur le site sont susceptibles d'être considérées comme visant un public non résident.
Dans sa Recommandation n° 99-02, la COB indique:
"La société qui choisit d'ouvrir un site Internet de promotion et / ou de commercialisation de produits de placement collectif ou de services de gestion sous mandat est tenue de veiller à ce que son offre respecte les règles en vigueur dans les territoires visés."
Encore faut-il savoir ce que l'on entend par «territoires visés», à partir du moment où un site Internet est susceptible d'être consulté dans le monde entier. En France, pour déterminer si un territoire particulier est visé par une offre sur Internet la COB se fonde sur plusieurs critères, non exclusifs des uns des autres. Ainsi, le contenu de l'information disponible, la langue, le plan ou l'arborescence du site, les liens établis à l'initiative de la société entre son site et d'autres sites, les conditions d'acceptation des ordres en provenance des résidents de pays étrangers, sont autant de critères analysés par la COB pour permettre d'appréhender le public visé et, par conséquent, le territoire visé par l'information financière diffusée sur un site.
Dans sa Recommandation 99-02, la COB précise: " *Lorsque le site vise les résidents d'autres territoires, la société s'enquiert des réglementations spécifiques à chaque territoire et veille à les respecter.*

Afin que les résidents des pays où il est possible de consulter le site ne soient pas induits en erreur, la société est invitée à préciser le champ géographique de son offre par un avertissement.

1.2. L'offre de produits off shores à des résidents français: le danger du démarchage:
Aux termes de l'article 23 de la loi du 23 décembre 1988 relative aux OPCVM, "*La constitution, la transformation, la fusion, la cession ou la liquidation d'un OPCVM sont soumises à l'agrément de la COB (...) Seront punis d'une amende de* 15.337 euros à 7666.871 euros *et de six*

mois à deux ans d'emprisonnement les dirigeants de droit ou de fait d'un organisme qui aura procédé à des placements collectifs en valeurs mobilières sans avoir été agréé ou qui aura poursuivi son activité malgré un retrait d'agrément."

A cette interdiction s'ajoute celle du démarchage financier effectué par des personnes non agrées, délit puni de trois ans d'emprisonnement, et de 383.435 euros d'amende.

Pour considérer s'il y a ou non démarchage, les autorités de marché se fondent sur une série d'indices relatifs à la nature de l'information donnée et aux techniques de sollicitation utilisées.

A priori, une information succincte, insuffisante pour qu'un investisseur puisse décider de contracter avec le fournisseur concerné sans demande d'information complémentaire, ne pourrait pas, semble-t-il, constituer une offre au sens légal du terme.

En revanche, un site contenant les informations figurant habituellement dans le prospectus d'un OPCVM, et indiquant les modalités de souscription ou d'acquisition des parts effectue un acte de commercialisation et doit par conséquent recueillir l'autorisation à la COB.

De même, le fait de publier une simple liste de produits "offshores" ne serait pas nécessairement considéré comme une offre de parts ou d'actions d'un OPCVM. En revanche, une information sur les performances et sur les modalités de souscription concernant des produits "offshore" non-autorisés en France, et qui figureraient au sein d'éléments concernant des produits agréés ou autorisés en France, serait susceptible d'être qualifié d'offre interdite en France.

1.3. La requalification de l'offre en appel public à l'épargne

La promotion d'instruments financiers par le biais d'un site Internet est susceptible d'être assimilée à un appel public à l'épargne définit *«par l'émission ou la cession d'instruments financiers dans le public en ayant recours soit à la publicité, soit au démarchage, soit à des établissements de crédit ou à des prestataires de service d'investissement»*.

Le simple renvoi, par le biais d'un lien hypertexte, vers un autre site diffusant ledit produit peut être assimilé à un appel public à l'épargne

2°) L'information sur les produits et les services proposés

2.1. La consistance de l'information:

Il est essentiel de permettre à l'investisseur de déterminer si le produit proposé sur Internet fait l'objet d'un agrément et d'une surveillance par une autorité compétente, et de faire la différence entre les produits faisant l'objet d'un placement privé ou les produits constitués dans une zone offshore, et les produits soumis à une norme légale (autorisation, déclaration préalable, ...).

Dans sa recommandation n° 99-02, la COB a déterminé très précisément la consistance de l'information devant accompagner chaque produit financier:

«—l'identité du produit, en particulier sa forme juridique, et la date d'agrément, de visa ou d'autorisation de commercialisation délivré par la Commission des opérations de bourse ,avec mention des éventuelles réserves, investissements ou mises en garde.

—l'identité des opérateurs (société de gestion - le cas échéant, gestionnaire par délégation -, dépositaire, conservateur, commissaire aux comptes, promoteurs personnes habilitées à recevoir les souscriptions et les rachats, correspondant centralisateur pour les OPCVM qui ne sont pas de droit français) ;

— la classification, l'orientation de gestion (politique d'investissement et restrictions spécifiques d'investissement), la nature des risques encourus et l'horizon de placement (ces éléments peuvent être complétés par des indications sur le type d'investisseur " cible ") ;

— l'ensemble des frais supportés par l'investisseur ou par l'OPCVM luimême, frais de gestion, de souscription et de rachat;

—les modalités de souscription et de rachat (notamment les modalités relatives au préavis ou au montant minimum à investir)»

La COB rappelle par ailleurs qu'une information librement consultable par les résidents français ne doit porter que sur des produits de placement collectif dont le régime n'interdit pas le démarchage ou la publicité en France.

2.2. Le contrôle de l'information:

La COB insiste sur la nécessité de permettre au public de se procurer facilement toute la documentation relative aux informations diffusées sur le site, que ces informations soient directement relatives aux caractéristiques du produit, ou relatives à ses performances.

Dans sa Recommandation 99-02, la COB insiste donc sur l'origine des informations, les conditions de leur mise à disposition et sur les systèmes de contrôle permettant de s'assurer que le souscripteur a sciemment renoncé à réclamer des documents papiers.

3°) Règles relatives à la souscription ou la signature du mandat

Les règles de conduite applicables à la fourniture de services d'investissement et à la commercialisation de produits financiers ont été déterminées par la Directive européenne sur les services d'investissement du 10 mai 1993.

Dans ses travaux préliminaires à la recommandation n°99-02, la COB a rappelé le caractère primordial, parmi les règles de bonne conduite, des règles relatives à la relation avec le client, ce d'autant que l'absence de contact direct ou «vocal» entre le client et le prestataire rend délicate la mise en œuvre de ces règles.

Pour la COB, deux des règles de bonne conduite, à savoir connaître son client et adapter sa prestation, doivent trouver une application concrète lors de la configuration des sites offrant un produit ou une service financier.

En ce qui concerne les précautions à prendre avant la souscription ou la signature du mandat, la COB rappelle que le recours à Internet doit être mutuellement bénéfique pour les parties concernées, qui doivent se prémunir dans la mesure du possible contre les risques liés à une utilisation mal maîtrisée.

Comme on peut le constater, faute de pouvoir contrôler l'activité «-transnationale» de l'offre de produits financiers sur Internet, la COB, comme l'ont fait d'autres autorités de marché dans d'autres pays, se préoccupe d'encadrer le plus précisément possible les rapports entre les établissements prestataires de services Internet et leurs clients «internautes», notamment par des recommandations.

Si l'harmonisation en matière bancaire et financière réalisée par les Etats de l'EEE devrait éviter que des entraves à la libre circulation des produits financiers soient rétablies en raison de l'émergence d'un nouveau moyen de communication, il ne faut toutefois pas négliger le risque de discrimination que des préconisations différentes entre les différents Etats européens peuvent faire naître et celui d'une absence de contrôle par une autorité nationale ou communautaire du respect des règles prudentielles.

QUESTION 15

Hormis la Banque de France, les autorités compétentes françaises n'ont aucun rapport institutionnalisé par la loi avec la Banque centrale européenne. Les relations sont de nature informelle.

QUESTION 16

Traditionnellement dévolu aux juges, le pouvoir de sanction en matière financière a peu à peu fait l'objet d'un transfert aux autorités administratives qui ont la faculté de prononcer des sanctions administratives et disciplinaires.

Ces sanctions, tout en étant distinctes des sanctions pénales, leur ressemblent par leur caractère coercitif (amendes, fermeture d'établissements, retrait d'agrément,...).

Ce pouvoir de sanction des autorités administratives a été jugé compatible avec l'article 6.1 de la Convention Européenne de Sauvegarde des Droits de l'Homme. La Cour Européenne des Droits de l'Homme ne s'oppose pas à ce qu'une autorité administrative indépendante soit investie d'un pouvoir de sanctions administratives assimilables à des sanctions pénales (arrêt Le Compte, Van Leuwen et De Mère, 23 juin 1981, n°1/1981/32/47-48).

Toutefois, la dévolution de ce pouvoir de sanction aux autorités administratives indépendantes a eu pour corollaire la judiciarisation croissante de ces autorités, qui doivent respecter un certain nombre de garanties procédurales posées tant par les textes internes régissant ces autorités, que par les principes posés par la CEDH.

Le **principe d'impartialité** est le plus fréquemment invoqué à l'appui des recours intentés contre les décisions des autorités administratives indépendantes.

Sur ce point, on note une divergence d'appréciation sur la portée de ce principe entre les juridictions judiciaires et les juridictions administratives.

Les juridictions administratives, qui ont à statuer sur les décisions de sanctions du CMF, considèrent que ces décisions de sanctions sont assimilables à des sanctions pénales, et que les recours fondés sur l'article 6.1 de la CEDH sont recevables. A ce titre, les conséquences de la présence au délibéré du Rapporteur ont ainsi été examinées. Pour les juridictions administratives, les pouvoirs limités du Rapporteur (il n'est pas à l'origine de la saisine, il ne participe pas à la formulation des griefs et n'a pas le pouvoir de classer l'affaire, ou au contraire d'élargir le cadre de sa saisine,...) permet à celui-ci d'être présent aux délibérés, même avec voie délibérative, sans que cette présence soit contraire aux principes fondamentaux de la CEDH, et notamment de son article 6.1 (Conseil d'Etat, sect. 20 octobre 2000 Société Habib Bank Limited; CE 22 novembre 2000, Société Crédit Agricole Cheuvreux).

Au contraire, le Juge Judiciaire, compétent pour connaître des recours contre les décisions individuelles de la COB, considère que la présence du Rapporteur aux délibérés et sa participation au vote ne permet pas de respecter le principe d'un procès impartial (Cour de Cassation, Assemblée Plénière, 5 février 1999).

En conséquence, la COB a modifié dans un premier temps son règlement intérieur pour mettre en conformité sa procédure avec cette exigence de la CEDH.

Mais c'est aussi l'ensemble de la procédure de sanction des manquements boursiers devant le Collège de la COB qui a été jugé contraire au droit à un procès impartial par la Cour d'Appel de Paris (C A Paris 1ère Chambre H, 7 mars 2000).

La Cour d'Appel de Paris a considéré qu'ayant successivement «*décidé la mise en accusation, formulé les griefs visant la personne poursuivie, statué sur la culpabilité et sanctionné cette dernière*», le Collège de la COB ne pouvait plus être considéré comme objectivement impartial.

Cet arrêt a conduit à réformer la procédure de sanction de la COB par deux décrets du 1er août 2000.

Ces décrets ont, en premier lieu, séparé les tâches entre le Président et le Directeur Général de la COB, et, en second lieu, modifié le statut du Rapporteur, qui reste un membre du Collège désigné à la demande exclusive du Directeur Général, par le Président, mais qui, après avoir élaboré puis présenté son rapport au Collège, ne délibère plus, ni même n'assiste aux délibérés.

Se pose par ailleurs le problème de l'application du **principe de la personnalité des peines** en cas de sanctions pécuniaires et disciplinaires.

En application de ce principe de personnalité des peines, le Juge Administratif sanctionne les décisions infligeant un blâme (sanction disciplinaire) à une société absorbante du fait des agissements de la société absorbée.

En revanche, le Juge Administratif considère que ne sont pas contraires à ce principes les sanctions pécuniaires(sanctions administratives) infligées à cette même société absorbante, toujours du fait des agissements de la société absorbée, au motif que, en droit des sociétés, la fusion a pour conséquence la transmission universelle du patrimoine de la société absorbée par la société absorbante.

Le Juge Judiciaire applique avec rigueur le principe de personnalité des peines, sans distinction selon la nature des sanctions prononcées.

Ainsi, la Cour d'Appel de Paris a eu à connaître de trois procédures de sanctions ouvertes par la COB à l'encontre d'une société pour manquement à son règlement 9807 relatif à l'information du public: la dissolution de ladite société par l'effet de sa scission en 7 sociétés nouvelles avait conduit la COB à notifier à ces dernières les griefs initialement retenus à l'encontre de la société primitive et à prononcer des sanctions pécuniaires à l'encontre de chacune des sept sociétés, en se fondant sur la règle de transmission universelle de patrimoine, applicable en cas de scission (article L 236-3 du Code de Commerce).

Ces décisions ont été annulées par un arrêt de la Cour d'Appel de Paris du 14 mai 1997, confirmé par la Chambre Commerciale de la Cour de Cassation (Cass. Com. 15 juin 1999).

Le Juge Judiciaire a écarté la notion de continuité économique, retenue par la COB pour justifier ses décisions de sanction dans la mesure où le sujet de droit du règlement en 90-02 est l'entreprise considérée comme une personne physique ou morale et non pas l'entreprise considérée comme une entité économique.

Selon le Juge Judiciaire, on ne peut déroger au principe général de la personnalité des poursuites et des sanctions posé par l'article 6.1 de la

CEDH, aux termes duquel il n'est pas possible d'incriminer une personne autre que l'auteur des manquements, sauf fraude à la loi.

Par ailleurs, les autorités administratives indépendantes sont également tenues de respecter l'article 8 de la CEDH, protégeant la vie privée, en respectant, entre autre, les règles de confidentialité et de secret professionnel, notamment à l'égard de l'administration fiscale. Si des dispositions ont adoptées afin de transmettre certaines informations aux autorités chargées de la lutte contre le blanchiment de l'argent, le droit d'accès et de rectification des informations transmises est garanti par les dispositions de la Loi Informatique et Libertés.

QUESTION 17

L'introduction de l'Euro aura sans aucun doute des incidences sur le secteur bancaire, non pas tant du point de vue du contrôle par les autorités compétentes, mais plutôt sur la situation des entreprises établies en France. Ainsi la comparaison des prix pourra être faite plus aisément, et les obligations auxquelles sont soumis les établissements de crédit établis en France, notamment au regard de certains droits reconnus aux clients (droit au compte, droit au formule de chèque gratuite, absence de rémunération des comptes à vue pour les résidents) vont peser de plus en plus lourd dans la compétitivité de ces établissements. De manière récurrente la question de la facturation des chèques est évoquée par les associations professionnelles, à laquelle s'opposent, de manière toute aussi récurrente, les associations de consommateurs.

Si l'harmonisation communautaire des règles comptables et de consolidation permet aux établissements bancaires communautaires d'être évalués sur des bases identiques, en revanche, les divergences des règles nationales en matière de protection des consommateurs entraîne des distorsions de concurrence et des discriminations à rebours que déplorent les associations professionnelles françaises.

GERMANY

Financial Services in the Era of the Euro and E-Commerce:

Does home country control work?

Rapporteur
Dr Adrian Glaesner

ZULASSUNG

Frage 1
Welche Verfahren bestehen für die Aufsichtsbehörden, um die zuständigen Behörden eines anderen Mitgliedstaates gemäss Art. 7 der Zweiten Bankrechtskoordinierungsrichtlinie zu konsultieren, (1) wenn ein Tochterunternehmen eines in einem anderen Mitgliedstaat zugelassenen Kreditinstituts errichtet wird, (2) wenn ein Tochterunternehmen des Mutterunternehmens eines in einem anderen Mitgliedstaat zugelassenen Kreditinstituts errichtet wird, (3) wenn das Kreditinstitut durch die gleichen natürlichen oder juristischen Personen wie ein in einem anderen Mitgliedstaat zugelassenes Kreditinstitut kontrolliert wird?

Die RL 89/646 (Zweite Richtlinie des Rates zur Koordinierung der Rechts- und Verwaltungsvorschriften über die Aufnahme und Ausübung der Tätigkeit der Kreditinstitute v. 15.12.1989) ist ebenso wie 6 weitere einschlägige Bankenrichtlinien[1] durch die Richtlinie 2000/12 v. 20.3.2000 über die Aufnahme und Ausübung der Tätigkeit der Kreditinstitute[2] (Abl. 2000 Nr. L 126/1) ersetzt worden.

Die Kodifizierungsrichtlinie bildet den EG-rechtlichen Rahmen für die Aufsicht über deutsche Banken. Gemäss Art. 12 Kodifizierungsrichtlinie, der mit Art. 7 der Zweiten Bankrechtskoordinierungsrichtlinie identisch ist, muss im Fall der Zulassung eines Kreditinstituts eine vorherige Konsultation der zuständigen Behörden des anderen Mitgliedstaates erfolgen, wenn ein Tochterunternehmen eines in einem anderen Mitgliedstaat zugelassenen Kreditinstituts errichtet wird, ein Tochterunternehmen des

Mutterunternehmens eines in einem anderen Mitgliedstaat zugelassenen Kreditinstituts errichtet wird, oder wenn das Kreditinstitut durch die gleichen natürlichen oder juristischen Personen wie ein in einem anderen Mitgliedstaat zugelassenes Kreditinstitut kontrolliert wird. Art. 28 Kodifizierungsrichtlinie sieht ausdrücklich vor, dass die zuständigen Behörden bei der Überwachung der Tätigkeit der Kreditinstitute zusammenarbeiten und die Informationen austauschen, die für die Ausübung der Aufsicht erforderlich sind.

Art. 7 der zweiten Bankrechtskoordinierungrichtlinie wurde durch §33b KWG umgesetzt. Er begründet die Konsultationspflicht mit den zuständigen Behörden des Herkunftsmitgliedstaats, ohne Einzelheiten zu regeln.

Das Bundesaufsichtsamt für das Kreditwesen hat mit den Aufsichtsbehörden fast aller EU-Mitgliedstaaten sowie der anderen Staaten des EWR (Ausnahmen: Irland und Lichtenstein) bilaterale Vereinbarungen über die Beaufsichtigung von Kreditinstituten –sog. Gemeinsame Standpunkte oder memoranda of understanding- abgeschlossen. Das erste derartige Abkommen ist 1992 zwischen dem Bundesaufsichtsamt für das Kreditwesen und der frz. Commission Bancaire und dem Comité des établissements de crédit geschlossen worden. In diesem Rahmen finden regelmässig bilaterale Konsultationen statt. Wichtiger Bestandteil der memoranda of understanding ist die Einräumung gegenseitiger Prüfungsrechte.

Die zum 01.05.2002 neugegründete Bundesanstalt für Finanzdienstleistungsaufsicht ist hervorgegangen aus der Zusammenlegung des Bundesaufsichtsamts für das Kreditwesen, des Bundesaufsichtsamts für das Versicherungswesen und des Bundesaufsichtsamtes für den Wertpapierhandel. Da das materielle Aufsichtsrecht für die drei Bereiche Bankenaufsicht, Versicherungsaufsicht und Wertpapierhandelsaufsicht hiervon unberührt geblieben ist, richten sich die Kompetenzen der Bundesanstalt für Finanzdienstleistungsaufsicht nach dem für den jeweiligen Sektor einschlägigen materiellen Recht: Kreditwesengesetz, Versicherungsaufsichtsgesetz und Wertpapierhandelsgesetz. Soweit die Beaufsichtigung des Bankensektors betroffen ist, tritt die Bundesanstalt für Finanzdienstleistungsaufsicht an die Stelle des Bundesaufsichtsamtes für das Kreditwesen.

Da der vorliegende Bericht auf die Bankenaufsicht beschränkt ist, wird die Funktion der Bundesanstalt für Finanzdienstleistungsaufsicht nur in bezug auf den Bankensektor geschildert werden.

Die Bundesanstalt für Finanzdienstleistungsaufsicht steht in engem Kontakt mit den anderen Aufsichtsbehörden in der EU, um Informationen auszutauschen, die den Erwerb von Beteiligungen, die Errichtung von Tochtergesellschaften, Eröffnung von Niederlassungen, die Eignung von Geschäftsleitern oder die Ausübung des grenzüberschreitenden

Dienstleistungsverkehrs von Einlagenkreditinstituten oder Wertpapierhandelsunternehmen betreffen.

Frage 2
Hat der vorherige Konsultationsprozess Anlass zu Schwierigkeiten gegeben?

Zu praktischen Erfahrungen der Bankenaufsicht im Zusammenhang mit dem Konsultationsprozess sind keine detaillierten Stellungnahme zu bekommen. Aus dem Jahresbericht des BAKred 2000 (der zuletzt erschienene) ergeben sich keine Anhaltspunkte für Schwierigkeiten in der Praxis.

Frage 3
Sind Fälle bekannt, in denen die zuständige Behörde aus einem der in Art. 5 der Zweiten Bankrechtskoordinierungsrichtlinie genannten Gründe die Zulassung verweigert hat?

Gem. Art.7 Abs.2 Kodifizierungsrichtlinie, der Art. 5 der Zweiten Bankrechtskoordinierungsrichtlinie ersetzt, verweigern die zuständigen Behörden die Zulassung, wenn sie nicht davon überzeugt sind, dass die das Kreditinstitut kontrollierenden Gesellschafter oder indirekten Anteilsinhaber den Anforderungen genügen, um eine solide und umsichtige Führung des Kreditinstituts zu gewährleisten.

Dementsprechend sieht §2b KWG vor, dass der Erwerb einer bedeutenden Beteiligung (10% oder mehr) dem BAFin und der Bundesbank angezeigt werden müssen. Gleichsam ist die Veränderung in einer bestehenden Beteiligung zu melden, wenn Schwellenwerte von 20, 33 oder 50% über- oder unterschritten werden oder die Kontrolle über das Institut erworben wird. Die Anzeige umfasst die Angabe der für die Beurteilung der Zuverlässigkeit der Anteilsinhaber notwendigen Tatsachen. Bei Anteilserwerb durch juristische Personen erstreckt sich die Prüfung der Zuverlässigkeit auch auf die Prüfung der Zuverlässigkeit der Inhaber, gesetzlicher Vertreter oder persönlich haftender Gesellschafter.

Versagungsgründe sind insbesondere die Unzuverlässigkeit des Anzeigenden bzw. der gesetzlichen Vertreter, die Gefährdung einer wirksamen Aufsicht durch den Beteiligungserwerb oder die Gefahr, dass aufgrund des Beteiligungserwerbs das Institut mit Sitz im Inland Tochterunternehmen eines ausländischen Instituts wird, das nicht wirksam beaufsichtigt wird oder dessen Aufsichtsbehörden zu einer befriedigenden Zusammenarbeit mit dem BAFin nicht bereit sind.

Praktische Relevanz hat die Vorschrift beispielsweise in Zusammenhang mit der versuchten Übernahme der Commerzbank durch eine Investorengruppe, die sich in der "Cobra-GmbH" zusammengeschlossen hatte, erlangt. Wegen der Unzuverlässigkeit eines ihrer geschäftsführenden Mitglieder hat die Aufsichtsbehörde –zuständig war das Bundesaufsichtsamt für das Kreditwesen- die Stimmrechtsausübung untersagt.

Daneben besteht gem. § 21 Wertpapierhandelsgesetz eine Meldepflicht an die Bundesanstalt für Finanzdienstleistungsaufsicht, wenn durch Erwerb, Veräusserung oder auf sonstige Weise die Schwellen von 5%, 10%, 25% 50% oder 75% der Stimmrechte an einer börsennotierten Gesellschaft erreicht, überschritten oder unterschritten werden.

Frage 4
Nach Zulassung durch die Behörden seines Heimatlandes ist ein Kreditinstitut nach Massgabe von Art. 18 der zweiten Bankrechtskoordinierungsrichtlinie berechtigt, die in der Anlage zur Richtlinie aufgeführten Tätigkeiten sowohl über eine Zweigstelle, als auch im Wege des Dienstleistungsverkehrs auszuüben.

a) Durch welche gesetzliche Regelungen ist Art.18 umgesetzt worden?

§24a KWG regelt das Prozedere in Zusammenhang mit der grenzüberschreitenden Errichtung von Niederlassungen und Erbringung von Dienstleistungen durch deutsche Einlagenkreditinstitute und Wertpapierhandelsunternehmen. Nach Durchführung des in der Zweiten Bankrechtskoordinierungsrichtlinie vorgesehenen Notifizierungsverfahrens sind die Einlagenkreditinstitute und Wertpapierhandelsunternehmen berechtigt, grenzüberschreitend Dienstleistungen zu erbringen bzw. Niederlassungen zu gründen.

Die Einlagenkreditinstitute bzw. Wertpapierhandelsunternehmen sind verpflichtet, Änderungen in den Verhältnissen, die Gegenstand der Anzeige waren, den Aufsichtsbehörden anzuzeigen.

b) Wie erfolgreich ist das Prinzip der Herkunftsmitgliedstaatkontrolle angewendet worden?

Aus den Veröffentlichungen der Aufsichtsbehörden ergeben sich keine Anhaltspunkte für Schwierigkeiten.

c) Gibt es Fälle, in denen ein Kreditinstitut auf der Grundlage seiner Zulassung im Herkunftsmitgliedstaat Tätigkeiten, die in der Anlage zur zweiten Bankrechtskoordinierungsrichtlinie genannt sind, in Deutschland ausüben darf, die einem in Deutschland zugelassenen Kreditinstitut verboten sind?

Nein. Die im Anhang I der Kodifizierungsrichtlinie aufgeführten Tätigkeiten, der Anhang II der Zweiten Bankrechtskoordinierungsrichtlinie entspricht, sind in Deutschland zugelassenen Kreditinstituten erlaubt.

Frage 5
Welchen Genehmigungserfordernissen unterliegt ein in einem anderen Mitgliedstaat zugelassenes Kreditinstitut mit Blick auf Tätigkeiten, die nicht von der Zweiten Bankrechtskoordinierungsrichtlinie gedeckt sind?

In Bezug auf Tätigkeiten, die nicht unter die Richtlinie fallen, und die auch nicht aufgrund anderer EG-rechtlicher Vorschriften privilegiert sind, gilt der allgemeine Genehmigungsvorbehalt des §32 KWG. Danach bedarf der Genehmigung der Bundesanstalt für Finanzdienstleistungsaufsicht, wer gewerbsmässig oder in einem Umfang, der einen in kaufmännischer Weise eingerichteten Geschäftsbetrieb erfordert, Bankgeschäfte betreibt oder Finanzdienstleistungen erbringt.

Frage 6
Gibt es Fälle, in denen derartige Vorschriften mit Gemeinschaftsrecht unvereinbar sein könnten?

So weit ersichtlich, keine. Die Befugnis der Mitgliedstaaten zur Aufrechterhaltung von nationalen Regelungen hinsichtlich bestimmter aufsichtsrechtlicher Sachverhalte ergibt sich allerdings aus dem Gesichtspunkt, dass diese Sachverhalte aus zwingenden Gründen des Allgemeininteresses geregelt werden müssen, dass keine abschliessende EG-rechtliche Regelung vorliegt und dass eine Kontrolle durch die Behörden des Herkunftsland nicht geleistet werden kann. Mit zunehmender Harmonisierung des Aufsichtsrecht reduziert sich daher der Raum für die Anwendung dieser Vorschriften.

DAS ALLGEMEININTERESSE

Frage 7
Gemäss Art. 21 der Zweiten Bankrechtskoordinierungsrichtlinie behält der Aufnahmemitgliedstaat bestimmte Befugnisse gegenüber in einem anderen Mitgliedstaat zugelassenen Kreditinstituten.

a) Welches sind die aus Gründen des Allgemeininteresses erlassenen Vorschriften?

Es gibt keinen numerus clausus dieser Vorschriften. Die Erbringung von

Dienstleistungen und die Errichtung von Niederlassungen unterliegen einer allgemeinen Aufsicht durch die Bundesanstalt für Finanzdienstleistungsaufsicht hinsichtlich der ordnungsgemässen Durchführung der Geschäfte. Die Bundesanstalt für Finanzdienstleistungsaufsicht hat die Kompetenz, gegen ungesetzliche Geschäfte einzuschreiten und die sofortige Einstellung der Geschäfte und deren Abwicklung anzuordnen (§§ 37, 44c KWG). Weitergehende Befugnisse hat die Bundesanstalt für Finanzdienstleistungsaufsicht gegenüber Niederlassungen ausländischer Unternehmen: diese unterliegen der Liquiditätskontrolle durch die deutschen Aufsichtsbehörden. Besteht die Gefahr für die Erfüllung der Verpflichtungen einer Niederlassung gegenüber seinen Gläubigern, reichen die Befugnisse bis hin zur Schliessungsanordnung.

b) Haben die zuständigen Behörden die ihnen gem. Art. 21 (5) der Zweiten Bankrechtskoordinierungsrichtlinie zustehenden Befugnisse ausgeübt?

Soweit ersichtlich, ist kein Fall bekannt geworden, in dem die Aufsichtsbehörden einem Kreditinstitut mit Zulassung in der Europäischen Union die Aufnahme neuer Geschäftstätigkeiten untersagt hätten.

c) Welche Rechtsschutzverfahren bestehen gegenüber Massnahmen der Aufsichtsbehörden?

Gegenüber Anordnungen der Bundesanstalt für Finanzdienstleistungsaufsicht ist nach Durchführung des Widerspruchsverfahrens der allgemeine Verwaltungsrechtsweg eröffnet. Allerdings ist darauf hinzuweisen, dass die Anordnungen gem. §49 KWG "sofort vollziehbar" sind. Das bedeutet, dass die Einlegung des Rechtsmittels das betroffene Institut nicht von der Verpflichtung befreit, die Anordnung zu befolgen.

d) Gibt es Präzedenzfälle für die Einlegung von Rechtsmitteln?

Soweit ersichtlich, sind keine Fälle von besonderem Interesse veröffentlicht worden.

DIE ERRICHTUNG VON NIEDERLASSUNGEN

Frage 8
Gibt es Schwierigkeiten in Zusammenhang mit der Errichtung von

Niederlassungen durch ein Kreditinstitut, wo Deutschland (a) der Herkunftsmitgliedstaat und (b) der Aufnahmemitgliedstaat des betroffenen Kreditinstituts ist?

Aus den veröffentlichten Stellungnahmen der Aufsichtsbehörden ergeben sich insoweit keine Anhaltspunkte.

DIE GRENZÜBERSCHREITENDE ERBRINGUNG VON DIENSTLEISTUNGEN

Frage 9

Gibt es Schwierigkeiten in Zusammenhang mit der grenzüberschreitenden Erbringung von Dienstleistungen durch ein Kreditinstitut, wo Deutschland (a) der Herkunftsmitgliedstaat und (b) der Aufnahmemitgliedstaat des betroffenen Kreditinstituts ist?

Aus den veröffentlichten Stellungnahmen der Aufsichtsbehörden ergeben sich insoweit keine Anhaltspunkte.

DIE ZUSTÄNDIGEN AUFSICHTSBEHÖRDEN

Frage 10

Welche sind in Deutschland die mit der Aufsicht über Kreditinstitute befassten Behörden und damit die "zuständigen Behörden" im Sinne der Zweiten Bankrechtskoordinierungsrichtlinie?

Die in Deutschland zuständigen Aufsichtsbehörden sind die Bundesanstalt für Finanzdienstleistungsaufsicht und die Deutsche Bundesbank. Wie zu Frage 1 bereits ausgeführt, ist die Bundesanstalt für Finanzdienstleistungsaufsicht die Nachfolgebehörde für die Bundesaufsichtsämter für das Kreditwesen, das Versicherungswesen und den Wertpapierhandel. Die Bundesanstalt für Finanzdienstleistungsaufsicht verfügt über hoheitliche Befugnisse zur Durchführung aufsichtsrechtlicher Massnahmen. Im Bereich der Bankenaufsicht arbeitet sie mit der Deutschen Bundesbank zusammen, der die laufende Überwachung der Institute obliegt.

Frage 11

Welche Rolle spielt die Deutsche Bundesbank in der Aufsicht über die Kreditinstitute?

Gem. § 7 KWG obliegt der Deutschen Bundesbank die laufende Überwachung der Institute. Hierzu bedient sie sich ihrer

Hauptverwaltungen (frühere Landeszentralbanken). Die laufende Überwachung umfasst insbesondere alle Massnahmen zur Überprüfung der angemessenen Eigenkapitalausstattung und die Auswertung der von den Instituten einzureichenden Unterlagen. Die Deutsche Bundesbank hat dabei die Richtlinien der Bundesanstalt für Finanzdienstleistungsaufsicht zu beachten, die diese im Einvernehmen mit der Deutschen Bundesbank erlässt. Die Kompetenz zum Erlass hoheitlicher Massnahmen hat dagegen ausschliesslich die Bundesanstalt für Finanzdienstleistungsaufsicht. Diese legt allerdings "in der Regel" ihren Massnahmen die von der Deutschen Bundesbank getroffenen Prüfungsfeststellungen und Bewertungen zugrunde.

Daneben sieht das KWG vor, dass bei der Festlegung der Grundsätze für die Beurteilung der angemessenen Eigenkapitalausstattung und Solvabilität die Bundesanstalt für Finanzdienstleistungsaufsicht "Einvernehmen" mit der Deutschen Bundesbank herzustellen hat. Auch die Verordnungsermächtigung des § 24 KWG sieht vor, dass das Bundesfinanzministerium die Verordnungskompetenz "im Benehmen" mit der Deutschen Bundesbank auszuüben habe.

Insgesamt kann man daher festhalten, dass die Deutsche Bundesbank im Bereich der vorbeugenden Überwachung der Institute die Vorarbeit leistet, die es der Bundesanstalt für Finanzdienstleistungsaufsicht erlaubt, die ggfs. erforderlichen hoheitlichen Massnahmen zu erlassen.

Frage 12

Wie wird in Deutschland die Notwendigkeit einer integrierten Finanzdienstleistungsaufsicht im Gegensatz zur Sektoraufsicht beurteilt?

Aufgrund des Gesetzes über die integrierte Finanzdienstleistungsaufsicht vom 22. April 2002 ist zum 1. Mai 2002 die Bundesanstalt für Finanzdienstleistungsaufsicht gegründet worden. Auch wenn das materielle Prüfungsrecht der drei Sektoren nicht konsolidiert worden ist und die Bundesanstalt für Finanzdienstleistungsaufsicht dementsprechend je nach Sektor auf verschiedenen rechtlichen Grundlagen (KWG, VAG und WphG) agiert, wurde doch erstmals eine staatliche Aufsichtsbehörde geschaffen, die sektorübergreifend die wichtigsten Teilnehmer des Finanzmarktes – Kreditinstitute, Finanzdienstleistungsinstitute und Versicherungsunternehmen – überwachen soll. Mit der Schaffung einer integrierten Allfinanzaufsicht sollte zum einen die Beaufsichtigung von Finanzprodukten unabhängig davon sichergestellt werden, ob es sich um Versicherungs- oder Bankprodukte handelt. In diesem Zusammenhang ist auf die insbesondere im asset management zu beobachtende Entwicklung hinzuweisen, dass Banken Produkte anbieten, die traditionell Versicherungsprodukte waren. Zum anderen ist zu beobachten, dass in

Deutschland wie in anderen europäischen Ländern auch Banken und Versicherungen sich verstärkt zu sektorübergreifenden Konzernen zusammenschliessen.

Aufgrund dieser Entwicklung bestand das Bedürfnis, durch die Entwicklung einer sektorübergreifenden Aufsicht auch die Finanzaufsicht an den veränderten Marktverhältnissen auszurichten. Gleichzeitig sollen damit Wettbewerbsverzerrungen vermieden werden, die aufgrund von Regelungsdifferenzen unter einer geteilten Aufsichtsstruktur entstehen könnten. Mit der Schaffung einer Allfinanzaufsichtsbehörde ist die Erwartung verbunden, dass sie im Rahmen eines einheitlichen Aufsichtskonzeptes gleiche Regeln für gleiche Risiken entwickelt und damit aufsichtliche Wettbewerbsgleichheit gewährleistet. Um die Funktionsfähigkeit des gesamten Finanzsektors sicherzustellen, verfolgt die Bundesanstalt für Finanzdienstleistungsaufsicht gleichermassen das Ziel der Solvenzsicherung von Banken und Versicherungen wie das Ziel des Schutzes von Kunden und Anlegern. Dabei entspricht es der allgemeinen Auffassung, dass die Finanzaufsicht nur im öffentlichen Interesse ausgeübt wird. Der einzelne Marktteilnehmer (Bürger oder Unternehmen) kann aus den aufsichtsrechtlichen Vorschriften kein subjektives öffentliches Recht auf "Durchführung" von finanzaufsichtsrechtlichen Massnahmen herleiten. In diesem Zusammenhang ist auf ein aktuelles Vorabentscheidungsverfahren hinzuweisen, in dem der Bundesgerichtshof dem EuGH die Frage vorgelegt hat, inwiefern diese Sichtweise aufrechterhalten werden kann im Lichte des inzwischen erreichten Umfangs an Harmonisierungsrichtlinien, die zu einem grossen Teil mit dem Schutz des Verbrauchers begründet worden sind.

Frage 13
Welche Rolle sollte die Europäische Zentralbank in der Finanzaufsicht spielen?

Die gem. Art. 105 Abs. 5 EGV vorgesehene Mitwirkung der EZB an der Finanzaufsicht wird, wie es auch durch Art. 25 EZB-Satzung zum Ausdruck kommt, als beratende Rolle angesehen. Dieses gilt jedenfalls so lange, wie der Rat nicht durch einstimmigen Beschluss der EZB nach Art. 105 Abs. 6 EGV "besondere Aufgaben im Zusammenhang mit der Aufsicht über Kreditinstitute und sonstige Finanzinstitute" überträgt. Aufgaben der Versicherungsaufsicht sind hiervon ausdrücklich ausgenommen.

Frage 14
In welchem Umfang sind die Schlussfolgerungen dieses Berichts durch die Einführung des Euro und die Entwicklung des e-commerce beeinflusst worden?

Weder die Einführung des Euro, noch die Entwicklung des e-commerce stellen das bisherige Konzept der Finanzaufsicht grundsätzlich in Frage. Allerdings führt die Entwicklung des e-commerce zu neuen aufsichtsrechtlichen Fragestellungen. Der Vertrieb von Finanzdienstleistungen über e-commerce macht es beispielsweise möglich, Geschäftsabläufe zwischen einem ausländischen Anbieter und seinem inländischen Kunden auf rein virtueller Basis abzuwickeln, ohne dass eine Tätigkeit im herkömmlichen Sinn auf dem Territorium des Kunden ausgeübt würde. Hieraus ergibt sich die Frage, wann eine die Erlaubnispflicht auslösende Tätigkeit vorliegt. Die bisherige Verwaltungspraxis nahm eine Erlaubnispflicht an, wenn "wesentliche Teilakte" im Gebiet der Bundesrepublik Deutschland erbracht wurden. In einer jüngeren Verlautbarung hat das Bundesaufsichtsamt für das Kreditwesen erklärt, dass "angesichts ... der zunehmenden Nutzung moderner Kommunikationsmittel für Zwecke des Fernabsatzes ... die Erlaubnispflicht heute selbst in den Fällen zu bejahen (ist), in denen sie, z. B. für das vereinzelte Werben inländischer Kunden durch Aktivitäten im Inland, in der Vergangenheit möglicherweise verneint wurde" (Verlautbarung des Bundesaufsichtsamts für das Kreditwesen v. 12.04.2002, Az II 7 [118751] 100). Hierin kommt zum Ausdruck, dass die aufgrund der technischen Entwicklungen schwerer fallende Abgrenzung zwischen Tätigkeiten, die noch nicht erlaubnispflichtig sind und Tätigkeiten, die dem Genehmigungsvorbehalt unterliegen, tendenziell zu Lasten der genehmigungsfreien Tätigkeiten getroffen wird.

Frage 15
Welche Beziehung besteht zwischen den zuständigen Aufsichtsbehörden und der Europäischen Zentralbank?

Die Deutsche Bundesbank wirkt im ESZB über die Mitgliedschaft ihres Präsidenten im EZB-Rat mit. Darüber hinaus ist sie auf Arbeitsebene in den vom EZB-Rat gebildeten Ausschüssen und Arbeitsgruppen vertreten.

Frage 16
Welchen Einfluss hat die Menschenrechtsgesetzgebung auf das Aufsichtsrecht?

Die Menschenrechtsgesetzgebung hat keinen nennenswerten Einfluss.

Frage 17
Haben sich bei der Einführung des Euro Unzulänglichkeiten in Zusammenhang mit der Beaufsichtigung von Kreditinstituten und das Bedürfnis nach einer weiteren Harmonisierung ergeben?

Nein.

ZUSAMMENFASSENDE THESEN

1. Der durch das Gemeinschaftsrecht mit der zweiten Bankrechtskoordinierungsrichtlinie und der sie ersetzenden Kodifizierungsrichtlinie vorgegebene Rahmen für die Einführung des Prinzips der Herkunftslandkontrolle wurde in Deutschland angemessen umgesetzt.
2. Aus Sicht der Aufsichtsbehörden liegt es nahe, die Ausgangsfrage positiv zu beantworten. Die Zusammenarbeit der Aufsichtsbehörden vollzieht sich in einem Rahmen, der aufsichtsrechtliche Mindeststandards garantiert, eine effiziente grenzüberschreitende Ausübung der Aufsicht ermöglicht und den Aufsichtsbehörden den Handlungsspielraum belässt, bestimmte für den Heimatmarkt wichtige Kontrollfunktionen (Liquiditätskontrolle, Einschreiten gegen ungesetzliche Geschäfte) weiterhin auszuüben.
3. Aus Sicht der betroffenen Unternehmen stellen sich die den Behörden des Gastlandes verbleibenden Kontrollbefugnisse als Beschränkungen in der Ausübung der Grundfreiheiten dar, die erhöhte Kosten ohne Schaffung von Mehrwert und damit Effizienzverluste bedeuten.
4. Aus gemeinschaftsrechtlicher Sicht ist festzuhalten, dass das für die Schaffung des Binnenmarktes geltende Prinzip "Mindestharmonisierung und gegenseitige Anerkennung" im Bereich der Finanzdienstleistungen nur unvollkommen umgesetzt worden ist.

NOTES

[1] RL 73/183/EWG
RL 77/780/EWG
RL 89/299/EWG
RL 89/647/EWG
RL 92/30/EWG
RL 92/121/EWG

[2] Im folgenden: **"Kodifizierungsrichtlinie"**

ITALY

Financial Services in the Era of the Euro and E-Commerce:

Does home country control work?

Rapporteurs
Sergio M. Carbone, Francesco Munari** and Paolo Terrile****

I. MEASURES IMPLEMENTING THE SECOND BANKING DIRECTIVE

The provisions of the Second Banking Directive – i.e. Council Directive 89/646/EEC of 15 December 1989 on the coordination of laws, regulations and administrative provisions relating to the taking up and pursuit of the business of credit institutions (OJ L 386 30.12.1989 p.1) were originally implemented by Italy with the Legislative Decree 14 December 1992 no. 481 (Italian Official Journal, Ordinary Supplement, 17 December 1992, no. 296).

At the present, however, these provisions are contained in the Legislative Decree 1 September 1995, no. 385, *Testo Unico delle leggi in materia bancaria e creditizia* (Italian Official Journal, Ordinary Supplement, 30 September 1993, no. 230), which consolidated legislation on banking activity (hereinafter referred to as the "D.Lgs. no. 385/95").

Other sources of regulation which are relevant for the adoption of the Second Banking Directive into Italian law can be found in second-level acts and provisions, aimed at implementing the rules of law set forth in statutory provisions. It should be noted that second-level legislation adopted to implement D.Lgs. no. 481/92 with respect to issues governed by the Second Baking Directive is mainly still in force even if the latter Decree has been repealed by D.Lgs. no. 385/95: the above pursuant to Art. 161.5 of D.Lgs.

* Full Professor of International Law at the University of Genoa.
** Full Professor of International Law at the University of Genoa.
*** Lecturer of International Economic Law at the University of Genoa.

no. 385/95, establishing that the provisions enacted by credit authorities pursuant to legal rules which were repealed or substituted by the Decree of 1995 remain valid until the entry in force of relevant new acts.

This is valid for instance for the Ministerial Decree 28 December 1992, which sets forth rules and principles concerning the controls on the activities of Italian subsidiaries of Community credit institutions. Indeed, Art. 55 of D.Lgs. no. 385/95 now provides that Banca d'Italia should conduct controls on the subsidiaries of Community banks pursuant to a resolution of the Interministerial Decree on Credit and Savings (*Comitato interministeriale per il credito ed il risparmio,* CICR); yet, such resolution has not been enacted, so that the above mentioned Ministerial Decree is still in force.

Rules and procedures which implement the framework envisaged by the Second Banking Directive are also set forth in the Instructions for the supervision of banks (*Istruzioni di Vigilanza per le banche*) which Banca d'Italia enacts pursuant to relevant provisions, in particular Arts. 4 and 5 of D.Lgs. no. 385/95 (hereinafter referred to as "Instructions"). Similarly, Art. 5 of the Ministerial Decree 28.12.1992 entrusts Banca d'Italia to enact the rules for its application, which can be found in the Instructions.

The provisions of the Second Banking Directive are now consolidated in Directive 2000/12/EC of the European Parliament and of the Council of 20 March 2000 relating to the taking up and pursuit of the business of credit institutions (OJ L 126 26.5.2000 p.1).

II. PROCEDURES FOR THE AUTHORISATION OF BANKS AFFILIATED TO OTHER COMMUNITY BANKS

The D.Lgs. no. 385/95 does not contain specific provisions addressing the scope of application of Art. 7 of Directive no. 89/647/EEC (now Art. 12 of Directive 2000/12/EC). The issue instead is expressly dealt by the Instructions.

More precisely, Title I (Subjects), Chapter 1 (Authorisation to Banking Activity), Section VIII (Affiliates to Foreign Banks), Par. 1 (Affiliates to Community Banks), specifies that the grant of an authorisation in favour of banking affiliates to Community banks is subject to the rules and procedures normally applicable for the grant of authorisation to banking activity (which are set forth at legislative level in Arts. 13 and 14 of D.Lgs. no. 385/95 and its implementing measures, and described in the same Chapter of the Instructions, under Sections I to VI). For the purpose of the relevant provisions of the Instructions, an "affiliate to a foreign bank" ("*filiazione di banca estera*") is meant to designate a national bank controlled also indirectly by a foreign bank or by natural and juridical persons, which control the foreign bank.

The consultative requirements of Art. 12 Directive 2000/12/EC are therefore accommodated in the framework of the rules and procedures which otherwise govern the grant of an authorization to banking activity. In this regard, the Instructions simply specify that in case of an authorization concerning an affiliate to a Community bank, Banca d'Italia issues the authorization with the prior consultation of the home Member State (competent authorities) of the bank, pursuant to Art. 7 of the Directive 2000/12/EC.

In this regard, it is worth noticing that these prior consultations take place during the process of authorisation and are carried out in an unstructured manner and without specific provisions regulating the procedures for the consultation.

According to the Report of Banca d'Italia on the activities of year 2001, there are ten banks affiliated to Community banks operating in Italy.

III. THE FRAMEWORK OF COOPERATION OF BANCA D'ITALIA WITH THE COMPETENT AUTHORITIES OF OTHER MEMBER SSTATES

The exchange of information among competent authorities takes place under specific Memoranda of Understanding bilaterally executed by Banca d'Italia with the competent national authorities of other Member States. These Memoranda are in particular aimed at defining the actual forms of cooperation between home and host Member States for the purpose of assuring an efficient conduct of the prudential supervision on subsidiaries and affiliates of Community banks. The Memoranda are normally based on specific principles:

—they define in details the tasks entrusted to and falling within the responsibility of the competent authority of the home Member State. This is important in respect of the controls on the liquidity of the bank, for which the responsibility of the home State is normally recognized: hence, the latter authority exerts the supervision on this point in the framework of the supervision on the overall financial stability of the credit institution (host State authorities retain residual power where controls on liquidity affect monetary policies);
—they address the necessity to maintain a continuous and reciprocal flow of information, through the establishment of periodical meetings and the possibility to have recourse to procedure for consultation on specific issues of supervision;
—without prejudice for the home State control principle, they set up mechanisms for the prudential supervision of market risk affecting banks because of the operation of their subsidiaries abroad;

—they include measures of cooperation for inspections and for the management of crises involving credit institutions which might present risks of propagation.

The above mentioned framework of cooperation is supported by the provisions of Art. 7.6 of D.Lgs. no. 385/95, according to which Banca d'Italia may cooperate with the competent authorities of Member States in order to favour the respective tasks and also through the exchange of information. Further statutory support can be found under Italian law in Art. 69 of D.Lgs. no. 385/95: with respect to the issue of cooperation, this provision establishes that Banca d'Italia may agree with the authorities of other EC Member States both modes of cooperation and the respective allocation of specific tasks on each authority regarding the prudential supervision on a consolidated basis of groups operating the diverse countries.

IV. REFUSAL TO GRANT AUTHORISATION ON THE GGROUNDS SET FORTH IN ART. 5 DIRECTIVE 89/646EEC (NOW ART. 7.1 AND 2 OF DIRECTIVE 2000/12/EC)

Pursuant to Art. 7.1 of Directive 2000/12/EC, competent authorities may not grant authorisation for the taking-up of the business of credit institutions before they have been informed about the identities of the shareholders or members, whether direct or indirect, natural or legal persons, that have qualifying holdings, as well as about the amounts of those holdings. In addition, Art. 7.2 provides that the competent authorities shall refuse authorisation if, taking into account the need to ensure the sound and prudent management of credit institutions, they are not satisfied as to the suitability of the abovementioned shareholders or members.

Italian law provisions concerning the control of the identity and suitability of shareholders are contained in Art. 14 D.Lgs. no. 385/95, pursuant to which Banca d'Italia may authorize the exercise of banking activity if the participants to the stock capital of the credit institution present (a) the requirements of honour envisaged under Art. 25 and (b) the conditions for the release of an authorization as set forth in Art. 19.

In respect of (a) above, the requirements of honour required by Art. 25 to participate in the capital of credit institutions have been established by the Department of Treasury through the Ministerial Decree 18 March 1998 no. 144: basically, shareholders should not be subject to criminal judgements and measures concerning facts which are not compatible with the exercise of banking activity.

In respect of (b) above, Art. 19 of the Decree establishes that Banca d'Italia must authorise the acquisition of "qualified participations" by any interested party in credit institutions, this qualified participation being either above 5% of the capital or a controlling participation.

Pursuant to these provisions, Banca d'Italia may apply the rules and requirements set forth by Art. 7 Directive 2000/12/EC (which are preconditions for the grant of an authorisation). To this regard, however, it should be noted that decisions to refuse authorisation are not officially published, opposed to decisions which grant it.

V. THE FREEDOM OF ESTABLISHMENT AND TO PROVIDE SERVICES IN ITALY BY COMMUNITY BANKS: THE MEASURES OF IMPLEMENTATION

Articles 18 of the Directive 89/646/EEC (now Art. 19 Directive 2000/12/EC) and the related provisions have been originally implemented under Italian law at a statutory level under D.Lgs. no. 481/92. As noted, these provisions are nowadays contained in D.Lgs. no. 385/95, more precisely in Articles 15 on subsidiaries (especially pars. 3 and 5) and 16 on service provisions (especially pars. 3 and 5). As also noted, Art. 55 of D.Lgs. no. 385/95 further entrusts to Banca d'Italia the task of controlling the activities of the subsidiaries of Community banks.

Other rules and procedures regulating the exercise of the freedoms of establishment and to provide services under Art. 19 Directive 2000/12/EC are contained in the Ministerial Decree 28.12.1992 and in the Instructions, under Title VII (Cooperative Credit Banks and Foreign Banks), Chapter 2 (Community Banks and Investment Undertakings in Italy).

VI. (FOLLOWS): THE APPLICATION OF THE HOME COUNTRY CONTROL PRINCIPLE

—The application of the home State control principle is affected by two different orders of considerations.

In the first place, within the cooperation framework set forth among the competent authorities it is not uncommon to find a specific regulation of the actual application of the home State control, at least with respect to a clear and express apportionment of the tasks among the concerned authorities (see above par.).

Secondly, the application of the home State control principle is affected by the extent of authority which the host State reserves for itself.

In implementing Art. 13.3 D.Lgs. n. 385/95, Art. 1.2 of the Ministerial Decree 28.12.1992 sets forth the principle according to which the subsidiaries of Community banks may exercise the activities admitted to the benefit of the mutual recognition subject to the rules protecting the general good in force in Italy. According to Art. 5 of same Decree, it is for Banca d'Italia to enact the rules for the implementation of said provision.

The Instructions hence establish the rules of Italian law which are applicable in general terms to the activities carried out by Community banks operating in Italy through a subsidiary or under the freedom to provide services.

Title VII, Chapter 2, Section 2, Paragraph 4 (Applicable Rules) contains the provisions of Italian law which are applicable to the subsidiaries established in Italy by Community banks. While the reproduction of the entire list does not appear appropriate, it seems that pursuant to a position taken by Banca d'Italia the activities of a subsidiary of a Community bank operating in Italy are subject to a significant series of national legal provisions (see Attachment A).

A similar approach is also taken with respect to the provisions of bank services by a Community bank in the Italian territory: Section IV (Provision of Services without Establishment) of the Instructions lists the provisions of Italian law by referring practically to the same list of the rules applicable to the subsidiary, with the only exclusion of the application of those rules strictly related with – and conceivable because – the existence of an establishment (see Attachment B).

In this connection, some perplexities can be expressed with respect to the compatibility of this approach with the intended purposes of the Second Banking Directive, as also articulated by the Commission Interpretative Communication 97/C 209/04 on the "Freedom to Provide Services and the Interest of the General Good in the Second Banking Directive". According to the Commission position, a credit institution operating in the context of the mutual recognition could be forced to bring its services in line with the legislation of the host country only if the measures relied against it are in the interest of the general good, and hence satisfy the four-folded rules of reason elaborated by the ECJ (see Part II, Par. B, of the Interpretative Communication). On the contrary, the requirements set out in the Instructions appear to go possibly beyond the limits summarised above.

VII. (FOLLOWS): CAPABILITIES OF ITALIAN BANKS TO PROVIDE THE SERVICES ADMITTED TO MUTUAL RECOGNITION

Under Italian legislation, the activities admitted to the mutual recognition under Annex I to Directive 89/646/EEC (now Annex I to Directive 2000/12/EC) – which are listed in Art. 1.2, lett. f), D.Lgs. no. 385/95 – can be exercised by Italian banks without limitation (see in this regard, Instructions, Title I (Subjects), Chapter I (Authorisation to Banking Activity), Section III (Program of Activity)). It is hence not possible that a credit institution of another Member State may provide, based on its home country authorisation, services admitted to the mutual recognition which Italian banks may not be authorised to provide.

VIII. THE EXERCISE OF ACTIVITIES NOT ADMITTED TO THE BENEFIT OF THE MUTUAL RECOGNITION

Art. 17 of the D.Lgs. no. 385/95 governs the exercise of activities not listed in the Annex I to Directive 2000/12/EC by Community banks.

According to this provision, Banca d'Italia regulates the exercise of activities which are not admitted to mutual recognition, and which are however carried out by the Community banks in the Italian territory, in accordance with the deliberation of CICR.

As of today, rules implementing this provision are still provided for in the Ministerial Decree 28.12.1992. Art. 4 of this Decree specifies that Banca d'Italia may authorise Community banks, through subsidiaries or in the framework of the freedom to provide services, to exercise in the Italian territory also activities different from those admitted to the benefit of mutual recognition, provided that (a) the relevant activities are actually exercised in the home Member State, and (b) the competent authority of the home Member State is informed of the intention of the bank to supply the relevant services also in the Italian territory. Furthermore, it is provided that, in evaluating the request, Banca d'Italia takes into account whether the activities may be exercised by banks authorised to operate in the Italian territory.

National laws and regulations which credit institutions authorised to carry out the above activities are required to comply are specified by the Instructions, which however make no difference whether the related banking activity falls or not within the scope of those admitted to the benefit of the mutual recognition. In particular, reference is made to Title VII, Chapter 2, Sections II (Par. 4) for activities rendered through the establishment of a subsidiary and to Title IV for the provision of services without an establishment (see par. above).

Doubts about the compatibility of the application of these national laws or regulations can be expressed with respect to proper application of the general good principle in the selection in general and preliminary terms of the rules applicable to Community banks.

IX. THE GENERAL GOOD: APPLICABLE LEGAL RULES

Provisions implementing Art. 21(5) Directive 89/646/EEC (now Art. 22(5) of Directive 2000/12/EC) are now contained in Arts. 55 and 79 D.Lgs. no. 385/95.

As noted above, Art. 55 D.Lgs. no. 385/95 entrusts Banca d'Italia with the tasks of operating controls on the subsidiaries of Community banks. In this regard, the matter is still regulated by the Ministerial Decree 28.12.1992, and specifically by its Art. 2 concerning the controls of the subsidiaries operation.

Art. 2.1 requires at the present that Banca d'Italia (a) assures the observance of the provisions on mandatory reserves and (b) evaluates the situation of liquidity of the subsidiaries, in cooperation with the competent Authorities of Member States.

Art. 2.2 provides that Banca d'Italia should communicate to each subsidiary the provisions regarding control applicable to it as well as the rules of general interests whose compliance by said subsidiary is monitored by Banca d'Italia.

Art. 79.1 D.Lgs. no. 385/95 provides that, in case of infringement by Community banks of provisions concerning the activity of subsidiaries or the provisions of services in the Italian territory, Banca d'Italia (a) may order the bank to terminate such infringement, while at the same time (b) request the competent home State authority the issuance of the acts which may be necessary.

The Instructions specify that the order to terminate the infringements is directed to the Community banks and, when activities of a subsidiary is involved, to the persons in charge of the subsidiary. The order is also communicated to the competent Authority of the home Member State to which, if necessary, the adoption of necessary acts is required.

Art. 79.2 further specifies that Banca d'Italia may adopt acts which it considers necessary, including the prohibition to initiate new operations and the closing of the subsidiary, when (a) the competent Authority does not take proper actions, (b) the infringements may prejudice the general good, or (c) in cases of urgency for the protection of the interests of customers and persons to which banking services are rendered.

n such situations, Banca d'Italia adopts the measures which are necessary to terminate the infringements, which may also include the decision to prohibit the pursuance of new operations or the order to close the subsidiary, provided that the competent authority has been prior informed about such decisions. Again, also these acts are directly issued by Banca d'Italia and notified to the Community bank and, in case they involve a subsidiary, to the persons in charge of the subsidiary. The European Commission and the competent Authority of the home Member State are also informed of the issuance of the relevant acts.

X. (FOLLOWS): THE APPEAL PROCEDURES AND JUDICIAL STANDARDS OF REVIEW

The addressees of any measures adopted pursuant to Art. 79.2 D.Lgs. no. 385/95 may petition Banca d'Italia with a motivated request to reconsider the situation and in such situation withdraw the measures. Banca d'Italia decides on the request within a 60-day period.

However, acts of Banca d'Italia can be challenged with the same procedures envisaged under Italian law for the opposition to viz. annulment of administrative acts, these procedures including also petitions addressed to administrative bodies and administrative courts. In particular, Art. 9 D.Lgs. no. 385/95 expressly provides for the possibility to challenge before CICR those acts adopted by Banca d'Italia which concern supervision activities. It should be noted, however, that this form of opposition is seldom employed, and judicial relief is mostly used.

In fact, the acts adopted by Banca d'Italia may be judicially challenged before administrative courts under the usual grounds, *i.e.* when acts are adopted (a) in violation of laws and regulations, (b) without proper authority, and (c) with excess of powers. The competent administrative court of first instance is the *Tribunale Amministrativo Regionale del Lazio*, whose decisions can be further appealed before the Consiglio di Stato. In recent times, Art. 7 of Law 21 July 2000 no. 205 (which amended Art. 33 of Legislative Decree 31 March 1998 no. 30) has attributed to administrative courts the exclusive jurisdiction on acts concerning prudential supervision of credit institutions.

The standard of review by administrative courts is that typical of those existing within civil law legal systems to challenge administrative acts. These acts are assisted by a presumption of legitimacy and correctness, and may be opposed on the three grounds summarised above which exclude the review of the merits of administrative acts. It is however worth mentioning that case law on the review of the decisions of regulatory authority is increasingly taking into consideration and emphasizing the duty of providing proper reasoning and motivation, hence granting private parties an adequate protection, while at the same time respecting the powers of the competent administrative authorities, in our case Banca d'Italia.

XI. THE ESTABLISHMENT OF BRANCHES

As noted above, rules concerning the right to establish branches by a credit institution in accordance with the framework of the Second Banking Directive are now contained in Arts. 15 and 16 D.Lgs. no. 385/95.

Art. 15.1 provides the possibility for Italian banks to establish subsidiaries in the territory of Italy and in other Member States. Banca d'Italia may however prohibit the establishment of new subsidiaries for reasons relating to the adequacy of organizational structure or the financial, economic, and patrimonial situation of the bank.

The Instructions elaborate the procedures and requirements for the exercise by Italian credit institution of the right to establish subsidiaries in other Member States. The relevant provisions are contained in Title III (Structure), Chapter II (Subsidiaries of Banks and Investments Services Undertakings), Section II (Subsidiaries of Banks).

It is worth noticing that, under Art. 1.2, lett. e), D.Lgs. no. 385/95, "Subsidiary" ("*Succursale*") is meant to designate an office constituting a part of a bank, lacking of autonomous legal personality, which carries out directly, in whole or in part, a banking activity. The Instructions further elaborate this notion for the purposes of applying the rules on the freedom of establishment. According to them, a "subsidiary" is meant to be a permanent point of operation, even though it does not operate in a continuously manner, which directly carries out with the clients, in whole or in part, the activity of the bank. In this regard, the definition excludes: (a) the equipment for "home banking activities" and automatic points of operation, such as Automated Teller Machines (ATM) and Point of Sale (POS) terminals, which are not presided by bank personnel; (b) administrative offices, even if they are accessible by the clients; (c) temporary points of operation at fairs, markets, exhibitions and shows of a occasional natures.

Neither Art. 1.2, lett. e), D.Lgs. no. 385/95, nor the Instructions replicate the provisions of Art. 1.1, point 3, of Directive 89/646/EEC (and Directive 2000/12/EC), which also specifies that more points of operation constituted in the same Member State by a credit institution having its legal seat in another Member State are to be considered as a single subsidiary. The apparent discrepancy among Community and national law is however resolved by the Instructions which expressly specify that the intention of a credit institution which is already established in a host Member State to open other subsidiaries therein is subject, pursuant to Art. 19.6 Directive 89/646/EEC (now 20.6 Directive 2000/12/EC), to the procedure concerning the modifications of the information previously communicated by the credit institution.

Italian Banks intending to establish a subsidiary in an EC Member State must file a preliminary communication with Banca d'Italia, stating:

—the Member State where the credit institution plans to establish a subsidiary;
—a programme of activity specifying the types of business which the credit institution intends to carry out in the host Member State. The bank must clearly indicate whether it intends to carry out activities not admitted to the benefit of the mutual recognition, being understood that, in such case, the exercise of those activities is anyway subject to the requirements of

the host Member State;
—the structural organisation of the subsidiary;
—the address of the subsidiary from which documents may be obtained;
—the name of those responsible for the management of the branch.

In addition, when the communication is filed by a bank which belongs to a banking group having a supervisory capital of less than Euro 100 millions (or an individual bank with a corresponding individual supervisory capital), the communication must also contain elements demonstrating the current existence of positive relations with customers residing or operating in the host Member State. The Instructions specify in details the terms of the procedure which is to be followed.

Banca d'Italia may prohibit the establishment of a subsidiary in Member State for reasons which pertain to the adequacy of the organisational structure or the financial, economic and patrimonial situation of the bank or of the related banking group. In this regard, the evaluation concerning of the organisational adequacy takes into account the increasing difficulties which the banks may face in assuring the efficacy of internal controls on subsidiaries operating abroad.

With respect to the establishment in Italy of subsidiaries of credit institutions belonging to other Member States, the relevant regime is offered by Art. 15.3 D.Lgs. no. 385/95. As prescribed by the Second Banking Directive, the establishment of a subsidiary is subject to a communication to Banca d'Italia by the Authority of the home Member State, provided that the subsidiaries may begin operation after the elapse of a two-month period from the said communication. It is expressly provided that Banca d'Italia (and, with respect to operation in investments services, the *Commissione Nazionale per le Società e la Borsa*, CONSOB) may specify to the competent Authority of the Member State and to the bank the conditions whose compliance is required for the operation of the subsidiaries consistently with the general good.

The relevant procedure is elaborated in details in Title VII, Chapter II of the Instructions. Specifically, Community banks that are going to operate for the first time in Italy through the establishment of a subsidiary need to notify such decision to the competing authority of their home Member State. The beginning of the subsidiary's operation is subject to the receipt by Banca d'Italia of the preventive communication of the host Member State, including the information required by Art. 19.2 of Directive 89/646/EEC (now art. 20.2 of Directive 2000/12/EC). The subsidiary may thereafter be established and operate in Italy either (a) upon receipt of a communication from Banca d'Italia or (b) after the elapse of a 60-day period from the receipt by Banca d'Italia of the communication of the home Member State competent authority.

The Community bank authorised to establish a subsidiary in Italy is in any case required to notify the date of the beginning of operation for the purpose of the registration in the registrar of banks authorised to operate in Italy, which is kept and operated by Banca d'Italia pursuant to Art. 13. Rules and procedures set forth for the implementation of the Second Banking Directive on the establishment of subsidiaries have performed so far in proper pursuance of the objectives expressed by the EC legislation. There is in this connection a common understanding that, to a significant extent, the Community rules and principles on the freedom of establishment and to provide services in banking sector have reasonably accomplished their goals. It is worth mentioning that this situation sharply contrasts with the difficulties characterizing the application and enforcement of the EC legislation on the freedom of establishment and to provide services in the field of investments services.

XII. THE FREEDOM TO PROVIDE SERVICES

Art. 16.1 D.Lgs. no. 385/95 provides the possibility for Italian banks to exercise in another Member State the activities admitted to the mutual recognition without the need to establish a subsidiary therein, subject to the procedures set forth by Banca d'Italia.

The Instructions contain the rules elaborated by Banca d'Italia for this purpose: reference is particularly made to the provisions contained in Title III, Chapter III (Provision of Services with Establishment Abroad). Preliminarily, they state the notion of services which is relevant for the purpose of the exercise of the related freedom. According to them, the "provisions of services without an establishment" ("*prestazione di servizi senza stabilimento*") define the exercise of banking and financial operations in the territory of a foreign State in the absence of subsidiaries and by means of a temporary organisation (provided that the offer of service carried out through actual – even though occasional – presence in the host State of the service provider personnel is compatible with the requirement of the temporary organization).

The Instructions expressly provide that services rendered by mail or through other means of communication (phone, fax, electronic network, etc.) fall within the rules applicable to the provision of services upon the concurrent presence of the following conditions:

(a) the service is rendered as a consequence of a commercial initiative, carried out by the service provider on the territory of the service consumers, that is not limited to a promotional activity but also include an invitation to execute a contract; and

(b) the offer of services is precedent to the physical movement of the service provider for the execution of relevant acts, or the contract concerning the provisions of services can be executed at distance, without the simultaneous presence of the service provider and the service consumer.

Other services, which are rendered without the movement of the service provided in the State of the service consumer, for which the above conditions are not met, are excluded from the application of the rules on the provisions of services without establishment and can be rendered without restraint.

The following activities are excluded by the Instructions from the application of the rules on the provisions of service without previous establishment, with the consequence that they fall within the scope of application of rules concerning the operation through subsidiaries:

(a) services rendered through Automatic Teller Machines, installed in the territory of the host State, where the personnel of the bank is present. However, if ATMs are not presided by the bank personnel, rules on the provision of services continue to apply;
(b) services rendered through independent intermediaries, provided the following conditions are met: the intermediaries (i) operate in an exclusive manner for a single bank, (ii) have the power to negotiate businesses with third parties, (iii) have the authority to bind the bank, and (iv) act in permanent manner. However, services rendered by independent intermediaries in the absence of the said conditions continue to be subject to the rules on the provision of services.

Pursuant to the Instructions, Italian banks interested in carrying out in other Member States and for the first time activities admitted to the mutual recognition under the freedom to provide services are required to file a communication to Banca d'Italia at least 30 days before the beginning of activities. The communication must in particular specify the Member State in which the credit institution intends to operate, the activities admitted to the mutual recognition which are meant to be carried out, and the modalities of operation of the activities. The Instructions set forth in details the relevant procedure in accordance with terms and conditions of Art. 20 Directive 89/646/EEC (now 21 Directive 2000/12/EC).

With respect to the freedom to provide services by banks located in other Member States, Art. 16.3 D.Lgs. no. 385/95 provides that Community banks may exercise the activities set forth in Art. 16.1 (see above) without the establishment of subsidiaries, provided that that Banca d'Italia has been previously informed by the competent Authority. According to the

Instructions, the interested bank may begin the activities from the moment in which Banca d'Italia receives a preventive communication from the competent Authority of the home Member State.

It is worth noticing that there seems to be a more significant discretion in favour of Member States in defining the modes of services provision which can be included in the exercise of the related freedom *vis-à-vis* modes of provision which imply the exercise of the right to establish subsidiaries. Although the Commission Interpretative Communication 97/C 209/04 offered a series of guidelines on modes of services provision (Part I, Par. B, of the Communication), discrepancies among the notion adopted in each Member States may in any case persist and affect the level of harmonization of the EC legislation, especially with the diffusion of e-commerce and technologies for distance communication.

In addition to that, it should be mentioned once again the comprehensive approach followed by Banca d'Italia in defining and listing the laws and regulations of Italian law which are considered applicable to the provision of services in Italy by Community banks. As already noted, the compatibility of such an approach with EC law can be debated with respect to the exercise of the right of establishment, and thus appears even more problematic with respect to the provision of services.

XIII. THE COMPETENT AUTHORITY: BANCA D'ITALIA

As already noted in the preceding paragraphs, the Italian authority empowered to supervise credit institutions is Banca d'Italia. Art. 4.1 D.Lgs. no. 385/95 entrusts in particular to Banca d'Italia the function of supervising credit institutions. Specifically, Banca d'Italia (a) formulates proposals for resolutions to be adopted by the CICR in matters concerning the regulation of banking activities and supervision, (b) issues regulations when provided for by the law, and (c) gives instructions and adopts any measure pertaining to its own competency.

In such capacity, Banca d'Italia is the competent authority for the purposes of the enforcement of the Second Banking Directive, and therefore, and inter alia, receives relevant communications, issues those acts related thereto, and performs the relevant controls consistently with the provisions of EC legislation.

In the banking services sector, Banca d'Italia does not share its prerogatives with other authorities. The approach is however different in the field of investment services, where Banca d'Italia has concurring competencies which the *Commissione Nazionale per le Società e la Borsa* (CONSOB), in respect of the regulation of investment undertakings.

The Legislative Decree 24 February 1998 no. 58 (*Testo unico in materia di intermediazione finanziaria*), which reformed the law governing investments markets and services, entrusts to Banca d'Italia the authority to supervise investments undertakings with respect to the reduction of risks and patrimonial stability (Art. 5.2 D.Lgs. no. 58/98). The scope of authority recognized to Banca d'Italia is deeply articulated into various specific prerogatives. It is in particular worth to mention that Banca d'Italia enacts the rules concerning (a) the patrimonial adequacy, (b) the reduction of risks in its different configurations, (c) the participation that can be detained, (d) the administrative and accounting organisation and (e) the internal controls (art. 6.1 D.Lgs. no. 58/98).

However, D.Lgs. no. 58/98 also attributes to the *Commissione Nazionale per le Società e la Borsa* the authority to supervise the activities of investments undertakings with respect to transparency and correctness of their conducts (art. 5.3). In this regard, for example, CONSOB is entrusted with the enactment of regulations concerning the procedures (also of an internal nature) regarding (i) the services rendered in favour of customers and the evidence of orders and operations, (ii) the conducts to be maintained in the relationships with service customers, with a view to reducing to a minimum conflict of interests, and (iii) the duties of information in the provisions of services.

However, rules on the access of undertakings to the provisions of investments services reflect the role of Banca d'Italia as competent regulatory authority in the banking sector. Indeed, while the power to authorize the provision of investment services by investment undertakings (the so called SIM-*Società di Investimento Mobiliare*) is attributed to CONSOB (Art. 19.1 D.Lgs. no. 58/98), Banca d'Italia is competent to issue authorisations to exercise investment services to those banks which are authorised to operate in Italy (Art. 19.4 D.Lgs. no. 58/98). Hence, depending on whether the investment services are offered by a bank or by another institution, the competent authority in the Italian legal system may vary between respectively Banca d'Italia and CONSOB.

However, it should be noted that, in any case, CONSOB maintains its authority to supervise the conducts of banks providing investment services, so that, in case of subsidiaries of Community Banks which intend to operate investment services, it is for CONSOB to state and enforce the laws and regulations pertaining to the relevant activities in the furtherance of the general good (see Art. 15.3 D.Lgs. no. 385/95).

XIV. THE INVOLVEMENT OF BANCA D'ITALIA IN PRUDENTIAL SUPERVISION

In Italy, prudential supervision of credit institutions has been constantly entrusted to Banca d'Italia, in its capacity of national central bank.

Its role has been highlighted already above, specifically as envisaged by relevant provisions of the D.Lgs. no. 385/95, and in particular those provisions regarding the supervision of banks' operations and activities within the Italian territory.

As already noted, Banca d'Italia has also competencies with respect to the prudential supervision of the activities of undertakings which render investment services.

XV. AN INTEGRATED SUPERVISORY AUTHORITY FOR THE FINANCIAL SERVICES' SECTOR?

The current situation in Italy is characterized by the simultaneous presence of several authorities for the financial services' sector.

As noted above, Banca d'Italia has supervisory authority upon bank activities, with respect to admission to these activities, prudential supervision, and regulation of banking activities.

The portion of the financial services' sector concerning investment services is however subject to a different regime, where both Banca d'Italia and CONSOB act, under different roles, as competent authorities. As noted, the scope of activity of the two authorities is defined by attributing to Banca d'Italia the power to regulate capital adequacy and stability of investment undertakings, while CONSOB is entrusted with the regulation of transparency and correctness of the conducts and behaviours of the investment undertakings.

In the field of investment services, CONSOB maintains the role as exclusive regulating authority in respect of regulation of markets and issuers of securities, consistently with powers and prerogatives whose scope is set forth by D.Lgs. no. 58/98.

Furthermore, the portion of the financial services' sector regarding insurance services is subject to a third authority, the *Istituto per la vigilanza sulle assicurazioni private e di interesse collettivo* (ISVAP), which supervises insurance companies and their activities. A different authority, the *Commissione di vigilanza sui fondi pensione* (COVIP), is entrusted with certain aspects of the regulation of pension funds.

The simultaneous presence of these authorities, exercising tasks and competencies that in certain situation may overlap (this appears to be especially true with respect to the competencies of Banca d'Italia and CONSOB) recently gave rise to a debate concerning the opportunity to integrate competencies in a single supervisory authority.

There is, in this regard, a common understanding that the simultaneous concurrences of the competencies of more authorities in the sector of financial services or in parts thereof may give rise to inefficiencies and cause in certain cases a duplication in controls and requirements applicable to the addressees of regulation, especially with respect to conglomerates.

Possible solutions to overcome these problems contemplate either the possibility to integrate the competencies in the sector of investment services into a single authority (whether by incorporating an authority into another, or by constituting a new authority merging the resources of existing ones), or – at least – to transfer the competencies on insurance services to one of the already existing authority.

However, a possible reform of the regime of the different portions of the financial services' sector appears premature. In this regard, it is worth noticing that the comprehensive reform of the investment services is still recent as it dates back of 1998, with the Legislative Decree no. 58 of 28 February 1998 (entered into force on July 1, 1998). In addition to that, reforms are going in any case to encounter resistances, also at political level, if aimed at depriving existing entities, especially the more prestigious ones, of any of their "traditional" powers and prerogatives.

XVI. A ROLE FOR ESCB IN PRUDENTIAL SUPERVISION?

It is well known that the European System of Central Banks (ESCB) is framed in such a way to exclude prudential supervision from the tasks attributed and transferred with exclusive authority to the European Central Bank.

To this purpose, it is worth recalling that, in the field of prudential supervision, Art. 105.5 of the EC Treaty entrusts the ESCB with the task to contribute to the smooth conduct of policies pursued by the competent authorities relating to the prudential supervision of credit institutions and the stability of the financial system. This choice seems to be a consistent application of the subsidiarity principle, so that the supervision of credit institutions has remained in the hands of the national central banks (see Art. 5 of the EC Treaty). In any case, it also reflects the approach previously followed by many Member States to entrust prudential supervision to entities other than the central banks.

Art. 105.6 of the EC Treaty specifies however that the Council may, acting unanimously on a proposal from the Commission and after consulting the ECB and receiving the assent of the European Parliament, confer upon the ECB specific tasks concerning policies relating to the prudential supervision of credit institutions and other financial institutions with the exception of insurance undertakings.

These provisions are then specified in further details by the Statute of the European System of Central Banks and the European Central Bank, where Art. 25.1 thereof indicates that the ECB may render opinions and be consulted by the Council, the Commission, and the competent authorities on the scope of application and implementation of the Community legislation concerning prudential supervision of credit institutions and the stability of the financial system.

Art. 25.2 of the ESCB Statute further provides that, in compliance with decisions of the Council pursuant to Art. 105.6 of the EC Treaty, the ECB may execute specific tasks concerning policies relating to the prudential supervision of credit institutions and other financial institutions, with the exception of insurance undertakings.

Within the framework of the balance of authorities and tasks on prudential supervision set forth in the above mentioned provisions, in the Italian debate there is not a clear and unanimous consent on the necessity that the ECB be entrusted with a more significant role in the prudential supervision of credit institutions.

Positions have been expressed that the simultaneous exercise of the monetary and prudential supervision functions by the ECB would be either detrimental or beneficial for the European system.

Those opposing the attribution of supervisory tasks to ECB have in particular outlined the risks that measures adopted in the application of one of the functions may conflict with the pursuance of the goals of the other policy.

On the contrary, other have expressed the view that a correct and efficient exercise of monetary policies by the ECB demands also the attribution to it of tasks of prudential supervision of banks. This view, in particular, appears to be influenced by the introduction of the Euro, as it reflects the assumption that the pursuance of the objectives of stability entrusted to the ECB may be put at risk by deficiencies and failures of the banking systems which prudential supervision is up to prevent, monitor and remedy. The argument may also find support in the increasing recognition that, especially within the EU and also as a consequence of technological development, banking activities are increasingly assuming a multinational character, which contrasts with limited territorial nature and force of the prudential supervision activities carried out by national authorities. Additionally, it has been noted that, in the framework of concurrent tasks and competencies of different authorities, there is a potential risks of strategic and opportunistic behaviours by national central banks in dealing with problems of lack of liquidity/insolvency.

In any case, however, it is also worth noticing that in the next future a transfer of prudential supervision authority to the ECB could be in any case be more likely resisted by the Member States where prudential supervision was previously entrusted to national central banks, whose competencies have been already reduced in favour of the ECB as result of the entry into operation of the ESCB.

In this connection, it should be observed that the relationships between Banca d'Italia and the ECB are inspired to good and fair cooperation, though they are certainly influenced by the transfer to the latter of significant competencies which were previously exercised by the former. And it is worth mentioning that ECB itself has released comments in favour of a Community framework of prudential supervision where the relevant tasks are entrusted to national central banks, within a coordination framework to be dealt at the ESCB level also in light of already existing and possible future means and modes of cooperation in the "Euro-system".

XVII. THE IMPACT OF HUMAN RIGHTS LEGISLATION

The debate which has developed in the United Kingdom on the impact of human rights legislation on laws and procedures concerning the regulation of financial services (especially with respect to adjudicative and enforcement jurisdictions of competent authorities) does not appear to have any relevance in Italy nor under Italian law.

While the expedite and summary character of decisions assumed by UK financial authorities was deemed by competent authorities to require significant adjustments in light of the human rights legislation, the same does not hold true for Italian legislation of financial and banking sector, where principles of due process are normally observed, as a result of the application of the fundamental principles of law embodied in the Italian legal system.

XVIII. FURTHER HARMONIZATION OF PRUDENTIAL SUPERVISION AT THE EU LEVEL AFTER THE INTRODUCTION OF THE EURO

While no particular inadequacies in the supervision of credit institutions have been highlighted by the introduction of the Euro, the latter may reasonably have an impact on the further enhancement of the transnational dimensions of the activities of undertakings which operate – also within the same conglomerates –in different countries and/or portions of the financial services' sector.

Such development takes place in a framework of prudential supervision in which the relevant tasks are entrusted to national central banks. To this regard, while radical reforms do not seem probable, nor even desirable, due consideration being taken also to the present priorities in the European Agenda (enlargement, institutional reform, and so on), one can nevertheless expect that the introduction of the Euro may indeed call for the setting up of institutional mechanism aimed at establishing a proper and efficient cooperation among supervisory authorities.

LUXEMBOURG

Financial Services in the Era of the Euro and E-Commerce:

Does home country control work?

Rapporteur
Isabelle Goubin

AUTHORIZATION

1. In the Grand-Duchy of Luxembourg, the Commission de surveillance du secteur financier (CSSF) is the banking supervisory authority. In the three cases listed in article 7 of the SBD, the CSSF consults the home country supervisor during the application process. The consultation takes place in a formal manner through an exchange of correspondance. This procedure does not preclude the CSSF from calling the home authority up to have an exchange of view on the suitability of the shareholders and/or the fitness and properness of the management of the applicant bank, if deemed necessary. The answer received from the home country authority is taken into account by the CSSF in the decision making process to grant a banking license.

It should be noted that the same procedure is applied if the applicant originates from a third country (non EU country). In this case, the objective of the consultation is twofold: to find out first, whether the home country supervisor applies generally accepted minimum banking supervision standards (i.e. the core principles for effective banking supervision defined by the Basle Committee on Banking Supervision) and second, whether the banking group of which the Luxembourg applicant bank is a part of falls under an adequate consolidated supervision. If the first condition were not fulfilled, the CSSF would refuse the banking license. If the second criterion were not met, the CSSF would avail itself of the right to impose additional/particular conditions to the applicant.

1. According to the CSSF, no problems have been experienced so far with the prior consultation process. The CSSF is of the opinion that the cooperation process between banking supervisory authorities within the EU works satisfactorily. Indeed, in the CSSF's experience, the responses from the consulted authorities are received within a reasonable timeframe and are precise enough to allow for an informed decision by the CSSF. In cases where additional information is deemed necessary, the CSSF contacts the supervisory authority concerned by phone and has so far always received the requested information.

2. The CSSF policy is to discourage the applicant to submit a formal application if the CSSF has reservations about the suitability of the shareholders of the applicant bank.

There have been instances in the past where the CSSF has strongly «recommended» to an applicant not to apply formally for a banking licence to the Minister. In the instances concerned, the applicant has followed the «advice» of the CSSF and has not introduced a formal request for a banking licence.

As a consequence, the Minister had never to refuse authorization to an applicant.

3. a) Article 18 of the SBD has been taken up in articles 30 and 31 of the Law of April 5, 1993 relating to the financial sector, as modified. The Law has entered into effect three days after its publication in the Mémorial (Official Journal of the Grand-Duchy of Luxembourg). Circular IML 93/100 has laid down in detail the conditions/criteria to be met by credit institutions branching in or providing services in Luxembourg.

b) EU credit institutions established in Luxembourg or providing services in Luxembourg are subject to home country supervision. The CSSF exercises a residual supervision with regard to liquidity, money laundering and rules of conduct. Futhermore, the CSSF requires branches to submit on a regular basis information regarding their balance sheet and off-balance sheet activities, and their profit and loss account.

The cooperation between the home supervisor and the CSSF has never given raise to concern in the CSSF's view. The CSSF has concluded bilateral MOUs with the banking supervisory authorities of all EU Member states which host branches of Luxembourg credit institutions or whose credit institutions have established branches in Luxembourg. Bilateral meetings between supervisory authorities take place on a regular basis, in most cases on an annual basis.

Moreover, the CSSF has concluded MOUs with other banking supervisory authorities to enhance the effectiveness of the consolidated supervision exercised over specific large pan-European financial groups.

According to the CSSF, the home country principle has applied effectively in cases where the CSSF is the host country supervisory authority. The CSSF's experience has, however, been less conclusive when the CSSF has been the home country supervisor. Several Luxembourg banks have for instance in the past given up the intention to establish a branch in Belgium due to the extensive regulatory requirements imposed by the Belgian authority on the grounds of the general good.

c) The situation referred to in the questionnaire cannot occur in Luxembourg to the extent that Luxembourg has a universal banking system. Banks licensed in Luxembourg are authorized to offer all types of financial services without any legal restriction. In particular, banks may offer the services listed in the annex of the SBD.

3. The list of financial activities in the annex to the SBD is quite extensive and encompasses all relevant services offered by credit institutions. The CSSF has so far never received an application for a banking license where the home country authorization covers an activity not listed in the annex to the SDB. The answer to this question is therefore an hypothetical one, setting out how the CSSF is likely to apply the national legislation.

Only the activities listed in the annex of the SBD do benefit from the European passeport. If an applicant bank intends to exercise an activity not listed in the annex to the SBD, the CSSF is likely to require the bank to meet the Luxembourg regulation with regard to the activity concerned. If the CSSF deemed the home country rules applicable to this activity equivalent to the Luxembourg rules, it would be likely to exempt the bank from abiding to the Luxembourg rules.

4. To our best knowledge, the Luxembourg legal and regulatory provisions applying to branches set up by EC credit institutions in Luxembourg or to EC credit institutions providing financial services in Luxembourg are compatible with the general provisions of Community law.

THE GENERAL GOOD

7. a) Article 21 (5) of the SBD has been taken up in article 46 (8) of the Law of April 5, 1993 relating to the financial sector, as modified.

b) So far the CSSF has never exercised the powers referred to in article 21 (5) of the SBD.

c) The credit institution may lodge within one month an appeal against the measures taken by the CSSF with the Administrative Court (Tribunal administratif).

d) Not applicable (see response under b) above).

THE ESTABLISHMENT OF BRANCHES

8. a) The CSSF has not experienced any difficulties when a Luxembourg credit institution has intended to establish or has established a branch in another EU Member state. Some Luxembourg credit institutions have, however, forgone the idea of establishing a branch in another EU Member state due to the extensive regulatory and supervisory requirements of the host country authority. It seems that in particular Belgian, and Italian authorities impose a heavy regulatory and reporting burden upon branches on the grounds of consumer and investor protection rules.

b) The CSSF has not experienced any difficulty as a host member state.

THE PROVISION OF CROSS-BORDER SERVICES

9. a) According to the information received from Luxembourg banks, some EU Member States require banks providing services on their territory to abide by the local rules in the same way as if they had set up a branch in their territory on the grounds of the general good. This practice is not only contrary to the jurisprudence of the European Court of Justice, but also constitutes a major obstacle to the free provision of services and hence to the realization of the Internal Market. Moreover, credit institutions are required to meet the local rules on consumer protection regardless of whether there exist equivalent rules in the home country or not.

In addition, host supervisor requirements with regard to credit institutions offering services via Internet are quite extensive in some instances. Thus some host country supervisors avail themselves of the right to look into the security features and the procedures and controls aimed at preventing operational and legal risks in place in credit institutions offering services via the Internet. One might question this approach to the extent that sound administrative and accounting procedures and adequate internal control mechanisms fall within the competence of the home country supervisor according to the SBD.

b) The CSSF has not experienced any difficulty as a host member state.

THE COMPETENT AUTHORITIES

10. The Commission de surveillance du secteur financier (CSSF) is the

competent autority in charge of the supervision of the banking sector in Luxembourg.

11. The Banque centrale du Luxembourg (BcL) is not involved in the prudential supervision of the banking sector. The law creating the BcL does not assign any specific mission to the BcL in this regard. The competence of the BcL with regard to banks derives from the provisions of the EU Treaty and the ECB/ESCB statutes. Therefore, the BcL as a member of the ESCB contributes to promoting the stability of the financial sector, has a competence for the oversight of payment systems and must regularly submit to the ECB banking statistics deemed necessary for monetary policy purposes.

12. The CSSF has been created by the law of December 23, 1998. The Law transfers the supervisory functions exercised by the BcL and by the Stock Exchange Commissioner to the CSSF. The CSSF is in charge of the supervision of credit institutions, investments firms and other professionals of the financial sector, investment funds, pension funds, financial markets, payment systems and securities settlement systems in which the BcL does not participate. The supervision of the insurance sector falls outside the competence of the CSSF and is entrusted to the Commissioner of the Insurance sector (Commissariat aux Assurances).

The institutional reform shows that the Luxembourg government has opted for an integrated supervisory model. This model is aimed at defining a unified legal framework and at promoting a coherent supervisory approach in the financial sector; it mitigates the risk of regulatory arbitrage. Furthermore, small countries like Luxembourg have an interest in merging supervisory functions into a single authority to keep costs to a minimum.

13. Neither the EU Treaty nor the ECB/ESCB statutes do confer to the European Central Bank any competence for the daily prudential supervision of banks. The ECB's mission is confined to the monitoring of macro-prudential issues that are relevant to the stability of the financial system. The operational supervision of individual credit institutions, the so called micro-prudential supervision, remains the responsibility of the national supervisory authorities and thus is outside the ECB's competence. The CSSF fully supports the division of tasks between the ECB/NCBs and the national banking supervisory authorities as set out in the Treaty and the ECB/ESCB statutes for the following reasons:

j) banking supervision is exercised in the public interest. It seems desirable to entrust this mission to an authority accountable to the government so that the management of the supervisory authority can be revoked by the government if needed. The ECB whose independence is enshrined in the Treaty does not fulfil this criterion;

k) banking supervision is best exercised at the national level. The proximity of the national authorities to the banks enhances the effectiveness of the supervision. Indeed, national authorities are most familiar with the local legal and regulatory provisions applicable to the banks and are therefore best placed to verify the banks' compliance with these rules;

l) the exercise of supervisory functions by a central bank can give rise to conflict of interests.

10. Neither the introduction of the Euro nor the growth of E-commerce have influenced these views.

11. The relationship of the CSSF with the ECB is limited to the participation of a representative of the CSSF in the Banking Supervision Committee set up by the ECB. The CSSF does not feel a need to establish a direct working relationship with the ECB, since the ECB has neither a competence for nor is it involved in the daily prudential supervision of banks.

12. The CSSF has not been affected so far by the human rights legislation. It should be noted that the credit institutions have a right of appeal against the decisions of the CSSF according to the Law of April 5, 1993 relating to the financial sector, as modified.

13. The introduction of the Euro has not highlighted any inadequacy in the banking supervision regime in Luxembourg. Further harmonization of consumer and investor protection rules at EU level seems, however, desirable so that credit institutions can fully benefit from the Internal Market.

NORWAY

Financial Services in the Era of the Euro and E-Commerce:

Does home country control work?

Rapporteur
Associate Professor, dr. juris Henrik Bull

GENERAL COMMENT

Norway, Iceland and Liechtenstein are associated to the European Community through the *Agreement on the European Economic Area* (the EEA Agreement). This Agreement i.a. extends the EC rules on the single market for financial services to these states, including all directives on banking, insurance and investment services, and also the E-commerce directive. However, the Economic and Monetary Union is not part of EEA.

AUTHORISATION

Question 1. *Procedures for prior consultation under Article 7 of the Second Banking Directive*

The procedures are informal. The Banking, Insurance and Securities Commission of Norway have entered into agreements, usually referred to as «Memoranda of Understanding», with the competent authorities of other states. The memoranda usually make a reference to the consultation procedure, but do not provide any details. Most cross-border establishments in the Norwegian financial services sector have been undertaken by credit institutions headquartered in other Nordic States, and the Nordic banking, insurance and securities commissions traditionally have a close co-

* Centre for European Law, University of Oslo, in collaboration with Mr. Kjell Arne Åsgården, The Banking, Insurance and Securities Commission of Norway

operation. A point of interest in the consultations is usually whether the parent undertaking has established itself in other states as well, and if so, to which extent the parent undertaking has been supportive of its subsidiary in case the subsidiary has experienced financial difficulties.

In addition to the consultation process between supervisory authorities, representatives of the parent undertaking are briefed by the Banking, Insurance and Securities Commission of Norway on their rights and obligations, as well as on the legislation applicable to the subsidiary.

Question 2: *Any problems with regard to the consultation procedure?*

Non. On the contrary, the consultations are usually quite frank and open.

Question 3: *Any cases of authorisation having been refused, in particular with regard to Article 5 of the Second Banking Directice?*

There have been no such cases.

Question 4: *Activities covered by Article 18 and listed in the Annex as services covered by home country control*
a) Implementation of Article 18 in Norwegian law

According to Act of 10 June 1988 No 40 on Financial Services and Financial Institutions, as amended, any credit institution headquartered in a State belonging to the European Economic Area and duly authorised and supervised by the authorities of that State, may pursue such activities in the Norwegian market as are covered by its home State authorisation, subject to the rules laid down in subordinate legislation pursuant to the said Act. Two Royal Decrees issued pursuant to the Act (2 may 1994 No 326 relating to branch offices in Norway and 7 July 1995 No 717 relating to direct supply of banking services from other EEA States) limits the right to market and supply services in Norway to the services mentioned in the Annex to the Second Banking Directive.

b) Effectiveness of the home country control principle

Obviously, Norwegian authorities are not fully informed of all steps that the competent authorities of the credit institution's home state take with regard to the institution's activities in Norway. This is particularly so with regard to cross-border supply of services. However, so far there have been no negative experience. As to branch offices, where Norwegian authorities are informed of on-the-spot verifications, cf. Article 15 of the Second Banking Directive, it is the impression of Norwegian authorities that home state authorities take their supervisory responsibility very seriously.

Norwegian authorities usually follow establishments abroad and cross-border services by Norwegian credit institutions closely, as such activity may often have a higher risk profile than activities in the Norwegian home market.

c) Any foreign credit institutions that provide services which are covered by the Annex to the Second Banking Directive, but which not allowed for Norwegian credit institutions?

This has not been an issue.

Question 5: *Activities not listed in the Annex*

There are no special rules on activities falling outside the list in the Annex. If the service in question may only be pursued in Norway on the basis of a banking licence, a Norwegian banking licence would be needed. As such a licence presupposes headquarters in Norway, the credit institution would have to set up a subsidiary in Norway.

However, the mere acceptance of Norwegian customers that themselves approach the institution, without the institution engaging itself in any form of marketing in Norway, would not necessitate a Norwegian banking licence. (There is no specific rule on this, but it must be presumed that the Norwegian banking legislation only applies to banking activities that may be said to take place in the Norwegian market. For all practical purposes this would mean that the credit institution would have to show a certain level of active presence in the Norwegian market before a banking licence is required.)

Furthermore, both the Act of 24 May 1961 No 2 relating to commercial banks and the above-mentioned Act on Financial Services and Financial Institutions allow foreign credit institutions (also from non-EEA States) to set up «representative offices» in Norway, upon a mere registration with the Banking, Insurance and Securities Commission of Norway. The border-line between the marketing activities that may be pursued through a representative office, and such marketing activities that would trigger the need for a full banking licence is not clear. Presumably, if the marketing is directed towards the general public, not only towards specific groups with special needs, a full banking licence would be needed.

Question 6: *Compatibility with the general provisions of Community law*

The European Court of Justice has consistently treated national licensing requirements as restrictions on establishment and the free movement of services and capital. The same would apply under the EEA Agreement, which in its «Main Part» contain the same general provisions as the EC Treaty (although based on the «pre-Maastrict» EC rules, in particular with regard to free movement of capital). Presumably, the need for a banking licence (or other licence) in order to engage in activities not covered by the Annex to the Second Banking Directive would be seen as a restriction. Whether or not it would also be an unlawful restriction would seem to depend on the activity in question as well as the requirements that would be part of the host state licensing regime, seen in conjunction with the requirements to which the activity in question would be subject under its home state legislation. To the extent that the host state requirements would be necessary and proportionate in order to safeguard general good considerations of the host state that would not be adequately protected by the home state regime, it would seem that the host state could impose a licensing regime. A requirement that a subsidiary must be set up in the host state would probably easily be deemed to be a disproportionate.

Question 7: *Powers of the host state authorities under Article 21 of the Second Banking Directive*

a) Legal rules adopted in Norway in the interest of the general good

Norwegian authorities have not enacted a consolidated and exhaustive list of Norwegian legal rules that credit institutions of other EEA States must respect in the interest of the general good. However, the two Royal Decrees mentioned in the answer to question 4 (a) are exhaustive with regard to which provisions of the Act relating to commercial banks (cf. question 5) and the Act on financial services and financial institutions (cf. question 4(a)) that apply to banks from other EEA states that are active in Norway. The Act of 19 June 1997 No 79 on securities trade and investment services contain a similar exhaustive list with regard to that law, which applies also to banks engaged in investment services. Generally speaking, only provisions that may be said to have a bearing on the institution's relationship with its customers, including marketing regulations, have been included.

In addition, the Act of 25 June 1999 No. 46 on contracts relating to banking services, have its own rules on applicable law with regard to consumer contracts. These rules make Norwegian law obligatory as the applicable law in most cases. Thus, the Acts goes further in protecting consumer interests than the Rome Convention on the Law Applicable to Contracts, which in the same circumstances only leads to the law of the consumer's country of residence being applicable in the absence of a choice-of-law clause in the contract, and, in case of such a clause, only guarantees the application of the mandatory rules of that law.

Outside those acts already mentioned, also other provisions of Norwegian law may apply to credit institutions of other EC/EEA states that are active in Norway. It is not necessarily spelt out in each case whether a specific rule applies in this way. This must then be determined according to the general principles on the application of Norwegian law, both of a private law nature and a public law nature, to actions and events with a cross-border element.

b) Have competent authorities exercised their rights under Article 21(5) of the Second Banking Directive and, if so, in what circumstances?

In one case, the Norwegian branch office of a credit institution from another EC/EEA state had problems in fulfilling Norwegian money laundering requirements on the presentation of ID cards or similar documentation when opening a new account. This was due to its general customer relationship policy. However, the problems were sorted out and the branch now follows Norwegian rules.

Otherwise, the experience is good.

c) Appeals procedures under Article 21(6)

A decision by the Banking, Insurance and Securities Commission of Norway pursuant to national provisions implementing Article 21 (4) and (5) of the Second Banking Directive falls under the general principle that any decision by a body of the executive branch of government may be subject to judicial review as to their legality (procedural errors, factual errors, errors of law etc.). In addition, any decision by the Commission may be brought before the Ministry of Finance for administrative review according to the general rules on such appeals to the body immediately superior to the body which made the initial decision. As the superior body, the Ministry may try all aspects of the case, including every aspect of the Commission's exercise of any discretionary powers that it may have under the relevant legislation.

d) Any case in which the right of appeal has been invoked?

There are no such cases under Article 21(6) of the Second Banking Directive.

THE ESTABLISHMENT OF BRANCHES

Question 8: *Any difficulties with regard to the establishment of branches where Norway is ...*
a) ...the home state?

Some years ago, what was clearly meant to be a branch office in another Scandinavian state, was presented to Norwegian authorities as a «representative office». It is not quite clear why this was done, but one may speculate that it was either due to lack of knowledge of the new EC/EEA rules, or in order to avoid the reporting requirements to which branches usually are made subject in the host state. However, when Norwegian authorities informed the credit institution of their opinion that this was a branch office, not a representative office, the credit institution amended their filing without protests.

b) … the host state?

The only example concerns an undertaking that was only engaged in currency exchange, both in its home state and with regard to the activity it wanted to pursue in Norway. When it was pointed out to the home state authority that this hardly qualified under the Second Banking Directive, nothing more was heard of the matter.

THE PROVISION OF CROSS-BORDER SERVICES

Question 9: *Any difficulties with regard to the provision of cross-border services where Norway is …*
a) … the home state?

No.

b) … the host state?

No, except for the fact that many, if not most, of the filings have been made «just in case» by credit institutions that do not really have any plans for being actively present in the Norwegian market.

THE COMPETENT AUTHORITIES

Question 10: *National authorities empowered to supervise credit institutions*

The Banking, Insurance and Securities Commission of Norway.

Question 11: *Any role for the Central Bank in prudential supervision?*

The Norwegian Central Bank supervises liquidity issues, but has otherwise has no responsibility for prudential supervision of credit institutions.

Statistical information which credit institutions are required to report, is reported to one and the same data base, to which both the Banking, Insurance and Securities Commission of Norway, the Norwegian Central Bank and the Central Bureau of Statistics have access.

Question 12: *An integrated supervisory authority for financial services?*

Norway has had an integrated supervisory authority for financial services since 1986. The experience is positive (there has never been a discussion to divide it up again.

Question 13: *Need for the European Central Bank to play a role in prudential supervision?*

Cf. *general comment* above: Norway remains outside the EU, but is part of the internal market for financial services through the EEA Agreement. To invest the European Central Bank with supranational powers to carry our prudential supervision of Norwegian credit institutions would cause constitutional problems. Apart from this, Norwegian authorities have no official policy with regard to the future role of the European Central Bank in prudential supervision. This is seen as an internal EU question.

Question 14: *View on this influenced by the introduction of the Euro and the growth of E-commerce?*

The growth of E-commerce does of course strengthen the case for a single European body for prudential supervision. With regard to the Euro, this is probably also so with regard to the EU Members States forming part of the Euro Zone. However, as pointed out in the answer to Question 13, with regard to Norway other considerations come into play.

Question 15: *Relationship between Norwegian authorities and the European Central Bank*

Not being a Member State of the EU, Norwegian authorities only have arrangements on mutual exchange of information with the European Central Bank. When officials of the Norwegian Central Bank meet officials of the European Central Bank, a representative of the Banking, Insurance and Securities Commission of Norway usually takes part in the meeting.

Question 16: *Human rights legislation*

Human rights legislation has not been an issue with regard to the supervision of financial institutions in Norway.

Question 17: *Has the introduction of the Euro highlighted any inadequacies with regard to the supervision of credit institutions or the need for further harmonisation?*

Cf. questions 13 and 15: Norway's position outside the EU means that Norwegian supervisory authorities are not in a good position to ascertain this.

SPAIN

Financial Services in the Era of the Euro and E-Commerce:

Does home country control work?

Rapporteurs
Luis M. Hinojosa Martínez and Carlos J. Moreiro González***

I. INTRODUCTION

After some token gestures during the first half of the XXth century,[3] the real process of internationalisation in the activities of the Spanish banks began modestly in the sixties and seventies and bloomed in the eighties and nineties. After the 1999 mergers, the two biggest Spanish banks have almost half of their commercial assets situated abroad.[4] The extraordinary development of the Spanish economy in the last twenty years, and in particular of the Spanish financial market, has made such a process possible.

The main foreign market for Spanish banks is Latin America,[5] and the second is Europe. Their presence in North America and in Asia is much less relevant. The reason for these choices is related to the principal motive for this exterior growth: the provision of services to the national client. Thus, the Spanish banks followed their main customers to those markets where for cultural reasons (Latin America) or for their geographical proximity (Europe) they could operate more conveniently.

The strategies used to spread throughout Europe have differed depending on each bank: while BSCH has preferred to establish strategic alliances with local partners in other Member States (Champalimaud in Portugal or Societé Général in France) or to buy participations in foreign entities

* Ph.D., LL.M. (London School of Economics) (Université Libre de Bruxelles), Professor of European Law in the University of Granada. Prof Hinojosa has drafted sections 1, 6, 7, 8 A), B), C) and D).

** Ph. D. (E.U.I. Florence), LL.M. (College of Europe, Bruges) Professor of European Law in the University Carlos III of Madrid. Prof. Moreiro has drafted sections 2, 3, 4 and 5.

(Commerzbank in Germany), BBVA group has opted for the creation of its own network of branches and subsidiaries (in spite of its participation in Banca Nazional del Lavoro or its alliance with the French insurance company Axa). Banco Popular has created its own subsidiary in France (together with Banco Comercial Portugues) and has entered into alliances with local partners in Germany and the Netherlands. Despite of their growing importance in the Spanish financial market, the Savings Banks (Cajas de Ahorro) have not developed a strategy of foreign expansion, probably because of the territorial basis of their activity, and also due to the legal limitations they face for the collection of resources in the capital markets.[6] There are also regulatory hurdles in the host Member States which render the competitive entry of the Spanish credit institutions in those markets more difficult.[7]

The penetration of the Spanish banking market by foreign credit institutions has proved to be a difficult task because of the existence of important barriers to entry.[8] The first of them is the saturation of the Spanish market, which has the most dense network of branches in Europe.[9] If we connect this reality with the fact that Spanish consumers choose their credit entity, in the first place, for its geographical proximity and, secondly, for family or personal tradition,[10] the result is that the Spanish banking market, at least at the retail level, is extremely difficult to break into. Most likely, this is the reason why the strategy most commonly used by banks from other European countries to enter that market has been the purchase of Spanish banks with a network of branches already in place.

In that context, one could ask whether the cross-border provision of banking services through internet may play a role in the transformation of the dynamics of this market. The truth is that some European Banks have managed to penetrate the Spanish retail banking market through the web.[11] The Spanish credit institutions also compete there but they do not control this medium, and their network of branches is not useful in such an environment. Nevertheless, there are some factors that limit the possibilities of growth in this market:[12] (a) the low profit margins because of increased competition, which is much harder on the web, (b) the lesser degree of client's fidelity in this market, (c) the promotional expenses in order to gain clients from traditional banking, and (d) the general tendency to the slow growth of banking business on the web. To these economic arguments we must add the legal complexities of electronic banking contracts.[13] Hopefully, the final approval of the Proposal for a Directive on the distant marketing of financial services[14] may help in the near future to solve some of the latter. In any case, it seems that we are dealing here with a long-term battle.

At the time of writing, the Spanish Parliament is discussing a draft law entitled "Measures for the reform of the financial system",[15] which could affect the issues discussed in this paper. Nevertheless, most of the proposed law presented by the Government is dedicated to the reform of the stock market and its supervision, following the allegations against the stock-broking firm *Gescartera*, which caused political turmoil some months ago. As concerns the *Ley* 26/1988, of July 29th, on the discipline and control of credit institutions in Spain, which is the main normative reference for this report, the only relevant changes impinge on electronic commerce and on the updating of the fines in case of infringement to that law. The proposed law also maintains the traditional division between the three sectors of the financial market: banking, insurance and stock markets.

For reasons of space, we should notice that in this report we will only deal with banks and savings banks (*bancos* and *cajas de ahorro*), the two most important credit institutions in Spain, and not with other credit entities of minor importance, such as credit co-operatives (*cooperativas de crédito*) or credit pools (*sociedades de garantía recíproca*).

II. AUTHORISATION

Answer to question 1.—Procedures, which are formal in nature, are ruled mainly by the Royal Decree 1245/1995 of 14th July, and by laws 3/1994, of 14th April and 26/1998, of 29th July.

Banco de España (hereinafter BdE), will send a letter to the authorities responsible for supervising the foreign credit institution in question. This letter is always written on a case-to-case basis.

Once the answer has been received, the BdE, shall issue a report that will send to the Ministry of Economy. The latter, is the competent authority that will entitle credit institutions to take up business in the country.

Answer to question 2.—Problems are of minor relevance. Only there may be some delays on receiving the answer to the letters. Although sometimes the Spanish Authorities must send the same letter twice, at the end there is always an answer from the competent authorities of the Member State in question.

Answer to question 3.—The Ministry of Economy has refused authorisation in several cases. Either when considering the need to guarantee sound and prudent management of the planned institution, or when the suitability of the shareholders, who are going to have a significant holding therein, is not considered adequate. This criteria is applied on an equal basis in every case and in full respect to the principle of non-discrimination (article 12 EC).

Spanish regulations on the constitution of credit institutions stress the importance of issues like the suitability of shareholders with significant holdings, and the soundness of accounting procedures. Therefore, article 4 of RD 1245/1995 states that a significant holding shall mean one that directly or indirectly amounts up to 5 percent or more of the capital or voting rights of a credit institution, or is enough feasible to make a significant influence thereover. The amount of 5 percent, which is under the limit fixed by the Second Banking Directive has been deemed to be adequate by the Spanish Administrative Courts (see LF n°3 of the Judgement of 31.5.2000 on case 0693/1997, Audiencia Nacional16-S.VI).

On the other hand, article 4 of RD 1245/1995 states that the aforesaid suitability shall be assessed on the basis "inter alia" of: the business and professional repute of the shareholders and the assets such shareholders have available to meet their commitments.

Answer to question 4.a.—Mainly by the implementation of articles 9 and 11 of the RD 1245/1995.

Answer to question 4.b.—The home country authorities request the BDE, to carry out the supervision. Once it has been accomplished the BDE, shall send them a report.

Answer to question 4.c.—No

Answer to question 5.—Article 51.2 of Law 26/1988, of 29th July and articles 9.2d), 10 and 11.1 of the RD 1245/1995.

The pursuing of the activities not listed in the Annex of the Second Banking Directive shall be conditional upon the BDE's prior authorisation. In the event that the activity concerned is prohibited or restricted for credit institutions, the BDE, shall notify such circumstance to the institution and to its home country authorities.

Answer to question 6.—No.

III. THE PROTECTION OF THE GENERAL GOOD

Answer to question 7.a.— There is no specific legislation establishing a list of measures to be enacted in the interest of the general good. Legal rules are adopted to cope with problems arising in different fields of the financial activity such as money laundering, e-commerce, consumer credit, the movement of capitals and payments with third countries, transparency, and so on.

On the other hand, article 2.2 of the RD 1245/1995 establishes a list of persons which are considered to lack "business and professional repute" for pursuing of banking activity: those with a criminal record or subject to criminal charges or those who, in the proceedings referred to by Title III of Book IV of Criminal Procedure Law, are subject to an order for oral proceedings to be opened in respect of offences for breaching the tax regulations, mistrust in the custody of documents, money laundering, misappropriation of public funds, disclosure of secrets and crimes against property, persons disqualified from holding positions in the civil service or in the administration or management of financial institutions, and undischarged bankrupts.

Last but not least, articles 3 to 6 of the Law 26/1988, of 29th July, establishes a list of very serious or minor breachments to the provisions on the taking up and pursuit of banking activities.

Answer to question 7.b.- Under article 7.6 of Law 13/1994, of 1st June (amended by Laws 66/1997 of 30th December, and 12/1998 of 28th April), the BDE, shall supervise the solvency activities and compliance with specific regulations of credit institutions. Thus, the BDE, has exercised its powers controlling the transparency of the activities pursued in Spain by credit institutions authorised in another Member State.

On the other hand, articles 18 and 23 bis of the Law 26/1998 of 29th July, gives powers to the BDE, for conducting proceedings and levy sanctions for serious and minor breachments to the banking legislation affecting credit institutions authorised in another Member State.

Up to date, there are no records of sanctions imposed by the BDE. Not even by the Council of Ministers or the Ministry of Economy, that keeps the power to levy sanctions for very serious breachments to the legal rules, adopted in the interest of the general good.

Answer to question 7.c.— Article 2.2 of Law 13/1994, and article 25.2 of Law 26/1988 establish that the sanctions imposed by the BDE, shall be subject to ordinary appeal to the Ministry of Economy.

On the other hand, article 2.3 of Law 13/1994 establishes that the Audiencia Nacional shall have sole jurisdiction in the case of appeals filed against acts adopted by the BDE, not subject to ordinary appeals, as well as against decisions of the Ministry of Economy on appeals filed against acts adopted by the BDE

The Spanish Constitutional Court and the Third Section of the Spanish Supreme Court keep competences for extraordinary appeals filed against cases sentenced by the Audiencia Nacional.

Answer to question 7.d.— As regards credit institutions, there is only one case judged by the Audiencia Nacional the 15th October 2001. The appeal number 0911/1997 Banque Paribas, S.A. c., Ministro de Economía y Hacienda17, which was rejected by the Court.

The Plaintiff invoked its right of appeal to avoid the payment of pecuniary sanctions imposed by the Ministry of Economy upon breachment of its obligations on internal accounting. The main ground for the sanctions was the fail to fulfil requirements on computer assistance to develop the bank activities linked to the stock exchange and the capital markets.

IV. THE ESTABLISHMENT OF BRANCHES

Answer to question 8.a.—There are no outstanding obstacles to be remarked. However, within the Spanish legal environment the administrative requirements for the establishment by Spanish credit institutions of branches abroad are highly demanding. Accordingly, the applications ..... must fulfil with several standards envisaged in article 9.3 of RD 1245/1995, and must be filed upon the procedure established by article 13 of the same RD.

Whenever an application is not fully in order, decisions could be delayed for more than three months up to the completion of all the administrative requirements. It shall be very exceptional a case of refusal by the BDE In this sense, article 13.2 of the above-mentioned RD says that "the application can only be refused by the BDE, if there are enough reasons to doubt the adequacy of the administrative structure or the financial situation of the credit institution, taking into account the activities envisaged, or when the programme of operations presented include activities for which the institution does not have authorisation".

Answer to question 8.— No serious difficulties have been experienced. However, short delays could be experienced before the beginning of the activities by branches of credit institutions authorised in another EU member state.

In this sense, articles 9.3 of RD 1245/1995, states that "the opening in Spain of such branches [...] shall be conditional upon the BDE's receiving a communication from the supervising authority of the credit institution containing at least the following information:

a) A programme of operations [...].
b) The address in Spain [...]
c) The names and professional records of those responsible for the management of the branch.
d) The amount of own funds and the solvency ratio of the credit institution [...]
e) The details of any deposit-guarantee scheme that may cover the deposits of the branch [...]"

On the other hand, the second paragraph of article 9.4 of the aforesaid RD, states that "Banco de España may set a waiting period of two months from the receipt of the communication [...]", in order to prepare the supervision of the branch in question.

Last but not least, the same provision specifies that "in the event that the activities described in the communication are referred to those which are not listed in Article 53 of Law 26/1988, 29th July, and the activity concerned is prohibited or restricted for credit institutions, the BDE, shall notify such circumstance to the institution and to its supervisory authority".

V. HUMAN RIGHTS AND CREDIT INSTITUTIONS

Answer to question 16.— There are no records of discrimination on grounds of sex, race, religion or whatsoever as regards the authorisation to be in charged of the administration of the Spanish credit institutions. Not even at the level of consumers of financial services (i.e., consumer credit, mortgage credit).

As regards the protection of personal data, the Spanish legislation implements the EC Directives rightly. However, there are some cases (of a sole internal nature), where plaintiff invoked human rights legislation in the appeal procedures.

There are several grounds for appealing, i.e., the right of hearing while pending an administrative proceeding against the plaintiff and the right to make depositions,18 principles of "res iudicata" and "non bis in idem",19 etc.

VI. THE PROVISION OF CROSS-BORDER SERVICES BY CREDIT INSTITUTIONS OF OTHER EU COUNTRIES IN SPAIN

Any credit institution of another Member State can provide the financial services listed in Art. 52 Ley 26/1988 (which basically reproduces Annex 1 of Directive 2000/12) in Spain, as soon as the BdE receives a communication from the supervisory authority in the Member State of origin[20]. This communication has to specify (as expressly established in Art. 21 of Directive 2000/12) which of the activities mentioned in the list are intended to be developed by the foreign credit institution. A new communication from the same authority will be needed if, in the future, the credit institution intends to provide any service included in Art. 52 Ley 26/1988, but not mentioned in the first communication. Obviously, Spanish law requires that the credit institution be authorised to carry out the same activities in the home Member State.

In any case, when developing their activities in Spain, the credit institutions of other Member States have to comply with the rules adopted in the interest of "general good", whatever their territorial scope[21], "when they are of application" (Art. 51 (2) Ley 26/1988).

The credit institutions of other Member States may open Representation Offices (*Oficinas de representación*) in the Spanish territory to help themselves in the cross-border provision of financial services. However, the opening of these offices has to be previously authorised by the BdE,[22] and these bureaux cannot be used for the deposit of funds or for any other activity of mediation. The Representation Office must be dedicated exclusively to providing information or to commercial promotion (Art. 10 RD 1245/1995). In return for the facility to open a Representation Office the range of activities that they are authorised to carry out is very limited.[23] All changes in the *status* of the office must be communicated to the BdE.

Spanish legislation also allows the utilisation of agents who act on behalf of a credit institution situated in a different Member State (Art. 22 RD 1245/1995). The agent can be a natural person or a Spanish credit institution with whom an agreement has been reached for such a representation. A complete list of those agents has to be sent every year to the BdE, indicating the powers conferred on each of them. Any change in this representation must also be immediately communicated to the BdE. In any case, the credit institution remains accountable for the fulfilment of the norms regulating the provision of the financial services by the agent, who cannot use its own bank accounts (to pay or to receive funds) in the operations.[24]

VII. THE PROVISION OF CROSS-BORDER SERVICES BY SPANISH CREDIT INSTITUTIONS IN OTHER EU COUNTRIES

The Spanish credit institutions which intend to provide cross-border financial services in other Member States must communicate that fact previously to the BdE, indicating the activities that they plan to engage in. The BdE will send this information to the competent authority in the host Member State within one month (Art. 15 RD 1245/1995). If a Spanish credit institution wants to open a Representation Office[25] in that Member State, it must inform the BdE even before presenting any application to the competent authority in the above-mentioned Member State. Furthermore, the Spanish entity has to continue informing the BdE of any change in the status or situation of that Representation Office.

VIII. THE PRUDENTIAL SUPERVISION OF CREDIT INSTITUTIONS IN SPAIN

a) The division of the role of supervision and the concept of "competent authority" for the purposes of supervision of credit institutions

The general competence to supervise the financial market corresponds to the Government. More concretely, the Ministry of Economy exercises this function, although some specific technical and independent organs have been created to enforce the rules promulgated by the Legislature. The financial market is divided for the purposes of supervision as in other Member States: the BdE controls credit institutions, the *Comisión Nacional del Mercado de Valores* (The National Stock-Market Commission, hereinafter CNMV) is in charge of investment societies, and the *Dirección General de Seguros* (General Directorate of Insurance) supervises insurance companies. The connection between the different sections of the financial market obliges these technical authorities to co-ordinate their activities among themselves, and with the political authority (the Government).

Nevertheless, this connection of the different sections of the financial market leads to an inevitable overlapping in the supervisory activities of the different authorities. For example, the fact that in Spain the credit institutions have the capacity to provide investment services causes a confluence of supervisory competencies between the BdE and the CNMV for such operations. Art. 88 of Ley 24/1988 (as modified by Ley 37/1998) tries to solve the problem by conferring the competence to supervise liquidity to the authority where the company is registered,[26] while the control of the functioning of the stock markets remains the sole responsibility of the CNMV. As a consequence, if a credit institution from a different Member State operates in the Spanish stock market, it will have to deal with three supervisory "competent authorities": the one in the State of origin (that controls its solvency), the BdE (competent to enforce the rules applicable to the credit institutions and adopted in the interest of general good), and the CNMV (in charge of the operation of the stock markets).

If we focus our attention on the credit market, the bulk of the supervisory activity is in the hands of the BdE, although it shares it to some extent with the Ministry of Economy and the Departments of Economy of the different Regional Governments (*Comunidades Autónomas*). In any case, we must clarify that the competencies of these latter Departments are limited to the activities of the Savings Banks (*Cajas de Ahorro*).[27]

The general regulation of the discipline and inspection of the credit entities in Spain is comprised in Ley 26/1988, which also applies to the branches of foreign banks operating in Spain, to the Spanish physical or legal persons controlling a credit entity in another Member State, and even to the persons directing the branches of foreign credit entities in Spain.

Since this Ley 26/1988, the power to register, control and inspect all credit institutions operating in Spain has been concentrated in the BdE. They have to provide it with different kinds of information, and the BdE may carry out ordinary inspections (for a routine control of the application of the banking legislation) or extraordinary inspections (when the BdE is interested in a special aspect of the activity of a particular credit institution). The BdE is also the public authority competent for the investigation and institution of proceedings against those entities violating the Spanish banking law, and for the application of sanctions to "minor" and "grave" infringements. The sanction of the "very grave" infringements corresponds to the Ministry of Economy[28] (except for the revocation of the authorisation to operate, which must be decided by the Government as a whole).

Although the BdE takes its decisions independently of the Government in the field of supervision, the rules applicable to this activity are different from those which guarantee its freedom of action in the application of the monetary policy.[29] Article 7 (4) of Ley 13/1994 (as modified by Ley 12/1998) guarantees that neither the Government nor other national or Community organ can give instructions to the BdE in relation to monetary policy, which is directed by the norms enacted and the decisions taken by the ECB. Besides, the BdE resolutions in this field put an end to the administrative procedure, and they can only be appealed in the Courts (the *Audiencia Nacional* or the ECJ, as the case may be). On the other hand, it is the Government who puts forward the law concerning the supervision of credit institutions in Spain, and the BdE decisions in this context may be appealed to the Ministry of Economy. Therefore, the Government exercises an indirect control over this supervisory function,[30] both by establishing the regulatory framework in which it has to be enforced, and by keeping the last word in control and inspection decisions.[31]

A much more thorny question arises over the division of supervisory competencies between the BdE and the Departments of Economy of the Regional Governments in relation to the Savings Banks (*Cajas de Ahorro*).[32] We find here a reproduction of the fight for power between the State (represented in the credit market by the BdE) and the Regions, which has resulted in a good number of cases before the Constitutional Court, some of them directly related to the supervision of the credit market.

As we have already mentioned, Article 149 (1) (11) sets out that the State enjoys the power to establish the "bases" for the regulation of credit, banks, and insurance. The use of the word "bases" to describe the State intervention indicates that this is a competence where the Regional Governments develop legislative and executive actions. Consistent with the Constitution, Article 7 (6) of Ley 13/1994 recognises the competence of the BdE to exercise its supervisory function over the credit institutions, "without prejudice to the prudential supervisory function of the Regions, within the framework of their competencies, and to the co-operation of the latter with the BdE". This not very clarifying provision has to be complemented with the Acts of Autonomy (*Estatutos de Autonomía*), where each Region assumes competencies over the credit institutions.[33] The normative development of these competencies has resulted in a proliferation of regional Acts applicable to the Savings Banks operating in each Region, drawing a tremendously complex legislative panorama.[34] In that context, Additional Section 1 of Ley 31/1985 shows rather wishful thinking when it "authorises" (we could even say promotes) the signing of conventions between the BdE and the Regions in order to delimit the responsibilities in the field of supervision.[35]

Article 42 of Ley 26/1988 establishes the distribution of competencies between the BdE and the Regions, and its content has been reviewed on several occasions by the Constitutional Court as a result of the appeals lodged by those Regions which considered that the distribution of competencies made by the State invaded their powers.[36] This provision can be summarised by saying that the Ley 26/1988 is declared "basic" in most of its content (this means that the Regions have to respect its terms, for example in relation to the classifications of offences, or the priority of competencies in favor of the State in certain cases), and reserves the power to sanction the infringements concerning the solvency of the credit entities or the monetary system to the BdE.[37] Besides, the Regions must communicate to the State (the BdE or the Ministry of Economy, depending on the issue) any information they might have in relation to the infringements which are of the exclusive competence of the central power. In parallel, the BdE will send to the Governments of the Regions any information it might have about the rest of the infringements set out in Ley 26/1988 (those that are not of its exclusive competence). In any case, if it is the Department of Economy of a Region who has instituted the proceedings for a "very grave" or a "grave" infringement, its decision on the case cannot be adopted without a previous report being made by the BdE.

In short, depending on the issue, and on the competencies assumed by that particular Region, the institution of proceedings and the determination of the sanction, may correspond to the BdE or to the Regional Government. This lack of systematisation can be identified as a political/technical barrier to the entry of other Member States' Savings Banks in the complex Spanish market. Fortunately, the norms and models of accounting in all credit institutions are established by the Ministry of Economy with unified criteria in the whole Spanish territory.[38]

b) The BdE's supervisory competencies

As in most modern supervisory systems, the rules applied by the BdE tend to guarantee a high standard of accounting transparency, rather than establishing a rigid and imperative model for the direction of the credit entities.[39] Thus, in the first place, the power to establish the rules of accounting and the models of financial statements for all credit institutions has been conferred on the BdE, and it has exercised this competence in Circular 4/1991, which has been modified on several occasions.[40] This regulation takes into account the Community Directives on the subject.[41]

The BdE is also the lender of last resort in the Spanish financial system, and it is the competent authority to decide on the necessity to intervene in a credit institution for its reorganisation or winding-up.[42] Equally, it has to see if there are "banking incompatibilities" by the key posts of the credit entities. In that context, if the BdE finds that these incompatibilities exist, it can propose to the Ministry of Economy the appointment of inspectors to control the activity of the financial entity concerned.[43]

As a part of the normal development of its supervisory activity, the BdE controls the acquisition of a qualifying participation (5% of the capital or of the voting rights) in credit entities,[44] the own funds ratio,[45] large exposures, the compulsory registration of entities, statutes, key posts and risks,[46] and the fulfilment of its regulations on transparency of operations and consumer protection.[47]

The flow of information from the credit institutions to the BdE is channelled through two different conduits: statistical control and inspections. The first takes place when the credit institutions regularly send the BdE the compulsory declarations established by law. This information may be completed after additional and more specific demands for information made by the BdE, if it considers it necessary for the development of its supervisory function. The inspections also adopt two different modalities: those called "ordinary" or "general", in which the BdE periodically checks the activity of the credit institutions,[48] and those known as "extraordinary", "special" or "monographic", in which the BdE focuses its investigation on a particular aspect of an institution's activity.[49] The special inspection may also test the system of internal control of the credit entity in order to observe its reaction in the face of different events in the financial market.[50] Additionally, it must be noticed that resistance to an inspection of the BdE is qualified as a very grave infringement under Art. 4 (h) of Ley 26/1988.

All these activities are complemented by the regulatory power of the BdE in the field of supervision through the *Circulares*. However, there is a limit to the use of this power: it can be exercised only when the Government, by law, has expressly authorised the BdE to use it in that particular ambit.[51]

The BdE is competent to exercise its supervisory power over any branch of the Spanish credit institutions (inside or outside the Spanish territory),[52] and over any branch of the credit institutions authorised in another Member State and operating in Spain. In relation to the latter, Article 43 *bis* of Ley 26/1988 specifies that the BdE can inspect these branches, in particular with regard to their liquidity, the application of its monetary policy, and the appropriate functioning of the payments system. In so doing, the BdE may request the same information that it asks of the Spanish entities. The BdE also has competence to watch over the risks undertaken by those foreign branches in the Spanish market in order to be able to inform the supervisory authority in the country of origin, and to ensure that the foreign branches behave "in conformity with the norms of general good". This open expression, not precisely defined in Spanish law, leaves great discretion to the BdE, which may apply to the branches of credit institutions authorised in other Member States the same regime that it uses for the Spanish entities with regard to solvency, monetary discipline and operation of the Spanish financial market.

c) The BdE's power to sanction

All credit institutions are subject to the same sanction regime in Spain, in spite of the fact that their conduct is ruled by different norms. This common standard is set up in Title I of Ley 26/1988.

The nature of this procedure is administrative, and that means that if the facts investigated by the BdE lead to the institution of a penal procedure, the administrative one will be suspended until the judges have finally decided upon the case.[53] Art. 294 of the Spanish Penal Code punishes with 6 months to 3 years of imprisonment (or a fine equivalent to 12 to 24 months)[54] the rejection or obstruction of the supervisory activity of the Administrative authorities, such as the BdE.[55] After the judicial resolution, the BdE must respect the finding of facts made in such a resolution. Another corollary of the administrative nature of the sanction procedures instituted by the BdE is that they do not deal with the civil or commercial consequences of the infringements. These have to be resolved through private independent actions in the Civil Courts.

Focusing on the procedure instituted by the BdE, we have already explained that the Ley 26/1988 distinguishes between "very grave" (Art. 4), "grave" (Art. 5) and "minor" (Art. 6) infringements. The penalties for these infringements are now being updated in the reform which the Spanish Parliament is presently discussing.[56] The prescription period for these offences also varies depending on their gravity: the very grave and grave infringements are prescribed in five years, and the minor ones in two.

The procedure remains unchanged in the above-mentioned reform, and the Executive Board of the BdE continues to be the competent authority for the institution of proceedings.[57] The same Executive Board decides on the sanction if it has found a grave or minor infringement; but if the facts are categorised as a very grave infringement, the expedient will be sent to the Ministry of Economy, who will definitively decide on the sanction[58] (except for the revocation of the authorisation, which has to be decided by the Government as a whole).[59] The institution of proceedings against the branches of credit institutions authorised in another Member State will be communicated to the supervisory authorities in the country of origin. If the result of the investigation leads to the imposition of sanctions for grave or very grave infringements, the decision is communicated to the same authorities and to the Commission.[60]

As we have already mentioned, the decisions of the BdE in the field of monetary policy and the issue of banknotes and coins put an end to the administrative procedure, and may only be appealed before the Courts (the Administrative Chamber of the *Audiencia Nacional*). On the other hand, the BdE's decisions in the field of supervision may be appealed before the Ministry of Economy. The resolutions of the latter may then be appealed before the Courts (again, the Administrative Chamber of the *Audiencia Nacional*).[61] The sanctions imposed by the BdE, the Ministry of Economy or the Government on the basis of Ley 26/1988 are "immediately executive".

d) The relationship between the BdE and the ECB and the future of the credit institutions supervision in the EU

The present regulation of the functioning of the BdE is set out in Ley 13/1994 (BdE Autonomy Act), which was enacted to fulfil the legal requirements of the monetary Union and prepare the BdE for its insertion in the ESCB. This law was later amended (by Ley 66/1997 and by Ley 12/1998) to adjust these rules more precisely to the effective starting-up of the third phase of the monetary Union.[62]

As drafted today, Art. 1 (3) of Ley 13/1994 says that "as a part of the ESCB the BdE is subject to the EC Treaty and the ESCB Statutes". After this obviousness, it is recalled that the BdE shall follow the guidelines and decisions issued by the ECB, in the context of the ESCB.

More interesting for this paper is the reform that Ley 12/1998 introduced in the content of Art. 7 (3) of Ley 13/1994, which defines the main functions to be developed by the BdE in the context of the ESCB. After setting out some of the competencies expressly provided by the Treaty for the Eurosystem, an open provision has been included which refers to "other functions derived from its position as a part of the ESCB". This norm would permit the assumption of powers by the BdE to enforce the supervisory rules enacted by the ECB, if the latter were assigned that competence in the future (Art. 105 (6) EC), without any need to modify of the Spanish legislation.

The BdE representatives regularly co-operate with their colleagues of other EU countries in the Banking Supervision Committee of the ECB.[63] The BdE does not take any official position about the options on the possible centralization of the supervisory functions at an European level, or between the inclusion of these competencies within the activity of the ECB, or the creation of an independent agency for this purpose. A general reference is usually made to the document published by the ECB in 2001 on "The role of Central Banks in prudential supervision",[64] where it is advised that central banking and supervision of credit entities should be concentrated in the same authority.

In any case, there seems to be a general feeling among the BdE's officials that the concentration of the supervisory function at an European level would be now premature. Although the need for enhanced co-operation between national authorities is always stressed, and the supervision of both the financial conglomerates and the cross-border provision of services via Internet[65] cause important regulatory concerns, it is submitted that further harmonisation of the supervisory regulations applied in the Member States should precede the above-mentioned unification.[66] The present Governor of the BdE recently published an article in which he added some more prerequisites for the establishment of a centralised model of supervision in the EU: the convergence of supervisory practices (not just of the rules), the strengthening of the exchange of information mechanisms, and further progress in political integration that would help to solve the distribution of the budgetary efforts between Member States when the European authority decides to intervene in a banking crisis.[67]

NOTES

[1] For example, the Banco de Bilbao opened a branch in Paris in 1902, and another one in London in the forties; the Banco de Santander established two representation offices in Latin America and one in London in the fifties; and the Banco Popular developed a modest network of branches in France during the sixties.

[2] According to the data provided by Sánchez Peinado, 46,93 % of the BSCH's commercial assets, and 40% of BBVA's commercial assets (E. SÁNCHEZ PEINADO, Internacionalización de la banca española. Evolución y resultados en los años noventa, in 794 Información Comercial Española 143-154, octubre 2001).

[3] Precisely because of their large exposure in countries like Peru, Brasil and, above all, Argentina, the profits of the Spanish Banks have been sharply reduced in 2001.

[4] On this issue, see J. GARCÍA ROA, Las Cajas de Ahorros españolas: cambios recientes, fusiones y otras estrategias de dimensionamiento, Madrid (1994).

[5] For example, on 17th April 2002, the French Banking Commission prohibited *CaixaBank* (48 branches and 70.000 clients in France), the French Subsidiary of *La Caixa*, to continue offering 2% interest as remuneration on its current accounts, because the legislation in that country does not allow for remuneration on this kind of accounts.

[6] The situation is even more difficult for the banks with their head offices outside the European Union. A recent report shows that they lost 7,81 million euros in Spain only in the first trimester of 2002 (El País, La banca extranjera pierde en España, 21.5.2002, p. 55).

[7] According to the ECB, in 1999 the number of branches and ATMs for each million inhabitants in Spain was 989 and 1062 respectively, while in France the figures were 411 and 535, in Germany 674 and 563, and in the United Kingdom 219 and 476.

[8] V. PÉREZ-DÍAZ/ J. C. RODRÍGUEZ/ E. CHULIA, Cajas y bancos: una experiencia de diversidad institucional, in 74-75 Papeles de Economía Española 269, (1998).

[9] That is the case of Evolve bank, owned by Lloyds TSB, and above all ING Direct, which belongs to the Dutch group ING.

[10] For a more comprehensive analysis of all these issues, see E. BERNAL JURADO, Estrategia de la banca española en la comercialización de servicios financieros a través de internet, in 2720 Boletín Económico de ICE 9-17, (marzo 2002).

[11] For a review of the regulation of electronic banking contracts in Spain, see I. RAMOS HERRANZ, Contratación bancaria electrónica, in G. A. BOTANA GARCÍA (Coord.) Comercio electrónico y protección de los consumidores 795, Madrid (2001).

[12] Proposal for a European Parliament and Council Directive concerning the distance marketing of consumer financial services and amending Council Directive 90/619/EEC and Directives 97/7/EC and 98/27/EC (COM (1998) 468, of 14.10.1998).

[13] *Proyecto de Ley* on the Measures for the Reform of the Financial System, published in the *Boletín Oficial de las Cortes Generales, serie* A, No. 69-1, of 8.3.2002

[14] The Audiencia Nacional is the National Court of Appeals

[15] Ministry of Economy

[16] Judgement of 5.6.1998 on case 5304/1995, CMG, TS-S.VII.

[17] Judgement of 7.2.2001 on case 0784/1998 de Diego Nafria, AN – S.VI.

[18] The BdE cannot impose here (as in the case of the establishment of a branch) a two-month waiting period in order to organise its supervisory function.

[19] This means that the norm may be state, regional or local.

[20] In the request, the financial entity has to specify the activities that it intends to develop in the office, the name and the record of the person who will be in charge.

[21] These Representation Offices are not banks in any sense, but they are often an useful instrument to explore the Spanish market, as a first step that may lead to the future creation of a branch or a subsidiary.

[22] Besides, there are some operations that Spanish law excludes from the agency contract, such as the provision of guarantees and warranties (Art. 22 (2) RD 1245/1995).

[23] We use this term with the meaning which has been given to it in the last section. Again, the information must include the list of activities that the office will develop in the host Member State.

[24] Here we can find a different spirit from that which prevails in Community legislation, because the latter always classifies the supervisory authorities with reference to the market/operation supervised. See on this issue F. ZUNZUNEGUI, Derecho del mercado financiero 101, Madrid (2000).

[25] The Regional Governments also have competencies in relation to other credit entities authorised for a specific and single activity, but we will not deal with that issue in this paper. For a review of the rules of supervision applicable to some of those entities, see R. POVEDA ANADÓN, Las entidades de crédito de ámbito oper-

ativo limitado: supervisión y control, in Derecho del Mercado Financiero 41-77, Madrid, 1994.

[26] Although it acts "at the request of the BdE" (Article 18 of Ley 26/1988, as modified by Ley 12/1998).

[27] This distinction between the monetary policy and the regulation of the credit market has its basis in the Spanish Constitution. Its Article 149 (1) (11ª) confers on the State exclusive competence (as against the Regional Governments) for the regulation of the monetary system, and for the establishment of the "bases" for the regulation credit, banks, and insurance. The use of the word "bases" indicates that the latter is a competence where the Regional Governments may intervene, while they have no possibility of action in relation to the regulation or enforcement of the monetary policy.

[28] J. GARCÍA-ANDRADE GÓMEZ, La posición jurídica del Banco de España en el SEBC 64-67, Madrid (2000).

[29] It should be mentioned that Additional Section 10 of Ley 26/1988 directly confers competence on the Government to supervise and inspect the "de facto providers" of financial services, who operate without registration. The Ministry of Economy can sanction the failure to provide information, or the delivery of false information, or the non co-operation with the inspection (which may be delegated to the BdE) with a fine that does not exceed 30.050 Euros.

[30] These problems also affect the supervision of other kinds of credit institutions, such as the *Sociedades de Garantía Recíproca*, the *Cooperativas de Crédito*, etc., but, as we have already said, we are not dealing with these minor entities in this paper.

[31] For a study of the regulation of this subject in the different Acts of Autonomy and the Spanish Constitution, together with an analysis of the concept of "bases" in the case-law of the Constitutional Court, see J. L. FUERTES SUÁREZ, La distribución de competencias entre el Estado y las Comunidades Autónomas en materia de ordenación del crédito y la Banca, in Estudios de Derecho Público Bancario 151-173, Madrid, (1987).

[32] See the critical comments of L. A. POMED SÁNCHEZ, Algunas reflexiones sobre los problemas actuales del derecho público bancario en España, in 62 Revista de Derecho Bancario y Bursátil 375, (1996).

[33] No formal agreements have been signed until now between the BdE and the Regions.

[34] Among the case-law of the Spanish Constitutional Court concerning the distribution of powers between the State and the Regions in relation to the credit entities, we consider of special interest the following judgements: 1/1982, of 28.1.1982; 48/1988, of 22.3.1988; 49/1988, of 22.3.1988; 178/1992, of 13.11.1992; 96/1996, of 30.5.1996; 235/1999, of 16.12.1999. For a comment and summary of some of these judgements, see A. JIMÉNEZ-BLANCO, El Banco de España y las entidades del mercado financiero, in A. ALONSO UREBA/ J. MARTÍNEZ-SIMANCAS (Dirs.), Derecho del mercado financiero 13-14, Madrid (1994).

[35] The power to sanction corresponds exclusively to the BdE in the case of the infringements listed in letters b), c) and f) of Art. 4 and g), h), i), k), and p) of Art. 5 of Ley 26/1988. The Constitutional Court has confirmed in its judgement 96/1996 the compatibility with the Spanish Constitution of this assignment of competencies,

but it has nuanced that in the case of Art. 5 p) (the infringement of the norms on accounting, formulation of balance sheets, and financial statements), when the entity competent to receive those documents is the Region, the latter shall also be competent to impose the sanctions attached to the infringement of those obligations. Therefore, we find here a paradoxical "exclusive" competence to sanction of the BdE which is not so exclusive. In the same judgement, the Court declared the partial unconstitutionality of Art. 42 Ley 26/1988 because this provision only recognised the competencies of the Regions in relation to Savings Banks and the Credit Cooperatives, ignoring their power to sanction other credit entities (FJ 22 and 23). In its more recent judgement 235/1999, the Constitutional Court recalled this partial unconstitutionality of Art. 42 and urged the legislative power to remedy the situation (FJ 13).

[36] Art. 48 (1) Ley 26/1988, whose constitutionality has been confirmed after judgements 386/1993 (FJ 3) and 96/1996 (FJ 14) of the Constitutional Court. The Ministry has delegated this power to the BdE.

[37] A. DE JUAN, El Banco de España y la supervisión del sistema bancario, in 18 Papeles de Economía Española 112, (1984).

[38] *Circulares* of the BdE No. 7/1991, 4/1992, 5/1992, 9/1992, 14/1992, 15/1992, 18/1992, 21/1992, 4/1993, 11/1993, 3/1994, 6/1994, 2/1995, 2/1996, 7/1996, 5/1997, 7/1998, 2/1999, 9/1999, 4/2000, 5/2000 y 4/2001. For a comment on this issue, see J. FERNÁNDEZ SANGUINO, Actividad de control de las entidades de crédito, 106 Partida doble 131-132 (diciembre 1999).

[39] Directive 86/635/EEC of 8.12.1986 on the annual accounts and consolidated accounts of banks and other financial institutions (OJ L 372, of 31.12.1986), and Directive 89/117/EEC of 13.2.1989 on the obligations of branches established in a Member State of credit institutions and financial institutions having their head offices outside that Member State regarding the publication of annual accounting documents (OJ L 44 of 16.2.1989).

[40] For a review of the Banks encountering financial difficulties and the cost that this has caused to the rest of the Spanish financial system, see the annual Memorias del Fondo de Garantía de Depósitos en Establecimientos Bancarios.

[41] Art. 12 of *Decreto* 702/1969.

[42] Title VI of Ley 26/1988.

[43] *Circular* 5/1993 of the BdE, modified several times. In relation to the monetary policy, Art. 66 (2)(e) of the new *Reglamento interno* of the BdE sets up the power of this institution to act against any violation of the minimum reserves and statistical information obligations established in Regulation (EC) No 2818/98 of the European Central Bank of 1 December 1998 on the application of minimum reserves and Regulation (EC) No 2819/98 of the European Central Bank of 1 December 1998 concerning the consolidated balance sheet of the monetary financial institutions sector (R. DE SANTILLÁN FRAILE, El Banco de España como parte integrante del SEBC: novedades en el Reglamento Interno del Banco de España aprobado por Resolución del Consejo de Gobierno del Banco de España de 28 de marzo de 2000, 197 Noticias de la UE 67 (junio 2001).

[44] See the *Circular* of the BdE 13/1988 on the key posts of the credit institutions, the *Circular* 7/1993 on the Special Registry of Statutes, and the *Circular* 3/1995 on the Risks Information Central (*Central de Información de Riesgos*).

[45] *Circular* of the BdE 8/1990, modified by *Circulares* No. 22/1992, 13/1993, 5/1994, 3/1996 , 4/1998, 3/1999, 1/2000 and 3/2001.

[46] Art. 17 (a) of *Decreto-ley* 18/1962, still in force although most of this *Decreto-ley* was abrogated by Ley 13/1994.

[47] Art. 17 (c) of *Decreto-ley* 18/1962.

[48] In any case, the BdE cannot sanction a bank simply because its internal system of control does not function diligently. The institution of proceedings needs as condition *sine qua non* the existence of an infringement of the law (See judgement of the Supreme Court [*Tribunal Supremo*] of 30.5.1995).

[49] Art. 3 (1) of Ley 13/1994 (as modified by Ley 12/1998). For a review of the difference in the independence of the BdE in relation to its regulatory power, depending on the matter (monetary or supervisory), see J. GARCÍA-ANDRADE GÓMEZ, La posición jurídica del Banco de España en el SEBC 68-69, Madrid (2000).

[50] The inspection of the BdE may equally reach any Spanish person controlling a credit institution in another Member State, within the framework of the cooperation with the supervisory authorities in that country (Art. 43 *bis* of Ley 26/1988).

[51] The same facts may give rise at the same time to a penal and an administrative sanction. The Spanish Constitutional Court has established that this possibility does not violate the *non bis in idem* principle when the legal good protected by those norms is different (see judgement 234/1991 [FJ 2]).

[52] In the Spanish penal code the fines are calculated on a daily rate, from a minimum of 1,20 _ and a maximum of 300_ per day (Art. 50 of the Spanish Penal Code).

[53] For a complete study of the penal consequences of this criminal offence, see J. MARTÍNEZ RUIZ, La tutela jurídico-penal de las potestades administrativas de supervisión e inspección de los mercados financieros, Madrid (2001).

[54] See Art. 40 of the *Proyecto de Ley* on the Measures for the Reform of the Financial System, published in the Boletín Oficial de las Cortes Generales, serie A, No. 69-1, of 8.3.2002. For a review of the amendments to this project presented by the different political groups, see the Boletín Oficial de las Cortes Generales, serie A, No. 69-12, of 17.5.2002.

[55] For an analysis of this procedure, see F. ZUNZUNEGUI, Derecho del mercado financiero 357-368, Madrid (2000).

[56] For a review of the sanctions applied by the BdE see the Memoria del Servicio de Reclamaciones del Banco de España, published each year. For an excellent summary of the cases until 1998, see J. FERNANDO ROBLES, Prácticas incorrectas y condiciones abusivas en las operaciones bancarias, Madrid (1998). The reports for 1999 and 2000 can be found in the web page of the BdE (www.bde.es).

[57] Art. 18 of Ley 26/1988. The supervisory authorities in the home State must be consulted before the revocation of the authorisation for a branch of a credit institution with its head office in another Member State.

[58] Art. 23 *bis* of Ley 26/1988.

[59] Art. 2 of Ley 13/1994, as modified by Ley 12/1998 and art. 25 of Ley 26/1988.

[60] For a comment, see L. POMED SÁNCHEZ, Dos reformas recientes de la ley de autonomía del Banco de España, 70 Revista de Derecho Bancario y Bursátil 586, (abril-junio 1998).

[61] For a review of the activities of the Banking Supervisión Committee since its creation in 1998, see M. GRANDE, The role of the Eurosystem in the field of prudential supervision and financial stability, 50 Euro 57, (2000).

[62] Available at *www.ecb.int*.

[63] A. GOUTZINIS, European Banks and the cross-border provision of services via the Internet: Commercial practices and regulatory concerns, 3 Journal of International Banking Regulation 208, (December 2001).

[64] F. J. PRIEGO, Enhanced Co-operation among Regulators and the Role of National Regulators in a Global Market. The Spanish Perspective 7-8, International Bar Association, Barcelona, 30.9.1999.

[65] J. CARUANA, La supervisión bancaria en la Unión Europea, 84-85 Papeles de Economía Española 42-43, (2000).

SWEDEN

Financial Services in the Era of the Euro and E-Commerce:

Does home country control work?

Rapporteurs
Lars Pehrson and Svante Johansson

AUTHORISATION

1. The Swedish acts contain nothing explicit on ”prior consultation”. However, the officer in charge at the Swedish Financial Supervisory Authority (the “SFSA”) will take contact with the applicant's home country authority if any questions arise or clarifications are deemed necessary.
2. No.
3. No.
4. (a) Article 18 has been entered into the acts regulating banks and other credit institutions.
4. (b) Quite effectively. The Swedish rules are basically only translations of the Directive's text and foreign credit institutions can, therefore, carry on business in Sweden in any way covered by the Directive.
4. (c) No, Swedish credit institutions may provide the services listed in the annex.
5. Any entity from a country within the EEA may carry out activities in Sweden in the same way as domestic players. For activities not listed in the Annex, the answer will, therefore, depend on the nature of the activities. A foreign credit institution will be allowed to carry out activities that a Swedish entity would be allowed to carry out without permission. If, on the other hand, the activity would require permission if carried out by a Swedish entity, a foreign credit institution would not be allowed to carry out that activity (except, of course, a permission is granted).
6. No.

THE GENERAL GOOD

7.(a) There is no specific rules regarding the general good in the Swedish acts. Swedish banks and credit institutions have to carry out their activities in a way that will safeguard the public's confidence. The SFSA also has the power to impose sanctions on credit institutions - Swedish or foreign - that act in an "inappropriate" way, which rule, of course, can be used to protect the general good.
7.(b) Not as far as can be judged by publicly available information.
7.(c) Decisions by the SFSA can be appealed to court.
7.(d) No.

THE ESTABLISHMENT OF BRANCHES

8. We are not aware of any particular mention-worthy legal problems in connection with the establishment of branches.

THE PROVISION OF CROSS-BORDER SERVICES

9. Regarding cross-border activities the Swedish acts are, to some extent, vague and can be hard to interpret, which can lead to practical inconveniences, but we have not experienced any real difficulties.

THE COMPETENT AUTHORITIES

10. The competent authority for the purpose of the Second Banking Directive is the SFSA, which is the single financial supervisory authority in Sweden, covering all financial business.
11. No.
12. As mentioned under 10 above, the SFSA is the single financial supervisory authority in Sweden, covering all financial business. We are not aware of any discussion aiming to change this structure.
13. There is no general consensus, but for the need of securing cooperation between national supervisory authorities, in which process the ECB can play an important role.
14. Sweden has not adopted the Euro. However, the introduction of the Euro and the growth of E-commerce have emphasised the above-mentioned need for cooperation between supervisory authorities.
15. No information available.
16. The European Convention on Human Rights and Fundamental

Freedoms has in Sweden the status of an act. However, we are not aware of any situation in which the Convention has affected the work of the SFSA.

17. No. Sweden has, as mentioned above under 14, not adopted the Euro.

SWITZERLAND

Financial Services in the Era of the Euro and E-Commerce:

Does home country control work?

Rapporteurs
*Stefan Hoffmann, Claude-Alain Margelisch, Markus Staub and Mireille Tissot**

* Swiss Bankers' Association

I. INTRODUCTION[1]

Switzerland is not a member of the European Union. As such, the questionnaire that was sent to members of FIDE is not relevant to Switzerland. Consequently, the authors of this report have taken a different approach, choosing to look at the situation with regard to supervision and electronic commerce within the framework of legal relations established between Switzerland and an EU member state. In other words, our analysis is based on the relationship between the EU and a third country.

We have endeavoured to retain the structure of the questionnaire as far as possible. To facilitate the reading of this report, we have also included a table of contents, which can be found at the beginning.

The relevant legal situation is that of 1 June 2002.

II. PRINCIPLES OF SUPERVISION FOR FOREIGN BANKS OFFERING SERVICES IN SWITZERLAND

1. General principles

The Swiss Federal Banking Commission (SFBC) is the primary vehicle for bank and financial market regulation and supervision in Switzerland. As an independent federal administrative agency, assigned to the Federal Department of Finance (FDF) in administrative terms only, the SFBC has developed over the years from a banking supervisory authority into an organisation charged with the supervision of extensive areas of the financial sector. Today, its duties and responsibilities are as follows:

- Supervision of banks
- Supervision of investment funds
- Supervision of central mortgage bond institutions
- Supervision of stock exchanges and brokers
- Supervision of the disclosure of holdings and public offers.

The SFBC monitors compliance with legal regulations, passes all necessary ordinances and decrees to this effect, and has an extensive right to information.

At the international level, the SFBC is a member of the Basle Committee on Banking Supervision, the Technical Committee of IOSCO and the Joint Forum on the Supervision of Financial Conglomerates.

A system of dual control

Two aspects of Swiss banking regulation and supervision that set

Switzerland apart from other countries are the system of dual control and the relatively high level of self-regulation.

The Swiss **system of dual control** is based on a clear division of responsibilities between the SFBC as the federal supervisory authority and private auditing firms recognised by the SFBC (statutory bank auditors). Auditing costs are passed on to the institutions being supervised.

The auditors and auditing firms recognised by the SFBC are legally bound to the institutions they audit by means of a contractual relationship under private law. The content of their auditing activities, however, is primarily defined by public law. As an "instrument" of the SFBC, the auditors exercise direct supervision by carrying out regular audits within the banks. In doing this, they fulfil a public duty, but do not have any official powers as such. They report the results of their audit to the SFBC. In addition, the SFBC occasionally carries out direct audits within the supervised banks.

As well as examining the annual accounts, the auditors check in particular whether the bank (or the securities dealer) is complying with the articles of association and regulations as well as the provisions of banking law, the directives issued by the SFBC and supervisory codes of conduct (see below). Since auditors play an important role in the system of control, they have to satisfy strict requirements. In particular, they must be completely independent from their clients, both financially and in terms of staff, and they have to be sufficiently qualified. This system of dual control has proven extremely effective in Swiss banking supervision. A working group of the SFBC is currently drafting legislation to incorporate the recommendations of the commission of experts for auditing (headed by Prof. P. Nobel, summary report dated December 2000).

Self-regulation

The second distinguishing feature of Swiss banking regulation concerns the importance of **self-regulation** in addition to government regulation. The Swiss Bankers' Association (SBA) issues its members with universally valid guidelines for certain areas of banking activity (codes of conduct). Compliance with these guidelines is checked as part of the statutory bank audit (see above). Key examples are the agreement on due diligence (Agreement on the Swiss banks' code of conduct with regard to the exercise of due diligence, CDB), the Portfolio Management Guidelines, the Risk Management Guidelines for Trading and for the Use of Derivatives, and the Code of Conduct for Securities Dealers. The Association also issues its members with recommendations on various areas of activity.

In the past, the high level of self-regulation has proven extremely effective. For many areas, self-regulation is more thorough and more cost-effective than government regulation.

2. *Approval procedure before the Federal Banking Commission*

The universal bank

Swiss financial legislation is based on the principle of the universal bank. In contrast to EU law, a banking establishment in Switzerland may offer its full range of products and services to clients as soon as it has received approval from the Federal Banking Commission (SFBC). Thus, contrary to Annex 1 of Directive 2000/12/EC of the European Parliament and of the Council of 20 March 2000 relating to the taking up and pursuit of the business of credit institutions, there is no specific descriptive list of financial activities in Swiss financial legislation.

Moreover, Article 2 of the Swiss Federal Law on Banks and Savings Banks (Banking Act, BA) specifies that the provisions of the law applicable to Swiss financial institutions shall apply by analogy to the subsidiaries, branches, agencies and permanent representatives of foreign banks in Switzerland. In other words, a foreign bank in Switzerland enjoys the same status as a universal bank.

Conditions required for a bank to exercise its activity in Switzerland

As in the European Union, a bank is required to obtain a licence prior to engaging in business operations in Switzerland. This licence will be granted if the bank provides the following evidence (Art. 3, para. 2 BA):

- *It must clearly define the scope of business*: on the basis of articles of association, by-laws, company contracts and business rules of the bank; it must also specify the geographical scope of its activities, which must be in line with its financial resources.
- *It must establish an adequate organisation*: by instituting, according to the scope or the importance of its business activities, the executive bodies as well as bodies for supervision and control. The authorities of these bodies must be clearly segregated in such a way as to ensure the effective supervision of the bank's management; the bank's actual management must be located in Switzerland.
- *The minimum share capital* of CHF 10 million (= around EUR 6.6 million) must be fully paid in.
- *The persons charged with the administration and management of the bank must enjoy a good reputation and present all the guarantees of proper business conduct*; this is a fundamental requirement in Switzerland in so far as it constitutes the measure not only of the bank's reputation but also of the Swiss Financial Centre as a whole. Consequently, applications for licences must contain details of the

nationality, domicile, significant shareholdings and any pending judicial or administrative proceedings of the bank's management. Incidentally, each person must submit a signed curriculum vitae, an extract from the Criminal Register and references.

The Federal Banking Commission has amassed a wide-ranging body of case law in this area, and has adopted a number of regulations on this basis which it has subsequently extended to the whole of the banking sector (for example, measures to be taken by banking establishments in order to prevent foreign heads of state from abusing the Swiss financial centre).

Moreover, persons within the bank who *possess qualified participations* (at least 10% of the capital or voting rights, held either directly or indirectly) must guarantee that their influence will not have a negative impact on a prudent business activity.

- *The persons entrusted with the management of the bank have their domicile in a place* which allows them to ensure management in a factual and responsible manner.

Additional conditions that foreign banks must satisfy

If a foreign bank is planning to commence activities in Switzerland, it must first satisfy the same conditions as a Swiss bank, as listed above. However, Swiss banking law demands that the following conditions be complied with as well:

- *Reciprocity must be guaranteed* by the countries in which foreigners possessing significant shareholdings are domiciled, except where there are international commitments.
- *The name of the bank* must not permit conclusions to be drawn or presumed about the Swiss nature of the establishment.
- *If the bank is a member of a group active in the financial sector*, it must-demonstrate that it is subject to appropriate consolidated supervision by foreign authorities.
- *The bank must inform the national bank* of the business it conducts as well as its relations outside Switzerland.

Granting licences – appeals

The licensing procedure with regard to the exercising of a banking activity in Switzerland is governed by the concept of constitutional freedom of trade and industry. It is thus unconnected to the law of concessions and the holding of a state monopoly whose activity may be delegated to third parties. As a result, the government may not intervene to regulate the number of players in the market. Thus, as soon as a bank fulfils the conditions necessary for granting a licence, it has a claim which it can assert vis-à-vis the supervisory authority. On the other hand, if at a later stage the conditions are no longer fulfilled, the licence is withdrawn.

As a general rule, the Federal Banking Commission makes an administrative decision when it issues a licence. In other words, it is the law on administrative procedure that applies. This means that even if the SFBC examines the licence application in an independent and official capacity, it must observe a number of provisions of administrative law, such as not abusing its assessment powers, granting the requesting banks the right to a hearing and to view the dossier. It must also indicate in its decision how the bank may appeal against a decision. Pursuant to Art. 24 BA, the decisions of the SFBC may be overturned by administrative appeal to the Federal Supreme Court, i.e. in the specific case where the SFBC does not grant a licence to bank which has requested the same. In this way, judicial control over the licensing procedure is ensured.

3. *Supervisory competence of the Swiss National Bank*

Monitoring of interbank payments

According to Swiss National Banking Law (NBL), the Swiss National Bank (SNB) has no authorisation to monitor financial institutions directly, unlike some foreign central banks. However, the SNB does assume monitoring functions indirectly, particularly in the area of non-cash payments.

Art. 2, para. 1 NBL lists among the primary responsibilities of the SNB "facilitating payment services". Moreover, Art. 14, para. 7 NBL authorises the SNB to provide giro, settlement and collection services. The SNB is chiefly involved in non-cash interbank payment services, because this is where it can make the greatest contribution to the security and efficiency of payment services, and because the SNB must be able to rely on a stable system of payments when implementing its monetary policy.

The Swiss Interbank Clearing payment system (SIC), is operated on behalf of the SNB by Swiss Interbank Clearing AG, a private company owned by the Swiss banks. However, the SNB does exercise considerable controls over the SIC. All changes and additions to the existing provisions require the approval of the SNB.

SIC is an electronic real-time gross settlement system. In such systems, payments are settled sequentially, i.e. on a gross basis, and debited from the giro accounts at the SNB. Credit transfers are only executed by SIC provided that the issuing bank has the corresponding funds available in its giro account at the SNB. If insufficient credit is available, the payment instruction is automatically held pending in a waiting list until the requisite coverage is provided by means of additional payments. Executed payment transactions are therefore irrevocable and final.

The banks settle large payment transactions and part of their mass payment transactions via SIC. Since November 2000 the Swiss Post Office has also been settling its money market transactions via SIC. The SNB supervises SIC and SIC participants.

SIC has a direct connection to SECOM, the securities clearing system operated by SIS SegaInterSettle. This connection ensures that delivery and payment occur simultaneously when securities and repo transactions are settled.

Cross-border euro payment services

When the third phase of European monetary union was launched at the beginning of 1999, the central banks of all EU countries introduced the TARGET system (Trans-European Automated Real-time Gross settlement Express Transfer) as a means of linking their national payment systems. TARGET facilitates the implementation of the monetary policy of the European Central Bank and cross-border payment services in the euro-zone. Only the payment systems of EU member states are permitted to join TARGET. The Swiss banks operate a special clearing bank in Frankfurt called Swiss Euro Clearing Bank (SECB) in order to obtain access to TARGET. The SECB reports directly to the German banking supervisory authorities. The euroSIC system employed by the SECB for settlement is used primarily for euro payments between Swiss banks, while most cross-border payments are still settled via correspondent banks.

Revision of the National Banking Law

Following the reform of the Federal Constitution (Art. 99) and the entry into force of the Federal Law on Currency and Payment Instruments, the National Banking Law (NBL) is now being revised as well. Between March and July 2001, the Federal Department of Finance carried out a consultative procedure regarding the complete revision of the NBL. The results of this consultative procedure were published in January 2002. The Federal Council will issue its communication to the Federal Chambers in mid-2002.

Monitoring and supervision of payment and settlement systems

According to the preliminary draft of the future National Banking Law (D-NBL), the SNB is to be given certain powers to monitor payment systems (Art. 18 D-NBL). These powers are based on a three-stage regulatory model: in the first stage, operators of payment systems will be subject to a statistical reporting obligation (Art 15, para. 2 D-NBL). Non-cash payment systems that settle payments to an open circle of recipients will have an extended duty of disclosure (Art. 18, para. 1, D-NBL). For non-cash payment systems where there is a risk to the stability of the financial system, the SNB can set up qualitative minimum requirements (Art. 18, para. 2, D-NBL). According to the commission of experts, the term "payment system" covers the money side of securities settlement systems, but not the securities side (report, page 126).

During consultation, this concept met with general approval. However, the banks and authorities complained that the revision of the NBL had not been used as an opportunity to explicitly subject the "securities side" (central archiving of securities as well as payment and settlement systems) to supervision in addition to payment services ("money side"), and in general to supervise the operation of key financial centre systems.

On 16 January 2002, therefore, the Federal Council decided in the communication to the revised NBL to authorise the SNB to monitor payment and securities settlement systems. In this connection, the coordination between the SNB and the SFBC is also explicitly regulated. The two have agreed to divide the complementary supervisory duties as follows: the SFBC will remain responsible for banking supervision, while the SNB will assume responsibility for monitoring the system. From the list in Art. 18, para. 2, D-NBL, it can be seen that the following points are classified as system monitoring:

- assessing operational security
- defining and checking the criteria for accepting system participants
- assessing the preventative measures to be taken in the event that system participants incur payment difficulties
- approving the method of payment used in the system.

According to the Swiss Federal Banking Act and the Securities Act, banking supervision covers, among other things:

- checking the guarantee of impeccable business conduct of the shareholders and those persons charged with the administration and management of the company (Art. 3, para. 2, letter c of the Banking Act; Art. 3, para. 2, letter b of the Securities Act; Art. 10, para. 2, letter d of the Securities Act)
- approving the company regulations and articles of association (Art. 3, para. 3 of the Banking Act) and the organisation (Art. 3, para. 2, letter a of the Banking Act, Art. 10, para. 2, letter a of the Securities Act).
- continuous supervisory activity (Art. 23bis, para. 1, 23ter, para. 1 of the Banking Act; Art. 35, paras. 1 and 3 of the Securities Act; Art. 56-58 of

the Investment Fund Act); in particular over areas such as shareholders' equity, risk diversification, the organisation, the internal control system, compliance, etc.

- dealing with the statutory bank auditors' reports (Art. 18 ff. of the Banking Act, Art. 43 ff. of the Banking Ordinance; Art. 17 ff. of the Securities Act)
- providing administrative assistance to domestic and foreign supervisory authorities (Art. 23^{sexies} of the Banking Act; Art. 38 of the Securities Act, Art. 63 of the Investment Fund Act).

4. *Instruments at the disposal of the Swiss supervisory authority*

Consolidated supervision within the meaning of Art. 4^{quinquies} BA

The Swiss banks have always been aware of the fact that efficient cooperation between the authorities of the host country and the authorities of the home country is an essential prerequisite for monitoring international banking operations. As early as May 1983, the Basle Committee set down the principles of supervision for banks abroad. Today, after the financial scandals which have taken place at BCCI and Barings Bank, no-one questions the fundamental importance of consolidated supervision.

The principle of consolidated supervision is anchored in Art. 4 ^{quinquies} BA, which specifies that banks, whose parent companies are supervised by banking or financial market supervisory authorities, may transmit information or documents not publicly available to their parent companies which are necessary for the purpose of consolidated supervision.

To prevent the system from being abused and in order to find a solution which complies with banking secrecy, Swiss legislation has made the provision of this information subject to the following conditions:

- Information must be used exclusively for internal control or direct supervision of banks or other financial intermediaries subject to licence
- The parent company and the supervisory authorities responsible for consolidated supervision are bound by official or professional secrecy
- The information may not be transmitted to third parties without the prior permission of the bank or on the basis of a blanket permission in a state treaty.

International administrative assistance

Judicial assistance governs cooperation between judicial authorities, while international administrative assistance concerns the cooperation between administrative supervisory authorities. In these two cases, legal guarantees ensure that the justified interests of the customers are not infringed.

In accordance with Art. 23 ^{sexies} BA, the Federal Banking Commission (SFBC) may provide foreign supervisory authorities with information not generally accessible to the public. The provision of this information, however, is subject to three conditions stipulated by law:

- Information must be used exclusively for internal control or direct supervision of banks or other financial intermediaries requiring authorisation
- The information provided may only be used for the direct supervision of banks and other financial intermediaries requiring authorisation. Information may not be passed on to the tax authorities
- The foreign authority may not transmit information to other authorities or public supervisory bodies without the prior consent of the SFBC or on the basis of a blanket permission contained in a treaty with a contracting state. The transmission of information to foreign criminal authorities is not permitted if there is no provision for judicial assistance in criminal matters between the states concerned. The purpose is to avoid circumvention of the rules regarding judicial assistance in criminal matters.

In particular, if the information to be given to a foreign supervisory authority concerns clients, the Federal law on administrative procedure applies, which means that any decision taken by the SFBC may be contested by the client by means of an administrative appeal before the Federal Supreme Court. Both the SFBC and the Federal Supreme Court must guarantee the client the right to a hearing as well as the right to view the dossier.

On-site inspections

In October 1996, a working group consisting of representatives of the Basle Committee on banking supervision and the Offshore Group of Banking Supervisors published recommendations for cross-border banking supervision. These recommendations incorporated proposals aimed at ensuring efficient supervision of the activities of international banks, notably by means of closer cooperation between banking supervisory authorities through on-site inspections.

The revised Banking Act, which entered into force on 1 October 1999, allows foreign supervisory authorities to carry out on-site inspections in Switzerland. However, these checks must be limited to the information needed to supervise the banks concerned on a consolidated basis; they are subject to the same rules as those which apply to international administrative assistance. Moreover, all the information requested by the foreign supervisory authorities which directly or indirectly concerns the management of client assets in particular must respect the right to appeal within the meaning of the law on administrative procedure. Finally, the banks can request that the foreign supervisory authorities be accompanied by the SFBC. These provisions have also been incorporated in the Securities Act.

5. *The future development of financial supervision in Switzerland*

Looking at the possible regulatory developments, it should be noted that Switzerland is currently evaluating the integration of financial market supervision. At the end of 2001, the Federal Council commissioned a group of experts to implement legislation following the summary report of the group of experts on financial market supervision (Zufferey). The chairman of this new commission of experts is Prof. U. Zimmerli from the University of Berne. In particular, the Zimmerli group has been instructed to draft a bill incorporating the recommendations of the Zufferey group, together with a report, by the end of 2002.

In terms of content, the bill must *first* contain proposals for the establishment of an integrated financial market supervisory authority which will assume the current duties of the Federal Banking Commission (SFBC) and the Federal Office of Private Insurance (FOPI). "Merging" the SFBC and FOPI into a single federal organisation, naturally together with existing specialisations, is to be encouraged because it offers the opportunity to exploit synergies and to ensure a more efficient flow of information; the integration of banking and insurance supervision is also in line with an international trend.

Secondly, the commission of experts is to draw up proposals to extend prudential supervision; it will check whether and to what extent little regulated or non-regulated categories of financial service providers can be subject to sufficient regulation and supervision (currency dealers, introducing brokers, independent asset managers).

Thirdly the commission will focus on drawing up legal provisions for the further differentiation and simplification of financial market regulation. A move away from the "one size fits all" principle in favour of sufficient differentiation or a functional regulatory approach ("same business, same risks, same rules") which is suitable for the heterogeneous Swiss banking sector, would be welcomed.

The *fourth* strategic thrust of the Zimmerli group is likely to be the necessity for additional legal provisions regarding the regulation and supervision of bancassurance groups and financial conglomerates. In connection with the creation of effective instruments, it is important to ensure competitive neutrality, i.e. in particular preventing distortions of competition between financial groups and financial conglomerates on the one hand and "pure" banks or insurance groups on the other.

III. E-COMMERCE

1. Introduction

This chapter deals with the supervision of cross-border banking services offered via the Internet when the bank is not represented in the consumer's country of domicile. Having touched on the cooperation between the supervisory authorities within the Basle Committee, we will now define the concepts of "bank", "e-banking" and "Internet banking".

We will then look at the principles of supervision for European Union banks offering products and services in Switzerland and, conversely, for Swiss banks offering their services in EU countries.

2. Cooperation between the supervisory authorities/the work of the Basle Committee

The Basle Committee on banking supervision, under the auspices of the Bank for International Settlements, has set up a working group to examine the issue of e-commerce (Electronic Banking Group). So far, this working group has dealt chiefly with the management of risks associated with electronic banking (see the report entitled "Risk Management Principles for Electronic Banking"[2], published in May 2001). Considering the rapid evolution of technology, the Basle Committee has, however, abandoned the idea of formulating mandatory principles in this area.

The Swiss Federal Banking Commission (SFBC) is represented in the working group of the Basle Committee on electronic banking services. In this context, in particular, the SFBC is in favour of a liberal solution which does not hamper the future development of financial services via the Internet. According to the SFBC, this solution should be based on the recognised principle of supervision in the home country. Proceedings following any infringements would then involve collaboration between the different supervisory authorities and criminal proceedings authorities. The SFBC's position is viewed with some scepticism. **This is explained further by the fact that the foreign supervisory authorities are increasingly being expressly asked to handle consumer protection issues and these may differ radically from the tasks of an authority primarily involved in prudential supervision.**[3]

Thus, the provision of cross-border banking services via the Internet is not covered in international treaties or, at the very least, by a prudential framework that is obligatory in nature and widely recognised by the international community.

3. *Definitions*

"Bank"

A "bank" cannot, in principle, begin operating until it has obtained the approval of the relevant supervisory authority. However, the banking activities subject to approval vary from country to country. In Switzerland, one activity in particular requires a banking licence, namely accepting deposits from the public on a professional basis or soliciting these publicly[4]. In comparison, German law makes provision for no less than twelve different activities requiring approval[5].

This amount of disparity causes complications for providers of cross-border online banking services, since they have to find out about the legislation of different countries and, if necessary, the practices of supervisory authorities. In this respect, it is worth investigating whether any banking services can be provided via the Internet without the need for a physical presence in the consumer's country of domicile and, if necessary, which supervisory authority is responsible for supervising banks who offer cross-border services.

"E-banking"/"Internet banking"

There are numerous definitions of "e-banking" or "online banking". We will use the definition of the Swiss Federal Banking Commission (SFBC). According to the SFBC, "The term "electronic banking" (also called "e-banking" and "online banking") denotes the provision of banking services via electronic channels such as the Internet (Internet banking) or mobile telephones (mobile banking, m-banking). Other phenomena that have already been around for some time, such as Bancomat or Telebanking ("PC banking", direct connection to the bank via telephone, formerly via Videotex), may be considered as forms of electronic banking. In the near future, other channels, e.g. television (TV banking), will be made available for distribution of financial services"[6]. We are limiting our analysis here to Internet banking, i.e. banking services provided via the Internet.

Advertising

If a bank does not have a permanent presence in a third country, it can solicit clients via distance marketing for commercial purposes (advertising and canvassing). It is therefore important to determine to what extent the presentation of banking services via the Internet may constitute "advertising" in the surfers' country of domicile where it is accessible and, if necessary, whether a banking licence is required from the relevant supervisory authority in order to advertise. Again, there are no recognised international standards covering these issues.

4. Principles of supervision for EU banks offering services in Switzerland

Principal aspects of the regulations in Switzerland/practices of the SFBC

As we said in point II.2, a foreign bank wishing to exercise its activities in Switzerland must fulfil the requirements of the Ordinance on Foreign Banks in Switzerland (OFB). Under the terms of Article 2 of the Ordinance, the foreign bank must require approval from the SFBC if it employs persons in Switzerland who, on a permanent and commercial basis, in or from within Switzerland,

a. enter into transactions, maintain customer accounts or legally bind the bank (branch);
b. are active in a manner other than mentioned under lit. a, namely if they forward clients orders to the foreign bank or if they represent the foreign bank for marketing or other purposes (representative office).

The activities that are not expressly mentioned in the OFB may, in principle, be considered as cross-border activities. Since these activities are not covered by any specific regulations, the SFBC accepts that foreign banks do not need to obtain a licence from it in order to exercise their activities in Switzerland via the Internet[7].

The SFBC Annual Report 1999 explains the approach of the supervisory authority as follows: "(...) Swiss law takes an extremely liberal stance to the matter. In fact, only providers who offer their financial services in or from Switzerland require a licence. Foreign providers who can only be reached in Switzerland via the Internet and who do not have a physical presence in the country (e.g. US Internet brokers) do not require any licence in Switzerland"[8].

On its web site, the SFBC confirms in these terms the position expressed in its Annual Report: "Banks and securities dealers based outside Switzerland are allowed to offer their products and services to Swiss clients via the Internet providing they have no physical presence in Switzerland (branch offices, agencies) and do not employ anyone locally (as representatives). However, they may designate a paying agent in Switzerland without prior approval"[9].

Moreover, the SFBC does not make any distinction between basic information, advertising and an offer to conclude transactions. Hence, "Advertising by foreign-based banks on the Internet or in the Swiss media is deemed permissible by the SFBC even when such advertising is deliberately targeted at Swiss clients and there is access to this advertising in Switzerland"[10].

However, if the foreign bank falsely leads people to believe in its advertisement that it is based in Switzerland - using for example an address in this country - the SFBC can inform the foreign supervisory authority on the basis of Article 2, para. 3 of the Ordinance on Foreign Banks in Switzerland. If this authority does not intervene, however, the SFBC has only limited means of coercion.

5. Principles of supervision for Swiss banks offering services abroad, in particular in the European Union

Principal aspects of the regulations in Switzerland / practices of the SFBC

There are no specific regulations in Switzerland governing the supervision of financial services offered electronically. The regulations in force for "ordinary" banking services apply equally to online products and services.

A bank subject to supervision in Switzerland may offer products and services to clients abroad via the Internet. It does not need to obtain a **specific** licence from the Federal Banking Commission (SFBC)[11]. In fact, there is no provision restricting or banning the offering of such services from Switzerland.

Moreover, the exercising of such an activity does not have to be declared. The SFBC considers that the corresponding bank is exercising its commercial activity in Switzerland. Thus, Article 3, para. 7 of the Federal Banking Act, under the terms of which banks organised according to Swiss law that envisage being active abroad by means of a subsidiary, branch, agency or representation must first inform the Swiss Federal Banking Commission of their intention, does not apply in this particular case.

The SFBC is currently working on new regulations to allow the opening of online accounts. These regulations should come into force sometime during 2003. By way of a temporary regulation, the SFBC issued in March 2001 a set of minimum standards governing the opening of accounts by correspondence and the supervision of accounts for banks and securities dealers operating exclusively on the Internet[12].

Principal aspects of the regulations in the European Union and in certain member states

European directives/GATS

Under the terms of Article 24, para. 3 of the *Directive relating to the taking up and pursuit of the business of credit institutions*[13], "the Community may, through agreements concluded in accordance with the Treaty with one or more third countries, agree to apply provisions which, on the basis of the principle of reciprocity, accord to branches of a credit institution having its head office outside the Community identical treatment throughout the territory of the Community". So far, however, the Community has not concluded a corresponding agreement with Switzerland. What is more, this provision does not relate to online banking services, which are carried on according to the freedom to provide services.

The *Directive on electronic commerce*[14] deals in particular with the conditions of access to the activity of information society services. In this respect, it stipulates the principle of supervision by the home country. However, the directive does not apply to service providers based in a third country (cf. "Whereas" 58 of the directive). Swiss banks wishing to offer their products and services online in the European Union cannot therefore claim any entitlement under this directive.

The *Common Position adopted by the Council on 19 December 2001 with a view to adopting the directive concerning the distance marketing of consumer financial services*[15] is aimed at harmonising, at the European level, the area of pre-contractual information and the right of withdrawal following conclusion of the contract. This directive, which is likely to be adopted during the course of 2002, is of considerable importance – albeit indirect – for service providers based outside the European Union. In fact, under the terms of Article 12, para. 1 of the Common Position, "Consumers may not waive the rights conferred on them by this Directive". Paragraph 2 of this same provision stipulates in addition that "Member States shall take the measures needed to ensure that the consumer does not lose the protection granted by this Directive by virtue of the choice of the law of a non-member country as the law applicable to the contract, if this contract has a close link with the territory of one or more Member States". There is good reason to assume that the directive will be based on the principle of minimum harmonisation. Consequently, the national legislation of member states which goes beyond the directive might continue to apply in certain circumstances. As in the past, service providers of third countries will have to take into account the national legislation of the different member states.

Moreover, according to the *Communication* on e-commerce and financial services of 7 February 2001[16], "Each Member State may define its policy with respect to those third country service providers, provided that policy conforms with international trade agreements. The Union may well need to develop a co-ordinated approach to third country providers"[17]. Up until now, this has not been the case. A bank subject to supervision in Switzerland which is not established in an EU member state must therefore satisfy the regulations and requirements of the supervisory authority of the different EU member states in which it wishes to offer products and services via the Internet.

Finally, the *General Agreement on Trade in Services* issued by the WTO, of which Switzerland is a member, would not necessarily solve this situation by invoking the "treatment of the most favoured nation" with regard to the European Union. In fact, there are exceptions to this agreement. Thus, under the terms of Article V of this Agreement (economic integration), the members of the WTO are authorised to participate in an agreement liberalising trade in services provided, in particular, that this agreement covers a substantial number of sectors and provides for the absence or elimination of discrimination between the states concerned.

Observation: no or limited access to the internal market

According to Article 2, para. 3 of the Federal Banking Act "The Federal Council is empowered, on the basis of reciprocal recognition of equivalent rules over banking activities and equivalent measures in the field of banking supervision, to enter into treaties with states which grant the possibility for banks from the contracting states to open a branch, agency or representation without the permission of the Banking Commission". It should be noted that the Federal Council has not made use of this competence.

In the absence of international accords governing this issue, Swiss banks wishing to offer their products and services online from Switzerland must satisfy the national legislation of the different states as well as the practice of the supervisory authorities of these states.

IV. CONCLUSION

In this report we have presented the basic principles of Swiss banking regulation and supervision. Naturally, this summary makes no claim to be complete. The objective was simply to present the basic principles relevant to e-commerce in a condensed form.

At this point, it must be emphasised once again that both the system of dual control with auditing firms as statutory bank auditors and the high level of self-regulation in Switzerland compared with other countries have proven extremely effective.

Secondly, this discussion has illustrated that Switzerland's financial market regulation and supervision is currently undergoing a transformation, and various reforms are in progress. The ongoing work of the Zimmerli commission of experts is just one example.

Specifically in the area of e-commerce, the following conclusions may be drawn: The provision of cross-border financial services via the Internet is not covered in international treaties or, at the very least, by a prudential framework that is obligatory in nature and widely recognised by the international community. Consequently, many supervisory authorities do not permit banks to access their own markets unless they first obtain a licence or place them under a reporting obligation, in conformity with their national legislation. The differences between the legal frameworks governing national supervisory authorities are a genuine problem for providers of financial products and services. Even if they have the appropriate licence from a supervisory authority in their home country, there is a considerable risk that they will be violating the principles of supervision in force in certain countries. This is particularly likely if their service offering can be accessed online, in unlimited form, around the world.

NOTES

[1] This report contains only the personal opinions of the authors and does not in any way engage the standpoint of the Swiss Bankers' Association.

[2] "Risk Management Principles for Electronic Banking", Basle Committee on banking supervision, Bank for International Settlements, May 2001, http://www.bri.org/publ/bcbs82.htm. See also the report of the International Organization of Securities Commissions (IOSCO): "Report on Securities Activity on the Internet II", June 2001, http://www.iosco.org/download/pdf/2001-securities_activity_internet.pdf.

[3] SFBC Annual Report 2001, Ch. 3.3, p. 242 ff.

[4] See Article 2a of the Banking Ordinance.

[5] See Article 1 of the German Banking Law.

[6] "Frequently asked questions / E-finance", Swiss Federal Banking Commission (SFBC), http://www.ebk.admin.ch/e/faq/faq4.htm

[7] Michael Kunz, Regulation of Electronic Banking in Switzerland, Schulthess Juristische Medien AG Zurich (2001), p. 50 ff.

[8] SFBC Annual Report 1999, p. 249.

[9] "Frequently asked questions/ E-finance", Federal Banking Commission (SFBC), cf supra, note 5.

[10] "Frequently asked questions/ E-finance", Federal Banking Commission (SFBC), cf supra, note 5.

[11] Michael Kunz, Virtuelle Banken und Effektenhändler, *Der Schweizer Treuhänder 1-2/01*, p. 57 ff. 16

[12] SFBC minimum standards applicable to banks and securities dealers operating exclusively on the Internet for the opening of accounts by correspondence and the supervision of accounts, March 2001.

[13] Directive 2000/12/EC of 20 March 2000 relating to the taking up and pursuit of the business of credit institutions, JOCE 26.05.2000, L.126.

[14] Directive 2000/31/EC on certain legal aspects of information society services, in particular electronic commerce, in the Internal Market (Directive on electronic commerce), *JOCE* 17.07.2000, L.178/1.

[15] Common Position (EC) No 16/2002 adopted by the Council on 19 December 2001 with a view to adopting Directive 2002/.../EC of the European Parliament and of the Council of ... concerning the distance marketing of consumer financial services and amending Council Directives 90/619/EEC, 97/7/EC and 98/27/EC, *JOCE* 5.3.2002, C 58 E/32.

[16] Communication COM (2001) 66 final from the Commission to the Council and the European Parliament on "e-commerce and financial services" of 7 February 2001, p. 7. The Communication is available at http://www.europa.eu.int/comm/internal_market/en/finances/general/ecom_en.pdf

[17] Communication from the Commission to the Council and the European Parliament on "e-commerce and financial services", p. 6.

UNITED KINGDOM

Financial Services in the Era of the Euro and E-Commerce:

Does home country control work?

Rapporteurs
*William Blair QC and Richard Brent**

Note: the questions largely relate to regulatory practice. The comments set out below represent our best understanding, and not necessarily our personal views.

AUTHORISATION

1. *What procedures exist for the competent authorities in your country to engage in the "prior consultation" envisaged by Article 7 of the Second Banking Directive on the authorisation of a credit institution which is (1) a subsidiary of a credit institution authorised in another Member State; (2) a subsidiary of the parent undertaking of a credit institution authorised in another Member State; or (3) controlled by the same persons as control a credit institution authorised in another Member State? Are those procedures formal or informal in nature?*

The obligation to consult, as envisaged by Article 7 of the Second Banking Directive, now Article 12 of the Consolidation Directive[1], is imposed on the Financial Services Authority, the UK's competent authority, by statute: see section 49(2) Financial Services and Markets Act 2000. It is also imposed where the FSA is considering the cancellation or variation of an existing UK authorisation.

Where there is a proposed acquisition by a credit institution authorised

* Verulam Buildings, Gray's Inn

in another Member State of a credit institution authorised in the UK, the Financial Services Authority is also under a statutory obligation to consult the home state regulator of the acquirer. This is laid down in Regulation 5(2) of The Financial Services and Markets Act 2000 (Consultation with Competent Authorities) Regulations 2001 (SI 2001/2509).]

2. *Have any and, if so, what problems been experienced with the prior consultation process?*

So far as it is known, no problems have been experienced with the prior consultation process.

3. *Are you aware of any cases where the competent authorities have refused authorisation, in particular in accordance with Article 5? If so, in what circumstances has authorisation been refused?*

We are not aware of any cases where authorisation has been refused, in particular, in accordance with Article 5 of the Second Banking Directive (now Article 7 of the Consolidation Directive), on the basis of the suitability of the shareholders and members of the subsidiary seeking authorisation. Such a refusal would now in theory be published in accordance with section 391 Financial Services and Markets Act 2000, although the FSA has a discretion as to the information that it considers appropriate to publish.

4. *Once authorised by its home country, a credit institution may, in accordance with Article 18, carry on any of the activities listed in the Annex either by the establishment of a branch or by way of the provision of services in any other Member State. In this regard:*
   - *(a) By what legislative or other means have the provisions of Article 18 been given effect in your country?*
   - *(b) How effectively has the home country control principle applied?*
   - *(c) Have there been cases in your country where a credit institution is able to provide (on the strength of its home country authorisation) particular services listed in the Annex which credit institutions subject to supervision by your competent authorities are not authorised to provide? If so, what are those services and has this given rise to any problems in practice?*

(a) Article 18 of the Second Banking Directive (now Article 18 of the Consolidation Directive) is implemented in the UK by means of section 31(1)(b) and Schedule 3 to the Financial Services and Markets Act 2000, which came into force on 1 December 2001. Part II of Schedule 3 sets out the conditions that have to be satisfied in the case of both the establishment of a branch and the provision of services. With regard to the establishment of a branch, the Financial Services Authority as the UK regulator must have received a notice from the firm's "home state" regulator that it has given consent to establish a branch in the UK (see Article 20(3) of the Consolidation Directive). The consent notice must comply with the requirements of that Directive (see Article 20(2)), and the FSA is then under an obligation to prepare for the firm's supervision and notify it of any UK rules with which the firm is obliged to comply. Similar requirements apply in relation to the provision of services by way of implementation of Article 21 of the Consolidation Directive. Further provision is made for the implementation of the Article 18 rights in Chapter 5 of the Authorisation Manual of the FSA Handbook. The Handbook comprises the FSA Rules, which the FSA is authorised to make under the Financial Services and Markets Act 2000.

(b) It is considered that the "home country control" principle has been very effective. It is thought to have benefited banks in that as a result they only have to comply with one set of prudential regulatory requirements. At the same time, it has brought benefits to the banking markets of "host" countries by making them more competitive.

In the past, there have been problems relating to the proper demarcation between "home" and "host" state regulatory control. However, the greatest concern in the UK arose prior to the introduction of "passport" rights under the Second Banking Directive. This was as a result of the collapse of BCCI in July 1991, which was *not* authorised in the UK by reason of the bank's exercise of its "passport" rights. Rather, it was authorised as a licensed deposit-taker under the Banking Act 1979 by the Bank of England in reliance (in accordance with section 3(5) of that Act) on the Luxembourg authorities' assurances as to the management of the business, and the prudence with which it was conducted. This authorisation continued under the Banking Act 1987 by reason of that Act's transitional provisions. As is well known, the collapse of BCCI gave rise to the concern that its supervision "fell" between two competent authorities. This was because it was registered in one jurisdiction, but effectively carried on business in another. This led to amendments to the First Banking Directive by means of European and Parliament Directive 95/26/EC. This provided, inter alia (see Article 3(2)), for the insertion of a new Article 2a requiring that Member States oblige credit institutions to have their head offices in the same Member States in which they have their registered office, and where a credit institution's registered office is outside the jurisdiction, that its head office is in the Member State where it actually carries on its business. This provision may now be found in Article 6(2) of the Consolidation Directive. It also provided, by the insertion of a sub-paragraph to Article 3(2) of the First Banking Directive, for competent authorities to refuse authorisation where the complex structures of the institution in question prevent the effective exercise of supervisory functions (Article 2 of 95/26/EC). See now Article 7 of the Consolidation Directive.

(c) In the UK, the authorisation of financial institutions by the competent authorities has historically been on a functional, rather than on an institutional, basis. Thus, prior to the coming into force of the Financial Services and Markets Act 2000, the business of "deposit-taking" required authorisation under the Banking Act 1987, and the conduct of "investment business" required authorisation under the Financial Services Act 1986. "Investment business" includes many of the activities specified in the Annex to the Second Banking Directive. The Financial Services and Markets Act 2000 has now abolished the system of "dual authorisation". Instead, it now requires all financial institutions (including credit institutions) to obtain a permission under Part IV of the Act to carry on regulated activities (which include the activities of credit institutions). However, the institution is only authorised to carry on those regulated activities that are in fact specified in the permission.

By contrast, the single market directives of which the Second Banking Directive is one, operate on an institutional basis. Thus where an institution falls within the definition of a "credit institution", in theory it may be permitted by the home state to carry out all of the activities listed in the Annex. The consequence of this is that where a credit institution in another Member State is authorised on such an institutional basis, it may be the case that it will be authorised to carry on more activities than, for example, a bank in the UK which is only authorised to carry on a deposit-taking business.

In practice, however, UK institutions will be authorised to carry on a number of activities. Thus, the theoretical "a-symmetry" between UK functionally-authorised institutions and those authorised on an institutional basis is unlikely to arise in practice to any great extent.

5. *In relation to activities not listed in the Annex, with what provisions of your national laws or regulations must a credit institution authorised by another Member State comply?*

If the activity falls within the definition of a "regulated activity" as set out in the Financial Services and Markets Act (Regulated Activities) Order 2001, one of two situations will obtain.

Where the particular credit institution is authorised by another Member State, and the provisions of the law of the home state afford equivalent protection to that under UK law or satisfy conditions laid down by a Community instrument for the co-ordination or approximation of laws relating to that activity, then, under Schedule 4 to the Financial Services and Markets Act 2000, it will have permission under UK law to carry out that regulated activity. By "equivalent protection" is meant that consumers are afforded protection that is equivalent to that afforded by the or under the Financial Services and Markets Act 2000 in relation to the particular activity. This is provided that written notice of intention to carry out such an activity in the UK is given to the FSA and is accompanied by the information specified by the FSA (including confirmation of authorisation in the home state). The activity must be carried out either through a UK branch or by providing services in the UK. The permission will be treated on the same terms as those which apply to that firm's home state authorisation. That is to say, it will reflect any limitations or requirements that are included in that authorisation.

Where such a Schedule 4 permission does not exist, and the activity is a "regulated activity", the firm will require what is termed a "top-up permission" under Part IV of the Financial Services and Markets Act 2000 as if it were a UK entity. In this case, it will be subject to the same terms and conditions, and same level of supervision, by the UK's competent authority as if it were a UK registered entity.

6. *Are there cases where such national laws or regulations may not in fact be compatible with the general provisions of Community law? If so, what are they?*

It is not generally considered that such regulation infringes general provisions of Community law such as those relating to the free provision of services. Nor do we know of any cases where such UK regulation has been challenged on the basis that they are contrary to the "free movement" principles of the EC Treaty. Given that the "equivalent protection" requirement relates to the protection of consumers, and Community law has historically recognised that "the banking sector is a particularly sensitive sector from the point of view of consumer protection"[2], prima facie such restrictions are justified, to use the language of the European Court of Justice, by "imperative reasons relating to the public interest". However, to the extent that in the future consumer protection measures become increasingly harmonised within the Community, and UK domestic measures exceed those protections, in theory they could be challengeable on the basis that they impose unnecessary or disproportionate restrictions.

THE GENERAL GOOD

7. *Under Article 21, host Member States retain certain powers over credit institutions authorised in another Member State. In this regard:*

(a) *What are the legal rules adopted in your country in the interest of the general good (see Article 21(5))?*

(b) Have the competent authorities exercised their powers under Article 21(5) and, if so, in what circumstances?
(c) What are the appeal procedures that exist (see Article 21(6))?
(d) Have there been cases where a credit institution invoked its right of appeal and, if so, how has the court approached the appeal?

(a) The measures adopted under what is now Article 22(5) of the Consolidation Directive in the "general good", and of which the "incoming" credit institution must be informed in accordance with Schedule 3 to the Financial Services and Markets Act 2000, fall into two categories. The first are those measures, particularly in relation to the protection of consumers, that form part of the general law. Thus such institutions will have to observe, for example, the provisions of the Consumer Credit Act 1974, which implements, but is also more stringent than, the Consumer Credit Directive[3]. The second consists of a sub-set of the rules set out in the FSA Handbook e.g. conduct of business rules, which authorised UK institutions have to observe as a condition of their authorisation. The rules with which such institutions have to comply are helpfully summarised in Annex 3 to Chapter 5 of the Authorisation Module of the FSA Handbook. The extent to which they apply principally depends on the extent to which the incoming firm operates by way of a branch or simply through the provision of services. In the latter case, many parts of the Handbook only apply if the firm carries on regulated activities *in the United Kingdom*. However, determining where the activity is conducted in the age of the internet and telephone banking may itself be problematic.

(b) No publicly available information exists as to whether the Financial Services Authority as the competent authority of a host state has exercised its powers under what is now Article 22(5) of the Consolidation Directive to prevent or punish irregularities that are committed by credit institutions authorised in other Member States on the basis that they are contrary to the UK's rules adopted in the "general good".

(c) The procedures set out in Article 22 of the Consolidation Directive are implemented in the UK by Part XIII of the Financial Services and Markets Act 2000. So far as "appeals" are concerned, they are first made (see section 197(8) of that Act) to the Financial Services and Markets Tribunal (which approaches the relevant decision de novo). It is fully independent of the FSA and is run by the Lord Chancellor's Department. Appeals lie from the Tribunal to the Court of Appeal on a point of law only (see section 137(1)).

(d) No such cases are known.

THE ESTABLISHMENT OF BRANCHES

8. *What, if any, difficulties been experienced with regard to the establishment of branches by a credit institution, where your country is (a) the home Member State and (b) the host Member State of the institution concerned (see Articles 19 and 21)?*

(a) We are not aware of any difficulties experienced with regard to the establishment by a UK authorised entity of branches in another Member State. However, certain formalities have to be complied with as a matter of UK law. They are set out at Part III of Schedule 3 to the Financial Services and Markets Act 2000. It is an offence for a UK firm to establish a branch in another Member State where it has failed to comply with the requirements of paragraph 19 of that Schedule (see paragraph 21).

(b) We are also unaware of any difficulties experienced by credit institutions authorised in other Member States that are seeking to establish branches in the UK. As at 30 November 2001, there were 95 European authorised institutions with UK branches authorised to take deposits in the UK.

THE PROVISION OF CROSS-BORDER SERVICES

9. *What, if any, difficulties been experienced with regard to the provision of cross-border services by a credit institution, where your country is (a) the home Member State and (b) the host Member State of the institution concerned (see Articles 20 and 21)?*

(a) We are not aware of any difficulties experienced with regard to the provision by a UK authorised entity of services to another Member State. However, as in the case of establishing branches in other Member States, certain formalities have to be complied with as a matter of UK law. They are also set out at Part III of Schedule 3 to the Financial Services and Markets Act 2000 (see paragraph 20). It is likewise an offence for a UK firm to provide cross-border services where it has failed to comply with the requirements of that Schedule (see paragraph 21).

(b) We are also unaware of any difficulties experienced by credit institutions authorised in other Member States providing cross-border services into the UK. As at 30 November 2001, there were 181 European authorised institutions entitled to accept deposits in the UK on a cross-border basis.

THE COMPETENT AUTHORITIES

10. *What are the national authorities empowered in your country to supervise credit institutions and which are, therefore, the "competent authorities" for the purposes of the Second Banking Directive?*

The Financial Services Authority is the UK's sole competent authority.

11. *Does the national central bank in your country have an involvement in prudential supervision and, if so, what is its role?*

The supervisory function exercised by the Bank of England over credit institutions was transferred to the Financial Services Authority by section 21(a) of the Bank of England Act 1998. The Bank of England remains responsible for the operation of monetary policy and for ensuring overall financial stability. Strong links between the Bank of England and the Financial Services Authority have been maintained as set out in a Memorandum of Understanding between the Treasury, the Bank of England and the Financial Services Authority. For example, the Chairman of the Financial Services Authority sits on the Court of the Bank of England, and the Deputy Governor of the Bank is a member of the Financial Services Authority Board. Provision is also made for the exchange of information between the Bank and the Financial Services Authority.

12. *What is the view in your country about the need for an integrated supervisory authority for the financial services sector as a whole rather than separate authorities for different parts of it, and why?*

In May 1997 the UK government decided in principle to create a unitary regulatory structure for the supervision of the financial services sector. This was a reaction to the increasing blurring of different types of financial institutions, and the need to regulate them in a consistent way. It was also perceived as a way of ensuring more effective and efficient regulation. In particular, it was considered that a single regulator would result in economies of scale and scope, clear and consistent objectives and clear lines of accountability. In the UK, nine regulatory bodies have now been subsumed by the single Financial Services Authority.

13. *What is the view in your country about the need for the European Central Bank to play a role in prudential supervision, and why?*

According to a paper published by an official of the FSA, the view in the UK (insofar as there is a collective view) is that the case for European

Central Bank supervision is not made out. This is said to be for two principal reasons. First, it is because Europe lacks the relevant structures for such supervision: the Treaty and the statutes that established the ECB do not provide for it to play such a role. But secondly, and perhaps more importantly, it can be argued that the development of financial conglomerates and increasing commercial integration point to the creation of single national regulators, such as the Financial Services Authority, that are better able to cope with their peers, rather than to the creation of a pan-EU supervisor of banks alone. In other words, a separate European banking supervisor would not properly reflect, and so not as effectively address, developments in the market that it would be regulating. At the same time the paper states that it is not considered that the criticisms made of national regulators, namely that they may have exclusively domestic mandates and suffer from a lack of independence from the political process, are justified. For example, the Financial Services Authority as a banking regulator is obliged under the Consolidation Directive to collaborate closely with the authorities of other Member States. Likewise, section 354 of the Financial Services and Markets Act 2000 requires the Financial Services Authority to share information with other authorities within the EEA (as well as without), where this is legally permissible. The FSA is also set up, and regarded as, an institution independent of government.

14. *To what extent, if at all, have those views been influenced by the introduction of the Euro and the growth of E-commerce, and why?*

These views on the role of the European Central Bank in the prudential supervision of banks are unlikely to be affected by the introduction of the euro and e-commerce. As to the euro, although London is a major trading centre, it remains outside the euro-zone. As to e-commerce, its growth is regarded as being a neutral factor with regard to the role of the ECB.

However, the growth of e-commerce, as is well-known, has affected the distinction drawn in the Consolidation Directive between "home" and "host" state control. Under the Consolidation Directive, where banks authorised in one Member State provide services or operate a branch in another, they must comply with the conduct of business rules of the host state. However, under the Electronic Commerce Directive[4], which applies to all services, including financial services, provided by the internet, the service provider, subject to certain derogations, has only to comply with the requirements of the Member State from where the service is provided (the "country of origin"). In other words, financial services may be provided across the EU from a single web-site that complies only with the country of origin rules.

The result is that, in theory at least, a customer in any given Member

State may be faced with one set of information and conditions (as laid down by domestic law) when purchasing from a financial entity established in that State, and another when purchasing over the internet. This situation therefore provides a further justification for those who seek greater levels of harmonisation in the provision of financial services in the EU, and in particular seek the harmonisation of "conduct of business" rules as well centralised prudential supervision.

Nonetheless, the UK's Financial Services Authority remains publicly committed to the existing concept of regulatory harmonisation i.e. to the mutual recognition of national regulatory systems built around harmonised core standards. It is against the higher degree of detailed standardisation that some Member States consider necessary. As to the UK government, in a paper published in 2000, it also remained committed to the principle of "home state" regulation. But it also importantly suggested that there should be a move towards "home state (or country of origin) regulation of conduct of business and consumer protection, combined with mutual recognition across the EU".

The FSA in its latest Annual Report has also indicated that the new European regulatory structure introduced for the securities market following the recommendations of the Lamfalussy Wise Men could be a useful model for banking regulation in Europe. By analogy, this would involve the creation of a "Committee of European Banking Supervisors" (on which representatives of national competent authorities would sit) to advise the Commission on banking policy issues, and a "European Banking Committee" (comprised of representatives of the Member States) to vote on draft technical implementing measures submitted by the Commission under implementing powers granted to the Commission by the Council under a framework regulation.

It is not inconceivable that the ECB might have a greater formal role in the prudential regulation of banks by participating in such structures. But the adoption of such structures by no means entails the ECB participating in them, and the FSA does not refer to the ECB being given any such role in its Annual Report.

It should also be noted that at the Brussels ECOFIN meeting of 7 May 2002 the Council invited the Economic and Financial Committee to report on possible structures for financial regulation and supervision, initially by July 2002, and finally by the end of September 2002. The arrangements on which it is to report have to be consistent with a number of principles, including "subsidiarity, since supervisory tasks are best performed as close as possible to supervised entities and since financial crises may have implications for public finances". This suggests that ECOFIN is not considering a transfer of prudential regulatory authority to the European Central Bank.

15. *What relationship do the competent authorities in your country have with the European Central Bank?*

The Financial Services Authority participates fully in the valuable work undertaken jointly by EU central banks and supervisors on financial stability matters through the Banking Supervision Committee under the auspices of the European Central Bank. The Governor of the Bank of England participates in the General Council of the ECB, but does not have a seat on the Governing Council (membership is restricted to euro-zone countries).

16. *How, if at all, has human rights legislation affected the competent authorities in your country?*

The European Convention on Human Rights was incorporated in the UK's domestic law by the Human Rights Act 1998 which came into effect in 2000. It was used by financial institutions to require safeguards in the various enforcement procedures intended to place limitations on regulatory discretion in decision making. These were imposed by amendments in the Financial Services and Markets Act 2000 as it was going through parliament.

An example is the role that human rights considerations played in the establishment of the Financial Services and Markets Tribunal. This hears cases referred to it by those wishing to contest the decisions of the Financial Services Authority. It is fully independent of the FSA (in compliance with the requirements imposed by Article 6 of the Convention), whereas its predecessor, the Financial Services Tribunal, established under the Financial Services Act 1986, was run by the Treasury, which also at the time had certain regulatory responsibilities. Further, in order to comply with Article 6 of the Convention, the new Tribunal has full jurisdiction to determine matters of fact (in draft, the Bill appeared to limit its jurisdiction over factual matters); and it will generally hold its hearings in public. In relation to market abuse proceedings, which some regard as criminal rather than civil, as a result of industry pressure the government made provision for free legal assistance in appropriate cases so as to comply with the additional requirements of Articles 6(2) and 6(3) of the Convention.

17. *Has the introduction of the Euro highlighted any inadequacies in your country in the supervision of credit institutions and the need for further harmonisation at the EU level?*

The development of a single capital market is of fundamental significance. The implications are only beginning to be worked out.

NOTES

[1] Directive 2000/12/EC of 20 March 2000.

[2] Case C-222/95 *Parodi v Banque H Albert de Barry et Cie* [1997] ECR I-3899, paragraph 22.

[3] Directive 87/102/EEC as amended.

[4] Directive 2000/31/EC of 8 June 2000.

QUESTIONNAIRE FOR TOPIC III

Cross Border Mergers in Company Law and Competition Law: Removing the Final Barriers

General Rapporteurs
Professor Guido Alpa and Professor Jan Wouters***

A. INTRODUCTION

Take overs are subject to rapidly developing regulatory regimes where European and national law are in complex interaction. Competition law and company law are important factors but so are, for instance, tax law, accounting law, and the regulation and organisation of the securities market and settlement system. Different national regimes create potential restrictions on the exercise of the fundamental freedoms of EC law, in particular the right of establishment and the right to provide services. Harmonisation of national rules is one way of reducing these restrictions but harmonisation cannot completely eliminate the restrictions posed by the remaining national jurisdictions and enforcement regimes. Since the present topic was adopted at the FIDE conference in Helsinki in 2000, major new proposals have been made in the field, including the First Report of the High Level Group of Company Law Experts (10 January 2002) and the Green Paper on the Review of the Merger Regulation (11 December 2001).

Different models are pursued in company law and competition law, and this may increase the tension at the enforcement level. It may cause problems both for regulators and for private parties.

In financial market regulation and company law, the jurisdiction remains in the member states, and there are proposals for further harmonisation of the relevant laws. Coordination between different national financial market authorities within one jurisdiction may be a considerable challenge in itself; the European dimension adds to this complexity. The discussion about establishing European regulatory bodies in the financial market field (as reflected for investment services in the Lamfalussy Report

* Rome
** Leuven

and for banking the German-British proposals) has not addressed the institutional regulatory aspect of take overs in particular. It may be possible that future European harmonisation of take over laws could take the form of a regulation (instead of a directive) as a consequence of the general development of European financial market regulation.

In competition law, mergers either fall under the European Commission's jurisdiction or that of the member states. Mergers with a Community dimension are filed with the European Commission under the EU Merger Regulation. Under the one-stop-shop principle national authorities cannot apply their own competition laws to the transactions (except in very limited circumstances). The criteria for what constitutes a Community dimension and the threshold test for clearance are presently under discussion. There are also recent initiatives for the coordination and harmonisation of national merger procedures.

In this Questionnaire the aim is to explore the remaining barriers to take overs in national jurisdictions and in the application of Community law. Focus is on the burden constituted by different national rules and enforcement regimes. No attempt is made to cover all issues but the aim is to collect relevant information that can serve as a background for a general discussion and assessment of the problems. The discussion should address not only procedural and substantive legal issues but the question of institutional reform and allocation of functions between member states and Community institutions.

B. THE COMPETITION REGIME

1. What is the view from your country[1] on the functioning of the threshold levels in Article 1(2) as well as the 2/3 rule in the Merger Regulation, and the proposal in the Commission's Green Paper for amendment of Article 1(3) to deal with the problems of multiple filings?
2. In light of the experiences made in your country, do member states have sufficient flexibility to call for mergers to be referred back under Article 9 of the Merger Regulation? In light of the proposal in the Commission's Green Paper, what is your view on the circumstances in which this power should be exercised?
3. Is the system of consultation between the European Commission and the national competition authorities (NCAs) working adequately? Does there need to be a better formalised system for consultation between NCAs directly involved either in the case of multiple filings outside the merger control regulation or in cases where more than one member state exercises the Article 9 request?

4. How does the test under the law of your country compare to that under the Merger Regulation? Should all member states adopt the same test as under the Merger Regulation, and should this EU test be the (US) 'significant lessening of competition' test rather than the present EU 'dominance' test?
5. Are the procedural and judicial safeguards adequate to protect parties from abuse of power by the competition authorities? How does the laws of your country compare to EC law in this respect?
6. Below are a number of questions relating to domestic law which may assist in a comparative analysis.
   a. Please provide an overview of the structure of and main features of the relevant domestic legislation and the institutional framework (who enforces it)? It may be helpful with some information about the role of private rights of action.
   b. What kinds of transactions are caught? Are joint ventures caught? What are the jurisdictional thresholds? Is it difficult to identify with sufficient certainty whether a filing is in fact required under national law? Are foreign-to-foreign mergers caught?
   c. Is the filing mandatory or voluntary? Who is responsible for filing? What is involved in the preparation of a filing? What are the deadlines for filing? What are the waiting periods and does implementation of the transaction have to be suspended?
   d. What are the issues and possible sanctions involved in closing before clearance? What is the timetable for clearance and can it be speeded up?
   e. Are there any special rules applicable to public takeover bids?
   f. What is the substantive test for clearance?
   g. To what extent are non-competition issues relevant to the review process?
   h. Is it possible to remedy competition issues?
   i. What are the typical steps during the investigation? What rights do complainants have? What publicity is given to the process? What are the opportunities for judicial review?
   j. What are the enforcement powers? How does administrative and civil sanctions compare with the EC regime? And what are the criminal sanctions, and are they used?
   k. Do the authorities cooperate with other antitrust authorities?
   l. Are there also rules on foreign investment, special sectors or other relevant approvals?
   m. Are there current proposals to change the legislation?

C. COMPANY LAW AND FINANCIAL MARKET REGULATORY REGIME

7. What will you identify as the main obstacles to take overs where a company[2] from your jurisdiction is either bidder or target and the other company is from another EU jurisdiction[3]?
8. Do hostile take overs by companies from other EU jurisdictions in fact take place in your country?
9. To what extents are there any sectors (utilities, financial institutions) that in practice are further protected from hostile take overs, or foreign[4] take overs in particular? Are there any policy statements or particular legal mechanisms that give effect to this protection, or is it a matter of informal mechanisms?[5]
10. What are the company law techniques of completing a take over or merger that are used in practice where one of the companies is from another EU jurisdiction? Please give particular attention to how this would differ from the usual completion of a take over or merger where both companies are from your jurisdiction. It would be useful if you could add a comment about the consequences on the techniques used of the taxation regime and of any differential tax treatment of take overs or mergers where one party is from another EU jurisdiction.
11. A duty on listed companies to disclose capital and control structures is proposed in *Issues Relating to Takeover Bids*, the First Report of the High Level Group of Company Law Experts (see p 25). Would this require amendments in the legislation in your country? How would these amendments in case be implemented (in primary company law, securities law, stock exchange regulations etc.)?
12. A so called break through rule after take over bids is another of the proposals in *Issues Relating to Takeover Bids*, the First Report of the High Level Group of Company Law Experts (see p 29). Would this require amendments in the legislation in your country? How would these amendments in case be implemented (in primary company law, securities law, stock exchange regulations etc.)?
13. In your view, would these two new rules as proposed have any material impact on the existing barriers to take overs in your country (or in others as seen from your point of view)? It would be helpful if you could demonstrate the impact, or lack of it, by going through one or more recent take over bids that failed in your country (or in some other member state, by a company from your country).
14. Below are a number of questions which may assist in a comparative analysis.
    a. What are the main features of the relevant domestic take over legislation constituting the company law and financial market regime, and who enforces it (independent regulators, regulatory bodies

with appeal to ministry, stock exchange)? What is the extent of intervention by the takeover regulator(s) – to what extent does the regulator have wide or general discretions to block and play a protectionist role (for example in its capacity as approver of the offer terms/documentation)?

b. Are there restrictions on a board taking action to frustrate a bid that has been made? When do the relevant restrictions start to apply – earlier than a formal announcement/filing of a bid? To what extent can shareholders approve the taking of frustrating action in advance of any bid?

c. Are there restrictions on the type of consideration that can be offered in a bid, for example securities only if these are listed in the target country's home state or the EU?

h. Are there effective compulsory acquisition procedures regarding a small non-accepting minority? Can a bidder make its offer conditional on achieving the number of shares required so it can operate a squeeze out?

e. Is there a principle of board neutrality? Can a target board align itself with a particular bidder/agree measures such as exclusivity arrangements to protect a particular deal?

f. Can a target board hand over information to a potential bidder?

g. Are structures permitted which concentrate control rights in the hands of minority shareholders? Are structures permitted which place limitations/restrictions on voting rights, caps for example on voting rights above a certain threshold?

h. Can restrictions be placed on the transferability of shares either by the issuer (in articles of association or by other means) or by arrangements between shareholders? Can a board delay registering transfers of shares?

i. What contractual barriers (including share holder agreements) to take over bids are in use in public companies (*eg* golden parachutes, change of control provisions triggering default of loan agreements, or wining up or change of control of joint ventures)? What are the prospects of review by courts on the basis of contract or company law and by regulators on the basis of securities laws or stock exchange regulations?

j. Are there current proposals to change the legislation relating to take overs?

D. FINAL ISSUES

1. In your view, what is the extent to which the complexity of the regula-

tory arrangements, within national jurisdictions and between the Commission and member states, present an obstacle to take overs?

2. Can you list some instances where different rules in the different regulatory systems have caused practical obstacles in a take over process? (One instance could be different time limits under the EC Merger Regulation and national merger rules on the one hand and under stock exchange rules on the other.)

F. FOR REFERENCE

Issues Relating to Takeover Bids First Report of the High Level Group of Company Law Experts (10 January 2002) http://www.europa.eu.int/comm/internal_market/en/company/company/news/hlg01-2002.pdf

Green Paper on the Review of Council Regulation (EEC) No 4064/89 COM(2001) 745/6 (11 December 2001) http://www.europa.eu.in / comm/competition/mergers/review/

NOTES

[1] The aim is not here to have an authoritative statement but a report which can contribute to the discussion. For EEA (non member) country rapporteurs, the subject of the question is intended to be the EEA regime. For non member (non EEA) countries, there are special issues. Country rapporteurs are welcome to limit their answers in the way they believe to be most helpful or interesting with the purpose of the questionnaire in mind.

[2] Focus is here mainly on listed companies but information about non listed and also non public companies will of interest if this is possible to provide.

[3] Here too the following applies. For EEA (non member) country rapporteurs, the subject of the question is intended to be the EEA regime. For non member (non EEA) countries, there are special issues. Country rapporteurs are welcome to limit their answers in the way they believe to be most helpful or interesting with the purpose of the questionnaire in mind.

[4] "Foreign" here includes both take overs from other member states and from non member states (or non EEA countries).

[5] In the case of banks or insurance companies, the relevant ministry and supervisor would be usually be able to block take overs on prudential grounds and their involvement would be difficult to review. Similar mechanisms would be in place for many utilities where state ownership often adds to the problems. An extensive review is not required, but it would be useful with an assessment of how such mechanisms function. If there have for instance not been any take over by a foreign bank, that is an interesting point.

AUSTRIA

Cross Border Mergers in Company Law and Competition Law: Removing the Final Barriers

The Austrian Perspective

Rapporteur
Ass.-Prof. Dr. Peter Stockenhuber[1]

A. THE COMPETITION REGIME

1. What is the view from your country on the functioning of the threshold levels in Article 1(2) as well as the 2/3 rule in the Merger Regulation, and the proposal in the Commission´s Green Paper for amendement of Article 1(3) to deal with the problems of mulitiple filings?

From the Austrian point of view, the threshold levels of Art. 1(2) and the 2/3 rule are functioning well. There is certainly room for discussion about the height of the turnover level and - sufficient working capacities of the Commission presupposing - some time in the future, these levels should be lowered. However, as far as the functioning of the present thresholds is concerned, there seems to be no reason for any criticism.

Concerning the Commission´s proposal for transferring mergers requiring multiple filings in three Member States into the Community´s jurisdiction, without doubt it seems that this approach is to be preferred to the present system of Art. 1 (3). It appears that this criterion of multiple filings would be more suitable to catch mergers with a Community dimension (from an economic point of view) than under the present system consisting of the five criteria of Art. 1 (3). However, it needs to be examined whether such a linkage between Community competence on the one hand and discretion of national legislators on the other is lawful under Community law.

The Commission´s proposal should be clarified in such a way that the final assessment of whether national merger criteria are in fact fulfilled is left to the national competition authorities. A review of the parties´ analysis of the merger criteria of different Member States would not only increase the workload of the Commission unnecessarily but would possibly also lead to divergent interpretations of national competition law by both the Commission and national authorities as well as causing considerable problems and uncertainties.

2. In light of the experience made in your country, do member states have sufficient flexibility to call for mergers to be refferred back under Article 9 of the Merger Regulation? In light of the proposal in the Commission´s green Paper, what is your view on the circumstances in which this power should be exercised?

So far there have been no Austrian calls for referrals of mergers pursuant to Art.9. There was only one case (Case No.IV/M.1221, Rewe/Meinl) in which an application for referral was considered by the Ministry of Economics but ultimately no referral application was put forward to the Commission due to political considerations.

The Commission´s proposal for simplification of the referral criteria is viewed positively and might even allow for a shortening of the deadlines for referral applications.

The Commission´s suggestion for *ex officio* referrals to national authorities without any preceding notice from the relevant Member State should however not be taken up. First, this seems to collide with the principle of subsidiarity (since the transfer of competence from an EU institution to a national authority seems to require the acceptance of the latter). Secondly, for political reasons, it might be more opportune for a Member State to have a merger satisfying the Art.9 criteria be dealt with by an „outside" institution, such as the Commission, rather than by a national authority (as was demonstrated by the Austrian Rewe/Meinl case).

3. Is the system of consultation between the European Commission and the national competition authorities (NCAs) working adequately? Does there need to be a better formalised system for consultation between NCAs directly involved either in the case of multiple filings outside the merger control regulation or in cases where more than one member state exercises the Article 9 request?

According to information given to the rapporteur by national competition authorities, the present system of consultation and information between the EC Commission and national institutions is rather intensive and works adequately. The cooperation and consultation system set up by national

European competition authorities is also working in a satisfactory manner and provides sufficient opportunities and possibilities for mutual contact and consultation. Further intensification can be expected from current efforts for improvement and from the new „Regulation 17“.

4. How does the test under the law of your country compare to that under the Merger Regulation? Should all member states adopt the same test as under the Merger Regulation, and should this EU test be the (US) „significant lessening of competition“ test rather than the present EU „dominance“ test?

At first sight the substantive test under Austrian merger law seems very similar to that under the EC-Merger Control Regulation (EC-MCR). According to the law, the Cartel Court must prohibit a merger if it leads to the *„creation or strenghtening of a dominant position“*. There are however three main differences.

First, the law defines what market position is to be regarded as „dominant“ through the use of qualitative and quantitative criteria. A dominant position exists, if an undertaking is a) *„exposed to no or no substantial competition“* or b) if it has *„in relation to its competitors an overreaching market position“* (based on the critieria financial power, relationships with other undertakings, access to supplier- and user-markets, circumstances which restrict market access for other undertakings) – i.e. qualitative criteria.

If an undertaking reaches certain market share-thresholds (30%; over 5% and exposure to competition from only two more competitors; over 5% and at the same time belonging to the four biggest undertakings which have a combined market share of at least 80%) in the whole of Austria or in a smaller relevant Austrian market, it has to prove, that the critertia a) and b) are not fullfilled (quantitative criteria).

An undertaking is also regarded as market dominant if it has c) *„in relation to its suppliers or users, an overreaching market position“* – i.e. qualitative criteria. Such a position is deemed to exist, if the suppliers or users depend on the maintenance of the business relation with the merging undertakings concerned in order to avoid grave economic disadvantages.

Secondly, contrary to the test under the EC-MCR, there is no criteria concerning the *„significant impediment of effective competition“*.

Thirdly, if the merger does not only create or strengthen a dominant position but also leads to *„an improvement of the conditions of competition, which surmont the disadvantages of market dominance“* or if it is *„necessary for the maintenance or improvement of the international competitiveness of the undertakings involved and is at the same time justified from a national economic point of view“*, the merger must be allowed by the Cartel Court.

As far as the test is concerned which should be used by the Member States it would - for obvious economical, administrative and simplification reasons - of course be helpful and welcome if the national tests were identical to the EU-test. However, since merger law is a very sensitive issue in most countries, it should ultimately be left to the Member States to decide if they want to alter their existing rules accordingly. Any EU-unification measures should therefore be based upon the unanimous approval of all Member States.

Regarding the question whether the present EU-test should be changed to the *„significant lessening of competition“*-test (US), the answer is clearly no. There are several reasons for this. First, the EU-test has widely been accepted and proven successful. Lawyers and undertakings know the meaning of this provision since the decisions of the Commission and the EU-Courts provide sufficiently clear guidelines. Secondly, the wording of the present EU-test already contains the element of *„significant impedement to effective competition“* anyway and academic literature has shown that this test-limb is very similar in meaning to *„the creation or strenghtening of a dominant position“* (the Commission itself also states in the Green Paper that an application of the SLC-test would only lead to slightly different results in most cases). Further, it must be doubted whether the US-test is superior to the present EU-test and whether it would result in an improvement of conditions of competiton in the EU-market which cannot be achieved by the „dominance test“, especially since the latter allows for sufficient flexibility and leaves enough room for adaption. Finally, several Member States have modelled their merger provisions on the EU-model (including the dominance test) and most competition authorities and lawyers have also looked to the interpretation of EU-law when construing their national laws. The convergence thus reached at a level below the Community thresholds would be put in jeopardy if the SLC-test was introduced. The (uncertain) gains from the introduction of the SLC-test would be disproportional to its negative effects. The convergence of European and American merger law alone does not seem to be a good enough reason for this change.

5. Are the procedural and judical safeguards adequate to protect parties from abuse of power by the competition authorities? How do the laws of your country compare to EC law in this respect?

As far as the merging parties are concerned, the law provides that they can appeal against decisions of the Cartel Court to the Upper-Cartel Court, which is basically a division of the Austrian Supreme Court. This seems sufficient protection against the abuse of power.

Competitors, users and suppliers as well as consumers have, however, no adequate rights to be heard in merger cases. Although they may be heard by the relevant authorities (Federal Competition Authority, Public Prosecutor in Cartel Matters) at the important pre-notification stage, they have no legal right to it. After a merger-notification has been made to the Cartel Court they may put forward their views about the proposed merger to the Court but - since they have no formal legal standing in merger cases - they have neither the possibility to actually instigate an examination procedure (or force the Federal Competition Authority or the Public Prosecutor in Cartel Matters to do so) nor to appeal against decisions of the Court.

Compared to EC Law, where complainants and under certain cirumstances even parties who did not take part in the proceedings before the Commission may appeal against decisions of the Commission, the legal protection offered by Austrian merger law to parties concerned by a merger is therefore less developed.

6. Below are a number of questions relating to domestic law which may assist in a comparative analysis

a) Please provide an overview of the structure of and main features of the relevant domestic legislation and the institutional framework (who enforces it)? It may be helpful with some information about the role of private rights of action.

Antitrust law in Austria is based on the Cartel Act 1988 (as amended) and the new Competition Act 2002. The recent reform of Austrian antitrust law which entered into force on 1 July 2002 has brought dramatic changes to the institutional structure of the authorities involved in antitrust procedures. In addition to the already existing Cartel Court (which takes all decisions in subject matters) three new institutions have been created:

1. Federal Competition Authority
2. Competition Commission
3. Public Prosecutor in Cartel Matters

The Federal Competition Authority (FCA) is an institution independent from the public administration. It consists of the General Director, the Deputy Director and a staff of 20 members. Its three main functions are

a) to play a leading role in the detection of violations of Austrian and EC antitrust provisions through the use of its investigative powers (the latter are a new phenomenon in Austrian antitrust law since until the recent reform no institution involved in antitrust proceedings, including the Cartel Court, was entrusted with such powers);

b) to start proceedings against violators before the Cartel Court (in merger cases the FCA and the Public Prosecutor in Cartel Matters are the only two institutions which can initiate examination procedures before the Cartel Court);
c) to cooperate with and support the EC Commission in its own antitrust proceedings.

The FCA has comprehensive legal standing in all antitrust and merger proceedings, may initiate examination proceedings in all matters provided for by the Cartel Act, may ask for judicial review of the Cartel Court´s decisions (even if the procedure was not initiated on its initiative) and has, in relation to mergers, a monopoly position (shared with the Public Prosecutor in Cartel Matters) in so far as only it (or the PP) can initiate an examination procedure in relation to a merger notified to the Cartel Court.

The Competition Commission (CompComm) has no decision making powers but serves as an advisory body to the FCA. It consists of eight independent expert members, four of which were nominated by the Minister of Economics and Labour for their expertise while the remaining four were nominated by political institutions (Austrian Chamber of Commerce, Austrian Chamber of Labour, Austrian Trade Unions, Representative Body of Farmers). The CompComm has a leading role in the execution and application of Austrian merger control provisions since it can recommend to the FCA to apply to the Cartel Court to start an examination procedure in relation to a notified merger (it must be pointed out that the Cartel Court cannot start an examination procedure in relation to a notified merger ex officio but only if a request to do so has been filed by the FCA or the Public Prosecutor in Cartel Matters). To secure the execution of this right any member of the CompComm may ask the FCA for access to the notification documents and for copies of it. Although the FCA is not bound to comply with the CompComm´s recommendation to file for the initiation of an examination procedure it forces the FCA - if the latter refuses to initiate examination proceedings - to justify towards the CompComm why it does not comply with the latter´s recommendation. The law then also requires the FCA to publish both the CompComm´s recommendation and its own reasons for non-compliance with it at its own homepage („*http://www.bwb.gv.at*") and in its annual competition report. It should be added, that a similar safeguarding procedure applies if the FCA has acted in accordance with a recommendation of the CompComm but intends to retract its application for examination of a merger at a later stage. In this case the FCA must present the CompComm with an opportunity to make a statement in relation to the proposed retraction before the withdrawl. Through this mechanism the law ensures - an active approach of the CompComm presupposing - that the important question of whether the

FCA initiates (or follows up) examination procedures in merger cases is not decided upon behind closed doors but under circumstances where a minimum of publicity and transparancy is guaranteed.

The Public Prosecutor in Cartel Matters (PP) is an institution under the control of the Ministry of Justice. Its function is *„to represent the public interest in competition matters"* before the Cartel Court. The legal position of the PP is very similar to the one held by the FCA; e.g. it also has comprehensive legal standing in all antitrust procedures and may ask for judicial review of the Cartel Courts decisions. Like the FCA it can also initiate an examination procedure in relation to a notified merger. However, the lawmakers intended the PP only to play a supplementary role to the FCA and - in merger cases - to act only, when the latter regards an application for examination of a notified merger as unnecessary due to the lack of competition concerns and this assessment does not comply with the government´s own assessment.

The Cartel Court continues to take all important decisions in antitrust matters. With the recent changes it has lost its capacity to initiate proceedings ex officio in all cartel-, abuse of dominat position- and merger-cases. It can now only start proceedings if applications are put forward by parties appling for antitrust exemptions, complainants or - in merger cases - the FCA or the PP. In cases where the imposition of a fine by the Cartel Court seems appropriate a request by the FCA or the PP is also required before the Cartel Court can impose such a fine. Finally it should be mentioned, that the dominant influence of political institutions in the Cartel Court´s composition has also been brought to an end by the recent reform. The majority of judges is now made up of professional judges and not, as before, of lay-men nominated by these political institutions.

As yet, mergers have not given rise to any private actions by competitors (or other market participants) on the basis of competition concerns. It seems very uncertain whether Austrian private law provides for any legal basis for claims based on the violation of merger control provisions. This may only be the case if a merger is regarded as an abuse of a dominant position (on the basis of the Continental Can decision of the ECJ).

b) What kinds of transactions are caught? Are joint ventures caught? What are the jurisdictional thresholds? Is it difficult to identify with sufficient certainty whether a filing is in fact required under national law? Are foreign-to-foreign mergers caught?

The transactions caught by the Austrian merger control provisions are listed in § 41 (1) Cartel Act:

—Acquisition of the whole or the substantial parts of an undertaking by another, particularly through merger (in the sense of the 3rd EU-Directive)

or certain types of transformation which result in the creation of a new legal personality;
—Lease of business premises;
—Acquisition of shares of a company, whether directly or indirectly, of 25% and 50%;
—The creation of personal identity of at least the half of the members of the governing or supervisory body of two or more companies;
—Any other connection between undertakings through which one undertaking can, directly or indirectly, exert decisive influence over another undertaking.

Certain joint ventures are caught under the Austrian merger regime. The legal definition of these is identical to the (earlier) definition of concentrative JVs under the EC-Merger Control Regulation before its amendement:

§ 41 (2) Cartel Act: „The creation of a joint venture performing on a lasting basis all the functions of an autonomous economic entity, and which does not give rise to coordination of the competitive behaviour of the parties amongst themselves or between them and the joint venture, constitutes a concentration.“

The jurisdictional thresholds are as follows:
—the combined relevant turnover (worldwide) of the involved undertakings must amount to 305 Mio Euro
—the combined relevant turnover in Austria of the involved undertakings must amount to 15.2 Mio Euro
—the turnover of at least two participating undertakings (worldwide) must amount to 2 Mio Euro (for the purposes of turnover-calculation in the media sector, the turnover of media undertakings or media services must be multiplied by the factor 200).

The definition of concentration, as well as the turnover critieria, are sufficiently clear so that in the majority of cases it is possible for the undertakings involved in a merger to determine whether a filing is necessary or not. However, there are still some unresolved questions in relation to the calculation of turnover when a company is part of a bigger concern/group (and the question arises, which connection must exist between separate undertakings so that they can be regarded as part of the same concern/group) and when state enterprises are involved.

There are no specific rules for foreign-to-foreign mergers; such mergers fall within the remit of the Austrian merger provisions if the relevant criteria are met.

c) Is the filing mandatory or voluntary? Who is responsible for filing? What is involved in the preparation of a filing? What are the deadlines for filing?

What are the waiting periods and does implementation of the transaction have to be suspended?

The filing of a merger fulfilling the relevant critieria and thresholds is mandatory under Austrian merger control provisions. The decision-making or governing representatives of an undertaking are - in relation to their company - responsible for filing; if the merger is carried out before approval, the undertakings (and not their representatives) involved may be fined.

The law stipulates only in rather rough terms what information must be included in a filing (detailed information regarding the circumstances which are relevant for the creation or strengthening of a dominant position, e.g. structure of each undertaking involved in the merger, turnover and market shares, general information concerning market structure). As a consequence the undertakings involved in a merger are left with some leeway for deciding which information they include in a merger notification. If the information provided seems insufficient, the Cartel Court can ask for more precise and detailed information. According to the new law, the Minister for Justice (in cooperation with the Minister for Economics and Labour) can now pass a regulation which contains more detailed provisions regarding form and contents of merger notifications. Until today no such regulation has been passed however.

The parties filing a merger must provide several copies of the filing documents and have to pay costs up to an amount of 29,000 Euro if the Federal Competition Authority or the Public Prosecutor in Cartel Matters apply for an examination of the merger.

The law provides for no filing deadline. Since the merger must not be carried out before approval (or before the issuance of a statement by the Cartel Court that no application for examination has been filed by the FCA or the PP) it is recommended to file as early as possible.

From the time the filing reaches the Cartel Court the maximum waiting period is five months. Within these five months the Cartel Court may examine the merger and the implementation of the merger must be suspended. However, the Cartel Court can only examine the merger within this time span if the Federal Competition Authority or the Public Prosecutor in Cartel Matters apply for an examination within four weeks after the filing documents have been sent to them by the Cartel Court. If in their view the proposed merger raises no competition concerns (maybe after alterations have been agreed between them and the parties of the merger) and as a consequence they choose not to apply for an examination within these four weeks, the Cartel Court has to issue a statement that no application for examination has been filed and the merger may be carried out. As a result, parties to a merger are advised to contact the FCA and the PP before the filing of a merger to clear any possible competition concerns; if this course of action is taken, the waiting period may be reduced to a few days (between the filing of the merger with the Cartel Court and the issuance of the statement mentioned above which can be issued after the FCA and the PP have waived their right to apply for an examination).

d) What are the issues and possible sanctions involved in closing before clearance? What is the timetable for clearance and can it be speeded up?

If a merger is implemented before the end of the waiting period, the underlying contracts are void. The undertakings involved may also be fined up to 10% of their worldwide turnover from the previous year.
As fas as the timetable for clearance and speeding-up possibilities are concerned please see *supra c)*.

e) Are there any special rules applicable to public takeover bids?

There are no special merger control provisions regarding public takeover bids.

f) What is the substantive test for clearance?

At first sight the substantive test under Austrian merger law seems rather similar to the one under the EC-Merger Control Regulation (EC-MCR): If a merger leads to the „*creation or strenghtening of a dominant position*“, the Cartel Court must prohibit the transaction.

However, contrary to the test under the EC-MCR there is no criteria concerning the „*significant impediment of effective competition*“. Furthermore, if the merger also leads to „*an improvement of the conditions of competition, which surmont the disadvantages of market dominance*“ or if it is „*necessary for the maintenance or improvement of the international competitiveness of the undertakings involved and is at the same time justified on a national economic point of view*“, the merger must be allowed by the Cartel Court (please see also answer to question 4 above).

g) To what extent are non-competition issues relevant to the review process?

As mentioned in *supra 4)* and *f)*, non-competition issues can play a role in the review process in so far as the Cartel Court must examine whether a merger maintains or improves the international competitiveness of the undertakings involved and „*is at the same time justified from a national economic point of view*“.

Apart from this, the law requires the consideration of a specific non-competition issue in the media sector. In this area the Cartel Court must not only examine whether a merger fullfils the „normal“ substantive criteria, but also if it can be expected that it will result in an *„impairment of media plurality“*.

Finally it should be mentioned that non-competition issues may also play a role in the initiation of a review process. The Competition Commission, which may recommend the filing of an application for examination to the the Federal Competition Authority, consists of eight members. Four of these members are nominated by political institutions (Austrian Chamber of Commerce, Austrian Chamber of Labour, Austrian Trade Unions, Representative Body of Farmers). Since one member only can give rise to a CC´s recommendation it seems that non-competition issues (such as consequences of a merger for the job situation in a specific sector or environmental concerns) may play a role for the initiation of a merger examination.

h) Is it possible to remedy competition issues?

As mentioned above in *supra c)*, it is advisable for the merging parties to contact the the Federal Competition Authority (and the Public Prosecutor in Cartel Matters) before the filing of a merger with the Cartel Court. If the FCA raises any competiton concerns at this early stage of the procedure, the parties may alter their original merger plans and thereby dispel the FCA´s (and the PP´s) doubts. Should the FCA be satisfied with the alterations, it (and the PP) may wave their right to file for an application for examination.

If an examination procedure is initiated by the the Federal Competition Authority or the Public Prosecutor in Cartel Matters, the parties may also propose alterations/modifications to the notified merger plan to the Cartel Court which the Court may include in its decision as conditions or obligations. If the circumstances subsequently change, the parties to the merger may apply to the Cartel Court for an alteration or the lifting of these conditions or obligations.

i) What are the typical steps during the investigation? What rights do complainants have? What publicity is given to the process? What are the opportunities for judicial review?

The typical steps during an investigation are collection of the main facts and market data surrounding a merger by the Federal Competition Authority or, if proceedings were initiated, by the Cartel Court via questioning of the parties involved in a merger, competitors and other market participants and expert witnesses. The Cartel Court may also gather legal expertise from listed antitrust experts and ask regulators and certain political institutions for their views on specific cases. The Cartel Court may finally ask the FCA to gather and provide necessary information and documents (such as market data) within the latter´s obligation to provide administrative aid.

Complainants have no formalised legal rights to be heard by the Federal Competition Authority, the Public Prosecutor in Cartel Matters or the Competition Commission. However, they are free to contact these institutions and inform them of their concerns or ask the FCA or the PP to file for an examination of a notified merger (the FCA or the PP are not obliged to comply with this request). Once a merger has been filed with the Cartel Court and the Court has published the merger in the Official Journal of the Vienna Gazette, undertakings whose economic or legal interests are affected by the merger may write to the Cartel Court about their concerns within 14 days of publication. They have no right however that any special treatment or attention is given to their statement.

There are some provisions which provide some degree of publicity during the process of a merger. The first measure of publicity is the requirement that the Cartel Court publishes the main features of a notified merger in the Official Journal of the Vienna Gazette (which is also accessible via internet free of charge). After this publication has taken place, the Competition Commission may ask the Federal Competition Authority for access to the file of the notified merger (the merger must be notified to the Cartel Court which then sends a copy of the notification documents to the FCA but not to the CompComm). It can then decide as to whether the notified merger raises competition concerns and whether a recommendation to the FCA to apply for an examination is appropriate. If such a recommendation is in fact issued by the CompCom and the FCA does not comply with it, the recommendation of the CompCom as well as the reasons of the FCA for its non-compliance with this recommendation must be published on the homepage[2] of the FCA. If, following an application for examination of a merger by the FCA or the PP, the Cartel Court reaches a decision about the merger, this decision will either be published in one or several law journals or can be obtained from any citizen (against costs). Last but not least, the Austrian Cartel Act provides for a „Cartel Register“ which is open to the public. All notifications and prohibitions of mergers must be recorded in this register; it also includes a collection of all notification documents.

Complainants have no legal standing in a merger procedure and have therefore no possibility for judicial review (if for example neither the FCA nor the PP decide not to file for an application of examination or if the Cartel Court allows a notified merger). If the Cartel Court reaches a decision, only the FCA or the PP (which have initiated the proceedings) have a right to judicial review.

j) What are the enforcement powers? How does administrative and civil sanctions compare with the EC regime? And what are the criminal sanctions, and are they used?

If a merger is carried out before approval of the Cartel Court (or before the issuance of a statement that no application for examination had been filed by the Federal Competition Authority or the Public Prosecutor in Cartel Matters), the law provides that the undertakings concerned may be fined by the Cartel Court between 10,000 and 1 Mio Euro or up to 10% of their worldwide turnover from the previous year. As far as the level of the administrative fine is concerned, Austrian merger control law is therefore almost identical to Art.14(2)a EC-MCR. The Cartel Court can however only impose a fine after a request by the FCA or the PP.

As far as civil law sanctions are involved, the law stipulates that the contracts underlying a merger are void if the merger is implemented before the end of the waiting period. If the merger is later allowed by the Cartel Court, the contracts become binding. Civil law sanctions are therefore very similar to Art.7 (5) EC-MCR. Austrian law however contains no exception similar to Art.7 (6) EC-MCR.

Since the new law came into force (1 July 2002), there are no longer criminal sanctions for the violation of merger control provisions. In any case they had previously never been used anyway (mainly due to the fact that mergers were never implemented before filing or approval by the Cartel Court).

k) Do the authorities cooperate with other antitrust authorities?

Yes; please see answer to question 3 above.

l) Are there also rules on foreign investment, special sectors or other relevant approvals?

There are special merger provisions for the media sector (please see *supra-b)* for the turnover-calculation and *suprag)* for the relevance of media plurality).

There are special competition rules in the regulated network industries (gas, electricity, telecommunication, railway) particularly in relation to questions regarding access to infrastructures (but no specific merger provisions). Notwithstanding the competence of the Cartel Court to apply normal antitrust law to these sectors, the questions mentioned are also dealt with by the relevant Regulators. As far as merger control is concerned, Austrian cartel law provides, that the Regulators of these sectors may make statements to the Cartel Court or may be asked by the Cartel Court for such statements in merger procedures. They have, however, no right to apply for examinations or to judicial review in merger cases.

The Austrian Cartel Act contains special merger provisions (exceptions) for the acquisition of shares by banks or financial institutions. Such transactions are not caught by the merger control provisions if the shares are only bought by the bank a) for the purpose of selling or b) for the purpose of rescuing a failing company or for the purpose of security over claims against such a company or c) if the shares are bought by a financial institution the only purpose of which is to aquire, to administer and to commercialise such holdings without - directly or indirectly - interfering in the government of these undertakings. The acquirer is required not to use his voting rights in order to influence the competitive behaviour of the company and must sell the shares in case a) within one year and in cases b) within one year after the ending of the rescuing- or security-purpose.

For other relevant approvals regarding the mergers/takeovers of banks or insurance companies please see answer to question 9. below.

m) Are there current proposals to change the legislation?

The last reform of the Austrian cartel law only entered into force on 1 July 2002. At the moment there are no known plans for change.

B. COMPANY LAW AND FINANCIAL MARKET REGULATORY REGIME

7. What will you identify as the main obstacles to takeovers where a company from your jurisdiction is either bidder or target and the other company is from another EU-jurisdiction?

Austrian company law and takeover law contains no specific barriers or hindrances to cross-border takeovers as compared to intra-Austrian takeovers/mergers.

Takeovers of Austrian companies by companies from other jurisdictions and national takeovers are faced however with the following three obstacles: a) the relatively high degree of state-ownership in some large listed companies (although it should be mentioned that the Austrian government has started a privatisation programme which will result in a considerable reduction of state holdings); b) the Austrian stakeholder landscape which is characterised on the one hand by a very high percentage of big institutional shareholders (banks, insurance companies etc) which are often connected via cross-shareholdings and on the other hand - compared to other countries - by the small amount of shares dispersed widely amongst the public[3]; c) the obligation of the acquirer of a controlling interest in an Austrian company listed on the Vienna Stock Exchange to make a mandatory cash offer (the price to be offered must comply with certain minimum requirements laid down in the Take Over Act) to all the shareholders of the target (please see 14 a) below).

If an Austrian company considers the takeover of a company from another EU-jurisdiction, the main obstacles (if any) will be contained in the law of the other Member State; Austrian law does not provide any obstacles in this respect.

8. Do hostile takeovers by companies from other EU jurisdictions in fact take place in your country?

Hostile takeovers are a very rare phenomenon in Austria. This is even more true for hostile takeovers of Austrian companies by companies from other EU or EFTA jurisdictions. The last case seems to have been the contested takeover of the Austrian Krems Chemie by the Finnish Neste Oy (regarded as friendly by the offeree´s board) and the Norwegian Dyno Industrier ASA (regarded as hostile by the offeree´s board) in 1997.

9. To what extent are there any sectors (utilities, financial institutions) that in practice are further protected from hostile takeovers, or foreign takeovers in particular? Are there any policy statements or particular legal mechanism that give effect to this protection, or is it a matter of informal mechanisms?

Provisions that need to be mentioned in this context regard financial institutions. According to the Austrian Banking Act, the merger between financial institutions as well as the acquisition (or divestiture) of shares in a financial institution by another up to (or below) the thresholds of 10%, 20%, 33% and 50% of the capital or voting rights need the specific approval of the Minister of Finance. Approval will be given if the normal criteria for a banking licence are fulfilled.

The second provision provides that anybody who intends to acquire shares of at least 10% of the capital or the voting rights of a financial institution (or intends to increase his holding of 20% to over 20%, 33% or 50%) has to notify the Minister of Finance of his intention. The Minister may then prohibit the acquisition if the acquirer does not seem to be fit to conduct the business of a financial institution in a proper and orderly manner or if the Minister of Finance may be hindered in conducting his supervisory duties due to the close affiliation of the financial institution with a certain human being or legal identity.

It should be noted that both provisions mentioned offer no specific protection from hostile or foreign takeovers in the banking sector but apply to mergers and the acquisition of shares in general.

Similar provisions apply to certain insurance companies according to the Austrian Insurance Supervision Act.

As far as utilities are concerned, some laws oblige the state to hold certain minimum amounts of shares, e.g. in the energy/electricity sector the Republic of Austria is required to hold 51% of the stakes in the „Verbund" (Austria´s largest electricity company).

Based on the fact that many foreign takeovers of Austrian companies have taken place in the past in all sectors of the economy there seem to be no formal mechanisms (apart from the ones mentioned) in place which could be used in a protectionist manner. Such mechanisms would certainly be contrary to public policy statements of the present (and past) governments.

10. What are the company law techniques of completing a takeover or merger that are used in practice where one of the companies is from another EU jurisdiction? Please give particular attention to how this would differ from the usual completion of a takeover or merger where both companies are from your jurisdiction.

In the majority of cases the company law technique used is a „share deal", e.g. the takeover is achieved via acquisition of a block of shares from a former shareholder (perhaps in conjunction with the acquisition of shares via the Stock Exchange) conferring a controlling interest to the acquirer (this includes cases in which the Austrian company is the target and the offeror from another jurisdiction and vice versa). If the company whose shares are acquired is an Austrian stock corporation listed on the Vienna Stock Exchange, the acquistion of control triggers the obligation to make a mandatory bid to all the shareholders of the target company. Voluntary public bids aimed at acquiring control over an Austrian company are rare.

If only Austrian companies are involved, formal mergers (in the sense of the 3rd EU-Directive) also take place; this technique is however mainly used for companies already belonging to the same group/concern and less often used for bringing independent companies together within one legal personality. The company law technique of a formal merger is not available to cross-border transactions.

One wideley reported and discussed example of a complex technique used for the takeover of an Austrian company by a company from another EU-jurisdiction is demonstrated by the friendly takeover of the Austrian „Bank Austria" (BA), listed on the Vienna Stock Exchange, by the German „HypoVereinsbank" (HVB), listed on the Frankfurter Stock Exchange. [4] This transaction included and combined many different company law techniques for restructuring a company. In the first phase of the transaction, BA transferred all its business operations to one of its non-listed subsidiaries (BA-new); this involved split-up- and merger-operations as well as a capital increase against contribution in kind. As a result of these actions, BA continued as a listed holding company with all its business concentrated in BA-new. In the second phase, BA contributed its shares in BA-new to the German HVB in exchange for shares of the latter. BA was now a shareholder in HVB while BA-new was now an Austrian subsidiary of HVB. During the third phase, BA was formally merged with its now sub-subsidiary BA-new and the shares of the German HVB owned by the Austrian BA were used directly to compensate the shareholders of BA for the loss of their shares. As a result of these transactions, the shareholders of an Austrian company thus became shareholders of a German company and the control over the business operation of an Austrian company was transferred to a German company. The latter was not under the control of a particular shareholder or group of shareholders as a result of which no mandatory bid had to be made under the Austrian Take Over Act to the shareholders of BA.

11. A duty on listed companies to disclose capital and control sturctures is proposed in *Issues Relating to Takeover Bids*, the First Report of the High Level Group of Company Law Experts (ss p 25). Would this require amendments in the legislation in your country? How would these amendments in case be implemented (in primary company law, securities law, stock exchange regulations etc.)?

The disclosure proposals made in *Issues Relating to Takeover Bids* would require only small changes since Austria law already provides for the disclosure of interests in companies. The Stock Exchange Act, for example, requires persons who acquire shares or increase or lower their holdings above or below certain thresholds in companies listed on the Vienna Stock Exchange to notify the Austrian Financial Market Authority and the Vienna Stock Exchange. Stock Corporations which experience considerable changes in the voting powers of their shareholders have to inform the public through announcement in the Official Journal of the Vienna Gazette. Other disclosure rules regard the publication of directors´ dealings and the publication of shareholdings in the annual reports of companies.

The changes (if any were needed at all) would most likely be implemented in the Stock Exchange Act and/or primary company law.

12. A so called break-through rule after takeover bids is another of the proposals in *Issues Relating to Takeover Bids*, the First Report of the High Level Group of Company Law Experts (ss p 29). Would this require

amendments in the legislation in your country? How would these amendments in case be implemented (in primary company law, securities law, stock exchange regulations etc.)?

Yes, the break-through rule would require amendments in primary company law (Stock Corporation Act) and/or the Take Over Act.

13. In your view, would these two new rules as proposed have any material impact on the existing barriers to takeovers in your country (or in others as seen from your point of view)? It would be helpful if you could demonstrate the impact, or lack of it, by going through one or more recent takeover bids that failed in your country (or in some other member state, by a company from your country).

If the disclosure proposal required any amendments to Austrian law at all (please see answer to question 11. above) they would still have no impact on the barriers to takeovers due to the nature of these obstacles (please see answer to question 7. above).

It might well be the case that the introduction of a break-through rule would lower the barriers to takeovers in Austria (please see answer to question 7. above). It seems however, that the maximum threshold of 75% of the risk bearing capital (as suggested in the *Issues Relating to Takeover Bids*, p. 31) would, in a considerable number of cases, be too high as to put an unwelcome bidder in Austria into a position to take advantage of the rule since the average size of the largest stock held in Austrian companies would often prevent him from reaching this threshold. The exact impact of such a rule depends therefore on its exact scope and on whether Austria would lower this threshold (as well as the majority requirements required for special resolutions).

There are no cases or instances known in which the existence of a break-through rule would have prevented a bid from failing (it should be added that there are no surveys or statistics about the quantity and quality of restrictive voting or control structures in Austrian companies which may frustrate a bid).

14. Below are a number of questions which may assist in a comparative analysis

a) What are the main features of the relevant domestic takeover legislation constituting the company law and financial market regime, and who enforces it (independent regulators, regulatory bodies with appeal to ministry, stock exchange)? What is the extent of intervention by the takeover regulator(s) - to what extent does the regulator have wide or

general discretions to block and play a protectionist role (for example in its capacity as approver of the offer terms/documentation)?

Austria´s takeover legislation is contained in the Take Over Act which entered into force on 1st January 1999[5]. It is applicable to Austrian companies whose equities (both with or without voting rights) are listed on the Vienna Stock Exchange and was modelled after the British „City Code on Takeovers and Mergers". The most important sections of the relevant proposal of the EU Directive on takeovers and mergers were also incorporated into the Take Over Act. It regulates both voluntary bids and mandatory bids in the context of changes in controlling interests in stock corporations.

The enforcement and surveillance of the law has been entrusted to an independent Takeover Commission set up at the offices of the Vienna Stock Exchange. It consists of twelve members (appointed for a period of five years) and is independent from the Stock Exchange as well as from the public administration. This regulatory authority fulfils both the function of arbitrator and court, as it has the task of issuing recommendations rapidly and of reaching formal decisions in its function as competent authority - including sanctions - regarding bidders, target companies and third parties. Recourse against formal decisions may only be lodged with the Constitutional Court.

The Take Over Act has been designed to deal with the following issues:

- Minimum standards for public bids are set up. The Act introduces procedural rules, e.g. information to be contained in the offer documents or the period during which a bid has to be open to acceptances. Additional rules are designed to prevent insider dealing via disclosure rules. The management of the offeree company may not frustrate the bid and has to communicate to the shareholders its views on whether the bid is fair and appropriate.
- A so-called mandatory bid is introduced: If control in a listed company is transferred (e.g. by the sale of a block of shares by the former controlling body), the acquirer shall make a cash bid to all holders of shares in the offeree company. Shareholders may choose to „exit" by divestment and liquidate their holdings rather than remain in the company controlled by the acquirer. Exceptions may be granted (e.g. if a controlling holding is acquired for the purposes of reconstruction).

The Take Over Act contains five general principles:

- Equal treatment of all shareholders, i.e. major shareholders and strategic shareholders must be treated in the same way as minority shareholders of freefloating stocks or institutional portfolio investors. The only exception applies in the case of a mandatory bid where a discount of 15% of the package price obtained by a majority shareholder is allowed. Stock corporations wishing to treat their shareholders equally may refrain from granting the discount by changing their articles of association.

- Transparency and sufficient time and information for the adressees of a bid. Shareholders should thereby be given the possibility to reach a well-founded decision whether or not to accept a voluntary offer or, in the case of a mandatory bid (after the change of a controlling interest), whether or not to leave the company or remain affiliated. Comprehensive information, that has been scrutinized by an independent expert for completeness and accurracy, must therefore be made available to them. The Takeover Commission has the right to examine the takeover prospectus of the offerer and, in the event of serious errors in content, it will announce these to the public or even bar the bid from being made.
- Impartiality and neutrality of the Management Board and the supervisory body of the target company. This aims to eliminate the preferential treatment of individual shareholders and the opportunity of members of the management to act in their own interest. Takeover defence measures after a bid has been made are only possible to a limited extent and only permissable after a new resolution has been passed at the general shareholders´ meeting.
- Avoidance of market distortion and insider dealings. If the secrecy of preparatory measures is no longer guaranteed at the bidding or target company, the bidder must make a public announcement on the takeover bid. This type of *ad hoc* reporting is subject to supervision by the Austrian Financial Market Authority.
- Rapid completion of takeovers. Various regulations concerning minimum and maximum periods aim at preventing takeover procedures from taking too long. Blocking times are designed to prevent one bidder from making several offers within a short period of time and from causing excessive disturbances within the target company.

As can be seen from the overview in the preceding paragraphs the intervention possibilities as well as the available discretion are quite far-reaching and can even result in the blocking of a bid (subject to judicial review). In the past 3 _ years, however, there has been no reason whatsoever to suspect that the independent Takeover Commission has acted in a biased manner, in particular on protectionist motives. Quite to the contrary, in the most important case since the beginning of its activity - the takeover of the Austrian „Bank Austria“ by the German „HypoVereinsbank“ (see answer to question 10. above) - it would have been possible for the Takeover

Commission to hinder the transaction (or at least make it more difficult for the parties) by deciding that the Take Over Act was applicable to this very complex friendly takeover (in this case the HVB would have had to make a cash offer which, according to newspaper reports, it was not willing to do and would probably have resulted in the abandoning of the transaction). It decided however that the Act was not applicable and, as a consequence, the transaction was able to be carried out as planned by the parties.

b) Are there restrictions on a board taking action to frustrate a bid that has been made? When do the relevant restrictions start to apply - earlier than a formal announcement/filing of a bid? To what extent can shareholders approve the taking of frustrating action in advance of any bid?

The Take Over Act obliges the board and the supervisory body of the offeree company to refrain from any act liable to frustrate the bid from the time the offeree company has become aware of the offeror´s intention to make a bid. This restriction does not apply where measures are based on a prior obligation of the adminstrative organs of the offeree company or on resolutions passed by the general meeting of shareholders after the intention of the offeror to make a bid has become known.

Whether at a time before the offeror´s intention to make a bid has become known a board may take frustrating action within its autonomous managing functions or only with the approval of the supervisory board or the shareholders (who are in this respect not limited in any way) depends on the kind of frustrating action the board is considering and is regulated by company law.

c) Are there restrictions on the type of consideration that can be offered in a bid, for example securities only if these are listed in the target country´s home state or the EU?

In the case of a mandatory bid, the law requires the bidder to offer the offeree´s shareholders payment in cash. Only in addition to the cash offer may he also offer an exchange for other securities as an alternative. There are no restrictions regarding the type of consideration in the case of a voluntary bid.

d) Are there effective compulsory acquistion procedures regarding a small non-accepting minority? Can a bidder make its offer conditional on achieving the number of shares required so it can operate a squezze out?

The Take Over Act itself provides no possibility for the acquirer to force non-accepting shareholders to sell their shares. However, company law provides that the holder of a 90% stake in a public or private company may acquire the business operation of the company (which will cease to exist after the end of the operation) if he offers a fair consideration in cash to the minority for the loss of their shares.[6]

The bidder can include a condition in his offer according to which he shall only be bound by it if he reaches a certain threshold of shares (e.g. 90%). Furthermore, in the case of voluntary offers, an offer by which the bidder may acquire a controlling interest shall be *ex lege* conditional on the offeror acquiring more the 50% of the voting right carried by ordinary shares.

e) Is there a principle of board neutrality? Can a target board align itself with a particular bidder/agree measures such as exclusivity arrangements to protect a particular deal?

Yes, please see answers to questions 14 a) and b) above for more information on the neutrality principle.

f) Can a target board hand over information to a potential bidder?

The Take Over Act contains no obligation according to which the board of the target must provide information to a potential bidder. It permits however that the target´s board enters into negotiations with a potential bidder even before a bid has been made public. Such negotiations will, in many cases, include the disclosure of at least some information regarding the circumstances of the potential target company. As far as these negotiations are permissable, duties of confidentiality are said to be set aside. It seems uncertain, however, whether this is true for all kinds of duties of confidentiality. It seems questionable for example if the Take Over Act´s provision allowing the target´s board to enter into negotiations with a potential bidder also allows it to disclose market sensitive information without the supervisory body´s consent.

g) Are structures permitted which concentrate control rights in the hands of minority shareholders? Are structures permitted which place limitations/restrictions on voting rights, caps for example on voting rights above a certain threshold?

While the Austrian Stock Corporation Act prohibits so-called multiple votes shares („*Mehrstimmrechtsaktien*"), it allows for the limitation of voting rights conferred by shares („*Höchststimmrechtsaktien*") and thus provides a mechanism by which control can be conferred on a minority shareholder.

h) Can restrictions be placed on the transferability of shares either by the issuer (in articles of association or by other means) or by arrangements between shareholders? Can a board delay registering transfer of shares?

Such restrictions can be contained in the articles of association of a company for personal shares („*Namensaktien*“) as well as in shareholder agreements.

i) What contractual barriers (including share holder agreements) to takeover bids are in use in public companies (eg golden parachutes, change of control provisions triggering default of loan agreements, or winding up or change of control of joint ventures)? What are the prospect of review by courts on the basis of contract or company law and by regulators on the basis of securities laws or stock exchange regulations?

The main contractual barriers to takeovers seem to be golden parachutes for the member of the board, the suspended sale of „crown jewels“ to a „white knight“ which would make the acquisition of the remaining business operations less attractive to a (potential) bidder, and the suspended purchase of certain undertakings which might cause antitrust problems to a successful bidder. These obstacles seem lawful under Austrian company, contract and takeover law and judicial review or litigation will, under normal circumstances, not lead to results according to which a successful bidder would not be bound by them (no decisions of the courts are known which would suggest a different outcome).

j) Are there current proposals to change the legislation relating to takeovers?

The Takeover Commission has proposed some changes. These relate to improvements to market information with the aim of avoiding market distortions especially in the phase before the announcement of a bid; greater harmonisation between company law in regard of mergers and splitting-up on the one hand and the takeover rules on the other; the improvement of the principle of equal treatment of all shareholders by abolishing the discount of 15% of the package price obtained by a majority shareholder in the case of a mandatory bid permissable under the present provisions.

C. FINAL ISSUES

15. In your view, what is the extent to which the complexity of the regulatory arrangements, within national jurisdictions and between the Commission and member states, present an obstacle to takeovers?

The complexity of the relevant regulatory arrangements and laws concerning mergers and takeovers definitely present difficulties to lawyers, investment banks, accountants and others involved in such transactions, particularly if they have not had to deal with these provisions before.

However, the Austrian Takeover Commission sees itself as an institution whose function also is to help and advise parties concerned with the interpretation of the relevant provisions. The same may be expected from the newly created Federal Competition Authority. Both institutions can be contacted before the beginning of a transaction by undertakings considering a public bid or a merger and can be asked e.g. for advice about past decisions and legal interpretations.

It must also be remembered that undertakings envolved in such transactions are in the vast majority of cases be assisted by highly specialised lawyers, banks etc. and the complexity of takeover law, antitrust law, company law, securities law and stock exchange regulations does therefore not present a hurdle to takeovers which cannot be overcome. This assessment does of cource not mean that greater harmonisation and coordination (particularly in regard of time limits) between these different fields of law were neither required nor welcome.

16. Can you list some instances where different rules in the different regulatory systems have caused practical obstacles in a takeover process? (One instance could be different time limits under the EC Merger Regulation and national merger rules on the one hand and under stock exchange rules on the other).

The Austrian Takeover Commission has found, that different regulatory systems, in particular different time schedules and time limits set by the Austrian Take Over Act on the one hand and National and European merger control regimes on the other (and indeed by other laws requiring takeover approvals by specific authorities, please see answer to question 9. above) have caused difficulties to the parties involved in takeovers/mergers and given rise to uncertainties as to how to proceed in the transactions envisaged. As a result it published an opinion which aims to assist parties concerned by advising on how to coordinate the necessary steps and on how to set the time spans eg on conditional offers.[7]

According to its opinion in the case „BA/HVB“ (please see answer to question 10 above) it also found that that some differences and disparities exist between merger law (in the sense of the 3rd EU-Directive) on the one hand and takeover law on the other as regards safeguarding mechanisms in the interest of minority shareholders. As a consequence it suggested amendments to the law in order reach greater harmonisation.

NOTES

[1] LL.M. (Edin) Institute of Commercial Law and Business Law, Faculty of Law, University of Vienna.

[2] The law requires the Federal Competition Authority to install a homepage („*http://www.bwb.gv.at*"). It does not however specify – apart from the publication of the Competition Commission´s recommendation and the reasons for non-compliance – which information has to be published in the internet.

[3] For reference to the extremly high ownership concentration in Austria see also the study of *Gugler/Kalss/Stomper/Zechner*, The Separation of Ownership and Control: An Austrian Perspective, European Corporate Governance Network (1997; as Part of a Survey of 7 European Countries submitted to the European Commission DG III). It showed that in the 600 largest corporations the average size of the largest stake is above 80%.

[4] A very detailed opinion of the Takeover Commission regarding this case is published in English at „*http://www.takeover.at/english/eframe.htm*" (GZ 2000/1/4-171).

[5] The description and overview in the answer to question 14.a) is based on information contained at the comprehensive homepage of the Austrian Takeover Commission „*http://www.takeover.at*" (in particular on an article by *K.Fuchs*, Austria´s New Takeover Act and the Takeover Commission, also published in: The Austrian Financial Markets - A Survey of Austria´s Capital Markets, Rev. Ed. 1999). It also contains the Take Over Act (in English).

[6] Amendments have been proposed according to which a „proper" squeeze out will be possible in the future (and in the course of which the company concerned will not cease to exist as under the present provisions referred to in the text).

[7] The Takeover Commison´s opinion (3 December 2001, GZ 2001/V/1) can be downloaded from „*http://www.takeover.at*".

BELGIUM

Cross Border Mergers in Company Law and Competition Law: Removing the Final Barriers

Rapporteurs
Geert A Zonnekeyn[1] *and Elke Janssens*[2]

I. GENERAL INTRODUCTION

This paper is a contribution to the XX Congress of the Fédération Internationale pour le Droit Européen ("FIDE") that will be held in London from 30 October 2002 to 2 November 2002. It takes the form of responses to a series of questions from the Congress's General Rapporteurs.

II. THE COMPETITION REGIME

Council Regulation (EEC) No. 4064/89 of 21 December 1989 "on the control of concentrations between undertakings", as amended (the "EC Merger Regulation")[3], which entered into force on 21 September 1990, provided the EC for the first time with an adequate instrument for the control of cross-border concentrations. Since then, more and more countries, including EC Member States such as Belgium, adopted their own merger control legislation.[4] The result is that the number of transactions requiring multiple filings in various jurisdictions has increased exponentially. In the case of cross border mergers, it is now routine in large transactions to cope with filing requirements in 20 to 30 and even 40 jurisdictions.

It is therefore essential, at EC level, to achieve a certain degree of harmonisation between the national merger regimes or, even more crucial, to accomplish that cross border mergers are dealt with by one and the same competition authority, be it the European Commission or one of the Member States' competition authorities. These are the cornerstones upon which an efficient enforcement of merger control within the EC ought to be built in order to remove the (final) barriers for dealing with cross border mergers in the EC.

The Commission's Green Paper on the review of the EC Merger Regulation[5] has contributed much to this debate but, as can be seen from the comments to the Green Paper, there is still a (long) way to go.[6]

1. Replies to the questionnaire

1. What is the view of your country on the functioning of the threshold levels in article 1(2) as well as the 2/3 rule in the Merger Regulation, and the proposal in the Commission's Green Paper for amendment of article 1(3) to deal with the problems of multiple filings?

General comments. The allocation of jurisdiction between the Commission and the Member States is certainly one of the most complex issues raised in the Green Paper. The allocation rule in the EC Merger Regulation is based on two alternative turnover thresholds. Article 1(2) of the EC Merger Regulation provides that a concentration has a "Community dimension" where: (i) the combined world-wide turnover of all the parties to the concentration exceeds 5 billion euro; (ii) the Community-wide turnover of at least two parties to the concentration exceeds 250 million euro; unless the parties to the concentration achieve more than two-thirds of their Community-wide turnover in one and the same Member State (the so-called "level 1 thresholds"). Under the 2/3 rule, contained in article 1(3) of the EC Merger Regulation, a concentration which does not meet the existing thresholds, will nevertheless have a "Community dimension" where: (i) the combined aggregate world-wide turnover of all the undertakings concerned is more than 2,500 million euro; (ii) the aggregate Community-wide turnover of each of at least two of the undertakings concerned is more than 100 million euro; (iii) in each of at least three Member States, the combined aggregate turnover of all the undertakings concerned is more than 100 million euro; and (iv) in each of at least three Member States included for the purpose of point (iii), the turnover of each of at least two of the undertakings concerned is more than 25 million euro; unless each of the undertakings concerned achieves more than two-thirds of its aggregate Community-wide turnover within one and the same Member State. These thresholds are often referred to as the "level 2 thresholds". Above these thresholds, the European Commission has sole jurisdiction. To adapt allocation of jurisdiction as efficient as possible, two parallel referral mechanisms were established, respectively in article 9 of the EC merger Regulation (the so-called German clause which implies a referral by the European Commission to one or more Member States) and in article 22 (the so-called Dutch clause which implies a referral by one or more Member States to the Commission).

The general turnover thresholds. Too low or too high? The threshold levels referred to in article 1(2) of the EC Merger Regulation seem to function well. However, some are of the opinion that these thresholds are either too low or too high. John Vickers, Director General of the Office of Fair Trading, for example, argued that since the adoption of the EC Merger Regulation the European price level has risen about 30%. Therefore, if the 5 billion euros threshold of 1990 had been price-index-linked, it would now be about 6.5 billion euros. In addition, if one would benchmark the threshold against nominal GDF (i.e. the income and expenditure of the whole economy), than 5 billion euros in 1990 would now be more than 7.5 billion euros, an increase over 50%.[7] Ulf Böge, President of the Bundeskartellamt, stated that "*[W]enn die Schwelle von 5 Mrd. Euro Umsatz nicht erreicht wird, sollte es auch bei Mehrfachanmeldungen nicht den Automatismus einer Zuständigkeit der EU-Kommission geben.*"[8]

Article 1(3) of the EC Merger Regulation. In its Green Paper, the European Commission proposes to amend the one-stop-shop threshold (article 1(3) of the EC Merger Regulation), which confers jurisdiction to the European Commission for mergers not reaching the first threshold but nevertheless producing effects in at least three Member States. Central to this proposal was the need to ensure an effective, efficient, fair and transparent control of concentrations at the most appropriate level. In practice, article 1(3) of the EC Merger Regulation failed to cover the majority of multiple notifications in EC Member States.[9]

However, it is doubtful whether these objectives will be achieved. The Commission's proposal would probably lead to increased administrative burden an reduced legal certainty. For example, under the current provisions of the EC Merger Regulation, the jurisdictional tests of national systems are irrelevant and notifying parties need only look to one set of turnover-based thresholds. The Green Paper fails to extend this benefit to a larger number of concentrations and will require parties to look to a large number of possible combinations of national merger systems when the tresholds of article 1(2) of the EC Merger Regulation are not met. If the juridictional test in the legal system of the EC Member States would be identical, the negative impact of the proposal would be greatly diminished. Such "harmonisation" has not yet been achieved to date and will not materialize in the near future.

There are other problems than having to cope with different jurisdictional tests. For example, the very definition of the concept "concentration" is not identical in all EC Member States. National competition authorities may therefore have jurisdiction over transactions which do not qualify as a concentration within the meaning of article 3 of the EC Merger Regulation. In addition, the triggering event for notification has not yet been harmonized within the EC Member States. Under the EC Merger Regulation, a concentration must be notified not more than a week after the conclusion of the agreement, or the announcement of the public bid, or the acquisition of a controlling interest whichever the earliest. This is later than some national merger control regimes provide.

Alternatives. Nothwithstanding the aforementioned abkjections to the Commission's proposal, it is clear that article 1, §3 of the EC Merger Regulation must be aùended so as to cover more transactions which would otherwise be subject to multiple filings in at least three EC Member States.

2. In light of the experiences made in your country, do Member States have sufficient flexibility to call for mergers to be referred back under article 9 of the Merger Regulation? In light of the proposal in the Commission's Green Paper, what is your view on the circumstances in which this power should be exercised?

Belgium has not yet made an official request to the Commission for a referral of a concentration under article 9 of the EC Merger Regulation. However, it contemplating to so with regard to an intended notification of Electrabel to the European Commission.

The Green Paper aims at facilitating and simplifying the referral mechanism under article 9 of the EC Merger Regulation. It is proposed to maintain only article 9(2)(b) but to facilitate its use by disjoining the referral request from evidence of a threat of creation or strengthening of dominance and/or by eliminating the need to establish that the relevant market is not a substantial part of the common market. Instead, it would be sufficient that the request establishes that the alleged effect on competition, which would justify the referral, does not extend to significant effects in terms of foreclosure, spill-over on related markets of greater geographic scope or similar cross-border effects. The Green Paper further proposes that the Commission should be able to refer a case or part of a case to national authorities where the same criteria as described above are fulfilled. Finally, there is also general discussion of the possibility that referrals to Member States would be dealt with under the same deadlines and procedure as cases handled at Commission level only. Each of these objectives will be addressed below.

Simplification of the referral criteria. Simplification of the current referral criteria in Article 9(2)(a) of the EC Merger Regulation would be welcome. This could be done by disjoining the criterion that there should be evidence of a threat of creation or strengthening of dominance and by eliminating the need to establish that the relevant market is not a substantial part of the common market. Both of these criteria have placed an unduly onerous burden on Member States requesting a referral.

Referrals by the Commission at its own initiative. Legal certainty and efficiency require that referrals back to Member States occur only rarely and in situations where it is clear that the Member States' authorities want to review a particular transaction and have good reasons for doing so.

Timing. Were the current referral criteria to be simplified, the deadline should still enable national authorities to verify whether the (amended) criteria for referral are met and would also help reduce delays to the notifying parties caused by such requests.

Harmonization of procedural rules and deadlines. Notifying parties should not be made worse off by the fact that their transaction has been referred to a national competition authority ("NCA"). However, the reality is that the divergence in national procedural and substantive rules and deadlines for the assessment of transactions means that they frequently are, in particular where only part of a transaction is referred to a NCA. This may raise concerns under the non-discrimination principle.

3. Is the system of consultation between the European Commission and the national competition authorities (NCA's) working adequately? Does there need to be a better formalised system for consultation between NCA's directly involved either in the case of a multiple filings outside the merger control regulation or in cases where more than one Member State exercises the Article 9 request?

Following an initiative by the Dutch Competition Authority (NMa) in April 2001, the association of European Competition Authorities ("the ECA") was established. The ECA is an informal association which serves as a forum where competition authorities operating within the EEA meet to discuss about the application and enforcement of competition rules and to improve the working relations amongst them. Within the ECA a working group dealing with issues related to multi-jurisdictional merger filings was set up. It was set up in response to signals from the business community that multi-jurisdictional filings involve considerable expenses and could lead to inconsistent outcomes of the investigations undertaken in the different jurisdictions.

The multi-jurisdictional mergers working group has focused on ways of reducing the burden of multiple filings for the companies involved by improving the cooperation between competition authorities. As a first step the working group has issued a Procedures Guide in relation to multi-jurisdictional mergers. The Procedures Guide, which has been approved by the ECA during the recent meeting in Athens in April 2002, sets out the practice of information exchange between ECA competition authorities, which was already taking place on a very informal basis, in the case of multiple merger notifications. If an ECA member receives a merger notification which has also been notified in one or more other ECA Authorities, that authority will notify the other ECA authorities of this fact by means of an "ECA notification". An example of an ECA notification is attached to the ECA Procedures Guide and includes, for instance, information on the transaction, the parties/sectors involved and the deadline by which a decision must be taken. This way the different investigating competition authorities will keep each other informed from an early stage and where possible will try to avoid inconsistent outcomes. The information exchanged for this purpose is mainly non-confidential information. Exchange of confidential information will only occur where it is possible under the relevant national legislation and if not only with a waiver by the parties involved in the merger. The mutual exchange of information with regard to multiple notifications of concentrations has also resulted in a situation where the working group has acted as a platform for coordinating joint requests for referrals, in accordance with article 22 of the EC Merger Control Regulation. For the first time since its introduction in 1998, a joint article 22 request was made in two recent EC merger cases.[10] For the first time since its introduction in 1998, a joint Article 22 request was made in two recent EU merger cases. The first case was recently approved following a detailed (second phase) investigation and subject to divestitures, while the Commission unconditionally approved the second case after a first-phase investigation. This is a remarkable result given the fact that a joint referral had never occurred before the working group was set up, due to practical problems such as the difficulty of knowing where the merger had been notified and how to coordinate the responses of the competition authorities involved.

Finally, the network has facilitated coordination between the NCAs with regard to other merger control-related issues, including advisory committee meetings. Overall, the informal cooperation of the ECA multi-jurisdictional merger network seems to have worked well and there would seem to be no need, at this particular time, for a formalized structure. To the contrary, it is felt that the informal structure may contribute to the effectiveness of the network.

4. How does the test under the law of your country compare to that under the Merger Regulation? Should all Member states adopt the same test as under the Merger Regulation, and should this EC test be the (US) "significant lessening of competition" test rather than the present EC "dominance" test?

The substantive test under the Belgian Competition Act reiterates the dominance test of Article 2 of EC Merger Regulation, *i.e.*, the Competition

Council assesses whether a concentration "*will create or strengthen a dominant position that would significantly impede effective competition on the Dutch market or a part thereof*".[11] Its application by the Competition Council also closely follows EC practice. In both concept and application, the Belgian substantive test thus conforms to EC law.

Harmonization of the substantive tests to assess concentrations within the Member States is essential to provide sufficient and clear legal certainty for cross-border transactions subject to multiple filing requirements. Accordingly, the Commission should strongly advocate harmonization of Member States' notification thresholds, information requirements, and substantive review standards. With regard to the substantive review standards, the Green Paper discusses the possibility that the Commission would replace the current dominance test for the assessment of concentrations under article 2 of the EC Merger Regulation with the concept of "substantial lessening of competition", which is the substantive standard in several major jurisdictions including the United States, Canada, Australia and South Africa.

Before analyzing whether there is a need to adopt the substantial lessening of competition ("SLC") test, it is important to establish what benefits might be expected if the SLC test replaced the dominance test.

Possible benefits of adopting the SLC test over the dominance test. First, it would help eliminate the potentially damaging consequences of divergence between competition authorities in the review of international mergers. Although countries may enact and enforce their own rules, when one country prohibits a merger on the basis of theories that other countries do not follow, there is a risk that important efficiencies may be sacrificed and benefits denied to consumers world-wide. Divergent substantive standards also increase the transaction costs associated with the merger clearance process and may deter mergers that would have been pro-competitive.

Second, the SLC test can be solidly rooted in economics.

Third, the outcome of the appeal against the Commission's *Airtours/First Choice*[12] decision also shows that there may be lacunae in the current *collective dominance* test applied by the Commission. The EC Merger Regulation only prohibits transactions that create or strengthen a collective dominant position, and not merely transactions that would lead to less competition between oligopolists. From an analytical point of view, the SLC test may be more suitable to capture the competition concerns in such cases.

Fourth, the application of an SLC test seems to be based on "commonsense". If the objective of merger control is to ensure that markets remain competitive, rather than to anticipate future abuses of dominance, it would seem that a SLC based test is to be preferred above the dominance test of article 2(3) of the EC Merger Regulation.

Arguments in favour of the retention of the current dominance test. Notwithstanding that the fact that the SLC test would generally appear to be a more suitable standard by which to review mergers and acquisitions, the prevailing view questions whether the benefits of replacing the current dominance test with an SLC test are sufficient to counterbalance the adverse results that would follow such a change.

Some arguments in favour of the retention of the current dominance test:

1. The dominance test has a long antecedence in EC competition law.
2. The European Commission has now generated a considerable amount of decision-making practice.
3. Many EC Member States have adopted the "dominance" concept as the substantive test.

It is further argued that the current wording of the EC Merger Regulation's substantive test leaves enough scope for incorporating an analysis of whether appropriately substantiated efficiencies are likely to counterbalance any potential anti-competitive effects that might otherwise follow from a reportable transaction. In addition, there is sufficient scope within the tests as now written in the EC Merger Regulation to incorporate the central elements of the SLC test into the Commission's analysis. Whatever test is applied, however, the Commission's and NCAs' retention of more economists to help ensure that their decisions are underpinned by rigorous economic analysis would be welcome.

5. Are the procedural and judicial safeguards adequate to protect parties from abuse of power by the competition authorities? How does the law of your country compare to EC law in this respect?

As will be further analysed under question 6 below, it is important to emphaise that the enforcement of Belgian competition law is built upon a dualistic structure. Investigation and decision-making are strictly separated.[13]

6. Below a number of questions relating to domestic law which may assist in a comparative analysis.

a. Please provide an overview of the structure and main features of the relevant domestic legislation and the institutional framework (who enforces it)? It may be helpful with some information about the role of private rights of action.

Genesis of the 1991 Belgian Competition Act. The Law of 5 August 1991 on the Protection of Economic Competition ("the 1991 Competition Act") entered into force on 1 April 1993[14] and replaced the Law of 27 May 1960 on Protection against the Abuse of Economic Power ("the 1960 Competition Act").[15] The 1960 Competition Act contained no general prohibition of anti-competitive agreements or concerted practices, comparable to Article 81 EC Treaty. As is apparent from its title, the 1960 Competition Act was based instead on a concept of limited intervention: the Belgian authorities only aimed to control the abusive exercise of economic power. The underlying policy was to allow cartels and concentrations, on the basis that they were necessary for Belgian industry to compete with a generally fiercer competition from abroad.

The changed philosophy vis-à-vis competition law of the 1991 Competition Act is very well reflected in the preparatory works. In 1960, the legislator was very concerned about the risks of a stringent competition policy on the ability of Belgian industry to compete abroad. In 1991, the legislator considered a general competition regime necessary to guarantee the right for industry to carry out its activities on the market of its choice within clear and precise limits and to create a framework for the beneficial effects of competition on the price and quality of products.

The 1991 Competition Act was substantially amended by two Acts of 26 April 1999.[16] To a large extent, the amendments were intended to remedy the inadequate functioning of the institutions established by the 1991 Competition Act. Another objective of the amendments was to make the enforcement of the 1991 Competition Act more balanced. Until the 1999 amendments, the Belgian competition authorities devoted most of their energy to the investigation of concentrations, giving relatively little attention to the investigation of restrictive practices. The 1999 amendments were introduced to change this situation. The amendments entered into force gradually between 27 April 1999 and 1 October 1999[17] and a consolidated version of the 1991 Competition act was later published in the *Belgian State Gazette*.[18]

Institutional framework. One of the original institutional features of the 1991 Competition Act is the dualism between the Competition Service and the Competition Council.[19] The decision-making process is in the hands of the Competition Council, an independent administrative court, or its Chairman. The Competition Service investigates competition cases, monitors the compliance with decisions taken by the Competition Council and acts as the latter's secretariat.[20]

The Competition Service and the Unit of Reporters. The Competition Service is a department within the Belgian Ministry of Economic Affairs. In 1999, it was reinforced with a unit of reporters, a newly created body of independent officials.[21] It is envisaged that four reporters will be designated.[22] The unit of reporters leads the investigation of competition cases and determines the order in which files shall be dealt with. They can give orders to the staff of the Competition Service, for example to carry out an investigation on which the final report (comparable to the statement of objections of the European Commission) will be based.

In order to allow the unit of reporters and the Competition Service to properly fulfil their investigatory duties, the Unit of Reporters has broad powers of investigation, including the right to issue binding requests for information and search warrants. Similarly, reporters are entrusted with all investigations into interim measures. Additionally, reporters are responsible for the drafting of investigation reports and their submission to the Competition Council.[23]

The Unit of Reporters instructs the Competition Service to carry out an investigation with regard to a particular case. The Competition Service prepares a report which is submitted to the Unit of Reporters. This report will be the basis for the statement of objections prepared by the Unit of Reporters.

The Competition Council. The Competition Council is an administrative tribunal with powers of decision-making, proposal and advice. It consists of twenty members, including a Chairman and a Vice-Chairman (both selected within the judiciary), eight members comprised of magistrates, members of the bar with a seniority of more than ten years, or persons lecturing law at an EC university and ten members appointed on the basis their proficiency in competition matters. Members are appointed for a period of six years.[24] Four members, including the Chairman and the Vice-Chairman, fulfil their tasks on a full time basis.[25]

The Competition Council receives all notifications relating to restrictive competition practices or negative clearances, establish the existence of restrictive practices, close a file, clear or prohibit concentrations, and impose fines and periodic penalty payments.[26]

Additionally, the Competition Council has the power to propose to the Minister of Economic affairs the adoption of block exemptions.[27] The Competition Council must also draw up an annual report on the application of the Competition Act.[28]

The Chairman of the Competition Council has certain prerogatives. The Chairman may order interim measures in cases which are under investigation[29] and can impose fines and periodic penalty payments in certain cases.[30] The Chairman may also take general or sectoral inquiries.[31] For each investigation, it is the Chairman who decides on the confidential treatment of documents and the possible non-disclosure of certain documents for reasons of business secrecy.[32]

The Competition Commission. The Competition Commission is a committee forming part of the Central Council for the Economy and is composed of representatives of employers and employees in industry. It has only advisory powers and plays no formal role in the decision making process.[33] The Competition Commission acts on its own initiative or at the request of the government or the Competition Council.

b. What kind of transactions are caught? Are joint ventures caught? What are the jurisdictional thresholds? Is it difficult to identify with sufficient certainty whether a filing is in fact required under national law? Are foreign-to-foreign mergers caught?

The notion of a concentration. Article 9, §1 of the 1991 Competition Act provides that a concentration occurs where:

- two previously independent undertakings merge; or
- an undertaking or a person already controlling an undertaking acquires direct or indirect control over the whole or parts of another undertaking;

Article 9, §2 of the 1991 Competition Act specifies that joint ventures performing, on a lasting basis, all the functions of an autonomous economic entity (the so-called "full-function joint ventures") constitute a concentration within the meaning of the Competition Act.[34] However, full-function joint ventures between undertakings which remain independent and which could lead to co-ordination of the behaviour of the parent companies are also assessed under article 2 of the Competition Act. Joint ventures that do not result in the creation of a full-function joint venture are not governed by the merger control procedure, but instead are reviewed exclusively under article 2 of the 1991 Competition Act.

This definition of concentration is similar to the definition under the EC Merger Regulation.

Control is defined as the power to exercise a decisive influence on the activities of the other undertaking, having regard to all factual and legal circumstances. For example, control is found to exists if an undertaking has:

- The ownership or right to use all or part of the assets of the other undertaking; and/or
- Rights or contracts which provide it with decisive influence on the composition and voting decisions of the organs of an undertaking.

Jurisdictional thresholds. Concentrations must be notified if the undertakings concerned have a combined turnover in Belgium of 40 million euro and at least two of the undertakings concerned have a turnover in Belgium of at least 15 million euro.[35]

The turnover test is replaced by the following test in relation to banks and insurance companies:[36]

- for banks: a test based on one-tenth of the total of the balance sheet; and
- for insurance companies: a test based on the value of the issued gross premiums.

Recent case law of the Competition Council seems to indicate that the relevant criteria for the geographical allocation of turnover is either the place of performance of the contract for the provision of services or the place where the product is sold, in case of sale.[37] This differs from the approach adopted by the EC Commission that traditionally considers that the location of turnover is determined by the location of the customer at the time of the transaction.[38]

Territorial application. The Belgian provisions on merger control apply to all concentrations between undertakings that meet the specified turnover thresholds in Belgium. This means that the Competition Act will apply, even in case of a merger of two foreign undertakings which either have subsidiaries in Belgium or even merely exporting to Belgium, if the turnover in Belgium of such undertakings exceeds the specified thresholds.

c. Is the filing mandatory or voluntary? Who is responsible for filing? What is involved in the preparation of a filing? What are the deadlines for filing? What are the waiting periods and does implementation of the transaction have to be suspended?

Mandatory notification. Notification of concentrations is mandatory where the above turnover thresholds are exceeded. The concentration must be notified to the Belgian Competition Council within one month of the signing of the agreement, publication of the purchase offer, the takeover or the acquisition of control. Parties may notify a draft agreement.

Procedure. An investigation by the Unit of Reporters is initiated upon notification by the parties; upon request of the Competition Council, acting *ex officio* or pursuant to a complaint by a third party; upon request of another government department; or upon request of the Court of Appeal in cases where the Court has been requested to give a preliminary ruling in matters pending before the Civil Courts involving a competition issue.

The Unit of Reporters must commence its investigation immediately upon receipt of a complete notification, or if the notification is incomplete, as soon as complete information is received. After having completed its investigation, and within 1 month after receipt of the complete notification, the Unit should submit its report, with a proposed decision, to the Competition Council. At least 15 days before the hearing by the Competition Council, the Unit should send a copy of the report to the notifying parties. Interested parties have a right to be heard by the Competition Council.

The Competition Council must issue a reasoned decision within 45 days after receipt of a complete notification that either the transaction falls within the scope of the 1991 Competition Act or that the transaction does not fall within the scope of the 1991 Competition Act.

If the transaction falls within the scope of the 1991 Competition Act, the Competition Council can:

a. Decide to declare the concentration admissible. The notifying parties can, until a decision has been taken by the Competition Council, change the conditions of the concentration. In that case, the Competition Council will take a decision on the thus modified concentration. If the notifying parties together control less than 25% of the relevant market, the concentration is declared admissible; or
b. Decide that serious doubts exist as to the admissibility of the concentration, and order the Unit of Reporters to start a second phase investigation.

If the Competition Council does not issue one of these decisions within 45 days, the merger is deemed admissible. If the Competition Council requests a further investigation, it must issue a final decision within a maximum period of 60 days from the date of the decision to start such investigation, failing which the merger is deemed admissible. The Competition Council may decide to declare the merger admissible subject to certain conditions and/or the acceptance of commitments by the notifying parties.

It is important to note that the first and second stage investigation deadlines can be extended upon explicit request by the parties, and maximum for the duration suggested by them.

Information required. The notification form CONC/C–1 requires both the acquired and acquiring parties to provide information and documents relevant to the transaction's potential anti-competitive effects, including a signed copy of the agreement; the last audited annual accounts; a copy of the by-laws and studies and reports which were drafted for the purposes of the transaction, analysing market shares, competition, potential sales growth, etc. The notifying parties should file ten confidential versions and one non-confidential version of the notification form CONC/C-1.

d. What are the issues and possible sanctions involved in closing before clearance? What is the timetable for clearance and can it be speeded up?

Sanctions. Generally, until the Competition Council has adopted a clearance decision, the parties are only permitted to take those measures to implement the concentration which result from the concentration as such and (i) are reversible and/or (ii) do not permanently alter the structure of the market. The Competition Council may impose a daily penalty ("dwangsom" or "astreinte") of up to 250,000 BEF on each of the undertakings concerned in case it decides to order the divestiture of companies merged without its prior approval. In addition, the Competition Council may impose the following fines:

A fine of up to 10% of the turnover of each of the undertakings concerned if prior to obtaining the Competition Council's decision, the parties took measures which affected the irreversibility of the merger or changed the market structure in a permanent way or the parties did not comply with a decision prohibiting the merger.

A fine of 20,000 to 1 million BEF (495.79 to 24,789.35 Euro) if a merger that falls under the Act has not been pre-notified, if the parties intentionally or negligently gave false or misleading information in a notification, or if they provided incomplete information or obstructed the investigation process.

Timetable. The procedure has been explained above. It is important to know that the Competition Council is prepared to speed up the procedure upon request of the notifying parties and taking into consideration the the particular circumstances of a case.

e. Are there any special rules applicable to public takeover bids?

The treatment of public takeover bids under the 1991 Competition Act mirrors that under the EC Merger Regulation. The implementation of a public bid is exempted from the prohibition against implementing an intended concentration before notification and a subsequent period of four weeks has passed, provided that the Competition Council is notified immediately and the acquiring party does not exercise its voting rights.

f. What is the substantive test for clearance?

The principal test as to whether or not the concentration will be declared admissible is similar to the test under the EC Merger Regulation. Article 10 §3 of the 1991 Competition Act provides that concentrations have to be declared admissible if they do not create or strengthen a dominant position as a result of which effective competition would be significantly impeded in the national market or in a substantial part thereof.

Article 10 §2 of the 1991 Competition Act specifies the criteria which the Competition Council may take into account in its assessment. These criteria are: the necessity to maintain and develop effective competition on the national market, on the basis of market structure and actual or potential competition, the market position of the undertakings concerned, their economic and financial power, the position of suppliers and customers, barriers to entry, the evolution of supply and demand, the consumer interest and possible pro-competitive efficiencies.

In the case of a structural joint venture, possible co-ordination between the parent companies will be assessed under article 2 of the 1991 Competition Act. Article 10, §5 of the 1991 Competition Act sets out, in terms identical to those of Article 2, §4 of the EC Merger Regulation, the basis of the Competition Council's assessment.

g. To what extent are non-competition clauses relevant to the review process?

Before the 1999 amendments, article 10, §3 of the 1991 Competition Act provided that concentrations which were found to create or reinforce a dominant position on the Belgian market, could nevertheless be authorised by the Competition Council where the latter had ascertained that their contribution to the improvement of production or distribution, the economic or technical progress or the improvements in the market structure outhweighed their negative impact on competition. In its evaluation, the Competition Council had to take account the general economic interest, the competitiveness of the economic sectors involvedcompared with international competition and the interests of the consumer.

This provision was abolished in 1999 and the "article 10, §3 test" is now replaced ith a broader test. Article 10, §6 of the 1991 Competition Act now provides that where the public interest so justifies, the Council of Ministers may, *ex officio* or upon request of the parties, clear a transaction that was declared inadmissible by the Competition Council. Also, the Council of Ministers may decide to lift in whole or in part the conditions and obligations imposed by the Competition Council.

h. Is it possible to remedy competition issues?

Modification of the conditions of the concentration. Article 33, §2, 1(a) of the Competition Act provides that the notifying parties may, at any stage during the first phase of the procedure, modify the conditions of the concentration. This possibility was included in the Competition Act in

1999. This modification was very important since prior to the insertion of that provision, the Competition Council only had the possibility either to approve the concentration unconditionally when there were no serious doubts as to its admissibility, or to open a second phase procedure in case there were serious doubts as to its admissibility. This explains why the Competition Council refused conditional clearance after the first phase of the procedure. In De Post/NV Hagefin/R. Ketels/A. Boodts, the Competition Service had proposed to approve a concentration subject to certain conditions.[39] The Competition Council refused to impose conditions and approved the concentration unconditionally.

The 1991 Competition Act does not provide for a time-limit as to when the notifying parties may modify the conditions of the concentration. In principle they may do so until the Competition Council has taken a final decision. This would imply that the notifying parties are allowed to modify the concentration even at the final hearing before the Competition Council. This would give the Competition Council practically no time to study the proposal of the notifying parties. It would have been better therefore to extend the first phase investigation under these circumstances and to oblige the notifying parties to propose their modifications to the Competition Council within a certain time-limit after the notification of the concentration. A possible solution under the current provisions of the Competition Act is that the notifying parties ask the Competition Council to extend the deadline of the first phase investigation in accordance with article 33, §3 of the Competition Act.[40]

Neither the EC Merger Regulation initially provided the European Commission with the necessary powers to impose conditions after a first phase investigation. This did not prevent the European Commission of doing so in practice. It was argued therefore that the acceptance of conditions during the first phase of the procedure was "illegal".[41] The EC Merger Regulation now explicitly provides that the European Commission may impose conditions during the first phase of the procedure.[42]

Conditions, obligations and commitments. Article 34, §1 of the Competition Act provides that the Competition Council is allowed to attach conditions and obligations to its clearance decision but only after a *second phase investigation. The possibility for* the notifying parties to modify the conditions of the concentration (see above) could serve as a kind of "substitute" since the Competition Council could ask the notifying parties to modify the concentration. Obviously, the Council would not be able to impose these modifications as a condition for approval of the concentration.

i. What are the typical steps during the investigation? What rights do

complainants have? What publicity is given to the process? What are the opportunities for judicial review?

In practice, similar to the European Commission, the Belgian competition authorities attach considerable importance to observations made by third parties. In its market testing of an notified transaction, the Unit of Reporters requests information from customers, suppliers, and competitors concerning the relevant markets and the transaction. After notification, the Competition Council publishes an announcement in the *Belgian Official Gazette*. Accordingly, third parties with direct interests may submit comments on the proposed transaction.

After having completed its investigation, and within 1 month after receipt of the complete notification, the Unit should submit its report, with a proposed decision, to the Competition Council. At least 15 days before the hearing by the Competition Council, the Unit should send a copy of the report to the notifying parties. Interested parties have a right to be heard by the Competition Council.

The Competition Council must issue a reasoned decision within 45 days after receipt of a complete notification that either the transaction falls within the scope of the 1991 Competition Act or that the transaction does not fall within the scope of the 1991 Competition Act.

Decisions of the Competition Council are published in the *Belgian Official Gazette* and on the Competition Council's website.

Judicial review. The decisions of the Competition Council are subject to appeal before the Brussels Court of Appeal. Such appeals do not have a suspensory effect. Appeals must be filed within 30 days of the publication of the decision in the *Belgian Official Gazette* or its notification to the parties concerned. This appeal may be filed by the notifying parties, by the Minister for Economic Affairs and by any interested third party which has requested to be heard by the Competition Council.

Furthermore, if the "general interest" so requires, the Council of Ministers ("Ministerraad" or "Conseil des Ministres") may, *ex officio* or upon request of the parties, clear a transaction that was declared inadmissible by the Competition Council. Also, the Council of Ministers may decide to lift in whole or in part the conditions and obligations imposed by the Competition Council.

In its assessment, the Council of Ministers will take into account the general interest, national security and the competitiveness of the industries concerned, while bearing in mind international competition, consumer interests and employment.

The Council of Ministers must take a decision within 30 days of notification of the Competition Council's decision. If the Council of Ministers has not taken a decision within this deadline, it is deemed not to have authorised the transaction.

An appeal against the decision by the Council of Ministers is possible before the Council of State ("Raad van State" or "Conseil d'Etat") within 30 days of the notification of the decision or its publication in the *Belgian Official Gazette*. Such appeals do not have a suspensory effect. If the Council of State decides to annul the Council of Minister's decision, the Council of Ministers can take a new decision within a further 30 days.

j. What are the enforcement powers? How does administrative and civil sanctions compare with the EC regime? And what are the criminal sanctions, and are they used?

Powers of investigation. Article 23 of the 1991 Competition Act gives the Unit of Reporters wide-ranging powers of investigation. In general, the Reporters have the power to collect information, receive dispositions and all written and oral statements, and can be informed of the content of all documents or items of information (including digitally stored data) which they consider necessary for the performance of their duties, irrespective of who is holding them. They are entitled to make copies thereof and gather information on the spot. Besides actively searching for information, the Reporters are also entitled to appoint experts and to determine their advisory tasks.

Reporters will initiate the investigation either on their own initiative or at the request of the undertakings concerned, a complainant, the Minister for Economic Affairs or the Minister for Small and Medium-sized Enterprises, supervisory authorities (e.g. in the banking or insurance sector) or the Competition Council. In order to respond adequately to preliminary questions raised by the national courts, the Court of Appeal in Brussels may also request investigations by the Unit of Reporters.

The two most important investigative tools are written requests for information and "on the spot" searches.

Written requests for information. Written requests for information must mention the legal basis and purpose of the request. As under EC competition law, the addressee is not legally obliged to respond to such a request. However, if the undertaking is uncooperative, either by not respecting the time limit or by giving incomplete, inaccurate or misleading information, the Unit of reporters may issue a decision which requires the undertaking concerned to reply to the request for information. In case of incomplete, inaccurate or misleading replies the failure to respect the time-limits, the Competition Council can impose a fine between 495 euro to 24,800 euro.

"On the spot" searches. "On the spot" searches can take place between 5 am and 6 pm in the premises of the undertakings concerned, and at the domicile of directors, managers and other employees. The Reporters can also search the offices and domicile of persons, internal or external, responsible for the commercial, accounting, administrative, fiscal and financial management of the undertakings concerned. In the latter case, and for all searches of domiciles, the Reporters will need to be in the possession of a warrant issued in advance by an investigating magistrate. If the Reporters have reasons to believe that the documents or other relevant information may be found at other premises, they are similarly entitled to search these other places. Under all circumstances, the officials must have a written warrant issued by the Unit of reporters and indicating the object and purpose of their assignment. On the spot searches (the so-called "dawn raids") are typically unannounced.

In pursuing their assignment, the officials will make copies of the documents in which they are interested. However, the 1991 Competition Act also entitles them to seize items and seal property. The duration of seizing items and sealing properties has been limited to 48 hours. In the accomplishment of their task, the officials may request police assistance.

All findings are officially recorded. Legal privilege is recognised under the same principles as under EC competition law.

Criminal sanctions. Criminal sanctions may be imposed upon natural persons. The criminal sanctions provided for in the 1991 Competition Act relate to the inappropriate use or disclosure of documents or information received under the provisions of the 1991 Competition Act. Such practices may be punished with a criminal fine of between 2,48 to 248 euro and/or a jail sentence between two months and five years.[43] Article 44 of the 1991 Competition Act does not specify the addressees of criminal sanctions. It could, therefore, apply to all entities involved in the procedure under the Competition Act, including the parties. Criminal sanctions can also be imposed in case of a violation of Article 23 §3 of the 1991 Competition Act ("on-the-spot-verifications") and of decisions referred to in Article 51 of the 1991 Competition Act ("blocking statutes").

k. Do the authorities co-operate with other antitrust authorities?

The Belgian competition authorities co-operate with other EC competition authorities through the network of European Competition Authorities, as well as the Advisory Committee. They also have regular contacts with other competition authorities and they participate in international fora such as the OECD and the WTO and the International Competition Network ("ICN").

l. Are there also rules on foreign investment, special sectors or other relevant approvals?

For an answer to these questions, the reader is referred to the analysis under questions 7 and 9 below.

m. Are there current proposals to change the legislation?

Pending proposals. There are currently two proposals pending to amend the 1991 Competition Act.

One proposal is aimed at establishing an exception for certain liberal professions with regard to the scope of application of the Competition Act by introducing a so-called "general interest exception".[44]

Another proposal is aimed at amending the notification thresholds for concentrations and to reduce the investigation period for concentrations. [45] The Bill refers to the current turnover thresholds, which are too low with the consequence that too many concentrations have to be notified without impact on the Belgian market. The Bill therefore proposes to increase the current turnover thresholds from respectively 40 million euro and 15 million euro to 100 million euro and 40 million euro. The investigation period would be reduced to 30 days as in most other EC Member States.

Reform of the merger control regime. There is currently a proposal pending that would substantially amend the merger control regime in Belgium. The proposal has been submitted to the Competition Council by the Minister for Economic Affairs for an official advice. It is too early to comment on the text of this proposal. Suffice it to say that the system would be modelled on the French merger control system.

III. COMPANY LAW AND FINANCIAL MARKET REGULATORY REGIME[46]

7. What will you identify as the main obstacles to takeovers where a company from your jurisdiction is either bidder or target and the other company is from another?

1. A company from another EU jurisdiction wishes to take over a Belgian company.

a. Barriers resulting from the corporate organisation of the target company. Some corporate forms result in a more difficult takeover. This is for example the case for a private limited company (*"besloten vennootschap met beperkte aansprakelijkheid/société privée à responsabilité limitée"*) or a partnership limited by shares ("*commanditaire vennootschap op aandelen/société en commandite par actions*"). In such companies, the director can be appointed in the Articles of Association, which makes his removal difficult. In co-operative companies ("*coöperatieve vennootschap/société coopérative*") shareholders can not be removed unless some specific enumerated reasons are fulfilled.

Private limited companies and co-operative companies only have registered shares, making it impossible to acquire shares in an anonymous manner.

b. Barriers resulting from the Articles of Association.
The obstacles to a takeover can be diverse and depend mainly on the Articles of Association of the target company.

First, the Articles of Association may set forth restrictions to the transferability of the shares. Pre-emption rights, take along clauses, rights of first refusal, approval rights and stand still provisions are common in Belgian companies.[47][48] However, the above mentioned restrictions will never be set forth in the Articles of Associations of listed companies.[49] Often major shareholders of listed companies have entered into a shareholders' agreement containing such provisions.

Companies can issue non voting shares giving right to a preferential dividend, which makes a takeover less interesting for a bidder[50]. Bonus shares can also be issued to protect the company against hostile takeovers. The Articles of Association of the company determine the rights and obligations of the holders of the bonus shares. Multiple voting rights per bonus shares are impossible. No more votes may be conferred to the issued bonus shares than one half of the number vested in the aggregate shares which represent the capital of the company. Furthermore, the votes of the holders of the bonus shares may not be counted at voting for more that 2/3rd of the number of votes cast for the shares which represent the capital[51].

The Articles of Association can limit the number of votes per shareholder[52]. It is not possible to create shares with multiple voting rights.

Specific majorities with respect to decisions, enumerated in the Articles of Association of the company, to be taken by the board of directors or general meeting of shareholders are also common (for example regarding the appointment of the board of directors, to take decisions related to the financing of the company). The Articles of Association can attach veto rights or special rights to the different categories of shares issued by the company (for example, a preferential right to dividends, the right to propose candidate for the nomination as a director).

c. Barriers resulting from the shareholding of the target.
A very efficient barrier protecting a company from a takeover is the incor-

poration of a holding company. The majority shareholders transfer their shares to this holding company, which is controlling the target company. Without the co-operation of this holding company it is impossible to acquire the control of the target company.

The same result is achieved by the incorporation of a foundation ("*administratiekantoor*"). Again the ownership of the shares is transferred to this foundation. The foundation issues certificates or depository receipts. The holders of these share certificates will have right to the financial and patrimonial rights and obligations related to the certified shares. Foundations are most of the time incorporated for tax reason and estate planning. It is not uncommon that the Articles of Association of such foundation limit the right to exchange depository receipts for underlying shares.

Control in a company can be exercised in an indirect manner through a cascade of companies. It may be difficult for a bidder to know who is actually controlling the target company. Transparency of the shareholding may be an issue in such case.

The target company may have issued "poisoned warrants" in favour of the majority shareholders in the past. These warrants can be exercised in case of a takeover[53]. By exercising the warrants, the shares acquired by the bidder will be diluted.

Shareholders' agreements can also provide in a shareholders' syndicate. The shareholders, which are part of this syndicate, will act through the president of the syndicate and will follow the common position of the syndicate. Essential to the syndicate are voting agreements between its members.

d. Barriers resulting from the position of the board of directors of the target company

The board of directors of the target company can decide on the hostile nature of the takeover and can try to frustrate the takeover. Since the board of directors generally represents the majority shareholders, the actions of the board of directors of the target will be determined by mutual agreement amongst these shareholders.

The board of directors can for example reduce the available shares by a redemption by the company of its own shares[54] or by building cross shareholdings with related companies[55]. The shares to be acquired by a bidder may be diluted by a capital increase of the company within the limits of the authorised capital[56].

Within certain limits, the board of directors of the target company can decide to proceed to the sale of the most attractive assets of the company. In some cases, put- or call option agreements are entered into with a third party or shareholder which can be exercised in the event of the takeover[57].

Often the board of directors will search for an alternative bidder ("white knight") if it considers the takeover not in the interest of the company.

e. Barriers related to the activities of the target company

Agreements with customers or suppliers frequently contain change of control clauses. This is also the case of financing or loan agreements. A bidder therefor has to take into account that agreements may be cancelled as a result of the takeover of the company[58].

In certain sectors, permits are required. The shareholding of the company can be an important element in the lapsing of a permit[59].

Sometimes the management agreements with the directors of the target company set forth in substantial fees in case of a revocation of their mandate as a result of a takeover ("golden parachutes"). The bidder can revoke the mandate of the directors *ad nutum*, but will have the obligation to pay these fees to the revoked directors.

f. Administrative barriers

In principle a foreign investor does not need a specific authorisation to invest in a Belgian company. However some formalities have to be fulfilled by a foreign company prior to the takeover.

In case of a public takeover bid over a Belgian company, whether or not stock quoted, several notifications are required. If a company wants to acquire an exclusive or joint control of a Belgian company which offers or has publicly offered its securities[60], its intention must be notified to the Belgian Banking and Finance Commission at least five days before the acquisition[61]. The purchaser will have to provide evidence that there are mechanisms ensuring the equal treatment of shareholders, the full information of the shareholders, the safeguard of the interest of all shareholders and the transparency and the proper functioning of the financial market. The Belgian Banking and Finance Commission will control whether these mechanisms are sufficient and can publish its comments on the transaction when the purchaser does not comply with these comments. If a purchaser acts in breach of these mechanisms the Belgian Banking and Finance Commission can suspend the transaction and the President of the Commercial Court can order the purchaser to stop all infringements[62].

If a company A becomes holder of voting securities[63], representing 5 or more percent of the total votes of the securities of a Belgian company listed on a stock exchange within the European Union, company A must immediately notify the Belgian company and the Belgian Banking and Finance Commission thereof. This notification is also required if company A increases its existing shareholdings above the thresholds of 5, 10, 15, 20, etc. percent or when, following a divestiture, its shareholding drops below the above mentioned thresholds. When a threshold of 20% is reached, the notification must also describe the future intentions of the purchaser regarding the company. Finally an acquisition or transfer of the direct or indirect legal or actual control of a Belgian company listed on a stock exchange within the European Union must also be disclosed[64].

Some scholars allege that the work council of the Belgian target has to be informed prior to any public announcement of the takeover of the company[65]. In general the work council should be informed about the economic, financial and social consequences of the takeover of the company. The work council has no decision-making power.

When a company wants to launch a public takeover bid on a Belgian company, it will have to comply with a rigid procedure that is described in the Royal Decree of November 8, 1989. A difference is made between a voluntary (chapter II of the Royal Decree of November 8, 1989) or a mandatory takeover bid (chapter III of the Royal Decree of November 8, 1989). With respect to the voluntary takeover bid, chapter II of the Royal Decree of November 8, 1989 does not expressly mention which companies it applies to. Therefore, the procedure of chapter II of the Royal Decree of November 8, 1989 is considered to be applicable to all companies (Belgian or foreign, stocked quoted or not) launching a public takeover bid on voting securities and other securities giving a right to subscribe to, to convert into or to acquire voting securities. The Belgian regulation is applicable and the Belgian authorities are competent from the moment the aforementioned securities are scattered in the public in Belgium. So when a Belgian company is listed on a foreign stock exchange or a foreign company is listed on the Brussels stock exchange or the securities of a foreign company are scattered in the public in Belgium, the Belgian authorities are competent and will apply the Belgian regulations.

In case of an acquisition of control at a price higher than the market price (control premium), the new controlling shareholder must proceed to a mandatory takeover bid. This means he must give the public the opportunity to sell their shares at the same price (or counter performance)[66] as the foregoing transaction[67]. Chapter III of the Royal Decree of November 8, 1989 regulates the mandatory takeover bid. As distinct from the voluntary takeover bid, the mandatory takeover bid is limited to Belgian companies that publicly offer or have publicly offered their securities[68]. The procedure to be followed is a burden for the company.

In the event of an acquisition of shares through a capital increase some formalities have to be accomplished, such as the execution of a notary deed, special reports of the board of directors and, possibly, the auditor. These documents must comply with the Belgian language regulation. For foreign company this may cause an administrative discomfort.

2. A Belgian company wants to take over a company from another EU jurisdiction

In principle, the takeover will be regulated by the law of the target company. There are no specific rules regarding the takeover of a foreign company by a Belgian company, except when its shares are scattered among the Belgian public (see above).

8. Do hostile takeovers by companies from other EU jurisdictions in fact take place in your country?

Yes, but not very regularly. Since in Belgium, most shares of, even stock quoted, companies, are held by one or more majority shareholders, takeovers are negotiated with the majority shareholder(s) (and thus friendly) and afterwards followed by a mandatory or voluntary public takeover bid.

Two cases of hostile takeover bids in 1988 are at the origin of the present regulation[69]. The first is the public takeover bid from AG Groep on the shares of Assubel-Leven. The board of directors of Assubel-Leven proposed another purchaser (AGF, Cobepa, Mosane and "Groep Brussel Lambert"). Finally, the different parties reached an agreement. The second is the hostile takeover bid by the French company Cerus on the Generale Maatschappij van België. This bid was frustrated by a number of companies gathered round Suez[70].

Another example is the public takeover bid of Fortis AG on the shares of the Generale Bank. ABN AMRO Holding, a Dutch company, made a counter offer, which was considered hostile by the board of directors of the Generale Bank. Again the hostile takeover bid did not succeed[71].

Several friendly public takeovers by companies from other EU jurisdictions did succeed (for example: the takeover bid of the American Premier Parks on Walibi[72]; from Suez Lyonnaise des Eaux and the Generale Maatschappij van België on Tractebel[73]; from Ford Capital BV on Ford Motor Company (Belgium)[74]; from AXA on Royale Belge[75]).

9. To what extent are there any sectors (utilities, financial institutions) that in practice are further protected from hostile takeovers, or foreign takeovers in particular? Are there any policy statements or particular legal mechanisms that give effect to this protection, or is it a matter of informal mechanisms?

Some sectors are governed by specific regulations, which in practice protect these industries from hostile or foreign takeovers. This is, for example, the case for credit institutions, insurance companies, investment companies, the energy sector, the food and drugs industry, etc.

With respect to credit institutions, a company wanting to takeover a Belgian credit institutions, must notify the Belgian Banking and Finance Commission in advance of its intention to acquire shares, if this acquisition would result in the purchaser holding directly or indirectly at least five percent of the capital or the voting rights[76]. This notification requirement also applies if a shareholder intends to increase its existing shareholdings above 10, 15, 20, etc. percent or intends to divest, its shareholding dropping below the above mentioned thresholds. The Belgian Banking and Finance Commission may object to the transaction within three months after receiving the notification, if the potential purchaser does not have the necessary qualities for a sane and prudent management of the credit institution[77]. In certain circumstances the Belgian Banking and Finance Commission also has to approve a merger of credit institutions[78]. This approval can only be refused for reasons of sane and prudent management of the credit institution within three months from the notification of the project[79].

A similar rule applies to insurance companies[80]. Again an investor intending to acquire directly or indirectly a participation of at least 10 percent of the capital or the voting rights or any other possibility to exercise significant influence over the management of an insurance company must notify in advance the Supervisory Agency for Insurance Companies. Any increase of an existing shareholdings above the thresholds of 10, 15, 20, etc. percent or disinvestment resulting in the dropping of the shareholding below the above mentioned thresholds must also be notified. Finally, the notification requirement also applies if the insurance company becomes an affiliate of another company. The Supervisory Agency for Insurance companies may object to the acquisition within three months after the notification, if the potential purchaser does not have the necessary qualities for a sane and prudent management of the insurance company[81]. The Supervisory Agency for Insurance Companies has to approve a transfer of rights and obligations by an insurance company established in Belgium or in a non E.U. country[82].

Investment companies are subject to a similar regulation[83]. Again a notification must be made to the Belgian Banking and Finance Commission of the intention of acquiring shares in a Belgian investment company resulting in the purchaser holding directly or indirectly at least five percent of the capital or the voting rights of the investment company. This notification requirement also applies if a shareholder intends to increase its existing shareholdings above 10, 15, 20, etc. percent or intends to disinvest, its shareholding dropping below the above mentioned thresholds. The Belgian Banking and Finance Commission may object to the transaction within three months after receiving the notification, if the potential purchaser does not have the necessary qualities for a sane and prudent management of the credit institution[84]. In certain circumstances the Belgian Banking and Finance Commission also has to approve a merger of investment companies[85]. This approval can only be refused for reasons of sane and prudent management of the credit institution within 3 months from the notification of the project[86].

In the energy sector, several regulations protect the market from hostile, foreign takeovers. In case of a significant change in the shareholding of the company managing the electricity distribution system, which could jeopardise the independence of the management of the system, the Minister can, after consultation and advice, revoke the permit of this company[87]. A similar rule applies in the event of a change of control, merger or split of a company holding a permit for the construction of a installation producing electricity[88]. These principles are also applied at the Flemish level[89]. Moreover, the company managing the distribution system may not, directly or indirectly, in whatever way, hold a participation in a producer, manager of a transmission permit or intermediary or in companies associated with or linked to the aforementioned companies[90]. The Walloon Government demands that 51 percent of the securities representing the capital of a company managing the distribution system is held by the municipalities or provinces[91]. At the Brussels level a combination of both rules exists[92].

10. What are the company law techniques of completing a takeover or merger that are used in practice where one of the companies is from another EU jurisdiction? Please give particular attention to how this would differ from the usual completion of a takeover or merger where both companies are from your jurisdiction. It would be useful if you could add a comment about the consequences on the techniques used of the taxation regime and of any differential tax treatment of takeovers or mergers where one party is from another EU jurisdiction.

3. Takeover of a Belgian company by a company from another EU jurisdiction

A takeover of a Belgian company can take different forms : (i) an acquisition of shares in a private or publicly held company through the acquisition of outstanding shares or the subscription of newly issued shares (i.e. a share deal); (ii) an acquisition of assets or a business (i.e. an asset deal); (iii) a co-operation by setting-up a joint venture; or (iv) a merger (see below).

a. An acquisition of shares

In case of a share deal, there will be a transfer of shares from the moment parties agree on the shares to be transferred and the price of these shares[93]. This transfer is enforceable against third parties when the purchaser physically holds the share certificates of bearer shares[94] or the transfer of registered shares is inscribed in the shareholders' register of the company[95]. There are no specific rules applicable in case of a transfer between a Belgian and a foreign company[96].

A foreign investor can also acquire shares by subscribing a capital increase. In Belgium, shareholders have a preferential right, which implies that shares to be subscribed for cash must first be offered to the existing shareholders in proportion to the amount of the capital the shares of these shareholders represent. The current shareholders will therefore either have to waive their preferential rights or their preferential right has to be limited or restricted[97] in order to permit the investor to subscribe to a capital increase. Again, the nationality of the investor is, in principle, not relevant.

From a tax point of view, a share deal is less favourable for the purchaser because there will be no stepped-up basis for a tax deductible depreciation of the underlying assets. The capital gains realised by the seller of shares in a Belgian company are in principle tax free if they did not belong to a Belgian permanent establishment or fixed place of business of the seller. However, exception is made for the gains on shares belonging to a substantial shareholding[98] in a Belgian company[99]. A 16,5% tax is due on the actually realised capital gains in case of a sale of a substantial shareholding to a foreign company.

In the event of a contribution to the capital of the target company a registration duty of 0,5% is due on the equity contribution.

b. An acquisition of assets

In case of an asset deal, distinction is made between two ways of transferring the assets: (i) the assets are transferred under Belgian civil law concerning transfers of assets; (ii) a universality of assets[100] or a branch of activities[101] can be transferred following a specific procedure which is described at Article 760 of the Belgian Company Code. If assets are transferred under Belgian civil law, the transfer must comply with the specific regulations applicable to each of the transferred assets[102]. This is a very time consuming procedure, but, in principle, no difference must be made between a transfer between two Belgian companies and a Belgian company and a foreign company. In the second case, the Belgian Company Code has established a specific procedure regarding the transfer of a universality of assets or a branch of activity. Most of the legal doctrine argues that these specific procedures do not apply to transactions in which a foreign company is involved. The important number of practical objections related to an application of this regulation to an international transaction supports this point of view.

An asset deal is, from a tax point of view, less interesting for the seller, since the sale is subject to a capital gains tax at the normal corporate income tax rate. In the event of a transfer of real property, transfer taxes are due. For the purchaser an asset deal has the advantage of creating a possibility to depreciate the acquired business assets on a stepped-up basis. The future gains and losses can also be calculated from the new stepped-up basis.

If the purchaser has no fixed place of business in Belgium, the Belgian tax authorities may not tax its business profits. Most of the time the purchased assets will constitute a permanent establishment of the foreign company, subject to Belgian corporate income tax. The purchaser will in such event be taxed on its Belgian source or earned income.

4. Takeover of a company from another EU jurisdiction by a Belgian company

The takeover is in principle regulated by the law of the country of the target company and will be supervised by the authorities of the country of the target company. However, it becomes more complicated if the securities of the target company are listed on the stock exchange of another country or are scattered among the public in different countries. Some authorities, amongst which the Belgian Banking and Finance Commission, interpret their competencies in a broad way and consider themselves competent from the moment the securities circulate among Belgian investors.

Of course the Belgian rules and regulations fully apply to the Belgian company.

5. Cross boarder mergers

The Belgian Company Code provides in two types of mergers : a merger by acquisition[103] and a merger by incorporation[104]. These procedures are however not applicable to cross border mergers. In case of a cross border merger, one of the two companies involved will have to be winded up. The assets and liabilities of this company are then being contributed to the surviving company[105].

From a tax point of view this means that all capital gains on the assets and liabilities of the acquired company will be subject to corporate income tax and all elements of the funds of the acquired company are treated as if they were distributed.

11. A duty on listed companies to disclose capital and control structures is proposed in Issues Relating to Takeover Bids, the First Report of the High Level Group of Company Law Experts (see p 25). Would this require amendments in the legislation in your country? How would these amendments in case be implemented (in primary company law, securities law, stock exchange regulations etc.)?

The duty to disclose fully the capital and control structures of listed companies, proposed in the First Report of the High Level Group of Company Law Experts, is more far-reaching than the current disclosure obligations in Belgium.

The Law of March 2, 1989 on the publication of major shareholdings in companies listed on a stock exchange and the regulation of public takeover bids[106], the Royal Decree of May 10 ,1989 on the publication of major shareholdings in companies listed on a stock exchange and the Belgian Company Code[107] already provide in a mandatory system of disclosure of significant shareholdings for Belgian companies whose securities are listed on a stock exchange in the European Union. On a voluntary base, companies whose securities are not listed on a E.U.-stock exchange can provide in a similar system in their Articles of Association[108].

A company acquiring or disposing of a number of securities in another (private[109]) company with the effect that its shareholding exceeds or falls below the threshold of 10 percent the shares or voting rights of that other company must notify that company of such acquisition or disposal[110].

In general, the Market Rules of Euronext Brussels provide that the issuer must ensure that all necessary information and facilities are available in Belgium to enable holders of listed securities to exercise their rights[111]. The Nasdaq Europe Rule Book states that the market authority can take all actions which it deems appropriate to ensure the integrity, security and fair dealing on Nasdaq Europe and to protect investors and the public interest[112]. At all times, the equal treatment of the shareholders has to be ensured by the company[113]. Listed companies also have the obligation to disclose any information regarding the exercise of shareholder's rights or of rights connected with the holding of securities and any information regarding the rights connected with the holding of securities[114,115].

The Report of the High Level Group of Company Law Experts on Issues related to Takeover Bids of January 10, 2002 enumerates some examples of information that should be disclosed. Most of this information is already available to the public in Belgium with respect to listed companies, but requires an active search by the shareholder[116]. It might be advisable to disclose (and regroup) this information in the annual report[117] of the company. It should be noted that many holders of bearer shares do not want to disclose the size of their shareholding and only vote at the meetings of shareholders with a small number of their shares. Without a voluntary disclosure of its participation, it will be very difficult to retrieve the composition of a shareholding of a company.

12. A so called break through rule after takeover bids is another of the proposals in Issues Relating to Takeover Bids, the First Report of the High Level Group of Company Law Experts (see p 29). Would this require

amendments in the legislation in your country? How would these amendments in case be implemented (in primary company law, securities law, stock exchange regulations etc.)?

The break through rule implies that the bidder, acquiring 75% of the share capital of a company, is able to control the affairs of the company.

In Belgium, an amendment of the Articles of Association of a company requires a quorum of attendance of 50% of the capital and a majority of 75% of the voting rights in the company[118]. This majority can be reinforced in the Articles of Association of the company. It is also possible that the Articles of Association provide in voting caps making it impossible to modify the Articles of Association of the company to the majority shareholder (holding more than 75% of the voting rights)[119]. Moreover, veto rights can be granted to a category of shares, allowing this category of shares to prevent a majority shareholder to amend the Articles of Association. Articles of Association also often provide in a right of proposal of candidates for the mandate of director by a category of shares[120].

An introduction of the break through rule in the Belgian system of law would, principally, require an amendment of the Company Code.

When organisations with a shareholding of public authorities are concerned, an amendment of the specific regulations applicable to this companies will be necessary. These companies are seldom subject to the general company law or the capital market regulations. Given the diversity of such companies, it is impossible to give some general principles as to the required amendments.

13. In your view, would these two new rules as proposed have any material impact on the existing barriers to takeovers in your country (or in others as seen from your point of view)? It would be helpful if you could demonstrate the impact, or lack of it, by going through one or more recent takeover bids that failed in your country (or in some other member state, by a company from your country).

Especially the break through rule would bring along an important change in the Belgian legal system. However, the impact on the chances of success of a hostile takeover bid will be negligible. As stated before, a hostile takeover bid is mostly frustrated by the board of directors of the target company, who will either look for a white knight, either proceed to a capital increase within the aforementioned limits[121]. The directive would not prohibit these actions.

In the event of a friendly takeover, the bidder will negotiate with the majority shareholders and will seldom need to use such a procedure.

14. Below are a number of questions which may assist in a comparative analysis.

a. What are the main features of the relevant domestic takeover legislation constituting the company law and financial market regime, and who enforces it (independent regulators, regulatory bodies with appeal to ministry, stock exchange)? What is the extent of intervention by the takeover regulator(s) – to what extent does the regulator have wide or general discretions to block and play a protectionist role (for example in its capacity as approver of the offer terms/documentation)?

In Belgium, the most important regulations in this respect are the Belgian Company Code, the Royal Decree n°185, the Royal Decree of July 7, 1999, the Law of March 2, 1989 and the Royal Decree of November 8, 1989. However other financial and case law as well as the recommendations of the competent authorities have contributed to the development of the takeover regulation. The main features of this body of rules are examined below when discussing the different authorities intervening in case of a public takeover.

The Banking and Finance Commission

The Banking and Finance Commission is a public institution whose decisions are taken in complete autonomy.

The tasks of the Belgian Banking and Finance Commission can be divided into three categories: (i) the supervision of financial intermediaries (in particular the prudential supervision of credit institutions and investment firms), and the supervision of investment advice companies and exchange offices; (ii) the supervision of financial information and of the markets for financial instruments; and (iii) the supervision of undertakings for collective investment.

As a part of its task to supervise the financial information and the markets for financial instruments, the Belgian Banking and Finance Commission supervises takeovers and changes in the control of public companies.

The Belgian Banking and Finance Commission's role is not confined to a literal implementation of the laws, decrees and regulations. Even though its legal powers have been considerably extended, the Belgian Banking and Finance Commission still attaches great importance to consultation with companies and their professional associations. In addition, the Belgian Banking and Finance Commission regularly contributes to the drafting of laws and decrees on financial and economic matters. In certain legally specified cases, it must be consulted.

In order to verify whether a transaction or an activity falls within the scope of the laws and regulations whose application the Banking and Finance Commission must supervise, it may require the persons or companies concerned to provide all necessary information. The Belgian Banking and Finance Commission has the power to make on-the-spot checks to verify the accuracy of the submitted information.

All regulatory decisions taken by the Belgian Banking and Finance Commission must be submitted for approval to the Minister of Finance, and, mostly, also to the Minister of Economy. As concerns the authority or institution to which appeals against the decisions of the Belgian Banking and Finance Commission have to be submitted, a distinction has to be made between decisions taken by the Belgian Banking Commission in individual cases and in its capacity as an administrative authority. Appeals against the decisions of the Belgian Banking and Finance Commission relating to individual cases have to be brought before the Minister of Finance. Decisions taken by the Belgian Banking and Finance Commission in its capacity as an administrative authority can be appealed against with the Council of State. The members and staff of the Banking and Finance Commission are bound by a duty of professional secrecy. A breach of this duty is punishable under criminal law.

a. *Intervention of the Belgian Banking and Finance Commission in the event of a (voluntary) takeover bid*

Anyone intending to make a takeover bid must notify the Belgian Banking and Finance Commission in advance. The notification must include the price and the main terms of the bid, as well as the indication that the bid is made in compliance with the regulations. Other prescribed information, including the draft prospectus and a document certifying that the necessary funds are available, shall have to be added to the notification. The Belgian Banking and Finance Commission must publish the notification no later than the day following the date of its receipt.

In certain circumstances, the Belgian Banking and Finance Commission may suspend publication of the notification of the takeover bid for a maximum of three days. This will be the case if it considers that its terms do not comply with the regulations, or that the fixed goals of the transaction can not be achieved. In such an event, the Belgian Banking and Finance Commission must inform the President of the Commercial Court, who will decide whether the bid complies with the regulations, and whether notification of the bid can be published.

From the date of publication, the bidder and the target company are prohibited from publishing any document or from making any declaration or statement which can mislead the public. All notices, advertisements, posters and any other document disclosing the transaction to the public must be submitted for the prior approval of the Belgian Banking and Finance Commission.

The board of directors of the target company must comply with certain rules of conduct. For instance, the defensive measures which it may take to frustrate the bid are restricted once the bid has been launched[122].

A takeover bid can only be launched once a prospectus, approved by the Belgian Banking and Finance Commission, has been published. The prospectus must provide securities holders of the target with the information, necessary to make an informed judgment on the transaction. The prospectus must mention the opinion of the board of directors of the target on the bid. The approval of the prospectus does not mean that the Belgian Banking and Finance Commission takes any position with regard to the price or appropriateness of the transaction: in other words, the Belgian Banking and Finance Commission will not express an opinion as to whether or not the bid is justified from an economic point of view, or as to whether it is in the investor's interest to accept the bid.

The Belgian Banking and Finance Commission will refuse to approve a prospectus where it is of the opinion that the terms of the bid may mislead the public as to the nature of the transaction or the rights attached to the securities. The bidder may launch an appeal with the Minister of Finance against this refusal.

The prospectus will be published in the form of a brochure and will be made available free of charge by the financial agent for the transaction. In addition, the bidder must publish in one or more newspapers where the public can obtain the prospectus.

After the prospectus has been published, any subsequent information in the form of notices, advertisements, posters or other documents must previously be submitted to the Belgian Banking and Finance Commission for its approval.

The bid must remain open for no less than ten, and no more than twenty days from the date on which the prospectus is published.

Other persons interested in the target company can make a counter-bid. This and any subsequent higher bids must offer a price which exceeds the most recent bid, counter-bid or higher bid by at least 5%. A counter-bid or higher bid is subject to the same procedure as the initial bid. The draft prospectus drawn up by the counter-bidder or higher bidder is transferred to the bidder by the Belgian Banking and Finance Commission. The bidder, counter-bidder and higher bidder must be placed on an equal footing as regards the information provided by the target company[123].

Where the Belgian Banking and Finance Commission considers that the transaction harms the interests of the securities holders, it may advise the President of the Commercial Court, so that the latter may order the persons responsible to put an end to the transaction.

b. *Intervention of the Belgian Banking and Finance Commission in the event of a change of control*

Anyone intending to acquire control of a company through the systematic purchase of securities on or outside the stock exchange, whether alone or in concert with another party, must notify the Belgian Banking and Finance Commission in advance.

The notification must be accompanied with information enabling the Belgian Banking and Finance Commission to determine whether the market will be adequately informed and whehter the principle of equal treatment for all shareholders will be complied with. In order to achieve these objectives, the Belgian Banking and Finance Commission may, if necessary, apprise the person submitting the notification of any observations. If that person fails to act upon these observations, the Belgian Banking and Finance Commission may make them public.

Where a premium has been paid to acquire control the public must have an unconditional right to sell all its securities at the same conditions[124]. This right is given to the public through either a takeover bid or a share-support operation[125].

The takeover bid must be made in compliance with the procedures provided for a voluntary takeover bid. As a result, the Belgian Banking and Finance Commission must, in this case too, approve the prospectus in advance, so as to ensure that shareholders receive complete and accurate information.

c. *Intervention of the Belgian Banking and Finance Commission in the event of a squeeze out bid*

Anyone intending to make a squeeze out bid[126] must notify the Belgian Banking and Finance Commission. The notification must include a report by an independent expert, an opinion from the board of directors of the company and a draft prospectus. When apprised of a squeeze out bid, the Belgian Banking and Finance Commission will publish it, indicating at the same time where the public can obtain the expert's report free of charge.

The difference between a squeeze out bid and a takeover bid is that any security that has not been presented by the end of the squeeze out bid is deemed to have been transferred to the bidder by law. This is why any shareholder concerned may within fifteen days of the publication of the notification submit their grievances to the Belgian Banking and Finance Commission. Such grievances may, for instance, relate to the evaluation of the securities and the price offered. At the expiry of that time period, the Belgian Banking and Finance Commission may send its remarks to the bidder and to the other parties concerned. If these remarks are not taken into account by the bidder, the Belgian Banking and Finance Commission may refuse to approve the prospectus. Where the Belgian Banking and Finance Commission considers that the transaction harms the interests of the holders of the securities, it may also request the President of the Commercial Court to order the persons responsible to put an end to the transaction[127].

The prospectus may only be published after it has been approved by the Belgian Banking and Finance Commission.

As soon as the squeeze out bid is notified to the Belgian Banking and Finance Commission, the bidder may no longer acquire securities under conditions differing from those of the bid, unless the bidder extends those conditions to all remaining minority shareholders.

Euronext Brussels

Euronext was created in September 2000 by the merger of the exchanges in Amsterdam, Brussels and Paris in response to the growing demand from the market, the political environment being favourable to further consolidation in the European capital market, and the desire to capitalise on greater liquidity and lower costs resulting from the introduction of the euro.

Euronext aims to provide a fair and orderly market with built-in safeguards for the quality of price formation. Members of Euronext are subject to a "rule book" including rules on how brokers should trade and how issuers should deal with price-sensitive information. Euronext, through its exchange operators, identifies, analyses and reports violations of the rules and regulations to the responsible authorities. Depending on the circumstances, it may intervene itself or report violations to the regulators.

Important in this regard is rule 3403/2 of the Market Rules of Euronext Brussels[128] which provides that the "*issuer shall ensure that all necessary information and facilities are available in Belgium to enable holders of listed securities to exercise their rights*".

In particular, any issuer shall have to disclose to the market all corporate information and documents, information regarding the listed securities, periodic financial information and price sensitive information required to be disclosed under the Royal Decree of July 3, 1996 on periodical information to be disclosed by issuers whose financial instruments are listed on the first market and new market of a stock exchange and the Royal Decree of July 3, 1996 on occasional information to be disclosed by issuers whose financial instruments are listed on the first market and new market of a stock exchange, at such a time and in such a manner as prescribed by these Royal Decrees.

A listed company will have to release all occasional information within the meaning of the Royal Decree of July 3, 1996 on occasional Information.

The control of that information is vested with the market authority of Euronext Brussels. This control is exercised *a posteriori*, i.e. the information must not be sent to the market authority prior to being released.

Two types of information are deemed to be occasional and have to be made public without delay : information regarding the exercise of the rights of the holders of securities of the company (Article 4 §1, 1°,2°,3°)[129] (i) and sensitive information[130] (ii).

When the given information does not conform to the rules as laid down in the Royal Decree of July 3, 1996 on occasional information, the market authority is entitled to require every necessary (additional) information from the company[131]. The market authority may notify to the company that : it does not furnish sufficient information to allow the public to properly appreciate all aspects concerning the company which are relevant to the public (i); it does not respect the required timing of publication (ii); or it does not treat its shareholders equally (iii)[132]. Then the market authority invites the company to make any observations on this notification within a determined period. If, after the expiry of this period and if the observations do not satisfy the market authority, the latter is entitled to publish this information on the account of the company.

The market authority can also require the publication of some specific information[133]. If the company does not publish the requested information, the market authority is entitled to publish it on the account of the company.

The market authority has the right to prescribe, as a sanction, that any information to be published be communicated to the market authority prior to its release to the public in order to exercise preventive control[134].

When the provided information is constantly insufficient, the market authority is entitled to suspend or radiate the listed shares from the quotation. When the market authority suspends the listed shares, this may not last more than two days.

However, the market authority may exempt the company from publishing any sensitive information if the publication of some data may prejudice its legitimate interests[135].

The non-compliance with the provisions on the Royal Decree of July 3, 1996 on occasional information is criminally sanctioned[136].

Nasdaq Europe

Nasdaq Europe is a pan-European exchange, which is independent from any national market place. The supervision of Nasdaq Europe is organised according to a two-tier structure. The first-line control is in the hands of the Nasdaq Europe market authority and the second-line control over the market authority and its procedures is entrusted to the Belgian Banking and Finance Commission[137].

The exchange is subject to the same legal framework as Euronext Brussels[138]. Further, the Nasdaq Europe Rule Book expressly provides that the market authority is competent for assuring the transparency, integrity and security of Nasdaq Europe, the equal treatment of the holders of the admitted financial instruments and the dissemination of information to the public[139]. In particular, the market authority has a right of injunction, which implies that it may order anyone to put an end to practices which disturb its functioning. This may, for example, be the case because the equal treatment and information of the shareholders and investors is jeopardised[140]. The market authority has a broad discretionary authority with respect to the continuing requirements related to the listed financial instruments[141].

Supervisory Agency for Insurance Companies

A public agency, the Supervisory Agency for Insurance Companies was introduced by the Act of 9 July 1975 regarding the supervision of insurance businesses. The Supervisory Agency for Insurance Companies is also responsible for supervising mortgage companies, pension funds and insurance brokers.

The Supervisory Agency for Insurance Companies examines, on a yearly basis, the overall financial situation of each insurance business to ascertain whether the firm is able to meet its insurance business commitments and liabilities. In order to achieve this objective, the financial supervision is aimed at ensuring that an insurance business is managed in a sound and prudent manner, more especially by examining the shareholding aspect. As a consequence thereof, any person holding or seeking to acquire 10% or more of shares of an insurance firm must notify the Supervisory Agency for Insurance Companies accordingly.

The Agency also ensures that insurance businesses comply with all regulations applicable to the aforementioned companies by sending out inspectors, who have the authority to examine the company's documents at its registered office.

The Agency is charged with the approval of (i) documentation in respect of Belgian and foreign firms (outside the European Economic Area); (ii) documentation concerned with insurance business carried on in Belgium by non-Belgian EEA firms ; and (iii) portfolio transfers, mergers, etc..

The Supervisory Agency for Insurance Companies is also responsible for registering insurance brokers and those companies in charge of distribution in insurance firms. The Supervisory Agency for Insurance Companies ensures that with regard to brokers, the legal requirements imposed on them are observed: professional knowledge, financial skill, professional integrity and civil liability cover.

In the event of a takeover of a company subject to the control of the Supervisory Agency for Insurance Companies, the latter shall intervene in the procedure.

b. Are there restrictions on a board taking action to frustrate a bid that has been made? When do the relevant restrictions start to apply – earlier than a formal announcement/filing of a bid? To what extent can shareholders approve the taking of frustrating action in advance of any bid?

There is no specific procedure concerning hostile takeover bids. However, from the moment a board of directors has been informed of a takeover bid by the Belgian Banking and Finance Commission, the board may not[142] :

(i) increase the capital by non-cash contributions or by cash contributions with restriction or exclusion of shareholders' pre-emptive rights;
(ii) issue securities with voting rights or warrants giving rights thereto, unless they are first offered to the shareholders on a *pro rata* basis;
(iii) adopt resolutions or carry out transactions which would materially affect the company's assets or liabilities, or enter into obligations without effective consideration.

These restrictions do not apply earlier than the formal notification of the bid by the Belgian Banking and Finance Commission to the board of directors.

The above does not apply to transactions that are already sufficiently advanced before the board is being informed of the bid by the Belgian Banking and Finance Commission. This means that the board of directors can pursue with:

(i) the performance of obligations validly entered into prior to the notification of the Belgian Banking and Finance Commission[143];
(ii) a capital increase, provided such increase has been authorised no longer than three years earlier by a majority of 75 percent of the shareholders, and provided that the securities issued at such occasion are fully paid-up and do not exceed 10 percent of the company's capital prior to the issue and provided that the issue price is at least equal to the bid price[144];
(iii) the acquisition of the company's own shares provided that such acquisition has been authorised no longer than three years before by a majority of 75 percent of the shareholders and that the board has established that the transaction is necessary to prevent an imminent serious prejudice to the company[145];
(iv) the sale of the company's "crown jewels", provided that the granting of

such purchase option to a third party is approved by the shareholders' meeting and that an abstract of the decision of the shareholders' meeting is filed with the clerk of the commercial court[146];

(v) the application of an approval clause in the Articles of Association of the target company or in a notarial deed concerning the issue of convertible bonds or bonds with warrants, provided that the refusal of approval of the transaction is based on a long-term and non-discriminatory application of the approval clause and the approval clause has been notified to the Belgian Banking and Finance Commission before the notification of the bid[147].

All the above mentioned actions have been approved by the shareholders prior to the bid.

c. Are there restrictions on the type of consideration that can be offered in a bid, for example securities only if these are listed in the target country's home state or the EU?

In the event of a public takeover bid the consideration can either be a cash consideration, either a share exchange or a combination of both. When a public takeover offer in exchange of securities, which are quoted on a Belgian regulated market, is made, the bidder must request the listing of the offered securities on that regulated Belgian market within one month after closure of the offer[148]. The Belgian Banking and Finance Commission can grant exceptions to this rule[149].

In the event of a squeeze out[150], it could be argued that the purchase price must be paid in cash.

d. Are there effective compulsory acquisition procedures regarding a small non-accepting minority? Can a bidder make its offer conditional on achieving the number of shares required so it can operate a squeeze out?

A distinction has to be made between a public and a private squeeze out. Whereas through a public squeeze out, securities holders are forced to hand over their securities to the bidder, they can not be forced to do so if it concerns a private squeeze out.

If a shareholder owns, directly or indirectly alone or in mutual consent, 95 percent of the securities of a target public company, it may launch a purchase offer on the remaining shares[151]. A similar rule applies if, as a result of a public takeover bid, the bidder holds 95% or more of the securities of a target company[152]. A specific procedure has to be complied with[153]. The securities, which are not offered by the minority shareholder after the closure of this offer, are considered transferred to the bidder by law[154].

If this purchase offer follows a public takeover bid, the bidder may reopen the bid under the same conditions as the initial bid for fifteen days following a simplified squeeze-out procedure. This possibility must however be explicitly provided for in the prospectus.

As concerns this transaction for private companies, a different procedure with a different outcome exists[155]. A private company aiming to acquire 100% of the shares of a target company, does not have to notify the Belgian Banking and Finance Commission thereof. Instead an extensive and written report has to be drawn up by the bidder[156] and by the certified auditor or accountant[157]. The board of directors of the target company has to establish a report giving its advice concerning the completeness and not-misleading information, its advice with respect to the report of the auditor and its advice with respect to the price. In case all securities are securities in registered form, the aforementioned reports have to be sent to the security holders by registered mail. The securities holders must react within 30 days from the sending of the aforementioned registered mail, to communicate in writing their objections. The bidder should decide either to maintain the initial offer or change offer in way beneficial to the securities holders. Decision of bidder to be sent by registered letter to the holders of securities within 15 days after the end date of the period of complaint. The offer can be accepted no less than 10 days but no more than 20 days after the date the bidder has disclosed final offer. In case securities holders object to the offer in writing, they can not be forced to hand over their securities.

At the end of the procedure, except for the securities of which the owners have explicitly and in written stated that they are not willing to hand over their securities before the period of acceptance of the offer has expired, securities that have not been offered shall be considered by law to be transmitted to the bidder upon payment of the purchase price into the *Deposito and Consignatiekas* ("*Caisse de Dépots et Consignation*").

Except for a mandatory takeover bid, a bidder can make its bid conditional on acquiring a minimum of securities. The draft prospectus included in the notification to the Belgian Banking and Finance Commission must expressly mention this possibility. When the minimum threshold mentioned in the prospectus is not reached, the bidder will not be obliged to acquire the securities that were offered to him. The bidder may acquire the securities if fewer securities have been tendered than the minimum number set out in the prospectus, if it has reserved itself the right to acquire them, even if the minimum number is not obtained, in the prospectus[158]. The public and the Belgian Banking and Finance Commission have to be informed by the bidder whether it makes this type of acquisition, indicating the number of securities acquired and held after acquisition[159].

e. Is there a principle of board neutrality? Can a target board align itself with a particular bidder/agree measures such as exclusivity arrangements to protect a particular deal?

There is no principle of neutrality of the board of directors of a target company. The Belgian Banking and Finance Commission notifies the public takeover bid to the board of directors of the target[160]. This notification includes the draft prospectus of the bidder. Within five days following the receipt of the notification, the board must inform the Belgian Banking and Finance Commission whether it finds the draft prospectus is complete and not misleading. The board will also give its opinion on the bid. The board will have to indicate whether it considers the bid to be in the interest of the shareholders, the creditors and the employees of the company; whether the board intends to invoke existing approval clauses or pre-emptive rights and whether the directors-shareholders will accept the offer[161].

The board of directors will often align itself with a particular bidder and will try to protect a particular deal. This protection can be established through different anti-takeover instruments that are used against one bidder and in favour of another bidder. Exclusiveness is not possible. Also in a friendly public takeover bid another bidder may make a counter or higher bid for the same securities[162]. The bidder, the counter bidder and the higher bidder must be treated equally with regard to the information disclosed by the target company[163]. The Belgian Banking and Finance Commission must also be notified of any contact between the bidder and the target company after receiving the notification of the bid[164]. By means of the opinion mentioned above, the board of directors can express its preference.

f. Can a target board hand over information to a potential bidder?

The disclosure and use of information with respect to the target company in order to buy or sell shares in this company may constitute insider trading, which is criminally sanctioned under Belgian law, as this information is considered to be privileged[165].

In order to qualify as privileged information, and data must have the following features[166]: (i) the information must not be public yet; (ii) the information must be sufficiently precise; (iii) the information must relate to one or several issuers of securities; (iv) if made public, the information should be likely to have a materially effect on the stock price of the securities in the target company.

Business plans, important strategic options and any negotiations or transactions that are not yet disclosed to the public would for example qualify as privileged information.

The board of directors of the target company must therefore refrain from disclosing privileged information to third party, unless such communication occurs in the normal exercise of its work, profession or function[167].

Any contact between the bidder and the target company after receiving the notification of the bid must be notified to the Belgian Banking and Finance Commission[168].

g. Are structures permitted which concentrate control rights in the hands of minority shareholders? Are structures permitted which place limitations/restrictions on voting rights, caps for example on voting rights above a certain threshold?

Yes, voting rights may be limited, provided that this limitation is applicable to all shareholders[169], the size of the shareholdings can be limited, non-voting shares[170] or preference shares can be issued. A veto or approval right can be granted to a category of shares[171].

Special majorities with respect to decisions enumerated in the Articles of Association of the company to be taken by the board of directors or general meeting of shareholders are also common (for example regarding the nomination of the board of directors, to take decisions related to the financing of the company). The Articles of Association can attach special rights to the different categories of shares issued by the company (for example, a preferential right to dividends, the right to propose candidate for the nomination as a director).

A wide variety of structures concentrating the control in the hands of certain shareholders exist. However, the Belgian Banking and Finance Commission and the market authority will guard the interests of the public.

h. Can restrictions be placed on the transferability of shares either by the issuer (in articles of association or by other means) or by arrangements between shareholders? Can a board delay registering transfers of shares?

The Articles of Association of the target company or the shareholders' agreements can contain restrictions on the transferability of the shares of a target company. Stand still provisions[172], pre-emptive rights, rights of first refusal and approval clauses[173] or take along rights[174] are common in Belgium. Companies listed on Euronext Brussels do not have such transferability restrictions in their Articles of Association, since the securities of listed companies should be freely transferable, but their major shareholders have often executed a shareholders' agreement containing such restrictions. Transfer restrictions in shareholders' agreements are not enforceable against third parties acting in good faith. If the third party is aware of the transfer restrictions, he should refrain from assisting contract parties in breaching their contractual obligation.

A board of directors can not refuse the registration of a transfer of shares of the company in its share register when the Articles of Association of the company and the applicable regulations have been complied with. However, if the board of directors refuses registration the only way to force them to registrar the transaction will be through a court action.

i. What contractual barriers (including shareholder agreements) to takeover bids are in use in public companies (eg golden parachutes, change of control provisions triggering default of loan agreements, or wining up or change of control of joint ventures)? What are the prospects of review by courts on the basis of contract or company law and by regulators on the basis of securities laws or stock exchange regulations?

Shareholders' agreements are common practice in public companies since most public companies are still controlled by the original shareholders (often one family). Pre-emptive rights, take-along rights, rights of first refusal and approval rights are customary. Joint ventures are often accompanied by a stand still engagement of its shareholders[175], but joint ventures are seldom public companies. Shareholders' agreement often also deal with a shareholders' syndicate or voting arrangements. In such event, proxy is given to the president of the syndicate or to one of the shareholders to represent the parties to the agreement at the meeting of shareholders.

Financing or loans granted by one of the shareholders may be linked to their shareholding. The same applies to other (commercial) agreements executed between the target company and one of its shareholders.

Sometimes the management agreements with the directors of the target company provide in substantial fees in case of a revocation of their mandate as a result of a takeover ("golden parachutes"). The bidder can revoke the mandate of the directors *ad nutum*, but will have the obligation to pay these fees to the revoked directors.

The prospects of review of the above mentioned barriers by court are nearly non existing. The principle of contractual freedom is still the guiding principle and only if a party abuses its right, a judge will intervene.

j. Are there current proposals to change the legislation relating to takeovers?

No, however when the 13th Directive on the Company Law concerning takeover bids shall have to be incorporated in the Belgian law, Belgium will of course need to amend its regulation on takeover bids.

NOTES

[1] Member of the Belgian Competition Council, Academic consultant European

Institute University of Ghent. Geert A. Zonnekeyn has written the chapter on competition law. The views expressed in this report are these of the author.

[2] Nauta Dutilh, Brussels Free University of Brussels, lke Janssens has written the chapter on company law.

[3] OJ L 395/1 of 30 December 1989. Regulation rectified by OJ L 257/13 of 21 September 1990 and OJ L 3/16 of 7 January 1997 and amended by the 1994 Act of Accession. The EC Merger Regulation was modified by Council Regulation (EC) No. 1310/97 of 30 June 1997, OJ L 180/1 of 9 July 1997 rectified by OJ L 199/69 of 26 July 1997 and OJ L 40/17 of 13 February 1998. For comments on the EC Merger Regulation, see e.g. C.J. Cook and C.S. Kerse, *E.C. Merger Control* (London, Sweet & Maxwell, 2000, 3rd ed.) 376 p. and B.E. Hawk and H.L. Huser, *European Community Merger Control: A Practitioner's Guide* (The Hague, Kluwer Law International, 1996) 511 p.

[4] A survey by White & Case, covering 130 jurisdictions, concluded that 67 countries now have merger control laws in place. As far as the EC is concerned, did the survey indicate that many of the Member States revised their laws or are bringing them into conformity with the EC Merger Regulation. While this trend helps to harmonize standards within the EC, it – somewhat paradoxically – can add to the burden on transactions too small to meet the EC filing thresholds. In such cases, parties may be required to file in various EC Member States where the deal may have a national impact. See *2001 Survey of Worldwide Merger Notification Requirements*.

[5] Green Paper on the Review of Council Regulation (EEC) No. 4064/89, COM(2001) 745/6 final of 11 December 2001.

[6] The summaries of the replies received on the Green Paper have been published on the DG COMP website (see http://europa.eu.int/comm/competition/mergers/review/comments.html).

[7] J. Vickers, "International Mergers: the View from a national Authority", in *Annual Proceedings of the Fordham Corporate Law Institute. International Antitrust Law & Policy*, B. E. Hawk (ed.) (Juris Publishing, Inc., New York, 2002), p. 203, at p. 213.

[8] Press release of 19 December 2001, "*Bundeskartellamt verweist Fusion Promatech/Sulzer an die Wettbewerbsbehörde in Brussel*".

[9] As the European Commission pointed out in its Green Paper, in 2000 there were only 20 notifications to the Commission under article 1(3) as against 75 notifications to three or more Member States.

[10] *See Promatech-Sulzer Textil* (Case COMP/M.2698) and *GEES-Unison* (Case COMP/M.2738).

[11] *See* Article 10, §3 of the 1991 Competition Act.

[12] Case IV/M.1524.

[13] For a further analysis of this dualistic system, see B. Ponet, "De Belgische Raad voor de Mededinging in het wijzigend mededingingslandschap", in L. Peeters, P. Matthyssens and I. Verbeek (eds.), *Stakeholder Synergie. Referaten van het Vijfentwintigste Vlaams Wetenschappelijk Economisch Congres* (Garant, Leuven, 2002), p. 521 and J. Steenbergen, "Decision-making in Competition Cases: the Investigator, the Prosecutor and the Judge", in Current and Future Perspectives on EC Competition Law, L. Gormley (ed.), (Kluwer Law International, The Hague, 1997) p. 101-108.

[14] Published in the *Belgian State Gazette* of 11 October 1991, p. 22493. For comments, see e.g. T. Chellingsworth and M. Van der Woude, Commentary on Belgian Merger Control, in *Merger Control in the EU*, P. Verloop. (ed.) (Kluwer Law International, The Hague, 1999), p. 71-116. J. Ratliff and E.A. Wright, "Belgian Competition Law - The Advent of Free Market Principles", W. Comp. (1992) p. 33-51; A. Vanderelst and F. Wijckmans, "The Belgian law of 5 August 1991 on the Protection of Economic Competition", ECLR (1992), p. 120-128; B. Van de Walle De Ghelcke and K. Platteau, "The New Belgian Competition Act", IBLJ (1993), p. 743-757; J. Ysewyn, "Uncertainty Relating to Merger Notification requirements under Belgian Competition Law", ECLR (1995) p. 323-326.

[15] Published in the *Belgian State Gazette* of 22 June 1960, p. 4674. For comments on the 1960 Competition Act, see e.g. L.P. Suetens, "Belgian Anti-Trust Law in Action", CMLRev. (1964-65) p. 325-339.

[16] Published in the *Belgian State Gazette* of 27 April 1999, p. 14118. Article 53 of the Competition Act was amended in August 2001, published in the *Belgian State Gazette* of 22 September 2001, p. 31916. For comments, see e.g. D. Szafran, La loi sur la protection de la concurrence économique. Réforme de 1999", JT (2000), p. 474; J. Steenbergen, "De wijzigingen van de Belgische Wet Mededinging", SEW (1999), p. 358; J. Steenlant, A. Vanderelst and F. Wijckmans, "De Gewijzigde Wet op de Mededinging: Een Tweede Kans?", TPR (2001), p. 703 and H. Swennen, "De wijziging van de Wet tot bescherming van de economische mededinging", TBH (1999), p. 372. For an anlysis of the provisions on merger control, see V. Dirckx, "Les Lois du 26 avril 1999 modifiant la Loi du 5 août 1991 sur la protection de la concurrence économique: quel impact sur les notifications de concentrations?", Daor (1999), p. 95. See also the various contributions in J. Stuyck and P. Wytinck (eds.), De hervormde Belgische Mededingingswet (Kluwer, Antwerpen, 2000) 177 p.

[17] The Act of 26 April 1999 (I) entered into force on 27 April 1999. The Act of 26 April 1999 (II) entered into force on 1 October 1999. Specific provisions entered into force at an earlier date. The new concentration control thresholds entered into force on 1 July 1999 (Royal decree of 7 May 1999, *Belgian State Gazette* of 1 July 1999, replaced by Royal Decree of 14 June 1999, *Belgian State Gazette* of 31 July 1999). A number of other provisions entered into force on 1 September 1999 (Royal Decree of 14 June 1999, *Belgian State Gazette* of 1 September 1999).

[18] Royal Decree of 14 June 1999, *Belgian State Gazette* of 1 September 1999, p. 32315. Unless otherwise indicated, hereinafter, references to articles of the 1991 Competition act are references to this officially consolidated version.

[19] On this subject, see J. Steenbergen, "Decision-making in Competition Cases: the Investigator, the Prosecutor and the Judge", in Current and Future Perspectives on EC Competition Law, L. Gormley (ed.), (Kluwer Law International, The Hague, 1997) p. 101-108.

[20] Article 14 §1 of the 1991 Competition Act.

[21] Article 14 §2 of the 1991 Competition Act.

[22] To date, only two reporters have officially been appointed.

[23] Article 14 §2 of the 1991 Competition Act. See also articles 23, 24 and 32bis of the 1991 Competition Act.

[24] Article 17 of the 1991Competition Act.

[25] Article 17, §4 of the 1991 Competition Act.
[26] Articles 29, §1, 30, 31, 33, 36 and 37 of the 1991 Competition Act.
[27] Article 28 of the 1991 Competition Act.
[28] Article 19, §5 of the 1991 Competition Act.
[29] Article 35 of the 1991 Competition Act.
[30] Article 40 of the 1991 Competition Act.
[31] Article 26 of the 1991 Competition Act.
[32] Articles 24 §1, 27 §1 and 32ter of the 1991 Competition Act.
[33] Article 21 of the 1991 Competition Act.
[34] For a definition of the concept "full-function joint ventures, see the Commission Notice on the concept of full-function joint ventures under Council Regulation (EEC) No 4064/89 on the control of concentrations between undertakings, OJ C 66/1 of 2 March 1998. For an early analysis of the Commission's practices on the treatment of full-function joint ventures, see F.E. González-Diaz, "Joint Ventures under EC Competition Law: the New Bounderies", in *Mélanges en Hommage À Michel Waelbroeck*, Vol. II (Bruylant, Brussels, 1999) p. 1019; J. Maillo, "Empresas en Participación Concentrativas y Artículo 81 del Tradado CE : Dos años aplicaión del articulo 2(4) des Reglamento CE dez control de las operaciones de concentración" (Universidad San-Pablu-CEU, 2001), 52 p.; M. Waelbroeck, "Le régime applicable aux Entreprises Communes en Droit Communautaire de la Concurrence depuis l'Entreé en Vigueur du Règlement (CE) No. 1310/97 du Conseil", in *Mélanges offerts à Pierre Van Ommeslaghe* (Bruylant, Brussels, 2000) p. 813 and G.A. Zonnekeyn, "The Treatment of Joint Ventures Under the Amended E.C. Merger Regulation", ECLR (1998), p. 414.
[35] Article 11 §1 of the 1991 Competition Act.
[36] Article 46 §3 (a) and (b) of the 1991 Competition Act.
[37] Decision of the Belgian Competition Council of 18 October 2000 in Case No. 2000-C/C-31, *De Beers Australia Holdings Pty Ltd./Ashton Mining Ltd*, published in the *Belgian Official Gazette* of 3 May 2001, p. 14375 and decision of the Belgian Competition Council of 8 November 2000 in Case No. 2000-C/C-35, *NV P&O Port Holdings/NV Antwerp Combined Terminals*, published in the *Belgian Official Gazette* of 3 May 2001, p. 14379. The approach followed by the Competition Council has been subject to criticism. See J. Ysewyn, "Overzicht van rechtspraak van de Raad voor de Mededinging in 1999-2000", TBH (2001), at pp. 644-645. See also the discussion in the annual Report of the Belgian Competition Council (2000), p. 29. For an overview of the Commission's practice, see M. Broberg, *The European Commission's Juridiction to Scrutinise Mergers* (Kluwer Law International, The Hague, 1998), p. 125-146.
[38] See Commission Notice on calculation of turnover under Council Regulation (EEC) No. 4064/89 on the control of concentrations between undertakings, *O.J.* C 66/25 of 2 March 1998, at para. 45-48.
[39] Decision of 15 September 1997, no. 97-C/C-20, *De Post/NV Hagefin/R.Ketels/A. Boodts*, *Belgian Official Gazette*, 22 October 1997, p. 28124.
[40] Parties did not have this possibility under the old provisions of the 1991 Competition Act. The tim-limits of the Competition act were considered to be of public order and could not be extended even with the explicit consent of the noti-

fying parties. See judgment of the Brussels Court of Appeal of 25 June 1997, *Société Callebaut AG/Société de participations monilieres/Compagnie Nationale a Portefeuilles v. Belgian State*, *Belgian Official Gazette*, 4 July 1997.

[41] See M.P. Broberg, "Commitments in Phase One Merger Proceedings: The Commission's Power to accept and enforce Phase One Commitments", CMLRev (1997), p. 845.

[42] Article 6, §2 of Council Regulation 4046/89, as amended.

[43] Article 44 of the 1991 Competition Act.

[44] Bill of 26 October 1999 to amend the Law of 5 August 1991 on the Protection of Economic Competition, *Parl. St. Senaat*, 1999-2000, no. 2-126/1.

[45] Bill of 6 September 2001 to amend the Law of 5 August 1991 on the Protection of Economic Competition, *Parl. St. Kamer*, 2000-2001, no. 1402/01.

[46] General remark: by company is meant a company limited by shares ("*naamloze vennootschap/société anonyme*"). If another corporate organisation is meant, this will be mentioned explicitly. A public company is a company limited by shares that publicly offers or offered its securities through a public offering or listing on a stock exchange in Belgium or abroad (Article 438 of the Belgian Company Code).

[47] An approval clause has to be notified to the Belgian Banking and Finance Commission. In the event of a public takeover bid, the board of directors of the target company will have the obligation to indicate whether it intends to invoke the existing approval clauses in the company's Articles of Association. The approval rights can be invoked by the board subsequently provided that there has been a long-term and non-discriminatory application of this approval clause (Article 512 of the Belgian Company Code).

[48] Following the notification of a public takeover bid, the board of directors must indicate to the Belgian Banking and Finance Commission whether it will exercise the pre-emption rights in the Articles of Association. If the pre-emption right is exercised, a proposal to the shareholders must be made, within five days after the closing of the bid, for the acquisition of the securities by one or more persons with regard to whom pre-emption rights have not been exercised or with respect to whom approval has been given at a price at least equal to the price of the bid or the counterbid (Article 511 of the Company Code).

[49] The market authority requires the freely transfer of shares before a company can be listed.

[50] Article 480 of the Belgian Company Code.

[51] Article 542 of the Belgian Company Code.

[52] Article 544 of the Belgian Company Code.

[53] The shares subscribed in such event must be registered and can not be transferred during one year. It is impossible to force the holders of the warrants to exercise their warrants (Article 500 of the Belgian Company Code).

[54] Article 620 and following of the Belgian Company Code. In principle a resolution of the meeting of shareholders is required if a company acquires it own shares. The Articles of Association may provide that no resolution of the meeting of shareholders is required if the acquisition is necessary to avoid an imminent serious prejudice to the company (such as a hostile takeover bid). The use of this mechanism is limited by the stringent rules governing the acquisition of own shares.

[55] Article 632 of the Belgian Company Code limits the cross shareholding to 10% of the voting rights in the companies.

[56] This possibility is limited in the event of a notification by the Belgian Banking and Finance Commission of a public takeover bid (Article 607 of the Belgian Company Code).

[57] Article 556 of the Belgian Company Code. Only the meeting of shareholders can approve such options and an abstract of the decision of the meeting must be filed with the clerk of the Commercial Court.

[58] In the event of a public takeover bid, such clauses can only be invoked if the meeting of shareholders has approved it and when it has been filed with the clerk of the Commercial Court before the notification of the bid to the company (Article 556 of the Belgian Company Code)

[59] See below, question 9.

[60] Meant is : the company whose securities are listed on the Belgian regulated markets or regularly traded at auctions organised periodically and companies whose securities are distributed publicly.

[61] Article 38 of the Royal Decree of November 8, 1989.

[62] Articles 15 – 17 of the Law of March 2, 1989.

[63] which may or may not represent the capital.

[64] Law of March 2, 1989 on the publication of major shareholdings in companies listed on a stock exchange and the regulation of public takeover bids.

[65] Article 11 of the Collective Bargaining Agreement of March 9, 1972.

[66] Or highest price or counter performance offered during the twelve months before it acquired control.

[67] Article 41, § 1 of the Royal Decree of November 8, 1989.

[68] More in particular is meant by companies that publicly offer or have publicly offered their securities : (i) companies whose securities are listed on a Belgian regulated market or whose securities are regularly traded at the periodic auctions of a stock exchange; and (ii) companies whose securities are held by more than 50 persons (Article 1, §2 of the Royal Decree of November 8, 1989).

[69] Report of the Belgian Banking and Finance Commission, 1989-1990, 75.

[70] A white knight was found (Suez) and the board of directors of the Generale Maatschappij doubled the subscribed capital of the company in favour of Suez.

[71] Report of the Belgian Banking and Finance Commission, 1997-1998, 112.

[72] Report of the Belgian Banking and Finance Commission, 1997-1998, 123.

[73] Report of the Belgian Banking and Finance Commission, 1999-2000, 79.

[74] Report of the Belgian Banking and Finance Commission, 1999-2000, 84.

[75] Report of the Belgian Banking and Finance Commission, 1997-1998, 119.

[76] Article 24 of the Law of March 22, 1993 on the status and control of credit institutions.

[77] Article 24, § 3 and § 7 of the Law of March 22, 1993.

[78] Articles 30 and 31 of the Law of March 22, 1993 : the Belgian Banking and Finance Commission must approve a merger of credit institutions or other institutions active in the financial sector, a transfer of all or part of the business or of all rights and obligations resulting from a credit institution's operations, and some similar operations.

[79] Article 30 of the Law of March 22, 1993. If the Belgian Banking and Finance Commission does not intervene within 3 months from the notification of the project, the approval is considered granted.

[80] Law of July 9, 1975 on the control of insurance companies.

[81] Article 23bis, § 1 of the Law of July 9, 1975 on the control of insurance companies.

[82] Article 74 of the Law of July 9, 1975.

[83] Law of April 6, 1995 on Secondary Markets, the Status and Control of Investment Companies, Intermediaries and Placement Advisors.

[84] Article 67, § 3 and § 7 of the Law of April 6, 1995.

[85] Articles 73 and 74 of the Law of April 6, 1995: the Belgian Banking and Finance Commission must approve a merger of investment companies or other institutions active in the financial sector, a transfer of all or part of the business or of all rights and obligations resulting from a investment company's operations, and some similar transactions.

[86] Article 73 of the Law of April 6, 1995. If the Belgian Banking and Finance Commission does not intervene within 3 months from the notification of the project, the approval is considered granted.

[87] Article 10, § 2 of the Law of April 29, 1999 regarding the organisation of the electricity market.

[88] Article 4, § 3, 3° 2 of the Law of April 29, 1999 and Article 10, § 1 of the Royal Decree of October 11, 2000.

[89] Article 6, 1° of the Flemish Decree of July 17, 2000 with respect to the significant change in the shareholding of a company managing the transmission system, Article 17, § 7 ° of the Flemish Decree of July 17, 2000 regarding the change of control, merger or split of the company holding a distribution permit and Article 20 of the Decision of the Flemish Government of June 15, 2001 concerning the distribution permits.

[90] Article 14, § 1 of the Decision of the Flemish Government of June 15, 2001 regarding the company managing the distribution grid.

[91] Article 7 of the Decree of the Walloon Government of April 12, 2001 and Article 26 of the Decision of the Walloon Government regarding the management of the distribution system.

[92] The permit of company managing the local distribution system can be withdrawn in case of an important change in the shareholding of this company which could jeopardise the independence of the management of the system (Article 3, § 3 of the Ordonnance of the Brussels Government of July 19, 2001) and the local transmission system is managed by a semi public organisation ("intercommunale") of which the communities are part (Article 6, § 4 and 8, § 2 of the Ordonnance of the Brussels Government of July 19, 2001).

[93] Article 1583 of the Belgian Civil Code.

[94] Article 2279 of the Belgian Civil Code.

[95] Article 504 of the Belgian Company Code.

[96] Regarding the rules applicable in case of a public takeover bid, see above.

[97] Article 598 and following of the Belgian Company Code.

[98] A substantial shareholding means that the seller (and its relatives or related

companies) holds more than 25% of the Belgian company at any time during the 5 years prior to the sale.

[99] Article 90 of the Belgian Income Tax Code.

[100] By a universality of goods is meant, all operational activities and related assets and liabilities of a company (Article 678 of the Belgian Company Code).

[101] A branch of activity is a unit which conducts a business activity autonomously from a technical and operational perspective and which is capable of functioning by itself (Article 680 of the Belgian Company Code).

[102] For example : for real estate a public deed must be established, a transfer of customer lists or contracts requires the consent of the customer, a transfer of registered intellectual property rights must be evidenced in a written document, etc.

[103] Article 671 of the Belgian Company Code.

[104] Article 672 of the Belgian Company Code.

[105] Of course the national law of the other company involved will have to be checked.

[106] Which is the result of the adoption of the directive on disclosure of major shareholdings of December 12, 1988 – 88/627 (PB L n° 348 dated December 17, 1988).

[107] Articles 514 and following of the Belgian Company Code.

[108] Article 515 of the Belgian Company Code.

[109] Such a notification is not mandatory when a notification under the Law of March 2, 1989 has been made.

[110] Article 632 of the Belgian Company Code.

[111] Rule 3403/2 of the Market Rules of Euronext Brussels as approved by Ministerial Decree of May 29, 2001.

[112] Rule 52.0.4 of the Nasdaq Europe Rule Book.

[113] Rule 3403/1 of the Market Rules of Euronext Brussels, Rule 33.0.0 of the Nasdaq Europe Rule Book and Article 2 of the Royal Decree of July 3, 1996 on occasional information to be disclosed by issuers whose instruments are listed on the first market and new market of a stock exchange.

[114] Such as, for example, the issue of securities of the same nature, subscriptions, waiver of rights and operations of conversion.

[115] Article 4, § 1 of the Royal Decree of July 3, 1996 on occasional information.

[116] The interested shareholder should consult the file of the company at the office of the clerk at the commercial court or the publication at the annexes of the Belgian Official Gazette. The prospectus published at the occasion of an issue of new securities also provides the enumerated information.

[117] Articles 82 and following of the Royal Decree of January 30, 2001 should be amended.

[118] Article 558 of the Belgian Company Code.

[119] Article 544 of the Belgian Company Code.

[120] A modification of the rights attached to a particular category of shares is only possible when a specific procedure is observed (Article 560 of the Belgian Company Code).

[121] In the Generale Bank case, the capital of the Generale Bank was increased by the board of directors within the limits of the authorized capital in favour of Fortis AG (Report of the Belgian Banking and Finance Commission 1997-1998, 115).

[122] See question 14.B below.

[123] See question 14.F below.

[124] I.e. where the price paid for the acquisition of those securities that conferred the control was higher than the market price at the time of acquisition.

[125] Meant is a procedure in which the price is maintained at a fixed level for at least fifteen days.

[126] By a squeeze out bid is meant the procedure creating the opportunity for a physical person or legal entity to acquire through a purchase offer all voting securities of a Belgian company, if it holds alone or in concert with another person 95% of the voting securities of that company (Article 32 of the Royal Decree of November 8, 1999 and Article 513 of the Belgian Company Code). A distinction ahs to be made between a public and a private squeeze out. See question 14.D below.

[127] See question 14.D below.

[128] As approved by the Ministerial Decree dated 29 May 2001.

[129] Information regarding the exercise of the rights of holders of securities of the company includes : any information regarding the exercise, by the holders of securities, of their shareholder's rights or of the rights connected with the holding of securities, including the date and the agenda of the general meeting (i); any information regarding the rights connected with the holding of securities (including but not limited to the notifications concerning the attribution and payment of dividends, the modifications to the conditions of or to the applicable interest rate, the issues of securities of same nature, the operations of attribution, subscription, waiver of rights and operations of conversion, in accordance with the concerned securities) (ii); and the appointment of any financial institution as representative of the company, where the holders of securities can exercise their financial rights, unless the company exercises itself the financial service in Belgium.

[130] Sensitive information means: every modification of the rights attached to the different categories of securities (i); or every fact or decision that, if made public, should influence in a sensitive way the price of the listed shares (ii). It is up to the company, under the control of the market authority, to decide whether the information is sensitive or not.

[131] Article 8 of the Royal Decree of July 3, 1996 on occasional information.

[132] Article 9 of the Royal Decree of July 3, 1996 on occasional informa ion.

[133] Article 10, §1 of the Royal Decree of July 3, 1996 on occasional information.

[134] Article 10, §2 of the Royal Decree of July 3, 1996 on occasional information.

[135] Article 5, §1 *in fine* of the Royal Decree of July 3, 1996 on occasional information and Rule 3404/1 of the Rulebook.

[136] Article 148, § 4, 10° of Law of April 6, 1995 on secondary markets, on the legal status and supervision of investment firms, on intermediaries and investment advisers.

[137] Nasdaq Europe NV is a Belgian company with registered seat in Brussels.

[138] The above mentioned Royal Decrees also apply. The disclosure of information is elaborated in Rule 55 of the Nasdaq Europe Rule Book.

[139] Rule 33.0.0 of the Nasdaq Europe Rule Book.

[140] Rule 34.0.0 and its instructions of the Nasdaq Europe Rule Book.

[141] Rule 51.0.1 of the Nasdaq Europe Rule Book.

[142] Articles 557 and 607 of the Belgian Company Code.
[143] Article 607, § 2, 1° of the Belgian Company Code.
[144] Article 607, § 2, 2° of the Belgian Company Code.
[145] Article 620 of the Belgian Company Code.
[146] Article 556 of the Belgian Company Code.
[147] Article 16 of the Royal Decree of November 8, 1989.
[148] Article 31 of the Royal Decree of November 8, 1989.
[149] For example when the bidder is a company listed on another stock exchange. See the share exchange offer of Accor on CIWLT (Report of the Belgian Banking and Finance Commission, 1994-1995, 110); the share exchange offer of AXA on Royale Belge (Report of the Belgian Banking and Finance Commission, 1997-1998, 121) and the share exchange offer of Premier Parks on Walibi (Report of the Belgian Banking and Finance Commission, 1997-1998, 123).
[150] Article 513 of the Belgian Company Code expressly provides that the securities which were not offered after the closure of takeover bid are considered as transferred to the bidder provided that the price is deposited with the Official receiver ("*Deposito- en Consignatiekas/Cassire de Dépôts et Consignations*"). Such a deposit would not be possible in the event of an exchange offer.
[151] Article 513, § 1 of the Belgian Company Code; See question 14.A above.
[152] Article 32 of the Royal Decree of November 8, 1989 forces a bidder to re-open the bid under the same conditions when he has acquired 90% of the securities of the company.
[153] A file including a draft prospectus, a report from an independent auditor with respect to the valuation methods applied by the bidder and a report of the board of directors with respect to the comprehensiveness and accuracy of the draft prospectus, the auditors report and indicating whether, in the opinion of the board, the squeeze out is in the interest of the company (the notification), must be submitted to the Belgian Banking and Finance Commission. The Belgian Banking and Finance Commission will publish the notification. The minority shareholders have one month to address their remarks to the Belgian Banking and Finance Commission. The Belgian Banking and Finance Commission can forward these remarks to the bidder, who, in such case, will have 15 days to amend its offer. The Belgian Banking and Finance Commission can then approve the prospectus. During a period of minimum 10 and maximum 20 days, starting as from the publication of the prospectus, the minority shareholders can either accept or refuse the offer.
[154] The consideration required for these securities will be kept by the official receiver *("Deposito- en Consignatiekas/Caisse de dépôts et consignations")* until the previous owners come forward.
[155] Article 513, § 2 of the Belgian Company Code.
[156] This report needs to include at least the following elements: (i) information related to the identity of the bidder, the number of securities in its possession at the time when the report is drafted; (ii) information related to the purchase offer, and (iii) information related to the target company.
[157] The written report of a certified auditor or accountant concerns the relevance, in view of the commonly used assessment rules, of the assessment rules used by the bidder for the valuation of the company and the justification of the price; also opinion as to whether the price safeguards the interests of the security holders.

[158] Article 28 of the Royal Decree of November 8, 1989.
[159] Article 29 of the Royal Decree of November 8, 1989.
[160] Article 14 of the Royal Decree of November 8, 1989.
[161] Article 15 of the Royal Decree of November 8, 1989.
[162] Article 34 of the Royal Decree of November 8, 1989.
[163] Article 36 of the Royal Decree of November 8, 1989.
[164] Article 9 of the Royal Decree of November 8, 1989.
[165] Articles 181 to 191 of the Act of 4 December 1990 on financial operations and financial markets.
[166] Article 181 of the Act of 4 December 1990.
[167] Article 183, 1° of the Act of 4 December 1990.
[168] Article 9 of the Royal Decree of November 8, 1989.
[169] Article 544 of the Belgian Company Code.
[170] Article 480 and following of the Belgian Company Code.
[171] Such rights may never lead to the non transferability of the shares of a company.
[172] Such restriction bars each transfer of shares. To be valid, the restriction has to be limited in time and has to be in the interest of the company (Article 510 of the Belgian Company Code).
[173] The restriction resulting from an approval clause or from a clause providing for a pre-emptive right may not result in a non transferability of more than 6 months from the date of request of approval or the invitation to exercise the pre-emptive right. In a public takeover bid, the use of a pre-emptive right or approval clause is restricted.
[174] A take-along right is an arrangement that a shareholder will not sell its shares without giving the other shareholders the right to participate in the sale. This right must also be justified in the interest of the company.
[175] Three to five years is accepted by the Belgian practice.

ANNEXE

	Public squeeze out	Private squeeze out	Tender offer
Scope of application	• Target: company limited by shares which has made a public offer of its securitiesin the sense of Article 438 of the Company Code or not • Bidder: each natural or legal person who, alone or jointly holds 95% or more of the voting securities of a public company limited by shares or a limited partnership with share capital • • Object: *all* remaining securities, irrespective of whether they represent the company's capital	• Target: public company limited by shares which has *not* made a public offer of its securities in the sense of Article 438 of the Company Code or not • Bidder: each natural or legal person who, alone or jointly holds 95% or more of the voting securities of a of a public company limited by shares or a limited partnership with share capital Object: *all* remaining securities, irrespective of whether they represent the company's capital	• Target: no specific requirements • Bidder: no specific requirements • Object: *all* voting securities or equivalent securities not yet in possession of the bidder
Procedure	Requirements related to the bidder: The bidder needs to, alone or jointly, hold 95% or more of the voting	Requirements related to the bidder: The bidder needs to, alone or jointly, hold 95% or more of the voting	Requirements related to the bidder: No specific requirements related to the bidder

Public squeeze out	Private squeeze out	Tender offer	
	securities of a public company limited by shares or a limited partnership with share capital, to be determined at the time *when the bidder notifies its intention to the BFC* to launch a public purchase offer	securities of a public company imited by shares or a limited partnership with share capital, to be determined at the time *when the bidder draws up the report* (see further)	
	The bidder has to agree to finalize the bid and the bidder can not acquire any securities on which the bid applies under other terms than the terms of the bid, unless the other terms are extended to all beneficiaries of the purchase offer	The bidder has to agree to finalize the bid and the bidder can not acquire any securities on which the bid applies under other terms than the terms of the bid, unless the other terms are extended to all beneficiaries of the purchase offer	
requirements related to the offer:	Relate to *all* securities of the target company which are not yet in possession of the bidding company	Idem	Relate to *all* securities or equivalent securitie is not yet in possession of the bidder
regular and credible offer:		regular and credible offer:	
	The requirements and the terms of the public offer need to be in conformity with the rules hereafter set		the requirements and the terms of the public offer need to be in conformity with the rules hereafter

Public squeeze out	Private squeeze out	Tender offer	
	forth: they need to be drafted in such a way that the that the interests of the security holders are safeguarded		set forth; in particular as regards the price, they have to enable the bidder the reach the intended purpose
	price has to be paid in cash		price not necessarily to be paid in cash
	determination of the price: price has to '*safeguard the interests of the securities holders*' *i.e.* price justified in view of the value of the company; no calculation of minority discount or minority premium but equal treatment of majority and minority security holders; price is not a compensation offer has to mention that every price increase, shall be beneficial to all security holders having accepted the offer prior to the change a firm offer: unless the bidder extends the purchase offer to all securities,	determination of the price: price has to take into account the *interests of the owners of the securities* *i.e.* .importance of equality of treatment	determination of the price: freely to be determined by the bidder

Public squeeze out	Private squeeze out	Tender offer	
	the bidder can not acquire securities at other terms and conditions than those exposed in the purchase offer (or following comments made by the BFC, change the offer to the benefit of the securities holders)		
	availability of funds: all necessary funds for the execution of the offer either need to be blocked on a bank account with any of the financial institutions in the sense of the law of 22 March 1993 or in the form of an irrevocable and unconditional credit, approved by such a financial institution, exclusively to be used for the payment of the securities holders	availability of funds: all necessary funds for the execution of the offer either need to be blocked on a bank account with any of the financial institutions or in the form of an irrevocable and unconditional credit, approved by such a financial institution, exclusively to be used for the payment of the securities holders	availability of funds: idem as public squeeze out
	intervention of intermediary the acceptance of the approvals and the payment of the price have to be guaranteed by a Belgian financial institution in the sense of the law of 22 March 1993		intervention of intermediary idem as public squeeze out

Public squeeze out	Private squeeze out	Tender offer
Pase I: Notification to the Banking and Finance Commission	Within 1 month before the commencement of the transaction. The notification must include, amongst others, the price, the conditions, most important rules for the offer and the information showing that the offer complies with Article 45 (see above) To be added to the notification: • draft prospectus • report of an independent expert, concerning the relevance, in view of the commonly used assessment rules, of the assessment rules used by the bidder for the valuation of the company and the justification of the price. Also opinion as to whether the price safeguards the interests of the security holders • advice of the Board of Directors of the target company	No notification to the Banking and Finance Commission **BUT:** • **extensive and written report drawn up by the bidder**: This report needs to include at least the following elements: • information related to the identity of the bidder, the number of securities in its possession at the time when the report is drafted; • information related to the purchase offer • information related to the target company • **Written report of a certified auditor or accountant,** concerning the relevance, in view of the commonly used assessment rules, of the assessment rules used by the bidder for the valuation of the company and the justification of the price. Also opinion as to whether the price safeguards the interests of the security holders

Public squeeze out	Private squeeze out	Tender offer	
	• copy of the request for admission directed to the Minister of Finance in case the bidder does not resort under the law of any of the EU member states	• **Advice of the board of directors of the target company:** three-folded advice, with respect the completeness and not-misleading information, its advice with	
Disclosure of the notifrication of the public purchase offer	By the BFC at the latest 1 day after the day on which the notification was received • Notification of the bid to the target company and the bidder • Possible intervention of the security holders: notification of objections to the BFC	respect to the report of the auditor and its advice with respect to the price • in case all securities are nominated securities, the aforementioned reports have to be sent to the security holders by registered mail • **Intervention of the envisaged securities holders** within 30days from the sending of the aforementioned registered mail: written objections • **possible reaction of the bidder:** either maintain the initial purchase offer or change offer in way beneficial to the securities holders	By the BFC at the latest 1 day after the day on which the notification was received • Notification of the bid to the target company and the bidder • Possible involvement of the Board of Directors of the target company: • Report of the Board of Directors if the information in the prospectus is not complete or misleading eventually to be notified to the BFC within 10 days from the receipt of the draft prospectus

Public squeeze out	Private squeeze out	Tender offer	
		• **decision of bidder** to be disclosed by the sending of registered letter to the holders of securities within 15 days after the end date of the period of complaint	
Phase II: Investigation by the Banking and Finance Commission	Investigation by the BFC of the terms of the public purchase offer as concerns their regularity and the quality of the information Approval of the prospectus or comments made by the BFC Disclosure of the prospectus	Not applicable	Investigation by the BFC of the terms of the public bid as concerns the quality of the information not misleading the public) Approval of the prospectus by the BFC Disclosure of the prospectus
Phase III: - Progress and termination of the Purchase offer or bid	• Duration of the offer A period of minimum 10 days and maximum 20 days has to be respected for the approval of the prospectus, as from the date of the disclosure of the prospectus • Termination of the offer Within 5 days after the	A period of minimum 10 days and maximum 20 days has to be respected for the approval of the Offer, as from the date the bidder has disclosed final offer	• Duration of the offer A period of minimum 10 days and maximum 20 days has to be respected for the approval of the prospectus, as from the date of the disclosure of the prospectus • Termination of the offer

Public squeeze out	Private squeeze out	Tender offer	
	termination of the offer: disclosure of the result by the bidder Note: During the procedure: supervision of the Banking and Finance Commission on the basis of the law of 2 March 1989		Note: Once the target company is the object of a tender offer, other interested parties can launch a counteroffer; the bidder may make a higher offer
Consequences	• At the end of the proceedings, any securities that have not been offered, shall be considered by law to be transmitted to the bidder upon payment of the purchase price into the Consignatiekas ("Caisse de Dépots") (Art. 60 RD). • At the end of the purchase offer, the company will no longer be considered to be a company which makes or has made a public offer of its securities unless bonds issued by the company are still publicly held.	• In case securities holders object the purchase offer in written way, they can not be forced to hand over their securities • At the end of the proceedings, except for the securities of which the owners have explicitly and in written stated that they are not willing to hand over their securities before the period of acceptance of the offer has expired, any securities that have not been offered shall be considered by law to be transmitted to that person upon payment of the purchase price into the Consignatiekas ("Caisse de Dépots")	

DENMARK

Cross Border Mergers in Company Law and Competition Law: Removing the Final Barriers

Rapporteurs
Morten Broberg[1] *and Søren Friis Hansen*[2]

B. THE COMPETITION REGIME

Question 1: What is the view from your country on the functioning of the threshold levels in Article 1(2) as well as the 2/3 rule in the Merger Regulation, and the proposal in the Commission's Green Paper for amendment of Article 1(3) to deal with the problems of multiple filings?

Answer: In the view of the Danish Competition Authority, neither the threshold levels in Article 1(2) nor the two-thirds rule should be amended. Rather than amending the present thresholds, the Danish Competition Authority proposes the consideration of a solution whereby the undertakings concerned should have the option either of making multiple notifications to the Member States concerned or of notifying the concentration to the Commission if the concentration is notifiable to the competition authorities of several Member States.

In the opinion of this rapporteur the threshold levels set out in Article 1(2) do not provide a fully satisfactory way of allocating jurisdiction. To a considerable extent this is due to the fact that group turnover does not constitute an adequate means of defining those concentrations that have real Community dimension.[3]

As for the present thresholds set out in Article 1(3), I fully agree with the Commission that these do not work. However, this does not mean that I agree with the Commission's proposal that the thresholds in Article 1(3) should be replaced by a rule whereby concentrations that fall within the scope of the merger control regimes of at least three Member States should instead be notified to the Commission. This view is based on the following observations:

- Turnover thresholds were originally chosen because they provided an objective and unambiguous allocation of jurisdiction. The drawback was that it was obvious that such thresholds would catch a number of concentrations lacking real Community dimension and, equally, that they would miss a significant number of concentrations which have real Community dimension. To introduce a dividing line like the one proposed by the Commission in the Green Paper would mean that the clear delimitation of jurisdiction through the use of turnover criteria would be lost. However, the maintenance of the thresholds in Article 1(2) would necessarily mean that the disadvantages of the turnover thresholds would not be removed. Hence, the Commission's proposal means that the advantages of the turnover thresholds would be lost while their disadvantages would remain.
- Making the Commission's jurisdiction conditional upon whether a concentration is caught by the merger control regimes of a given number of Member States implies that the jurisdiction of the Commission may be altered unilaterally by the Member States. If just one of the Member States expands or diminishes the scope of its merger control regime, this may directly affect the number of concentrations that are notifiable in three Member States. This may have an immediate effect on the jurisdiction of the other Member States.
- An obvious problem in relation to the Commission's proposal is how to establish quickly, efficiently and correctly whether a concentration falls within the scope of a national merger control regime. The Commission has proposed a non-opposition procedure, under which the notifying parties must show the national merger control regimes to which the concentration must be notified. The Member States will then have a certain amount of time in which to oppose the findings of the notifying parties. If no opposition is raised, the Commission may rely on the findings of the notifying parties. Such a system is likely to cause considerable problems in practice.
- Even though the national merger control regimes have undergone a "soft harmonisation" during the past decade, substantial differences persist. Further harmonisation would therefore be highly desirable, if the Commission's proposal were to be adopted. This is particularly so in respect of the definition of a concentration and in respect of when a concentration is notifiable.
- The Commission's proposal requires a concentration to be notifiable in at least three Member States. It is difficult to see any convincing reasons why the Commission has set the limit at three rather than two Member States. Before the 1997 revision of the Merger Regulation, the Commission tabled a proposal very similar to the present one. At that time, however, the Commission proposed that it should have jurisdic-

tion when a concentration would be notifiable in only two Member States.

- In support of the need for the proposed revision, the Commission points to the likely expansion of the Community by 10 new Member States. However, the expansion of the Community to 25 Member States would necessarily mean that the proposed new rule on jurisdiction would lead to even more arbitrary results than is the case today, and it would lead to increased forum shopping.
- Finally, it is remarkable that the Commission appears not to have considered the problem relating to the EEA-Agreement. Hence it seems that the present system for establishing jurisdiction in either the EEA (Norway, Iceland and Liechtenstein) or in the Community will continue. This means, for instance, that a concentration that is notifiable in Finland, Sweden and Denmark will be transferred to the Commission, whereas a concentration that is notifiable in Finland, Sweden and Norway will not.

In the opinion of this rapporteur a better (though not perfect) solution would be to abolish the thresholds set out in Article 1(3), to lower the thresholds in Article 1(2) and to supplement Article 1(2) with a *de minimis* rule.[4]

Question 2: In light of the experiences made in your country, do Member States have sufficient flexibility to call for mergers to be referred back under Article 9 of the Merger Regulation? In light of the proposal in the Commission's Green Paper, what is your view on the circumstances in which this power should be exercised?

Answer: The Danish Competition Authority has no objections to the flexibility of the present referral system under Article 9 of the Merger Regulation. Moreover, the Competition Authority supports the proposal that guidelines on Article 9 referrals should be introduced[5] and that the Commission should be given the power to refer a case to the national competition authorities.[6]

Question 3: Is the system of consultation between the European Commission and the national competition authorities (NCAs) working adequately? Does there need to be a better formalised system for consultation between NCAs directly involved either in the case of multiple filings outside the Merger Regulation or in cases where more than one Member State exercise the Article 9 request?

Answer: The Danish Competition Authority has only very limited experience in the field of referred mergers. However, the experience so far has been very positive.

Where several Member State competition authorities have parallel jurisdiction over the same concentration, a formalised system is desirable. Indeed, a working group under the ECA (European Competition Authorities) has started work to remedy the problems relating to the exchange of information between the competition authorities in cases of multi-jurisdictional mergers.

Question 4: How does the test under the law of your country compare to that under the Merger Regulation? Should all Member States adopt the same test as under the Merger Regulation, and should this EU test be the (US) 'significant lessening of competition' test rather than the present EU 'dominance' test?

Answer: The Danish test is the same as that in the Merger Regulation, i.e. a concentration will only be prohibited if it creates or strengthens a dominant position whereby effective competition in the market is significantly impeded.

In the view of this rapporteur the actual merger control test applied by the different Member States should be a matter for the individual Member States. This best accords with the principle of subsidiarity. Obviously, this may cause problems where a concentration has effects in several Member States, but nevertheless falls to be vetted by the national merger control regimes. In principle, concentrations which obviously have real Community dimension should be vetted by the Commission rather than by Member State competition authorities. The correct solution would therefore seem to be to transfer such concentrations to the Commission for examination.

Question 5: Are the procedural and judicial safeguards adequate to protect parties from abuse of power by the competition authorities? How does the laws of your country compare to EC law in this respect?

Answer: Under the Danish merger control scheme, the main safeguard against abuse of power is the possibility of appealing against the decision of the Competition Council to the Competition Appeals Tribunal. Moreover, decisions of the Competition Appeals Tribunal may be challenged before the ordinary courts. The value of these safeguards is somewhat diminished, however, by the fact that proposed concentrations are often under a considerable time-pressure so it may not make sense to appeal against a decision. Another limit on the use of this safeguard is that the competition authorities generally have a wide ranging discretion.

As for procedural and judicial safeguards, the main difference between the regime set up under the Merger Regulation and the Danish merger regime appears to be that the Danish scheme does not include a hearing officer.

Question 6a: Please provide an overview of the structure of and main features of the relevant domestic legislation and the institutional framework (who enforces it)? It may be helpful with some information about the role of private rights of action.

Answer: Denmark has virtually copied the Community's merger control system. Hence, the Danish system requires that concentrations that fulfil certain turnover thresholds must obtain prior approval from the Danish Competition Authority before closing. As with the Merger Regulation, the Danish system operates a two-phase procedure. In the first phase, the Competition Authority must decide whether the merger merits a full scale examination, and if so, a second phase investigation is initiated. The clearance decision may be made conditional upon the parties fulfilling certain conditions.

Question 6b: What kinds of transaction are caught? Are joint ventures caught? What are the jurisdictional thresholds? Is it difficult to identify with sufficient certainty whether a filing is in fact required under national law? Are foreign-to-foreign mergers caught?

Answer: All concentrations fulfilling the turnover thresholds set out below are caught. The Danish definition of a concentration has been taken from the Merger Regulation (as amended by Regulation 1310/97). As with the Merger Regulation, the Danish merger control regime therefore also covers full-functionjoint ventures.

The jurisdictional thresholds are as follows:

I. A. Where the combined aggregate turnover in Denmark of the parties to the transactions is 3.8 billion Danish Kroner (approx.: 510 million Euro) or more;

and

B. The aggregate turnover in Denmark of each of at least two of the parties is 300 million Danish Kroner (approx.: 40 million Euro) or more:

or, alternatively,

II. A. Where the aggregate turnover in Denmark of at least one of the parties is 3.8 billion Danish Kroner (approx.: 510 million Euro) or more;

and

B. The aggregate world-wide turnover of at least one of the other parties is 3.8 billion Danish Kroner (approx.: 510 million Euro) or more.

As the Danish merger regime is a virtual copy of the Community regime, establishing whether a transaction must be notified is fairly straightforward. Also, the case law generated under Community law is persuasive authority in the interpretation of Danish law.

Foreign-to-foreign mergers which fulfil the above turnover thresholds are also notifiable. Hence if, for instance, two undertakings set up a full-function joint venture in Japan, and one of these undertakings belongs to a group that generates a turnover of more than 3.8 billion Danish Kroner in Denmark, and the other undertaking belongs to a group that generates more than 3.8 billion Danish Kroner world-wide, the transaction will be notifiable (unless it also has a Community dimension).

Question 6c: Is the filing mandatory or voluntary? Who is responsible for filing? What is involved in the preparation of the filing? What are the deadlines for filing? What are the waiting periods and does implementation of the transaction have to be suspended?

Answer: Filing is mandatory. The undertakings involved in the concentration are responsible for submitting the filing. Even though the Danish Competition Authority requires appreciably less information than the Commission requires in its Form CO, preparing the filing can still be an onerous task. The undertakings concerned must fill in a Form K2. Form K2 first of all requires the undertakings concerned to provide information about the relevant markets and about the undertakings acting in these markets.

Filing must be made within one week of the earliest of the following:

(i) the conclusion of the agreement,
(ii) the announcement of a public bid, or
(iii) the acquisition of a controlling interest.

As a clear principal rule, a transaction may not be implemented before it has been approved by the authorities. There are two exceptions to this rule. First, in the case of a public bid, the bidder may complete the transaction, but must observe certain restrictions on the exercise of the voting rights thus acquired. Second, the Competition Council has the power to grant an exemption.

The waiting periods are as follows:

The Competition Council must decide whether to approve the transaction or to initiate a full investigation within four weeks from the receipt of a completed notification.

If there is to be a full investigation, the Competition Council has a further three months in which to reach a final decision. These deadlines may only be extended in exceptional circumstances.

Question 6d: What are the issues and possible sanctions involved in closing before clearance? What is the timetable for clearance and can it be speeded up?

Answer: The conclusion of a transaction before it has been cleared by the authorities is a criminal offence, punishable by a fine.

The timetable for clearance has been set out in the answer to question 6c above. The undertakings concerned may speed up the process by contacting the Competition Authority before notifying, in order to assure that the notification will be completed, by responding swiftly to requests from the Competition Authority, and by being prepared to offer undertakings to remedy the Authority's possible concerns as to the effects of the transaction.

Question 6e: Are there any special rules applicable to public takeover bids?

Answer: Public takeover bids are subject to the same rules as are other concentrations.

Question 6f: What is the substantive test for clearance?

Answer: The Danish merger control regime operates a two-pronged substantive test which has been taken from the Merger Regulation. Hence, a concentration must be prohibited if it creates or strengthens a dominant position whereby competition is significantly impeded. The substantive test is thus based on a dominance test.

Question 6g: To what extent are non-competition issues relevant to the review process?

Answer: In principle the substantive test under the Danish merger control regime is purely a competition-based one. Obviously, there is no guarantee that non-competition issues (such as the need to secure jobs or to protect a "national champion") will never be taken into account.

Question 6h: Is it possible to remedy competition issues?

Answer: The Danish merger control regime, like the Community's, provides the parties with the possibility of addressing competition concerns during the review process.

Question 6i: What are the typical steps during the investigation? What rights do complainants have? What publicity is given to the process? What are the opportunities for judicial review?

Answer: In principle, the investigation by the Danish Competition Authority begins when it receives a notification of a concentration. During the four week long first phase, the Authority carries out a preliminary investigation in order to ascertain whether the concentration gives rise to competition concerns. Only if, on the basis of the first phase examination, the Competition Authority finds that the concentration gives rise to competition concerns, will the three month long second phase investigation be initiated. During this second phase, the Authority must carry out an in-depth examination. The Competition Council must reach a final decision on the basis of this examination.

Third parties have very limited rights. The Danish Competition Act expressly provides that in merger cases third parties may not appeal to the Competition Appeals Tribunal against a decision of the Competition Council. However, provided that a third party has the requisite *locus standi*, he may challenge such a decision before the ordinary courts.

Publicity is very limited during the review process. The Danish Competition Act explicitly excludes the application of the Law on Public Access to Documents to the field of competition. This means that there is only limited publicity during the review process. Parties to a concentration do have access to the files, however.

Decisions by the Competition Council may be appealed to the Competition Appeals Tribunal. Decisions by the Competition Appeals Tribunal may be appealed to the ordinary courts.

Question 6j: What are the enforcement powers? How does administrative and civil sanctions compare with the EC regime? And what are the criminal sanctions and are they used?

Answer: Two types of enforcement powers are available in case of infringement of the Competition Act. If a person fails to provide information requested by the Competition Council or fails to comply with a condition or an order issued under the powers of the Act, the Council may impose periodic penalty payments. Other infringements, such as failing to notify a concentration or carrying on with a concentration that has been prohibited, are considered to be criminal offences. In these situations the case will be handed over to the public prosecutor who may bring the case before the criminal courts. Those prosecuted may be punishable by fine.

Question 6k: Do the authorities cooperate with other antitrust authorities?

Answer: The Danish Competition Authority has entered into an agreement with the competition authorities of Norway and Iceland on co-operation in competition cases.

Question 6l: Are there also rules on foreign investment, special sectors or other relevant approvals?

Answer: In Denmark only a single set of rules applies to substantive competition assessment.[7] Hence, no special rules apply to foreign investments or special sectors.

Question 6m: Are there current proposals to change the legislation?

Answer: No.

C. COMPANY LAW AND FINANCIAL MARKET REGULATORY REGIME

Question 7: What will you identify as the main obstacles to take overs where a company from your jurisdiction is either bidder or target and the other company is from another EU jurisdiction?

Answer: In Denmark the phenomenon of 'takeovers' was pretty well unknown until around 1990. Since then there have been a number of studies of the market for corporate control in Denmark. These studies have revealed a number of general factors which characterise the Danish business environment and the Danish securities market, and which constitute potential obstacles to a company or person wishing to take over a Danish company. It should be emphasised that there are variations between individual Danish companies, and that the obstacles to takeovers referred to are thus not characteristic of all Danish companies.

Under Danish law it is permitted to divide the share capital of a company into different classes of shares, so that the voting rights of individual classes of shares differ. This can mean that a person who owns a minority of a company's shares can nevertheless control a majority of the votes which can be given at a general meeting of the company (see Question 14g below).

In the Danish business environment, in a relatively large proportion of companies the controlling shareholder is a trust fund. Carlsberg and Novo Nordisk are examples of Danish companies where the parent company is a trust fund. Frequently the trust deed requires that the trust fund maintain a given proportion of the share capital of the production companies which are part of the corporate group. Thus, the Carlsberg Fund must own a controlling shareholding in the production company Carlsberg Bryggerier A/S. Takeovers are thus frequently excluded in companies which are controlled by a trust fund.

In general Danish companies typically have highly concentrated ownership. This means that the takeover of a Danish company can often only take place by agreement with the controlling shareholder. The proportion of the total listed share capital in Denmark which is owned by institutional investors is about 25%.

The obstacles to takeovers referred to above are, as indicated, general factors existing in the Danish business environment. There do not appear to be any general legal issues which make the takeover of Danish companies problematic in cases where the acquiring company is domiciled in another EU or EEA Member State.

There are about 35,000 public limited companies (aktieselskaber) in Denmark. These companies are subject to the provisions of the Act on public limited companies (referred to here as ASL). Of these Danish public limited companies, about 250 are listed on the Copenhagen Stock Exchange. The most widespread form of company is the private limited company (anpartselskab). About 65,000 private limited companies are registered in Denmark. The private limited company is the usual form of incorporation for small and medium size businesses with a limited number of owners, which is why this form of company has only a very modest part to play in connection with takeovers in Denmark. The great majority of takeovers in Denmark thus concern public limited companies.

Question 8: Do hostile take overs by companies from other EU jurisdictions in fact take place in your country?

Answer: From 1990 to 2002 there were a large number of takeovers of Danish companies. Most of these were takeovers which took place with the co-operation of the managements of the companies involved. The number of attempted hostile takeovers has thus been relatively modest. A significant number of these attempted hostile takeovers have been initiated by foreign companies, of which, in turn, most have been domiciled in other EU or EEA Member States.

In 1999 the Danish government carried out a study of the ownership structure of Danish businesses. It was shown that the number of company mergers and acquisitions which involved a Danish company and a company from another EU Member State was between 200 and 350 a year between 1986 and 1998. Of these, the number of takeovers in which a Danish company was the target company was between 50 and 100 a year.[8]

Question 9: To what extents are there any sectors (utilities, financial institutions) that in practice are further protected from hostile take overs, or foreign take overs in particular? Are there any policy statements or particular legal mechanisms that give effect to this protection, or is it a matter of informal mechanisms?

Answer: Throughout the 1990s the Danish State privatised a number of large national enterprises. These privatisations involved the reconstruction of the nationalised business into a public limited company, whereupon the State sold its shareholding in whole or in part. There have been cases where foreign companies have acquired control of privatised companies. For example, the controlling shareholding in the national telecommunications company (Teledanmark) was transferred from the Danish State to an American company in 1997.

There have also been cases where Danish banks have been taken over by foreign banks. Thus, in 2001, Svenska Handelsbanken made a voluntary and an obligatory takeover offer to the other shareholders in the Danish bank Midtbank.

Under Danish law, a finance company is understood to include stockbroking companies, insurance companies, banks and savings institutions, cf. ß 2.1 in the Act on finance companies[9]. In Denmark, finance companies are under the supervision of a central authority, the Financial Supervisory Authority. Before a person or a company acquires a qualifying share of the votes or capital of a Danish finance company, the acquisition shall be notified to and approved by the Financial Supervisory Authority, cf. ß 11 in the Act on finance companies.

In the electricity supply sector, a significant proportion of Danish companies are owned by Danish local government authorities. The Act which governs Danish electricity supply companies includes a provision under which, if a local government authority sells its share in an electricity supply company, whether in whole or in part, it can only recover the original capital investment. If there is a net profit from the sale, this shall be set off against the local governments authority's contribution from the State[10]. This means that a significant indirect obstacle has been put in the way of takeovers of Danish electricity supply companies, as there is no incentive for the seller to relinquish control of the company. This indirect obstacle applies equally to Danish and to foreign companies.

Question 10: What are the company law techniques of completing a take over or merger that are used in practice where one of the companies is from another EU jurisdiction? Please give particular attention to how this would differ from the usual completion of a take over or merger where both companies are from your jurisdiction. It would be useful if you could add a

comment about the consequences on the techniques used of the taxation regime and of any differential tax treatment of take overs or mergers where one party is from another EU jurisdiction.

Answer: In practice, takeovers are most frequently carried out by the acquirer making a voluntary offer to buy shares in the target company. The acquirer will hereby often acquire a sufficient proportion of the shares in the target company to trigger a requirement to make an obligatory takeover offer (see Question 14a below).

If the acquirer gets ownership of 90% or more of the shares in the target company, the acquirer will frequently make a compulsory purchase of shares from the remaining minority shareholders in the company, who may not have accepted the offer made (see Question 14d below). Where the acquired company is listed on the stock exchange, it shall be de-listed after the acquisition.

Where a takeover involves an exchange of shares, the shareholders in the acquired company are, for tax purposes, regarded as having acquired the shares in the acquiring company on the same date and for the same amount as the exchanged shares, cf. ß 13 in the Act on advance corporation tax[11]. The share exchange does not thus trigger any immediate taxation of the shareholders of the acquired company. The provision in the Act on advance corporation tax applies when both the acquiring and the acquired companies are domiciled in an EU Member State or are companies which are domiciled in a country outside the EU and which correspond to a Danish public or private limited company. Thus, Danish law does not distinguish between foreigners and Danes in connection with the tax treatment of share exchanges.

In connection with the merger of two large banks, the merger was executed in such a way that the shareholders of the holding company of the company which was to be taken over were offered shares in the holding company of the acquiring company. Following the share exchange, there was a series of mergers between the subsidiary companies of the two concerns.

Question 11: A duty on listed companies to disclose capital and control structures is proposed in Issues Relating to Takeover Bids, the First Report of the High Level Group of Company Law Experts (see p 25). Would this require amendments in the legislation in your country? How would these amendments in case be implemented (in primary company law, securities law, stock exchange regulations etc.)?

Answer: The group of experts appointed by the Commission has suggested that the publication of certain information should be required. Most of the information concerned is already covered by the requirements for publication under existing Danish law. Publication is thus obligatory to the extent that the decisions in question can only be made in accordance with provisions in the company's articles of association.

As for information about share ownership, Danish law already has a requirement that major shareholders shall allow their shareholding to be made public (ASL ß 28a and ß 29 in the Act on the trade in securities – VÊrdipapirhanselsloven – referred to here as VHL). There is no obligation for members of the management to publicise their shareholdings in the company, unless they are covered by the rules on major shareholders. Such an obligation would therefore be novel in Danish law.

Under Danish law, the division of shares into different classes of shares must be authorised by the articles of association, so, for this reason, this information is already publicly available. The acquisition by a company of its own shares can only be carried out by the board of directors when authorised to do so by the general meeting of the company, and under the authority of the articles of Association, so that the capacity of the management to buy the company's own shares shall be made public under existing law.

Existing Danish law does not have a requirement for the publication of rules on the appointment and dismissal of members of the management, or of agreements which come into effect upon the change of control over the company. Any requirement for the publication of such information would thus require an amendment to the law.

It is clear that the collective publication of the information in question under the rules of the stock exchange would give a potential investor quicker and easier access to this information, compared with current Danish law, under which the available information must be obtained from various different sources.

Question 12: A so called break through rule after take over bids is another of the proposals in Issues Relating to Takeover Bids, the First Report of the High Level Group of Company Law Experts (see p 29). Would this require amendments in the legislation in your country? How would these amendments in case be implemented (in primary company law, securities law, stock exchange regulations etc.)?

Answer: A Break Through Rule in connection with takeover bids, as suggested by the group of experts appointed by the Commission, could only be implemented in Denmark following an amendment to Danish legislation. Any such amendment must at least cover the provisions in ß 31 of VHL concerning takeover bids. Since the rules on the division of share capital into different classes of shares is authorised by ASL, the implementation of a Break Through Rule would also require an amendment of this Act.

It should be added that the introduction of a Break Through Rule, as proposed by the group of experts, would cause a number of special problems in Danish law. Under the Danish Constitution, the Danish State may expropriate the property of its citizens, upon the payment of reasonable compensation, where the public weal requires this (ß 73 of the Constitution). The latest proposal for the Fifth Company Law Directive included a general prohibition of the division of share capital into different classes of shares. The Danish view is that the repeal of the existing Danish rules allowing the division of share capital into different classes of shares would amount to expropriation of the property of the owners of shares with strongly weighted voting rights.

There is a corresponding problem in relation to the proposed Break Through Rule. There can thus be no doubt that a shareholder, who controls a voting majority in a company which has different classes of shares by virtue of possession of shares with strongly weighted voting rights, will be able to claim compensation from the Danish State under the constitutional rules on expropriation, if the shareholder in question loses his voting majority through the implementation of a Break Through Rule.

Question 13: In your view, would these two new rules as proposed have any material impact on the existing barriers to take overs in your country (or in others as seen from your point of view)? It would be helpful if you could demonstrate the impact, or lack of it, by going through one or more recent take over bids that failed in your country (or in some other member state, by a company from your country).

Answer: As argued below (in answers to Questions 14g and 14h), the possibility of dividing the share capital into different classes of shares is a defence against takeovers which is relatively frequently used in Danish companies. In fact, it is a highly effective defence. There can therefore be no doubt that the introduction of a Break Through Rule into Danish law would make a significant difference to the possibility of carrying out takeovers of Danish companies.

Question 14a:What are the main features of the relevant domestic take over legislation constituting the company law and financial market regime, and who enforces it (independent regulators, regulatory bodies with appeal to ministry, stock exchange)? What is the extent of intervention by the takeover regulator(s) – to what extent does the regulator have wide or general discretions to block and play a protectionist role (for example in its capacity as approver of the offer terms/documentation)?

Answer: In 1996, a reform of the Danish stock exchange rules was carried out. A number of different sets of rules which regulate the activities of the different actors on the financial market as well as the issuing companies were gathered together in the VHL.[12]

There are special provisions on takeover bids in §§ 31 and 32 of the VHL. These provisions are supplemented by a statutory instrument, which contains more detailed rules for making takeover bids.[13]

Where there is a direct or indirect transfer of a shareholding in a company which has one or more classes of shares listed on the Copenhagen Stock Exchange, then, under certain conditions, the person or company acquiring the shares shall give all other shareholders an offer to dispose of their shares on the same terms.

The criteria used in § 31 of VHL which determine whether the acquirer of shares is obliged to make a takeover bid, are, for all practical purposes, the same as the company law definition of a concern which is in § 2 of ASL, and which is based on the Seventh Company Law Directive. However, the provision on effective control (VHL § 31.1.5)) is different.

A takeover bid must be made if a person or company acquires a controlling influence on a company and comes to possess more than one third of the voting rights. The possession of a majority of the voting rights automatically triggers the obligation to make a takeover bid (VHL § 1.1.1)). Where a person or company possesses between 33.4% and 50% of the voting rights in a company which is listed on the Copenhagen Stock Exchange, that person or company can be required to make a takeover bid. There can also be an obligation to make a takeover bid where two or more shareholders act in concert to obtain control of a listed company.

The obligation to make a takeover bid applies to all who acquire a controlling shareholding in a company which is listed on the Copenhagen Stock Exchange, regardless of whether they are natural or legal persons, and regardless of their nationality.

In connection with the making of an obligatory takeover bid, the acquirer of shares shall prepare and publish a special offer document. There are detailed minimum requirements for the content of the offer document, cf. the statutory instrument on takeovers, § 3.1) to 15).

Likewise, a special offer document shall be prepared where a person or company, not having an obligation to do so under VHL § 31, makes a public bid to acquire shares in a company whose shares are listed on the Copenhagen Stock Exchange, cf. VHL § 32 (on voluntary bids).

An infringement of the obligation to make a takeover bid can be punished by a fine. The obligation is enforced by the Financial Supervisory Authority and the Securities Council. The Copenhagen Stock Exchange has a duty to ensure that the rules on the obligation to make a bid are complied with (VHL § 31). In cases where a minority shareholder believes that a major shareholder has disregarded the obligation to make a takeover bid, then the minority shareholder in question can bring civil proceedings with a view to having a takeover bid made, cf., for example, the decision of the Supreme Court in the case reported in UfR 1999.727H.

Apart from the cases where a bid does not satisfy the minimum requirements for the content of an offer document, neither the Copenhagen Stock Exchange nor the other authorities have any authority to block the making of a bid.

The rules on the making of takeover bids can conflict with the rules on the compulsory redemption of the shares of minority shareholders (see Question 14d below). This is, for example, the case where, before an obligatory bid has been made or before the deadline for the acceptance of such a bid, a shareholder has acquired 90% of the target company's shares. It is the established practice of the Copenhagen Stock Exchange that where, in connection with the making of a voluntary bid, a shareholder obtains such control over a company that this triggers a duty to make an obligatory takeover bid on identical terms, then that shareholder is required to make a takeover bid under the provisions of VHL § 31, regardless of the fact that the shareholder in question could initiate compulsory acquisition under the provisions of ASL §20b. The remaining minority shareholders can, however, freely choose whether they wish to accept the takeover bid made, or whether they wish their shares to be compulsorily acquired in accordance with the rules in ASL § 20d.

There are a number of **exceptions** to the obligation to make a takeover bid.

In general, when shares are transferred as the result of inheritance, a gift or through the recovery of debt, this does not give rise to a requirement to make a takeover bid.

A transfer of shares which takes place within the same group of companies does not involve a duty to make a takeover bid. This is in accordance with the statutory instrument on takeovers, § 1.6. Correspondingly, it is the practice of the Copenhagen Stock Exchange that there is no duty to make a takeover bid when a transfer of shares takes place within a group of persons who, under the rules in the VHL, are considered as one owner. For example, this will be the case where shares are transferred between family members who have previously acted and voted as if they were a single shareholder. Furthermore, a shareholder who already controls a voting majority in a company is not required to make a takeover bid where that person acquires further shares in order to consolidate his position.

A shareholder can obtain possession of a controlling shareholding in other ways than through the actual purchase of shares. A *merger* does not, on the face of it, give rise to an obligation to make a takeover bid. However, in practice, the Copenhagen Stock Exchange has assumed that a merger which is made with a view to avoiding the obligation to make a takeover bid will be covered by the rules on takeover bids.

Another situation which can lead to a change in the control over a company is when there is an issue of shares. Under Danish law, there is an assumption that there is a right to subscribe for shares when shares are issued by means of cash subscription (ASL § 30). However, the company general meeting can decide to vary the right to subscribe, just the right to subscribe does not apply when there is an issue of shares for non-cash consideration. A share issue made without a right for existing shareholders to subscribe could lead to a change of the control over the company. The practice of the Copenhagen Stock Exchange has established that, in general, a share issue does not trigger an obligation to make a takeover bid, unless the share issue is made with a view to avoiding the obligation to make a takeover bid.

Question 14b: Are there restrictions on a board taking action to frustrate a bid that has been made? When do the relevant restrictions start to apply – earlier than a formal announcement/filing of a bid? To what extent can shareholders approve the taking of frustrating action in advance of any bid?

Answer: Where a takeover bid is made in accordance with the rules in the VHL, the board of directors of the target company shall prepare a report on the offer for the shareholders (the statutory instrument on takeovers ß 7.) This report shall be made public before the end of the first half of the offer period. Apart from this, there are no special rules concerning the duties of the management when a takeover bid is made for a company. Under Danish law the actions of the company's management are thus governed by ordinary company law rules.

In accordance with the general duty of the management to protect the interests of the shareholders, the management may not actively oppose a takeover bid which can be regarded as advantageous for the shareholders of the company. However, there is nothing to prevent the management from trying to obtain a competing bid. Agreements on changes to the conditions for members of the management can be made in connection with takeover bids, though it must be presumed that information about such agreements is given to the shareholders. It would be contrary to the management's duty of loyalty towards the shareholders if the management sought to secure for itself special privileges in connection with the takeover of a company.

Question 14c: Are there restrictions on the type of consideration that can be offered in a bid, for example securities only if these are listed in the target country's home state or the EU?

Answer: There are no general restrictions on the offeror's consideration paid for the shares to be acquired. Thus shares can be offered in exchange for shares in the target company. The primary rule is that the offeror shall offer the same consideration to the other shareholders as has been given in payment for the shares already acquired (the statutory instrument on takeovers, § 5.4). However, the offeror can always fulfil his obligations by making a cash payment for the shares of the shareholders in the target company.

Question 14d: Are there effective compulsory acquisition procedures regarding a small non-accepting minority? Can a bidder make its offer conditional on achieving the number of shares required so it can operate a squeeze out?

Answer: Under ASL § 20b, a shareholder who owns more than 90% of the shares in a company to which there are attached at least 90% of the total voting rights in the company, can compulsorily acquire the remaining shares. A decision to make such compulsory acquisition shall be made by the majority shareholder and the board of directors of the company. If agreement cannot be reached between the majority shareholder and the minority shareholders on the share price, this shall be settled by an impartial valuer. Under these same conditions any minority shareholder can require that the majority shareholder shall redeem his shares (ASL § 20d).

Question 14e: Is there a principle of board neutrality? Can a target board align itself with a particular bidder/agree measures such as exclusivity arrangements to protect a particular deal?

Answer: Under Danish law, the board of directors of a company has a duty, faithfully to look after the interests of the company. However, there is no requirement that the board of directors shall be neutral in relation to any takeover offer. As stated above, most takeovers in Denmark have been carried out in co-operation with the target company. In these cases the board of directors usually make a recommendation about the offer made.

Question 14f: Can a target board hand over information to a potential bidder?

Answer: Under Danish law, the management of a company has a duty of confidentiality. A member of a company's management who, without authorisation, passes on confidential information, is liable to punishment (ASL § 161). The management of a company can enter into negotiations with other companies on merger or takeover. As part of these negotiations it is permitted to exchange confidential information between the managements of the companies involved.

Where a person, who possesses information which has not been made public, passes this on, or where there is trading in a company's shares on the basis of such information, this will amount to an infringement of the prohibition against insider dealing.

Question 14g: Are structures permitted which concentrate control rights in the hands of minority shareholders? Are structures permitted which place limitations/restrictions on voting rights, caps for example on voting rights above a certain threshold?

Answer: existing Danish law it is permitted, where authorised by the company's articles of association, to divide the share capital into different classes of shares, with different rights attaching to the individual classes. In practice the shares of the different classes are often referred to as 'A shares' and 'B shares' etc. It is thus permissible for the voting rights of a company's shares to differ, so that some shares may be given greater voting rights than shares in other classes of shares. It is permissible for the voting rights to differ by a ratio of up to 1:10 (ASL § 67), and this is the proportion which is used by most of the companies which have different classes of shares.

The possibility of dividing the share capital into different classes of shares thus means that a shareholder who owns a modest proportion of the share capital can possess a majority of the voting rights. However, where a decision is taken by the general meeting of a company to change the articles of association, the shareholders with weaker voting rights are protected, since such a decision must be supported by both 2/3rds of the votes cast and by 2/3rds of the capital represented at the general meeting (ASL § 78).

There are no restrictions on the capacity to divide the share capital into different classes of shares as far as companies listed on the Copenhagen Stock Exchange are concerned. It is possible for just one of a company's classes of shares to be listed on the stock exchange, though the general rule is that all classes of shares are required to be listed.

The question of the appropriateness of the co-existence of different classes of shares has been the subject of intense debate in Denmark in recent years. It has been noted that there has been a tendency that, among newly listed companies on the Copenhagen Stock Exchange, very few have their share capital divided between different classes of shares, and that some companies which have already been listed have removed their existing divisions into classes of shares.

In 1999, a committee drawn from different government departments concluded that there is no particular need to do away with the existing possibility of dividing share capital into different classes. The committee found that this is a question which is best left to the market.[14]

However, in the Danish report on Corporate Governance, the committee recommended that listed companies should do away with divisions into different classes of shares. Under the rules which apply to issuers of securities on the Copenhagen Stock Exchange, the Stock Exchange recommends that, in their annual reports, listed companies should abide by the recommendations contained in the report referred to.

In general, under Danish law it is possible to introduce voting limits or ownership limits through appropriate provisions in the articles of association. A decision to introduce an ownership limit must be made at a general meeting with at least a 9/10ths majority (ASL § 79.2). Although it is not possible to introduce restrictions on the sale of shares which are listed on the Copenhagen Stock Exchange (see Question 14h), under the practice of the Stock Exchange it is accepted that the articles of association can include ownership limits in companies which are listed on the Stock Exchange, as long as the limit for the proportion of shares which may be owned by a single shareholder is not set at below 10%. In practice, such ownership limits are often found in the articles of association of banks.

Question 14h: Can restrictions be placed on the transferability of shares either by the issuer (in articles of association or by other means) or by arrangements between shareholders? Can a board delay registering transfers of shares?

Answer: It is possible to introduce restrictions on the sale of a company's shares in its articles of association. Under Danish law there are no limits with regard to the types of restrictions on sales which can be made. In practice this kind of provision is used in relation to two specific types of restriction on sales.

The shareholders of a company can be given a prior right to acquire the company's shares (ASL § 19). The articles of association can contain a provision about the price that shall be paid for the shares. If the price determined under the provisions of the articles of association would lead to an obviously unreasonable price, this can be set aside by the courts.

There can also be a requirement that the company shall approve all purchasers of the company's shares. In practice it is the board of directors which is given the power to approve new shareholders.

As for shares which are listed on the Copenhagen Stock Exchange, these may not be subject to restrictions on their sale in the articles of association. It is possible to make a provision in a shareholder agreement to restrict the sale of shares which are listed on the Stock Exchange, but such a shareholder agreement must be made public where the shareholders covered by the agreement together own more than 5% of the company's share capital (the statutory instrument on takeovers § 10).

There is nothing to stop a company having several classes of shares, of which only one is listed. There can be provisions in the articles of association restricting sales of shares in non-listed classes of shares. As the non-listed classes of shares will often include the voting majority in the company (see Question 14g), this combination constitutes a significant obstacle to a hostile takeover of the company.

Shareholder agreements which involve a restriction on the sale of non-listed shares can be freely entered into. Such shareholder agreements are subject to the same requirements for publication as apply to corresponding agreements on listed shares. The requirement for making public shareholder agreements which involve a restriction on sale of shares thus applies if at least one of the company's classes of shares is listed on the Copenhagen Stock Exchange.

According to the practice of the Stock Exchange, it is not required that the text of any shareholder agreement should be made public. It is sufficient that the main points of the agreement should be made public.

Question 14i: What contractual barriers (including share holder agreements) to take over bids are in use in public companies (eg golden parachutes, change of control provisions triggering default of loan agreements, or winding up or change of control of joint ventures)? What are the prospects of review by courts on the basis of contract or company law and by regulators on the basis of securities laws or stock exchange regulations?

Answer: Under Danish law, it is permitted to make agreements providing that the members of the management shall be granted a special severance package if there should be a change of control of the company. Such agreements are assumed to be lawful, and are only subject to such limitations as apply under the general company law rules. This means that the rewards of the management shall be reasonable, and that any agreement may not lead to members of the management being given terms which would constitute a clearly unreasonable advantage for the management, at the expense of the company.

Question 14j: Are there current proposals to change the legislation relating to take overs?

Answer: The Danish rules on takeover bids were laid down in law in 1996 as part of the stock exchange reform. The provisions of VHL ß 31 were amended by Act No. 250 of 23rd April 1999, because the acquisition of a controlling shareholding in the national telecommunications company (Teledanmark) by an American company had not triggered a requirement for the making of a takeover bid under the original rules concerning obligatory takeover bids.

There are no current plans to change the Danish rules on takeover bids.

D. FINAL ISSUES

Question 15: In your view, what is the extent to which the complexity of the regulatory arrangements, within national jurisdictions and between the Commission and Member States, present an obstacle to take overs?

Answer: In our view, one of the main obstacles created by the complexity of the regulatory arrangements is the additional uncertainty which it introduces into the process. Another problem arises where it is necessary to notify a concentration to several authorities since these will normally require different information, in different formats and in different languages. This puts a significant extra burden on the parties at a time when their human resources will normally be fully occupied with the commercial aspects of the transaction.

Question 16: Can you list some instances where different rules in the different regulatory systems have caused practical obstacles in a take over process? (One instance could be different time limits under the EC Merger Regulation and national merger rules on the one hand and under stock exchange rules on the other).

Answer: We have submitted question 16 to a number of lawyers practising in the field of merger control. The main problems identified are:

I. Incompatibility between the time limits laid down under the competition rules and the time limits provided under stock exchange rules. This problem is particularly exacerbated where a notified transaction enters an in-depth (second phase) examination with the competition authorities.

II. Most national merger control regimes operate under strict time limits. However, some merger control regimes (such as the Brazilian) continue to be very slow, and this obviously creates problems. (Closing a deal "without Brazil" is therefore not uncommon).

III. The information requirements differ between the different merger control regimes making it necessary to adapt the notification to the requirements of each regime. Moreover, in some cases the information requirements appear to be particularly heavy. This is not least so *vis-à-vis* notifications to the Commission under Form CO (see section 5.4 thereof) and to the American authorities under the Hart-Scott-Rodino Act (see Item 4c thereof).

IV. The language requirements differ from one regime to another. In some instances the Danish Competition Authority has accepted a notification made in English, thereby easing the burden where a notification must be made to a number of different merger control regimes.

V. During a hostile take-over bid it may be difficult (or even impossible) to obtain the necessary information to file a merger notification. In some jurisdictions (though not in Denmark) this may create a catch-22-like situation. This is so where, on the one hand, there is no possibility of acquiring control over a target without prior approval from the competition authorities while, on the other hand, the bidder is unable to get access to the information that is required to make a complete notification without first obtaining control over the target.

The practitioners asked found that the American Hart-Scott-Rodino Act provides a fine solution to this problem as it enables the bidder to notify the transaction providing only the information that is available to this party. Thereupon the American competition agency will require the target to submit the necessary information concerning that party. In this way a complete notification may be made and a final decision may be taken by the relevant competition agency even though the bidder has no access to the pertinent information *vis-‡-vis* the target.

NOTES

[1] Lecturer, ph.d., Faculty of Law, University of Copenhagen, Studiegaarden, Studiestraede 6, DK-1455 Copenhagen K, Denmark. Responsible for parts B and D.

[2] Professor, Lic.jur., Department of Accounting, Finance & Law, University of Southern Denmark, Campusvej 55, DK-5230 Odense M, Denmark. Responsible for parts C and D.

[3] On this point, see further my criticism of the present thresholds (together with suggestions for improvement thereof) in Morten Broberg, 'The European Commission's Jurisdiction to Scrutinise Mergers', 1st edition, Kluwer Law International, The Hague 1998, chapter 10.

[4] A more elaborate exposition of my criticism of the proposal put forward in the Commission's Green Paper may be found in my article "Muddying the Clear Waters - On the Commission's proposal for a new delimitation of jurisdiction in the field of merger control", which will be published in the September 2002 issue of the *European Competition Law Review*.

[5] See the Green Paper, para. 81.

[6] See the Green Paper, para. 81, letter b). The Danish Competition Authority adds, however, that the Commission should contact the national competition authority in question before making such referral.

[7] Certain types of concentrations require approval by authorities other than the Competition Council, e.g. concentrations in the financial sector. These approvals are not made on the basis of a substantive competition assessment.

[8] Cf. Debatoplæg om aktivt ejerskab (1999), p. 290.

[9] Cf. Act No. 501 of 7th June 2001.

[10] Cf. ß 37 in the Act on electricity supply (Consolidated Act No. 767 of 28th August 2001).

[11] Cf. Consolidated Act No. 796 of 10th September 2001.

[12] Cf. Consolidated Act No. 168 of 14th March 2001.

[13] Cf. Order No. 827 of 10th November 1999.

[14] Cf. Debatoplæg om aktivt ejerskab, published in 1999. The report is available on www.fm.dk.

FINLAND

Cross Border Mergers in Company Law and Competition Law: Removing the Final Barriers

Rapporteurs
Mr Ari Keinänen, Mr Arttu Mentula, and Mr Henrik Hinders[1]

THE COMPETITION REGIME

1. What is the view from your country[2] on the functioning of the threshold levels in Article 1(2) as well as the 2/3 rule in the Merger Regulation, and the proposal in the Commission's Green Paper for amendment of Article 1(3) to deal with the problems of multiple filings?

The threshold levels set out in Article 1(2) and the 2/3 rule in the Merger Regulation are functioning well from the Finnish point of view. As to Article 1(3), it has not worked in a way as the intention was when this amendment was implemented in the Merger Regulation. Therefore, any amendments to Article 1(3), which would reduce the number of multiple filings, would be welcomed.

2. In light of the experiences made in your country, do member states have sufficient flexibility to call for mergers to be referred back under Article 9 of the Merger Regulation? In light of the proposal in the Commission's Green Paper, what is your view on the circumstances in which this power should be exercised?

The Finnish Competition Authority ('FCA') made a partial referral request under Article 9 of the Merger Regulation to the Commission in the Metsäliitto/Vapo case. The Commission referred thereafter the case partially with its decision made on 8 February 2001 to the FCA according to the FCA's request. This is the first time so far the FCA has used the referral mechanism set out in Article 9 of the Merger Regulation. On the other hand, it may be assumed that in other possible referrals the FCA considered that the Commission's own investigations would be sufficient.

The Commission's power to refer cases should be exercised in exceptional circumstances, because the referral normally generates extra costs and prolongs the decision process. In its Green Paper, the Commission has proposed that it should be able to refer cases at its own initiative to national authorities. It is questionable whether the Commission should be granted this power. There is a risk that the Commission could refer cases to the national competition authorities depending also on the Commission's workload.

3. Is the system of consultation between the European Commission and the national competition authorities (NCAs) working adequately? Does there need to be a better formalised system for consultation between NCAs directly involved either in the case of multiple filings outside the merger control regulation or in cases where more than one member state exercises the Article 9 request?

The system of consultation between the Commission and the FCA is working adequately. The FCA has entered into an informal network called European Competition Authority ('ECA') which is set up by the head of national European competition authorities. Within the ECA, there is one working group which deals with merger control issues. For example, the case handlers in each country can be in contact with each other taking, however, into account the applicable confidentiality obligations. A better formalised system for consultation between the NCAs would make the communication between the authorities more transparent also in relation to the notifying parties.

4. How does the test under the law of your country compare to that under the Merger Regulation? Should all member states adopt the same test as under the Merger Regulation, and should this EU test be the (US) 'significant lessening of competition' test rather than the present EU 'dominance' test?

The dominance test is also being used under the Finnish merger control regulation. All member states should adopt the same test which should be the dominance test. There is already lots of case-law concerning the dominance test and therefore it is also easier for the companies in practice assess whether the contemplated transaction might face competition problems. The dominance test already provides with the NCAs an adequate 'tool' to investigate different kinds of transactions. It can be also more difficult for the FCA to block a merger under the dominance test than under the SLC test.

5. Are the procedural and judicial safeguards adequate to protect parties from abuse of power by the competition authorities? How does the laws of your country compare to EC law in this respect?

The Finnish legislation as regards to merger control and the current practice of the competition authorities adequately protects parties from abuse of power by the competition authorities. If the FCA is going to propose to the Market Court that a transaction should be prohibited, the separate and independent Market Court has to investigate whether the FCA's request is founded. It is the Market Court which decides upon the proposal of the FCA whether the transaction should be prohibited from the competition law point of view. The situation could be different if the FCA could itself in the first place make a decision to prohibit a merger and the parties to the concentration could first thereafter appeal to the Market Court.

6. Below are a number of questions relating to domestic law which may assist in a comparative analysis.

a. Please provide an overview of the structure of and main features of the relevant domestic legislation and the institutional framework (who enforces it)? It may be helpful with some information about the role of private rights of action.

Finnish provisions on the control of concentrations ('merger control') came into force on 1 October 1998. The provisions are included in Chapter 3a of the Act on Competition Restrictions 480/1992 ('Competition Act'), which sets out the main substantive rules for the Finnish merger control. These provisions are supplemented by the Ministry of Trade and Industry's decision on the obligation to notify concentrations (499/1998), which includes the notification form, and on the calculation of turnover of the parties to a concentration (498/1998).

Notification of a concentration to the FCA is mandatory. The FCA may propose to the Market Court (former Competition Council) that a concentration shall be prohibited or order it to be dissolved or attach conditions on the implementation of the concentration, if as a result of it a dominant position will arise or be strengthened which significantly impedes competition in the Finnish market or in a substantial part of it. Also cross border mergers fall within the scope of the Competition Act in the event that the worldwide turnover thresholds mentioned below in point b. will be met and the object of the acquisition, or the corporation part of the same group, the merging entity or the joint venture to be established conducts business in Finland. Penalty payments can be imposed upon the undertakings which fail to notify or which implement the transaction before the clearance.

b. What kinds of transactions are caught? Are joint ventures caught? What are the jurisdictional thresholds? Is it difficult to identify with sufficient certainty whether a filing is in fact required under national law? Are foreign-to-foreign mergers caught?

The acquisition of control, the acquisition of entire business operations or a part thereof, the merger or the creation of a joint venture to perform on a lasting basis all the functions of an autonomous economic unit ('full-function joint venture') fall within the scope of the merger control provisions of the Competition Act. Non-full function joint ventures do not necessarily fall outside the application of the Competition Act and they may require an exemption or negative clearance.

The merger control applies only to a concentration where the turnover thresholds set out in the Competition Act are exceeded and where the object of the acquisition, merging entity or proposed joint venture, or any entity or foundation related to them, conducts business in Finland. The merger control provisions apply to a concentration in which the combined worldwide turnover of the parties to it exceeds approximately 336 million Euros and the worldwide turnover of at least two parties exceeds 25.2 million Euros. There is also a special two-year rule in addition to the similar two-year rule as in the Merger Regulation according to which the turnover of the target shall also include the turnovers of all corporations operating within the same industry in Finland where the acquirer has acquired control during the preceding two years.

It can sometimes be difficult to identify with sufficient certainty whether filing is required under the merger regulation. With regard to the foreign-to-foreign mergers, these transactions are also caught and they may fall within the merger control even in those cases where the target company has hardly any physical presence in the Finnish market since there is no threshold for the turnover accrued solely from the Finnish market. It is, however, possible to ask the FCA's opinion whether the transaction has to be filed with the FCA.

c. Is the filing mandatory or voluntary? Who is responsible for filing? What is involved in the preparation of a filing? What are the deadlines for filing? What are the waiting periods and does implementation of the transaction have to be suspended?

The filing is mandatory. The acquirer(s) of control or business operations, the merging parties and the founders of a joint venture are responsible for filing. The preparation of the filing requires that the merger control form, which requires lots of detailed information, has to be filled in. It is also often advisable to have a pre-notification meeting with the FCA in order to discuss whether the cross border transaction falls within the scope of the Finnish merger control and that the FCA may reduce the possible amount of data needed in the notification form. In these pre-notification discussions, it can also be possible that the FCA might informally indicate whether the contemplated transaction can cause any competition problems.

A concentration shall be notified to the FCA within one (1) week from the acquisition of control, the acquisition of business operations or a part thereof, the announcement of a public bid referred to in the Securities Markets Act, the decision to merge the merging companies or the decision to set up the joint venture at a founding meeting. One should also note that in the cases of acquisition of control or business assets the one-week notification period starts normally from the signing of a binding agreement.

The concentration shall not be implemented prior to a final decision or other approval by the competition authorities. Under special circumstances, it may be possible to apply for an exemption from the FCA in order to implement the deal partly before the clearance.

d. What are the issues and possible sanctions involved in closing before clearance? What is the timetable for clearance and can it be speeded up?

Any undertaking, which closed the deal before the clearance by the competition authorities may face a penalty payment of between approximately 841 Euros and approximately 673,000 Euros. In exceptional cases, a penalty payment up to 10% of the previous year's worldwide turnover may be imposed. One should also note that the FCA interprets the merger control provisions in a way that the prohibition to implement the transactions concerns also those parts of the transaction which are situated outside Finland, which might affect the planning of the closing time schedule also in other countries. The Market Court may also upon the proposal of the FCA order a transaction to be dissolved.

If the FCA does not start an in-depth investigation within one (1) month of the receipt of the notification, the concentration shall be deemed accepted (first phase). However, the time shall not start to run if the notification submitted is fundamentally incomplete. If the FCA decides to undertake an in-depth investigation, it shall then within three (3) months make its decision from the date of making the decision to initiate further investigations (second phase). The Market Court may extend this period by two (2) months. During the second phase, the FCA has the competence to either approve a concentration or propose to the Market Court its prohibition. The Market Court has to make its decision within three (3) months.

It can sometimes be possible to speed up the clearance by the FCA. This concerns transactions in which there is real hurry to close the transaction and there are hardly any competition effects in the Finnish market. The speeding up of for the clearance depends normally also on the workload of the FCA.

e. Are there any special rules applicable to public takeover bids?

A concentration shall be filed with the FCA within one week from the announcement of a public bid referred to in the Securities Markets Act, even though the succeeding of the public bid would be unsure. As a rule, the parties shall not implement the concentration during the waiting period. However, there is a special rule applicable to public bids according to which the prohibition to implement the deal does not prevent the enforcement of a public bid.

f. What is the substantive test for clearance?

According to the Competition Act, the substantive test for clearance is the dominance test. The Market Court may upon the proposal of the FCA prohibit or order an existing concentration to be dissolved or attach conditions on its implementation, if as a result of it a dominant position will arise or be strengthened which significantly impedes competition in the Finnish market or in a substantial part of it.

g. To what extent are non-competition issues relevant to the review process?

Non-competition issues are not normally relevant to the review process.

h. Is it possible to remedy competition issues?

It can be possible to remedy competition issues. If there are competition law problems related to the contemplated transaction, the parties to the concentration can propose to the FCA remedies which would remove the FCA's concerns.

i. What are the typical steps during the investigation? What rights do complainants have? What publicity is given to the process? What are the opportunities for judicial review?

As to the typical steps during the investigation, the FCA conducts its own market test. In practice, the FCA sends e.g. questionnaires to the main customers and competitors of the parties involved in order to assess the competition impacts of the transaction. Based on the data received from the market and through its own investigations, the FCA will define the relevant markets and the parties market shares in those markets. If it is unlikely that there are competition problems involved, it is not normally necessary to define the relevant market in a precise way. With regard to phase two investigations, it is typical that the FCA and the parties will have several meetings in order to discuss about the definition of the relevant market, competition problems, possible undertakings and other similar issues.

The Finnish Supreme Administrative Court concluded in its decision of 4 July, 2002 (224/2/02) concerning the Sonera/Loimaan Seudun Puhelin case that the complainants, which were not parties to the concentration, did not have the right to appeal to the Competition Council (now Market Court) and thereby revoked the Competition Council's decision. The Competition Council had concluded that two of the complainants had right to appeal since they had direct interest in the merger with connection in safeguarding competition in the market place. Of course, the complainants are still in general able to express their views of the contemplated transaction by contacting the FCA during the FCA's investigations, but their right to appeal is very limited.

The filing of a notification will be registered at the FCA. Accordingly, the pending of a notification is public information. Otherwise, the process is confidential (including e.g. possible pre-notification discussions). During the investigation, the FCA may give a public announcement of the stage of the decision-making process, but does not normally indicate its final decision. The FCA will later publish a public version of the merger control decision.

j. What are the enforcement powers? How does administrative and civil sanctions compare with the EC regime? And what are the criminal sanctions, and are they used?

Upon the proposal of the FCA, the Market Court may prohibit or order that an existing corporation be dissolved or it may attach conditions on its implementation. An undertaking which fails to notify or implements a concentration in breach of the merger control provisions shall be imposed a penalty payment referred to in point d. above, unless the infringement is to be considered minor or the imposing of a penalty payment would otherwise be considered unjustified as regards to safeguarding competition.

A person who on purpose gives wrong information to competition authorities may be ordered to pay criminal fines different from the administrative penalty payments imposed on the companies or be sent to prison. With regard to the merger control issues, the criminal sanctions have not been used so far.

k. Do the authorities cooperate with other antitrust authorities?

Yes. See point 3 above.

l. Are there also rules on foreign investment, special sectors or other relevant approvals?

There are no rules on foreign investment. The merger control provisions apply also to all foreign investments, which meet the thresholds set out in the merger regulation.

With regard to special sectors, there is a special provision concerning the electricity market. The Market Court may upon the proposal of the FCA prohibit a concentration in the electricity market which would give the parties a combined share of more than 25% on a national level in the transmission of electricity at 400 V. This provision may prevent any undertaking from controlling more than one quarter of the total Finnish electricity distribution.

There are also special provisions concerning insurance companies and other financial institutions referred to in the merger control provisions in which cases the approval of the Insurance Supervisory Authority has to be also obtained. However, the notification to the FCA is not necessary if the Insurance Supervisory Authority has requested a statement from the FCA and the FCA concludes in its statement that it does not oppose the approval of the concentration.

m. Are there current proposals to change the legislation?

No.

COMPANY LAW AND FINANCIAL MARKET REGULATORY REGIME

The below answers are provided with respect to situations where the target company is a Finnish listed company. In case the bidder is a Finnish company and the target company is from another jurisdiction, the Finnish regulations are, in the main, not applicable.

7. What will you identify as the main obstacles to take overs where a company[3] from your jurisdiction is either bidder or target and the other company is from another EU jurisdiction[4]?

In the Finnish securities regulations the nationality of the bidder is not of the essence when the target company is a Finnish listed company.

Respectively, should the bidder be a Finnish company or person and the target company from another EU jurisdiction, the Finnish securities regulations do not include any provisions which could been seen as an obstacle to a take over.

However, the main obstacles to any take overs may be so-called 'poison pill' provisions which are included in the articles of association in a number of Finnish listed companies as well as share voting caps that gives control over the company to a small group of shareholders. By a 'poison pill' is meant e.g. a provision in the articles of association according to which any shareholder who reaches or exceeds, (typically) the ownership of 30% or 50% of all the shares in the company, is liable to redeem the shares held by the other shareholders at their request. Finally, it could be mentioned as an eventual obstacle to take overs that the Finnish state is a majority shareholder in a number of Finnish listed companies in the sense that there are particular laws under which the Finnish state is obliged to own a certain proportion in the Finnish listed companies. As an example could be mentioned the energy corporation Fortum Plc.

8. Do hostile take overs by companies from other EU jurisdictions in fact take place in your country?

Yes, but they are rare. The Finnish law does not include any definition on the concept of 'hostile'. It should be noted that take overs of Finnish companies have usually been conducted as 'friendly', i.e. take over is promoted or not frustrated by the board of the target company.

9. To what extents are there any sectors (utilities, financial institutions) that in practice are further protected from hostile take overs, or foreign[5] take overs in particular? Are there any policy statements or particular legal mechanisms that give effect to this protection, or is it a matter of informal mechanisms?[6]

Under the Act on the monitoring of foreigners' corporate acquisitions in Finland, acquisition of ownership of one-third or more of the voting rights in significant Finnish companies (more than 1000 employees or assets or annual turnover exceeding EUR 168 million on consolidated basis) may be restricted by Finnish government should the government deem that the acquisition would endanger a significant national interest. However, the aforementioned does not apply on foreign persons or entities from another member state of the EEA or the OECD. Accordingly, in practice the referred act becomes very rarely applicable.

Further, under the Act on Credit Institutions, anyone who intends to acquire a qualified holding (at least 10 % of the aggregate votes, share capital or co-operative capital of the credit institution) in a credit institution shall notify the Finnish Financial Supervision Authority ('FSA') thereof in advance. The FSA may, within tree months of the receipt of the aforementioned notification object to the acquisition of the holding if the information obtained on the reliability or suitability of the holders or other information makes it likely that the holding would operate to the detriment of the prudent and sound management of the credit institution. The Insurance Companies Act contains quite similar provisions as to acquiring of control in insurance corporations and mutual insurance companies.

Lastly, as mentioned earlier, the fact that the Finnish state is, by law, a major shareholder in a number of listed companies may be deemed as a protective measure.

10. What are the company law techniques of completing a take over or merger that are used in practice where one of the companies is from another EU jurisdiction? Please give particular attention to how this would differ from the usual completion of a take over or merger where both companies are from your jurisdiction. It would be useful if you could add a comment about the consequences on the techniques used of the taxation regime and of any differential tax treatment of take overs or mergers where one party is from another EU jurisdiction.

A take over or merger is usually completed through a public bid or by mutual decisions of the general meetings of the involved companies to merge. As to the public tender offer, the decision of a bid shall be published immediately as well as served upon the company that has issued the securities subject to the bid and to the Helsinki Stock Exchange. Before the entry into force of the bid, the bidder shall publish and, for the period the bid is open, have available for the public tender document ('Prospectus'), which shall contain essential and sufficient information enabling an informed assessment of the merits of the bidder. Furthermore, at the close of the tender period, the bidder shall without delay publish the portion of ownership and voting rights that he may acquire in the target company by acquiring the securities offered for sale on the basis of the tender offer and taking into account any securities he has otherwise acquired and previously held.

As to the mergers, the Companies Act does not recognize a 'cross border' merger in the sense the merger is defined in the said Act (in a merger between two or more Finnish companies all of the assets and rights as well as obligations and liabilities of the merging companies will, by operation of law, be transferred as an universal succession to the recipient company upon the completion of the merger). Therefore, mergers where the other company is from abroad are usually completed through a public bid. As an alternative, the bid may be addressed to the actual business of the company (which is usually, in fact, conducted in the subsidiaries of the listed company) after which the combination is conducted through sharing the control over the business together with the said listed company.

As to the tax consequences in connection with a public bid, it should be noted that transfer tax is imposed on share transfers at the rate of 1,6 per cent of the transfer price. However, should the seller and the purchaser not be resident in Finland or if the share transfer takes place as a stock exchange trade on the Helsinki Stock Exchange, transfer tax is not levied. The tax, if payable, is usually paid by the purchaser and it is payable within two months of the date of the share purchase. As to the selling individuals (resident in Finland) it should be noted that capital gains arising from the sales of shares are taxed as capital income. Respectively, incomes arising from the sale of shares by companies resident in Finland are included as part of their gross income. However, subject to certain qualifications, a sale is not taxable if it is completed through a share exchange transaction in which the bidder acquires at least 50 per cent of the shares and votes of the target company and issues its new shares as consideration.

11. A duty on listed companies to disclose capital and control structures is proposed in *Issues Relating to Takeover Bids*, the First Report of the High Level Group of Company Law Experts (see p 25). Would this require amendments in the legislation in your country? How would these amendments in case be implemented (in primary company law, securities law, stock exchange regulations etc.)?

Yes. As mentioned in the Issues Relating to Takeover Bids, First Report of the High Level Group of Company Law Experts ('Report') disclosure of some of the elements are already required under existing directives which has been duly implemented into the Finnish legislation. Therefore, the main emphasis as to the eventual amendments to the legislation would be in combining the different elements of disclosure to be disclosed in combined coherent way (in e.g. annual reports) as recommended in the Report. At the moment the duty to disclose is regulated mainly in the Securities Markets Act so it would seem most practical that the required amendments would be implemented into the same act.

12. A so called break through rule after take over bids is another of the proposals in *Issues Relating to Takeover Bids*, the First Report of the High Level Group of Company Law Experts (see p 29). Would this require amendments in the legislation in your country? How would these amendments in case be implemented (in primary company law, securities law, stock exchange regulations etc.)?

Yes. It would appear evident that the 'break through' rule should be implemented in the Companies Act since it would have a substantial effect on the rights of the other shareholders in the company.

13. In your view, would these two new rules as proposed have any material impact on the existing barriers to take overs in your country (or in others as seen from your point of view)? It would be helpful if you could demonstrate the impact, or lack of it, by going through one or more recent take over bids that failed in your country (or in some other member state, by a company from your country).

It would seem that the 'duty to disclose' rule would not have a material impact since the information as to the capital and control structures is already, in essential parts, available for a potential bidder. Instead, the 'break through' rule would have a material impact because the Finnish law does not at the moment include such a provision.

14. Below are a number of questions which may assist in a comparative analysis.

a. What are the main features of the relevant domestic take over legislation constituting the company law and financial market regime, and who enforces it (independent regulators, regulatory bodies with appeal to ministry, stock exchange)? What is the extent of intervention by the takeover regulator(s) – to what extent does the regulator have wide or general discretions to block and play a protectionist role (for example in its capacity as approver of the offer terms/documentation)?

As to the Finnish take over regulations the Securities Markets Act and the Companies Act as well as regulations and guidelines issued by the FSA and rules of the Helsinki Stock Exchange are important. In Finland there is not any specific 'Takeover Panel' who would oversee the take overs. The take over documents (e.g. an offer document) have to be approved by the FSA. The requirements for the substance of the aforementioned documents are included in the Securities Markets Act and in the statements issued by the FSA. The Finnish authorities do not at the moment have any particular role or powers to block or play a protectionist role as to the take overs as long as the relevant regulations are followed when making a bid. Should the takeover not be made in accordance with the relevant laws and regulations, it may be challenged in a public court.

b. Are there restrictions on a board taking action to frustrate a bid that has been made? When do the relevant restrictions start to apply ñ earlier than

a formal announcement/filing of a bid? To what extent can shareholders approve the taking of frustrating action in advance of any bid?

Owing to the fact that the Finnish law does not provide any specific regulations regulating the duties of the board of the target company in a bid situation, under law the board has no thereto related express duties. From the general duties under the Companies Act follows that the board shall duly and carefully consider any offer to be made and thereby act in the best interests of the company, and particularly, in the best interest of the shareholders of the company. Accordingly, under the Finnish law there is nothing that would expressly restrict the board from frustrating a bid. However, it should be noted that most of the methods (as issuance of new shares) to frustrate a bid require a decision which is to be made in a general meeting of the company by the shareholders.

c. Are there restrictions on the type of consideration that can be offered in a bid, for example securities only if these are listed in the target country's home state or the EU?

No. However, should the consideration be something else than money the offer shall contain essential and sufficient information enabling an informed assessment of the offered consideration.

d. Are there effective compulsory acquisition procedures regarding a small non-accepting minority? Can a bidder make its offer conditional on achieving the number of shares required so it can operate a squeeze out?

Yes. According to the Securities Markets Act if one acquires more than two thirds of the total voting rights of the company after the share of the company or a security entitling one to a share of the company has been admitted to public trade one shall be under a duty to redeem also the remaining shares and securities. Under the said Act the offer may be made conditional on achieving the aforementioned threshold (or any other percentage of the ownership). Furthermore, under the Companies Act a shareholder holding more than 90% of the shares and of the total voting power in the company shall have the right to redeem the shares held by other shareholders (squeeze out).

e. Is there a principle of board neutrality? Can a target board align itself with a particular bidder/agree measures such as exclusivity arrangements to protect a particular deal?

See answer to the question in point b.

f. Can a target board hand over information to a potential bidder?

The Finnish law does not contain any specific regulations regulating the right of any limited company to give information of the company to a potential bidder. Further, the law does not provide any express prohibition to allow a due diligence even in a listed company. Accordingly, in case of a planned bid the board of the target company may give information of the company or allow a possibility to conduct a due diligence investigation to the bidder, but the board is not obligated to do so. From the general duties under the Companies Act follows that the board shall duly and carefully consider any request of information of the company and decide would giving the information or allowing the investigation be in the best interests of the company, and particularly, in the best interest of the shareholders of the company. Furthermore, the board has to take into account the relevant insider regulations.

g. Are structures permitted which concentrate control rights in the hands of minority shareholders? Are structures permitted which place limitations/restrictions on voting rights, caps for example on voting rights above a certain threshold?

Yes, in practice this is made by the use of voting caps. The referred structures are permitted under the Finnish law but are, however, subject to certain restrictions.

h. Can restrictions be placed on the transferability of shares either by the issuer (in articles of association or by other means) or by arrangements between shareholders? Can a board delay registering transfers of shares?

No. If the company is listed on the Helsinki Stock Exchange the transferability of the shares may not be restricted in the articles of association. This restrictions does not apply to eventual shareholder agreements or other arrangements between shareholders.

i. What contractual barriers (including shareholder agreements) to take over bids are in use in public companies (e.g. golden parachutes, change of control provisions triggering default of loan agreements, or wining up or change of control of joint ventures)? What are the prospects of review by courts on the basis of contract or company law and by regulators on the basis of securities laws or stock exchange regulations?

Shareholder agreements, golden parachutes and other such arrangements are used in public companies but their purposes are not usually to prevent hostile take overs as e.g. to remunerate directors or to protect lenders.

As to the contractual barriers to take over bids it should be noted that they may be invalid if their enforcements would be dishonourable and unworthy as defined in the Finnish law. Moreover, the invalidity of such contractual barriers might be based on a violation of the principle of equal treatment of the shareholders.

j. Are there current proposals to change the legislation relating to take overs?

Not expressly relating to take overs. However, a work group has been set to prepare an eventual general reform of the Companies Act which may have some relevance as to the take overs.

D. FINAL ISSUES

15. In your view, what is the extent to which the complexity of the regulatory arrangements, within national jurisdictions and between the Commission and member states, present an obstacle to take overs?

In our view the complexity of the regulatory arrangements does not constitute any obstacle to the take overs where professional advisers are used to review the aspects of different laws and regulations.

16. Can you list some instances where different rules in the different regulatory systems have caused practical obstacles in a take over process? (One instance could be different time limits under the EC Merger Regulation and national merger rules on the one hand and under stock exchange rules on the other.)

We are not aware of any particular obstacles in this respect. The relevant time limits to be followed in a bid can be set relatively freely by the bidder.

F. FOR REFERENCE

Issues Relating to Takeover Bids First Report of the High Level Group of Company Law experts (10 January 200) http://www.europa.eu.int/comm/internal_market/en/company/news/hlg01-2002.pdf

Green Paper on the Review of Council Regulation (EEC) No 4064/89 COM(2001) 745/6 (11 December 2001) http://www.europa.eu.int/comm/competition/mergers/review/

NOTES

[1] Ari Keinänen, Partner, Mergers and Acquisitions Group; Mr. Arttu 1entula, Partner, EU and Competition Law Group; and Mr. Henrik Hinders, Associate, Mergers and Acquisitions Group at Merilampi Marttila Laitasalo's Helsinki office (www.mmllaw.fi).

[2] The aim is not here to have an authoritative statement but a report which can contribute to the discussion. For EEA (non member) country rapporteurs, the subject of the question is intended to be the EEA regime. For non member (non EEA) countries, there are special issues. Country rapporteurs are welcome to limit their answers in the way they believe to be most helpful or interesting with the purpose of the questionnaire in mind.

[3] Focus is here mainly on listed companies but information about non listed and also non public companies will of interest if this is possible to provide.

[4] Here too the following applies. For EEA (non member) country rapporteurs, the subject of the question is intended to be the EEA regime. For non member (non EEA) countries, there are special issues. Country rapporteurs are welcome to limit their answers in the way they believe to be most helpful or interesting with the purpose of the questionnaire in mind.

[5] 'Foreign' here includes both take overs from other member states and from non member states (or non EEA countries).

[6] In the case of banks or insurance companies, the relevant ministry and supervisor would be usually be able to block take overs on prudential grounds and their involvement would be difficult to review. Similar mechanisms would be in place for many utilities where state ownership often adds to the problems. An extensive review is not required, but it would be useful with an assessment of how such mechanisms function. If there have for instance not been any take over by a foreign bank, that is an interesting point.

FRANCE

Les concentrations transfrontières au regard de la régulation financière et du droit de la concurrence: Les derniers obstacles à lever

Rapporteurs
Dr Nicolas Charbit[1] *and Me. Michel Debroux*[2]

Auteurs
Régulation financière : Me. Jacques Buhart, Me. Thierry Aballéa, Avocats, Coudert Frères, Paris
Droit de la concurrence : Dr. Nicolas Charbit, Me. Michel Debroux
Droit social : Me. Caroline Thomelet, Avocat, Groupe Thesis, Paris

Contributeurs
Christophe Barthelemy (Directeur juridique EDF)
Françoise Blanquet (Magistrate, Commission Européenne)
François-Emile Brocard (Avocat, doctorant)
Noël Chahid Nouraï (Conseiller d'Etat en disponibilité)
Xavier Delcros (Professeur Université de Sceaux, Avocat, Delcros)
Dimitri Delesalle (Avocat, Rambaud Martel)
Mirko Hayat (Chambre de Commerce Internationale de Paris)
David de Giles (Avocat, Backer & McKenzie)
Anne Houtin-Adam (Chambre de Commerce Internationale de Paris)
Laurence Idot (Professeur Paris I)
Olivier de Juvigny (Avocat, Rambaud Martel)
Pierre Kirch (Avocat, Moquet Borde)
Stanislas Martin (Chef du Bureau B3, DGCCRF)
Maggy Pariente (Ma'tre de conférences, Université Paris I)
Lucien Rapp (Professeur Université Toulouse, Avocat, Serra-Leavy-Cazals)
Stéphane Rodrigues (Ma'tre de conférences, Paris I, Avocat, Klein Goddard)
Joëlle Simon (Directrice juridique du MEDEF)
François Souty (Conseil de la concurrence)

[1] Chargé d'enseignement, Université Paris I - Panthéon Sorbonne Secrétaire général adjoint de l'Association des Juristes Européens
[2] Avocat, Associé, Clifford Chance, Paris

A. INTRODUCTION

Le présent rapport a été préparé par les membres et sympathisants de l'Association des Juristes Européens, association qui représente en France la FIDE. A la suite de la communication des sujets par le secrétariat FIDE début 2001, Monsieur Marco Darmon, Président de l'AJE, a organisé un large appel à candidatures auprès des membres afin de préparer la participation française au XX Congrès. C'est ainsi qu'ont pu être organisées, sous la coordination des deux co-rapporteurs, huit séances de travail portant chacune sur un des thèmes suivants :

- *Les obstacles, les blocages et les solutions afférant à la libre circulation des sociétés dans l'Union européenne,* par Maggy Pariente, Ma'tre de conférences à l'Université de Paris I (25 octobre 2001).
- *Les obstacles tenant au droit fiscal*, par Noël Chahid Nouraï, Conseiller d'Etat en disponibilité, et M. Mirko Hayat, responsable de la fiscalité internationale à la CCIP (22 novembre 2001).
- *La citoyenneté européenne des sociétés,* par Me. Stéphane Rodrigues, Ma'tre de conférences à l'Université de Paris I, Avocat, Klein Goddard (3 décembre 2001).
- *Les obstacles propres au droit boursier,* par Me Olivier de Juvigny et Dimitri Delesalle, Avocats, Rambaud Martel, et M. François-Emile Brocard, doctorant, Avocat (24 janvier 2002).
- *Les limites de la Société européenne,* par Mme Françoise Blanquet, Magistrate, Commission Européenne, Mme Joëlle Simon, Directrice juridique du MEDEF, et Mme Anne Houtin, Directrice adjoint DGAEI à la CCIP (13 février 2002).
- *La coopération internationale en matière de concentrations*, par Mme Laurence Idot, Professeur à l'Université de Paris I, et M. François Souty, responsable des aspects de coopération internationale au Conseil de la concurrence (27 mars 2002).
- *La coopération entre autorités nationales de concurrence européennes et le nouveau régime de la loi NRE,* par Stanislas Martin, chef du bureau des concentrations à la DGCCRF, Me David de Giles, Avocat,

Backer & McKenzie, et Me Pierre Kirch, Avocat, Moquet Borde (4 avril 2002).

- *Service public et concentrations transfrontières,* par les Professeurs Xavier Delcros, Université de Sceaux, Lucien Rapp, Université de Toulouse, M. Christophe Barthelemy, Directeur juridique EDF, et Me Michel Debroux (10 avril 2002).

Le présent rapport ne peut malheureusement retracer la richesse de ces contributions, qui ont donné lieu pour certaines, à des conférences et des publications scientifiques. En effet, les délais nécessaires à la communication du questionnaire FIDE n'ayant pas permis de planifier ces séances de travail selon la grille de lecture adopté par les rapporteurs généraux, il a été jugé préférable d'organiser un programme de travail indépendant autour des thèmes pressentis.

L'ensemble des intervenants à ces séances de travail ont ainsi indirectement participé à l'élaboration du présent rapport. Leur nom appara't ainsi en tant que contributeurs. Le rapport leur a été préalablement communiqué pour information. Les auteurs de ce rapport sont pour la section relative à la régulation financière, Me. Jacques Buhart et Me. Thierry Aballéa, Avocats, Coudert Frères, et pour la section droit social, Me. Caroline Thomelet, Avocat, Thesis. Les deux co-rapporteurs du groupe de travail, Dr. Nicolas Charbit et Me. Michel Debroux ont rédigé la section relative au droit de la concurrence. Les conclusions du rapport doivent donc être directement attribués à ces auteurs.

B. LES OBSTACLES TENANT AU DROIT DE LA CONCURRENCE

1. What is the view from your country on the functioning of the threshold levels in Article 1(2) as well as the 2/3 rule in the Merger Regulation, and the proposal in the Commission's Green Paper for amendment of Article 1(3) to deal with the problems of multiple filings?

La toute première observation tient à l'importance supposée de cette question. Il ressort en effet des études du groupe de travail que, bien que la Commission insiste tout particulièrement sur cette question des seuils, les entreprises n'en font plus une question prioritaire comme en 1989 et 1997, préférant porter leurs critiques sur les questions d'ordre procédural. Ainsi, la question du champ d'application du guichet unique ne constitue plus pour les opérateurs français la question première du Règlement concentrations, quand bien même la proposition de la Commission ait bien sûr donné lieu à des réactions de principe.

Deux positions se dégagent, elles peuvent néanmoins se concilier. Pour certains, la compétence exclusive de la Commission européenne pour toute opération nécessitant une notification dans au moins trois des Etats membres est de nature à simplifier les contraintes des entreprises. L'étude statistique des opérations contrôlées plaide sans discussion en faveur de l'extension du guichet unique (en ce sens, voir *Ph. Corruble, Dix ans d'application du Règlement concentration par la Commission européenne, Une analyse juridique des statistiques, Gaz. Europ. Pal. , 31 mai 2001, p. 5*). Pour ceux-là, l'ensemble des propositions de la Commission quant aux règles de compétence doit être accueillie favorablement (Rapport CCIP, pp. 12-14).

D'autres font valoir un point de vue plus nuancé. Les seuils de l'article 1.3 n'ont que tardivement commencé à effectivement fonctionner ; il est donc trop tôt pour les remettre en cause, l'analyse statistique de leur mise en œuvre fournie par la Commission apparaissant insuffisante. La suppression des seuils de l'article 1.3 suggérée par la Commission pourrait entra'ner, loin de l'effet recherché, une augmentation sensible de l'insécurité juridique en raison des différences existant encore entre les différentes législations nationales de contrôle des concentrations. Cette remarque conduit à la conclusion selon laquelle les seuils de l'article 1.3 ne devraient pas faire l'objet d'une suppression (Rapport AFEC, p. 9). Enfin, certains parmi cette seconde tendance ont proposé de rendre facultative et non plus obligatoire la règle des trois Etats membres proposée par la Commission, cela revenant à confier une possibilité de renvoi au niveau communautaire en cas d'accord entre autorités nationales de concurrence (Rapport MEDEF).

Soutenant ces premières réflexions, le groupe de travail prend position en faveur d'une suppression des seuils de l'article 1.3 et d'une compétence unique de la Commission en cas de pluri-notification dans au moins trois Etats membres. Ce point de vue se fonde sur l'impératif de simplification de la réglementation communautaire, trop souvent critiquée comme source de complexité supplémentaire par une partie de l'opinion française. En outre, le rapprochement du citoyen et de l'Europe passe par l'accessibilité et l'intelligibilité du droit qui constitue une forme de l'objectif constitutionnel français de sécurité juridique *(Cons. const., 16 déc. 1999, RTDC n°1/2000, p. 186, note N. Molfessis)*. En tout état de cause, le groupe de travail rejoint les différentes opinions recueillies en soulignant qu'une telle évolution devrait être l'occasion, non d'un simple renforcement des pouvoirs de la Commission, mais d'une meilleure concertation entre la Commission et les autorités de régulation des Etats membres. Cela suppose de la part des Etats membres, une meilleure coordination des méthodes d'analyse de l'effet concurrentiel des concentrations.

Un risque a cependant été souligné par une partie du groupe : la règle des trois Etats membres doit être appréciée au regard de la proposition de la Commission d'un renvoi article 9 à sa propre initiative (système dit *call option*). Concrètement, avec l'élargissement de surcro't, la Commission risque de crouler sous les notifications du fait de la règle des trois Etats membres. Pour se décharger, elle sera tenté d'user de l'article 9 pour renvoyer aux Etats membres les dossiers ayant le moins d'intérêt pour elle (principe de subsidiarité bien compris). Au final, les entreprises pourraient ne plus avoir de guichet unique, mais subiraient un rallongement des délais de l'ordre d'un mois par rapport à la situation actuelle. De ce point de vue, la réforme pourrait ne pas constituer un grand progrès.

2. In light of the experiences made in your country, do member states have sufficient flexibility to call for mergers to be referred back under Article 9 of the Merger Regulation? In light of the proposal in the Commission's Green Paper, what is your view on the circumstances in which this power should be exercised?

Le Ministre de l'économie a eu recours à la procédure de l'article 9 du Règlement communautaire à environ dix reprises, l'exemple le plus récent étant celui de la prise de contrôle d'une partie des actifs de la société Moulinex par la société SEB, autorisée par décision du 8 juillet 2002. Il faut souligner que dans cette décision, le Ministre a fait usage de la théorie de l'« entreprise défaillante » (« *failing company defence* ») pour justifier l'autorisation accordée sans aucune condition ou engagement, alors que la Commission européenne, qui avait approuvé cette même opération le 8 janvier 2002, avait assorti sa décision de conditions et n'avait pas eu recours à la théorie de l' « entreprise défaillante ». Pour autant, il ne semble pas qu'il faille voir là une divergence d'analyse, la France ayant considéré que la *failing company defence* trouvait à s'appliquer sur le marché français, alors que la Commission n'a pas souhaité l'examiner en phase I pour les autres marchés, mais a semblé a priori l'écarter pour les pays européens autres que la France. La décision "6-2" (autorisation avec engagements) de la Commission a été attaquée devant le TPICE par des concurrents de Seb, Conair et Philips. Parmi les moyens soulevés par Philips, le fait que la décision 6-2 ne concerne pas la France, du fait de la décision de renvoi, est contestée au motif notamment que la Commission n'aurait pas démontré que les autorités nationales étaient mieux placées que la Commission pour traiter de marché français.

Dans la plupart des cas de renvoi au titre de l'article 9 du Règlement, l'opération de concentration est soumise pour avis au Conseil de la concurrence, ce qui n'est que la conséquence logique de l'identification d'un risque de création ou renforcement d'une position dominante - critère posée par l'article 9 du Règlement - qui correspond assez largement au critère d'identification d'un risque d'atteinte à la concurrence, posé par l'article L.430-5 C. com., qui constitue le critère préalable à la saisine du Conseil de la concurrence.

Il existe toutefois quelques rares exemple de renvoi au titre de l'article 9 du Règlement qui n'ont pas été suivi d'une saisine du Conseil de la concurrence : il s'agit de l'acquisition du contrôle conjoint par la Compagnie Nationale de Navigation et Sogelfa, une filiale d'Elf Aquitaine, de la Compagnie Industrielle Maritime (CIM). Approuvée partiellement par la Commission européenne le 1er décembre 1997 (aff. IV/M.1021), cette opération a été ensuite approuvée par le Ministre le 6 janvier 1998, à la suite d'engagements souscrits par les parties en phase I. Les opérations *Total/Fina* et *TotalFina/Elf* n'ont pas non plus fait l'objet d'une saisine, non plus que *CSME/SMA/Rock*.

Au vu de l'expérience française, les autorités nationales paraissent disposer d'une certaine flexibilité pour obtenir le renvoi d'une concentration au titre de l'article 9, flexibilité renforcée par (i) la pratique des renvois partiels par la Commission (dont la légitimité peut être contestée dans la mesure où ils ne sont pas expressément prévus par le texte, voir AFEC, p. 10), et (ii) la souplesse d'appréciation de la Commission dans la démonstration, par l'Etat membre, de l'existence d'un risque de création ou de renforcement d'une position dominante.

A cet égard, la proposition de la Commission de remplacer l'obligation de démonstration d'un tel risque, par une simple « affirmation motivée » ne ferait du point de vue du groupe de travail qu'officialiser la pratique actuelle. Mais cette proposition suscite une question de droit interne que n'aborde pas le Livre Vert : les entreprises ne devraient-elles pas se voir reconna'tre le droit de contester cette « affirmation motivée » dans la mesure où elle pourrait s'apparenter à un jugement préalable porté sur l'opération, sans qu'elles ne puissent disposer des éléments nécessaires, du temps et d'un accès au dossier lui permettant de contester celui ? Cette questions soulève d'importants enjeux en termes de respect des droits de la défense auxquels il conviendrait de répondre si cette proposition du Livre Vert devait être adoptée.

La procédure de renvoi prévue à l'article 9 étant une exception au principe de « guichet unique » et étant susceptible d'entra'ner des coûts et des délais supplémentaires, ainsi qu'un degré d'incertitude juridique accru (notamment en cas de renvois partiels auprès de plusieurs autorités nationales, comme ce fut le cas dans l'opération *Carrefour/Promodès*), cette procédure devrait être assez strictement encadrée et, lorsqu'elle est mise en œuvre, simplifiée. En ce sens, la proposition de réduire de trois à deux semaines le délai pendant lequel les Etats membres peuvent demander l'application de l'article 9 doit être favorablement accueillie.

La proposition de renvoi à l'initiative de la Commission para't conforme au principe de subsidiarité, mais se heurte au principe du guichet unique. De plus, l'équilibre du contrôle des concentrations communautaires repose sur le principe de compétence exclusive et non de subsidiarité. La proposition ne devrait donc être mise en œuvre que si un seul Etat est concerné ; à défaut, les inconvénients pratiques de cette atteinte au guichet unique pour les entreprises deviendraient considérables (cf. AFEC, p. 11).

3. Is the system of consultation between the European Commission and the national competition authorities (NCAs) working adequately? Does there need to be a better formalised system for consultation between NCAs directly involved either in the case of multiple filings outside the merger control regulation or in cases where more than one member state exercises the Article 9 request?

Il est sans doute difficile d'exprimer une opinion définitive sur le caractère adéquat des consultations entre la Commission et le réseau des autorités nationales, dans la mesure où ces consultations n'ont été formalisées que récemment ; en outre, dans le cas de la France, la réforme du régime de contrôle des concentrations est intervenue trop récemment pour que l'on puisse juger de l'efficacité des consultations entre la DGCCRF et la Commission.

Il est certain toutefois que ces consultations sont utiles sur le plan pratique, en particulier dans les cas de notifications multiples ou de renvois au titre de l'article 9 par plusieurs Etats membres, mais il faudrait s'assurer que les entreprises et leurs conseils soient informés de ces consultations et puissent disposer d'éléments leurs permettant d'exprimer leur point de vue dans le respect de leurs droits. A ce jour, le groupe de travail déplore que rien ne garantit une telle information. A noter que le site Internet de la DGCCRF reproduit l'accord passé entre les membres de l'ECA *(procedural guide)* prévoyant un système de *waivers* lors de la transmission d'informations relevant du secret des affaires.

4. How does the test under the law of your country compare to that under the Merger Regulation? Should all member states adopt the same test as under the Merger Regulation, and should this EU test be the (US) 'significant lessening of competition' test rather than the present EU 'dominance' test?

Dans le cadre de la phase I du contrôle, le Ministre de l'économie doit tenir compte de « l'atteinte à la concurrence », critère critiqué par la doctrine car particulièrement vague et constituant une zone d'insécurité juridique pour les entreprises *(L. Idot, La deuxième partie de la loi NRE, JCPG n° 36, 5 septembre 2001, p. 1615)*. Le Ministre a l'obligation de passer en phase II et de saisir le Conseil de la concurrence s'il estime que l'opération est de nature à porter atteinte à la concurrence et que les engagements ne suffisent pas à y remédier.

Le Conseil examine alors si l'opération est de nature à porter une telle atteinte « notamment par création ou renforcement d'une position dominante... » (Art. L. 430-6, al. 1, Cod. Com.). La loi sur les Nouvelles Régulations Economiques du 15 mai 2001 (dite loi NRE) a ajouté à cet article le critère du « renforcement d'une puissance d'achat qui place les fournisseurs en situation de dépendance économique », disposition destinée à permettre un contrôle plus strict des concentrations dans la grande distribution *(P. de la Laurencie et al., Rev. Lamy Droit économique, juillet 2001, n° 129).*

Enfin, le Conseil appréciera ensuite si l'opération apporte au progrès économique une contribution suffisante pour compenser les atteintes à la concurrence. Ainsi, à la différence essentielle du droit communautaire, l'appréciation du bilan concurrentiel est suivie d'un bilan économique, spécificité française (Art. L. 430-6, Cod. Com.).

Autre spécificité française liée au critère d'appréciation d'une concentration, les injonctions imposées par le Ministre doivent être *« de nature à apporter au progrès économique et social une contribution suffisante pour compenser les atteintes à la concurrence »* (Art. L. 430-7, III, al. 1, 2ème tiret, Cod. Com.). Ainsi, est réintroduit dans le contrôle des concentrations un critère social permettant de prendre en compte le nombre d'emplois supprimés ou sauvegardés.

En dépit de ces différences, on peut estimer que le critère français est pour l'essentiel proche du critère communautaire, l'appréciation du bilan concurrentiel étant principalement fondé sur le critère de la création ou du renforcement d'une position dominante, expression reprenant les termes mêmes du Règlement n° 4064/89.

Les opinions recueillies par le groupe s'accordent à penser que la différence entre le critère communautaire et le critère américain de réduction substantielle de la concurrence est d'ordre sémantique (voir not. *J. Ysewin, The new world of Merger Task Force, Competition, Janv. 2002 ; CCIP, p. 33 ; AFEC, p. 24).* En effet, si la rédaction des dispositions diffèrent sensiblement, la pratique de la MTF permet d'englober l'analyse faite par la FTC, notamment grâce au développement du contrôle de la position dominante oligopolistique. Certes, selon certaines opinions, l'annulation de la décision *Airtours/First Choice* par le Tribunal de première instance des Communautés européennes pourrait en partie remettre en cause le rapprochement fonctionnel qui s'est opéré dans le contrôle communautaire et nord-américain des concentrations. Le groupe de travail conclut donc avec la majorité des praticiens français quant à l'inutilité de la modification proposée. Tout au contraire, la modification de ce critère pourrait entra'ner une insécurité juridique quant à la prévisibilité des solutions.

En revanche, les recherches du groupe de travail ont révélé une critique sévère à l'encontre de l'évolution progressive de la pratique décisionnelle de la MTF. Selon certains, l'analyse concurrentielle de la Commission manquerait de clarté et de rigueur économique, notamment lorsque celle-ci est appelée à appréhender des concepts économiques comme ceux de position dominante collective (voir plus haut), d'effet de gamme ou de réduction de la concurrence potentielle. A cet égard, il appara't souhaitable que la Commission précise son analyse de l'application du critère à ces situations par le biais de Lignes directrices (AFEC, p. 27). Le véritable enjeu du Livre Blanc sur les critères d'appréciation du contrôle réside ainsi plus dans une clarification de mise en œuvre du critère afin de rendre plus prédictibles les solutions, plutôt que dans la modification de ce critère qui fait l'objet d'un consensus français et semble-t-il, international. C'est pourquoi le groupe de travail accueille favorablement cette proposition de rédaction de lignes directrices relatives à l'application du critère de création ou renforcement d'une position dominante, à l'instar de la FTC ou de la pratique de la Direction générale de la concurrence et de la consommation et de la répression des fraudes (DGCCRF, Méthode d'analyse pour le contrôle des concentrations, 1992, Etudes DGCCRF, document qui demande lui-même à être mis à jour à la suite de la loi NRE).

Pour autant, le groupe de travail n'estime pas opportun que soit instaurée au sein de la MTF une cellule d'économistes sur le modèle du Bureau of Economics de la FTC. En effet, en raison des fortes différences culturelles existant entre juristes et économistes et la ségrégation fonctionnelle qu'il pourrait en résulter, il semble qu'il soit préférable que les équipes de rapporteurs soient composées à la fois de fonctionnaires économistes et de fonctionnaires juristes (au moins un pour trois). La création d'une cellule ad hoc s'opposerait précisément à l'effet recherché d'introduction d'une meilleures prise en compte de l'économique dans les décisions.

5. Are the procedural and judicial safeguards adequate to protect parties from abuse of power by the competition authorities? How does the laws of your country compare to EC law in this respect?

Contrairement à la situation communautaire, le contrôle des concentrations peut impliquer, en France, deux autorités, mais les décisions en matière de concentrations n'appartiennent toutefois qu'au seul Ministre de l'économie qui, même lorsqu'il décide de saisir le Conseil de la concurrence pour avis ("examen de phase II") n'est pas lié par l'avis rendu par ce dernier.

Comme toute décision administrative, les décisions rendues par le Ministre en matière de contrôle des concentrations sont susceptibles de recours devant le juge administratif. Ce droit de recours est ouvert non seulement aux parties, mais aussi à tout tiers démontrant qu'il a intérêt à agir. Aux termes de l'article R. 311-1 (9°) du Code de justice administrative, *"Le Conseil d'État est compétent pour conna'tre en premier et dernier ressort [...] des recours dirigés contre les décisions ministérielles prises en matière de contrôle des concentrations économiques".*

Les arrêts du Conseil d'Etat en matière de contrôle des concentrations sont peu nombreux et, à ce jour, seules deux décisions du Ministre ont été annulées sur des motifs de procédure (*INTERBREW*, 9 avril 1999, pour violation du principe du contradictoire vis-à-vis de tiers, et *KORAMIC*, 31 mai 2000, pour violation du principe du contradictoire vis-à-vis des vendeurs). Il faut distinguer selon que le recours porte sur une décision d'autorisation ou sur une décision d'interdiction. Selon les conclusions du commissaire du gouvernement dans l'arrêt "*Coca-Cola*" du 9 avril 1999 :

- le juge n'exerce qu'un contrôle restreint sur la décision du Ministre de ne pas saisir le Conseil de la concurrence (et d'ainsi autoriser une opération),
- mais il exerce un plein contrôle de proportionnalité lorsqu'il est saisi d'un arrêté du Ministre (interdiction ou autorisation assortie d'injonctions ou prescriptions). Le pouvoir du Ministre est ici assimilé à un pouvoir de police économique, la légalité d'une décision est subordonnée à sa proportionnalité.

En cas d'annulation d'une décision prise en matière de contrôle des concentrations, un avis du Conseil d'Etat du 15 juillet 1999 a précisé qu'il appartient alors au Ministre de statuer sur l'opération à la date de son nouvel examen, "en prenant en considération les circonstances de droit et de fait existant à la date d'adoption de la nouvelle décision à prendre". L'article 10 du décret du 30 avril 2002 a repris cette solution, et prévoit que les parties soumettent une notification "actualisée" dans un délai de deux mois suivant la date du jugement.

En pratique, les délais d'instruction et de jugement des recours sont considérablement plus brefs qu'à l'ordinaire, les juridictions compétentes traitant les affaires de concentrations en « urgence signalée » : il faut compter environ 6 à 9 mois entre la date du recours et l'adoption de l'arrêt du Conseil d'Etat, à comparer à des délais d'environ 2 ans en matière d'excès de pouvoir.

Il faut encore souligner que les autorités de la concurrence françaises disposent d'un pouvoir d'appréciation très large en matière de constatation du caractère complet ou non d'un dossier, notamment en ce qui concerne les marchés pertinents ; ce pouvoir d'appréciation est à présent reconnu explicitement dans le décret du 30 avril 2002 (article 3). Par ce biais, les autorités de la concurrence peuvent inviter –voire contraindre– les parties à communiquer des informations relatives à des marchés définis selon les souhaits des autorités, parfois en contradiction avec les définitions de marché présentées par les parties. Ainsi, ce pouvoir discrétionnaire va au-delà de la simple gestion administrative du dossier et permet aux autorités de concurrence d'influencer l'approche de fond adoptée par les parties. Un contrôle juridictionnel est toutefois possible, et a notamment été exercé par le Conseil d'Etat dans la décision du 6 octobre 2000 « Pernod-Ricard » (dite *Coca-Cola II*).

6. Below are a number of questions relating to domestic law which may assist in a comparative analysis.

a. please provide an overview of the structure of and main features of the relevant domestic legislation and the institutional framework (who enforces it)? It may be helpful with some information about the role of private rights of action.

Le droit français des concentrations a connu récemment une réforme fondamentale, issue de la loi dite "NRE" du 15 mai 2001, dont les dispositions relatives au contrôle des concentrations ont été précisées dans un décret du 30 avril 2002, et sont entrées en vigueur le 18 mai 2002. Le droit français a été largement aligné sur le droit communautaire, les principales innovations du nouveau régime français étant :

- les seuils exprimés en parts de marché sont supprimés, seuls les seuils exprimés en chiffre d'affaires étant pris en compte (cf. infra *b.*) ;
- la notification des opérations de concentration relevant du droit français est à présent obligatoire et non plus volontaire ;
- l'opération ne peut être mise en œuvre avant l'obtention de l'autorisation ministérielle (période suspensive).

L'examen du dossier est effectué par les services de la Direction Générale de la Concurrence, de la Consommation et de la Répression des Fraudes ("DGCCRF"), qui dépendent du Ministre de l'économie et des finances ; la décision appartient au Ministre de l'économie et des finances, qui peut décider, à l'issue de la première phase d'examen, d'autoriser l'opération, avec ou sans conditions, ou qui peut soumettre l'opération à l'avis consultatif du Conseil de la concurrence, déclenchant ainsi la seconde phase de l'opération. Des engagements peuvent être proposés par les parties, tant en phase I qu'en phase II.

Dans un délai maximal de 5 jours après le dépôt du dossier de notification, les tiers sont informés de la notification par le biais d'un avis publié sur le site Internet de la DGCCRF ; ils peuvent formuler des commentaires lors du test de marché (« *market testing* ») réalisé par la DGCCRF et, comme il a été vu ci-dessus (question n° 5), ils peuvent former un recours contre les décisions du Ministre, à la condition d'apporter la preuve de leur intérêt à agir.

b. What kinds of transactions are caught? Are joint ventures caught? What are the jurisdictional thresholds? Is it difficult to identify with sufficient certainty whether a filing is in fact required under national law? Are foreign-to-foreign mergers caught?

Exactement de la même façon que le droit communautaire, le droit français considère désormais qu'une opération de concentration est réalisée:

- en cas de fusion entre deux ou plusieurs entreprises antérieurement indépendantes;
- en cas de prise de contrôle d'une entreprise par une ou plusieurs autres. Comme en droit communautaire, le contrôle découle des droits, contrats ou autres moyens qui confèrent, seul ou conjointement et compte tenu des circonstances de fait ou de droit, la possibilité d'exercer une influence déterminante sur l'activité d'une entreprise;
- en cas de création d'une entreprise commune de plein exercice (c'est-à-dire une entreprise qui accomplit de manière durable toutes les fonctions d'une entité économique autonome).

Les opérations de concentration entre entreprises étrangères (*"foreign-to-foreign")* peuvent relever du contrôle français si les seuils juridictionnels sont atteints, à savoir :

- lorsque deux au moins des parties à la concentration ont réalisé l'année précédant l'opération, individuellement, un chiffre d'affaires hors taxes en France supérieur à 15 millions d'euros;
- et que l'ensemble des parties a réalisé durant l'année précédant l'opération, un chiffre d'affaires hors taxes mondial cumulé supérieur à 150 millions d'euros.

Pour le calcul de ces seuils en chiffres d'affaires, le décret du 30 avril 2002 se contente de renvoyer expressément à l'article 5 du Règlement communautaire, mesure utile et bienvenue sur le plan pratique, qui illustre le lien de plus en plus étroit entre dispositions nationales et communautaires du contrôle des concentrations. Il faut souligner que le niveau très bas de ces seuils a déjà entra'né une augmentation très considérable du nombre d'opérations notifiées.

c. Is the filing mandatory or voluntary? Who is responsible for filing? What is involved in the preparation of a filing? What are the deadlines for filing? What are the waiting periods and does implementation of the transaction have to be suspended?

La notification est obligatoire ; elle incombe à l'acquéreur en cas de prise de contrôle exclusif, à l'ensemble des entreprises en cas de fusion ou, en cas d'entreprise commune conjointement contrôlée, à l'ensemble des sociétés exerçant le contrôle.

Il n'y a pas de délai pour effectuer la notification, qui peut survenir dès que les parties se sont "irrévocablement engagées", mais dans la mesure où l'opération ne peut pas être mise en œuvre avant l'obtention d'une autorisation, il est de l'intérêt des parties de notifier aussi rapidement que possible.

d. What are the issues and possible sanctions involved in closing before clearance? What is the timetable for clearance and can it be speeded up?

Le nouveau régime interdit la réalisation de l'opération avant la délivrance de l'autorisation ministérielle, sous peine de sanctions prévues à l'article L.430-8 Cod com. (injonction de revenir à la situation antérieure et possibilité d'infliger une sanction pécuniaire pouvant s'élever à 5 % du chiffre d'affaires hors taxe réalisé par la ou les entreprise(s) à qui incombait l'obligation de notifier).

De la même manière que le Règlement communautaire l'a prévu à l'article 7.4, le second alinéa de l'article L.430-4 a en effet prévu un régime de dérogation dans des cas exceptionnels, « en cas de nécessité particulière dûment motivée ». La DGCCRF a précisé que ce type de dérogation peut se concevoir lorsque les parties doivent procéder à la réalisation effective de l'opération alors que la procédure de contrôle n'est pas terminée (par exemple dans le cas du prononcé d'un plan de reprise, dans le cadre d'un redressement judiciaire, où le jugement prononçant le plan de cession doit être mis en œuvre sans délai).

Lorsqu'une opération a été notifiée, le Ministre dispose d'un délai de cinq semaines au lieu de deux mois précédemment, à compter de la délivrance de l'accusé de réception qui constate le caractère complet du dossier de notification, pour rendre une décision. En l'absence de décision à l'expiration de ce délai, les parties bénéficient d'une autorisation tacite. A ce stade de la procédure (« phase I »), le Ministre peut prendre trois types de décision :

- autoriser l'opération sans condition ;
- autoriser l'opération, à la condition que les entreprises aient souscrit des engagements de nature à résoudre les problèmes de concurrence soulevés par l'opération (la remise d'engagements par les parties plus de deux semaines après la notification complète porte le délai initial de cinq à huit semaines au maximum, afin d'en permettre l'étude et éventuellement le test auprès de tiers) ;

- saisir, pour avis, le Conseil de la concurrence de l'opération, déclenchant ainsi la « phase II ».

La phase d'examen approfondi peut durer un maximum de quatre mois supplémentaires à compter de la saisine du Conseil de la concurrence. Le Conseil de la concurrence rend son avis (purement consultatif) au Ministre, à l'issue d'une procédure contradictoire qui lui permet d'établir un bilan concurrentiel de l'opération apprécié au regard de la contribution au progrès économique éventuellement apportée par cette même opération. Le Conseil doit rendre son avis trois mois après la saisine. Le Ministre dispose alors de quatre semaines pour rendre sa décision (ce délai pouvant être augmenté de trois semaines si des engagements sont proposés plus d'une semaine après la remise de l'avis). Le Ministre peut :

- autoriser l'opération, avec ou sans engagements de la part des entreprises, comme en première phase ;
- autoriser l'opération, mais en assortissant cette autorisation d'injonctions de nature à remédier aux atteintes à la concurrence ou de prescriptions de nature à apporter au progrès économique et social une contribution suffisante pour compenser ces atteintes à la concurrence ;
- interdire l'opération.

Dans ces deux derniers cas, la décision prend la forme d'un arrêté pris conjointement par le Ministre chargé de l'économie et le Ministre en charge du secteur concerné. Il n'existe pas de moyen pour accélérer ce processus ; il convient toutefois de souligner qu'après deux mois d'application du nouveau régime, il est possible de constater que, dans les cas « simples », la DGCCRF s'efforce d'adopter ses décisions dans un délai plus court que le délai maximal de cinq semaines en phase I. Mais rien ne garantit que cette tendance sera confirmée à l'avenir, tant elle dépend du nombre de dossiers en cours d'examen et des ressources en personnel –limitées – des services compétents.

e. Are there any special rules applicable to public takeover bids?

L'article 6 du décret du 30 avril 2002 apporte une solution similaire, en pratique, à l'article 7.3 du Règlement communautaire : l'article 6 précise qu'en cas d'opération de bourse (OPA/OPE), la « réalisation effective » de l'opération est réputée intervenir non pas au moment où sont échangés les titres, mais seulement au moment où sont exercés les droits ainsi transférés. Ainsi, l'existence d'une procédure de contrôle de la concentration ne fait pas obstacle à l'échange des titres proprement dit, restant compatible avec le calendrier de l'opération de bourse. Toutefois, aucune disposition ne permet de résoudre la situation où l'opération serait interdite après que l'échange de titres ait été effectué *(voir infra. Réponse à la Question n° 15/16).*

f. What is the substantive test for clearance?

Voir supra. la réponse à la Question n° 4 ci-dessus : le critère d'analyse est celui de « l'atteinte à la concurrence », qui correspond assez largement, en pratique, au critère communautaire de « création ou renforcement d'une position dominante », mais qui est toutefois plus large que ce dernier et qui peut contribuer à donner un pouvoir d'appréciation plus important au Ministre de l'économie et des finances.

g. To what extent are non-competition issues relevant to the review process?

Le processus d'analyse porte essentiellement sur les considérations liées au droit de la concurrence, mais d'autres facteurs jouent aussi un rôle non négligeable, dans la mesure où la décision ultime appartient au Ministre de l'économie et que l'expérience montre que des considérations de politique industrielle ou des considérations sociales (maintien d'emplois, etc.) peuvent être prises en compte. En outre, lorsque le Conseil de la concurrence est saisi pour avis, dans le cadre d'une phase II, il lui incombe de prendre en considération « la compétitivité des entreprises en cause au regard de la concurrence internationale » (article L.430-6 du code de commerce).

h. Is it possible to remedy competition issues?

La possibilité de proposer des engagements visant à remédier à des risques d'atteinte à la concurrence existait déjà avant la réforme du régime français, mais elle a été formalisée et systématisée dans le nouveau texte qui a aligné la pratique française sur la pratique communautaire. Les engagements peuvent être proposés tant en phase I qu'en phase II ; selon la date à laquelle ils sont proposés, ils peuvent entra'ner un report des délais de la procédure, afin de permettre à la DGCCRF d'évaluer ces éléments et, le cas échéant, de les « tester » auprès du marché.

i. What are the typical steps during the investigation? What rights do complainants have? What publicity is given to the process? What are the opportunities for judicial review?

Les étapes essentielles sont les suivantes :

- Avant la notification : les contacts informels de pré-notification sont devenus une pratique courante et sont très recommandés, notamment pour s'assurer que la DGCCRF considère le dossier complet ; il n'est pas rare de transmettre une copie du projet de dossier de notification dans le cadre de ces contacts informels.
- Quelques jours après la notification (maximum cinq jours), les tiers sont informés de la notification par le biais d'un avis publié sur le site Internet de la Direction Générale de la Concurrence, de la Consommation et de la Répression des Fraudes ("DGCCRF") ; l'avis contient un appel public à commentaires, dans un délai généralement fixé à une dizaine de jours.
- Pendant la phase I, la DGCCRF procède, lorsque le dossier le justifie, à un « test de marché » ; toujours pendant cette phase I, il est possible pour les parties de proposer des engagements pour remédier à un risque d'atteinte à la concurrence.
- En cas de phase II, la procédure d'examen du dossier par le Conseil de la concurrence est contradictoire, et les parties peuvent formuler des observations. Toutefois, le Conseil peut entendre des tiers en l'absence des parties, de même que les comités d'entreprise, à leur demande.
- A la fin de la phase I ou de la phase II, lorsque le Ministre a adopté sa décision, il publie un bref « avis » indiquant le sens de sa décision dans un délai de 5 jours ouvrables (article 7 du décret du 30 avril 2002). L'article 9 de ce décret prévoit également une publication *in extenso* de la décision dans la revue spécialisée (le « BOCCRF »), mais sans qu'aucun délai soit précisément édicté. Il faut noter que les entreprises disposent, à compter de la notification d'une décision, d'un délai de 15 jours pour indiquer au Ministre les décisions relevant du secret des affaires, ce qui permet d'occulter les informations *"sensibles"* lors de la publication au BOCCRF (article 8 du décret).

Les possibilités de recours ont été décrites ci-dessus (voir réponse à la question n° 5).

j. What are the enforcement powers? How does administrative and civil sanctions compare with the EC regime? And what are the criminal sanctions, and are they used?

Les sanctions du non-respect des obligations imposées par la loi sont fixées à l'article L.430-8 du Code de commerce ; elles sont très proches des sanctions prévues par les dispositions communautaires :

"I. - Si une opération de concentration a été réalisée sans être notifiée, le Ministre chargé de l'économie peut infliger aux personnes auxquelles incombait la charge de la notification une sanction pécuniaire dont le montant maximum s'élève, pour les personnes morales, à 5% de leur chiffre d'affaires hors taxes réalisé en France lors du dernier exercice clos, augmenté, le cas échéant, de celui qu'a réalisé en France durant la même période la partie acquise, et, pour les personnes physiques, à 1,5 million d'euros. En outre, le Ministre enjoint sous astreinte aux parties de notifier l'opération, à moins de revenir à l'état antérieur à la concentration. Il peut également saisir le Conseil de la concurrence sans attendre la notification. La procédure prévue aux articles L. 430-5 à L. 430-7 est alors applicable."

"II. - Si une opération de concentration notifiée et ne bénéficiant pas de la dérogation prévue au deuxième alinéa de l'article L. 430-4 a été réalisée avant l'intervention de la décision prévue au premier alinéa du même article, le Ministre chargé de l'économie peut infliger aux personnes ayant procédé à la notification une sanction pécuniaire qui ne peut dépasser le montant défini au I."

"III. - En cas d'omission ou de déclaration inexacte dans une notification, le Ministre chargé de l'économie peut infliger aux personnes ayant procédé à la notification une sanction pécuniaire qui ne peut dépasser le montant défini au I. Cette sanction peut s'accompagner du retrait de la décision ayant autorisé la réalisation de l'opération. A moins de revenir à l'état antérieur à la concentration, les parties sont alors tenues de notifier de nouveau l'opération dans un délai d'un mois à compter du retrait de la décision, sauf à encourir les sanctions prévues au I."

"IV. - S'il estime que les parties n'ont pas exécuté dans les délais fixés une injonction, une prescription ou un engagement, le Ministre chargé de l'économie peut saisir pour avis le Conseil de la concurrence. Si l'avis du Conseil de la concurrence constate l'inexécution, le Ministre chargé de l'économie et, le cas échéant, le Ministre chargé du secteur économique concerné peuvent :

- Retirer la décision ayant autorisé la réalisation de l'opération. A moins de revenir à l'état antérieur à la concentration, les parties sont tenues de notifier de nouveau l'opération dans un délai d'un mois à compter du retrait de la décision, sauf à encourir les sanctions prévues au I ;
- Enjoindre sous astreinte aux parties auxquelles incombait l'obligation non exécutée d'exécuter dans un délai qu'ils fixent les injonctions, prescriptions ou engagements.

En outre, le Ministre chargé de l'économie peut infliger aux personnes auxquelles incombait l'obligation non exécutée une sanction pécuniaire qui ne peut dépasser le montant défini au I."

L'article 11 du décret du 30 avril 2002 prévoit que les astreintes prononcées en application de l'article L.430-8 ne peuvent excéder un montant maximal de 20 000 euros par jour de retard. Il n'y a pas de sanctions pénales prévues pour une infraction à ces dispositions.

Par ailleurs, l'article L. 430-9 du Code de commerce tel qu'insitué par la loi NRE permet désormais au Conseil de la concurrence de demander au Ministre de l'économie, postérieurement à la phase de contrôle des concentrations, de réexaminer le rapprochement en cause parce qu'il s'est finalement traduit par l'exploitation abusive d'une situation de domination. Le Conseil a fait usage pour la première fois de cette nouvelle prérogative, dans une décision du 11 juillet 2002 *Compagnie générale des eaux /Lyonnaise des eaux,* relative à la situation de la concurrence dans les secteurs de l'eau potable et de l'assainissement. Ainsi, le Conseil a demandé au Ministre de l'économie le réexamen de la constitution, à laquelle il ne s'était pas opposé, d'entreprises communes par la Compagnie générale des eaux et la Lyonnaise des eaux, réexamen susceptible d'aller jusqu'au démantèlement de ces filiales communes au regard notamment de la mise en commun des moyens par ces entreprises pour répondre à des appels à concurrence.

k. Do the authorities cooperate with other antitrust authorities?

La réponse est positive : la DGCCRF fait partie du réseau des autorités nationales de concurrence *(« international competition network »).*

l. Are there also rules on foreign investment, special sectors or other relevant approvals?

Il n'y a pas de règles particulières s'appliquant aux investissements étrangers du moins en matière de contrôle des opérations de concentrations (pour les autres opérations, le régime d'investissements des étrangers est essentiellement déclaratif). En revanche, des dispositions particulières existent dans le secteur des médias. La loi NRE du 15 mai 2001 a modifié l'article 41-4 loi du 30 septembre 1986 relative à la liberté de communication ; désormais, les entreprises fournissant des services de communication audiovisuelle sont soumises au contrôle des concentrations. La seule spécificité en la matière tient à ce que le Conseil de la concurrence, lorsqu'il est saisi pour avis d'un projet de concentration concernant de telles entreprises, doit recueillir l'avis du CSA.

Par ailleurs, la soumission éventuelle des établissements de crédit au contrôle français des concentrations demeure largement débattue: de nombreux auteurs considèrent en effet que ces établissements, s'ils sont soumis au contrôle communautaire des concentrations, échappent au contrôle national. Il faut toutefois nuancer cette approche par deux rappels : tout d'abord, le contrôle national des concentrations s'applique aux activités non-bancaires des établissements de crédit, et ensuite, s'agissant des activités bancaires, les autorités françaises de la concurrence pourraient invoquer l'article 22(3) du Règlement communautaire pour soumettre à la Commission européenne une opération de concentration où des établissements de crédit seraient des entreprises concernées.

m. Are there current proposals to change the legislation?

Dans la mesure où la réforme française est très récente, il est peu probable que des changements fondamentaux intervienne rapidement, à l'exception peut-être d'une modification à la hausse des seuils de chiffre d'affaires. Ces derniers sont en effet particulièrement bas, et il existe un risque que les services de la DGCCRF ne soient pas dans un proche future en mesure de consacrer les ressources suffisantes aux dossiers complexes s'ils doivent faire face à une augmentation significative du nombre de dossiers « simples ». Il faut également souligner que la DGCCRF devrait publier, dans le courant du mois de septembre 2002, un projet de « lignes directrices » dans l'application du contrôle des concentrations, qui fera l'objet d'une consultation publique avant la publication de la version définitive, fin 2002.

C. LES OBSTACLES TENANT A LA RÉGULATION FINANCIERE

7. What will you identify as the main obstacles to take overs where a company from your jurisdiction is either bidder or target and the other company is from another EU jurisdiction ?

Pour les opérations de contrôle quelle que soit leur nature, des règles impératives régissent certains secteurs imposant ainsi des contraintes supplémentaire à un acquéreur étranger même communautaire. Certains réglementations sectorielles imposent des conditions directement ou indirectement plus contraignantes pour une société communautaire (cf. infra Question 9). Plus généralement, de réelles difficultés s'opposent aux fusions (au sens juridique du terme) entre une société d'un Etat membre de l'Union Européenne (« Etat Membre ») et une société française pour des raisons essentiellement liées à l'application des règles de droit international privé. L'unanimité requise pour le changement de nationalité consécutif au transfert du siège social de la société cible dans le pays de l'acquéreur comme les difficultés rencontrées pour la transmission universelle de patrimoine sont des obstacles pour les fusions (id. cf. infra Question 9). S'agissant des sociétés cotées, certaines mesures de défenses anti-OPA(E) interdisent ou créent des difficultés majeures pour l'initiateur quelle que soit sa nationalité mais à partir de règles françaises qui peuvent être atypiques au regard d'autres législations. Il s'agit notamment de la structure de la société en commandite, de l'identification des actionnaires ou de l'action privilégiée de l'Etat (infra Question 14, i-j).

8. Do hostile take overs by companies from other EU jurisdictions in fact take place in your country?

Ces dernières années, peu d'opérations hostiles ont eu lieu en France avec des émetteurs d'origine intra communautaire. L'opération initiée par l'assureur italien Generali sur les AGF en 1997 est la dernière offre majeure correspondant à ce critère. Elle s'est résolue par l'intervention de l'assureur allemand Allianz qui, après que l'Etat ait donné son aval à l'opération projetée le 9 février 1998, a pris le contrôle des AGF en 1998 par le biais d'une OPA amicale.

9. To what extents are there any sectors (utilities, financial institutions) that in practice are further protected from hostile take overs, or foreign take overs in particular? Are there any policy statements or particular legal mechanisms that give effect to this protection, or is it a matter of informal mechanisms?

En principe, les investissements étrangers en France sont libres et ne donnent lieu qu'à une déclaration administrative *a posteriori*, sauf s'il s'agit d'opérations intervenant dans des domaines sensibles pour lesquels un contrôle préalable subsiste. Les investissements étrangers même communautaires dans les secteurs de l'activité économique considérés comme sensibles, car affectant des intérêts publics essentiels, ne peuvent être réalisés qu'avec l'autorisation préalable du Ministre de l'économie, des finances et de l'Industrie. Sont concernés (art. L 1513 Code monétaire et financier) :

- les investissements effectués dans des activités participant en France, même à titre occasionnel, à l'exercice de l'autorité publique, activités dont le régime s'oppose aux prises de contrôle (notaires, certains aspects des missions des commissaires priseurs...) ;
- les investissements de nature à mettre en cause l'ordre public, la santé publique (ex. laboratoires pharmaceutiques) ou la sécurité publique, ainsi que ceux réalisés dans des activités de recherche, de production ou de commerce d'armes, de munitions, de poudres et substances explosives destinées à des fins militaires ou de matériel de guerre.

Cependant, la CJCE a déclaré contraire au principe de libre circulation des capitaux, les dispositions de l'art. L 1513 Code monétaire et financier dans une question préjudicielle du Conseil d'Etat relative à l'application de l'article 58 § 1-b), ex-article 73 D § 1 du Traité CE (CJCE 14 mars 2000, C-54/99, *Association Eglise de scientologie*). La CJCE a en effet estimé qu'en l'absence de définition suffisamment précise de ces notions, les investisseurs ne peuvent conna'tre les situations dans lesquelles une autorisation est nécessaire ; dès lors, la CJCE a conclu que cette atteinte au principe de liberté de circulation n'est pas justifié.

Dans certains secteurs, les prises de contrôle doivent également faire face à des problèmes en raison de la réglementation qui leur est propre. On peut évoquer le cas des sociétés pour lesquelles des qualifications professionnelles (diplômes nationaux) sont imposées aux dirigeants ou aux actionnaires (laboratoires d'analyse médicale, fabrication et vente en gros de produits pharmaceutiques et sociétés de gestion de portefeuille notamment). Soulignons néanmoins que les contraintes imposées aux investisseurs étrangers ont majoritairement disparu pour les sociétés des Etats Membres dans le cadre de l'harmonisation permanente du droit communautaire.

En ce qui concerne les opérations visant des banques françaises, il est important de souligner le rôle déterminant que joue le CECEI («Comité des Etablissements de Crédit et des Entreprises d'Investissement») dans la validation des restructurations bancaires. Le CECEI prend des décisions ou accorde les autorisations ou dérogations individuelles prévues par les dispositions législatives et réglementaires applicables aux établissements de crédit et aux entreprises d'investissement, à l'exception de celles relevant de la Commissions bancaire (Lois du 24 janvier 1984 et du 2 juillet 1996). A la suite de l'affaire *BNP-Paribas-Société Générale*, certains lui reprochent de s'être attribué un véritable pouvoir d'appréciation de l'opportunité économique de l'opération créant ainsi une insécurité juridique. Rien ne permet d'affirmer que le CECEI ne reproduira pas une telle appréciation d'opportunité pour une opération réalisée à l'initiative d'une société communautaire.

Dans le secteur des médias, les actions d'une société titulaire d'une autorisation d'émettre, délivrée par le CSA (Conseil Supérieur de l'Audiovisuel), sont nominatives. La réglementation interdit, par principe, aux personnes de nationalité étrangère (hors Union Européenne) de détenir plus de 20% du capital ou des droits de vote d'une société titulaire d'une autorisation d'émettre. En matière de presse, l'acquisition directe ou indirecte de plus de 20% du capital social ou des droits de vote d'une entreprise de presse au sens de la loi est interdite. Cette limitation ne s'applique qu'aux publications en langue française et ne concerne que les prises de participation.

Enfin pour les télécommunications, l'autorisation nécessaire pour l'établissement et l'exploitation d'un réseau ouvert au public, lorsqu'elle concerne un réseau utilisant des fréquences radioélectriques, ne peut être accordée à une société dans laquelle plus de 20% du capital social ou des droits de vote sont détenus, directement ou indirectement, par des personnes de nationalité étrangère hors Union Européenne). De même, aucune personne de nationalité étrangère ne peut procéder à une acquisition ayant pour effet de porter, directement ou indirectement, la part détenue par des personnes de nationalité étrangère à plus de 20% du capital social ou des droits de vote dans les assemblées générales d'une société titulaire d'une telle autorisation.

Cependant, la validité du seuil des 20 % opposée aux investisseurs étrangers (hors Union Européenne) appara't douteuse et son application tombée en désuétude. En effet, depuis l'entrée en vigueur de l'Accord de Marrakech du 15 avril 1994 (1er janvier 1998 en France) ayant institué l'OMC, les participations indirectes d'investisseurs non européens sont libéralisées, même si le texte de l'article L 33-1 du Code des postes et télécommunications n'a pas été corrigé depuis lors. Ce nouvel état du droit semble devoir autoriser un montage communautaire permettant aux investisseurs étrangers d'"européaniser" leurs capitaux en intercalant un véhicule juridique communautaire entre eux et la société-cible ; ce montage a été validé par les autorités administratives françaises pour autant que le véhicule juridique communautaire satisfasse aux trois critères suivants : constitution selon les lois d'un Etat-membre, siège social (qui n'a pas besoin d'être celui du principal établissement) sur le territoire de l'un des Etats-membres, exigence d'un lien effectif et continu avec l'économie d'un Etat-membre. Ce montage courant en matière de télécommunications semble pouvoir s'appliquer aux autres secteurs couverts par l'Accord de Marrakech.

10. What are the company law techniques of completing a take over or mer that are used in practice where one of the companies is from another EU jurisdiction? Please give particular attention to how this would differ from the usual completion of a take over or merger where both companies are from your jurisdiction. It would be useful if you could add a comment about the consequences on the techniques used of the taxation regime and of any differential tax treatment of take overs or mergers where one party is from another EU jurisdiction.

Il existe en France différents schémas permettant la prise de contrôle ou l'acquisition d'une société. Pour la majeure partie des opérations, l'implication d'une société étrangère dans ces opérations ne constitue pas un obstacle de principe pour la bonne fin de l'opération sauf dans le cas des fusions.

- Tant les aspects juridiques que fiscaux doivent être revus pour les fusions.

  Sur le plan fiscal, la fusion absorption d'une société d'un Etat Membre par une société française est réalisée selon les mêmes modalités qu'une opération locale. En revanche, la fusion absorption d'une société française par une société d'un Etat Membre se traduit par la constitution en France d'un établissement stable de la société européenne et doit faire l'objet d'un agrément préalable délivré par l'administration fiscale. Dans cette hypothèse, l'opération doit être économiquement justifiée, ne doit pas avoir pour objectif principal ou un de ses objectifs principaux la fraude ou l'évasion fiscale et les modalités de réalisation de l'opération doivent permettre une imposition future des plus-values en France. Pour les fusions intracommunautaires, l'administration fiscale française devrait approuver l'opération dès lors que la société issue de l'opération s'engage à respecter les dispositions fiscales françaises sécurisant l'imposition à terme des plus-values réalisées (Loi de finance pour 2002).

Sur le plan juridique, les fusions sont réalisées par transmission universelle du patrimoine de la société absorbée à la société absorbante ou à une société nouvelle. La complexité des opérations de fusion est accentuée par leur nature intracommunautaire et l'approche de législations de certains Etats Membres qui interdisent les fusions transnationales.

Les règles du droit international privé qui déterminent la loi applicable au projet de fusion donnent compétence à la *lex societatis*. Chaque étape de la fusion est soumis, soit à la loi française, soit à la loi étrangère en fonction de la société concernée à cette étape (application distributive des lois en présence). En cas de fusion absorption, la loi de la société absorbante doit être appliquée pour déterminer les règles propres à l'augmentation de capital devant permettre l'entrée dans le capital des actionnaires de la société absorbée. La *lex societatis* trouvera à s'appliquer dans chaque société lorsqu'il s'agira pour chacune d'elle de déterminer les règles de quorum et de majorité applicable pour la décision des actionnaires de procéder à la fusion. Dans d'autres cas, l'application distributive des lois en présence est impossible, il conviendra alors d'appliquer cumulativement les deux lois des sociétés. En pratique, cela revient à cumuler les exigences ou à tout le moins d'appliquer la plus sévère des deux lois. Par exemple, la loi française admet que le traité de fusion soit passé par acte sous seing privé, alors que le droit portugais et le droit espagnol imposent un acte en la forme authentique. Dans une telle hypothèse, il sera fait application de la loi la plus contraignante, à savoir celle exigeant la rédaction d'un acte authentique.

Enfin, dans certains cas, l'implication d'une société étrangère (communautaire ou non) rendra en pratique l'opération de fusion impossible. L'absorption d'une société française par une société étrangère est en pratique quasiment impossible. L'absorption de la société française s'analyse en droit français comme un transfert de siège social avec pour conséquence un changement de nationalité. Ce changement de nationalité crée une modification des obligations légales pesant sur les actionnaires et est, à ce titre, soumis à la décision unanime des actionnaires. Sauf à ce que la société française soit une filiale à 100%, il est très difficile de procéder à une telle opération.

Dans ce contexte, la fusion est souvent en pratique écartée au profit d'opérations poursuivant le même objectif sous une autre forme.

- Ainsi, pour l'acquisition de l'activité d'une cible -cotée ou non, sont utilisées les techniques de l'apport partiel d'actif ou d'acquisition de fonds de commerce.

L'apport par une société française d'une branche d'activité à une société d'un Etat Membre doit être approuvé par l'administration fiscale afin de bénéficier du régime spécial des fusions. La société française devra en particulier conserver les titres reçus en rémunération des actifs apportés pendant au moins trois ans et s'engager à calculer les plus-values de cession ultérieure de ces titres par référence à la valeur d'inscription desdits actifs à son bilan (Loi de finance pour 2002).

L'apport par une société d'un Etat Membre de sa succursale française à une société française peut être réalisé dans le cadre du régime fiscal de faveur sans demande d'agrément si les deux conditions précitées sont remplies (engagement de conservation des titres et modalités de calcul ultérieur des plus-values de cession). Si ces deux conditions ne sont pas respectées, l'opération devra être approuvée par l'administration fiscale française qui pourra exiger de la société communautaire qu'elle cède les titres reçus en contrepartie de l'apport à une société holding française qui s'engagera elle-même à respecter les engagements précités.

L'apport par une société française à une société d'un Etat Membre de titres est assimilé à une branche d'activité autonome et doit être approuvé par l'administration fiscale française qui subordonne l'application du régime fiscal de faveur au respect des deux conditions précitées. En outre, la société communautaire bénéficiaire de l'apport devra conserver les titres reçus lors de l'apport tant que la société française apporteuse conserve elle-même les titres reçus en rémunération de son apport.

- L'acquisition des titres d'une cible cotée passe par la réalisation d'OPA(E) et OPR ou achat d'un bloc de contrôle hors marché avec garantie de cours. L'acquisition des titres d'une cible non cotée est réalisée au travers d'une acquisition d'un bloc de contrôle de la cible par échange de titres ou paiement en numéraire, l'opération pouvant être réalisée par le biais d'un LBO.

11. A duty on listed companies to disclose capital and control structures is proposed in Issues Relating to Takeover Bids, the First Report of the High Level Group of Company Law Experts (see p 25). Would this require amendments in the legislation in your country? How would these amendments in case be implemented (in primary company law, securities law, stock exchange regulations etc.)?

La loi française impose un principe général d'information (article 412-1 du Code monétaire et financier) complété par des règlements COB qui en précisent l'étendue et la nature. Ainsi l'information qui doit être fournie au public est appréciée sous l'angle de la pertinence qu'elle revêt aux yeux des investisseurs.

On peut noter que dès 1999, la COB conseillait les sociétés cotées de diffuser sur leur site Internet tous les documents visés ou approuvés par ses soins (Recommandation 98-05). Dorénavant, les émetteurs d'offre doivent impérativement adresser une version électronique du prospectus à la COB afin que cette dernière assure sa diffusion sur son site Internet (Règlement COB 2002-01). En outre la COB recommande également aux émetteurs de s'abstenir de répondre à des interrogations individuelles de participants aux forums de discussion sur Internet dans le souci d'éviter toute atteinte à l'égalité de traitement des investisseurs (Recommandation 2000-02).

En ce qui concerne les dirigeants des sociétés cotées, la recommandation 2002-01 les invite à déclarer systématiquement les transactions réalisées par leurs soins sur les titres de la société qu'ils dirigent. Pendant une offre, les dirigeants doivent aviser la COB de tout acte autre que de gestion courante sauf ceux expressément autorisés par l'assemblée générale extraordinaire pendant l'offre (Règlement COB 2002-04). Les clauses prévoyant des conditions préférentielles de cession ou d'acquisition de sociétés cotées des conventions transmises au CMF sont présentées dans les notes d'information.

La modification de la législation afin de prendre en compte les propositions du groupe d'expert pré-cité visant à préciser les informations qui doivent être diffusées pourrait être réalisée par voie de modification des règlements COB validée par arrêté ministériel.

12. A so called break through rule after take over bids is another of the proposals in Issues Relating to Takeover Bids, the First Report of the High Level Group of Company Law Experts (see p 29). Would this require amendments in the legislation in your country? How would these amendments in case be implemented (in primary company law, securities law, stock exchange regulations etc.)?

Ces propositions visent à s'opposer aux défenses anti-OPA (statuts, pactes d'actionnaires, structure de détention, décisions prises pendant l'offre) dans le souci de permettre aux seuls actionnaires de décider de la suite à donner à l'offre. Si de telles dispositions étaient adoptées au niveau communautaire, le législateur français devraient alors les transposer dans la loi, et les autorités de marché modifier les dispositions réglementaires en conséquence.

Cependant, certains en France doutent de l'opportunité de ces éventuelles futures dispositions au regard de l'intérêt de la société dans le contexte des offres à caractère purement spéculatif sans logique industrielle. De ce point de vue, cette hypothèse rend légitime des mesures anti-OPA destinées à préserver les intérêts de la société, même au détriment des intérêts des actionnaires

Dans ce contexte, il est intéressant de noter que la validité de certaines mesures anti-OPA prises pendant l'offre par une assemblée générale ou le rachat d'actions (pour une offre exclusivement réglée en numéraire et à condition qu'il s'agisse d'un programme de rachat d'actions déjà en cours avec une prorogation expresse pendant une offre visée dans la résolution l'assemblée générale) est actuellement expressément reconnue par le récent Règlement COB 2002-04 sur les OPA.

13. In your view, would these two new rules as proposed have any material impact on the existing barriers to take overs in your country (or in others as seen from your point of view)? It would be helpful if you could demonstrate the impact, or lack of it, by going through one or more recent take over bids that failed in your country (or in some other member state, by a company from your country).

En ce qui concerne les fusions transfrontalières intra-communautaires, les propositions ne peuvent modifier les problèmes soulevés par l'application distributive des lois des sociétés en cause ou l'unanimité requise par la loi française en cas de changement de siège social entra'nant la modification de la nationalité de la société cible française. Ces questions pourraient être résolues par l'adoption d'un nouveau projet de société européenne.

Même si les praticiens trouvent des mécanismes alternatifs pour réaliser des opérations transfrontalières qui ne sont pas définies comme des fusions sur le plan juridique, la transmission universelle de patrimoine que permettent les fusions reste un atout majeur qui ne peut pas véritablement être reproduit pas des solutions alternatives. Mais en tout état de cause, même les fusions de sociétés cotées françaises rencontrent l'obstacle de la COB et du CMF qui s'opposent à de telles fusions.

En ce qui concerne les OPA(E), la modification des règles telles que proposées par le groupe des experts favoriserait les opérations autant pour les société françaises que celles des Etats Membres dans la mesure où les obstacles pour ces dernières sont essentiellement concentrés au niveau des secteurs réglementés.

14. Below are a number of questions which may assist in a comparative analysis.

a. What are the main features of the relevant domestic take over legislation constituting the company law and financial market regime, and who enforces it (independent regulators, regulatory bodies with appeal to ministry, stock exchange)? What is the extent of intervention by the

takeover regulator(s) – to what extent does the regulator have wide or general discretions to block and play a protectionist role (for example in its capacity as approver of the offer terms/documentation)?

Les deux autorités de marché sont le CMF (« Conseil des Marchés Financiers ») et la COB (« Commission des Opérations de Bourse »). Le CMF fixe les principes généraux d'organisation et de fonctionnement des marchés réglementés d'instruments financiers et contrôle la régularité des opérations effectuées sur un marché réglementé. Il réglemente et approuve les opérations sur titres financiers. Le règlement CMF définit les règles régissant les offres publiques faites en France et portant sur des instruments financiers admis sur un marché négocié.

La COB est une autorité administrative indépendante dont la mission consiste en la protection de l'épargne publique, à assurer le bon fonctionnement des marchés d'instruments financiers et à veiller à l'information des investisseurs. Elle contrôle l'information financière des sociétés cotées et agrée les produits et les entreprises de gestion d'actifs.

L'avant-projet de loi du 7 février 2001 (n° 2920) portant réforme des autorités financières vise à instituer une autorité unique, l'Autorité des marchés financiers (« AMF ») qui se substituera à la COB et au CMF. Bien que ce texte ait été préparée par l'ancienne majorité parlementaire, il, le nouveau Ministre de l'économie et des finances envisageait courant juillet 2002 de le reprendre.

b. Are there restrictions on a board taking action to frustrate a bid that has been made? When do the relevant restrictions start to apply – earlier than a formal announcement/filing of a bid? To what extent can shareholders approve the taking of frustrating action in advance any bid?

Par principe, le conseil d'administration doit avoir une délégation préalable de l'assemblée générale pour décider de mesures anti-OPA qui ne peuvent intervenir qu'une fois l'opération déclenchée. Les actionnaires peuvent décider de prendre toute mesure utile pour contrer une telle offre au préalable.

c. Are there restrictions on the type of consideration that can be offered in a bid, for example securities only if these are listed in the target country's home state or the EU?

L'initiateur peut offrir aux actionnaires de la société visée :

- ses propres actions, résultat d'une augmentation ou de la remise d'actions acquises dans le cadre d'un programme de rachat d'actions,

- des action d'une société tierce par rapport à l'initiateur, action de filiales de l'initiateur,
- tout type de valeur mobilière (certificat de valeur garantie, action à émettre, Obligations Remboursables en Actions...)
- une soulte,
- une combinaison de ce qui précède.

Les titres remis aux actionnaires de la société visée peuvent être ceux d'une société française ou étrangère.

d. Are there effective compulsory acquisition procedures regarding a small n-accepting minority? Can a bidder make its offer conditional on achieving the number of shares required so it can operate a squeeze out?

d.1 Are there effective compulsory acquisition procedures regarding a small non-accepting minority?

Les associés, par principe, ont un droit de conserver leurs titres et ne doivent pas être contraints de les céder contre leur gré. Néanmoins, ce principe subit quelques exceptions distinctes selon que les sociétés sont cotées ou non.

Pour les sociétés non cotées, la loi autorise, pour les statuts des sociétés par actions simplifiées, l'inscription dans les statuts des clauses d'exclusion des actionnaires dès lors que ces mentions précisent également les modalités d'éviction des actionnaires. Pour les sociétés anonymes, une telle décision doit être approuvée au préalable par l'assemblée générale selon les modalités inscrites dans les statuts ou déterminées par l'assemblée générale décidant sur l'opération de rachat forcé. La loi ne prévoit rien pour les autres types de sociétés non cotées et la réponse dépend donc des circonstances de fait.

Pour les sociétés cotées, la procédure du retrait obligatoire, qui constitue la suite d'une offre publique de retrait, est prévue par les textes. Il convient à partir du seuil de détention de 95% des droits de vote (seul ou de concert), de déposer une offre de retrait qui sera visée par le CMF et à laquelle la COB ne présentera pas d'opposition suite à la valorisation des actions par un expert indépendant. L'initiateur de l'OPR, suivie d'une procédure de retrait obligatoire, s'engage au rachat des actions présentées par les minoritaires.

d.2 Can a bidder make its offer conditional on achieving the number of shares required so it can operate a squeeze out?

L'initiateur d'une OPA peut conditionner son offre à l'obtention d'un certain pourcentage du capital ou des droits de vote. A défaut d'atteindre le pourcentage annoncé, l'offre devient caduque. Afin d'éviter ce risque, le schéma classique consiste à organiser une OPA conditionnée par l'obtention de 50% des droits de vote suivie d'une OPA simplifiée pour viser l'objectif du seuil de détention de 95% nécessaire à l'organisation d'une offre de retrait. L'OPR est ensuite prolongée par un retrait obligatoire afin de sortir de la cote.

e. Is there a principle of board neutrality? Can a target board align itself with a particular bidder/agree measures such as exclusivity arrangements to protect a particular deal?

Le principe de la neutralité du Conseil d'Administration relève implicitement de l'obligation de loyauté, d'intégrité et de transparence sur les opérations tel visé dans le Règlement COB 2002-04 (cf. infra Question 14.f) pendant les phases préliminaires de l'opération.

Dès lors que la COB a apposé son visa sur la note d'information établie par le candidat acquéreur, la société cible doit déposer auprès de la COB une note d'information dans les 5 jours de bourse de la réception de la note de l'initiateur. Cette note doit préciser notamment l'avis motivé du conseil d'administration sur l'intérêt ou les risques que présente l'offre pour la société visée et pour ses actionnaires et les conditions de vote dans lesquelles l'avis a été rendu, les administrateurs pouvant demander qu'il soit fait état de leur identité et position.

Néanmoins, rien ne s'oppose à ce que l'initiateur de l'offre puisse proposer aux actionnaires principaux des modalités pour agir de concert, ou inversement que les actionnaires principaux se rapprochent de l'initiateur.

f. Can a target board hand over information to a potential bidder?

Le principe visé par la COB en matière d'offres publiques est celui du respect du libre jeu de des offres et des surenchères, tant du point de vue des initiateurs que des sociétés cibles. Le Règlement n° 2002-04 de la COB précise que « *toute personne doit agir dans le respect du libre jeu des offres et des surenchères, de l'égalité de traitement ou d'information des détenteurs de titres des sociétés concernées, de la transparence et l'intégrité du marché, de la loyauté dans les transactions et de la compétition. (...) Si les dirigeants des sociétés concernées décident d'accomplir des actes autres que ceux de gestion courante, les dirigeants de la société visée doit en aviser la Commission afin de lui permettre de veiller à l'information du public et de faire le cas échéant conna'tre son appréciation* ». La COB veille donc sur l'égalité de l'information, principe qui interdit à la cible de faire profiter un « chevalier blanc » d'informations dont l'initiateur ou le marché n'aurait pas eu connaissance. Différentes règles doivent être prises en compte dans ce contexte :

- les délits d'initiés vis à vis du candidat acquéreur ;
- la divulgation d'information privilégiée ;
- le respect de l'égalité d'information vis à vis des minoritaires : en effet malgré leur droit d'information régi par certaines dispositions légales impératives, ils ont accès à beaucoup moins d'informations pertinentes que les candidats acquéreurs, même dans l'hypothèse où ces derniers ne donnent aucune suite à leur projet.

Cependant et compte tenu de ce qui précède, un candidat acquéreur ne saurait présenter une offre sans recueillir des informations pertinentes de la société cible. Dans cet esprit et conscient des règles qui s'imposent à eux, la mise à disposition des informations nécessaires à l'offre doit se faire à travers les principes suivants (qui n'exonèrent pas les candidats acquéreurs et la cible de leur responsabilité) :

- principe d'égalité d'accès à l'information entre les candidats acquéreurs, même si celui-ci n'est pas juridiquement protégé,
- confidentialité sur les informations reçues par les candidats ,
- lettre d'intention traduisant une volonté explicite d'acquisition,
- engagement d'abstention à agir sur les titres de la cible.

En décembre 2001, la COB a lancé une consultation de place sur la transmission d'informations privilégiées à l'occasion de la mise en place de data room sous la forme d'un projet de recommandation. En mars 2002, la COB a présenté la synthèse de la consultation de place, de laquelle il ressort une grande variété de positions sur ce point. La consultation n'avait pas donné lieu à une recommandation de l'autorité courant juillet 2002.

g. Are structures permitted which concentrate control rights in the hands of minority shareholders? Are structures permitted which place limitations/restrictions on voting rights, caps for example on voting rights above a certain threshold?

En France, les sociétés en commandite par actions, les sociétés par actions simplifiées et les sociétés civiles de gestion de patrimoine sont utilisées pour ce type d'effet de leviers. Par extension les structures de holding, la combinaison avec les conventions de vote et les actions à droit de vote double ainsi que les obligations convertibles en action permettent également cet objectif.

h. Can restrictions be placed on the transferability of shares either by the issuer (in articles of association or by other means) or by arrangements between shareholders? Can a board delay registering transfers of shares?

h. 1. Can restrictions be placed on the transferability of shares either by the issuer (in articles of association or by other means)?

Il convient de distinguer entre les sociétés cotées et les sociétés non cotées encore appelées sociétés fermées.

- s'agissant des sociétés cotées, les limitations à la libre cessibilité des actions serait difficilement compatibles avec la rapidité des transactions boursières. Néanmoins au plan des principes, l'article L.228-25 du Code de commerce autorise en la réglementant strictement la procédure d'agrément cession d'actions de sociétés cotées. Au plan pratique, les clauses limitant la libre cessibilité sont appelées à dispara'tre pour toutes le sociétés qui demanderont l'admission de leurs actions aux négociations sur un marché réglementé français. En effet, l'entreprise de marché qui gère ces marchés réglementés (articles P 1.1.17 et 1.1.28 du règlement Euronext Paris) subordonne son accord pour cette admission à la suppression de toute clause statutaire pouvant limiter la libre négociation des titres.
- s'agissant de sociétés non cotées, l'émetteur peut prévoir dans ses statuts, en fonction de la forme sociale retenue un certain nombre d'hypothèse organisant la cession des titres :
- clause d'agrément simple : à noter qu'elles ne sont pas applicables en cas de cession entre actionnaires.
- clause d'agrément particulière : ces clauses visent à soumettre à la procédure d'agrément toute modification intervenue dans le capital social ou des droits de vote d'un actionnaire personne morale ; ainsi à défaut d'agrément du nouveau détenteur de capital de la personne morale actionnaire, l'émetteur pourra faire en sorte que les actions de cet actionnaire soient acquises soit par l'émetteur lui-même soit par des tiers agréés.
- clause de preemption : elles sont applicables aux cessions entre actionnaires
- clause d'inaliénabilité : les statuts de sociétés par actions simplifiées peuvent interdire aux associés de céder leurs titres pendant une durée déterminée, durée qui ne saurait excéder 10 ans.
- clause d'exclusion : les statuts de l'émetteur peuvent prévoir des cas d'exclusion d'un associé et fixer les conditions de cession de ses actions.

h.2. Can restrictions be placed on the transferability of shares by arrangements between shareholders?

Les actionnaires d'un société, certains d'entre eux seulement peuvent organiser, lorsque les statuts ne le prévoient pas, la limitation à la libre cession des actions. Cela peut résulter d'un choix et d'une décision stratégiques dont les conséquences produisent des effets juridiques différents selon que cette limitation est statutaire ou non ; cela peut résulter de dispositions impératives (cf. ci-dessus le règlement Euronext) et les accords entre actionnaires restent le seul moyen d'encadrer et réglementer la cession des titres.

Ces types d'accords existent pour les sociétés cotées et non cotées. Dans le premier cas, une législation particulière leur est applicable. En effet, toute clause d'un pacte d'actionnaire comportant des conditions préférentielles de cession ou d'acquisition d'actions admises sur un marché réglementé doit faire l'objet de mesure de publicité : transmission de ladite clause au CMF et publicité des principales dispositions. A défaut de transmission, les effets de la clause sont suspendus en période d'offre publique sur les titres qui ont sont l'objet et les parties déliées de leurs engagements pendant cette période. De la même manière, en cas de dépôt d'une offre publique, les accords susceptibles d'avoir une incidence sur l'appréciation de ladite offre, conclus soit par les actionnaires de la société visée soit des personnes agissant de concert doivent être notifiés par leur signataire au CMF, à la COB et au conseil d'administration de la société concernée.

h.3. Can a board delay registering transfers of shares?

S'agissant des sociétés cotées, dés réception de l'ordre de vente ou d'achat, l'établissement teneur de comptes est tenu de le comptabiliser. A ce stade, le rôle du conseil d'administration est plus limité.

S'agissant des sociétés non cotées, aucune disposition particulière ne régit les modalités d'inscription en compte des valeurs mobilières, ce sont les statuts qui doivent en aménager les modalités. L'Association Nationale des Sociétés par Actions (ANSA) a défini un cahier des charges que les sociétés ont la liberté de suivre ou non. De façon synthétique, les opérations sur les valeurs mobilières doivent être retracées chronologiquement dans un journal général (appelé également registre de mouvements de titres) et dans des comptes individuels d'actionnaires (qui donne pour chaque actionnaire sa situation personnelle).

C'est au président qu'il appartient de comptabiliser les opérations intervenues sur les actions, après que le titulaire l'en ait informé. La comptabilisation des opérations doit intervenir dans un délai de six jours à compter de l'information du président. La demande de comptabilisation d'une opération par le titulaire doit être accompagnée de tous les documents justificatifs attestant de la réalisation définitive de l'opération.

Le président ne saurait comptabiliser une opération sans s'assurer que cédant et cessionnaire ont respecté le cas échéant les clauses statutaires d'agrément ou de préemption, à défaut sa responsabilité pourrait être engagée, dans la mesure où l'inscription en compte vaut justification de la propriété (quand bien même ne s'agirait-il que d'une présomption simple). La société émettrice doit donc vérifier que le donneur a la capacité et le pouvoir de d'effectuer le mouvement de titres, sinon l'instruction de mouvement serait nulle.

i. What contractual barriers (including shareholder agreements) to take over bids are in use in public companies (eg golden parachutes, change of control provisions triggering default of loan agreements, or wining up or change of control of joint ventures)? What are the prospects of review by courts on the basis of contract or company law and by regulators on the basis of securities laws or stock exchange regulations?

Parmi les mesures préventives contractuelles, les statuts peuvent prévoir des obligations de déclaration de franchissement de seuils dès 0,5 % du capital qui viennent ainsi s'ajouter aux seuils réglementaires. De plus les statuts peuvent imposer la procédure de titres au porteur identifiables afin de parfaitement identifier les actionnaires. Cette procédure est généralement mise en place afin d'identifier l'actionnariat à la date de clôture de l'exercice et avant l'assemblée générale ordinaire d'approbation des comptes.

La ma'trise du capital social peut également être exercée au travers des pactes d'actionnaires avec des engagements de ne pas répondre favorablement à une offre hostile, un droit de préemption exercé au prix de l'offre hostile, ou des engagements d'inaliénabilité dans certaines conditions et/ou des engagements de non-agression signés par les actionnaires minoritaires.

Il est possible dans une certaine mesure de créer des catégories d'actions différentes permettant l'instauration de droits de vote doubles et la limitation du nombre de droits de vote (action spécifique ou *golden share)*. Les actions privilégiées détenues par l'Etat dans des sociétés comme TotalFina-Elf interdisent de fait toute prise de contrôle des sociétés privatisées concernées. Cependant, la France a été condamnée par la CJCE le 4 juin 2002 (C 483/99) pour non-respect du principe de libre circulation des capitaux en raison de l'action spécifique détenue par l'Etat français dans la société Elf Aquitaine. Cette action spécifique figure dans les dispositions du décret n°93-1298 du 13 décembre 1993 et impose notamment l'approbation préalable par le Ministre de l'économie de tout franchissement à la hausse des seuils de détention directe et indirecte de titres du dixième, du cinquième ou du tiers du capital ou des droits de vote de la société. Le principe même de l'action privilégiée n'est pas remis en cause par la CJCE, ce qui laisse l'opportunité à l'Etat français d'adapter les dispositions incriminées en prévoyant des critères suffisamment précis et objectifs pour l'approbation des opérations visées afin de conserver une partie de leur efficacité en tant que mesure anti-OPA. Courant juillet, Seul un règlement européen devrait pouvoir résoudre la question des actions spécifiques des Etats dans certaines sociétés.

D'autres actions peuvent être prises comme la réunion d'un noyau d'actionnaires au sein d'une holding, le lancement d'un programme de rachat d'actions, l'émission de titres sans droit de vote, toutes les mesures visant à renforcer l'auto contrôle, et les participations croisées.

Il est également possible de déléguer par l'assemblée des actionnaires au conseil d'administration l'autorisation de procéder à une augmentation de capital ou d'organiser une assemblée générale extraordinaire des actionnaires en cours d'offre (cf. supra Question 12 pour le dernier Règlement COB sur les OPA).

La fidélisation de l'actionnariat par les droits de vote double, les primes aux actionnaires stables et la majoration de dividendes incitent ces derniers à conserver le contrôle tel qu'il existe.

La société en commandite par action ou l'insertion de clause relatives à un changement de contrôle dans les contrats commerciaux ou financiers et dans les filiales communes sont des mesures qui visent également à s'opposer aux offres hostiles.

Le faible nombre d'opérations hostiles en France peut également s'expliquer par le poids de l'actionnariat salarié dans certaines grandes sociétés cotées (Société Générale par exemple) pour lesquelles l'initiateur d'une offre pourrait être confronté à une opposition d'actionnaires salariés qui est un facteur de risque considérable quant au succès de son opération.

j. Are there current proposals to change the legislation relating to take overs?

Comme précisé ci-dessus la COB devrait encadrer l'organisation des data rooms mais aucune date n'a été précisée suite à la synthèse de la consultation sur ce thème. La fusion de la COB et du CMF pourrait avoir lieu dans un avenir proche. Le CMF envisagerait par ailleurs de conditionner toute offre publique à l'autorisation préalable des autorités de concurrence.

D. AUTRES « OBSTACLES » : DROIT SOCIAL

Si les obstacles tenant à la régulation financière et au droit de la concurrence sont reconnus, il convient également, dans le contexte du droit français, d'insister sur les obstacles tenant au droit social (au sens du droit du travail et de la sécurité sociale salarié). Les procédures de droit social (recrutement, exécution du contrat de travail, licenciements...) et les coûts sociaux (charges sociales directes et indirectes, formation, financement des comités d'entreprises...) ainsi que les droits individuels et collectifs diffèrent sensiblement entre Etats concernés et constituent dans le cas français un obstacle de première importance devant participer à ce titre à la réflexion lancée par la FIDE.

Ces obstacles tenant au droit social interne ne font à ce jour pour l'essentiel que l'objet de déclarations de principes ou de tentatives de réglementation ou d'harmonisation au niveau communautaire. La confrontation de ces deux séries de disposition a conduit le groupe à conclure en faveur de l'instauration de conditions d'égalité de traitement des salariés en cas de concentration transfrontalière.

Il convient d'abord de préciser brièvement les conditions d'applicabilité du droit social français. Toute personne quelque soit sa nationalité résidant en France bénéficie des dispositions du droit interne. Une protection sociale complète doit être assurée. C'est une règle d'ordre public. Le principe posé est donc celui de la territorialité d'application des textes ; ce principe n'admet pas l'application du droit d'un autre Etat sur le territoire. Il existe cependant des exceptions qui tiennent principalement au cas de détachement, le droit communautaire du travail permettant sous certaines réserves aux citoyens d'un autre Etat de rester soumis aux dispositions du droit de leur pays même s'ils résident et travaillent en France pendant quelques mois.

En tout état de cause, tout opérateur économique partie à une concentration transfrontières doit informer les institutions représentatives du personnel, les comités d'hygiène et de sécurité, le comité d'entreprise - voire dans certains cas les organisations syndicales directement - et les institutions élues ou désignées dans l'établissement, l'entreprise, le groupe (comité de Groupe, comité d'entreprise européen) ou l'unité économique et sociale (dans le cas d'une pluralité d'entreprises ne constituant pas un groupe). Cette information concerne l'impact de la concentration sur l'organisation générale de l'entreprise et du travail et sur la formation professionnelle. Cette information concerne également les conséquences d'une décision prise dans un Etat dans les autres Etats de l'Union Européenne (voir affaire Renault Vilvorde).

L'information doit être préalable à la mise en oeuvre du projet, particulièrement si celui-ci peut avoir des conséquences sur la situation de l'emploi. La loi NRE pré-citée ainsi que la loi de modernisation sociale de janvier 2002 ont conforté et accentué le rôle du comité d'entreprise en permettant à celui-ci de demander à inclure des projets de résolutions soumises à l'assemblée générale de l'entreprise et organisant la consultation de celui-ci sur la politique de l'emploi et les projets de licenciement. La loi de modernisation sociale prévoit également la présence de salariés dans les conseils de surveillances ou d'administration si les salariés possèdent 3% au moins du capital.

Le droit communautaire tente de régler certaines de ces difficultés qui constituent autant d'obstacles aux concentrations transfrontières. Ainsi, le Traité d'Amsterdam a renforcé le principe de l'égalité de traitement entre les personnes travaillant dans un même Etat membre. De plus, les règlements relatifs aux règles de sécurité sociale (Règlements n° 1408/71 et suivants), applicables aux travailleurs migrants, permettent de régler un conflit de statut (travailleur salarié ou non salarié), de durée de présence dans un autre Etat membre, et donc de droit applicable (droit français, droit du pays d'origine). La directive n° 94/45 relative aux accords instituant les comité d'entreprise Européen a été transposée en droit français et indique quel est le rôle du comité d'entreprise européen

La directive 96/71 CE du 16 décembre 1996 JOCE L 18 du 21 janvier 1997 s'intéresse au détachement dans le cadre d'une prestation de service et insiste sur l'application du droit du pays d'accueil. Enfin, la directive n° 2001/23 a procédé à la codification de la directive du 14 février 1977 concernant le rapprochement des législations des Etats Membres relatives au maintien des droits des travailleurs en cas de transfert d'entreprises, d'établissements ou de parties d'entreprises ou d'établissements.

En dépit de l'existence de ces textes, facteur facilitatif des obstacles de droit social en matière de concentrations transfrontières, les experts du groupe de travail estiment que l'état du droit communautaire qui a pourtant pour objet de protéger les salariés de chaque Etat et de réaliser l'égalité de traitement de tous les salariés travaillant dans un même Etat, n'a pas permis à ce jour de réaliser la pleine égalité de traitement en cas de concentration transfrontalière. De plus, l'état du droit ne permet pas de réaliser la pleine égalité de traitement des entreprises elles-mêmes, les règles de chaque pays étant particulièrement complexes et substantiellement différentes. Le groupe de travail appelle donc à une meilleure prise en compte des obstacles tenant au droit social par l'instauration de nouveaux instruments communautaires et souligne la nécessité de progrès dans l'harmonisation des dispositions d'ordre social.

E. REMARQUES FINALES

15-16. In your view, what is the extent to which the complexity of the regulatory arrangements, within national jurisdictions and between the Commission and member states, present an obstacle to take overs? Can you list some instances where different rules in the different regulatory systems have caused practical obstacles in a take over process?

Le groupe de travail a porté son attention sur la question résultant de la confrontation des calendriers tenant au contrôle de concurrence et au contrôle boursier.

En premier lieu, il convient de noter qu'à la suite d'un oubli du législateur français, la récente loi NRE pré-citée ne contenait pas de disposition équivalente à l'article 7.3 du Règlement. On sait que cette disposition a pour objet de rendre automatiquement possible, contrairement au principe du gel d'une opération de concentration pendant son examen par la Commission, la poursuite de l'acquisition ou l'échange des titres pourvu que l'acquéreur n'exerce pas les droits de vote attachés aux participations acquises, ou bien ne le fasse qu'en vue de sauvegarder la valeur de son investissement mais uniquement à condition d'y avoir été expressément autorisée par la Commission.

A la suite de la loi NRE, le nouvel article L 430-4 du code de commerce prévoit, à l'instar du Règlement n°4064/89, que la réalisation effective d'une opération notifiée ne peut intervenir qu'avec l'accord du Ministre, mais dispose également que : « *En cas de nécessité dûment motivée, les parties qui ont procédé à la notification peuvent demander au Ministre chargé de l'économie une dérogation leur permettant de procéder à la réalisation effective de l'opération de tout ou partie de la concentration sans attendre la décision [du Ministre] et sans préjudice de celle-ci* ». L'inconvénient de cette rédaction est de rendre non-automatique la dérogation de simple poursuite d'acquisition des titres, contrairement au droit communautaire.

Cette critique ayant été immédiatement soulevée par les praticiens et la doctrine – notamment à l'occasion d'une réunion ouverte au public du groupe de travail - le décret d'application n° 2002-689 du 30 avril 2002 est parvenu à un résultat similaire que le Règlement n°4064/89 en retardant la prise en compte de la date de la réalisation effective de l'opération dans le cas des OPA/OPE. En effet, l'article 6 de ce décret dispose que : « *Lorsqu'une concentration est réalisée par achat ou échange de titres sur un marché réglementé, sa réalisation effective, au sens de l'article L 430-4 du Code de commerce, intervient lorsque sont exercés les droits attachés aux titres. L'absence de décision du Ministre ne fait pas obstacle au transfert desdits titres* ». Ainsi, quand bien même l'acquisition de titres sur le marché boursier permettra d'obtenir le contrôle, cette prise de contrôle ne sera pas considérée valoir réalisation effective de la concentration : seul l'exercice des titres sera considéré comme réalisation effective de l'opération.

En définitive, le rattrapage astucieux mais acrobatique de la loi par le décret conduit à un résultat dont on s'accorde à considérer qu'il rend similaires les régimes français et communautaire de contrôle des concentrations en matière d'OPA/OPE (en ce sens, *P. Arhel, Le décret NRE, Contrats, Concurrence, Consommation, juin 2002, p. 11).*

En second lieu, le groupe de travail a examiné les récente décisions de la Commission *Tetra-Laval/Sidel,* et *Schneider Electric/Legrand*, décision de toute première importance pour la France. On sait en effet que ces affaires ont pour la première fois vu se réaliser le risque depuis longtemps pressenti de contradiction frontale entre les décisions rendues aux termes du contrôle de droit financier et de droit de la concurrence.

Le problème est bien connu : alors que la réglementation financière contraint à rendre irrévocable une OPA/OPE afin de garantir les droits des actionnaires qui prennent le risque d'apporter leur titre (article 5-1-4 du règlement général du Conseil des marchés financiers), à l'inverse le droit de la concurrence, afin de permettre l'étude de l'impact concurrentiel par les autorités de concurrence, non seulement contraint de rendre révocable une opération de concentration, mais encore interdit la réalisation effective de l'opération notifiée. La difficulté provient de ce que le calendrier boursier anticipe le calendrier concurrence. Ainsi, alors qu'une OPA/OPE aura été déclarée irrévocable, il est possible qu'une décision négative d'une autorité de concurrence s'oppose à la réalisation effective de cette opération. L'acquéreur malchanceux devra donc revendre les titres acquis, et ce au prix d'une très sensible décote. C'est ce qui s'est passé dans les deux affaires précitées. Ni le droit communautaire, ni le droit français ne contienne actuellement de dispositifs pour limiter les conséquences de ce décalage ; certaines suggestions peuvent être tirés des expériences étrangères (*F-E. Brocard, Le contrôle des concentrations en cas d'offre publique, Gaz. Europ. Pal., à para'tre).*

On peut estimer que cette question relève plus de la réglementation financière que du droit de la concurrence. Ainsi, elle devra être débattue au niveau communautaire à l'occasion de la nouvelle proposition de 13ème directive sur les OPA/OPE. Au niveau français, l'Association de défense des actionnaires minoritaires a préconisé l'adoption d'un système inspiré de la réglementation américaine où le projet annoncé par l'initiateur devrait attendre pour ouvrir la période d'offre d'avoir obtenu l'autorisation des autorités de concurrence compétentes. Le groupe de travail a estimé que cette proposition contribuerait à ralentir à l'excès toutes les procédures boursières, au détriment de l'effet de surprise souvent recherché par les OPA/OPE, et alors que les cas de contradiction des deux régimes de contrôle demeurent exceptionnel.

D'autres propositions ont pu être faites. Ainsi, une proposition de loi relative à certaines adaptations du droit boursier avait été déposée par le sénateur Marini le 20 décembre 2001 devant le Sénat. Cette proposition maintenait le principe de l'irrévocabilité de l'offre tout en introduisant une exception à ce principe dans le cas d'une décision négative d'une autorité de concurrence. Cette proposition ayant été déposée au bureau du Sénat, les élections présidentielles de mai 2002 et la fin de la XI législature ne l'ont pas affecté. Le Sénat peut en poursuivre l'examen et, le moment venu, transmettre le texte à la nouvelle Assemblée. Le groupe s'est dans son ensemble montré favorable à l'adoption d'une telle proposition.

Enfin, le groupe de travail a relevé une forme d'obstacle relevant de la disparité des législations française et communautaire distinct du problème évoqué ci-dessus (cf. Q. 10, 13).

En effet, les montages alternatifs aux opérations de fusion sont souvent plus complexes à mettre en oeuvre. A titre d'exemple, , le 3 septembre 1997 Sema Group, une société de droit anglais (« public limited company ») et la Financière Sema (société de droit français) ont fusionné par absorption de la Financière Sema par Sema Group. L'opération a été rendue complexe par le fait que le principe du transfert universel du patrimoine de l'absorbée semble être un mécanisme inconnu en Grande-Bretagne. Or, en raison de ce mécanisme, Sema Group devait être amenée à détenir ses propres actions, puisque les actifs de la Financière Sema étaient composés pour l'essentiel de titres Sema Group. Mais à de rares exceptions près, qui n'étaient pas applicables en l'espèce, le droit britannique semble interdire strictement qu'une société puisse détenir ses propres actions. Afin de résoudre ce conflit de loi, il a été procédé à l'annulation des actions Sema Group détenues par la Financière Sema et à une augmentation simultanée du capital de Sema Group réservée aux actionnaires de la Financière Sema. La Financière Sema a donc transféré son patrimoine à Sema Group, alors que ce dernier ne comportait plus les titres Sema Group mais seulement quelques actifs mineurs. On notera qu'il s'agit d'une opération facilitée par une réalisation au sein d'un même groupe de sociétés.

Il conviendrait donc de réformer le droit communautaire afin de permettre aux acteurs d'utiliser la technique des fusions sur le plan transfrontalier intra-communautaire comme ils l'utilisent généralement sur le plan national.

GERMANY

Cross Border Mergers in Company Law and Competition Law: Removing the Final Barriers

Rapporteur
Dr Werner Berg[1]

B. THE COMPETITION REGIME

1. What is the view from your country[2] on the functioning of the threshold levels in Article 1(2) as well as the 2/3 rule in the Merger Regulation, and the proposal in the Commission's Green Paper for amendment of Article 1(3) to deal with the problems of multiple filings?

Die in Art. 1 Abs. 2 der Fusionskontrollverordnung[3] (FKVO) enthaltenen Kriterien enthalten eine sachgerechte und praktikable Zuständigkeitsabgrenzung zwischen der EG-Kommission und den Mitgliedstaaten. Die Umsatzschwellen haben sich als handhabbares Zuständigkeitskriterium bewährt. Allerdings wäre ihre Absenkung eine Möglichkeit, komplizierte Reformen des Art. 1 Abs. 3 FKVO zu vermeiden (dazu sogleich). Die 2/3-Regel verkörpert den Gedanken, dass ein Zusammenschluss dort geprüft werden soll, wo der wirtschaftliche (und damit auch wettbewerbliche) Schwerpunkt der beteiligten Unternehmen liegt. Insofern besteht kein Änderungsbedarf.

Nach dem Vorschlag der Kommission im Grünbuch zur FKVO soll die Kommission automatisch zuständig sein, wenn ein Zusammenschluss in mindestens drei Mitgliedstaaten anmeldepflichtig ist.[4] Dem damit verbundenen Ziel der Kommission, Mehrfachanmeldungen zu vermeiden, indem sie der Kommissionszuständigkeit zugeführt werden, wird ausdrücklich zugestimmt. Allerdings bestehen Zweifel an der Tragfähigkeit der vorgeschlagenen Änderung. Wie die Kommission selbst feststellt, sind die Aufgreifkriterien der nationalen Fusionskontrollregelungen nach wie vor sehr unterschiedlich ausgestaltet. So lässt sich das Anmeldeerfordernis etwa in den Ländern, in denen Marktanteilsschwellen gelten (Griechenland, Portugal, Spanien, Vereinigtes Königreich) nicht ohne genauere Untersuchungen klären. Ferner führt das Auswirkungsprinzip (vgl. etwa § 130 Abs. 2 Gesetz gegen Wettbewerbsbeschränkungen, GWB) dazu, dass jedenfalls solange erhebliche Unsicherheiten über das Anmeldeerfordernis bestehen können, bis die jeweilige nationale Behörde, wie von der Kommission vorgeschlagen, zum Anmeldeerfordernis Stellung genommen hat. Die Klärung dieser Zweifelsfragen kann nicht nur zu erheblichen Zeitverzögerungen führen, die eine Verlängerung der Frist nach Art. 4 Abs. 1 FKVO erforderte, sondern hätte auch Unklarheiten im Rechtsschutz für die Unternehmen zur Folge. Die Stellungnahmen der nationalen Behörden könnten wohl nur vor nationalen Gerichten angegriffen werden, deren Entscheidungen geeignet wären, die Zuständigkeit der Kommission rückwirkend zu begründen oder entfallen zu lassen. Weitere Probleme resultieren aus den unterschiedlichen Zusammenschlussbegriffen der einzelnen Fusionskontrollregelungen. So stellt nach dem GWB im Gegensatz zur FKVO der Erwerb von 25% der Anteile am Kapital oder den Stimmrechten an einem anderen Unternehmen einen Zusammenschluss dar (§ 37 Abs. 1 Nr. 3 lit. b))[5]. Auf Gemeinschaftsebene würden solche Transaktionen, soweit sie nicht mit dem Erwerb der Kontrolle über das andere Unternehmen einhergehen, nach Art. 81 EG geprüft.

Da eine Vollharmonisierung der nationalen Fusionskontrollregelungen weder wünschenswert noch realistisch ist, wäre eine Absenkung der Schwellenwerte des Art. 1 Abs. 2 FKVO (bei gleichzeitiger Streichung des Art. 1 Abs. 3 FKVO) die einfachste und praktikabelste Lösung. Die dadurch bedingte erweiterte Zuständigkeit der Kommission könnte durch wirksamere Verweisungsvorschriften eingeschränkt werden. Durch dieses Modell würden auch zeitaufwendige Mehrfachbefassungen der Mitgliedstaaten (Feststellung der Anmeldebedürftigkeit durch die Mitgliedstaaten, Anmeldung bei der Kommission, Verweisung an die Mitgliedstaaten) vermieden.

2. In light of the experiences made in your country, do member states have sufficient flexibility to call for mergers to be referred back under Article 9 of the Merger Regulation? In light of the proposal in the Commission's Green Paper, what is your view on the circumstances in which this power should be exercised?

Die Voraussetzungen für die Verweisung eines Zusammenschlusses an die Mitgliedstaaten sind eng. Art. 9 FKVO enthält zwei Alternativen, nach denen Mitgliedstaaten die Verweisung eines Zusammenschlusses beantragen können: Nach Abs. 2 lit. a) muss der Mitgliedstaat, der eine Verweisung beantragt, geltend machen, dass der Zusammenschluss eine beherrschende Stellung auf einem gesonderten Markt zu begründen oder zu verstärken droht. Selbst wenn dieser „*prima facie*" Nachweis gelingt, steht die Verweisung im Ermessen der Kommission. In einer gemeinsamen Protokollerklärung haben Rat und Kommission jedoch festgehalten, dass Zusammenschlüsse, die eine beherrschende Stellung in einem wesentlichen Teil des Gemeinsamen Marktes zu begründen oder zu verstärken drohen, nur in Ausnahmefällen an die Mitgliedstaaten verwiesen werden sollen.[6]

Für eine Verweisung nach Art. 9 Abs. 2 lit. b) ist erforderlich, dass der Zusammenschluss den Wettbewerb auf einem Markt in dem betreffenden Mitgliedstaat beeinträchtigt, der einen gesonderten Markt bildet und keinen wesentlichen Teil des Gemeinsamen Marktes darstellt. Aufgrund der weiten Auslegung des Tatbestandsmerkmals „wesentlicher Teil des Gemeinsamen Marktes" durch die Kommission und die Gemeinschaftsgerichte[7] kommt eine Verweisung hier nur in Betracht, wenn wirklich eng begrenzte regionale Märkte innerhalb eines Mitgliedstaates betroffen sind.[8] Für die Behandlung dieser Wettbewerbsprobleme fehlt der Kommission nach Art. 2 FKVO, der ebenfalls auf den Gemeinsamen Markt oder einen wesentlichen Teil desselben abstellt, ohnehin die Kompetenz.

Die absolute Zahl der Verweisungen hat sich ab 1997 merklich erhöht und hat 2002 schon zur Jahreshälfte den Vorjahreswert erreicht.[9] An dieser Steigerung[10] hatte die zum 1. März 1998 in Kraft getretene zweite Verweisungsalternative praktisch keinen Anteil.

Aus der Sicht der betroffenen Unternehmen ist die enge Begrenzung der Verweisungen nachdrücklich zu begrüßen. Verweisungen verlängern das Verfahren, ziehen erheblichen Mehraufwand nach sich und sind begrenzt vorhersehbar. Sie nehmen den Unternehmen den größten Vorteil der einheitlichen Entscheidung für die gesamte EU (bzw. den gesamten EWR; „*one-stop-shop*"). Dies gilt namentlich für Teilverweisungen und solche an mehrere Mitgliedstaaten. Akzeptabel wäre eine Ausdehnung der Verweisungsmöglichkeiten daher nur als Korrektiv zu einer erweiterten Kompetenz der Kommission (s. oben Ziffer 1.).

Der Kommission ist insoweit zuzustimmen, als sie auf das Kriterium der drohenden Marktbeherrschung verzichten will. Die Ermittlung drohender Marktbeherrschung ist zeitaufwendig und an sich kein Kriterium für die Zuständigkeitsverteilung. Im Übrigen ist auch bisher nicht ganz klar, welche Anforderungen an den „*prima facie*"-Nachweis drohender Marktbeherrschung gestellt werden. Hier war die Kommission bisweilen sehr großzügig.[11] Richtiger erscheint es, bei glaubhaft dargelegter Beeinträchtigung des Wettbewerbs in dem betreffenden Mitgliedstaat, die Zuständigkeit anhand der geographischen Auswirkung des Zusammenschlusses abzugrenzen. Die Kommission sollte Zusammenschlüsse mit rein regionalen Auswirkungen innerhalb eines

Mitgliedstaates an diesen verweisen, unabhängig davon ob die betroffene Region einen wesentlichen Teil des gemeinsamen Marktes darstellt. Dasselbe sollte für Zusammenschlüsse gelten, die rein nationale Märkte betreffen, die gesonderte Märkte darstellen und keine spürbaren Auswirkungen darüber hinaus haben. Gehen die Wirkungen des Zusammenschlusses über einzelne Mitgliedstaaten hinaus oder entwickeln sich Märkte zu europäischen, so sollte dieser Zusammenschluss von der Kommission beurteilt werden. Genaue Leitlinien für die Verweisungspraxis wären insbesondere unter dem Aspekt erhöhter Rechtssicherheit sehr willkommen. Sie sollten u.a. die Praxis der Kommission bei der Anwendung der Verweisungskriterien detailliert darstellen und zur Beteiligung der Parteien und Dritter im Verweisungsverfahren Stellung nehmen. Die von der Kommission vorgeschlagene Verkürzung der Antragsfrist durch den Mitgliedstaat von drei auf zwei Wochen wäre zu begrüßen, ist aber nicht zwingend notwendig. Eine Verweisung von Amts wegen durch die Kommission erscheint nicht erforderlich. Das Gleiche gilt für den Vorschlag, statt des nationalen Kartellrechts in Verweisungsfällen immer die FKVO anzuwenden. Die Verfahrensdauer nach deutschem Recht beträgt bis zu vier Monaten und steht im Einklang mit der Frist nach Art. 9 Abs. 6 FKVO.

3. Is the system of consultation between the European Commission and the national competition authorities (NCAs) working adequately? Does there need to be a better formalised system for consultation between NCAs directly involved either in the case of multiple filings outside the merger control regulation or in cases where more than one member state exercises the Article 9 request?

Diese Frage ist für einen Rechtsanwalt schwer zu beantworten. Defizite der Kooperation zwischen der Kommission und den nationalen Kartellbehörden werden im Rahmen von EG-Fusionskontrollverfahren namentlich bei der Verhandlung von Abhilfemaßnahmen sichtbar. Sowohl in der ersten als auch in der zweiten Prüfungsphase führen die Konsultationen zwischen der Kommission und den Mitgliedstaaten bisweilen zu Verzögerungen im Verfahren mit der Folge, dass die Möglichkeit der Unternehmen, ihre angebotenen Abhilfemaßnahmen „nachzubessern“, eingeschränkt wird oder ganz entfällt.

Grundsätzlich zu begrüßen ist die verstärkte Zusammenarbeit der Mitgliedstaaten nach Art. 22 Abs. 3 FKVO.[12] Die Verweisung an die Kommission führt zu einer einheitlichen Entscheidung über den Zusammenschluss. Der geringe Gebrauch, der von dieser Vorschrift in der Vergangenheit gemacht wurde, sowie die mit ihr verbundenen Anwendungs- und Auslegungsprobleme[13] lassen Art. 22 Abs. 3 FKVO aber nicht geeignet erscheinen, das Problem der Mehrfachanmeldungen alleine zu lösen.

4. How does the test under the law of your country compare to that under the Merger Regulation? Should all member states adopt the same test as under the Merger Regulation, and should this EU test be the (US) 'significant lessening of competition' test rather than the present EU 'dominance' test?

Nach dem GWB ist ein Zusammenschluss durch das Bundeskartellamt zu untersagen, wenn zu erwarten ist, dass dieser eine marktbeherrschende Stellung begründet oder verstärkt, es sei denn, die beteiligten Unternehmen weisen nach, dass durch den Zusammenschluss auch Verbesserungen der Wettbewerbsbedingungen eintreten und dass diese Verbesserungen die Nachteile der Marktbeherrschung überwiegen (§ 36 Abs. 1 GWB). Marktbeherrschend sind nach der Legaldefinition in § 19 Abs. 2 GWB ein oder mehrere Unternehmen dann, wenn es überhaupt keine Wettbewerber gibt, die Unternehmen keinem wesentlichen Wettbewerb ausgesetzt sind oder eine im Verhältnis zu ihren Wettbewerbern überragende Marktstellung haben, die sie in die Lage versetzt, sich unabhängig von Wettbewerbern, Kunden und anderen Marktteilnehmern zu verhalten. § 19 Abs. 3 GWB enthält eine Marktbeherrschungsvermutung bei bestimmten Marktanteilen. Die Fusionskontrollverordnung stellt auf die Begründung oder Verstärkung einer marktbeherrschenden Stellung ab, durch die wirksamer Wettbewerb im Gemeinsamen Markt oder einem wesentlichen Teil desselben erheblich behindert würde (Art. 2 Absätze 2, 3 FKVO). GWB und FKVO decken sich daher jedenfalls im Hinblick auf das Eingriffskriterium der Entstehung oder Verstärkung einer marktbeherrschenden Stellung.

Es wäre sicher wünschenswert, dass alle EU-Mitgliedstaaten einheitliche Kriterien zur Beurteilung von Zusammenschlüssen in ihren Fusionskontrollregelungen festlegten. Allerdings zeigt bereits der Vergleich der deutschen mit der EG-Fusionskontrolle, dass der „Marktbeherrschungstest" nur einen Teil der Prüfung ausmacht. Während in Deutschland eine (weitreichende) Marktbeherrschungsvermutung gilt, muss die Kommission die Marktbeherrschung im vollem Umfang nachweisen. Andererseits können auf Grund der Abwägungsklausel in § 36 Abs. 1 GWB unter bestimmten Voraussetzungen Marktbeherrschungseffekte hingenommen werden. Die FKVO wurde bislang überwiegend restriktiver interpretiert, obwohl das Kriterium „*durch die wirksamer Wettbewerb im Gemeinsamen Markt oder einem wesentlichen Teil desselben erheblich behindert würde*" ebenfalls Raum für eine solche Interpretation ließe.

Im Übrigen böte die einheitliche Verwendung des

Marktbeherrschungskriteriums oder des „*Substantial Lessening of Competition*"-Tests (SLC-Test) in der EU jedenfalls für sich genommen noch keine Gewähr für materiell-rechtlich einheitliche Fusionskontrollregelungen. Einerseits bestehen zwischen den Staaten, die das Marktbeherrschungskriterium ins Zentrum ihrer Zusammenschlusskontrolle stellen, und solchen, die den SLC-Test anwenden, erhebliche Übereinstimmungen. So ist die Frage nach der Marktstärke ein zentrales Kriterium unter dem SLC-Test in den USA.[14] Das Gleiche gilt etwa für Australien und Neuseeland.[15] Andererseits bestehen zwischen den Fusionskontrollregelungen der Staaten, die den SLC-Test anwenden, teilweise erhebliche Unterschiede (etwa im Hinblick auf die Bedeutung, die der Marktkonzentration oder anderen Kriterien beigemessen werden).[16]

Im Übrigen wendet die weit überwiegende Mehrheit der EU-Mitgliedstaaten und der Beitrittsländer den Marktbeherrschungstest an (vgl. u.a. das neue polnische bzw. tschechische Kartellrecht). Insgesamt erscheint die Vereinheitlichung materieller Prüfungskriterien zwischen der EU und ihren Mitgliedstaaten im gegenwärtigen Stadium weniger wichtig als die effiziente Kooperation im konkreten Fall.[17] Die Erfahrung zeigt, dass die tatsächlichen Divergenzen in konkreten Zusammenschlüssen geringer sind als es bei der theoretischen Erörterung der anzuwendenden Prüfungskriterien der Fall wäre.[18]

5. Are the procedural and judicial safeguards adequate to protect parties from abuse of power by the competition authorities? How does the laws of your country compare to EC law in this respect?

Die Verfahrensrechte nach dem GWB und nach der FKVO sind sich (jedenfalls in ihrer Papierform) sehr ähnlich. Nach § 40 Abs. 1 GWB muss das Bundeskartellamt den Zusammenschlussbeteiligten binnen eines Monats ab Eingang der vollständigen Anmeldung mitteilen, dass das Hauptprüfungsverfahren eingeleitet wird (sog. „Monatbrief"). Nach § 40 Abs. 2 GWB hat das Amt binnen einer Frist von vier Monaten seit Eingang der vollständigen Anmeldung durch Verfügung zu entscheiden, ob ein Zusammenschluss untersagt oder freigegeben wird. Beide Fristen sind verfahrensrechtliche Ausschlussfristen, deren Ablauf das Recht auf Untersagung erlöschen lässt. Die FKVO kennt vergleichbare Fristen (erste Phase: ein Monat; zweite Phase: vier Monate), mit deren Ablauf eine Freigabe fingiert wird (Art. 10 Abs. 6 FKVO).

Wenn das Bundeskartellamt beabsichtigt, einen Zusammenschluss zu untersagen, sendet es den Parteien eine „Abmahnung", in der die voraussichtlichen Entscheidungsgründe mitgeteilt werden. Dieses Instrument dient dem rechtlichen Gehör und ist mit der „Mitteilung der Beschwerdepunkte" nach der FKVO vergleichbar. Nach § 56 Abs. 1 GWB hat die

Kartellbehörde den Beteiligten Gelegenheit zur Stellungnahme zu geben und sie zu einer mündlichen Verhandlung zu laden (vgl. Art. 18 Abs. 1 FKVO). Die Beteiligten haben nach deutschem Recht Akteneinsichtsrecht (vgl. § 29 VwVfG). Es bezieht sich nicht nur auf die eigentlichen Verfahrensakte, sondern auf alle Akte, die mit dem Gegenstand des Verfahrens in Zusammenhang stehen und für die Entscheidung von Bedeutung sein können. Nach der FKVO erhalten die Verfahrensbeteiligten (also auch betroffene Dritte) Akteneinsicht in der zweiten Phase (Art. 18 Abs. 3 FKVO).[19]

Gegen Verfügungen des Bundeskartellamts wie z.B. gegen Untersagungsentscheidungen oder bedingte Freigabeentscheidungen ist Beschwerde an das OLG Düsseldorf zulässig (§ 63 Absätze 1 und 4 GWB). Die Beschwerde ist nach § 66 Abs. 1 GWB binnen einer Frist von einem Monat ab Zustellung der angefochtenen Verfügung beim Bundeskartellamt schriftlich einzureichen. Ob eine der Freigabeentscheidung angeschlossene Auflage oder Bedingung nach deutschem Recht selbständig angefochten werden kann, ist umstritten.[20] Gegen die Entscheidung des OLG Düsseldorf ist Rechtsbeschwerde an den BGH möglich. Außer in den Fällen des § 74 Abs. 4 GWB bedarf sie der Zulassung (§ 74 Abs. 1 GWB; zu den Zulassungsgründen vgl. § 74 Abs. 2 GWB).

Im EG-Fusionskontrollverfahren kann nach Art. 230 Abs. 4 EG Nichtigkeitsklage gegen Untersagungsentscheidungen oder die Erteilung von Auflagen und Bedingungen beim EuG erhoben werden. Gegen dessen Entscheidung steht den Parteien das Rechtsmittel zum EuGH offen. Obwohl die Rechtsmittelbefugnisse auf deutscher und europäischer Ebene sehr ähnlich ausgestaltet sind, waren die Rechte der Parteien in der deutschen Fusionskontrolle bislang praktisch wirksamer geschützt, denn die Verfahrensdauer in der deutschen Fusionskontrolle war erheblich kürzer als auf EU-Ebene.[21] Eine Annäherung könnte durch die Einführung des beschleunigten Verfahrens vor den Gemeinschaftsgerichten erfolgen, dessen Wirksamkeit sich aber noch erweisen muss.[22]

Nach deutschem Recht haben Beschwerden gegenüber Freigabeentscheidungen keine aufschiebende Wirkung (§ 64 Abs. 1 GWB). Die Vollziehung kann jedoch vom Beschwerdegericht ausgesetzt werden, wenn dies im öffentlichen Interesse oder im überwiegenden Interesse eines Beteiligten geboten ist (§ 65 Abs. 3 Satz 2 GWB). Dies soll erfolgen, wenn die Vollziehung für den Beschwerdeführer eine unbillige, nicht durch überwiegende öffentliche Interessen gebotene Härte zur Folge hätte (§ 65 Abs. 3 Satz 2 i. V. m. § 65 Abs. 3 Satz 1 Nr. 3 GWB). Im Übrigen kann das Beschwerdegericht einstweilige Anordnungen zur vorläufigen Regelung eines Rechtszustandes treffen (§ 64 Abs. 3 i. V. m. § 60 GWB). Unter sehr engen Voraussetzungen[23] kann es sogar den Vollzug eines untersagten Zusammenschlussvorhabens gestatten.[24]

Insgesamt enthält das deutsche Recht somit eine Reihe von materiellen und verfahrensmäßigen Vorkehrungen, mit denen Verfahrensmissbrauch durch die Behörden wirksam vorgebeugt wird.

6. Below are a number of questions relating to domestic law which may assist in a comparative analysis.

a) Please provide an overview of the structure of and main features of the relevant domestic legislation and the institutional framework (who enforces it)? It may be helpful with some information about the role of private rights of action.

Die Fusionskontrolle wurde in Deutschland im Jahre 1973 eingeführt. Die einschlägigen gesetzlichen Regelungen finden sich im 7. Abschnitt des GWB (§§ 35 bis 43), einem Gesetz aus dem Jahr 1958 in der Fassung der 6. GWB-Novelle von 1998. Das Kapitel zur Fusionskontrolle enthält spezielle Vorschriften zu den Aufgreifschwellen, der materiellen Beurteilung von Zusammenschlüssen, Zusammenschlusstatbeständen, Anmelde- und Anzeigepflichten, zum Verfahren etc. Im Übrigen (etwa für die Definition der Marktbeherrschung oder die Beteiligung am Verfahren) gelten die allgemeinen Vorschriften des GWB.

Für Maßnahmen der Fusionskontrolle ist das Bundeskartellamt, eine selbständige Bundesoberbehörde mit Sitz in Bonn, ausschließlich zuständig (§ 48 Abs. 2 GWB). Eine Ausnahme stellt die Ministererlaubnis nach § 42 GWB dar. Sie obliegt dem Bundeswirtschaftsminister.

Zu den Rechten privater Dritter in der Fusionskontrolle wird auf die Ausführungen zu Ziffer 6. i) verwiesen.

b) What kinds of transactions are caught? Are joint ventures caught? What are the jurisdictional thresholds? Is it difficult to identify with sufficient certainty whether a filing is in fact required under national law? Are foreign-to-foreign mergers caught?

Nach § 37 GWB gelten folgende Unternehmensverbindungen als Zusammenschlüsse:

- Der Erwerb des Vermögens eines anderen Unternehmens ganz oder zu einem wesentlichen Teil;
- der Erwerb der unmittelbaren oder mittelbaren Kontrolle durch ein oder mehrere Unternehmen über die Gesamtheit oder Teile eines oder mehrerer anderer Unternehmen;
- der Erwerb von Anteilen an einem anderen Unternehmen, wenn diese Anteile allein oder zusammen mit sonstigen, dem anderen Unternehmen

bereits gehörenden Anteilen 50% oder 25% des Kapitals oder der Stimmrechte des anderen Unternehmens erreichen oder übersteigen;
- jede sonstige Verbindung von Unternehmen, auf Grund deren ein oder mehrere Unternehmen unmittelbar oder mittelbar einen wettbewerblich erheblichen Einfluss auf ein anderes Unternehmen ausüben können.

Gemeinschaftsunternehmen sind vom Anwendungsbereich des GWB umfasst (vgl. insbesondere § 37 Abs. 1 Nr. 3 Satz 3). Zusammenschlüsse sind kontrollpflichtig, wenn im letzten Geschäftsjahr vor dem Zusammenschluss die beteiligten Unternehmen insgesamt weltweit Umsatzerlöse von mehr als 500 Millionen Euro und mindestens ein beteiligtes Unternehmen im Inland Umsatzerlöse von mehr als 25 Millionen Euro erzielt haben. Trotz Erreichens dieser Umsatzschwellen ist eine Anmeldung entbehrlich, wenn ein unabhängiges Unternehmen erworben wird, das im vorangegangenen Geschäftsjahr Umsätze von weniger als 10 Millionen Euro hatte (§ 35 Abs. 2 Nr. 1 GWB). Eine Anmeldung ist auch nicht erforderlich, soweit ein sog. Bagatellmarkt betroffen ist (Jahresumsatz von weniger als 15 Millionen Euro; § 35 Abs. 2 Nr. 2 GWB).

Häufig lässt sich relativ problemlos und mit hinreichender Zuverlässigkeit sagen, ob eine Anmeldung erforderlich ist. Probleme ergeben sich jedoch bisweilen bei der Prüfung der Inlandsauswirkung von Auslandszusammenschlüssen, die nach § 130 Abs. 2 GWB Voraussetzung für die Geltung des GWB und damit für die Anmeldepflicht ist, und der vorstehend erörterten Bagatellmarktklausel (§ 35 Abs. 2 Nr. 2 GWB). Zur genaueren Bestimmung, wann eine Inlandsauswirkung im Sinne von § 130 Abs. 2 GWB vorliegt, hat das Bundeskartellamt ein Merkblatt herausgegeben, das die Beurteilung erleichtert.[25]

c) Is the filing mandatory or voluntary? Who is responsible for filing? What is involved in the preparation of a filing? What are the deadlines for filing? What are the waiting periods and does implementation of the transaction have to be suspended?

Zusammenschlüsse, die die Voraussetzungen nach dem GWB erfüllen (s. oben Ziffer 6. a) und b)), müssen beim Bundeskartellamt angemeldet werden (§ 39 Abs. 1 GWB). Eine als solche sanktionierte Anmeldepflicht existiert nicht, Zusammenschlüsse dürfen aber vor ihrer Freigabe nicht vollzogen werden (§ 41 Abs. 1 GWB). Unter engen Voraussetzungen kann das Bundeskartellamt vom Vollzugsverbot befreien (§ 41 Abs. 2 GWB). Zur Anmeldung verpflichtet sind die am Zusammenschluss beteiligten Unternehmen und in den Fällen des Vermögens- oder Anteilserwerbs auch der Veräußerer (§ 39 Abs. 2 GWB).

Eine vollständige Anmeldung muss bestimmte Angaben über die

Struktur des Zusammenschlusses sowie über die am Zusammenschluss beteiligten Unternehmen enthalten. Nach § 39 Abs. 3 GWB muss die Anmeldung u.a. Angaben über die Art des Geschäftsbetriebes, die Umsatzerlöse, die Marktanteile einschließlich deren Berechnungsgrundlage, sofern diese mindestens 20% erreichen, die Höhe der erworbenen Anteile sowie die Kontaktdetails einer im Inland zustellungsbevollmächtigten Person enthalten. In der Praxis verzichtet das Bundeskartellamt aber häufig auf Angaben, die für die Beurteilung des Zusammenschlusses nicht von Bedeutung sind. Anmeldungen zum Bundeskartellamt sind in der Regel ungleich kürzer als solche nach dem Formblatt CO zur Kommission. Nach § 39 Abs. 6 GWB haben die beteiligten Unternehmen dem Bundeskartellamt den Vollzug des Zusammenschlusses unverzüglich anzuzeigen.

d) What are the issues and possible sanctions involved in closing before clearance? What is the timetable for clearance and can it be speeded up?

Nach § 41 Abs. 1 GWB dürfen Unternehmen einen Zusammenschluss nicht vollziehen oder am Vollzug mitwirken, solange er nicht freigegeben ist. Dem Vollzugsverbot unterfallen alle Rechtshandlungen, die für die privatrechtliche Erfüllung des Zusammenschlusstatbestandes konstitutiv sind, sowie alle Handlungen, die die wirtschaftlichen Wirkungen des Zusammenschlusses vorwegnehmen. Der Verstoß gegen das Vollzugsverbot ist eine Ordnungswidrigkeit, die mit einer Geldbuße bis zu 500.000 Euro und über diesen Betrag hinaus bis zur dreifachen Höhe des durch die Zuwiderhandlung erlangten Mehrerlöses geahndet werden kann (§ 81 Abs. 1 Nr. 1 i. V. m. Abs. 2 GWB). Das gegen das Vollzugsverbot verstoßende Rechtsgeschäft ist schwebend unwirksam. Das Geschäft wird nachträglich wirksam, und zwar mit Rückwirkung, wenn ein dann stattfindendes Fusionskontrollverfahren durch Freigabe positiv abgeschlossen wird. Das Bundeskartellamt kann auf Antrag Befreiungen vom Vollzugsverbot erteilen. Eine Befreiung vom Vollzugsverbot steht jedoch im Ermessen der Behörde und erfordert in jedem Fall das Vorliegen wichtiger Gründe wie z.B. das Entstehen eines schweren Schadens für eines der beteiligten Unternehmen oder für Dritte für den Fall des Zuwartens mit der Durchführung des Zusammenschlusses. Die Befreiung kann jederzeit, auch vor der Anmeldung, erteilt und mit Bedingungen und Auflagen versehen werden (§ 41 Abs. 2 GWB).

In den kontrollpflichtigen Fällen verfügt das Bundeskartellamt grundsätzlich über einen Zeitraum von vier Monaten für den Abschluss des Prüfungsverfahrens (Kommissionsverfahren: fünf Monate). Das Bundeskartellamt darf einen Zusammenschluss nur untersagen, wenn es den anmeldenden Unternehmen innerhalb einer Frist von einem Monat ab

Beginn des Fristlaufes mitteilt, dass es in die Prüfung des Zusammenschlusses (Hauptprüfverfahren) eingetreten ist (§ 40 Abs. 1 GWB). Diese Mitteilung (sog. „Monatsbrief") ergeht formlos und stellt keine Verfügung dar. Sie hat nur den Zweck, dem Bundeskartellamt die volle viermonatige Prüfungsfrist zu erhalten; materielle Voraussetzung ist lediglich, dass eine weitere Prüfung des Zusammenschlusses erforderlich ist. Die Monatsfrist ist eine Ausschlussfrist, bei deren Nichteinhaltung der Zusammenschluss automatisch freigegeben ist (s. oben Ziffer 5.). Das Gleiche gilt für die Gesamtprüfungsfrist von vier Monaten seit Eingang der Anmeldung. Das Bundeskartellamt ist grundsätzlich nicht dazu verpflichtet, die Monatsfrist bis zum Erlass des Monatsbriefes auszuschöpfen. Das Gleiche gilt für die Frist von vier Monaten.

e) Are there any special rules applicable to public takeover bids?

Es bestehen keine besonderen kartellrechtlichen Bestimmungen für öffentliche Übernahmeangebote.

f) What is the substantive test for clearance?

Für die materiellen Prüfkriterien in der deutschen Fusionskontrolle wird auf die Ausführungen zu Ziffer 4. verwiesen.

g) To what extent are non-competition issues relevant to the review process?

Gesichtspunkte außerhalb des Wettbewerbsrechts kommen im Verfahren zur Erteilung einer Ministererlaubnis zum Tragen. Nach § 42 Abs. 1 GWB kann der Bundesminister für Wirtschaft auf Antrag die Erlaubnis zu einem vom Bundeskartellamt untersagten Zusammenschluss erteilen, wenn die Wettbewerbsbeschränkung von gesamtwirtschaftlichen Vorteilen des Zusammenschlusses aufgewogen wird oder der Zusammenschluss durch ein überragendes Interesse der Allgemeinheit gerechtfertigt ist. Gesamtwirtschaftliche Vorteile können z.B. sein die Erhaltung eines volkswirtschaftlich besonders wertvollen technischen Potentials oder Know-hows, die Lösung von Strukturkrisen, die Sanierung der beteiligten Unternehmen sowie die Stärkung der internationalen Wettbewerbsfähigkeit. Als Interessen der Allgemeinheit können sozialpolitische Gründe wie insbesondere die Sicherung von Arbeitsplätzen oder regional-, militär- und gesundheitspolitische Gründe von Bedeutung sein. Nach § 42 Abs. 2 Satz 2 GWB ist im Ministererlaubnisverfahren auch die Wettbewerbsfähigkeit der beteiligten Unternehmen auf ausländischen Märkten zu berücksichtigen. Dabei geht es um die Erhaltung bereits beste hender Wettbewerbsfähigkeit, aber auch um die Möglichkeit, durch erhöhte Wettbewerbsfähigkeit auf ausländischen Märkten die Marktposition der beteiligten Unternehmen zu verbessern. Jüngstes Beispiel für die Anwendung von § 42 Abs. 1 GWB ist die Ministererlaubnis zugunsten von E.ON für den Erwerb der Kontrolle über die Ruhrgas AG (Zusammenschlüsse E.ON/Gelsenberg bzw. E.ON/Bergemann).

h) Is it possible to remedy competition issues?

Ja. Nach § 40 Abs. 3 GWB kann die Freigabe eines Zusammenschlusses mit Bedingungen und Auflagen verbunden werden. Diese dürfen sich jedoch nach § 40 Abs. 3 GWB nicht darauf richten, die beteiligten Unternehmen einer laufenden Verhaltenskontrolle zu unterziehen.

i) What are the typical steps during the investigation? What rights do complainants have? What publicity is given to the process? What are the opportunities for judicial review?

Nach Einreichen der Anmeldung wird das Bundeskartellamt zunächst prüfen, ob die Anmeldung vollständig ist. Sollte die Anmeldung unvollständig sein, wird das Bundeskartellamt soweit es die Angaben benötigt um Ergänzung bitten. Erst wenn die vollständigen Angaben vorliegen, werden die Fristen ausgelöst. Sodann wird das Bundeskartellamt prüfen, ob die vorgelegten Informationen ausreichen, um den Zusammenschluss zu beurteilen. Ist dies nicht der Fall, wird es weitere Informationen von den Parteien, ggf. auch von Dritten einholen. Wenn der Zusammenschluss augenscheinlich keine substantiellen Wettbewerbsprobleme in Deutschland mit sich bringt, wird das Amt den Zusammenschluss vor Ablauf der Monatsfrist per Schreiben genehmigen. Dieses Genehmigungsschreiben kann nicht angefochten werden.[26]

Bestehen hingegen Bedenken, dass der Zusammenschluss eine marktbeherrschende Stellung begründet oder verstärkt oder fehlen noch erhebliche Informationen, wird das Bundeskartellamt binnen der Monatsfrist die beteiligten Parteien durch den sog. „Monatsbrief" davon in Kenntnis setzen, dass es in die Prüfung des Zusammenschlusses (Hauptprüfungsverfahren) eingetreten ist. Nach Ablauf einer Frist von vier Monaten seit Eingang der Anmeldung wird das Bundeskartellamt den Zusammenschluss untersagen oder (gegebenenfalls unter Auflagen und Bedingungen) genehmigen. Sowohl Genehmigungs- als auch Untersagungsentscheidungen sind formale Verwaltungsakte, die zu begründen sind und Gegenstand richterlicher Kontrolle sein können.

Am Zusammenschluss Beteiligte können eine Untersagungsentscheidung, aber auch eine bedingte oder mit Auflagen versehene Entscheidung anfechten. Ob Auflagen oder Bedingungen selbständig angefochten werden können, ist umstritten (s. oben Ziffer 5.). Dritte können eine Anfechtungsbeschwerde nach § 63 Abs. 1 GWB erheben. Nach § 63 Abs. 2 GWB sind beschwerdeberechtigt aber nur die am Verfahren vor der Kartellbehörde Beteiligten (§ 54 Abs. 2 GWB). Dritte sind also nur anfechtungsberechtigt, wenn sie sich nach § 54 Abs. 2 Nr. 3 zu dem Verwaltungsverfahren haben beiladen lassen.

Details der Anmeldung werden grundsätzlich nicht veröffentlicht. Bedeutende Zusammenschlussentscheidungen des Bundeskartellamt werden durch Pressemitteilungen bekannt gemacht oder im Tätigkeitsbericht des Amtes, der alle zwei Jahre erscheint, veröffentlicht. Alle Entscheidungen, die nach Durchführung eines Hauptprüfungsverfahrens getroffen werden, müssen im Bundesanzeiger veröffentlicht werden. Das Gleiche gilt für die Vollzugsanzeige (§ 43 GWB). Geschäftsgeheimnisse werden vor der Veröffentlichung entfernt.

j) What are the enforcement powers? How does administrative and civil sanctions compare with the EC regime? And what are the criminal sanctions, and are they used?

Wenn die gesetzlichen Voraussetzungen für eine Untersagung erfüllt sind, wird das Bundeskartellamt den Zusammenschluss untersagen (§ 36 Abs. 1 GWB). Es kann ferner die Entflechtung eines Zusammenschlusses anordnen, der bereits vollzogen wurde (§ 41 Abs. 3 GWB). Zur Durchsetzung seiner Anordnung kann das Bundeskartellamt Zwangsgelder festsetzen, die Ausübung von Stimmrechten untersagen oder einen Treuhänder bestellen, der die Auflösung des Zusammenschlusses herbeiführt (§ 41 Abs. 4 GWB).

Sowohl nach dem GWB als auch nach der FKVO können die Parteien bei bestimmten Zuwiderhandlungen mit einem Bußgeld belegt werden. Strafrechtliche Sanktionen sind im GWB und in der FKVO nicht vorgesehen.[27]

Nach Art. 14 Abs. 1 FKVO können für das Unterlassen der Anmeldung oder für falsche Angaben Geldbußen in Höhe von 1.000 bis 50.000 Euro verhängt werden. Verstöße gegen das Vollzugsverbot können nach Art. 14 Abs. 2 FKVO mit Geldbußen bis zu 10% des Gesamtumsatzes geahndet werden. Ferner gewährt Art. 15 FKVO der Kommission die Möglichkeit, bestimmte Verhaltensweisen, etwa die Auskunftserteilung, durch Zwangsgelder durchzusetzen.

Für die Sanktionen nach deutschem Recht wird auf die Ausführungen zu Ziffer 6. d) verwiesen. Ferner hat das Bundeskartellamt die Möglichkeit, Bußgelder für falsche Auskünfte, unrichtige oder unvollständige Angaben bei der Anmeldung, deren Verspätung oder Unterlassung oder die fehlende oder unrichtige Vollzugsanzeige bis zur Höhe von 25.000 Euro zu verhän gen (§ 81 Abs. 1 Nr. 4, 7, 8 i. V. m. Abs. 2 GWB).

k) Do the authorities cooperate with other antitrust authorities?

Ja. Das Bundeskartellamt ist unter anderem Mitglied im Verbund der "European Competition Authorities" (ECA). ECA ist ein Diskussionsforum der Wettbewerbsbehörden der Länder im Europäischen Wirtschaftsraum sowie der Europäischen Kommission und der EFTA-Überwachungsbehörde. Das seit April 2001 bestehende Forum hat sich vorgenommen, die Zusammenarbeit der Behörden zu verbessern und damit zu einer wirksamen Durchsetzung des jeweiligen nationalen wie des europäischen Wettbewerbsrechts beizutragen. Seit September 2001 unterrichten sich die nationalen Behörden gegenseitig über alle Fusionsfälle, die in mehreren ECA-Ländern anmeldepflichtig sind (Mehrfachnotifzierungen). Die gegenseitige Unterrichtung hat auch dazu beigetragen, dass erstmals mehrere nationale Wettbewerbsbehörden gemeinsam Fusionsfälle gemäß Art. 22 der FKVO an die Europäische Kommission verwiesen haben.[28]

Ferner ist das Bundeskartellamt Gründungsmitglied des International Competition Network (ICN), einem internationalen Diskussionsforum der Wettbewerbsbehörden, dessen Eröffnungskonferenz am 28./29. September 2002 in Neapel stattfinden wird. ICN soll für einen weltumspannenden Austausch zwischen den Kartellbehörden sorgen.

l) Are there also rules on foreign investment, special sectors or other relevant approvals?

Für Kreditinstitute, Finanzinstitute und Versicherungsunternehmen besteht in Art. 37 Abs. 3 GWB eine Ausnahmebestimmung, nach der im Falle des Anteilserwerbes an einem anderen Unternehmen zum Zweck der Veräußerung kein Zusammenschluss vorliegt, solange die Stimmrechte aus den Anteilen nicht ausgeübt werden und die Veräußerung innerhalb eines Jahres erfolgt.

m) Are there current proposals to change the legislation?

Die jüngste (bedeutende) Reform des GWB fand im Jahre 1998 statt und trat am 1. Januar 1999 in Kraft. Infolge der Einführung der europäischen Einheitswährung wurden die im GWB angegebenen Geldbeträge auf einer 2:1 Basis umgerechnet. Weitere Gesetzesänderungen sind derzeit nicht geplant.

C. COMPANY LAW AND FINANCIAL MARKET REGULATORY REGIME

7. What will you identify as the main obstacles to take overs where a

company29 from your jurisdiction is either bidder or target and the other company is from another EU jurisdiction[30]?

Für die Übernahme einer börsennotierten Gesellschaft mit Sitz in Deutschland gilt seit 1. Januar 2002 das Wertpapiererwerbs- und Übernahmegesetz (WpÜG).[31] Die Regelungen des WpÜG differenzieren nicht zwischen öffentlichen Angeboten von deutschen Bietern, solchen von Bietern aus einem anderen Staat des Europäischen Wirtschaftsraums (EWR) oder Bietern aus anderen Staaten.
Ein öffentliches Übernahmeangebot ist danach genauen Vorschriften über das Angebot (Angebotsunterlage, Gegenleistung, Angebotsänderung, Haftung etc.) und das Verfahren unterworfen. Das WpÜG soll ausweislich der Begründung des Regierungsentwurfes Leitlinien für ein faires und geordnetes Angebotsverfahren schaffen, ohne dabei Unternehmensübernahmen zu fördern oder zu verhindern.[32] Diesem Ziel wird das Gesetz im Wesentlichen gerecht. Dennoch enthält das WpÜG einige Regelungen, die für Bieter Übernahmehindernisse darstellen können. Zwar darf der Vorstand der Zielgesellschaft grundsätzlich keine Handlungen vornehmen, durch die der Erfolg des Angebots verhindert werden könnte (sog. „Neutralitätspflicht"; § 33 Abs. 1 Satz 1 WpÜG). Dies gilt allerdings nicht

> „für Handlungen, die auch ein ordentlicher und gewissenhafter Geschäftsleiter einer Gesellschaft, die nicht von einem Übernahmeangebot betroffen ist, vorgenommen hätte, für die Suche nach einem konkurrierenden Angebot sowie für Handlungen, denen der Aufsichtsrat der Zielgesellschaft zugestimmt hat." (§ 33 Abs. 1 Satz 2 WpÜG)

Außerdem kann die Hauptversammlung den Vorstand durch sog. „Vorratsbeschluss", der 18 Monate gültig ist und mit 75% des bei der Beschlussfassung vertretenen Grundkapitals gefasst wird, zur Vornahme von Abwehrmaßnahmen ermächtigen (§ 33 Abs. 2 WpÜG). Praktisch bedeutsam dürfte vor allem die letzte Alternative nach § 33 Abs. 1 Satz 2 WpÜG werden. Mit Genehmigung des Aufsichtsrates kann der Vorstand Maßnahmen ergreifen (etwa wichtige Unternehmensteile veräußern), um die Übernahme abzuwehren. Allerdings ist nach der BGH-Rechtsprechung die Zustimmung der Hauptversammlung erforderlich, wenn die Handlung einen schwerwiegenden Eingriff in die Rechte und Interessen der Aktionäre darstellt.[33] Diese Kriterien dürften auch hier zur Anwendung kommen. Auch die Suche nach einem *white knight* könnte Übernahmen im Einzelfall erheblich verteuern oder gar vereiteln. Demgegenüber dürften Vorratsbeschlüsse eher selten sein, weil der Vorstand damit gegenüber der Hauptversammlung seine Befürchtung offen legen müsste, übernommen zu werden. Da die genaue Abgrenzung dessen, was als Handlung eines ordentlichen und gewissenhaften Geschäftsleiters anzusehen ist, unklar ist, dürfte auch diese Ausnahme nur geringe praktische Bedeutung erlangen. Der Vorstand der Zielgesellschaft wird in dieser Situation wahrscheinlich bestrebt sein, sein Handeln vom Aufsichtsrat genehmigen zu lassen.

Ein weiteres Übernahmehindernis stellt das Pflichtangebot nach § 35 ff. WpÜG dar. Wer Kontrolle (d.h. im WpÜG 30% oder mehr der Stimmrechte) an der Zielgesellschaft erlangt, ist verpflichtet, dies unter Angabe der Höhe seines Stimmrechtsanteils unverzüglich zu veröffentlichen und nach Abgabe einer Angebotsunterlage ein Angebot zu veröffentlichen (§ 35 WpÜG). Das Angebot muss sich auf alle noch nicht vom Bieter gehaltenen Aktien erstrecken (§§ 32, 39 WpÜG). Da ein Pflichtangebot nicht nur für Zielgesellschaften abgegeben werden muss, deren unmittelbare Kontrolle erworben wurde, sondern auch auf solche, über die mittelbare Kontrolle besteht, kann dies in Fällen verflochtener Beteilungen des Zielunternehmens zur Abgabe mehrerer Pflichtangebote führen.[34] Der Bieter kann auf Antrag vom Pflichtangebot befreit werden, wenn er etwa trotz Überschreitens der 30%-Schwelle keine Kontrolle über das Zielunternehmen erlangt hat.[35]

In einem Pflichtangebot muss als Gegenleistung der höchste Preis gezahlt werden, den ein Bieter während der drei Monate vor Kontrollerlangung gezahlt hat.[36] Dies schließt den Erwerb großer Aktienpakete ein, für die regelmäßig ein Paketzuschlag gezahlt wird. Dies verteuert die Transaktion für den Bieter und erschwert Übernahmeangebote.

Eine gesellschaftsrechtliche Sonderregel, die die Übernahme des betreffenden Unternehmens erschwert, existiert in Deutschland nur noch in Form des sog. VW-Gesetzes[37], das den kontrollierenden Einfluss des Landes Niedersachsen an der VW AG sichert. Da solche Sonderregeln in einer Reihe anderer Mitgliedstaaten noch bestehen, stellen sie für deutsche Unternehmen erhebliche Hindernisse bei Übernahmen von Gesellschaften in diesen Mitgliedstaaten dar.

8. Do hostile take overs by companies from other EU jurisdictions in fact take place in your country?

Ja, allerdings wurden alle Beispiele „feindlich“ begonnen, aber „freundlich“ beendet. Jüngere Beispiele sind die feindlichen Übernahmen der Mannesmann AG (Deutschland) durch Vodaphone Airtouch plc (Vereinigtes Königreich) und von der Kamps AG (Deutschland) durch Barilla (Italien).

9. To what extents are there any sectors (utilities, financial institutions) that in practice are further protected from hostile take overs, or foreign[38] take overs in particular? Are there any policy statements or particular legal

mechanisms that give effect to this protection, or is it a matter of informal mechanisms?[39]

Besondere Regelungen existieren in Deutschland für Banken und Versicherungen. Nach § 2b KWG muss jeder, der beabsichtigt, eine bedeutende Beteiligung an einem Kreditinstitut zu erwerben, der Bundesanstalt für Finanzdienstleistungsaufsicht (BAFin) und der Deutschen Bundesbank die Höhe der beabsichtigten Beteiligung unverzüglich anzeigen. Die BAFin kann innerhalb von drei Monaten nach Eingang der Anzeige den beabsichtigten Erwerb der bedeutenden Beteiligung oder ihre Erhöhung untersagen, wenn Tatsachen vorliegen, aus denen sich ergibt, dass der Anzeigende oder, wenn er juristische Person oder Personenhandelsgesellschaft ist, gesetzliche Vertreter oder persönlich haftende Gesellschafter nicht zuverlässig ist. Ferner muss der Erwerber ein Inhaberkontrollverfahren beim Prüfungsverband deutscher Banken durchführen, wenn die Zielgesellschaft am Einlagensicherungsfonds des Bundesverbands deutscher Banken[40] mitwirkt. Dieses Verfahren beruht nicht auf gesetzlichen Vorgaben, sondern auf dem Statut des Einlagensicherungsfonds und soll dessen Funktionsfähigkeit sichern. Verstöße gegen Mitwirkungspflichten nach dem Statut des Einlagensicherungsfonds können zum Ausschluss von der Mitwirkung am Einlagensicherungsfonds führen.

Nach § 104 Versicherungsaufsichtsgesetz (VAG) hat derjenige, der beabsichtigt, eine bedeutende Beteiligung (gemäß § 7a Abs. 2 Satz 3 VAG mindestens 10% des Nennkapitals oder der Stimmrechte einer Versicherungsaktiengesellschaft) an einem Erstversicherungsunternehmen zu erwerben, der Aufsichtsbehörde die Höhe der beabsichtigten Beteiligung unverzüglich anzuzeigen. Die Aufsichtsbehörde kann den beabsichtigten Erwerb der bedeutenden Beteiligung oder ihre Erhöhung unter bestimmten Voraussetzungen untersagen.[41] Ferner besteht für das Versicherungsunternehmen nach § 13d Abs. 4 VAG eine Anzeigepflicht für den Erwerb oder die Aufgabe einer bedeutenden Beteiligung am eigenen Versicherungsunternehmen, das Erreichen sowie Über- oder Unterschreiten der Beteiligungsschwellen von 20%, 33% und 50% der Stimmrechte oder des Nennkapitals sowie für die Tatsache, dass das Unternehmen Tochterunternehmen eines anderen Unternehmens wird.

10. What are the company law techniques of completing a take over or merger that are used in practice where one of the companies is from another EU jurisdiction? Please give particular attention to how this would differ from the usual completion of a take over or merger where both companies are from your jurisdiction. It would be useful if you could add a comment

about the consequences on the techniques used of the taxation regime and of any differential tax treatment of take overs or mergers where one party is from another EU jurisdiction.

Das WpÜG differenziert nicht zwischen Übernahmen durch inländische Bieter und solchen durch Bieter aus anderen EU-Mitgliedstaaten. Hier wird der Zusammenschluss aufgrund des Erwerbs von Anteilen erreicht.

Ferner gibt es auch die Möglichkeit eines Zusammenschlusses durch Verschmelzung im Sinne von § 1 Abs. 1 Nr. 1, § 2 des deutschen Umwandlungsgesetzes[42]. Diese Möglichkeit steht nur Unternehmen mit Sitz in der Bundesrepublik Deutschland zur Verfügung.

Es sei darauf hingewiesen, dass seit etwa einem Jahr die Veräußerung von Beteiligungen an Kapitalgesellschaften durch Kapitalgesellschaften in Deutschland steuerfrei ist.

11. A duty on listed companies to disclose capital and control structures is proposed in Issues Relating to Takeover Bids, the First Report of the High Level Group of Company Law Experts (see p 25). Would this require amendments in the legislation in your country? How would these amendments in case be implemented (in primary company law, securities law, stock exchange regulations etc.)?

Nach § 21 Wertpapierhandelsgesetz (WpHG) ist derjenige, der durch Erwerb, Veräußerung oder auf sonstige Weise 5%, 10%, 25%, 50% oder 75% der Stimmrechte an einer börsennotierten Gesellschaft erreicht, überschreitet oder unterschreitet, verpflichtet, die betreffende Gesellschaft sowie die BAFin schriftlich darüber zu informieren. Die börsennotierte Gesellschaft ist ihrerseits verpflichtet, Mitteilungen nach § 21 Abs. 1 WpHG in einem überregionalen Börsenpflichtblatt zu veröffentlichen. Sind die Aktien der börsennotierten Gesellschaft an einer Börse in einem anderen Mitgliedstaat der EU oder einem Vertragsstaat des EWR zum amtlichen Handel zugelassen, so muss die Gesellschaft die Informationen auch in einem Börsenpflichtblatt dieses Staates veröffentlichen oder, sofern das Recht dieses Staates eine andere Form der Unterrichtung des Publikums vorschreibt, in dieser anderen Form vornehmen. Die Veröffentlichung muss in einer Sprache abgefasst werden, die in diesem Staat für solche Veröffentlichungen zugelassen ist (§ 25 Abs. 1 und 2 WpHG). Die BAFin befreit auf schriftlichen Antrag die börsennotierte Gesellschaft von diesen Veröffentlichungspflichten, wenn die Veröffentlichung dem öffentlichen Interesse zuwiderlaufen oder der Gesellschaft erheblichen Schaden zufügen würde, sofern im letzteren Fall die Nichtveröffentlichung nicht zu einem Irrtum des Publikums über die für die Beurteilung der betreffenden Wertpapiere wesentlichen Tatsachen und Umstände führen kann (§ 25 Abs.

4 WpHG). Eine Veröffentlichungspflicht in einem überregionalen Börsenpflichtblatt in Deutschland trifft auch Gesellschaften mit Sitz im Ausland, deren Aktien zum amtlichen Handel an einer inländischen Börse zugelassen sind, wenn die in § 21 Abs. 1 Satz 1 WpHG genannten Stimmrechtsveränderungen eintreten (§ 26 Abs. 1 WpHG). § 26 Abs. 3 WpHG berücksichtigt die Vorgaben der Richtlinie 88/627/EWG des Rates vom 12. Dezember 1988 über die bei Erwerb und Veräußerung einer bedeutenden Beteiligung an einer börsennotierten Gesellschaft zu veröffentlichenden Informationen[43]. Danach besteht für Gesellschaften mit Sitz in einem anderen Mitgliedstaat der EU oder einem EWR-Vertragsstaat, deren Aktien sowohl an einer Börse im Sitzstaat als auch an einer deutschen Börse zum amtlichen Handel zugelassen sind, die Veröffentlichungspflicht, die das Recht des Sitzstaates aufgrund von Art. 10 der Richtlinie 88/627/EWG vorschreibt. Die Veröffentlichung muss in Deutschland in einem überregionalen Börsenpflichtblatt in deutscher Sprache vorgenommen werden.[44]

Die Stimmrechtsanteile sind in einer Stimmrechtsdatenbank auf der Internet-Seite der BAFin veröffentlicht: www.BAFIN.de.

Ferner besteht für den Emittenten von Wertpapieren, die zum Handel an einer inländischen Börse zugelassen sind, die Pflicht zur Veröffentlichung und Mitteilung kursbeeinflussender Tatsachen (§ 15 WpHG), und seit dem 1. Juli 2002 sind Geschäfte mit Wertpapieren der eigenen Gesellschaft durch Vorstands- und Aufsichtsratsmitglieder börsennotierter Gesellschaften und ihrer Ehepartner, eingetragenen Lebenspartner und Verwandten ersten Grades von diesen zu veröffentlichen (sogenannte *„directors dealings“*; § 15a WpHG). Für Kapitalgesellschaften (Aktiengesellschaften, Kommanditgesellschaften auf Aktien und Gesellschaften mit beschränkter Haftung) sieht das Handelsgesetzbuch (HGB) eine Pflicht zur Erstellung eines Jahresabschlusses vor (§§ 325 ff. HGB). Darin sind u.a. die Anteile der Gesellschaft an verbundenen Unternehmen anzugeben (vgl. § 327 Nr. 1 HGB). Emittenten zugelassener Aktien sind nach § 40 Börsengesetz zusätzlich verpflichtet, innerhalb des Geschäftsjahres regelmäßig mindestens einen Zwischenbericht zu veröffentlichen, der anhand von Zahlenangaben und Erläuterungen ein den tatsächlichen Verhältnissen entsprechendes Bild der Finanzlage und des allgemeinen Geschäftsganges des Emittenten im Berichtszeitraum vermittelt.

Unterhalb der gesetzlichen Normierung bestehen weitere Veröffentlichungspflichten, die den Emittenten durch die Börse auferlegt werden. Dazu gehört etwa die strukturierte Quartalsberichterstattung am Neuen Markt, die eine Segmentberichterstattung einschließt.

Ob der Vorschlag der „High Level Group of Company Law Experts“ eine Änderung des deutschen Rechtes nach sich ziehen würde, hängt somit von der konkreten Ausgestaltung der neuen Gesetzgebungsinitiative ab. Die grundsätzliche Idee beider Vorschläge ist im deutschen Recht bereits verwirklicht. Erforderliche Änderungen würden wahrscheinlich in denjenigen gesetzlichen Vorschriften vorgenommen, in denen diese Vorschläge im Grundsatz bereits verwirklicht sind (siehe oben).

12. A so called break through rule after take over bids is another of the proposals in Issues Relating to Takeover Bids, the First Report of the High Level Group of Company Law Experts (see p 29). Would this require amendments in the legislation in your country? How would these amendments in case be implemented (in primary company law, securities law, stock exchange regulations etc.)?

Die „*break through rule*" könnte im WpÜG verankert werden. Das Aktiengesetz müsste entsprechend angepasst werden. Es müsste ein Mechanismus eingebaut werden, der es erlaubt, nach einem erfolgreichen Übernahmeangebot, also einem Angebot, das zur Kontrolle durch den Erwerber führt, eventuelle Vorkehrungen gegen feindliche Übernahmen in der Satzung der Gesellschaft aufzuheben. Für Satzungsänderungen ist zur Zeit nach zwingendem Recht ein Beschluss der Hauptversammlung mit (in der Regel) einer Mehrheit von _ der abgegebenen Stimmen erforderlich. Soweit die „*break through rule*" durch europäisches Gemeinschaftsrecht eingeführt würde, müsste auch das sogenannte VW-Gesetz diesem Mechanismus unterworfen werden. Daher müsste im WpÜG entweder ausdrücklich normiert werden, dass die „*break through rule*" auch gesetzlich normierte Sonderrechte durchbricht, oder es müsste im VW-Gesetz ein entsprechender Vorbehalt aufgenommen werden. Schließlich stellt sich die Frage, ob die „*break through rule*" auch die Abberufung des Aufsichtsrates, dem Organ zur Kontrolle der Geschäftsführung, ermöglichen soll. Wäre dies der Fall, so müsste das Aktiengesetz auch insoweit geändert werden.

13. In your view, would these two new rules as proposed have any material impact on the existing barriers to take overs in your country (or in others as seen from your point of view)? It would be helpful if you could demonstrate the impact, or lack of it, by going through one or more recent take over bids that failed in your country (or in some other member state, by a company from your country).

Die Einführung von Vorschriften zur Offenlegung von Kapital- und Kontrollstrukturen (soweit dies nicht bereits geschehen ist) hätte für Übernahmen in Deutschland nur geringe Auswirkungen. Wie gezeigt (s. oben zu Ziffer 11.) bestehen in Deutschland bereits weitgehende Offenbarungspflichten für Kapitalbeteiligungen. Damit sind auch Kontrollstrukturen weitgehend nachvollziehbar. Die Einführung einer

„*break through rule*" hätte vor allem zur Folge, dass die Beschränkungen im VW-Gesetz aufgehoben würden. Flächendeckende und weitreichende weitere Folgen hätte diese Neuerung nur, wenn generell nach einem erfolgreichen Übernahmeangebot eine Satzungsänderung zur Beseitigung von Abwehrmaßnahmen mit erleichterten formellen Anforderungen ermöglicht würde, insbesondere mit einer geringeren Mehrheit für Beschlüsse der Hauptversammlung.

14. Below are a number of questions which may assist in a comparative analysis.

a) What are the main features of the relevant domestic take over legislation constituting the company law and financial market regime, and who enforces it (independent regulators, regulatory bodies with appeal to ministry, stock exchange)? What is the extent of intervention by the takeover regulator(s) – to what extent does the regulator have wide or general discretions to block and play a protectionist role (for example in its capacity as approver of the offer terms/documentation)?

Nach deutschem Übernahmerecht ist der Bieter verpflichtet, seine Entscheidung zur Abgabe eines Angebotes zu veröffentlichen (§ 10 WpÜG). Spätestens vier Wochen nach der Veröffentlichung der Entscheidung zur Abgabe eines Angebotes muss der Bieter der BAFin die Angebotsunterlage einreichen (§ 14 WpÜG). Die BAFin prüft die Angebotsunterlage. Sie muss die in § 11 Abs. 2 WpÜG aufgeführten Inhalte enthalten. Dazu gehören Angaben zu Art und Höhe der für die Wertpapiere der Zielgesellschaft gebotenen Gegenleistung, zu den Bedingungen, von denen die Wirksamkeit des Angebots abhängt und zum Beginn und Ende der Annahmefrist. Weitere Anforderungen an den Inhalt der Angebotsunterlage ergeben sich aus § 2 der WpÜG-AngebotsVO.[45] Die BAFin hat das Angebot zu untersagen, wenn die Angebotsunterlage nicht die gesetzlich erforderlichen Angaben enthält, die in ihr enthaltenen Angaben gegen gesetzliche Vorschriften verstoßen oder der Bieter gar keine Angebotsunterlage übermittelt hat oder die Angebotsunterlage nicht veröffentlicht hat. Ferner *kann* die BAFin das Angebot untersagen, wenn der Bieter die Veröffentlichung nicht in der vorgeschriebenen Form vornimmt (§ 15 Abs. 2 WpÜG).

Das Angebot muss bindend sein (vgl. § 17 WpÜG) und darf – außer dem Vorbehalt der Zustimmung der Gesellschaftsversammlung – nicht von Bedingungen abhängig gemacht werden, deren Eintritt der Bieter ausschließlich selbst herbeiführen kann. Dasselbe gilt für Widerrufs- oder Rücktrittsvorbehalte (§ 18 WpÜG). Genaue Vorschriften bestehen auch für die zu erbringende Gegenleistung (§ 31 WpÜG). Die Annahmefrist für das Angebot darf grundsätzlich vier Wochen nicht unter- und zehn Wochen nicht überschreiten (§ 16 Abs. 1 Satz 1 WpÜG). Bei Übernahmeangeboten haben die Aktionäre, die das Angebot noch nicht angenommen haben, nach Bekanntgabe der Annahmequote noch zwei weitere Wochen Zeit, das Angebot anzunehmen (§ 16 Abs. 2 Satz 1 WpÜG). Änderungen des Angebots sind nur im beschränkten Umfang möglich (Erhöhung der Gegenleistung, Änderung der Gegenleistung, Verringerung des Mindestanteils, von dessen Erwerb der Bieter die Wirksamkeit des Angebots abhängig gemacht hat, Bedingungsverzicht; vgl. § 21 WpÜG).

Interventionsmöglichkeiten der BAFin bestehen insbesondere im Rahmen der Prüfung der Angebotsunterlagen. Die differenzierten gesetzlichen Anforderungen an die Angebotsunterlage könnten der BAFin – rein theoretisch – eine Handhabe geben, Übernahmeangebote zu behindern. Allerdings besteht derzeit kein Anlass, dies tatsächlich zu vermuten. Im Übrigen besitzt die BAFin Ermittlungsbefugnisse nach § 40 WpÜG. Danach hat der Bieter Auskünfte zu erteilen und Unterlagen vorzulegen, die die BAFin zur Überwachung der Einhaltung der gesetzlichen Pflichten benötigt.

b) Are there restrictions on a board taking action to frustrate a bid that has been made? When do the relevant restrictions start to apply – earlier than a formal announcement/filing of a bid? To what extent can shareholders approve the taking of frustrating action in advance of any bid?

Für diese Frage wird auf die Ausführungen zu Ziffer 7 verwiesen.

c) Are there restrictions on the type of consideration that can be offered in a bid, for example securities only if these are listed in the target country's home state or the EU?

Bei einem Übernahmeangebot muss die Gegenleistung grundsätzlich entweder in einer Geldleistung in Euro oder in liquiden Aktien bestehen, die zum Handel an einem organisierten Markt (vgl. § 2 Abs. 7 WpÜG) im EWR zugelassen sind. Soweit die Aktien, die der Bieter erwerben will, Stimmrecht gewähren, müssen die als Gegenleistung angebotenen Aktien ebenfalls stimmberechtigt sein (§ 31 Abs. 2 WpÜG). Der Bieter ist verpflichtet, den Minderheitsaktionären der Zielgesellschaft zumindest wahlweise als Gegenleistung eine Geldleistung in Euro anzubieten, sofern er oder mit ihm gemeinsam handelnde Personen oder deren Tochterunternehmen während eines Zeitraums von drei Monaten vor dem Übernahmeangebot mehr als 5 % oder während des Übernahmeverfahrens mehr als 1 % der Anteile der Zielgesellschaft gegen Geld erwerben.

d) Are there effective compulsory acquisition procedures regarding a small non-accepting minority? Can a bidder make its offer conditional on achieving the number of shares required so it can operate a squeeze out?

Mit Einführung des WpÜG hat der deutsche Gesetzgeber Regelungen zum Ausschluss von Minderheitsaktionären (sogenannte „*Squeeze out*"-Bestimmungen) in das Aktiengesetz eingefügt.[46] Ferner kann ein Aktionär, der am Grundkapital einer Aktiengesellschaft oder einer Kommanditgesellschaft auf Aktien zu mindestens 95% beteiligt ist, die Aktien der Minderheitsaktionäre gegen deren Willen gegen Gewährung einer angemessenen Barabfindung erwerben. Die Barabfindung muss die Verhältnisse der Gesellschaft im Zeitpunkt der Beschlussfassung ihrer Hauptversammlung berücksichtigen (§ 327b Aktiengesetz). Der Erwerb der Aktien der Minderheitsaktionäre erfolgt durch Hauptver-sammlungsbeschluss und dessen Eintragung im Handelsregister (§§ 327c bis 327e Aktiengesetz). Anfechtungsklagen gegen den Übertragungsbeschluss können nicht darauf gestützt werden, dass die festgelegte Barabfindung nicht angemessen ist (§ 327f Abs. 1 Satz 1 Aktiengesetz). Stattdessen kann die Höhe der Abfindung auf Antrag jedes ausgeschiedenen Aktionärs vom Gericht nach § 306 Aktiengesetz überprüft werden. Die Kosten dieses Verfahrens trägt der Hauptaktionär (§ 306 Abs. 7 Satz 7 Aktiengesetz).

Ein Bieter kann die Wirksamkeit seines Angebotes davon abhängig machen, dass er einen Mindestanteil der Wertpapiere an der Zielgesellschaft erwirbt (Umkehrschluss aus § 21 Abs. 1 Nr. 3 WpÜG). Daher kann er sein Angebot auch davon abhängig machen, dass er 95% des Kapitalanteils der Zielgesellschaft erwirbt und daher befugt ist, einen *Squeeze out* durchzuführen.

e) Is there a principle of board neutrality? Can a target board align itself with a particular bidder/agree measures such as exclusivity arrangements to protect a particular deal?

Das WpÜG enthält einen Neutralitätspflicht des Vorstandes in § 33 Abs. 1 Satz 1 (vgl. oben zu Ziffer 7.). Der Vorstand der Zielgesellschaft kann zwar nach einem konkurrierenden Angebot suchen (§ 33 Abs. 1 Satz 2 WpÜG), er kann jedoch dieses Angebot nur soweit unterstützen, als dies als Handlung eines ordentlichen und gewissenhaften Geschäftsleiters einer Gesellschaft angesehen werden könnte oder es vom Aufsichtsrat konsentiert ist (§ 33 Abs. 1 Satz 2 WpÜG; vgl. die Ausführungen zu Ziffer 7.). Als Handlung eines ordentlichen und gewissenhaften Geschäftsleiters soll nach der Begründung des Regierungsentwurfs auch die Weiterführung bereits eingeschlagener Unternehmensstrategien gelten.[47] Bestand also bereits eine Strategie zur Übernahme durch ein anderes Unternehmen, so dürfte insoweit eine Unterstützung des Vorstandes möglich sein.

f) Can a target board hand over information to a potential bidder?

Das WpÜG selbst enthält keine Vorschriften, die die Übermittlung von Informationen an potentielle Bieter verbietet. Für die Übermittlung solcher Informationen hat der Vorstand daher die ihm obliegenden allgemeinen Sorgfaltspflichten (vgl. § 93 Aktiengesetz) sowie die Insiderregeln der §§ 12 ff. WpHG zu beachten.

g) Are structures permitted which concentrate control rights in the hands of minority shareholders? Are structures permitted which place limitations/restrictions on voting rights, caps for example on voting rights above a certain threshold?

Im deutschen Aktienrecht sind solche Strukturen nicht möglich. Mehrstimmrechte sind nach § 12 Abs. 2 Aktiengesetz unzulässig. Höchststimmrechte sind im deutschen Aktienrecht ebenfalls nicht vorgesehen. Nur im VW-Gesetz sind sie ausnahmsweise gesetzlich normiert.

h) Can restrictions be placed on the transferability of shares either by the issuer (in articles of association or by other means) or by arrangements between shareholders? Can a board delay registering transfers of shares?

Es ist zulässig, die Übertragung von Namensaktien an die Zustimmung der Gesellschaft (vertreten durch den Vorstand), des Aufsichtsrats oder der Hauptversammlung zu binden (§ 68 Abs. 2 AktG). Einzelne Aktionäre können sich außerhalb der Satzung in den Grenzen der Vertragsfreiheit gegenseitig verpflichten, nicht über Aktien zu verfügen.

i) What contractual barriers (including share holder agreements) to take over bids are in use in public companies (eg golden parachutes, change of control provisions triggering default of loan agreements, or wining up or change of control of joint ventures)? What are the prospects of review by courts on the basis of contract or company law and by regulators on the basis of securities laws or stock exchange regulations?

In Deutschland existieren solche Bestimmungen nicht.

j) Are there current proposals to change the legislation relating to take overs?

Nein. Das Wertpapierübernahmegesetz trat am 1. Januar 2002 gerade erst in Kraft.

D. FINAL ISSUES

15. In your view, what is the extent to which the complexity of the regulatory arrangements, within national jurisdictions and between the Commission and member states, present an obstacle to take overs?

Ein Hindernis besteht darin, dass die Materie nur in einem Teil der Mitgliedsländer überhaupt gesetzlich geregelt ist. Schließlich sind die Aktienrechte der Mitgliedsländer sehr verschieden, so dass ein Vergleich nur der Regelungen über Übernahmen nicht ausreicht, um festzustellen, ob es Hindernisse gibt, die aus der Eigenart des jeweiligen Aktienrechts entstehen. In der Bundesrepublik ist eine solche Eigenart z.B. das duale System der Verwaltung durch Vorstand und Aufsichtsrat.

16. Can you list some instances where different rules in the different regulatory systems have caused practical obstacles in a take over process? (One instance could be different time limits under the EC Merger Regulation and national merger rules on the one hand and under stock exchange rules on the other.)

Solche Beispiele sind mir für Übernahmen innerhalb der EU nicht bekannt.

NOTES

[1] Alle Antworten stellen rein persönliche Ansichten des Berichterstatters dar und sind weder offizielle Stellungnahmen deutscher öffentlicher Stellen noch eine solche der Wissenschaftlichen Gesellschaft für Europarecht. Der Berichterstatter dankt allen Juristen der Sozietät GLEISS LUTZ, die ihm Hinweise für die Beantwortung der Fragen gegeben haben, namentlich Dr. Ralf Thaeter für seine Anregungen und die Durchsicht des gesellschaftsrechtlichen Teils des Fragebogens und Michael Schedl für seine Unterstützung bei der Erstellung des Manuskripts.

[2] The aim is not here to have an authoritative statement but a report which can contribute to the discussion. For EEA (non member) country rapporteurs, the subject of the question is intended to be the EEA regime. For non member (non EEA) countries, there are special issues. Country rapporteurs are welcome to limit their answers in the way they believe to be most helpful or interesting with the purpose of the questionnaire in mind.

[3] Verordnung (EWG) Nr. 4064/89 des Rates vom 21.12.1989 über die Kontrolle von Unternehmenszusammenschlüssen, ABl. Nr. L 395 vom 30.12.1989, S. 1, berichtigte Fassung in ABl. Nr. L 257 vom 21.9.1990, S. 1, zuletzt geändert durch Verordnung (EG) Nr. 1310/97 des Rates vom 30.6.1997, ABl. Nr. L 180 vom 9.7.1997, S. 1.

[4] Grünbuch über die Revision der Verordnung (EWG) Nr. 4064/89 des Rates vom 11.12.2001, KOM(2001) 745/6 endgültig, Rn. 57.

[5] Ebensolche Regelungen enthalten die Wettbewerbsgesetze Irlands und Österreichs.

[6] Abgedruckt in WuW 1990, S. 240.

[7] Die Gebiete der einzelnen Mitgliedstaaten gelten ohne Weiteres als wesentliche Teile des Gemeinsamen Marktes (str. für Luxemburg, bejaht in einem Verfahren nach Art. 86 EWGV von GA Warner, Schlussanträge in der Rs. 77/77, BP/Kommission, Slg. 1978, 1513, 1537). Dasselbe kann für einzelne Regionen oder bestimmte Teile größerer Mitgliedstaaten gelten und wurde etwa für den Hafen von Genua vom EuGH bejaht, vgl. Rs. C-179/90, Porto di Genova/Gabrielli, Slg. 1991, I-5889 Rn. 15 und Rs. C-18/93, Corsica Ferries, Slg. 1994, I-1783 Rn. 41.

[8] Vgl. COMP/M.2730 - Connex/DNVBVG. Der Zusammenschluss betraf öffentliche Nahverkehrsdienste.

[9] Verweisungsentscheidungen: 1990 bis 1995: 0 bis 1 pro Jahr, 1996: 3, 1997 bis 2001: 4 bis 7, 2002 (bis 30.6.): 7.

[10] Relativ zur Zahl der angemeldeten Zusammenschlüsse gesehen nahm die Zahl der Verweisungen nach 1997 kontinuierlich ab und dürfte erst 2002 den Wert von 1997 übersteigen.

[11] Vgl. COMP/M.2760 - Nehlsen/Rethmann/swb/BEG.

[12] Vgl. Fälle COMP/M.2698 Promatech/Sulzer und COMP/M.2738 GES/Unison. Diese Fälle waren von sieben Mitgliedstaaten der EU gemeinsam an die Kommission verwiesen worden.

[13] So ist etwa unklar, welche Ereignisse die Frist nach Art. 22 Abs. 4 FKVO auslösen.

[14] Siehe Punkt 2.0 der *Horizontal Merger Guidelines*. Den Begriff der Marktmacht definieren sie als die Möglichkeit, sich anders zu verhalten, als es unter den Bedingungen wirksamen Wettbewerbs zu erwarten wäre. Damit wird aber im Rahmen des SLC-Tests genau jener „wettbewerblich nicht kontrollierte Verhaltensspielraum" geprüft, mit dem die marktbeherrschende Stellung im Rahmen der europäischen Fusionskontrolle üblicherweise definiert wird.

[15] Vgl. das Diskussionspapier des Bundeskartellamts „Das Untersagungskriterium in der Fusionskontrolle - Marktbeherrschende Stellung versus Substantial Lessening of Competition"; abzurufen unter „www.bundeskartellamt.de/Diskussions beitrage.html".

[16] Vgl. Fn. .

[17] Wie die Kommission selbst in Rn. 169 des Grünbuches andeutet, ist dieser Paradigmenwechsel im Grünbuch auch nicht ausreichend erörtert.

[18] Vgl. dazu International Competition Policy Advisory Committee (to the Attorney General and the Assistant Attorney General for Antitrust); Final Report of 28 February 2000, p. 51.

[19] Vgl. auch die Mitteilung der Kommission über interne Verfahrensvorschriften für die Behandlung von Anträgen auf Akteneinsicht.

[20] Vgl. Immenga/Mestmäcker, GWB-Kommentar, 3. Aufl. 2001, § 40 Rn. 72.

[21] Verfahren vor den Gemeinschaftsgerichten dauern etwa zwei Jahre pro Instanz, Verfahren in Deutschland liegen in der Regel bei unter einem Jahr für die erste Instanz und etwas über einem Jahr für das Rechtsmittel.

[22] Vgl. Mitteilung über die Änderung der Verfahrensordnung des Gerichts erster Instanz zur Beschleunigung der Verfahren, ABl. Nr. L 322 vom 19.12.2000, S. 4.

[23] Voraussetzungen sind ernsthafte Zweifel an der Rechtmäßigkeit der Untersagungsverfügung und Drohen eines außergewöhnlichen und irreparablen Schadens bei Fortgelten des Vollzugsverbotes.

[24] Vgl. KG WuW/E 2571 Gaslöschanlagen.

[25] Merkblatt zur Inlandsauswirkung vom Januar 1999, zu finden auf der Homepage des Bundeskartellamtes: „www.Bundeskartellamt.de".

[26] Bechtold, GWB-Kommentar, 2. Aufl. 1999, § 40 Rn. 6.

[27] Art. 14 Abs. 4 FKVO bestimmt ausdrücklich, dass die Entscheidungen in Art. 14 Abs. 1 und 2 FKVO nicht strafrechtlicher Art sind. Ob dies für den extrem weiten Rahmen des Art. 14 Abs. 2 FKVO materiell tatsächlich zutrifft, sei hier dahingestellt.

[28] Vgl. oben Fn. .

[29] Focus is here mainly on listed companies but information about non listed and also non public companies will be of interest if this is possible to provide.

[30] Here too the following applies. For EEA (non member) country rapporteurs, the subject of the question is intended to be the EEA regime. For non member (non EEA) countries, there are special issues. Country rapporteurs are welcome to limit their answers in the way they believe to be most helpful or interesting with the purpose of the questionnaire in mind.

[31] Gesetz zur Regelung von öffentlichen Angeboten zum Erwerb von Wertpapieren und von Unternehmensübernahmen vom 20.12.2001, BGBl. I, S. 3822.

[32] Regierungsentwurf, BT-Drs. 14/7034, S. 28.

[33] Sog. Holzmüller-Fälle, BGH NJW 1982, S. 1703.

[34] Vgl. dazu aber § 9 Satz 2 Nr. 3 der Verordnung über den Inhalt der Angebotsunterlage vom 27.12.2001, BGBl. I, S. 4263 (WpÜG-AngebotsVO). Danach kann auf Antrag eine Befreiung vom Pflichtangebot gewährt werden, wenn auf Grund der Erlangung der Kontrolle über eine Muttergesellschaft mittelbare Kontrolle an deren Tochtergesellschaft erlangt wurde und der Buchwert der Beteiligung an der Tochtergesellschaft weniger als 20% des buchmäßigen Aktivvermögens der Muttergesellschaft beträgt.

[35] Für weitere Ausnahmen vom Pflichtangebot vgl. §§ 36, 37 WpÜG.

[36] Vgl. § 4 WpÜG-AngebotsVO.

[37] Gesetz über die Überführung der Anteilsrechte an der Volkswagenwerk Gesellschaft mit beschränkter Haftung in private Hand, BGBl. I 1960, S. 585.

[38] "Foreign" here includes both take overs from other member states and from non member states (or non EEA countries).

[39] In the case of banks or insurance companies, the relevant ministry and supervisor would be usually be able to block take overs on prudential grounds and their involvement would be difficult to review. Similar mechanisms would be in place for many utilities where state ownership often adds to the problems. An extensive review is not required, but it would be useful with an assessment of how such mechanisms function. If there have for instance not been any take over by a foreign bank, that is an interesting point.

[40] Der Einlagensicherungsfonds sichert als freiwillige privatrechtliche Sicherungseinrichtung Kundeneinlagen bei den im Bundesverband deutscher Banken zusammengeschlossenen deutschen Privatbanken.

41 § 104 Abs. 1a Satz 1 VAG lautet: „Die Aufsichtsbehörde kann [...] den beabsichtigten Erwerb der bedeutenden Beteiligung oder ihre Erhöhung untersagen, wenn Tatsachen die Annahme rechtfertigen, dass
1. der Anzeigende [...] nicht zuverlässig oder aus anderen Gründen nicht den im Interesse einer soliden und umsichtigen Führung des Erstversicherungsunternehmens zu stellenden Ansprüchen genügt,
2. das Erstversicherungsunternehmen durch die Begründung oder Erhöhung der Beteiligung mit dem Inhaber der bedeutenden Beteiligung in einen Unternehmensverbund eingebunden würde, der durch die Struktur des Beteiligungsgeflechts oder durch mangelhafte wirtschaftliche Transparenz eine wirksame Aufsicht über das Versicherungsunternehmen beeinträchtigen kann, oder
3. das Erstversicherungsunternehmen durch die Begründung oder Erhöhung der bedeutenden Beteiligung Tochterunternehmen eines Versicherungsunternehmens eines Drittstaats [...] würde, das im Staat seines Sitzes oder seiner Hauptverwaltung nicht wirksam beaufsichtigt wird oder dessen zuständige Aufsichtsstelle zu einer befriedigenden Zusammenarbeit nicht bereit ist."

42 Umwandlungsgesetz vom 28.10.1994 (BGBl. I, S. 3210 zuletzt geändert am 23.3.2002, BGBl. I, S. 1163).

43 ABl. Nr. L 348 vom 17.12.1988, S. 62.

44 Die Schwellenwerte für die Mitteilungspflicht der meldepflichtigen Personen nach Art. 4 der Richtlinie 88/627/EWG weichen von denjenigen nach § 21 Abs. 1 WpHG ab. Solche Abweichungen sind nach Art. 3 und Art. 4 Abs. 1 der Richtlinie 88/627/EWG zulässig.

45 Verordnung über den Inhalt der Angebotsunterlage, die Gegenleistung bei Übernahmeangeboten und Pflichtangeboten und die Befreiung von der Verpflichtung zur Veröffentlichung und zur Abgabe eines Angebots vom 27.12.2001, BGBl. I, S. 4263.

46 Art. 7 des Gesetzes zur Regelung von öffentlichen Angeboten zum Erwerb von Wertpapieren und von Unternehmensübernahmen vom 20.12.2001, BGBl. I, S. 3822.

47 Regierungsentwurf, BT-Drs. 14/7034, S. 58.

NETHERLANDS

Cross Border Mergers in Company Law and Competition Law: Removing the Final Barriers

Rapporteurs
Robbert O. Snelders and Maurits Dolmans[1]

This article is a contribution to the XX Congress of the Fédération Internationale pour le Droit Européen ("FIDE") that will be held in London from October 30, 2002 through November 2, 2002. It takes the form of responses to a series of questions from the Congress's General Rapporteurs. These questions aim to explore remaining barriers to takeovers in the various Member States of the European Union. The article is organized as follows. Section A examines possible obstacles to cross-border M&A activity from the perspective of Dutch merger control law. Section B examines any such obstacles inherent in Dutch company law and/or Dutch capital market regulation. Finally, Section C offers a brief conclusion.

A. THE COMPETITION REGIME

1. What is the view of your country on the functioning of the threshold levels in Article 1(2) as well as the 2/3 rule in the Merger Regulation, and the proposal in the Commission's Green Paper for amendment of Article 1(3) to deal with the problems of multiple filings?

There are few legal commentators that address the functioning of the thresholds levels of the EC Merger Regulation, other than to support the principle of one-stop-shopping and the apparent failure of Article 1(3) to achieve its objective of subjecting multiple national filings to EC jurisdiction.[2] The Commission's recent proposals to reform Article 1 of the EC Merger Regulation, however, have been subject to criticism. Jurisdictional thresholds based on objective, clear-cut turnover tests are the most capable of providing the clear legal certainty that the business community requires.

The frustrations sometimes associated with multi-country filings should not be addressed by creating a more complex and less objective system for case allocation. The revised thresholds proposed by the Commission may create more problems than they would resolve. A better step toward reducing the burdens associated with multi-jurisdictional filings would be to harmonize Member States' notification thresholds, information requirements, and substantive review standards.

The Commission's proposal to expand its jurisdiction. The Commission takes the position that Article 1(3) of the EC Merger Regulation has not achieved its objective of conferring Commission competence over transactions that require notification in multiple Member States. In the Commission's view, Article 1(3) should be amended to ensure "*effective application of Community competition rules to cases with a cross-border interest, while, in a balanced way, reducing the administrative burden for the involved companies.*" The Green Paper suggests amending Article 1 of the EC Merger Regulation to grant automatic Community competence over cases subject to notification in three or more Member States. The proposal also envisages that the relevant Member States would confirm the parties' conclusions on the application of the national thresholds on the basis of which Commission jurisdiction would be conferred.

The Commission is the body best suited to review transactions that raise predominantly cross-border issues, and the Commission's "one-stop-shopping" procedure often offers companies significant advantages over multi-country filings.[3] In particular, multiple national filings may involve higher transactional costs and can create difficulties of timing and legal certainty. These burdens are likely to become much more acute as candidate countries join the Community. Support exists for changes that would allow more companies to voluntarily take advantage of a single European merger review procedure.[4]

However, it is not obvious that the Green Paper's multiple filing proposal would necessarily result in more transactions that have a genuine Community interest being notified to the Commission. Many Member States have low thresholds for merger review that do not depend on meaningful effects on competition within their national territory, still less on any cross-border effects. This situation would likely be compounded by further accessions to the EU, since several candidate countries have very low thresholds based on worldwide (*e.g.*, the Czech Republic and the Slovak Republic) or national (*e.g.*, Bulgaria and Romania) turnover that are satisfied by many transactions. Further, it is also questionable whether establishing Community jurisdiction should be done on the basis of national thresholds.

While there may be some justification for presuming Community interest under the current Member State turnover thresholds listed in Article

1(3)(a)-(b) of the EC Merger Regulation, the mere fact that a transaction would need to be notified in three Member States is almost certainly a less reliable indicator of Community interest. This means that, under the proposal, the Commission would have to be prepared to deal with many more notifications, many of which would raise no material competition issues. This would not be a useful deployment of Commission resources. Thus, it would be better if the Commission were to foster consensus among the Member States and candidate countries on the need to: (i) apply reasonable monetary threshold requirements, (ii) repeal current thresholds based on market shares, and (iii) base competence only on demonstrable effects on competition within the jurisdiction.

More fundamentally, there are practical difficulties associated with the Green Paper's proposal that may severely limit its usefulness and could even create greater uncertainty than presently exists. First, as the Green Paper acknowledges, certain Member States' merger control rules are based on criteria that are neither objective nor readily ascertainable. For example, market share thresholds for notification currently exist in Greece, Portugal, Spain, and the United Kingdom, as well as in several candidate countries (*i.e.*, Bulgaria, Cyprus, Latvia, Poland, Slovakia, and Slovenia). Many of these jurisdictions have widely differing policies on the issue of market definition, ranging from the sophisticated to the very rudimentary. The prospect of having mandatory jurisdictional alternatives determined on the basis of separate market definition assessments by the merging parties, national competition authorities, and the Commission is not attractive. The following three examples illustrate some of the potential difficulties.

(i) Consider a case where the merging parties took the view that Commission notification was required based on their assessment that their shares in the relevant markets triggered at least three Member State reporting thresholds. Following the Commission's review, a subsequent Commission decision finding that the relevant markets or shares were different could affect the parties' initial jurisdictional assessment, potentially removing the Commission's competence to review the transaction and resulting in severe delay.

(ii) Consider a case where the parties conclude that filing is required in two Member States, but not in a third Member State that relies on market share thresholds as a basis for jurisdiction. Based on this assessment, they would file in the two Member States only. If later, however, the third Member State concludes that its thresholds were satisfied and that the transaction should have been reported, the parties could find themselves both (a) exposed to fines for a failure to notify under the EC Merger Regulation; and (b) having expended unnecessary time and effort in two national proceedings, presumably pre-empted by the Commission's mandatory jurisdiction triggered by the third Member State's market definition determination.

(iii) Given Member States' propensity to define geographic markets along national lines, a concentration may fall under the Commission's jurisdiction based on the assessment of national market shares. If the Commission's review finds, however, that the relevant geographic market is wider than national and that market shares as a result would be lower, the basis for the Commission's jurisdiction would be voided.

In most such cases, the Green Paper's proposed procedure for confirmation of the parties' jurisdictional assessment would not remove the potential for confusion and delay. Amending the proposal to give merging parties the option (but not the obligation) to notify the transaction to the Commission under this multiple filing threshold would solve the second problem identified above, because a contrary market definition finding by the third Member State would not affect the jurisdiction of the two Member States in which notifications had been filed (*i.e.*, the situation would be no different than at present). However, non-exclusive Commission jurisdiction under a multiple filing threshold would not resolve the first problem identified above; Commission findings on market definition contrary to the merging parties' position could still eliminate Commission jurisdiction (as the proposed threshold would not be met) and could force the parties to re-start the review process before the national authorities.

Secondly, further problem arises from voluntary notification regimes such as currently applicable in the United Kingdom. In our view, in cases where a transaction meets the reporting thresholds in two Member States having mandatory notification regimes and in a third Member State with a voluntary regime, the parties should remain free to choose whether they would have notified in that third Member State or not (and thus whether the Commission's jurisdictional threshold is satisfied or not). The Commission should explicitly address this issue in order to eliminate any possible doubt.

Other approaches may be more effective. If the Commission is minded to adopt the Green Paper's multiple filing proposal, a number of potential areas of uncertainty need to be addressed. For example, some confusion could arise as to when a transaction that is reportable to the Commission under the "three Member States" test would become reportable. Most Member States either have no specific triggering event, the only condition being that a notifiable transaction cannot be closed without prior approval, or have triggering events that correspond to those in Article 4(1) of the EC Merger Regulation. We assume that the triggering event for concentrations reportable under this threshold would be the same as for any other transaction reportable under the EC Merger Regulation. For the avoidance of doubt, however, the Commission should clarify that the new threshold would be satisfied if the transaction is in theory reportable to three different national competition authorities (*i.e.*, without the need for the respective national triggering events, if any, to have occurred). It should also be made clear that any applicable deadlines for filing at the national or EU level and any sanctions in this regard would not apply until it was clear in which jurisdiction(s) the notifying parties should file.

Conclusion. In sum, there are a number of practical and legal difficulties associated with the Green Paper's proposal that could ultimately jeopardize its effectiveness. Some of these problems could be mitigated if the parties to transactions otherwise subject to notification in three or more Member States retained discretion to choose either a single Commission notification or multiple Member State notifications. Nonetheless, significant difficulties would remain. On balance, the procedural difficulties associated with the proposed reform make it likely to create more problems than it solves. A better step toward reducing the burdens associated with multi-jurisdictional filings would be for the Commission to advocate greater harmonization of Member States' notification thresholds, information requirements, and substantive review standards.

2. In light of experiences in your country, do member states have sufficient flexibility to call for mergers to be referred back under Article 9 of the Merger Regulation? In light of the proposal in the Commission's Green Paper, what is your view on the circumstances in which this power should be exercised?

Under the procedure in the Netherlands, the Minister of Economic Affairs, as the representative of the Government, is competent to request a referral to the Dutch Competition Authority (*Nederlandse Mededingingsautoriteit*, the "NMa"). To date, experience remains limited in the Netherlands in respect of referrals under Article 9 of Council Regulation 4064/89, as the Netherlands has only requested and been granted an Article 9 referral on a single occasion.[5] Moreover, little has been published concerning the Netherlands' ability and exercise of the ability to request such referrals. Some criticism has been expressed, however, in connection with a perceived lack of transparency in the Commission's decisional practice to refer cases back to Member States, also querying whether the increased use of the referral will diminish the EC Merger Regulation's principle of one-stop-shopping.[6]

The Commission believes that the referral mechanism of Article 9 of the EC Merger Regulation should be simplified. It proposes to maintain only Article 9(2)(b), but to facilitate its use by disjoining the referral request from evidence of a threat of creation or strengthening of dominance and/or by eliminating the need to establish that the relevant market is not a substantial part of the common market. Instead, it would be sufficient that the request establishes that the alleged effect on competition does not extend to significant effects in terms of foreclosure, spill-over on related markets of greater geographic scope, or similar cross-border effects. The Green Paper further proposes that the Commission should be able to make a referral of its own initiative under analogous criteria *i.e.*, without a request from the Member State(s). There is also general discussion of the possibility that referrals to Member States would be dealt with under the same deadlines and procedure as cases handled at Commission level only. Each of these points is addressed below.

(i) *Simplification of the referral criteria.* Simplification of the current referral criteria in Article 9(2)(a) of the EC Merger Regulation would be welcome.[7] This could be done by disjoining the criterion that there should be evidence of a threat of creation or strengthening of dominance and by eliminating the need to establish that the relevant market is not a substantial part of the common market. Both of these criteria have placed an unduly onerous burden on Member States requesting a referral. In particular, it seems unfair to require a Member State in possession of only a notification to produce evidence within three weeks of a conclusion that the Commission would take considerably longer to reach with more information in its possession. Likewise, the effect on various local or national markets has become unnecessarily complicated; it should be sufficient that there are no cross-border or spill-over effects.

(ii) *Referrals by the Commission at its own initiative.* Little support exists for this proposal.[8] Legal certainty and speed of process require that referrals back to Member States occur only rarely and in situations where it is clear that the Member States' authorities want to review a particular transaction and have good reasons for doing so.

(iii) *Timing.* Were the current referral criteria to be simplified, the deadline should still enable national authorities to verify whether the (amended) criteria for referral are met and would also help reduce delays to the notifying parties caused by such requests.

(iv) *Harmonization of procedural rules and deadlines.* Broad agreement exists with the comment in the Green Paper that notifying parties should not be made worse off by the fact that their transaction has been referred to a national competition authority ("NCA"). However, the reality is that the divergence in national procedural and substantive rules and deadlines for the assessment of transactions means that they frequently are, in particular where only part of a transaction is referred to a NCA. This may raise concerns under the non-discrimination principle.

3. Is the system of consultation between the European Commission and the national competition authorities (NCAs) working adequately? Does there need to be a better formalised system for consultation between NCAs directly involved either in the case of multiple filings outside the merger control regulation or in cases where more than one member state exercises the Article 9 request?

Cooperation between the Commission and the NCAs.[9] In general, cooperation between the Commission and the NCAs appears to perform adequately. However, the level of cooperation between the Commission and the NCAs could still be strengthened. In particular, the Commission could involve the Member States to a greater extent in its decision-making process; and the Commission has recently failed to accord the Member States sufficient time and attention in considering increasingly complex second-phase cases. As the Green Paper readily acknowledges, the Commission must work under strict deadlines in a second-phase investigation, which can become a constraint in complex cases where the Commission is only able to produce a statement of objections well after the initiation of the second-phase proceedings. This pressure has the result that the role of the Member States has come under increasing pressure. In that regard, recent experience in Brussels in second-phase cases has shown that the Commission has already concluded its position before consulting the Member States, thus preempting any meaningful dialogue between the Member States and the Commission.

Cooperation among NCAs. Cooperation between NCAs has been significantly expanded recently. Following an initiative by the NMa in April 2001, the NCAs established the association of European Competition Authorities (the "ECA").[10] The ECA is an informal association that serves as a forum where competition authorities operating within the EEA (European Economic Area) meet to discuss the application and enforcement of competition rules and the improvement of working relations amongst them. Since the establishment of the ECA network, the NCAs have in particular cooperated with regard to multi-jurisdictional concentrations. In response to comments from the business community, a network was created within the ECA dealing specifically with issues related to multi-jurisdictional merger notifications.

The ECA multi-jurisdictional mergers network has focused on reducing the burden of multiple filings by improving cooperation among competition authorities. As a first step, the network has issued a Procedures Guide concerning multi-jurisdictional mergers. If an ECA member receives a merger notification that was also notified to one or more other ECA authorities, that authority will notify the other ECA authorities. Such notification includes, among other things, information on the transaction,[11] the parties/sectors involved, and the deadline by which a decision must be taken. This way the different competition authorities will strive to coordinate from an early stage, and where possible will try to avoid inconsistent results.

The ECA multi-jurisdictional merger network has also facilitated the coordination of joint requests under Article 22 of the EC Merger Regulation. For the first time since its introduction in 1998, a joint Article 22 request was made in two recent EU merger cases.[12] For the first time since its introduction in 1998, a joint Article 22 request was made in two recent EU merger cases. The first case was recently approved following a detailed (second phase) investigation and subject to divestitures, while the Commission unconditionally approved the second case after a first-phase investigation. A joint referral had never occurred before the ECA network was set up, apparently due to practical problems including difficulties related to a lack of transparency regarding the countries where the concentration had been notified and the coordination of the responses of the NCAs involved.

Finally, the network has facilitated coordination between the NCAs with regard to other merger control-related issues, including advisory committee meetings. Overall, the informal cooperation of the ECA multi-jurisdictional merger network seems to have worked well and there would seem to be no need, at this particular time, for a formalized structure. To the contrary, it is felt that the informal structure may contribute to the effectiveness of the network.

4. How does the test under the law of your country compare to that under the Merger Regulation? Should all member states adopt the same test as under the Merger Regulation, and should this EU test be the (US) "significant lessening of competition" test rather than the present EU "dominance" test?

The substantive test under the Dutch Competition Act (*Mededingingswet*, "the Competition Act") reiterates the dominance test of Article 2 of EC Merger Regulation, *i.e.*, the NMa assesses whether a concentration "will create or strengthen a dominant position that would significantly impede effective competition on the Dutch market or a part thereof".[13] Its application by the NMa also closely follows EC practice. In both concept and application, the Dutch substantive test thus conforms to EC law.

Harmonization of the substantive tests to assess concentrations within the Member States is important to provide sufficient and clear legal certainty for cross-border transactions subject to multiple filing requirements. Accordingly, the Commission should strongly advocate harmonization of Member States' notification thresholds, information requirements, and substantive review standards. As to the latter, the Green Paper discusses the possibility that the Commission would replace the current dominance test for the assessment of concentrations under Article 2 of the EC Merger Regulation with the concept of "substantial lessening of competition", which is the substantive standard in several major jurisdictions including the United States, Canada, and Australia.

Before analyzing whether it would be desirable to adopt the substantial lessening of competition ("SLC") test, an important threshold issue is to establish what benefits might be expected if the SLC test replaced the dominance test.

a Possible benefits of adopting the SLC test over the dominance test

Two principal arguments have been advanced in favor of adopting the SLC test for EU merger review. First, it would help eliminate the potentially damaging consequences of divergence between major jurisdictions in the review of international mergers. Although jurisdictions are of course entitled to enact and enforce their own rules, when one jurisdiction blocks a merger on the basis of theories that other jurisdictions do not endorse, there is a risk that important efficiencies may be sacrificed and benefits denied to consumers world-wide. Divergent substantive standards also increase the transaction costs associated with the merger clearance process and may deter mergers that would have been pro-competitive and efficiency-enhancing. It should also be remembered that substantive divergence ultimately undermines the political consensus supporting antitrust enforcement, and thereby, the integrity of the enforcement system. If the aim is for a convergence of outcomes, then beginning from the same substantive test would seem to be a significant step in the right direction.

Second, a number of economists have expressed the view that dominance has important limitations as a substantive test for the review of mergers and acquisitions. The SLC test is a more appropriate, economics-based tool to assess the competitive effect of mergers and acquisitions, since it allows greater emphasis to be placed on inter-firm competitive dynamics, empirical evidence, and economic analysis, permits greater identification of the competition problems and associated remedies, and allows greater scope for the use of efficiency analysis. It has also been argued that the SLC test would impel the Commission to focus less on whether (potentially less efficient) competitors could be marginalized by a merger and more on whether the effects on competition are good or bad from a consumer perspective in the form of lower prices. These considerations, *inter alia*, led the Director-

General of Fair Trading with the Office of Fair Trading to state as follows:[14]

"Dominance is not an ideal test for considering the impact of a merger on competition. Narrowly interpreted it would be far too permissive. The Commission has therefore been creative in applying the dominance test, particularly when looking at oligopolistic markets. But the concept of joint or collective dominance is not without difficulties."

The outcome of the appeal against the Commission's *Airtours/First Choice*[15] decision also shows that there may be lacunae in the current *collective dominance* test applied by the Commission. The EC Merger Regulation only prohibits transactions that create or strengthen a collective dominant position, and not merely transactions that would lead to less competition between oligopolists. From an analytical point of view, the SLC test may be more suitable to capture the competition concerns in such cases.

In addition to possible limitations in the assessment of joint or collective dominance, the SLC test may also have discernible advantages over the dominance test in regard to certain issues of *single-firm dominance*. Two examples help to illustrate the issue.

(i) First, consider a proposed merger between the #2 and #3 firms in a 3-firm market where the shares are 60%/20%/20%. Since the combined entity would remain much smaller than the market leader, it would be difficult to argue that it would become individually dominant. Moreover, if market conditions are not conducive to oligopoly behavior (*e.g.*, there is "lumpy" demand or a lack of price transparency), it may be impossible to apply a convincing collective dominance analysis. Nevertheless, based on the high level of market concentration, significant competitive concerns could arise. A similar fact-pattern arose in the recent *Heinz/Beech-Nut* baby food transaction that the U.S. Federal Trade Commission challenged successfully.[16] In that case, there was a clear market leader and vigorous competition between merging #2 and #3 parties to be the second baby food producer on supermarket shelves. (For various reasons, there are seldom more than two baby food brands on supermarket shelves.) In this situation, the merger of #2 and #3 was bound to lessen competition, and was, accordingly, challenged by the FTC. This fact-pattern would not be caught by any reasonable concept of dominance.

(ii) Second, consider a proposed merger between two competitors in a differentiated product market whose products are particularly close substitutes for each other. As a result of the elimination of direct competition between the merging parties, such a transaction could

> enable the parties to raise prices, even if the combined entity would not be the largest player or have a market share indicative of individual dominance. To deal with such "unilateral effects" considerations, it might be possible to define narrower markets, to treat a low market share and other factors as evidence of dominance, or to argue that there would be collective dominance post-transaction. However, none of these approaches properly captures the economically objectionable feature of the transaction.

The Green Paper postulates a similar example, but adds that the Commission "*has not so far encountered a situation of this kind*" (Green Paper, ¶ 166). This may be true, but, as explained above, the situation is far from implausible, and it should be clear that the concept of dominance has, properly applied, limited utility in this context.

SLC may also have advantages over the current dominance test in the context of certain *vertical concentrations*. The focus of the Commission's analysis of vertical mergers has, rightly, been on the possibilities for the vertically integrated merged entity to foreclose rivals by raising their costs or denying them access to some input also used by the vertically integrated entity's downstream operations. However, the Commission's decisional practice suggests that, even where a firm acquires a dominant position in an upstream market that would allow it to impose discriminatory conditions on its horizontal competitors in a downstream market, the Commission will not find the creation of a dominant position in the downstream market unless its market share (along with other factors) in the downstream market itself indicates a dominant position.[17] While, as a general matter, it is correct to identify vertical concerns only where the merged entity has market power on both the upstream and downstream markets, it is also clear that a threshold that requires dominance in both the upstream and downstream markets may not fully capture the economically injurious features of vertical concentrations. The U.S. Department of Justice's Non-Horizontal Merger Guidelines explain that competitive concerns may arise in situations that fall short of dominance:

> "Entry through the acquisition of a relatively small firm in the market may have a competitive effect comparable to new entry. Small firms frequently play peripheral roles in collusive interactions, and the particular advantages of the acquiring firm may convert a fringe firm into a significant factor in the market. The Department is unlikely to challenge a potential competition merger when the acquired firm has a market share of five percent or less. Other things being equal, the Department is increasingly likely to challenge a merger as the market share of the acquired firm increases above the threshold."[18]

Thus, an SLC test may be more apt to analyze issues of foreclosure and the other effects of a vertical concentration on the structure of distinct, but related, markets, than one based on dominance.

In conclusion, in certain cases there are material differences between the dominance and SLC tests, and the SLC test may be a more appropriate, economics-based tool to assess mergers and acquisitions.

b. The benefits of the SLC test do not outweigh the considerable uncertainty and other disadvantages associated with a change

Notwithstanding that the fact that the SLC test would generally appear to be a more suitable standard by which to review mergers and acquisitions, the prevailing view questions whether the benefits of replacing the current dominance test with an SLC test are sufficient to counterbalance the adverse results that would follow such a change.[19] In particular, it is debated whether there are material differences between the fundamental economic principles applied by the Commission using the dominance test and the major jurisdictions using the SLC test. It is also clear that both the SLC and dominance tests are not static concepts, but have evolved, and will continue to evolve, over time. More fundamentally, it is postulated that whatever advantages the SLC test may have over the current dominance test are far outweighed by the uncertainty and other disadvantages that would be created were the substantive test under the EC Merger Regulation to be changed at this stage. These issues are developed in greater detail below.

The substantial degree of de facto convergence that already exists between the EU and other major jurisdictions is unlikely to materially increase if the EU adopted the SLC test. The principal argument in favor of adopting the SLC test is that it would facilitate substantive convergence with other major merger review jurisdictions, increase legal certainty, reduce the burden on notifying parties, and make it clearer how and why regulators differ in their treatment of the same transaction. However, this argument overstates the practical impact that changing the wording of the substantive test for clearance would have. It also ignores the fact that several factors have contributed to the EU's achieving a substantial degree of *de facto* convergence with other major jurisdictions. In particular:

(i) *Market definition.* The Commission's Notice on the definition of the relevant market is very similar to the U.S. Department of Justice and Federal Trade Commission Horizontal Merger Guidelines (the "U.S. Guidelines"),[20] as numerous commentators have noted.[21] As a result, differences in market definition between the EU and the United States and Canada have been rare.

(ii) *Principles of substantive analysis.* The unilateral effects and coordinated interaction tests described under the U.S. Guidelines are very similar to the single firm dominance and collective dominance tests applied under the EC Merger Regulation. Indeed, the U.S. Guidelines define a "substantial lessening of competition" as "creating or enhancing market power", which is very similar to "creating or strengthening a dominant position". Thus, the EU's view is similar to other major jurisdictions' analyses of international mergers in all but a few exceptional cases. Where differences have arisen, these have been primarily attributable to differences in the application of common underlying principles to a given transaction. For example, in the *GE/Honeywell* transaction, the fact that the EU and the United States reached opposing conclusions was almost certainly not a function of the wording of their respective substantive tests for merger review, but more likely reflected different philosophies on the application of the underlying principles and their assessment of the future effects of the transaction on the market.[22] Convergence is not necessary for its own sake and, if there are differences in the underlying economic approach between the EU and other jurisdictions, these will not be resolved by their adopting substantive tests with similar wording.

(iii) *Bilateral cooperation.* Under the Cooperation Agreements signed between the EU and the United States, and Canada, the agencies share, on a regular and continuing basis, views and information about particular transactions, coordinate the timing of the review process to the extent feasible, and generally achieve consistent or complementary remedies. In addition, both the U.S. agencies and the Commission are devoting substantial resources to using their Joint Merger Working Group to facilitate even greater convergence on issues such as conglomerate mergers, process and timing, and principles of assessment, including several issues raised by the Green Paper.[23]

It is not obvious that there are major lacunae in the current dominance test. Experience under the EC Merger Regulation has shown that the current dominance test is a sufficiently flexible tool to capture a wide range potentially anti-competitive effects of mergers and acquisitions. There is general support for the Green Paper's statement that "*experience in applying the dominance test has not revealed major loopholes in the scope of the test.*" For example, when the EC Merger Regulation was adopted, there was considerable debate as to whether an increase in concentration, and the threat of coordinated action, could be challenged. The Community Courts have now made it clear in the *Kali und Salz* and *Gencor* cases that collective dominance can be challenged under the EC Merger Regulation. Thus, the Commission has brought cases based on an oligopoly theory where concentration involves reduction of a three-firm market to two (*Gencor*) and a four-firm market to three (*Airtours*). Likewise, the dominance test has proved capable of capturing conglomerate issues and vertical foreclosure concerns in circumstances where the market shares may not themselves have been indicative of dominance.[24]

Dominance has a long antecedent in Community competition law and uncertainty would be created by the adoption of the SLC test. Dominance has a long antecedent in Community competition law (*e.g.*, Article 82 EC, Article 66(2) ECSC), and a substantial body of jurisprudence has developed in the last decade under the EC Merger Regulation. There would be legal uncertainty if the relevance of the jurisprudence created by the Commission under the EC Merger Regulation were to be called into question by the adoption of the SLC test. Were the existing body of Commission decisional practice and the jurisprudence of the Community Courts to be discarded at this stage, it may take a further decade or more before an equally settled replacement body of jurisprudence under the SLC test would evolve. That would be unsatisfactory. *A contrario*, if the existing jurisprudence were deemed still to be applicable, it is difficult to see any convincing reason for changing to the SLC test at all.

Uncertainty could in part be remedied by the adoption of clear guidelines on the Commission's application of the SLC test. However, notifying parties and their legal advisers attach importance to the predictability and transparency of the principles by which the Commission assesses notified operations, and would therefore be troubled by any short- to medium-term uncertainty in the process. Finally, there are concerns that the concept of dominance under the EC Merger Regulation has resulted in a cross-contamination of the jurisprudence under Article 82 EC. Even if these concerns were valid – and we believe that they are – they are not a reason to change the current dominance test under the EC Merger Regulation. That assessment should be guided only by what test is the most suitable for merger review, and not by ancillary considerations. Finally, many Member States have enshrined the dominance test in their national competition laws. While we do not believe that this is a reason in itself against adoption of the SLC test, the risk that an increasing number of referrals by national authorities to the Commission, and by the Commission to national authorities, would be assessed according to different substantive principles is tangible and is perhaps a further reason for maintaining the current position.

Conclusion. Regarding the *dominance vs. substantial lessening of competition test,* the SLC test may have some advantages over the current dominance standard. In particular, the SLC test may be better suited to deal with: (i) certain cases involving oligopolies (*e.g.*, there may be reasonable objections to certain transactions that would lead to less competition between oligopolists, even if no collective dominant position could be established); (ii) certain transactions that could lead to price increases as a result of elimination of direct competition between the parties, even if no dominant position is created or strengthened (*e.g.*, a merger between the second- and third-largest firms in a market not conducive to oligopoly behavior); and (iii) certain vertical transactions.

Nevertheless, the benefits of amending the EC Merger Regulation to incorporate an SLC test are probably outweighed by the uncertainty and other disadvantages that would follow from such a change. Moreover, the fundamental economic concepts upon which appropriate merger analysis should be based are common to both the dominance and SLC tests. The current wording of the EC Merger Regulation's substantive test leaves ample scope for incorporating a robust analysis of whether appropriately substantiated efficiencies are likely to counterbalance any potential anti-competitive effects that might otherwise follow from a reportable transaction. However, Article 2(1)(b) and/or Article 2(3) might benefit from more specific wording on this issue, not least because the Commission has not rigorously applied these provisions in the context of efficiencies. Furthermore, there is sufficient scope within the tests as now written in the EC Merger Regulation to incorporate the central elements of the SLC test into the Commission's analysis. Whatever test is applied, however, the Commission's and NCAs' retention of more economists to help ensure that their decisions are underpinned by rigorous economic analysis would be welcome.

5. Are the procedural and judicial safeguards adequate to protect parties from abuse of power by the competition authorities? How do the laws of your country compare to EC law in this respect?

As discussed under 6(i) below, the Dutch Competition Act provides for a two-phase filing procedure similar to the EC Merger Regulation. As in the EC procedure, and in particular, the second phase of the merger review process, there are some fundamental shortcomings in the current administrative procedure that encroach on the due process rights of the notifying undertakings.[25] The principal due process concern in the current system is that the NMa states the case against a notified concentration and decides how far it is proved. There is no independent assessment of the case's merits and the strength of the evidence.

The lack of independent review contrasts with the position in a number of other Member States' merger control regimes.[26] In short, the same body should not act as investigator, prosecutor, and judge in reviewing concentrations that may have considerable implications for the Dutch (or even international) economy.

The second concern is the judicial review by the District Court of Rotterdam (Chamber of Administrative Law) (*Rechtbank Rotterdam,*

Sector Bestuursrecht) and, on appeal, by the Court of Appeal for Trade and Industry in The Hague *(College van beroep voor het bedrijfsleven)*. Delays in judicial review of NMa merger control decisions can be a significant issue, since the courts will rarely be in a position to rule within a period that would allow the parties to reconstitute the transaction.

There would be distinct benefits in switching to a system whereby the NMa would be required to convince an independent tribunal of the merits of its case. This would most likely mean that, if it wished to oppose a transaction, the NMa would initially bring proceedings against the merging parties in the District Court of Rotterdam or before a newly created administrative tribunal within the NMa (similar to the administrative law judge system within the U.S. Federal Trade Commission). Either reform would likely involve an amendment of the Act, which could be done as part of the revisions following from the current consultation period.

Under the U.S. system, for instance, competition authorities must initiate proceedings before a Federal Court in order to block a merger. The prospect of independent judicial review exerts discipline on agency decision-making at all stages, irrespective of whether the transaction is ultimately challenged or abandoned. A number of senior officials within the DOJ and FTC have confirmed this, including the current Deputy Assistant Attorney-General of the Antitrust Division of the U.S. Department of Justice:

> "If we decide in the U.S. to challenge a merger, we know we may have to go to court to convince a federal judge, by the preponderance of the evidence after an evidentiary hearing, that the merger may substantially lessen competition. This means that we know our witnesses will be exposed to the crucible of cross-examination before an independent fact-finder... *After just six weeks at the agency, I cannot overstate how much knowing we may have to prove our case to an independent fact-finder disciplines our decision-making.*"[27] (Emphasis added)

There are many desirable elements of the current Dutch system that have worked well, and the majority of these could be successfully retained in a reformed system along the lines outlined above. Only exceptionally would the NMa be required under a reformed system to bring the matter before an independent tribunal, since experience has shown that it is only likely to challenge a transaction in rare cases.

In the absence of institutional and judicial reform, we believe that the following measures could help improve the safeguards in the existing system, without fully remedying, however, the defects identified above:

(i) *Role for an independent adviser.* There would be benefits in allowing an independent adviser to publicly review the substance of the NMa's case. If the NMa's conclusions are different to those of the independent adviser, there would be value in requiring the NMa to state clearly why its conclusions differ. As a practical matter, such a change would require that the independent adviser not be notionally attached to the NMa and that he or she have sufficient resources to perform the tasks allocated.

(ii) *Formal deadline or best practice guidelines for issuance of the "preliminary assessment"*. A problem in second-phase proceedings tends to be that the parties' have little time to engage the NMa in substantive discussion concerning its findings. At the same time, the parties need to decide to offer undertakings to meet the concerns identified. It is therefore important that the NMa has a meaningful period to assess parties' submissions and to have further discussions with the parties, before the issue of remedies needs to be addressed. We would favor a clear deadline for the NMa to identify competitive concerns, or, at a very minimum, best practice guidelines.

(iii) *Greater transparency on the role of third parties.* In response to increasing concerns as to the level of third party access, we consider it critical that all information provided by third parties be made available to the notifying parties. At present, there is no consistent practice with regard to recording emails, telephone conversations, and other informal meetings or communications between third parties and the NMa out of respect for the rights of defense.

6. Below are a number of questions relating to domestic law which may assist in a comparative analysis.

a. Please provide an overview of the structure of and main features of the relevant domestic legislation and the institutional framework (who enforces it)? It may be helpful to include some information about the role of private rights of action.

The principal legislation. The relevant domestic legislation is the Competition Act of May 22, 1997. The Competition Act entered into force on January 1, 1998. It is closely modeled on EC competition law, and EC rules and precedent serve to interpret the Competition Act.[28] The Competition Act covers behavioral conduct (identical to Articles 81 and 82 of the EC Treaty); merger control rules (modeled on EC Merger Regulation); and provides certain enforcement powers. The general rules on administrative procedure in the General Act on Administrative Law (*Algemene wet bestuursrecht*) of June 4, 1992, also cover enforcement of the Competition Act.[29]

Competent authority. The authority responsible for merger review is the NMa.[30] The NMa operates as a department within the Ministry of Economic Affairs (*Ministerie van Economische Zaken*) and its Minister has the power to overrule the NMa's decisions in individual cases. On January 31, 2002, the Lower House of Parliament (*Tweede Kamer*) adopted a bill that would convert the NMa into an independent administrative agency (*zelfstandig bestuursorgaan*). The (amended) bill is currently pending before the Upper House of Parliament (*Eerste Kamer*).[31]

b. What kinds of transactions are caught? Are joint ventures caught? What are the jurisdictional thresholds? Is it difficult to identify with sufficient certainty whether a filing is in fact required under national law? Are foreign-to-foreign mergers caught?

Jurisdiction. The Competition Act applies to "concentrations". A concentration arises in the following circumstances:

(i) two or more undertakings merge (*i.e.*, a statutory merger);
(ii) one or more undertakings acquire direct or indirect "control" of the whole or parts of one or more other undertakings; or
(iii) a joint venture is established which performs on a lasting basis all the functions of an autonomous economic entity and which does not give rise to a coordination of the competitive behavior of the parent companies.

As under EU law, "control" is defined as the ability to exercise a decisive influence on the activities of an undertaking on the basis of actual or legal circumstances. This does not refer to day-to-day management, but to decisions concerning an undertaking's strategic commercial interests in the longer term. Minority shareholdings, contractual rights, and other means that give rise to "control" also give rise to a concentration. Also in this regard, the NMa closely follows EC precedent, in particular the Commission Notice on the concept of control under the EC Merger Regulation. If an undertaking is governed by the "large company" regime (*structuurregime)*,[32] the NMa does not consider this to imply that the majority shareholders cannot have decisive influence within the meaning of the Competition Act.

Thresholds. A concentration must be notified to the NMa if certain objective, easily assessable turnover criteria are met:

(i) the combined aggregate worldwide turnover of all participating undertakings exceeded (113,450,000 in the last calendar year; and
(ii) the aggregate Dutch turnover of each of at least two of the undertakings concerned exceeded (30 million in the last calendar year.[33]

As under EU law, where the acquisition consists of the acquisition of parts of a business, only the turnover relating to the acquisition of these parts must be taken into account. Turnover is calculated based on the provisions set forth by the Competition Act and the Book 2 of the Dutch Civil Code, which again largely mimic EC law.[34] Foreign-to-foreign transactions require notification in the Netherlands if a concentration satisfies the above thresholds. No physical presence in the Netherlands of the undertakings concerned is required; meeting the thresholds equates to the concentration having an effect on competition in the Netherlands.

Joint ventures. Dutch merger control law still incorporates the pre-1998 treatment of joint ventures under the EC Merger Regulation.[35] Accordingly, a distinction is made between concentrative and cooperative joint ventures. The former are joint ventures performing on a lasting basis all the functions of an autonomous economic entity which do not give rise to the coordination of the competitive behavior of the parent companies. Cooperative joint ventures are not subject to the merger notification rules. Full-function joint ventures, on the other hand, require notification if the thresholds are satisfied. Other joint venture operations, such as structural cooperative joint ventures, are governed by the provisions of Article 6 of the Competition Act, which closely follows Article 81 of the EC Treaty. A recent review of the Competition Act identified that the treatment of joint ventures under Dutch merger control law should be brought into line with EC law, *i.e.*, subjecting cooperative joint ventures to merger control instead of behavioral competition review.

c. Is the filing mandatory or voluntary? Who is responsible for filing? What is involved in the preparation of a filing? What are the deadlines for filing? What are the waiting periods and does implementation of the transaction have to be suspended?

Mandatory pre-merger control. The Competition Act requires notification where the thresholds, as described above, are met. In the case of a (statutory) merger, the merging undertakings have to notify the transaction. Where an undertaking acquires control of (part of) another undertaking, the obligation to notify applies both to the acquiring undertaking and the seller (although, in practice, the acquirer will typically submit the notification). In the case of a public bid, the bidder must notify the concentration. There are currently no filing fees. The signing of an agreement or the acquisition of a controlling interest is not necessary for notification; a concrete intention to undertake a transaction is sufficient.

Procedure. The Competition Act provides for a two-phase filing procedure. In the first phase, the NMa must decide whether a license (*vergunning*) authorizing the concentration is required within four weeks starting from the day after the receipt of the notification (provided that day is not a

Saturday, a Sunday, or a public holiday). Accordingly, the parties are prohibited from closing their transaction for four weeks pending the NMa's review.[36] If the NMa decides that a license is required, an in-depth investigation is required. To begin the second phase, the parties (or party) concerned will have to submit a separate application. The NMa must decide on the license application within 13 weeks following receipt of that notification.[37]

A breach of the obligation to implement a transaction with prior approval may void the concentration in respect of the Netherlands. Under Dutch civil law, this entails that the concentration and all its effects must be reversed. In addition, the NMa can impose administrative sanctions.

Information required. Implementing Royal Decrees (*koninklijke besluiten)* provide, *inter alia*, for the notification forms that must be used for the first-phase notification and the second-phase license application. The first-phase notification form is loosely modelled on Form CO (the EU filing form) and requests information on the undertakings concerned, including their business activities and the relevant sectors; information on the corporate groups; financial information; a description of the concentration and supporting documentation; the most recent documents showing the intent to effect the concentration; and the powers of attorney by the undertakings concerned to the designated representative(s). With respect to substantive information, the form requests a description of and market data for any relevant market where the products or services of the undertakings concerned overlap. Parties must also submit market research reports, and, if there is an overlap between the parties' activities, information on the major competitors and customers and trade organizations. Moreover, parties must indicate whether there are any ancillary restraints. If there are affected markets, parties should provide both value and volume based market share data. The second-phase license application form mirrors the detail required by Form CO.

d. What are the issues and possible sanctions involved in closing before clearance? What is the timetable for clearance and can it be sped up?

As noted above, implementing a concentration before the NMa has been notified of, and cleared, a transaction may result in the nullity of the transaction under Dutch law. In addition, the NMa can impose administrative penalties, including fines of up to a maximum of (22,500, on each party responsible for filing, as well as order, backed by periodic penalty agreements, to cease or reverse the infringement.

Upon receipt of the notification, the NMa must decide within four weeks to clear the transaction or refer the notification to an in-depth second stage license investigation. This period will start running the day after the receipt of the notification, provided this day is not a Saturday, Sunday, or public holiday. The period for review is suspended while the NMa request further information from the parties to the concentration. There is, in general, no possibility of speeding up the process other than by discussing the envisaged transaction in pre-notification meetings because the NMa requires some time to market test the proposed concentration. Suspension of the 4-week and 13-week periods can be minimized by providing the requested information as soon as possible and by anticipating additional questions.

The NMa has issued a decision with policy rules setting out a simplified procedure.[38] If a notification fulfils the requirements of the simplified procedure notice, the NMa may issue a short-form decision. The NMa will normally issue such a decision if: (i) there are no objections from third parties, (ii) it is clear that Dutch merger control is applicable, and (iii) it is clear that the concentration does give not rise to any competitive issues. Qualifying for simplified procedure treatment may speed up the notification process, and as a result, the notifying party could obtain a decision within two or three weeks. The requirements concerning the provision of data and information for such concentrations, however, remain the same.

e. Are there any special rules applicable to public takeover bids?

The treatment of public takeover bids under the Competition Act mimics that under the EC Merger Regulation. The implementation of a public bid is exempted from the prohibition against implementing an intended concentration before notification and a subsequent period of four weeks has passed, provided that the NMa is notified immediately and the acquiring party does not exercise its voting rights.

f. What is the substantive test for clearance?

A proposed concentration requires a license where the NMa considers that it is likely that it "will give rise to or strengthen a dominant position which significantly impedes competition in the Netherlands or in any part of it". A license will be granted if the NMa concludes, following a second-phase investigation, that such a threat will not materialize. In practice, the NMa's interpretation of the dominance test closely follows that established in EC precedent. Accordingly, the substantive assessment is, in concept and application, similar to that undertaken by the Commission under EC Merger Regulation.

g. To what extent are non-competition issues relevant to the review process?

The relevance of non-competition issues in Dutch competition law, be it merger control or behavioral conduct, is much debated. The general opinion holds that Dutch competition law, following in the footsteps of EC law, is unclear on this point, but that it provides at least a certain margin for the NMa to weigh non-competition interests as long as these interest increase consumer welfare. Moreover, commentators in Dutch literature consider that "economic interest" is an expansive concept that can include, for example, public health and employment. At the same time, these commentators are cautious that such an approach should not open the door to all sorts of social interests.[39] In any event, the Minister of Economic Affairs may, upon request, overrule the NMa and allow a transaction on general interest grounds. Such grounds may be economic or non-economic, but must outweigh the expected detriment to competition. The Minister of Economic Affairs has, to date, not exercised this power.

h. Is it possible to remedy competition issues?

The Competition Act does not provide for the possibility of remedies during the first-phase investigation.[40] However, in practice parties can try to satisfy the requirements of the NMa by amending the concentration and re-notifying it, similar to the practice under the EC Merger Regulation pre its amendment in 1998 to incorporate the opportunity for notifying parties to offer undertakings during the first phase.[41] A recent review of the Competition Act concluded that it should be amended to include the possibility of remedies in the first-phase.

The NMa may attach conditions to the granting of a license following the second-phase investigation, including the amendment of a transaction. Similar to the EC procedure, it is up to the parties to offer and determine the scope of any remedies during the license application procedure. Contrary to the EC procedure, there are no legal deadlines to offer undertakings. The NMa has announced that it will issue (draft) guidelines concerning remedies in the course of 2002.[42]

i. What are the typical steps during the investigation? What rights do complainants have? What publicity is given to the process? What are the opportunities for judicial review?

In practice, similar to the EC Commission, the NMa attaches significant importance to observations made by third parties. In its market testing of an notified transaction, the NMa requests information from customers, suppliers, and competitors concerning the relevant markets and the transaction. After notification, and after the filing of an application for a license, the NMa publishes an announcement in the Dutch Official Journal (*Staatsblad*). Accordingly, third parties with direct interests may submit comments on the proposed transaction to the NMa. Although not obliged to do so, eight weeks after the application for a license is filed in the second phase, the NMa will communicate its preliminary assessment in writing to the undertakings concerned and to affected third parties (similar to the Statement of Objections under EC procedure). The undertakings involved are invited to respond to the preliminary assessment. Approximately two weeks after the NMa's assessment is communicated to the parties, an oral hearing will be arranged, which is presided over by an independent adviser and may be attended by third parties. Decisions of the NMa, including a decision that a license is required, are published on the NMa's website and in [**ADD**].

j. What are the enforcement powers? How does administrative and civil sanctions compare with the EC regime? And what are the criminal sanctions, and are they used?

The NMa's enforcement powers are largely similar to that of the EC Commission, although the maximum fines are generally lower. (The head of the NMa has suggested that maximum fines should be increased to ensure sufficient deterrence.)[43] The Competition Act does not provide for criminal sanctions, nor are there any current legislative proposals to introduce criminal sanctions.[44]

Enforcement powers. If a concentration is implemented in breach of the standstill obligation, it is null and void and the NMa may required the concentration to be reversed within a specified time-limit. The NMa may also impose administrative sanctions, including fines and periodic penalty payments. A maximum fine of (4,500 may be imposed for non-compliance with regulations or a failure to comply with the information requirements in relation to a request for a license. The NMa may impose fines of up to (22,500 for providing inaccurate or incomplete information, non-compliance with the regulations for a concentration license, and a number of other infringements. In addition to the imposition of administrative fines, the NMa may impose interim measures sanctioned by penalties. If the NMa concludes that a concentration would create or strengthen a dominant position, it will prohibit the concentration or approve it following undertakings to remedy the identified concerns.

Judicial review. Appeals against NMa decisions are to be filed to the District Court of Rotterdam (Chamber of Administrative Law) within six weeks of the decision.[45] The judgment of the District Court may be further appealed to the Court of Appeal for Trade and Industry in The Hague. Any person whose interests are directly affected may appeal against a decision. The Minister of Economic Affairs may, in response to a request, grant a license for an envisaged concentration even though the NMa has refused to grant one. Decisions of the Minister are subject to judicial review.

k. Do the authorities cooperate with other antitrust authorities?

The NMa cooperates with other EU antitrust authorities through the network of European Competition Authorities, as well as the Advisory Committee. The NMa also has regular contacts with the U.S. antitrust agencies, among others, and with the OESO.

l. Are there also rules on foreign investment, special sectors or other relevant approvals?

As discussed in more detail in response to Questions 7 and 9 below, there are no rules on foreign investment and Dutch law in principle does not discriminate against foreign investors. However, residency or EU nationality requirements apply to the shipping, aviation, and defense industries. In addition, certain businesses need to be conducted in a specific legal form and certain formalities need to be complied with. In the areas of banking, insurance, and investment services, the Minister of Finance (*Minister van Financiën)* must give his prior approval before a "qualified interest" may be obtained in, or sometimes by, a Dutch bank, insurance company, securities intermediary, or stock exchange. Such approval may be refused only on a limited number of grounds and is subject to legal review.

m. Are there current proposals to change the legislation?

There are no current defined proposals to amend the Competition Act (other than the amendments corresponding to the proposed reform of the NMa). The Ministry of Economic Affairs recently commissioned an independent evaluation of the experience under the Competition Act, which concluded that Dutch merger control functions well.[46]

The review identified three areas of improvement that essentially would harmonize certain aspects of Dutch merger control to the standard of the EC Merger Regulation. As such, these amendments, if adopted, will increase transparency for business. The areas are:

(i) subjecting cooperative joint ventures to merger control review, *i.e.*, conforming the treatment of joint ventures to the EC Merger Regulation following its 1998 amendment;
(ii) the possibility to offer undertakings to remedy competitive concerns identified following a first-phase investigation, *i.e.*, implementing the same amendment concerning the use of undertakings to conclude a first-phase investigation as under the EC Merger Regulation in its 1998 amendment; and
(iii) the strengthening of certain aspects of procedure, including the use of

oral hearings, adopting legal deadlines to offer remedies, the imposition of remedies, and the NMa's exercise of the ability to request supplemental information.

B. COMPANY LAW AND FINANCIAL MARKET REGULATORY REGIME

1. Introduction

This Section addresses Dutch company and securities laws relevant to cross-border acquisitions of widely held Dutch public limited liability companies (*naamloze vennnootschappen,* or "NVs") with a primary listing on the stock exchange of Euronext Amsterdam N.V. ("Euronext"). It is organized as follows. First, it summarizes certain key aspects of Dutch company law, in particular, as they affect anti-takeover measures. Second, it identifies several proposed changes to Dutch company law that would have implications for domestic and cross-border M&A. Finally, it responds to a series of questions from the Congress's General Rapporteurs.

Dutch company law — traditionally characterized by the so-called "stakeholder model" — is in the midst of change. Global competition for capital, the rise of the institutional investor, and international debate on corporate governance standards have focused attention on shareholder value. Two resulting trends can be identified. First, shareholders in Dutch companies are more aggressively asserting their rights in Dutch courts. Second, recently proposed legislative changes, if adopted, would increase shareholder influence over management and move the Netherlands from one side of the "corporate governance continuum" — the consensus-driven "stakeholder model" — to a more Anglo-American-style "shareholder model".

These developments may be expected to reduce some of the existing obstacles to domestic and cross-border acquisitions of NVs — and may foreshadow greater changes to the regulation of M&A activity in the Netherlands, such as those proposed in the Report of the High Level Group of Company Law Experts on Issues Related to Takeover Bids (named after its chairman Mr. Jaap Winter, the "Winter Report").

2. Overview of Dutch Company law affecting Cross-Border Mergers and Acquisitions

Two key characteristics of Dutch company law are relevant in assessing possible obstacles to cross-border acquisitions of NVs. The first is the so-called "large company" regime (*structuurregime*), which is mandatory for NVs meeting certain size thresholds but may also be adopted by smaller NVs. The second is a traditional tolerance of a variety of anti-takeover measures. Both characteristics find their roots in a "stakeholder model" of the company, which seeks to protect the interests not only of the company's shareholders but also of a variety of other stakeholders (including, for example, employees and creditors).

a. The "large company" regime

Since 1971, every "large company" (*structuurvennootschap*) in the Netherlands has been subject to a special company law regime. Subject to certain exceptions,[47] an NV is subject to the "large company" regime if it meets the following three criteria for three consecutive years:

(i) the NV's issued capital (plus reserves) equals at least (13 million;
(ii) the NV (or another company in the NV's corporate group) has established a works council (*ondernemingsraad)* pursuant to mandatory Dutch law;[48] and
(iii) the NV, together with other companies in the NV's corporate group, employs at least 100 persons in the Netherlands.

"Large companies" are required to have a two-tier board structure: (i) a management board, which is responsible for day-to-day management, and (ii) a supervisory board, which oversees and advises the management board. The supervisory board of a "large company" has the following key powers: xxvii to appoint, suspend, or dismiss any member of the management board;

(i) to appoint, suspend, or dismiss any member of the management board;
(ii) to adopt the annual accounts;
(iii) to approve certain management resolutions (*e.g.,* concerning corporate structure, the issuance of additional shares, the approval of material corporate transactions, or management resolutions with significant consequences for employees); and
(iv) to appoint supervisory board members through a system of co-optation (*i.e.,* a system in which the supervisory board members are appointed by the supervisory board).

The "large company" regime has in practice shielded NVs from takeovers, since the supervisory board holds key powers typically reserved for shareholders and shareholders cannot dismiss the supervisory board. The supervisory board's power of co-optation, in particular, has enabled supervisory (and management) boards to "weather" shareholder opposition. Even though the "large company" regime does not stop a bidder from acquiring a significant part or all of the shares of a target NV, it does prevent a bidder from exercising control over the target NV. It makes an NV a less attractive target and may, therefore, dissuade takeovers. For this reason, many NVs that are excepted from the "large company" regime have voluntarily elected to be governed by this regime (so that they are insulated from shareholder pressures).

b. Tolerance of anti-takeover measures

Dutch company and securities laws — including Exhibit X to the Euronext Listing and Issuing Rules (*Fondsenreglement*) — allows NVs to adopt a wide range of anti-takeover measures. Next to the voluntary adoption of the "large company" regime, the following three anti-takeover measures are the most commonly employed:[49]

(i) *Issuance of depositary receipts.* Approximately 20% of all NVs at Euronext are listed through so-called depositary receipts (*certificaten van aandelen*).[50] Depositary receipts are listed instruments issued by a special-purpose foundation (*administratiekantoor*), which carry rights to the beneficial ownership of underlying shares in an NV held by the foundation. They are either fully exchangeable for the underlying shares or, as is more common, exchangeable for a certain maximum percentage of the underlying shares, as prescribed in the NV's Articles of Association, usually 1% (the "X%-rule"). Crucially, it is the foundation and not the holders of the depositary receipts that exercises the voting rights associated with the underlying shares.[51]

    The foundation's Articles of Association typically instruct the foundation's board to vote the shares in the best interests of the NV, its business, and all of those involved therein. In practice, the foundation's board often includes current and/or former members of the NV's management — which has created a general perception that foundation boards are "management friendly". In recent years, foundations have shown an increased willingness to allow the holders of depositary receipts to exercise voting rights through powers of attorney. Nonetheless, few holders of depositary receipts actually exercise voting rights (mostly they are as inactive as shareholders and do not attend shareholder meetings), so the foundation's aggregate voting power remains largely with its board.

(ii) *Issuance of preference shares.* Preference shares (*preferente aandelen*) are shares carrying normal voting rights that an NV issues to a special-purpose foundation to dilute the voting power of other shareholders. Dutch law permits NVs to issue preference shares against payment of only 25% of their nominal value. The power to issue preference shares is often delegated to the management or supervisory board for a period of up to 18 months, thus allowing it to fend off any unwelcome bidder for the NV.[52] Some NVs have issued (or granted a call option on) up to 50% of the total voting rights in the NV to such a foundation. In practice, the mere threat of a management or supervisory board being able to issue such shares can be sufficient to successfully fend off a hostile bid. In many instances, the device is structured in such a way that the actual issuance of the preference shares is outside the control of the NV, *i.e.*, through a grant to a foundation of a call option over the shares.

(iii) *Issuance of priority shares.* Priority shares (*prioriteitsaandelen*) carry certain exclusive rights concerning the NV's business. These may include the exclusive power: (a) to propose an amendment to the NV's Articles of Association, (b) to approve the issuance of additional shares, and (c) to make binding nominations for the NV's management and supervisory boards (in the event that the "large company" regime does not apply). As an anti-takeover device, priority shares are commonly issued to special-purpose foundations or to former or current members of the NV's management.

In recent years, shareholders have increasingly challenged management boards that they felt did not deliver sufficient value for shareholders. Shareholders have sued NVs for alleged corporate mismanagement *(wanbeleid)*, and recent court judgments in the Gucci[53] and Rodamco[54] cases have shown an increased willingness by the courts to scrutinize the deployment of anti-takeover measures (in particular, the issuance of preference shares) by an NV's management board. These cases show a reassessment of the discretion traditionally permitted to management to adopt and maintain anti-takeover measures and a growing recognition that such measures, if abused, allow management to act in its own interests rather than the interests of the NV's shareholders and other stakeholders.

3. *Proposed Legislative Changes*

The increasing focus on management accountability to shareholders has led to a number of legislative proposals that seek to increase the rights of shareholders and holders of depositary receipts. The major proposals are discussed below.

a. Changes to the "large company" regime

On January 8, 2002, the Government presented Parliament with a proposal to amend the "large company" regime (*Wet tot wijziging van boek 2 van het Burgerlijk Wetboek in verband met de aanpassing van de structuurregeling*).[55] The proposed changes cover the following matters:

(i) *Appointment and removal of supervisory board members.* The supervisory board would be required to (a) notify the general meeting of shareholders and the works council of any vacancy on the board at least two months before such vacancy must be filled, and (b) provide the general meeting of shareholders with a nominee for each vacancy. The works council would have the right to present to the supervisory board candidates for nomination for at least one-third of the vacancies, which the supervisory board can only reject on limited grounds and any objection must be approved by the Enterprise Chamber of the Amsterdam Court of Appeal (*Ondernemingskamer van het gerechtshof te Amsterdam,* the "Enterprise Chamber"). The general meeting of shareholders (with a two-thirds majority of the votes cast, representing at least one-third of the issued share capital) would be empowered to reject candidates proposed by the supervisory board for the vacant supervisory board seats (including any nominee proposed by the supervisory board on the works council's request).[56] Most importantly, the general meeting of shareholders by the same qualified majority would be able to dismiss the entire supervisory board[57] — but not any of its individual members[58] — with immediate effect. In that circumstance, the Enterprise Chamber would have to appoint a temporary supervisory board that would select and present new supervisory board candidates.

(ii) *Increased powers for the general meeting of shareholders.*[59] The general meeting of shareholders would have the right (a) to approve certain management board resolutions which affect the identity or the character of the NV or its business (*e.g.*, formation or termination of material joint ventures, transfer of all or substantially all of the NV's business, or the acquisition or disposition of an interest in another legal entity representing at least one-third of the net equity value of the NV),[60] and (b) to adopt the annual accounts. In addition, shareholders representing at least 1% of the issued share capital (instead of the current statutory threshold of 10%) or holding an interest in the NV with a market value in excess of (50 million would be entitled to put certain issues on the agenda of the general meeting of shareholders.

(iii) *Voting rights for holders of depositary receipts.* Holders of depositary receipts would be given the right to demand an exclusive (*privatieve)* power of attorney to exercise the voting rights associated with the underlying shares. The issuing foundation could refuse to provide or if provided could subsequently revoke such power of attorney only if

(a) a public offer for the underlying shares has been made, (b) the depositary receipt holder, acting alone or in concert with others, represents 25% or more of the NV's issued share capital, or (c) the issuing foundation believes that the holder of the depositary receipt would cast a vote that would seriously prejudice the best interests of the NV or the NV's business. The foundation could not refuse to provide a power of attorney and could not revoke one, however, if a majority of the foundation's board is comprised of current or former members of the NV's management or supervisory boards, employees of the NV and/or its group companies, and/or regular advisors of the NV.

b. Changes to anti-takeover measures

The use of anti-takeover measures has been the subject of discussion in the Netherlands for over 15 years. In 1989, the Association for the Securities Trade (*Vereniging voor de Effectenhandel*), a predecessor of Euronext, and the Listed Companies Association (*Vereniging van Effecten Uitgevende Ondernemingen*) reached agreement on the permissible use of anti-takeover measures (*i.e.*, Exhibit X) but agreed to commence more thorough discussions about their use. After many years of intense negotiation and lobbying, the Government in 1997 presented Parliament with the draft Act on Break-Through Measures (*Wetsvoorstel tot invoering van de mogelijkheid tot het treffen van bijzondere maatregelen door de ondernemingskamer over de zeggenschap in de naamloze vennootschap*).[61] Criticism of the draft Act and developments in the general corporate governance debate in the Netherlands led to a delay in its adoption. To date, the draft Act has not been adopted and its content remains the subject of debate.

Under the proposed break-through rule, a shareholder of an NV may request the Enterprise Chamber to remove certain anti-takeover measures if the shareholder:

(i) holds at least 70% of the NV's issued capital;[62]
(ii) notified the NV of its shareholding; and
(iii) has held such shares for 12 consecutive months.

In making the break-through request, the shareholder would be required to state its intentions concerning the NV, its proposed composition of the management and supervisory boards, and the measures it considers necessary to remove any relevant takeover defenses. The Enterprise Chamber would then have to appoint a panel of three experts, who must report on the shareholder's intentions and the consequences of revoking the anti-takeover measures. The Enterprise Chamber could refuse to grant relief or make any relief subject to additional conditions, such as requiring the requesting shareholder to launch a bid for all remaining outstanding shares.

The proposed break-through rule before the Parliament is broader in scope than the break-through rule proposed in the Winter Report, as further discussed below in our responses to Questions 12 and 13. It would allow, for example, the cancellation of shares, the annulment of board resolutions and resolutions of the general meeting of shareholders, and the dismissal of members of the management and supervisory boards. The principal difference, however, is the one-year waiting period in the Dutch proposal, which has been subject to fierce criticism. It would force a bidder/majority shareholder to maintain his investment for 12 months, thus giving the NV's management ample opportunity to frustrate the majority shareholder's attempt to obtain full control over the NV. More generally, as discussed in our response to Question 12, we believe that there are considerable problems associated with the introduction of a break-through rule, either as proposed by the Government or the Winter Report.

c. Introduction of a mandatory bid

There is currently no statutory obligation to launch a bid after acquiring a certain percentage of the issued securities of an NV. The Netherlands is, to our knowledge, the only Member State whose laws do not provide for a mandatory bid.[63] However, this may change in the near future. On January 30, 2002, the Minister of Finance published a consultation document regarding the introduction of a mandatory bid rule in the Netherlands and the relationship between such a rule and the break-through measures proposed in the draft Act on Break-Through Measures.[64]

4. Response to specific questions

7. What would you identify as the main obstacles to takeovers where a company from your jurisdiction is either bidder or target and the other company is from another EU jurisdiction?

In considering the main obstacles to takeovers in the Netherlands,[65] a useful distinction may be made between general obstacles under company law, securities laws and other government rules and regulations, and specific obstacles in the form of anti-takeover measures.

Obstacles under company and securities laws. The completion of the acquisition of shares in the capital of an NV for cash consideration requires — at a minimum — the completion of the following steps:[66]

(i) *Corporate approvals.* A distinction may be made between the acquisition of newly issued shares from an NV and the acquisition of previously issued shares from its shareholders. An acquisition of newly issued shares requires the approval of the NV's general meeting of shareholders (unless the power to issue shares has been delegated to the management or supervisory boards). In addition, approval of the management and supervisory boards may be important in case preference shares, priority shares, or depositary receipts for shares have been issued to special-purpose foundations, as these foundations tend to support the proposals of the management board.

(ii) *Offering memorandum.* Under the 1995 Act on the Supervision of Securities Trade (*Wet toezicht effectenverkeer 1995,* the "Securities Act"), the bidder must make available to the NV's shareholders an offering memorandum (*biedingsbericht)* in accordance with the 1995 Decree on the Supervision of Securities Trade *(Besluit toezicht effectenverkeer 1995,* the "Decree"). In addition, both the bidder and the NV have obligations to disclose certain information to the public.

(iii) *Trade union consultation.* Under the 2000 Merger Code for the protection of the interests of employees (*SER-besluit Fusiegedragsregels 2000 ter bescherming van de belangen van werknemers,* the "Merger Code"),[67] the NV's management board must inform relevant trade unions of any proposed takeover before it makes any public announcements.[68] In addition, the NV's management board must discuss the proposed merger and its consequences with the trade unions at a time when the trade unions' opinion can still have a substantial influence on the NV's decision whether to consummate the merger (in any event, before the bidder and the NV enter into any definitive agreement (in a friendly takeover) or before the bidder may announce any bid (in a hostile takeover)).[69] If the trade unions consider that the NV has violated the Merger Code, they may petition the Merger Code Adjudication Committee (*geschillencommissie*) established under the Merger Code.[70] The only remedy, however, that the Merger Code Adjudication Committee offers if it concludes that an NV has violated the Merger Code, is the publication of its findings.

(iv) *Works council consultation.* Under the Works Council Act (*Wet op de ondernemingsraden)*, the NV's management board must consult the works council and obtain its advice concerning any proposed takeover. The management board must consult the works council at a time when the opinion of the works council can still have a substantial influence on the NV's decision on the takeover (in any event, before the bidder and the NV enter into any definitive agreement). If the works council opposes the takeover, the NV may not proceed with the execution of any final decision on the takeover for a period of one month, during which time the works council may decide to petition the Enterprise Chamber. If the Enterprise Chamber finds that, taking into account all interests concerned, the NV could not reasonably have come to the decision it took, the Enterprise Chamber may, on request of the works council, order the NV to cancel its decision (in whole or in part) or to mitigate certain of the consequences resulting from the takeover. Such orders, however, may not interfere with the rights of any third party.

The above steps differ depending on whether the bidder opts to offer shares instead of cash[71] or opts for an assets deal[72] or a statutory merger.[73]

Regulatory obstacles. Regulatory obstacles include, among others:

(i) *Nationality and residency requirements.* As discussed in more detail in our response to Question 9, there are Dutch or EU nationality and residency requirements set forth in the statutes governing the shipping and aviation sectors, which affect acquisitions of control by non-EU persons over NVs with operations in these sectors.
(ii) *Antitrust approvals.* If the target and the bidder reach certain turnover thresholds, prior NMa approval is required. (For an extensive discussion of these thresholds, see the first Section of this Report.)
(iii) *Other approval requirements.* As discussed in more detail in our response to Question 9, there are governmental or regulatory approval requirements in the finance, insurance, and utilities sectors.

Specific anti-takeover measures. Anti-takeover measures that may be employed by NVs include, among others:

(i) voluntary adoption of the "large company" regime;
(ii) issuance of depositary receipts, often in combination with the X%-rule;
(iii) granting to a special-purpose foundation of a call option over preference shares;
(iv) issuance of priority shares, including golden shares, or shares that give special nomination rights for the appointment of members of the management and supervisory boards;
(v) quorum and supermajority requirements in the NV's Articles of Association;
(vi) "pyramid structures";[74]
(vii) seeking a "white knight";[75]
(viii) "crown jewel" lock-ups;[76]
(ix) "golden parachutes";[77]

(x) change of control clauses in important agreements (*e.g.*, financing documents) or issuance of "poison debt";[78] and
(xi) creation of a "Pacman" defense.[79]

While certain measures (such as the measures mentioned under (ii), (iii), (vi), (vii), and (xi)) prevent the bidder from acquiring a majority of the outstanding shares, other measures prevent the bidder from exercising effective control over the company (such as the measures mentioned under (i), (iv), and (v)). In addition, others aim at making an acquisition less attractive (see measures under (viii), (ix), and (x)).

In case of friendly takeovers, anti-takeover measures do not present a real obstacle for two reasons. First, during the pre-bid negotiation, the bidder and the NV typically agree to a standstill, which makes it unnecessary for the NV to invoke additional takeover defenses. Secondly, with the cooperation of the NV's management, any anti-takeover measures that were put in place before the takeover negotiations started can be removed (*e.g.*, any depositary receipts may be exchanged for the underlying shares; the Articles of Association may be amended to remove any X%-rule, the "large company" regime (if adopted voluntarily), or any special quorum, supermajority requirements, or special nomination rights).

The situation is different with respect to hostile takeovers, where the bidder lacks the support of the NV's management and/or supervisory boards. In those circumstances, it is practically impossible to overcome takeover defenses. As there has been no negotiated standstill, the NV can, and often will invoke takeover defenses. Sometimes, these *ad hoc* measures are difficult to overcome, in particular, if they involve third parties. In addition, even if the bidder were to obtain a majority of the outstanding shares or depositary receipts, it would often lack control over the NV. Without support of the management and/or supervisory boards, the bidder would not be able to remove the implemented takeover defenses that prevent it from exercising effective control.

All of the above applies equally to both Dutch and non-Dutch bidders.

Winter Report measures. The board neutrality rule and the break-through rule as proposed by the Winter Report, if adopted in their current form, would lead to some change in the Dutch corporate landscape, but they would not result in a complete ban on takeover defenses.

The board neutrality rule[80] would only affect the adoption of a limited number of takeover defenses, such as the search for a "white knight" and the "Pacman" defense. Certain authors are of the opinion that the pre-bid grant of a call option over preference shares would also be affected.[81] In contrast, the break-through rule proposed by the Winter Report would affect more takeover defenses, such as the voluntary adoption of the "large company" regime, the issuance of priority shares, and quorum and supermajority requirements in the NV's Articles of Association. The takeover defense of issuing depositary receipts, however, would, not be affected, which could limit the impact of the break-through rule for a significant number of NVs (since the voting rights attached to the underlying shares would continue to be exercised by the special-purpose foundation).[82]

The break-through rule as proposed by the draft Act on Break-Through Measures (discussed in detail in our response to Question 12) would affect more takeover defenses than the rule proposed in the Winter Report (such as the use of depositary receipts). However, under the draft Act it is not certain that the Enterprise Chamber will grant the bidder the requested break-through.

Nevertheless, the introduction of the board neutrality rule and the break-through rule (whether in the form proposed by the Winter Report or by the draft Act on Break-Through Measures) would not affect certain other defenses, such as "pyramid structures", "crown jewel" lock-ups, and change of control clauses. In addition, NVs could switch to more structural defenses, such as the engagement of core shareholders (*e.g.*, cross-shareholdings by friendly shareholders).

8. Do hostile takeovers by companies from other EU jurisdictions in fact take place in your country?

We are not aware of any case where an NV has been the subject of a successful hostile takeover by a Dutch or non-Dutch bidder. We are, however, aware of a number of hostile takeover attempts that have failed for a variety of reasons that include the barriers identified in the Introduction and our response to Question 7. In addition, it is likely that a number of contemplated hostile takeover attempts have simply never materialized due to the freedom permitted, and the anti-takeover measures available to, an NV's management to fend off a hostile bid.

9. To what extent are there any sectors (utilities, financial institutions) that in practice are further protected from hostile takeovers, or foreign takeovers in particular? Are there any policy statements or particular legal mechanisms that give effect to this protection, or is it a matter of informal mechanisms?

Although Dutch law in principle does not discriminate against non-Dutch investors, there are two statutory methods through which certain sectors could be protected from cross-border takeovers (whether friendly or hostile): (i) Dutch or EU nationality or residency requirements, and (ii) governmental or regulatory approval requirements.

Nationality and residency requirements. There are Dutch nationality and residency requirements set forth in the statutes governing the shipping[83] and aviation[84] sectors, which affect acquisitions of control by non-EU persons over NVs with operations in these sectors.

In addition, in the aviation sector, we believe that acquisitions of control by non-Dutch EU acquirors is also impeded, as a practical matter, because the bilateral aviation treaties — which have been entered into by the Netherlands with many non-European countries to provide landing slots for their respective domestic carriers — typically require that a carrier be controlled by Dutch nationals or the Dutch State in order to obtain the benefits provided by the treaties. As a result, a Dutch target carrier — or another EU target carrier since this issue applies equally to carriers located in other Member States — may lose critical landing slots upon being acquired by an entity controlled by nationals of another Member State.

Furthermore, in the defense sector, contractual change of control clauses incorporating Dutch residency requirements may act as a barrier to cross-border acquisitions of certain Dutch companies, a substantial part of whose business involves the supply of military goods and services to the Government. These clauses could enable the Government to terminate the relevant supply contract upon a non-Dutch party acquiring control over a Dutch supplier.

Approval requirements. There are governmental or regulatory approval requirements in the finance, insurance, and utilities sectors.

In the finance and insurance sectors, prior approval is required from the competent authority for the acquisition of a "qualified interest" (*gekwalificeerde deelneming)*, of 5% or 10%, in a credit institution,[85] investment firm,[86] stock exchange,[87] or insurance company.[88] Such approval can be refused only on a limited number of statutory grounds and is subject to judicial review.

In the electricity and gas sectors, prior approval is required from the Minister of Economic Affairs for a transfer of (i) shares in a licensed electricity or gas distributor or grid operator, or (ii) the title to the grid (*netwerk)*.[89] Under the relevant provisions, such approval may be withheld if the acquiror of the shares or the grid is not a Dutch local government (or an entity directly or indirectly controlled by a Dutch local government). The policy guidelines[90] relating to these provisions, further state that such approval will be withheld if, *inter alia*, title to the grid is not retained by, or transferred to, a Dutch local government.[91]

We have not identified any other Dutch laws, regulations or relevant policy statements that could shield NVs active in any particular sector of the Dutch economy from takeovers by non-Dutch acquirors. We note, however, that the Dutch State has various controlling shareholdings in key Dutch listed and non-listed companies, including in the telecommunication (KPN N.V.), post (TPG N.V.), and aviation sectors (KLM N.V. and N.V.

Luchthaven Schiphol, the owner and operator of the Amsterdam airport). The Articles of Association of such companies, under normal company law rules, often grant the Dutch State specific voting rights enabling it to act to protect the public interest.

Although the Government has recently indicated that it intends to manage each of its various shareholdings solely in its capacity as a shareholder (instead of as a government) with the interests of the public perceived to be served by such NVs being safeguarded in other ways (through legislation),[92] this new stance would not prevent the Government, for example, from deciding not to tender its shares to a non-Dutch bidder solely for political concerns. As a result, depending on the circumstances and the parties involved at the time of any such bid, proposed takeovers of these companies by non-Dutch bidders may be more difficult to accomplish.

10. What are the company law techniques of completing a takeover or merger that are used in practice where one of the companies is from another EU jurisdiction? Please give particular attention to how this would differ from the usual completion of a takeover or merger where both companies are from your jurisdiction. It would be useful if you could add a comment about the consequences on the techniques used of the taxation regime and of any differential tax treatment of takeovers or mergers where one party is from another EU jurisdiction.

Generally, there are three methods of acquiring an NV's business: (i) acquiring the shares of the NV (*aandelenfusie*), (ii) a statutory merger of the acquiror and the NV (*juridische fusie*), and (iii) acquiring the assets and assuming the liabilities of the NV (*bedrijfsfusie*).

Share acquisitions. The method most commonly used to acquire an NV is the acquisition (directly or through an affiliate or special-purpose vehicle) of the shares of the NV through a public offer or a privately negotiated sale. The Securities Act allows three types of public offers: (i) offers to acquire all issued shares of the target at a fixed price or exchange ratio and open to all holders of the target's shares (a "firm offer" (*vast bod*)); (ii) offers to acquire up to 30% of the issued shares of the target and open, on a pro rata basis, to all holders of the target's shares (a "partial offer" (*partieel bod*)); and (iii) offers to acquire up to 30% of the issued shares of the target and inviting all holders of the target's shares to tender such shares, on a pro rata basis, to the bidder at a price to be determined by each individual holder (a "tender offer" (*tenderbod*)). Private share acquisitions typically follow the pattern of such acquisitions in other EU jurisdictions, *i.e.*, the acquiror acquires from the selling shareholder(s) all or a majority of the shares in the NV or the NV's key subsidiaries, in exchange for cash and/or shares of the acquiror.

Share acquisitions do not give an advantage to Dutch acquirors over non-Dutch acquirors.

Statutory mergers. Although a statutory merger is currently used more in a corporate restructuring than an M&A-context, we consider it another key-method of acquiring an NV and expect to see an increasing number of statutory mergers in the friendly takeover-context in the years to come. The merger provisions in Part 7 of Book 2 of the Dutch Civil Code are based on the Third Company Law Directive and permit "direct" and "forward triangular" *(driehoeksfusie)* mergers. In a "direct" merger, one legal entity (the disappearing entity) merges into another legal entity (the surviving entity). In a "forward triangular" merger, one legal entity (the disappearing entity) merges into a subsidiary or a special-purpose vehicle of the acquiror, with the shareholders of the disappearing entity acquiring, by operation of law, shares in the acquiror. Dutch company law does not permit "direct" or "forward triangular" mergers involving non-Dutch legal entities.[93] (The proposed Tenth Company Law Directive would have permitted EU cross-border mergers but has not been adopted.[94])

The inability of using a statutory merger may disadvantage non-Dutch acquirors in various ways.

First, a Dutch acquiror, by acquiring a sufficient percentage of the NV's shares (possibly even less than 50%), may be able to control the general meeting of shareholders of the target NV, allowing it to effect a "direct" or "forward triangular" merger and a "freeze-out" of the remaining shareholders of the target (unless the NV's Articles of Association contain specific quorum and majority requirements). In contrast, a non-Dutch acquiror, in a share acquisition, would not be able to consolidate an NV's business or effect such a "freeze-out" unless it managed to acquire at least 95% of the shares of the target, allowing it to initiate buy-out proceedings (discussed below in our response to Question 14).

Secondly, a statutory merger may create certain important tax benefits (that a Dutch acquiror could take advantage of) if the acquisition is financed in whole or in part by debt. For example, a "forward triangular" merger would allow the Dutch acquiror to create a fiscal unity (*fiscale eenheid*)[95] with the merged subsidiary enabling it to set-off losses of the acquiror (taking into account the interest payments on the debt) against profits of the merged subsidiary.

Asset acquisitions. This method is commonly used when an acquiror does not desire to assume all of the target's liabilities or when the acquiror wishes to benefit from a stepped-up tax basis. We note that Dutch law does not recognize the concept of universal succession of a business (such as, for instance, the *fonds de commerce* under French law and the *azienda* under Italian law), so the assets and liabilities being acquired must each be transferred separately to the acquiror in accordance with the appropriate method of transfer.

Asset acquisitions do not give an advantage to Dutch acquirors over non-Dutch acquirors.

11. A duty on listed companies to disclose capital and control structures is proposed in Issues Relating to Takeover Bids, the First Report of the High Level Group of Company Law Experts. Would this require amendments to the legislation in your country? How would these amendments be implemented (in company law, securities law, stock exchange regulations, etc.)?

Current disclosure obligations under Dutch law reveal to a large extent the ownership and control structures of NVs. It may, however, be time-consuming[96] to obtain such information, as it is disseminated through various sources, and sources may not always be up-to-date.[97]

Disclosure obligations under Dutch law on NVs, their board members, and their shareholders are as follows:[98]

(i) The 1996 Trade Register Act (*Handelsregisterwet 1996)*, the 1996 Trade Register Rules (*Handelsregisterbesluit 1995)*, and Book 2 of the Dutch Civil Code[99] require the members of the management board of an NV to file the following information with the Trade Register (*Handelsregister)* at the relevant Chamber of Commerce (*Kamer van Koophandel)*: (a) the number of authorized, issued, and paid-up shares; (b) the different classes of shares, if any; (c) the identity of the sole shareholder of the NV, if applicable; (d) the personal data of all management and supervisory board members and, with respect to members of the management board, whether they are authorized to represent the NV solely or jointly; (e) the number of employees employed by the NV; (f) the NV's deed of incorporation, including its Articles of Association[100] and any subsequent amendments; and (g) the NV's annual report[101] and annual accounts, together with certain additional data, such as an auditors' letter and a list of the persons authorized to exercise particular control rights over the NV under the NV's Articles of Association. All the information filed with the Trade Register is available to the public.

(ii) The Euronext Listing and Issuing Rules subject NVs to a prospectus obligation upon the offering of shares. The prospectus is made available to the public, free of charge, by the NV, the paying agent, or Euronext, and contains detailed information on the company's capital structure (including information on convertible securities) and the company's control structure. Dutch residents may consult prospectuses through Euronext's website during and after completion of the share issue. In addition, Euronext rules and regulations require NV's to regularly update previously disclosed information in the press. This includes the obligation to publish changes in the structure of the company's capital, amendments to the rights attached to different classes of shares, and any fact or circumstance that may have a significant influence on the price of the listed securities.

(iii) The 1996 Act on the Disclosure of Major Holdings requires shareholders to disclose the acquisition or disposition of certain securities meeting certain size thresholds to the NV and to the Netherlands Authority for the Financial Markets (*Autoriteit Financiële Markten,* the "Financial Markets Authority"), the competent authority under this Act and the Securities Act.[102] In addition, members of the management and supervisory boards must report trades in securities of the NV (or its affiliates) to the Financial Markets Authority. The information is published in a register that is accessible on-line.[103]

Given these existing disclosure obligations under Dutch law, the disclosure obligations proposed by the Winter Report,[104] if adopted in their current form, would require only minor amendments to Dutch legislation, *i.e.,* amendments obligating the disclosure of (i) "pyramid structures" and circular and cross-shareholdings, (ii) the institution of Employee Share Ownership Plan ("ESOPs") and the control thereof,[105] and (iii) change of control provisions in key agreements. The Winter Report's recommendation that an NV's information be disclosed in a combined and coherent way would, however, require more substantial amendments.

These amendments could be implemented in company law, securities laws, and/or the Euronext Listing and Issuing Rules. We believe that any changes to the content of disclosures and any provisions mandating the combined and coherent disclosure of information would best be placed in the securities laws, in particular the 1996 Act on the Disclosure of Major Holdings. Reference could be made to the existing disclosure mechanism under this Act. In addition, the Financial Markets Authority, seems best equipped to monitor compliance with the disclosure obligations.

Finally, we note that the Winter Report's specific recommendations on disclosure requirements were subsequently incorporated in an independently prepared consultation paper circulated on May 8, 2002 by the Commission's Directorate General for the Internal Market, which paper outlines concrete proposals for broad disclosure obligations for listed companies.[106] Specifically, these proposals would:

(i) increase the frequency of financial reporting (to at least four times a year) and provide that a listed company's annual report be published publicly within three months of the end of each financial year;[107]

(ii) broaden the scope of the information to be published by listed companies under continuing disclosure obligations;[108] and

(iii) approve additional ways in which information may be disseminated.[109]

As the disclosure obligations proposed in the consultation paper are considerably wider in scope than those recommended by the Winter Report, if such obligations were adopted at EU level or in the Netherlands, they would result in more substantial legislative amendments than those outlined above.[110]

12. A so-called break-through rule after takeover bids is another of the proposals in Issues Relating to Takeover Bids, the First Report of the High Level Group of Company Law Experts. Would this require amendments in the legislation in your country? How would these amendments be implemented (in company law, securities law, stock exchange regulations, etc.)?

In the absence of a Dutch rule on break-through measures, the adoption of the break-through rule, as proposed by the Winter Report, would require amendments to Dutch law. These amendments would likely be incorporated in Dutch company law (Book 2 of the Dutch Civil Code).

If the draft Act on Break-Through Measures (see Introduction) were to be adopted by Parliament, however, Dutch law — which allows substantial asymmetry in voting rights — would differ in the following respects from the break-through rule as proposed by the Winter Report:[111]

(i) *Period.* The draft Act on Break-Through Measures only relates to the situation post-closing, after the bidder/majority shareholder has acquired at least 70% of the capital of the target, whereas the Winter Report also proposes a board-neutrality rule for the pre-closing period. In the pre-closing period, *i.e.*, the period before the acquisition of a majority stake, the bidder has little protection under Dutch law against takeover defenses invoked by the target NV, although the lack of a board neutrality rule is to some extent mitigated by the method of calculating compliance with the 70% threshold. Under the draft Act on Break-Through Measures, any shares which the NV issued after it received notice from the bidder/majority shareholder that it acquired 70% of the NV's capital are excluded, as are any preference shares or other shares primarily issued to protect the NV, whenever such shares were issued.

(ii) *Timing.* The draft Act on Break-Through Measures only allows a break-through after the expiration of a one-year waiting period following satisfaction of the 70% threshold. Under the Winter Report, however, a successful bidder may immediately upon the acquisition of the threshold percentage of risk-bearing capital invoke a break-through. The one year waiting period — a result of a compromise between the Association for the Securities Trade and the Listed Companies Association — has been fiercely criticized, as it provides the NV's management board with ample opportunity and time to frustrate the goal of the bidder/majority shareholder, for example, by seeking a "white knight", selling "crown jewels", or installing "golden parachutes".

(iii) *Procedure.* Under the draft Act on Break-Through Measures, the bidder/majority shareholder must file a petition with the Enterprise Chamber stating its intentions concerning the NV, its proposed composition of the management and supervisory boards, and the measures it considers necessary to remove any relevant anti-takeover measures.[112] The Enterprise Chamber then appoints a panel of three experts, who report on that shareholder's intentions and the consequences of revoking the takeover defenses. The Enterprise Chamber may refuse measures of the first category[113] (*i.e.,* measures aimed at giving the petitioner influence on the composition of management and supervisory boards through its vote in the general meeting of shareholders) if the NV proves that it is likely that the petitioner's intentions fundamentally violate the NV's interests or that it could be reasonably expected that the petitioner would not act in accordance with general principles of reasonableness and fairness. Such intentions and expectations are presumed to exist if the petitioner:

(a) has not fulfilled obligations to disclose its shareholding;
(b) has seriously violated public offer rules;
(c) has, through its conduct, seriously violated the interests of the NV;
(d) has, without economic necessity, terminated or endangered the existence of other enterprises under its influence; or
(e) has not tried sufficiently hard to reach agreement with the NV's management.

Besides these factors being vague and of potentially wide application, it is difficult to see the reason for the link between these factors and the refusal of relief in all cases. Nevertheless, the scope to make such presumptions renders the outcome of any court proceedings less certain.

Under the Winter Report, by contrast, a bidder who has reached the required threshold, has the right to convene a general meeting of shareholders on short notice, in which he has the right to exercise voting rights in proportion to his holding of risk-bearing capital. The ability to cause any takeover measures to be removed is not dependent upon any judicial approval of the bidder's future intentions or past conduct.

(iv) *Scope.* The measures proposed by the draft Act on Break-Through Measures are broader in scope than those proposed in the Winter Report. The Winter Report limits break-through measures to amendments to the NV's Articles of Association. Under the draft Act, however, the Enterprise Chamber may not only make amendments to the NV's Articles of Association but may also order a special-purpose foundation that has issued depositary receipts to exchange them fully for the underlying shares (overriding any provisions to the contrary), cancel preference and priority shares, and annul any board or shareholder resolutions.

As a result, even if the draft Act on Break-Through Measures were to be enacted prior to the adoption of the break-through rule proposed by the Winter Report, amendments to Dutch law would still be necessary to implement those recommendations fully. Since the draft Act is proposed to be included in Part 8 of Book 2 of the Dutch Civil Code concerning Dispute Regulation and the Right of Inquiry (*Geschillenregeling en het recht van enquête*), it is likely that the Winter Report recommendations, whether implemented before or after enacting the draft Act, would be included in that same Part.

13. In your view, would these two new rules as proposed have any material impact on the existing barriers to takeovers in your country (or in others as seen from your point of view)? It would be helpful if you could demonstrate the impact, or lack of it, by going through one or more recent takeover bids that failed in your country (or in some other member state, by a company from your country).

The response to this Question differs for the proposed additional disclosure obligations concerning capital and control structures, and the proposed break-through rule. In our view, the proposed additional disclosure obligations are unlikely to have a material impact on cross-border acquisitions of NVs. While such obligations would facilitate the collection of information on capital and control structures, such information is already largely available under current rules.

On the other hand, the introduction of a break-through rule — in particular, in combination with a board neutrality rule, as proposed in the Winter Report — may be expected to encourage hostile takeover bids. At this stage, it is unclear whether a break-through rule will be included in a new proposal for the Thirteenth Company Law Directive on takeover bids. Moreover, it may be questioned whether such rules would achieve their stated objective of leveling the playing field for takeovers within Europe. The following considerations suggest that the proposals might well produce market distortions and other unintended effects.

(i) *Selectivity.* The proposed break-through rule overrides certain voting asymmetries and other takeover obstacles contained in the target's Articles of Association as well as certain resolutions of the board and the general meeting of shareholders. It does not, however, remove (and may be incapable of setting aside) a series of mechanisms with equivalent effect (*e.g.*, "pyramid structures", voting agreements among incumbent shareholders, or control restrictions inherent in protective corporate governance structures provided by law, such as the "large company" regime).

(ii) *No level playing field within Europe.* The resulting selectivity is likely to play out differently among Member States depending on prevailing mechanisms rooted in different corporate and share ownership traditions. In other words, the proposed break-through rule is too selective to achieve a level playing field. It may produce new distortions. There is a risk that it would cause a shift from takeover defenses within its scope to defenses outside of its scope. The latter include mechanisms that are arguably more harmful to market efficiency and transparency (*e.g.*, "pyramid structures").[114]

(iii) *No level playing field with the United States.* Although outside the scope of this report, the proposed break-through rule (as well as the proposed proportionality rule) may widen rather than narrow the gap between the European and U.S. "markets for corporate control", which goes against the sense of increased globalization of the economy. The question is whether, in a longer-term perspective, it is strategically wise to turn Europe into a substantially more open takeover environment than the United States.

(iv) *Other harmful collateral effects.* The break-through rule proposed by the Winter Report may produce other undesirable side effects and market distortions:

(a) Especially when coupled with the proposed board neutrality rule, they would facilitate unfriendly takeover bids and reduce the incentive for negotiated transactions that, by and large, are more likely to produce more balanced solutions taking into account the interests of all stakeholders. There is a significant risk that corporate raids would concentrate on companies that have share ownership structures with asymmetrical voting rights, as such raids may be attracted by the perceived "hidden value" purportedly suppressed by those voting structures.

(b) More generally, those provisions, especially in combination with the proposed board neutrality rule, would effectively place a "for sale" sign on EU-listed companies and, again, particularly those with asymmetrical voting structures. It is important to recognize the very real costs and inefficiencies in managing a company if it is continuously thought of as being for sale.

(c) The proposed break-through rule could cause increased difficulties for EU companies in raising funds as it would become harder to persuade investors to accept shares with preferential dividend and voting rights in compensation for the increased risk. More generally, companies having multiple classes of shares may face increased equity pricing uncertainties in the market.

The recent Gucci and Rodamco cases illustrate that the proposed board neutrality and break-through rules in their current form would not have a significant impact on takeovers in the Netherlands if the mandatory bid rule is not introduced simultaneously. Neither Gucci N.V. ("Gucci") nor Rodamco North America N.V. ("Rodamco") had any takeover defenses in place. In the case of Gucci, LVMH acquired a significant minority stake in Gucci (34% of the shares) and announced that, although it did not intend to launch a public bid for all remaining outstanding shares, it wanted to appoint a member to Gucci's supervisory board. As the acquired significant minority stake effectively enabled LVMH to control Gucci's general meeting of shareholders, the Gucci board felt compelled to invoke two takeover defenses: first the implementation of an ESOP, and, secondly, a transaction with a "white knight".

In the case of Rodamco, Westfield acquired 24% of Rodamco's outstanding shares from the Dutch pension fund ABP (ABP kept approximately 6% of Rodamco's shares). Following its acquisition of this significant minority stake, Westfield requested that Rodamco's management board change its strategy and call a general meeting of shareholders in which the shareholders could vote on the dismissal of the members of the management and supervisory boards and on the appointment of Westfield's candidates. Prior to its request, Westfield had indicated to Rodamco that it was not planning to make a public bid for all outstanding Rodamco shares. Since Westfield (together with ABP) effectively controlled the general meeting of shareholders, the Rodamco board decided to issue shares, and grant an option to acquire additional shares, to a special-purpose foundation as takeover defenses.

If these cases had occurred following the introduction of the proposed board neutrality and break-through rules, the board neutrality rule would not have been triggered in either case, as LVMH and Westfield each refused to make a public bid for all outstanding shares, although each effectively controlled the general meeting of shareholders. This refusal to make a public bid would have been prevented had there been a mandatory bid rule with sufficiently low thresholds, for example, for bidders that alone or acting in concert hold 30% of the outstanding shares. Furthermore, through introduction of the board neutrality and break-through rules, Gucci and Rodamco would have been prevented from invoking post-bid takeover defenses, and pre-bid takeover defenses could have been removed.

14. Below are a number of questions which may assist in a comparative analysis.

a. What are the main features of the relevant domestic takeover legislation constituting the company law and financial market regime, and who enforces it (independent regulators, regulatory bodies with appeal to ministry, stock exchange)? What is the extent of intervention by the takeover regulator(s) — to what extent does the regulator have wide or general discretion to block and play a protectionist role (for example, in its capacity as approver of the offer terms/documentation)?

Domestic takeover legislation. There are two sets of rules that are relevant to takeovers in the Netherlands, both of which entered into force on September 5, 2001.

First, the Securities Act — and its implementing rules in the Decree — apply to public offers by Dutch and non-Dutch bidders for voting securities that are listed on a recognized stock exchange in the Netherlands (*i.e.*, Euronext) or that are "regularly traded in the Netherlands" (*i.e.*, in the over-the-counter market or on an electronic trading platform) or for depositary receipts of, or other securities convertible into, voting securities.

Secondly, there is a body of "soft law" rules contained in the Merger Code. In the event of an offer to acquire all issued securities of the target where (i) the bidder holds 50% or less of the securities of the target, (ii) the bidder or the target has at least 50 employees in the Netherlands, and (iii) the transaction would have a significant impact in the Netherlands, the bidder and the target are required to consult the relevant trade unions, if any, before reaching any agreement (if the bid is friendly) or launch of the bid (if the bid is hostile).[115]

Role of "supervisors". There are two bodies that play a role in the enforcement of the above-identified sets of rules: the Financial Markets Authority and the Merger Code Adjudication Committee.

The Financial Markets Authority is an independent legal body, responsible for supervision of the Securities Act with wide investigatory and enforcement powers. The Financial Markets Authority does not approve the terms and conditions of any bid but has a ten day statutory period to review the offering memorandum describing the terms of a bid and may require the inclusion of additional information. In addition, the Financial Markets Authority has the general power to issue instructions aimed at securing the adequate functioning of the securities markets and the protection of investors. Even though the Financial Markets Authority could, in theory, use these powers to delay or obstruct a bid, its discretion is limited and in most cases, subject to judicial review.[116] Moreover, it is our impression that, in the limited period of time during which the Financial Markets Authority has held these powers (since September 5, 2001), it has exercised its powers in an objective and non-discriminatory manner and has not favored or disfavored non-Dutch bidders.

The Merger Code Adjudication Committee, a special dispute resolution committee established by the Social and Economic Council, is empowered to hear complaints of alleged infringements of the Merger Code that are brought by trade unions or other parties involved in a proposed merger. Although the only possible sanction of the Merger Code Adjudication Committee is publication of its findings, bidders typically comply with the requirements of the Merger Code.[117]

b. Are there restrictions on a board taking action to frustrate a bid that has been made? When do the relevant restrictions start to apply — earlier than a formal announcement/filing of a bid? To what extent can shareholders approve the taking of frustrating action in advance of any bid?

An NV is, in principle, free to take any measures to prevent an unwelcome shareholder securing a dominant or substantial degree of control over the NV. When faced with a bid, the management board and supervisory board are required to consider the interests of all stakeholders in the NV. They do not owe an overriding fiduciary duty to shareholders.

Each of the four most common anti-takeover devices (*i.e.*, (i) the issuance of depositary receipts, (ii) the issuance of preference shares, (iii) the issuance of priority shares, and (iv) the voluntary adoption of the "large company" regime) must be authorized by the general meeting of shareholders of the NV at some stage, either through the Articles of Association of the NV or, in the case of priority of preference shares, through the adoption of a resolution authorizing the management board to issue such shares. All four measures may be implemented prior to the launch of a bid. In the case of preference shares, the issuance may be structured so that the actual issuance of the shares is outside the control of the NV (*i.e.*, through the grant of a call option over the shares to a special-purpose foundation).

The most common anti-takeover defense launched in light of a hostile bid is the issuance of, or the threat of issuing, preference shares. In light of the Gucci and Rodamco cases — although these cases have to be seen in their particular factual context — it can be said that the issuance of preference shares to a foundation is permitted provided that (i) the issuance is aimed at temporarily "neutralizing" the increasing influence of the bidder who, the management board believes, may not act in the best interests of the company (including, the interests of the other shareholders), (ii) is at costs that are not too burdensome to (indirectly, the shareholders of) the NV, (iii) while the bidder is offered a fair opportunity to present its plans concerning the target to the target's shareholders, and (iv) the management board of the target is willing and in fact engages in talks with the bidder.

In addition, or as an alternative to issuing preference shares, the management board may decide to seek a "white knight" or to convince the NV's shareholders that the bidder's offer is insufficient. Such actions may be combined with an undertaking on the part of the management board to distribute any excess cash to shareholders, to restructure the NV, or to alter the NV's strategic direction (including commitments to make particular divestitures or acquisitions).

c. Are there restrictions on the type of consideration that can be offered in a bid, for example securities only if these are listed in the target country's home state or the EU?

Except in the case of a "tender offer", where the consideration offered must be in cash, a bidder may offer shareholders cash or securities or a combination of both. There is no requirement that any securities offered be listed securities.

d. Are there effective compulsory acquisition procedures regarding a small non-accepting minority? Can a bidder make its offer conditional on achieving the number of shares required so it can operate a squeeze out?

There are two effective methods to "freeze out" minority shareholders:

Buy-out procedure. A shareholder who holds at least 95% of the issued capital of an NV may initiate a buy-out procedure before the Enterprise Chamber requiring all other shareholders to transfer their shares to such shareholder at a price which is set by the Enterprise Chamber. The procedure typically takes between six to 12 months, but sometimes even longer if, for instance, one of the parties appeals the decision of the Enterprise Chamber to the Dutch Supreme Court (*Hoge Raad*). The Winter Report takes the view that the price offered in a takeover bid should be presumed to be a fair price if the bid has been accepted by shareholders holding 90% or more of the share capital with respect to which the bid has been made. If such a presumption were incorporated into Dutch company law, we believe that it would speed-up a buy-out procedure significantly.

Freeze-out merger. A shareholder who holds a sufficient number of shares, to be able to cause an amendment to the Articles of Association of the NV, may, unless the Articles of Association require a particular qualified majority vote in the case of a proposed merger, cause the target to

merge into the bidder, provided that the bidder (which may be a special-purpose vehicle) is also a Dutch legal entity — see also our discussion of "forward triangular" mergers in our response to Question 10. A freeze-out merger can be effected within six weeks.
In both cases, a bid can be made conditional upon the number of tendered shares being sufficient to commence a buy-out procedure or to cause the target to enter into a freeze-out merger.

e. Is there a principle of board neutrality? Can a target board align itself with a particular bidder or agree to measures such as exclusivity arrangements to protect a particular deal?

There is no board neutrality rule. Under Dutch company law, the management and supervisory boards are each under an obligation to act in the best interests of the NV, including the interests of all stakeholders (including employees, shareholders, and creditors), implying that each board should consider in good faith any competing bid or alternative proposal concerning the NV (such as any proposals aimed at keeping the company independent). Although entering into a lock-up or break-up fee arrangement that permanently forecloses a third-party bid or alternative proposal might be inconsistent with this duty, the propriety of the actions of the management and supervisory boards must be assessed in context. In certain circumstances, we believe that foreclosing other bids or proposals through the adoption of such measures may be justified (for example, if the NV simply has no time left to shop the NV around or to consider alternative proposals).

f. Can a target board hand over information to a potential bidder?

In a friendly bid, it is common practice for a bidder to be given the opportunity to perform a limited due diligence investigation. This investigation is sometimes followed by a more extensive due diligence inquiry after the public announcement of a bid. A target would normally require a bidder to enter into a confidentiality agreement (including a standstill provision) before the target shared any confidential information with the bidder. Both the target and the bidder would have to observe the strict Dutch insider trading laws which prohibit both the disclosure of, and trading on, inside information. In practice, parties often consult the Financial Markets Authority and the public prosecutor to seek confirmation that these prohibitions do not apply to their specific situation.

g. Are structures permitted which concentrate control rights in the hands of minority shareholders? Are structures permitted which place

limitations/restrictions on voting rights, for example caps on voting rights above a certain threshold?

Dutch company law does not permit non-voting shares or multiple-voting shares.[118] As discussed in the Introduction, however, Dutch company law does allow a number of structures in which key control rights are concentrated in the hands of minority shareholders (*e.g.*, through the issuance of priority shares) or a special-purpose foundation (*e.g.*, through the issuance of depositary receipts or preference shares).

In addition, there are a number of permitted corporate structures in which voting rights are not proportional to the shareholders' economic investments. For instance, Dutch company law permits an NV to issue two classes of shares with substantially different nominal values but identical economic rights and obligations. The voting rights are, subject to some limited exceptions, always proportional to the nominal value of the shares. Consequently, by issuing two classes of shares at the same price but with one class of shares with a high nominal value (such as EUR 1,000) and the other class of shares with a low nominal value (such as EUR 0.01), control can be exercised by a party holding a small number of the shares with the high nominal value.

h. Can restrictions be placed on the transferability of shares either by the issuer (in Articles of Association or by other means) or by arrangements between shareholders? Can a board delay registering transfers of shares?

Transfer restrictions (*blokkeringsregelingen*) which require the prior approval of, for example, an NV's management board, can only be placed on non-listed registered shares (as opposed to bearer shares), although no transfer restriction may make a proposed transfer impossible or unduly burdensome. Shareholders are free to enter into an agreement preventing one or more shareholders tendering their shares to another shareholder, but the existence of such an agreement would not void a transfer to a third party if the transferee had no knowledge of the shareholders' agreement. In addition, we do not believe that the provisions of such arrangements would be unenforceable, as is the case in Italy,[119] in light of an offer to acquire all issued (voting) securities of a target.

A transfer cannot be delayed by the NV's management board as there is no legal requirement that a transfer be registered by the board in order for it to become effective.

i. What contractual barriers (including shareholder agreements) to takeover bids are in use in public companies (e.g., "golden parachutes", change of control provisions triggering default of loan agreements, or wind-

ing up or change of control of joint ventures)? What are the prospects of review by courts on the basis of contract or company law and by regulators on the basis of securities laws or stock exchange regulations?

There are a large number of "contractual barriers" which might be triggered upon the launch of a bid or upon a change of control, including "golden parachutes" for key personnel (generally considered to be valid so long as the amounts to be paid out are not excessive and there are no "single triggering" events), change of control clauses in various contracts (including loan agreements, joint venture agreements, leases or any other key contracts), and break-up fee arrangements (generally considered to be valid provided that the arrangement has the purpose of compensating the non-terminating party for its reasonable costs). In general, management boards of NVs have considerable discretion to adopt such "contractual barriers" and the limited case law and publications from legal commentators suggest that Dutch courts would only step in to remove a "barrier" (on the basis that its adoption constituted corporate mismanagement or was *ultra vires*) if there had been no commercial justification for its erection and it had been erected solely to deter a third party from launching a bid or presenting an alternative proposal by destroying the target's value (*e.g.*, through "crown jewel" arrangements or by having the target run up significant unnecessary costs).

j. Are there current proposals to change the legislation relating to takeovers?

As discussed in the Introduction and in our response to the Questions, various legislative proposals are pending or expected in the area of takeovers and corporate governance:

(i) the Government launched a public consultation on January 30, 2002, concerning the introduction of a mandatory bid;
(ii) the Government set up at the beginning of 2002 a committee consisting of international experts to study possible ways to implement an effective proxy-solicitation system;
(iii) the current public offer rules, contained in the Decree, are being reviewed and a draft Decree amending the current rules is expected to be published in 2003;
(iv) a proposal is pending to reform the "large company" regime;
(v) a proposal is pending to grant voting rights to holders of depositary receipts and to introduce a requirement that shareholders vote on major corporate resolutions that would affect the nature of an NV's business; and

(vi) a proposal is pending concerning the removal of anti-takeover measures.

C. CONCLUSION

Dutch merger control rules do not, in our view, present serious obstacles to cross-border transactions that do not have appreciable adverse competitive effects. Dutch merger control is administered competently and without bias. As always, there is room for improvement – mainly on procedural issues. More fundamentally, the burdens associated with multi-jurisdictional filings could be further alleviated through the harmonization of Member States' notification thresholds, information requirements, and substantive review standards.

Dutch company law presents a greater number of issues relevant to cross-border takeovers. The "large company" regime under Dutch company law makes an NV a less attractive target and may, therefore, dissuade takeovers. Governmental or regulatory approvals for takeovers are required in a number of industry sectors, including finance, insurance, and utilities. Dutch or EU nationality and residency requirements apply in the shipping and aviation sectors. Finally, the Dutch State maintains controlling shareholdings in key Dutch listed and non-listed companies in the telecommunications, postal, and aviation sectors. With some possible exceptions, however, these arrangements would appear to meet the criteria developed by the European Court of Justice in the application of the EC Treaty's provisions on the freedom of establishment and the free movement of capital.

Finally, Dutch legal and business culture have traditionally been tolerant of the use of a variety of anti-takeover measures. Specific anti-takeover measures employed by Dutch NVs are practically impossible to overcome. Recent political debate and case law, however, show that this tolerance is fading as the Netherlands shifts from a consensus-driven "stakeholder model" to a more Anglo-American-style "shareholder model". This may be expected to reduce some of the existing obstacles to domestic and cross-border acquisitions of NVs — and may foreshadow greater changes to the regulation of M&A activity in the Netherlands.

NOTES

[1] Cleary, Gottlieb, Steen & Hamilton, Brussels. The authors are enormously indebted to their colleagues Peter Werdmuller, Jan Meyers, Annet van Hooft, Adriaan Koch, Rogier Groen, Robert O'Donoghue, Thomas Cox, Chris Cook, and Harlan Cohen. The authors bear sole responsibility for any errors.

[2] *See* the official Dutch response to the Green Paper by the Minister of Economic Affairs (*Minister van Economische Zaken*) in a letter to Commissioner Monti, pp. 1-2.

[3] *Ibid.*.

[4] *Ibid.*.

[5] *See Vendex/KBB*, Case IV/1060. The case involved a significant proposed concentration related to a number of markets within the non-food retail sector in the Netherlands.

[6] *See* E.H. Pijnacker Hordijk, *Towards the tenth anniversary of the EC merger regulation; and interim report*, SEW 4, April 1999, pp. 125-127; *Also*, S.E.M. Hooijman, *Verslag van de de vergadering van de Nederlandse Vereniging voor Europees Recht, 10 jaar fusiecontrole in de Europese Gemeenschap*, May 28, 1999.

[7] *See* the official Dutch response to the Green Paper by the Minister of Economic Affairs in a letter to Commissioner Monti, p. 3.

[8] *Ibid.*

[9] *See* P.M.A.L. Plompen, *Samenwerking van de D-G NMa met andere mededingingsautoriteiten*, Markt en Mededinging 1998, nr. 2, pp. 49-54.

[10] *See* S. Plas, Actualiteiten Mededingingsrecht 2002, p. 84; NMa's website; and NMa's 2001 Annual Report, p. 13.

[11] The information exchanged for this purpose is mainly non-confidential information. Exchange of confidential information will only occur where it is possible under the relevant national legislation, and if not, only with a confidentiality waiver by the parties involved.

[12] *See Promatech-Sulzer Textil*, Case COMP/M.2698; *GEES-Unison*, Case COMP/M.2738.

[13] *See* Article 41(2) of the Competition Act.

[14] John Vickers, *International Mergers: The View From A National Authority*, speech at 28th Annual Conference on International Antitrust Law and Policy, Fordham University School of Law, New York, October 25, 2001.

[15] Case IV/M.1524.

[16] *FTC v. H.J. Heinz & Co.*, D.C. Circuit Docket No. 00-5362 (decided April 27, 2001); *see also* P.J. Slot, *Over Herfindahl-Hirschman-Index en Efficiency*, Markt en Mededinging 2001, nr. 4, pp. 127-128.

[17] *See Nordic Satellite Distribution*, Case IV/M.490, ¶ 164.

[18] *See* Section 4.134.

[19] *See* the official Dutch response to the Green Paper by the Minister of Economic Affairs in a letter to Commissioner Monti, p. 4.

[20] U.S. Department of Justice and Federal Trade Commission, Horizontal Merger Guidelines, 4 Trade Reg. Rep. (CCH), ¶¶ 13,104 (1992) (with April 8, 1997 revision to § 4).

[21] *See, e.g.*, Simon Baker and Lawrence Wu, *Applying the Market Definition Guidelines of the European Commission* 1998 E.C.L.R. 273.

[22] The EU and the United States reached opposing conclusions on five key issues: (i) whether GE could be said to have a "dominant" position in the global market for aircraft engines; (ii) whether bundling of avionics and non-avionics systems with aircraft engines was likely, and likely to be a successful exclusionary strategy;

(iii) whether GE's vertical integration into aircraft leasing could give rise to realistic foreclosure concerns; (iv) whether cross-subsidization through GE's overall financial strength would harm competition by enabling Honeywell to invest more in R&D and offer its customers lower prices than its rivals could; and (v) whether these price cuts would harm competition by forcing rivals to exit the market. On all of these issues, the EU said "yes" and the United States said "no."

[23] *See* William J. Kolasky, Deputy Assistant Attorney-General of the Antitrust Division of the U.S. Department of Justice, *U.S. and EU competition policy: cartels, mergers, and beyond*, speech at Council for the United States and Italy Bi-Annual Conference, January 25, 2002.

[24] *See General Electric/Honeywell, Case COMP/M.2220*; and *Neste/IVO*, Case IV/M.931. In that case, there was a proposed merger between Finland's only supplier of natural gas and its leading provider of electricity (with 60-70% of the wholesale market). Approximately 10% of Finland's electricity production uses natural gas. Despite this low figure, the Commission found that "*the merged entity would as a result of the vertical links between natural gas and electricity production be in a position to successfully adopt market strategies that would not have been possible prior to the concentration.*" First, by raising the price of gas (thereby increasing the costs for competing electricity producers) the firm could successfully increase electricity prices. Second, the firm could control future investment in electricity generation because any potential new entrant would effectively be "*dependent on his largest competitor for supplies of fuel.*" Accordingly, the Commission found that the transaction would create or strengthen a dominant position on the Finnish market for wholesale sales of electricity.

[25] *Compare*, the official Dutch response to the Green Paper by the Minister of Economic Affairs (*Minister van Economische Zaken*) in a letter to Commissioner Monti, pp. 5-6.

[26] The following Member States' merger control regimes have a two-stage decision-making process or independent evaluation of the initial objections to a merger or acquisition: Belgium, Finland, Germany, Spain, Sweden, and the United Kingdom. Other jurisdictions make a distinction between the fact-gathering and decisional stages (*e.g.*, Ireland), but are typically taken by political institutions such as the Ministry of Economics, which would not receive substantial support.

[27] *See* William J. Kolasky, Deputy Assistant Attorney-General of the Antitrust Division of the U.S. Department of Justice, *Conglomerate mergers and range effects: it's a long way from Chicago to Brussels*, speech at George Mason University Symposium, November 9, 2001.

[28] *See*, generally, P.J. Slot, *De Europeesrechtelijke achtergronden van de mededingingswet*, Mededingingsmonografieën Deel 1 De Nederlandse Mededingingswet in perspectief, pp. 17-34.

[29] On differences in procedure between the Act and the EC Merger Regulation, *see* M. van der Woude, *De procedure voor de NMa: 'zeker geen Europese kloon'*, Markt & Mededinging 1998, nr. 3, pp. 84-90.

[30] Within the NMa's structure are also organized certain sector-specific supervisory bodies, including the electricity watchdog (*Dienst toezicht en uitvoering Energie*, "Dte"). It is intended that the currently independent supervisory authority

for the telecommunications sector (the *Onafhankelijke Post en Telecommunicatie Autoriteit*, "OPTA"), be reorganized as a separate chamber within the NMa by 2005, or possibly earlier, following a recent joint proposal by the NMa and OPTA. *See* the joint NMa and OPTA press release 02-24, July 10, 2002, available in English at www.nma-org.nl/english, under "press releases". *See also* A.T. Ottow and I.M. Spong, *De sectorspecifieke toezichthouders en het kamermodel NMa*, Markt & Mededinging 2002, nr. 4, pp. 128-134, for a critique of the position of OPTA and DTe following the adoption of the proposal.

[31] For commentaries on the reform of the NMa, *see, e.g.*, S.E. Zijlstra, *Moet de NMa een zelfstandig bestuursorgaan worden?*, Markt & Mededinging 2000, nr. 4, pp. 154-157; Y.E. de Muynck, *Verzelfstandiging van de NMa: kritiek onterecht*, Actualiteiten Mededingingsrecht 2001, pp. 75-77; J. van Leerdam, *Bij verzelfstandiging past rechtspersoonlijkheid NMa*, Markt & Mededinging, 2001, nr. 6; E.H. Pijnacker Hordijk, *Noodzaak voor duidelijke en sterke ministeriële verantwoordelijkheid voor de Mededingingsbelei*d *(redactionee*l), Markt & Mededinging, 2001, nr. 6; P.J.M. Koning and N.U.N. van den Euvel-Kien *Formeel mededingingsrech*t, 2000, p. 289; and J.K. de Pree, Het Financieele Dagblad, August 16, 2001.

[32] The "large company" regime is discussed in the second Section of this report.

[33] This second limb of the turnover thresholds was raised in 2001 from NLG 30 million to (30 million, *inter alia*, to free capacity at the NMa to focus on more complex cases and to relieve the burden on medium and small undertakings.

[34] *See, e.g.*, G. Leuverink, *Omzetberekening bij concentratiecontroles*, Actualiteiten Mededingingsrecht 2002, nr. 2, pp. 24-25.

[35] *See* F.O.W. Vogelaar, *Van Joint Ventures, mededinging en de nieuwe eeuw*, Markt en Mededinging 2001, nr. 4, pp. 129-144, for a discussion of the NMa's approach to cooperative joint ventures.

[36] *See* R.J. van Dam, *'Als elke dag telt', fatale beslistermijnen in de Mededingingswet*, Markt en Mededinging, 2001, nr. 7, pp. 259-264. There are two exceptions to this rule. First, implementing a public bid is allowed provided that (i) the NMa is notified immediately and (ii) the acquirer does not exercise its voting rights. Second, the NMa may for serious reasons, such as irreparable harm, grant a dispensation from the prohibition at the request of one of the notifying parties. Such dispensation is, however, rare.

[37] The four-week and 13-week periods will be suspended from the day on which the NMa requires further information from the notifying parties until the day on which such information is provided. In practice, additional information is frequently requested

[38] Decision of August 4, 2000, available on NMa's website.

[39] *See*, generally, K.J.M. Mortelmans and J.W. van de Gronden, *Mededinging en niet-economische belangen*, in Mededingingsmonografieën Deel 4; and NMa's 2001 Annual Report, at p. 13.

[40] As discussed below, a recent review has concluded that the Act should be amended in this respect to explicitly allow the offering of undertakings during the first-phase. *See* Berenschot, *Syntheserapport Evaluatie Mededingingswet*, May 30, 2002, pp. 40-41.

[41] *See* Y.E. de Muynck, *"Remedies" in de vorm van gewijzigde meldingen*, Actualiteiten Mededingingsrecht 2001, Nr. 3, pp. 61-65; and NMa's 2001 Annual Report, p. 36. For case-law *see e.g., Remy Cointreau/Bols*, Case No. 2124; *Grand Dorado/Center Parcs*, Case 2209.

[42] *See* NMa's 2001 Annual Report, p. 36.

[43] A.W. Kist, *"De NMa in haar vierde jaar"*, Markt & Mededinging 2001, nr. 1.

[44] A contrary view that criminal sanctions should be considered was expressed by M.R. Mok, *Het voorstel-Mededingingswet*, TVVS 1996, p. 157.

[45] *See, e.g.*, Wegener e.a. v. D-g NMa (District Court of Rotterdam, September 20, 2000), and the note of P.P.J. van Ginneken in Markt & Mededinging, 2001, nr. 1.

[46] *See* for more detail, Berenschot, *Syntheserapport Evaluatie Mededingingswet*, May 30, 2002, pp. 40-41.

[47] For example, there is an exception for NVs that operate as holding companies of corporate groups that employ a majority of their personnel outside the Netherlands.

[48] A works council, which is generally required if a business employs 50 or more employees on a regular basis, consists of a chairman and a number of members elected by and among the NV's employees. It represents the employees *vis-à-vis* the NV's management. The works council must be consulted on certain decisions intended to be taken by the NV's management (*e.g.*, decisions relating to the transfer of control over, the cessation of or a significant change in the NV's business or any part of it; any substantial change in the organization of the NV's business; and the entering into or termination of, for example, joint ventures), the intended appointment or dismissal of a member of the management board, and must provide its prior approval for any decision relating to the determination, modification, or revocation of the employment conditions and employee benefits. In case of disputes, both the NV's management and the works council can initiate court proceedings to have certain "corporate action" approved or blocked.

[49] Exhibit X places certain restrictions on the use and combination of these three anti-takeover measures. An NV can only implement two of the three measures and the composition of the boards of the special-purpose foundations need to meet a certain level of independence *vis-à-vis* the board of the NV.

[50] *See* D.F.M.M. Zaman and W.J. Oostwouder, *Over certificaten mét en aandelen zónder stemrecht*, Ondernemingsrecht 2001-15, p. 442.

[51] Holders of depositary receipts may, however, attend and take part in general meetings of shareholders.

[52] This delegation to the management board of the power to issue preference shares is usually renewed at each annual general meeting of shareholders.

[53] LVMH Moët Henessy Louis Vuitton SA, *et al*/Gucci Group N.V., Stichting Belangen Werknemers, Pinault-Printemps-Redoute S.A., *et al*, Hof Amsterdam (Ondernemingskamer), March 8, 2001, NJ 2001, p. 224.

[54] Vereniging van Effectenbezitters/Rodamco North America N.V. and Westfield European Investments Pty Ltd, Hof Amsterdam (Ondernemingskamer), March 22, 2002, JOR 2002, p. 82.

[55] *See Tweede Kamer* 2001-2002, 28179 (a copy of the proposal, in Dutch, can be downloaded from www.overheid.nl/op).

[56] In light of the proposed amendments to the "large company" regime, several NVs and, in particular, a number of multinationals (including Ahold N.V., Getronics N.V., Numico N.V. and Wolters-Kluwer N.V.) that had voluntarily adopted the "large company" regime, have dismantled the regime and amended their Articles of Association to the effect that members of the supervisory board are no longer appointed through co-optation. Instead, the Articles of Association include a system of binding nominations by the supervisory board. The general meeting of shareholders may overrule a binding nomination of the supervisory board by a two-thirds majority of the votes cast, representing at least one-half (instead of one-third) of the issued share capital. Neither the works council nor the general meeting of shareholders has a right to present candidates for nomination to the supervisory board. These multinationals defend the dismantling on the argument that a majority of their employees are based outside the Netherlands and that they find it problematic that a works council, which, in practice, solely comprises Dutch employees, has such a large influence over the composition of the supervisory board. *See also* L. Timmerman, *De politieke haalbaarheid van het Wetsvoorstel aanpassing structuurregeling*, Ondernemingsrecht 2002-3/4, p. 106.

[57] Any resolution to that effect must be properly reasoned and may only be adopted if the intended dismissal has been put on the agenda of the general meeting of shareholders, and both the management board and the works council have been duly notified.

[58] Although the shareholders at the general meeting of shareholders cannot dismiss an individual member, shareholders may ask the competent court to dismiss an individual member, which request can only be granted on a limited number of grounds.

[59] *See* for a critique of this proposal M.W. Josephus Jitta, *Schuitje varen, theetje drinken, varen wij door het polderland*, Ondernemingsrecht 2002-3/4, pp. 74-82.

[60] Failure to obtain prior approval will not render the transaction null and void, but may result in the liability of members of the management board, and in certain cases also members of the supervisory board, *vis-à-vis* the NV.

[61] *See Tweede Kamer* 1997 - 2002, 25732 (A copy of the proposal, in Dutch, can be downloaded from www.overheid.nl/op).

[62] In calculating compliance with the 70% threshold, any shares which the NV issued after it received a notification from the shareholder that it acquired 70% of the NV's issued capital, are excluded. Likewise, certain kinds of shares such as preference shares and fully paid-up shares that were mainly issued to protect the NV such as priority shares, whenever issued, are not taken into account.

[63] In the introduction to the consultation document released by the Minister of Finance on January 30, 2002, the Government states that Greece and the Netherlands are the only two remaining Member States without a mandatory bid rule. In fact, the Greek Capital Market Commission, the Greek securities regulator, already introduced a mandatory bid rule in 2000 requiring a shareholder holding an interest of 50% or more in a Greek listed entity to launch a bid for the remaining outstanding voting securities (*see Public Offer for the Purchase of Transferable Securities*, Greek Capital Market Commission Decision 1/195 of July 19, 2000, which entered into force on August 22, 2000).

[64] A copy of the consultation document and the reactions, all in Dutch, can be downloaded from the website of the Ministry of Finance www.minfin.nl.

[65] We do not consider possible obstacles if a Dutch NV intends to acquire a non-Dutch target, since those will largely be a function of foreign law. Under Dutch law, a NV wishing to make a foreign acquisition must obtain the necessary corporate approvals and consult with the trade unions and works council (see below). There is no trade union consultation obligation if the takeover does not affect the bidder's Dutch employees.

[66] Although filings under the 1996 Act on the Disclosure of Major Holdings (*Wet melding zeggenschap in ter beurze genoteerde vennootschappen 1996*) may be considered an obstacle to creeping acquisitions, they are not included in this list.

[67] The Merger Code is issued by the Social and Economic Council (*Sociaal-Economische Raad*; the "SER"), a tripartite body comprised of representatives of the Government, trade unions, and employers.

[68] The obligation for the NV's management board to consult the trade unions only exists if the NV employs at least 50 employees. Under the Merger Code, the NV must consult the following trade unions: (i) trade unions of which at least one member is a member of the NV's works council, (ii) trade unions involved in the negotiation of collective bargaining agreements binding on the NV, and (iii) trade unions that have been regularly active for the NV's employees in the two year period before the takeover.

[69] At the same time as the NV informs the trade unions, it must also inform the SER.

[70] The Merger Code Adjudication Committee consists of representatives of trade unions and employer organizations and independent members.

[71] If a non-Dutch bidder offers shares, it may also be subject to non-Dutch securities laws.

[72] In the event of an asset transfer, Dutch securities laws do not apply and no offering memorandum is necessary. If the asset transaction involves all of the NV's assets, as further discussed in our response to Question 10, the view of most Dutch legal commentators is that such a transaction requires the prior approval of the general meeting of shareholders.

[73] In the event of a statutory merger, as further discussed in our response to Question 10, the general meeting of shareholders of each of the target NV and the bidder NV would have to approve such merger.

[74] A pyramid structure is a group structure characterized by a chain of control using several holding companies. The ultimate shareholders control each company in the chain by majority or controlling minority interests. As a result the ultimate shareholders may control the whole chain up to and including the company at the bottom on the basis of a small total investment.

[75] A person or company that rescues the target of an unfriendly takeover bid by, for instance, acquiring a controlling interest in the target or by making a competing offer for the shares in the target.

[76] An anti-takeover measure in which a target company sells its most valuable asset (the "crown jewel") to a third party so that the target will be less attractive to an unfriendly bidder.

[77] An employment contract provision that grants members of management lucrative severance benefits — including long-term salary guarantees or bonuses — if control of the company changes hands.

[78] Debt that allows an investor to redeem the security before maturity if the issuer of the debt becomes the target of a hostile takeover. "Poison debt" makes it expensive for the bidder to buy the target because the bidder will have to raise cash to pay off the holders of the debt.

[79] An anti-takeover measure by which the target attempts to take over the bidder by making a cash offer for the bidder company's shares; the name derives from a video game popular in the 1980s, the object of which was to gobble up the enemy.

[80] The board neutrality rule is intended to prevent the board of a target company from autonomously adopting defensive measures once a bid has been announced. It requires a target's board to seek shareholder approval on any action intended to frustrate the bid.

[81] W.J. Slagter, L. Timmerman, D.C. Buijs, G. van Solinge, and M.P. Nieuwe Weme are of the opinion that an issuance of preference shares pursuant to a call option would violate the board neutrality rule. Others, including, P.J. Dortmond, M.J.G.C. Raaijmakers, and M. van Olffen, disagree. *See* L.J. Hijmans van den Bergh and G. van Solinge, *Implementatie van de 13e Richtlijn*, p. 106.

[82] According to the Rapport Honée/Timmerman 2000, 56% of Dutch listed companies use preference shares: L.J. Hijmans van den Bergh and G. van Solinge, *supra* note 80, p. 106.

[83] Pursuant to Article 311 of the Commercial Code (*Wetboek van Koophandel*), a seagoing vessel (*zeeschip*) is Dutch if, among other things, it is at least two-thirds owned by individuals or entities from an EU or EEA Member State, who are active in the shipping industry in the Netherlands.

[84] Pursuant to Articles 16 and 16a of the Act on Aviation (*Luchtvaartwet*), a Dutch aviation operating license is only granted if the intended licensee has its principal place of business and registered office in the Netherlands. Pursuant to Article 4, ¶2 of Council Regulation 2407/92/EEC on licensing of air carriers, it is a condition of an operating license that the licensee is at all times effectively controlled by Member States or nationals of such States.

[85] *See* Article 24 of the 1992 Act on the Supervision of the Credit System (*Wet toezicht kredietwezen 1992*).

[86] *See* Article 16 of the Securities Act.

[87] *See* Article 26a of the Securities Act.

[88] *See* Article 175 of the 1993 Act on the Supervision of the Insurance System (*Wet toezicht verzekeringsbedrijf 1993*).

[89] *See* Article 93 of the 1998 Electricity Act (*Electriciteitswet 1998*) and Article 85 of the Gas Act (*Gaswet*)·

[90] *See* Policy guidelines concerning the privatization of energy-distribution enterprises of July 10, 2001 (*Beleidsregels privatisering energiedistributiebedrijven van 10 juli 2001*). (A copy of the text, in Dutch, can be downloaded from www.overheid.nl/op).

[91] A number of legal commentators have expressed the view that the provisions of the policy guidelines and proposed amendments implementing the policy guide-

lines to the 1998 Electricity Act and Gas Act do not meet the criteria developed by the European Court of Justice in the "golden share" cases (*i.e.*, *Commission v Portugal*, Case C-367/98; *Commission v France*, C-483/99; and *Commission v Belgium*, C-503/99) on the basis that (i) the criteria to be applied to a decision of the Minister of Economic Affairs are not specifically expressed, and (ii) the condition that legal ownership of grids is to be held by Dutch local governments or entities controlled by Dutch local governments constitutes a breach of the principle of proportionality. *See* W.J. Oostwouder, *Het gouden aandeel is dood, leve het gouden aandeel?*, Vennootschap & Onderneming, June 2002, p. 98; W. Koster, *Europees Hof scherpt regels voor gouden aandeel aan*, Het Financieele Dagblad, June 8, 2002.

[92] *See* letter of the Minister of Finance to the Parliament dated December 12, 2001 (*Nota deelnemingenbeleid Rijksoverheid*). (A copy of the text, in Dutch, can be downloaded from www.minfin.nl).

[93] This is the view of most legal commentators *See, e.g.*, G. van Solinge, *Grensoverschrijdende juridische fusie*, 1994, pp. 173, 320. *See also*, P. van Schilfgaarde, *Van de BV en de NV*, 2001 p. 337. P. Vlas, Rechtspersonen, Praktijkreeks IPR, 1999, p. 158, however, takes the view that a cross-border merger should be allowed provided that the relevant jurisdictions each have provisions on statutory mergers.

[94] Proposal for a Tenth Council Directive based on Article 54(3)(g) of the Treaty concerning cross-border mergers of public limited companies of December 14, 1984, COM (84/727 final, 85/C 23/08). This proposal contained rules relating to mergers between companies from different Member States.

[95] Under Dutch tax law, a fiscal unity can be created if at least 99% of the shares in the subsidiary is held by the parent NV and the companies are consolidated. Under proposed legislation that is expected to enter into force on January 1, 2003, this percentage will be reduced to 95%.

[96] Recently proposed changes to Directive 68/151/EEC ("First Company Law Directive") should — to some extent — make company information more easily and rapidly available to the public while at the same time simplifying the disclosure formalities required from companies. The proposal would, if it were adopted, require that the Member States make possible the filing of company documents and particulars by electronic means as of January 1, 2005. Copies of those documents would be accessible to the public by electronic means. The proposed amendment would not alter the original list of documents and particulars that must be disclosed, nor the original provisions whereby Member States must determine by which persons the disclosure formalities are to be carried out. For an electronic copy of the proposal, *see* http://europa.eu.int/comm/internalmarket/en/company/company/news/index.htm.

[97] *See Kritiek op vaker melden van belangen*, Het Financieele Dagblad, June 11, 2002.

[98] Additional (and specific) disclosure and/or reporting obligations may apply to companies active in certain industries (*e.g.*, banking and insurance).

[99] These sources implement Directives 68/151/EEC, 77/91/EEC, 78/660/EEC, and 83/349/EEC ("First, Second, Fourth, and the Seventh Company Law Directives" respectively).

[100] An NV's Articles of Association contain, among others, the following information: (i) whether the NV has different classes of shares, and if so, the rights attached to each class; (ii) whether the power to issue shares has been delegated to the management board and for what period of time; (iii) the manner in which members of the management board are appointed (*i.e.*, by way of binding nomination of certain class(es) of shareholders or by a simple or qualified majority of all shareholders); (iv) the manner in which the members of the supervisory board are appointed, and, related to this, if the NV is subject to the "large company" regime; (v) decisions that the management board cannot adopt without prior supervisory board approval or shareholder approval; and (vi) whether there are limitations on the ownership of shares (*e.g.*, the X%-rule).

[101] An NV's annual report not only contains useful information on the past and expected course of business of the NV, but, pursuant to the Euronext Issuing and Listing Rules, also information on any anti-takeover devices involving the use of preference shares, priority shares, or depositary receipts. For example, it indicates to whom the NV has issued preference shares, with whom it has concluded subscription agreements for such shares, and who are the board members of any foundation to which the NV has issued (or granted a call option on) preference shares. It also indicates the names of the members who are on the board of any foundation that has issued depositary receipts as well as the natural or legal persons ultimately responsible for casting votes on priority shares. Pursuant to the draft Act on Disclosure of Directors' Remuneration and Share Ownership (*Wetsvoorstel openbaarmaking van de bezoldiging en het aandelenbezit van bestuurders*), in the near future, an NV's annual accounts will also report the salary of each management and supervisory board member, any agreed termination payments (including "golden parachutes"), and the number of the NV's shares or other securities that each board member holds.

102 The 1996 Act on the Disclosure of Major Holdings implements Directive 88/627/EEC on the information to be published when a major holding in a listed company is acquired or disposed of. This directive and two other directives (i.e., Directive 79/279/EEC on coordinating the conditions for the admission of securities to official stock exchange listing and Directive 82/121/EEC on information to be published on a regular basis by companies the shares of which have been admitted to an official stock exchange listing) were consolidated into EC Directive 2001/34/EEC on the admission of securities to official stock exchange listing and on information to be published on those securities. This last directive is currently under review as part of the EC Commission's "transparency agenda". The Commission is also preparing a directive on insider dealing and market manipulation and a directive on the prospectus to be published when securities are offered to the public or admitted to trading, both of which would impose additional and continuing disclosures.

[103] *See* www.autoriteit-fm.nl.

[104] The Winter Report recommends that listed companies in all Member States be required to disclose their capital and control structures, for instance in their annual reports, their listing particulars and in prospectuses required to be published upon the issue of new securities. In addition, listed companies should be under a contin-

uing disclosure obligation and companies should be encouraged to use their websites as a medium to disclose information to shareholders. The information to be disclosed should, among others, include: (i) direct and indirect significant shareholdings, including holdings through "pyramid structures" and circular and cross-shareholdings; (ii) board members' and employees' shareholdings and rights to acquire shares; (iii) ESOP control mechanisms, if the employees do not control the plan themselves; (iv) a description of all classes of shares (including non-listed shares) and the rights and obligations that attach to these shares; (v) holders of shares with special control rights and a description of their rights; (vi) a description of the rules applicable to the appointment and removal of board members and the amendments to the Articles of Association; and (vii) a description of the powers of the management board, in particular whether the board may issue and cancel shares. *See* The Winter Report, p. 25.

[105] Often NVs include the aggregate number of options granted to employees and their conditions in their annual accounts, in accordance with the Peters Commission Corporate Governance Guidelines. *See* S.C.J.J. Kortmann, N.E.D. Faber, and E. Loesberg, Corporate governance in perspectief, 1998, p. 372.

[106] *See* http://europa.eu.int/comm/internal_market/en/finances/mobil/transparency/index.htm for a general discussion of the EU's "transparency agenda", and p. 8 of the May 8, 2002 consultation paper for a fuller description of the proposed disclosure obligations.

[107] *See* pp. 4, 5 and 6 of the May 8, 2002 consultation paper. The proposals include (i) quarterly interim reporting within two months after the end of the quarter, and (ii) a maximum publication period of three months for the annual report (currently this is five months, or under special circumstances, 13 months). In addition, with reference to the recommendations included in the Winter Report, the consultation paper proposes to include the following information in the annual report: (a) amounts, content, and identity of holders of shares with special control rights and a description of their rights (under the Euronext Issuing and Listing Rules this information is already included into the annual accounts); (b) description of the rules applicable to the appointment, dismissal and the powers of board members, in particular for issuing shares, and the amendment of the Articles of Association (currently this information is available in the NV's Articles of Association); (c) description of ESOPs, in particular a description of the control mechanism if they are controlled by a third person on behalf of the employees (currently, in accordance with the Peters Corporate Governance Report recommendations, certain basic information regarding ESOPs may be found in the annual accounts); and (d) information about the number of shares and the right to acquire shares (stock options), held by management (currently the aggregate number of shares and stock options owned by management are included in the annual accounts, pursuant to company law and the Peters Corporate Governance Reports. In the near future the number of shares and stock options are to be included on an individual basis into the annual accounts under the draft Act on Director's Remuneration and Share Ownership).

[108] With respect to continuing disclosure obligations, in particular the obligation to publish price sensitive information, the consultation paper refers to the Market Abuse Directive which is expected to require NVs to publish all inside information

immediately. It also proposes to upgrade the disclosure of voting and capital structures and to that effect envisages, among others, the following changes: (i) lower thresholds (starting at 5% and also introducing thresholds of 15% and 30%) to trigger the disclosure obligations regarding the acquisition or disposal of major holdings in companies; (ii) shorter time periods to inform the public that thresholds have been met; (iii) disclosure of voting rights under financial instruments that confer the right to acquire or sell shares; and (iv) disclosure of the contents of shareholders agreements as a whole.

[109] NV's should have the possibility to disclose information not only via press but also via electronic means. In addition the consultation paper proposes to introduce a central filing as an additional means for NV's to disclose information.

[110] The proposals included in the May 8, 2002 consultation paper are preliminary and no draft Directive has been prepared yet. It is unlikely that the proposed draft regulation will be implemented into Dutch law in the near future.

[111] In essence, the Winter Report seeks to eliminate takeover defenses that rely on asymmetries between the voting and economic rights associated with shares. To that end, it proposes rules that would override disproportionate shareholder voting rights in takeover situations. These override provisions would require votes to be counted strictly in proportion to the shareholders' interests in risk-bearing capital. They would have a pre-closing and a post-closing component. Pre-closing, a proportionality rule would apply at any general meeting of shareholders convened to vote on defensive action against a takeover bid. It would override multiple voting rights, voting caps, voting rights given to securities that are not part of risk-bearing capital (possibly including "golden shares"), and other features that deviate from strict proportionality between risk-bearing capital and voting rights. Post-closing, the Winter Report recommends a break-through rule that would enable a successful bidder that has acquired some threshold controlling stake of the share capital (not to exceed 75%) to reverse any mechanisms contained in the target NV's Articles of Association or other constitutional documents that would prevent it from exercising its proportionate voting rights (multiple voting rights, voting caps, voting rights given to securities that are not part of risk-bearing capital, and arguably, supermajority voting requirements in excess of those required by law) or its core control rights (exclusive right of a class of shares to make binding nominations for appointment of board members, staggered appointments of board members, appointments of board members for fixed terms, *etc.*).

[112] These measures (which may also be taken with respect to certain of the NV's Dutch subsidiaries) can be divided into two categories. The first category contains measures aimed at giving the petitioner influence (*e.g.*, through a court order to exchange depositary receipts for shares, to cancel preference shares that have been issued without pre-emptive rights, to undo a voluntary adoption of the "large company" regime, or to amend the NV's Articles of Association to allow shareholders the power to appoint and to dismiss the members of the management and supervisory boards). The court would have to grant these measures unless the NV proves that it is likely that the requesting shareholder's intentions would fundamentally violate the NV's interests or that it could be reasonably expected that the requesting shareholder would not act in accordance with general principles of

reasonableness and fairness. The second category contains measures aimed at providing the petitioner with control over the NV other than through the general meeting of shareholders and which may have more direct and far reaching consequences for other stakeholders (*e.g.*, cancellation of priority shares, annulment of board or shareholder resolutions, or amendments to the Articles of Association other than amendments enabling shareholders to appoint the members of the management and supervisory boards). The court could only take those measures in circumstances where, after taking into account the other stakeholders' interests, it would be unreasonable and unfair to refuse them.

[113] *Ibid.*

[114] The Winter Report, p. 39, states that the Group "believes [that] pyramid structures should remain outside the scope of the break-through rule. They pose general problems also outside the context of a takeover bid. They undermine the transparency of the ownership structure of listed companies; they affect the pricing mechanism with regard to listed shares at all levels in the structure; they make control over companies belonging to such groups substantially incontestable, even when they are listed, or at least they make the acquisition of control of such companies extremely expensive; and finally, they create minority shareholders at several levels who directly and indirectly in total hold the majority of the risk bearing capital but are unable to exercise control at any level."

[115] In addition, a Dutch bidder must consult its works council before launching a bid while certain board actions of the Dutch target (*e.g.*, the issuance of preference shares to a foundation) may also be subject to prior works council consultation. *See*, *e.g.*, R.A.A. Duk, *Onvriendelijke overname en ondernemingsraad*, A-T-D, Opstellen aangeboden aan Prof. mr. P. van Schilfgaarde, 2000.

[116] Any decision of the Financial Markets Authority (including the refusal to take a decision) concerning a public offer is subject to a right of appeal before the Trade and Industry Appeal Tribunal (*College voor het beroeps- en bedrijfsleven*). Any decision of the Trade and Industry Appeal Tribunal is final.

[117] Since the adoption by Euronext of the Euronext Rule Book on October 29, 2001, members of Euronext (*toegelaten instellingen*) are no longer under an obligation to refuse to co-operate with a bidder who fails to comply with the provisions in the Merger Code. In theory, there is no penalty on violating the Merger Code, but in practice, we believe that members of Euronext most likely will not be willing to assist a bidder that, for instance, refuses to enter into trade union consultations.

[118] Dutch company law does, however, allow structures in which an NV's Articles of Association limit the number of votes that a shareholder may cast provided that shareholders who own the same *amount* of shares (as opposed to *number* of shares) may cast the same number of votes, and the Articles of Association do not favor the holders of larger amounts of shares over the holders of smaller amounts of shares. In addition, Dutch company law allows structures in which (i) a shareholder does not receive more than six votes if the authorized capital is divided into 100 or more shares, or (ii) a shareholder does not receive more than three votes if the authorized capital is divided into less than 100 shares.

[119] *See* Article 123(3) of the Legislative Decree No. 58 of February 28, 1998, the Unified Financial Act (*Testo Unico dell'Intermediazione Finanziaria*).

NORWAY

Cross Border Mergers in Company Law and Competition Law: Removing the Final Barriers

Rapporteurs
*Asle Aarbakke and Helge Stemshaug**

B. THE COMPETITION REGIME

1. What is the view from your country[1] on the functioning of the threshold levels in Article 1(2) as well as the 2/3 rule in the Merger Regulation, and the proposal in the Commission's Green Paper for amendment of Article 1(3) to deal with the problems of multiple filings?

The discussion concerning the threshold levels and the 2/3 rule has limited impact within the EFTA pillar of the EEA regime. Following the EU membership of Sweden, Finland and Austria, it is unlikely that there will ever be any future transactions meeting the thresholds in Article 1 solely within the EFTA pillar, and, thus, having an EFTA dimension notifiable to the EFTA Surveillance Authority (ESA). From an EFTA-EEA perspective, the importance of the threshold levels is therefore limited within the EFTA pillar, in absence of an EEA dimension with respect to the jurisdiction criteria.

As it is also unlikely that any transaction would require parallel national notifications in Norway, Iceland and Liechtenstein, without also having a Community dimension pursuant to the current Article 1 or the Commission's proposal for amendment of Article 1(3), in which the decisive criterion for establishing Community interest would be based on the fact that a merger gives rise to three or more national notification requirements, the proposal would have little impact on transactions within the EFTA pillar. Again, the reason is the absence of an EEA dimension with respect to the jurisdictional criteria.

2. In light of the experiences made in your country, do member states have sufficient flexibility to call for mergers to be referred back under Article 9 of the Merger Regulation? In light of the proposal in the Commission's Green Paper, what is your view on the circumstances in which this power should be exercised?

With respect to the degree of flexibility to request referral of cases under Article 9, the experiences made in Norway have so far been limited. Within the EFTA-pillar of the EEA regime it is also unlikely that a referral issue will ever arise, c.f. section 1 above.

However, the referral mechanism under Article 9 of the Merger Regulation was successfully applied in a recent case concerning the merger between the two Norwegian companies Aker Maritime AS and Kværner ASA. As the concentration had a Community dimension according to the Merger Regulation, notification to the Commission was filed 14 December 2001. On the same date the Commission received a request for partial referral from the Norwegian competition authorities, pursuant to Article 6 of Protocol 24 to the EEA Agreement and Article 9 of the Merger Regulation. As requested, the Commission decided 23 January 2002 to refer the case to the Norwegian competition authorities with respect to the market for engineering, procurement and construction (EPC) contracts and the market for maintenance, modification and operation (MMO) contracts. As both Aker Maritime and Kværner were major contractors within the oil and gas industry on the Norwegian continental shelf, the case was regarded of considerable political and social importance in Norway. Furthermore, Norwegian competition authorities were considered to hold high competence with respect to the offshore industry in general and were also better placed as to the gathering of relevant market information. On 11 February 2002 the Norwegian competition authorities adopted its decision that the merger would not give rise to anti-competitive effects contrary to Norwegian competition law (decision A2002-1). Although the referral issue unavoidably would have had certain impact upon the timing of the process, the case was thus cleared by the competition authorities within less than two months from the time of the notification to the Commission.

In our view, a simplification of the criteria for referral, disjoining the referral request from evidence of a threat of creation or strengthening of dominance, as proposed in the Commission's Green Paper, would, obviously, to some degree provide improved flexibility of the referral mechanism. However, the Norwegian Aker Maritime-Kværner case demonstrates, in our opinion, that also the current referral mechanism in Article 9 gives the necessary flexibility with respect to allocation of competence in merger control, provided that the referral issue is treated with due efficiency by both national competition authorities and the Commission. The case also illustrates the importance of particular considerations - in terms of the markets concerned or other circumstances owing to the activities of the merging companies - being taken into account by the competition authorities, as early as possible in the notification process. Furthermore, the treatment of the Aker Maritime-Kværner case may to some extent indicate that the three-week deadline for submitting a referral request is at least sufficient. In conclusion, it is our view that the issue of flexibility of the current referral mechanism is to a large extent a matter of priority of the competition authorities involved.

Although it is obviously important to ensure that the referral mechanism provides sufficient flexibility to national competition authorities, and the Commission's proposal to disjoin the referral issue from evidence of a threat of creation or strengthening of dominance would represent a step forward in this concern, it is, in our view, equally important to ensure that the power of referral may not be exercised unless the national competition authorities involved are undoubtedly better placed to review the possible effects on competition of the transaction in question. This would imply that the power of referral should be exercised solely if alleged effects on competition would primarily occur within the boarders of the Member State concerned.

3. Is the system of consultation between the European Commission and the national competition authorities (NCAs) working adequately? Does there need to be a better formalised system for consultation between NCAs directly involved either in the case of multiple filings outside the merger control regulation or in cases where more than one member state exercises the Article 9 request?

The system for consultation between the competition authorities may be evaluated respectively from the view of national competition authorities and from the view of the companies being subject to an investigation under the merger control rules. We are not in a position to address the views of the Norwegian competition authorities.

However, based on our experience as legal advisors to companies concerned, it is our opinion that the consultation system may to some extent benefit from an increased transparency towards the parties to the transaction concerned. Transparency would not necessarily have to extend to the further details of each consultation. For the purposes of effectively gathering the relevant market information, and safeguarding a sufficient degree of contradiction in the process, the parties concerned should, however, as a minimum, be informed as to which authorities that are being consulted with respect to the transaction. Such transparency is equally important whether the consultation involves the Commission, or national competition authorities only.

4. How does the test under the law of your country compare to that under the Merger Regulation? Should all member states adopt the same test as under the Merger Regulation, and should this EU test be the (US) 'significant lessening of competition' test rather than the present EU 'dominance' test?

Under Norwegian competition law the substantive test for clearance is a 'significant lessening of competition' test, in which efficiency considerations will also be taken into account (c.f. section 6 (f) below).

In our view, there appear to be only marginal substantive diversities between the 'significant lessening of competition' test and the 'dominance' test, and a possible harmonisation of the national rules within the EEA member states with respect to the substantive test for clearance will therefore in practice have limited impact on the legal uncertainty in cases of multiple filings. Thus, to effectively deal with the problems of multiple filings, it would in our opinion be more important to procure harmonisation of the national notification criteria, in particular in terms of the kind of transactions that should be notified (concentrations), the companies that are relevant for calculation of turnover, and the further rules on calculation of turnover as well as the time limits.

5. Are the procedural and judicial safeguards adequate to protect parties from abuse of power by the competition authorities? How does the law of your country compare to EC law in this respect?

Under Norwegian law, any decision adopted by the Norwegian Competition Authority (the "NCA") may be appealed to the Ministry of Labour and Government Administration (the "Ministry"), c.f. section 6 (i) below. Appeal decisions by the Ministry have in a limited number of cases been adopted to a large degree on basis of broader political and social considerations, which are relevant to the Ministry's decision, whereas the extent of the judicial review has in practice been somewhat limited in so far as the alleged effects on competition are concerned. For the parties concerned, this practice may to some extent give rise to legal uncertainty, depending *inter alia* on the political and social importance of the case. As there are no definite time limits for the Ministry's treatment of a case, experience also indicates that an administrative review procedure may be long lasting. Approximately 50 per cent of all prohibiting decisions/clearance on conditions decisions, a total of about 15 cases, have been appealed to the Ministry since 1994.

Decisions made by the NCA and/or the Ministry may also be subject to judicial review before Norwegian courts, c.f. section 6 (i) below. Contrary to the right of administrative appeal before the Ministry, the right of judicial review before the courts has not been used in any competition case so far, since the Competition Act came into force in 1994. The object of the right is also somewhat limited; in so far as a judicial review cannot comprise the legal assessment by the NCA and/or the Ministry on whether an intervention is required under the law to prevent the anti-competitive effects of the transaction concerned (see section 6 (a) below regarding the structure and main features of merger control under the Norwegian competition act and section 6 (i) regarding *inter alia* judicial review).

As regards the form of procedure applicable to the treatment of a case by the NCA (c.f. also section 6 (i) below), the rules do not provide any right of formal hearing before a decision is made, nor are the parties concerned entitled to request hearing of any third parties. The treatment of a case will involve hearing of the parties concerned, though such hearing may be limited to written statements submitted by the parties. When the NCA is charged with both evaluation of the evidence and making the final decision, there is an inherent risk that evidence can me misinterpreted. These aspects may in our view indicate that the current form of procedure would benefit from certain amendments, *inter alia* in terms of the rules to safeguard contradiction of the parties concerned.

6. Below are a number of questions relating to domestic law, which may assist in a comparative analysis.

a. Please provide an overview of the structure of and main features of the relevant domestic legislation and the institutional framework (who enforces it)? It may be helpful with some information about the role of private rights of action.

The main features of Norwegian merger control legislation are contained in Section 3-11 of the Competition Act of 1993 (the "Competition Act"), which is enforced by the Norwegian Competition Authority (Konkurransetilsynet) (hereinafter the "NCA"). An English translation of the Competition Act is available at www.konkurransetilsynet.no.

Under Section 3-11, the NCA may intervene in respect of "acquisitions of enterprises" which result in "the creation or strengthening of a significant restriction of competition", in so far as such effects on competition are deemed contrary to the purpose of the Act, which, pursuant to Section 1-1, is "the efficient utilisation of society's resources through workable competition".

Decisions of the NCA may be appealed to the Ministry of Labour and

Government Administration (the "Ministry"). Norwegian courts may only review NCA's and the Ministry's interpretation of the Act, its application of the procedural rules and whether it has abused the procedural rules.

b. What kinds of transactions are caught? Are joint ventures caught? What are the jurisdictional thresholds? Is it difficult to identify with sufficient certainty whether a filing is in fact required under national law? Are foreign-to-foreign mergers caught?

The Act sets out a list of events covered by the concept of 'acquisition of enterprises', namely:

- mergers;
- acquisition of stocks or shares, and;
- acquisition of parts of a business (assets).

Acquisition of assets constituting an independent business is also deemed to be covered by the Act.

Acquisition of stocks or shares is subject to merger control under the Act, even if there is no change of control. Thus, also acquisition of minority shareholdings without getting *de facto* control, will constitute an "acquisition of enterprise" under the Act.

Joint ventures are subject to merger control under the Act, provided that the joint venture is acting as an independent market operator. If the joint venture is regarded strictly as a cooperation vehicle between independent parent companies, the joint venture is not subject to merger control, but to the general competition rules contained in the Act.

The joint venture must be established on a lasting basis in order to be considered as an independent market operator. Furthermore, it must to a significant degree control its own market behaviour. EU jurisprudence will be relevant when deciding when a joint venture is deemed to be subject to Section 3-11.

There are no jurisdictional thresholds under Section 3-11 of the Act. However, the NCA has issued guidelines stating that, as a general rule, it will only investigate transactions where the combined market share of the parties to the transaction exceeds 40 per cent, or where the combined market share of the three largest market participants (including the combined market share of the parties) exceeds 60 per cent. These guidelines are however not binding on the NCA.

Filing is voluntary and will not in any circumstance be required under Norwegian law, c.f. section (c) below. However, depending on the concentration concerned, it may be difficult to identify with sufficient degree of certainty whether the transaction is such that it most likely would be investigated in any case by the NCA, and, thus, whether a voluntary filing would be preferable from the perspective of the parties concerned, c.f. section (c) below on time limits applicable.

The merger control provision in Section 3-11 covers all transactions affecting the Norwegian markets, and thus potentially covers foreign-to-foreign mergers. So far, however, the NCA has not intervened in any foreign-to-foreign mergers.

c. Is the filing mandatory or voluntary? Who is responsible for filing? What is involved in the preparation of a filing? What are the deadlines for filing? What are the waiting periods and does implementation of the transaction have to be suspended?

There is no mandatory filing requirement under the Act. A voluntary filing can be made pursuant to Section 3-11, having the effect of forcing the NCA to decide within three months after filing whether or not to investigate the case further. Otherwise, the NCA may delay its decision for six months from the date of the final agreement. The latter time limit (i.e. six months) also applies if the NCA, on basis of a voluntary filing, informs the parties within the three-month time limit that further investigations will be initiated.

As filing is voluntary, no party has responsibility for filing. There are no filing fees.

There are no formal requirements for voluntary filings. If a voluntary filing is made, it should however contain information about the transaction, the parties involved, ownership, the relevant market(s), market shares and other market participants. In cases where the NCA decides to initiate further investigations, more detailed information will be required. The level of detail of the information submitted in a voluntary filing should be assessed depending upon whether the transaction otherwise is likely to be subject to further investigations.

As filing is voluntary, there are also no deadlines for filing or sanctions for not filing. To obtain the full benefit of a voluntary filing, the parties are recommended to notify as soon as a final agreement is concluded. The NCA have in some circumstances also accepted notifications submitted before final agreement has been concluded.

Irrespective of whether a voluntary filing is made, there is no waiting period or suspension of implementation under the Act. However, if the NCA has reason to believe that the acquisition may create or strengthen a significant restriction of competition, and considers it necessary in order to accomplish a potential intervention against the acquisition, the NCA is empowered to prohibit the implementation of the transaction temporarily or to lay down other restrictions. The provision, granting such power to the

NCA, came into force in May 2000 and is merely applicable to exceptions. The provision has so far been applied by the NCA in one case only.

d. What are the issues and possible sanctions involved in closing before clearance? What is the timetable for clearance and can it be speeded up?

If the NCA has not adopted a decision prohibiting implementation during investigation, c.f. (c) above, there is no waiting period or suspension of implementation, and subsequently no penalties for closing before clearance. If, on the other hand, the NCA has ordered the parties to suspend implementation during investigation, closing before clearance will be a criminal offence and may result in fines or imprisonment (c.f. (j) below).

The NCA has the power to intervene against a transaction for a period of six months after the date of the final agreement. The period may be extended up to one year if 'special circumstances' exist.

A clearance decision may however be obtained within three months from filing if a voluntary filing is submitted to the NCA. A voluntary filing has the effect of forcing the NCA to decide within three months whether or not it will investigate the merger further. If the NCA does not react within the three-month period, the transaction is considered cleared and the NCA may not intervene against the merger at a later stage. If, however, the NCA informs the parties three months after notification that it will investigate the case further, the normal time period applies, i.e. six months from the date of the final agreement.

e. Are there any special rules applicable to public takeover bids?

There are no special rules relating to public takeover bids in the Act.

f. What is the substantive test for clearance?

The substantive test for clearance is a 'significant lessening of competition' test, in which the NCA will evaluate whether or not the transaction will create or strengthen a significant restriction of competition. According to the NCA's guidelines, the test involves three stages:

The NCA will initially define the relevant markets affected by the transaction and calculate the market shares of the parties. If the combined market shares of the parties exceed 40 per cent, or the market shares of the three largest market players, including the parties to the concentration, exceed 60 per cent, the NCA will normally proceed to analyse further whether or not the transaction will create or strengthen a significant restriction on competition.

Where these market shares thresholds are not met, the transaction will normally be cleared without further investigation. The market share thresholds above are nevertheless not binding on the NCA.

As a second step, the NCA will evaluate whether or not the transaction will create or strengthen a significant restriction of competition. In this assessment the NCA will consider whether, as a result of the transaction, the parties either alone or in combination with other market players will be able to exercise market power (single firm dominance or collective dominance) in the affected markets.

As the object of the Act is to achieve the efficient utilisation of society's resources, the NCA will not intervene in a transaction that creates efficiency gains outweighing the detriment to competition. Only efficiency gains that result directly from the implementation of the transaction, and which will be realised within a two-year period, will be taken into account. Economies of scale and the rationalisation of administrative or other overlapping functions in the undertakings concerned will normally be considered as efficiency gains.

g. To what extent are non-competition issues relevant to the review process?

The main role of the NCA is to ensure effective competition in Norway. The object of the Act is to achieve the efficient utilisation of society's resources. Thus, the NCA will not intervene if a transaction creates efficiency gains that outweigh the detriment to competition. Apart from efficiency gains, only competition issues are relevant to the NCA's assessment under Section 3-11. Where an intervention from the NCA is appealed to the Ministry, political and social considerations may, however, be of significant importance. Past experiences show that e.g. the effect on employment and on rural society may play a role when the Ministry has accepted anti-competitive mergers having other benefits prohibited by the NCA.

i. Is it possible to remedy competition issues?

Negotiations between the NCA and the parties with the aim of finding an amicable solution are obligatory as part of an investigation. In the course of these negotiations it may be possible to remedy competition issues by giving undertakings. The undertakings must reduce or remove the negative effects on competition in a way that is acceptable to the NCA. Both structural and behavioural remedies may be accepted. There are no formal time limits within which the parties must propose remedies.

Remedies proposed by the parties may be stipulated as conditions of clearance by the NCA.

j. What are the typical steps during the investigation? What rights do complainants have? What publicity is given to the process? What are the opportunities for judicial review?

The NCA will normally start its investigation under Section 3-11 of the Act by requesting the parties to provide all information relevant to the transaction. Such requests will normally include information about all relevant agreements, minutes of board meetings, the parties' definition of relevant markets, the combined market shares of the parties, the market shares of the main competitors, the name and size of the most important customers and suppliers as well as other information which may be of particular interest to the transaction in question.

Normally the NCA will contact customers, suppliers and competitors and invite them to submit market information and to give their assessment of whether or not the transaction will create restrictions in the relevant markets. No time-limits or formal procedures exist for contact between the NCA and third parties. The parties concerned have no formal right to request hearing of particular third parties.

If the NCA, on the basis of the information received, concludes that the transaction will create or strengthen a significant restriction of competition, it will provide the parties with a draft decision, and invite them to start negotiations in order to find an amicable solution.

If, after the negotiations, the parties have not proposed undertakings or taken other actions sufficient to resolve the negative effects of the transaction, the NCA will make a final decision, which may amount to outright prohibition or to a conditional clearance.

Private parties may submit complaints to the NCA. The NCA is not obliged to initiate any investigation of such complaints. Complainants and other interested parties, including the media, may request access to the NCA's files, including any voluntary notification, though business secrets and certain other types of information are exempt from scrutiny.

As regards publicity, the NCA normally publicises the fact that it has received a voluntary filing or that it is investigating a merger, and issues press releases in some cases. In addition, customers, suppliers and competitors are informed about the transaction and are invited to give their views on its effect on the relevant markets. Furthermore, complainants and other interested parties may request access to files, apart from parts containing business secrets.

With respect to judicial review, all decisions of the NCA are subject to administrative review by the Ministry. Appeals must be filed within three weeks from the date of the NCA's decision. There are no requirements as to the content of the appeal, except that it must be made clear that it is an appeal, and it should be made in writing. Decisions of the NCA and the Ministry may also be appealed to the Norwegian courts.

Norwegian courts may only review the NCA's and the Ministry's interpretation of the Act, their application of the procedural rules and whether they have abused their powers, but not their evaluation of whether or not an intervention under Section 3-11 is warranted to combat the negative effects of the transaction. There is no time limit for launching an appeal, apart from the general limitation period for claims.

j. What are the enforcement powers? How does administrative and civil sanctions compare with the EC regime? And what are the criminal sanctions, and are they used?

The NCA may prohibit a merger if it is found to create or strengthen a restriction on competition contrary to the purpose of the Act. If the NCA decides to clear a merger, it may attach such conditions to its decision as it regards necessary to remedy the negative effects of the transaction. It may require divestiture of shares, or the sale of the whole or parts of a company or of assets.

Non-compliance with decisions of the NCA is a criminal offence, and may result in fines or imprisonment of up to three years (six years in aggravated circumstances). The same applies to failure to provide information or the submission of incorrect or misleading information. Since non-compliance is a criminal offence, the NCA will refer the case to the police for prosecution. The NCA may in addition impose periodic penalty payments in order to ensure compliance with its decisions. The size of the penalty payment is determined by the NCA, and there are no statutory upper or lower limits. The NCA may also, separately or in addition to criminal proceedings, require the parties to relinquish all gains derived from infringements under the Act. Where it is impossible to establish the size of the gain, the amount may be determined approximately.

In 2002, the NCA has so far (August) prohibited one acquisition and attached conditions to one clearance decision. Both acquisitions affect the wholesale market of electrical power. Both decisions have been appealed to the Ministry.

In 2000 and 2001, the NCA did not prohibit any acquisitions or mergers. However, the NCA attached conditions to two clearance decisions both in 2000 and 2001. In one of the cases, the Ministry modified the conditions in its appeal decision.

k. Do the authorities cooperate with other antitrust authorities?

The NCA cooperates with the European Commission and with the EFTA Surveillance Authority in accordance with the EEA Agreement, which provides for rules on cooperation equivalent to the EU rules.

For the purposes of meeting Norway´s obligations to foreign states or international organisations under international agreements, the Act empowers the NCA to exchange confidential information with foreign competition authorities where the information is necessary to promote the competition rules of Norway or of the state or organisation in question. Norway, Denmark and Iceland entered into an agreement on March 16, 2001 enabling exchange of confidential information also in merger cases. The Act also empowers the NCA to make requests for information on behalf of foreign competition authorities. For the purpose of meeting Norway's obligations to foreign states or international organisations under international agreements, the NCA may request information from both individuals and undertakings.

l. Are there also rules on foreign investment, special sectors or other relevant approvals?

There are no general rules on foreign investments in Norway. However, in respect of mergers and acquisitions in special sectors such as banking, insurance, shipping, mining, power, media, telecommunications, oil and gas and agriculture, there are regulations that apply in addition to the Act. Some of the rules involve mandatory filing and clearance before transactions can be implemented.

Until July 2002, the Norwegian Business Acquisition Act 1994 ('the Acquisition Act') provided for a general notification requirement for acquisitions of shares or assets in Norwegian companies or businesses, provided that certain requirements with respect to both the number of shares bought and the size of the business were met. The Acquisition Act has now been repealed. As a consequence of the repeal, transactions entered into on or after July 1 2002 are no longer subject to any general notification requirement in Norway.

An acquisition of shares or assets may still trigger a notification requirement or be subject to a concession pursuant to other specific legislation.

Pursuant to the Concession Act 1974 ('the Concession Act'), all acquisitions of real property in Norway require government approval, unless otherwise stated in the Concession Act (eg, acquisitions of developed property no larger than 20,000 square metres). Further, acquisitions of more than one-third, or of at least one-half or two-thirds, of the share capital or assets in a company that owns (or has a tenancy or a beneficial right to) such real property, will require a corresponding approval.

However, if a transaction was subject to notification under the Acquisition Act, a specific approval under the Concession Act was not necessary, provided that the real property that the target business owned was not used for or regulated to agricultural purposes. However, after the repeal of the Acquisition Act this exception will no longer be applicable. Hence, acquisitions of shares or assets in Norwegian companies or businesses owning (or having a tenancy or a beneficial right to) real property of 20,000 square metres or more, or used or regulated for agricultural purposes, will normally require approval pursuant to the Concession Act.

However, the acquirer of a company or business whose acquisition is subject to approval under the Concession Act may apply for an exemption from such obligation. The Ministry of Agriculture has stated that an exemption will normally be granted for acquisitions that were previously subject to the Acquisition Act (and therefore did not need an approval under the Concession Act).

A Green Paper dated May 15 2002, proposes replacing the existing Concession Act with a new act. The proposal includes i.a. amendments that in practice will exempt most transactions previously subject to the Acquisition Act. If the government maintains their proposals after the hearing, the proposal will be sent to Parliament. An effective date for the potential new act is not expected before the beginning of 2004.

m. Are there current proposals to change the legislation?

In November 2000 the Norwegian government appointed a committee to review the current competition Act, including the merger provisions. The committee shall present its proposal for new regulations within November 2002.

C. COMPANY LAW AND FINANCIAL MARKET REGULATORY REGIME

7. What will you identify as the main obstacles to take overs where a company[2] from your jurisdiction is either bidder or target and the other company is from another EU jurisdiction3?

Norwegian company law contains restrictions on a company's ability to grant loans etc to its shareholders, which limit the possibility to finance a take-over by funds from the target company and/or companies in the target company's group. There are two kinds of limits, of which particularly the second one in practice is considered an important obstacles to take-overs.

First, there is a general limitation on a company's ability to grant loans etc to its shareholders or companies controlled by a shareholder. Such loans etc may, at the outset, only be granted within the limits specified for distribution of dividends and only to the extent adequate security is pledged for the company's claim for repayment. Loans etc to Norwegian parent companies are exempt. There is also an exemption for loans etc to parent companies belonging in the EEA provided, however, that the EEA parent company is subject to equally strict or stricter rules on loans etc to shareholders as those contained in Norwegian legislation. As most EEA states have less strict rules within this field, most EEA parent companies will not qualify for the exemption and consequently the limitations apply.

Secondly, Norwegian company law prohibits Norwegian companies from making assets available, grant loans or pledge security in connection with the acquisition of shares in the company or in a group company. The provision is inspired by section 23 of the second company law directive, but has a much wider scope inter alia since it prohibits refinancing for a certain time after an acquisition. However, lawful distributions from the company, typically in the form of dividends, are normally not caught by the provision. The provision is equally applicable to Norwegian and foreign bidders, and constitutes in both events an important obstacle to take-overs.

As for the financial market regulations, particularly two rules should be mentioned. These rules are not obstacles to take-overs as such, but effectively limit the possibility to conduct a "cheap" take-over.

First, a person or company whose holding of shares, call options, convertible bonds etc in a listed company reaches, goes beyond or falls below 1/10, 1/5, 1/3, 1/2, 2/3, 9/10 of the share capital or an equivalent part of the votes that may be cast in the company, is obliged to notify the stock exchange of this event once an agreement to sell or purchase shares etc has been concluded. The information will then be made publicly available by the exchange. These rules imply that it is difficult to gain control in a company without paying a "premium" to the market.

Secondly, Norwegian law contains a mandatory offer obligation which also has the effect of preventing "cheap" take-overs. The mandatory offer obligation is triggered when a shareholder becomes the owner of shares representing more than 40% of the votes in a listed company. Rules on consolidation apply, and even the achievement of indirect control may trigger the obligation. In such case the shareholder needs to notify the exchange and the company and. Moreover, he will have to, within a period of four weeks, either sell the shares exceeding the threshold or make an offer to purchase all the shares of the company. A mandatory offer must be unconditional and must comprise all the shares of the company, including shares with limited or no voting rights. The offer price shall be at least as high as the highest payment the offerer has made or agreed in the period six months prior to the point at which the mandatory offer obligation was triggered. If it is clear that the market price when the mandatory offer obligation is triggered is higher than the price resulting from the first sentence, the offer price shall be at least as high as the market price. The consideration must always be offered in cash, but the offeror may additionally give the shareholders a right to accept other forms of settlement. The offer shall be backed by a guarantee from an approved financial institution. The offer shall state a time-limit for shareholders to accept the offer, which must be between 4 and 6 weeks. The offer must be made in an offer document which must satisfy a number of requirements, and which is to be approved by the exchange.

8. Do hostile take overs by companies from other EU jurisdictions in fact take place in your country?

Yes, from time to time although hostile take-overs were apparently more common some years ago.

9. To what extents are there any sectors (utilities, financial institutions) that in practice are further protected from hostile take overs, or foreign[4] take overs in particular? Are there any policy statements or particular legal mechanisms that give effect to this protection, or is it a matter of informal mechanisms?[5]

The acquisition of shares – in most cases only above certain thresholds – in certain types of companies, requires a concession from public authorities. This is the case for financial institutions, energy companies (including transmission companies) and companies engaged in fisheries and fish and shellfish farming. The relevant rules are to be found in statutory provisions, and are applicable regardless of whether the purchaser is domestic or foreign, and regardless of whether the acquisition is considered hostile or not.

Such requirements do from time to time prevent take-overs. A foreign company recently tried to acquire a Norwegian financial institution through a voluntary bid. The relevant authority would only grant the concession if the bidder got more than 90% acceptance, as this would enable the bidder to become the sole owner through a squeeze out of the remaining minority shareholders (see answer to question 14 d regarding squeeze-outs). The bid was accepted by approximately 88% of the share capital, the remaining share capital mainly being owned by another Norwegian financial institution which opposed the transaction. As the threshold level was not reached and it was therefore not possible to obtain the concession the bid was eventually withdrawn.

Until recently, a more general regime of public approval was in force when someone acquired 1/3, 1/2 and 2/3 of the shares/votes in certain larger companies. It was not necessary for the acquirer to apply for a concession, but the Ministry of Trade and Industry was to be notified of any such acquisitions and had the possibility to intervene and not approve the acquisition – or to approve it subject to certain conditions. During the period this regime was in force, we are not aware of any incidents where the Ministry refused to approve an acquisition but there were some examples of conditional approvals. This general regime was abolished with effect from 1 July 2002.

10. What are the company law techniques of completing a take over or merger that are used in practice where one of the companies is from another EU jurisdiction? Please give particular attention to how this would differ from the usual completion of a take over or merger where both companies are from your jurisdiction. It would be useful if you could add a comment about the consequences on the techniques used of the taxation regime and of any differential tax treatment of take overs or mergers where one party is from another EU jurisdiction.

When both the purchaser and the target are Norwegian companies, the purchaser have the choice to leave the target company as a separate company in the purchasers group, or to merge or demerge the target company with the purchasing company or another company in the purchaser's group. In the first case, integration with the existing activities of the purchasing company will have to be carried out through transfers and transactions between the target company and other group companies. If either the purchaser or the target is a foreign company, this is the only means of integration available, as the choice of merging or demerging the target company is not available. Attempts to implement "mergers by agreement" where a Norwegian company is involved, have so far not been successful and are not likely to be so in the future.

11. A duty on listed companies to disclose capital and control structures is proposed in *Issues Relating to Takeover Bids*, the First Report of the High Level Group of Company Law Experts (see p 25). Would this require amendments in the legislation in your country? How would these amendments in case be implemented (in primary company law, securities law, stock exchange regulations etc.)?

Information on capital and control structures is available in various ways under the current Norwegian legislation.

All Norwegian companies are registered in a central Register of Business Enterprises. The register keeps an updated copy of the companies' articles of association, which shows, inter alia, the share capital and the number of shares as well as any restrictions on voting or transfer of shares. The register also contains information on any existing powers of attorney to increase the share capital, to acquire the company's own shares, etc. The information held by the Register is public and may be obtained by anyone.

All public limited liability companies are to keep a register of shareholders with the Norwegian Registry of Securities. The register of shareholders is to be available to anybody.

All Norwegian companies are under an obligation to provide information on the capital structure in their annual accounts. This includes information on the share capital and the number of shares and, where applicable, on classes of shares and subscription rights. Provisions in the articles of association regarding voting rights are also to be mentioned. Moreover, the annual accounts are to contain information on the 20 largest shareholders and the size of their shareholdings. Information on shareholders with a shareholding of less than 1% may be omitted. The annual accounts are also to contain information on shareholdings by the managing director and members of the board of directors. The annual accounts of larger companies are also to contain information on shareholdings by leading employees, as well on shareholdings by persons and companies related to any of the said persons.

In any prospectus, listed companies are always required to disclose information on the capital structure, as well as information on the 20 largest shareholders, determined on the basis of both capital and votes. To the extent this is known to a company, prospectuses are also required to disclose information on shareholders who exercise joint control etc over the company. It would seem that the current requirements are essentially in line with the recommendations contained on pages 25-26 of the *Issues Relating to Takeover Bids*, the First Report of the High Level Group of Company Law Experts.

A person or company whose holding of shares, call options, convertible bonds etc in a listed company reaches, goes beyond or falls below 1/10, 1/5, 1/3, 1/2, 2/3, 9/10 of the share capital or an equivalent part of the votes that may be cast in the company, is obliged to notify the stock exchange of this event once an agreement to sell or purchase shares etc has been concluded. The information will then be made publicly available by the exchange. Rules on consolidation apply for the purpose of determining whether the said thresholds are passed. A notification shall, inter alia, contain information on the exact size of the shareholding. It may, but need not, contain information on whether or not the purchaser intends to buy additional shares. There is currently a pending proposal to lower the lowest threshold from 1/10 to 1/20.

Members of the board of directors, the managing director, leading employees et al of a listed company, are always required to notify the exchange of any transactions they or affiliated persons or companies are involved in. Such information is made publicly available by the exchange.

To conclude: The current Norwegian legislation seems essentially in line with the recommendations regarding disclosure. To the extent amendments are necessary, it would depend on the circumstances what instruments need to be amended. Provisions on annual accounts are contained in the Accounting Act, provisions on prospectuses are mainly contained in the Securities Trading Act and in the stock exchange regulations, whereas provisions on shareholders' obligations to notify the exchange of transactions they are involved in are contained in the Securities Trading Act.

12. A so called break through rule after take over bids is another of the proposals in *Issues Relating to Takeover Bids*, the First Report of the High Level Group of Company Law Experts (see p 29). Would this require amendments in the legislation in your country? How would these amendments in case be implemented (in primary company law, securities law, stock exchange regulations etc.)?

Under the current Norwegian legislation an offeror would be bound by and have to comply with various defense mechanisms provided for by the articles of association of a company. There is no possibility of "breaking through" such provisions in other ways than through an amendment of the articles, and such an amendment would have to be adopted in compliance with the current regime. Hence, voting restrictions etc would have to be respected.

It follows that the proposed break through rule would require amendments to Norwegian legislation. It would presumably be most appropriate to implement such a rule in the Securities Trading Act.

13. In your view, would these two new rules as proposed have any material impact on the existing barriers to take overs in your country (or in others as seen from your point of view)? It would be helpful if you could demonstrate the impact, or lack of it, by going through one or more recent take over bids that failed in your country (or in some other member state, by a company from your country).

As has been explained above, Norwegian rules on disclosure are already to a great extent in line with the current proposal. Therefore, the material impact would be limited.

By contrast, the proposed break-through rule would be entirely new to Norwegian law. Nevertheless, it is questionable whether the impact will be great. In our impression, and save for special sectors where statutory limitations apply (see answer to question 9), restrictions on voting rights etc are not very common in companies listed in Norway and rarely constitute a major barrier to take-overs. Hence, in all likelihood the impact of the proposed rule would accordingly be fairly limited.

14. Below are a number of questions which may assist in a comparative analysis.

a. What are the main features of the relevant domestic take over legislation constituting the company law and financial market regime, and who enforces it (independent regulators, regulatory bodies with appeal to ministry, stock exchange)? What is the extent of intervention by the takeover regulator(s) – to what extent does the regulator have wide or general discretions to block and play a protectionist role (for example in its capacity as approver of the offer terms/documentation)?

Many of the main features have been addressed in answer to other questions. In the following a brief summary is provided.

Main features of company law include:

- fairly rich opportunities to limit voting rights and the transferability of shares through provisions of the articles of association or by agreement. Listed companies are subject to a stricter regime.
- limited possibilities to use the funds of a target company for the financing or refinancing of an acquisition.
- rights and obligations of a board in connection with a take over are to a limited extent specified, and therefore need to be determined on the basis of the "interest of the company" and similar general principles.
- where one shareholder holds more than 90% of the shares/votes in a company, a mutual right for the majority and minority shareholders to demand that the minority's shareholding be transferred to the majority shareholder.

All Norwegian companies are registered in a central Register of Business Enterprises. The information held by the register – which includes inter alia the articles of association, powers of attorney for the board to increase the share capital or to issue convertible bonds, the names of board members etc – is publicly available. The Register controls the legality of resolutions etc that are filed for registration. Apart from that, there is no public or private body entrusted with the task of supervising the implementation of company law provisions for non-listed companies.

In the annual accounts companies are required to disclose various information about inter alia capital and ownership structures. In addition to auditing the annual accounts, the company's auditor is also required to give confirmations in connection with various transactions, such as amendments to the share capital, mergers and demergers, etc. In this respect, the auditor has a kind of supervisory function.

As for the financial market legislation, the following main features should be mentioned:

- companies listed with a Norwegian exchange are subject to fairly wide duties of disclosure. Companies are required to notify the exchange of circumstances which are significant to the quotation. Information is also to be given in prospectuses of various kinds.

- shareholders are under an obligation to disclose information on transactions that causes the person's holding of shares and/or rights to shares to reach or pass certain threshold levels, currently 1/10, 1/5, 1/3, 1/2, 2/3 and 9/10 of the share capital/voting rights. There is a pending proposal to lower the lowest threshold to 1/20.
- when a person/company through acquisition becomes the owner of more than 40% of the shares in a listed company, a mandatory offer obligation is triggered. This implies, in brief, that the shareholder concerned must make an offer to acquire all the shares in the company at a price at least as high as the highest price paid by the offeror during the preceding six-month period. Mandatory offers must offer cash consolidation, and are required to be unconditional. The offer document needs to be approved by the exchange.
- voluntary offers in listed companies are subject to certain formal requirements and need to be approved by the exchange. Voluntary offers may be conditional, for instance upon a certain degree of acceptance, that a public permission is obtained, etc.
- fairly strict rules on insider trading in listed companies apply.
- a register of primary insiders is kept and such insiders are required to disclose any transactions they or affiliated persons or companies take part in.

The exchange is entrusted with the primary responsibility for supervising and executing the said financial market legislation. The Banking, Insurance and Securities Commission ("Kredittilsynet") is a public body which is also entrusted with various tasks within this field.

b. Are there restrictions on a board taking action to frustrate a bid that has been made? When do the relevant restrictions start to apply – earlier than a formal announcement/filing of a bid? To what extent can shareholders approve the taking of frustrating action in advance of any bid?

The general limitations on the conduct of the board are to be found in company law. The board may not adopt measures which are capable of giving certain shareholders or other parties an unfair advantage at the expense of other shareholders or the company. Moreover, the board is under a general obligation to act in the "interest of the company". However, there is no general consensus as to what interest are covered by this concept, nor as to how the various interests are to be reconciled. Still, it is clear that the board may not frustrate a bid purely out of concern for its own interest and the positions of the board members. It is equally clear that board may take steps to frustrate a bid even though the general meeting has not granted the board any advance power to do so. In fact, since the board is to pursue the interests of the company, it may be permissible for the board to frustrate a bid even in situations where the majority of the shareholders are positive to the bid. This could be the case if the board has reasonable grounds to believe that a takeover will be prejudicial to the interests of the company.

In connection with mandatory offers, but not voluntary offers, more specific limitations apply as to what measures may be adopted by the board and management. The limitations are set out in the Securities Trading Act, and become effective from the time when the board is informed of the bid, and last until the bid lapses and the result is clear. During this period the board and management may not: (1) issue shares or other financial instruments in the company or a subsidiary, (2) merge the company or subsidiary, (3) sell or purchase substantial areas of operation of the company or its subsidiaries, or other dispositions of material significance for the nature or scope of its operations, or (4) purchase or sell the company's own shares. The said limitations to not apply to dispositions which are part of the company's normal ongoing business operations, or cases where the general meeting has empowered the board of directors or manager effectively in charge to make the decisions in question with buy-out situations specifically in mind.

c. Are there restrictions on the type of consideration that can be offered in a bid, for example securities only if these are listed in the target country's home state or the EU?

A mandatory offer must always offer consideration in cash, but may additionally grant the recipients a choice to accept a different kind of consideration. The consideration must in any event be backed by a guarantee provided by an approved financial institution.

There are no specific provisions on what consideration may be offered in a voluntary offer.

Both mandatory and voluntary offers are to be approved by the exchange, and the exchange might, in principle, refuse to approve an offer due to the type of consideration that is offered. We are not aware of any examples that this has happened though.

d. Are there effective compulsory acquisition procedures regarding a small non-accepting minority? Can a bidder make its offer conditional on achieving the number of shares required so it can operate a squeeze out?

If a parent company, directly or through a subsidiary, holds more than 90%

of the shares/votes in a subsidiary, the board of directors of the parent company may decide that the parent company is to take over the remaining shares in the subsidiary. Conversely, each of the remaining shareholders in the subsidiary is entitled to demand that the parent company take over the shares.

The parent company must offer the shareholders a redemption price. If the offer is made in writing to all shareholders with a known address and is also made public by the insertion of a notice in the Norwegian Official Gazette and in a newspaper which is widely read in the area in which the registered office of the company is located, a deadline may be fixed within which the individual shareholder may make objections to or reject the offer. If no such objection is received by the company before the expiry of the deadline, the shareholder shall be regarded as having accepted the offer.

In the absence of an amicable agreement or acceptance of an offer, the redemption price shall be fixed by an appraisement, which is normally to carried out for the account of the parent company.

If a parent company has decided to take over shares, the parent company is to be registered as the owner of the shares in the register of shareholders, provided that the parent company has paid the total offer price into a separate account in a bank which is authorised to carry on banking activities in Norway. Hence, the parent company does not have to await the outcome of any valuation proceedings in order to become owner of the shares.

In a voluntary offer the offeror may make its offer conditional upon achieving the number of shares required so it can operate a squeeze out. Mandatory offers must be unconditional, and a similar condition is therefore not possible for such offers.

e. Is there a principle of board neutrality? Can a target board align itself with a particular bidder/agree measures such as exclusivity arrangements to protect a particular deal?

As described above in answer to question 14 b, the board is under a general obligation to act in the "interest of the company" and is not permitted to adopt measures which are capable of giving certain shareholders or others an unfair advantage at the expense of other shareholders or the company. Within those fairly vague limits, the board may, in principle, act in support of one particular bidder if this is considered beneficial for the company.

f. Can a target board hand over information to a potential bidder?

The Norwegian Securities Trading Act contains fairly strict rules on insider trading applicable to financial instruments which are or are to be listed. These rules will effectively limit a target board's possibility to hand over information which is not already publicly available and which is relevant for the quotation of the financial instrument to a potential offeror.

The general principle of equal treatment of shareholders applicable to all companies will also limit the target board's possibility to hand over information.

For non-listed companies, the board's general obligation to act in the "interest of the company" and the prohibition against measures which are capable of giving certain shareholders or others an unfair advantage at the expense of other shareholders or the company, impose limitations on the possibility to hand over information to a potential bidder. It is not strictly forbidden to hand over information if this is considered to be in the interest of the company, but the board must exercise due care in determining how and to what extent this is permissible. One possible approach would be to use an independent advisor as a kind of "intermediary". The advisor could then, for instance, give a declaration of confidentiality, and would only be permitted to reveal to the potential offeror his conclusions as to whether or not given criteria are satisfied.

The above-mentioned limitations apply to information which is not publicly available. It is recalled that various sorts of information are indeed publicly available and in such cases the board can freely hand over the information. This is for instance the situation with regard to who are the shareholders of a company.

g. Are structures permitted which concentrate control rights in the hands of minority shareholders? Are structures permitted which place limitations/restrictions on voting rights, caps for example on voting rights above a certain threshold?

Although as a starting point one share carry one vote, various voting right restrictions may be established through provisions of the articles of association of a company. The articles of association may contain provisions on voting right restrictions attached to a person, for instance in the form that no shareholder, or group of shareholders, may vote for more than a given percentage of the total votes that may be cast. The articles of association may also provide that the shares in a class of shares are not to carry voting rights or are to carry limited voting power. A provision of the latter kind must be approved by the Ministry of Trade and Industry if the total nominal value of the shares in a company with such voting right restrictions constitutes more than half the share capital of the company. Except for that, there are no specific limitations as to what voting right restrictions may be implemented through provisions of the articles of association. However, it should be noted that voting right restrictions are not fully effective in all respects. Hence, a voting right restriction which is attached to a share or person is of no significance in relation to provisions in the public limited liability companies act which grant rights to each shareholder or to shareholders owning or representing a certain part of the share capital. The same applies in relation to provisions which, in order for a resolution to be adopted, require that a certain part of the share capital which is represented at the general meeting votes in favour thereof.

Even for listed companies, there are no specific limitations with regard to maintaining or implementing voting right restrictions in the articles of association. The exchange may react or intervene if voting right restrictions are deemed to restrict the transferability of the shares in violation of the general listing criteria (see the answer to question 14 h), but such interventions are fairly rare.

It follows from what is said that Norwegian law permits the establishment of structures that confer the control to minority shareholders, and this is the case even for listed companies within certain limits. However, although permitted the general impression is that voting right restrictions are not very common in listed companies, and far less common than they used to be.

h. Can restrictions be placed on the transferability of shares either by the issuer (in articles of association or by other means) or by arrangements between shareholders? Can a board delay registering transfers of shares?

From a company law perspective various restrictions on the transferability of shares may be provided for in the articles of association. The articles may for instance provide that any transfer of shares requires the consent of the board, that a shareholder or share transferee must have certain qualifications, or that there is to be a right of preemption in the event of a transfer.

Restrictions on the transferability of shares may also be established through agreements among some or all shareholders of a company.

According to the stock exchange regulations general conditions for the listing of shares are that the shares are assumed to be of public interest and that they are likely to be the object of regular trading. The regulations also state that listed shares are "in principle" to be freely transferable. A company with restrictions on the transferability of its shares is under an obligation to inform the exchange of any such restrictions, whether established by the articles of association or by agreement. Although restrictions on the transferability are not entirely forbidden, the exchange normally takes a strict approach towards such restrictions when assessing whether the said criteria are satisfied.

In cases where restrictions on the transferability are provided for in the articles of association, the board may delay registration of transfers of shares within specified time-limits to give effect to the applicable provision. In other cases, the board is not entitled to delay registration of a transfer.

i. What contractual barriers (including share holder agreements) to take over bids are in use in public companies (eg golden parachutes, change of control provisions triggering default of loan agreements, or wining up or change of control of joint ventures)? What are the prospects of review by courts on the basis of contract or company law and by regulators on the basis of securities laws or stock exchange regulations?

All the said types of contractual barriers are commonly used in Norway, separately or in any combination. All companies are to a certain extent required to disclose information on such arrangement in their annual accounts. Listed companies are under a stricter obligation to disclose such information to the exchange and in prospectuses. The exchange will supervise listed companies to ensure that such barriers are not in conflict with the general listing criteria (see answer to question 14 h).

j. Are there current proposals to change the legislation relating to take overs?

One proposed amendment to the Securities Trading Act regarding disclosure of transactions is mentioned elsewhere.

D. FINAL ISSUES

15. In your view, what is the extent to which the complexity of the regulatory arrangements, within national jurisdictions and between the Commission and member states, present an obstacle to take overs?

Take-overs of listed companies are normally carried out with the assistance of local counsel and the complexity of the regulatory arrangement is therefore normally not a problem.

16. Can you list some instances where different rules in the different regulatory systems have caused practical obstacles in a take over process? (One instance could be different time limits under the EC Merger Regulation and national merger rules on the one hand and under stock exchange rules on the other.)

NOTES

* Bugge, Arentz-Hansen & Rasmussen, Oslo, Norway

[1] The aim is not here to have an authoritative statement but a report which can

contribute to the discussion. For EEA (non member) country rapporteurs, the subject of the question is intended to be the EEA regime. For non member (non EEA) countries, there are special issues. Country rapporteurs are welcome to limit their answers in the way they believe to be most helpful or interesting with the purpose of the questionnaire in mind.

[2] Focus is here mainly on listed companies but information about non listed and also non public companies will of interest if this is possible to provide.

[3] Here too the following applies. For EEA (non member) country rapporteurs, the subject of the question is intended to be the EEA regime. For non member (non EEA) countries, there are special issues. Country rapporteurs are welcome to limit their answers in the way they believe to be most helpful or interesting with the purpose of the questionnaire in mind.

[4] "Foreign" here includes both take overs from other member states and from non member states (or non EEA countries).

[5] In the case of banks or insurance companies, the relevant ministry and supervisor would be usually be able to block take overs on prudential grounds and their involvement would be difficult to review. Similar mechanisms would be in place for many utilities where state ownership often adds to the problems. An extensive review is not required, but it would be useful with an assessment of how such mechanisms function. If there have for instance not been any take over by a foreign bank, that is an interesting point.

UNITED KINGDOM

Freshfields Bruckhaus Deringer's Response to Questionnaire for Topic III (Cross Border Mergers in Company Law and Competition Law)

Rapporteur
Paul Lomas

I. THE COMPETITION REGIME

1. What is the view from your country[1] on the functioning of the threshold levels in Article 1(2) as well as the 2/3 rule in the Merger Regulation, and the proposal in the Commission's Green Paper for amendment of Article 1(3) to deal with the problems of multiple filings?

The views of UK stakeholders who responded to the issue of jurisdiction in the Commission's Green Paper were varied. However respondents have broadly agreed with the Commission that the thresholds of Article 1(2) of the Merger Regulation, as well as the 2/3 rule, function satisfactorily and there is no need to modify these provisions. This is, for instance, the view of the Department of Trade and Industry ('DTI'), which stated in its response to the Green Paper that changes to the basic turnover thresholds of Article 1(2) do not appear justified and that retaining the 2/3 rule is entirely consistent with the principle of subsidiarity.

With regard to the Commission's proposals about Article 1(3) of the Merger Regulation however, there has been greater and more diverse comment. In relation to this Article, the Commission states that it has not achieved its objective of conferring Commission competence over cases that affect three or more Member States. The Commission considers that altering the five criteria of Article 1(3) (or modifying Article 22) are unlikely to provide any significant improvement in this respect. In order to address the problem of merging parties having to make multiple filings with a number of national competition authorities ('NCAs'), it proposes to introduce automatic Community competence over cases subject to multiple filing requirements in three or more national jurisdictions. This proposal, which enforces the Merger Regulation's 'onestopshop' approach, is attractive to many. There are, however, a number of issues which the Commission will need to consider in order for the 'three Member State' rule to work in practice:

- For instance, procedural and substantive national laws are not currently uniform nor all based on objectively quantifiable criteria (such as turnover or assets located in the jurisdiction concerned). For example, market share or "share of supply" tests are used in a number of Member States (i.e. the UK, Spain, Portugal and Greece) to determine jurisdiction of the NCA. The subjective nature of such a test means that determining jurisdiction is not necessarily a simple or quick exercise. As a consequence, parties may experience unwelcome delay when applying the 'three Member State' rule. In any event, to provide certainty, the Commission's suggestion that NCAs confirm within a short deadline whether they have jurisdiction would be required.
- Where parties fail to notify the Commission, the Commission might need to request confirmation from three or more Member States that they have jurisdiction. Timing would be an issue here too, as it would not be desirable to allow, say, two Member States to start investigating the transaction while the Commission is arguing that a third also has jurisdiction and that it should therefore itself take over the case. It is also anomalous that triggering the jurisdiction of a voluntary merger regime (as in the UK) could result in a mandatory filing under the Merger Regulation.
- To avoid issues relating to jurisdiction rather than substance dominating affairs it would be sensible if notifying parties be allowed, if they all agree, to opt voluntarily for Commission jurisdiction but not to make it obligatory. This would also ensure that cases which trigger three national merger regimes but only have an impact on competition in a single distinct national market would be reviewed by the NCA best placed to do so (and would be a way of shortcutting the Article 9 referral process (see 2 below)).

On balance, the concept of the 'three Member State' rule is attractive because it provides a 'one-stop-shop'. However, as indicated, a number of inherent difficulties with the rule still need to be considered and addressed by the Commission, as acknowledged by the Commission. The European Competition Commissioner, Mari Monti recently said in relation to Article 1(3) that 'the validity of many [respondents'] concerns has to be acknowledged, and so we are actively reflecting on what form the Commission's ultimate proposal might take, in the light of the feedback we have received'[2].

2. In light of the experiences made in your country, do member states have sufficient flexibility to call for mergers to be referred back under Article 9 of the Merger Regulation? In light of the proposal in the Commission's Green Paper, what is your view on the circumstances in which this power should be exercised?

There have since 1991 been ten cases of referrals back to the UK under Article 9 of the Merger Regulation (six were 'partial' and four were 'full' referrals). Notably, however, there have been three cases where the UK government's request for a referral has been unsuccessful[3]. In the light of this experience, the UK authorities have not always had the flexibility to review mergers which they consider warrant scrutiny at a national level.

The Commission considers that the referral mechanism of Article 9 should be simplified and its operation made more predictable. The Commission's proposal is namely to require only that an Article 9 request should provide evidence of an *effect* on competition in a distinct national market (i.e. without the need to show evidence of a threat of creation or strengthening of dominance and/or by eliminating the need to establish that the relevant market is not a substantial part of the common market).

Such a simplification as proposed by the Commission has obvious attractions. However, it does run the risk of increasing the number of politically motivated requests for referral, thereby undermining the significant benefits offered by the Merger Regulation's 'onestopshop'. The criteria for referral therefore need to be very clear and strict as otherwise companies may too frequently find themselves notifying to the Commission and then finding that they have to deal instead with one or more NCAs, with all the uncertainty, delay and double work that this may involve.

On the one hand, it is important that companies are not able to opt for what they may see as the convenience of the Merger Regulation procedure in cases in which the geographic scope of the competition concerns is clearly local or national: the Commission should make a clear policy statement that there is a presumption that concentrations having an effect on national or local markets should be dealt with by NCAs. Where there are national or distinct markets within a Member State then the Commission should retain jurisdiction only where there is Community interest in doing so, or where the market is in the process of changing from being national to European.

On the other hand, with ever-increasing economic integration across the Community, the number of cases in which there are no significant cross-border effects will be decreasing, and where there are such effects the Commission should retain jurisdiction.

To ensure that a more flexible version of Article 9 is predictable and transparent, a guideline to explain the application of the Article's criteria, as suggested by the Commission, is imperative.

3. Is the system of consultation between the European Commission and the national competition authorities (NCAs) working adequately? Does there need to be a better formalised system for consultation between NCAs directly involved either in the case of multiple filings outside the merger control regulation or in cases where more than one member state exercises the Article 9 request?

As referred to in the Commission's Green Paper[4], there has been a recent initiative by the competition authorities of the Member States for closer cooperation in dealing with, among other things, merger cases that are notified in more than one country. Recent experience shows that as a result of the newly created Association of European Competition Authorities ('AECA') the system of consultation between the European Commission and NCAs and NCAs themselves is certainly working and to the benefit of European companies. By way of example, there have been two joint referrals under Article 22 of the Merger Regulation. The UK, Germany, Italy, Spain, France, Portugal and Austria jointly referred the merger of *Promatech/Sulzer* to the Commission in December 2001 and February 2002. In April 2002, the Commission launched a Phase II investigation into the case but cleared it on 24 July 2002 subject to Promatech making certain divestments. Similarly, the UK, Germany, Italy, Spain, France and Greece jointly referred the merger of *General Electric Engine Services/Unison Industries* to the Commission in February/March 2002. This was granted unconditional approval by the Commission in April 2002.

There is not however any official information regarding the AECA. It is understood that members meet every two months to discuss closer cooperation (including topics such as information exchanges and confidentiality) and the Commission is invited to attend. The AECA also has an internet site which encourages, for instance, communication between authorities and discussions on mergers.

If the successful cooperation of and consultation amongst the AECA continues there may be no need for a more formalised system. It would however perhaps be helpful for the AECA to publish some information regarding its working.

4. How does the test under the law of your country compare to that under the Merger Regulation? Should all member states adopt the same test as under the Merger Regulation, and should this EU test be the (US) 'significant lessening of competition' test rather than the present EU 'dominance' test?

The UK's jurisdictional merger control tests are set out in the response to question 6(b) below. This explains that the current jurisdictional thresholds depend on a market share test or on assets one, compared with the turnover tests which establish a "Community dimension" under the Merger Regulation (see however the response to question 6(m) below which explains that, under the Enterprise Bill's proposed changes to legislation, the assets test will be replaced with a turnover test).

Under the UK's regime, a merger will qualify for investigation by the Office of Fair Trading ('OFT') where, among other things, two or more enterprises 'cease to be distinct' (see the response to question 6(b) below for details). This concept is broadly similar to that of a 'concentration' under the Merger Regulation.

Under UK legislation, enterprises will 'cease to be distinct' where they are brought under common ownership or control or one ceases to carry on business as a result of arrangements between them. 'Control' covers a range of possibilities from acquisition of the 'ability materially to influence the policy' of an enterprise (a 15% holding and, in exceptional circumstances, sometimes less may be sufficient) to the acquisition of a controlling interest. Control for the purposes of the Merger Regulation means the ability to exercise 'decisive influence' and can include the acquisition of a minority shareholding (a 19.9% shareholding can be used as a 'rule of thumb' but other factors such commercial and structural ones will also have a bearing).

The UK's current substantive test for clearance is currently 'public interest' primarily on competition grounds (see the response to question 6(f) below for details and the response to question 6(m) for proposed changes to the UK's legislation), in contrast to the Merger Regulation's test of whether a concentration creates or strengthens a dominant position as a result of which effective competition would be significantly impeded in the Common Market or in a substantial part of it.

There is obviously a lot to be said for harmonisation of national merger control regimes (not least in the context of the 'three Member State' rule discussed at question 1 above) but the reality of this is undoubtedly a long way off.

The amendment of the EU's current substantive test of 'dominance' to the (US) significant lessening of competition ('SLC') test is discussed in the Commission's Green Paper. Opinion over this is divided. For instance, the UK DTI's response to the Green Paper endorsed such an amendment (unsurprisingly, given the proposal under the UK Enterprise Bill to replace the existing UK 'public interest' test with that of a SLC test – see the response to question 6(m) for details). The DTI stated that the SLC test is "fundamentally better adapted to merger control, primarily because it is directly grounded in economic analysis and the impact of a merger on competition in a way that the concept of dominance is not. It is also a more flexible test than dominance, making it particularly well suited to tackling oligopolistic markets". The DTI also cited two specific reasons why a move to a SLC test would be beneficial in the context of the Merger Regulation. First, it would bring the Regulation into line with other important international merger control regimes, including that of the USA and secondly, the DTI sees real benefits in introducing a clear separation between the competition test in the Merger Regulation and the concept of dominance under Article 82 of the Treaty.

On the other hand, others believe that rather than focus on the 'SLC v dominance' debate it would be more appropriate to clarify the law on collective dominance (particularly in the light of the *Airtours/First Choice* judgement) to increase transparency and predictability in the Community review process. Indeed, that judgment may well cause the Commission to reconsider whether now is the time to move to a SLC test.

5. Are the procedural and judicial safeguards adequate to protect parties from abuse of power by the competition authorities? How does the laws of your country compare to EC law in this respect?

English law contains two main remedies to control anti-trust authorities: the Courts and the specialist Competition Commission Appeal Tribunal ('CCAT') created by the Competition Act 1998 (the 'Act'). Appeal lies from the CCAT to the Appeal Court on a matter of law. In essence, the Act conformed English domestic competition law, but not merger control, with EC law, incorporating (by virtue of section 60) decisions of EC substantive law.

The Act also brought about structural change in the previous Monopolies and Mergers Commission and introduced the CCAT, the first and current President of which is Sir Christopher Bellamy, formally a judge in the CFI. The CCAT draws on the traditions both of Community law and the Common law. Currently, it does not exercise any powers over decisions taken by the competition authorities in the field of mergers. Thus, the comments below are derived from experience of the CCAT's practice in the non-merger area. This is relevant because, under reforms currently before Parliament, its powers will be extended to deal with mergers.

The reforms are contained in the Enterprise Bill, which (as described elsewhere and in particular in response to question 6(m)) provides for a greater degree of independence generally from political intervention in merger decisions. As part of this reform, the CCAT (which will be renamed the Competition Appeal Tribunal ('CAT')) will gain greater independence from the Competition Commission, partially to address concerns as to the need for independent tribunals pursuant to Article 6 of the European Convention on Human Rights (as implemented in English law by the Human Rights Act 1998). In that new role, it will hear reviews of decisions taken by either the OFT or at the second investigatory stage by the Competition Commission.

The existence of two parallel systems, one specialist, and the other generalist, but with much wider jurisdiction and powers, is capable of creating jurisprudential difficulties. These may be exacerbated when reform of Regulation 17 is implemented, bringing greater stress on the system. To date, the Courts have generally deferred to either the EC authorities or domestic authorities (as the case may be) where similar substantive decisions are being considered by both (*Synstar Computer Services (UK) Ltd. v ICL (Sorbus) Ltd.* [2001] C.P. Rep. 98; *MTV Europe v BMG Records (UK) Ltd.* [1997] 1 CMLR 867; *Iberian Trading UK v BPB Industries*, [1997] ICR 164; *Morgan Stanley Dean Witter Bank Ltd. v Visa International Service Association*). However, such issues do not commonly arise in a merger context.

The issue of control of power arises both at the procedural and the substantive level. There is also the question of interim measures or interim injunctive relief against either type of decision, which will be considered first.

The Courts have a wide-ranging injunction jurisdiction, exercisable in accordance with the principles of *American Cyanamid v. Ethicon* ([1975] AC 396): essentially that there should be an arguable case (or a serious issue to be tried), that the loss should not be capable of being remedied in damages (so that some behavioural remedy is required) and that the balance of convenience favours intervention.

These principles give rise to considerable problems in practice. First in the merger context, the interference by means of an injunction is usually dispositive of a matter in practice. The Courts then require a threshold of proof based around a sufficient likelihood of success (*NWL Ltd. v Woods*, [1979] 1 WLR 1294), which can be difficult to substantiate in the limited procedures associated with interlocutory proceedings.

Secondly, the balance of convenience test is usually operated to give great weight to not interfering in the operation of capital markets and the interests of shareholders (*R v Panel on Take-overs and Mergers, ex p. Datafin* ([1987] QB 815; *R v Panel on Take-overs and Mergers, ex p. Guinness plc* ([1990] 1 QB 815); *Plessey Co v GEC Siemens*).

These doctrines make it very difficult to obtain interlocutory support for a challenge to anything other than procedural or jurisdictional issues. Conversely the Courts have great flexibility as to their own procedures (including speed of hearing) and remedies. This means that, subject to the above constraints, it is possible to obtain a very fast and flexible response.

In its short existence to date, the CCAT seems to be adopting similar principles. In practice, and practical application, they are not radically different from those that would apply under classic interim measures applications at the EC level. Indeed, in *NAPP Pharmaceutical Holdings Ltd. v The Director General of Fair Trading*, Case 1000/1/1/01(IR), the principles in cases such as *American Cyanamid*, were stated to provide useful and relevant analogies, but to not in themselves be necessarily determinative of the issues likely to arise in relation to interim measures applications before the CCAT. Instead, the nearest comparable situation was considered to be that of an application to the Court of First Instance for interim relief, pending an appeal against a decision taken by the Commission.

Turning to issues of final consideration of a competition authority's powers, as mentioned above, the Courts have been reluctant to intervene in the evaluation of substantive competition issues by specialist bodies. This applies not only in the case of proceedings which are being simultaneously conducted in both tribunals, in the sense of which tribunal should be accorded preference, but also to a review by the Courts of the merits of a decision by a competition authority. Quite apart from the deference to the specialist tribunal where there are parallel processes, the Courts have recognised the value of the expertise of the specialist bodies and shown some reluctance to interfere retrospectively in their processes and decisions.

The Courts' powers in this area derive from their judicial review powers. However, these powers only permit the Courts to overturn an administrative act in certain circumstances. These include legal error, substantial error in the decision-making process (e.g. considering irrelevant factors) and the concept of *Wednesbury* unreasonableness (that, loosely, a decision that is so unreasonable that no reasonable official could have made it, cannot stand). It is evident that it is difficult to apply such powers to an alleged substantive error based on the responsible evaluation by a specialist body of factual and economic evidence in a highly judgmental area.

Thus, although a challenge to a decision is possible (see the case currently before the ECJ of a challenge to a decision of the MMC, *R v Monopolies and Mergers Commission, ex p. Milk Marque* ([2000] COD 329), it is difficult to succeed in most circumstances.

In the merger context, under the regime, which will be brought in by the Enterprise Bill, the new CAT will have a broader role than before, and in particular, will have powers to hear appeals from decisions of either the OFT or the Competition Commission in the merger area. In the future, therefore, there will be a statutory right of appeal from a merger decision of the competition authorities to the CAT. The Enterprise Bill specifically provides that the principles to be applied in that review are those of English judicial review (as briefly described above) and it will not therefore be a review on the merits. However, given the degree of relevant technical expertise that the CAT will have in the general competition area, it seems likely that whatever the legal test, it is likely to be more interventionist than the High Court would be.

The CAT will therefore resemble in some respects the CFI when considering decisions of the Commission in the merger area. However, it remains to be seen how much the review test under the Bill will be interpreted to apply the same threshold as the CFI currently does. In addition, the CAT will be free from the rules of procedure and other process constraints on the CFI, and will be likely to be able to move more quickly and flexibly, delivering a decision on matters of substance in a shorter time.

A particular difficulty arises with the current regime under the Act and it remains to be seen how that will evolve in the context of the merger regime. It is currently only possible to appeal decisions of the Director General (section 46). This gives rise to particular problems in that important decisions, particularly on matters of due process, can be taken otherwise than by way of formal decision, leaving parties without a remedy otherwise than by way of approach to the Courts. This issue potentially might also arise under the Enterprise Bill.

The Court system is reasonably tolerant of the right of third parties to intervene and/or challenge decisions. They need only show *locus standi*: a sufficient interest in the subject matter of the decision challenged. Under the procedures of the Act, third parties currently have very limited rights because of the requirement under section 47 for a third party to request the DGFT to withdraw or vary his decision before having a right of appeal. The resulting loss of judicial protection has, however, been recognised and the Enterprise Bill will rectify this by replacing section 47 with a new version that removes this requirement. Moreover, as regards merger decisions, the Enterprise Bill specifically gives wide rights of access. Finally, the responsibility for determining whether a third party has sufficient interest to make an appeal will, in the future, lie with the CAT. Thus it seems likely that the issue of the protection of third party interests will be resolved.

The current position in Scotland and Northern Ireland, is that a decision of the competition authorities, including the Secretary of State, is potentially judicially reviewable in the relevant jurisdiction (to the extent that the parties do not wish to avail themselves of judicial review proceedings in England), if there is a specific issue relating to that jurisdiction. Judicial review proceedings in Scotland or Northern Ireland follow local principles as to both procedure and substantive law. In future, the CAT's jurisdiction will apply to decisions involving connections with Scotland and Northern Ireland, but in appropriate circumstances an appeal will lie to the relevant Appeal Court.

Thus, it can fairly be said that the UK does have judicial protection in this area. Its scope and nature is broadly equivalent to that of the EC processes. In certain respects, the UK system is preferable in that there are more diverse remedies and the prospect of faster resolution (c.f. the problems arising from the *Airtours* decision and the delays inherent in the challenge in *GEC/Westinghouse*). There are still inherent tensions in the need for a fast decision but one which is balanced, right and fair and takes account of all interests, including those of shareholders, in a highly charged commercial environment where there is the risk of unmeritorious challenge as well as a need for judicial protection.

6. Below are a number of questions relating to domestic law which may assist in a comparative analysis.

(a)Please provide an overview of the structure of and main features of the relevant domestic legislation and the institutional framework (who enforces it)? It may be helpful with some information about the role of private rights of action.

The primary legal basis for merger control in the UK is the Fair Trading Act 1973 ('FTA'). The FTA establishes a tripartite administrative procedure for merger control involving the Secretary of State for Trade and Industry ('Secretary of State'), the Director-General of Fair Trading ('DGFT') and the Competition Commission ('CC').

Broadly, the FTA enables the Secretary of State to determine whether or not to refer qualifying mergers to the CC for investigation. The DGFT, head of the OFT, advises the Secretary of State in this matter. Only a small percentage of qualifying mergers are actually referred to the CC for investigation. On a referral, the CC investigates to determine whether or not a merger operates or may be expected to operate against the public interest. However, it is the Secretary of State who, in the case of an adverse report, ultimately decides whether to prohibit the merger, to impose some other remedy or whether to clear it unconditionally.

The FTA therefore currently confers overall responsibility for merger control on the Secretary of State. She ultimately decides whether to clear a merger or to refer it to the CC for investigation. She also determines, following an adverse report, whether a merger can proceed and, if so, on what terms. The DGFT plays an advisory role. His functions include a specific duty to monitor mergers and to make appropriate recommendations to the Secretary of State. The CC's role is an investigative one. It must investigate mergers referred to it and report on its findings. It cannot investigate mergers on its own initiative.

There is no statutory right of appeal from a recommendation of the CC or a decision made under the FTA by the Secretary of State (but see the response to question 6(i) ("what are the opportunities for judicial review"?)).

The Enterprise Bill, published on 26 March 2002, will fundamentally alter the institutional framework of the current merger regime (see the response to question 6(m) below).

(b) What kinds of transactions are caught?

The Secretary of State may refer to the CC 'a merger situation qualifying for investigation' which will arise when the following conditions are satisfied:

- two or more enterprises cease to be distinct or there are arrangements in progress or in contemplation which will lead to enterprises ceasing to be distinct; and
- at least one of these enterprises is carried on by, or is under the control of, a body corporate incorporated in the UK (including UK subsidiaries of foreign companies); and
- either the merger has not yet taken place or has taken place within the last four months; and
- the transaction meets the jurisdictional thresholds described below.

Two enterprises will 'cease to be distinct' either if they are brought under common ownership or control or if one ceases to carry on business as a result of arrangements between them. Enterprises will be regarded as being under common control where they are enterprises of interconnected bodies corporate (i.e. parent and subsidiary, or sister subsidiaries); enterprises carried on by two or more bodies corporate of which one and the same person or group of persons has control; or an enterprise carried on by a body corporate and an enterprise carried on by a person or group of persons having control of that body corporate. A person or group of persons will also be treated as having control of an enterprise where they have the ability to control or materially to influence the policy of that enterprise.

Are joint ventures caught?

The application of the criteria set out above will apply to many joint ventures. In the case of joint ventures which involve a shift of control or influence over an identifiable 'enterprise' a merger situation qualifying for investigation may arise, provided that either the assets or the market share criteria (see below) are satisfied.

What are the jurisdictional thresholds?

The FTA provides alternative thresholds based on market share and assets:

- the 'share of supply' test is satisfied only when the merger itself creates or enhances a 25 per cent share of supply or purchases in the UK (or in a substantial part of it). Where one company already has a 25 per cent share of a particular market and the other has no share of that market, this threshold will not apply; or

- the gross value of the assets taken over must exceed £70 million (approximately €109 million at the relevant rate of £1 = €1.55 applicable in July 2002). This is determined by adding together the book value of all the tangible and intangible assets of the target (after depreciation) including investments and current assets, whether within the UK or not, but with no deduction for liabilities of any kind.

In general, the FTA will not apply to any transaction which falls under the jurisdiction of the Merger Regulation.

Is it difficult to identify with sufficient certainty whether a filing is in fact required under national law?

There are often occasions when, due to the subjective nature of the FTA's 'share of supply' test and the need to consider the market in question, it is difficult to determine whether a filing with the OFT is required. In cases which lack certainty, merging parties often take advantage of approaching the OFT for informal advice or confidential guidance (see the response to question 6(i) ("what publicity is given to the process?")). Notably, however, the move to an alternative objective (and low) turnover test (see the response to question 6(m) below) is likely to lessen the number of cases which lack certainty with regard to filing.

Are foreign-to-foreign mergers caught?

The assets test is applied on a world-wide basis and only one UK-related enterprise need be involved. The OFT's guidance is that 'a merger between two foreign companies may still qualify for investigation where either company controls any enterprise which is carried on or incorporated in the UK'. Therefore an overseas company with a subsidiary incorporated in the UK or a branch or a division in the UK will be regarded as satisfying the requirement of a UK link. An appropriate test to apply (although not one which has been specifically endorsed by the OFT) is that used in UK tax statutes. This test distinguishes between carrying on business 'in' and 'with' the UK. Accordingly, a non-UK established enterprise whose only trading links with the UK comprises the sale of goods to customers located in the UK would not be regarded as carrying on business in the UK provided that it did not negotiate or conclude the sales contracts within the UK.

The test can lead to a significant number of cases in which foreign-to-foreign mergers technically qualify for investigation.

(c) Is the filing mandatory or voluntary?

Filing in the UK is voluntary and will remain so post the changes proposed in the Enterprise Bill (but see the response to question 6(l) below for the filing rules for special sectors such as newspapers). However, in practice a large number of deals are pre-notified to give the parties legal certainty since the OFT can, and regularly does, review mergers on its own initiative (as a result of either monitoring the press for merger announcements or a third party drawing a merger to its attention).

Who is responsible for filing?

Either form of filing (see below) may be given by any person carrying on an enterprise to which the notified arrangements relate. Such a person may authorise, in writing, another to act on its behalf. It is not necessary for Merger Notices or submissions to be made jointly.

What is involved in the preparation of a filing?

Filing may be done either by use of a pro-forma merger notice ('Merger Notice') or by a submission in any format. In practice, a Merger Notice is advantageous since, in this instance the Secretary of State must decide within the fixed period (usually 20 working days see below) whether or not to refer the merger to the CC. Informal advice or confidential guidance may be sought (see the response to question 6(i) ("what publicity is given to the process?") below) prior to notification.

The OFT has published guidance on the kind of information which is generally required in order for it to take a view of whether a merger situation is likely to qualify for investigation and, if so, its possible effect on competition and the public interest. In addition to a full description of the transaction and proposed timetable, it requires information on the merging enterprises' market shares in the UK or a substantial part of it. In order to assess market definition, information is sought on demand-side substitutability, supply-side substitutability and the geographic market. Information on horizontal overlaps, vertical links and entry barriers will also be relevant.

Copies of the latest relevant annual reports and accounts and, in certain cases a pro-forma balance sheet for the merging enterprises and, where appropriate, copies of press releases and of any offer document or listing particulars produced in connection with the proposal should accompany the Merger Notice. A Merger Notice must also be accompanied by the correct fee in order to be valid. The level of fees payable for either a Merger Notice or a submission varies according to the size of the acquisition and ranges from £5,000 (approximately €8,000) to £15,000 (approximately €23,000). As from June 2001, certain small and medium-sized firms are exempt from the payment of fees. With a Merger Notice, the fee is payable upon filing. With a submission, the fee is payable when the Secretary of State announces her decision.

Although not specifically required, where a submission is made to the OFT, similar information should be provided as in a Merger Notice.

The time required to complete a Merger Notice or draft a submission depends on the complexity of the case and the ability of the parties to collate the relevant information promptly.

What are the deadlines for filing?

Since there is no obligation to notify a merger, there are no filing deadlines and no sanctions apply if no notification is made. Where parties do not seek clearance, however, they take the risk that, whether or not third parties complain, the OFT may investigate the merger on its own initiative (for a maximum of four months following a completed transaction becoming public) and the further risk that divestment or conditions for clearance could be ordered following an adverse CC report.

What are the waiting periods and does implementation of the transaction have to be suspended?

Where a Merger Notice is submitted, the initial statutory period for the OFT's consideration is 20 working days, beginning with the first day after the Merger Notice has been received by the OFT and any relevant fee has been paid. The period may be extended by 15 working days.

The timetable for dealing with a submission is less specific. The stated aim of the DTI and the OFT is that the Secretary of State should reach a decision on 90 per cent of mergers within 45 working days from receipt by the OFT of a 'satisfactory submission'. Where a merger is referred by the Secretary of State to the CC for investigation the reference must specify a period (of not more than six months) within which the CC must report. In practice, the usual period is three, and exceptionally four, months. An extension of up to three months may be requested. Following the CC's report, the Secretary of State will aim to reach a decision in 80 per cent of cases within 20 working days of receipt of the CC's report.

Since notification is voluntary, there are no real impediments to the completion of a merger while it is being considered by the OFT (but see the response to question 6(d) below and note that if a Merger Notice is submitted, parties cannot close the transaction and retain the benefit of the statutory timetable but can move onto the nonstatutory basis). In practice, however, constraints may be imposed by the nature of the offer, for example, if the City Code on Takeovers and Mergers ('the Takeover Code') applies (see the response to question 6(e) below). Furthermore, if a reference is made to the CC, it is then unlawful, except with the consent of the Secretary of State, for any party to the reference or one of its group or associated companies (in each case incorporated or carrying on business in the UK) to acquire an interest in shares in a company to which the reference relates, unless the interest is acquired pursuant to a pre-existing contractual obligation. The consent of the Secretary of State is rarely granted.

(d) What are the issues and possible sanctions involved in closing before clearance?

Since the UK regime is a voluntary one, there is no bar to completing unless the merger is referred to the CC. However, where a merger is completed without clearance, the parties run the risk that the OFT may investigate the merger and the further risk that, if the merger is referred to the CC, the Secretary of State will usually request the DGFT to seek interim undertakings to restrain the parties from acting in a way which might prejudice the outcome of the CC's inquiry or the Secretary of State's subsequent action. Such undertakings usually require the merged companies not to take further steps to integrate the businesses until the outcome of the CC investigation has been made public. It is also unlawful to acquire any further shares in each other (see the response to question 6(c) ("what are the waiting periods and does implementation of the transaction have to be suspended?") above). Furthermore, if the merger is completed and is subsequently referred to the CC, the CC could recommend divestment or conditions for clearance.

What is the timetable for clearance and can it be speeded up?

See the response to question 6(c) above which sets out the relevant timetables. Parties have no specific ability to speed up the relevant timetables although their cooperation with the OFT/CC will prevent any unnecessary delays.

(e) Are there any special rules applicable to public takeover bids?

If the merger involves the purchase of a listed or unlisted public company that is resident in the UK, the Takeover Code requires that the bid should lapse at the point when the merger is referred to the CC or to Phase II proceedings under the Merger Regulation. Upon such lapse, the bidder and the shareholders of the target company will no longer be bound by acceptances of the offer made prior to the reference to the CC or the decision under Article 6(1)(c) of the Merger Regulation. The bid may however be revived (within a certain timeframe) if, subsequently, it is cleared by the CC or the Secretary of State allows it to proceed subject to certain undertakings being given or a clearance decision is made pursuant to the Merger Regulation.

(f) What is the substantive test for clearance?

The grounds upon which the DGFT advises the Secretary of State and the grounds upon which the Secretary of State may make a CC reference, are not exhaustively defined in the FTA. In practice, a first instance view on a 'public interest' test is taken. 'Public interest' as defined in section 84 FTA is construed as a matter of policy as competition. The usual relevant competition factors may be taken into account, such as the market share of the new enterprise created by the merger; the market shares and competitive strengths of competitors; barriers to entry; advantages over competitors (intellectual property rights, for example); the availability of substitute products; and the position of buyers or suppliers in the relevant market.

When a merger is referred to the CC, the test applied by the CC in deciding whether or not to recommend clearance is whether the merger situation operates, or may be expected to operate, against the public interest. The term 'public interest' is non-exhaustively defined in the FTA and allows the CC to take into account 'all matters which appear to them in the particular circumstances to be relevant'. The list of relevant factors includes maintaining and promoting effective competition in the supply of goods and services in the UK; promoting the interests of consumers; promoting cost reduction and the development of new techniques and products; facilitating the entry of new competitors; the balanced distribution of industry and employment in the UK; and maintaining and promoting competitive activity in markets outside the UK.

In practice competition has, in recent years, been the most important factor taken into account in CC investigations. It seems that the public interest test is broad enough to allow the CC to take efficiencies into account or to accept a failing firm defence.

See also the response to question 6(m) below which sets out the proposed changes to the public interest test.

(g) To what extent are non-competition issues relevant to the review process?

Given the central role afforded to the Secretary of State and the broad public interest test set out in the FTA, non-competition issues have, on occasion, been relevant in the review process. Thus reports have, for example, taken into account matters such as overseas control, employment, regional issues and public security and defence. The predominant issue has, however, in recent years been competition. Notably, in the case of Richard Desmond's takeover of the Express newspaper group, the OFT's report to the Secretary of State recommended that the merger be cleared on competition grounds and stated that the OFT was 'not wellplaced ... to asses the noncompetition issues which have been raised in this case'.

Further, the UK government is proposing to limit the opportunity for Ministerial intervention and to replace the public interest test with a competition-based test (see the response to question 6(m) below).

(h) Is it possible to remedy competition issues?

Undertakings may be offered to remedy any possible detriment to the public interest at two different stages. First, parties may be able to prevent a reference to the CC by offering appropriate undertakings. Second, undertakings may be offered to the Secretary of State following a CC investigation to remedy any adverse findings identified.

The Secretary of State may accept formal written undertakings instead of making a reference to the CC. Proposed undertakings are published in draft form, together with the advice from the DGFT, and third parties may submit comments. Although in principle a broad range of undertakings could be offered at this stage, in practice structural remedies are favoured over behavioural remedies since the latter require long-term monitoring.

Following a reference to the CC, it may conclude that action should be taken to remedy adverse effects and make recommendations as to such action. The DGFT also advises the Secretary of State on remedies, which may be different to those proposed by the CC. Although the Secretary of State will take account of the recommendations or advice received from the CC and DGFT, she is not bound by them and may decide to impose different remedies. The DGFT is usually charged with seeking appropriate remedies consistent with the Secretary of State's decision.

The *Interbrew/Bass* case was notable in that it gave rise to the first successful challenge regarding remedies imposed by the CC and the Secretary of State (namely the divestment of the UK business of Bass Brewers to a buyer approved by the DGFT). In a landmark judgement by the High Court on 25 May 2001 it was ruled that the CC had failed to give Interbrew the chance to explore alternative plans to ease concerns of reduced competition and the question of remedies was remitted to the Secretary of State (with assistance from the DGFT) for reconsideration. The result was that Interbrew was ordered to sell only the Carling business portion of Bass Brewers (this was completed on 4 February 2002).

Under the proposed changes to depoliticise the merger review process, the CC will take decisions as to remedies, without the Secretary of State's involvement (see the response to question 6(m) below).

(i) What are the typical steps during the investigation?

Following notification of a qualifying merger, the OFT may require clarification or may request further information. Where competition or other public interest issues are raised, the OFT will generally meet with the parties to discuss their concerns.

The OFT will invariably seek third party comments. When the OFT receives a Merger Notice or a submission, it will announce the proposed merger on the London Stock Exchange's Regulatory News Service and give third parties an opportunity to comment within a certain period. It may also issue a supplementary press release or make an announcement in the trade press. As well as publishing a general request for representations, the OFT may contact competitors, major customers or suppliers and will maintain the confidentiality of any information so provided.

Where the OFT concludes that substantive competition or other public interest issues arise it will convene a meeting of the Mergers Panel, a non-statutory body on which all interested government departments are represented. Having taken views of the Mergers Panel into account, the DGFT will submit written recommendations to the Secretary of State.

The Secretary of State is not obliged to follow the DGFT's advice and, although she generally does, there have been a number of notable exceptions in the past. The policy of the current Secretary of State is, however, to accept the advice of the DGFT, save in exceptional circumstances. This policy is a precursor to the change in law under which the DGFT will make the reference decision (see the response to question 6(m) below). The DGFT's advice to the Secretary of State regarding cases which are referred to the CC and those of an important nature is published. The Secretary of State may either clear the merger or refer it to the CC. The time allowed for an inquiry by the CC is six months, extendable by a further period of three months. Usually the Secretary of State will allow three months for the CC to complete its inquiry. The Secretary of State aims to publish the CC's report within 20 working days in 80 per cent of cases.

What rights do complainants have?

Where the OFT is informed of a prospective merger, third parties are generally given an opportunity to comment. As referred to above, in addition to publishing a general request for representations, competitors, major customers or suppliers may be contacted by the OFT. Any information provided by third parties will be confidential.

Where a merger has been referred to the CC, the CC will also request third party views by placing advertisements in newspaper or trade press. As part of the 'open government' initiative, CC procedure now includes a number of steps which contribute towards transparency. For example, the CC will consider whether a public or joint hearing is appropriate and a verbatim transcript will be made available to participants. Issues and remedies letters will be made available not only to the parties but details will also be published for consultation on the CC's website (http://www.competition-commission.org.uk). A summary of views appears in the CC's published report (although parties have no right to inspect the OFT's or CC's files). Third parties also have the opportunity to give their comments when the DGFT is negotiating undertakings either in lieu of or following a reference.

What publicity is given to the process?

Current government policy is to make the merger clearance process more transparent. The OFT publicly announces its intention to seek third party views and it is intended that in significant cases the DGFT will publish his advice to the Secretary of State on whether or not to refer a merger to the CC.

Once a merger has been referred to the CC, comments will be invited via an announcement in newspapers and trade press. The CC may decide to hold a public hearing, in which case a transcript may be published. At the time an 'issues' letter is sent to the parties, the CC normally publishes a statement on its website and issues a press release informing the public of the matters of concern which it is considering. The CC will also invite comments on appropriate remedies to address the issues identified and in some cases has published a statement of remedies which it might recommend if it were to reach an adverse conclusion.

The DGFT publishes draft undertakings and invites comments when he is negotiating remedies either in lieu of or following a reference to the CC. In addition, press releases are issued by the Secretary of State in relation to clearances and referrals.

There is, however, a procedure for obtaining 'confidential guidance' whereby one or more of the parties to a proposed merger may seek an indication, given in confidence, from the Secretary of State as to whether the transaction would be likely to be referred to the CC if it were to proceed. This procedure is an informal practice developed and recognised over a number of years. It involves an evaluation by the OFT but, because of confidentiality, without the views of third parties. Guidance is qualified accordingly. Sometimes no outcome can be expressed on the information available and without the benefit of third party views. Decisions on confidential guidance are not binding upon the Secretary of State.

What are the opportunities for judicial review?

There is no statutory right of appeal from a recommendation of the CC or a decision made under the FTA by the Secretary of State. Such categories of decision-making are, however, subject to narrow rights of judicial review for example, on grounds of illegality (unlawfulness), irrationality (unreasonableness) or procedural impropriety (unfairness). Consequently, the High Court does not act as a court of appeal for the procedure but will simply review the merits of the decision-making process. The first, and only, successful application for judicial review of a decision made under the FTA merger provisions was *Interbrew/Bass* in 2001.

The Enterprise Bill will grant a power to review decisions taken in connection with merger references to the specialist Competition Appeals Tribunal (see the response to question 6(m) below).

(j) What are the enforcement powers?

If the CC concludes that the merger may not be expected to operate against the public interest, the Secretary of State is not entitled to intervene. If the CC finds, by a two-thirds majority of the investigating panel, against the merger or that it should be allowed only if remedial action is taken, the Secretary of State has a discretion either to block the merger or to permit it, conditionally or unconditionally. She has power to make a wide variety of orders following an adverse CC report but in practice undertakings are normally accepted rather than orders imposed. Where a merger has already been completed, the same powers exist and divestment can be ordered where appropriate.

How does administrative and civil sanctions compare with the EC regime?

Failure to comply with an order made by the Secretary of State (as referred to above) would result in the relevant companies being liable for contempt of court. To date this has never happened.

Under the EC regime, where a concentration has already been implemented and is subsequently prohibited, the Commission may also require divestment or any other action that may be appropriate in order to restore conditions of effective competition.

In addition, the Commission has the power to impose fines on undertakings for failure to comply with their obligations under the Merger Regulation. In particular, failure to suspend implementation of a merger pending examination or putting into effect a merger prohibited by the Commission may expose the companies concerned to fines of up to 10 per cent of their aggregate turnover. The Commission may also impose periodic penalty payments in certain circumstances.

The Commission may revoke its clearance decision (whether granted in first or second phase) where a breach of undertakings is committed or where the decision is based on incorrect information.

And what are the criminal sanctions, and are they used?

There are no criminal sanctions under the FTA (but see the proposed changes under the Enterprise Bill referred to in the response to question 6(m) below).

(k) Do the authorities cooperate with other antitrust authorities?

The OFT does cooperate with other competition authorities, both formally and informally, but in each case subject to restrictions on the exchange of confidential information. The framework for cooperation by the Member States in relation to agreements notified under the Merger Regulation is set out in the regulation itself. As a competent authority in the UK, the OFT receives details of all mergers notified in Brussels. It examines each case, consults with other government departments as necessary and provides the UK's view to the Merger Task Force where appropriate. The OFT also represents the UK at hearings convened by the Merger Task Force and attends Advisory Committee meetings.

Although there is no formal agreement to cooperate as between the EU national competition authorities themselves, perhaps the most tangible evidence of cooperation came in September 1997 when the OFT announced its participation in a system allowing notification of mergers in each of France, the UK and Germany on a voluntary common form. The authorities of all three countries will accept the form where a merger is to be examined in more than one of the countries and the parties will be notified within a month if more examination is needed. The OFT has expressed disappointment that the common notification form is rarely used and has pointed out that it offers the active goodwill of the authorities in cooperating in the analysis and processing of a merger.

Early in 2000, the then Secretary of State, Stephen Byers, asserted that with increasing globalisation, there is a good case for improving cooperation and information exchanges between the national competition authorities. Although the Government has proposed legislation to allow sharing of information between competition authorities, information gained from merger investigations will be excluded.

(l) Are there also rules on foreign investment, special sectors or other relevant approvals?

There are no rules against foreign investment in the FTA. However, the broad public interest test set out in the FTA has enabled account to be taken, in the past, of the fact that control of a UK company will be passing overseas. In *The Government of Kuwait/British Petroleum*, for example, the Monopolies and Mergers Commission (now the CC) concluded that the Government of Kuwait's acquisition of BP would operate against the public interest. These types of factors may be relevant where industries of vital national interest (such as defence or oil) are at issue.

The Industry Act 1975, however, makes special provision for cases involving the acquisition of 'important UK manufacturing undertakings by non-UK persons' (as yet unused). The Broadcasting Act 1990 (as amended) imposes restrictions and prohibitions on nationality grounds on the persons who can hold licences for radio and television services.

There are special provisions of the FTA applicable to newspaper mergers. Broadly, the preliminary vetting of newspaper mergers is carried out by the Department of Trade and Industry. With certain exceptions, newspaper mergers are automatically referred to the CC. A purchaser may not complete a newspaper merger and take the CC risk: a transfer of a newspaper business without the Secretary of State's prior written consent is unlawful and void and penalties can be imposed on those knowingly concerned in, or privy to, such a transfer. The public interest criteria applied by the CC include consideration of the effect of merger on the need for accurate presentation of news and free expression of opinion.

In addition to the provisions of the FTA, special account must be taken of mergers in certain other sectors. For example, the Water Industry Act 1991 contains a special regime for the control – in particular the automatic reference to the CC – of mergers between certain water companies. While this principle will remain, the procedural provisions on water mergers are to be modified by the Enterprise Bill to bring them into line with more general procedural developments (see the response to question 6(m) below). A number of other special statutory provisions apply in the media and banking sectors that may impact upon mergers and acquisitions.

(m) Are there current proposals to change the legislation?

Patricia Hewitt came to office as the Secretary of State for Trade and Industry following the general election in June 2001. Soon after the election, the Government announced a broad package of reforms aimed at raising productivity in the UK. These reforms include sweeping changes to the competition regime which the government considers to be at the heart of its strategy to close the productivity gap with the UK's competitors. A White Paper on competition policy was published on 31 July 2001 and the Enterprise Bill was published on 26 March 2002. It is anticipated that the Bill will be in force by Spring 2003. Part 3 of the Enterprise Bill deals with the reform of the current merger regime and takes forward the Government's earlier consultation on its reform. The key changes are that political involvement in merger cases will be reduced and a new substantive test for appraisal will be introduced. A competition based test will replace the current public interest test. In the future, therefore, decisions should be clearer, more predictable and, generally, apolitical, taken by those best qualified to act (the independent competition authorities).

If adopted in their current form the new rules for decision making should work in the following way:

- Save in cases involving defined public interest issues the OFT will have the duty to refer relevant mergers to the CC where it believes that they have resulted, or may be expected to result, in a substantial lessening of competition within any UK market. The Government has decided to adopt the substantial lessening of competition test, already used in a number of countries, including the US, rather than the current EC dominance test.
- A merger will be 'relevant' (and hence may be referred) where 'two or more enterprises have ceased to be distinct' and *either* the value of the turnover in the UK of the enterprise being taken over exceeds £45 million *or* where the merger would result in the new merged entity having, or exceeding, a 25% share of supply of goods or services in the UK or in a substantial part of the UK. The Bill thus retains the current share of supply test but replaces the assets test with a turnover test.
- The OFT will not be obliged to make a reference if: the market involved is of insufficient importance; suitable undertakings are accepted from the parties by the OFT *in lieu* of a reference to the CC; or if customer benefits outweigh any substantial lessening of competition[5]. Relevant customer benefits are narrowly defined in the Bill but include efficiencies, in the form of lower prices, higher quality, greater choice or greater innovation in a UK market.
- On referral of a merger the CC will have to determine whether a relevant merger situation has been, or will be, created which has resulted, or may be expected to result, in a substantial lessening of competition within any market or markets in the UK. Where an anti-competitive outcome is identified the CC must decide, taking account of any relevant customer benefits, whether it should itself take action, or recommend taking of action by others, to remedy, mitigate or prevent the substantial lessening of competition.
- It will essentially be for the CC and OFT to enforce remedies. The role of the Secretary of State will be confined to cases involving public interest issues (the only one of which currently specified is 'national security') or special interest grounds.

- The new Competition Appeals Tribunal (which will take over the functions of the current Appeals Tribunal of the CC and will acquire some new functions under the Bill) will have power to review decisions taken in connection with a merger reference. In determining such an application, which is to be made within three months from the date of the decision to which it relates, the Competition Appeals Tribunal is to apply "the same principles as would by applied by a court on an application for judicial review".
- The Bill provides, in accordance with the UK government's desire to crack down on serious infringements of the competition rules, for the introduction of a criminal offence for individuals who engage in cartel agreements. The Bill divorces the offence from any infringement of the EC or UK competition rules and provides for an additional extraditable offence to apply to individuals who *dishonestly* agree with one or more persons to make or implement horizontal agreements to fix prices, share markets, limit production or rig bids. The new offence is to be backed up with severe sanctions of prison sentences of up to five years and/or fines. The UK government takes the view that these kinds of sanctions are more likely to concentrate the mind of directors and other employees than corporate fines (which may still be applicable in concurrent civil proceedings).
- The Bill contains a number of other miscellaneous and supplementary changes to the current system. For example, it introduces a new statutory maximum period of 24 weeks (extendable in special cases for a period of up to 8 weeks) within which the CC will be obliged to publish its report on merger cases and confers power on the CC to impose monetary penalties on persons for non-compliance with orders for the production of documents or information.
- Changes are also to be introduced to the water mergers regime with the objective of aligning, in so far as it is possible, the procedural regime for mergers between water enterprises with the new general regime (while maintaining the automatic reference of mergers between certain water companies to the CC). For example, the assets test will be replaced with a turnover test when determining whether a merger between water enterprises qualifies for a mandatory reference, the responsibility for making such decisions will be transferred from the Secretary of State to the OFT, the responsibility for final decisions on what remedies should be applied in the event of an adverse finding will be transferred from the Secretary of State to the CC and in the case of a completed water merger, the time period in which the OFT will have to make a reference will be reduced from 6 to 4 months from the date of the merger taking place.

7. What will you identify as the main obstacles to takeovers where a company[2] from your jurisdiction is either bidder or target and the other company is from another EU jurisdiction[3]?

There are no formal barriers to a bidder offering just cash for a UK listed company. Where the consideration also involves securities there are more difficulties but not necessarily obstacles (see answer to Question 15 below). The City Code (see Question 10 below) operates effectively to ensure that shareholders decide on the merits of an offer – a process that is further facilitated by the shares in most UK listed companies being widely held and traded by unconnected institutional investors.

UK listed companies must seek shareholder consent for all transactions (including mergers) over a certain size-assessed by reference to a number of financial tests (e.g. if consideration to market capitalisation exceeds 25%). There is no exactly equivalent rule in any other European jurisdiction.

8. Do hostile takeovers by companies from other EU jurisdictions in fact take place in your country?

Yes. Hostile bids are not, compared with recommended bids, very common but are still more frequent than in other European jurisdictions. Lafarge of France unsuccessfully made an initial hostile offer for Blue Circle. Most market observers however thought it was Lafarge's unwillingness to pay more which resulted in its offer being unsuccessful. Lafarge subsequently made a recommended successful offer for Blue Circle. Lafarge had previously made a successful hostile bid for Redland. OM of Sweden unsuccessfully made a hostile bid for the London Stock Exchange (an unlisted company). There have also been successful hostile bids from outside the EU such as AMP for Pearl.

9. To what extents are there any sectors (utilities, financial institutions) that in practice are further protected from hostile takeovers, or foreign[4] takeovers in particular? Are there any policy statements or particular legal mechanisms that give effect to this protection, or is it a matter of informal mechanisms?[5]

All of the following industries are subject to additional regulatory constraints (none of which draw a distinction between hostile or recommended transactions or, with the exception of certain media, UK, EU or other overseas bidders):

- Coal/steel
- Airlines
- Newspapers
- Broadcasting
- Banks
- Consumer credit businesses
- Financial services businesses
- Insurance businesses
- Oil
- Electricity/water/gas/telecoms
- Gaming
- Lloyds brokers or underwriting agencies.

There is little or no recent evidence of nationalistic policies. Indeed many regulated water and electricity companies have, for instance, been taken over by German, French and US bidders. There is also very little State ownership of UK listed companies which further de-politicises the process. Bids for UK commercial banks by overseas bidders have not been experienced but this might as much be because of the lack of synergies in cross-border banking deals as anything else. Hostile bids for UK banks are possible – see the bids by The Royal Bank of Scotland and The Bank of Scotland for NatWest. Many of the UK's investment banks have been taken over by overseas companies (for instance Warburgs by UBS and Kleinwort Benson by Dresdner).

10. What are the company law techniques of completing a takeover or merger that are used in practice where one of the companies is from another EU jurisdiction? Pleas give particular attention to how this would differ from the usual completion of a takeover or merger where both companies are from your jurisdiction. It would be useful if you could add a comment about the consequences on the techniques used of the taxation regime and of any differential tax treatment of takeovers or mergers where one party is from another EU jurisdiction.

The usual form of takeover involves the bidder making a general offer to all target shareholders on the register of members to acquire their shares. Shareholders are sent an offer document containing information on the bidder and its offer with a form of acceptance or instructions on how to accept the offer electronically. A bidder has to secure acceptances over shares representing at least 50 per cent of the target's share capital in order to succeed with the bid. This 50 per cent can include market purchases.

Another way of achieving a change of control of a public company is to use a statutory mechanism known as a scheme of arrangement. This is a process involving court approval which allows a company to change its capital structure and agree matters with its shareholders; it is not a US or continental style merger where one company ceases to exist. Under a scheme the target's shareholders could agree that their existing shares be cancelled and reissued to the bidder, or transferred to the bidder, in consideration for the payment of cash or the issue of new shares by the bidder.

The target company would apply to court which may then convene a meeting of shareholders. At the meeting a majority in number representing three-quarters in value of members voting must approve the scheme. The scheme then requires the sanction of the court. Once the scheme has been approved all shareholders are bound by it.

A scheme of arrangement has certain advantages over an offer, including the fact that it should avoid a half per cent stamp duty charge that will be payable on a general offer. Additionally, the bidder is certain to acquire 100 per cent of the target company shares on completion. A scheme does however require a higher approval level than an offer as it requires approval by a majority in number representing 75 per cent in value of the shareholders voting at the meeting (or the relevant class meeting). On a takeover offer the bidder has only to secure acceptances over 50 per cent of the voting shares. However the fact that a scheme, if successful, will guarantee that all shareholders of the target are bound is sometimes seen as crucial.

A scheme can only be used if the bid is recommended because it requires the active assistance of the target's directors. Schemes are also inflexible because of the court's involvement. It is not easy to improve the terms, for example, if a rival bidder appears.

Generally speaking, most takeovers are implemented by way of a takeover offer but schemes are common for transactions with long timetables and also where it is desirable and necessary to avoid US securities registration requirements. The choice between offer and scheme typically does not depend on whether the bidder is from another EU jurisdiction or not. E.On's acquisition of Powergen and the acquisition of Saatchi by Publicis (German and French bidders respectively) were both accomplished using a scheme of arrangement.

There is little differential tax treatment of takeovers and mergers where one party is from another EU jurisdiction or even a non-EU jurisdiction. The three main tax considerations are:

- Tax on the target shareholders – very generally speaking this depends on whether a gain (or loss) is realised which is usually when the offer consideration is in the form of cash but not when the consideration is in the form of securities regardless of the country of incorporation of the issuer of those securities.
- Stamp duty - Transfers of shares in an English company are subject to

stamp duty which is payable at a rate which is equivalent to 0.5%. In a scheme of arrangement which involves the cancellation of shares there is no transfer so stamp duty is not payable. Stamp duty is payable whether the consideration is in the form of cash or shares and regardless of the nationality of the bidder.

- Where securities are offered as consideration, the tax payable by the holder after completion of the offer on receipt of dividends, capital repayments etc. This will differ between different countries – largely depending on double tax treaties.

11. A duty on listed companies to disclose capital and control structures is proposed in Issues Relating to Takeover Bids, the First Report of the High Level Group of Company Law Experts (see p 25). Would this require amendments in the legislation in your country? How would these amendments in case be implemented (in primary company law, securities law, stock exchange regulations etc.)?

It is possible that encouraging companies to make disclosure more explicit, prominent or easily available (e.g. via websites) may require changes but as a general proposition very little will have to change in the UK because the rights attaching to shares have to be publicly filed, all shareholders with interests in excess of 3% or more have to declare their interest to the Company and the Company in turn must declare this publicly and in their annual reports. Further, certain arrangements between shareholders must also be reported to the Company and publicly disclosed. The changes could be via UK Listing Authority rules (subject to the Prospectus Directive) or via Companies Act legislation.

12. A so called break through rule after take over bids is another of the proposals in Issues Relating to Takeover Bids, the First Report of the High Level Group of Company Law Experts (see p 29). Would this require amendments in the legislation in your country? How would these amendments in case be implemented (in primary company law, securities law, stock exchange regulations etc.)?

The so-called break-through rule would require amendments in primary company law – it is thought that UK Listing Authority regulation changes would not be sufficient. It is for debate in the UK as elsewhere whether it is possible to deprive those who currently have voting control of that right.

13. In your view, would these two new rules as proposed have any material impact on the existing barriers to takeovers in your country (or in others as seen from your point of view)? It would be helpful if you could demon-

strate the impact, or lack of it, by going through one or more recent take over bids that failed in your country (or in some other member state, by a company from your country).

For the reasons stated above and below – see 14(g) – it is thought that the break-through rule would make very little difference in the UK due to the relatively small number of companies with restricted voting / control structures. This reflects the relatively diverse holdings of shares by unconnected institutions in most companies. To the extent that recent bids have failed in the UK this is largely been because independent shareholders have not been persuaded of the value of the consideration.

14. Below are a number of questions which may assist in a comparative analysis.

a. What are the main features of the relevant domestic take over legislation constituting the company law and financial market regime, and who enforces it (independent regulators, regulatory bodies with appeal to ministry, stock exchange)? What is the extent of intervention by the takeover regulator(s) – to what extent does the regulator have wide or general discretions to block and play a protectionist role (for example in its capacity as approver of the offer terms/documentation)?

Takeovers in the UK are governed by the City Code on Takeovers and Mergers (the City Code). The City Code applies to offers for public companies resident in the UK, the Channel Islands and the Isle of Man (whether or not their shares are listed). The City Code also applies to mergers and statutory schemes of arrangement involving a change of control of a UK public company. The City Code does not apply to private companies unless there has been some marketing of their shares to the public in the previous 10 years.

The City Code is a non-statutory set of rules developed by the UK Takeover Panel to reflect more than 20 years' practical experience of takeovers. The City Code consists of 10 general principles and 38 detailed rules. The general principles are essential to an understanding of how the City Code works. The most fundamental principle is that all shareholders must be treated equally.

A number of statutory rules also apply during takeovers. For example, there are criminal restrictions on insider dealing and the making of misleading statements and market manipulation. There is also a new civil prohibition on market abuse.

The UK Listing Authority's listing rules (the Listing Rules) will not usually be relevant unless the bidder's shares are listed on the London Stock

Exchange's market for listed securities or if it is offering securities as part of the takeover which will be listed in London.

Although a non-statutory body, the Takeover Panel's rulings are invariably complied with. The Takeover Panel prides itself (justifiably) on its speed, efficiency, consistency and confidentiality. The Takeover Panel's standing has been reinforced by the UK courts' decision not to interfere with Takeover Panel rulings or decisions during the course of a bid. Accordingly, while it is theoretically possible for there to be judicial review of Takeover Panel rulings, there is virtually no litigation in the context of UK takeovers. A new market abuse regime has recently been introduced in the UK, increasing the scope for litigation during bids. However, the Financial Services Authority, which will enforce the new regime, regards the Takeover Panel as the prime regulator during bids.

The Takeover Code is designed principally to ensure fair and equal treatment of all shareholders in relation to takeovers and to provide an orderly framework within which takeovers are conducted. Generally speaking the Takeover Panel does not approve nor review takeover documentation. It is also not responsible for reviewing or approving the offer price – other than when an offer is made for more than one class of security e.g. a security convertible into ordinary shares where it does have a role in ensuring that price is a comparable one to the basic offer. The Takeover Panel also polices the conditionality of offers. However none of the above really enable the Takeover Panel to act in a protectionist role nor can we think of any recent examples when they might have been said to have done so. Further, the Takeover Panel does not take jurisdiction over takeovers of UK public companies which are not managed in the UK nor, historically, has it taken jurisdiction over structures involving dual listed holding companies although this is likely to change.

b. Are there restrictions on a board taking action to frustrate a bid that has been made? When do the relevant restrictions start to apply – earlier than a formal announcement/filing of a bid? To what extent can shareholders approve the taking of frustrating action in advance of any bid?

The directors of the target are not allowed to take any action which could frustrate the making of a bid. This applies from the time the directors reasonably believe a bid might be imminent (Rule 21 of the City Code).

What the Takeover Panel will regard as frustrating action goes beyond what might be expected. Not only will poison pill type contractual arrangements and material disposals or acquisitions be covered but also issues of shares or options and contracts otherwise than in the ordinary course of business. Entering into or amending directors' employment contracts is also regarded as frustrating action.

The target board can, however, invite shareholders to approve what would otherwise be frustrating action. The philosophy of the City Code is that it is up to target shareholders to decide the outcome of an offer and shareholders can therefore be asked to approve any defensive action the board thinks appropriate. Institutional shareholders are, however, generally reluctant to agree to any measure which would eliminate the possibility of a bid.

For most listed companies, the shareholding base is fairly widespread with the majority, often more than 90%, held by a wide range of institutional shareholders. Generally the approach of such institutional shareholders is to oppose any measures which reduce the possibility of a bid being made and, should a bid be made, that they should decide on the merits or otherwise of the relevant offer. Accordingly, shareholders do not typically approve poison-pill type provisions in the UK either before (even though Rule 21 does not apply at that time) or during an offer.

c. Are there restrictions on the type of consideration that can be offered in a bid, for example securities only if these are listed in the target country's home state or the EU?

A bidder will often offer shares or other securities as consideration for the offer. It may offer shares alone, as an alternative to cash or a mixture of cash and shares. A UK target shareholder would usually expect these shares to be listed on the London Stock Exchange's market for listed securities or traded on the UK Alternative Investment Market. There are however increasing numbers of bids including shares listed on an overseas exchange. Whilst there is no legal obstacle to this, settlement and trading can cause difficulties particularly for non-institutional investors.

Accepting shares or other paper consideration may have tax advantages for target shareholders who will usually be able to 'roll over' any capital gain they have made on their shares in the target. A cash offer is often accompanied by a loan note alternative for this reason. Loan notes are a form of unsecured, typically unlisted debenture issued to enable shareholders to postpone their capital gains tax liability.

There will be no need for a prospectus provided the bid is made to all target shareholders. If the bidder's shares are (or are to be) officially listed and the number of new shares to be issued equals 10 per cent or more of its current issued share capital, it will have to publish listing particulars.

d. Are there effective compulsory acquisition procedures regarding a small non-accepting minority? Can a bidder make its offer conditional on achieving the number of shares required so it can operate a squeeze out?

The Companies Act provides a procedure for the compulsory acquisition of the shares of any minority shareholders following a takeover offer. Provided the bidder secures 90 per cent acceptances of the shares to which the offer relates (excluding shares held by the bidder or its associates at the time the offer document is posted) it will have the right to compulsorily acquire or 'squeeze out' the remaining shareholders.

This level has to be achieved within four months of the date the original offer document was posted. Within two months of achieving the 90 per cent level, the bidder may give notice in accordance with the Companies Act that it wishes to purchase compulsorily those shares on the same terms (i.e. identical form of consideration) as the original offer. Subject to certain minority rights, completion of this statutory procedure takes six weeks.

Shareholders have the right to object to the acquisition of their shares by applying to the court within six weeks of the date the relevant notice was given. In practice, however, this right is rarely exercised and is almost never successful.

It is possible to make the offer conditional on 90% acceptances of the shares to which the offer relates and for the bidder to lapse the offer if this condition is not satisfied. Typically the bidder will have the right to waive the acceptance condition down to no less than 50%. It is very rare for a successful bidder, i.e. one that has successfully reached more than 50%, subsequently not to reach 90% and complete the compulsory squeeze-out. If a scheme of arrangement is used then once the scheme becomes effective – following the relevant shareholder votes and court approval – it is binding on all shareholders whether or not they voted in favour.

e. Is there a principle of board neutrality? Can a target board align itself with a particular bidder/agree measures such as exclusivity arrangements to protect a particular deal?

There is no strict concept of board neutrality in the sense that one bidder can be favoured over another. However, directors of a target company must act bona fide in the best interests of the company and not use their powers for an improper purpose. This principle is enhanced by the City Code which requires target directors, when advising shareholders, to act only in their capacities as directors and not to have regard to personal or family shareholdings or their relationships with their company. It also reminds directors to consider carefully any commitment which would restrict their freedom to advise shareholders in the future.

The target directors are obliged by the City Code to circulate their views on any offer to shareholders and to obtain independent advice.

Subject to acting bone fide in the best interests of the Company, it is possible for the Target Board to agree exclusivity arrangements if they think it is in the interest of the Company to do so. They can also agree break-fees

– very broadly up to 1% of market value. They cannot, however, bind themselves to make a positive recommendation in favour of the offer regardless of circumstances. Their duty in relation to recommendations to shareholders is an on-going one which has to be exercised in accordance with their fiduciary duties throughout of the offer process.

f. Can a target board hand over information to a potential bidder?

Yes – provided that if such information is price sensitive it must make it clear to the bidder that the information is price sensitive, must be kept confidential and that no dealings in the targets may take place whilst such information remains price sensitive.

Under the City Code the target will have to provide any bone fide bidder or potential bidder with information it has given to any other bidder. This rule applies even if the other potential bidder is hostile or a competitor of the target. The Takeover Panel will, however, permit the target to insist on a confidentiality agreement.

g. Are structures permitted which concentrate control rights in the hands of minority shareholders? Are structures permitted which place limitations/restrictions on voting rights, caps for example on voting rights above a certain threshold?

Yes – but these are increasingly rare. There are a small handful of listed companies which have voting and non-voting shares where the economic rights are identical. The number of UK listed companies with this sort of structure has declined considerably over the last few years.

There are few companies which place limitations / restrictions on voting rights. These include certain defence companies where overseas holders are typically restricted to 15% of the voting rights and a few former building societies which have a voting threshold of 15% for a single shareholder (together with concert parties) for the first five years after their conversion into banks.

h. Can restrictions be placed on the transferability of shares either by the issuer (in articles of association or by other means) or by arrangements between shareholders? Can a board delay registering transfers of shares?

No in the case of the issuer. Under the Listing Rules securities must be freely transferable to be listed. It is, however, possible to have a restriction on the right of transfer if the holder has not complied with the notice under section 212 of the Companies Act 1985 – a provision which enables a company to enquire about all those who have interests (in the widest legal sense) in its shares. It is technically possible to have restrictions on transfers of partly paid securities but these are extremely rare. It would be an improper use of powers for directors to delay the registration of transfers.

Whilst it is possible for shareholders to agree restrictions between themselves it is thought that this is very uncommon probably because of the widespread ownership of shares between institutions and the fact that agreements of this sort can lead to additional disclosure obligations under the Companies Act and may – depending on the provisions – result in the parties being parties acting in concert for purposes of the City Code which would then potentially give rise to mandatory bid obligations if further shares were bought.

i. What contractual barriers (including share holder agreements) to takeover bids are in use in public companies (e.g. golden parachutes, change of control provisions triggering default of loan agreements, or wining up or change of control of joint ventures)? What are the prospects of review by courts on the basis of contract or company law and by regulators on the basis of securities laws or stock exchange regulations?

These are rare. Whilst loan agreements, joint venture agreements and other material contracts may have change of control clauses in them, it is not generally thought to be a proper use of power by directors to agree to such provisions in order to prevent or discourage a bid for the company. Likewise golden parachutes for directors do exist, but they have to be negotiated in good faith as part of the relevant directors' remuneration package rather than as a barrier to a takeover. Such provisions also constitute frustrating action – see answer to Question 14(b) above.

j. Are there current proposals to change the legislation relating to takeovers?

No, apart from a proposal to include transactions involving the creation of dual listed holding companies within the City Code and subject only to any changes necessary as a result of the introduction of further directives such as, possibly, the market abuse directive.

D. FINAL ISSUES

15. In your view, what is the extent to which the complexity of the regulatory arrangements, within national jurisdictions and between the Commission and member states, present an obstacle to takeovers?

Barriers tend to be greater for takeovers where the consideration is in the form of securities where such consideration:

- is likely to result in different after tax receipts for shareholders
- will probably not fall within the local stock index requiring compulsory disposal by index tracker funds
- may be difficult to trade/settle in the local market.

These factors combined with a tendency for sales in a target's home market and a corresponding flow-back to the bidder's market continue to make share for share transactions more difficult.

16. Can you list some instances where different rules in the different regulatory systems have caused practical obstacles in a take over process? (One instance could be different time limits under the EC Merger Regulation and national merger rules on the one hand and under stock exchange rules on the other.)

From a UK perspective the timetables and procedures are sufficiently well developed to accommodate anti-trust and other regulatory delays (in contrast, for instance, with the positions in France and Spain). In particular the use of pre-conditional offers under which the offers are only made once relevant anti-trust clearances are achieved are now common.

The City Code only expressly allows delays as result of the UK or EC anti-trust processes. However, in practice it is possible to accommodate the US procedures in particular – whether under Hart Scott Rodino, SEC review or specific regulatory clearances in some industries. These procedures can also be used to cover other jurisdictions including where the transaction does not fall within the Merger Regulation.

These rules are better developed in respect of Anglo-US transactions which have been more common. Likewise some of the differences in regulation – particularly US disclosure rules which can cause difficulties in the UK because of the need for formal reports on profit forecast for instance – are better developed in the US than European context.

Potential problem areas in relation to European transactions are the mismatch between different jurisdictions on the need for share valuations and, potentially, where conditionally of offers is restricted by local regulation but the UK bidder needs shareholder approval in order to makes its offer.

NOTES

[1] Focus is here mainly on listed companies but information about non listed and also non public companies will be of interest and is included where this has been possible to provide.

[2] Here too the following applies. For EEA (non member) country rapporteurs, the subject of the question is intended to be the EEA regime. For non-member (non EEA) countries, there are special issues. Country rapporteurs are welcome to limit their answers in the way they believe to be most helpful or interesting with the purpose of the questionnaire in mind.

[3] "Foreign" here includes both takeovers from other member states and from non-member states (or non EEA countries).

[4] In the case of banks or insurance companies, the relevant ministry and supervisor would be usually be able to block takeovers on prudential grounds and their involvement would be difficult to review. Similar mechanisms would be in place for many utilities where state ownership often adds to the problems. An extensive review is not required, but it would be useful with an assessment of how such mechanisms function. If there have for instance not been any take over by a foreign bank, that is an interesting point.

[5] The aim is not here to have an authoritative statement but a report which can contribute to the discussion. For EEA (non member) country rapporteurs, the subject of the question is intended to be the EEA regime. For non member (non EEA) countries, there are special issues. Country rapporteurs are welcome to limit their answers in the way they believe to be most helpful or interesting with the purpose of the questionnaire in mind.

[6] Speech entitled "Review of the EC Merger Regulation – Roadmap for the reform project" given on 4 June 2002 at the Conference on Reform of European Merger Control at the British Chamber of Commerce in Brussels.

[7] On 11 January 1999, the UK government asked for *Electricity de France/London Electricity* to be referred to the UK in accordance with Article 9 of the Merger Regulation, however the request was unsuccessful (and the merger was cleared by the Commission after a Phase I investigation). On 2 June 1999, the UK government asked for *Exxon/Mobil* to be referred to the UK, in accordance with Article 9 of the Merger Regulation, however the request was unsuccessful (the merger was cleared (with undertakings) by the Commission after a Phase II investigation). On 18 April 2000, the UK government asked for *Nabisco/United Biscuits* to be referred to the UK, in accordance with Article 9 of the Merger Regulation, however the request was unsuccessful (after the deal was modified to avoid Nabisco controlling both UB and Horizon, another biscuit maker. This modification removed competition concerns and therefore there was no need to refer the case to the UK. The merger was cleared (with undertakings) by the Commission after a Phase I investigation).

[8] Paragraph 28.

[9] Section 21 Enterprise Bill.